ENCYCLOPEDIA OF
Erotic
Literature

ENCYCLOPEDIA OF
Erotic
Literature

1

A–K
INDEX

Gaëtan Brulotte
John Phillips

EDITORS

 Routledge
Taylor & Francis Group
New York   London

Routledge is an imprint of the
Taylor & Francis Group, an informa business

Routledge
Taylor & Francis Group
270 Madison Avenue
New York, NY 10016

Routledge
Taylor & Francis Group
2 Park Square
Milton Park, Abingdon
Oxon OX14 4RN

© 2006 by Taylor & Francis Group, LLC
Routledge is an imprint of Taylor & Francis Group, an Informa business

Printed in the United States of America on acid-free paper
10 9 8 7 6 5 4 3 2 1

International Standard Book Number-10: 1-57958-441-1 (Hardcover)
International Standard Book Number-13: 978-1-57958-441-2 (Hardcover)

Library of Congress Cataloging-in-Publication Data

Encyclopedia of erotic literature / Gaëtan Brulotte, John Phillips, editors.
   p. cm.
  ISBN-13: 978-1-57958-441-2 (alk. paper)
  ISBN-10: 1-57958-441-1 (alk. paper)
  1. Erotic literature--Encyclopedias. I. Brulotte, Gaëtan. II. Phillips, John. 1950-

PN56.E7E53 2006
809'.9353803--dc22
                                           2006040224

Visit the Taylor & Francis Web site at
http://www.taylorandfrancis.com

and the Routledge Web site at
http://www.routledge-ny.com

TABLE OF CONTENTS

ADVISORS

Sarane Alexandrian
Superieur Inconnu

Peter Brown
Trinity College, Oxford

Peter Cryle
University of Queensland

Joan DeJean
University of Pennsylvania

Michel Delon
Université de Paris-Sorbonne (Paris IV)

Eve Fishburn
University of North London

Lucienne Frappier-Mazur
University of Pennsylvania

Jay A. Gertzman
University of Bradford

Owen Heathcote
University of Bradford

Maxim Jakubowski
University of Colorado at Boulder

Patrick J. Kearney
University of Colorado at Boulder

Peter Michelson
University of Colorado at Boulder

Jane Mills
Australian Film Television and Radio School

Michael Perkins
University of Essex

Ken Plummer
University of Essex

Gerald Prince
University of Pennsylvania

Everett K. Rowson
New York University

Clifford J. Scheiner
Institute for Advanced Study of Human Sexuality

Joseph Slade III
Ohio University

Douglas Wile
CUNY–Brooklyn College

INTRODUCTION

'I authorize the publication and sale of all libertine books and immoral works; for I esteem them most essential to human felicity and welfare, instrumental to the progress of philosophy, indispensable to the eradication of prejudices, and in every sense conducive to the increase of human knowledge and understanding.' (Marquis de Sade, *Juliette*)

Erotic literature is a global cultural expression represented in nearly all literary forms from the ancient world to the present. Recognizing its rich scope and cultural importance, scholars from around the world are drawn to the genre and the study of erotic literature is now a vast and emerging field. In these two volumes, the *Encyclopedia of Erotic Literature* invites the reader to embark on the scholarly exploration of a genre that traverses the horizon of human sexual experience, transforming our understanding of such experience and the experience of literature as well.

In an interview in 2002, the late French philosopher, Jacques Derrida was asked, if he were to watch a documentary about a philosopher—Heidegger, Kant, or Hegel—what would he wish to see in it. He replied 'Their sex-lives... because it is not something they talk about.'[1] The intellectual tradition of the Judeo-Christian West has repressed its sex-life in much the same way as the philosophers Derrida had in mind, and yet, the poets and story-tellers of West and East alike have never stopped talking about sex. This encyclopedia is the first of its kind: a comprehensive discussion and scholarly analysis of those innumerable works, written in many different languages throughout our known history, in which 'sex-talk' is the dominant discourse. The history of this discourse is as old as the history of writing itself.

During the six years since its inception, this project has attracted considerable intellectual interest from all over the globe. Leading scholars in the world's most renowned universities have acted as advisors from an early stage, as well as contributing many of the 546 entries that make up the two volumes of the work. The total number of contributors exceeds 400.

The conceptual framework determining the general organization of contents prior to its distribution in alphabetical order was divided into four categories: Historical Overviews, Topics and Themes, Literary Surveys, Writers and Works. Historical Overviews are categorized by language/geographical or cultural area and ideally include all literary genres (e.g. the Ancient World or French Canadian Literature); Topics and Themes focus on a predominant or general subject in the field (e.g. Libertinism or Necrophilia) or a critical approach (such as Feminism or Queer Theory); Literary Surveys address genres, or publication issues (Pulp Fiction or Bibliographies, for instance), Writers and Works include individual entries on authors or works —whether attributed or anonymous—(D.H. Lawrence or *Jin Ping Mei*, for example), which address their relation to the history of the genre as a whole, and evaluate their contribution to it. Each entry offers a set of bibliographical references and suggested further readings. With very few exceptions, the length of entries varies from a minimum of 1000 words to a maximum of 8000 words, according to the relative importance of the subject-matter.

We have tried to be as inclusive as possible, but as with all undertakings of this size and scope, there are inevitable omissions. Limitations of space regrettably dictate that lines have constantly to be drawn. Audio-visual works (paintings, photos, films), for example, have not been included, since this is an encyclopedia of the erotic *in literature*. On the other hand, if there are a larger number of entries relating to literature in French, it is because French and Francophone writers have contributed more than any other linguistic culture to the development of the erotic genre. The eminent author and publisher, Jean-Jacques Pauvert has called this phenomenon 'l'exception française'[2], the French exception.

Nonetheless, the *Encyclopedia of Erotic Literature* aims to be universal in scope, both geographically and historically, and to reflect current research in the field. The work is principally intended as a valuable resource for all those studying, researching, or teaching any aspect of erotic literature and/or the history of sexuality. Eschewing technical language wherever possible, it will also appeal to the general reader with an interest in exploring this subject.

QUESTIONS OF DEFINITION

Our definition of erotic literature is a universal one, not a judgmental one, encompassing all fictional genres (the novel, poetry, the short-story, drama and some Eastern forms) but also essays, autobiographies, treatises, and sex manuals from a wide range of cultures. Erotic literature is defined here as works in which sexuality and/or sexual desire has a dominant presence. All types of sexuality are included in this definition. When consulting existing reference works and dictionaries on the subject, and the very few specialized histories of the genre, one is struck by the difficulty scholars have encountered in differentiating erotic literature from pornography or from love stories containing sexually explicit passages. Neither of the existing terms, erotic or pornographic, is neutral. But generally speaking the former is usually taken to refer to an acceptable form of sexual representation, while the latter designates a form that is socially or politically unacceptable. Both terms are therefore infected with a degree of judgmentalism that we sought to avoid in an attempt to provide the richest and widest range of literatures to the reader that reflect the abundant diversity within the genre. The distinction between the erotic and the pornographic depends on arguments and stereotypes that are fundamentally subjective, and that are psychological, ethical, feminist, or aesthetic in nature. Legal rulings are themselves influenced and determined by such arguments which are always culturally and temporally relative.

The psychological point of view is wholly related to reader response. According to this point of view, erotica arouses the individual reader, while pornography does not. This distinction is clearly confusing, since pornography can arouse a reader as much as so-called erotica. Webster's English Dictionary defines 'pornography' as 'a portrayal of erotic behavior designed to cause sexual excitement.' Homosexual literature will not arouse everyone but is part of what we call erotic literature. Literary depictions of necrophilia may not arouse most readers but belong to the erotic tradition. The consensus of scholarship during the last quarter century is that such a literary genre cannot be defined according to the individual reader's desire, since each person has his/her own 'sexual template' as modern psychology calls it. Indeed, many erotic texts do not seek to arouse at all.

From an ethical viewpoint, pornography is what other people find erotic, presupposing the existence of a sexual norm according to which one group of persons judge and reject what they dislike. This argument raises the delicate question of 'perversion', since pornography has frequently been associated with 'perverted' sexuality, i.e. with a sexuality or sexual orientation that is different from one's own. The psychoanalytical concept of 'perversion' tends to construct a sexual norm from the standpoint of which there are deviations. Freud defined 'perversion' as any sexual activity that is not intercourse: hence oral sex is 'perverted', so is masturbation, and so forth. In this view most human sexual habits and erotic inclinations turn out to be 'perverted'. However, the notion of 'perversion' has been revisited by modern anthropologists and historians who have demonstrated the temporal and cultural relativity of the concept. When Pierre Klossowski in twentieth century France writes of a husband who enjoys giving his wife to other men, some may consider this gesture 'perverted'. For the Inuit, on the other hand, such behavior is simply the expression of conventions of hospitality.

The sociological perspective defines eroticism as the pornography of the dominant social class. In this view, eroticism has aristocratic associations, while pornography is a lower-class activity. Thus, pornography but not eroticism may represent a threat to the status quo. Yet, as numerous entries demonstrate, the eroticism of 'high literature' is just as capable of subversion as more popular forms of writing about sex. Erotic works by philosophers during the French Enlightenment, for example, arguably helped to pave the way for the French Revolution. Throughout history, in fact, erotic writings generally can be said to have had a socially leveling influence.

The gender of the author is another spurious yardstick, by which the pornography/eroticism distinction is sometimes measured. In this perspective, men produce pornography while women 'write the erotic'. This argument falters when confronted with anonymity, or the extensive use of pseudonyms. Moreover, some authors employ strategies to make believe that the narrator is male or female, creating confusion as to the author's sex or gender. And what are we to think of the many novels by women in contemporary France that are as explicit or as sexually violent as anything authored by a man? Pro-censorship feminists regard any depiction of sexual behavior which degrades and abuses women as pornographic. Such views are highly subjective, and beg the question of what constitutes degradation or abuse, but if the author of the text or image is male, his gender is itself grounds to condemn him in their eyes. Andrea Dworkin, for example, suggests that 'Male power is the *raison d'être* of pornography: the degradation of the female is the means of achieving this power.'[3] A recent ruling by the Canadian Supreme Court, masterminded by Dworkin and her fellow anti-pornographer campaigner, Catherine MacKinnon, defines the related concept of obscenity according to the harm it does to women's pursuit of equality.[4] Yet, much extreme sexual material, such as gay male 'porn', does not represent women at all.

Legal definitions are no more helpful, as they tend to depend on aesthetic norms which vary from culture to culture, and from period to period. In particular, the way in which obscenity is defined has changed considerably over the centuries. Concepts of obscenity are central to anti-pornography legislation in Britain and the USA, as well as in France. In Britain, the law currently defines obscenity as 'anything that may deprave or corrupt persons who are likely to read, see or hear the matter contained or embodied in it'[5]. In the USA, the so-called 'Miller Test' is still the

predominant legal definition of obscenity. According to this test, which originated in a 1973 case tried before the American Supreme Court, Miller v. California, there are three criteria: 1) does a work as a whole appeal to 'prurient interest'?; 2) does it depict or describe sexual conduct in a 'patently offensive way'?; 3) does it lack serious literary, artistic, political or scientific value'?[6]

These definitions of obscenity are dangerously vague, since they all depend upon the inescapable subjectivity and cultural relativity of other terms, such as 'indecent', 'deprave', 'corrupt', 'prurient', 'offensive', 'value', 'harm', 'equality', embedded in them. In the French law of the last two centuries, the concept of 'bonnes moeurs' (which roughly translates as 'public decency') is equally vague and culturally relative, as the history of censorship clearly shows — how many of us would consider Flaubert's *Madame Bovary* or the racier pieces in Baudelaire's best known collection of poems, *Les fleurs du mal* (*The Flowers of Evil*), a threat to public morals now?

All of the above arguments fail to produce a satisfactory distinction between the erotic and the pornographic. In antiquity, the word 'pornographos' bore little relation to our contemporary notion of pornography as writing or images that aim to arouse sexually, since it merely denoted a type of biography, 'the lives of the courtesans', which was not necessarily obscene in content.[7] In fact, it was not until the nineteenth century that the dictionary definition of the word was widened to include 'the expression or suggestion of obscene or unchaste subjects in literature or art'[8], and began, therefore, to assume a pejorative meaning.

The etymology of the word, 'obscenity', by contrast, is dubious. Its modern definition of 'indecent' or 'lewd' is preceded by the archaic meaning of 'repulsive' or 'filthy' (OED). Some recent commentators have suggested that the word originally meant 'off the scene', referring, in other words, to actions in the classical theatre that were too shocking to take place 'on stage' in full view of the audience.[9] What all of these definitions have in common is their subjective basis, for what is 'repulsive' or 'shocking' to some will not be so to others. When used in a sexual context, moreover, the word reveals a profoundly negative attitude to the sexual functions and to sexual pleasure. For Susan Sontag,

'It's just these assumptions that are challenged by the French tradition represented by Sade, Lautréamont, Bataille, and the authors of *Story of O* and *The Image*. Their assumption seems to be that 'the obscene' is a primal notion of human consciousness, something much more profound than the backwash of a sick society's aversion to the body.'[10]

Like 'pornography', then, 'obscenity' has acquired a negative charge in a Western culture, conditioned by the puritanism of Christianity, a negativity which legal definitions have reinforced. For Jacques Derrida, each term of such binaries as 'eroticism' and 'pornography', or 'eroticism' and 'obscenity' is already infected with its opposite, and so becomes ultimately undecidable, a signifier whose signified cannot be finally fixed. In view of these linguistic and conceptual slippages, then, and while accepting that even the word 'eroticism' can never be entirely neutral, the decision was taken at an early stage to discourage the use of 'pornography' and 'obscenity' as terms most likely to convey negative impressions. Thus, they are employed sparingly, and always within a clear historical and cultural context. The term 'erotic literature' also benefits from a more stable meaning throughout history and is more inclusive of the variety of works this encyclopedia covers.

One last point on this issue of definition: the dangers of too broad a definition of eroticism were apparent from the outset, and it was thought that to define any work containing sexual scenes as erotic would be to invite entries on practically the whole of World literature.

CORPUS AND CONTENT

Our selected corpus reveals above all a remarkable diversity in the types of sexuality represented (heterosexuality, homosexuality, sado-masochism, fetishism, incest, etc). This sexual diversity is equally matched by the diversity of literary forms in which these sexualities are represented, from pure dialogue to classical narrative, from the epistolary novel to prose poetry. Style too ranges from the highly metaphorical to the extremely crude. Thus, eroticism is found as much in literary masterpieces as in pulp fiction. This diversity may surprise some readers, since it has often been argued that erotic texts are mediocre in quality and repetitive in form and subject-matter. On the contrary, readers will discover here that erotic literature is far more diverse

than generally believed. Indeed, much erotic writing belongs to the literary avant-garde, thanks to a readiness to experiment and innovate on formal levels. Many of the works discussed are also of considerable philosophical and socio-historical interest, conveying a wealth of fascinating information about the history and evolution of intimacy and the social mores surrounding it, offering insights on rites and taboos, on the history of attitudes to the body, and many other cultural practices.

As for the familiar charge that this is a literature aimed only at the male voyeur, erotic texts frequently appeal to all of the senses, from the evocation of the sensation of bodily touch, taste and smells to the screams, whispers and silences that can accompany the sex-act. Such descriptions speak as much to women as to men. This is a literature that is more likely to undermine than to reinforce conventional thinking and social stereotypes. The traditional unity of the person and the body that our western culture has constructed over the centuries is, for example, repeatedly put into question by a writing that foregrounds bodily pleasure.[11] Erotic writing constantly renews itself, finding new ways of staging and figuring desire. Differences of race or ethnicity tend to be effaced in pursuit of the solitary goal of sexual satisfaction.

Erotic works do sometimes project a utopian vision of the world, which they picture as liberated from all its current limitations. But in doing so, they point to the difficulties associated with such idealism, and raise important philosophical questions in relation to concepts of freedom and the other.

It will have become clear by now that the aims of erotic literature cannot be reduced to sexual arousal alone. Indeed, these texts are inspired by a multiplicity of objectives, social, political, and moral, embracing themes and forms that are just as diverse as those of any other literary genre. The literary depiction of sexuality offers essential insights into every aspect of the human condition. Although eroticism is ostensibly linked to materialist views of life, the body has served throughout history as the central focus of a search that ever seeks to transcend it, reaching out to mythical, metaphysical and spiritual dimensions. In this sense, all erotic texts address issues of both life and death—orgasm in French is popularly described as 'la petite mort'—since, as Freud demonstrated, Eros (the life force) and

Thanatos (the death drive) are inextricably bound up with each other... which amounts to saying that the sexual impulse is a fundamental expression of the human story in all its facets.

The twentieth century authors and thinkers, Georges Bataille and Michel Foucault both believed that sexuality was *the* major problem facing mankind, and yet, for mainly political and religious reasons, the study of erotic expression has largely been suppressed, as much in the academy as in society generally. It is true that the recent rise of 'Sexuality and Gender Studies' in universities has given academics permission to read and teach erotic works, but only within the politically correct context of feminism or queer theory. The two volumes of this encyclopedia represent a much wider critical interest on the part of the hundreds of scholars, men and women, of all ethnicities, genders, and sexualities, teaching and researching in universities on every continent, and under every kind of political regime. Others will hopefully follow the lead that they have taken here.

How to Use This Book

The *Encyclopedia of Erotic Literature* is composed of over 500 signed scholarly essays of 1000 to 8000 words in length. Researchers will find the encyclopedia's **A to Z format** easily navigable. Scholars seeking multiple entries within a specific area of inquiry will find the **thematic table of contents** of great value. There one can browse all of the entries concerning authors and works employing a specific *language* (i.e. Indian languages), *historical overviews* of specific nations, regions and periods (i.e. German: twentieth and twenty-first centuries), *literary surveys* of specific genres and trends (i.e. science fiction and fantasy) and entries exploring discrete concepts (i.e. prostitution) grouped as *topics and themes*. Nearly all of the entries concerning individual works or an entire body of work will be followed by a **capsule biography** of the author. Major articles contain a list of **References and Further Reading**, including sources used by the writer and editor as well as additional items that may be of interest to the reader. And a thorough, **analytical index** will instantly open the work up to every reader.

Gaëtan Brulotte
John Phillips

Biographical note on editors:

Gaëtan Brulotte is Distinguished University Professor of French and Francophone Literature at the University of South Florida in Tampa, U.S.A. He has published extensively on the subject of erotic literature, including a critically acclaimed book *Oeuvres de chair. Figures du discours érotique*.

John Phillips is Professor of French Literature and Culture at London Metropolitan University. He has published extensively on eighteenth and twentieth century French literature and on twentieth century film. His latest books are *The Marquis de Sade: A Very Short Introduction* and *Transgender on Screen*.

Notes

1 *Derrida*, a documentary by Kirby Dick and Ziering Kofman (Jane Doe Films Inc, 2002)
2 Pauvert, Jean-Jacques. *L'Amour à la française ou l'exception étrange*. Editions du Rocher, 1997.
3 *Pornography: Men Possessing Women*. New York: Perigee Books, 1981, p. 32.
4 See ibid., p. 54.
5 The Obscene Publications Act, 1959.
6 See Linda Williams, 'Second Thoughts on Hard Core. American Obscenity Law and the Scapegoating of Deviance' in *Dirty Looks. Women, Pornography, Power* (BFI Publishing, 1993), pp. 46–61; this reference, pp. 48–9.
7 See Linda Williams, 'A Provoking Agent. The Pornography and Performance Art of Annie Sprinkle' in Gibson & Gibson (eds), *Dirty Looks. Women, Pornography, Power* (BFI Publishing, 1993), pp. 176–91; this ref., pp. 181–2.
8 Quoted by Stephen Heath, *The Sexual Fix* (London & Basingstoke: MacMillan, 1982), pp. 105–6.
9 See Linda Williams, 'Second Thoughts on Hard Core. American Obscenity Law and the Scapegoating of Deviance' in Roma Gibson & Pamela Church Gibson (eds), *Dirty Looks. Women, Pornography, Power* (BFI Publishing, 1993), pp. 46–61; this ref., p. 47, n. 1.
10 Susan Sontag, 'The Pornographic Imagination' in Douglas A. Hughes (ed.), *Perspectives on Pornography* (New York: MacMillan, St. Martin's Press, 1970), pp. 131–69; this ref., pp. 153–54.
11 This unity is typically cerebral rather than physical, as Descartes's famous 'Cogito ergo sum' illustrates. The modern French critic and semiologist, Roland Barthes has drawn attention to the relative lack of philosophers of pleasure in the Western tradition and dreamed of writing a history of all the pleasures that societies have resisted, as well as of a history of desire (*Oeuvres complètes*. Paris, Seuil, 1995–2002: IV, 244, 255; V, 555)

LIST OF CONTRIBUTORS

Ivan Adamovic Independent Scholar

Jad Adams Independent Scholar

Jon Adams University of California at Riverside

Jonathan Alexander University of Cincinnati

Sarane Alexandrian Superieur Inconnu

Karen Alkalay-Gut Tel Aviv University

Evangelia Anagnostou-Laoutides University of Reading

Eric Annandale Independent Scholar

Sinan Antoon Dartmouth College

Brian James Baer Kent State University

Roger W. Baines University of East Anglia

Scott Bates University of the South

Hervé Baudry Coimbra University

Heike Bauer Independent Scholar

Gerd Bayer Case Western Reserve University

Edith J. Benkov San Diego State University

Juda Charles Bennett College of New Jersey

Patricia Berney Independent Scholar

Marc-André Bernier Université du Québec à Trois Rivières

Sarah Berry University of Hull

Anne Berthelot University of Connecticut

David Biale University of California at Davis

Lawrence J. Birken Ball State University

Caroline Blinder Goldsmiths College

Eliot Borenstein New York University

Serge Bourjea Centre d'étude du XXème siècle

Pablo Brescia Independent Scholar

Pollie Bromilow University of Liverpool

Diane Brown Macalaster College

Gaëtan Brulotte University of South Florida

Vern L. Bullough Independent Scholar

Gerald J. Butler San Diego State University

Madeline Camara University of South Florida

Rebecca Chalker Independent Scholar

Anthony H. Chambers Arizona State University

Philippe Che Université de Provence

Pamela Cheek University of New Mexico

Margaret Childs Independent Scholar

William J. Cloonan Florida State University

Peter Cogman University of Southampton

Paul Cooke University of Exeter

Michael G. Cornelius Wilson College

Jordi Cornellà-Detrell Lancaster University

Sébastien Côté Université de Montréal

Maurice Couturier Université de Nice-Sophia Antipolis

David Coward University of Leeds

Linda Craig University of East London

Michael Cronin Dublin City University

Ivan Crozier University College London

Peter Cryle University of Queensland

Louise Curth University of Exeter

Monica S. Cyrino University of New Mexico

Mark Darlow University of Nottingham

Ann Davies University of Newcastle

Dick Davis Independent Scholar

Herbert De Ley University of Illinois at Urbana-Champaign

Philip Deacon University of Sheffield

Sara Munson Deats University of South Florida

Camilla Decarnin Independent Scholar

Laura Desmond University of Chicago

Alexandra Destais Caen's University

James Diedrick Albion College

Sarah Donachie University of Newcastle upon Tyne

Wendy Doniger University of Chicago

David Dorais Independent Scholar

Florence W. Dore Kent State University

Lisa Downing Queen Mary, University of London

LIST OF CONTRIBUTORS

Nathalie Dumas Université d'Ottawa

Ted Emery Dickinson College

Michel Erman Université de Bourgogne

Matt Escobar Independent Scholar

Graham Falconer University of Toronto

Tracy Ferrell University of Colorado at Boulder

Alexandra Fitts University of Alaska Fairbanks

Charles Forsdick University of Liverpool

Claude Fouillade New Mexico State University

David O. Frantz Ohio State University

Lucienne Frappier-Mazur Independent Scholar

Patrick Paul Garlinger Northwestern University

Daniel Garrison Northwestern University

Tom Genrich Independent Scholar

Jay A. Gertzman Independent Scholar

Ruth Gilbert University of Southampton

James R. Giles Northern Illinois University

Bernadette Ginestet Independent Scholar

Philippe R. Girard McNeese State University

René Godenne Independent Scholar

S.E. Gontarski Florida State University

Sarah Gordon Utah State University

Robert E. Goss Metropolitan Community Church in the Valley

Nancy M. Grace College of Wooster

Mark Graybill Widener University

Mary Green University of Manchester

Susan Griffiths University of Cambridge

Terry Hale University of Hull

L. Grant Hamby Independent Scholar

Joseph Harris St Catharine's College-University of Cambridge

Jennifer Harrison College of William and Mary

Owen Heathcote University of Bradford

Rosmarin Heidenreich University of Manitoba

Leon-Francois Hoffman Princeton University

Earl Ingersoll SUNY at Brockport

Ben Jacob Independent Scholar

Karla Jay Pace University

Dominique Jeannerod University College Dublin

Toni Johnson-Woods University of Queensland

Dafydd Johnston University of Wales, Swansea

Jean Jonassaint Duke University

David Houston Jones University of Bristol

Miriam Jones University of New Brunswick, Saint John

Pierre Kaser Université de Provence

Thomas Kavanagh Independent Scholar

Michael Kearney Independent Scholar

Patrick J. Kearney Independent Scholar

Debra Kelly University of Westminster

LIST OF CONTRIBUTORS

Hubert Kennedy Independent Scholar

Brian Gordon Kennelly Webster University

R. Brandon Kershner Independent Scholar

Angela Kimyongür University of Hull

Faye Kleeman University of Colorado at Boulder

Jesse R. Knutson University of Chicago

Marc Kober Independent Scholar

Arne Koch University of Kansas

Adam Carl Komisaruk West Virginia University

Max D. Kramer Columbia University

Ricardo Krauel Princeton University

Selim S. Kuru University of Washington, Seattle

Christophe Lagier California State University Los Angeles

E.M. Langille St. Francis Xavier University

Patrick Wald Lasowski Université de Paris VIII

Evelyne Ledoux-Beaugrand Université de Montréal

Judith Yaross Lee Ohio University

Inger Leemans University of Utrecht

Gwendolyn Leick Chelsea College of Art and Design, University of the Arts, London

L. Scott Lerner Franklin & Marshall College

Alain Lescart University of Connecticut

André Lévy Université de Bordeaux

Darby Lewes Lycoming College

Tod Linafelt Georgetown University

Mark Llewellyn University of Wales

Loïc L. Lominé Cheltenham and Gloucester College of Higher Education

Thomas L. Long Thomas Nelson Community College

Edward Lucie-Smith Independent Scholar

Jean Mainil Northwestern University

Merja Makinen Middlesex University

Trina R. Mamoon University of Alaska Fairbanks

Lou Marinoff City College of New York

Chad Martin University of Natal

Diane E. Marting University of Mississippi

Ulrich Marzolph Enzyklopädie des Märchens

Sophia A. McClennen The Pennsylvania State University

Mark McHarry Independent Scholar

Becky R. McLaughlin University of South Alabama

Mark McLelland University of Queensland

Natania Meeker University of Southern California

Nola Merckel University of East Anglia

Jason A. Merrill Michigan State University

Peter Michelson University of Colorado at Boulder

Olivia Milburn University of London

Meredith Miller Independent Scholar

Carolina Miranda University of Hull

Katia Mitova Independent Scholar

Dominic Montserrat Open University

LIST OF CONTRIBUTORS

Ian Moulton Arizona State University West

Bradford Mudge University of Colorado at Denver

Mihaela Mudure Babes-Bolyai University

Elizabeth Newton Independent Scholar

Dany Nobus Brunel University

Scott B. Noegel University of Washington

Benedict O'Donohoe University of the West of England

Francis O'Gorman University of Leeds

Efstratia Oktapoda-Lu Independent Scholar

Dominique Paquet Independent Scholar

Julie Paquet University of Ottawa

Lizabeth Paravisini-Gebert Vassar College

John Parkin University of Bristol

Imogen Parsons Independent Scholar

Julie Peakman University College London

Dominique Péloquin Université Laval

Victor Peppard University of South Florida

John Perivolaris University of Manchester

Michael Perkins Independent Scholar

Chris Perriam University of Manchester

Ina Pfitzner Independent Scholar

John Phillips London Metropolitan University

Patrick Pollard Birkbeck College, University of London

Elizabeth Porges Watson Independent Scholar

Karl Posso The University of Edinburgh

Carrie A. Prettiman Cedar Crest College

Mark Pritchard Independent Scholar

Kirsten Pullen Independent Scholar

Walter P. Rankin George Mason University

Ajay Rao University of Chicago

Kokila Ravi Atlanta Metropolitan College

Mireille Ribiere Independent Scholar

Doug Rice California State University, Sacramento

Keith Richards Wake Forest University

Lee Anne Richardson Georgia State University

Michael Richardson Waseda University

Santiago Rodríguez Guerrero-Strachan Independent Scholar

Leyla Rouhi Williams College

Everett K. Rowson New York University

Cristina Ruiz Serrano The University College of the Cariboo

Frank A. Runcie Université de Montréal

Lorena Russell University of North Carolina at Asheville

Elizabeth Sabiston Independent Scholar

Pierre Saint-Amand Brown University

Lori Saint-Martin Independent Scholar

Elise Salaün Independent Scholar

Sarah Salih University of East Anglia

Tilde Sankovitch Independent Scholar

Angels Santa Universidad de Lleida

Chittaranjan Satapathy Independent Scholar

Andrew Schonebaum Barnard College

Paul A. Scott University of Kansas

Renée Scott University of North Florida

Paul A. Scott University of Kansas

Laurence Senelick Independent Scholar

Dorothy Severin University of Liverpool

Namascar Shaktini Florida Atlantic University

Sachie Shioya Independent Scholar

Debra Shostak College of Wooster

Gérard Siary University of Montpellier

Lisa Sigel DePaul University

Anne Simon Independent Scholar

Abigail Lee Six Royal Holloway, University of London

Joseph Slade III Ohio University

Marie-Agnès Sourieau Independent Scholar

Paul Sprachman Rutgers University

Philip Stewart Duke University

Julie Taddeo Independent Scholar

Jill Terry Independent Scholar

Morten Thing Roskilde Universitetsbibliotek

Lyn Thomas London Metropolitan University

Hannah Thompson University of London

Michael Tilby Selwyn College, Cambridge

Steven Totosy de Zepetnek Independent Scholar

Adrian Tudor University of Hull

James Turner University of California, Berkeley

Richard van Leeuwen Independent Scholar

Agnès Vannouvong Université de Marne-la-Vallée

Dimitris Vardoulakis Independent Scholar

Helen Vassallo University of Exeter

Sage Vivant Custom Erotica Source

Radu Voinescu Independent Scholar

Geoffrey Wall University of York

Ruth Wallach University of Southern California

Keith E. Welsh Webster University

Seth Whidden Villanova University

Frederick H. White Memorial Univerity

Barbara White Advanced Studies in English

Douglas Wile Brooklyn College CUNY

Terry J. Wilfong University of Michigan

Gordon Williams University of Wales, Lampeter

Jane Winston Northwestern University

Gina Wisker Anglia Polytechnic University

Gregory Woods Nottingham Trent University

Derek Wright Independent Scholar

I-Hsien Wu Columbia University

Markus Wust University of Alberta

Marilyn Yalom Independent Scholar

A TO Z LIST OF ENTRIES

THEMATIC TABLE OF CONTENTS

THEMATIC TABLE OF CONTENTS

French: Nineteenth Century

French: Twentieth Century

ABÉLARD AND HÉLOÏSE

Abélard

1079–1142
Dialectician, theologian, and philosopher

Héloïse

1101–1164
Abbess, epistolarian

Most of what is known about Abélard's life, and to a lesser extent about that of Héloïse, was written around 1133 by Abélard in his *Historia calamitatum* [*The Story of My Calamities*]. From it we learn that he was born in the small village of Le Pallet near Nantes in southern Brittany in 1079. He studied under scholastic theologians such as Guillaume de Champeaux (?–1121) and Anselme de Laon (c. 1050–1117), then taught rhetoric and dialectics in Paris and at the cathedral school of Notre Dame, where he obtained a chair in 1113. While in Paris, he met Héloïse and became her teacher at the request of her uncle, Canon Fulbert. Their clandestine and passionate love affair soon developed. Abélard was not able to maintain the quality of his teaching and, after Fulbert became aware of the relationship, the lovers were sepa-

rated. When Héloïse found out that she was pregnant, she fled with Abélard to his sister's house, where their son, Astrolabe, was born. Abélard then convinced Fulbert to let him marry his niece. At first, Héloïse refused marriage, considering this to be both dangerous and disgraceful for Abélard. But they returned to Paris and were married secretly. Eventually their wedding became public knowledge and Abélard was forced to take Héloïse to an abbey in Argenteuil, where she had been raised and educated. He settled in the nearby Saint-Denis monastery.

Thinking that Abélard had turned Héloïse into a nun to get rid of her, Fulbert ordered his kinsmen to have him castrated. At Saint-Denis, Abélard fell into a conflict with the abbot and other members of the congregation over their lack of monastic discipline. When students requested that he start teaching again, he decided to teach both the Holy Scriptures and philosophy. The study of secular books added to the attacks against Abélard. He wrote a controversial essay that insisted on understanding the meaning of words rather than accepting their superfluous mention, adding that this was necessary because nothing could be believed unless it was understood. A council convened against him ruled in favor of burning of the book and his persecution by his abbot and brethren. Abélard decided to retire to a remote area outside of Troyes, where soon students sought him out again. When Héloïse and her nuns were expelled from Argenteuil by a vengeful Suger (1081–1155), the abbot at Saint-Denis, Abélard gave her the land for a convent of the Paraclete order.

Abélard was charged with heresy for his comments concerning the Holy Trinity and the unity of God in 1121 and in 1140, the latter at a council headed by Bernard de Clairvaux (1090–1153). Peter the Venerable (c. 1092–1156) sided with Abélard and offered to welcome him at Cluny afterward. Upon the death of Abélard at Chalôn-sur-Saône, Peter wrote Héloïse a long letter that described his last few days. Peter also had Abélard's body transferred, as he had expressly wished in a letter to Héloïse, to the convent where she lived until her death in 1163 or 1164. They were buried in the same tomb. Their remains were reburied inside the Père-Lachaise cemetery in 1817.

Abélard's seeming aloofness limited the influence he had over his contemporaries, except for Pierre Lombard (1100–1160) and his student, who contributed greatly to his impact on thirteenth-century theologians and philosophers.

Writings

The *Historia calamitatum* was not meant to start a dialogue between Abélard and Héloïse, as it was addressed to an unknown recipient. It may indicate that Abélard was trying to avoid rekindling the passionate Héloïse by contacting her. Indeed, he recalls what took place between them while they were supposed to be studying, including the sweetness he felt when he struck Héloïse with blows to hide any suspicions outsiders may have had. However, Héloïse saw the *Historia* and responded to Abélard. Her correspondence to Abélard consists of three letters. In the first, she asks Abélard to write to her as he did when they were lovers; she recalls the many songs he wrote that made her name familiar to everyone. In her second letter, she takes upon herself full responsibility for what happened to Abelard. She admits also that she cannot forget the pleasures of love that are still vibrant in her mind even at times when she should be focused on a religious service. She thinks of their

lovemaking during the day. In her third letter, she asks Abélard to teach her about the origins of her nuns' order and to write rules for it. Her letters seem to follow a pattern in which she attempts to gauge his feelings toward her—going as far as to recall a surreptitious instance of lovemaking in a dark corner of her convent's refectory; and upon Abélard's lack of like response, she then seems to decide to limit the dialogue overwhelmingly to church matters. Héloïse's openness and explicitness make her the more vibrant character. Unfortunately, the letters that Abélard and Héloïse wrote in the early part of their relationship have not survived, and what is available of the songs written by Abélard—while recalling the precepts of courtly love—are not sufficient to confirm a discourse that in the *Historia calamitatum* is only marginally erotic.

Theological Writings

These writings include *Sic et non,* a series of excerpts arranged in favor of or against theological opinions; *Tractatus de unitate et trinitate divina* (condemned at the Council of Sens); *Introductio in theologia;* and *Dialogus inter philosophum, judaeum, et christianum.*

Philosophical Writings

Abelard's major philosophical writings are *Dialectica,* a logical treatise in four books; *Liber divisionum et definitionum*; and a moral treatise, *Scito Teipsum, seu ethica.*

CLAUDE J. FOUILLADE

Selected Works

The Letters of Abelard and Heloise. Translated and edited by Betty Radice and M.T. Clanchy. New York: Penguin Classics, 2003.

Clanchy, M.T. *Abelard: A Medieval Life.* Oxford and Malden, Mass: Blackwell, 1997.

The Cambridge Companion to Abelard. Edited by Jeffrey E. Brower and Kevin Guilford. Cambridge: Cambridge UP, 2004.

Ericson, Donald E. *Abelard and Heloise: Their Lives, Their Love, Their Letters.* New York: Bennett-Edwards, c .1990.

Gilson, Etienne. *Heloise and Abelard.* Ann Arbor: University of Michigan Press, 1968.

Marenbon, John. *The Philosophy of Peter Abelard.* Cambridge: Cambridge UP, 1997.

Pernoud, Regine. *Héloïse et Abélard.* London: Collins, 1973.

ABU NUWAS, AL-HASAN

c. 747–815
Arab poet

Abu Nuwas is not only one of the most important writers in Arabic literature, but also a major figure in the history of Arabic-language erotic writing. Part of a great flowering of culture in the early Abbasid period (749–945), Abu Nuwas used and built on traditional poetic forms to create an extraordinarily elegant, allusive, and vivid body of poetry. The forthright eroticism of Abu Nuwas's poems, with their frank celebration of the drinking of wine and the love of young men, captured the imaginations of much of the pleasure-loving elites of Baghdad, including the Abbasid caliph, al-Amin. Because they dealt with pleasures forbidden to strict Muslims, Abu Nuwas's poems shocked and scandalized the devout, who considered the works blasphemous. Abu Nuwas knew his Qur'an and other religious literature, though, and interwove religious allusions throughout his writings, as if to confound his critics. His writings also contain much that is self-mocking, morose, and even repentant, as if to show the range of experiences through which pursuit of pleasure can take a person.

The different accounts of Abu Nuwas's death show something of his reputation in life: He is variously described as dying in prison (incarcerated for a blasphemous poem), in the home of a tavern keeper, and in the house of a notable Shi'ite family that later assisted in the collection of his poems. Abu Nuwas enjoyed a considerable afterlife as a character in Arabic popular literature, most notably in the *Thousand and One Nights,* where he frequently appears as a court jester to Harun al-Rashid. But it was as an author of erotic verse that he was primarily remembered. Alternately held up and reviled by later writers as the poet par excellence of homoerotic desire in Arabic, Abu Nuwas's poems were widely cited and quoted long after his death. He inspired later writers of erotic poetry in Arabic, the popularity of his work fluctuating both with changing poetic fashions and with changing sexual mores. Abu Nuwas's erotic writings are currently enjoying a revival of interest among modern readers.

The *Diwan* of Abu Nuwas

Abu Nuwas's poetry is known primarily from a posthumous compilation known as the *Diwan.* The most reliable versions of the *Diwan* were compiled by al-Suli and Hamza al-Isbahani; the latter is the most extensive collection, containing almost 1,500 poems. The *Diwan* covers a wide variety of subjects, including hunting, panegyrics, lamentations, and satires—but the two major categories for which Abu Nuwas is best known can be classed as erotic: the love poems and the wine poems. Indeed, the categories often overlap, for wine and love are most often mixed in Abu Nuwas's poetry: Wine is shown as an aid to seduction, and the young men who bring the wine are quite often the objects of sexual advances (not always successful). This juxtaposition has the effect also of bringing together two forbidden pleasures into one situation. Although much of Abu Nuwas's erotic verse is addressed to young men, there are also a number of erotic poems in the *Diwan* addressed to women, which may have been even more shocking to Abu Nuwas's contemporaries. Wine itself in the poems is often personified as a woman, although in this capacity she acts more often than not simply as a facilitator of sexual activity between men; female musicians function in similar roles in the poems. Abu Nuwas's work is forthright and even self-deprecating about the hazards of both wine and seduction, and his accounts of rejection and the aftereffects of too much drinking are given with wry humor.

Typically, Abu Nuwas's erotic poems are narratives; the beginning of the poem often sets up a situation in which a narrator will encounter a handsome youth. The narrator brings the reader into this situation—in effect we sit next to him at a drinking party; for example, seeing what he sees as he admires the young man serving the wine, the youth's beauties being described at great length. This is often followed by an account of the seduction of the young man, sometimes with a considerable contrast in tone: In some poems the narrator goes from gentle admiration to clearly forcing himself on a young man of inferior status or strength, while there is sometimes outright payment for sexual favors. Such poems sometimes conclude on a note of regret—at the hangover of the following morning or the narrator's sexual impetuosity. Shorter poems in the *Diwan* are often less narratives than homages to desirable young men, enumerating their beauties and good qualities and planning how to win their favors. Each of the poems is unique, however, and fitting them too closely into a pattern detracts from the author's considerable inventiveness.

Abu Nuwas's language in his erotic poems is often veiled and allusive: the desired young men are described as fawns or gazelles, and sexual activity is frequently described metaphorically rather than explicitly. In one account of the seduction of a cupbearer, the narrator uses the metaphors of a military campaign to describe his sexual conquest—the young man is hit by a battering ram and fixed with a spear, and concedes the narrator's victory over him, but then asks for restitution. Yet Abu Nuwas is also sometimes quite frank in his descriptions of sexual activity between men, and these explicit accounts scandalized his more prudish contemporaries.

Abu Nuwas's poetic seductions were often unsuccessful or inconclusive; indeed, unachieved desire seems to spur on his poetic efforts. So, in a poem to a Christian cupbearer—many of Abu Nuwas's cupbearers are Christians, since they have no religious restrictions on the serving of wine—the speaker wants to be the young man's priest, his Bible, his eucharist, and the bubbles in his sacramental wine in order to get closer to him. Throughout his entire body of work, Abu Nuwas is concerned with style and effect; at its best, his poetry is highly evocative of moods, emotions, and passions, and nowhere is this more evident than in his erotic verse.

Biography

Abu Nuwas was born Hani' al-Hakami in al-Ahwaz (in the Iranian province of Khuzistan) between 747 and 762. His early education was in Basra, then later in Kufa. He studied poetry first with the poet Waliba b. al-Hubab (who may have also been his first lover), and later with the poet Khalaf al-Ahmar; he also studied Qur'an and *hadith*, as well as grammar. He moved to Baghdad, initially failed to get caliphal support, and was briefly exiled to Egypt. Eventually, he found favor with the caliph al-Amin, who was his patron and friend until Abu Nuwas's death in Baghdad between 813 and 815.

T.G. WILFONG

Selected Works

Abu Nuwas. *Diwan des Abu Nuwas*, edited by Ewald Wagner and Gregor Schoeler (4 vols.). Stuttgart: Franz Steiner Verlag, 1958–1988.

Wormhoudt, Arthur. *The Diwan of Abu Nuwas al Hasan ibn Hani al Hakami.* Oskaloosa, Iowa: William Penn College, 1974.

Bey, Hakim. *O Tribe that Loves Boys: The Poetry of Abu Nuwas.* Utrecht: Abu Nuwas Society, 1993.

Further Reading

Kennedy, Philip F. *The Wine Song in Classical Arabic Poetry: Abu Nuwas and the Literary Tradition.* Oxford: Clarendon Press, 1997.

Montgomery, James E. "Revelry and Remorse: A Poem of Abu Nuwas," *Journal of Arabic Literature* 25 (1994): 116–134.

———. "For the Love of a Christian Boy: A Song by Abu Nuwas," *Journal of Arabic Literature* 27 (1996): 115–124.

Schoeler, G. "Banshar b. burd, Abu 'l-'Atahiya and Abu Nuwas," in *Abbasid Belles-Lettres*, edited by Julia Ashtiany et al. Cambridge: Cambridge University Press, 1990.

Wagner, Ewald. *Abu Nuwas: Eine Studie zur Arabischen Literatur der Frühen 'Abbasidenzeit.* Wiesbaden: Franz Steiner Verlag, 1965.

———. entry on Abu Nuwas in *Encyclopedia of Islam*, edited by C.E. Bosworth, E. van Donzel, B. Lewis, and Ch. Pellat (2nd ed., 11 vols.). Leiden: Brill, 1954–2001.

Wright, J.W., Jr. "Masculine Allusion and the Structure of Satire in Early 'Abbasid Poetry," in *Homoeroticism in Classical Arabic Literature*, edited by J. W. Wright, Jr., and Everett K. Rowson. New York: Columbia University Press, 1997.

ACKER, KATHY

1947–1997
American novelist

Most of Kathy Acker's novels are written in the first person in a style of an abject dis-autobiographical plagiarism. In *Kathy Goes to Haiti*, for example, she invents an "I" that is a multiplicity of individuals from her life and from literary history and then uses her own "I" to travel through shocking explorations of sex in a deliberately arousing and, at times, disgusting manner. In *The Black Tarantula*, the inverse happens. Here the narrator becomes the main character in the porn books that she is copying. In *The Adult Life of Toulouse Lautrec by Henri Toulouse Lautrec*, the narrator is male for one page, then abruptly becomes female. It is in this book that Acker plagiarizes a passage from Harold Robbins' *The Pirate*. She includes it in a section called "I Want to Be Raped Every Night. Story of a Rich Woman." Acker transforms Robbins' soft-core, nearly romantic porn and recontextualizes it through intensifying the sexuality of the language, thus revealing the hidden structures of oppression in Robbins' novel. Later she does a similar shifting of text in *Great Expectations*, where she reimagines Dickens' tale and where again her protagonist, Peter, changes sex in order to experience fucking differently. Repeatedly Acker masks her I/eye in order to push past established limitations of sex. She becomes Pier Pasolini as Romeo in order to critique a woman's loss of subjectivity for experiencing sex. By tearing away at and reconstructing her autobiographical identities, which come through reading as well as experiencing the wor(l)d directly, Acker casts into doubt the image men have constructed for women to obey. Her strippers, her whores, her mothers, her stepdaughters seek new choices and act on them. The myth of romantic love is repeatedly dismantled in order to transform the lives of her characters and her readers alike. *In Memoriam to Identity* most clearly challenges this myth. Here, as in her other works, fucking is the only way to know that you are alive.

Throughout her writing Acker explodes the Bush-era notion of family values. "DOWN WITH THE FAMILY," Acker writes in *Politics*, "THE FAMILY IS THE WORST EVIL IN THIS COUNTRY." Her characters are haunted by ruptured desires in the family. In *I Dreamt I Was a Nymphomaniac Imagining*, the narrator recounts a "repulsively hetero" dream four times. While going crazy restraining herself, she seeks always to "do something wilder." She moves rapidly from one intense sex scene to another. In one she is fucking her sister when her sister's boyfriend walks in and tells them to do it in the bedroom, out of sight. Mothers reject daughters, fathers abandon daughters, and stepfathers attempt to rape.

But Acker never denies her characters' desires. She does not simplify the dynamics of desires, and her adolescent female characters have as much desire as the older men who seem to be only using these adolescents. Such a violent dynamic is most clearly created in *Blood and Guts in High School*. In the opening scene Janey begs her father not to leave her for another woman. Through the rest of the book, Janey battles other institutions that deny her access to power. *Don Quixote* begins with an abortion, a loss of body and self, but also a renaming of old myths and a staking claim to other desires. The misogyny of male texts is silenced from the outset, and Kathy, the narrator, embarks on a series of sexual escapades that eventually brings her to a feminine poetics of image and language. In this book, Acker literally fucks the writing of the past that had denied her a point of entry.

In her later works, Acker's main intention is to destroy the Great Tradition of the literary past. She does so in order to make other means of travel possible. *In Memoriam to Identity, Empire of the Senseless,* and *Pussy, King of Pirates* all wander across strange nomadic territories that cannot contain desire and language. Much of this is done to escape being caged by phallologocentric languages of denial. Even as the assaults on the female body continue in these narratives, Acker makes liberation possible through a language that means something to the female characters.

Acker's narrators look directly into and through bodies of desire in ways that shock traditions of reading and invent political realities that rage against the law of genre. Her novels, thus, create trouble for traditional approaches. Feminists who want to celebrate her for calling into question patriarchy and its violence against women are disturbed by her "vulgar" language. Postmodern academics blush when referring to her obsessive use of the words "cock" and "cunt" or of her intimate descriptions of perverse sex acts. Readers outside the academy want to celebrate Acker's riot grrrl attitude, which unfortunately allows for a misrecognition of the more profound and provocative nature of Acker's novels. Still, Acker's greatest importance as a political philosopher is that her work is read in so many places. Academics write dissertations, punk bands (most importantly The Mekons and Tribe 8) collaborated with her in live and recorded performances, bands of pirate girls publish 'zines, and gender fuck-ups write in minor languages that Acker's work made possible. Acker needs to be read as our modern-day de Sade, as a philosopher of the boudoir, who has made books dangerous once again—dangerous not because this is a woman writing explicit sex in obscene language, but because her writing breaks apart the infrastructure of capitalism and patriarchy.

Biography

Kathy Acker was born in 1947 in New York City where she was tutored at a private all-girls' school. After college, Acker worked in the sex industry. Later she taught at a number of art schools. She wrote several novels, three plays, a screenplay, and many theoretical essays on culture, politics, and sexuality. Acker's writing changed dramatically in the mid-1970s when she was introduced to contemporary French critical theory (especially the philosophy of Gilles Deleuze, Julia Kristeva, and Michel Foucault). Her influences include the writing of Gertrude Stein, William S. Burroughs, Georges Bataille, Marquis de Sade, Antonin Artaud, and Jean Genet.

DOUG RICE

Selected Works

Algeria: A Series of Invocations Because Nothing Else Works. 1984
Blood and Guts in High School. 1984
Don Quixote, Which Was a Dream. 1986
Empire of the Senseless. 1988
Essential Acker: The Selected Writing of Kathy Acker. Edited by Kathy Scholder and Dennis Cooper, 2002
Eurydice in the Underworld. 1997
Great Expectations. 1982
Hannibal Lecter, My Father. 1991
Hello, I'm Erica Jong. 1982
In Memoriam to Identity. 1990
Literal Madness: Three Novels: Kathy Goes to Haiti (1978); *My Death My Life by Pier Paolo Pasolini* (1984); *Florida* (1978). 1988
My Mother, Demonology. 1993
Politics. 1972; reprinted in *Avant-Pop: Fiction for a Daydream Nation,* edited by Larry McCaffery. 1993
Portrait of an Eye: Three Novels: The Childlike Life of the Black Tarantula by the Black Tarantula (1975); *I Dreamt I Was a Nymphomaniac: Imagining* (1974); *The Adult Life of Toulouse Lautrec* (1975). 1992
Pussy, King of the Pirates. 1996
Pussycat Fever, illustrated by Diane DiMassa and Freddie Baer. 1995
Rip-off Red, Girl Detective and the Burning Bombing of America. 2002
Variety (screenplay). Film directed by Bette Gordon. 1985

Further Reading

Brennan, Karen. "The Geography of Enunciation: Hysterical Pastiche in Kathy Acker's Fiction." *Boundary 2: An International Journal of Literature and Culture* 21.2, 1994.
Brown, Terry. "Longing to Long: Kathy Acker and the Politics of Pain." *Lit: Literature Interpretation Theory* 2.3, 1991.
Curtin, Maureen F. *Skin Tropes and Identities in Woolf, Ellison, Pynchon, and Acker.* Forthcoming.
De Zwaan, Victoria. *Interpreting Radical Metaphor in the Experimental Fictions of Donald Barthelme, Thomas Pynchon, and Kathy Acker.* Lewiston, NY: Edwin Mellen Press, 2002.
Dick, Leslie. "Feminism, Writing, Postmodernism," in *From My Guy to Sci-Fi: Genre and Women's Writing in the Postmodern World.* Edited by Helen Carr. London: Pandora, 1989.
Juno, Andrea. "Interview with Kathy Acker," in *Angry Women: Re/Search #13.* San Francisco: Re/Search, 1991
"Kathy Acker Issue." *Review of Contemporary Fiction* 9.3, 1989.
Kennedy, Colleen. "Simulating Sex and Imagining Mothers." *American Literary History* 4.1, 1992.
McCaffery, Larry. "The Artists of Hell: Kathy Acker and Punk Aesthetics." In *Breaking the Sequence: Women's Experimental Fiction.* Edited by Ellen G. Friedman and Miriam Fuchs. Princeton, NJ: Princeton University Press, 1985.

———. "The Path of Abjection: An Interview with Kathy Acker." In *Some Other Frequency: Interviews with Innovative American Authors.* Philadelphia: University of Pennsylvania Press, 1996.

Peters, Greg Lewis. "Dominance and Subversion: The Horizontal Sublime and Erotic Empowerment in the Works of Kathy Acker." In *State of the Fantastic: Studies in the Theory and Practice of Fantastic Literature and Film.* Edited by Nicholas Ruddick. Westport, CT: Greenwood, 1992.

Pitchford, Nicola. *Tactical Readings: Feminist Postmodernism in the Novels of Kathy Acker and Angela Carter.* Lewisburg, PA: Bucknell University Press, 2002.

Redding, Arthur F. "Bruises, Roses: Masochism and the Writing of Kathy Acker." In *Contemporary Literature* 35.2, 1994.

Shaviro, Steven. *Doom Patrols.* New York: Serpent's Tail, 1997.

Siegel, Carol. "Postmodern Women Novelists Review Victorian Male Masochism," *Genders* 11, 1991.

Walsh, Richard. "The Quest for Love and the Writing of Female Desire in Kathy Acker's *Don Quixote.*" *Critique: Studies in Contemporary Fiction* 32.3, 1991.

ADMIRABLE DISCOURSES OF THE PLAIN GIRL

Classical Chinese sex manual
c. 1566

There is some disagreement about the translation of the Chinese title *Sunü miaolun.* It was rendered as *The Admirable Discourses of the Plain Girl* by Robert van Gulik and as *The Wondrous Discourse of Su Nü* by Douglas Wile. The text in Chinese, preserved in a unique Japanese manuscript written around 1880, is copied among the ten "secret books" in van Gulik's *Erotic Prints of the Ming Period,* where the work is described and partially translated. Ten years later, with passages discreetly translated into Latin, it was included in *Sexual Life in Ancient China.* Van Gulik had also discovered a woodblock print from the Genroku era (1592–1596) of a Japanese translation by Manase Dôson (1507–1594). The Chinese preface offers no key to who the author might be, though we know it could not have been written later than 1566. Akira Ishihara suggested that the handbook could be linked to a much earlier tradition going back to the Song period (960–1279).

Whatever the case, the *Discourse* cannot be said to be simply a patchwork of extracts from the selections of sexual classics copied into the *Ishimpô* [*Essence of Medical Prescriptions*] compiled by Tamba Yasuyori between 982 and 984. Though belonging to the same tradition of Chinese sexological thought, the handbook differs from other texts by its excess of details. Both concise and comprehensive, the work belongs to a later state of Chinese society, when Confucian ideology weighed more heavily. Whether or not readers consider it a practical treatise of sexual hygiene for the married male, it offers a wide range of wise advice for both partners. However serious the intent may have been, its use in Japan seems to have had a playful side.

Content

The text is made up of rather short questions put by the mythical Yellow Emperor to the Plain Girl, who answers at length and with irrefutable authority on how to satisfy feminine sexual urges. Altogether the volume contains nearly ten thousand characters divided into the following eight chapters, or *pian:*

1. "Basic Principles," reminding that *yin* and *yang* are present in both sexes. "Indeed! Union of man and woman pertains to the Way made of a *yin* and a *yang.* Therefore there is a *yang* within a *yin* and the reverse. *Yin* and *yang,* man and woman: So is the way of heaven and earth."

2. "Nine Postures," each related to different animals and described more fully than

in earlier books, though the eighth requires two women. The names of the postures are: (1) Dragon Flying, (2) Tiger Approaching, (3) Monkey Attacking, (4) Cicada Clinging, (5) Turtle Rising, (6) Phoenix Soaring, (7) Rabbit Licking, (8) Fishes Nibbling, (9) Cranes Entwining.

3. "Shallow and Deep (Thrusts)," in which it is advised that "one must not be too hasty nor too slow. . . . It is of critical import to avoid too deep penetration or it may injure the five viscera. If penetration reaches the "valley seed," it injures the liver and one will suffer from clouded vision, caked ears, and discomfort in the four limbs." The *valley seed* is some five inches inside, as described on the preceding page.

4. "Five Desires and Five Injuries"—*five desires* means the signs of the five stages of mounting desire in women; *five injuries,* the five untimely or faulty ways a man can injure his partner's lungs, heart, liver, kidneys, spleen; in addition are described the ten feminine movements accompanying the different stage of her arousal and complete satisfaction.

5. "The Most Important Relationship," which deals with how to maintain conjugal harmony and obtain children.

6. "Thickness and Length"—of the male organ, which is irrelevant because "deriving pleasure from intercourse is a matter of inner feeling."

7. "Nourishing Longevity," in which it is advised to beware of too frequent ejaculation; nothing is said about a battle of sexes for each partner's longevity.

8. "The Four Stages [for man] and the Nine Arrivals [for woman]," in which it is said: "If the man wishes to fathom the woman's inner feelings, he must start to excite her interest by cracking jokes and stimulate her feelings by moving hands and feet. . . . To have intercourse when the four stages have not yet been reached nor the nine arrivals achieved is sure to bring disaster."

Thus well instructed and properly prepared for sexual harmony, the Yellow Emperor ascended to Heaven at the age of one hundred twenty, "together with the Plain Girl."

Impact

It is difficult to assess the impact in China of a work that had vanished without a trace until its discovery in Japan in the mid-twentieth century. Still its tenor fits well within the trends of thought in sixteenth-century China, where the claims of "feelings" were asserted by a growing number of Confucian scholars rejecting any attempt to extinguish them. The stronger drive was love. In 1598 Tang Xianzu (1550–1616) wrote in introducing his play *The Peony Pavilion* [*Mudan ting*]: "Love is of source unknown, yet it grows ever deeper. The living may die of it, by its power the dead live again."

Though handbooks of sexual import disappeared from China, they may have left an underground tradition of practical knowledge which may surface in the future.

ANDRÉ LÉVY

Editions

Gulik, Robert van. *Erotic Colours: Prints of the Ming Period, with an Essay on Chinese Sex Life from the Han to the Ch'ing Dynasty, B.C. 206–A.D. 1644* (vol. 2), three volumes. Tokyo: Privately published, 1951.

Translations

Wile, Douglas. "The Wondrous Discourse of Su Nü." In *Art of the Bedchamber, the Chinese Sexual Yoga Classics, including Women's Solo Meditation Texts* (pp. 122–133). Albany: State University of New York Press, 1992.
Santangelo, Paolo. *Il meraviglioso discorso della Fanciulla Pura: Piccola biblioteca dell'eros.* Milan: ES Srl, 1993.
Lévy, André. *Le sublime discours de la fille candide: Manuel d'érotologie chinoise.* Arles: Phillipe Picquier, 2000.

Further Reading

Gulik, Robert van. *Sexual Life in Ancient China: A Preliminary Survey of Chinese Sex and Society from ca. 1500 B.C. till 1644 A.D.* Leiden: E. J. Brill, 1961.
Ishihara, Akira, and Levy, Howard. *The Tao of Sex: An Annotated Translation of the Twenty-eight Sections of the* Essence of Medical Prescriptions (*Ishimpô*). Tokyo and New York: Shibundo and Harper & Row, 1968.

AFRICAN LANGUAGES: ALGERIA (MAGHREB)

Different ethnicities, religions, and cultures have shaped Algeria since antiquity. This has deeply influenced the interaction between sexes, and as a consequence, writings about them. According to Rachid Boudjedra, "there are very strong pagan residues" in present-day Algeria. The polemic of eroticism versus religion is nothing new: The Berbers rebelled time after time against what they saw as sexual repression in both Christianity and Islam. After becoming a Christian and a Church father, the first world-famous Berber writer, Augustine of Hippo Regius (today Annaba), 354–430, relentlessly chastised local pagan promiscuity. His fellow Berbers mostly ignored his sermons and epistles and quickly reverted to polytheism and free love. Three centuries later, the Arab historian Ibn Khaldun recorded the continued existence of sexual freedom. In the twelfth century, Sufism, a mystical form of Islam dominated by ecstatic manifestations expressed in the physical language of trance and open to both men and women, helped shape Algerian views of the body. In the Sufi tradition, physical love is an essential component of the alliance with God, as stated by its grand master, Ibn Arabi (1165–1240) in his *Treatise on Love.*

When French colonization took up its *mission civilisatrice,* it did not apply it only to the natives. It also aimed at enforcing moral codes of conduct in poor and uneducated immigrants, which would turn Algeria into a Mediterranean mainstay of the "New France" that nineteenth-century puritanical society wanted to create. Yet the "pied noir" (Algerian immigrant) proletariat quickly delighted in the adventures of their picaresque antihero Cagayous, a character very much in the tradition of the Roman comedies decried by the Augustinian Berber church (Musette, alias Auguste Robinet). Later on, the Algerian-born Albert Camus was attacked for the pagan sensuality of his texts, and especially for the sexual narrative in his short story "The Adulterous Woman," in which a French woman escapes her hotel room and has a passionate "adulterous" encounter with the desert. During the recent bloody years of Algerian turmoil at the end of the twentieth century, several writers, such as Rachid Boudjedra and Anouar Benmalek, have chosen to pit eroticism against Islamic terrorism. As a result, Boudjedra has been facing the death sentence of a religious *fatwa* for pornography, among other accusations, since 1983.

Only in the context of this recurrent struggle between puritanical and relaxed tendencies in Algeria can one decipher the complex interplay of religious taboos and iconoclastic rebellion in contemporary literature, and in particular the use of eroticism by francophone Algerian authors. If, according to Hédi Abdel-Jaouad, sexuality is a frequently treated subject in Algerian literature, Algerian francophone writers have always struggled to find their voice between tradition and transgression. The choice of writing in French might have provided a bracketed space where one could challenge the puritanical rigidity of society.

Facing social and religious taboos, narratives about the body have changed over time, passing from self-censorship to overt rebellion. Several trends stand out: Authors who started their literary careers before the beginning of the war for independence, such as Mouloud Ferraoun, Mouloud Mammeri, Mohamed Dib, and Kateb Yacine, denounced the oppression of Algerian society by French colonization, but also the sexual divorce between genders and the dreadful consequences of sexual repression enforced by Algerian families themselves. Sex in the narrative works of this first period often has two faces: light and darkness. Dark themes of rape—of the country/sexual rape/incest/arranged marriages treated as "legal rapes"— are counterbalanced by luminous, poetic descriptions of female beauty. For Mohamed Dib and Kateb Yacine, the female body is the center of sensuality and beauty, as well as a metaphor for the new country to come. Eroticism is an antidote for national and sexual repression. At that point in Algerian francophone literature, female characters were rarely in charge of their own sexuality, as they are in Mouloud Ferraoun's and Malek Haddad's novels. The pagan Berber heritage is represented in this generation by Jean Sénac, a gay poet who fought for Algerian independence and wrote lyrical poetic paeans to sexual freedom.

Writers who started their careers during the war of liberation, such as Assia Djebar and Mourad Bourboune, represent a more heterogeneous group of writers. Djebar also counterposes the dark side of rape (colonization and "legal rape") to a luminous one, represented by eroticism as both a union and a voyage. Her female characters often transgress taboos of traditional marital and sexual relations. Mourad Bourboune represents the pagan sensuality in this generation; in his *Pagan Pilgrimage* he evokes his personal version of Genesis: In the beginning was the body and God is the creation of man.

Algerian independence was marked by a strong desire for the relaxing of traditional codes of conduct. Writers who started their careers in the aftermath of independence, such as Nabile Fares, Rabah Belamri, Rachid Mimouni, Rachid Boudjedra, and Tahar Djaout, have chosen to continue the fight for freedom in the individual realm. Like Djebar, Fares describes eroticism as a complete union and a voyage. He also openly denounces the hegemony of religious morals in a society still permeated by paganism. Belamri shows desire as transcendence. Mimouni condemns Algerian society for the damage done to love and sex by the rapid return to a puritanical order. Boudjedra claims the heritage of heresy and eroticism in pre-Islamic poetry, and opts for iconoclastic

and paroxystic transgression of social and sexual codes. In his novels, sex is often treated as vengeance against the tyranny of patriarchal fathers and of religion. Djaout was assassinated for relentlessly using his pen to fight for freedom.

More recently, female novelists, such as Zoulika Boukortt, Nina Bouraoui, Aïcha Lemsine, Leïla Marouane, Yamina Mechakra, and Leïla Sebbar, have written, often with lyric exuberance, about female innermost feelings and desire. For many of them, writing and eroticism are intertwined. Franco-Algerian writer Nina Bouraoui, born five years after independence, who has written about her own homosexuality, seems to sum up the fascination for eroticism found in francophone Algerian writing when she notes that "words make love on the page."

BERNADETTE GINESTET

Further Reading

Bouhdiba, Abdelwahab. *La Sexualité en Islam*. Paris: PUF, 1982.

Chebel, Malek. *Le Corps dans la tradition du Maghreb*. Paris: PUF, 1984.

———, *Le Corps en Islam*. Paris: PUF, 1999.

Corbin, Henry. *L'Imagination créatrice dans le soufisme d'Ibn Arabi* (1958). Paris: Flammarion, 1993.

Dressel, Annette. *Ecriture et espace dans l'univers de Nabile Fares*. DNR Paris 13 (Charles Bonn), 1989.

Gafaiti, Hafid. *Rachid Boudjedra ou la passion de la modernité*. Paris: Denöel, 1987.

Kheridi, Rym. *Ecriture de l'impuissance*. DEA Lyon 2 (Charles Bonne), 1993.

Pelletier, Renée. *Femmes d'Islam ou le sexe interdit*. Paris: Denoël/Gonthier, 1980.

Sardier, Anne-Marie. *La Femme et son corps dans l'oeuvre d'Assia Djebar*. D# Paris 13 (Jacqueline Arnaud), 1985.

Sedgwick, Mark J. *Sufism: The Essentials*. Cairo: American University in Cairo Press, 2001.

Soukehal, Rabah. *Le Roman algérien de langue francaise*. Paris: Publisud, 2003.

Tosso-Rodinis, Giuliana. *Fêtes et défaites d'Eros dans l'oeuvre de Rachid Boudjedra*. Paris: L'Harmattan, 1994.

AFRICAN LANGUAGES: TUNISIA (MAGHREB)

Eroticism in Tunisian literature—indeed, in Maghrebian literature in general—can be traced back to Mouhammad al-Nafzâwî in the fifteenth century, around the time of the Tunisian founder of modern sociology, Ibn Khaldun (b. 1332) and of Chaucer in England. Al-Nafzâwî's work is entitled *La Prairie parfumée où s'ébattent les plaisirs* [*The Perfumed Garden*], composed between 1410 and 1434. A Berber from the south, around Tozeur, al-Nafzâwî lived and composed his work in Tunis, at the request or command of the vizier of the sultan of Tunis. A work of erotology, when it reached Europe in the nineteenth century, it was characterized as pornographic. For the Arabs, on the other hand, as Khawan writes, erotology was viewed as a science, *'ilm al-bâh* (40). They were, in fact, practicing a form of psychoanalysis.

La Prairie parfumée offers its readers a kind of earthly Paradise where the reader's pleasure and imagination are given free rein, as defined by the Arabic word *al-khâtir* (45). Body and soul act in harmony. Khawan insists on the distinction between eroticism and pornography, which is its exact opposite, since the former is above all rupture and disharmony (45). Al-Nafzâwî stresses the physical harmony between man and woman, adding a "thousand and one" medical hints (46–7). The work stresses the pleasure of the woman, who will feel naturally drawn to the sexual act, to coitus. Al-Nafzâwî's style is poetic, and by that very fact, pure. Khawan calls the text a "fine-cut jewel" (*joyau finement ciselé*) (49). Sexuality becomes an art, a "poetic transfiguration" leading to wonder (48).

In his seminal work, *L'Amour et l'Occident* [Love in the Western World]. Denis de Rougemont contrasts Eastern and Western attitudes toward love and sexuality. Although by "East" he specifies the Far East, many readers apply his theories to the Middle East and North Africa as well. In the East, he writes, "human love has usually been regarded as mere pleasure and

physical enjoyment" (63). In the West, on the other hand (as the result of a perversion of Christianity), the courtly, or romantic, love tradition has dominated the imagination since the Middle Ages, which was the time of al-Nafzâwî in the Maghreb. For the Westerner, romantic love/passion is exclusive of marriage. It demands total consummation, or fusion, which can occur only through death (e.g., Tristan and Isolde, Romeo and Juliet, Cathy and Heathcliff). De Rougemont advocates Christian love, or agape, which indicates an equal partnership, as opposed to eros, or passion.

Henry de Montherlant's antihero, Costals, in *Les Lépreuses*, in part 4 of *Les Jeunes filles,* embroiders on the East-West antithesis. He claims that the history of Judeo-Christian civilization is "that of efforts made by woman so that man be diminished and suffer, so that he becomes her equal" (237). The Orient, on the other hand, bases its view of women on biological realities that are deemed to make them subservient to masculine wisdom: "In the Occident, dominated by women, the cult of suffering. In the Orient, where man is the master, the cult of wisdom" (237). The Occidental male thus sees the Oriental notions of sexual *plaisir* and *jouissance* as based on female inferiority—a view not borne out by the works of al-Nafzâwî or of contemporary Tunisian writers like Abdelwahab Meddeb and Hédi Bouraoui.

In 1986 Meddeb's *Phantasia* offered a striking example of eroticism in Tunisian fiction. The Maghrebian protagonist/narrator, seeking his identity in Paris, the former colonizer, embarks on a quest for the ideal woman, embodied in one Aya. A prolonged, detailed ten-page description elaborates on the consummation of their love. Tahar ben Jelloun notes that for the narrator, total love and death are inextricably intertwined: "a violent eroticism linked to bodily agony, as Georges Bataille has said of eroticism" (*Le Monde*, September 12, 1986)—and as de

Rougemont has written of the love-death theme in the Occident.

Meddeb's description attempts to blur the line between sexuality and poetry. The lovemaking is Dionysiac, drawing on the wine forbidden to a strict Muslim. The narrator enumerates Aya's erogenous zones as if he were writing a poem on a body-text. Amidst all the sexual acrobatics, at times readers feel as they were reading Henry Miller, without the sense of humor. But the detailed description is supposed to result in the reader's pleasure. Meddeb dedicates this scene to Ibn Arabi, who saw coitus as "a spiritual realization embodied by the most accomplished of prophets, Mohammed" (181).

A postmodernist variation on the theme of eroticism appears in the novels of the Tunisian Hédi Bouraoui, who makes his home in Canada and has experienced and absorbed the cultures of three continents. *La Pharaone* is a quest for origins, Egypt being in many ways the cradle of Western civilization. A modern Maghrebian scholar, Barka Bousiris, visits Egypt in search of—he knows not what. Obsessed with the female pharaoh Hatchepsut, who succeeded her husband, took upon herself male attributes, and has been called the Queen Who Would Be King, Barka fulfills his own destiny. He is more and more drawn to the ancient world, to the dismay of his former lover, the Occidental Francine from France. Finally, he is apparently crushed under a statue of Hatchepsut, but the body disappears. Then, the pharaone takes over the narrative when her tablets, her "scriberies" in hieroglyphics, are discovered in Barka's hotel room after his death (236). The tablets introduce the thematic word *amourir* and the love-death motif which dominates the text. Francine begins to identify with her ancient rival and to recognize that Barka and Hatchepsut have achieved total fusion, through death and throughout eternity (229).

Barka may be the reincarnation of the scribe Kabar, who was Hatchepsut's love but whom she could not marry because he was a commoner. She created the values of Western civilization, before Akhnaten, before the Greeks and Romans. This same "goddess" of humanism nonetheless fell madly in love with her scribe, "the other half of her being" (244). But all too human, she succumbs to sexual jealousy, without real foundation, and orders Kabar killed, only to repent immediately and to await death

anxiously in order to rejoin Kabar. There are no sexual acrobatics here, but an eroticism contingent on memory and creativity. Hatchepsut, whose motto, "Make love, not war" (242), anticipates modern times, dreams of having Kabar return to earth, presumably as Barka, unconscious of his fate, to be reunited with her in love-death (*amourir*).

But the most explicitly erotic scene in the novel is that describing the wedding night of Ayman, the Copt, and Imane, the Muslim, who seems to be a latter-day Hatchepsut. Her defloration is presented poetically, metaphorically: "Penetration dissolves anguish verging on immortality, a pearl of blood in glorious pyrotechnics" (170). These two represent the future on earth, not an otherworldly fusion. As Francine points out, Barka led them all to the past in order to prepare the future (239).

In *La Femme d'entre les lignes,* it becomes very clear that coitus is being used as a metaphor for poetry. *Amourir* becomes *migramour* in the later novel. The wandering narrator, Tunisian in origin, a latter-day Ulysses, has attracted a reader, the Italian journalist Lisa, sight unseen. Finally they meet when he attends a conference in Rome. He imagines Lisa slipping between the sheets, and there is an embedded pun on *entre les lignes* and *entre les draps* [between the lines/ between the sheets]. The metaphor becomes explicit when the protagonist senses that Lisa slips between the sheets "pour bien être dans tes pages" [to be in your pages] (22). They find pleasure "between the lines," in the euphoria of blanks (62). As in the *nouveau roman*, the reader does not know if the whole love affair is real or a phantasm, for the body always blends into the "body-text" (64). Lisa disappears finally, in reaction to the narrator, who has tried to create her in his own image (84), and is transformed into Palimpseste (on whom much has been written). But not only does Palimpseste supplant Lisa, she turns the tables on the narrator, causing him to metamorphose into his own fictional personage, Virebaroud. *La Femme d'entre les lignes* is a love story, but the erotic charge is between writer and reader, personified by the protagonists but reflecting the author and ourselves as readers.

In the next novel, *Sept portes pour une brûlance,* which is probably the most erotic of them all, the female protagonist once again, like Palimpseste, turns the tables by narrating her own tale of passion for a man whom we never see and who never answers her letters. The tale takes the form of poetry found when an outside narrator (who is Tunisian) is presented with a bag of letters, unsigned, undated, chaotic, fragmented, but burning, unified by ardor and lyricism. The heroine expresses herself unrestrainedly, in a language both erotic and poetic, with frequent references to the biblical, Solomonic Song of Songs. The physical sex act is described viscerally in direct, simple language, without shame or rational control. The very anonymity and dislocation of the text makes it into a love story stripped to essences and generalized. The letters could have been addressed to any man by any woman. Therefore, the tale could have been lived by all of us, the readers, male and female alike (16).

From the Middle Ages to postmodernism, Tunisian writers have challenged stereotypes about the male/female dynamic in the Maghreb, have shown empathy with the female point of view—it is no accident that Tunisia has a long history of support for women's issues—and have moved comfortably from the realistically erotic to the poetic and metaphorical.

ELIZABETH SABISTON

Further Reading

Al-Nafzâwî, Mouhammad. *La Prairie parfumée où s'ébattent les plaisirs,* translated by René R. Khawan. Paris: Phébus, 1976.

Bouraoui, Hédi. *La Femme d'entre les lignes.* Toronto: Éditions du Gref, 2002.

———. *La Pharaone.* Tunis: Éditions L'Or du Temps, 1998.

———. *Sept portes pour une brûlance.* Ottawa: Vermillon, 2005.

Meddeb, Abdelwahab. *Phantasia.* Paris: Sindbad, 1986.

Montherlant, Henry de. *Les jeunes filles: Les lépreuses.* Paris: Gallimard, 1939.

Rougemont, Denis de. *Love in the Western World* [*L'Amour et l'Occident*]. New York: Doubleday, 1956 (orig. publ. 1939; translated 1940).

AGUSTINI, DELMIRA

1866–1914
Uruguayan poet

Los cálices vacíos

An anomaly within Spanish-American letters and often misunderstood, Delmira Agustini's lyric poetry has nevertheless become canonical in Spanish. In universities her erotic poems are taught, and in editions and reviews they are praised by the critics. But her nonerotic works are separated from the erotic ones and only the former are taught in the schools. Some titles of her erotic poetry make plain the decadent themes and aesthetic imagery of her eroticism: "Amor" [Love], "El intruso" [The Intruder], "El vampiro" [The Vampire], "La serpentina" [Serpentine], "Fiera de amor" [Beast of Love, my own translation], "Mis amores" [My Loves], and "Rebelión" [Rebellion]. Agustini's less well known erotic poems include her prayer to Blind Father Eros, "Plegaria" [Entreaty]; "A Eros" [To Eros]; "Boca a boca" [Mouth to Mouth]; and her series called the "El rosario de Eros" [The Rosary of Eros]. Despite her inclusion in the school curriculum and her wide name recognition in Spanish-American literary circles, Delmira Agustini has only recently been analyzed seriously and at length. These new in-depth studies have concluded that her uniqueness consists of a consistently female, sometimes gender-bending, perspective on heterosexual love.

The poems' erotic subject matter (and occasionally, their complexity) contributed to the greatness of the Uruguayan's legacy, but undoubtedly also to the paucity of translations and interpretations. An additional obstruction to Agustini's renown has been her place within Latin American literary history. Like other women writers from near her time, such as

13

Alfonsina Storni, Juana de Ibarbourou, and Gabriela Mistral, Agustini expresses more social concerns and employs greater simplicity of language than had been typical in Spanish-American *modernismo*, an international poetic style similar to French symbolism. Yet her poetry did not differ radically enough from *modernismo* in style and subject matter for it to be called *vanguardista* [avant-garde], in the manner of one of the series of splinter movements that followed *modernismo*. Hence Agustini has been deemed a *posmodernista*, an unhappy term that does not recognize her or her group's special qualities or innovations. In contrast to these difficulties for the studious, her late-modernist phraseology and decadent, even Gothic, imagery early attracted a steadily increasing international attention. Some evidence of this growing popularity transcending Spanish is that a volume of her verse has recently become available in English for the first time (2003, Southern Illinois University Press).

Agustini's eroticism—emanating from the strengths of a physically enjoyed, female body—appears alongside countervailing forces of feminine weakness, both in her life and in her poetry. Born among Montevideo's moneyed elite, she managed to have both a bohemian intellectual life, where the erotic was seen as fashionable, and a life constrained by chaperones and other sexist strategies of traditional bourgeois society. Doted on by her parents—who arguably overprotected their gifted daughter—the poet wrote scandalous verses they loved. Agustini's lyric was unceasingly promoted by her father, who, evidence suggests, wanted his daughter to conform to the standards of her day by going to her wedding day a virgin. Her parallel, radical life of the mind presented difficulties to her after she left her parents' home and married. After only one month of marriage, the young Delmira returned to her parents' home, decrying her new groom's "vulgarity." Family connections arranged for her one of the first legal divorces in Uruguay. However, she continued to see her ex-husband sporadically, unbeknownst to her family, apparently for sex. During one of these clandestine meetings, her ex-spouse shot and killed her and then himself. Accounts of the circumstances of her death at age 28 were published in newspapers, sometimes with the picture of her bleeding body, all over the continent.

More than a half century of poor editions, including an "official edition" published by the Uruguayan government that had to be recalled due to its numerous errors, has also inhibited the study of Delmira Agustini's erotic poems. In 1993 Magdalena García Pinto's Cátedra edition of the *Poesías completas*, appeared the first edition truly worthy of the adjective "complete." It includes an introduction which painstakingly traces the brutal history of the production and reception of her lyric, from the murder that ended her creative activity and prevented the author's own re-editing of her works, to the metaphorically violent, patriarchal discourse that continues to deny that she could have known what she was doing. The editor reminds readers how some historians of literature have insisted that Agustini was some sort of idiot savant who wrote intuitively and beyond her own capabilities. García Pinto's fine republishing of the originals and her feminist perspective signal that perhaps the disarray of the author's manuscripts, the neglect by interpreters and translators, and even the masculinist prejudice of some scholars may finally be coming to an end. In 1999 Alejandro Cáceres published an even more thoroughly edited critical edition within Uruguay (Editorial de la Plaza) that has had limited distribution. In 2003 Cáceres published the above-mentioned English translation. Although prior to the 1990s several book-length studies had been devoted to her life and works, this number has doubled within the last ten years and seems to be only increasing.

Regarding the meaning of her erotic poems, opinions diverge. One critic, writing in an underground newspaper in Montevideo, exemplified the stance of most outside and many inside Uruguay: that Agustini's poetry espouses a radical sexual liberation. On the other hand, traditional and conservative readers in Uruguay suggest that Agustini was writing about the soul's ecstasy in God rather than the body's pleasures. Her Catholic and religious imagery (in poems like "Plegaria" or those in the "El rosario de Eros" series) feeds both sides of the debate. It is clear to most readers, however, that Agustini's spiritual themes do not overwhelm the erotic in her poems and that the often contrasted elements feed one another. Her poetry may thematize corporeal sexuality more than spiritual love, but it is characterized by the mixing of the two. Scholars whose writings contain examples of measured evaluation, such as Sylvia Molloy and Angel Rama, have recognized Agustini's alternation of the pose of sexual assertiveness with that of a shrinking violet as one of the "tretas del débil," that is, a strategy of resistance used by those with little else to combat the power that others wield over them. While a strict Manichaean interpretation of her physicality and spirituality and of her passion and restraint satisfies few, the gaps, contradictions, oppositions, and paradoxes that appear when one examines Agustini's eroticism encourage tentative pronouncements on its overall nature.

To evaluate Agustini's importance as an erotic poet, it has always been necessary to pay attention to her life—true even for critics whose theoretical apparatus aims to be strictly formal and textual. Despite recent progress in critical analysis, it is still generally true that the best evidence for Agustini's popularity in Uruguay, and therefore evidence for how she has been read, can be found in the fascination with her life, in large part because her books were unavailable or only partially extant. It is paradoxical that the popular tendency to know details of Agustini's biography but few of her poems, while unfortunate in nearly every other way, has privileged Agustini as a subject for feminists. For instance, Molloy and Rama, each in distinct ways, speak of Agustini's need to produce performances of extreme behaviors in her writings because she was an intelligent woman taught to obey the constraints placed on wealthy women in Montevideo at the beginning of the twentieth century. A fiery expression of rebellion in one poem becomes a decadent obsequiousness in another. Here is the first stanza of "Otra estirpe" [Another Lineage], slightly modified from Cáceres' translation:

Eros, quiero guiarte, Padre ciego . . .
Pido a tus manos todopoderosas,
Su cuerpo excelso derramado en fuego
Sobre mi cuerpo desmayado en rosas!

[Eros, I want to guide you, blind Father . . .
From your almighty hand I ask for
His sublime body {spilling over with} fire
Upon my body faint in roses!]

The poetic voice's extraordinary strength of resolution at one moment is betrayed by her body. The voice first presumes to have the particular knowledge and control to guide the god of love, but then it falls weak at the moment her body is covered by her lover's.

Agustini's eroticism expresses an idealism and an antibourgeois morality, tinged with overtones of social criticism. Her female voice replays myths and literary topoi from the woman's point of view. She is the swan who rapes like Zeus and yet is female; she is the swan poet of the Decadents, but clearly a female esthete. Furthermore, her poems tell of accessing special, spiritual, and esoteric knowledge through the physicality of her female body. Her language partakes of a poetic vocabulary also rich in sonority, allusion, and rhyme; at the same time, she leads her generation with free verse. The poet's eroticism imbues her voice with a singular tone and spirit because its strength is always female, and what she might have called her "superiority of spirit" never imitates the masculine so much as it seems uniquely inspired by the experience of repression and oppression as a woman. The female voice is not feminist for having comprehended the struggles of other women and men to live in freedom or with justice—we do not know the extent to which she did understand the suffering of others—but she did claim the rights of pleasure and desire for women. This accomplishment alone makes her oeuvre worthy of greater recognition.

Biography

Delmira Agustini was born in Montevideo, Uruguay, in 1886. She published her first book of poems, *El libro blanco (frágil)*, in 1907. She died in 1914, at the age of 28, shot in the head by her husband of two months. They were in the process of divorce.

DIANE E. MARTING

Selected Works

El libro blanco (frágil). Montevideo: O.M. Bertani, 1907.
Cantos de la mañana. Montevideo: O.M. Bertani, 1910.
Los cálices vacíos (poesías). Montevideo: O.M. Bertani, 1913.
El rosario de Eros. Vol. I, *Obras completas de Delmira Agustini*. Montevideo: Máximo García, 1924.
Los astros del abismo. Vol. II, *Obras completas de Delmira Agustini*. Montevideo: Máximo García, 1924.

ALAS, LEOPOLDO

Cáceres, Alejandro, ed. *Delmira Agustini: Poesías completas*. Montevideo: Editorial de la Plaza, 1999.
———. ed. and trans., *Selected Poetry of Delmira Agustini: Poetics of Eros*. Southern Illinois University Press, 2003.
García Pinto, Magdalena, ed. *Poesías completas*. Madrid: Cátedra, 1993.

References and Further Reading

Benvenuto, Ofelia Machado de. *Delmira Agustini*. Montevideo: Ministerio de Instrucción Publica, 1944.
Escaja, Tina (compiler). *Delmira Agustini y el modernismo: nuevas propuestas de género*. Rosario, Argentina: Beatriz Viterbo, 2000.
———. *Salomé decapitada: Delmira Agustini y la literatura finisecular de la fragmentación*. New York: Rodopi, 2002.
Kirkpatrick, Gwen. "The Limits of Modernismo: Delmira Agustini y Julio Herrera y Reissig," *Romance Quarterly* 36.3 (1989): 307–314.
López Jiménez, Yvette. "Delmira Agustini (1886–1914), Uruguay," translated by Dwight García. In *Spanish American Women Writers: A Bio-Bibliographical Source Book* (pp. 1–8), edited by Diane E. Marting. New York: Greenwood, 1990.
Marting, Diane E., ed. *Women Writers of Spanish America: An Annotated Bio-Bibliographical Guide*. Bibliographies and Indexes in Women's Studies 5. New York: Greenwood, 1987.
Molloy, Sylvia. "Dos lecturas del cisne: Rubén Darío y Delmira Agustini." In *La sartén por el mango: encuentro de escritoras latinoamericanas* (pp. 57–69), edited by Patricia Elena González and Eliana Ortega. Río Piedras, Puerto Rico: Ediciones Huracán, 1984.
Rodríguez Monegal, Emir. *Sexo y poesia en el 900 uruguayo*. Montevideo: Editorial Alfa, 1969.
Silva, Clara, *Genio y figura de Delmira Agustini*. Buenos Aires: Editorial Universitaria de Buenos Aires, 1968.
———. *Pasión y gloria de Delmira Agustini*. Buenos Aires: Losada, 1972.
Stephens, Doris T. *Delmira Agustini and the Quest for Transcendence*. Montevideo: Editorial Géminis, 1975.
Varas, Patricia. "Lo erótico y la liberación del ser femenino en la poesía de Delmira Agustini," *Hispanic Journal* 15 (Spring 1994): 165–184.
Vidal, Jorge Media, et al. *Delmira Agustini, seis ensayos críticos*. Montevideo: Editorial Ciencias, 1982.

ALAS, LEOPOLDO

1852–1901
Spanish novelist and short story writer

La regenta

La regenta [*The Judge's or Magistrate's Wife*] is the principal novel by Leopoldo Alas (also known as "Clarín"), himself one of the major authors and critics of late-nineteenth-century Spanish prose. Ana Ozores, the *regenta* of the title, is a desperately bored and sexually frustrated married woman living in Vetusta (a fictional re-creation of Oviedo in the Spanish province of Asturias). Ana becomes the subject of adulterous desires on the part of her confessor, Fermín de Pas, a high-ranking priest, and the local Don Juan, Alvaro Mesía. Mesía proposes to seduce Ana; the designs of de Pas are less clear but are certainly sexual in intent. At the end of the novel, Mesía succeeds in his plans and de Pas finds out and subsequently spurns Ana when she returns to him for confession.

Although the motivation for the plot lies in the possibility of adulterous sex, the culminating seduction actually occurs "offstage" between chapters Twenty-Eight and Twenty-Nine. This structure offers the reader a sense of elongated foreplay before the sexual event itself that mirrors the general sense of eroticism, which in turn forms a backdrop for the novel's main action. Vetustan high society shows for the most part a prurient interest in the sexual lives of its members, including the three main characters, and treats the seduction of Ana as a spectator sport. The eroticism of the Vetustans is unhealthy and jaded, as characters continually seek sexual novelty—Mesía himself pursues Ana as a sop to his sated but fading sexual prowess. As Noël Valis has observed, Alas draws strong parallels between lust and greed: Banquets and dinners are occasions for flirting and the parade of lascivious desires, as with, for example, the meal held in honor of the atheist don Pompeyo Guimarán, where Mesía holds forth on his past seductions while his male audience listens greedily. Ana's friend Visitación's sticky habit of munching on sweets comes to reflect the high level of salivation that occurs when confronted with either food or sex—as also with Ana's aunts, who fatten her up while drooling over her sexual potential. The dinners held by Vegallana and his wife provide further opportunities for erotic romping and games, flirting and touching.

In this unhealthily prurient society, Ana, as the pure (in fact, virginal) wife with religious leanings, acts throughout as the focus for vicarious eroticism and voyeurism. Many of the characters look to Ana as a means of fulfilling vicarious sexual desires. This attitude toward her obtains from her very birth, the result of a love match between her father, a gentleman, and her mother, a seamstress—Vetustan society frequently equates the profession of seamstress with that of a dancer, and thus by implication a kept woman or prostitute. Ana's very origins are thus tainted with sexuality, and the taint persists during her childhood: An early and innocent incident when she runs away with a young boy, Germán, is perverted by her elders into a sign of precocious sexuality, as emphasized by her governess Camila and her lover, who looks forward to enjoying the benefits of Ana's developing sexuality. Ana's aunts not only salivate over her but act as procuresses, displaying Ana in the hope of making her a good marriage but in the process laying her open to the lascivious commentaries of others. Ana also becomes the object of voyeurism not only for the reader but for the Vetustans when she walks barefoot before everyone in the Easter procession. Even the town vamp Obdulia finds Ana's feet sexually attractive, hinting at Obdulia's homoerotic tendencies. This voyeuristic atmosphere encompasses the reader: Ana herself is on occasion displayed for the reader as an object of erotic desire, as she lies naked on her tiger skin rug like an artist's model. Her tactile pleasure in both the rug and the cool sheets of her bed suggests autoeroticism.

Much of the novel's action focuses on Vetusta's cathedral, and its priests and acolytes are not immune to the pervasive atmosphere of rotten eroticism. In particular Alas stresses de Pas as a sensual man, in contrast to Mesía, where the emphasis is placed on the Vetustan Don Juan's waning sexual reserves. De Pas's mother Paula keeps him supplied with a series of maids to attend to his needs, including, it is implied, his sexual desires. Alas hints broadly at this in the scene where de Pas and his current maid Teresa share a biscuit dipped in chocolate for breakfast: De Pas bites off one half of the biscuit and then presents the other half to Teresa, who bites in her turn. De Pas later has a sexual liaison with Petra, Ana's maid, who schemes to replace Teresa in de Pas's household and allows herself to be seduced by both de Pas and later Mesía as part of her scheme (which proves successful). Alas also offers a vignette of de Pas as he bites into a rosebud, and subsequently develops the motif in unhealthy directions as de Pas perceives girls at their catechism class in terms of roses in various stages of growth, some of them ripe for picking. Most of the priests do not share de Pas's sensuousness any more than they share in his excellent physique (Alas at one point describes him looking at his own powerful naked torso in the mirror), but they do comment maliciously and lasciviously on his relationship with Ana.

The novel's final scene sums up the sordid nature of eroticism in Vetustan society. As Ana lies unconscious in the cathedral after de Pas's final rejection of her, the acolyte Celedonio takes the opportunity to kiss her. This restores her consciousness, and she is aware of a sensation of a toadlike clamminess on her lips. Celedonio's effeminate nature and thus dubious sexuality, coupled with the sheer unpleasantness of the toad image, comes to represent the overall unhealthy attitude to sexual matters displayed by Vetustan society, an attitude of which Ana appears to become conscious only with this final insult. Alas offers us an eroticism designed to disgust as well as titillate.

Biography

Leopoldo Alas was born in Zamora, Spain, on April 25, 1852. He studied law in Oviedo and became a law professor there in 1883. His novels include *La regenta* (1884) and *Su único hijo* (1890). His collections of stories include *Pipá* (1886), *Doña Berta, cuervo, superchería* (1892), *El señor* (1893), *Cuentos morales* (1896), *El gallo de Sócrates* (1901), and *Doctor Sutilis* (1916). He died in Oviedo on June 13, 1901.

ANN DAVIES

Selected Works

Spanish

La regenta, 2 vols, Barcelona: Daniel Cortezo, 1884–1885.
———, 2 vols., Madrid: F. Fe, 1901.
———, 2 vols., Barcelona: Maucci, 1908.
———, 2 vols., Buenos Aires: Emecé, 1946.
———, Madrid: Biblioteca Nueva, 1947.
———, edited by José María Martínez Cachero. Barcelona: Planeta, 1963.
———, Madrid: Alianza, 1966.
———, Mexico City: Porrúa, 1972.
———, 2 vols., edited by Ganzalo Sobejano and José María. Madrid: Clásicos Castalia, 1981.

English

La regenta. Translated by John Rutherford. Harmondsworth, UK: Penguin, 1984.

Further Reading

Charnon-Deutsch, Lou. "Voyeurism, Pornography and *La regenta*," *Modern Language Studies* 19/4 (1989): 93–101.
Labanyi, Jo. "City, Country and Adultery in *La regenta*," *Bulletin of Hispanic Studies* 63 (1986): 53–65.
Rutherford, John. *Leopoldo Alas:* La regenta. London: Grant and Cutler, 1974.
Sinclair, Alison. *Dislocations of Desire: Gender, Identity and Strategy in* La regenta. Chapel Hill: University of North Carolina, Department of Romance Languages, 1998.
Valis, Noël. *The Decadent Vision of Leopoldo Alas: a Study of* La regenta y Su único hijo. Baton Rouge: Louisiana State University Press, 1981.
———, ed. *Malevolent Insemination and Other Essays on Clarín*. Ann Arbor: University of Michigan Press, 1990.

ALBERT-BIROT, PIERRE

1876–1967
French poet and dramatist

Albert-Birot's vast, six-volume *Les six livres de Grabinoulor* is an unpunctuated prose epic that cannot be classified in its entirety as a work of erotic literature, but there are several episodes amongst the many adventures and encounters of its eponymous hero, Grabinoulor, that engage him in scenes of an erotic nature, particularly in the early volumes. These volumes, begun toward the end of the First World War and continued in the 1920s, share much of the sensuality and exuberant love of life of Albert-Birot's poetry of the period (notably *La Joie des sept couleurs* and *La Lune, ou le livre des poèmes*).

From the opening words, when Grabinoulor awakes to find that "it wasn't only his mind that was reaching out to life in virile expectation," the main protagonist exhibits a healthy sexual appetite both as participant and as observer. Indeed: "Every morning Grabinoulor was in the habit of honouring his wife and that was why the street when he belonged to him when he walked so his hands his eyes his lips took her breast her belly her hips and all her curves" (I,3). The eroticism of the female body is celebrated further in this volume with the visual "Poems to the Flesh" (I,8) in the shapes of lips, breast, and bellies engraved on the Tower of Life that Grabinoulor "the pagan" built in the preceding chapter. The curved lines that represent these forms are associated throughout Albert-Birot's work (in prose, poetry, and painting) with the life force. The Tower also has a poem in the shape of a large phallus, "The poet salutes the divine ejaculator," and one representing the female sexual organs, "Everything disappears when the black triangle appears." These visual poems are interspersed throughout the chapter with a lyrical celebration of the sexual act: "In the morning the male opens his eyes his gaze expands to encompass the breasts of the sleeping female life is blonde white and pink and the male's vigour rises in the lower part of his beautiful belly." Grabinoulor's marital status does not preclude sudden sexual encounters, including those with the young girls on bicycles in the first volume (I,2), and in the second book with the little girl Paulette, whose naked body he has been admiring in the park and whom he introduces to sexual pleasure (II,29); nor is it any barrier to the enjoyment of a long episode of lovemaking with Mademoiselle Irène (II,25).

In the first book Grabinoulor is also an indulgent observer of the sexual activity of others, from passing moments including a queen and a cowherd, a marchioness and a "luxury hotel negro" to a king and a shepherdess (I,6) to a more extended episode in which he intervenes to find a lover for Eugénie, his voluptuous childhood friend (I,26). In the second book, Grabinoulor is a courteous host when the Angel Gabriel spends twelve hours in Paris, largely comprised of eating, drinking, and sex (II,20). In a later volume, Grabinoulor is able to witness the defloration of Eve by Adam, whom he finds in an Eden characterized by rampant disorder (IV,15). Adam and Eve are recurring characters in Albert-Birot's work, and Eve often stimulates sexual desire. In these later volumes the sexual allusions are often recounted with humor, such as in the fifth book, where Grabinoulor notes the two young lovers who "take each other" as they photograph themselves (V,13), or the young bride who is embarrassed by the presence of God if he is really everywhere (idem.); or in the fourth book, where Furibar, the hero's frequent companion (and antithesis in many ways) carries off Virginity, who falls in love with Grabi (IV,7). Tellingly perhaps, Grabi eventually invents "pure coitus" through the eyes, since sex is only a simulacrum of possession (V,8). Nonetheless, throughout the whole text Eros forms part of the system of excess that ensures the constant generation of the narrative. This economy of excess represents the ethical and political stance of the text's hero, who takes a position against all the inhibiting forces that oppress human nature and prevent pleasure. In his transgression of all laws, Grabinoulor upholds the sovereignty of desire against any threat, notably that of Monsieur Oscar Thanatou.

Biography

Albert-Birot was born in Angoulême, France, April 22, 1876. He attended the lycée there (now called Guez-de-Balzac) and the art school in Bordeaux. In Paris he worked in the sculptor Falguière's studio and was successful in the Paris salons in the early part of the century. He fathered four children with Suzanne Bottini, whom he never married and who left him in 1909. He later married twice: Germaine de Surville, a musician, in 1913 (died 1931) and Arlette Lafont in 1962. During the First World War Albert-Birot came to the forefront of the French avant-garde with the founding and editing of the literary journal *SIC* (1916–1919), in which he published, amongst others, the Italian Futurist poets and artists and the future Surrealists, André Breton, Louis Aragon, and Philippe Soupault. It was, however, the meeting with Guillaume Apollinaire that was to prove crucial, and the staging of *Les Mamelles de Tirésias* in 1917 came to fruition under the auspices of *SIC*. In this period Albert-Birot turned his attention from the visual arts (figurative, cubist and abstract painting, and sculpture) to poetry and to his masterpiece *Grabinoulor* (begun in 1918), both of which would occupy him for the rest of his life. His interest in theater led him to write several plays, and he was involved in dramatic productions in the 1920s. His withdrawal from the Parisian artistic scene led to a long period of neglect by the literary establishment, although he continued to publish poetry and to write *Grabinoulor* until the end of his long life. The full six volumes of *Grabinoulor* were finally published in 1991, nearly 35 years after a peaceful death in Paris, July 25, 1967.

DEBRA KELLY

Selected Works

Prose

Les Six livres de Grabinoulor. 1991
First Book of Grabinoulor (translated by Barbara Wright). 1986
Les Mémoires d'Adam et les pages d'Eve. (1943, 1948), 1986
Rémy Floche, employé. 1987
Autobiographie, suivi de Moi et moi. 1988
Le Catalogue de l'antiquaire. 1993

Theater

Matoum et Tévibar and *Larountala.* A "polydrama" in two parts (1919). *Théâtre I,* 1977.

Poetry

Trente et un poèmes de poche (1917). 1967, 1987
La Joie des sept couleurs (1919). 1967, 1987
La Lune, ou le livre des poèmes (1924). 1992
Poèmes à l'autre moi (1927). 1981
La Panthère noire (1938). 1982

Les Amusements naturels (1945), 1984
Le Train bleu, 1970

Further Reading

Follain, Jean. "Pierre Albert-Birot," in *Poètes d'aujourd'hui*. Paris: Seghers, 1967.

Kelly, Debra. *Pierre Albert-Birot. A Poetics in Movement, A Poetics of Movement*. London: Associated University Presses, 1997.
Le Dimna, Nicole. *Jeux et enjeux chez Pierre Albert-Birot*. Chieti: Maria Solfanelli, 1989.
Lentengre, Marie-Louise. *Pierre Albert-Birot. L'Invention de soi*. Paris: Jean-Michel Place, 1993.

ALCRIPE, PHILIPPE D'

1530/1–1581
French Benedictine monk and satirist

La nouvelle fabrique des excellents traicts de verité [*The New Factory of Excellent Traits of Truth*] is Philippe d'Alcripe's only surviving work, probably first published in 1579. Alcripe spared time from his vocation to write this comical set of tall tales numbering ninety-nine (perhaps in deliberate parody of the *Decameron* or the *Cent nouvelles nouvelles*). The ironic title implies fabrication, and the insistence on truth amounts to deliberate antiphrase. Such patterns extend a tradition of fables and liars' accounts whose classical antecedents include Aesop and more especially Lucian. Using written but also oral sources, and owing much to Rabelais, the collection lacks virtually all the didactic and spiritual dimensions of *Pantagruel and Gargantua,* concentrating instead on thematic variety and amusement for their own sake. This is not to say that the author was uneducated—borrowings from Pliny alone bear witness to his classical erudition; however, his avowed aim is to divert rather than instruct or inspire, a point perhaps held against him by his contemporaries and fellow monks.

The collection's erotic themes reflect medieval antifeminism in recounting the discomfiture and humiliation of women: A peasant relieving herself is frozen into a duck pond by her own urine; two whores are blown by the wind to the top of Rouen Cathedral, where they hang upside down, so revealing their *y gregeois*; a young wife, sick with constipation, is so ashamed at the prospect of an enema that she farts, so alleviating her condition, but also knocking over and befouling the apothecary in attendance. Acts of comic violence against men include the tale of a cutpurse pickpocket who inadvertently removes a victim's scrotum rather than his money bag and is executed by strangulation within the day. Meanwhile, the standard motif of cuckoldry returns at least once, in the story of a townsman's wife who offers her favors to an army captain. The husband's vengeance is brutal: He impales the lovers on a spit, then carries them through the streets to the chambers of a judge who had refused to intervene in the affair. In other tales, lusty cockerels and bitches in heat recall the importance of sex in the animal kingdom, while a swineherd who has lost a sow down a hole finds that cavity with the alacrity of a newly wed husband.

Alcripe's erotic themes are not always vulgar, however. The tale of three young men who dance the night away with a trio of fairies met by chance in a forest avoids explicit references to sex ("I dare not tell you what they did . . . "), focusing instead on the unfortunate consequences of the three wishes granted them by their magical partners. Moreover, the longest story (eight pages in the critical edition) recounts the seemingly chaste desire of a scholar for the daughter of the Sultan of Babylon. Enamored of her portrait, he sends her a message tied to a swallow, then receives in return, and via the same messenger, a ring which renders him invisible, so gaining him access to her bedchamber. No further details of the liaison follow. Hence, alongside a coarse and indelicate eroticism, Rabelaisian in the popular sense, we find various themes relating to courtly love, as well as the moral admonitions which traditionally accompany them: "Youth wastes itself daily on the kisses of *folamour*"; "a *folamour* blinds all humanity," etc. One cannot determine how seriously meant these morals are, nor yet how truly deferential or how critical are the various rhymes on womanhood with which other tales conclude. "Were woman's power the equal of her will, the world would be a violent place indeed"; "She is the hardest beast to master, if not to mount!"

Biography

Born Philippe le Picard in Lyons, Normandy, he received a monastic education and spent his adult life as one of the 20 or so monks manning the Cistercian Abbey of Mortemer (near Lisors, in the Eure) during a particularly dangerous period of the French Religious Wars. Pious and intellectually unambitious, he can in no way be reliably confirmed as that drunken vulgarian which tradition formerly described. His latter years were vitiated by a paralysis brought to an end by his death.

JOHN PARKIN

Bibliography

Alcripe, Philippe d'. *La nouvelle fabrique des excellents traicts de vérité*, critical edition by Françoise Joukovsky. Geneva: Droz, 1983.
Pérouse, Gabriel-A. In *Nouvelles françaises du XVIe siècle: Images de la vie du temps*. Geneva: Droz, 1977, and *Poétiques du Burlesque*. Paris: Champion, 1998.
The Tall Tale and Philippe d'Alcripe: An Analysis of the Tall Tale Genre with Particular Reference to Philippe d'Alcripe's La nouvelle fabrique des excellents traits de vérité, *Together with an Annotated Translation of the Work*. Translated by Gerald Thomas. Memorial University of Newfoundland, 1977.

AMARU

Eighth century Indian author

The *Amaruçataka* is a collection of one hundred or so detached Sanskrit erotic verses from sometime before the ninth century CE. This *terminus ante quem* is established by its citation in the ninth-century *Dhvanyâloka* of Ânandavardhana, but beyond this we know virtually nothing of its date, provenance, or authorship, as is the case with so many Sanskrit poems of any antiquity. It was composed in perhaps the seventh or eighth century, and quite possibly represents the work of more than one author. The *Amaruçataka* has been one of the most popular and widely circulated collections of Sanskrit court poetry. Its representation of courtly erotic life is quintessentially evocative and haunting. The verses are so many crystallizations of the games and wars of love, the torments and transports offered by the polygamous and promiscuous world of the early Indian court.

The verses of the *Amaruçataka* are characteristically dense. Each stanza presents an entire world of intrigue for whose decoding a commentary is almost always indispensable. The stanzas are monuments to the power of the detached Sanskrit verse (what in Sanskrit is termed *muktaka* or *subhâßita*) to compress content. A well-known example of an entire narrative woven into a few lines of poetry is verse sixteen of the western recension:

The pet parrot listened to the words the husband and wife were whispering last night. In the morning, the wife heard them being repeated before her in-laws in shrill tones. Agonized with shame, she invents a muzzle for his speech: Pretending to feed the creature a pomegranate fruit, she stuffs a ruby from her ear in his beak.

The numerous commentaries on the work testify to its density, but also to its popularity. Likewise bearing testimony to its popularity and traffic are the several regional versions of the collection: Bengali, Southern, Western, and Mixed. Only about half the verses are common to all the versions (Lienhard, 1983). The poem has been amply illustrated, and species of tantalizing illuminated manuscripts abound. Notable are the Oriya miniatures published by the Orissa Lalit Kala Akademi (see Further Reading below).

Romantic love in Sanskrit poetry is a dark and morbid thing. The emphasis in description is on anger and anguish; on separation (*viraha*), as opposed to enjoyment in union (*sambhoga*). Fantasized joys take precedence over real ones; feigned emotions over true feelings. Though the picture of love is dark, with endless descriptions of abandoned lovers wasting away in states of near hallucinatory psychosis, there is ample room for comedy and wit. Much of the humor revolves around the young wife (*navoḍhā* or *mughdhā*) stumbling as she learns the tricks for manipulating her beloved, or around the attempts of the slighted and estranged beloved (*kalahāntaritā*) to torture her lover back into her arms:

> Somehow, girlfriend, in play anger, I told him "get lost." No sooner had the stonehearted fellow got up from the bed and left in fury. Now my heart, its shame annihilated, longs for that cruel man whose love was rashly cast off. What can I do? (15)

Conversely, much of the poetry asks, what would a man not do for love? It depicts seemingly endless scenes of men groveling at the feet of ladies enraged at their adulterous escapades (sometimes even having been accidentally called by the name of another woman). In this verse the angry beloved finally relents:

> Her anger somewhat abated, she held her moonlike face in her hand, while I, all my stratagems abandoned, took only to groveling at her feet. Suddenly from the pouch in the corner of her eye, which held the glorious banner of her eyelash, a tear long retained was let go, tumbling on her breast and telling her mercy. (25)

Whether conducing to joy or sorrow, the *Amaruśataka* represents a world of multiple passions, where monogamy seems almost a noncategory:

> "Bowing at my feet, you try to conceal the mark on your chest from hugging her breasts smeared with thick sandal-paste!" As soon as she said this, I replied "What?!" and suddenly embraced her passionately so as to rub it off. In a rush of pleasure, she forgot the whole thing. (26)

There are many fantastic tales of Amaru's life, though as is the case with most Sanskrit works of any antiquity, knowledge of the historical Amaru, if indeed there was one, is lost to us. According to one legend, he slept with a hundred women and transmitted the experiences into a hundred verses. According to another tradition, the great exponent of nondualist metaphysics (*advaitavedānta*) Śaṅkarācārya entered the body of the king Amaru and thus studied the lore of eroticism without defiling himself. A number of manuscript colophons thus treat Śaṅkarācārya as the true author of the text, and on this basis the commentator Ravicandra attempted to interpret the verses of the *Amaruśataka* in terms of metaphysical theory (Lienhard, 93).

Whatever one makes of these traditions, the centrality of the *Amaruśataka* to the history of Sanskrit literature is beyond dispute. The text marks one of the first such collections of independent erotic stanzas known to us. This genre of poetic miniature etching took off in Sanskrit. Amaru's notable interlocutors and successors include *Bhartṛhari* of the *Śatakatrayī* (c. fourth century?), *Bilhaṇa* of *Caurapañcāśikā* fame (c. eleventh century), and Govardhana of the *Aryāsaptaśatī* (c. twelfth–thirteenth centuries). The list seems endless. Echoes of Amaru's haunting stanzas flood the works of all his predecessors. The tradition of Sanskrit erotic poetry marks one of the greatest contributions of Sanskrit to world literature and world reflection on the joy and horror of amorous attachment and detachment. In a significant sense, the early Indian theory of love was elaborated in the verses of poets and not in the pedantic discussions of scholars. Sanskrit poets delineated for the world a perfect neurosis with a capacity to transport and entrap in a way that offered continuous perspective on what it meant to be a human being. Thus the eroticism of this tradition came in a later period to represent and allegorize the highest spiritual and metaphysical dynamics open to conceptualization.

JESSE ROSS KNUTSON

Further Reading

Amaruçatakam. Bhubaneshwar: Orissa Lalit Kala Akademi, 1984.

Bharttṛhari and *Bilhaṇa. The Hermit and the Love Thief*, translated by Barbara Stoler-Miller. New York: Penguin Classics, 1991.

Bonner, Rahul. *Sexual Dynamics in the Amaruçataka.* University of Chicago Dissertation, 1991.

Lienhard, Siegfried. *A History of Classical Poetry: Sanskrit—Pali—Prakrit.* Vol. 3, *History of Indian Literature*, edited by Jan Gonda. Wiesbaden: Harrassowitz, 1983.

Love Lyrics by Amaru, Bhartṛhari, and *Bilhaṇa. Translated by Greg Bailey and Richard Gombrich.* New York: New York University Press and JJC Foundation, 2005.

AMIS, MARTIN

1949–

British novelist and essayist

Martin Amis is the author of satirical novels, short stories, and essays that unflinchingly document the devaluation of love and eroticism in the postmodern West. "Modern life . . . is so mediated that authentic experience is much harder to find," Amis told an interviewer in 1991. "We've all got this idea of what [life] should be like—from movies, from pornography." Amis's male characters ferociously pursue what a character in *Success* calls "socio-sexual self-betterment," but fulfillment is always beyond their reach. Trapped in the echo chamber of self-consciousness, they instead testify to the ways in which the cultural logic of capitalism militates against intimacy. Describing his seduction of Rachel Noyes in *The Rachel Papers*, Charles Highway strikes a chord that echoes throughout Amis's fiction:

> Only her little brown head was visible. I kissed that for a while, knowing from a variety of sources that this will do more for you than any occult caress. The result was satisfactory. My hands, however, were still behaving like prototype hands, marketed before certain snags had been dealt with. So when I introduced one beneath the blankets, I gave it time to warm and settle before sending it down her stomach. Panties? Panties. I threw back the top sheet, my head a whirlpool of notes, directives, memos, hints, pointers, random scribblings. (p.158)

Charles's reference to "prototype hands," like his subsequent use of "marketed," "directives,"

and "memos," demonstrates that his most intimate thoughts and actions are conditioned by a commodity fetishism that penetrates even the unconscious. Amis's most memorable characters are similarly driven and deformed by mass-mediated desire. John Self, the protagonist and narrator of *Money: A Suicide Note,* is "addicted to the twentieth century," and wallows in the consumerist vices of alcohol, cigarettes, and pornography ("Pornography isn't really erotic," Amis said in a 1984 interview, "it's carnal; it's a frippery for the jaded, and jadedness is . . . an enemy of eroticism"). Keith Talent, the small-time cheat and big-time adulterer of *London Fields,* whose libido is "all factoid and tabloid," represents a *reductio ad absurdum* of such addictions. His onanistic pursuits illustrate the observation of another character in the novel that "if love was dead or gone then the self was just self, and had nothing to do all day but work on sex. Oh, and hate. And death."

In addition to fiction, Amis has written a series of reviews, essays, and profiles exploring the social implications of sexual liberation and shifting gender relations. These include columns on strip clubs and pornographic magazines published in the *New Statesman* under the pseudonym "Bruno Holbrook"; reviews of novels that have expanded the boundaries of sexual representation (William Burroughs's *Queer,* Vladimir Nabokov's *Lolita,* Philip Roth's *The Dying Animal*); and a series of essays on such topics as AIDS, masculinity, *Playboy* founder Hugh Hefner, the singer Madonna, and the pornographic film industry. "Making Sense of AIDS," a detailed and sensitive essay on the AIDS crisis written for *The Observer* in 1985, was one of the first such articles to appear in the mainstream British press. "The Return of the Male" (1991), an essay on the poet Robert Bly's *Iron John: A Book About Men,* skewers Bly's mythopoeic machismo, mocks the cult of male privilege and embraces feminism as one important manifestation of a movement toward greater gender equity, "intensified by the contemporary search for role and guise and form." Like all of Amis's nonfiction, these essays demonstrate that behind the frenzied, cruel, self-obsessed, and often misogynist males that dominate his novels stands an author possessing a far wider range of emotional and moral responses.

In a 1996 interview, Amis compared his own "moral scheme" to that of his father, the noted author Kingsley Amis, observing that while his father prized decency, the positive values in his own books "are always represented by innocence, by a child." *Experience: A Memoir* (2000), an extended rumination on the complex relationship between innocence and experience, illuminates the sources of this outlook, as well as the reasons why innocence is typically conspicuous by its absence in Amis's fiction. In 1973, the same year his first novel appeared, Amis's beloved cousin Lucy Partington went missing; it was later discovered that she had been sexually tortured and killed by the serial murderer Frederick West. In 1975 Amis entered into an affair with a married woman which produced a daughter whose paternity Amis did not publicly acknowledge for nearly 20 years. As Amis writes in *Experience,* these facts help account for the "stream of lost or wandering daughters" who begin appearing in his fiction from *Success* onward. Amis eventually established a close relationship with this first daughter, and *Experience* itself is ultimately a narrative of affirmation, including the joys of romantic love and erotic passion. But as he has filtered these experiences through the genre of satire, which requires and thrives on negative emotion, they have generated fiction in which characters are agents or objects of perverse desires and designs, and sexuality is the enemy of innocence. This often produces wickedly funny comedy: Marmaduke in *London Fields* is a grotesque representation of Oedipal rivalry, a sexually precocious child determined to displace his father in his mother's affections.

But it seldom produces life-affirming representations of eroticism. Instead, sexuality typically appears in Amis's satirical fiction as another name for narcissism, for domination, for the corruption of innocence.

Biography

Martin Amis was born in 1949 in Oxford, England, the son of Kingsley Amis. His first novel, *The Rachel Papers,* was published in 1973 to wide critical acclaim (it won the Somerset Maugham Award in 1974). He has written nine novels, one screenplay (for *Saturn 3*), two collections of stories, and six works of nonfiction. His nonfiction has appeared in leading newspapers and magazines on both sides of the Atlantic, and he has served as fiction and poetry editor of the *Times Literary Supplement* and literary editor of the *New Statesman.*

JAMES DIEDRICK

Selected Works

The Rachel Papers. London: Jonathan Cape, 1973; New York: Alfred A. Knopf, 1974; New York: Vintage, 1992.

Dead Babies. London: Jonathan Cape, 1975; New York: Knopf, 1976; New York: Vintage, 1992. Republished as *Dark Secrets*, St. Albans: Triad/Panther, 1977.

Success. London: Jonathan Cape, 1978; New York: Harmony, 1987; New York: Vintage, 1992.

Other People: A Mystery Story. London: Jonathan Cape, 1981; New York: Viking, 1981; New York, Vintage, 1994.

Money: A Suicide Note. London: Jonathan Cape, 1984; New York: Viking, 1985; New York: Penguin, 1986.

The Moronic Inferno and Other Visits to America. London: Jonathan Cape, 1986; New York: Viking, 1987; New York: Penguin, 1987.

London Fields. London: Jonathan Cape, 1989; New York: Harmony, 1990; Toronto: Lester and Orpen Dennys, 1989; New York: Vintage, 1991.

Visiting Mrs. Nabokov and Other Excursions. London: Jonathan Cape, 1993; New York: Harmony, February 1994; Toronto: Knopf Canada, 1993.

Night Train. London: Jonathan Cape, 1997; New York: Harmony, February 1998; Toronto: Knopf Canada, 1997; New York: Vintage, 1999.

Heavy Water and Other Stories. London: Jonathan Cape, 1998; New York: Harmony, 1999; New York: Vintage, 1999.

Experience: A Memoir. London: Jonathan Cape, 2000; New York: Hyperion/Talk Miramax Books, 2000; Toronto: Knopf Canada, 2000; New York: Vintage, 2002.

The War Against Cliché: Essays and Reviews, 1971–2000. London: Jonathan Cape, 2001; New York: Hyperion/Talk Miramax Books, 2001.

Koba the Dread: Laughter and the Twenty Million. London: Jonathan Cape, 2002; New York: Hyperion/Talk Miramax Books, 2002.

"Vernon," *Penthouse* (London), December 1980: 57–62, 131. Republished as "Let Me Count the Times," *Granta* 4 (1981): 193–207; rpt. in *Heavy Water and Other Stories*, 75–93.

Nonfiction

Essays

"The Bodies in Question." *The Observer*, 18 February 1979, 11. Essay on pornography.

"The Utopian Woman." *The Observer Magazine*, 15 April 1984, 54–55. Profile of feminist Gloria Steinem; rpt. in *The Moronic Inferno*, 138–143.

"Making Sense of AIDS." *The Observer*, 23 June 1985: 17–18. Essay on AIDS; rpt. in *The Moronic Inferno*, 187–198.

"Mr. Hefner and the Desperate Pursuit of Happiness." *The Observer Magazine*, 22 September 1985, 12–16; rpt. *The Moronic Inferno*, 170–180. Profile of *Playboy* publisher Hugh Hefner.

"The Great American Mix." *The Observer*, 16 February 1986, 29. Essay on "sex, drink, and celebrity" among American writers, including Saul Bellow, Joseph Heller, Norman Mailer, Philip Roth, and Gore Vidal.

"H is for Homosexual." In *Hockney's Alphabet: Drawings by David Hockney*, edited by Stephen Spender. New York: Random House, 1991, 23–24. A short (two-page) rumination on homosexuality.

"Return of the Male." *London Review of Books*, 5 December 1991, 3; rpt. *The War Against Cliché*, 3–9. Review-essay analyzing *Iron John: A Book About Men*, by Robert Bly; *The Way Men Think: Intellect, Intimacy and the Erotic Imagination*, by Liam Hudson and Bernadine Jacot; and *Utne Reader. Men, It's Time to Pull Together: The Politics of Masculinity*. Collected in *War Against Cliché* (WAC).

"Lolita Reconsidered." *Atlantic*, September 1992: 109–120; rpt. in WAC, 471–490. Essay on Vladimir Nabokov's *Lolita*.

"Madonna Exposed." *The Observer Magazine*, 11 October 1992: 22–37; rpt. in *Visiting Mrs. Nabokov and Other Essays*, 255–264. Essay on the publicity machine surrounding Madonna and her book *Sex*.

"My Imagination and I." In *Power and the Throne: The Monarchy Debate*, edited by Anthony Barnett. London: Vintage, 1994, 79–80. Recounts a "sex dream" about the Duchess of York.

"Sex in America." *Talk*, February 2001, 98–103, 133–135. Essay on the Los Angeles pornography industry.

Reviews

"Organ Duets." *Times Literary Supplement*, 4 August 1972, 909 (published anonymously). Review of Alan Friedman's *Hermaphrodeity*.

"A Big Boob." *The Observer*, 25 March 1973, 36. Review of Philip Roth's *The Breast*.

"Unisex Me Here." *New Statesman*, 6 July 1973, 28–29. Review of David Bowie concert at the Hammersmith Odeon.

"Fleshpots" (by "Bruno Holbrook"). *New Statesman*, 14 September 1973: 362. Essay on London strip clubs.

"The Coming Thing." *New Statesman*, 28 September 1973: 438; rpt. in WAC, 57–58. Reviews *The Best of Forum*, ed. Albert Z. Freedman.

"Coming in Handy" (by "Bruno Holbrook"). *New Statesman*, 14 December 1973, 922–923. Essay on pornographic magazines.

"Rhetoric of Ghosts." *The Observer*, 3 March 1974, 37. Review of William Burroughs's *Exterminator!*

"Isadora's Complaint." *The Observer*, 21 April 1974: 37. Review of Erica Jong's *Fear of Flying*.

"Miss Emmanuelle." *New Statesman*, 23 August 1974, 264–265. Review of French soft-core film.

"Soft Cor." *New Statesman*, 13 February 1976, 199–200. Review of Richard Wortley's *Erotic Movies*.

"X to Grind." *New Statesman*, 3 September 1976, 321. Review of pornographic film *From Noon Till Three*.

"The Week Rape Came into Its Own." *Sunday Times*, 30 January 1977, 38. Review of *Act of Rape* (BBC-2).

"No Satisfaction." *New Statesman*, 13 January 1978: 50–51; rpt. in *The Moronic Inferno*, 42–45. Review of Philip Roth's *The Professor of Desire*.

"Getting Laid Comfortably." *The Observer*, 29 June 1980: 28; rpt. in *The Moronic Inferno*, 184–186. Review of Gay Talese's *Thy Neighbor's Wife*.

"Chicken Raunch." *The Observer*, 3 October 1982, 40. Review of drive-in brothel documentary *At the Chicken Ranch* (ITV) and cohabitation documentary *Couples* (BBC-1).

"Mother Nature and the Plague." *The Observer*, 1 May 1983, 36. Review of AIDS documentary *Killer in the Village* (Horizon).

"American Nightmare." *The Observer*, 29 April 1984, 23. Review of William Burroughs's *The Place of Dead Roads*.

"Impossible Love." *The Observer*, 20 April 1986: 24; rpt. in WAC, 302–304. Review of William Burroughs's *Queer*.

"What He Learned in Bed." *New York Times Book Review*, 30 August 1992: 1, 21; rpt. in WAC, 59–62. Review of Richard Rhodes's *Making Love: An Erotic Odyssey*.

"Over-Sexed and Over Here." *Sunday Times*, 24 September 1995: 7.3; rpt. in WAC, 294–297. Review of Philip Roth's *Sabbath's Theatre*.

"The Breasts." Review of Philip Roth's *The Dying Animal*. *Talk*, May 2001, 111–112.

Further Reading

Diedrick, James. *Understanding Martin Amis*. Columbia: University of South Carolina Press, 1995, 2002.

Doan, Laura L. "'Sexy Greedy Is the Late Eighties': Power Systems in Amis's *Money* and Churchill's *Serious Money*." *Minnesota Review* 34–35 (1990): 69–80.

Haffenden, John. "Martin Amis." In *Novelists in Interview*. London: Methuen, 1985, 1–24.

Mars-Jones, Adam. *Venus Envy: On the WOMB and the BOMB*. London: Chatto & Windus, 1990.

Morrison, Susan. "The Wit and Fury of Martin Amis," *Rolling Stone*, 17 May 1990, 95–102.

Wachtel, Eleanor. "Eleanor Wachtel with Martin Amis," *The Malahat Review*, March 1996, 43–58.

Wood, James. "Martin Amis: The English Imprisonment," in *The Broken Estate: Essays on Literature and Belief*. London: Jonathan Cape, 1999, 186–199.

ANDREEV, LEONID

1871-1919
Russian story writer and dramatist

Major Works: "The Abyss" and "In the Fog"

Andreev's involvement in erotic or "pornographic" literature occupied only a small part of his literary oeuvre. However, his two stories "The Abyss" (*Bezdna*) and "In the Fog" (*V tumane*) can be read as a transition between high-brow literature dealing with sexual topics (Lev Tolstoi's *Kreutzer Sonata* [*Kreitserova sonata*], 1889) and the "boulevard" or so-called pornographic literature of Mikhail Artsybashiev's *Sanin* (1907), Anastasiia Verbitskaia's *Keys to Happiness* [*Kliuchi shchast'ia*, 1909–13] and many others.

Andreev published "The Abyss" in the January 10, 1902, issue of *Courier*. The story begins with young Nemovetskii accompanying Zindaida Nikolaevna on a walk on the outskirts of town. With the approach of evening, the two adolescents begin their return home but have trouble finding the way. Eventually, they come upon a group of men who attack Nemovetskii and rape Zina. Upon gaining consciousness, Nemovetskii finds Zina, who is alive but comatose, and then proceeds to rape her.

"In the Fog" was published in the December 1902 issue of *A Journal for Everyone* [*Zhurnal dlia vsekh*] and tells the story of the young schoolboy Pavel, who has contracted a venereal disease from a prostitute. Pavel is ashamed and feels that he is unworthy of human contact, though tortured by his desire for lofty love with his sister's friend. Further tension is created by the inability of Pavel and his father to connect personally, denying Pavel an emotional catharsis and driving him out onto the street late one evening. Here he is propositioned by a prostitute, and the two return to her room. Pavel's guilt and the prostitute's drunkenness cloud their interaction, which leads to a fight in which Pavel stabs and kills the prostitute and then himself.

These two stories created a storm of protest among the reading public. Andreev wanted to portray the complexity of the ego, which contains brutal elements that can unexpectedly emerge and influence the individual. However, this demonstration of evil was interpreted as advocacy of it, and many argued that Andreev was slandering the noble, idealistic Russian youth. Andreev and his stories became the focal point for a larger debate that raged in the popular press. Even the wife of Tolstoi, Sophia Andreevna, wrote a letter to the editor of the *New Time* [*Novoe Vremia*] in which she thanked the paper for characterizing Andreev as an erotomaniac and claimed that the author infected the reading public and Russian youth with baseness. This attack from Sophia Andreevna seemed particularly unfair to Andreev, as he felt that "The Abyss" had followed in the tradition of Tolstoi's *Kreutzer Sonata*, going so far as to call his story the illegitimate daughter of Tolstoi's text.

However harsh the critics, Andreev found defenders as well, especially among the younger generation. Many university students wrote to newspapers suggesting that Andreev benefited the reader by showing without adornment the brute which exists in mankind. Andreev was also defended by such literary giants as Chekhov and

Gor'kii, who congratulated the author on presenting the moral agonies of sexual life to the reading public. This seemed all the more relevant, as "In the Fog" had been inspired by a news brief about a young man who had killed two prostitutes. It was Andreev's desire to understand the motivation for such actions that had led to his writing the story.

Andreev had written other works dealing with brutal crimes of passion ("The Lie" [*Lozh*], 1901, and "The Thought" [*Mysl'*], 1902), but it was "The Abyss" and "In the Fog" that acted as lightning rods in the ongoing debate concerning literary distinctions between high-brow erotic literature, as exemplified by Tolstoi and Mikhail Kuzmin (*Wings* [*Kryl'ia*], 1907), and pornographic boulevard literature by Artsybashiev, Verbitskaia, and many others. Since Tolstoi was beyond moral reproach, it fell to Andreev to be classified as a transitional writer for erotic literary trends in Russia at the turn of the century.

Biography

Son of a provincial land surveyor, Leonid Nikolaevich Andreev lost his father at an early age and spent his youth in difficult material conditions, supporting his mother and siblings. For his entire life, he displayed chaotic behavior, in the form of drinking binges, suicidal tendencies, and scandalous comportment. Although he held a law degree from Moscow University (1897), Andreev concentrated on writing court reports, topical satire, and short stories for the Moscow newspaper *Courier* (*Kur'er*). Andreev's first real literary success came with the story "Once It Was" (*Zhili-byli*), published in 1901 in the journal *Life* (*Zhizn'*). By this time, Maksim Gor'kii had befriended the young writer and introduced him into the *Wednesday* (*Sreda*) literary circle, whose members offered valuable literary and personal support and guidance. It was at this time that Andreev achieved incredible financial and literary success, mainly for his short stories. Andreev's participation in the *Wednesday* circle

diminished after going abroad at the end of 1905, and his friendship with Gor'kii degenerated into open hostility after 1907. Andreev moved from Gor'kii's publishing house Knowledge (*Znanie*) to Sweetbriar (*Shipovnik*) at this time and edited several of their literary almanacs, drawing himself closer to the writers of the Russian Symbolist movement.

In 1907–08, Andreev relocated to St. Petersburg and then to a house north of the capital—a region which was captured by Finnish forces after the revolution. At this time, Andreev directed his literary energies toward the stage. He was able to maintain his popular success with audiences, although literary critics received his works less and less favorably.

During World War I, Andreev's anti-German patriotism and his financial problems led to work on the pro-war newspaper *Russian Will* (*Russkaia volia*). He actively opposed the Bolshevik seizure of power in October 1917 and even wrote a passionate plea to the Western world to save Russia from the tyranny of Bolshevism. Andreev died in 1919 of a stroke without enough money for burial expenses, leaving behind a wife and five children.

FREDERICK H. WHITE

Selected Works

Sobranie sochinenii v 6 tomakh. Moscow: Khudozhestvennaia Literatura, 1990–96.
Visions: Stories and Photographs. Edited and with an introduction by Olga Andreyev. San Diego: Harcourt Brace Jovanovich, 1987.

Further Reading

Engelstein, Laura. *The Keys to Happiness: Sex and the Search for Modernity in Fin-de-Siècle Russia.* Ithaca, NY: Cornell University Press, 1992.
Iezuitova, L. *Tvorchestvo Leonida Andreeva, 1892–1906.* Leningrad: Iz-vo Leningradskogo Universiteta, 1976.
Kaun, Alexander. *Leonid Andreev: A Critical Study.* 1924; reprinted, New York: AMS Press, 1970.
Newcombe, Josephine M. *Leonid Andreev.* New York: Ungar, 1973.
Woodward, James B. *Leonid Andreyev: A Study.* Oxford: Clarendon Press, 1969.

ANGEL, ALBALUCÍA

1939–
Colombian novelist

Angel is considered by critics to be one of the most important Latin American feminist writers of the second half of the twentieth century. Her work is best known for the exploration of the repression of female sexuality in patriarchal societies. Her fiction is known for the frankness of its depiction of male violence against women and the analysis of female homosexuality as a path to women's control over their bodies. Angel was still in her twenties, in 1968, when she published her first novel, *Los girasoles en invierno* [Sunflowers in Winter], an episodic, disjointed tale set in the cafés and streets of Paris, in which she explores the ways in which her heroine, Alejandra, is forced to suppress her own beliefs and accept the limitations placed on women in a patriarchal society. Angel's heartrending portrait of women trapped in the tedium of traditional roles and her heroine's search for an escape from the thralldom of womanhood marks this first experimental novel as one of the earliest avowedly feminist novels in Latin America. The novel also opened a space for Angel among the writers of the Latin American literary "Boom" of the 1960s and 70s.

Angel's second novel, *Dos veces Alicia,* published in 1972 and set in London, offers a feminist rewriting of the traditional detective novel, in which the ambivalent situation of the female protagonist/detective recalls the duality of the figure of Alice in Lewis Carroll's *Alice in Wonderland,* a book that Angel acknowledges as having had a profound impact on her writing. Through an acutely self-conscious narrative, filled with commentary on the process of the text's creation, Alicia, the protagonist, challenges the doctor who has determined that Mrs. Wilson died of natural causes and embarks on her own investigation, in what critics have called a metaphor for the deconstruction of masculine authority.

In 1976, Angel published her third novel, *Estaba la pájara pinta sentada en el verde limón*

[The Spotted Bird Was Sitting on the Green Lemon Tree], a semiautobiographical tale set during the period known as La Violencia in Colombia (1947–1958), when civil war left about 400,000 dead. In this complex tale, where the reader must make sense of various intertwined plot lines, the character of Ana emerges as a clear protagonist, a girl living with the experience of having been brutally raped as a child by one of her father's laborers, a rape that prefigures the rape of hundreds of women as a political act during La Violencia. As a result of this assault, Ana experiences her society as a space of powerlessness for women, whose bodies are prey to sexual violence as an expression of the political and economic power enjoyed by men of all classes. Her rape by a laborer, a peasant working for her father, erases the illusion of any protection that class may offer a young girl like herself, the daughter of a landlord, from the sexual aggression of any man. Since Ana's plight ultimately has its roots in a political system that fails to protect women from male sexual aggression, Angel offers a political solution, as Ana joins a guerrilla movement that offers a possibility of a political transformation and a path to a different kind of sexual experience. *Estaba la pájara pinta* has been described as Angel's "most profound confrontation with Colombian reality," an accurate description for a novel that incorporates historical documentation, testimony, and an attempt to bring forth aspects of the country's history that have long been censored.

Angel's fourth novel, *Misiá señora* (1982), addresses fully the topic of female homosexuality that had hovered like a dark cloud over her young protagonist in *Estaba la pájara pinta*, where it was identified with sin and guilt. *Misiá señora* follows the heroine, Mariana, from childhood through an oppressive marriage and then to madness, focusing on her struggles against the homosexual desires that she seeks unsuccessfully to repress. The exploration of these desires supplies the erotic component of the novel.

Told through stream of consciousness by a narrator who finds in a descent into madness the only possibility of escape from an oppressive patriarchal system, the novel explores a woman's struggle for the right to control her own body.

Angel's fifth novel, *Las andariegas,* was published in 1984. Conceived as fragmented narratives written in a style close to that of concrete poetry, and inspired by Monique Wittig's *Les Guerrillères,* the novel recounts the lives of women throughout history who have battled against the established order. Angel's female warriors are presented as travelers through whom she seeks to elaborate a new history for women, rooted in a homosocial female society. The novel can be read as a celebration of the liberating potential of lesbian love.

In addition to her novels, Angel has published one collection of tales, *¡Oh, Gloria inmarcesible!* (1979), an interesting experimental text that takes the reader on a voyage of discovery of Colombia's natural geography and multicultural and multiracial society and of the problems of drug trafficking and traditional gender roles. She is also the author of two unpublished plays, *La manzaza de piedra* (1983) and *Siete lunas y un espejo* (1991). In 2004, Albalucía Angel published a book of poems, *Cantos y encantamiento de la lluvia.* She lectures frequently on feminist topics in international venues.

Biography

Albalucía Angel was born in Pereira, Colombia, in 1939, the daughter of a well-to-do family from the coffee-producing region of Quindío. She studied literature and art at the University of the Andes and in universities in Paris and Rome. Before she began her career as a writer, she earned a living as a folk singer in Europe. Since the 1970s she has lived in Europe, primarily in Great Britain, and the geography of her literary work echoes that of the countries where she has lived and traveled. Her brief marriage to iconoclastic Chilean writer Mauricio Wacquez ended in divorce.

LIZABETH PARAVISINI-GEBERT

Selected Works

Cantos y encantamiento de la lluvia. Bogotá: Apidama, 2004.
Dos veces Alicia. Barcelona: Seix Barral, 1972.
Estaba la pájara pinta sentada en el verde limón. Barcelona: Argos Vergara, 1984.
Las andariegas. Barcelona: Argos Vergara, 1984.
Los girasoles en invierno. Bogotá: Editorial Linotipia Bolívar, 1970.
Misiá señora. Barcelona: Argos Vergara, 1982.
¡Oh gloria inmarcesible!: Cuentos. Bogotá: Instituto Colombiano de Cultura, 1979.

Further Reading

Araújo, Helena. "Ejemplos de la 'niña impura' en Silvina Ocampo y Albalucía Angel," *Hispamérica* 13:38 (1984): 27–35.
Díaz-Ortiz, Oscar A. "G. Alvarez Gardeazábal y A. Angel: Insubordinación del género sexual para establecer una identidad gay," in *Literatura y cultura: Narrativa colombiana del siglo XX, I: La nación moderna* (pp. 225–257), edited by María Mercedes Jaramillo, Betty Osorio, and Angela Robledo. Bogotá: Ministerio de Cultura, 2000.
Lindsay, Claire. *Locating Latin American Women Writers: Cristina Peri Rossi, Rosario Ferré, Albalucía Angel, and Isabel Allende.* New York: Peter Lang, 2003.
———. "Wish You Weren't Here: The Politics of Travel" in Albalucía Angel's *¡Oh gloria inmarcesible!."* *Studies in Travel Writing* 7:1 (2003): 83–98.
Mora, Gabriela. "Albalucía Angel recuerda sus años de formación," *Alba de América* 18: 33–34 (1999): 403–418.
Taylor, Claire. *Bodies and Texts: Configurations of Identity in the Works of Griselda Gambaro, Albalucía Angel, and Laura Esquivel.* Leeds, England: Maney Publications for the Modern Humanities Research Association, 2003.
Ugalde, Sharon Keefe. "Between 'In Longer' and 'Not Yet': Woman's Space in *Misiá Señora,"* *Revista de Estudios Colombianos* 1 (1986): 23–28.

ANTICLERICALISM

The seventeenth and eighteenth centuries witnessed a change in the attitude toward the Catholic Church. Historically, the influence of the clergy was not restricted to religion; its presence was apparent in many secular bodies, including political, educational, and economic organizations. There had always been a continuous power struggle to curtail or destroy religious control in society; however, the seventeenth century saw the rise of a powerful weapon to this effect: eroticism in literature. This continued into the eighteenth century with the evolution of the libertine novel, where libertine culture signified the sexual freedom of the French aristocracy and the opposition to the strict moral, religious, and social codes enforced by the Church. An example of a late-libertine author is the Marquis de Sade. Notorious for his portrayal of obscene cruelty, sadism, and perverse sexual acts, many of his works are anticlerical in their nature, including *The 120 Days of Sodom* (1785) and *Justine, ou les malheurs de la vertu* (1791), which was revised over a ten-year period in three different versions—the first begun during de Sade's imprisonment in the Bastille.

In the three-volume *Bibliography of Prohibited Books* by Pisanus Fraxi (pseudonym of Henry Ashbee), there are listed examples of earlier works detailing illicit sexual liaisons between priests and nuns. Such titles include *The Cloisters Laid Open, or Adventures of the Priests and Nuns* (there is no date of publication of this work) and *The Nunns Complaint Against the Fryars,* published in 1676 as an English translation of an original French work entitled *Factum pour les religieuses* (1668). *The Nunns Complaint* is described as a novel that portrays the perversion of friars, detailing amongst other acts of impiousness "secret entries into the nunnery, and riotous and licentious conduct there; marriages with the nuns; wasting the revenue of the convent; general tyranny and injustice towards the sisters" (Pisanus Fraxi, vol. 2., 193).

The Enlightenment brought anticlerical literature to the fore. As Sánchez (1972, 57) writes:

The intellectual revolution of the seventeenth and eighteenth centuries broke sharply with the anticlerical tradition of the past. It is true that the *philosophes* (the enlightened thinkers) made many of the same criticisms which had been made ever since the anticlerical revolution of the twelfth century: the clergy were criticized for their obscurantism, their superstition, their greed, and their inability to practice what they preached. The *philosophes* varied this traditional criticism slightly by offering rational proof, for they were admirers of the scientific revolution. Even so, some new criticisms were made. These aimed at the clergy's otherworldliness, and in these attacks the difference from traditional anticlericalism became noticeable.

The anticlerical literature of the Enlightenment was different from earlier works due to the fact that in addition to being anticlerical it was also notably anti-Christian. In short, it not only attacked religious institutions and the clergy, but also launched an assault on the Christian faith. As a result, anticlerical literature of the Enlightenment was prominent in countries that were devoutly Catholic, including France and Spain. Many works aimed to represent religion as a violent, sadistic, and corrupt institution that violated the civil rights of people, especially the rights and purity of women.

There are many works that portray young women, particularly nuns and novices, as objects of erotic fantasy and desire or as tragic individuals who are nothing more than prostitutes and sex slaves for religious figures. Well-known examples include Denis Diderot's novel *La religeuse* (begun in 1760, though not published until 1796), which describes the life of Suzanne Simonin and her experiences in three different convents after being forced to become a nun by her family, and Matthew Lewis's *The Monk,* completed in 1796. Prior to writing *The Monk,* Lewis had seen some anticlerical dramatic productions, including *Les victimes cloîtrées* and *Camille, ou le souterrain,* both of which contained erotic scenes that influenced his novel. *The Monk* portrays the virtuous, beautiful, and young Antonia, who is ruthlessly raped and eventually killed by the monk Ambrosio. Unrepentant for his crimes, Ambrosio blames Antonia's beauty for leading him to violate her. During the course of the novel, Ambrosio is also seduced and tempted by the demonic Mathilda, a further testimony to the weakness of religious figures in anticlerical literature. Indeed, religious personages are often portrayed as figures of immorality; consider Frollo in Victor Hugo's *Notre Dame de Paris* (1831).

A later example of anticlerical literature, relatively unknown by comparison with the foregoing, is *The Awful Disclosures of Maria Monk*, published in 1835. A notable anti-Catholic work, it was written as a direct assault upon the Catholic religious establishments of Canada. The novel describes Maria's experiences at the Hôtel Dieu Nunnery at Montreal. Used as a sex object by the local priests, she is informed by her superior that the debauchery of the priests is justified: Forbidden to marry and denied the pleasures of the flesh, they live assiduous, yet lonely and isolated lives for the benefit of others, and so deserve to be "rewarded." The true extent of the depravity becomes apparent with Maria's discovery of a mass grave for illegitimate babies in the convent's cellars. In the preface to the novel, Maria observes: "It would distress the reader, should I repeat the dreams with which I am often terrified at night; . . . often I imagine myself present at the repetition of the worst scenes that I have hinted at or described. Sometimes I stand at the secret place of interment in the cellar; sometimes I think I can hear the shrieks of the helpless females in the hands of the atrocious men; and sometimes almost seem actually to look again upon the calm and placid features of St. Frances, as she appeared when surrounded by her murderers" (Anon., *Awful Disclosures*, preface, vi).

Other notable examples from the key 1860s-1870s period listed in the *Bibliography of Prohibited Books* include:

- Two works by French author Émile Alexis. *Les immoralités des prêtres catholiques* [*Immoralities of the Catholic Priests*] was first published in 1868 and republished in 1870 as *Crimes, attentats et immoralités du clergé catholique moderne* [*Crimes, Attacks, and Immoralities of the Modern Catholic Clergy*], in order to increase sales. It is described by Pisanus as "not directed against religion in general, nor even against priestcraft as a whole, but only against that part of the body whose conduct has proved to be immoral" (vol. 2, 201). The other work by Alexis is *Horreurs, massacres et crimes des papes* [*Horrors, Massacres, and Crimes of the Popes*], 1868.

- Works set in convents, including *The Pastimes of a Convent*, published in 1798, which was later republished under the title *The Amorous History and Adventures of Raymond de B—, and Father Andouillard*; and *Nunnery Tales*, published in 1866.

- *Le Prêtre, la femme et le confessional*, which was published in English as *The Priest, the Woman, and the Confessional* in 1874.

SARAH BERRY

References and Further Reading

Anon. *The Awful Disclosures of Maria Monk* and the *Mysteries of a Convent Exposed*. Philadelphia: E.B. Peterson, 1836.

Anon. *The True History of Maria Monk*. London: Catholic Truth Society, 1938.

Cryle, Peter, and O'Connell, Lisa, eds. *Libertine Enlightenment: Sex, Liberty and Licence in the Eighteenth Century*. Basingstoke, UK: Palgrave Macmillan, 2004.

Diderot, Denis. *La Réligeuse*, edited by Heather Lloyd. London: Bristol Classical Press, 2000.

Hugo, Victor. *Notre-Dame de Paris*. London: Penguin Books Ltd., 1978.

Kendrick, Walter. *The Secret Museum: Pornography in Modern Culture*. Berkeley and Los Angeles: University of California Press, 1996.

Lewis, Matthew. *The Monk*, in *Four Gothic Novels*. Oxford: Oxford University Press, 1994.

Marquis de Sade. *Justine, Philosophy in the Bedroom and Other Writings*. London: Arrow, 1991.

———. *The 120 days of Sodom, and Other Writings*, compiled and translated by Austryn Wainhouse and Richard Seaver. London: Arrow, 1990.

Pisanus Fraxi [H.S. Ashbee]. *Bibliography of Prohibited Books* (3 vols.), with introduction by G. Legman. New York: Brussel, 1962.

Sánchez, José. *Anticlericalism: A Brief History*. Notre Dame, IN: University of Notre Dame Press, 1972.

Summers, Montague. *The Gothic Quest: A History of the Gothic Novel*. London: Fortune Press, 1968.

Wright, Angela. "European Disruptions of the Idealized Woman: Matthew Lewis's *The Monk* and the Marquis de Sade's *La Nouvelle Justine*," in Avril Horner, ed., *European Gothic: A Spirited Exchange, 1760–1960*. Manchester: Manchester University Press, 2002.

APHRODISIACS

Named after the Greek goddess of love, Aphrodite, aphrodisiacs are substances consumed before or during lovemaking which are thought to enhance desire and pleasure. Scientists often question whether the supposed effects occur with any regularity, but erotic literature does not reflect those doubts.

In erotic stories, irritants usually have an aphrodisiacal function. The most striking in this regard, referred to regularly from the eighteenth century onward, is cantharides, often called "Spanish fly." It is not in fact a fly at all, but a small black beetle, *Cantharis vesicatoria,* which is crushed into a black powder and swallowed. Cantharides has in fact long been known to be quite dangerous. Even in very small doses, it causes burning of the urinary tract. The great French *Encyclopédie* of the eighteenth century calls it a poison. But there was erotic appeal in absorbing small quantities of poison, and the burning sensation within was taken to be a powerful sign of desire.

In libertine novels of the mid- to late eighteenth century, cantharides is just one of a class of substances used. Amber was another, as was aniseed. *Diabolini,* from Naples, were dark, small, and hot. In general, according to the literature of northern and western Europe, the warm, Mediterranean countries were the natural sources of almost everything aphrodisiacal. In the novels of writers such as Andréa de Nerciat, cantharides and diabolini are served up in libertine festivities as *bonbons,* or sweets. He calls them "charming poisons." But during the nineteenth century, the poisonous aspect became progressively more important, at the expense of the charm. There is in fact an escalation in the literary use of aphrodisiacs, and an aggravation of their effects. A powerful myth attributes the origins of the whole thing to de Sade. The young marquis had caused a scandal in 1772, in Marseilles, by giving black confectionery to some prostitutes, who became ill as a result. In the eyes of aristocratic libertines, and even in the view of de Sade's virtuous wife, this was only an unfortunate miscalculation of effects. But for the many writers of the nineteenth century who were haunted by de Sade's image, aphrodisiacs, and cantharides in particular, were the very substance of his influence. The diabolical marquis could thus be blamed (or credited) for disseminating through France, and thence through Europe, the black substance of poisonous desire.

The connection between sexual excitement and the risk of death by poison is made, for example, in Alfred de Musset's *Gamiani, ou deux nuits d'excès* (1833). Cantharides is used there as a stimulant, along with others, during an orgy involving a group of nuns. But the story's conclusion goes beyond this, as Gamiani, desperately seeking a remedy for chronically unsatisfied desire, brings about her own end with a "burning poison" which causes her to die in a violent spasm of pleasure. In the course of the nineteenth century, the role of aphrodisiacs in French erotic stories evolved further.

Toward the end of the century, there was an increasing preoccupation with links between sexuality and illness, and many novels on the generic borders of erotic literature managed to represent desire and pleasure while also expressing anxiety about their effects on the characters' health. There were more drastic venereal health concerns in the late nineteenth century, most notably the widespread presence of syphilis. But everyday erotic literature paid great attention to diet. Hot things were now often sourced to the Orient, rather than the Mediterranean. Chili, curry, pepper, cummin, even peppermint were all said to have the dangerous effect of heightening desire by gnawing away at the body from within. Under the effects of spicy diets, characters came to suffer from a desire too acute to be satisfied by any standard forms of pleasure. Drugs such as ether were also said to contribute to the same effect, producing pathological desire that could result eventually in death.

Certain women, especially of the East, were talked about as being dangerous to European men because their breath, their touch, their perfume, their very substance were thought to be erotically contagious. For fearful and excited writers of the fin-de-siècle, Oriental women were often seen as walking aphrodisiacs. Even for the anxious and the prurient, there was a thrill in aphrodisiacs, but it was, as literally as possible, the thrill of playing with fire, the intimate thrill of putting fiery substances inside one's body.

PETER CRYLE

Further Reading

Cryle, Peter. "The Substance of Desire: Towards a Thematic History of the Aphrodisiac in Nineteenth-Century French Fiction," *Nottingham French Studies* 37/1 (Spring 1998): 27–49.

Lever, Maurice. *Donatien Alphonse François marquis de Sade*. Paris: Fayard, 1991.

Taberner, Peter V. *Aphrodisiacs: The Science and the Myth*. Philadelphia: University of Pennsylvania Press, 1985.

Novels of the nineteenth century in which aphrodisiacs play a role include:

Belot, Adolphe. *Mademoiselle Giraud, ma femme*. Paris: Dentu, 1870.

Besse, Louis. *La Fille de Gamiani: journal d'une prostituée*. Paris: Albin Michel, 1906.

Dubut de Laforest, Jean-Louis. "Mademoiselle Tantale," in *Pathologie sociale*. Paris: Dupont, 1897.

Duo, Pierre. *Inassouvie*. Paris: Brossier, 1889.

Joze, Victor. *La Cantharide*. Paris: Fort, c.1900.

Maizeroy, René. *Deux Amies*. Paris: Havard, 1885.

Musset, Alfred de. "Gamiani, ou deux nuits d'excès," in *L'Erotisme romantique*, edited by J.-J. Pauvert. Paris: Carrere, 1984.

Reschal, Antonin. *Le Journal d'un amant*. Paris: Offenstadt, 1902.

APOLLINAIRE, GUILLAUME

1880–1918
French poet and prose writer

As a precocious adolescent, Apollinaire was well versed in the erotica of the *fin–de–siècle*, which Mario Praz in *The Romantic Agony* has called an age in which there reigned a vogue for "exotic perversions," including *sadisme à l'anglaise* ("English-style sadism," i.e., flogging) and the dark excesses of the "Slav soul." It was indeed a period much interested in flagellation, a taste for which Apollinaire apparently acquired from his Polish mother, who had a quick hand with a whip, and which he exploited in his own active sex life and in the best of his two pornographic novels, *The Eleven Thousand Rods*. He was also well read in the classics of erotic literature, a knowledge which served him well when he edited a series of anthologies of works by de Sade, Aretino, Baffo, Nerciat, Mirabeau, etc., for the Bibliothèque des Curieux from 1909 to 1912. He compiled secretly the first catalogue of the Bibliothèque nationale's collection of banned books, its "Enfer" in 1913, and edited a major collection of nineteenth-century erotic poems in 1910 called *Germain Amplecas* (*cas* is a slang word from the Italian *cazzo*, meaning "prick" and "shit").

Along with erotica, the *fin–de–siècle* was also a period when myths of theosophy were popular among intellectuals as a result of the influence of advanced Bible criticism, Jewish mysticism and the Cabala, and Rosicrucianism, as well as the serious study among ethnologists of comparative religions and folklore. In all of these studies Apollinaire was well versed, considering them valuable as poetic sources. The influence of Nietzsche was pervasive in the avant-garde circles in which he and friends, like the artist Pablo Picasso and the fantasist Alfred Jarry, moved— especially Nietzsche's dictum in *Europe Artiste* "We have killed God, we must become gods ourselves." Like Nietzsche, they favored the pre-Socratic Greek philosophers and placed their own aesthetic attempts at transcendency under the mythic aegis of Pythagoras, Dionysus, Orpheus, Pan, and Amphion. They were attempting to become new Orpheuses, new Nietzschean Antichrists themselves. They particularly celebrated the love-death (*Liebestot* or *petite mort*) between the poet-sun-Eros-Christ-phallus-phoenix and the Muse-night-Psyche-Mary-womb-siren, out of which the work of art is born. The artist thus becomes a kind of erotic savior, imposing his vision on a hostile world. In Apollinaire's poems and prose works, he variously portrays himself as Merlin the Enchanter, Pan, Ixion, Orpheus, Amphion, Christ, a holy clown, and a cosmopolitan, wandering god; his Muse is Viviane, the Sirens, Hera, Eurydice, Lilith, Eve, Salome, the Virgin Mary, Mary Magdalen, de Sade's Juliette, the Fair Rosemonde, and a number of beautiful passersby, from midinettes to prostitutes. Their offspring are his works of art.

On a personal, sexual level, these theories translated into a doctrine of apocalyptic salvation through the complete possession of a woman, both vulval and anal, stimulated by flagellation. To Apollinaire as to other, more serious theosophists, there was a cosmic unity between man-sun-penis and woman-night-vagina (or anus), the human experience being a microcosm of the universe (*Letters to Lou*, 1915). As in de Sade's statement, "Outside of the ass there is no salvation" (*Juliette,* IV), based on Alexis Piron's earlier saying, "Outside of the cunt there is no salvation" ("Ode to Priapus"), Apollinaire fashioned an absolute, mythic ethos from physical sexuality. Included in this ethos was his advocacy of the repopulation of France in view of the depredations of the Franco-Prussian War and World War I. Both in his minor pornographic novel, *The Exploits of a Young Don Juan,* and in his surrealistic farce, "The Breasts of Tiresias," he championed free love and female fertility as essential aspects of human eroticism.

On an aesthetic level, in the two little reviews he edited, and in his prolific journalistic writings from 1903 until his death in 1918, Apollinaire attempted to propagate these ideas. His principal aim was to bring together a "popular front" of modernism among all the arts, which he thought would result in a utopian age, a new erotic renaissance, in which poets and artists would be the prophetic leaders and role models. This age would be secular and would include the discoveries of science along with those of the arts. Together, they would unite the traditional order, sexuality, and beauty of French culture with the adventurism and futuristic explorations of the avant-garde. Although his vision of this

unity was somewhat compromised in the last years of his life by a certain amount of jingoism and antifeminism aggravated by his war experience, Apollinaire's modernistic ideas strongly influenced the surrealist movement of 1924–39, and his books soon were serving as revolutionary treatises throughout the artistic world.

The Eleven Thousand Rods

One of the Marquis de Sade's most influential pornographic works, *The 120 Days of Sodom,* written at the end of the eighteenth century, was not published in France until 1904. It is not surprising, therefore, that Apollinaire's most sadistic novel, *Les onze mille verges,* should arrive anonymously in the Paris underground two years later (1906–07). Incorporating much of de Sade's cruelty, black humor, and emphasis on bisexuality and anal intercourse, as well as providing a burlesque catalogue of the possibilities of sexual experience, Apollinaire's work is obviously a spin-off of de Sade's. It also resembles the latter's *Juliette* in being highly picaresque, full of libidinous, fantastic characters from various countries in Europe, with a priapic Romanian hospodar (a provincial governor in the Ottoman Empire) as its antihero and a wildly promiscuous French whore, Culculine d'Ancône (from *cul,* "ass," and *enconner,* "to put the prick in the cunt"), as one of its principal female protagonists. These characters embark on voyages into areas much in the news in the early years of the twentieth century, particularly into revolutionary Serbia and Siberia during the Russo-Japanese War. Like his patriotic Polish mother, Apollinaire detested Russia and was enthusiastically on the side of the Japanese in that conflict, unlike most of the mainstream French media. He had written columns for the socialist-anarchist newspaper *L'Européen* and shared the editors' revolutionary antagonism toward the tyrannical czarist regime. There were articles in the paper on Russian atrocities both in the war and on the home front (e.g., in the suppression of peasant uprisings), usually involving soldiers and workers being flogged to death by officers and landowners. It was appropriate, therefore, that Apollinaire's "one great unholy orgy," as the surrealist Robert Desnos called the novel, should feature "the dull thud of birch rods on robust and over-ripe flesh." Desnos also wrote that the work displays "the essentially modern role of masochism and the whip." Another surrealist, Louis Aragon, wrote that "it displays all the bitchery [*chiennerie*] of our century."

The title of the work is a pun on *verges* ("rods" or "scourges") and *vierges* ("virgins") and originates in the medieval legend of 11,000 virgins martyred by the Huns at Cologne. It also relates to a proverbial expression for a would-be womanizer, "a man in love with the 11,000 virgins." The main character in the book, the wealthy Romanian hospodar Mony Vibescu (*Mony* = "prick" in Romanian; *Vibescu* = French slang for "Dickfuckass"), an insatiable priapist, boasts that he can copulate twenty times in a row. His failure to accomplish this heroic feat results finally in his death under the scourges of 11,000 Japanese soldiers! As he dies, his body nothing but a formless mass of sausage meat, "his wide-open, glassy eyes seemed to contemplate the divine majesty of the great beyond."

As Aragon wrote in an introduction to the book, "Obviously, all that is not really very serious." Robert Desnos stated in his turn that "it was more poetic than erotic." And it is true that there are a number of burlesque episodes, parodies of French poets, and wild punning passages where the author seems drunk on his own verbiage, exotic customs and vocabulary, and bawdy jokes taken from books on European and Asiatic folklore. In addition, Apollinaire brings together some of the basic styles of the erotic classics with which he was so familiar. Not only does he set forth a de Sade–like compendium of the forms and positions of love, but he includes obscene punning names like those of André de Nerciat, the scholarly erudition of Mirabeau, incestuous episodes as in the novels of Rétif de la Bretonne, and bawdy dialogues among low-life types like those of Aretino, Zoppino, and Rétif. Yet he mentioned to friends that he wrote the book strictly for money; and after his arrest in 1911 as a suspect for the notorious theft of the *Mona Lisa* from the Louvre (he was innocent and soon released, but the affair seriously depressed him and aggravated the danger of his expulsion from France as a radical alien), he carefully hid his copy of the work in his library, toned down his campaign for erotic freedom, and increasingly became an outspoken French patriot.

Nevertheless, the multiple episodes of sadism, masochism, fetishism, saphism, transvestism, masturbation, homosexuality, incest, blasphemy, scatology, urolagnia, coprolagnia, coprolalia, necrophilia, pedophilia, gerontophilia, and zoophilia turn the work ultimately from a "not really serious" piece of Rabelaisian satire into something of an apocalypse of world sexuality, emphasizing the violence of revolution (in Serbia) and the sadistic chaos of a particularly bloody war in Russia. While Apollinaire's book was being written, Leo Tolstoy published *La guerre Russo-Japonaise,* in which he stated, "Hundreds of thousands of human beings are hunting each other down like wild beasts on earth and sea to kill each other, to mutilate each other, to torture each other as cruelly as possible." Thus it is not a coincidence that Mony Vibescu's most violent, most nauseating deeds, those involving torture and mutilation, make of him a Russian war hero. Indeed, several of the most violent incidents in the book were taken from reports in mainstream newspapers of the time, leading to the conclusion that the novel, almost in spite of itself and under all its satirical and comic episodes, is an ironic commentary on the terrible consequences of excessive sexuality and the gratuitous violence of war. It reveals a Manichaean dialogue between the light and the dark, between the cruel and the joyous sides of Apollinaire's philosophy of universal eroticism, a dualism which is not uncommon in the art and letters of the twentieth century and may be found in the eroticism of Bataille, Aragon, Artaud, Hemingway, Faulkner, Joyce, and many others. It is significant, for example, that Apollinaire's close friend Picasso, "that woman hater" (as Apollinaire once called him), maintained that *The Eleven Thousand Rods* was Apollinaire's best creation!

In addition, Apollinaire, like another friend and influence, the philosopher-novelist Remy de Gourmont, found a scientific basis for sexual excess. They were both fascinated by Émile Fabre's pioneering studies of insect life, and both believed that the murderous sex lives of certain insects paralleled those of men and women. In a letter dated October 14, 1915, Apollinaire wrote his fiancée that he had amused himself by attaching human names to Fabre's insects, giving them "a terrifying aspect of overly real humanity à la Marquis de Sade." Many of the episodes of *Les onze mille verges* thus fall into Gourmont's category of sex as *more bestiarum* (in the manner of animals).

A few years after writing *Les Onze mille verges,* Apollinaire edited an anthology of some of de Sade's more moderate passages, along with the works of other classic eroticists from the sixteenth and eighteenth centuries, and quickly became widely known as one of the principal European apologists for erotica in general and for "the Divine Marquis" in particular. In his introduction to de Sade, he called him "the freest spirit that has lived until now" and went so far as to refer to Juliette, de Sade's cruel and insatiable heroine, as "the new woman, . . . a being of whom we have as yet no idea, who is detaching herself from humanity, who will have wings, and who will renew the universe."

The Exploits of a Young Don Juan

Picaresque stories of the sexual initiation of randy adolescents go back to the ancient Greeks and constitute a stock-in-trade of nineteenth-century pornography. Apollinaire's obscene novel about a promiscuous sixteen-year-old boy named Roger (the name was chosen for its bawdy English meanings) is thus more conventional than *The Eleven Thousand Rods.* It is also more poorly written, and even though it was not published until 1911, it could well have been the first composed of the two. It contains some autobiographical allusions, and its sexuality is somewhat puerile, in keeping with the age of its protagonist. Its setting, moreover, is partly based on Apollinaire's yearlong sojourn as a tutor of French in a large German country house in 1901–02 when he was twenty-one years old. Perhaps he began writing it at that time in his frustration at being unable to bed his fellow tutor, the attractive English governess, Annie Playden (although they were probably stand-up lovers). He was also surrounded by a largely feminine household which included his pupil, an attractive young German girl. The novel deals largely with incest, a lifetime obsession of Apollinaire's, which partly stemmed from not knowing his father (Picasso thought he was a son of the pope) and from his love-hate relationship with his tempestuous Slavic mother.

Other influences besides de Sade (he probably hadn't yet read *The 120 Days*) were nineteenth-century "coming of age" pornographic novels, and especially the erotic dialogues and themes of incest in the works of another favorite eighteenth-century author, Rétif de la Bretonne. He particularly found fascinating Rétif's most pornographic novel, *The Anti-Justine.* Like Picasso, who sketched Alice Derain reading Rétif's book, Apollinaire was in rebellion against his strict Catholic upbringing, which led him to relish the novel's remarkably obscene and blasphemous celebration of the sexual relations between a father and a daughter (in a famous passage, she prays to "sweet Jesus the good fucker and pimp" of Mary Magdalene and "the sodomizer of Saint John"). And although Rétif ostensibly wrote the work to counter the cruelty of de Sade's pornographic writings, his book contains several sadistic episodes, just as Apollinaire's recurrent misogyny led him to include sadistic elements in his own pornographic works.

In *The Exploits of a Young Don Juan,* Roger recounts in the first person his first sexual experiences in a large country château. After discovering masturbation while looking at medical pictures, he first sleeps with the bailiff's pregnant wife, then deflowers his seventeen-year-old sister, Berthe, during her menstrual period. He then moves on to sex with Kate the maid, with the bailiff's wife's sister-in-law, with a servant Ursula, with a kitchen girl Babette, with Ursula again, and finally with his oldest sister, Élise, and with his aunt, Marguerite. Some of this lovemaking is preceded by spanking, and a certain amount of scatology is included, along with traditional puerile episodes of voyeurism and eavesdropping (at the confessional, in the maidservants' dormitory), in keeping with the adolescent subject matter. In all, a fairly wide range of sexual activity is explored in Apollinaire's usual picturesque, idiomatic vocabulary. Yet the episodes become monotonous by the end, as if the author were losing interest in his subject. Finally the book is brought to a close by the summary relation of three pregnancies and births, those of Ursula, Marguerite, and Élise, along with Roger's hope that he will have many more children.

The young Don Juan's final comment is that he is accomplishing his patriotic duty by augmenting the population of his country! This sounds outrageously satirical at first after the relation of so many self-indulgent orgies, yet it is echoed by several passages in other works of Apollinaire. In the final analysis, we are forced to take seriously Apollinaire's conception of repopulation as an inextricable element in his neo–de Sadean philosophy of pan-eroticism.

If free love is responsible for many babies, so much the better!

Alcools

Alcools (1913) was the first of Apollinaire's two main collections of poetry, works that bridged the transition from nineteenth-century, neo-Swedenborgian "angelism" in the symbolist poems of Nerval, Baudelaire, Rimbaud, and Mallarmé, to the more Freudian and revolutionary surrealist poems of the 1920s and 1930s. Its thematic structure is based on the poet's mythic picture of himself as an orphic, messianic figure wandering through modern European cities and landscapes experiencing the joys and sorrows of erotic, transcendent love. The *alcools* of the title flow through the book both as the intoxicating products of picturesque cafés and as the poetic vistas of the enchanting rivers that Apollinaire knew and loved, particularly the Rhone, the Rhine, and the Seine. They summarize the Dionysian-Apollonian dance of life and death that he experienced as an indefatigable *flâneur* ("walker-spectator"), his participation in the fascinating adventures of Eros and Anteros, their ecstasy and pain, and their infusion of light and shadow, fire and water. The book ends with the orphic lines, "I am drunk from drinking the entire universe / . . . / Listen to my songs of universal drunkenness."

The book opens in Paris on the edge of the Seine with the poem "Zone," which heralds the poetic and scientific glories of the twentieth century while chronicling at the same time the poet's own tragic loss of love in the departure of his mistress, the artist Marie Laurencin. He becomes a Christ-figure, crucified by love, and the famous final image of the poem is that of a beheaded (castrated), blood-red sun at dawn. Yet the book ends, again on the edge of the Seine, with the revolutionary Unanimist poem "Vendémiaire" [Vintage Month], a triumphant, Whitmanesque hymn to the poet-god and his privileged place at the center of an alcoholic universe. Apollinaire's beloved Paris becomes a kind of New Jerusalem to which the other drunken cities where the poet has lived—Rome, Nice, Lyons, and Cologne—pay homage. Thus the book is framed by two great poems, the first ending with an ironic sunrise at the poet's tragic demise ("Zone"), and the second ending with a sunrise at the dawn of a new apocalyptic age, a

"wine festival" of cosmopolitan poetry in utopian Paris ("Vendémiaire").

Other well-known poems in *Alcools* relate to love's loss in autumn and the melancholy passing of time; most famous are the haunting "Le pont Mirabeau" [Mirabeau Bridge] and the epic "La chanson du mal-aimé" [The Song of the Poorly Beloved]. The latter is a balladic, autobiographical work that takes the poet from London to Paris and includes ancient and modern legends, folklore, and lyrical refrains reminiscent of the "Testaments" of François Villon. It also contains the famous "seven swords" passage, seven fascinating, enigmatic stanzas that name and describe seven swords in the poet's heart that probably represent seven phases of the poet's sex life.

Besides the poems of love's loss, *Alcools* contains a number of poems of messianic transcendency. The most powerful of these are "Cortège," in which Apollinaire hymns himself as the product of all past experience; "Le Brasier" [The Brazier], in which he rises from Paris in a cosmic voyage to the heavens, where he unites with his dream of beauty like the mythic King Ixion uniting with his dream of the Mother Goddess; and finally "Les Fiançailles" [Betrothal], dedicated to Picasso and probably influenced by Picasso's artistic renewal in his seminal painting "Les Demoiselles d'Avignon" (1906–07). In this last work, the poet passes from his early Mariolatry to his crucifixion, when he loses both his friends and his former poetic truths, to finally his solar resurrection on Easter Day. The poem ends on the poet's rebirth as a new Knight Templar, a phallus- and Phoenix-like resurrection which makes him, like Picasso, the apocalyptic architect of a new temple of art.

Calligrammes, Letters to Lou, Tender as Memory

Apollinaire's other main poetry collection, *Calligrammes,* was published a few months before his death in 1918; the title is his term for concrete poems, a number of which are included in the work. The book consists of poems written largely out of his war experience, many of them composed under fire in the front-line trenches near Rheims. It begins with several free-verse poems from the period immediately preceding the war.

These poems relate to cosmopolitan, modernist ideas of poetry, sex, and art and feature lines inspired by paintings of Picasso, Delaunay, and Chagall. The first section also contains several experimental poems such as "Lettre-Océan," a simultaneous poem-telegram containing sights and sounds of Paris, and "Monday, Christine Street," a collage of bits of conversation heard in a café. There is also a long, prophetic work begun before the war and completed in 1917, "Les Collines" [The Hills], an important summary of the poet's life and creative achievements. The poem ends with a call to other poet-prophets to bring the old, classic world of order into the new world of adventurous art. These last three poems had a major influence on young Dadaists and surrealists after 1918, as did Apollinaire's revolutionary technique of doing away with all punctuation in the work, as he did in *Alcools.*

Following the prewar section come the war poems, which constitute a unique record of life and love in battle. There is probably nothing like them in any literature: journalistic, joyous, and erotic, they celebrate life in the front lines and the fantastic spectacle of war with its priapic canons, blazing ejaculations, and labyrinth of lascivious, female trenches. Out of this fabulous "love-death of nations," the utopian age of the future will be born. The allied victors of the war will realize all joys, "Women Games Factories Commerce/ Industry Agriculture Metal/Fire Crystal Speed/ Voice Gaze Touch . . ." ("War").

Many of these poems from the war zone were written to Apollinaire's various loves on the home front and are full of frank eroticism, paeans to "the nine holes of the (beloved's) body." They also provide an accurate record of his fellow soldiers' bawdy songs, jokes, and obscene vocabulary. Yet Apollinaire's most erotic writings out of his army experience are contained in two collections of letters, *Letters to Lou* and *Tender as Memory.* These two collections constitute a subtext to *Calligrammes,* the background of many of the best war poems. The first collection contains the letters and poems to his mistress Louise de Coligny, a wild party girl like his mother, a woman so turned on to eroticism—including anal sex and flagellation—that she comes close to Apollinaire's ideal woman of the future, de Sade's insatiable Juliette. The second collection has as its main theme the epistolary seduction of a virginal schoolteacher/ penpal, Madeleine Pagès, whom the poet had met only once on a train. The increasing heat of this correspondance, excited by the enforced chastity of a soldier's life in the trenches and the blossoming sexuality of a repressed schoolteacher, gradually rises to passionate outpourings from both camps, with the result that Madeleine eventually becomes Apollinaire's frank and totally submissive fiancée—entirely by mail! These two astonishingly intimate collections of letters, composed under the most difficult wartime conditions, besides giving a valuable blow-by-blow description of life on the western front, reveal in minute detail Apollinaire's wide experience in all matters pertaining to sexuality. They also provide impressive evidence of qualities he was famous for as a leading impresario of the avantgarde in Paris: his seductive enthusiasm and charm, his wit and humor, his astounding memory, his creative fluency, his inventive techniques, and the depth and breadth of his literary knowledge. All of these qualities were complemented by a broad and deep scholarship, which served to support his orphic philosophy of universal eroticism.

Yet Apollinaire's wide-ranging erudition and profound knowledge of foreign cultures and languages often make his works difficult to understand. For all their exotic vocabulary and references, however, they are never dull or overly academic; indeed, the poet was regarded by his contemporaries as a master of musicality and lyrical intoxication, purveyor of a mysterious beauty akin to the symbolists Gérard de Nerval and Arthur Rimbaud. As for his scholarship, most of his contemporaries agreed with his friend Gertrude Stein that it was a social and literary plus: "Guillaume was extraordinarily brilliant and no matter what subject was started, if he knew anything about it or not, he quickly saw the whole meaning of the thing and elaborated it by his wit and fancy carrying it further than anybody knowing anything about it could have done, and oddly enough generally correctly" (Stein, *The Autobiography of Alice B. Toklas,* 1933).

Apollinaire's erotic vocabulary is particularly rich. It includes French, British, Italian, German, and Slavic slang, Latin and medieval sayings, picturesque idioms, hundreds of euphemisms, poetic phrases, proverbs, and complex puns, the latter of which often fall into the category of what French critics call "calembours créateurs," *creative* puns. These are words and phrases that carry both a lyrical charge and a philosophical subtext.

A famous example of his punning profundity is the poem in *Alcools* "Chantre" [Choir-director, cantor]. The complete poem consists of one line, "Et l'unique cordeau des trompettes marines" [And the single cord of the trumpet marines]. All the words have witty, cosmic overtones. The *trompette marine* is both a large ancestor of the bass viol with a single string and a Mediterranean conch, thus both a stringed instrument and a wind instrument. *Cordeau,* "cord," contains several puns on terms for the penis (*cor, corde, cordon*) and relates to the sea trumpets sounded by water sprites in classical seascapes—it is a *cor d'eau* ("water horn") and a *corps d'eau* ("body of water"). The trumpet marine/conch is a symbol of the vulva, like the trumpet marine/horn which originally got its name from the German for "Mary's trumpet" (it was often played by nuns; the term was mistranslated by both the French and the British). In seventeenth-century occult writings, the huge instrument was both a symbol of the universe and of the body of man, both played upon by God.

Thus in one alexandrine line full of creative puns, Apollinaire, the godlike *chantre,* or poet/choir leader, both directs and plays on the single string of his instrument. The instrument resounds with all the male and female, aerial, terrestrial, and oceanic forces of the cosmos. While playing on the body of his mistress, Marie Laurencin, he is playing at the same time on Mary, the mother, daughter, and spouse of God. His phallic, microcosmic *uni-vers,* which means "one line" in French, thereby contains the macrocosmic *universe!*

Apollinaire's most frequent erotic terms and metaphors relate to the penis and the vulva. Many of these are of foreign origin. For the penis, there are *mony* (Romanian), *Roger, rod, cock, willy, horn* (English), *cazzo* (Italian), *lul* (Belgian), *Hans* (German), *phalle, priape* (Latin), *muleta* (Spanish), *IOD* (Hebrew), *Pata* (Turkish), and more than 150 French expressions, some of them of his own invention. For the vulva, there are *kteïs* (Greek), *tiz* (Arabian), *kunia* (Czech), *hole, queynte* (English), *quoniam* (Latin), and more than 130 French terms. In addition, there are no lack of expressions for breasts and nipples (more than 80 terms), a woman's body (more than 60), the anus (35), the clitoris (15), and various expressions for the testicles, buttocks, pubis, menses, excrements, ejaculation, and vaginal discharge, as well as for various kinds of lovers (e.g., more than 25 terms for a prostitute) and the many postures and acts of love. But the most interesting metaphors are often the most poetic, as for example, for the vulva of his penpal, Madeleine Soulas, which he had never seen, "a submarine garden of algae, coral, and sea urchins, of arborescent desires" (letter of October 9, 1915). Or for a penis in anal intercourse: "a bear cub stealing a honeycomb" ("6th Secret Poem" to Madeleine). Overall, Apollinaire's erotic vocabulary may be ranked in size and variety along with that of Aristophanes, Rabelais, Shakespeare, Mirabeau, de Sade, Joyce, and Genet as one of the richest in Western literature.

Apollinaire's "Carte du tendre" (map of the country of Love) is at the same time humorous, beautiful, ugly, poetic, cruel, and mysterious. He believed that the joyous and melancholy union of Psyche with Eros was the beginning and the end of the world, the full meaning of existence. In the *Chroniques d'art* of January 26, 1911, he wrote, "Love is not only French art, but Art itself, universal Art." *Poetry* to him had the Greek meaning of *creation,* the poet's re-creation or recasting in works of art of the orphic meaning of the universe, the cosmic force that "moves the sun and the other stars" (a quote from Dante he used in *Alcools*). His poems are pantheistic microcosms that reflect the larger reality, and if they are full of erotic puns and exotic phrases, the puns and phrases are like the ancient Greek *herms,* phallic mileposts to guide the reader to the center of that reality. This center is yonic and ineffable. In the poems' ultimate stage, "All is only a rapid flame / Flowered by the adorable rose / From which rises an exquisite perfume" (last stanza of "Les collines").

Biography

Apollinaire was born Wilhelm Albert Vladimir Alexander Apollinaris Kostrowitzky in Rome, Italy, August 25, 1880, to a young Polish woman and (probably) an Italian aristocrat. He was educated at Monaco, Cannes, and Nice,

1887–97, mostly in private Catholic schools. After short sojourns in Lyons, Paris, and Stavelot, Belgium, he settled in Paris in 1899, then left Paris to spend a year in the Rhineland as tutor to an aristocratic German family 1901–02, and toured Germany, Czechoslovakia, and Austria with the family. He lived in Paris the rest of his life except for a year in the army during World War I (1915). From 1907 to 1918, Apollinaire became a major apologist for the avant-garde art movements Fauvism, Cubism, Orphism, and surrealism ("the School of Paris") and for modernist poetry in the years of transition from symbolism to surrealism. His two influential poetry collections were *Alcools* (1913) and *Calligrammes* (1918), and he wrote a collection of short stories, *L'hérésiarque et cie* [*The Heresiarch and Company*], 1911; a book of art criticism, *Les artistes cubistes*, 1913; a fictional autobiography, *Le poète assassiné*, 1917; and a play, "Les Mamelles de Tirésias" [The Breasts of Tirésias], 1917. He was wounded by shrapnel in the temple in the trenches near Rheims on March 17, 1916, and was trepanned in Paris on May 2. He married Jacqueline Kolb in May 1918. Apollinaire died of influenza and the effects of his wound on November 9, 1918.

SCOTT BATES

Selected Works

Les onze mille verges (published anonymously). 1907; reprinted with a preface by Michel Décaudin, Paris: Pauvert, 1979; translated as *The Debauched Hospodar*, Los Angeles: Holloway House, 1967; as *Les Onze mille verges, or The Amorous Adventures of Prince Mony Vibescu*, translated by Nina Rootes, introduction by Richard N. Coe, New York: Taplinger, 1979.
Les exploits d'un jeune Don Juan (published anonymously). 1911?; reprinted with a preface by Michel Décaudin, Paris: Pauvert, 1977; translated as *Memoirs of a Young Rakehell*, Los Angeles: Holloway House, 1967 (in the same volume as *The Debauched Hospodar*).

L'Hérésiarque et cie. Paris: Stock, 1910; translated by Rémy Inglis Hall as *The Heresiarch and Company*, Garden City, NY: Doubleday, 1965.
Alcools, poèmes (1898–1913). Paris: Mercure de France, 1913; translated by William Meredith, New York: Doubleday, 1964; translated by Anne Hyde Greet, Berkeley and Los Angeles: University of California Press, 1965.
Calligrammes. Paris: Mercure de France, 1918; translated by Anne Hyde Greet with preface by S.I. Lockerbie, Berkeley, Los Angeles, London: University of California Press, 1980.
Le poète assassiné. Paris: L'Édition, Bibliothèque des Curieux, 1916; translated by Ron Padgett as *The Poet Assassinated*, London: Rupert Hart-Davis, 1968.
Tendre comme le souvenir. Paris: Gallimard, 1952.
Lettres à Lou. Edited by Michel Décaudin. Paris: Gallimard, 1969.
Apollinaire on Art: Essays and Reviews 1902–1918. Edited by LeRoy C. Breunig, translated by Susan Suleiman. New York: Viking Press, 1972.
Oeuvres poétiques. Edited by Marcel Adéma and Michel Décaudin, introduction by André Billy. Paris: Gallimard, Éditions de la Pléiade, 1977.
Oeuvres en prose complètes, 3 vols. Edited by Pierre Caizergues and Michel Décaudin. Paris: Gallimard, Éditions de la Pléiade, 1993.

Further Reading

Adéma, Marcel. *Guillaume Apollinaire le mal-aimé*. Paris: Pion, 1952; translated as Apollinaire by Denise Folliot. New York: Grove Press, 1955.
Bates, Scott. *Guillaume Apollinaire*, 2nd ed., rev. Boston: Twayne, 1989.
Breunig, LeRoy C. *Guillaume Apollinaire*. New York and London: Columbia University Press, 1969.
Davies, Margaret. *Apollinaire*. London: Oliver and Boyd, 1964; New York: St. Martin's Press, 1964.
Praz, Mario. *The Romantic Agony*, translated by Angus Davidson. London: Oxford University Press, 1933. Originally published as *Carne, la morte e il diavolo nella letteratura romantica*.
Shattuck, Roger. *The Banquet Years*. New York: Harcourt, Brace, 1955.
Steegmuller, Francis. *Apollinaire, Poet among the Painters*. New York: Farrar, Strauss, 1963.

APULEIUS

c.125 CE
Roman orator and philosopher

The book for which Apuleius is now chiefly remembered is the *Metamorphoses,* or *The Golden Ass.* The subtitle "Golden" ("Aureus") may contain an allusion to Pythagorean philosophy, might possibly be an indicator of the esteem in which the novel was held in antiquity, or could constitute an ironic allusion to the epic quest for the mythological Golden Fleece of Jason and the Argonauts as told in the *Argonautica,* a poem by Apollonius of Rhodes (third century BCE). It is the only Latin novel which survives complete, and consists of a series of imbricated tales told by a variety of different characters, including the Ass himself. In form it belongs to what were known as "Milesian Tales," being a collection of stories somewhat similar to the style of the *Arabian Nights* or Boccaccio's *Decameron* but set in a picaresque framework as the Ass moves from one disreputable or dangerous situation to another. It is in turn bawdy, humorous, melodramatic, mock-heroic, romantic, and mystical.

The basic plot is provided by the story of the adventures of a young man, who, through his uncontrolled curiosity, is transformed by witchcraft into an ass. After many adventures, he finally regains his human shape through the intervention of the goddess Isis and her brother Osiris and participates in the celebration of their mystic rites, recognizing his duty of worship and celibacy. The most famous inserted tale in the *Metamorphoses* is the story of Cupid and Psyche (IV.28–VI.24). This may be read as an allegory of the Soul (Psyche), who, sad and tormented while separated from her Master (Cupid, or Eros), regains perfection and happiness when reunited with Love. There is a parallelism with the plight of the Ass, whose curiosity causes his tragedy and who finally achieves salvation. "Cupid and Psyche" is, perhaps rather incongruously, told by an old hag, who is eventually murdered by the robbers she serves. She recounts how Venus, the Goddess of Love, is annoyed at the fame of Psyche's beauty, which threatens to rival her own, and so sends her son Cupid to persecute the girl. Cupid, however, falls in love with her and does not tell his mother. Their love is consummated in the dark, for Psyche must not see her husband. Her envious sisters, alleging that she is mating with a snake (for so an oracle has seemed to indicate), persuade her to light a candle. But a drop of hot wax wakes Cupid up and tragedy seems about to occur. Venus, now furious as she learns the truth, berates Cupid and sets impossible tasks for Psyche to perform, but Psyche accomplishes all she is told to do, being rescued from eternal sleep by Cupid. Jupiter, the King of the Gods, resolves that Cupid's cunning will be cured by matrimony. The child which is born of this union is called Pleasure (Voluptas). The story is highly charged with allegory and, among other things, illustrates the hag's contention that what we see, including what we dream, often signifies the opposite of what it apparently means. Despite being told by a lecherous old woman, this erotic tale is narrated chastely. Many of the other stories are not so restrained. They may be divided into two categories: those which concern the Ass himself, and those which are recounted by other individuals. Among the former we find the episode of Lucius's original misfortune: He sees in magic the possibility of erotic and other adventures (II.6). He is sexually aroused by Photis, the servant girl (II.7), and energetically makes love to her all night long on a couch. Having avoided Byrrhena, the predatory wife of his host, he witnesses with Photis the magic transformation of her mistress, and on trying the special ointment turns into an ass. A number of his subsequent adventures involve avoiding physical abuse, pain, and several unpleasant threats of imminent castration or death. A youth malevolently asserts that the Ass will go after anything: marriageable women, girls, boys, in the hope of sodomizing them (VII.21). But this is in fact untrue. Eventually, however, a woman, attracted by the size of his member, does make lustful advances to him and sets up a situation in private where she can gratify her desire. Surrounded by soft cushions and beautiful furnishings, they taste the delights of Venus despite the Ass's fear that his organ might prove too large (X.19–22). As a result, his owner decides to arrange a display where the Ass will couple with a multiple murderess, a condemned woman of the lowest sort, in the arena. The public's anticipation is, sadly, disappointed as the Ass makes his escape before he can be gored to death while locked in a bestial embrace (X.23–35). On an earlier occasion, he becomes the property of a band of wandering priests of Cybele, renowned for the orgiastic nature of their worship. The devotees are all castrated effeminates, eager for the services of a well-hung country lad whom they prefer to the Ass (VIII.26–29). Among the stories told by other characters, one features a corpse who says he was murdered by his adulterous wife (II.23–30); in another, a certain Thrasyllus attempts to seduce Charite, who eventually tricks and blinds him before committing suicide on her husband's tomb (VIII.1–14).

Four interrelated stories play on the theme of the lustful wife who outwits her cuckolded husband. In the first, a lover hides in a storage jar and is then replaced there by the husband while the adulterous pair sit on top and enjoy each other (IX.5–7). The second is about a lover who flees in haste, leaving behind a sandal which he nevertheless wittily explains away and calms the husband's suspicious jealousy (IX.17–21). In the third, to which the Ass is actually witness, a baker's wife welcomes her youthful lover, who has to be hidden under an inverted tub. When the Ass deliberately treads on his protruding fingers he is discovered, the baker takes him off, and, saying that what his wife enjoys should be shared, sodomizes him before having him soundly whipped (IX.22–23, 26–28). Inserted in this tale is the story of the fuller who discovers his wife's infidelity when the lover sneezes in his hiding place (IX.24–25). Unrelated to these, but still displaying a high degree of misogyny in the portrait of an insatiably lustful wicked woman, is the story of incest between a wife and her stepson (X.2–12). A false poison frustrates her foul designs and reveals her schemes. If all these women are shown in a disreputable light, it has also to be remembered that the nature of an ass is composed of lust, grossness, and lazy deceitfulness. The *Metamorphoses* takes us through these human states before reaching a final moral apotheosis (XI.15).

Biography

Apuleius was born into a prosperous family in Madaurus (North Africa). He was educated at Carthage, Rome, and Athens, thereafter becoming a priest of the Imperial Cult and a public speaker.

PATRICK POLLARD

Selected Works

Metamorphoses. Edited and translated by J.A. Hanson. Cambridge, MA: Harvard University Press, 1989.
The Transformations of Lucius, otherwise known as the Golden Ass. Translated by Robert Graves. Harmondsworth: Penguin, 1950.

Further Reading

Cooper, G. "Sexual and Ethical Reversal in Apuleius: The *Metamorphoses* as Anti-Epic," *Latomus* 168 (1980), pp. 436–466.
Hägg, E.H. *The Novel in Antiquity.* Oxford: OUP 1983.
James, P. *Unity in Diversity: A Study of Apuleius' Metamorphoses.* Hildesheim: G. Olms, 1987.
Konstan, D. *Sexual Symmetry: Love in the Ancient Novel and Related Genres.* Princeton, NJ: Princeton University Press, 1994.
Schlam, C.C. *The Metamorphoses of Apuleius.* London: Duckworth, 1992.
Scobie, A. *Aspects of the Ancient Romance and Its Heritage: Essays on Apuleius, Petronius and the Greek Romances.* Meisenheim am Glan, 1969.
Tatum, J. *Apuleius and the Golden Ass.* Ithaca, NY: Cornell University Press, 1979.
Walsh, P.G. *The Roman Novel.* Cambridge: CUP, 1970.
Winkler, J.J. *Auctor and Actor: A Narratological Reading of Apuleius' Golden Ass.* Berkeley and Los Angeles, CA: University of California Press, 1985.

ARABIC: MIDDLE AGES TO NINETEENTH CENTURY

The vast corpus of premodern Arabic writing is anything but reticent about matters of love and sex. Nostalgia for a lost love is a prominent theme already in the earliest preserved Arabic poetry, from the sixth century, and throughout the following millennium the independent love lyric enjoyed a central place in the poetic canon, undergoing developments that expanded its thematic range to include everything from the earthy and puckish to the desperately ethereal. Anthologists and prose essayists also turned their attention to the phenomenon of sexual love, producing a stream over the centuries of some two dozen monographs on "love theory," rich in psychological insight and providing the outside observer with a trove of sociological evidence. While this literature generally avoided explicit discussion or description of sex, the latter enjoyed its own well-defined and fully condoned literary space. In both poetry and prose, the forthright treatment of sexual matters was assiduously cultivated, in a variety of forms and with a variety of intentions, including amusement, shock, education, and sexual stimulation, all recognized as legitimate literary objectives. This broad range of literature included, but was by no means limited to, a genre of "erotica" in the narrow sense—that is, monographic treatments of sexual matters for which "explicitness" was a defining feature.

Both continuity and dynamism are givens in a literary tradition that extends over a millennium, and any overview of an important segment of that tradition must cope with both. For the survey presented here, chronology has been given precedence over typology, with the imposition of a very rough periodization meant to highlight developments over time, although continuity in the maintenance of specific genres will be apparent enough, not to mention the handing down, century by century, of a corpus of canonized poetry and anecdote. For its first three centuries, until about the 800, the Arabic literature

we have is essentially an oral tradition and, unless we count the Qur'ān, a poetic one. Ninth-century philologists carefully recorded this tradition as they knew it, and despite the inevitable uncertainties about authenticity, the result is a corpus of poetry extending back well into the sixth century, several generations before the advent of Islam in 610–622.

Pre-Islamic Arabic poetry was a highly developed art form, with a complex system of meter, rhyme, and thematics. Its most prestigious genre, the *qaṣīda* (ode), consisted of a monorhymed poem of some 50 to 100 lines with a fairly rigid sequence of themes: an initial reminiscence about a former love affair (the *nasīb*), followed by a description of the poet's journey on a camel, and then, the point of the poem, a section praising himself, his tribe, or (a harbinger of later developments) a patron. The *nasīb* was most commonly evoked by a chance visit to an abandoned campsite in the desert, the scene of the now-remembered tryst; the poet might describe the beauty of his lost beloved but would usually focus on his own emotions. Specific descriptions of what went on are relatively rare, although the most famous of these poets, Imru' al-Qays, notoriously described the way he made love to a nursing mother who had her infant at her side.

The *qaṣīda* eschewed any use of obscenity, but obscenity was certainly a recognized concept, and it turns up here and there in poetry of the genre recognized as the *qaṣīda*'s obverse, *hijā'*, "dispraise" or attack poetry. In *hijā'*, rival tribes, or specific members of them, were assaulted for all sorts of reasons, including their sexual immorality; and slurs on enemies' wives, mothers, and sisters, describing their (usually fictional) sexual escapades in the grossest terms, were a sanctioned component of such attacks.

The ninth-century philologists also preserved a fair amount of more general lore about pre-Islamic Arabian society, whose accuracy is, however, highly questionable, both because of doubts about its transmission (not being anchored by the specific wording of poetry) and because of the intervening advent of Islam, which gave later scholars every reason to paint the mores of pre-Islamic society in dark colors. This lore includes lurid descriptions of pre-Islamic Arabian prostitution; lists of famous fornicators of the period, as well as active and passive homosexuals (a topic untouched by the poetry altogether); and identification of the princess Hind, daughter of al-Nu'mān and a Christian, as the "first" Arab lesbian, whose devotion to her lover al-Zarqā' led to her founding of a nunnery to which she retired after her lover's death.

With God's revelations (in what was to become the Qur'ān) to the Prophet Muḥammad in Mecca and Medina in the early seventh century, Arabian society was transformed. Relations between the sexes were regularized, in carefully defined forms of marriage (including polygamy, with a maximum of four wives) and concubinage (unlimited); a firm line was drawn between licit and illicit sexual behavior (with adultery punishable by stoning and premarital fornication by flogging); and homosexual behavior was (rather ambiguously) condemned. Neither the Qur'ān nor handed-down traditions about the Prophet's words and deeds (the *ḥadīth*) have much to say, however, about *talking* (or writing) about sex. According to some accounts, the Prophet resorted to euphemism in referring to sexual pleasure ("tasting his or her little honey"); but others, defending the use of the Arabic equivalent of "four-letter" words, place them in the mouths of both the Prophet himself and his most highly esteemed Companions—in the proper context (one Companion is quoted repeatedly in the following centuries as saying that "obscenity" in speech is only objectionable when women are present). Again, questionable "lore" fills in some details about sexual practices at the time, including both greater independence among Medinan women (as compared with Meccans) and their greater sexual conservatism (e.g., opposition to anal intercourse, practiced by some Meccan immigrants to the city); the Prophet is reported to have objected to an institutionalized form of male transvestism only when one such transvestite, assumed to be impervious to women's sexual charms, betrayed too intimate a knowledge of them when describing a

prospective bride to an interested third party; but all such accounts are highly colored by later cultural developments.

In fact the Arabs' world changed radically after the death of the Prophet, as their Muslim armies conquered the Sasanian empire of Iran and Iraq in its entirety and deprived the Byzantine empire of its Syrian and Egyptian provinces. During the following century Arab warriors and their families put down roots in these foreign, sedentary societies, ruling over them and attempting to keep themselves segregated from them, but inevitably gradually succumbing to massive cultural influence from them. Our Arabic sources for this period—still oral, and still primarily poetic—do not yet betray much of an effect from this influence, but they do manifest important literary developments. Abuse poetry (*hijā'*) enjoyed an efflorescence, and the use of scurrilous sexual attacks on the victims' womenfolk became a commonplace in the invective of the famous poets Jarīr (d. 729) and al-Farazdaq (d. 728), as well as many others. At the same time, the poetry of love, separating from its status as a component of the *qaṣīda*, became a genre on its own, in two forms. On the one hand, nostalgia yielded to sweet despair among some Bedouin poets, who composed plangent lyrics about their hopeless passion for a thwarted love that drove them to madness or even an early death; this trend, which was to have a rich (and heavily romanticized) future, was dubbed "'Udhrī," after the 'Udhra tribe that was particularly associated with it. On the other hand, some urban poets, most notably 'Umar b. Abī Rabī'a (d. c. 720) in Medina, composed light and charming lyrics about their flirtations with the local girls, a style with an equally impressive future before it. Both of these styles of *ghazal* (love lyric) were quite chaste—specific references to sexuality were inappropriate, although a little raciness here and there was acceptable in the "urban" genre.

Again, the historically dubious anecdotal evidence preserved by later authors gives us a fuller picture, specifically of the "gilded" society of Mecca and Medina in the first century of Islam, when political power—the caliphate—had moved away (to Damascus), but the aristocrats of the holy cities gained enormous wealth from both their ascribed status and the economic impact of the annual pilgrimage. We hear a great deal about the lives of pleasure and indeed decadence led by these aristocrats, with intimations of freewheeling sexual lifestyles going well beyond the modest license reflected in the verse of 'Umar b. Abī Rabī'a and his fellow poets; representative of this material are the many stories about Ḥubbā, a Medinan prostitute and self-professed expert on sexual technique, whose detailed advice to brides (and bridegrooms) was to be quoted for many centuries.

But things seem to have gone yet further in the provinces, and specifically in the city of al-Kūfa, in Iraq, where a third school of love poetry can be discerned, one that moved in the direction of explicit articulation of sexuality. A group of Kūfan poets, at the opposite pole from 'Udhrī chastity, began to compose poems celebrating their sexual liaisons, as well as the joys of wine, both of which were in defiance of Islamic norms. It is here that we find the first articulation of what was quickly to become the important literary genre of *mujūn*, or "libertinism," antinomian poetry (and prose) that thumbed its nose at Islam and preached a message of pure hedonism—and equally quickly achieved acceptance as a *literary* phenomenon that did not, as such, endanger the mores of actual society. This trend was boosted further by the Damascene caliph al-Walīd b. Yazīd (d. 744), notorious for his attention to pleasures and inattention to affairs of state but famous as well for his seductive poetry about wine and women.

In 750 the Umayyad dynasty of caliphs in Damascus was overthrown by a revolutionary movement originating in eastern Iran, that of the 'Abbāsids, who assumed control of the Islamic state and shifted the center of power to the east, establishing their new capital in Baghdad in 762. This political revolution had profound cultural repercussions as well. With interaction, intermarriage, and the sheer passage of time, the conquering Arabs could no longer hold themselves aloof from the sedentary societies of the former Byzantine and Sasanian provinces they controlled; and the shift of power to the east assured a new dominance of Persian cultural norms over the evolving Islamic society.

Although it is difficult to pinpoint the exact correlation between political and literary events, it is clear that Arabic literature underwent a profound shift at this point as well, one aspect of which is enshrined in Arabic literary history as the advent of the "New" (*muḥdath*) poets. The former canons of Bedouin poetry—weeping over a deserted encampment, for instance—were not only abandoned but mocked, and the reality of city life was emphatically affirmed; at the same time a new and more precious literary style was instituted. In love poetry, the earthy Kūfan style was further developed, while the Udhrī style of breathless longing for an impossible love was taken to new (and acknowledgedly artificial) heights by the poet al-'Abbās b. al-Aḥnaf (d. c. 805). The Bedouin 'Udhrī poets of a century earlier became the subjects of legend, and an apparently totally fictitious poet, al-Majnūn ("the Madman"), was enshrined as their leader, complete with a corpus of verse attributed to him. What had been a Bedouin trend became a (somewhat brittle) urban fashion.

But even more extreme innovations were also taking place. The most brilliant poet of the new generation in Baghdad, Abū Nuwās (d. c. 815), had no use for Udhrī verse, but cultivated rather the Kūfan tradition of antinomianism. Not only did he become the most celebrated Arabic (and Islamic) poet of the joys of forbidden wine; he also established homoeroticism as a suitable, and quickly dominant, form of love (and sex) poetry. Later redactors of his collected verse divided his love poetry into three groups: heterosexual, homosexual, and libertine (*mujūn*). Poems in the first two categories celebrated the beauty of the beloved, complained (never too seriously) about his or her standoffishness and cruelty, and described the poet's woeful state, or they amusingly, and elegantly, recounted a light flirtation. By definition such love lyrics (*ghazal*) never made direct reference to sex, although a certain amount of innuendo could be appropriate. In Abū Nuwās's *mujūn* poetry, on the other hand, the point was to be as explicit—humorously and sometimes shockingly—as possible. Flirtation becomes seduction—one of the poet's favorite themes is the seduction of a young Christian boy in a tavern or monastery—and sometimes we are told even the number of thrusts involved in their lovemaking. One long poem describes the seduction of a professional singing slave girl, with whom the poet was able to reach orgasm only by imagining her as a boy. A few depict orgies, voyeurism, and other such activities.

Abū Nuwās was an important trendsetter in many ways, not least in institutionalizing *mujūn* poetry as an acceptable genre. Inevitably, some of his contemporaries and successors attempted to outdo him and devoted verses to such topics as loving descriptions of male and female genitalia; one poet made a specialty of writing elegies (*rithā'*) on his (putatively) uncooperative penis. The tradition of attack poetry (*hijā'*) also became even coarser, with the grossest sexual activities attributed to the poet's enemies. Of course, not all poets pursued all the available genres, but some of those most prominent for their panegyrics and elegies, such as Ibn al-Rūmī (d. 896), composed *mujūn* and *hijā'* with equal gusto. Virtually all of them included love lyrics in their work, and most celebrated both hetero-erotic and homoerotic passion.

But the early ninth century also witnessed the initiation of a serious written Arabic prose literature. Partly under the influence of a translation movement from Greek, Syriac, and Middle Persian, Arab authors embraced the concept of an authored monograph with a fixed text, and a flood of books ensued. Much of this early prose literature has been lost, but we are fortunate to have a sizable portion of the oeuvre of the most outstanding and prolific author of the day, al-Jāḥiẓ (d. 868). Al-Jāḥiẓ's interests were all-encompassing, and emphatically included love and sex. His essay collections *Love and Women* and *The Difference Between Men and Women* are unfortunately preserved only in fragments, but his work on *Singing Slave Girls* survives intact, presenting us with a characteristically sardonic picture of this institution of Baghdad high society. While casting his discussion in the form of a spirited defense of their trade by the owners and trainers of these professional entertainers, he manages to convey as well the negative side—the slave girls' gold-digging ways and the fuzziness of the line that kept many of them just this side of prostitution.

As is often the case with al-Jāḥiẓ, it is difficult to put a neat generic label on his *Singing Slave Girls*. Two other works, however, clearly fall into the category of *mujūn*, given their predominantly humorous purpose and their constant recourse to explicit discussion of sex. Both are debates about the relative merits of women and boys as sex partners for men, a topic known already in Greek literature (although the path of influence on the Arabic is impossible to trace) and one that was to continue to attract other Arabic authors for centuries to come. The *Boasting Match Between Sodomites and Fornicators*

actually begins with a defense of writing about frivolous topics and the use of obscene language, then presents a series of arguments comparing the physical pleasures of vaginal and anal sex, the beauties of women and boys, and so forth, together with an odd digression on eunuchs. The champion of heterosexual sex seems to win the debate, but not unambiguously. The situation is clearer in the *Superiority of the Belly to the Back*, in which al-Jāḥiẓ tries to turn a young colleague away from what he sees as his errant pursuit of homoerotic delights, employing mostly rhetorical arguments but also condemning sodomy flatly as unnatural vice—but without abandoning a jocular tone throughout.

Al-Jāḥiẓ has much more to say about sex and the sexes in his other works, notably in his multivolume *Book of Animals,* where his tendency to digress leads him to indulge in particular his obsession with eunuchs. Numerous other prose writers of the period included significant erotological material in their works as well, especially in the form of humorous anecdotes (ranging from short jokes to lengthy narratives) that were assiduously collected in anthologies, one of the most distinctive prose genres developed under the overall rubric of *adab,* or belles-lettres.

But a separate genre of erotica, in the narrower sense, also appeared in the ninth century. Unfortunately, all the early exemplars of what was to become an established tradition are lost, and we know of them only from later citations and bibliographical references. In particular, the invaluable late-tenth-century *Index,* a work composed by a Baghdad bookseller incorporating authors and titles with supplementary information about every book in Arabic of which he was aware, offers quite a lot of information about this early erotica. Referring to such works precisely as "sex books" (*kutub al-bāh*), he lists their titles under a rubric that indicates clearly enough an extensive debt to foreign influences as well as their explicitly prurient intentions: "Titles of books composed about sexual intercourse, Persian, Indian, Greek, and Arabic, in the form of sexually stimulating discourse."

Of the three Persian books listed, that of *Bunyāndakht* can be identified from extensive later quotations as advice for women on sexual matters proffered by a woman named Bunyāndakht, including detailed instructions for effectively stimulating a man in bed. The second, the book of *Bahrāmdakht,* does not appear in later sources and may be a garbled duplicate of *Bunyāndakht.* The title of the third, the book of *Bunyān Nafs,* is uncertain, appearing elsewhere as *Bunyāqis* or *Bunyāfis,* but it appears to be a man's name, with the author addressing such issues as women's preferences in penis sizes and shapes, the necessity for men to tell lies in order to conquer women, and why old women hate younger women more than old men hate younger men.

The two Indian books listed in the *Index* are apparently two different versions ("big" and "small") of the *Alfīya,* whose title ("The Thousander") is explained by other sources as referring to an Indian woman whose sexual expertise she owed to experiencing sexual intercourse with a thousand different men. This work is probably the same as that of Harqaṭ (or Harūṭ?) son of Ṭamas the Indian (al-Hindī), usually referred to simply as "The Indian," which is quoted extensively in a number of other sources, notably in the *Encyclopedia of Pleasure* (discussed below), where several such quotations closely parallel material in the *Kamasutra.* Topics discussed by The Indian in preserved citations include the kinds of women one should and should not marry; the parameters of possible penis size, with nicknames for large, medium, and small; appropriate grooming for both sexes; and the stimulating effects of talking during sexual intercourse.

The *Index* lists only one Greek sex book, that of Marṭūs the Greek, which seems likely to be the same as that of Arīṭās (or Arṭiyās) the Greek referred to several times in the *Encyclopedia of Pleasure,* where it is said to overlap heavily with the book of The Indian and is quoted for descriptions of male and female genitals and techniques for achieving simultaneous orgasm, and its approval of jealousy so long as it it is not excessive. Who the author of this book might actually be remains to be determined, but as a "stimulating" work, it was apparently generically distinct from both the medical sex book of Rufus of Ephesus (second century CE) and the medico-physiognomical work of his contemporary Polemon, both of which were translated into Arabic and left significant traces in the later erotological tradition.

In fact, under the stimulus of the Greek tradition—including, crucially, a major section of the pseudo-Aristotelian *Problemata,* dealing with various sexual questions—a number of Arabic physicians and philosophers composed works on sexual intercourse (*bāh*) that, unlike their more literary counterparts, have survived. We have a brief work of this nature by the "first Arab philosopher," al-Kindī (d. *c.* 865), dealing mostly with problems of impotence and various drugs purported to cure it; a reworking of the section on sex in the *Problemata* by al-Kindī's contemporary 'Īsā ibn Māssa, entitled *Questions on Reproduction, Offspring, and Sexual Intercourse;* and two works by the Christian Qusṭā ibn Lūqā (d. 912), one again focused on impotence problems but the other casting its nets more widely, with discussions of the age of puberty for males and females, the dangers for health of both excessive sexual activity and abstinence, and the peculiar sexuality of eunuchs. A generation later the celebrated physician al-Rāzī (d. *c.* 925) composed both a *Book on Sexual Intercourse,* very much along the lines of Qusṭā's broader work, with sections on the dangers of excess, the means to correct them, and an array of drugs and other treatments for male sexual problems, and a monograph, unique in the Arabic tradition, on what he calls *The Hidden Disease,* attempting to provide a physiological explanation for the phenomenon of passive male homosexuality, that is, adult men who derive sexual satisfaction from being penetrated anally by other men. Many of these ideas reappear in the *Canon* of Avicenna (d. 1037), which in Latin translation was to have a profound influence on medical thinking in medieval and early modern Europe.

The *Index,* in its section on medicine, notes some of these works, as well as a few others, including a work on coitus by the celebrated translator Ḥunayn b. Isḥāq (d. 873) that seems not to have survived; but such medical works are clearly considered to be generically distinct from the "lust-inducing" literary works listed for the Persians, Indians, Greeks, and Arabs. For the Arabs (presumably meaning original works, rather than translations, although foreign influence is clearly not irrelevant), the *Index* offers seven titles. Again, two of these are "big" and "small" versions of a single work, the *Book of Barjān and Ḥubāḥib,* by Abū Ḥassān al-Namlī (d. *c.* 860), which appears to have been quite popular. In the numerous citations from the book by later authors, the two women named in the title, apparently Persians, offer answers to a wide variety of questions posed by a nameless king, mainly on things a man would like to know about a woman's sexuality, and with a particular concern about the timing of male and female orgasms and what to do when they are not simultaneous. Al-Namlī has also an independent entry elsewhere in the *Index,* where it is recorded that he composed works on *Passive Sodomy, Lesbianism,* and *The Donkey-Renter's Speech to the Grocer's Daughter* [or *Slave Girl*], all of which have disappeared without a trace.

Of the remaining five titles offered by the *Index,* three are otherwise unknown: *The Free Woman and the Slave Woman, The Woman in Power Named "Playful" and the Sodomite Ḥusayn,* and *Beloved Slave Girls.* The last of these may well have dealt with lore about lesbian relationships, since elsewhere in the book the same vocabulary is used to refer to some dozen (completely lost) works on famous lesbian couples. The fourth, on *Lesbians and Passive Sodomites,* by the well-known court buffoon Abū l-'Anbas al-Ṣaymarī (d. 888), is known from extensive citations in later works and was clearly a typical "libertine" (*mujūn*) compilation of titillating anecdotes and other material; his other works (again, completely lost) include, according to the *Index's* own entry on him, a monograph on masturbation, a collection of anecdotes about pimps, and a book on *The Superiority of the Anus to the Mouth.*

It is surprising that the fifth of the *Index's* titles of Arabic erotica, the sex book by Ibn Ḥājib al-Nu'mān (d. 962), a contemporary of the *Index's* author, has not survived. Cited by the latter under the title *The Discourse of Ibn al-Dukkānī,* but more generally known as the *Book of Women,* it is singled out by the twelfth-century erotologist al-Samaw'al b. Yaḥyā as one of the two most effective works of this nature at stimulating a man's flagging sex drive, the other being the *Encyclopedia of Pleasure.* Oddly missing from the *Index's* list of erotica, but included in a separate entry elsewhere in the book, are the works of the obscure Ibn al-Shāh al-Ṭāhirī (early tenth century?), which included *Boys, Women, Passive Sodomy and Its Pleasures, Masturbation,* and *Taking Turns* (at homosexual anal intercourse).

The loss of all these early works is perhaps due in part to their relatively low prestige, but it would be quite erroneous to think of them as either "underground" or even "popular" literature; their authors (and translators) were certainly full-fledged literati, and these works would have circulated like any other books. The primary reason for their disappearance is, rather, that they served as mines for later authors, and as the material they contained was increasingly recycled, newer (and perhaps more comprehensive and sophisticated) works simply drove out the older ones, and demand for fresh copies of the latter dried up. A milestone in this process was certainly reached with the *Encyclopedia of Pleasure* by the rather obscure late-tenth-century author 'Alī ibn Naṣr al-Kātib, which is the earliest Arabic work of erotica to be preserved intact, and in many ways the most interesting and impressive of all.

It is most unfortunate that this important book has not yet been published in full; we have only an English translation (with many problems) that appeared in the 1960s, and an uncritical edition of the second two-thirds of the Arabic text (but presented as if complete) from 2001. At least seven manuscripts of the work are known to exist, two of which serve as the basis for the following description. It certainly lives up to its title, being truly encyclopedic in nature. Drawing on a very wide variety of sources, the author manages to examine the phenomenon of sex from many different angles, including anatomical, medical, lexicographical, psychological, sociological, and of course literary. A brief introduction opens with the standard pious formulae expected of any book in this culture, but it praises God for, in particular, having created sex and made it pleasurable, as well as having raised human beings above the animal kingdom so that they may practice more elevated (and pleasurable) forms of sexual interaction. Not surprisingly, the work is presented basically as a didactic one, instructing the reader in the ethics and etiquette of sex. The audience is assumed to be male (if not necessarily exclusively so), and the subordination of women to men is mentioned but not stressed. Rather it is the pursuit of harmony between the sexes that is said to be most important, and (pseudo-)Socrates is quoted as saying, "Sexual intercourse without companionability is uncouth." In an age when living an "elegant" lifestyle was an often articulated ideal, this book is intended to show how one can behave "elegantly" in the realm of sex.

In fact, of course, not everything included is so very refined, and it is probably fair to say that the author's real intention was to offer the reader both a tour of pleasure and a guide for maximizing same. Some passages are clearly meant to be sexually arousing; many others are humorous; many are soberly analytical. Poetry looms large—thousands of poems by dozens of poets are cited—as does anecdote; but 'Alī ibn Naṣr also speaks in his own voice over long stretches of the work. Especially striking is his attempt to present a coherent sociology of sexual relations, in a way not really found elsewhere in the Arabic tradition.

A somewhat detailed survey of the contents of the *Encyclopedia* will serve to illustrate almost all the themes and particular concerns of the entire erotic tradition, while highlighting some of the areas in which this work is exceptional. It is reasonably well organized, if not tightly so. Of the 43 chapters, the first 3 are devoted to sexual intercourse in general: its Arabic terminology (42 nouns, 45 verbs, with discussion of nuances), its merits and benefits (abstinence is argued to be unhealthy), and its phenomenology (answering such questions as why it is pleasurable, why people find it shameful, and why drunkards cannot perform; this chapter is taken in its entirety from the pseudo-Aristotelian *Problemata*). Chapters 4–6 discuss the male and female genital organs, the approach being again terminological (12 words for penis, 26 for vagina), literary (many poems describing each are quoted), and medical (mostly from Galen). The literary chapter includes two debates, one between the vagina and the penis (attributed to al-Jāḥiẓ, but not found in his extant works), the other between males and females as sex partners (from an otherwise unknown source).

Chapters 7–10 turn to forms of love "passion"—that is, bilateral sexual relations—and appear to be the real focal point of the book. Chapter 7 divides these into three types: male-female, male-male, and female-female (with a mini-debate, in verse, on which of the three is best), then adds a fourth, masturbation, with documentation of the occurrence of all four in the animal kingdom. Masturbation is set aside, however, since the author tells us he has devoted a separate monograph (otherwise unknown) to the topic, entitled *The Alchemy of Sex* (with an explanation of techniques "both with and without instruments"). A discussion is then added

about the controversy over whether sexual consummation enhances or destroys love passion, which gives the author the opportunity to retail a large quantity of poetry on both sides, with the Udhrī tradition well represented on the anti-sex side. A different fourth type is then proposed—what would today be called bisexuality—but the author refuses to give these people their own chapter, since they are relatively few, he says, and lack a name in Arabic, although he does find a few apposite verses to quote. Those whose tastes *do* run to both sexes, he suggests, might try eunuchs, who combine the attractions of each.

Chapter 8 deals with male-female relations, and the female role is divided into (1) woman as legal partner, (2) woman as mistress, and (3) woman as prey. Legal partnerships are also of three types: marriage with inheritance, marriage without inheritance, and concubinage; marriage without inheritance is *mut'a*, usually translated as "temporary marriage," a relationship recognized by Shī'ī Islam but violently opposed by Sunnīs, and the author's Shī'īte allegiance is here clearly revealed (and emphasized throughout the rest of the book, where approving discussions of *mut'a* keep recurring, at places both appropriate and inappropriate). Mistresses come in two types: professional singers (numerous poems and anecdotes are adduced) and "others," but the so-called others are problematic, since they inevitably have male relatives attempting to protect their honor. As for woman as prey, the author makes much of the superiority of the hunting of human beings to that of animals, the most important of the hunter's tools being love letters (the author puts in a plug for his separate work on the subject, unfortunately lost), although wine is also helpful.

In chapter Nine, 'Alī ibn Naṣr turns to male-male relations, beginning with an etymological discussion of the term for active sodomite (*lūṭī*) and concluding, correctly, that it actually comes from the name "Lot." The sodomites' claim that they are actually hypermasculine (since they sexually dominate males, not just females) is presented as an introduction to two more debates on the comparative advantages of boys or women as sex partners, the first long and elaborate (with boys winning in the end) and the second truncated, but in verse. A male is said to have a relationship with another male in one of three ways: as a *lūṭī*, a *baghghā'*, or a *ḥalaqī*. This is problematic; while a *lūṭī* is unambiguously someone who takes the active role in homosexual anal intercourse, *baghghā'* and *ḥalaqī* are ordinarily considered synonyms for one who takes the passive role, for sexual (as opposed to, say, monetary) reasons. 'Alī ibn Naṣr insists that he is not going to discuss the *baghghā'*, because it is too shameful a topic—he seems to mean here the truly committed adult male passive—but he gives a unique description of the *ḥalaqī* as someone who either enjoys *both* roles, because of his excessive lustfulness, or finds that he needs the sexual stimulation of the passive role in order (then) to perform actively.

*Lūṭī*s are then said to disagree about three things: (1) whether beardless or recently bearded boys are to be preferred (the former being the standard preference, and the whole controversy being enormously productive of poetry); (2) whether one should practice true anal or only intercrural (between the thighs) intercourse (the chief argument for the latter being its status as a lesser sin in Islamic law); and (3) whether one should grasp the boy's penis while penetrating him (which may or may not affect the *lūṭī*'s sense of his unimpugned masculinity). On the other side of the relationship, the boy may relate to his partner in one of three ways: as a beloved (in which case he behaves just like a female, except that he can also be a "friend" to his lover in a way a female cannot); as a "valet" (that is, a slaveboy acting as a personal attendant, whose owner conceals from the public the sexual nature of their relationship); or as a "visitor," which may mean simply a pickup, and under this category the author takes the occasion to offer a lengthy disquisition on (passive) male prostitution, with numerous humorous anecdotes. Further anecdotes about *lūṭī*s, and a discussion of the claim that *women* prefer their partners beardless, round out the chapter.

Chapter 10 proceeds to the subject of female-female relations. Medieval Muslim men in general seem to have found this phenomenon genuinely bewildering, and 'Alī ibn Naṣr is no exception. This chapter draws very heavily on Abū l-'Anbas's lost *Lesbians and Passive Sodomites* and directs the reader to it for further information. The chapter is concerned primarily with *explaining* lesbianism, first in physiological terms (either a vagina too long to be satisfyingly penetrated by a penis, or some other more radical

abnormality, the latter explanation attributed to al-Kindī; Galen is also referred to) and then in practical ones (fear of defloration and scandal, or of pregnancy). A long series of anecdotes then retails a favorite male theme, the lesbian "converted" to heterosexuality once she discovers its joys; many of these are in verse, addressed by converts to their still benighted former lovers. As throughout the Arabic tradition, the treatment here of lesbianism is limited, bemused, and emphatically from a male perspective.

Chapter 11, on physiognomy (e.g., how to tell from physical features who—male or female—is particularly lustful), functions as a sort of transition, and for the first time draws heavily and explicitly on earlier works of erotica, Greek, Persian, and Indian. Chapters 12–14 look at women as sex partners, addressing such questions as, what is the ideal woman like, both physically and in terms of character? and how do women differ in their approach to sex, their degree of sexual desire, and their skill in bed? Again extensive appeals are made to earlier works, including *Bunyāndakht*'s claim that women's lust is nine times as strong as that of men. An excursus on the permutations involved in matching male and female genital size (complete with a chart) and their strength of desire is attributed to The Indian—and is in fact an expanded paraphrase of a passage from the *Kamasutra*. Chapter 15 considers the question of heterosexual anal intercourse—a very high profile topic throughout the Arabic erotological tradition—noting the common (if not entirely justified) belief that one of the schools of Islamic law (the Mālikī) condones it and suggesting that while some women consent to it to avoid pregnancy, others do so because they enjoy it.

Having described what women are like, in chapters 16 and 17 'Alī ibn Naṣr turns to how to get them, first in general (sexual technique looms large, but reference to women's dislike of men's gray hair affords the opportunity to sample the abundant poetic corpus on that topic) and then specifically through the use of a go-between. Chapters 18 through 20 focus on the marriage bed—advance preparations (good grooming for men is recommended), foreplay (with a disquisition on cunnilingus, unusual for the Arabic tradition), and the effectiveness of lascivious wriggling and sex talk during intercourse.

The following chapters are devoted to ways of enhancing the sexual experience. Chapters 21 through 24 are mostly medical, offering detailed recipes for various aphrodisiacs, as well as a few nonpharmocological strategies; Chapters 25 and 26 consider appropriate times and circumstances for sex. Chapter 27 is entitled "Description of the Nasty Way of Doing It and Lewd Sex," and seems to be where the author has decided to deposit the most blatantly erotic material at his disposal. In Chapter 28 he turns to sex positions, which he divides into five main categories with 32 subdivisions, 16 of them involving anal intercourse. Fellatio is noted in passing as one of several aberrant practices for which some Indians are known. Chapter 29 assesses positions medically (some of them are harmful) and also ethically, the author stressing that positions that humiliate a *wife* (if not a concubine) are to be avoided. Chapter 30 completes the marriage-bed section by discussing the need for proper ritual ablutions after completion of the sex act.

In chapters 31 through 33 'Alī ibn Naṣr returns to medical considerations, listing various treatments to prevent pregnancy, combat the ill effects of excessive indulgence, and cure impotence. Chapter 34 is dedicated to nonmedical "strategems" for achieving such aims as quickening or retarding ejaculation and arousing a woman's desire. Special attention is given to success at "creeping" (*dabīb*), which is sexual molestation of a sleeping boy or slave girl in the wake of a drinking party when everyone has passed out—numerous anecdotes and poems are provided in illustration of this practice. More briefly, *Bunyāndakht* is quoted on how a wife should manage each of three types of husband—(1) the proper mate, (2) the autocrat (one who is too jealous), and (3) the cuckold (one who is not jealous enough).

The remainder of the book concerns itself with a variety of secondary matters. Chapter 35, entitled "*Fatwā*s About Sex," consists of long quotations from the authoritative Persian, Indian, and Greek sources, all cast in the form of answers to specific questions. The Persians (*Bunyāqis* and *Bunyāndakht*) address, among other things, men's and women's preferences in the size and shape of their mates' genitals. The Indians debate whether women ejaculate and attempt to explain the different pattern in their

pace of sexual excitement from that of men; here again the text closely parallels a passage in the *Kamasutra*. For the Greeks, the author cites the book of (the unidentified) "Arṭiyās" for various opinions on both male and female ejaculation. Chapter 36, adopting quite a different tone, reproduces a long series of humorous exchanges, in poetry and prose, mostly between men and their saucy mistresses, as well as more straightforward jokes. This is followed up, in the brief Chapter 37, by examples of a sort of humorous code employed by lovers, or flirters, to communicate surreptitiously with each other.

Jealousy is the subject of Chapter 38, a general discussion and some poetry being supplemented by a series of recipes for potions to keep women faithful. Chapter 39, on pimping, is almost entirely literary and humorous. Chapter 40, "On the Advantages of a Nonvirgin over a Virgin," consists of a debate between the two (with the nonvirgin winning) taken directly from the (otherwise unknown) book of that title by a certain Yazdajird ibn Nahmak (presumably a Persian). Chapter 41, on animal sexuality, is equally derivative, being made up exclusively of snippets from al-Jāḥiẓ's *Book of Animals*. The author returns briefly to the question of the size of genitals in Chapter 42, recounting an experiment he himself undertook to determine the volume of the average penis and quoting Galen on that of the average uterus. Chapter 43, "Miscellaneous Topics," concludes the book with various anecdotes on eunuchs, bestiality, and prostitution, mixed with recipes for "restoring" virginity and "curing" passive sodomites, and much else besides.

In selecting the topics for inclusion in his *Encyclopedia*, 'Alī ibn Naṣr was inevitably guided in large part by the texts he had at hand. While the work itself cannot be considered one of libertinism, or *mujūn*, a vast quantity of *mujūn* poetry and anecdotes were available, and he made the most of it. Literary (and, less clearly, sociological) conventions dictated the prominence of certain themes in this material, and accordingly we find 'Alī ibn Naṣr dwelling at length on, for example, boy-versus-girl debates, beards, the treachery of singing slave girls, heterosexual anal intercourse, creeping, and gray hair. Over the past two centuries all these had developed into standard *mujūn* topics, and in 'Alī ibn Naṣr's own day (the late tenth century) a second wave of *mujūn* fashionability can be detected in the literature, tinged with a distinct *nostalgie de la boue.* The most famous exponent of this trend was unquestionably the Baghdad poet Ibn al-Ḥajjāj (d. 1000), who, besides an impressive corpus of serious poetry, released a flood of obscene verses that went beyond anything seen before, most notably perhaps for their inclusion of a large dose of scatology. Straightforward (but extremely graphic) seduction poems alternate with such novelties as a lengthy arbitration by his personified penis between the competing claims of a slave girl's vagina and her anus; and constant references to anal intercourse (almost always heterosexual) are laced with deliberately disgusting references to excrement. Equally common are changes rung on the common phrase "my feces in your beard" (the approximate equivalent of "kiss my ass").

Other poets, notably Ibn Sukkara (d. 995), followed Ibn al-Ḥajjāj's lead and enjoyed great popularity with the cultured wazīr and Maecenas, the Ṣāḥib Ibn 'Abbād (d. 995), who in addition to his own scurrilous verses commissioned the composition of a lengthy ode by the poet Abū Dulaf detailing the lifestyles, predilections, and argot of the loose international confederation of beggars, thieves, and lowlifes generally known as the Banū Sāsān. Somewhat the same spirit pervades the *Maqāmāt,* a new form of prestige prose literature consisting of picaresque vignettes cast in a highly rhetorical rhymed prose, originated by Badī' al-Zamān al-Hamadhānī (d. 1008). It is true, however, that the protagonist of most of Badī' al-Zamān's sketches is much more interested in money than in sex, and their erotic component is comparatively small; the same pattern continued to hold for later *maqāma* collections, right down to the twentieth century, although there was usually a place for a sexual escapade or two, as for example a homosexual tryst in one of the *maqāmas* of Ibn Nāqiyā (d. 1092) or an attempted one in another by Ibn Sharaf (d. 1067). But the acknowledged master of the genre, al-Ḥarīrī (d. 1122), avoided *mujūn* almost entirely.

Richer in erotic content are some of the major anthologies of the period. An outstanding example is the *Quotable Quotes* of al-Rāghib al-Iṣfahānī (early eleventh century), a handbook of short poems and anecdotes on every conceivable subject, one of whose 16 chapters offers an extraordinarily concentrated series of quotable bits

of *mujūn.* Al-Rāghib here divides his subject matter into four broad categories, with numerous subheadings, each comprising between one and six relevant snippets. The first category deals with "active sodomy, male prostitution, passive sodomy, male transvestism, masturbation, creeping, pimping, and heterosexual fornication," with some 53 subheadings, ranging from "He Who Is Caught in the Act of Active Pederasty and Justifies Himself with a Qur'ānic Verse" to "Boasts by Transvestites About Their Specialty" to "The Clever Pimp." The second category is about genitalia and intercourse, with 39 subheadings, including "Loss of Bowel Control During Intercourse" and "Dildos." The third category, on lesbianism, has only five subheadings, including arguments for and against it and descriptions of lesbian sexual practices. Finally comes a section on farting, with 14 subdivisions, including one on riddles about it—the one common component of *mujūn* not associated directly with sex. This chapter by no means exhausts the erotic content of al-Rāghib's book, since there is also a completely separate chapter on marriage and related matters (with subsections on marriage and divorce, dowries, chastity, and jealousy and cuckoldry), but the material there is considerably tamer. Even tamer is a third chapter, on love poetry (*ghazal*), in which representative verses illustrate the standard themes of the genre—and which may serve as a salutory reminder that by no means are all treatments of erotic themes in Arabic literature aggressively sexual.

Mujūn material comparable (and sometimes virtually identical) to that in al-Rāghib's book may be found in many other anthologies of this and subsequent periods, sometimes in unlikely places. For example, the *Scattering of Pearls* of al-Ābī (d. 1030), a seven-volume collection exclusively of prose pieces (omitting all poetry), includes selections of jokes, organized by topic, at the end of each volume, as a form of comic relief from the serious tone of most of the work; these include jokes by and about libertine women and slave girls, womanizers and fornicators of both sexes, male transvestites, active sodomites, passive sodomites, and male libertines. A slightly later work, *Euphemisms* by al-Jurjānī (d. 1089), devotes its first chapter to sex, with subdivisions on fornication; sexual intercourse, the penis, and impotence; virginity; heterosexual anal intercourse; male prostitution and active sodomy; intercrural intercourse, male masturbation, and lesbianism; passive sodomy; jealousy; and pimping.

But the most extravagant example of *mujūn* literature from this (and perhaps any) period is certainly the *Sketch of Abū l-Qāsim al-Baghdādī*, by the otherwise unknown Abū l-Muṭahhar al-Azdī (probably mid-eleventh century). This unique work, which reads like a script, although its actual dramatic status is not entirely clear, depicts a single day in the life of its protagonist, a Baghdadi rascal visiting the Iranian city of Isfahan who crashes a drinking party and proceeds to wreak havoc. Having insinuated himself as a Qur'ān reciter and elegizer on the death of the Prophet's grandson al-Ḥusayn, he quickly reveals himself as a wastrel, insults the entire company one by one—accusing them in gross terms of various sexual vices—and launches into a long and elaborate comparison of Baghdad and Isfahan, to the discredit of the latter. After a chaotic game of chess and dinner, the wine is brought out, and as the party gets progressively drunker he alternately praises and attacks his companions, attempts to seduce the female singer and then the male cupbearer, launches into an extended tirade against the male singer, and finally falls asleep; the next morning he simply recites some pious phrases, bids the company farewell, and departs. In the course of this extended debauch, Abū l-Qāsim manages to quote vast quantities of obscene poetry and, to a lesser extent, anecdotes, touching on virtually all the multifarious themes inherent to the genre.

At the opposite extreme from such libertine literature, the tenth and eleventh centuries also witnessed extensive developments in the tradition of writing about a purer, more romantic, even ethereal sort of love. Already at the end of the ninth century, a major scholar of Islamic law, Muḥammad ibn Dāwūd al-Ẓāhirī (d. 910), had put together an anthology of chaste love poetry, entitled the *Book of the Flower,* organized in such a way as to present a coherent theory of how courtly love should progress; at the same time, being himself (by all accounts) in love (chastely) with another man, he succeeded in canonizing the incorporation of homoerotic love into this "higher" stratum of the Arabic treatment of erotic relationships (at the expense of abandoning all hope of ever sexually consummating such a relationship, something unthinkable in terms of Islamic law).

The *Book of the Flower* was, however, only one of three influential treatises on love produced at the time, advocating incompatible views of what it should be. A second, the *Embroidered* by al-Washshā' (d. 937), offered a distinctly more worldly general guide to stylish living, of which having elegant but not too serious affairs (strictly heterosexual) was an important part; characteristically, al-Washshā' also composed a manual for writing love letters. A third author, the pious al-Kharā'iṭī (d. 939), in his *Malady of Hearts,* inveighed against the power of sexual passion to lead the good Muslim astray but managed in the course of his disquisition to review much of the literature of 'Udhrī passion; while holding out a loving, stable marriage as the ideal, he made significant concessions to the thwarted passion advocated by Muḥammad ibn Dāwūd as ideal, although to be sure without the homoerotic component.

Ultimately, it was Muḥammad b. Dāwūd's romanticism that was to prove most influential in the romantic love tradition, and he stands at the head of a long series of works on "love theory" composed over the following millennium. Of these, the most attractive, and best known in the West, if not the most influential within the Arabic literary tradition, is the *Ring of the Dove* of Ibn Ḥazm (d. 1064), an extremely prominent Spanish (Andalusian) scholar otherwise known primarily for his legal and ethical writings. What makes Ibn Ḥazm's book particularly compelling is his insistence on restricting his anecdotal accounts to stories about his friends and acquaintances (sometimes suppressing their names), rather than retailing inherited material from other times and places; thus, even though the conventions of love poetry dominate the discussion, the anecdotes are telling evidence for the degree to which art influenced life in eleventh-century Andalusia (and undoubtedly elsewhere). A committed heterosexual himself, Ibn Ḥazm has no qualms about recounting the homosexual passions of others; he does, however, conclude his book with paired sermons against the immorality of both heterosexual and homosexual fornication. The degree to which (if at all) Ibn Ḥazm has something to tell us about Arabic influences on medieval European courtly love remains a hotly debated topic.

Later books on love theory—there are some two dozen, extending well into the eighteenth century—mostly restricted themselves to ringing changes on inherited materials, supplemented by the ongoing production of new love lyrics and anecdotes. Among the better-known examples of the genre are the *Lovers Devastated by Passion* of al-Sarrāj (d. 1106) and the *Martyrs of Love* of Mughulṭāy (d. 1361). A secondary stream continued the more pious stance of al-Kharā'iṭī, notable contributions being the *Condemnation of Passion* by Ibn al-Jawzī (d. 1200) and the *Garden of Lovers* of Ibn Qayyim al-Jawzīya (d. 1350). While all these works take sexual love as their subject matter, they are generally very careful to avoid any explicit references to sexuality itself, except, to some extent, in passages dedicated to the condemnation of actual sexual immorality.

The love lyric (*ghazal*) retained or even increased its domination of poetic production after the eleventh century and up to the nineteenth, in what is often called the postclassical age of Arabic literature. Among the developments that can be noted in this poorly researched area are a shift in balance between homoerotic and heteroerotic verse heavily in favor of the former, and, more generally, an increasing artificiality or even brittleness of tone, in accord with broader literary trends in the late Middle Ages and early modern times. A case in point of the latter is the increasing popularity of epigrams, two- to four-line poems describing the beauty of a given boy or woman and playing off some characteristic (e.g., a physical trait, ethnicity, profession) in a witty and often punning fashion. The first known anthology of such epigrams is the unpublished *Book of Boys,* later known as *A Thousand Boys,* by al-Tha'ālibī (d. 1038), but they became particularly fashionable in the fourteenth and fifteenth centuries. A typical example is the *Pastures for Gazelles on Beautiful Girls and Boys* by al-Nawājī (d. 1455), who seems also to be the first to have devoted an anthology exclusively to poetry about beards, with an untranslatable title that can only approximately be rendered as *Running Riot with Descriptions of Downy Beards.* More broadly based encyclopedias also continued to incorporate sections anthologizing *ghazal* (not just epigrams), as well as *mujūn.*

One especially important development in the love lyric, originating in Spain and attaining wide popularity in the twelfth century, was the appearance of strophic poetry, as opposed to the hitherto unchallenged monorhyme verse. This came in two forms. The *muwashshah,* in classical Arabic but often with noncanonical meter, features up to five separately rhymed stanzas, separated by monorhymed refrain verses and ending with a final line, the *kharja,* that is often couched in colloquial Arabic or Romance. Although the *muwashshah* came to be employed for a variety of genres (including panegyric), its first and natural subject was love, mostly reflecting standard thematic conventions—except in the *kharja,* which was often a sort of punch line, with a deflating or mocking message. The *zajal,* on the other hand, while structurally similar to the *muwashshah,* was composed entirely in the vernacular, and more often than not inclined thematically toward *mujūn.* Its most famous representative was Ibn Quzmān (d. 1160), whose bawdy lyrics, often depicting the seduction of both boys and women, evoke a lightness of touch relatively rare in the *mujūn* tradition.

Both *muwashshah* and *zajal* were originally forms of so-called popular literature, whose gradual (and incomplete) incorporation into the "high" literary tradition, particularly with the spread of their pursuit to the East, is difficult to trace and assess. This question is, however, a broader one, since the use of these popular forms, themes, and materials of all sorts was a growing phenomenon in the later medieval period. A particularly tricky example, but important in the *mujūn* tradition and thus to the history of Arabic erotica, are the shadow plays of Ibn Dāniyāl (d. 1310). The shadow play itself, with two-dimensional articulated figures held against a backlit translucent screen, was certainly a known form of popular entertainment from at least the eleventh century. Presumably of a generally ribald nature, it would not have had set written scripts, or at least not texts thought worthy of copying by respectable littérateurs. Ibn Dāniyāl's three plays form a unique exception, and it is difficult to pronounce either specifically on whether they were intended for performance or more generally on their generic (and societal) status. With their wit and adroit manipulation of language from *all* registers, from the high classical idiom to the lowest vernacular, they certainly qualify as art. All three plays deal extensively with erotic themes—one presenting itself as a mocking response to a governmental anti-vice campaign, a second offering a parade of street entertainers with all sorts of prurient interests, and a third detailing a homosexual affair and concluding with a series of poetry-spouting representatives of such various sexual practices as transvestism, masturbation, and creeping.

The thirteenth and fourteenth centuries also witnessed a second efflorescence in Arabic erotica in the narrow, monographic sense, after an apparently relatively fallow period in the wake of the *Encyclopedia of Pleasure.* The only identifiable work of this nature from the eleventh century is *Cohabitation and Coitus, on the Various Sorts of Sexual Intercourse* by the Egyptian historian al-Musabbiḥī (d. 1030), which seems to have disappeared without a trace. But then in the late twelfth century appeared two major texts, one more general and the other more specifically medical. Al-Samaw'al b. Yaḥyā (d. 1180), a Baghdadi convert from Judaism, seems to have followed very roughly the structure of the *Encyclopedia of Pleasure* in his *Pleasure Park for Friends on Companionship with Their Beloveds,* although the parts of this work that are accessible in print offer no direct textual evidence for such influence. It is divided into two parts, the first theoretical and the second practical, each with twelve chapters. Under theory, the first three chapters deal with sex in general, its positive and negative sides, frequency of practicing it, and why it is pleasurable. The next two treat impediments to sexual activity, either natural (impotence) or psychological (why some lovers decline to consummate their relationship—the 'Udhrī theme that sex destroys love). Chapter 6 explains why some men prefer boys to women and why some women prefer lesbianism; none of the reasons given for either are novel, except perhaps for the suggestions that some exceptionally masculine women desire to take the active role in sex and others are forced to have recourse to lesbian sex by the stringency of their seclusion. Chapter 7, however, on why sexual desire varies so much, includes a justification for such seclusion; and Chapter 8, also reflecting rather conservative views, explains why pious people do not turn away from sex altogether. The last four chapters discuss the etiquette of sexual relations, what one should look for in buying slaves (drawing from an established independent genre of writing on this topic), marriage and desirable and undesirable qualities in brides, and the rather different rules for taking mistresses. The tone throughout is considerably more sober than that of 'Alī ibn Naṣr's book, and citations from

poetry and anecdote, while not entirely missing, are kept to a minimum. The second, practical half of the work is almost entirely medical in nature, offering prescriptions for treating impotence, penile warts, premature ejaculation, and other maladies; recipes for aphrodisiacs; and concoctions to prevent pregnancy, induce abortion, and block the sex drive. The one malady al-Samaw'al despairs of curing is love passion (*'ishq*) itself.

At about the same time, the physician Jalāl al-Dīn al-Shayzarī (d. 1193), who was patronized by Saladin, composed his *Clarification of the Secrets of Sexual Intercourse,* whose content is almost entirely pharmocological. The work's two parts, each with ten chapters, deal with the "secrets of men" and "secrets of women," respectively. The recipes for men are said to increase sexual power and pleasure, as well as penis size, to promote or prevent pregnancy, and (the final chapter) to decrease sexual desire. Those for women are mostly cosmetic, promising to improve the complexion, promote weight gain, ensure good body odor, and narrow the vagina. References to former authorities are sparse and mostly medical (particularly Galen); the *Encyclopedia of Pleasure* is explicitly cited once, but in fact drawn on more heavily (if extremely selectively). Al-Shayzarī also wrote a book of love theory (although it includes, surprisingly, one chapter on *mujūn*), *The Garden of Hearts and Pleasure Park of Lover and Beloved,* which remains unpublished.

Several other purely medical sex books appeared in the course of the thirteenth and fourteenth centuries. One, *Sexual Hygiene,* was written by the famous Jewish physician, philosopher, and legal scholar Maimonides (d. 1204), who apparently also wrote a different work on sexual intercourse in Hebrew. Another, by the scientist and polymath Nāṣir al-Dīn al-Ṭūsī (d. 1273), was composed for the ailing son of a sultan, with numerous prescriptions meant to increase potency and sexual desire, but also including medicaments promising both to promote pregnancy and to inhibit it. But the sexological "star" of the thirteenth century was unquestionably the Tunisian Shihāb al-Dīn al-Tīfāshī (d. 1253), who composed at least three and possibly four influential works. Of these, one, the *Epistle on What Men and Women Need in Practicing Sexual Intercourse,* is again almost entirely pharmocological, this time with primary emphasis on the woman's cosmetic, medical, and psychological needs; the author's primary source (although he nowhere acknowledges it) is al-Shayzarī's *Clarification*. A second work, the *Book of the Forewing on the Etiquette of Sex,* is lost and known only from a few citations in later works, which suggest that it was primarily sociological in orientation and replete with anecdotes. The third, however, the *Delight of Hearts on What Cannot Be Found in Any Other Book,* is a major contribution to the genre.

What makes the *Delight of Hearts* stand out is its liveliness and immediacy, the originality of its structure, and its unabashed intention both to amuse the reader and to stimulate him (or her) sexually. It is unquestionably a work of *mujūn;* and, while relying heavily on by now well-worn poetry and anecdotes from the past, it leavens these with quite a number of contemporary accounts, gleaned by the author from his acquaintances in North Africa, Egypt, and Syria (with names sometimes but not always suppressed). The *mujūn* tone is quickly established in the first of the work's twelve chapters, which in fact has nothing to do with sex but presents the merits of "slapping" (*ṣaf*) in a pseudo-serious manner. For whatever reason, slapping someone on the back of the neck was generally considered uproariously funny in medieval Arabic societies, to the point that professional "slap takers" functioned as salaried buffoons in royal courts. Al-Tīfāshī's tongue-in-cheek analysis of this phenomenon serves as a signal that what is to come is going to embellish the material, delightful in itself, with a persistently ironic overlay that will only add to the fun.

Contrary to all his predecessors, al-Tīfāshī begins, in chapter Two, with panderers. These are carefully divided into 22 categories, 12 of them pandering women and 10 pandering men, the panderers themselves being women (10), men (10), transvestite men (1), or eunuchs (1). Each category is given a name, and the particular rules of the game are elucidated. This analytic section is followed up with an extensive selection of (traditional) "anecdotes and jokes about panderers," establishing an organizational pattern which recurs throughout the book. Chapter 3 explains how to be a proper (male) fornicator and how a female prostitute should behave, with Chapter 4 supplying both a list of seven kinds of whore and appropriate anecdotes (and poetry) on whoredom, and Chapter 5 adding yet more anecdotes

about fornicators. Giving equal time, as it were, Chapter 6 explains how to be a proper active sodomite, and how a male (passive) prostitute should behave, with the requisite anecdotes and poetry collected in Chapters 7 ("beardless male prostitutes") and 8 ("active sodomites"). Chapter 9 deals with creeping; here the primary prerequisite, we are told, is to have a small penis (an anecdote illustrates the point), and a detailed list of ten pieces of equipment (including scissors to cut the boy's trousers open) is followed by a profusion of anecdotes, both homosexual and heterosexual, traditional and contemporary. Chapter 10, on heterosexual anal intercourse, offers little that is unexpected; but Chapter 11, a rich and lengthy treatment of lesbianism, adopts a position that is on the whole more sympathetic than usual, with an entire section on arguments in its favor, as well as several extremely lubricious descriptions of lesbian sexual practices. Chapter 12, on transvestites (*mukhannathūn;* in this period perhaps better translated as "effeminates" or even simply "passive sodomites"), is the longest in the book. It includes, besides the anticipated wealth of traditional anecdotes and poetry, an entire series of contemporary stories (some simply humorous, others startlingly lascivious), an extended interview with a contemporary Baghdadi *mukhannath* about his taste in penises, and, in an unexpected conclusion, the entire text of al-Rāzī's medical monograph on *The Hidden Disease.*

The fourth work attributed to al-Tīfāshī, *The Old Man's Return to His Youth in Sexual Prowess,* is rather a puzzle. Unquestionably the most famous, or notorious, sex book in the contemporary Arab world (the *Perfumed Garden,* discussed below, is far more celebrated in the West than in the Middle East), this work is attributed in the extant manuscripts both to al-Tīfāshī and to Ibn Kamāl Pāshā (d. 1533), a well-known Ottoman author who, however, more likely simply translated it into Turkish, or, possibly, produced an abridgement of it in the original Arabic. On the other hand, al-Tīfāshī's authorship seems equally questionable, since the text we have (with considerable variation among the manuscripts) includes a number of anecdotes datable to at least a generation or two after his death, which are almost certainly not interpolations. Since virtually the entire text of al-Tīfāshī's medical *Epistle* is reproduced in *The Old Man's Return,* one possible solution to this problem would be to posit a somewhat later, unknown author for the latter, with the erroneous ascription to al-Tīfāshī being due to the close relationship between the two works; but further research will be needed to resolve these difficulties.

While lacking the verve that characterizes al-Tīfāshī's *Delight of Hearts, The Old Man's Return* does, with its extensive exploitation of the entire previous erotological tradition, represent a sort of culmination thereof, which perhaps accounts for its popularity. Its most fundamental debt is to al-Shayzarī's *Clarification,* but this is only one of seven basic sources obligingly listed in its introduction, the others being the *Book of Barjān and Ḥubāḥib,* al-Namlī's *Book of Sexual Intercourse* (this is a problem, since al-Namlī is otherwise known in the tradition only as the author of the *Book of Barjān and Ḥubāḥib*), Ibn Ḥājib al-Nūmān's *Book of Singing Slave Girls* (usually referred to as his *Book of Women*), al-Musabbiḥī's *Cohabitation and Coitus,* and *Wedding and Brides,* attributed (certainly wrongly) to al-Jāḥiẓ, a text much in the popular genre whose history has not yet been investigated. Whether the author had direct, or only indirect, access to the book of The Indian, whom he repeatedly cites, also remains to be determined.

Like al-Shayzarī, the author of *The Old Man's Return* divides his book into two parts, the first dealing with men and the second with women, each part comprising in this case 30 chapters. Part one begins with a discussion of male genitalia, then turns to a general consideration of sexual intercourse, with several chapters (mostly on the dire effects of overindulgence) lifted from al-Rāzī's medical *Book of Sexual Intercourse.* Virtually the entire remainder of this part (Chapters 8 through 29) is pharmacological, although there is a significant admixture of more purely magical remedies for the various sexual problems from which men may suffer. Only in the final chapter, "The Divisions of People's Objects of Love and Passion," does the author turn to broader considerations, although even here he restricts himself essentially to reproducing a rather garbled version of the Greek *Problemata* discussion of why some men have recourse to passive sodomy. Part 2 begins with a general discussion of women's charms and ways one can determine their degree of lustfulness, but then again turns to medical, cosmetic, and pharmological subjects, the focus of

Chapters 3 through 17. At that point, however, the work veers in a much more literary direction and begins to look more like a *mujūn* treatise. Chapter 18, on "different types of intercourse," quotes The Indian on a series of positions; Chapter 19, on "strategems," specifies the tools needed by the creeper (in a male homosexual context, despite this being the part of the work on women); Chapter 20, on "stories," offers an elaborate frame story with ten slave girls recounting their sexual adventures; and the remaining chapters deal in a wholly conventional way, replete with traditional anecdotes, with such topics as pandering, sexual etiquette, anal intercourse with women, and foreplay, extensive quotations from The Indian being a prominent feature throughout.

Considerably more restrained, although not wholly divorced from the *mujūn* tradition, is *The Gift of the Bride and Garden of Souls* by the Algerian al-Tijānī (d. after 1310), a work wholly dedicated to the subject of women (and avoiding the topic of homosexuality, male or female, almost altogether). In his introduction this author takes pains to distinguish his book—one of "scholarship and analysis"—from those of "light entertainment," by which he surely means the sort of thing composed by al-Tīfāshī (although the latter's *Forewing* is in fact the one erotological work he does quote). His many sources, which he scrupulously identifies, tend to run toward treatises on Islamic law and ethics, although mainstream belletristic works also figure prominently. Generically, the book appears to be rather a hybrid, despite its lucid organization. Having declared women to be "the greatest of pleasures" and described their general characteristics in his first chapter (of 25), al-Tijānī organizes the following ten chapters around the topic of marriage (choice of bride, dowry, wedding banquet, rights of spouses), with a single follow-up chapter on concubines. (Marriage guides are not a well-defined genre in Arabic literature, but a few somewhat parallel texts do exist.) The author then shifts his attention to "beauty," relying heavily on literary sources in the next eight chapters to detail women's physical attributes, including such components as age, virginity, complexion, weight, and stature, and dividing his twentieth chapter, on specific features, into 20 subsections, covering the woman's body from top to bottom, beginning with hair, forehead, and eyebrows, and ending with buttocks, legs, and feet. A section is included on the vagina, but even there the material presented is relatively mild. Only in the concluding five chapters (sexual intercourse in general, lascivious sounds and motions during intercourse, anal intercourse, jealousy, and jokes) does some truly libertine material appear, drawn, however, from more general earlier works rather than specifically erotic ones.

Much more conventional, but by no means unoriginal, is a work from the other end of the Arab world, the *Intelligent Man's Guide to Keeping Company with the Beloved* by the obscure Yemeni author Ibn Falīta (d. after 1363). Placing his work squarely within the erotological tradition, Ibn Falīta says he has read many sex books but has noted that they leave out a great deal, which his book is meant to supply. He explicitly leaves aside all medical aspects of the subject, as well as the more chaste love tradition, saying he is interested in "pleasure with the present beloved rather than preoccupation with seeking the absent one." While the topics covered are mostly in fact the usual ones, the author is true to his promise in offering primarily unique material, much of it the fruit of his own observations, and relatively little even of the poetry and anecdotes he includes have parallels in earlier erotic works. His first three chapters (of fourteen) cover marriage and sexual relations in general, with a particular emphasis on women's unbridled lubricity. Then come chapters on what women like and dislike in men, and what men like and dislike in women. Chapters 6 through 8, on various topics related directly to sexual desire and the sex act itself, are rather a hodgepodge, managing to touch on impotence, voyeurism, different types of vaginas (with a detailed list), sexual positions (with a particular concern for problems of the very obese and hunchbacks), masturbation, and dildos. Chapter 9 examines lesbianism, and the following two chapters present yet another debate on the relative merits of boys (Chapter 10) and women (Chapter 11) as sex partners for men. The final three chapters are devoted to panderers, women's wiles, and a potpourri of jokes and verses that do not fit anywhere else. Examples of the sort of unexpected content with which Ibn Falīta fills his book are an extensive discussion of the importance of kissing, especially during sexual intercourse, and a striking account of

two elderly men of his acquaintance who had maintained a close sexual relationship throughout their lives from their adolescent years.

For all its explicitness, and considerable entertainment value, Ibn Falīta's book seems on the whole to put didactic considerations to the fore and nowhere to present passages intended purely as sexual stimulation. In this respect it contrasts both with al-Tīfāshī's *Delight of Hearts* and with a slightly later work, by another Tunisian, the *Perfumed Garden* of al-Nafzāwī (early fifteenth century). The exceptional fame this book has attained in the West, due to the publication of French and English translations in the late nineteenth century, seems not to reflect any comparable status in the Arab world, although it has enjoyed some popularity there as well. The extant manuscripts of the work appear to reflect at least two different recensions, or perhaps merely an unusually extreme susceptibility to interpolation; most but not all of the passages unique to the longer version represent borrowings, probably direct, from Ibn Falīta's *Guide*. Al-Nafzāwī speaks himself in his introduction of having revised the work, at his patron's request, by adding supplementary medical information, and in fact the medical chapters sit rather ill with the primarily anecdotal and extremely lubricious content of the rest; but that is a different question, and none of the known manuscripts seem to reflect such a purported earlier version.

Be that as it may, the *Perfumed Garden,* in both versions, is characterized by a rather jejune presentation of basic information, to which is added, often rather awkwardly, quite a number of exceptionally long anecdotes, unparalleled elsewhere in the literature, whose intention is partly humor but mostly titillation. The first nine of its 21 chapters cover exactly the sort of topics one would expect: desirable and undesirable features in men and women; sexual intercourse, techniques and positions, harmful aspects; and terms for male and female genitalia. The accompanying stories, whose general tone and blatant fictionality are reminiscent of parts of *The Thousand and One Nights* (but far more obscene than anything in the latter), contribute little to the (shorter) contexts in which they are embedded and seem rather themselves to be the book's main point. After a perfunctory chapter on names for the penis of various animals, this pattern of succinct exposition combined with fairly elaborate anecdotes reasserts itself in two chapters on women's wiles and the variety of their sexual desires. The following brief eight chapters turn to medical topics (aphrodisiacs, abortificients, penis enlargers, etc.) and consist mostly of recipes, with no accompanying anecdotes at all. The concluding chapter, again on aphrodisiacs, offers five recipes, in the midst of which it inserts, with only a perfunctory attempt at justification, a long story about how four men, interrupting a lesbian orgy of one hundred virgins, managed to convert them all to heterosexuality.

The kinds of stories included in the *Perfumed Garden* give the distinct impression of a trend downward, toward the popular genre, in late medieval Arabic erotica, which may or may not be supported by further research into the following Ottoman period, thus far barely investigated. On the other hand, the extensive erotic writings of a major scholar of the late fifteenth century suggest that such topics were in no danger of losing their respectability in the high-brow tradition. The Egyptian al-Suyūṭī (d. 1505), famed for his unmatched productivity (he published well over 500 works) if not his originality, devoted at least eight and possibly more monographs to this field. Of these, the most substantial is *The Sash, on the Merits of Sexual Intercourse,* divided into seven parts: traditions handed down from the Prophet and his companions (covering various issues regarding both marriage and sex); lexicography (very long lists of synonyms for sexual intercourse, male and female genitalia, and lascivious movements during intercourse); anecdotes (mostly gleaned from standard belletristic works); rhymed prose and poetry (chiefly descriptions—both chaste and explicitly sexual—of beautiful women); anatomy (citing both medical and erotological sources); medicine (mostly a series of extracts from al-Rāzī's *Book on Sexual Intercourse*); and sexual intercourse in general (relying heavily on the *Encyclopedia of Pleasure*), with an appendix on sexual habits of animals. While by no means avoiding the explicitly lubricious, the work quotes so very widely from the broader literary tradition that its overall tone seems relatively mild, if by no means chaste. The author presents it as a drastic abridgement (one-tenth the length) of a larger work of his composition entitled *The Smiles of the Pretty and Beauty Marks of the Comely,* which seems to be irretrievably lost. He also composed a supplement to the *Sash,* called *Luxuriant Thickets of Anecdotes About Coitus,* which, as published, is both more lascivious than the former work and more indebted to erotological predecessors, although some major questions about both the text and its attribution remain to be investigated.

Al-Suyūṭī's more modest works include a brief marriage manual, presented as an antidote to the loose morals of contemporary women; a word study of the term *ghunj,* meaning lascivious sounds and motions during intercourse (divided into sections on terminology, religious traditions, anecdotes, and poetry, with acknowledged indebtedness to al-Tīfāshī and al-Tijānī, among others); and a literary tour de force in which representatives of 20 different professions present detailed descriptions of their wedding nights, employing technical terms of their craft as metaphors in doing so. Extant in manuscript, but not yet published, are two short opuscules on sexual terminology and legal questions concerning "the entry of the glans penis into the vagina," as well as a comic sermon on the penis.

The Arabic literature of the sixteenth through nineteenth centuries has traditionally been viewed as a vast wasteland of banal imitation of earlier glories, further marred by an obsessive preoccupation with rhetorical excess at the expense of either meaningful content or valid aesthetic objectives. While this view has come under increasing attack, a lack of adequate scholarly research precludes offering anything but the most impressionistic observations about the Arabic erotica of this period. Certainly works in the traditional mold continued to be produced, although none seem to have attained particular fame. Many titles noted by manuscript catalogues are anonymous; where authors are named they are obscure. Both medical works (mostly on aphrodisiacs, including at least one in verse) and anecdotal collections are known. One of these works, very much in the traditional mode, by the unknown and undatable 'Umar al-Ḥalabī (seventeenth century?), entitled *The Pleasure Park of Littérateurs and Consolation of Intimates,* found a French translator in 1893 but has had little impact in either the West or the East, and the Arabic original remains unedited.

One important trend in Arabic writing during the Ottoman period was the production and copying of texts of popular literature, generally composed in semicolloquial Arabic and considered unworthy of the attention of the educated classes. The most important representative of this literature (but by no means the only one) is the *Thousand and One Nights,* whose erotic component is far from negligible. Not only the frame story itself (presenting Shahrazād's dilemma as the result of her husband's despair over the unfaithfulness of wives) but also a significant proportion of the nested stories turn on sexual themes; on the whole, these seem—not surprisingly—to track rather well with what is to be found in the high-brow erotic literature, with which, in works like the *Perfumed Garden,* there is in fact significant overlap.

Aside from the somewhat greater prominence of popular fiction, it is probably safe to say that the pursuit of erotic themes, both in an ongoing *mujūn* tradition of poetry and anecdote and in a monographic literature devoted exclusively to sexual topics, continued unabated in Arabic Ottoman literature until the mid-nineteenth century, when the massive impact of Western colonialism changed all the rules and permanently disrupted the literary tradition. In the previous millennium, Arabic literature offered a remarkably open, rich, and variegated corpus of erotica, in which religious and ethical considerations, humorous exuberance, sociological analysis, and an unfettered celebration of the power of the word to stimulate both the imagination and the hormones were all given free play.

EVERETT K. ROWSON

Further Reading

'Alī ibn Naṣr al-Kātib, Abul Ḥasan. *Encyclopedia of Pleasure.* Translation Adnan Jarkas and Salah Addin Khawwam. Toronto: Aleppo Publishing, 1977.

Bauer, Thomas. *Liebe und Liebesdichtung in der arabischen Welt des 9. und 10. Jahrhunderts* [Love and Love Poetry in the Arab World of the Ninth and Tenth Centuries]. Wiesbaden: Harrassowitz, 1998.

Bell, Joseph Norment. *Love Theory in Later Hanbalite Islam.* Albany: SUNY Press, 1979.

Bouhdiba, Abedelwahab. *Sexuality in Islam.* London: Saqi Books, 1998.

Bousquet, G.H. *L'Ethique sexuelle de l'Islam* [Sexual Ethics in Islam]. Paris, 1966.

Declich, Lorenzo. "L'Erotologia araba: Profilo bibliografico [Arabic Erotology: A Bibliographic Profile]," *Rivista degli studi orientali* 68 (1994–95), 249–65.

Giffen, Lois Anita. *Theory of Profane Love among the Arabs: The Development of the Genre.* New York: NYU Press, 1971.

Ibn Falīta. *Rushd al-labīb ilā mu'āsharat al-ḥabīb* [The Intelligent Man's Guide to Keeping Company with the Beloved], edited and German translation by Ghadhban Al-Bayati (1–3, 1976); Adnan Husni-Pascha (4, 1975); J.E. Yousif (5, 1977); Boulus Al-Khouri (6.1, 1975); Abdul Khador Abdul Hassan (6.2, 1983M); Adnan Zeni (6.3, 1978); Mohamed Zouher Djabri (9–11, 1968); Elian Sabbagh (12–14, 1973), all Erlangen dissertations; *An Intelligent Man's Guide to the Art of Coition,* translated by Adnan Jarkas and Salah Addin Khawwam, Toronto: Aleppo Publishing, 1977.

Irwin, Robert. *The Arabian Nights: A Companion.* London, 1994.

'Īsā b. Māssa. *Masā'il fī al-nasl wa al-dhurrīya wa al-gimā'* [Questions on Reproduction, Progeny, and Sexual Intercourse], edited and German translation by Mohamed Walid Anbari (1971), Erlangen dissertation.

Kindī, al-, *K. al-bāh* [Book of Sexual Intercourse], edited and Italian translation by Giuseppe Celentano, "Due scritti medici di al-Kindī [Two Medical Texts by al-Kindī]," *Istituto Orientalie di Napoli, supplemento n. 18 agli annali* 39 (1979), facs. 1, 11–36

Leemans, Mitchke. Siḥāq *en Sekse: Lesbische Seksualiteit in Middeleeuws Arabische Literatur* [Siḥāq and Sex: Lesbian Sexuality in Medieval Arabic Literature]. Doctoral dissertation, 1996, Utrecht.

López-Baralt, Luce. *Un Kama Sutra español* [A Spanish Kama Sutra]. Madrid, 1992.

Malti-Douglas, Fedwa. *Woman's Body, Woman's Word: Gender and Discourse in Arabo-Islamic Writing* Princeton, NJ: Princeton University Press, 1991.

Marsot, Afaf Lutfi al-Sayyid, ed. *Society and the Sexes in Medieval Islam* (Sixth Giorgio Levi Della Vida Biennial Conference). Malibu, CA: Undena, 1979.

Meisami, Julie Scott. "Arabic *Mujūn* Poetry: The Literary Dimension." In *Verse and the Fair Sex: Studies in Arabic Poetry and the Representation of Women in Arabic Literature,* edited by F. De Jong, Utrecht, 8–30.

Munajjid, al-, Ṣalāḥ al-Dīn. *al-Ḥayāh al-jinsīya 'ind al-'arab* [Sexual Life Among the Arabs], 2nd ed. Beirut: Dār al-Kitāb al-Jadīd, 1975.

Murray, Stephen O., & Will Roscoe. *Islamic Homosexualities: Culture, History, and Literature.* New York: NYU Press, 1997.

Nafzāwī, al-, *al-Rawḍ al-'āṭir fī nuzhat al-khāṭir* [The Perfumed Garden of Sensual Delight]. Edited by Jamāl Jum'a, London: Riad El-Rayyes, 1990; *The Perfumed Garden of Sensual Delight,* translated by Jim Colville, London and New York: Kegan Paul International, 1999.

Nathan, Bassem. "Medieval Arabic Medical Views on Male Homosexuality," *Journal of Homosexuality* 26 (1994), 37–39.

Qusṭā b. Lūqā. *Kitāb fī l-bāh* [Book on Sexual Intercourse], edited and German translation by Najdat Ali Barhoum (1974), Erlangen dissertation.

———. *Kitāb fī l-bāh wa-mā yuḥtāju ilayhi min tadbīr al-badan fī sti'mālihi* [Book on Sexual Intercourse and the Bodily Regimen Required in Practicing It], edited and German translation by Gauss Haydar (part I, 1973), F. Abdo (part II, 1978), Erlangen dissertations.

Rāzī, al-. *Risāla fī l-bāh* [Epistle on Sexual Intercourse], edited by Hishām ‘Abd al-‘Azīz & ‘Ādil ‘Abd al-Ḥamīd, *Thalāth makhṭūṭāt nādira fī l-jins* (pp. 149–176). Cairo and London: Dār al-Khayyāl, 1999.

Rosenthal, F. "Ar -Rāzī on the Hidden Illness," *Bulletin of the History of Medicine* 52 (1978), 45–60.

Rowson, Everett K. "The Categorization of Gender and Sexual Irregularity in Medieval Arabic Vice Lists." In *Body Guards: The Cultural Politics of Gender Ambiguity*. Edited by Julia Epstein and Kristina Straub (pp. 50–79). New York and London: Routledge, 1991.

———. "Middle Eastern Literature: Arabic." In *The Gay and Lesbian Literary Heritage*, edited by Claude J. Summers (pp. 481–485). New York, 1995.

Samaw'al b. Yaḥyā, al-. *Nuzhat al-aṣḥāb fī mu‘āsharat al-aḥbāb* [Pleasure Parks for Friends on Companionship with Their Beloveds]. Edited and German translation by Taher Haddad (I.6–8, 1976), Fadi MansourL (II.1–5, 1975), Kamal Hallak (II.6, 1973), Erlangen dissertations.

Shayzarī, al-. *al-Īḍāḥ fī asrār al-nikāḥ* [Clarification of the Secrets of Sexual Intercourse]. Edited by Muḥammad Sa‘īd al-Ṭurayḥī. Beirut: Dār al-Qāri', 1986.

Suyūṭī, al-. *al-Wishāḥ fī fawā'id al-nikāḥ* [The Sash, on the Merits of Sexual Intercourse]. Edited by Ṭal‘at Ḥasan ‘Abd al-Qawī. Damascus: Dār al-Kitāb al-‘Arabī, 2001.

———. *Nawāḍir al-ayk fī ma'rifat al-nayk* [Luxuriant Thickets of Knowledge About Coitus]. Edited by Ṭal'at Ḥasan ‘Abd al-Qawī. Damascus: Dār al-Kitāb al-‘Arabī, 2001.

Tīfāshī, al-. *Nuzhat al-albāb fīmā lā yūjad fī kitāb* [The Delight of Hearts on What Cannot Be Found in Any Other Book]. French translation by R.R. Khawam, *Les Délices des coeurs*, Paris: Éditions Phébus, 1981; partial English translation (from the French) by E.A. Lacey, *The Delight of Hearts*, San Francisco: Gay Sunshine Press, 1988.

———. *Risāla fīmā yaḥtāj ilayh al-rijāl wa-l-nisā' fī isti'māl al-bāh minmā yaḍurr wa-yanfa'* [Epistle on What Men and Women Need in Practicing Sexual Intercourse]. Edited and German translation by by Hassan Mohamed El-Haw (1970), Erlangen dissertation.

——— (?). *Rujū' al-shaykh ilā ṣibāh fī l-qūwa ‘alā l-bāh* [The Old Man's Return to His Youth in Sexual Prowess], edited by Ṭal'at Ḥasan ‘Abd al-Qawī, Damascus: Dār al-Kitāb al-‘Arabī, n. d.; *The Old Man Young Again, Literally Translated from the Arabic by an English Bohemian*, anonymous translation, Paris, 1898.

Tijānī, al-. *Tuḥfat al-‘arūs wa-rawḍat al-nufūs* [The Gift of the Bride and Garden of Souls], edited by Jalīl al-‘Aṭīya. London: Riad El-Rayyes, 1992.

Ṭūsī, Nasīr al-Dīn, al-. *Kitāb al-Bāb al-bāhīya wa-l-tarākīb al-sulṭānīya* [Book of Sexual Discourse and Majestic Prescriptions], edited and German translation by Ghassan Ammari (1974), Erlangen dissertation.

‘Umar al-Ḥalabī. *Nuzhat al-udabā' wa-salwat al-qurabā'* [The Pleasure Park of Littérateurs and Consolation of Intimates]. French translation by Paul de Régla, *Théologie musulmane. El Ktab des lois secrètes de l'amour*. Paris, 1893; reprinted Paris, 1993.

Wright, J.W., Jr., and Everett K. Rowson, eds. *Homoeroticism in Classical Arabic Literature*. New York: Columbia University Press, 1997.

ARCAN, NELLY

1975–

French Canadian novelist

Nelly Arcan is the author of *Putain* and *Folle*. With *Putain* she made a notable entry onto the literary scene, both in France and in Quebec. The novel was first published by Editions du Seuil, winning her a place among the rare Quebecois authors whose first novel saw the light of day through a major French publisher.

With brutal and despaired writing that gives her texts a throbbing force, Arcan depicts not only sexuality, exhibited without shame, but also the immense despair of a narrator who simultaneously seeks and loses herself through sex. This sexuality, omnipresent throughout her texts, assumes an industrial form and presents itself effectively as labor, where the narrator is defined as a sex worker. She expends herself through this work in which money received in exchange for her sexual services compensates for her consumption. Her literary works recount the whole industry of sex, from prostitution to porn cinemas, and through erotic photographs in the Internet that preoccupy Arcan.

In *Putain,* she depicts a former escort who spits out her hatred and disgust for her customers as well as for the diktat of the image that turns women into enemies in the race for the title of the most beautiful and the most desired.

Bearing the form of litany, the account, built with long, breathless sentences, does not seek to rouse desire in the reader, who is implicated in and engulfed by the narrator's violence. Known only through an alias, Cynthia—the prostitute's name is borrowed from her older sister, who died at a young age—this narrator remains anonymous. Through the story, Arcan ventures beyond the specifics of the escort experience, relating a family history. Between the religious bigotry of her father, busy hunting down the devil, a bedridden mother reduced to the state of a larva, and the phantom of her deceased sister, the narrator attempts to find her place. Her exacerbated sexuality is both a way of breaking with her childhood's religious upbringing and of hurling a primal sort of scream back at her parents, her mother, in particular, who persists in ignoring her presence. Through these repeated screams and this excessive pleasure, she perhaps seeks to please her clients, but also to thus awaken her catatonic mother to her daughter's very existence.

The same narrator, driven by the will to be the goddess of the boulevard, on whom all gazes and desires converge, is also at the center of *Folle* [*Mad*], the author's second work. In this chronicle of a suicide, announced in a letter addressed to the man who has left her, the narrator—this time explicitly named Nelly Arcan—is constantly in search of a glance that would make her exist. If, in *Putain*, the man/woman relations are treated from the perspective of prostitution, Arcan in *Folle* approaches them through an amorous encounter. However, this encounter, doomed from the start, the end of which is announced at the beginning, remains subject to the leeches of the sex industry, which goes so far as to pervert the amorous discourse itself, invading it with pornographic vocabulary. There are intruders between the narrator and her lover; her former clients invade while he, the lover, finds pleasure with the Net girls, inevitably ruining their relationship.

The critical reception of Arcan's work was strongly tainted by the question of autobiography. Some reviews insisted on the autobiographical character of her work and presented it as factual truth rather than fiction. Having been more interested in hearing the author's reflections on the intricacies of the escort occupation rather than on the writing process, they have often overlooked the literary qualities of *Putain*

and *Folle*. However, the work of Arcan may be better described as *autofiction* in the general sense of the term, i.e., an account that uses the author's life as basic material without necessarily sticking to the historical or prosaic facts. Just as Nelly Arcan reveals herself to the public while remaining masked behind a pseudonym, in an inextricable way her accounts intertwine truth and fiction and, in one gesture, conceal what they allow to reveal.

The space occupied by sexuality in the work of Arcan places her alongside such French authors as Catherine Millet and Virginie Despentes. Often qualified as sulfurous, these writers depict female sexuality in detail and endeavor to smash the taboos regarding the representation of the female body. Following the example of her contemporaries, Arcan seems to have heard Héléne Cixous's call during the 1970s, inviting women in her manifesto, *The Laugh of Medusa*, to write their body and to thus reappropriate it.

But some 30 years later, in the work of Arcan, the female body is no longer a territory to reconquer, nor is it a place to find pleasure. On the contrary, here sexuality is inextricably related to death and to the loss of oneself. The fragile identity that the narrator attempts to consolidate by taking command of her speech is unceasingly shaken by sexuality, which appears to her primarily as the pawn for her existence. Her race to be the most beautiful, the most desirable, i.e., the most consumable, however, sets her in the role of the perpetual substitute. For, the prostitute that she becomes is not there for herself but is always called upon to replace another. The appropriation of her dead sister's name highlights this role of a replacement. Thus, not only is another person named in her place, but, concomitantly, the dead is questioned. In *Folle,* the narrator once again finds that she is at odds with herself. And from this conflict her madness is born: Mad with jealousy and with not being chosen as the goddess of desire, the narrator knows herself to be loved by her companion because of her borrowed name, Nelly, which has the quaint sound of the name of one of the man's former girlfriend.

In the image of the unstable identity of the narrator, the body proves to be a malleable object that must be incessantly fashioned to respond to the requirements of femininity and male desire. However, even though Arcan adopts a moralizing tone when it comes to warning against the icons of "perfect" femininity, her narrator adheres to this doctrine of beauty and physical perfection and is obsessed with her appearance and the effect she has on men. Arcan thus explores the feminine archetypes: Between the figure of the whore and the rejected lover driven to madness, a woman is caught in the endlessly recurring scission between body and spirit, striving to exist through her mind as well as through her sex.

Biography

Born in Quebec, Canada, in 1975, Arcan studied literature at the Université du Québec in Montréal, where she received a master's degree with a thesis on *Memoirs of My Nervous Illness* by Daniel Paul Schreber.

EVELYNE LEDOUX-BEAUGRAND

Selected Works

Folle. Paris: Editions du Seuil, 2004.
Putain [*Whore*]. Translated by Bruce Benderson. New York: Black Cat, 2005.

Further Reading

Cixous, Hélène. "The Laugh of Medusa," *Signs* 1 (1976), translated by Keith Cohen and Paula Cohen: 875–893.
Dupré, Louise. "Women's Writing in Quebec: From Rhetoric to New Social Propositions," in *The Rhetoric of Canadian Writing* edited by Conny Steenman-Marcusse. Amsterdam, Netherlands: Rodopi, 2002.
Hughes, Alex, & Kate Ince, eds. *French Erotic Fiction: Women's Desiring Writing: 1880–1990*. Oxford: Berg, 1996.
Morello, Nathalie, & Catherine Rodgers, eds. *Nouvelles écrivaines, nouvelles voix?* Amsterdam and New York: Rodopi, 2002.

ARETINISTS

Of the Italians who were doing for sexuality in the way of literary exposure and redefinition what Machiavelli had already done for politics, the most influential was undoubtedly Pietro Aretino. The prince in Lodge's *Margarite of America* (1596) keeps both "*Macheuils* prince" and Aretino's *Ragionamenti* [*Dialogues*] in his pocket. Aretino was equally associated with the notorious sexual postures designed by Giulio Romano and engraved by Raimondi, for which he supplied a set of *Sonetti lussuriosi* [*Lascivious Sonnets*] in 1527. Burton, *Anatomy of Melancholy* 3.2.2.4, aligns these postures with those of several women of antiquity: Astyannassa, maid of Helen of Troy; Philaenis of Samos; and Elephantis; the latter's work, according to Suetonius, being one of the visual stimulants which the emperor Tiberius brought to Capri. Jonson's Epicure Mammon (*Alchemist* II.ii.43–45), imagining his chamber "Fill'd with such pictures, as TIBERIVS tooke / From ELEPHANTIS: and dull ARETINE / But coldly imitated," still manages to hint that the imitations gesture mockingly toward a supposed classical tradition. As visual images, they had an international currency which could transcend linguistic barriers. But, for cultural and political reasons—Protestant England identified Italy not only with artistic innovation but with papal threat—Italian was the most studied of the continental vernaculars amongst educated Elizabethans, providing a significant domestic market for the London editions of Aretino. Although Italian lost ground to Spanish as a result of Philip II's aggressive policies, the interactive spread of literacy and cheap print facilitated Aretino's displacement of Ovid as the most favored erotic model for the British during the seventeenth century.

Aretino would have had an appeal not only as a symbol of sexual enlightenment but as critic of Rome. In the dedication to his *Sonnetti,* his insistence that the penis should be worn as a badge of honor directly challenges the Church's view, as articulated by St. Augustine, that the loincloth is a badge of the Fall. Effectively, he popularizes that libertinism latent in Pomponazzi which would take vigorous root in seventeenth-century France and thence influence Charles II and his modish following. Interestingly, Gabriel Harvey, *Pierce's Supererogation* (1593, p.47), links Pomponazzi as "poysonous Philosopher" with Machiavelli and Aretino, respectively poisonous politician and ribald. Harvey upbraids Thomas Nashe for following Aretino in exploring "veneriall machiauelisme." Nashe brackets Ovid and Aretino as upholders of Whoredom's throne, and the twin influence is apparent in his *Choise of Valentines*. Although it had only manuscript currency, Davies of Hereford, *Wits Bedlam* (1617, p.206), notes its popularity as well as its alternative title, "Nashes choosing Valentines; To wit, his *Dildo* knowne to euery Trull"; Tomalin's whore using a dildo when he suffers first from the disability described in Ovid's Elegy III.vi and then premature ejaculation.

In wedding an Aretine spirit to his neo-Ovidian verse form, Nashe anticipates that mid-seventeenth-century explosion of pornography, when Aretino's *Ragionamenti* and Giulio's pictures were major inspirations. That Aretino's sonnets had lapsed from view has less to do with their sodomitical bent than with the way that print, rendering verse's memorial aids redundant, allowed prose to usurp many of its functions. His device of subversive gossips imparting their sexual experience had already a firm place in such English writing as *A Talk of Ten Wives on Their Husbands' Ware* (c.1460) and Dunbar's *Tua mariit wemen and the wedo*. But the focus on marital problems and irregularities tended to shift to commercial sex under the impact of print and Reformation. Thus *The New Brawle Or, Rosemary-Lane against Turnmill Street* (1654), an exchange of insults between husband and wife, its dialogue form and scandalous tone both recalling Aretino, has more to do with whoring than marriage. Even before Doll appears, John complains that she "makes Hornes at me, bids me go look under the candle-stick" (i.e., where her clients leave their fee), her neighbors being Damrose Page and others of the brothel sorority.

In *Ragionamenti* marriage loses out to prostitution as a career for the whore Nanna's daughter Pippa. Also considered is the convent, but that hardly differs from the brothel; Aretino's anticlericalism being as influential as his racy language. The hackneyed figure of pestle pounding in mortar is refurbished when Nanna in frustration actually uses a pestle as dildo. This recalls Shakespeare's way of getting fresh mileage from tired old Petrarchisms in "My mistress' eyes are nothing like the sun." But here again Aretino led, versifying that while the mistress's breath hardly matches the odors of India or Sheba, and her eyes are neither Love's dwelling nor source of the sun's splendor, she can still charm a hermit. Aretino's book appeared as two parts in 1534 and 1536, the second commenting on reception of the first. Those orgiastic convent pictures, insists Nanna, were not malicious; she could have delivered a much more damaging exposé had she wished. But she is very conscious that print, new enough to require delicate negotiations with the oral, has brought alarming possibilities for breach of confidence. Hence, with some unscrupulous idler ever ready with his pen, instruction of Pippa will also alert future clients to the whore's wiles.

This crux, ignored by Markham's *Famovs Whore* (1609), who "knew all *Aretine* by rot" and passed on "his book-rules ... / To euery ignorant, yet wanton louer," provides justification for the writer purporting to treat unseemly topics as moral warning. Striking illustration is provided by an anglicizing of Nanna's discourse on prostitution. Although much of Nanna's activity might be accepted as ingenious pranks, Aretino allows neither her zest nor her witty resourcefulness to excuse her relentless pursuit of profit, exploiting people's good nature as well as their greed and gullibility. There are moments when even Antonia—herself riddled with an incurable pox—is shocked by the revelations, and begs Nanna to desist. But Aretine satire disappears and Markham-style repentance and moralizing conclude *The Crafty Whore* (1658). Part of this date has been trimmed in the unique surviving copy, but Naumann proposes dates outside publisher Henry Marsh's active life span. Besides, there is an advertisement appended to Montelion, *Don Juan Lamberto* (1661), valuably identifying the translator as R. H. (presumably Richard Head, who around this date produced the lost *Venus' Cabinet Unlock'd*, while in 1665 Marsh handled his *English Rogue*). That lost title accompanies *The Crafty Whore* in *A Strange and True Conference Between Two Notorious Bawds Damarose Page and Pris. Fotheringham* (1660), as desiderata for a brothel library. This dialogue, like a companion piece, *Strange and True Newes from Jack-a-Newberries Six Windmills,* focuses on Fotheringham's chuck-office, clearly the talk of dissolute London in 1660. Fotheringham's trick was to stand on her head, legs astride to allow "her Cully-Rumpers to chuck half crowns" into her commodity. Both dialogues itemize house regulations, a burlesque of brothel ordinances. The second, which orders that inmates must never "refuse to do the deed of nature either backwards or any other of *Peter Aretines* postures," was allegedly written by Aretino and sold by Rodericus a Castro, Spanish convert to Judaism and pioneer in gynecology.

It was the bitterness of the continental religious wars invading Britain which brought the flood of obscenity adumbrated by Nashe some half-century earlier. Sexual defamation was an obvious weapon for the civil war propagandist. Thus an allegation that "a holy Rebell" buggered a horse (*Mercurius Aulicus* 51, 16 December 1643) brought the rejoinder from *Mercurius Britanicus* 19 (28 December 1643) about royalists "keeping Mares for *breeding* Cavaliers on, and they may do it as lawfully as the Ladies of honour may keep Stallions and Monkies, and their Bishops Sheegoates and Ganimedes." *A Dialogue Between Mistris Macquerella, a Suburb Bawd, Ms Scolopendra, a Noted Curtezan, and Mr Pimpinello an Usher* (1650) was occasioned by the Commonwealth's act "for suppressing the detestable sins of incest, adultery and fornication." Despite the bawd's reassurances about "a nine dayes wonder," Scolopendra decides to head for Venice (Aretino's literary home, celebrated for its courtesans). The political gibe is missing from *The Wandring Whores Complaint for Want of Trading* (1663), which rehearses different problems: "The *Coffeehouses* have dry'd up all our Customers like Spunges.... Besides, there is so many privat Whores that a common wandring whore can get no imployment." *Strange Newes from Bartholomew-Fair Or, The Wandring-Whore Discovered* "by Peter Aretine" (1661) represents the fair's "Py-women" as whores who "have long since ... read *Aretine* both in Print and Picture," as *Mercurius Fumigosus* 13 (23 August 1654) puts it.

When Everard Guilpin, *Skialetheia* (1596, p.64), alludes to "*Aretines* aduenturous wandring whore," he means Lorenzo Venier's mock-heroic *Puttana errante* (c. 1531), commended by Aretino and frequently ascribed to him. This Renaissance *Eskimo Nell*, spiked with anticlericalism, is not to be confused with the (late?)-sixteenth-century *Piacevol ragionamento de*

l'Aretino [Aretino's Pleasant Discourse], which acquired the *Puttana errante* [Wandering Whore] title when appended to a 1660 edition of Aretino. It is heavily concerned with postures, making *The Ladies Champion* (1660) condemn "*Peter Aretine* for inventing the six and thirty several ways and postures of occupying." Its title and characters were quickly appropriated by John Garfield for his scurrilous serial, *The Wandring Whore*. The Ladies Champion, ostensibly attacking him as a "woman-hater, and enemy to multiplication" and supplying free advertisement. Ambiguity persists as the "Champion," feigning identity with John Heydon through adopting his pseudonym "Eugenius Theodidactus," accuses him of writing *The Wandring Whore*. The latter's author is also blamed for another serial, *Select City Quaeries*, while the wrong man (presumably Garfield) has been imprisoned for writing the *Whore*. The mesh of relationships draws tighter when *Strange and True Conference*, insulting Heydon in much the same terms as the *Champion*'s, receives advance notice in *Whore* II, suggesting that it was written by Garfield or a crony.

Quaeries 3 dubs Betty Lucas "*La Puttana Errante*"; but *The Wandring Whore* appends extensive lists of current professionals, indicating that there was no shortage of streetwalking candidates. The *Whore* staggered through six issues, containing details not only of traders but of their tricks. Grotesquerie peaks in the first issue, where Fotheringham's immodest posture was imitated while "Rhenish wine was [poured] into the Dutch wenches two holes till she roar'd" because of its "smarting and searching quality." Another tried the experiment with sack, "poured in on one side ... and suck'd out on the other, which is a new fashioned Cup for roaring boyes to drink in." These roarers laid a drunken whore "belly naked upon a Table, ... sticking a Candle in her Comodity, and drinking healths over the dead drunk party, til the merciless Candle fir'd her fur-bush quite away, the flame whereof was quickly abated by drawing a codpiece engine, and giving her two or three Coolers." The last (1663) issue, "Written by Peter Aretine," visits the Sesto Bridge district, haunt of prostitutes in Aretino's Rome. It also introduces Eubulus, hitherto supposedly a silent Aretinesque recorder, as one who has translated "*Peter Aretines Postures* into English" (presumably this serial echo of *Puttana errante*).

Aretino's last dialogue, where midwife and wet nurse discuss the art of bawding, probably inspired the lost *English Bawd* as well as *The London Bawd,* surviving in a fourth (1711) edition. The latter recalls Aretino's comparison of a doctor's bedside manner with a bawd's need to be ready with a hundred little tales, as the dialogue threatens to collapse under the weight of anecdote. But this does allow the bawd to retrieve her character, showing herself, like the Prohibition bootlegger, to be providing a public service; not only in cooling the spark's amorous ardor but in alleviating the frustration of mismatched wives. (This gibe at city husbands is more a London than an Aretine touch.) Another important bawd book, *The Whore's Rhetoric,* although based on Pallavicino's *La rettorica delle puttane* (1642), becomes Aretine dialogue. Like Pippa, Dorothea is an apt pupil; and her anxiety about losing her virginity is a direct borrowing. Warnings against lapsing into love and displaying envy of other women are similarly appropriated, while whole pages on handling superannuated clients follow *Ragionamenti* almost verbatim. Pallavicino's parody of the Jesuit Suarez has vanished, though it is this mockery of rhetorical procedures which explains why he was frequently assumed to be the author of *L'Alcibiade,* ambiguously signed "D.P.A.," viz., "di Padre Antonio" [Rocco] (or "Pietro Aretino"), published 1652 after lengthy manuscript circulation. London's fashionable set had absorbed Italian homoeroticism by the 1590s, and a later generation must have discovered Rocco's original, though it remained untranslated. The roles of pedagogue and seducer blur through reliance on rhetoric. The pupil's eventual sodomizing, a near-burlesque of that other scholastic method of applying rod to arse, becomes the ultimate teaching mode, recalling ancient associations of semen with brain matter and anticipating Chorier's punning suggestion of intellectual benefit from losing virginity: *mentula/mentis* (of the mind).

Rocco lacks Pallavicino's anticlericalism, something Aretino sponsored in works as diverse as Leti's pope-baiting *Puttanismo romano* [*History of the Whores and Whoredom of the Popes, Cardinals, and Clergy of Rome*] and Barrin's *Venus in the Cloister.* Leti's book, which Buet reissued with a new dialogue between Pasquin and Marforio (the two statues in Rome on which satires were hung), under a false London imprint in 1669, appeared in English the

following year. Leti suggests that prelates favor bardashes over harlots because they are more discreet and allegedly free from pox: What price church neutrality if one becomes "a Frenchman both in blood and constitution"? Wealth and status await the "Sodomitical boys ... for their great services done to those that take a pride to have their standing-chambers in the Arsehole of Rome" (*Culiseo,* popular arsehole/Colosseum quibble, also occurs in *Ragionamenti*). Sexual struggles to influence papal elections could be eliminated by making "the Popedom Hereditary; which might be done by the Popes taking a Wife; and so neither the Ingles, nor Whores would have any pretence to the *Vatican.*"

French and English texts of *Venus in the Cloister* appeared simultaneously in 1682, ascribed to "l'Abbé du Prat." The pattern of two young women, the elder instructing her junior, is borrowed from two other books which are required reading for the nuns. One is *L'Escole des filles* [*School of Venus*], perceptively termed insipid, though the other, Chorier's *Aloisia Sigea* is recognized as more accomplished and more dangerous. Angelica tells Agnes that the monks offer practical instruction far more efficacious than anything she can. When denied conjunction, the nuns ply glass instruments "oftner than their Beads," while the monks wage "*The War of Five against One.*" A sexual elite, founder-members including both bishop and supposed author Prat, grotesquely title themselves "Knights of the *Grate,* or of St. Lawrence," with double allusion to flames of passion and the grate providing access to the nuns. One wears a reliquary against his heart containing pubic hair of all those he has enjoyed. From Chorier comes a dynamic use of dialogue (non-Aretine, but perfected earlier in Rojas's *Celestina,* a courtly tale switching emphasis from lovers to go-between). Thus Angelica's talk is interspersed with lesbian caresses and spanking (after Agnes has become enflamed by hearing how teaching duties offer scope to visit pupils' "back apartments").

Millot and l'Ange's *L'Escole des filles* (1655) avoids such diversions. Although Fanchon is rapidly aided to lose her virginity by her more precocious cousin, Susanne's lore about flogsters, castrati, and dildos is all secondhand; and she is so late with her hints on contraception that it is well that she claims acquaintance with an effective abortifacient. Indeed Dunton,

Athenianism (1710), reckons this "lewd, vile and abominable Book ... a meer Novice" compared with some of the unnatural practices currently adopted to thwart pregnancy. Pepys, encountering it on 13 January 1668, thought it "rather worse then *putana errante*," abandoning his idea of getting his wife to translate it (first mention of an English version is in a 1680 court record). It is notable for shifting from an atmosphere of commercial sex to that of youthful ardor, producing frisson through Fanchon's combination of naïveté and knowingness. Despite a paucity of nonsexual detail, the ambience is clearly that of middle-class comfort. There is no reason, beyond that which brought Pepys to solitary orgasm, to engage with Fanchon's predicament, as there is, for instance, in Ward's *Rise and Fall of Madam Coming-Sir: Or, An Unfortunate Slip from the Tavern-Bar into the Surgeons Powdering-Tub* (1703), where the grim battle for economic survival allows the protagonist, lacking the support of parents or friends, both to teach a moral lesson and (despite Ward's facetiousness) to arouse sympathy. Lacking social comment, *L'Escole des filles* offers mild subversion, setting education by peers above the teaching of the church and advocating marriage as cover for extramarital activity. If the fragments quoted from a 1745 trial transcript by Donald Thomas are typical, English versions were both more pithy and more subversive than the original.

Chorier's *Aloisia Sigea* is amply subversive, reducing morality to reputation. Power is the theme: Husbands control wives but are themselves duped, as wives control their lovers using the leverage of law and religion as well as sex. Chorier sticks to a privileged milieu, recognizing with Aretino that the poor have neither time nor energy for sexual variation. His central character Tullia is doubtless the inspiration for Barrin's Angelica in finding religion, like other social forms, a matter of policy. Her friend Sempronia's sinister manipulations anticipate those of Laclos's Madame de Merteuil, though the cynical Chorier exacts no retribution. His Latin text exploits a new French descriptive spareness and enters English with one dialogue rendered in a manuscript commonplace book dated 1676, though the date may be that of either translation or source. Reference in the first scene of

Ravenscroft's *London Cuckolds* (1682) to "the beastly, bawdy translated book called the *Schoole of Women*" probably alludes to the 1680 French translation entitled *L'Academie des dames* (Foxon) and constitutes no evidence for a 1682 English version (Naumann, Wagner), especially as Ravenscroft's play was produced the previous year. An Englishing entitled *A Dialogue Between a Married Lady and a Maid* was prosecuted in 1684, Tom Brown, *The Reasons of Mr. Bays Changing His Religion* (1688), condemning Dryden because bits of his Lucretius are fit "*only to keep company with* Culpeppers Midwife, *or the* English *Translation of* Aloysia Sigea." While the book's main influence lies elsewhere, it occupies a climactic position in the English Aretine context and was still viewed as "the father or mother" of her pornographic collection by an English whore in the 1830s *Bagnio Miscellany*.

GORDON WILLIAMS

Selected Works

The Crafty Whore. Edited and translated by Daniela de Filippis. Naples: Liguori, 1998.
Garfield, John. *The Wandring Whore*, in *Marriage, Sex, and the Family in England 1660–1800* (a 44-volume facsimile series, edited by Randolph Trumbach). New York and London: Garland, 1986.
Millot, Michel, & Jean L'Ange. *The School of Venus*, translated by Donald Thomas. London: Panther, 1972.
Nashe, Thomas. *The Works*. Edited by R. B. McKerrow with corrections by F.P. Wilson. Oxford: Blackwell, 1966.
Piacevol ragionamento de l'Aretino, Il. Dialogo di Giulia e di Madalena. Edited by Claudio Galderisi. Rome: Salerno, 1987.
The Whore's Rhetorick. London: Holland, 1960.

Further Reading

Foxon, David. *Libertine Literature in England, 1660–1745*, reprinted with revisions (from *The Book Collector*, 1963), 1964.
Kearney, Patrick J. *A History of Erotic Literature*. London: Macmillan, 1982.
Naumann, Peter. *Keyhole und Candle*. Heidelberg: Winter, 1976.
Thompson, Roger. *Unfit for Modest Ears*. London: Macmillan, 1979.
Wagner, Peter. *Eros Revived: Erotica of the Enlightenment in England and America*. London: Secker and Warburg, 1988.

ARETINO, PIETRO

1492–1556
Italian poet, novelist, and essayist

Pietro Aretino, one of the most influential and financially successful men of letters in sixteenth-century Italy, is an almost mythical figure in the history of European erotic writing. He first gained notoriety in Rome in the mid-1520s with the *Sonetti lussuriosi*, a series of "lustful sonnets" he wrote to accompany 16 erotic engravings produced by Marcantonio Raimondi after drawings by Giulio Romano. The sonnets describe sexual activities and desires in clear, nonmetaphoric language, and although they were quickly suppressed, they became notorious throughout Europe. Although Aretino's name was synonymous with erotic writing and pictures well into the nineteenth century, the majority of his texts were not, in fact, erotic. After the sonnets and some other early poems, his major erotic work was the *Ragionamenti*, or *Dialogues*, written in Venice in the mid-1530s.

Aretino first attained public notoriety after the death of Leo X in 1522, when he wrote a series of satirical poems opposing the election of the foreign Pope Adrian VI and supporting the candidacy of his new patron, Cardinal Giuliano de' Medici, the future Clement VII. These poems, often quite bawdy and crude, were known as "pasquinades," because they were affixed anonymously to a battered old statue near Piazza Navona called Pasquino. It is unlikely that Aretino initiated this practice, which persisted throughout the sixteenth century and beyond, but more than anyone else he was identified with the poems. Indeed, when Adrian VI took power, Aretino found it prudent to leave the city.

The *Sonetti lussuriosi*

Adrian was pope for only two years, and Aretino returned to Rome after the election of his patron as Pope Clement VII in 1523. But he was soon in the midst of a new controversy. His friend Raimondi, a renowned Italian engraver,

was imprisoned by the pope's counselor, Giovanni Matteo Giberti, for having made the 16 erotic prints based on Romano. The court of Clement VII was not at all prudish. But while erotic drawings and paintings might be tolerated and even enjoyed within the relatively closed aristocratic world of the court, erotic *engravings,* which could be printed in large quantity, sold in the marketplace, and widely disseminated beyond the court, were another matter altogether. At a time when Lutheran criticism of papal corruption was spreading all over Europe, the Pope could not afford to have such materials associated with the Vatican.

Aretino petitioned the pope for Raimondi's release, and then, once his friend was safely out of jail, he wrote a series of 16 erotic sonnets—the *Sonetti*—to accompany the engravings. Together, the sonnets and engravings were known as *I modi* (the modes or postures) because each portrayed a man and a woman having intercourse in a different position. The history of the sonnets' dissemination is very difficult to trace with any accuracy, because the printing took place surreptitiously and most copies have been destroyed. At first, the sonnets probably circulated in manuscript, written by hand on the printed sheets of the engravings. While it was long thought that an edition of poems and engravings was printed in Rome in 1525, Bette Talvacchia has argued convincingly that the first printed edition was probably produced in Venice in 1527. No copies of this edition are known to exist. The earliest surviving edition is another one, probably printed in Venice the same year, but with crude woodcuts replacing the elegant engravings. Only one of the original 16 engravings is now extant.

Aretino's sonnets are the most important and influential erotic texts of the sixteenth century, not because of their content—significant though it is—but because of their sheer notoriety. Few copies were printed, and almost none survived the papacy's attempt to suppress them; but although few people read them, everyone heard of them. As time passed, the role of Raimondi and

Romano was largely forgotten, and the engravings became known as "Aretine's pictures," a phrase which was soon synonymous with erotic art or text of any kind. In Shakespeare's day, "aretine" was an English adjective and "to aretinize" was an English verb. In Elizabethan England, Aretino became an almost mythical figure of erotic excess. John Donne included him in a list of damned Catholic innovators, including Machiavelli; Ben Jonson used him as a model for his most famous character, Volpone; Thomas Nashe, a ranting satirist, took to calling himself "the English Aretine."

Raimondi's engravings are groundbreaking in that they depict naked couples having sex without recourse to any mythological trappings. The figures are clearly men and women, not gods and nymphs. Similarly, the language of Aretino's sonnets is straightforward and slangy rather than elevated and formal. Sex is described using crude everyday words without the aid of elaborate metaphors. As befits poems written to explicate images, the sonnets are more descriptive than narrative. They are almost all written in dialogue form—the men and women in the pictures converse as they have sex. They tell each other what they like and what they don't like. They celebrate their pleasures and make fun of their rivals. The couples engage in both vaginal and anal intercourse; neither practice is declared superior. The sonnets do not propose any hierarchy of positions or claim that any one position is natural. There is no depiction of oral sex or manual stimulation without penetration. The fundamental purpose of the poems would appear to be a celebration of the pleasures of heterosexual intercourse.

But in this case, appearances are deceiving. The sonnets cannot be understood outside of the political context which produced them. Aretino's writing of the sonnets was a slap in the face to those who had imprisoned Raimondi, and constituted a serious attempt to embarrass the papal court at a time of heightened social and political tension. Not only was Luther's revolt against Church authority gaining strength throughout Europe, the pope was also on the verge of war with the Holy Roman Emperor, Charles V—a conflict which would lead to the sack of Rome two years later. Aretino was no Protestant, but he was outraged at the mistreatment of his friend and the hypocrisy of the papal court. In a public letter written to justify his

writing of the sonnets, he contrasts official persecution of *I modi* with tolerance of corruption:

> What harm is there in seeing a man mount a woman? ... The thing nature gave us to preserve the race ... has produced all the ... Titians, and the Michelangelos; and after them the Popes, the Emperors, and the Kings... And so we should consecrate special vigils and feast-days in its honor, and not enclose it in a scrap of cloth or silk. One's hands should rightly be kept hidden, because they wager money, sign false testimony, lend usuriously, gesture obscenely, rend, destroy, strike blows, wound, and kill. (*Selected Letters*, p. 156)

Here Aretino ironically praises the penis, but in the sonnets, female genitalia receive equal praise and attention. In most cases, the speeches are equally divided between male and female speakers. While some of the engravings stress the man's aggressive strength, as a group the sonnets do not suggest masculine domination of the sexual encounter. In several sonnets the woman directs the man on how best to please her. And although the sex in some is fairly rough, none of the sonnets represents a rape. In most, both partners seem to take equal sexual pleasure. The following exchange from the first sonnet is typical:

> [He]: Let's fuck, my love, let's fuck quickly,
> Since we are all born to fuck.
> If you adore the cock, I love the cunt....
> [She]: But let's stop babbling and ram your cock
> All the way to my heart.
> (Sonnet 1, lines 1–3, 12–13)

Aretino's audacity in supporting Raimondi infuriated many at court, especially Papal Secretary Giberti, the official who had imprisoned Raimondi. On the night of July 28, 1525, Aretino was attacked by Achille della Volta, a gentleman in Giberti's service, and left for dead with serious injuries in his chest and hand. As soon as he had recovered enough to travel, Aretino left Rome. After a year or so spent mostly in Mantua, he settled in Venice in 1527.

That same year, Aretino wrote a *pronostico*, or prophecy, a parody of the many astrological almanacs published at the time. Rather than predicting astrological events, Aretino predicted political ones. The text does not survive, but it seems that in his attack on his former patron, the pope, he predicted that the Holy Roman Emperor would send an army to sack Rome. When a few months later his prophecy was substantially fulfilled, Aretino's reputation as a critic of official abuses was assured. By this time, his outspoken nature had already earned him the nickname "Il flagello dei principi" [The scourge of princes] and he adopted the Latin motto "Veritas odium parit" [The truth brings forth hatred].

Venice, an independent and powerful republic which was also the largest center of printing in Europe, gave Aretino a safe haven in which to live and write. There was little regulation of the press in Venice in the mid-sixteenth century, and as long as Aretino refrained from criticizing the republic, he could safely say almost anything he wanted to. A gifted polemicist and shrewd manipulator, he proceeded to amass a substantial fortune by encouraging various rulers to bid for his services. He received large sums of money from the Marquis of Mantua by promising to write an epic poem in his praise, which was never quite finished. In 1533, King Francis I of France hoped to buy Aretino's favor by sending him a three-pound gold chain with links in the form of tongues and bearing the motto "Lingua eius loquetur mendacium" [His tongue will speak lies]. Aretino continued to support Francis' rivals, but proudly wore the chain. After 1536 he received a generous annuity from Emperor Charles V. In the 1540s, he was also wooed by the court of King Henry VIII of England, who hoped he might make a good Protestant polemicist. Like Francis, Henry was disappointed.

The *Dialogues*

Aretino's most substantial erotic work is the *Ragionamenti*, or *Dialogues*, which was published in two parts in 1534 and 1536. Each part of the dialogues is divided into three books, each book devoted to a day's discussion, and for this reason the work is also sometimes referred to as the *Sei giornate* [Six Days]. The *Ragionamenti* is notorious for its explicit descriptions of sexual activity of all sorts: heterosexual intercourse, sex between men, lesbian sex, masturbation, anal sex, group sex, and voyeurism. As with many erotic Renaissance texts, however, there is little mention of oral sex.

The first part of the *Ragionamenti* is a dialogue between two Roman courtesans. Nanna, the older and more experienced of the two, is trying to decide how to raise her daughter Pippa, and she discusses Pippa's future with her friend Antonia. Both Nanna and Antonia agree that as a young woman Pippa has only three options in life: She must become a nun, a wife, or a whore. In her time, Nanna has been all three, and Antonia encourages her to recount her experiences so they can compare the three vocations and make the right choice for Pippa. Nanna spends the first day describing her experiences as a nun in a convent where she was placed by her parents as a young girl, the second day talking about her marriage to an impotent old man, and the third day recounting her lucrative career as a Roman courtesan.

At the end of the three days' discussion, the choice for Pippa is clear. Antonia concludes:

> The nun betrays her sacred vows and the married woman murders the holy bond of matrimony, but the whore violates neither her monastery nor her husband; indeed she acts like a soldier who is paid to do evil, and when doing it, she does not believe that she is, for her shop sells what it has to sell.... Go freely with Pippa and make a whore of her right off. (Rosenthal translation, p. 102)

The second volume of the *Ragionamenti* continues the discussion: On the fourth day, Nanna advises Pippa of her future profession; on the fifth day, Nanna warns her daughter about men's cruelty; and on the sixth day, mother and daughter listen as a midwife teaches a wet nurse how to become a procuress. The last day in particular has a desultory feel to it, and although Aretino did publish other volumes of dialogues, they are unrelated to the first two volumes and are not particularly erotic in nature.

As with the *Sonetti lussuriosi*, the *Ragionamenti* cannot be understood if one ignores its political context. Almost all the graphic sex for which the text is renowned comes at the very beginning, in the description of Nanna's experience as a virgin inducted into a convent. The life of monks and nuns is portrayed as a lustful, gluttonous, perverse, and selfish pursuit of pleasure. Pretending to renounce the world, the clergy are in fact the greatest sensualists of all. This criticism of monastic hypocrisy is reminiscent of a long medieval tradition of anticlerical stories, yet Aretino goes beyond his models both in the explicitness of his erotic description and the ferocity of his critique. In the fourteenth century, when Boccaccio and Chaucer wrote their tales of bawdy clerics, there was no Protestant alternative to the Catholic Church. When Aretino was writing the *Dialogues,* monasteries were being abolished all over northern Europe. At no time did Aretino ever seriously support Protestant reform—on the contrary, he allied himself with the Catholic imperial court of Charles V and wrote popular Catholic devotional texts. But he had a grudge against the pope, and the first "day" of the *Dialogues* is clearly a continuation of the antipapal polemic Aretino had pursued since his expulsion from Rome. Whatever his intention, harsh criticism of the abuses of the Church by Catholic writers was necessarily inflammatory, and could not help but weaken the Catholic cause in the early years of the Reformation.

Arriving at the convent, the innocent Nanna is treated to a gluttonous banquet, at the end of which Venetian dildos made of hollow glass are distributed to all the nuns. She is then taken to a room decorated with erotic paintings and soon discovers that she can peek into several other rooms through holes in the walls. Peering through the cracks, Nanna views a panopticon of sexual activity: Nuns engage in lesbian sex; monks bugger each other; monks and nuns have sex in couples and in groups. Nanna first learns how to use her own dildo (finding it cold, she urinates in it to warm it up), and then has sex with one of the prelates. This pattern of sexual initiation—voyeurism followed by masturbation followed by intercourse—was repeated in countless European erotic texts in the following centuries.

Pulled out of the convent after being beaten to a pulp by her clerical lover, Nanna is married off to an ugly, impotent, wealthy old man. She fakes her virginity by putting an egg filled with chicken's blood in her vagina, and then spends her time as a wife thinking of clever ways to commit adultery. The shocking description of orgiastic sex in the first book more or less vanishes in the second. In tone and content, Book Two is similar to the bawdy tales of Boccaccio's *Decameron.* The emphasis is on the funny tricks the wives play on their foolish husbands, not on steamy descriptions of the sex they finally get.

After her decrepit husband dies, Nanna goes back to her mother, who disguises her so that no one will know that she has been married, and then shrewdly markets her daughter as a virgin prostitute. The third book deals with Nanna's career as a courtesan and all the tricks she uses

to get money out her clients. Ironically, of all the women in the *Dialogues,* the whores are the least concerned with sex. Aretino's nuns live for sex, his wives for freedom, and his whores for money. "There wasn't a single man who slept with me," Nanna boasts, "who didn't part with a piece of his hide" (p. 127).

The dialogues are profoundly ambiguous in their portrayal of women. Courtesans are ironically celebrated for their cleverness and lack of hypocrisy, but they are simultaneously attacked for their selfishness and trickery. Separate editions of the third book of the *Ragionamenti* were published all over Europe in French, Latin, Spanish, and English translations as a warning against the wiles of wicked women. Editors added moralistic prefaces to ensure that readers would see Nanna and Antonia as subhuman predators.

Taken as a whole, however, the dialogues are hard to read as a simple attack on whores. They recognize that women's social and sexual options are severely limited and that women become whores for practical social reasons. They are also clear that financially successful courtesans like Nanna are not normative: "For one Nanna who knows how to have her land bathed by the fructifying sun, there are thousands of whores who end their days in the poorhouse" (p. 134). And the battle of the sexes in the *Dialogues* is clearly an unfair contest. As Nanna says, "I could tell of tens, dozens, scores of whores who ended up ... in hospitals, kitchens, or on the streets ... thanks to having whored for this man or that; but nobody will ever show me a man who, due to the whores, became a ... coachman, ... lackey, ... or mendicant" (p. 269).

Like Chaucer's Wife of Bath, Nanna is at once a nightmare of the antifeminist imagination and a proto-feminist heroine. Like her great contemporaries Gargantua, Pantagruel, and Falstaff, she is both grotesque and sublime. And like Aretino himself, she is clever, vindictive, and manipulative. Indeed, Aretino's greatest character may well also be his best self-portrait.

In the *Dialogues,* the greatest sin is hypocrisy, followed closely by stupidity. Like Boccaccio before him, Aretino accepts sex and physical pleasures as a predictable part of the natural world. For Aretino, whores are better than nuns or wives because they are not hypocrites. Like soldiers, they are doing an ugly but necessary job. Like merchants, they sell their wares to supply a social demand. The greatness of the *Dialogues* lies in its ruthless honesty, its irony, and its refusal to moralize. Aretino's social vision is extremely acute, and his text is one of the most remarkable and insightful works on the status of women in the sixteenth century.

The *Ragionamenti* was only a small part of Aretino's prolific writing during his time in Venice. He wrote some other satirical dialogues, several comic plays—some still highly regarded—and a series of devotional books with titles like *Three Books of the Humanity of Christ* (1535) and *The Life of the Virgin Mary* (1539). His popular translation of the *Seven Penitential Psalms* (1534) influenced other vernacular translations as far away as England. Over the period 1538–1557, Aretino published six volumes of his letters—thus becoming the first vernacular writer in Europe to publish his correspondence. He was known as a perceptive art critic and served as a business agent for his friend Titian, facilitating sales of Titian's paintings to Italian and European courts. In return, Titian painted his portrait twice.

In Venice, Aretino lived in a palatial house on the Grand Canal near the Rialto, full of courtesans and male secretaries, several of whom seem to have been his lovers. Though he never married, he had two daughters (Adria, 1537, and Austria, 1547), of whom he was very fond. Rumors of the licentiousness of his household were common, and in 1538 accusations of blasphemy and sodomy led him to leave Venice for a time. His provocative personality and polemical writing involved him in a series of literary feuds and scandals with rival writers such as Niccolò Franco and Anton Francesco Doni. He tended to win.

After Julius III, also from Arezzo, acceded to the papal throne in 1549, Aretino journeyed to Rome one last time in hopes of being made a cardinal. He had to settle for the honorary post of Gonfaloniere (standard bearer of the Catholic Church) of Arezzo and induction into the order of St. Peter. Two years after his death, in 1558, all of his books, devotional, political, and erotic, were placed on the Index of Prohibited Books by the Catholic Church. His reputation as a writer and art critic immediately went into eclipse. In the popular imagination, he was reduced to a caricature of sexual perversion, just as Machiavelli became a caricature of political amorality.

Only in the late twentieth century did the extent and nature of Aretino's achievement as a writer, art critic, and cultural figure come to be seriously reevaluated.

Given Aretino's notoriety and the fact that all his works were banned, it is not surprising that over the years many erotic texts were misattributed to him. John Wolfe, an Elizabethan printer, published an Italian edition of the *Ragionamenti* in London in 1584, which also included two other erotic texts not by Aretino: the *Ragionamenti di Zoppino* [*Zoppino's Dialogues*], an anonymous survey of famous Roman courtesans; and the *Commento di Ser Agresto* [*Ser Agresto's Commentary*], a bawdy academic dialogue by Annibale Caro. Perhaps the three texts most often misattributed to Aretino are the erotic and misogynist poems *La puttana errante* [*The Wandering Whore*] and *La trentuna di Zaffetta* [*The Rape of Zaffetta*], both by his pupil Lorenzo Veniero, and the anonymous prose dialogue known as *La puttana errante, or the Dialogue of Julia and Maddalena*, printed in the same volume as the *Ragionamenti* in an edition published in Amsterdam in the 1660s. *The Dialogue of Julia and Maddalena* is modeled closely on Aretino's *Dialogues*, though with none of its irony and subversive wit. It recounts the story of a young girl's initiation into prostitution and ends with an extensive list of sexual positions, with comic names such as "Moorish Style," "The Sleeping Boy," and "Riding the Donkey."

Although such misattributions have made Aretino's role in the history of European erotic writing seem larger than it was, he is nonetheless a crucial figure. Both Aretino's poetry and his *Dialogues* brought an unparalleled simplicity of language and explicitness of description to erotic writing. As noted earlier, the poems and engravings of *I modi* were the first modern European work to take sexual pleasure as their primary subject matter, without any philosophical gloss or mythological trappings. After centuries of scholarly neglect, Aretino's importance as a major cultural figure in sixteenth-century Italy is being strongly reaffirmed. A reevaluation of his achievement which balances his erotic writing with his significance as a social satirist, art critic, and influential man of letters is essential for a better understanding of the history of sexuality in the Renaissance.

Biography

Pietro Aretino was born in Arezzo, Italy, April 19/20, 1492, the son of a shoemaker. The name "Aretino" is not a family name—it simply means "from the town of Arezzo." Aretino's family origins and early career are somewhat unclear. In any case, his father soon deserted the family, and Pietro was raised by Luigi Bacci, a local nobleman who knew his mother. Aretino left Arezzo for Perugia in his early teens (c. 1507), apparently to apprentice as a painter, and he seems to have wandered around Italy for several years before entering the service of Agostino Chigi, the powerful Sienese banker, in Rome in 1517. Chigi's household was one of the most luxurious and sophisticated in Rome and offered Aretino the opportunity of coming in contact with many of the most renowned figures in the city, including the painter Raphael and the Medici Pope Leo X, who soon took Aretino into his own service.

Aretino was at the court of Pope Leo X from 1518 to 1521, then was in the service of Cardinal Giuliano de' Medici, later Pope Clement VII, from 1522 to 1525, before settling in Venice in 1527. There he rented a house on the Grand Canal, near the Rialto, 1529–1551. He received a gold chain from King Francis I of France in 1533, then an annuity from Emperor Charles V after 1536, and was named Gonfaloniere of Arezzo and Cavaliere of San Pietro by Pope Julius III in 1550. Aretino died in Venice on the evening of October 21, 1556, when he succumbed to an attack of apoplexy while talking with friends.

IAN FREDERICK MOULTON

Selected Works

Sonetti lussuriosi, c. 1525, as *I Modi: The Sixteen Pleasures: An Erotic Album of the Italian Renaissance.* Edited and translated by Lynn Lawner, 1988.
Ragionamenti, 1535, 1537, as *Aretino's Dialogues.* Translated by Raymond Rosenthal, 1971, 1994.
Selected Letters. Edited and translated by George Bull, 1976.

Further Reading

Frantz, David O. *Festum voluptatis: A Study of Renaissance Erotica.* Columbus: Ohio State University Press, 1989.
Freedman, Luba. *Titian's Portraits through Aretino's Lens.* University Park, PA: Penn State University Press, 1995.
Hunt, Lynn, ed. *The Invention of Pornography: Obscenity and the Origins of Modernity.* New York: Zone Books, 1993.
Hutton, Edward. *Pietro Aretino: The Scourge of Princes.* London: Constable, 1922.
Kendrick, Walter. *The Secret Museum: Pornography in Modern Culture.* Berkeley and Los Angeles: University of California Press, 1996.
Moulton, Ian Frederick. *Before Pornography: Erotic Writing in Early Modern England.* New York: Oxford University Press, 2000.
Pietro Aretino nel cinquecentenario della nascita (2 vols.). Rome: Salerno, 1995 (contains many essays in English).
Ruggiero, Guido. "Marriage, Love, Sex, and Renaissance Civic Morality," in *Sexuality and Gender in Early Modern Europe* (pp. 10–30), edited by James Grantham Turner. New York: Cambridge University Press, 1993.
Talvacchia, Bette. *Taking Positions: On the Erotic in Renaissance Culture.* Princeton, NJ: Princeton University Press, 1999.

ARGENS, JEAN-BAPTISTE DE BOYER MARQUIS D'

1703–1771
French novelist

The major work attributed to Argens is *Thérèse philosophe,* whose reputation was promoted by no less than the Marquis de Sade. Comparing Argens's work to other erotic novels of the period (*L'académie des dames, Histoire de Dom Bougre, L'éducation de Laure*), de Sade pointed out the superiority of his Provençal compatriot who was finally inspired to write an "immoral book." But despite de Sade's enthusiasm, attribution of the work to the Marquis d'Argens remains unproven. The surest confirmation of this attribution came from Guillaume Pigeard de Gurbert, who relied on a series of clues and echoes of phrases found in Argens's *Mémoires,* as well as *Lettres juives* and *Lettres cabalistiques. Thérèse philosophe* has also been attributed to Diderot, as well as to Arles de Montigny, who was involved in the clandestine production of the book. The date of 1748 for that production suggests that the novel first appeared that same year. But, as with every aspect of the novel, this date remains debatable. Combing the archives of the Bastille police, François Moureau traced the steps in the publication of the book and its underground printing. In December of 1748, the printing of the book and its engravings was completed, and Montigny, who for months had claimed to be in possession of the unpublished manuscript, was looking forward to selling the copies. *Thérèse philosophe* underwent several printings in the eighteenth century, and nearly a dozen illustrated editions were printed before the Revolution. Robert Darnton has shown how this work dominated bestseller lists until the end of the *ancien régime.* From this historian of the book we also learn how the publication of *Thérèse philosophe* coincided with the publication of the great works that ushered in the Age of Enlightenment and with the explosion of erotic literature, in his estimation a result of the simultaneous surge of free thinking and moral license.

A word must be said about the novel's subtitle, *Mémoires pour servir à l'histoire du P. Dirrag et Mademoiselle Eradice* [*Memoirs to Serve as a History of Father Dirrag and Mademoiselle Eradice*]. This subtitle is in part responsible for the attribution to Boyer d'Argens, who records in his *Mémoires* a contemporary event that was the stuff of scandal. The first part of the novel recounts the crux of the affair, in which a pious young woman of twenty years, Marie-Catherine Cadière, becomes involved with a Jesuit priest, Jean-Baptiste Girard, the rector of the naval chaplain's seminary at Toulon. The scenario draws on a notorious trial of the year 1730–1731, in which the young woman accused her confessor of sorcery, spiritual incest, and sexual abuse. Narrowly acquitted by the Aix Parliament on October 12, 1731, the priest escaped being

burned at the stake. What Argens recycles in his novel is the story of seduction by the Reverend Father, with its whiff of witchery. These characters borrowed from real life are thinly disguised by the anagrammatic names in Argens's text: Cadière becomes Eradice, Girard becomes Dirrag, and the site of the original affair, Toulon, becomes Volnot, located in the province of Vencerop (Provence).

Thérèse philosophe follows the typical pattern of a libertine initiation. The novel can be read as the pornographic version of a traditional coming-of-age novel. Thérèse is set upon the path toward realizing her potential up to the final revelation that caps the novel. The sexually precocious girl engages at the age of seven in pleasures usually reserved for a fifteen-year-old. Her mother tries to wean her from her compulsive and deleterious habit of self-stimulation. The story of Thérèse is that of reconciling the heroine to her "temperament"—that is, to the health of her body, the inverse of cachexia. In fact, the novel seems to result from a collage of four different narratives that end up involving the narrator. First there is the story of Eradice; second, the narrative recounting the sexual adventures of Madame C. and Abbé T.; third, the story, told in an unusual style, of Madame Bois-Laurier, a prostitute (the story of this courtesan could stand virtually on its own, with its picaresque, carnivalesque adventures and bawdy tales far removed from the more reserved style of the previous two stories); and fourth, the story of Thérèse's meeting with a count whose mistress she becomes and to whom the narrative is addressed. In the end Thérèse's apotheosis assumes the style of the first parts: Once again the text consecrates the meeting of sex and philosophy. These four seemingly disparate pieces can be seen as connected by their significance in Thérèse's development. They explain *a posteriori* the heroine's progress from her initial naiveté to her eloquent affirmation at the end of the novel.

Thérèse's initiation begins when she stays in a convent, where she meets the couple Eradice and Dirrag. The lovemaking she witnesses while hidden in a small closet is presented to her as a virtual ceremony. The nun receives instruction from the old priest, who cinches Eradice's devotion by persuading her to believe in the existence of a sacred cord, the cord of St. Francis, for which he ends up substituting his own sexual organ. In this programmatic episode, the narrator is confronted with the power of the erotic imagination. Thérèse "dreams" about the fetishized cord, which the text closely associates with Eradice's mystical ecstasy. Thérèse embraces the sacrilegious scenario as her own, for her own pleasure. The cord itself becomes, by association, an arousing object, which Thérèse keeps in mind even as she substitutes her bed poster in order to achieve pleasure. This cord, the first erotic object to be offered to Thérèse, will take on a primitive, associative function. The story of Eradice and Dirrag sets in motion the heroine's phantasmagorical delirium, the mystical ecstasy that had initially brought her to erotic satisfaction. At the beginning, the novel superimposes forbidden erotic images: snake, apple, terrifying firmament (hell), which become objects of arousal—hand and finger. The young heroine experiences only this frustrated and forbidden pleasure, marked with the sign of terror.

Dirrag's discourse, under the guise of spiritualism (he constantly plies Eradice with the commandments *forget yourself, let yourself go*) is however imbued with a free-floating materialism. Darnton sees Dirrag's lessons as indistinguishable from those of La Mettrie, and the seductive technology employed by the father is like a materialist application of the spiritual exercises (the chemical solution used to create stigmata, a dildo offered as a sacred relic, coitus experienced as religious ecstasy).

The second phase of Thérèse's initiation is entrusted to another couple, Madame C. and Abbé T., through a meeting arranged by her mother. This episode, a bucolic summer idyll, continues the voyeuristic structure of the novel. The optical machine previously used as a vantage point to observe Father Dirrag and Eradice is replaced by a series of observation posts: a "copse" from which Thérèse inspects her new friends (she hides there not only to watch them but "to hear them"), or the gap between the wall and a couch upon which the couple engages in sex, whence she watches and listens. This time Argens mixes the erotic tableaus with philosophical lessons. This is one of the elements that most resembles the structure of de Sade's work: the alternation between scenes of lechery and disquisitions. The Abbé takes on the role of Thérèse's new "confessor." In this part of the book, Argens exposes the principal materialist

theses of the novel. Thérèse gains from the "enlightenment" of her friends. The narrator notes with enthusiasm that "Madame C. was satisfied with my way of thinking and reasoning, and she was happy to guide me step by step to clear and undeniable proofs." Thérèse emerges from her state of illusion and sees "the shadows of her mind" dissipate. Through her contact with these two mentors, the heroine discovers the exercise of reason. She finds herself at ease in philosophical discourse, in the discussion of "moral and religious matters, metaphysical subjects." The Abbé mentions a series of precepts which reveal a conservative epicurean bent: an apology for virginity, the restriction of intercourse to marriage, and respect for social conventions and the public good. Nature is presented as sovereign, reigning over our passions. Abbé T. insists on debunking religious institutions as created by men out of the fears and hopes of mankind. God himself is subject to mechanical laws— "the principles of movement that He has established in everything that exists." The clichés of materialist discourse are all enumerated here, shades of La Mettrie's *L'Homme machine* [*Man a Machine*] and, as regards the criticism of religion, an anonymous text published in 1743 under the title *Examen de la religion dont on cherche l'éclaircissement de bonne foi* [*Examination of Religion to Seek Honest Clarity*].

As for the childhood masturbation that was harmful to Thérèse (through her obsessively self-gratifying hand), here it is converted into a natural instrument of pleasure. This is the project undertaken by her two instructors. Thérèse discovers the virtues of the hand, learning, by example, from the skillful finger of the Abbé. In Argens's text, touch is the sense that mediates the other senses (especially sight). The hand is certainly the most active organ in the novel. A machine par excellence, the nerve center for all organic functions, it circulates and distributes the entire range of erotic functions. The first contraceptive lessons begin at this stage of the narrative: Thérèse is well informed of the dangers of penetration and of unwanted pregnancy. This episode of enlightenment affirms the narrator's will to learn. The heroine is not merely a passive observer; she soon puts the Abbé's principles in writing.

The third stage in Thérèse's initiation coincides with her meeting with Bois-Laurier. The text presents this narrative of her life in a quasi-autonomous form. Bois-Laurier's account belongs to a genre typical of courtesans' memoirs. Her first name, moreover, is Manon, in an ironic and depraved nod to Prévost's famous heroine. Bois-Laurier, a retired prostitute whom Thérèse encounters in Paris shortly after the death of her mother, quickly becomes a surrogate mother. No longer a remonstrating mother, ruled by a fear of the senses, Bois-Laurier is on the contrary an enthusiastic instigator of Thérèse's initiation to pleasure. In the heroine's eyes, she naturalizes whoredom. Argens's Manon also shares with de Sade's major *débauchées* a common physiological trait: Like Durand and Martaine, Manon is barred from intercourse, "fastidiously" sealed by a "nervous membrane." But Argens inverts this flaw, or "irregularity," through the invention of sexual acts of unbridled imagination. Bois-Laurier's obstacle forces her partners to find pleasure through a series of inanimate devices. Mirrors, music, bizarre choreography, transvestism are all part of the menu of proffered "tricks." Thérèse will discover "male whims," the infinite variety of sexual acts, new positions to add to Aretino's catalogue. Indeed, what distinguishes the courtesan is this imaginative response to the impulses of nature. The actors in the scenarios recounted by Bois-Laurier find fabulous substitutes (dildo, whips). Sexual pleasure is also the occasion for laughter, another indulgence Thérèse discovers with Bois-Laurier as the two engage in "all sorts of follies." In fact, freed from any sense of guilt, sex becomes an occasion for shared laughter. At the same time, Argens inverts the relation with Thérèse's mentor. The philosophical upper hand reverts to Thérèse in this episode. Bois-Laurier, the narrator confides, "was not surprised at my moral, metaphysical, and religious awareness." It is noteworthy that if female homosexuality is celebrated in laughter and folly, the story of Bois-Laurier finds sodomy a stumbling block. In a text that is otherwise preoccupied with the relativity of sexual morality, she condemns as categorically abhorrent the "taste" of those she calls "monsters," whom she deems "the enemies of our sex."

Having reached maturity through her reasoned mastery of pleasure, the heroine meets a count at Bois-Laurier's, who will put the finishing touches on her libertine education. This character, presented as a paragon of the Enlightenment man, joins Thérèse in furthering her materialist instruction, to which he naturally brings a depth of libertine experience. Becoming the narrator's benefactor, he uses his erotic library and bawdy pornographic collection as tools of seduction. If Thérèse's actions still emulate the tableaus placed before her, this time the moves are "sophisticated": They are guided by the mind. She also becomes a reader and consumer of erotic novels, some of whose titles are mentioned in the text: *Le portier des Chartreux, La tourière des Carmélites, L'académie des dames, Thémidore, Fertillon.* Finally she can progress to the act, to the experience of pleasure.

In the end Argens also leads the heroine's hand to another exercise. The masturbating finger no longer follows a mechanical instinct; it becomes a tool in service of a discipline of pleasure. It involves Thérèse in a prophylactic regime: "I had seized the shaft I held it lightly in my hand... in which it bridged the space that brought it closer to pleasure." The Count himself is an expert at "external ejaculation" as preached by Abbé T., recommended for the effective and risk-free repetition of pleasure. The balance of happiness is possible only when these conditions are realized: "no fuss, no children, no worry."

Argens thus ends his heroine's enlightened phase. He brings her to the apex of her "determination," in the sought-after apotheosis of the senses. If Thérèse started out as a machine, propelled by her "temperament," at the end of the narrative she is a thinking, desiring machine. She has found the path to her desire and the means to act upon it. At last, reason informs the intelligence of the passions. Thérèse has become a *philosopher.*

Thérèse's emancipation brings Robert Darnton to consider the question of the text's feminism. Anachronism notwithstanding, he proposes a nuanced examination of this perspective. Indeed, at the end Thérèse has fully assumed the narrative voice, exceeding the simple role of listener that she has held all along. The final contract between Thérèse and the Count reflects the terms put forth by him (he offers to share his retirement property not far from Paris and guarantees her 2,000 livres). But Thérèse imposes her independence to the very end, demanding the right to pursue her own pleasure, to govern her own body.

Catherine Cusset finds even more irony in the ending. For her, the text ultimately upsets the self-aggrandizement of the male sex. She recalls the miserable sex of Bois-Laurier's anecdotes, with its dephallicized agents. Argens's novel thus quashes the male fantasy of omnipotence and counters it with the two women's laughter, just as in the end Thérèse's hand overmasters the Count's conquering sex.

In this sense, *Thérèse philosophe* writes an original story that slips the bonds imposed on the heroine by the typical pornographic novel. Thérèse's emancipation is that of a narrator who no longer "resists" writing, who no longer fears reflection, who joyfully embraces the first-person verb: "Ecrivons!" [I'll write!] The caption on the frontispiece of the novel ("Pleasure and philosophy bring happiness to the sensible man; he embraces pleasure with taste, he loves philosophy with reason") brings sex and philosophy together for man by joining taste with the love of reason. This is the same ground that Thérèse covers as she reaches the height of pleasure and writes in the happy assurance of reason. She then discovers her true mission, that of transmitting and divulging "truths." She wants to change, "by example and by reason," the way others think.

Biography

Jean-Baptiste de Boyer d'Argens was born in Aix on June 27, 1703, to a venerable Provençal family. His father, Pierre-Jean de Boyer, Lord of Éguilles, served as an attorney at the Parliament in Aix. After a colorful and adventurous youth (including trips to Algiers, Tunis, and Constantinople), the Marquis d'Argens joined the army, but his military career was cut short by a horseback riding accident. In 1735 he left for the Netherlands. That same year he published his *Memoirs* and embarked on a new career as a novelist. Argens also tried his hand at a more serious genre: His interest in the mores and customs of both ancient and modern peoples bore fruit in the publication of *Lettres juives* (1736), *Lettres cabalistiques* (1737), and *Lettres chinoises* (1739). At Voltaire's suggestion, Argens accepted an invitation from Frederick II of Prussia, arriving in Berlin in 1742 as the king's

chamberlain. Argens's Berlin years saw a number of publications, including *Réflexions historiques et critiques sur le goût* (1743) and *Réflexions sur les différentes écoles de peinture* (1752). Overcome by the ills of old age and the tyranny of Frederick II, he left Potsdam in 1769, returning to his family and his native Provence, where he built a country house named My Repose. Argens died at his sister's home on January 12, 1771.

PIERRE SAINT-AMAND
Translated from the French by
Jennifer Curtiss Gage

Selected Works

Thérèse philosophe, ou Mémoires pour servir à l'histoire du P. Dirrag et de Mademoiselle Eradice. The Hague, 1748; Paris?, 1780?; London, 1796.
Thérèse philosophe. Geneva-Paris: Slatkine, 1981 (presentation by Jacques Duprilot); in *L'Enfer de la Bibliothèque Nationale*, vol. V, Paris: Fayard, 1986 (presentation by Philippe Roger); Paris: Actes Sud, 1992 (presentation by Guillaume Pigeard de Gurbert); in *Romans libertins du XVIIIe siècle*, Paris: Laffont, 1993 (presentation by Raymond Trousson); in *Romanciers libertins du XVIIIe siècle*, Paris: Gallimard, "Pléiade," 2000 (presentation by Pierre Saint-Amand); Saint-Étienne: Publications de l'Université de Saint-Étienne, 2000 (presentation by François Moureau).
Mémoires de Monsieur le marquis d'Argens avec quelques lettres sur divers sujets. London, 1735.
Lettres juives. The Hague, 1736–1738.
Lettres cabalistiques. The Hague, 1737–1738.
La Philosophie du bon sens. London, 1737.
Lettres chinoises. The Hague, 1739–1740.
Réflexions historiques et critiques sur le goût. Amsterdam, 1743.
Réflexions critiques sur les différentes écoles de peinture. Paris, 1752.

References and Further Reading

Lynn Hunt, ed. *The Invention of Obscenity.* New York: Zone Books, 1993.
Cryle, Peter. *Geometry in the Boudoir.* Ithaca, NY: Cornell University Press, 1994.
Cusset, Catherine. *No Tomorrow.* Charlottesville and London: University of Virginia Press, 1999.
Darnton, Robert. *The Forbidden Best-Sellers of Pre-Revolutionary France.* New York: Norton, 1995.

ART OF THE BEDCHAMBER LITERATURE

The Chinese "Art of the Bedchamber" literature, a corpus of about a dozen received texts spanning two thousand years, represents a unique system of sex for health, harmony, pleasure, and eugenics. It shares borders on the right with medical sexology, which is chiefly concerned with sexual dysfunction and therapeutics, and sexual alchemy on the left, which is exclusively concerned with cultivating the physiological elixir of immortality.

Recovery and Reconstruction of the Texts

The theoretical foundations of the bedroom arts literature are prefigured in the earliest medical classics, *The Yellow Emperor's Inner Classic, Plain Questions* [*Huangdi neijing suwen*] and *Spiritual Pivot* [*Lingshu*]; in historical works, such as the *Zuo Commentary* [*Zuozhuan*] and *Spring and Autumn Annals of Lü* [*Lüshi chunqiu*]; and in philosophical works, such as the *Zhuangzi* and *Liezi,* all of which counsel moderation in the bedroom. Specialized medical works devoted exclusively to this theme include Zhu Danxi's *Treatise on Sexual Desire* [*Seyu pian*] and Zhao Xian's *Restraining Desires* [*Guayu*]. The bedroom arts literature, after occupying a rubric of its own in the official dynastic history of the Han (206–220 CE) and sharing a section with "Medical Works" in the Sui (581–618) and Tang (618–907), finally landed under "Daoist Works" in the *History of the Song* (960–1279). None of the titles listed in the *History of the Former Han* have survived, but unknown to the Chinese themselves, fragments were preserved in a Japanese collection of Chinese medical literature, the *Ishimpo* (982–984). Chinese scholar Ye Dehui [1864–1927] made this discovery in Japan and concluded that titles and fragments in chapter 28 of the *Ishimpo*, "Fangnei" [*Art of the Bedchamber*], closely corresponded to those listed in the *History of the Sui*. Piecing the fragments together, he was able to reconstruct four of these texts and published them in his 1903 *Shadow of the Double Plum Trees Collection* [*Shuangmei jingan congshu*]. Following this, Robert van Gulik's 1952 *Erotic Color Prints of the Ming* brought additional medical sexology and sexual alchemy texts to scholarly attention, the Mawangdui manuscripts gave us two complete sex handbooks of early second century BCE vintage, and Wile introduced a number of new texts from the Ming sexual alchemy tradition.

The Cultural and Empirical Foundations of the Bedroom Arts

It would be difficult to say whether the biology of human reproduction has done more to shape human culture or human culture has done more to shape human sexuality. Nevertheless, the classic Chinese sex manuals, written by and for men, are the elaboration of certain shared cultural assumptions, which might be conveniently summarized as the response to a series of perceived dilemmas:

1. Sexual arousal suffuses the body with a "divine wind," "living *qi*," or "spiritual enlightenment," but ejaculation brings "weariness, heavy joints, drowsiness in the eyes, parched throat, and buzzing in the ears." The ephemeral high is followed by a languorous low. Ejaculation equals enervation, not relaxation: A paradigm of tension/release is rejected for one of fullness/emptiness.

2. The more we spend the essence that creates new life, the more we shorten our own lives. Sexual potency declines with age; in fact, aging itself is the direct result of sexual expenditure. Before puberty, we are blessed with abundant *yang* (positive) energy, without lust or leakage.

3. Men are like fire, easily aroused and easily extinguished, whereas women are like

water, slow to heat up but more sustainable. This is a fundamental asymmetry between the sexes.

4. Ejaculation causes depletion, but abstinence causes physiological and psychological aberrations: atrophy of sexual fitness and obsessive thinking. The side effects of abstinence—masturbation, spermatorrhea, and nocturnal emissions—are worse than the disease of incontinence. In fact, long abstinence, punctuated by occasional ejaculation, results in "violent vacuity" that can actually be fatal.

5. Lovemaking creates harmonization and bonding between partners, but ejaculation leads to loss of interest and somnolence. Shared sexual satisfaction is the foundation of family solidarity, but satiety sets up a slide into disgust and shame.

6. Homeostasis between the heart (the seat of intellection) and kidney (the seat of sexual essence), or physiological fire-and-water principles, can be maintained only when the mind is calm and the semen is stable. A deficiency of water (semen) through frequent ejaculation allows the fire of desire to rage unchecked and leads to sex addiction, premature ejaculation, spermatorrhea, and nocturnal emission. Stability of sexual essence requires frequent, full arousal without ejaculation, not a disengaged or passive state.

7. Wives, concubines, courtesans, slave girls, and maids, collected as trophies of wealth, may end up being psychological, financial, and sexual burdens. The pleasures of polygamy may soon evaporate in the heat of jealousies and the responsibility to keep everyone satisfied.

The collective cultural solution to all of the above dilemmas is *coitus reservatus:* The measure of sexual prowess is not the ability to ejaculate repeatedly but to withhold climax and satisfy multiple partners. Repression of climax does not lead to frustration but to the prolongation of pleasure: trading in the precarious peak for the safe plateau. This is the esthetic of anticlimax that in Chinese painting, poetry, and music is called "blandness" (*pingdan*). Moreover, going beyond saving to profit, the man who induces his partner to release her sexual essence through orgasm, while restraining his own, may absorb her energy, thereby doubling his gain. Secondary potencies of sexual energy can also be absorbed from breath, saliva, and breasts. All of the texts counsel multiplying the number of partners to maximize the profit and warn that women can easily turn the tables in this contest. Therefore, men must strive heroically to discipline themselves not to ejaculate and to conceal this art from their partners. A man's primary loyalty must be to his parents, and every time he ejaculates, he gives away part of his inheritance and becomes a slave to his wife. If menstruation brings disorder and pollution to the community, ejaculation decapitates the patriarchy. Men must also regulate their sex lives in relation to the macrocosm, hence the dictum, "Thrice a month in spring, twice in summer, once in autumn, and none in winter" expresses the idea that *yang* energy is most easily replenished in the spring and summer and should be hoarded in the fall and winter.

From our earliest records, the Chinese bedroom arts have been inseparable from medicine. The regulation of sex life was as fundamental to health as eating and sleeping, and sexual energy (*jing*) was one of the three pillars of physiology, the other two being vital energy (*qi*) and spirit (*shen*). *Jing* is both semen and the energy residing therein; in its prenatal aspect it is pure life-giving potential, and in its postnatal aspect it is material, requiring supplementation and subject to corruption and instability. The second-century BCE *Ten Questions* [*Shiwen*] says, "Nothing is more important for the *qi* of man than the *jing* of the penis." The great Tang physician Sun Simiao puts the conventional wisdom in the mouth of the immortal Peng Zu in his *Supplement to Prescriptions Worth a Thousand Measures of Gold* [*Qianjin yifang*]: "The superior man sleeps in a separate bed, and the average sleeps under a separate quilt. A hundred doses of medicine are not as good as sleeping alone. Satiety at night costs one day of life, intoxication one month, but sex a year." *Jing* is stored in the kidneys, which in traditional medicine takes in the urogenital system but is also linked to the bones, marrow, brain, teeth, and hair. The kidneys are also the locus of the "gate of life" (*mingmen*), which is the seat of the "ministerial fire," "lesser heart," or the fire principle in the midst of water, *yang* in *yin*. The heart (seat of the spirit) and kidney (the seat of water) form an axis of influence such that agitation of the heart (emotions, desires) causes the kidney to lose seminal essence, while deficient seminal essence, in turn, causes clouding of the spirit. The aspect of consciousness centered in the kidneys is "will," which explains postcoital enervation. A final function of the kidney is to absorb the *qi* of the lungs during respiration, a function enhanced by deep abdominal breathing during intromission.

The Structure and Content of the Handbooks of Sex

In reconstructing the ancient manuals from fragments found in the *Ishimpo,* Ye Dehui's methodology was to derive a template based on a typical sequence of topics. A literary device used by nearly all the handbooks of sex is to structure them as a series of dialogues between a mythical emperor, usually the Yellow Emperor, and goddess initiatresses, immortals, or other legendary figures. Two exceptions are the *Dong Xüan zi,* which consists of the highly poetic and flowery pronouncements of a pseudonymous author, and the *True Classic of Perfect Union* [Jiji zhenjing], which is framed as an extended metaphor on the "art of war" in the bedroom.

Most of the bedroom-arts texts begin with a passage on the cosmological or ethical significance of the sex act. The *Secrets of the Jade Chamber* [Yufang bijue] opens with, "One yin and one yang are called the dao; intercourse and procreation are its function"; the *Dong Xüan zi* with, "One must imitate heaven and pattern oneself on earth, take yin as compass and yang as square"; and the *Exposition of Cultivating the True Essence* [Xiuzhen yanyi] with, "Without sexual intercourse, there would be no means of achieving harmony of the heart and oneness of spirit, which would be a perversion of human relationships." Alternatively, some begin with a personal predicament put in the mouth of the Yellow Emperor, such as in *The Classic of Su Nü* [Su Nü jing], "My *qi* is weak and out of harmony. There is no joy in my heart, and I live in constant fear"; or a generalized health syndrome, such as in the *Benefits of the Bedchamber* [Fangzhong buyi], "It has been said that before the age of forty men give free rein to their passions, but after forty suddenly become aware that their strength is declining."

The bedroom-arts narratives now proceed to a section proclaiming the paramount value of

sexual essence, such as in *The Dangers and Benefits of Intercourse with Women* [Yunu sunyi], "The dao [of longevity] takes jing as its treasure," or in the *Benefits of the Bedchamber,* "After forty, a man must constantly strengthen his jing, nourish and not waste it." Generally, this is bolstered by a warning of the consequences of incontinence, as in the *Prescriptions of Su Nü* [Su Nü fang], "Because of the danger of shortening one's life, a man must practice self-control and not think only of lust for women," and *Dangers and Benefits*, "A single act of intercourse causes one to lose a year of life, which cannot be regained by any amount of self-cultivation."

The next question usually posed by the mythical interlocutor is how to go about securing one's sexual essence. The answers include having partners who are not too beautiful, who are ignorant of the *dao,* and who are frequently changed, as well as the following general advice from the *Classic of Su Nü:* "Settle the *qi,* calm the mind, and harmonize the emotions. When the 'three *qi*' are awakened and the spirit is focused, then when you are neither cold nor hot, neither hungry nor full, completely settle the whole body. Now relax, penetrate shallowly, and move slowly with infrequent thrusts and withdrawals. In this way the woman will be satisfied and the man will retain his vigor."

The texts next take up the question of emotional harmonization between the partners and the need for artful foreplay. The *Dong Xüan zi* says, "He clasps her slender waist and caresses her jade body. Expressing their joy and speaking of deep attachment, of one heart and one mind, they now embrace and then clasp, their two bodies beating against each other and their lips pressed together."

Progressing to the more technical side of foreplay, the texts now begin to address the question of how the man should prepare himself for intromission, how to fully stimulate the woman, and how to monitor the signs of her arousal. The stages of arousal in the man are analyzed in one of our earliest received texts, the *Discourse on the Highest Dao Under Heaven* [Tianxia zhidao tan], and echoed in similar formulations in the later literature, "If the penis is enraged but not large, the flesh has not yet been aroused. If it is large but not stiff, the sinews have not yet been aroused. If it is stiff but not hot, the *qi* has not yet been aroused." The signs of arousal in the woman are analyzed in even greater detail. Beginning with the *Uniting Yin and Yang* [*He yinyang*] in the second century BCE, the observable phenomena of arousal are usually formulated as the "five signs": facial flushing, erection of nipples, salivating, vaginal secretion, and parched throat. Beyond these are the "five desires," including breath retention, flaring nostrils and parted lips, quivering, perspiration, and stiffening of the body, which tell the man that his partner seeks greater intensity. The "ten movements" allow the man to read the woman's body language and respond appropriately; for example, "Fifth, when she raises her legs to encircle him, it means that she desires deeper penetration." Some formulations of the signs of arousal are more medically based; for example, the "nine *qi*" trace the arousal process through a sequence of organ systems, as in *The Classic of Su Nü*, "When her 'yin gate' becomes slippery and wet, it means that her 'kidney *qi*' has arrived. When in the throes of passion she bites the man, it means that her 'bone *qi*' has arrived." There are also audible cues that are catalogued in *Uniting Yin and Yang*, including suspension of breath, inhalation, exhalation, panting, and teeth gnashing.

The signs of arousal are typically followed by a menu of postures, angles, depths, and tempos for intercourse. These are often presented as zoomorphic choreography, such as the "nine methods" or "thirty-six postures'": flying dragon, tiger stance, monkey's attack, and so forth. The *Dong Xüan zi* also describes a number of modes of "attack," such as, "a fierce general breaking through the enemy's ranks," "rising and suddenly plunging like a wild horse that has jumped into a mountain stream," or "rising slowly and pushing deliberately like a freezing snake entering its hole."

Next comes a catalogue of the advantages and disadvantages of various kinds of congress, usually summarized as the "eight benefits" and "seven ills." The "benefits" are often couched as therapeutic prescriptions, as for example in *Uniting Yin and Yang*: "One arousal without orgasm makes the ears and eyes sharp and bright. Two and the voice is clear," and the *Classic of Su Nü:* "The fourth benefit is called 'strengthening the bones.' Have the woman lie on her side, bend her left knee and stretch out her right thigh. The man lies on top and stabs her. Carry out five times nine strokes and, when

the count is finished, stop. This regulates the joints of the man's body and cures blocked menses in women. Practice five times daily for ten days, and one will be cured." The "seven ills" document and address various conditions arising from untimely relations. For example, "The third ill is called 'weak pulse.' Those who suffer 'weak pulse' force themselves to ejaculate even though the penis is not hard. If one engages in intercourse when the *qi* is exhausted, or one is full from eating, this injures the spleen and causes digestive problems, impotence, and insufficiency of *jing*. To remedy this, have the woman lie on her back and wrap her legs around the man's thighs... Have the woman perform the movements herself, and when her *jing* comes forth, stop. The man should refrain from orgasm." Some versions are based on concrete physiological changes, such as the *Classic of Su Nü*'s "five signs of a man's decline," which gauge the man's condition from the consistency of the semen or the force of ejaculation. For example, the third sign is that "[t]he semen turns foul smelling, which indicates damage to the sinews."

This, in turn, is followed by an argument for the advantages of *coitus reservatus*. The *Wondrous Discourse of Su Nü* [*Su Nü miaolun*] states, "By regulating the breath and 'borrowing water to control fire,' one can strengthen the 'true treasure' and go the whole night without ejaculating. After long practice one can achieve longevity and be free of illness." The consequences of violating this advice are luridly described in *Benefits and Harm*, "Licentiousness shortening a man's lifespan is not the work of ghosts or gods, but the result of base and vulgar impulses. When they feel the *jing* aroused and the urge to ejaculate, they try to please their partners. They expend all their strength insatiably. This does not promote their mutual health, but rather engenders harm. Some are shocked into insanity or experience 'emaciation-thirst' disease."

Ejaculation-control techniques range from mental abstraction and visualization, to practicing self-control with "ugly stoves," to modulating stimulation by the "nine shallow–one deep" thrusting pattern, to acupressure at the perineum, to breath synchronization with thrusts and withdrawals, to microcosmic orbit *qi* circulation. Beyond this, all of the bedroom-arts texts prescribe tables of optimum ejaculation frequency. There is a progression from the

Ma Wang dui texts in the second century BCE, which state, "When the *jing* is replete, one must ejaculate"; to the Sui dynasty's *Classic of Su Nü,* which allows twice per day at sixteen and twenty and once per day at thirty; to the *Wondrous Discourse* of the Ming, which allows once in thirty days at twenty. Thus there is a steady shift to lower frequency and from regarding a man's highest sexual power to be in adolescence and early manhood to regarding his peak to be in early middle age.

Eugenics and taboos go hand-in-hand in the sex manuals. The *Classic of Su Nü* documents the "nine misfortunes," which are based primarily on astrological and environmental factors, such as, "The third is children born during eclipses of the sun, who will suffer deformity or injury. The fourth is children conceived during thunder and lightning, when heaven is angry and threatening. These will easily succumb to insanity." *The Prescriptions of Su Nü* correlates the taboos with the ills, so for example, "The first set of taboos relate to the last or first days of the moon, the first or last quarter of the moon, the full moon, and the six *ding* days of the sexegenary cycle. Intercourse on these days will damage the *jing* of one's progeny, make a man impotent in the face of the enemy [women], [and] cause frequent spontaneous erections, red or yellow coloration of the urine, spermatorrhea, and early death." There are also positive steps one can take to enhance conception and secure fit heirs. The *Wondrous Discourse of Su Nü* lists three causes of infertility in men and three in women, including cold and deficient *jing* in men and sealed cervix in women.

One of the minor topics taken up in these texts is sexual physiognomy, or the art of ascertaining a woman's sexual fitness from her outward appearance. The *Secrets of the Jade Chamber* says, "One must choose young girls who have not yet borne children and who are amply covered with flesh. They should have silken hair and small eyes, with the whites and pupils clearly defined.... Their private parts and underarms should be free of hair, but if hair is present, it should be fine and glossy." The list of traits to be avoided is even longer, and includes "tangled hair, a fearful countenance, malletlike neck, prominent larynx, irregular teeth, husky voice, large mouth, high nose bridge, lack of clarity in the eyes, facial hair, large joints, yellowish hair, scant flesh, and pubic hair that is copious, coarse, and growing contrariwise. To consort with these types of women can only rob a man and do him harm."

How can women use the art of the bedchamber to their advantage? The *Secrets of the Jade Chamber* says, "It is not only *yang* that can be cultivated but *yin,* too. The Queen Mother of the West cultivated her *yin* and attained the *dao.* As soon as she had intercourse with a man, he would immediately take sick, while her complexion would become radiant.... If a woman knows the way of cultivating her *yin* and causing the two *qi* to unite harmoniously, then it may be transformed into a male child. If she is not having intercourse for the sake of offspring, she can divert the fluids to flow back into the hundred vessels."

One of the medical problems traceable to unbalanced sex life is "ghost sex." This condition afflicts involuntary celibates who are seduced by incubi and succubi that surpass mortal partners in their charms. Addictive and frequently fatal, ghost sex can be cured by sexual therapy involving prolonged, gentle intercourse without orgasm.

Appended formularies conclude most of the bedroom arts texts with prescriptions for various kinds of sexual dysfunction or general health problems traceable to sexual excess or abstinence. The *Prescriptions of Su Nü* offers five formulas, one for each of the four seasons and one for the whole year. More specific formulas treat impotence; premature ejaculation; spermatorrhea; diminutive penis; hypotonia, or trauma of the vagina; and lumbar pain.

Conclusion

Sex is not sinful, but a microcosm of the mating of Heaven and earth. The *History of the Former Han* calls sex "the highest expression of natural feeling, the realm of the highest dao," placing sex at the very center of human experience and spirituality. Surveying the bedroom-arts literature, there are no richer documents for the study of traditional Chinese culture. All the intellectual assets of the civilization are deployed here: medicine, meditation, mythology, philosophy, military science, alchemy, and poetry. The epicurean ideal that pleasure is the goal of life, and moderation maximizes pleasure, led the Chinese to make a yoga of sex. Written in a celebratory but cautionary tone, and containing equal parts of science, art, and argument, this literature vibrates with the tension between joy and phobia. Predating the *Kama Sutra* by centuries and exerting an unmistakable influence on Tantric practices, the Chinese bedroom-arts literature holds a unique place in the history of world sexology. Though perhaps too transpersonal for some modern Western tastes, there is much in the realm of both technique and transcendence that can expand the sexual imagination.

DOUGLAS WILE

Selected Works

Goldin, Paul. *The Culture of Sex in Ancient China.* Honolulu: University of Hawaii Press, 2002.

Gulik, R.H. van *Sexual Life in Ancient China.* Leiden: E.J. Brill, 1961.
Harper, Donald. "The Sexual Arts of Ancient China As Described in a Manuscript of the Second Century B. C." *Harvard Journal of Asiatic Studies* 47 (1987): 539–593.
Li Ling and Keith McMahon. "The Contents and Terminology of the Mawangdui Texts on the Arts of the Bedchamber." *Early China* 17 (1992): 145–185.
Needham, Joseph. *Science and Civilization in China* (Vol. 2, pp. 146–152) (Vol. 5, pp. 184–218). Cambridge: Cambridge University Press, 1962, 1986.
Schipper, Kristofer. *The Taoist Body.* Translated by Karen Duval. Berkeley and Los Angeles: University of California Press, 1993.
Wile, Douglas. *Art of the Bedchamber: The Chinese Sexual Yoga Classics, Including Women's Solo Meditation Texts.* Albany, NY: State University of New York Press, 1992.

ARTAUD, ANTONIN

1896–1948
French dramatist

In 1920, suffering from nervous disorders that had plagued him since childhood, Antonin Artaud went to Paris, where he was placed in the care of psychiatrist Dr. Toulouse. He received great support and encouragement in Paris. He was even made coeditor of Dr. Toulouse's own periodical *Demain,* which enabled him to develop his critical writing. With an aim of becoming a film actor, he took small roles in various Parisian theatrical productions. Through theater, he met Romanian actress Génica Athanasiou, with whom he had his first serious, sexual relationship. The relationship ended in 1927, due to his increasing drug addiction and unsuccessful attempts at detoxification. Athanasiou eventually left him for filmmaker Jean Grémillon. Artaud was devastated.

In 1924, Artaud joined the surrealist movement. He became the director of the *centrale surréaliste* and was involved in the group's periodical *La Révolution surréaliste.* After contributing to the second issue, he was made editor of the third issue, writing the majority of it himself. As a surrealist, he was "associated with a group that despised rationalism" (Hayman, 9). He viewed surrealism as a means to liberate the human spirit and everything that resembled it. Moreover, surrealism, he believed, was a revolt against language and traditional literature: "He felt nothing but contempt for the literary artistry which disguises human misery by hanging ornaments on it" (Hayman, 11).

Much of Artaud's work is characterized by its anti-Catholic nature (in 1930 he even wrote his own version of Lewis's *The Monk*). Earlier examples of his anti-Catholic writings can be found in the third edition of the *Révolution surréaliste.* This edition addressed the end of the Christian era. Along with other works, Artaud included his new version of the *Addresse au Pape:*

1. I repudiate my baptism.
2. I shit on the name Christian.
3. I masturbate on the holy cross....
4. It was I (and not Jesus Christ) who was crucified at Golgotha for rising up against god and his christ, because I am a man and god and his christ are only ideas which, besides, have been marked by

humanity's dirty hands.
(Hayman, 11–12, citing Artaud).

In July 1931 Artaud saw a production by a group of Balinese actors. This sparked a major event in his career, as he began to formulate ideas for his *Le théâtre de la cruauté* [*The Theater of Cruelty*], arguably his greatest achievement. With the emphasis on the director rather than the playwright, his aim was to explore the relationship between life, theater, and cruelty. His concept was that theater should embrace a nonverbal language, one of gesticulation and physical movements. He wanted to enact the release of emotion through theater with actors crying out and screaming during performances. The overall effect was surrealist, with the focus on the body.

Artaud was "drawn to the non-human—as a means of sterilizing fantasies that were erotic in origin" (Hayman, 95). He explored the darker side of human nature, often breaking social boundaries and moral codes. In *Les cenci* (1935), his first major production for *Le théâtre de la cruauté,* his own character says, "There is no life, no death, no God, no incest, no contrition, no crime in my existence. I obey my own law, of which I am my own master—and all the worse for those who are caught and sunk without trace in my inferno. My rule, my intent, is to seek out and to practise evil. I cannot resist the forces burning with violence inside me" (Artaud, *Collected,* 4:123). Perversion and brutality are also characteristic, as is the violation of the body and soul. For example, having been raped by her father in *Les cenci*, Beatrice says, "Everything is tainted. Everything. My body is sullied, but my soul is defiled. There is no part for me where I can hide" (Artaud, *Collected*, 4:139).

Artaud greatly admired the writings of the Marquis de Sade. In his first manifesto of *Le Théâtre de la cruauté,* he expressed a desire to stage a de Sade story, hoping to project all its eroticism on stage. In a review of *Les cenci*, it was also observed that "[t]he combination of furious blasphemies with atheism were reminiscent of the Marquis de Sade" (Hayman, 98). The Sadean aspect of Artaud's work is characterized by its sadistic nature. For instance, his production *La pierre philosophale* [*The Philosopher's Stone*], which bears the date 1930–31, portrays limbs being supposedly dismembered

and dummies being butchered by a psychotic doctor. Direct references to parts of the body, particularly the female reproductive organs, are also reminiscent of de Sade, and are one of the main reasons why Artaud's work has often been labeled as erotic.

In 1937, Artaud suffered a nervous breakdown and was subsequently institutionalized. He remained in various mental institutions until 1946. During this nine-year period, he was at times confined to a cell, suffering from malnutrition and subjected to over 50 electric shock treatments. After his discharge, he deplored the cruelty and violence that he had experienced in the name of psychiatry, even claiming to have been physically assaulted by a male nurse. He composed *Aliénation et magiave noire* [*Madness and Black Magic*] as a testimony to his experiences.

Biography

Antonin Artaud was born in Marseilles in 1896. In early childhood, he survived a severe attack of meningitis but was left with serious nervous disorders. He was admitted several times to a sanatorium for depression throughout his adolescence. During these stays, he became familiar with the works of Baudelaire and Poe, whose influence can be seen in his early writings. In May 1919, Artaud was prescribed opium, which led to a lifelong addiction. By January 1948, Artaud's health was rapidly declining, and after seeing a specialist he was diagnosed with an inoperable cancer. Two months later, he was found dead. His death was suggested as suicide, although this was never proved. Subsequently, he received a non-Catholic burial service, which he would have preferred.

SARAH BERRY

Selected Works

Collected Works (4 vols.). Translated and with an introduction by V. Corti. London: Calder and Boyars, 1960.
Artaud on Theatre. Edited by Claude Schumacher. London: Methuen Drama, 1989.

Further Reading

Barber, Stephen. *Antonin Artaud Blows and Bombs*. London: Faber and Faber, 1993.

Biro, Adam, and René Passeron, eds. *Dictionnaire général du Surréalisme et de ses environs*. Paris: Presses Universitaires de France, 1982.

Brau, Jean-Louis. *Antonin Artaud*. Paris: Table Ronde, 1971.

Hayman, Ronald. *Artaud and After*. Oxford: Oxford University Press, 1977.

Sellin, Eric. *The Dramatic Concepts of Antonin Artaud*. Chicago: University of Chicago Press, 1968.

ARTSYBASHEV, MIKHAIL

1878–1927

Russian novelist, short-story writer, and playwright

Powerfully influenced by Dostoevskii, Tolstoi, and Andreev, Artsybashev's fiction offers an awkward yoking of suicide, murder, and sexual violence to an optimistic love of nature. His first important story, "Pasha Tumanov" (1901), in which a high school student who fails an exam shoots the headmaster and then himself amidst the beauty of a summer's day, was suppressed by the censor and did not appear until 1906. "Kuprian'" (1902) concerns a horse thief whom the author admires for his strength and passion; "Uzhas" [Horror 1905] describes a brutal rape in hair-raising detail.

Artsybashev finally caught the attention of the greater reading public with his first novel, *The Death of Ivan Landé* [*Smert' Ivana Lande*] (1904), a derivative attempt to create "a perfectly beautiful human being" à la Dostoevski's Prince Myshkin. Like his best-known novel, *Sanin,* a charge of pornography was also lodged against the novel *On the Brink* [*U poslednei cherty*] (1911–12), which tells of a suicide epidemic among the intellectuals of a provincial town. Other works, *Millions* [*Milliony*] (1908), a Dostoevskian study of a millionaire's isolation, and *The Worker Shevyrëv* [*Rabochiy Shevryrev*, 1911], were treated respectfully by the critics.

Artsybashev achieved widespread if controversial fame from his novel *Sanin,* begun in 1902, originally published in installments in *Sovremennoe Mir* in 1906–7, and then quickly distributed in a separate edition. The second edition was confiscated, and the author accused of pornography. Translated into many languages, *Sanin* caused a sensation wherever it was read. Criminal proceedings in Berlin and Munich ended in acquittal, however, and the Russian courts never got around to the case.

In its time a sensational best seller, read and discussed avidly by the intelligentsia, the bourgeoisie, and especially students, not only in Russia but throughout central and eastern Europe, *Sanin* is an uneasy blend of realism, eroticism, and tendentiousness. It echoed the calls for radical individualism, personal freedom from morality, and sexual nihilism that came in the wake of the failed revolution of 1905.

The protagonist Sanin is an amoral Nietzschean superhero, above the common herd, who spurns both emotional and intellectual ideals. A crude materialist with powerful muscles and strong appetites, he subscribes to Zarathustra's apothegm, "You're going after women? Don't forget the whip." In his cynicism and lechery, he also resembles the antiheroic underground man of Dostoevskii Sanin's message is that only natural impulses, untainted by social convention, are pure and real. Anything else, especially hypocritical bourgeois codes of respectability and honor, is specious and artificial. To be true to oneself is to set no limit to one's desires. Individualism is to be sought in sensual pleasure, peasant customs, nature, and death.

The action unfolds in and around stifling provincial towns, populated by disaffected and indolent young men and repressed, yet superficially emancipated young women. Although many readers view Sanin's aggressive behavior toward women as misogynistic, Artsybashev sometimes portrays these relations as a comradely complicity in erotic transgression. Sanin's actions occasionally belie the conventional pattern of sexual dominance and subordination he preaches in his long-winded discussions, so that the novel has been read by feminists as a condemnation of ruthless male conquest and the degradation of women and as a defense of equality in sexual relations.

Oddly, although it promotes hedonism, *Sanin* steers clear of the pleasure principle in its prose. It is crudely written, regularly bogging down in tedious, didactic dialogues which belabor the author's points. The liberal critic Korney Chukovsky complained that its literary quality and erotic appeal were vitiated by the argumentative tone. If its message is individualism, its medium is monotony. The characters are either inhibited or untrammeled. Sanin's final leap from a moving train into an open field "to meet the rising sun" is more the result of Chekhovian boredom than of high spirits.

Nonetheless, *Sanin* proved a provocation to thinkers of all factions. Leo Tolstoi dismissed it as an expression of "the vilest animal impulses," as did Maksim Gorki. Conservatives railed against it as pornography, while the younger generation avidly debated it and tried to put its lessons into practice. As D.S. Mirsky remarked, "The author of *Sanin* cannot be exculpated from having contributed to the moral deterioration of Russian society, especially of provincial schoolgirls." It was widely circulated among Russia's Jews in Yiddish translation, and Sholem Aleichem's story "Sanny" tells of a Jewish girl whose attempt to live up to *Sanin* leads to her suicide. The novel was dramatized in 1911 as *How to Live*. It was also one of the first books banned by the Bolsheviks after the October Revolution, an action which deeply embittered Artsybashev.

At the height of his popularity, between the Russian revolutions of 1905 and 1917, Artsybashev intuitively condensed the mood of the age, vulgarizing themes and characters from his more illustrious colleagues. A deadly pessimism and stridency crept into his later writing, leading one wag to refer to Artsybashev's characters as "the Club of Suicides."

Plays

Artsybashev's prewar plays enjoyed some success on Moscow and St. Petersburg stages. Influenced strongly by Ibsen, Strindberg, and Hamsun, these well-carpentered if morbid melodramas deal with the "sex war" and the double standard. *Jealousy* [*Revnost'*, 1913] concerns the writer Sergei Petrovich, tormented by the provocative behavior of his wife. Owing to her upbringing, she is insufferably wanton without actually being unfaithful. Her loose behavior is misread by a libidinous Caucasian prince, whose advances, though rebuffed, seem to confirm Sergei's suspicions. He strangles his wife, who is blameless in all but appearance. *Enemies* [*Vragi*, 1917] is based on the incompatibility of the sexes—men wishing for a harem, women for an ideal lover. All couples have to lie to make their marriages work and therefore end up hating one another. This idea also animates *The Law of the Savage* [*Zakon dikariia*, 1917], in which a lawyer is killed in a duel he undertakes to safeguard the honor of a wife he doesn't love. Alternately hysterical and preachy in tone, these plays disclose an underlying misogyny and a lugubrious view of human sexual relations.

Biography

Mikhail Petrovich Artsybashev was born October 24, 1878 (Old Style calendar), in Izium, Russia, into a family of minor landowners—son of the district police captain and, on his mother's side, great-grandson of the Polish patriot Kosciuszko. The lush green forests, sunny fields, and smooth-running river of the southern Russian hamlet of Akhtyrka, where he grew up, are regularly evoked in his writing. Artsybashev's schooling stopped at the fifth grade of the *gymnasium,* and, at sixteen, he began to place stories in provincial newspapers.

After a two-year marriage ended in separation, Artsybashev moved to St. Petersburg, where lack of a diploma prevented his admission to the Academy of Arts. While earning a living as a caricaturist and land-council clerk, he continued to paint and write. He emigrated to Warsaw in 1923, where he became coeditor of an anti-Bolshevik newspaper. Deteriorating health and financial distress kept him from writing anything significant prior to his death on March 3, 1927.

LAURENCE SENELICK

Selected Works

Sobranie sochanenii, 10 vols., 1905–17; selected stories in English as *The Millionaire*, translated by Percy Pinkerton, 1915; as *Tales of the Revolution*, translated by Percy Pinkerton, 1917.

Sanin, 1909; as *Sanine, a Russian Love Novel*, translated by Percy Pinkerton, 1923, 1925, 1926, 1931, 1932, 1969; as *Sanin*, translated by Michael R. Katz, 2001.

U poslednei cherty: Roman, 1911; as *Breaking-Point*, 1915.

Revnost', 1913; *Vragi*, 1917; as *Jealousy, Enemies, The Law of the Savage, with an Introductory Essay on Marriage*. Translated by Mme A. Strindberg, Maxim Levitski, and W.F. Adams, 1923.

Zhena. 1913.

Mstitel': Sbornik rasskazov. 1913.

Voina, 1914; as *War, a Play in 4 Acts*, translated by Thomas Seltzer, 1916; as *War: A Play in Four Acts*, translated by Percy Pinkerton, 1923, 1932.

"Evrei: Rasskaz." 1915; as "The Jew: a Story," in M. Gorky, ed., *The Shield*, 1917.

Dikie: povest'. 1922; as *The Savage*, translated by G. Canning and Mme A. Strindberg, 1924, 1951.

D'iavol: Tragicheskoi fars v 4 deistviiakh. 1925, 1977.

Teni utra: romani, povesti, rasskazy. 1990.

Further Reading

Achkasov, Aleksei. *Artsybashevskii 'Sanin' i okolo polovogo voprosa*. Moscow: D. P. Efimov, 1908.

Danilin, N. *'Sanin' v svete russkoi kritike*, Moscow: Zaria, 1908.

Engelstein, Laura. *The Keys to Happiness. Sex and the Search for Modernity in Fin-de-siècle Russia*, Ithaca and London: Cornell University Press, 1992.

Luker, Nicholas J.L. *In Defence of a Reputation: Essays on the Early Prose of Mikhail Artsybashev*. Nottingham: Astra Press, 1990.

Novopolin, G.S. *Pornograficheskii élement v russkoi literature*. St Petersburg: M. M. Stasiulevich, 1909.

O'Dell, Sally. *Mikhail Petrovich Artsybashev (1878–1927) a Centennial Presentation and Assessment*. Nottingham: Astra Press, 1980.

O'Dell, Sally, and Nicholas J. Luker. *Mikhail Artsybashev: A Comprehensive Bibliography*. Nottingham: Astra Press, 1983.

Omel'chenko, A.P. *Svobodnaia liubov' i sem'ia: 'Sanin', kak vopros nashego vremeni*. St Petersburg: Pos'ev, 1908.

Pachmuss, Temira. "Mikhail Artsybashev in the Criticism of Zinaida Gippius," *Slavonic and East European Review* 44 (1966): 76–87.

ASHBEE, HENRY SPENCER

1834–1900

English bibliographer and novelist

The author of *My Secret Life*, a 4,200-page narrative purporting to be the sexual autobiography of a Victorian gentleman, is listed as "anonymous" in most reference works. Circumstantial evidence, however, has increasingly pointed to Henry Spencer Ashbee, the Victorian businessman and erotic bibliophile. If Ashbee did not write the text, cultural historians would have to invent someone very much like him to account for its existence: a wealthy member of a male network comprising authors and publishers with the power, privilege, and leisure required for such clandestine projects; a man like the poet Algernon Charles Swinburne, the politician Richard Monckton Milnes (Lord Houghton), the Orientalist Sir Richard Burton, or the publisher of *My Secret Life*, "Charles Carrington"

(the pseudonym of Harry Ferdinando)—all of whom Ashbee counted as friends. The ambiguity concerning the book's authorship is in many ways salutary, since it focuses attention where it belongs: on the cultural production, circulation, and significance of pornography in the late nineteenth century. As Michel Foucault observes in "The Author Function," "writing is primarily concerned with creating an opening where the writing subject endlessly disappears". In the case of *My Secret Life*, this gap is filled by a desiring male subject who speaks literal volumes about Victorian ideologies of gender, power, and sexuality.

My Secret Life

If Ashbee wrote *My Secret Life*, it is likely he began it in the 1880s. In 1857, when he was in

87

his mid-twenties and already a connoisseur of erotica, the Obscene Publications Act led to a clampdown that drove the trade underground. As the century progressed, erotica publishing in English shifted to the Continent, particularly Paris and Amsterdam, and there was a brisk trade in smuggling books into Britain. Peter Mendes has established that *My Secret Life* was printed in Amsterdam between approximately 1888 and 1894, most likely by the Belgian publisher Auguste Brancart. It is not possible to establish how many copies were issued, although certainly more than the six claimed in the preface to the book's index: "It is in print in eleven volumes, of which six copies only have been struck off and the type then broken up". In 1901 the so-called Charles Carrington published the first six chapters of the book as *The Dawn of Sensuality* and a year later issued a catalogue announcing for sale the entire book, running to eleven volumes. Today only four complete sets of *My Secret Life* are known to exist apart from the copy in the British Library: one at the Kinsey Institute for Research in Sex, Gender and Reproduction (Indiana University, Bloomington) and three in the hands of private collectors in London, Hamburg, and Switzerland (Gibson).

The relative sexual openness of the 1960s increased interest in Ashbee and *My Secret Life*. Gershon Legman was the first to argue, in 1962, that Ashbee was almost certainly the author of *My Secret Life* (an expanded version of the essay containing this claim appears as the introduction to the complete Grove Press edition of the book, published in two volumes in 1966). Ashbee's three erotic bibliographies, published in expensive, limited editions during his lifetime and known to only a small coterie of collectors, reappeared in a facsimile edition in 1966. In 1964 Steven Marcus returned their author to prominence in *The Other Victorians*, devoting one chapter to Ashbee's bibliographies and two chapters to *My Secret Life*. Marcus does not identify Ashbee as the author of *My Secret Life*, but he does read the narrative as a true history of its author's erotic life. Subsequent critics of *My Secret Life* depart from Marcus on this point and view the text as fiction. In the words of James Kincaid, who also declines naming Ashbee as author, *My Secret Life* is "a picaresque (or post-modern) novel" which "operates as a subversive version of genteel fic-

tion and its main motor: how sheer tenacity and good luck can overcome the odds, master the obstacles created by class, modesty, and money".

In the 1970s Ashbee's granddaughter granted Ian Gibson access to Ashbee's diaries, and these helped convince Gibson that Ashbee wrote *My Secret Life*. Although no trace of the original manuscript seems to exist, and no confirmatory written documentation has come to light, Gibson finds the circumstantial evidence overwhelming. He presents this case in considerable detail in chapter 5 of *The Erotomaniac*, ranging from stylistic similarities linking the book with Ashbee's diaries and *Travels in Tunisia* to "numerous broad similarities" between Walter, the narrator of *My Secret Life*, and Ashbee himself. Among the latter, Gibson cites their common love of billiards, southern climates, and classification, as well as their shared class arrogance and snobbism: Both men express irritation when the lower classes become too familiar or fail to comply with their desires. In addition, *My Secret Life* constitutes a violent attack against Victorian hypocrisy and sexual repression, against the "ultra-squeamishness and hyper-prudery" lamented by Ashbee/Fraxi in his introduction to the *Index librorum prohibitorum*. The author of *My Secret Life*, like Ashbee/Fraxi, is outraged by the British refusal to tell children the truth about their bodies. Twice, for instance, Walter jeers at the "parsley-bed" theory of reproductive biology.

My Secret Life implicitly argues the case for uninhibited sex in a society in which "this act of mighty power and eternal endowments" is termed "foul, bestial, abominable!" and "may not be mentioned or talked about." As Walter puts it:

> It seems to me, that both men and women may be straight, and fair in all they do, be as good and useful members of society as others, yet take their chief delight in carnal pleasures. I am sure that it is so with hundreds of thousands of men, in the middle and upper classes, who are good husbands and fathers, yet who don't put a half of their sperm into their wives' cunts, and indulge in all the varieties, refinements, and eccentricities of lust habitually. But women can't act similarly without deteriorating.

Like Ashbee's friends Swinburne and Burton, Walter is openly contemptuous of Christianity, holding it responsible for "the absurd finical notions about nudity and the necessities of nature, which my own countrymen have". He also often employs comic irony in mounting his assaults on conventional pieties. Following a long treatise on copulation, he proposes that this passage "may be read usefully after evening family prayers also, by older members of the family as well, to whom at times it may serve as an aphrodisiac, and it will spare many young, but full grown people, trouble and loss of time in searching for knowledge which ought to be known to all, but which owing to a false morality, is a subject put aside as improper". Elsewhere he adapts the Anglican liturgy to his own vision of eternal concupiscence: "As in the beginning, now and ever it will be—Fucking".

Once readers step outside his masculinist and upper-class frame of reference, of course, they discover that Walter lives in a world of unequally distributed carnal pleasures. As Kincaid has written, "[E]xcept for the time with prostitutes, he is pretty much devoting his life to a career of sexual harassment; when he isn't, that is, actually committing rape". Of the 1,200 women Walter says he has had intercourse with, many are from the lower classes, many are poor, and many would qualify as children under current legal definitions (the age of consent for females in Britain was thirteen until 1885, when it increased to fifteen). In this connection it is worth mentioning that *My Secret Life* was being compiled while a four-part investigation into child prostitution was appearing in the *Pall Mall Gazette*. "The Maiden Tribute of Modern Babylon," written by the paper's editor W.T. Stead, appeared in the issues of July 6, 7, 8, 9, and 10, 1885, and contained two sections headed "Why the cries of the victims were not heard" and "Strapping girls down." Although Walter does not directly refer to Stead's revelations, he does dismissively allude to the series. After deflowering Phoebe, Walter informs us, "She'd felt my stiff prick, I'd fucked her again, she had given down her maiden tribute to mix with her ravisher's, and our spendings had mingled in our pleasure". This passage also captures the narrator's unthinking and misguided assumption, expressed throughout *My Secret Life*, that females automatically experience orgasms through the kind of penetrative sex that is pleasurable to the male—and that their orgasms are always accompanied by ejaculation.

In addition to its status as erotic fantasy, *My Secret Life* is an important document in Victorian social history. Walter may be a fictional persona, but many of his observations correspond to those recorded by such urban sociologists as Henry Mayhew and Bracebridge Hemyng. Mayhew's *London Labour and the London Poor* (1861–1862) contains a chapter on prostitution written by Hemyng that reports on an interrogation of an Irish brothel keeper:

> She was intensely civil to the inspector, who had once convicted her for allowing three women to sleep in one bed, and she was fined five pounds, all which she told us with the most tedious circumstantiality, vowing, as "shure as the Almighty God was sitting on his throne," she did it out of charity, or she wishes she might never speak no more. "These gals," she said, "comes to me in the night and swears (as I knows to be true) they has no place where to put their heads, and foxes they has holes, likewise birds of the air, which it's a mortial [sic] shame as they is better provided for an against than them that's flesh and blood Christians".

Walter too has an acute ear for dialogue, as in this description of his reunion with the Irish prostitute "Big-Eyed Betsy Johnson":

> She was always lascivious. "Your fucking is delicious, me dear. You still do it well." On my preparing to leave, "Why sure, and you're not going after doing it once, and all these years since I've seen you? I recollect you, when I had to tell you you had done enough for your money. Ah, I'm older, but sugar me if you go yet," said she, clutching hold of my prick. So we fucked again, and again, for I could not resist her.

Except for the self-glorifying detail that Walter embeds in his account, the two passages are remarkably similar.

When Walter is in his twenties, he records that his "erotic fancies took the desire for a young lass," and his extended account of his meetings with the fifteen-year old Kitty is one of the most revealing in the book. He says of her that "there was a frankness, openness, and freshness ... which delighted me" and records their many conversations, beginning with this one:

> "How long have you been gay?" "I ain't gay," said she, astonished. "Yes you are." "No I ain't." "You let men fuck you don't you?" "Yes, but I ain't gay." "What do you call gay?" "Why the gals who come out regular of a night, dressed up, and gets their livings by it." I was amused. "Don't you?" "No.

Mother keeps me.'' ''What is your father?'' ''Got none; he's dead three months back,—mother works and keeps us. She is a charwoman, and goes out on odd jobs.'' ''Don't you work?'' ''Not now,'' said she in a confused way; ''mother does not want me to; I takes care of the others.'' ''What others?'' ''The young ones.'' ''How many?'' ''Two, —one's a boy, and one's a gal.'' ''How old?'' ''Sister's about six, and brother's nearly eight, —but what do you ask me all this for?'' ''Only for amusement, —then you are in mourning for your father?'' ''Yes, it's shabby, ain't it? I wish I could have nice clothes. I've got nice boots, —ain't they?'' —cocking up one leg— ''a lady gave 'em me when father died, —they are my best.''

For the privileged Walter, Kitty's situation is mainly a source of ''amusement,'' but when she explains her motives in entering prostitution, her perspective is more sobering:

She said, ''I buy things to eat; I can't eat what mother gives us. She is poor, and works very hard; she'd give us more, but she can't; so I buy foods, and gives the others what mother gives me; they don't know better, —if mother's there, I eat some; sometimes we have only gruel and salt; if we have a fire we toast the bread, but I can't eat it if I am not dreadful hungry.'' ''What do you like?'' ''Pies and sausage-rolls,'' said the girl, smacking her lips and laughing. ''Oh! My eye, ain't they prime, —oh!'' ''That's what you went gay for?'' ''I'm not gay,'' said she sulkily. ''What, what you let men fuck you for?'' ''Yes.'' ''Sausage-rolls''? ''Yes, meat-pies and pastry too.''

The contrast between Walter's leisured pursuit of Kitty and her own more urgent economic needs casts a harsh light on class divisions and the sex trade in Victorian London.

Beyond its importance as social history, *My Secret Life* has great value for students of the Victorian novel. Many of the passages in the narrative literally flesh out the sexual subtexts in Dickens's novels—for instance, from the activities of the prostitute Nancy in *Oliver Twist* to the coarse appetites of Major Bagstock in *Dombey and Son*. Moreover, the nonchalance of Walter concerning Kitty's plight highlights the extent to which the novel as Dickens and others conceived it was a moral instrument, meant to rouse middle-class readers from such complacency. In chapter 15 of *Bleak House*, the governess Esther Summerson and her employer John Jarndyce visit a family of orphaned children whose father they had known and whose lives parallel those of Kitty and her siblings in significant ways. Charley, the older sister in

Bleak House, goes out to do washing rather than prostituting herself; but aside from this difference, her life of poverty and privation is identical to Kitty's. The difference between the two tellings is one of affect: Dickens has Esther and Jarndyce identify with these children and express outrage at their situation, whereas Walter feels vaguely superior to Kitty and is happy that she is at his disposal. Dickens emphasizes the web of moral causality and responsibility that unites the most cosseted with the most destitute; Walter is untroubled by the disparity between his economic condition and that of Kitty (Marcus, p.105–09).

In this sense, *My Secret Life* exists in a supplementary relationship to the mainstream Victorian novel generally, and to Dickens's novels in particular. Self-interest predominates in the narrative, just as the laissez-faire economic theory that alarmed Dickens and many of his fellow novelists predominated in the nineteenth century. Walter is thus more representative of prevailing social attitudes than are the Oliver Twists and Esther Summersons of Dickens's fictional worlds, who oppose utilitarian calculations in all their forms. ''Fucking is the greatest pleasure of life, and the woman who delays getting it for years, loses much'', Walter avers, and he sets about producing his version of the greatest good for the greatest number. He approaches sex like Ashbee himself approached free trade—with an enthusiastic entrepreneurial spirit, energetic productivity, and an eager willingness to exploit women, children, and the working class. Like David Copperfield, Walter turns out to be the hero of his own life—a confessional hero who turns sex into text, extracting the maximum surplus value from his erotic experiences. If the nineteenth century witnessed ''the transformation of sex into discourse,'' as Michel Foucault writes in *The History of Sexuality*, Ashbee and Walter were two of its greatest alchemists.

Biography

Born in 1834 in Kent, Henry Spencer Ashbee was a successful London businessman, travel writer, and family man. He left school at sixteen and went straight into trade. After making a financially advantageous marriage at twenty-eight, he became manager of a profitable textile business, a member of several City companies,

London clubs, and national societies, and an extensive traveler. In 1865 he moved with his family to 46 Upper Bedford Place in Bloomsbury, just off Russell Square, where he remained for 20 years. The British Library was only a few minutes away, which must have appealed to Ashbee, who became a confirmed bibliophile in his thirties. Distinguished by a passion for genteel flagellation, he became his era's preeminent bibliographer of forbidden literature, beginning with the lavishly produced *Index librorum prohibitorum* (1877), published under the scatological pseudonym "Pisanus Fraxi." This volume was followed by *Centuria Librorum Absconditorum* in 1879 and *Catena Librorum Tacendorum* in 1885. By the time Ashbee published his *Bibliography of Tunisia from the Earliest Times to the End of 1888* under his own name in 1889, it was an open secret that he was also Pisanus Fraxi, Britain's reigning authority on erotica. Indeed, as Ian Gibson demonstrates in *The Erotomaniac: The Life of Henry Spencer Ashbee,* the only thing that made the activities of Ashbee and his like-minded friends "secret" was that they took place out of the view of wives, children, and economic subordinates—except those prostitutes and mistresses who serviced their fantasies. When Ashbee died in 1900, he bequeathed to the British Museum a library running to thousands of volumes, which included the most extensive collection of private erotica ever to come into the public domain.

JAMES DIEDRICK

Selected Works

Index Librorum Prohibitorum: Being Notes Bio-, Biblio-, Iconographical and Critical, on Curious and Uncommon Books. London, 1877.
Centuria Librorum Absconditorum: Being Notes Bio- Biblio- Iconographical and Critical, on Curious and Uncommon Books. London, 1879.
Catena Librorum Tacendorum: Being Notes Bio- Biblio- Iconographical and Critical, on Curious and Uncommon Books. London, 1885.
A Bibliography of Tunisia from the Earliest Times to the End of 1888. London, 1889.
Quintin Craufurd. Paris, 1891.
An Iconography of Don Quixote, 1605–1895. London, 1895.

Editions

Anon. *My Secret Life.* Introduction by Gershon Legman, 2 vols., with continuous pagination. New York: Grove Press, 1966 (the first open and unabridged publication of the book).
Ashbee, H.S. *A Complete Guide to Forbidden Books* [facsimile edition of *Index Librorum Prohibitorum, Centuria Librorum Absconditorum,* and *Catena Librorum Tacendorum*], edited by E.S. Sullivan. North Hollywood, CA: Brandon House, 1966.
Kronhausen, Phyllis, and Eberhard Kronhausen. *The English Casanova: A Presentation of his Unique Memoirs 'My Secret Life,'* 2 vols. London: Polybooks 2nd reprint, 1967.

Further Reading

Foucault, Michel. *The History of Sexuality: An Introduction* (vol. 1). Translated by Robert Hurley. New York: Vintage Books, 1978.
———. "What Is an Author?" Translated by Donald F. Bouchard & Sherry Simon, in *Language, Counter-Memory, Practice* (pp. 124–127), edited by Donald F. Bouchard. Ithaca, NY: Cornell University Press, 1977.
Gibson, Ian. *The Erotomaniac: The Secret Life of Henry Spencer Ashbee.* Cambridge, MA: Da Capo, 2001.
Hyde, H. Montgomery. *A History of Pornography.* New York: Farrar Straus and Giroux, 1965.
Kincaid, James R. "Introduction," *My Secret Life: An Erotic Diary of Victorian London,* edited and abridged by James Kincaid & Richard Tithecott. New York: Signet, 1996.
Kronhausen, Eberhard, and Phyllis Kronhausen. *Pornography and the Law: The Psychology of Erotic Realism and Pornography.* 2nd ed. New York: Ballantine Books, 1964.
———. Eberhard, and Phyllis Kronhausen, *Erotic Fantasies; A Study of the Sexual Imagination.* New York: Grove Press, 1970.
Legman, Gershon. "'Pisanus Fraxi' and His Books," introduction to *Bibliography of Prohibited Books ... By Pisanus Fraxi* (pp. 5–51). New York: Jack Brussel, 1952 (a 3-volume reprint of *Index Librorum Prohibitorum, Centuria Librorum Absconditorum,* and *Catena Librorum Tacendorum*).
Marcus, Steven. *The Other Victorians.* New York: Basic Books, 1964.
Mayhew, Henry. *London Labour and the London Poor,* 4 vols. New York: Dover, 1968.
Mendes, Peter. *Clandestine Erotic Fiction in English, 1800–1930: A Bibliographical Study.* Aldershot, UK: Ashgate, 1993.
Sutherland, John. *Offensive Literature: Decensorship in Britain, 1960–1982.* New York: Barnes & Noble, 1982.
Walkowitz, Judith R. *Prostitution and Victorian Society: Women, Class, and the State.* Cambridge: Cambridge University Press, 1980.

AUDEN, W.H.

1907–1973
British poet

"The Platonic Blow"

"The Platonic Blow" (or "A Day for a Lay" or "The Gobble Poem," as it has also been called) is the best-known and most substantial of a small number of erotic poems Auden wrote, not for publication but for the private amusement of close friends. In a letter to Chester Kallman on December 13, 1948, Auden wrote: "Deciding that there ought to be one in the Auden Corpus, I am writing a purely pornographic poem, *The Platonic Blow*. You should do one on the other Major Act. Covici would print them together privately on rubber paper for dirty old millionaires at immense profit to us both. (Illustrations by [Paul] Cadmus?)"

The poem is about Auden's favourite sexual activity, fellatio; the "other Major Act" he refers to, more to Kallman's taste, was anal intercourse. One reason for his writing it was to show Norman Holmes Pearson of Yale University, with whom he was about to coedit a poetry anthology, the kind of person he was. In this sense, it is a clear statement not only of personal interest, but even of basic identity.

After the poem had been published, against his will, by the arts magazine *Fuck You,* in New York in 1965, Auden complained to Monroe Spears: "[I]n depressed moods I feel it is the *only* poem by me which the Hippies have read" (November 18, 1967). It was also published by a magazine more appropriately called *Suck.* Among friends, Auden openly acknowledged authorship of it. The British politician Tom Driberg recalled an occasion when, visiting the poet for lunch in New York, he was given a privileged reading. Auden also read part of it from a hot tub at a spa on Ischia to the visiting German student Peter Adam, later a distinguished broadcaster. Auden even once admitted to the mainstream press that the poem was his (*Daily Telegraph Magazine*, August 9, 1968). However,

when *Avant-Garde* magazine published it in March 1970, again without permission, and even had the courteous nerve to send the poet a fee, Auden returned the check and repudiated authorship.

Like so much of his verse, "The Platonic Blow" is a technical tour de force. It adopts a syncopated measure Auden found in the Arthurian cycle *Taliessin through Logres* (1938) by the British Roman Catholic poet Charles Williams. He made more polished use of the form, later, in the second section of "Memorial for the City" (1949), which is dedicated to the memory of Williams. Auden's obvious pleasure in the erotic poem derives as much from the wickedness of its sexually explicit parody of a deeply serious, spiritual book as from the sexual narrative itself.

The poem consists of 34 stanzas of four lines each, rhymed ABAB. The lines range in length from 10 to 16 syllables, but they all have five insistent stresses. The vocabulary combines unexpected archaisms ("lofty," "beheld") and apparently inappropriate formal expressions ("sutures," "ineffably," "capacious," "indwelling," "voluminous") with the erotic demotic ("cock," "arse," "knob," "hard-on," "spunk"). The insistency of his internal rhymes ("fresh flesh," "the charms of arms," "the shock of his cock," "quick to my licking," "sluices of his juices," "the notch of his crotch," "spouted in gouts") and half-rhymes ("slot of the spout," "curls and whorls") seems clumsy at first, but soon gathers momentum in vivid mimesis of the act they represent.

The narrative itself is entirely conventional, in a literal sense slavishly following pornographic precedent. Spoken from the point of view of the adoring fellator, it follows a familiar route from the picking-up of an attractive stranger to consummation and ejaculation. Faced with the body of a young man, the speaker is at a rhapsodic pitch throughout. The object of his attention corresponds with Auden's ideal image of the American dreamboat: "Present address: next door. / Half Polish, half Irish. The youngest

From Illinois. / Profession: mechanic. Name: Bud. Age: twenty-four." He is blond. To an extent, it does not matter whether this boy is actually homosexual. Auden believed, in any case, that straight American men did not really care for sexual intercourse with women: they just wanted to get blown while reading the newspaper. His fantasy was to be the one who did that favor.

In this written version of the fantasy, however, the blown man reciprocates. Before the speaker can begin sucking him, without being asked, Bud undresses fully. When the speaker, too, has undressed, they kiss. He fucks the speaker intercrurally. The speaker then explores the whole of his body, including his armpits and arse. Bud even has a voice of his own: When the speaker finally gets around to sucking him, he "hoarsely" says: "That's lovely! ... Go on! Go on!" Later, he whimpers expressively, "Oh!" and as he is about to ejaculate, "O Jesus!" This man is, then, a cooperative version of Auden's American stereotype, a young man who seems unashamed to involve himself in a mutual homosexual act but who ultimately submits to the imperative of the exploring mouth and becomes completely passive in the face of its unrelenting onslaught.

According to Harold Norse, who had firsthand experience, Auden was actually an inept fellator, regardless of his enthusiasm for the act: "The more feverishly he labored, the less I responded." There is no such discomfort in "The Platonic Blow." Only the gay Japanese poet Mutsuo Takahashi's long poem "Ode" outdoes it in exuberant celebration of the fellator's art.

Biography

Wystan Hugh Auden was born on February 21, 1907, and was educated at Gresham's School, Holt, and Christ Church College, Oxford. He was actively, if discreetly, homosexual from an early age. Although in 1935 he married Erika Mann, he did so to help her escape Nazi Germany, and the marriage was never consummated. In January 1939, he left Britain for the United States with Christopher Isherwood. Chester Kallman, the eighteen-year-old boy who would become his lover, met him after attending a poetry reading he gave in New York on April 6, 1939. Auden died in Vienna on September 29, 1973.

GREGORY WOODS

Selected Works

Auden, W.H. "The Platonic Blow," *Fuck You: A Magazine of the Arts* 1 (March 1965).
"The Gobble Poem." *Suck: The First European Sex Paper* 1 (October 1969).
"A Day for a Lay." *Avant-Garde* 11 (March 1970).
Collected Poems. London: Faber, 1976.

Further Reading

Carpenter, Humphrey. *W.H. Auden: A Biography*. London: Allen & Unwin, 1981.
Norse, Harold. *Memoirs of a Bastard Angel*. London: Bloomsbury, 1990.
Woods, Gregory. "W.H. Auden." In *Articulate Flesh: Male Homo-eroticism and Modern Poetry*. New Haven and London: Yale University Press, 1987.

AUTOBIOGRAPHY OF A FLEA

The subtitle of this work is: *Recounting all his Experiences of the Human, and Superhuman, Kind, both Male and Female; with his Curious Connections, Backbitings, and Tickling Touches; the whole scratched together and arranged for the Delectation of the Delicate, and for the Information of the Inquisitive, etc., etc*

The initial press run of *The Autobiography of a Flea* was limited to 150 copies, under the false imprint of "The Phlebotomical Society, Cytheria, 1789"; in reality: c. 1885 for Lazenby/Avery. A question hangs over its authorship. *Galitzine* refers to its author as "un avocat anglais, bien connu à Londres" [an advocate well known in London], suggested to be Frederick Popham Pike (Mendes, p. 128), the only barrister known to be writing pornography at this time, and a member of William Dugdale's coterie (which included Sellon, Campbell, Potter, and Sala) from the 1860s until his death in September 1877. Other contenders for its authorship include Frederick Hankey, who died in 1882, Henry Spencer Ashbee, and Stanislas de Rodes.

Written from the view of an onlooking flea, the work tells the exploits of the libidinous adventures of Bella, a young girl, and a monastery of corrupt monks, the work being essentially anti-Catholic. The novel is quite well written, with detailed full-length descriptions, good scene setting, and tension buildups.

The story starts with descriptions of the fourteen-year-old Bella. She is introduced in the terminology common to its genre: "her soft bosom was already budding into those proportions which delight the other sex," "her skin as soft and as warm as velvet," her head held "coquettishly as a queen." Particular attributes are admired, with the writer venerating her "pretty little foot," "swelling thighs," "beautiful belly," and "mystic grotto."

Bella follows the path of other inquisitive protagonists of the period, yet she shows little of the modesty often portrayed in fictional virgins. "When are you going to explain and show me all those funny things you told me about?" she asks. Although a virgin, when her paramour, Charlie, kisses her, Bella makes no resistance; she even aids and returns her lover's caresses. He puts his hand up her petticoats, all the while encouraged by Bella. "'Touch it,'" she whispers to him, "'you may.'" She throws back her head and abandons herself to enjoyment of the experience, telling him, "What delightful sensations you give me."

Although she wants to explore her sexuality, is described as "glowing with the unwonted impulse stealing over her," and is an active participant, she is still described as submissive: "[S]he lay the delicious victim of whomsoever had the instant chance to reap her favours and cull her delicate young rose."

Through a "raging torrent of desire" she loses her virginity, but the unlucky lovers are caught by an irate priest, a handsome man of forty-five, with "a pair of brilliant eyes, which, black as jet, threw around fierce glances of passionate resentment." His torrent of rhetoric serves to make him look ridiculous and pious: "For you miserable girl, I can only express the utmost horror and my most righteous indignation. Forgetful alike of the precepts of the holy mother church, careless of your honour, you have allowed this wicked and presumptuous boy to pluck the forbidden fruit! What now remains for you? Scorned by your friends from your uncle's house, you will herd with the beasts of the filed, and exiled, as by Nebuchadnezzar of old, shunned as contamination by your species, you will be glad to gather a miserable sustenance in the highways." This initial indignation by the priest highlights the later hypocrisies of the church and its clergy as they introduce Bella to frenzied sex.

The priest, Father Ambrose, arranges for Bella to come to his sacristy the following day; meanwhile he will consult with the Blessed Virgin. The next day he tells Bella how she can atone for her sins:

> You will swim in a sea of sensual pleasure, without incurring the penalties of illicit love. Your absolution will follow each occasion of your yielding your sweet body to the gratification of the church, through her ministers, and you will be rewarded and sustained in the pious works by witnessing—nay, Bella, by sharing fully those intense and fervent emotions the delicious enjoyment of your beautiful person must provoke.

Bella feels pleasure and surprise while "she became fully aware of the enormous protuberance of the front of the holy Father's silk cassock." She did not seem at all abashed when he uncovered it, and in her face "there was nothing mingled with it of alarm or apprehension."

The scene then explores cunnilingus and fellatio and the tale moves on to a full penetration scene, which is described as torture to her: "With a faint shriek of physical anguish, Bella felt that her ravisher had burst through all the resistance which her youth had opposed to the entry of his member, and the torture of the forcible insertion of such a mass bore down the prurient sensations with which she had commenced to support the attack."

The following week, she goes back to do more "penitence." At the end of her copulation with the priest, two more priests spring forth, the elder one stating, "This is against the rules and privileges, which enact that all such game shall be in common." They had been watching through the keyhole and now want her for themselves. The younger newcomer was unattractive but this only increased her passion: "He was short and stout, but built with shoulders broad enough for a Hercules. The child had caught a sort of lewd madness; his ugliness only served further to rouse her sensual desires."

Following a path of increased sexual degradation, scene by scene, sodomy, homosexuality, and incest are explored. Bella's uncle masturbates Father Ambrose: "[D]eliberately taking it in his hand, he manipulated the huge shaft with evident satisfaction,"—then, taking Bella, the uncle spells out the incestuous nature of his act: "Yes, Bella, into the belly of my brother's child."

Once her uncle is involved, Bella experiences fear, dread, horror, and disgust. Despite enjoying the priests, she does not want her uncle's advances, but she cannot escape his clutches. He enters her bed at midnight suddenly and with vigor, increasing the feelings of intrusion into her private space. It takes 80 pages and many scenes before Bella's own sexuality eventually awakens; she has "become a woman of violent passions and unrestrained lust."

In another scene, we see the farcical Father Clement floating around clandestinely at night in his flowing monk's robe with its ample cowl. During Father Clement's attempts to seduce Bella, he accidentally finds himself with a Madame Verbouc. As he assaults her, Monsieur Verbouc enters and we are given a somewhat comic descriptive scene of the monk being caught midflow. Fleeing as fast as he can, he is pursued by the irate husband: "Dodging as well as he could the cuts which Mons. Verbouc aimed at him, and keeping the hood of his frock over his features to avoid detection, he rushes toward the window by which he entered, then taking a headlong leap he made good his escape in the darkness, followed by the infuriated husband."

In a later scene, Bella returns to the young farming lad she encountered earlier, and he and his father want to have sex with her. She is frightened but does not put up much resistance. The boy exclaims: "I want you to see father's cock; my gum! you ought to see his cods, too." The tale explores homosexual incest between father and son. After his father has taken Bella, "Tim, with true filial care, proceeded to wipe it [his father's penis] tenderly and return it, pendant and swollen with its late excitement, within his father's shirt breeches." The father masturbates the son before he enters Bella—this seems to happen frequently, and the boy enjoys it, as he explains, "Father frigs me and I like it." Even stranger, after having Bella, Tim cannot "spend." The father blames himself for masturbating the boy too frequently: "It's the frigging. I frig him so often that he misses it now."

This book incorporates the gamut of sexual experience—fellatio, cunnilingus, and incestuous relationships: between father, son, and daughter, and including incestuous homosexuality and sodomy.

JULIE PEAKMAN

Editions

First edition, London. "1789" [1885]; reprints c. 1886, c. 1887, c. 1890, c. 1895, 1901, c. 1915, c. 1921, "1901" [c. 1930].

Further Reading

Kearney, Patrick. *The Private Case: An Annotated Bibliography of the Private Case Erotic Collection in the British (Museum) Library* (pp. 104–106). London: Jay Landesman, 1981.

Mendes, Peter. *Clandestine Erotic Literature in English, 1800–1930* (pp. 127–130). London: Scholar Press, 1993.

AVANTURES SATYRIQUES DE FLORINDE, LES

1625
Anonymous

Who wrote *Les avantures satyriques de Florinde habitant de la Basse Région de la Lune* (hence *Florinde*)? It is usually catalogued as having an anonymous author. However, Bertrand Guégan, in the introduction to the 1928 edition, discusses possible authors. The three most interesting of all these possibilities are discussed below.

Certain elements of the text suggest to Guégan that *Florinde* is not by a French writer, and he suggests the name of Henry de Codony (or Codoni). This is based on the initials *C* and *I* before the text, which Guégan interprets to stand for Codony, Italian. Also, in the text, the author mentions that he is Italian and a favorite of the French king Louis XIII. This also fits with what is known of Codony's life. He was acquainted with Tristan l'Hermite, who led a picaresque life reminiscent of Florinde's. Additionally, he spent some time in jail. This may indicate why *Florinde* remains an anonymous text, because its author did not want to risk further punishment.

It so happens that in 1625 a ballet (*Les fées de la forêt de Saint-Germain*) was performed at the Louvre. This ballet included the character of an aged fairy, as does *Florinde,* danced by a certain Delfin (a name most assuredly based on the Italian anagram, R. Delfino, or Florinde in French). Nothing else is available about Delfin.

Of all the possible authors suggested by Guégan, the best known is Charles Sorel (1599–1674). Sorel wrote *Histoire comique de Francion* (1623), a text he modified, corrected, and toned down in subsequent editions from 1626 (the year following the original publication of *Florinde*) to 1641. Attributing *Florinde* to Sorel stems from the language and scenes found in the *Histoire comique de Francion,* which can remind one of some of those found in *Florinde.* The similarity in the structure of the titles has certainly contributed to this suggestion. Yet, vocabulary selection seems to indicate that different authors wrote the two texts.

Florinde is divided into five parts (*livres*) written in prose and in verse. It tells the adventures of Florinde as he travels through a country that evokes a bucolic Greece in an undetermined age. Florinde himself is compared to Ulysses and, at some point, seeks the help of the goddess Diana. At times, one is also reminded of the landscapes described in the French *romans précieux* of the same period. Additionally, Florinde is not a common name. It appears in Voltaire's *Essai sur les moeurs* (chapter XXVII) as the name of the daughter of Count Julien who may have been raped by Rodrigue.

Most of *Florinde* takes place around the town of Ephèse, as well as the castle of Assotie, where the witch (*magicienne*) Upérorque reigns. In the first part, Florinde runs into trouble because of his many feminine acquaintances. What starts as jealousy will bring upon Florinde the wrath of Upérorque wherever he may be. He must flee but cannot avoid the attack of a monster on a beach.

In the second part, the forces of evil organize against Florinde. He is able to escape through a tunnel with the help of a gentle nymph. In the process, he meets an old hermit who will protect Florinde from Upérorque and one of her accomplices by giving him a holy reliquary.

In the third book, as a storm rages by, Florinde finds refuge with his traveling companions in a cave, where they meet three nymphs and an old woman who turns out to be a witch. They escape and later are attacked by demons. They spend the night in an inn. Florinde befriends the wife of the absent innkeeper and they retire to her bedchamber. Her husband returns unexpectedly, and as often happens to Florinde, his lovemaking is interrupted. He manages to escape again.

Several conversations take place at the beginning of the fourth part. The initial one discusses how a virgin makes love for the first time. Another mentions what happens when a woman finds her lover in bed with her maid. As for Florinde, he wonders whether he should get involved or wait for a better opportunity. He decides to get involved with Coryne. They meet in Gontade. The text then provides a detailed description of their lovemaking.

In the last book, Florinde spends a fair amount of time with his friend, Piston, who lives in a beautiful house with exquisitely designed gardens. Florinde overhears the conversation between a mother and daughter. She wants to sell her daughter's virginity several times and turn her into a whore. Florinde eventually reaches the residence of witches. Inside, he finds several young women and an old witch who fills the room with a foul-smelling vapor. Florinde apparently kills a lion that attacks him, but he soon discovers that he has killed a man wearing a lion's pelt. Soon thereafter, Florinde is visited in a dream by a woman. He realizes that she is Philosophy. She has come to cure him of deep-rooted, unpleasant-smelling ulcers. She also convinces Florinde that "he must reform his life and despise the dirty voluptuousness the seeking of which, so filled with difficulties, sometimes gives repentance at the same time as sexual release" (*Florinde*, p. 139. Translated from the French by Claude Fouillade).

Florinde resolves to leave all this bitterness behind. When he finds himself close to Ephèse, his reason overcomes his heart and he decides to return to France. He sails around the *Isles Aériennes*. In the end, Florinde decides to settle in Paris, a town in which he finds that life is pleasant to live, and has himself naturalized "a true Frenchman."

The author of *Florinde* is undoubtedly a learned *libertin* (P. Pia suggests that *Florinde* contains reminiscences of the *Dialogues des courtisanes* and the *Euphormion*). To this list should be added the sixteenth-century classic *Lazarillo de Tormes*. Both poems and prose in this work are filled with double entendres, whose meaning has been lost through the centuries, the allusion to the *basse région de la lune* notwithstanding. It has also been suggested that *Florinde* hints at the attacks that were made against the "libertine scoundrels" of the time. Yet, *Florinde* research proposes that Upérorque is a personification of the Roman Catholic Church; it further suggests that other *magiciennes* are muses that work to bring about the ruin of mankind.

CLAUDE FOUILLADE

Selected Works

Les Avantures satyriques de Florinde habitant de la basse région de la lune. From a manuscript of 1625, with etchings by J.-E. Laboureur, introduction by Bertrand Guégan. Paris: Au Cabinet du Livre, 1928.

Further Reading

Minazzoli, Gilbert, ed. *Dictionnaire des oeuvres érotiques: Domaine francais*, with a preface by Pascal Pia. Paris: Mercure de France, 1971.
Minazzoli, Gilbert, ed. *Dictionnaire des oeuvres érotiques: Domaine francais, table de renvois, répertoire des auteurs et des oeuvres*, with a preface by Pascal Pia. Paris: Robert Laffont, 2001.

B

BABEL, ISAAC EMMANUILOVICH

1895–1939
Russian-Jewish short story writer, dramatist, and screenwriter

Isaac Emmanuilovich Babel, author of many short stories, two plays, several screenplays, and numerous newspaper articles, must be considered, after Chekhov and Bunin, one of the greatest, if not the greatest Russian short story writer of the 20th century and arguably the greatest Russian erotic writer of that period. His prose style combines laconism with bright, original imagery, and his stories from all periods are suffused with a playful and provocative eroticism that takes many forms. In several stories there is a clear link between seduction and the act of artistic creation.

In "Guy de Maupassant," 1932, the narrator uses Maupassant's story "L'aveu" together with a made-up story about himself as means of seducing Raisa Benderskaia, whose only passion in life is the French author. "My First Fee," 1939, also features a made-up story. The narrator tells about himself as a male prostitute to overcome his initial inability to perform and win the sympathy of the prostitute Vera, who is so taken with the story that she engages him in a night of lesbian sex. The switching of sex roles is ironic, as the narrator, who was looking for his first sexual engagement, ends up pretending he is a male prostitute and receives the love a woman gives to another woman. Babel's description of their night of love is perhaps the most exuberant of its kind in all of Russian literature: "Now tell me, I would like to ask you about this—have you ever seen how country carpenters build a house for their fellow carpenter, how hot and fast and gaily the chips fly from the log they are planning? That night a thirty-year old woman taught me the tricks of her trade. I learned secrets that night you will never learn; I experienced a love you will never experience; I heard the works of a woman meant for another woman. I have forgotten them. It is beyond us to remember them" (my translation from *Sochineniia* 2, 252).

Sex by transaction figures prominently in Babel. In "Fee" the narrator in effect trades his story for sex, as Vera refuses the fee they had agreed on. In "A Hardworking Woman," 1928, Anelia makes a deal to have sex with three officers for two pounds of sugar but stops in the middle with the third man. In a related story,

"At Our Father Makhno's," 1923, however, violence takes the place of transaction, as six men rape a young woman. "The Kiss," 1937, an echo of a Chekhov story with the same title, ends when the narrator, whose lover keeps asking when he will take her and her family away with him from the front, does not hold up his end of an implicit bargain and leaves her after a night of love.

Voyeurism is found in a number of stories, most graphically in "Through a Crack," 1917, where the narrator arranges with the proprietor of a brothel to watch young women and their clients having sex. In later stories voyeurism appears in a subtler form, as for example in "My First Love," 1925, in which the ten-year-old narrator is in love with his neighbor's wife. As is evident from titles such as "First Fee" and "First Love," initiations, sexual and otherwise, are an important theme in Babel.

Some of Babel's best erotic passages are associated with a woman taking pity on a man, as happens in "First Fee." In "Doudou," 1917, a French nurse has sex with a dying officer as a kind of final act of tender mercy. She is fired for this but does not regret her action. The reader may sense the motive of male sexual wish fulfillment in passages like this one.

Heterosexual eroticism is predominant in Babel, but there are some fascinating instances of homosexual eroticism as well. In "My First Goose," 1920, the narrator is entranced with the beauty of Savitsky's gigantic body. "He smelled of perfume and the cloying cool of soap. His long legs looked like girls sheathed to the shoulders in shining jackboots" (*Sochineniia* 2). The image of girls may act here as a heterosexual cover for the homoeroticism that would have been considered more "risky" by contemporary readers and critics. Similarly, at the end of the story the narrator lies sleeping, legs entangled with those of the other soldiers, all the while dreaming of women. "The Awakening," 1931, also contains suggestions of homoeroticism, as the narrator is envious of the bronze tans of the local boys and their ability to swim. He loves their coach and mentor Smolich, "as only a young boy who is sick with hysteria and headaches can love an athlete" (*Sochineniia* 2).

The sudden switches in sexual roles in Babel are emblematic of his whole fictional world, where one's identity is always being tested, and where it may be revealed in the most unexpected ways. Eroticism is an essential feature of Babel's prose, and as with his other central themes, he continually plays variations on his various erotic themes in all kinds of different contexts.

Biography

Born in the largely Jewish Moldavanka district of Odessa, June 30, 1894. Studied English, French, and German at a commercial school and Hebrew at home; read a great deal, especially French literature. Wrote his first stories in French. Graduated from a commercial institute in Kiev, 1915. Charged with writing pornography ("Through the Window"), 1917 (charges mooted by the Revolution). Married Evgenia Borisovna Gronfein, 1919; father of scholar Nathalie Babel. Wrote sketches for Maxim Gorkii's newspaper, 1919. Worked as a newspaper correspondent during the Civil War on the Polish front with the Red Army's First Cavalry, 1920. First became known with publication of *Red Cavalry* stories, 1923–24. Had relationship with Tamara Kashirina (later Tamara Ivanova), 1925–26; father of artist Mikhail Ivanov. Visited France, where wife Evgenia emigrated, from 1927 to 1935. Set up household with Antonina Nikolaevna Pirozhkova, 1935; father of Lydia. Knew French writers André Gide and André Malraux. Offered contract for collected works, 1938. Arrested May 15, 1939; falsely charged with spying for France and Austria and being a terrorist. Shot in prison January 27, 1940. Exonerated, 1954.

VICTOR PEPPARD

Selected Works

Collected Stories by Isaac Babel. Introduction by Lionel Trilling. Edited and translated by Walter Morison. New York: Criterion Books, 1955.

Isaac Babel, The Lonely Years: 1925–1939: Unpublished Stories and Correspondence. Edited and introduced by Nathalie Babel. Revised 1995.

You Must Know Everything. Edited by Nathalie Babel. New York: Farrar, Straus and Giroux, 1966.

Sochinenia [*Works*]. Compiled by A. N. Pirozhkova. Commentary by S. N. Povartsova. 2 vols. Moscow: Khudozhestvennaia literatura, 1990.

1920 Diary [of Isaac Babel]. Edited and introduced by Carol J. Avins. Translated by H. T. Willetts. New Haven, CT: Yale University Press, 1995.

The Complete Works of Issac Babel. Edited by Nathalie Babel. Translated with notes by Peter Constantine.

Introduction by Cynthia Ozick. Chronology of Babel's life by Gregory Freidin. New York: Norton, 2002.

Further Reading

Bloom, Harold (ed., with introduction). *Isaac Babel, Modern Critical Views*. New York: Chelsea House Publishers, 1987.

Carden, Patricia. *The Art of Isaac Babel*. Ithaca and London: Cornell University Press, 1973.

Ehre, Milton. *Isaac Babel: Twayne's World Author Series*. Boston: Twayne Publishers, 1986.

Falen, James. *Isaac Babel, Russian Master of the Short Story*. Knoxville: University of Tennessee Press, 1974.

Hallett, Richard William. *Isaac Babel: Modern Literature Monographs*. New York: Ungar, 1973.

Luplow, Carol. *Isaac Babel's Red Cavalry*. Ann Arbor: Ardis, 1982.

Mann, Robert. *The Dionysian Art of Isaac Babel*. Oakland: Barbary Coast Books, 1994.

Pirozhkova, Antonina. *At His Side: The Last Years of Isaac Babel*. Translated by Anne Frydman and Robert L. Busch. South Royalton, VT: Steerforth Press, 1996.

Vospominania o Babele [Reminiscences about Babel]. Compiled by A. N. Pirozhkova and N. N. Urgeneva, with articles by Lev Slavin, Pirozhkova, Urgeneva. Moscow: Izdatel'stvo Knizhnaia palata, 1989.

Zholkovsky, A. K., and M. B. Iampolsky. *Babel* (in Russian). Moscow: Carte Blanche, 1994.

BAI, XINGJIAN

?–826 CE
Chinese poet and novelist

Tiandi yinyang jianohuan dale fu [*Prose Poem on the Supreme Joy of the Sexual Union of Yin and Yang, Heaven and Earth*]

The text of the *Tiendi yinyang jiaohuan dale fu*, quite apart from its unique content, has had a long and checkered history. Written in the late eighth or early ninth century by Bai Xingjian, the only received copy was immured around 1000 CE in the Cave of a Thousand Buddhas at Dunhuang on the Silk Road. Temple guardian Wang Yuanlu (d. 1931) discovered the work in a secret cache of thousands of scrolls, selling many to Aurel Stein (1861–1911) in 1907 and Paul Pelliot (1879–1945) in 1908, a fact regarded as an act of cultural preservation in the West and cultural piracy in China.

Spirited to the Bibliotheque Nationale in Paris, the text was kept under lock and key by Pelliot, much to the chagrin of other Sinologists, until a visiting Chinese dignitary, naval secretary and Hebei viceroy Duan Fang (1861–1911) was allowed to examine and photograph it. Shortly thereafter, in 1913, Lo Zhenyu (1866–1940) published a collotype reproduction in Beijing as part of his *Manuscripts from the Dunhuang Caves* [*Dunhuang shishi yishu*]. Ye Dehui (1864–1927) published an annotated edition in 1914 in his *Twin Plum Tree Shadows* collection [*Shuangmeijinga congshu*], and Robert van Gulik made further emendations in his 1951 *Erotic Colour Prints of the Ming Period*. The Dunhuang manuscripts bear the name Bai Xingjian (d. *c.* 826), younger brother of major Tang poet Bai Juyi, an attribution questioned only by the pseudonymous author of the colophon appended to the 1913 collotype edition.

As a literary genre, the fu—a prose-poem or poetical essay—was gestated during the Warring States period (475–221 BCE), perfected during the Han dynasty (206 BCE–220 CE), and continued into the Tang dynasty (618–907) to serve as a vehicle for extended meditations in an elegant yet loose verse form. Although the *fu* sometimes degenerated into mere literary tour de force, the *Prose Poem on the Supreme Joy* is original in its subject matter and serious in its purpose, and in spite of numerous scribal errors, rewards the reader with many vivid passages evoking the entire scope of sexual experience. It offers a rare alternative to the didactic purpose of sex handbooks and sexual alchemy on the one hand and the often cynical and perverse tone of pornographic novels on the other.

The first two sections set the stage by proclaiming the cosmic, social, and psychological significance of the sex act. Sex is the microcosmic enactment of the mating of heaven and earth, yin and yang; it is the most fundamental of human bonds, the object of our greatest desire, and the source of our highest pleasure. Section 3 describes the conception, constitutions, and maturation of males and females. At puberty, "her warm moist complexion resembles jade ... her hands are as pure as snow," and with thoughts turning to love, it is time to consult a matchmaker. Painted in auspicious red tones, the fourth section describes the wedding night, on which as bride and groom repair to a room suffused with "red light," the groom reveals his "crimson bird" and loosens his bride's "vermilion trousers." As he "raises her feet and caresses her buttocks," she clasps his "jade stalk" and the couple consummate "the union of yin and yang" that will bind them together forever.

The fifth section, the longest, is an exposition of the infinite possibilities in lovemaking. Temporally, it may be moonlight or daylight, spatially a tall pavilion or open window, and inspiration may come from the handbooks of sex or erotic paintings. Her gossamer and embroidered garments are shed and the gentleman drinks in her beauty with hands and eyes. He may place her feet on his shoulders or pull her skirt above her belly. Deep kisses and tight embraces cause his "jade stalk to be enraged" and her "nether lips to part." As her scented secretions flow, he thrusts from above and below, left and right, from the "zither strings" at one-inch depth to the "grain seed" at five inches. He may penetrate shallowly, "like a suckling infant," or deeply, "like a freezing snake slithering into its hole." When she makes purring sounds, her skin is flushed and hair disheveled, he will be moved to even greater efforts as his seminal essence penetrates all the way to her womb. Languid and lubricious with secretions, maidservants wash her with scented water, help her change her gown, and repair her coif and makeup.

The sixth section displays the more varied palate of pleasures that the gentleman of leisure may explore with his seductive and talented concubines. He experiments with more acrobatic positions, anal intercourse, and fellatio, together with female prone and female superior postures. But in the end, he observes the bedroom arts' injunction to "return the essence and withhold emission; inhale a breath and swallow the saliva."

The seventh section is a sexual symphony in four movements based on the four seasons. In spring, couples sport in the women's quarters, like orioles and swallows mating in the woods. In summer, nature's luxuriance casts its reflections on the bedchamber, or the couple may dally in the gardens or pools. In autumn, fans are put away, bed curtains are drawn, and strings play a somber tune. In the winter, lovers surround themselves with embroidered quilts, woolen carpets, sandalwood incense, hot wine, and charcoal braziers. In the season of old age, though weak and withered, couples find it even easier to perfect the bedroom arts.

The eighth section describes the sex life of the emperor amidst his legions of secondary wives, concubines, courtesans, musicians, dancers, singers, and slave girls. As a diversion, his Majesty randomizes his favors by riding about the palace grounds in a goat cart, while eager women hang bamboo leaves on their door latches to attract the goat. The author mentions that the ancient ideal of the emperor sporting with nine lesser wives each night, culminating in coition for procreation with the empress at the end of each month, had lapsed by Tang times and that in the absence of protocol, all 3,000 women openly vied for the privilege of his bed, adding wryly that "the bodies of these myriad women are served up to this or that man."

Section 9 describes the loneliness of single men and the longing of travelers for lovers far away, their loss of appetite, wanness, pining, sleeplessness, and dreams. Section 10 describes forbidden fruit and stolen moments, when bold men steal into the women's quarters to find shy virgins too frightened to cry, married women who feign sleep and offer no resistance, and welcoming women who come to a bad end. These unceremonious assignations and surreptitious trysts in unconventional settings, for all their fear and trembling, can be far more exciting than tamer sessions in one's own bed. The eleventh section describes the love of lower-class women, citing famous men like Guo Pu and Ruan Xian, who were not ashamed to proclaim their love for their maidservants. Section 12 describes ugly, unkempt, foulmouthed, and malodorous women, such as the wives of men like Liang Hong and Xu Yun. Section 13 describes temptations of nuns who forsake their vows and willingly accept the advances of noblemen, famous scholars, priests, and tall foreign monks with great members. The fourteenth section deals with male homosexual relations by chronicling notorious emperors and their famous favorites. The truncated last section begins with the lives of rough country people before ending in lacuna.

Summarizing the significance of the *Prose Poem on the Supreme Joy* in Chinese literature and in the history of world erotic literature, it is the only received full-length treatment of human sexuality in a literary form from the imperial period. Philosophically, it accepts sexual desire and sexual behavior as natural, without any suggestion that repression or abstinence has a legitimate role in ethical or spiritual practice. As a literary work, its main theme is the celebration of sex for all strata, all ages, and all circumstances, but its panoramic sweep also takes in the suffering of deprivation, though remaining mute on the subject of widowhood. While not questioning the institutions of polygamy, concubinage, and slavery, it focuses mainly on mutually pleasurable relations but does not neglect the vulnerability of women preyed upon in their quarters by opportunistic men. There is implied criticism of the hypocrisy of Buddhist monks and nuns and the irony of the imbalance of thousands of women serving one emperor. As a typical literatus of the period, the author demonstrates a grasp of the language and

principles of the handbooks of sex, a knowledge of the sexual peccadillos of famous persons in earlier times, and mastery of poetic descriptions of lovemaking against the background of nature and the refined lifestyle of the upper class. The work confirms the scholarly consensus that the Tang was a period of relative sexual freedom that preceded the Song, when the Neo-Confucian cult of chaste widowhood and prudery held sway for the next thousand years.

Biography

Younger brother of major Tang poet Bai Juyi, Xingjian was an outstanding author in his own right. According to his biographies in the *Old Tang History* and *New Tang History,* he was a *jinshi* licentiate, holder of numerous official posts, and author of the famous Tang novel *The Story of Li Wa* [*Li Wa zhuan*].

DOUGLAS WILE

Editions

"Tiandi yinyang jiaohuan dale fu," in *Dunhuang shishi yishu*, 1913; *Shuangmei jingan congshu*, 1914; *Erotic Colour Prints of the Ming Dynasty*, 1951; *Sexual Life in Ancient China*, 1961.

Further Reading

Liu Dalin. *Zhongguo gudai xing wenhua.* Yinchuan: Ningxia renmin chubanshe, 1993.
Van Gulik, R. H. *Erotic Colour Prints of the Ming Period.* Tokyo: privately printed, 1951; *Sexual Life in Ancient China*, Leiden: E. J. Brill, 1961.

BALZAC, HONORÉ DE

1799–1850
French novelist and dramatist

Throughout his writings, Balzac's literary allusiveness reveals a deep fascination with the Western erotic canon. He claimed that the *Satyricon* was the Roman equivalent of one of

his own *scènes de la vie privée,* while lamenting in the *Avant-Propos* to *La comédie humaine* (1842), that Petronius's satire excited his curiosity more than it satisfied it. One of his most memorable creations, Valérie Marneffe in *La Cousine Bette* (1846), is described by him in the wake of Laclos's erotic masterpiece *Les liaisons dangereuses* as a "bourgeois Madame de Merteuil." Other works recalled by him from the eighteenth-century libertine tradition include Louvet de Couvray's *Les amours du chevalier de Faublas.* One of his early pseudonymous works of fiction, *Jean-Louis, ou la fille trouvée,* was devised in conscious imitation of Pigault-Lebrun's licentious *romans gais.* The features of Laurence Sterne's writings that made them such an important source of inspiration for Balzac were several but included Sterne's gift for witty sexual innuendo. The practice of Sterne and of Balzac's acknowledged predecessor Rabelais (Balzac's fellow native of Touraine) were explicitly recalled in many of his early works and were the predominant literary influence on the *Physiologie du mariage* (1830), a composition the scabrous nature of which made it necessary for it to be attributed to a "young bachelor" and to be preceded by the warning "Ladies not admitted." This was followed by a series of tales (*Les contes drolatiques,* 1832–37) which imitated Rabelaisian subject matter and attempted to revive, albeit with scant philological exactitude, Rabelais's sixteenth-century French. Only the first three *dixains* were ever completed.

Balzac's exploration of sexual love and desire was, however, by no means restricted to a continuation of established erotic genres. In *La fille aux yeux d'or* (1835), the voluptuary and dandy de Marsay proclaims: "Everyone speaks of the immorality of *Les liaisons dangereuses* and that other book that has a maid's name for its title [the transparent reference here is to de Sade's *Justine,* a novel responsible for the name borne by the maids in both *La peau de chagrin* (1831) and *Petites misères de la vie conjugale* (1842)], but there exists a horrible and appalling book that is sordid, corrupt and always open, a book that will never be closed, the vast book that is the world we inhabit, to say nothing of another book a thousand times more dangerous and which consists of all the things men whisper, or ladies utter behind their fans, to each other every evening at the ball." There could hardly be a more eloquent description of Balzac's *Human Comedy,* which, in addition to highlighting the economic and political workings of early-nineteenth-century France, is a vast sexual comedy. To the fore is the author's unrivalled insight into feminine psychology. (His great objection to Walter Scott, whose work in other respects he so admired, was his puritanical depiction of

passion.) The institution of marriage and its social and psychological significance are dissected by him with unerring dexterity. The contrasting female types in the *Comédie humaine* are remarkable for their range. There are studies of naive virgins and wives devoid of sexuality, as well as sexually aware wives who are unhappy or unfaithful. In the provincial novel *La vieille fille* (1837), the middle-aged Mademoiselle Cormon's virginity is an encumbrance to her. The sexual ignorance she displays in her desperate hunt for a husband is treated in a comic mode, though there is a sting in the tail: She ends up choosing a suitor who is impotent. The unwilling sexual repression of the eponymous protagonist of *La cousine Bette,* on the other hand, leads to paroxysms of jealousy and a violent expression of hatred and spite, while in *Le lys dans la vallée* (1835) Félix de Vandenesse is ensnared by de Marsay's mistress, the man-eating Lady Dudley. Lesbianism is hinted at in *La cousine Bette* and treated more explicitly in *La fille aux yeux d'or,* a work that may well have its origin in George Sand's relationship with the actress Marie Dorval. The courtesans who play such a prominent part in the *Comédie humaine* come from different backgrounds and each possess a distinct character. As the contemporary critic Jules Janin put it, with all the venom of professional envy, "Woman is Monsieur de Balzac's invention."

While many of Balzac's male characters have a public life in business, politics, journalism or letters, they too are remarkable for their sharply differentiated sexuality. The range of sexual appetite and attraction they exhibit is knowingly communicated to the reader. Both individually and collectively, Balzac's heterosexual males are condemned never to find satisfaction. They oscillate in their attraction to complementary female types, thereby situating the sexual ideal in promiscuity rather than a monogamous relationship. The extreme cases include Baron Hulot's priapism (not pedophilia, as is sometimes stated) in *La cousine Bette.* The bourgeois parvenu, in contrast to his libertine seniors, is, on the other hand, pilloried for seeking value for money. Male homosexuality features prominently. In the closing pages of *Illusions perdues* (1837–43), a scene much admired by Proust, the central figure in the *Comédie humaine,* the eloquent and predatory ex-convict Vautrin, picks up the suicidal Lucien de Rubempré. His homosexual nature, already apparent from his befriending of Rastignac in *Le père Goriot* (1835), becomes more explicit in *Splendeurs et misères des courtisanes* (1845–55). *Le cousin Pons* (1847) features the homosocial bonding of Pons and Schmucke. Balzac is no less suggestive in his depiction of sexuality's twilight zones, as can be seen from the numerous examples of a transference of gender characteristics. M. de Valois's studied art of flirtation in *La vieille fille* might be thought to place him in opposition to his impotent rival, yet the contrast is subtly complicated by the ambiguity present in the depiction of him as a "ladies' man." The short story *Sarrasine* (1831) depicts the indeterminate sexuality of a castrato, while the Swedenborgian *Séraphîta* (1835) features the ideal figure of the androgyne. *Une passion dans le désert* (1837), which relates a solider's infatuation with a female panther, has been seen as a study of sexual aberration but, as Herbert J. Hunt has pointed out, is much more likely to be "a [humorous] comparison between the felinity of women and the femininity of panthers."

There emerges from all of Balzac's novels, but in the complex myth that is constructed around sexual excess and sexual abstinence in *La peau de chagrin* (1831) in particular, an acute sense of the problematic nature of sexual desire and its incompatibility with the fabric of society's institutions. Examples of virtuous or idealized love are rare and, in the exemplary case of Henriette de Mortsauf in *Le lys dans la vallée*, ends, revealingly, in her death. *La muse du département* (1843) has a bitter lesson for Dinah de la Baudraye, who misreads the significance of the journalist Lousteau's vacation affair with her and duly pays the price: The relationship is doomed, and she has no choice but to return to her impotent husband.

There are signs that incestual feelings (brother/sister in *la fille aux yeux d'or*, father-daughter in *Le père Goriot*) enjoy a privileged status in the author's *imaginaire*. The novels indeed offer rich pickings for the psychoanalytic critic, who will also find much to ponder in the author's own biography. Beginning with his early, requited, passion for Madame de Berny, Balzac was attracted to women who were more than old enough to be his mother (his relationship with his actual mother remained notoriously difficult). His affair with Madame Hanska was conducted more by correspondence than in the flesh. She was already in her ninth year of widowhood when, in the year of his own death, they were married. There were contemporary rumors that he enjoyed at least one homosexual relationship (for example, with Jules Sandeau; or with his groom Anchises, of whom there is a telling reflection in the pretty groom who appears in *La maison Nucingen*, 1838).

Biography

Born in Tours, May 20, 1799. Boarded at *pension* in Tours, 1804–07; educated by the Oratorians in Vendôme, 1807–13; at the Collège de Tours, 1814; the Institution Lepitre, Paris, 1814; and the Lycée Charlemagne, Paris 1815–16; enrolled Faculty of Law, Paris and worked as lawyer's clerk, 1816–19. Gained law degree but abandoned law for literature, 1819. Completed first literary work, *Cromwell,* a five-act verse tragedy (unpublished), 1819. Began lasting relationship with 45-year-old Laure de Berny ("La Dilecta"), 1822. Published popular fiction with Liberal overtones under pseudonyms Lord R'Hoone and Horace de Saint-Aubin (partly in collaboration with others), 1822–24. Began love affair with the 42-year-old Duchesse d'Abrantès, 1825; helped her write the first volumes of her memoirs. In business as printer, 1826–28; ended in financial ruin. Publication of *Le dernier chouan,* the earliest of his works to be included in *La comédie humaine;* death of father (Bernard-François Balzac), 1829. Prolific output as journalist and author of short stories ("scenes of private life" and philosophical tales), 1829–32, after which devoted increasingly to novels. Failed relationship with the Marquise de Castries, 1831–32. Began correspondence with admirer from Ukraine, Mme Eveline Hanska ("L'Etrangère"), 1832. Converted to neo-legitimism, partly to please Mme de Castries, 1832. Met Mme Hanska in Switzerland, 1833. Relationship with Maria du Fresnay; second meeting with Mme Hanska (now his mistress) in Geneva, 1833–34. Birth of daughter by Marie, 1834. Met Mme Hanska in Vienna, 1835 (eight years elapsed before they met again). Birth of probable son (by Sarah, Countess Guidoboni-Visconti); death of Mme de Berny, 1835. Visited Italy with Caroline Marbouty disguised as pageboy, 1836. Extensive travels in Italy, 1837. President of the Société des gens de lettres, 1839 (honorary president, 1841). Staged *Vautrin* (immediately banned) in Paris, 1840. Relationship with housekeeper, Louise Breugniot (known as Mme de Brugnol), 1840. Visited Touraine and Brittany, probably with Hélène de Valette, 1841. Publication of the "Avant-Propos de *La comédie humaine*," 1842. Met recently widowed Mme Hanska in St Petersburg; returned via Germany and Belgium, 1843. Chevalier de la Légion d'honneur, 1845. Traveled extensively with Mme Hanska in Europe, 1845–46; stillbirth of their child, 1846. Lived with her in Paris for part of 1847; and in Ukraine, 1847–48. Returned to Paris alone; failed to be elected to the Académie française, 1848 and 1849. Returned to Ukraine, 1848–50. Severe bouts of illness, 1849–50. Married Mme Hanska, 1850. Died in Paris, August 18, 1850, survived by wife and mother.

MICHAEL TILBY

Selected Works

(date of publication is that of the first edition in book form)

Jean Louis, ou la fille trouvée. 1822
Physiologie du mariage, 1830; as *The Physiology of Marriage*
Sarrasine. 1831; as *Sarrasine*
La peau de chagrin. 1831; as *The Magic Skin, The Fatal Skin*, or *The Wild Ass's Skin*
Etude de femme. 1831; as *Study of Woman* or *A Study of a Woman*
Le curé de Tours. 1832; as *The Abbé Birotteau* or *The Vicar of Tours*
Les contes drolatiques. 1832–37; as *Droll Stories*
La femme de trente ans. 1832–42; as *The Woman of Thirty*
Eugénie Grandet. 1833; as *Eugénie Grandet* or *Eugenie Grandet*
La duchesse de Langeais. 1834; as *The Duchesse de Langeais*
Le contrat de mariage. 1834–35; as *A Marriage Settlement* or *The Marriage Contract*
La fille aux yeux d'or. 1835; as *The Girl with the Golden Eyes* or *The Girl with Golden Eyes*
Le père Goriot. 1835; as *Daddy Goriot; or Unrequited Affection, Père Goriot, Old Man Goriot*, or *Old Goriot*
Séraphîta. 1835; as *Séraphîta*
Le lys dans la vallée. 1836; as *The Lily of the Valley* or *The Lily in the Valley*
Une passion dans le désert. 1837; as *A Passion in the Desert*
La vieille fille. 1837; as *An Old Maid* or *The Jealousies of a Country Town*
Illusions perdues. 1837–43; as *Lost Illusions*
La maison Nucingen. 1838; as *The Firm of Nucingen* or *Nucingen and Co.*
Une fille d'Eve. 1839; as *A Daughter of Eve*
Béatrix. 1839–45; as *Béatrix* or *Beatrix: Love in Duress*
Autre étude de femme. 1842; as *Another Study of Woman*

Mémoires de jeunes mariées. 1842; as *Memoirs of Two Young Married Women, Letters of Two Brides*, or *The Two Young Brides*
La muse du département. 1843–44; as *The Muse of the Department*
Honorine. 1844; as *Honorine*
Modeste Mignon. 1844; as *Modeste Mignon*
Petites misères de la vie conjugale. 1845–46; as *Pinpricks of Married Life*
Splendeurs et misères des courtisanes. 1845–55; as *A Harlot's Progress* or *A Harlot High and Low*
La cousine Bette. 1847; as *Cousin Bette, Cousine Bette*, or *Cousin Betty.*
Le cousin Pons. 1847; as *Cousin Pons*

Further Reading

Abramovici, Jean-Christophe. "Cronos écrivain: jeunesse et vieillesse dans les *Contes drolatiques*." In *L'Année balzacienne 1999*, 47–58.
Bar, Francis. "Archaïsme et originalité dans les *Contes drolatiques*." In *L'Année balzacienne 1971*, 189–203.
Baron, Anne-Marie. *Le Fils prodige. L'inconscient de 'La Comédie humaine'.* Paris: Nathan, 1993.
———. *Balzac, ou l'auguste mensonge.* Paris: Nathan, 1998.
Barthes, Roland. *S/Z.* Paris: Seuil, 1970; translated by Richard Miller, London: Jonathan Cape, 1975.
Beizer, Janet L. *Family Plots: Balzac's Narrative Generations.* New Haven, CT: Yale University Press, 1986.
Bernheimer, Charles. "Cashing in on Hearts of Gold: Balzac and Sue." In *Figures of Ill Repute: Representing Prostitution in Nineteenth-Century France.* Cambridge, MA: Harvard University Press, 1985.
Berthier, Philippe. "Balzac du côté de Sodome." In *L'Année balzacienne 1979*, 147–77.
Bichard-Thomine, Marie-Claire. "Le projet des *Contes drolatiques* d'après leurs prologues." In *L'Année balzacienne 1995*, 151–64.
Bolster, Richard. *Stendhal, Balzac et le féminisme romantique.* Paris: Minard, 1970.
Bordas, Eric. "Chronotopes balzaciens. Enonciation topographique de l'Histoire dans les *Contes drolatiques*." *Poétique* 121 (February 2000), 3–20.
———. "L'ordre du temps drolatique." In Nicole Mozet and Paule Petitier (eds), *Balzac dans l'histoire*, 209–21. Paris: SEDES, 2001.
———. "Quand l'écriture d'une préface se dédouble. L'Avertissement et le Prologue des *Contes drolatiques* de Balzac." *Neophilologus*, 82 (1998), 369–83.
Bornet, Richard. "La structure symbolique de *Séraphîta* et le mythe de l'androgyne." In *L'Année balzacienne 1973*, 235–52.
Brua, Edmond. "*La Filandière*, allégorie politique." In *L'Année balzacienne 1973*, 55–74.
Césari, Paul. *Etude critique des passions dans l'oeuvre de Balzac.* Paris: Les Presses modernes, 1938.
Chollet, Roland. "De *Dezesperance d'amour* à la Duchesse de Langeais." In *L'Année balzacienne 1965*, 93–120.
———. "Le second dixain des contes drolatiques." In *L'Année balzacienne 1966*, 85–126.

———. "La jouvence de l'archaïsme." In *L'Année balzacienne 1995*, 135–50.

Citron, Pierre. "Interprétation de *Sarrasine*." In *L'Année balzacienne 1972*, 81–95.

———. "Le rêve asiatique de Balzac." In *L'Année balzacienne 1968*, 303–36.

———. "Sur deux zones obscures de la psychologie de Balzac." In *L'Année balzacienne 1967*, 3–27.

Coquillat, Michelle. "Mme de Mortsauf: la femme-sexe." In *La Poétique du mâle*. Paris: Gallimard, 1982.

Danger, Pierre. *L'Eros balzacien. Structures du désir dans 'La comédie humaine'*. Paris: Corti, 1989.

Delattre, Geneviève, "De *Séraphîta* à *La fille aux yeux d'or*. Conjonction et disjonction des contraires." In *L'Année balzacienne 1970*, 183–226.

Delon, Michel. "Le boudoir balzacien." In *L'Année balzacienne 1998*, 227–45.

Drevon, Marguerite and Jeannine Guichardet. "Fameux sexorama." In *L'Année balzacienne 1972*, 257–74.

Faillie, Marie-Henriette. *La femme et le code civil dans 'La comédie humaine' d'Honoré de Balzac*. Paris: Didier, 1968.

Farrant, Tim. *Balzac's Shorter Fictions. Genesis and Genre*. Oxford: Oxford University Press, 2002.

Felman, Shoshana. "Rereading Femininity," *Yale French Studies* 62 (1981), 19–44.

Frappier-Mazur, Lucienne. "Balzac et l'androgyne. Personnages, symboles et métaphores androgynes dans *La Comédie humaine*." In *L'Année balzacienne 1973*, 253–77.

Frappier-Mazur, Lucienne, and Jean-Marie Roulin (eds.). *L'Erotique balzacienne*. Paris: SEDES, 2001.

Gerstenkorn, Jacques. "Du légitimisme drolatique: *Le Prosne du ioyeulx curé de Meudon*." In *L'Année balzacienne 1988*, 291–303.

Gun, Willem Hendrikus van der. *La courtisane romantique et son rôle dans 'La Comédie humaine' de Balzac*. Assen: van Gorcum, 1963.

Hannoosh, Michele. "La femme, la ville, le réalisme: fondements épistémologiques dans le Paris de Balzac." *Romanic Review* 82.2 (March 1991), 127–45.

Heathcote, Owen. "The Engendering of Violence and the Violation of Gender in Honoré de Balzac's *La fille aux yeux d'or*." *Romance Studies* 22 (Autumn 1993), 99–112.

Hoffmann, Léon-François. "Eros en filigrane: *Le curé de Tours*." In *L'Année balzacienne 1967*, 89–105.

———. "Mignonne et Paquita." In *L'Année balzacienne 1964*, 181–86.

Jameson, Fredric. "Realism and Desire: Balzac and the Problem of the Subject." Chap. 3 in *The Political Unconscious: Narrative as a Socially Symbolic Act*. Ithaca, NY: Cornell University Press; London: Methuen, 1981.

Kelly, Dorothy. "Gender and Rhetoric: Balzac's Clichés." Chap. 2 in *Fictional Genders. Role and Representation in Nineteenth-Century French Narrative*. Lincoln, NE, and London: University of Nebraska Press, 1989.

———. "The Primal Scene of Castration, Voyeurism, and *La fille aux yeux d'or*" and "Romanticism, Voyeurism amd the Unveiling of Woman: Sexual/Textual Ambiguity in *La peau de chagrin Telling Glances*."

Chaps. 3 and 5, respectively, in *Voyeurism in the French Novel*. New Brunswick, NJ: Rutgers University Press, 1992.

Knight, Diana. "Reading as an Old Maid: *La cousine Bette* and Compulsory Heterosexuality." *Quinquereme* 12.1 (January 1989): 67–79.

Le Yaouanc, Moïse. "La physiologie du plaisir selon la *Physiologie du mariage*. Lectures et principes d'un jeune célibataire." In *L'Année balzacienne 1969*, 165–82.

———, "Le plaisir dans les récits balzaciens." In *L'Année balzacienne 1972*, 275–308; *L'Année balzacienne 1973*, 201–33.

Lucey, Michael. "Balzac's Queer Cousins and Their Friends." In *Novel Gazing: Queer Readings in Fiction*, Edited by Eve Kosofsky, 167–98. Durham, NC: Duke University Press, 1997.

Massant, Raymond. "Balzac disciple de Rabelais et maître du conte drolatique." In *Balzac et le Touraine*. Tours: Imprimerie Gibert-Clarey, 1950.

———. "A propos des *Contes drolatiques*: réalités et fictions dans *La Belle Impéria*." *Revue des sciences humaines* (January-June 1950): 49–69.

Matlock, Jann. "Pathological Masterplots: Hysteria, Sexuality, and the Balzacian Novel." In *Scenes of Seduction. Prostitution, Hysteria, and Reading Difference in Nineteenth-Century France*. New York: Columbia University Press, 1994.

Michel, Arlette. *Le Mariage et l'amour dans l'oeuvre romanesque d'Honoré de Balzac*. 4 vols. Lille: Atelier de reproduction des thèses de l'université de Lille III, 1976.

———. *Le mariage chez Honoré de Balzac: Amour et féminisme*. Paris: Les Belles Lettres, 1978.

Milner, Max. "Des dispositifs voyeuristes dans le récit balzacien." In *Balzac, une poétique du roman*, Edited by Stéphane Vachon, 157–71. Saint Denis: Presses universitaires de Vincennes; Montreal: XYZ, 1996.

Mortimer, Armine Kotin. "Le corset de *La Vieille Fille*." In *L'Oeuvre d'identité. Essai sur le romantisme de Nodier à Baudelaire*, Edited by Didier Maleuvre and Catherine Nesci, 39–48. Montreal: Départment d'études françaises, Université de Montréal, 1996.

Mounoud-Anglés, Christiane. *Balzac et ses lectrices. L'affaire du courrier des lectrices de Balzac. Auteur lecteur: l'invention réciproque*. Paris: INDIGO, côté-femmes, 1994.

Mozet, Nicole. *Balzac au pluriel*. Paris: Presses universitaires de France, 1990.

Nesci, Catherine. "Etude drolatique de femmes. Figures et fonction de la féminité dans les *Contes drolatiques*." In *L'Année balzacienne 1985*, 265–84.

———. *La femme mode d'emploi. Balzac de la 'Physiologie du mariage' à 'La Comédie humaine'*. Lexington, KY: French Forum Publishers, 1992.

———. "*Le succube* ou l'itinéraire de Tours en Orient." Essai sur les lieux du poétique balzacien." In *L'Année balzacienne 1984*, 263–95.

Noiray, Jacques. "Images de la machine et imaginaire de la femme chez Balzac." In *L'Année balzacienne 1999 (I)*, 177–88.

Pasco, Allan H. "Death Wish" In *Sick Heroes. French Society and Literature in the Romantic Age, 1750–1850*. Exeter: University of Exeter Press, 1997.

Prendergast, Christopher. "Antithesis and Ambiguity." In *Balzac: Fiction and Melodrama*. London: Edward Arnold, 1978.

Regard, Maurice. "Balzac et Sade." In *L'Année balzacienne 1971*, 3–16.

Riffaterre, Michael. "Contraintes de lecture: l'humour balzacien." *L'Esprit createur* 24.2 (Summer 1984): 12–22.

Robb, Graham. *Balzac*. London and Basingstoke: Picador, 1994.

Rousset, Jean. "*La Comédie humaine* comme répertoire." In *Leurs yeux se rencontrent. La scène de première vue dans le roman*. Paris: Corti, 1981.

Saylor, Douglas B. *The Sadomasochistic Homotext: Readings in Sade, Balzac, and Proust*. New York: Peter Lang, 1993.

Schuerewegen, Franc. "Pour effleurer le sexe: A propos d'*Honorine* de Balzac." *Studia neophilologica* 55.2 (1983): 193–97.

Serres, Michel. *L'Hermaphrodite. Sarrasine sculpteur*. Paris: Flammarion, 1987.

Vachon, Stéphane. "La robe et les armes." In *Balzac ou la tentation de l'impossible*, Edited by Raymond Mahieu and Franc Schuerewegen, 179–90. Paris: SEDES, 1998.

Valentin, Eberhard. "*Le Frère d'armes*, examen de l'archaïsme d'un conte drolatique." In *L'Année balzacienne 1974*, 69–90.

Vanoncini, André. "*La Duchesse de Langeais* ou la mise à mort de l'objet textuel." *Travaux de littérature* 4 (1991): 209–15.

BAN, JIEYU

c. 48–6 BCE
Chinese poet

Ban Jieyu, a poet of Han dynasty (202 BCE–9 CE), is accredited with two *fu* poems, although Kang-I Sun Chang and Haun Saussy have recently cast doubt on her authorship of "Dao su fu" [Rhapsody on Pounding Silk] in *Women Writers of Traditional China: An Anthology of Poetry and Criticism*. The traditional *fu* poem is usually referred to as "rhyme prose" or "rhapsody": Its introduction is in prose, the main body of the poem is based on rhymed verse most of the time, and the conclusion reverts to a prose format. Both introduction and conclusion can take the form of a question or an answer. It is not limited to descriptions and can be used to express philosophical ideas as well as personal emotions. Her "Zi dao fu" [Rhapsody of Self-Commiseration] recalls happy episodes ("Basking in the sage sovereign's generous grace" and "I received highest favor in the Storied Lodge") and sad ones ("Where, still in swaddling clothes, my infant sons met disaster" and "My lord no longer favors me with his presence—who could feel honor in this?") of Ban Jieyu's life. It also harks back to the time when she moved to the Palace of Eternal Trust with the Empress Dowager ("I am hidden in the dark palace, secluded and still") and mentions titles of poems that hint at her displeasure with the ruthless conduct of the ones she considers usurpers, Zhao Feiyan and her sister. She also expresses her desire to please and fulfill the emperor and repay her devotion when she states:

Whether awake or asleep, I sighed repeatedly;
I'd loosen my sash and reflect on myself.
I spread out paintings of women to serve as guiding mirrors. (ll. 11–13)

The third poem, attributed by some to Ban Jieyu is known as "Yuan ge xing" [Song of Resentment]. In it one finds allusive language that shows Ban Jieyu's regret at having lost the affection and interest of the emperor when she recalls a "fan of conjointed bliss" which "goes in and out of my lord's breast and sleeve." Her sorrow at losing his sexual attention is expressed in metaphoric terms that are reminiscent of the process often used in later Chinese erotic anthologies such as *The Jade Terrace Anthology*, commissioned by Emperor Jianwen Di (503–551 CE) of the Liang dynasty.

Biography

Ban Jieyu (Pinyin transcriptions rather than the old Wade-Giles are used throughout; Ban

Jieyu replaces Pan Chieh-yu) is related to Guwutu (604 BCE–?), "nurtured from tiger" in ancient Chinese. Later on, the family chose the Chu name Ban ("striped") for its close association with the same animal. The Ban family eventually moved to an area north of the Great Wall, where its descendants prospered and gained fame; thus the Ban family was able to acquire official ranks at the court. In *Lienu zhuan* [*Traditions of Exemplary Women*], Liu Xiang (79–8 BCE) describes Ban Jieyu as a woman with penetrating intelligence who could write well. She attracted the attention of Emperor Cheng Liu Ao (32–7 BCE), was given an important position in the palace, and was eventually elevated to the rank of consort: *Jieyu* describes her as the imperial concubine. The emperor liked to chat with her when he visited the inner circle and felt comfortable to be around her, especially as he had his mother's approval for doing so. As she was so talented, many people wished for several generations that their daughters might be as bright and intelligent. She came to the favorable notice of the Grand Empress Dowager Wang.

In his introduction to the chapter in the *Han shu* [*The History of the Former Han Dynasty*], written by the historian Ban Gu (32–92 CE), that deals with Emperor Cheng, Homer H. Dubs provides additional information about the life of Ban Jieyu in the imperial palace. As Emperor Cheng's children with his first wife, Empress Xu, all died in infancy, he started to spend more time with his concubines, because according to Confucius, one of the most important duties of a filial son was to father a male heir, even more so in the case of an emperor. First among his concubines he favored Ban Jieyu, a relative of Ban Gu, who had entered the harem as a junior maid but soon rose to the second rank of *favorite beauty*. She remained the emperor's prime favorite for many years and bore him two children. Although sources available agree that one was a male child, there is disagreement regarding the sex of the second child. Both died at a very early age.

Ban Jieyu had to be concerned about how the emperor would be seen, as many sources comment on her refusal to ride with the emperor in his cart; she based her decision on ancient paintings that showed decadent rulers of the Xia, Shang, and Zhou dynasties spending most of their time riding with their concubines when they should have been seen with famous people.

As the emperor wished to secure an heir, Ban Jieyu introduced him to one of her maids, who also became a favorite beauty. Thereafter, Emperor Cheng became so attracted to a dancer known as Flying Swallow (Zhao Feiyan) that he made her part of his harem and she soon replaced Ban Jieyu for the affection of the emperor.

Toward the end of the reign of Emperor Cheng, palace intrigues and accusations increased. The empress became estranged from the emperor, and Zhao Feiyan accused her of performing sorcery against him. Eventually, several members of the court, including the empress's sister, were executed. Ban Jieyu, although accused of being an accomplice, was able to prove through her eloquence that she had not been a participant. In 16 BCE, Zhao Feiyan became empress, and Ban Jieyu came to realize that life at court would soon become untenable for her. She asked permission to leave the harem and to be allowed to care as a lowly servant for the empress dowager in the Palace of Eternal Trust. After the death of Emperor Cheng, she was further removed from the intrigues of the court when she became part of the staff of his funeral park, a position she held until her death.

CLAUDE FOUILLADE

Further Reading

David R. Knechtges. *The Han Rhapsody: A Study of the Fu of Yang Hsiung (53 B.C.–A.D. 18)*. Cambridge: Cambridge University Press, 1976.

New Songs from A Jade Terrace: An Anthology of Early Chinese Love Poetry. Translated with annotations and an introduction by Anne Birrell. London and Boston: Allen & Unwin, 1982.

Pan Ku. *The History of the Former Han Dynasty*. Vol. 2, *First Division: The Imperial Annals*, Chaps. VI–X. A critical edition with annotations by Homer H. Dubs with Pan Lo Chi and Jen Tai. Baltimore: Waverly Press, 1938–1955.

Women Writers of Traditional China: An Anthology of Poetry and Criticism. Edited by Kang-i Sun Chang and Haun Saussy. Stanford, CA: Stanford University Press, 1999.

BARBEY D'AUREVILLY, JULES-AMÉDÉE

1808–1889
French novelist and critic

Les Diaboliques [The She-Devils]

Upon its publication in 1874, Barbey d'Aure-villy's collection of novellas was threatened with prosecution for outrage to public morality. Barbey withdrew the volume from sale, not wanting what he saw as a metaphysical challenge to contemporary attitudes to be bracketed with pornography. It was republished in 1882 after the end of the period of "moral order" of the 1870s and with the relaxation of censorship in 1881.

The six stories all present variations on a conversational frame: an aristocratic salon, a bedroom, in which a speaker gradually unfolds a tale set in a closed world; a small town in Normandy, a Spanish castle, that leads to a violent and surprising climax.

The opening tale, "Le rideau cramoisi" ["The Crimson Curtain"], sets the pattern: The narrator is traveling by night with the vicomte de Brassard, renowned for his military heroism and amorous conquests. As their coach pauses in a small town, a lit window prompts Brassard to retell his first affair. At the age of seventeen, inexperienced in love and war, he was billeted with an elderly couple; their young daughter initiated an intensely physical but totally word-less affair with the officer, crossing her parents' bedroom to visit him every other night until, after six months, she died abruptly in his arms, leaving him panic stricken. The other tales evoke similarly transgressive passions: In "Le Dessous de cartes d'une partie de whist" ["The Underside of the Cards at a Game of Whist"], the aloof Scotsman Marmor de Karkoël has an affair not just with the comtesse de Stasseville, but with her daughter; after the death of both women (the daughter perhaps poisoned) and the departure of Marmor, adultery and incest are completed

with the implication of infanticide when a child's body is found concealed in a flower-tub. The women are strong-willed but deceptive in appearance. A prostitute in a sordid quarter of Paris reveals herself to her client as a Spanish duchess, seeking revenge on her husband by degrading his name: In a jealous rage he had had his cousin, for whom she was consumed with an idolatrous but unconsummated passion, strangled before her and his heart thrown to his dogs. The final scenes are excessive in their combination of physical violence and symbolic profanation. In "A un dîner d'athées" [At a Dinner of Atheists], set in a French garrison in Spain, major Ydow is provoked by his mistress, nicknamed La Pudica because of her virtuous blushes but in reality predatory, sensual, and promiscuous; they fight over the embalmed heart of the child he had thought was his; then, in a possessive rage, he uses the pommel of his sabre to seal her vulva with the wax with which she had been sealing a letter—refusing her sexual autonomy, punishing her with a male symbol of power—and then is run through by Mesnilgrand (a former lover of La Pudica) who has overheard the scene hidden in the cupboard.

Barbey's preface to the first edition claimed that the morality of the collection lay in evoking horror for the scenes depicted. But what Barbey achieves is rather to challenge what he sees as the tepid conformity and banality of the nineteenth century, with its confidence in progress, democracy, and science. His lucid, passionate figures, untroubled by guilt, notably the virile women, defy the limiting conventions of their world. Their "hideous energy" arouses a paradoxical admiration and underlines the persistence of the diabolical in "this time of progress and civilisation." The physical horrors remind the reader that for Barbey the true horrors are in the mind and the soul. Transgression, as Mesnilgrand points out to a diner who has entertained the atheists with a tale of how he threw the consecrated host into a pigsty, has no force without a framework of belief.

The recurrent references to the devil and the diabolical (the French title could mean "Diabolical Tales" as well as "She-Devils") point to the element in human nature that reason cannot pin down: Sexuality and death are intertwined, and at the heart of the stories lies an enigma. Whose is the child whose body is hidden in the flower-tub? What drives Alberte in her reckless affair with Brassard? The narrative offers only "a glimpse of Hell through a cellar window," carefully prepared and delayed, as the narrator constructs a series of stories within stories. In the climax the details (in "A un dîner d'athées," allusions to candles, to porches and openings, to sabres) fall into place, as in a jigsaw. The tales end abruptly, precluding any attempt to find out "what happened next" or to fill in the gaps.

Ce qui ne meurt pas

Barbey completed his novel *Germaine* in 1833 but failed to find a publisher both in 1835 and, after revision, in 1845; a third reworking, *Ce qui ne meurt pas* [*What Never Dies*], was published in 1884. It explores through analysis and dialogue the developing passions between three characters in an isolated Norman chateau: Allan de Cynthry, a beautiful orphan of seventeen; the aloof widow Yseult de Scudemor; and her tomboy daughter of thirteen, Camille. Out of pity, Yseult yields to Allan's adolescent passion, knowing that it will not last; indeed, within two years Allan falls for Camille, whose pregnancy precipitates their marriage. But Yseult is also pregnant by Allan: The discovery of Yseult's child (both half-sister and husband's child) destroys Camille's happiness and precipitates Yseult's death. For all the characters love proves impossible, as it transgresses barriers (age, kinship, marriage); for each character a previous love (for Yseult, a schoolgirl lesbian attachment and an affair with her husband's nephew) undermines reciprocity in a present relationship; and, unlike sterile pity, which "does not die," passion is sensual and transient. Although essentially psychological, the variations on semi-incestuous passion and certain scenes—Allan's desire reawakening as he watches Yseult in bed, Camille undressing for an unmoved Allan on their wedding night—proved audacious in 1835. They were no longer shocking by the 1880s.

Biography

Born in Saint-Sauveur-le-Vicomte, Normandy, November 2, 1808. Educated in Valognes, staying with a liberal and freethinking uncle, then at Collège Stanislas, Paris, 1827–29; studied at the Faculty of Law, Caen, 1829–33. Moved to Paris. Struggled with little success to gain a living as a political and literary critic, collaborating with several reviews and newspapers; became known as a flamboyant dandy, but rapidly exhausted an inheritance. From 1846 his initial rebellion against his backward-looking family shifted to ultraroyalist and Catholic views, and his controversially reactionary and provocative political and literary journalism brought him notoriety; he gradually became known as a novelist (*Le Chevalier des Touches*, 1863). From 1871 stayed increasingly in Valognes. Suffering from liver disease, he fell seriously ill in 1888 and died after a hemorrhage, in Paris, April 23, 1889.

PETER COGMAN

Editions

Les Diaboliques. Paris: Dentu, 1874; Paris, Lemerre, 1882; Edited by Jacques-Henry Bornecque, Paris: Garnier, 1963; in *Œuvres romanesques complètes*, Edited by Jacques Petit, 2 vols, Paris: Gallimard, 1964; Edited by Michel Crouzet, Paris: Imprimerie Nationale, 1989, as *Weird Women*, no translator named, London and Paris: Lutetian Society, 1900; as *Les Diaboliques*, translated by Ernest Boyd, New York: Knopf, 1925; as *Les Diaboliques*, no translator named, London: Elek, 1947; as *The She-Devils*, translated by Jean Kimber, London: Oxford University Press, 1964.

Ce qui ne meurt pas. Paris, Lemerre, 1884; in *Œuvres romanesques complètes*, Edited by Jacques Petit, 2 vols, Paris: Gallimard, 1964; as *What Never Dies*, translated by Sebastian Melmoth (doubtfully attributed to Oscar Wilde), Paris: privately printed (by "Charles Carrington" [Harry Ferdinando]), 1902.

Selected Works

Une vieille maîtresse. 1851
L'Ensorcelée. 1854; as *Bewitched*, translated by Louise Collier Willcox. 1928
Le chevalier des Touches. 1864
Un prêtre marié. 1865
Une page d'histoire. 1882
Le cachet d'onyx (written 1830). 1919

Further Reading

Bellemin-Noël, J. *Diaboliques au divan*. Toulouse: Ombres, 1991.

Bernheimer, Charles. *Figures of Ill-repute*. Cambridge, MA: Harvard University Press, 1989.

Berthier, Philippe. *Barbey d'Aurevilly et l'imagination*. Geneva: Droz, 1978.

Berthier, Philippe. *Un écriture du désir*. Paris: Champion, 1987.

Chartier, Armand B. *Barbey d'Aurevilly*. Boston: Twayne, 1977.

Hirschi, Andrée. "Le 'Procès' des *Diaboliques*." *Revue des Lettres Modernes* (1974): 403–408; *Barbey d'Aurevilly 9: l'histoire des "Diaboliques"*, 6–64.

Milner, Max. "Identification psychanalytique de la perversion dans *Les Diaboliques*." In *Barbey d'Aurevilly cent ans après (1889–1999)*, Edited by Philippe Berthier, 313–325. Geneva: Droz, 1990.

Rogers, Brian. *The Novels and Stories of Barbey d'Aurevilly*. Geneva: Droz, 1967.

Sivert, Eileen Boyd. "Narration and Exhibitionism in *Le Rideau cramoisi*." *Romanic Review* 70 (1979): 146–58.

Tranouez, Pierre. *Fascination et narration dans l'œuvre romanesque de Barbey d'Aurevilly: La scène capitale*. Paris: Minard, 1987.

BATAILLE, GEORGES

1897–1962

French novelist and philosopher

Georges Bataille is impossible to categorize as a writer: Whatever the subject or the discipline to which a particular work of his may be said to belong, Bataille could not really be categorized as a sociologist, a philosopher or an economist, since his whole work emerges from the same source and responds to similar demands. Underlying all of his concerns is a fascination with the dynamic between the life force (represented most particularly by the erotic impulse) and the pull of death. His teachers were the Russian philosopher Leon Chestov, who stimulated in him above all an interest in Nietzsche; the sociologist Marcel Mauss, who caused him to question conventional views of the economic relationships between people in society; and Alexandre Kojève, the Hegelian philosopher, who encouraged his interest in the social organization of society. He was above all influenced by Nietzsche, not simply philosophically, but in the way he lived his life: Like Nietzsche, Bataille considered philosophy as emerging from the experience of life and not from the contemplation of abstract theories. In addition, he was notable as an editor of journals, being responsible for *Documents* (1929–30), *Acéphale* (1936–9) and *Critique* (1946–62), having founded both *Acéphale* and *Critique*, the latter of which was still being published in 2002.

Bataille was also the author of several novels, or perhaps more accurately, narrative texts, in which eroticism is to the fore and which contribute to what may be considered pornographic literature. It is important to insist on the fact that they are "pornographic" rather than "erotic," since Bataille insisted on their unrespectable quality; indeed, he regarded literature itself as accursed, and its works as being "evil," a theme explored in his study *Literature and Evil* (1955). It would be wrong, however, to see these works as set apart from his theoretical texts. Rather, they explore the same themes in different ways, enriching and sometimes commenting upon the themes he raised in his more "respectable" works. Having said this, though, a tension is still maintained between the "respectable" and "unrespectable" texts: During his lifetime, Bataille published most of his novels under pseudonyms and never publicly acknowledged having written them. This tension is central to his understanding of the basis of the erotic relation.

It is important to appreciate that Bataille was a serious writer concerned with fundamental issues. This is as true of his supposedly pornographic literature as it is of his theoretical texts. His novels are "pornographic" not in the sense of being titillating or exploitative, but because they are rending and unbearable and speak of things that should not be spoken of, yet have to be spoken of—a paradox that is central to Bataille's philosophy. Sex is obscene because it is linked to death, which cannot be spoken about and is itself obscene because it undermines the stability and security of life. The fundamental framework of all of his writing is an exploration of what it means to be human and the nature of existence, especially in terms of how people live with one another. His work as a whole may be said to be concerned with one overarching question: How do we come to terms with the fact of our limits and live with the realization that we are discontinuous beings ultimately consigned to death and oblivion?

Central to this is the notion of communication. In order to survive in society, we need to communicate with our fellow beings. Bataille was firmly opposed to the doctrine of individualism that informs so much of Western thinking. He believed that the individual is no more than a concretization of forms and has no existence in and of itself. We are fundamentally social and material beings whose reality is formed by the demands society makes of us. We may accept or fight against such demands, but we cannot ignore them. Birth is a violent process, tearing us from the continuity of the universe, where all things are undifferentiated, and casting us into a world marked by difference. We need to come to terms with the fact that what surrounds us is alien to us. It imposes conditions on us, forces us to take certain paths while disqualifying others, and never allows us to relax into what we are, whatever that may be. We are therefore separated, at a fundamental level, both from ourselves and from others.

Sexual relationships are the locus of experience in which this separation is most acutely and intensely felt. In sexual union, we are drawn to what will annihilate us. It is important to realize that Bataille is not at all an advocate of sexual freedom. Far from it, sexuality is anguish; it defines our torment even as it promises to alleviate it. In its most intense form, in love, this anguish becomes unbearable, especially when we are faced with the loss of what we have loved. The sexual act itself encapsulates this sense of anguish: Drawn into a momentary unity with the other, we are paradoxically forced to confront the essential separateness against which this apparent unity is measured. This is the essential meaning of the "petite mort" experienced in orgasm. "Sexual satisfaction," for Bataille, could be only a fundamental evasion, if not a contradiction in terms.

Eroticism is therefore the cornerstone of Bataille's thinking. It is, far more than language or culture, what distinguishes us from beasts, who experience only functional sexuality and remain within a relative continuity of being. Eroticism is thus linked with death, or rather with the consciousness of death: It is because we, unlike other animals, are aware of the fact that we shall die that our being is so fundamentally anguished. Consciousness itself, then, is founded in knowledge of death: We become aware of ourselves as separated beings when we learn that one day we shall no longer live, that we shall return to the continuity from which we were expelled in being born and that, in the process, all sense of ourselves as individualized, integral beings—so important to us in our existence as social beings—will be lost.

A fascination with form and materiality therefore lies at the heart of Bataille's interrogation. In a very short early text, he posited the idea of the "formless" as that which defies meaning and so subverts everything we cherish in the world. Matter in itself is in fact formless and assumes a form only through the human engagement with it. But there is something accursed about this engagement, since by transforming matter in this way, we become uneasy about the real nature of the material world, which escapes us (this is the conventional separation between nature and culture, but conceived in such a way that culture is seen as a deception we tell ourselves to hide from our true nature, which is brute matter). His materialism emerges from this notion: He was not a common materialist in the sense that he believed that there is only one material world, but rather he asserted materialism as the condition of our existence as human beings, in the process brandishing materialism as a weapon against all "idealism" (by which he meant any belief that makes it possible to transcend the human condition). He termed this conception "base materialism," since it takes us to our roots, which are precisely what we try to deny through a concern for the future and some form of "salvation": These are simply vain attempts to evade the inevitable. This notion, subversive of cultural forms, strips us of our dignity: We are nothing but formless matter pretending to be something we are not.

From this perspective, sexual desire in Bataille is traumatic and overpowering. Its basis is to be found not in an instinctive will to propagate the species (indeed, eroticism is even the antithesis of the will to reproduce), nor is it a libidinous urge for pleasure or power. Not that these do not exist, but they are not of its essence. Desire, rather, is something akin to the death drive of Freudian psychology: an elementary urge to return to the lost continuity of existence and to experience the baseness at the core of our reality as material beings. As such, it challenges our sense of personal identity and the responsibility we owe to society.

Eroticism is thus transgressive of social norms, bringing into question what binds us together in society. In this, like all transgressive forms—festivals, initiation rituals, sacrificial practices, wars—it affirms, even as it challenges, social structures: It does not, as such, represent a rebellion against society. Indeed, for Bataille, the whole social structure relies precisely upon such transgressive moments that bring it into question only in order to strengthen it.

These are the themes that are worked through, in interweaving ways, in both Bataille's theoretical and literary writings, which represent a powerful interrogation of what it means to be present in the world and how our identity is formed through an engagement with forces that are alien to us (these may be social forms, other people, or the life force itself).

The Story of the Eye (1928)

The Story of the Eye was Bataille's first major published work, but never during his lifetime did he publicly acknowledge having written it. It appeared clandestinely in 1928 under the name of Lord Auch in an edition of only 134 copies. Yet it is probably now the book for which he is best known.

Like most of Bataille's stories, it is a tale of sexual initiation. In it, his own adolescent fears and desires are projected onto an imagined scenario. The unnamed narrator and his girlfriend Simone are sixteen at the beginning of the story. They indulge in sexual games together, though without actually copulating. One day while they are on a cliff top, a pure girl, Marcelle, happens by, and they draw her into their games. Marcelle becomes a kind of touchstone for their desire, almost an emissary whose mission is to quicken and extend their transgressive instincts. In the end she seems to offer herself as something of a

sacrificial victim, who, in dying, through suicide, finally allows the young lovers to consummate their love, which they do before desecrating the corpse of the young woman. Escaping to Spain, the narrator and Simone encounter a rich Englishman, Sir Edmund. Together, they attend a bullfight in Madrid. Sir Edmund offers Simone, at her request, a plate containing bull's balls. As she inserts one of them into her vagina, the bullfighter Granero is struck by a bull, and his eye is cast out of its socket. Still intoxicated with the horror of this scene, they travel next day to Seville. Passing by the church of Don Juan, they decide to enter and Simone enjoins a priest to hear her confession. While confessing, Simone is also masturbating and then challenges the priest, whom she sexually abuses. Finally, while in the process of fucking Simone, the priest is martyred by Sir Edmund. After having performed profanities with the corpse of the priest, including cutting out one of his eyes, which Simone tries to insert into her anus, they make their way incognito through Andalusia, the two men dressed as priests, before setting sail at Gibraltar.

Like all of Bataille's fictions, *The Story of the Eye* is about sexual fascination taken in its most disturbing aspects. It is fundamentally the story of Simone, a capricious young woman who carries the events along by her refusal of all constraint. The unnamed narrator is enraptured by Simone's immorality. Saying that she is immoral, however, tells only half the story: This is an "immorality" that is active and contagious, going beyond human bounds; it serves no ends but is a disinterested immorality, an immorality that immolates. Like a devouring sun goddess (almost all of Bataille's heroines share the quality that they are as much forces of nature as women), she consumes everything in her path.

There is a childlike quality to *The Story of the Eye*—and this because of, rather than despite, its erotic qualities. The cruelty, at least, is that of children, or perhaps of children emerging into adolescence while retaining the innocence of childhood. For it is—and this is not the least of its qualities—a profoundly innocent book, an innocence which is that of fairy stories (and of course, fairy stories can be written only by adults).

At the same time, this innocence is marked by trauma, the trauma that faces all humans as they learn of the reality of sex and death. Simone confronts this trauma—and she alone is an active character in the story, the others being either victims, observers, or catalysts—not by adapting herself to it, but by following the logic of its realization to its extreme. It is this that makes her a goddess as well as retains her as a child: She refuses the injunction to become a human by restraining her urges in the interests of society.

But the story is at the same time the dream, or the nightmare, of the narrator, who is carried along rather than seduced by Simone. This has an element of Nietzschean eternal return, for it is an adolescent dream; not the dream of an adolescent, but rather a dream that recurs and repeats itself throughout the life cycle, presenting a temptation (which is the temptation of adolescence) to enter the realm of the impossible, retaining the innocence of childhood within the framework of adult desires, while rejecting the responsibilities that come with adulthood.

A curious thing about this is that it is so totally contrary to Bataille's own adolescence. Far from living a life of extreme libidinous unconstraint, Bataille appears not even to have sowed any conventional wild oats. On the contrary, he seems to have gone to the other extreme, devoting himself to a life of pious rectitude with the intention of becoming a priest. Having been brought up without religion, his adolescent rebellion was to become a Catholic. He appears to have renounced Christianity sometime around 1922, when he was already twenty-five (Bataille later said that he rejected Christianity because it had caused "a woman he loved to shed tears"), but the crucial event may have been when he witnessed the death of the bullfighter Granero in the ring, an event that plays a key role in *The Story of the Eye*. Bataille wrote *The Story of the Eye* at a time of personal crisis. Turning violently against religion and plunging into a life of debauchery, having become fascinated by the works of Nietzsche, Bataille had perhaps in one bound reached the point Nietzsche reached in 1889 when he went insane. Faced with a void, he did not, however, become mad. Instead he became a writer, and *The Story of the Eye* was the first fruit of this new confidence. It might even be said, developing the theme of eternal return, to be Bataille's attempt to rewrite his adolescence, or perhaps, more accurately, to write it over, like a palimpsest, so re-creating his own identity.

Bataille credited the psychoanalyst Adrien Borel, under whom he undertook analysis, with

providing him with the assurance necessary to write a book. He had previously, in 1926, written *W.C.*, a work at once "of violent opposition to any form of dignity" and "a shriek of horror," as he described it, which he had destroyed. *The Story of the Eye* has the sense of deliverance, but it is a deliverance through laceration. Bataille could come to terms with his "sickness"—a sickness of the soul that could never be cured or even communicated because it was a sickness of existence itself—only by means of violent catharsis, which is precisely what writing meant to him and of which *The Story of the Eye* sets the standard.

Blue of Noon (1935)

Le bleu du ciel was written at the beginning of 1935 (though published only in 1957) at a moment of transformation in Bataille's life, when his first marriage was breaking up and he was losing any hope in political solutions to the problems of existence.

It begins in London, where the narrator, Henri Troppmann, having split up with his wife, Edith, leaving her and the two children in Brighton, is staying at the Savoy with a rich German woman called Dorothea, whom he calls Dirty. Dirty, drunk, calls for the maid and elevator attendant and, giving them a massive tip, subjects them to a nauseous performance in which she urinates on the carpet and verbally abuses them. Back in Paris, Troppmann meets up with Lazare, a young revolutionary, "ugly and conspicuously filthy," with whom he constantly argues but who becomes his confidante. Later, he is introduced to another woman, Xenie, at dinner. Caressing her thigh, he digs a fork into her leg, drawing blood. The next day, he feels ill. He visits Lazare, who is with her father-in-law. The three of them discuss politics before Troppmann, disgusted by their conversation, which seems meaningless to him, leaves, walking home in the pouring rain. He becomes seriously ill and is confined to his room. Xenie visits him and agrees to stay with him, to the annoyance of his mother-in-law, with whom he is living. Their talk is mostly of death: she is drawn to him but feels that their relationship will cause her to die. Troppmann speaks of his necrophiliac urges, confiding in her that when his mother died he had performed an obscene act in the presence of her corpse. He seduces

Xenie but has the feeling that he is making love with a corpse.

We next encounter Troppmann in Barcelona, a city on the point of insurrection. He meets a friend, Michel. They talk about Lazare, who is planning to attack a prison with a group of revolutionaries. Being terrified at the thought of meeting Lazare, Troppmann calls Xenie, asking her to join him in Barcelona. While she is on her way, he receives a letter from Dirty. Trying to contact her, he learns that she is catching a plane to Barcelona to be with him. The next day, he meets Xenie at the train station but leaves her with Michel while he goes to meet Dirty at the airport: She looks terrible and is apparently seriously ill. In his room, she tells him of going into a church in Vienna and lying outstretched on the ground, arms outstretched. Xenie comes to the room in a frantic state. He is desperate to prevent her from disturbing Dirty and has to force her to leave. Next day, Xenie returns, accompanied by Lazare. He learns that Michel has been killed in street fighting. Troppmann and Dirty remain in Barcelona for some months until her money runs out, when he accompanies her to Germany. Near Trier, they make love in a graveyard. When they reach Trier, disheveled and covered in mud, a little boy stares at them. He imagines that this little boy might have been the young Karl Marx (who was born in Trier). The next day they travel on to Frankfurt, where they will part. Against the background of Nazi regimentation, he catches the train back to Paris.

Le bleu du ciel is marked by a sense of impending tragedy. All hope appears to have been abandoned. The characters all seem to be on the point of crying, when they are not about to vomit, and all seem to be contemplating death. The only exception, Lazare, the fanatical revolutionary, is portrayed as dangerously naive. The most "realist" of Bataille's novels (at least to the extent that it takes place in a recognizable locale with direct links to events and characters in Bataille's life and can, although misleadingly, be analyzed as a *roman à clef*), it eludes any easy categorization. In a world on the point of collapse, sexuality is the only thing that vivifies life, but the characters are impotent, destined to a sterile future in which death alone has sovereignty.

Le bleu du ciel is a tormented book. If all of Bataille's fiction has a tormented quality, no others are so unrelenting in their treatment of

it. As his most directly autobiographical story, we are justified in regarding this torment as being carried over from his own life at the time. The story is also distinguished from his others insofar as the crisis to which it gives voice emerges from the problems of everyday living rather than from anguish over the predicament at the heart of human existence. His other books may more accurately be described as lacerated rather than tormented, and the distinction is fundamental to understanding the significance of *Le bleu du ciel*.

The eroticism of the book cannot be detached from its political content. While not at all a work of "sexual politics," the breakdown in sexual relationships the story details seems to parallel the breakdown in the political situation. Bataille had apparently taken the name of Troppmann from a murderer executed in 1870 for having killed his parents and his six brothers and sisters. As "too much of a man," in his impotence and lack of purpose, he appears to reflect an inability to act that would characterize the politics of the time, a crisis of virility that would lead to the terrible conflagrations of the Spanish civil war and world war. Even the women (in virtually all of Bataille's other fiction, the women are the active characters, who make things happen) seem strangely subdued and lacking in energy, despite the political engagement of both Lazare and Xenie.

The book is also a record of separation; not only had his marriage failed, so too had his belief in the efficacy of political activity been shattered. Bataille would continue to be politically active until the beginning of the Second World War, but his political activity would henceforth be drained of hope: The rising clouds of fascism—ever-present throughout the book—were largely responsible for this crisis, since, as Bataille analyzed it, fascism responded to elemental human compulsions that could lead to only the worst and which communism appeared unable to satisfy (and of which capitalism was incapable even of perceiving the necessity).

After he had written *Le bleu du ciel,* the double crisis that had given rise to it would be temporarily resolved in Bataille's life, or at least put on hold. During 1935, he fell in love with Colette Peignot, with whom he had his most intense relationship, both sexually and intellectually. In the same year, he also formed Contre-Attaque, an antifascist, anti–Popular

Front political group. When this collapsed, he established the College of Sociology and a secret society, Acéphale, devoted to strange rituals to confront the lack of significant myths in contemporary life. With the coming of war, these groups fell apart. Even more significantly, Colette Peignot died in 1938, leaving Bataille bereft and in solitude.

Le bleu du ciel is a portent of this collapse. Troppmann seems oppressed by the immensity of the sky, something emphasized by the fact that the story takes us across a Europe about to be devastated, as Bataille's personal life too was to be devastated.

Madame Edwarda (1941)

Madame Edwarda tells the story of a meeting with God, in the guise of a whore, or, quite simply, a woman. It was another book that Bataille never publicly acknowledged writing and which was published under the name of Pierre Angélique (the first two editions were issued with false dates and places of publication). Wandering through the deserted streets around rue Poissonnière and rue Saint-Denis, with solitude and darkness completing his drunkenness, the unnamed narrator desires to be as naked as the night. Attracted by the light of a brothel, he enters and chooses Madame Edwarda from among a group of prostitutes. As he caresses her, he feels himself abandoned, as though he is in the presence of God. In this moment when he feels enclosed by night, Madame Edwarda opens her legs and her "tatters [hardly a euphemism, but rather an intensification of the obscenity of revealing her sexual parts] looked at me, hairy and pink, full of life like a repulsive octopus." She forces him to look at her sexual parts and then to kiss them, telling him that she is indeed God. When he has paid the brothel keeper, Madame Edwarda takes him upstairs to a room lined with mirrors. They may or may not have sex, then Edwarda insists they go out. In the streets, beneath the porte Saint-Denis, a strange ritual takes place between them. This culminates when a taxi comes by. Edwarda, naked, reveals her sexual parts to the driver, and they have sex, watched by the narrator.

Madame Edwarda is one of the most intense and concentrated stories ever written. Barely ten pages long, it contains more real content than most stories of ten times its length. Its intensity is such that it is difficult to write about: In writing the text, the author (and we should recall that this is Pierre Angélique, who should not be confused with Georges Bataille, who wrote a preface to the 1954 edition—Bataille's play upon authorship takes its most complex form with this book) is describing the "impossible," something that can be only experienced and dissolves if subjected to discursive language. Consequently, his writing here is troubled and becomes incoherent in places.

Like all of the characters in Bataille's work, the narrator is interested neither in pleasure nor in satisfying a physical urge in the sexual encounter. He enters the brothel to get away from the solitude of night, attracted by its light. His experience there is comparable to that of the Hindu devotee who enters a temple to be in the presence of divinity; to be *seen* by the deity. It is also an encounter with the mother goddess—she might be Medusa or Durga—in her terrible aspect. But the invitation to look directly at her most intimate parts, recalls ancient mystery cults, or Tantric practices, in which the female sexual organs are worshipped, and looking upon them is part of an initiation ritual. This impossible encounter on a Parisian night is all the more powerful for having been unanticipated.

The Dead Man (1944)

All of Bataille's work is marked by death. In this story (if that is what it can be called), death takes its most explicit form. Published only in 1967, the story concerns a woman, Marie, whose lover Edouard has just died. Naked as he had asked her to be when he was dying, she keeps vigil over his body. Putting on an overcoat, she goes into the forest and then to the village inn. Hesitating for a while, she enters and orders a drink, offering herself and getting drunk. She dances and has sex with a farmhand, Pierrot, but is more drawn to a diabolical, ratlike dwarf, the Count, who appears in the inn later. She urinates over him for his pleasure, and at dawn they leave for her home to rejoin the corpse of Edouard. On the way, Marie listens to the singing of the birds in the forest. In the house, the Count undresses. He goes to join Marie in the room with the corpse of Edouard, but as he does so she electrocutes herself. After watching the hearse with the two coffins pass by, the Count throws himself into the canal.

The Dead Man essentially recounts an initiation ritual into death. The structure of the story appears to be established as a sacrilegious parody of the stations of the cross to Calvary, with Edouard and the Count, respectively, representing the aspects of Christ dead and resurrected—although it is actually Marie who is the crucified one, subject to self immolation. A variation on Bataille's familiar themes, in this story the woman acts as an emissary of death, initiating it and making it active (here she too may be compared to Christ, but a reversed Christ, offering oblivion rather than salvation).

Like *Madame Edwarda*, a short but intense story, *The Dead Man* is the most obscene and unbearable of Bataille's narratives, with an obscenity that is the obscenity of death. Although the war is not mentioned in it, the story is permeated by the atmosphere of war and ends with all three of the main characters dead.

L'Abbé C. (1950)

In *L'Abbé C.* we are again confronted with a triad of characters. In this story we actually have twin brothers, Charles and Robert, and a woman, Eponine. Set in 1942 under the Nazi occupation (although this presence is barely hinted at in the story), we are given a narrative fragmented in its structure. The main part of the story is written by Charles, prefaced by an unnamed editor, a friend of the brothers. This unnamed editor concludes the story.

We are introduced to the characters some time after Robert (the Abbé C. of the title) has returned to his hometown, where his brother still lives. As a child, Robert had been close friends with a girl, Eponine. When, aged thirteen, she had started to sleep around, Robert had broken off his friendship with her and refused even to acknowledge her existence. This also estranged him from his brother. The story starts some ten years later. Robert has become a priest, while Charles lives a debauched life, and Eponine is a prostitute. In her hatred of Robert ("if she saw him on the street she would laugh and, like someone gaily whistling for his dog, click her tongue and call out to him: 'Virgin!'"), Eponine is determined to seduce him, and enlists Charles to help her. They meet when climbing a tower next to the church. The climb is precipitous, and

Charles almost falls, nearly taking Robert with him; the temptation of suicide, causing the death of his brother in the process, is not far away from his thoughts. Isolated from the world in the tower, the tensions between them are exacerbated with the arrival of Eponine's mother, who berates her daughter for going out naked under her coat. When a gust of wind momentarily blows open her coat, Robert is traumatized by a glimpse of her nudity. Next day when he visits him, Robert tells Charles that he is seriously ill, but Charles insists he must go to Eponine. He refuses, and Eponine, furious with Charles for having failed in his task, gives herself to the local butcher.

The following Sunday, Robert is persuaded to perform high mass. Charles attends, as does Eponine, along with two prostitute friends, Rosie and Raymonde. They sit in the front row. While taking mass, Robert is seemingly so disturbed by their presence that he collapses. Apparently gravely ill, Robert is cared for by nuns. One evening, while Charles and Eponine are making love, someone relieves himself on her doorstep. At first it is believed that the butcher is responsible, but they discover that it was Robert who did it while secretly watching their lovemaking. Robert vanishes, and Charles later discovers that Robert went on to live a debauched life with the two prostitutes, Rosie and Raymonde, until arrested by the Gestapo for his resistance activities. Tortured, he betrays Charles and Eponine immediately but gives away none of his resistance comrades under the worst tortures before he dies. The Gestapo arrests Eponine, who dies at their hands, but Charles left home and so evades capture. Having discovered the truth of his betrayal from Robert's former cellmate, Charles deposits the manuscript with the editor, insisting that he must arrange for it to be published. A few weeks later, Charles commits suicide.

L'Abbé C. is a closed narrative. It "conceals the very thing it was supposed to make known". As much might be said of most of Bataille's writing, but in this book the "concealing what was supposed to be revealed" is most fully realized within narrative terms. At the end, we know that the three central characters are all dead. If we are struck by the capriciousness of the characters, it is a caprice marked by compulsion; there is nothing arbitrary about it: Their tormenting of one another is a form of love. In tormenting one another, too, they are tormenting themselves. As with all of Bataille's characters, they are bound together by some mysterious pact of which they know nothing, other than that they cannot resolve it and consequently it tears them apart.

The two brothers mirror and complete one another; as twins they have chosen different paths, but no matter what they do, they are inseparable. If Robert is a coward, a sanctimonious and hypocritical man with desires he is unable to control, at least he has the imagination to recognize his weaknesses, whereas Charles, in surrendering to libertinism, seems to surrender any active life, being at the mercy of events and unable to act in any direction, even as a hypocrite. They represent a similitude of characteristics, not an opposition, manifesting incompatible feelings that nevertheless make up a perfect whole. This makes each of them individually incomplete, but, more than this, uncompletable, since what each lacks is contained within the other: Charles, the libertine, is impotent; Robert, the priest who has given himself to God and to chastity, is a surging mass of desires. Neither has a genuine identity but is defined by an absent self which is unknowable to them. In consequence neither man is able to respond to the challenge Eponine issues to them. This woman, *eponymous* as she is, is defined in relation to the two men (L'Abbé C. is "the abc" and may refer to both men, since besides being two halves of the same person, they seem to be rudimentary people, containing the essential elements of what constitutes a human being, but in an underdeveloped form), who together sum up the trepidation of men confronted with the principle of femininity. At one point, Charles even imagines himself as Eponine in bed with Robert, and there is a certain suggestion that the characters, at some level, are interchangeable with one another, since none has a clear identity but seems to act only on an imperative of or to bring forth a reaction from the others. It is this that gives the story its particular quality: There is no opposition between the characters, but rather a similitude that holds them bound to one another and unable to act on their own behalf.

My Mother (1955)

My Mother was written in the mid-fifties but remained uncompleted and was published only

posthumously in 1967. It appears that had Bataille published it, it would have been under the pseudonym of Pierre Angélique (the author of *Madame Edwarda*), whose story it tells. At the beginning, Pierre's father has just died. Pierre, seventeen years old, is a pious young man, who has largely been brought up by his grandmother and has lived with his parents for only the previous three years. He does not regret the death—he even rejoices in it—as his father, whom he saw as a drunkard, abused his wife, Hélène, Pierre's mother. On the evening before the funeral, Hélène reveals a side of herself that Pierre has never seen before: she shows that she is a debauched woman, as she wants him to know that she is repugnant and yet, in spite of this, to love her to the point of death. He learns that she had been a child of nature, running naked in the woods, and that his father, coming across her there, had raped her. When she became pregnant, they were forced to marry. But it was she who had corrupted him, and they lived a debauched life together, of which Pierre was completely unaware. She undertakes to initiate her son in the same way. First she shows him obscene photographs, at which he masturbates. This is an act that exposes to Pierre a side of himself he had kept hidden or been unaware of and it overpowers all of his pious thoughts. Unable to go to his confessor (something which would have been a betrayal of his mother), far from feeling ashamed, he is "proud as a savage" at his sins. Recalling a maxim from La Rochefoucauld that "neither the sun nor death can be looked at directly," he has the sense that knowledge of his mother's crimes, far from repelling him, had caused him to elevate her into God. Another character enters upon the scene, forming the triadic relation that is characteristic of virtually all of the situations in Bataille's fiction. This is Réa, Hélène's lover, who acts as the intermediary between Pierre and his mother, engaging him in sexual excess. Réa also serves to provide a breakwater, something like the sword that lies between Tristan and Iseult, preventing physical consummation with his mother, which was really the sign of the impossible. Another of Hélène's lovers, Hansi, enters the picture when Hélène and Réa leave together for Egypt. A new triad is formed by the introduction of Loulou, Hansi's maid. One day, Hélène and Réa return unexpectedly, finding Hansi and Pierre naked. This makes possible the final transgression, when Pierre and his mother make love. Afterward, Hélène kills herself, Réa becomes a nun, and Hansi marries another man. Pierre is left alone in his loss.

Bataille planned that *My Mother* would constitute, with *Madame Edwarda* and another story, *Charlotte d'Ingerville* (of which only a fragment remains), a trilogy providing a kind of autobiography of Pierre Angélique, which Bataille intended to call *Divinus deus*.

It would be wrong to think of *My Mother* as a novel about incest. There is no sexual desire between Pierre and his mother; their physical relations are rather determined by the rules of an initiation ritual, the necessary culmination of which is a transgression which is an experience of the impossible. Hélène, although she is his mother, is not a mortal woman, she "was of another world," and it is their final coupling, like that of the devotee of a mystery cult, that serves to give Pierre a glimpse of the "other world" that is the impossible. She is less his mother than a succubus who responds to his hidden temptations, and he is less her son than a fact of nature tied to her by something more powerful than any biological link: "You are not my son, but the fruit of my anguish in the woods" she says at one point.

Pierre himself is torn between two worlds. This "angelic stone" combines, like an alchemical emblem, the elements of earth and air, for, as always with Bataille, names are significant and imbue characters with an identity that constrains them within certain limits which they need to understand if they are to learn to unravel the secret paths that lead toward the impossible. The initiation is necessary to draw Pierre away from the path of piety and righteousness, in which he is trapped in illusions, seeking a perfection he projects upon his mother. Revealing her true nature, the mother also separates Pierre from Christian illusions of transcendence and salvation. This mother is not simply a god, but a *sun god*, giving with no expectation of return but implacable and terrifying in her demands. Like Madame Edwarda she has many of the characteristics of Durga, or Kali, in her ferocious form.

But there is also a sense in which the relation between Pierre and Hélène is itself an illusion, one more puzzle in a quest for self-realization. Pierre comes to accept that he does not love his mother; he adores her. The distinction is crucial. This adoration, in fact, stands in the way of love.

The woman he loves is Hansi, and he realizes that this love is something his mother will never accept. This makes the ultimate transgression all the more crucial: Pierre must "know" his mother completely, in order to kill her within himself. This is his betrayal of her: He casts her out of himself and she must die. Even this is insufficient to realize his love for Hansi: She will marry another. In the final analysis, he is alone.

But not for long. In the sketch of the next part of the trilogy, another initiatrice will appear: Charlotte d'Ingerville, who seems to be something of an amalgam of Hansi and Hélène; indeed, she too has been initiated by the latter. He meets her in a church, where he has gone to "acknowledge" his sins (his debauchery with Réa, Hansi, and Loulou; his making love with his mother). This is not a confession, but another transgressive act: to acknowledge crimes that were more divine than the church. Charlotte tells him to leave a light on in his room and she will come to him at midnight. She informs him about the form by which his mother "initiated" her in the woods. Later, in Paris, Charlotte is arrested when drunk and appears to be dying. The story ends there and we can only conjecture how it would have continued.

Clearly *My Mother* and *Charlotte d'Ingerville* were conceived by Bataille as leads into *Madame Edwarda*. Pierre is led through a whole series of stages of initiation by different women whose overall trajectory is difficult to discern due both to the fragmentary nature of the narratives and to the fact that as the final stage of the process, *Madame Edwarda* is so perfectly formed and yet seems to have an existence to the side of the other stories, being rather a culmination of them.

In his stories, Bataille explores a world of "lacerated" being, a favorite word of Bataille's referring to the identity of people and their relationships with one another, indicating that we are not secure in the nature of what we are and that it is our erotic relationships that reveal this most starkly. There is an unsparing quality to Bataille's work. For him eroticism is nefarious, having a violent and shattering quality—certainly nothing about it is reassuring. As has been emphasized, it is indissolubly allied with, and indeed is an intimation of, death, even setting itself up against life. There is something of the Chthonic quality to Bataille's viewpoint, which brings him close to the Manichaean attitude that saw the world of matter and everything associated with it, including life itself, as the product of evil. Eroticism does not serve fertility, but dissolution, tearing open the person and revealing the absence of being that lies at its heart.

At the same time, however, there is a plenitude and expansiveness in Bataille's conception. In perhaps his most widely quoted passage, he defined eroticism as "assenting to life up to the point of death"; it is "the assenting to life even in death." This is the curse that is placed upon sexuality, which makes the sexual act both rending and desirable, since it reveals our vulnerability just as it seems we are satisfying our yearnings. And yet it is at the same time a profound affirmation of being. If eroticism strips us bare, it also opens us up to something greater, to the universal flow, making it possible for us to live. In eroticism, we dissolve our personality within that of another. In this respect, the Manichaean element in Bataille's thinking is overturned, for if Bataille considers matter evil, he does not seek escape from it, but rather to plunge into it, since it is part of the principle of life that must be accepted on its own terms.

This goes against that received wisdom of genetics which asserts that life serves life and that the purpose of life is to reproduce itself. On the contrary, Bataille asserts that life serves death and that far from wishing to preserve itself, life has a stronger urge to expend itself; this marks its complicity with death. Here is the horror of being—more deeply inscribed than that with which Conrad concluded *Heart of Darkness*—but it is a horror that, far from repelling Bataille, attracts him, for it is horror only because it violates our sense of personal security, tearing us apart and revealing what we truly are. Instead of denying the evil of the universe or striving to overcome it, the need, for Bataille, was to confront it.

These themes are extensively developed in various theoretical works. In three books conceived of as a kind of trilogy, to be called *La Somme athéologique*, there are no "characters" as such and the themes are approached in a way that is fundamentally philosophical in nature, but the same issues are raised as in the novels, and in a similarly digressive form, so that to draw a distinction between them and the novels is not always a simple matter. These books are *Inner Experience* (1943), described as a "journey to the ends of the possible"; *Guilty* (1944); and

On Nietzsche (1945), which pays homage to Bataille's spiritual mentor. All were written during wartime and give voice to a deep anxiety that is less connected to the war as such than to Bataille's inner state, in which the nature and force of sexual attraction and the erotic relation are central. Rather than being a participant in a war, Bataille once said that he was himself war.

One of the most striking aspects of Bataille's work was the link he made between eroticism and the economy. He first made this link in an essay published in 1933, "The Notion of Expenditure," in which he asserted that society (at least modern society) was founded in a denial of the natural exuberance of the world. Instead of accepting this natural exuberance, we try to master it in order to provide ourselves with security and shelter from the hostile world surrounding us. This leads us to make scarcity the principle that determines not simply our economic activity, but every aspect of our behavior. Bataille, in contrast, believed that our productive activity naturally created surpluses, and the principal problem was how to expend such surplus. He developed this argument further in his book *The Accursed Share*, published in 1949, in which he looked at the ways in which societies had historically sought to control this natural exuberance of which eroticism—an example of pure expenditure—was one of the main expressions.

The Accursed Share was also conceived as a trilogy, but like so many of Bataille's projects, it was never completed (although we do have texts of the two other parts that appear to be almost in a finished form). The second volume, *The History of Eroticism* (written in 1951, but unpublished in Bataille's lifetime), directly ties eroticism into his argument and was the first of three works in which Bataille directly confronted eroticism sociologically. It was followed by *Eroticism* (1957), arguably Bataille's masterpiece, and *The Tears of Eros* (1961), his last work, which largely applies the argument of *Eroticism* to the history of art. These books work as theoretical elaborations of the themes to be found in his novels and need to be read in conjunction with them. Bataille's work as a whole is marked by its probing and unflinching quality, and he explored eroticism, both in his fictional works and in his theoretical texts, not as something salacious or titillating, and certainly not as something distracting, but in a way that placed its understanding at the heart of existence and of what it means to live in the world. His conclusions are hardly comforting, but nor are they derisive. He believed that looking at the horror of existence full in the face was the only way to be able to come to terms with it.

Biography

Born in Billon, Puy-de-Dome, in central France, Georges Bataille was a largely self-taught philosopher and sociologist who wrote works on economic and political theory, religion, and the history of art.

MICHAEL RICHARDSON

Selected Works in English. Translator

Manet. Austryn Wainhouse and James Emmons. Geneva: Skira; London: Macmillan, 1955.

Prehistoric Painting: Lascaux or the Birth of Art. Austryn Wainhouse. Geneva: Skira; London: Macmillan, 1955.

The Beast At Heaven's Gate [*Madame Edwarda*]. Austryn Wainhouse. Paris: Olympia Press, 1956.

Eroticism. Mary Dalwood. London: Calder & Boyars, 1962; San Francisco: City Lights, 1986; London: Marion Boyars, 1987.

My Mother. Austryn Wainhouse. London: Jonathan Cape, 1972.

Literature and Evil. Alastair Hamilton. London: Calder & Boyars, 1973.

The Story of the Eye. Joachim Neugroschel. New York: Urizen Books, 1977; London: Marion Boyars, 1979; Harmondsworth: Penguin, 1982.

Blue of Noon. Harry Matthews. London: Marion Boyars, 1979.

L'Abbé C. Philip A. Facey. London: Marion Boyars, 1983.

Visions of Excess: Selected Writings 1927–1939. Allan Stoekl. Manchester, UK: Manchester University Press, 1985.

Writings on Laughter, Sacrifice, Nietzsche, Un-Knowing. Annette Michelson. *October* 36 (Spring 1986).

Inner Experience. Leslie Anne Boldt. Albany: State University of New York, 1988.

Guilty. Bruce Boone. Venice, CA: Lapis Press, 1988.

The Accursed Share. Robert Hurley. New York: Zone Books, 1988.

Theory of Religion. Robert Hurley. New York: Zone Books, 1988.

The Tears of Eros. John Connor. San Francisco: City Lights, 1989.

My Mother, Madame Edwarda, The Dead Man. Austryn Wainhouse. London: Marion Boyars, 1989.

The Impossible. Robert Hurley. San Francisco: City Lights, 1991.

The Trial of Gilles de Rais. Robert Robinson. Los Angeles: Amok, 1991.

On Nietzsche. Bruce Boone. London: Athlone Press, 1992.

The Absence of Myth. Michael Richardson. London: Verso, 1994.

Essential Writings. Edited by Michael Richardson. London: Sage, 1998.

The Bataille Reader. Edited by Fred Botting and Scott Wilson. Oxford: Blackwell, 1998.

The Unfinished System of Nonknowledge. Stuart Kendall and Michelle Kendall. Minneapolis: University of Minnesota Press, 2001.

Further Reading

Botting, Fred, and Scott Wilson. *Bataille*. New York: Palgrave, 2001.

Champagne, Roland A. *Georges Bataille*. New York: Twayne, 1998.

Hegarty, Paul. *Georges Bataille, Cultural Theorist*. London: Sage, 2000.

Hollier, Denis. *Beyond Architecture*. Translated by Betsy Wing. Cambridge, MA: MIT Press, 1990.

Hussey, Andrew. *The Inner Scar: The Mysticism of Georges Bataille*. Amsterdam: Rodopi, 2000.

Land, Nick. *The Taste for Annihilation: Georges Bataille and Violent Nihilism*. London: Routledge, 1992.

Libertson, Joseph. *Proximity: Levinas, Blanchot, Bataille and Communication*. The Hague: Martinus Nihoff, 1982.

Pefanis, Julian. *Heterology and the Postmodern: Bataille, Baudrillard, Lyotard*. Durham and London: Duke University Press, 1991.

Richardson, Michael. *Georges Bataille*. London: Routledge, 1994.

Richman, Michèle. *Beyond the Gift: Reading Georges Bataille*. Baltimore: Johns Hopkins Press, 1982.

Shaviro, Steven. *Passion and Excess: Blanchot, Bataille, and Literary Theory*. Tallahassee: Florida State University Press, 1990.

Surya, Michel. *Georges Bataille, An Intellectual Biography*. Translated by Krzysztof Fijałkowski and Michael Richardson. London: Verso, 2002.

BAUDELAIRE, CHARLES (PIERRE)

1821–1867
French poet, short story writer, and essayist

Baudelaire is remembered for his art and literary criticism, his translations, and his experimental prose poetry (the *Petits poèmes en prose*), as well as for his verse poetry. His essay on the phenomenology and aesthetics of urban life (*Le peintre de la vie moderne* [*The Painter of Modern Life*], 1863) has made his name synonymous with the philosophy of modernity.

Les Fleurs du mal (1855)

As well as providing a unique bridge between the Romantic and Symbolist aesthetic and philosophical schools, and pioneering innovation in poetic form and subject matter, Baudelaire's verse collection, *Les fleurs du mal* [*The Flowers of Evil*] stands as an encyclopedic and imaginative catalogue of the varieties of sexual feeling, desire, and expression. Echoing de Sade's impressive catalogue of perversions in *Les 120 Journées de Sodome* [*The Hundred and Twenty Days of Sodom*] (1874–5) and anticipating works of sexology such as Krafft-Ebing's by three decades, Baudelaire's work exemplifies the mid-nineteenth-century European taste for perverse and extreme expressions of the erotic imagination.

Baudelaire's writing, like that of de Sade before him, is fueled by a desire to challenge the delusions of the complacent reader (in this case the educated middle classes) regarding the "good" in human nature. *Les fleurs du mal* opens with Baudelaire's famous address, "Au lecteur," which invites the reader to suspend moral judgment of what follows in favor of unflinching self-examination. Baudelaire suggests that the forbidden desires of which he will speak ("le viol, le poison, le poignard, l'incendie" [rape and poison, the blade and arson]) are not foreign to the average reader, but indeed central to the human condition. For their refusal to confront their own propensity to crime, Baudelaire's bourgeois peers are denounced in the final line of the poem as "hypocrites lecteurs" [hypocrite readers].

Baudelaire's contention that the middle classes would be shocked by his work proved apt. On publication of *Les fleurs du mal,* the poet faced a charge of outraging public decency and was fined 300 francs by the Sixième Chambre Correctionelle. Six of his poems, treating the themes of lesbianism, morbidity, sadistic wounding, and fetishistic sex, were condemned by the court for their salacious and blasphemous content. All six poems were subsequently published in Belgium in 1866 under the title *Les épaves* and were included in subsequent editions of *Les fleurs du mal.*

Baudelaire's erotic poems feature a dizzy array of sexual personae and protagonists. The figure of the lesbian is a particularly important one for Baudelaire, reflected by the fact that early drafts of *Les fleurs du mal* went under the working title *Les lesbiennes* (1845–7). As indicated by the title of the poem "Femmes damnées" [Damned Women], the lesbian woman was a figure rejected by society and God, a marginal subject. In this, she provides (like beggars, widows, and the poor in other poems) a figure of identification for the self-styled *poète maudit* [cursed poet], who saw himself as both rejected by, and superior to, the common herd. As well as being a figure of identification, the lesbian is a source of fascination for Baudelaire in her role of erotic adventurer. She is seen to be capable of infinite pleasures, about which he is pruriently curious. Predictably, perhaps, of the three poems that Baudelaire penned about lesbians, "Femmes damnées," which focuses on their outcast and wretched status and "soifs inassouvies" [unslaked thirsts], was not banned, while "Lesbos" and "Femmes damnées: Delphine et Hyppolyte," which treat instead the incomparable pleasures of lesbian sex, provoked the condemnation of the court.

In other poems, Baudelaire's ambivalent attitude toward the female sex is revealed in scenarios of domination, torture, and punishment.

As the title of Georges Blin's 1948 study of Baudelaire would suggest, sadism and its counterpart masochism are central thematic features of Baudelaire's verse. The poetic "I" of *Les fleurs du mal* explores and expresses at different moments desires that are both sadistic and masochistic. In poems such as "A celle qui est trop gaie" [Against Her Levity] and "A une madone" [To a Madonna], he fantasises about inflicting murderous sexual wounds on the beautiful women he desires. In the latter case, he mixes blasphemy with sadism, as the woman described embodies the qualities of the Madonna. In a powerful climax, the poet unsheathes seven knives, representing seven sins, which he plunges into her heart.

On the other hand, in "L'Idéal" [The Ideal], the poet masochistically desires a strong, punishing woman, a *femme fatale*, seen when he declares: "Ce qu'il faut à ce cœur profond comme un abîme, / C'est vous, Lady Macbeth, âme puissante au crime" [This heart is cavernous and it requires / Lady Macbeth and an aptitude for crime]. Baudelaire's poetry demonstrates an extraordinary awareness, then, of the ways in which the two desires are the flipsides of each other, inextricably linked in the human psyche. In "L'Héautontimorouménos" [The Self-Tormentor, after a play by Terence], we see this idea expressed in the striking formulation "Je suis la plaie et le couteau ! / Je suis le soufflet et la joue !" [I am the knife and the wound it deals / I am the slap and the cheek]. The erotic ideal of being simultaneously the one who inflicts suffering and the one on whom suffering is inflicted is a theme that runs through Baudelaire's writing.

Not all of Baudelaire's poems are so charged with the violence of desire, whether sadistic or masochistic. In "Une nuit que j'étais près d'une affreuse juive..." [I spent the night with a gruesome Jewish whore] and "Je t'adore à l'égal de la voûte nocturne..." [Urn of stilled sorrows, I worship you], the erotic encounter is described in terms that are suggestive of coldness, sleep, or death; a barely disguised necrophilic fantasy. Similarly, perhaps, in poems which focus fetishisticallly on body parts, such as "La chevelure" [The Head of Hair], or on inanimate objects, such as "Les Bijoux" [Jewels], the erotic experience described is to all intents and purposes solitary, inward-looking, and masturbatory rather than concerned with sexual intersubjectivity.

Traditional scholarship on Baudelaire's erotic poems tended to group them into cycles corresponding to his love affairs or periods of infatuation with three women (Jeanne Duval, Mme Sabatier, and Marie Daubrun). Psychoanalytic scholars have been drawn instead to analyze the varieties of perverse desire visible in the collection, as explored briefly above, as revelatory symptoms of the neurotic fantasies of both the poet and his culture. In an important work of 1977, Leo Bersani reads *Les fleurs du mal* as exemplary of a certain kind of erotic subjectivity characterized by "psychical mobility," that is, by a series of shifting, self-undermining desires. Such critical works draw attention to the ways in which Baudelaire voices ideas about the self which pave the way for Freud's insights into the unconscious and the privileged place he will accord to the interplay of destructive and erotic instincts.

Biography

Born in Paris and educated at the Collège Royal de Lyon (1832–6) and the Collège Louis-le-Grand, from which he was expelled in 1839. Traveled to Mauritius and Réunion between 1841 and 1842, after which he returned to Paris. In 1848 he fought on the barricades during the *journées de février* and the *journées de juin* and aligned himself with the resistance against the military coup of Louis-Napoleon Bonaparte in 1851. Left France for Belgium in 1864, after failing to be elected to the Academie française. In 1866, having suffered several strokes, he returned to Paris, where he spent the last year of his life in a nursing home. Died in 1867 of a degenerative illness, probably syphilis related.

LISA DOWNING

Editions

Baudelaire, Charles. *Œuvres complètes*. Edited by Claude Pichois. 2 vols. Paris: Pléiade/Gallimard, 1975–76.
Les Fleurs du Mal: The Complete Text of The Flowers of Evil *in a New Translation by Richard Howard*. Brighton: Harvester, 1982.

Selected Works

Salon de 1845.
Salon de 1846.
La Fanfarlo, 1847.

Histoires extraordinaires, 1856, and *Nouvelles histoires extraordinaires*, 1857 (translations of short stories by Edgar Allan Poe)
Les Paradis artificiels. 1860
Salon de 1859
Le Peintre de la vie moderne. 1863
Petits poèmes en prose (*Le Spleen de Paris*). 1869 (published posthumously)

Further Reading

Bataille, Georges. *La littérature et le mal*. Paris, Gallimard, 1957; as *Literature and Evil*, translated by Alastair Hamilton, London: Marion Boyars, 1990.
Benjamin, Walter. *Charles Baudelaire: A Lyric Poet in the Era of High Capitalism*. Translated by Harry Zohn. London, NLB, 1973.
Bersani, Leo. *Baudelaire and Freud*. Berkley and Los Angeles: University of California Press, 1977.
Blin, Georges. *Le sadisme de Baudelaire*. Paris: Corti, 1948.
Fairlie, Alison. *Baudelaire: Les fleurs du mal*, London, Arnold, 1960.
Laforgue, René. *L'Échec de Baudelaire: Etude psychanalytique sur la névrose de Charles Baudelaire*. Paris, Denoël et Steel, 1931.
Paglia, Camille. "Cults of Sex and Beauty: Gautier Baudelaire and Huysmans." In *Sexual Personae*. New York: Yale University Press, 1991.
Sartre, Jean-Paul. *Baudelaire*. Paris, Gallimard, 1947; as *Baudelaire*, translated by Martin Turnell. New York: New Directions, 1967.
Ward Jouve, Nicole. *Baudelaire: A Fire to Conquer Darkness*. London: Macmillan, 1990.

BÉALU, MARCEL

1908–1993
French novelist

Passage de la bête

The venomous charm of this novel lies in Eva's dark side, which is unknown to her husband Simon, her daughter Carine, or even herself. This aspect of her personality grows until it darkens the character's fate. Indeed, Eva falls in love with Laura, a young rider. A feverish and sudden affair begins, and ends tragically: Simon kills his rival, and then his wife commits suicide. The sapphic relationship lasts more than three years, and Simon suffers from sexual frustration and jealousy. The plot is based on an adulterous love triangle, a classic plot, with a unique variation: It is not the man who betrays, but the woman, who, because her lover is another woman, feels it is not as wrong.

The reasons for Eva's passion for Laura are explained gradually, and the story manages to explore what in 1969 was still the scarcely dealt with theme of lesbian love. Moreover, it is interesting to follow a masculine point of view that does not proclaim lesbianism as a conquest but presents it as a moral defect, in the strict line of André Breton's opinion of masculine homosexuality. The author does criticize this point of view—clinical and scientific studies do not give any satisfactory explanation for lesbianism. The author emphasizes the shallowness of sexuality in a heterosexual couple where there is no love. In fact, the novel reveals two more important aspects. First, the author finds the best of his inspiration in the evocation of the sensuous relationship that is developing between the two seductive women. The author knows how to communicate the emotions associated with voyeurism to his readers. In particular, the natural sense of ignorance that men feel about a sexual pleasure that can be experienced without them is strongly felt. Secondly, the author demonstrates his mastery of a fantasy art elaborated from an ordinary situation that falls in an apparent unreality. Marcel Béalu is very often inspired by dreams or reverie. Indeed, an obsessive reverie is the starting point of the story, as the heroine, Eva, lets her imagination wander around two disturbing phenomena: She hears a thunderous noise, which is nothing but galloping horses who come from the nearby seafront stud farm. Then, she sees the vision of a beautiful horse being

BÉALU, MARCEL

ridden bareback by a naked, sun-tanned equestrian. This rider is Laura, a daring Amazon and the owner of the stud farm. The lady and the horse ride into the sea foam. The animal and the naked woman are indistinguishable in Eva's mind, but she is not clearly aware of it.

The theme of the beast is repeated in a synthetic way when the husband, Simon, faced with the difficulties of his life with Eva, feels as if an invisible beast were lying on the roof of his house, crushing it little by little. At several points in the story, the vision of the horse is said to be an infernal one, because Eva cannot forget it, and it is at the heart of the crisis that disrupts their conjugal happiness.

Before meeting Laura, it is the horse that Eva sees, just awakening from her reverie. And the encounter with the magnificent horse is for her like a romantic rendezvous. She strokes his fur, and immediately, Laura is in front of her. Laura and the horse are made of the same "carnal gold." The transfer from the horse to the lady is therefore easy. As for Laura, she professes to love men, women, and animals. Laura swims naked in the sea and sucks Eva's shaved armpit. She protects her by laying her body on her and controls her as if she were a stubborn animal. They lie stomach to stomach, and their breasts are compared to four pigeons in a single nest. The sapphic scenes are described poetically—for example, fingers are compared to "a game of quick flames from the offered neck to the breast." Hands and lips are compared to water.

Marcel Béalu is well known for his use of cruel literary games, playing with a mixture of innocence and cruelty. Laura decides to make Simon jealous of the pleasure she gives to Eva, letting him hear his wife cry with pleasure, and she succeeds in giving her "the small pearl," the drop that appears on Eva's lips. This expression was taught to Eva by Simon. He has to wait and sleep near Eva without having sex with her. He desires her body, especially when he looks at her armpit, or feels her shoulder at night. Simon feels like raping his wife and, later on, imagines taking his revenge on Laura by organizing a gang rape of her.

His carnal sufferings are compared to a "blood thorn stuck at the center of him." Spying on the sexual encounters of his wife with Laura, he accepts becoming the "broken mirror" of their pleasure. He often goes to Paris, in order to read books on lesbianism, and meets prostitutes. Meanwhile, Eva has violent dreams where she takes part in orgies in a church, with other people wearing masks. In another significant dream, a monstrous black-haired beast is killed—and here she may be dreaming of her own body. According to Simon, the body is a beast, but this beast is in quest of a nest and is looking for a soul. He dreams of recovering the perfumed armpits of Eva, and "the rustle of fresh mint around her sex, before she bursts in pleasure." He has not heard or smelled this for three years. One day, he meets the two women on horseback while he is driving his "D.S." and thinks about running them down with his metal beast. He abandons the idea this time, but later on, his jealousy drives him to murder Laura, and as result, he loses Eva.

Biography

Born in Selles-sur-Cher, in 1908, he died in Paris in 1993. As a friend of Max Jacob, he inherited a love of for style, and an eccentric imagination. André Pieyre de Mandiargues praised his surreal romanticism and his talent for writing fantasy short stories. He was the longtime owner of an antiquarian bookshop, Le Pont traversé, near the Jardin du Luxembourg in Paris.

MARC KOBER

Selected Works

L'Araignée d'eau, followed by Contes du demi-sommeil. Paris: Belfond, 1969.
La grande marée. Paris: Belfond, 1973.
La mort à Benidorm. Paris: P. Fanlac, 1985.
Le bruit du moulin. Paris: Corti, 1986.
Erréros. Paris: Fata Morgana, 1983.

Further Reading

Le regard oblique: Marcel Béalu. Interview with M. France Azar and Jean-Michel Place. Paris, 1993.

126

BEAUVOIR, SIMONE DE

1908–1986
French novelist, essayist and playwright

Simone de Beauvoir was the leading figure of French feminism. Her lifelong relationship with Jean-Paul Sartre was based on "essential" love and allowed "contingent" love affairs. Her free and open relationship with Sartre, built on intellectual dialogue and freedom, identified her as an emancipated modern woman. During the 1940s, at a time when France was ideologically conservative, she wrote *The Second Sex* (1949). Now hailed as one of the founding texts of French feminism, it provoked many negative reactions at the time; Albert Camus, for instance, considered the book an "insult to the Latin male."

Two images of me are current, she wrote: "I am a mad woman, an eccentric, my morals are extremely dissolute; in 1945, a communist woman told the story that during my youth in Rouen, I had been seen dancing naked on the tops of barrels. I have assiduously practiced every vice; my life is a perpetual orgy, etc. Or flat heels, tight bun, I am a chieftainess, a lady manager, a schoolmistress (in the pejorative sense given to this word by the right). I spend my existence with books and sitting at my worktable, pure intellect…. Apparently a combination of these two portraits involves no contradiction…. The essential is the figure I cut should be abnormal" (*The Force of Circumstances*, 647–8).

This ironic twofold representation conveys the image of conventional social rigidity and conversely attests to total freedom. This duality reflects the position of Simone de Beauvoir on the question of eroticism; on the one hand, she reduces eroticism to physical coldness in her novels, and, on the other hand, she thoroughly enjoys the theoretical exploration of freedom and looks at the questions of body and sexuality with no taboos.

Her autobiographical novels, along with her memoirs, *Memoirs of a Dutiful Daughter* (1958), *The Prime of Life* (1960), *The Force of Circumstances* (1963), relate the evolution of

woman from teenage to adulthood. In her books, she perceives the relation to the body through a certain degree of puritanism. In *The Prime of Life* she recalls being shocked by the casual way "Camille [one of Sartre's lovers] used her body. But was it her emancipation, she asked, or my puritan upbringing that should be blamed for this?" (62). She continues, including Sartre in her observations: "We detested the idea of eroticism—which Malraux used so plentifully in *Man's fate*—because it implied a specialized approach that at once overinflated sex and somehow cheapened it. Hemingway's lovers were in love all the time, body and soul: actions, emotions, and words were all equally permeated with sexuality, and when they gave themselves to desire, to pleasure, it bound them together in their totality" (144).

This statement makes perfect sense taking into account the striking fact that eroticism is absent in her own fictional or autobiographical works. Such is the case in her first novel, *She Came to Stay*, a love triangle involving Pierre, Elisabeth, and Xavière. The female protagonist is immediately identified by her physical coldness. "How cold you are!" her young lover Guimiot tells her. Physical love is here described as an act with no passion:

> Guimiot was consciously doing his job as a male. How could she tolerate these services rendered, ironic as they were?… Guimiot's mouth wore a grimace of pleasure and his eyes were drawn up at the corners. At this moment, he was thinking only of his pleasure, with the avidity of an animal. She closed her eyes once more, and a scorching humiliation swept over her. She was anxious for it to end. (90)

The female character, persona erotica *a priori*, is portrayed as a passive, frigid woman closed to carnal pleasure. She is also reduced to being a prey. Reading *The Second Sex* brings clarity to this reification. De Beauvoir writes, "woman is always frustrated as an active individual. She does not envy man his organ of possession, she envies his prey." These words, which reveal the relationship to the desired woman in her rapport to the masculine world, make her an object of devouring consumption. This devouring process reaches its ultimate end in *She Came to Stay* when Xavière, the centerpiece of the love triangle, is murdered.

In the chapter entitled, "The Sexual Initiation," the "erotic experience" is depicted as a brutal moment. "It is a decisive event that makes a break with the past" (*The Second Sex*, 371). The erotic experience for man is defined as an act for which erection is the principle and coition the end. Taking as premise the opposition between the two organs, the clitoris and the vagina, she comes to the conclusion that "at the stage of childhood the former is the center of female sex feeling... and woman retains her erotic independence all her life." De Beauvoir then takes a step further and develops the fairly questionable concept of a "becoming woman": "Woman is penetrated and fecundated by way of the vagina, which becomes an erotic center only through the intervention of the male, and thus always constitutes a violation. Formerly it was by a real or simulated rape that a woman was torn from her childhood and hurled into wifehood." The female erotic experience is thus for de Beauvoir an inescapable fate imposed upon woman. "This world, she claimed, always belonged to males: none of the justifications brought to us appeared satisfactory"; the only way out for women is freedom.

If in her novels, she veils her relation to flesh and eroticism behind a restrained language, she alludes rather crudely to eroticism in her epistolary works. The glutinous metaphor de Beauvoir uses to describe a night she spent with a young lover is edifying in this respect: "Pathetic night—passionate, sickening like foie gras" (*Letters to Sartre*). De Beauvoir was indeed not shy about her bisexuality and had affairs with her female students. She writes:

> If I were a man, maybe I should be a very wicked one, because I surely should enjoy to make love to young girls and having them love me.... When I was a teacher, they often fell in love with me and sometimes I enjoyed it a bit and even three or four times, I really cared a little for it and I happened to behave very badly. (*Letters to Nelson Algren*, 135)

The absence of, or silence on, eroticism in her novels compared with the frank sexual freedom she demonstrates in her letters is striking. The discrepancy between her private life and the ideological stances she endorses (i.e., her total silence about the question of lesbianism) could be construed as existential materialism. How could woman, being *a priori* the Other of man, possibly construct her own identity as a free subject by way of her love for another woman? This untenable situation, along with the burden of social conventions, made it impossible for existentialist Simone de Beauvoir to express herself clearly on the question of lesbianism. De Beauvoir proceeded with veiled words, as she did when, for instance, she recalled her friend Zaza for whom she "felt noncodified feelings."

Even if her fictional work is far from describing a paradise of pleasures, her epistolary and theoretical writings tackle the questions of the body and its meanings. By expressing her views on these questions, she overturns the received ideas of society and rethinks the locus of the body, in particular the female body. As such, the work of Simone de Beauvoir paves the way to contemporary feminism, while subverting bourgeois moral values.

Biography

Simone Lucie-Ernestine-Marie-Bertrand de Beauvoir was born on January 9, 1908, in Paris to Georges Bertrand and Françoise (Brasseur) de Beauvoir. She studied at the Sorbonne, where she met Jean-Paul Sartre in 1929. In the coming decades she became revered as one of the foremost thinkers in French history and one of the most influential figures in 20th-century feminism. De Beauvoir died of pneumonia on April 14, 1986.

AGNÈS VANNOUVONG

Translated from the French by Nadia Louar

Selected Works

The Prime of Life. Cleveland, OH: World Publishing Company, 1962.
She Came to Stay. New York: Norton, 1990.
Memoirs of a Dutiful Daughter. Cleveland, OH: World Publishing Company, 1959.
The Force of Circumstances. New York: Putnam, 1965.
Letters to Sartre. New York: Arcade, 1992.
The Second Sex. New York: Alfred A. Knopf, 1975.
A Transatlantic Love Affair: Letters to Nelson Algren. New York: New Press, 1998.

BECKFORD, WILLIAM

1760–1844
English novelist and travel writer

Vathek

William Beckford claimed in 1838 that he had rushed off *Vathek* in three days, inspired by his twenty-first birthday and Christmas celebrations in 1781. There is evidence to suggest, however, that there were experimental drafts of *Vathek* (originally written in French) by 1778 and that the draft, which was begun immediately after the Christmas festivities, was not completed until the summer of 1782.

Beckford entrusted the translation of *Vathek* into English to the Reverend Samuel Henley, an orientalist, whom he first met at his Christmas party, whilst he continued working on the *Episodes,* intended as an epilogue to *Vathek.* In these, five royals who appear at the end of the novel recount in turn why they were to suffer everlasting torment. Losing patience with the delays caused by Beckford's absorption in the *Episodes,* Henley published *Vathek* himself in 1786 without mention of Beckford's authorship. Rather, he offered it as a translation of an authentic Arabian tale and provided copious sets of scholarly footnotes to accompany and validate the text. Beckford published an inferior French version in Paris in 1787 that lacked Henley's careful and sensitive editing of Beckford's original.

Vathek, son of Carathis, is the ninth Caliph of the Abassides. The Giaour, an evil Indian magician, offers to guide Vathek to the Palace of Subterranean Fire of Elbis, where he could possess the treasures of the Pre-Adamite Sultans and the Talismans of Soliman that control the world, in exchange for renouncing his God, Mahomet [*sic*]. With an insatiable desire for the knowledge of all things, Vathek readily agrees and, having first sacrificed 50 beautiful boys as proof of his fealty, sets off with his entourage for the ruins of Istakhar, which lead to the Halls of Elbis.

En route, he stays with the Emir Fakreddin, a devout follower of Mahomet, and falls in love with Nouronihar, the Emir's daughter. Nouronihar is betrothed to the Emir's thirteen-year-old exquisitely beautiful nephew Gulchenrouz. Determined to keep Vathek from his daughter, the Emir arranges for the betrothed couple to be given a powder that gives them the appearance of death. In this state, they are taken to the cave of Meimoune, where their servants trick them into believing that they are really dead and must do penance for their indolent lives. Believing Nouronihar dead and broken by grief, Vathek renounces the Giaour and begs forgiveness of Mahomet, vowing to pay daily homage to Nouronihar. Yet Nouronihar and Vathek meet by accident and, discovering that Nouronihar has also been offered the riches of the subterranean palace in a vision, the pair set off for Istakhar, spurning one last opportunity to return to Mahomet. Punished in the subterranean palace for their unrestrained passions and desire for divine as well as mortal knowledge, the lovers are condemned to hopelessness and an eternity of solitary wanderings in hatred and anguish, unable to enjoy the knowledge of all things or the possession of the treasures that surround them. As Nouronihar and Vathek await the final torment of having their hearts eternally engulfed in flames, they listen to four princes and a princess tell what has brought them to the same fate (the stories intended for the *Episodes*). By the end of the novel, only Gulchenrouz finds happiness, for he, like the 50 sacrificial boys, is saved by a Genius who loves and protects children. Living above the clouds, the boys and Gulchenrouz are blessed by the Genius with the happiness of everlasting childhood and innocence.

The eroticism of *Vathek* lies in the air of eighteenth-century Western orientalism and decadence that pervades the novel. Vathek, like his subjects, is addicted to sensuality, overindulgence, sexual pleasure, and gourmandizing. In order to gratify his senses, Vathek builds five palaces overlooking his city of Samarah, each dedicated to one of the senses and including the Retreat of Mirth, where seductive women pleasure whomever the Caliph commands. The novel abounds with reference to opulent furnishings, mouthwatering delicacies, heady fragrances, and sexual pleasure. Yet alongside this hedonism lies a casual indifference to suffering, as when Carathis, described as the wickedest of women, commands her one-eyed Negro mutes to strangle citizens of Samarah as part of her oblation to the Giaour.

The novel also contains strong homoerotic and pedophilic elements, which find resonance in Beckford's own sexuality. In 1779, Beckford fell in love with William, the eleven-year-old son of the 2nd Viscount Courtenay, becoming his lover in 1781. This has led some critics to regard *Vathek* as a *roman-a-clef,* with Vathek and Gulchenrouz as fictional counterparts to Beckford and William Courtenay. Another reading has seen *Vathek* in terms of an "autobiographical allegory" that enabled Beckford to explore his feelings of guilt over his recent seduction of Courtenay (Timothy Mowl, *William Beckford*).

The homoeroticism in *Vathek* works on two levels. There is simple admiration of youthful beauty, as when the Caliph sleeps on silk cushions with two young pages beside him. It also finds expression in the descriptions of Gulchenrouz's girlish effeminacy and the grace and suppleness of the 50 naked competitors as they prepare for the games preceding their oblation. The homoeroticism also works at a more sinister level. Vathek is himself naked as he plays with the boys, having given parts of his dress to them as prizes before sacrificing the innocents to the Giaour's voracious appetite. As Carathis recognizes, the Giaour finds "nothing so delicious... as the heart of a delicate boy palpitating with the first tumults of love," and it is for this reason that she wishes to offer Gulchenrouz as a supreme sacrifice to him. A careful reading of *Vathek* reveals a subplot in which the powers of Good and Evil do battle for the lives and bodies of these sacrificial victims. Good, in the form of a Genius whose life is devoted to the protection of children, wins, keeping the children forever safe above the clouds. There is something uncomfortable, however, about Beckford's fantasy of a Genius with a "fondness for the company of children" and the power to grant eternal boyhood. Denied their manhood, the youths merely exist to satisfy an older man's desire to be always surrounded by beautiful and loving boys.

Biography

Beckford was born September 29, 1760, probably at Fonthill in Wiltshire, where he was also educated. In 1783, Beckford, a bisexual, married Lady Margaret Gordon, by whom he had two daughters. Beckford wrote novels, biography, and retrospectives on his youthful travels. He traveled widely in Europe, including Switzerland, Portugal, Spain, and Italy, prompted in part by a self-imposed exile to avoid scandal at home over a homosexual affair. At one time, known as the wealthiest man in England, Beckford was an avid art collector and aesthete, who built Fonthill Abbey near Bath, an extravagant mansion which famously fell down in 1825. Beckford died at Bath on May 2, 1844. His first novel, *Vathek*, an Arabian/gothic-style tale, was published in England in 1786.

BARBARA WHITE

Editions

Vathek. Oxford: Oxford University Press, 1983; London: Creation Books, 2000.

Selected Works

Biographical Memoirs of Extraordinary Painters. 1780
Dreams, Waking Thoughts, and Incidents. 1783
Modern Novel Writing, or The Elegant Enthusiast. 1796
Azemia. 1797
Italy, with Sketches of Spain and Portugal. 1834
Recollections of an Excursion to the Monasteries of Alcobaca and Batalha in 1794. 1835
The Episodes of Vathek. 1912
Liber Veritatis and *The Vision.* 1930

Further Reading

Boyd, Alexander. *England's Wealthiest Son.* London: Centaur Press, 1962.
Brockman, H.A.N. *The Caliph of Fonthill.* London: Werner Laurie, 1956.
Lees-Milne, James. *William Beckford.* Tisbury, Wiltshire: Compton Russell, 1976.
Malcolm, Jack, ed. *Vathek and Other Stories: A William Beckford Reader.* London: Pickering and Chatto, 1994.
Mowl, Timothy. *William Beckford: Composing for Mozart.* London: John Murray, 1998.

BELEN (NELLY KAPLAN)

1936–
Argentine short story writer and novelist

Passionate about the cinema, Nelly Kaplan became the assistant to legendary director Abel Gance, working with him on his monumental films *Magirama* (1955–6) and *Austerlitz* (1960), and was second-unit director of *Cyrano et d'Artagnon* (1963). She also become close friends with André Breton and Philippe Soupault.

Publishing three slim volumes of short stories under the name Belen in the early 1960s, which were gathered in one volume, *Le réservoir des sens* in 1966, she also became a filmmaker in her own right in 1961, with a short film, *Gustave Moreau.* A series of short documentaries, mostly about painters, followed, notably *A la source, la femme aimée,* which, based on secret notebooks of André Masson, was severely cut by the French censor. In 1968 she made her first feature film, *La Fiancée du pirate* and has since made several other films for the cinema and television. In 1971 she published a "ciné-roman," *Le collier de ptyx* under her own name. This was followed by a novel, *Mémories d'une liseuse de draps,* published in 1973 under the name Belen. The latter was revised and reissued in 1998 with a different title, *Un manteau de fou rire,* along with a new novel, *Aux orchidées sauvages.* In the meantime, new editions of *Le réservoir des sens* had appeared in 1988, augmented with new stories, and in 1995, when it was accompanied by a longer story, *La gardienne du temps.* In 2005 she published another novel, *Cuisses de grenouille.*

Mémoires d'une liseuse de draps is presented as the autobiography of the young woman who wrote *Le réservoir des sens* (the earlier collection of stories had come with an inserted biographical notice announcing that she was writing her memoirs). Belen is born of a sailor (or pirate) and an unknown mother. Spending an idyllic childhood as a daughter of the sea aboard her father's ship, the *Sperma,* doted upon by the loving crew, her only childhood friend is a lion named Griffy. When she is eight, she receives her name, conferred on her in the course of a lubricious ritual when she first becomes aware of her sexuality. Reaching the Galápagos Islands, she finds that her friends there have been massacred by agents of the sinister CIA (Company of American Indies), thus destroying the revolutionary community devoted to erotic and political freedom that had been established by Jaguar Bronstein. When she is kidnapped by the reactionaries, the CIA's evil head José Acero Stalin orders that she be executed by being cast into the sea, but the *Sperma* is following behind and her friends are able to save her. The *Sperma* manages to evade the CIA, and during her formative years, Belen participates in the triumphant revolutionary movement in Angola. Arriving in Amsterdam when she is sixteen, it is time for her initiation as a woman. She is asked to choose the man who will take her virginity and decides that her father should be her first lover. The ritual is performed in a strange apartment in Amsterdam, but as they are returning to their ship, they are apprehended by Acero's men. Belen is captured and her father is killed, while the *Sperma* is set on fire. The other crew members lie low, but Griffy is captured and sent to an animal sanctuary. Escaping to the China Seas after seducing the millionaire Van Ryn Susy, who is in Acero's pay, Belen finds refuge in a pleasure district in Shanghai, where she becomes aware of her strange gift: the ability to read the future in the deposits men leave on the bedclothes. Her fame spreads and she becomes fabulously rich. Learning that Griffy is held prisoner in Persia, she goes to try to rescue him. Persia at this time is under the control of the Great Matriarchy, whose representatives are sympathetic but unable to help as Griffy is being held by a group of religious fanatics, who intend to sacrifice him. Belen, therefore, must rescue the lion on her own, in which task she succeeds. Momentarily united with Griffy (woman and lion couple in their excitement at being together again) and the other members of the crew, she discovers that José Acero is in Buenos Aires and travels there, in the guise of the adventuress Léonie d'Ashby, and lures him into a seductive trap in order to kill him. Her mission accomplished, she retires to an island in the Sargasso Sea, where she writes the stories contained in *Le réservoir des sens*.

Mémoires d'une liseuse de draps (reissued in 1998 under its original prepublication title, *Un manteau de fou rire*) is a novel fully within the surrealist tradition, taking as its point of departure Fourier's proposition that "passions are proportionate to destinies." If it contains a wealth of allusions and references which may not be immediately apparent to the general reader, it can nevertheless be read as a pure adventure story, albeit one that is both provocative and insolent in its tone and situations. Its transgressive aspect is shown in Belen's openness to a range of sexual encounters, which caused some trouble with the censors at the time of its first publication in 1973.

The novel encapsulates the themes that run through all of Kaplan's substantial oeuvre of writing and films. Commitment to freedom means that freedom of the senses as much as political freedom is at stake; it is the freedom of revolt, the freedom not to succumb to anything that is sordid in life. But this freedom is as far as can be from that supposedly defended by our political masters in today's world. It is a freedom that bears the black flag and is essentially the freedom to *feel*. It is also a powerful celebration of the possible. *Voyeur* and *voyeuse*, she is equally committed to the pleasures of sight as an opening up of potentialities of existence. "Eroticists of the world unite," she once proclaimed. "You have only your chains to lose and a whole wide sensual world to gain."

Biography

Born in Buenos Aires, Nelly Kaplan bought a one-way ticket to France in 1952 and has since settled in Paris.

MICHAEL RICHARDSON

Selected Works

Stories

Le Réservoir des sens. Paris: Le Jeune Parque, 1966; Paris: Jean-Jacques Pauvert, 1988; as *Le réservoir des sens, suivi de La Gardienne du temps*, Paris: Le Castor Astral, 1995.

Le Collier de Ptyx. Paris: Jean-Jacques Pauvert, 1971.

Belen, *Mémoires d'une liseuse de draps*. Paris: Jean-Jacques Pauvert, 1973.

Aux Orchidées sauvages. Paris: La Différence, 1998.

Un Manteau de fou rire. Paris: La Différence, 1998.

Ils furent une étrange comète. Paris: Le Castor Astral, 2002.

Cuisses de grenouille. Paris: Maren Sell, 2005.

Films

Gustave Moreau. 1961

Rudolphe Bresdin. 1962

Abel Gance hier et demain. 1962

A la source, la femme aimée. 1964

Dessins et merveilles. 1965

La nouvelle orangerie. 1966

Les années 25. 1966

Le régard Picasso. 1967

La fiancée du pirate. 1968

Papa, les petits bateaux. 1971

Néa. 1976

Charles et Lucie. 1979

Abel Gance et son Napoléon. 1983

Pattes de velours. 1985

Plaisir d'amour. 1991

She has also written several films for TV, directed by Jean Chapot, and wrote the screenplay for *Il faut vivre dangereusement*, a film directed by Claude Makowski.

Further Reading

Colaux, Denys-Louis. *Nelly Kaplan: Portrait d'une flibustière*. Paris: Dreamland, 2002.

Sebbag, Georges. *Le Point sublime: Breton/Rimbaud/ Kaplan*. Paris: Jean-Michel Place, 1997.

BELOT, ADOLPHE

1829–1890
French novelist

Born November 6, 1829, in Pointe à Pitre to a rich Creole family of Guadeloupe, Adolphe Belot came to France to study law. After graduation, he registered as a lawyer with the bar of Nancy but never pleaded a case. In 1855, he launched himself into the literature, publishing a novel, *Châtiment* [*Punishment*], which passed unnoticed. He consequently wanted to try his luck in the theater, initially with a one-act comedy, *A la campagne* [*In the Countryside*], then with a three-act comedy, *Le testament de César Girodet* [*César Girodet's Testament*], which premiered on September 30, 1859, at the Odéon. It played more than 200 times and was included in the repertory of the Comédie Française. This success encouraged Belot to settle in Paris and produce other theater plays: *Un secret de famille* [*A Family Secret*] (1859), *La vengeance du mari* [*Husband's Revenge*] (1860), *Les maris à système* [*Husbands with System*] (1862), among others. During this same period, he also published serial novels and short stories. He was decorated with the Legion of Honor in April 1867. A year later, he presented *Le drame de la rue de la Paix* [*The Drama of Rue de la Paix*] at the Odéon. Up to this point, his career as a successful writer was unblemished by any scandal.

It is then he entrusted to *Le Figaro* his new novel, *Mademoiselle Giraud ma femme* [*Miss Giraud My Wife*], which was serialized in the newspaper in the autumn of 1869. This was the story of a man who marries a young girl but does not succeed in consummating the marriage, for she always refuses him. Suspicious that she has a lover, he follows her and finds that she is having a sapphic affair with an aristocrat, the Countess de Blengy. The story climaxes with the man killing the lesbian seductress and being acquitted.

This novel was no praise of feminine homosexuality; on the contrary, it had an admonitory tone. Nevertheless, when the hero catches his spouse and the countess in a room, some *Figaro* subscribers protested. The editor had to interrupt the publishing of the serial, on December 22, 1869, apologizing as follows: "It is dangerous to treat such scabrous subjects in a newspaper." However, he declared in conclusion: "We advise those of our readers whom the adventures of Mademoiselle Giraud did not startle overmuch and who desire to know the end that it will appear in the volume at the end of next month."

Adolphe Belot could not have wished for better publicity. *Mademoiselle Giraud ma femme* was a triumph that survived the Second Empire and flourished under the Third Republic. This novel has had 63 editions in 15 years. That of 1879 was prefaced by Emile Zola (who signed his preface "Thérèse Raquin," the name of his recent heroine). Adolphe Belot needed only to continue in this vein, which was what the public henceforth expected of him. He became the urbane novelist of passionate dramas, narrating tragic adulteries that finished with a killing or a suicide. His next novel, *La femme de feu* [*The Woman of Fire*] (1872), which had 47 editions, recounted an adultery the denouement of which was a double death. In two years (1875–1876) he wrote the four novels of his cycle *Les mystères mondains* [*The Urbane Mysteries*], comprising (besides the volume bearing that title) *Les baigneuses de Trouville* [*Bathers of Trouville*], *Folies de jeunesse* [*Madness of Youth*], and *Une maison centrale de femmes* [*A Central House for Women*].

Many bourgeois women readers made him their favorite author, as he dealt with matters of sexuality through allusion, without entering into embarrassing details. The scenes in his novels were situated in environments that captivated this readership: Trouville, a fashionable town for sea bathing, or the prison for women at Clermont, where his heroine Carmen Lelièvre is confined for kidnapping.

The daring reputation of Adolphe Belot increased with *La femme de glace* [*The Woman of Ice*] (1878), the hero of which, Henri Vandelle, has an ardent mistress he continues to see after getting married; but, from rancor, she no longer responds to his caresses, remaining "straight, impassible in his arms, being content with defying him with her gaze and smiling ironically." He becomes mad with frustration and kills her, then commits suicide.

Belot knew how to combine love and adventure in his novel trilogy, *La sultane parisienne, La fièvre de l'inconnu* [*Fever of the Unknown*] and *La vénus noire* [*The Black Venus*]. Baroness de Guéran, widow of an explorer, suggests to three men wanting to marry her that they accompany her on an expedition to Africa: "What shall I give you in exchange? My eternal friendship to two of you; perhaps my love to the third. Who will be the third? That is what I don't know". Over the course of their African adventures, until their encounter with Queen Walinda, the baroness falls in love with one of the three suitors. Another of Belot's success was *La bouche de Madame X* [*Madam X's Mouth*] (1882), with 154 editions, in which the male protagonist attempts to conquer a married woman, obsessed by her beautiful mouth. Belot wrote sequels to some of his novels. In 1883, *Reine de beauté* [*Beauty Queen*] had as a sequel *La princesse Sofia*, and in 1885, *Une affolée d'amour* [*Striken by Love*] was complemented by *La couleuvre* [*The Grass-snake*]. In the latter, we find the Duchess de Limour, an exalted and lucid lover, who "loves like a madwoman and thinks like the wisest woman."

Adolphe Belot was so famous that the Monte-Carlo Casino allocated him two thousand francs per year simply to be there during the season at one of the gaming tables—only his presence attracted a crowd of players. His observations on this environment inspired him to write *Une joueuse* [*A Player*] (1897) and *Une lune de miel à Monte-Carlo* [*Honeymoon in Monte Carlo*] (1887). He traveled to Brazil, to the United States, to Africa and Asia; his voyage to Cambodia allowed him to reveal, in *Cent femmes pour un homme* [*A Hundred Women for One Man*] (1889), numerous details on the harem of King Norodom I.

In 1883, Belot divorced his wife under conditions that amused all Paris. So that his wife could have custody of their two daughters, Belot had to be culpable in the divorce. Therefore, the couple decided that he would be caught by the police commissioner in bed with another woman. This called for several sessions before it succeeded: Sometimes the commissioner did not appear; sometimes the prostitute hired for the role ran away when ascertaining the adultery. Edmont de Goncourt was scandalized in his newspaper over "this contrived divorce, devised by wife and the husband."

After his divorce, in a playful mood, seeking new challenge: or needing to express his sexuality more plainly than in his official literature, Belot began to write erotic novels which he signed "A.B." The first of them, *L'Education d'une demi-vierge* [*Education of a Half-Virgin*] (1883), tells the story of a divorced woman, Lucienne d'Avenel, who decides to become an urbane prostitute, in company with her daughter Edmée, to whom she teaches the advantages of the job. The lavish parties given by the mother and the initiation of Edmée give place to very lascivious scenes with humorous touches.

In 1889, *La maison à plaisirs* [*The House of Pleasures*] (frequently reedited under the title *La passion de Gilberte* [*Gilberte's Passion*]) was one of A.B.'s novels that became a best–seller. The Gay Bibliography gives this abstract: "Voluptuous scenes take place in the boudoirs of one of those urbane rendez–vous houses that abound in Paris, to create easy relations for persons of both sexes in search of love, pleasures." A catalogue of the same year points out "pictures of an incredible lubricity, the accuracy of which can be guessed in minor details."

In *La canonisation de Jeanne d'Arc* [*Canonization of Joan of Arc*] (1890), A.B. narrates, in a manner as much spiritual as lascivious, "a soirée fin-de-siècle." The Countess de Liancourt, with her mother's help, is organizing a prodigious Parisian orgy in honor of Jeanne d'Arc, with the same care for protocol as for a charity celebration. In the middle of the orgy, a one-act erotic play, "L'Art de payer sa couturière" [*The Art of Paying Her Dressmaker*] is enacted by three women and two men, allowing the assistants to take a break and arouse themselves in new frolics.

La canonisation de Jeanne d'Arc was the last novel Belot wrote as A.B. before his death on December 17, 1890, in Paris. That same year, as Adolphe Belot, he published his last novel, *Chère adorée* [*Dear Precious*]. It is remarkable that Adolphe Belot, who during his lifetime had more success than Flaubert and Maupassant, has been almost completely forgotten since then. One does not even find his name in present-day French literary dictionaries.

On the other hand, A.B. continues to be an admired author of erotic literature. At his death, he left some works unpublished, and the efforts of his fans brought to light, in 1894, *Les heures érotiques modernes* [*Modern Erotic Hours*], including *La petite bourgeoise* [*The Petty Bourgeois*], *Le rat* [*The Rat*], and *Bouillie de maïs* [*Corn Mash*], which the clandestine editor qualified as "pretty short stories of a famous writer"; *Les péchés de Minette* [*Minette's Sins*], "by the author of *La passion de Gilberte*" (an indirect manner of designating A.B.) ("A young woman newly married meets the man of her dreams, a man who is at the same time a true lover, and who initiates his charming half in all the practices of libertinism"); and *La Chandelle de Sixte-Quint* [*The Candle of Sixtus the Fifth*], "by the author of *La maison à plaisirs*," which told the story of a condom through those using it.

In 1896., *Les stations de l'amour* [*The Love Stations*], the last novel signed A.B. certainly the best of Belot's posthumously published erotic novels. The novel consists of the letters of a husband, the engineer Léo, traveling on business in Calcutta, and his wife Cécile, back home in Paris, who inform each other about their adventures, because they want "a modernistic ménage" (as was the expression then). They swear to forgive each other their infidelities, provided that they tell each other "all, with details and without reserve." Léo narrates his sexual games with Dora, the daughter of Sir Duncan Simpson, general superintendent of the public works, and with her girl friends, Flora and Maud, in four-way lovemaking. True to Belot's commitment to creating atmosphere in his novels, the manner of describing the customs of India gives the story an exotic charm. For her part, Cécile confesses to Léo how she initiated a sapphic affair with her servant Thérèse and took pleasure with Gérard, a friend of her husband's, and Adrien, a young man she met in a restaurant.

The first edition of *Les stations* (subtitled *An Amorous Story of A Married Couple Momentarily Separated, and Rendering Their Mutual*

Freedom in Terms of Love) had only 125 copies printed, in Holland, accompanied by 62 free prints. This is a jewel of the curiosa of the nineteenth century. Among the editions, that of 1934 has a preface by Louis Perceau confirming that A.B. was Adolphe Belot.

Thereafter, from 1903 to 1912, three more works were speculatively attribute to A.B.: *Toute la lyre* [*All the Lyre*], *Select-Luxure* [*The House of Pleasures*], and *La luxure en ménage* [*The Lechery in Ménage*] (1912). We once again encounter Belot's first heroine, Lucienne d'Auvenel, who in *Toute la lyre* makes love in an automobile with three partners (in the eight chapter, entitled "In the Car! Chassé-croisé of sexes. An Orgy at 60 per Hour"), but such cars did not exist during Belot's time. Most of *Select-Luxure* happens in a boarding school, where we once again meet Edmée and where all the pupils devote themselves to sapphism. Lucienne introduces her daughter to her lover Daniel, who teaches her all that a man can offer. At last, *La luxure en ménage* was summarized as a story of "incest without a veil, a research into all voluptuousness, all enjoyment, between brother and sister, mother and daughter, ignoring social conventions, prejudice, scruples." It is unliked that the latter two books are by Adolphe Belot. There would not have been a wait of more than twenty years after his death before publishing them. Additional, they lack the elegance of Belot's style, which rendered his bold stories even more exciting.

The dichotomy of Adolphe Belot/A.B. is not a Jekyll and Hyde. Belot he simply amused himself by writing novels for "aware adults," so as not to be a prisoner of his conventional genre writing.

SARANE ALEXANDRIAN

Bibliography

Vapereau, G. *Dictionnaire universel des contemporains* [Universal Dictionary of the Contemporaries]. Vol. 1. Paris: Hachette, 1893.
La Grande Encyclopédie, inventaire raisonné des sciences, des lettres et des arts, par une société de savants et de gens de lettres, sous la direction d'André Berthelot [... reasoned dictionary of sciences, letters and arts, by a savant and people of letters, under the direction of André Berthelot]. Vol. 5. Paris: Société anonyme de la Grande Encyclopédie, 1891.
Helpey (pseudonym of Louis Perceau, bibliophile of Poitou). "Notice sur Adolphe Belot." In *Les Stations*

de l'amour, Bénarès, *Aux dépens des Bayadères* [*On the Bayaderes' Expense*], n.d. (This book was clandestinely published in Paris by Maurice Duflou in 1934).

Alexandrian, S. "La double vie d'Adolphe Belot." In *L'Erotisme au XIXe siècle*. Paris: Jean-Claude Lattès, 1993.

Cabeen, D. "Adolphe Belot." In *A Critical Bibliography of French Literature: The Nineteenth Century*, edited by D. Bagueley, 584–86. Syracuse, NY: Syracuse University Press, 1994.

BÉRANGER, PIERRE JEAN DE

1780–1857
French poet and songwriter

Chansons érotiques

Although no precise information is available concerning the composition of this collection of erotic songs by France's best-known *chansonnier,* they almost certainly date from the beginning of his career, i.e., before the catastrophic events of 1815—Waterloo and the ensuing return of the Bourbons—persuaded him to turn to the political satire for which he is now primarily remembered. Since 1813, Béranger had been a member of the *Caveau moderne,* an association of poets and songwriters who held monthly meetings in a well-known café, the Rocher de Cancale, primarily in order to sing the praises of Eros and Bacchus. The first collected *Chansons érotiques* appeared in 1829 as a supplement to the two-volume Baudoin edition of the previous year, i.e., at a time when Béranger was at the height of his considerable fame. He had already been in prison twice, in 1821 and again in 1828, for publishing works offensive to public morality, although not, we should note in passing, for obscenity: On both occasions, what had worried the authorities was his outspoken criticism of the Church and the royal family. (The second prison sentence was accompanied by a substantial fine, 10,000 francs, largely paid for by public subscription.) The contents of this supplement were reissued in a four-volume edition published in 1829 by Tarlier in Brussels and Perrotin in Paris. In 1834, Perrotin issued the first collected edition of Béranger's complete works in four octavo volumes, shortly followed, apparently without the author's permission, by a new supplement, subtitled *Chansons érotiques.* This volume contained 48 songs, 20 of which had not been collected in earlier editions.

At this stage of his life, Béranger was living in honorable retirement; the liberal cause for which he had struggled valiantly for 15 years had triumphed in the July Revolution of 1830. His best-known song, *Le roi d'Yvetot,* had been praised by no less an authority than Goethe as an example of an almost perfect poem; Stendhal regarded him as France's greatest living poet, and he was on familiar terms with writers of the calibre of Lamartine, Chateaubriand, and, notwithstanding his persistent sniping at the Catholic Church, Lamennais. In these circumstances, as a pillar of *petit bourgeois* respectability and with a reputation in Europe as the authentic "voice of the people," Béranger was understandably reluctant to have his readers reminded of the bawdy songs of his youth. The erotic poems of the 1834 supplement were consequently omitted from all subsequent editions published by Perrotin during his lifetime, notably the two-volume *Oeuvres complètes* of 1847. (Later publishers, after the poet's death in 1857, were less scrupulous; in 1864 and 1875, two collections similarly entitled *Les gaités de Béranger* and containing "the best erotic and satirical songs not included in his so-called complete works" were published purportedly in Amsterdam [actually Brussels] and Villafranca, respectively; but since they contain many songs not in fact by Béranger, the present discussion will be limited to the contents of the so-called supplement to the 1834 Perrotin edition).

With a century and a half of hindsight, and if we are prepared to admit that Béranger deserved neither the extravagant praise heaped upon him during his lifetime nor the neglect or downright hostility shown toward his poems by later generations, it now seems clear that the poet was being overscrupulous in excluding the *chansons érotiques* from his complete works, since, although cruder in subject matter and expression, they are not fundamentally different in spirit from his better-known and more accessible songs. The opening poem, *La romance de Mademoiselle Justine,* takes a familiar cliché of medieval romance—the knight who embarks on a crusade because he is rejected by a cruel mistress—and inverts it: "Why don't you come up to my bedroom, gentlemen? I have many, many charms, come, feel them, I'll be nice to you, I'll be very, very nice to you." *Le grand marcheur* [The Great Walker], like many of the songs, depends on a not particularly subtle double entendre in the refrain: "Leste et gai, j'enfile, j'enfile, j'enfile / J'enfile droit mon chemin" (the French verb *enfiler* means both to go or turn down, as in "I went down Regent Street," and to insert; so, freely translated, our Great Walker says something like: "As I make my way / Down life's highway / When I meet a maid / Who's not too staid / I push along [I push it in] / I push along [I push it in].") *Le lavement,* written in broad peasant dialect, makes far from original play with the administration of an enema: "You needn't be afraid, all the ladies in Paris do it this way." The narrator of *La petite ouvrière* discovers that "Mummy was right: True happiness lies in our fingertips." The abbess of a convent, in a poem of that name, after urging her charges to go forth and fight the good fight, bringing pleasure to all manner of men, as she had done for a good 20 years, proceeds to detail the various ways in which they should go about their task.

Many of the songs depend on this kind of catalogue effect; thus the sentry in *Le tour de ronde,* dutifully patrolling the castle walls, finds a courting couple at every corner pursuing with equal diligence their nightly pleasures, so he can report: "All's well, we can sleep in peace." Other songs are structured around a repeated phrase, often culminating in a volte-face in the closing lines; for example, *Un mot de plus, ou le séducteur indécent* consists of a dialogue between the seducer and the object of his desires: As he makes increasingly improper suggestions, the lady replies, first: "One more word, Sir, and I shall leave," then "One more word, Sir, and I shall blush," then "One more word, Sir, and I'll die," then, in the penultimate stanza, "One more word, Sir, and I'll come"; but, not unusually for Béranger, whose men tend to be only human, whereas his women are generally indefatigable, it is he, not she, who comes ("And that's the end of my song"), giving the final word to the lady: "Ah, said Lison, why finish so soon / Do it again, I want to remember it."

From this brief sampling, it is clear that puritanical readers as well as strict Catholics would find much to offend them in the *chansons érotiques.* Béranger had an excellent ear for popular speech, as evidenced by the racy exchanges in *L'Anneau de mariage* between the newly wed Joseph and the High Priest, who advises him "not to worry" should an angel happen to turn up at the marriage bedside. But for those who are comfortable with Boccaccio or with Chaucer's *Wife of Bath* or the text of Carl Orff's *Carmina Burana,* these little studied chansons are well worth revisiting. The pleasures they describe, admittedly limited in scope and somewhat repetitious, are shared equally by both parties, and, in terms of nineteenth-century French literary history, are a refreshing contrast to the mawkish sentimentality of Lamartine and Musset, or the disturbing and, at least for some critics, fundamentally misogynous sadomasochism of Baudelaire.

Biography

Pierre-Jean de Béranger was born August 19, 1780, in Paris. He was never formally educated and learned French grammar from a friend who was a printer. In 1802 he became a clerk at the University of Paris and did hack writing for hire. He gained sudden widespread fame after the publication of his own songs and poems, which were highly critical of the government set up under the restored Bourbon monarchy. The controversy they engendered led to his dismissal from his post and three months' imprisonment. He died in Paris on July 16, 1857.

GRAHAM FALCONER

Further Reading

Brivois, Jules. *Bibliographie de l'oeuvre de P-J de Béranger*. Paris: Conquet, 1876. Repr. Leipzig, 1974.
Poètes d'aujourd'hui series. Paris: P Seghers, 1971.

Touchard, Jean. *La gloire de Béranger*. Vol 1, 133–48. Paris: A. Colin, 1968.
Since the *chansons* were intended to be sung rather than read, it should be noted that several selections appeared in the 1970s on the Chants du Monde and Vega/Decca labels, although their availability is now somewhat sporadic.

BERG, JEAN[NE] DE

1930–
French novelist

In 1956, under the male pen name Jean de Berg, Catherine Ratskian published *L'Image* [*The Image*], a novel that echoes *Story of O,* which had been published three years earlier under the pseudonym Pauline Réage: Both are extremely well crafted erotic novels with heavy sadomasochistic themes and multiple descriptive tableaus stemming from these practices. Narrated by the male "Jean" character, *L'Image* describes his gradual involvement in a lesbian sadomasochistic relationship: His friend Claire, a mature woman, has taken Anne, a young woman, as a subservient lover. She invites Jean to assist in Anne's domination. Jean complies with pleasure and eventually ends up dominating Claire as well. The story closes on that last event. The book was published by cutting-edge publisher Jérome Lindon from Editions de Minuit. Lindon published the majority of the works of the "new novelist" movement, including those by his friend and leader of the movement, Alain Robbe-Grillet. Like *Story of O, L'Image* was not only successful, but also controversial and censored; its preface was written by a famous contemporary intellectual or author; and it was adapted to film in the 70s.

The treasure hunt and guessing game to try and unmask the author of *L'Image* and determine his or her gender fascinated the French literati and literature aficionados until the end of the twentieth century. The preface to *L'Image*

is signed with the initials P.R., which were attributed to Pauline Réage, the author of the then scandalous *Story of O.* The first name of the pseudonym and main character of the book, Jean, is the first name of Paulhan, Pauline Réage's famous intellectual lover. Some scholars long suspected in fact that Alain Robbe-Grillet himself was the author of the preface, although current English editions still wrongly attribute it to Pauline Réage. The idea that the book itself might also have been written by him was even considered.

Catherine Robbe-Grillet has finally admitted being the author of *L'Image* under the pseudonym Jean de Berg, and she privately admits that her husband is indeed the author of the preface. Alain Robbe-Grillet confirmed this fact in *Angélique; ou, L'enchantement* in 1986, explaining precisely how the hoax was set as a prank on Jean Paulhan with the help of Jérome Lindon. In fact Alain Robbe-Grillet had already partially revealed the truth about this literary masquerade when he chose the name Robert de Berg for one of his characters in *Topologie d'une cité fantôme* [*Topology of a Phantom City*], a collage novel from 1976. Robert de Berg's half-sister's name is "Djinn," which is a homonym of the name "Jean" in English and is also the title of another one of his books, which was written as a French teaching method for students of French in California universities in 1981.

Almost 30 years after *L'Image,* in 1985 Catherine Robbe-Grillet published *Cérémonies de femmes* [*Women's Rites*], subtitled *Essays in* the *Erotic Imagination. Cérémonies* is essentially a description and reflection of her own sadomasochistic erotic games, tracking her progress as a dominatrix in New York City and then Paris. It was printed under the pen name Jeanne de Berg, an apparent female counterpart to Jean de Berg. The book describes multiple partners and elaborate theatrical settings and includes a dialogue with a female friend of the narrative voice, Marie, asking questions about Jeanne's sadoerotic games.

Cérémonies came to the forefront when a chic, veiled Jeanne de Berg appeared on French television to publicize the book the year of its publication. Catherine played the part of a mysterious guest on the most famous French literary TV show at that time, the very popular *Apostophes,* watched by millions of francophone people worldwide. By then, the secret was already out—most of the audience already knew that it was indeed Catherine Robbe-Grillet who sat under the veil. However, Bernard Pivot, the fashionable host of the show, decided to play along and pretend that nobody knew the real identity of the veiled woman, even though he announced that this female author was the wife of a prominent contemporary French writer.

Both *L'Image* and *Cérémonies de femmes* have caught the attention of feminist critics. Claudine Brécourt-Villars in 1985 decoded Jean de Berg as an anagram of "Je bande R.G." [I have a hard-on, R.G.] and declared that the novel could not possibly have been written by a female. Both Alain and Catherine Robbe-Grillet have refuted the anagram hypothesis. Susan Sontag in *The Pornographic Imagination* praises both *Story of O* and *L'Image* as belonging to literature and ranking higher than Oscar Wilde's *Teleny, or the Earl of Rochester's Sodom.* In the scholarly article "Performance Anxieties and Theatrical Perversions: Jeanne de Berg's *Cérémonies de Femmes,*" Gwendolyn Wells looks for parodical intent in the novel, but her study is inconclusive: The book might be read as criticizing pornography as a form but, in any case, does not subvert the traditional phallic signs of power.

Biography

Born in Paris in 1930, Catherine Robbe-Grillet (née Catherine Ratskian, aka Jean[ne] de Berg) studied in a Catholic high school, Notre-Dame-de-Sion, and then, for her higher education, at HEC (Ecole des Hautes Etudes Commerciales). She married the controversial novel theoretician, novelist, and film director Alain Robbe-Grillet October 23, 1957, in Neuilly-sur-Seine. In 1961, en route to Tokyo, they survived a plane crash in Hamburg.

CHRISTOPHE LAGIER

Selected Works

Under the name Jean(ne) de Berg

L'Image. Paris: Minuit, 1956.
The Image. Translated from the French by Patsy Southgate. New York: Grove Press, 1966; New York: Creation Books, 2004 (no mention of translator).
Cérémonies de femmes. Paris: Grasset et Fasquelle, 1985.
Women's Rites. Translated from the French by Anselm Hollo. New York : Grove Press, 1987.

Further Readings

Under the name Catherine Robbe-Grillet

Entretiens avec Jeanne de Berg [Interview with Jeanne de Berg]. Brussels: 2002.
Jeune Mariée [Newly-wed]. *Journal 1957–1962.* Paris: Fayard, 2004.

Others

Brécourt-Villars, Claudine, ed. *Ecrire d'amour: anthologie de textes érotiqes féminins (1799–1984).* Paris: Ramsay, 1985.
Marin La Meslée, Valérie. "Rendez-vous avec Catherine Robbe-Grillet." *Magazine littéraire* 402 (October 2001): 36–38.
Sontag, Susan. "The Pornographic Imagination." In *Styles of Radical Wills.* New York: Delta Publishing, 1978.
Wells, Gwendolyn. "Performance Anxieties and Theatrical Perversions: Jeanne de Berg's *Cérémonies de femmes.*" In *Alteratives* (Festschrift for Jean Alter), Edited by Warren Motte and Gerald Prince, 215–29. Collection "French Forum Monographs," #82. Lexington, KY: French Forum Publishers, 1993.

BESTIALITY

Unlike some other themes of eroticism, such as flagellation, defloration, and the sexual imbroglio of the clergy, whose thematic emergence in erotic literature dominates specific historical periods and well-defined geographical areas, literary representations of sexual intercourse between human beings and nonhuman animals are not restricted to any given time and place. Regardless of cultural and linguistic context, spanning the entire history of erotica and cutting across the three main literary genres (prose, poetry, drama), bestiality, or what is sometimes referred to as *zoophilia,* seems to constitute a universal characteristic of the human sexual imagination. In addition, bestiality is one of the few erotic modalities that has lent itself easily to full integration within the narrative structure and stylistic requirements of all varieties of literary description. From satirical parable to entertaining limerick, from belles-lettres to the cheapest pornography, and from connoisseur edition to mass-market pulp fiction, bestiality has been able to adapt itself effortlessly to each and every niche of expression, often conditioning the erotic qualities of a textual composition all by itself.

One of the oldest documents sporting a scene of bestiality is Apuleius' *Asinus Aureus* [*The Golden Ass*] (second century CE), in which a young man, after being accidentally transformed into a donkey instead of a bird, sees himself faced with the daunting task of satisfying a noble and wealthy lady. The young man's initial anxiety about the size of his organ quickly turns into a fear that he may not be able to fulfil his mistress's ardent desire; but after a long night of adventurous excess, the woman decides to pay in advance for yet another encounter with her favorite lover. Similar examples of women lusting after the sexual prowess of animals abound in the grand symphony of erotic literature and pervade creations as semiotically diverse as the *Thousand and One Nights,* Saint-Just's *Organt* (1789), Andrea de Nerciat's *Le diable au corps* (1803), Jerzy Kosinski's *Steps* (1969), and Alberto

Moravia's *La cosa* (1984). The only variation on the theme of female bestiality in these works is found in the nature of the sexually active animal, yet even here the choice appears to be fairly limited, ranging (in order of preference) from donkeys to horses to dogs to apes.

Whereas the sexological and forensic reports of bestiality consist predominantly of sexual activities between male human beings and female animals, the distribution of gender is inversely proportionate within literary representations, such that women are endowed with irresistible seductive talents and unquenchable sexual appetites. One possible explanation for this remarkable shift of perspective could be that most literary accounts of cross-species sexual acts have been produced by men, so that the theme of a woman enjoying wild sex with animals epitomizes, more than anything else, the creative outcome of a male fantasy, in which the male author may unconsciously identify with the inexhaustible lascivious beast. In Pierre Béarn's *La bête* (1989), a male rendition of the erotic recollections of a woman, the penis of the adult man seducing the twelve-year-old girl is even explicitly designated as "the beast." Yet sometimes the zoophilic woman makes it crystal-clear that animals are much better lovers than their human counterparts, leaving the man in a state of jealousy, anger, and confusion. In Alfred de Musset's *Gamiani* (1833), for instance, Baron Alcide is forced to witness how Countess Gamiani suddenly disappears into an adjacent room in order to surrender herself completely to the frantic movements of an enormous dog. A similar theme occurs in Robinson Jeffers' poem *Roan Stallion,* although here the woman eventually kills her stallion-lover, after the latter murders her husband.

Much less frequent than the vignettes of male animals coupling with female humans are the literary versions of men initiating and enjoying bestial activities. When they do occur, they are often presented as guilt-ridden tales of youthful sexual exploration, as in the celebrated Dutch writer Jan Wolkers' *De hond met de blauwe tong* [*The Dog with the Blue Tongue*] (1964). Two notable exceptions to this pattern in the prose genre appear in Bernard Noël's *Le Château de Cène* (1969) and, although situated in a completely different league of creation, in Maurice Rheims's *O de mer* (1963). In the former novel, the male protagonist gives in to a forcefully imposed session of mutual fellatio with two dogs, whereas in the latter text a fisherman wallows himself pleasurably in the shiny wet tentacles of a female octopus. In the drama genre, a unique example of a man pursuing a horse appears in Fernando Arrabal's *Bestialité érotique* (1969).

What men seem to appreciate in their female animal partners is less a high degree of sexual performance and more the stereotypical features of the receptive woman: perennial accessibility, lack of resistance, physical warmth, and bodily softness. Whereas bestial women, at least in the male imagination, purportedly enjoy the aggressive beast in the weak man or, slightly more annoyingly, the beast instead of the man, the classic zoophilic man apparently fancies the obsequious woman in the wild beast. In substituting an animal for a human partner, both women and men are in search of the qualities which the opposite sex of their own species does not possess. For women the beastliness of the other triggers a picture of ultramasculinity (vigor and virility), whilst for men this beastliness conceals

a conventional image of suprafemininity (tenderness and commitment).

DANY NOBUS

Further Reading

Creager, Angela N.H., and William Chester Jordan. *The Animal/Human Boundary: Historical Perspectives*. Rochester, NY: University of Rochester Press, 2002.

Curnutt, Jordan. *Animals and the Law: A Sourcebook*. Santa Barbara, CA: ABC-Clio, 2001.

Dekkers, Midas. *Dearest Pet: On Bestiality*. Translated by Paul Vincent. London and New York: Verso, 2000.

Dubois-Dessaule, Gaston. *Bestiality: An Historical, Medical, Legal and Literary Study* (no translator given). New York: Panurge Press, 1933.

Edkins, D., ed. *Animal Attractions: A Tribute to the Love Between People and Animals*. New York: Harry N Abrams, 1995.

Grassberger, R. *Die Unzucht mit Tieren*. Vienna and New York: Springer Verlag, 1968.

Masters, R.E.L. *Forbidden Sexual Behavior and Morality: An Objective Reexamination of Perverse Sex Practices in Different Cultures*. New York: Julian Press, 1964.

Matthews, Mark. *The Horseman: Obsessions of a Zoophile*. New York: Prometheus Books, 1994.

Niemöller, A. *Bestiality and the Law: A Resume of the Law and Punishments for Bestiality with Typical Cases from the Fifteenth Century to the Present*. Girard, KS: Haldeman-Julius Publications, 1946.

Salisbury, Joyce E. *The Beast Within: Animals in the Middle Ages*. New York and London: Routledge, 1994.

Villeneuve, Roland. *Le musée de la bestialité*. Paris: Editions Azur, 1969.

Von Hentig, Hans. *Soziologie der zoophilen Neigung*. Stuttgart: Ferdinand Enke, 1962.

BI YU LOU [*THE JADES PAVILION*]

Medieval Chinese novel

For most Chinese novels written in the vernacular and published during the late Ming (1368–1644) and early Qing (1644–1911) periods, it is difficult, in some cases impossible, to identify the author and the date of publication. *Bi Yu Lou* is no exception to the rule. The writer of its foreword, also unknown, promotes the novel by saying it warns against dissoluteness, but above all contains erotic developments

which are far more elaborate than anything written on the subject ever before. Yet, despite its own undeniable qualities, *The Jades Pavilion* [*Bi Yu Lou*] is still far from outdoing the earlier works it directly draws its inspiration from.

Of the latter, the three most outstanding and obvious ones are definitely the *Jin Ping Mei* [*The Plum in the Golden Vase*], the *Huanxi yuanjia* [*Enemies Enamored*] and the *Rou putuan* [*The Carnal Prayer Mat*, published in 1657]. The first title shows how the names of the three main female characters can be combined to form title. From the second, a collection of tales published in Hangzhou in 1640, the *Bi Yu Lou* amongst other things borrows the pattern of a husband deceived by the friend in whose care he has entrusted his wife (a plot which serves as the basis of the *Huanxi yuanjia*'s nineteenth tale). And from the third one, it borrows the idea of an ill-endowed husband appealing to a master's *ars erotica* to have his penis lengthened and toned up; but whereas in Li Yu's work the hero was given the transplant of a dog's penis—an operation which turned him into a bedroom athlete—here the main character, Wang Baishun, undergoes a plant therapy which is supposed to enhance his capacities so as to satisfy the legitimate demands of his wife and also allow him some extramarital affairs. The stratagem by which Mrs Feng, the matchmaker, provides her client with a forsaken wife moreover happens to be exactly the same rotten trick as the one used in "The Pearl-Sewn Shirt," the very first tale (and a famous one) to appear in the first of the three collections that Feng Menglong (1574–1646) compiled between 1620 and 1627 under the title *San Yan* [Three Words]. As far as borrowings are concerned in the *Bi Yu Lou,* one may also think of such novels as the *Zhaoyang qushi* [The Lascivious History of Zhaoyang], built on the apparition of a she-fox spirit. Here, these sensual and disquieting characters are not only the cause of men's unrest, but also the instruments of retribution for acts that are often narrated with plenty of shocking details.

When Mr. Wang decides to go to the capital to have his genitalia improved and thus avoid the ire of his demanding wife Zhang Bilian, he entrusts her to his best friend Wu Neng. The latter soon cuckolds him with complete peace of mind, until a righter of wrongs one day catches the lovers red-handed and kills him. The ensuing court trial spares the avenger, who finds himself only banished, while Bilian's honor is also treated gently: She gets away with a mere sermon given by a very open-minded official. Once he's back home after a few months away, Wang Baishun makes use of his new genitals with his wife. He soon ends up unknowingly buying Wu Neng's daughter as a maid, and although the death of his friend fortuitously comes to his ears after a while, its true cause remains concealed from him. In the meantime,

he has an affair with a beauty on the occasion of stirring erotic dreams, and decides to marry her. But as the fiancée happens to be dead already, the matchmaker in charge suggests that he should marry another young beauty (and the neglected wife of a merchant constantly away on business) named Yulou. However, the ghost of the dead fiancée soon comes back to haunt Wang Baishun, demanding care from her originally promised one: She explains that she is a she-fox spirit and expects him to help her avoid the fateful end which is awaiting her. But when the time comes, Baishun doesn't keep his word, thereby dooming himself to suffer the revenge of the evil creature, who has miraculously managed to come back unscathed from her ordeal. And soon the punishment arrives: The return of Yulou's husband seals the tragic fate of Wang Baishun the lover. To cap it all, the once cuckolded merchant ends up marrying the wife of the cuckolder whom he has killed; Baishun's former sexual partners will from then on live with the merchant in perfect harmony, as equals. The epilogue, quite lenient toward a woman who has knowingly been unfaithful to her husband, as well as the general tone of the novel, both suggest an author who seems to be particularly well–disposed toward the fair sex. Likewise, he shows great sympathy for the merchant, who is far better treated in the novel than the scholars who are accused of the most reprehensible wrongdoings. Could it be that he was willing to please a specific audience, at a time when novels in vernacular Chinese were starting to be circulated more widely than before?

Indeed, the author of the *Bi Yu Lou* spared no effort to write a novel in which sex scenes are threaded together with steady rhythm: Only four chapters do not contain any explicitly erotic passages. Yet, he nonetheless remains notably moderate, depicting strictly heterosexual lovemaking between a man and his wife, and between each of them and their lover—the only bending of the rules being the relation between Baishun and the she-fox demon on the occasion of erotic dreams. As for the postures used during the lovemaking, they do not vary much, but leave room for the expression of a certain sensibility: Partners kiss on the mouth, and breasts are caressed and occasionally licked; the wife does not hesitate to blow the flute with her husband's penis so as to enhance her own desire; and all along, men pay special attention to their partners' small bound feet. Vaginal secretions also play an important part in the economy of love relations, though the author thoroughly avoids indulging in the display of a so-called erotic science. The sexuality here depicted is both healthy and sportsmanlike, and aims entirely at the satisfaction of the legitimate desires of the characters, who make use of their bodies as they like and with whom they please. Their sensual desire arises from the sight of bodies and is heightened by the consumption of alcohol, which literally flows throughout the novel.

The author's account moreover denounces practices that were very common in those days and which sometimes led masters to sexually

abuse their young maids. In the novel, the maid eventually passes away after being roughly deflowered. Those qualities may well have seduced the readership of that time and may also have inspired the writing of the *Huanxi langshi* [The Lascivious History of Pleasure], a short novel in 12 chapters which, as is the case for the *Bi Yu Lou*, remains anonymous and undated.

PIERRE KASER
Translated from the French by Victor Thibout

Translation of the *Bi Yu Lou*

Le Pavillon des Jades. Translated by Aloïs Tatu. Edited by Pierre Kaser. Arles: Editions Philippe Picquier, collection "Le pavillon des corps curieux," 2003.

BLASONS DU CORPS

The French word *blason* (blazon) is originally a heraldic term denoting a coat of arms, as well as its description. In the late 15th and 16th centuries, the heraldic meaning was extended to indicate a usually brief versified text, generally accompanied by an illustration, describing a wide range of subjects. The most interesting manifestation ot the poetic *blason* is to be found in the 16th-century subgenre of the *blasons du corps féminin,* which evoke separate parts of women's bodies in imaginative, erotically charged, metaphorical terms.

The context for the poetic practice of depicting distinct elements of the female form is situated, for the French poets of the Renaissance, in earlier literary traditions, and most significantly in the new anatomical treatises which stress the importance of dissection—i.e., of fragmentation and penetration—as a tool of exploration and knowledge, not only in the medical field but also in the wider scientific and intellectual sphere. The notion of the fragment, allied with an urge toward discovery and appropriation, partakes of the glamour of the "new" and encourages a titillating intensity focused on a singular, brilliantly appealing object.

The first *blason anatomique* was written by Clement Marot, one of the *Grands-Rhétoriqueurs*, closely connected with the court of Francis I. In 1535 he composed the *Blason du tétin* [Blazon of the Breast] and thus launches a literary fashion destined to enjoy an immense popularity through the century. Inspired and solicited by Marot, a spate of poets—some (such as Maurice Sceve) well-known authors from prominent cultural centers, others obscure provincials—follow his example, and already from 1536 on groups of *blasons* are included in larger poetic compilations. For the first time in 1543 a distinct volume under the title *Blasons anatomiques du corps fémenin* is published in Paris, comprising 37 poems, by 15 named and 8 anonymous authors. The multiple printings in the 16th century testify to the collection's success. In keeping with the taste for illustrated books, woodcuts accompany a number of the *blasons,* but, artistically rudimentary, they lack the amorous eloquence of the texts.

The *blasons du corps* are astrophic poems, mostly composed in octosyllabic verse. They vary widely in length, tone, and poetic virtuosity, but they all have in common their engagement with a single part of a woman's body, from the hair to the feet, including the most private parts. Typically the blasoned object is named copiously throughout the text, often at the start of each line, thus suggesting the anaphoric implorations of a profane litany, as the poet addresses himself to his selected idol in terms of adoration and supplication.

It is the presence of the poet/lover that creates the erotic space in which the object of desire is enthroned and, through the use of concatenated metaphors, transformed into multiple avatars of the author's needs and imaginings. Although a comic, occasionally scatological, note may be struck, and a ludic tone is often present, the majority of the poems evince a grave, ardently passionate mode of expression as the poet seeks to lose himself in the dangerous sexual space—images of secrecy, of peril, of entering abound—where he aspires to touch, to smell, to taste the seductive object he has created by seeing and dismembering a woman's body. The poet's implicit stance is both that of the dissecting conqueror and that of the conquered victim, since he must suffer the at times punishing dominance of his self-imposed obsession. Fetishistic, sadomasochistic, and voyeuristic overtones color the texts and confer upon them a manifest aura of sexual daring.

A variant on the *blasons* follows closely upon their invention, namely that of the *contreblasons* (counterblazons), which address the same body parts, but in terms of denigration. Again Marot leads the way with his *Contreblason du tetin,* in which the previously exalted breast is now described as ugly and repulsive. However, this "anti-model" intended by Marot to be read in jocular contrast to "the real thing" is followed by very few poets. Indeed, the greatest number of *contreblasons* are composed by one author, La Hueterie, who seeks not to emulate Marot, but rather to condemn the anatomical *blasons.* In this condemnation he is not alone; not surprisingly, the *blasons* scandalized a number of righteous critics who called them indecent and sinful.

While the known *blasonneurs* are all male, certain women poets of the period, such as Louise Labé and Catherine des Roches, engage in a practice akin to that of the *blason*'s detailed amorous description, without, however, the singular focus of the *blason;* at the same time they subvert certain conventions of the genre, and

thus deconstruct the language of male desire in order to reconstruct it in a female mode.

In the second half of the 16th century the use of the designation *blason* affixed to a love poem disappeared, although *Pleiade* poets, such as Ronsard, continue to draw on the thematic possibilities initiated by Marot and his followers. In Renaissance England the lineaments of the French *blason* appear as poetic topoi and figures, embedded in more extensive textualizations of a woman's presence.

Although from the 17th century on the *blasons anatomiques,* now considered a dubious minor genre, tended to be excluded from anthologies and literary surveys, a renewed interest in their textual and historical existence was manifested in the 19th and 20th centuries by a number of editions and studies, and since the last quarter of the 20th century, various critical/theoretical approaches have been applied to them. Psychoanalytical (Freudian, Lacanian) readings have scrutinized the unconscious of the texts; feminist interpretations have examined the misogyny implied in the reification and morselization of the female body; the problematics of gender representation and of sexual politics, intersecting with cultural and rhetorical traditions, have been investigated; New Historicism has analyzed the poems as symptomatic of early modern society, a world marked by fragmentation. The *blasons du corps* thus assume a multiplicity of meanings, all springing from their seemingly simple (descriptive, evocative) as well as from their complex (obsessive, dramatic) discourses, and from their compelling erotic authority.

TILDE SANKOVITCH

Editions

Guegan, B. *Blasons anatomiques du corps fémenin.* Paris: Les Paralleles, 1931.
Lambert, Jean-Clarence. *Les blasons du corps feminin.* Paris: Balland, 1967.
Schmidt, Albert-Marie. in *Poètes du XVIe siecle.* Paris: Gallimard, 1953.

Further Reading

Hillman, David, and Carla Mazzio, eds. *The Body in Parts: Fantasies of Corporeality in Early Modern Europe.* New York and London: Routledge, 1997.
Jones, Ann Rosalind. "Petrarchism with a Difference," in *A New History of French Literature,* ed. Denis Hollier. Cambridge, MA: Harvard University Press, 1989.

Kritzman, Lawrence D. *The Rhetoric of Sexuality and the Literature of the French Renaissance*. Cambridge: Cambridge University Press, 1991.

Pike, Robert E. "The 'Blasons' in French Literature of the Sixteenth Century," *Romanic Review* 27 (1936): 223–47.

Saunders, Alison. *The Sixteenth-Century Blason Poetique*. Bern: Peter Lang, 1981.

Sawday, Jonathan. *The Body Emblazoned: Dissection and the Human Body in Renaissance Culture*. London: Routledge, 1995.

Sorsby, Karen. *Representations of the Body in French Renaissance Poetry*. New York: Peter Lang, 1999.

Tomarken, Annette and Edward. "The Rise of the Sixteenth Century *blason*," *Symposium* 29 (1975): 139–63.

Vickers, Nancy J. "Diana Described: Scattered Woman and Scattered Rhyme," *Critical Inquiry* 8 (1981): 265–79.

"Members Only: Marot's Anatomical Blazons." In *The Body in Parts: Fantasies of Corporeality in Early Modern Europe*, Edited by David Hillman and Carla Mazzio. New York and London: Routledge, 1997.

Williams, Grant. "Disarticulating Fantasies: Figures of Speech, Vices and the Blazon in Renaissance English Rhetoric." *Rhetoric Society Quarterly* 29 (1999): 43–53.

Wilson, Dudley B. *Descriptive Poetry in France from Blason to Baroque*. Manchester: Manchester University Press, 1967.

BLESSEBOIS, PIERRE CORNEILLE

c. 1646–c. 1700
French novelist and dramatist

Pierre Corneille Blessebois was born with the forenames Pierre Alexis, but later abandoned these. He also abjured his Protestantism, much to the chagrin of his mother. His interest in religion was shared by other libertine writers (such as Théophile de Viau), many of whom were unjustly criticized on the grounds of impiety and atheism, when their attacks were often focused on religious hypocrisy and excess rather than faith itself. Blessebois wrote two religious tragedies, though these may have served as a means of flaunting his Catholic credentials after the Revocation of the Edict of Nantes (1685) in order to allay any suspicion of attachment to his former religion. He also changed his name to the more literary-sounding Pierre Corneille Blessebois, and its first recorded use coincides with his writing debut with a manuscript entitled *Les aventures dans le parc d'Alençon* [*Adventures in Alençon's Park*] (1668), which was circulated among a select local readership. This novel dealt with the question of whether love is caused by nature or nurture, though this philosophical undercurrent is tempered by the work detailing the sexual peccadilloes of certain inhabitants of the town of the work's title. The scandal caused by the tale's explicit erotic content and its fundamental critique of a seemingly malicious God, compounded by Blessebois's mother's distress, obliged him to return to Verneuil.

His next novel was also semi-autobiographical, *Le rut, ou la pudeur éteinte* [*The Rutting Season, or Spent Modesty*] (1676), a work of revenge parodying his mistress, Marthe Le Hayer, for having reported him to the authorities. Blessebois thinly disguised her as Amarante, a sexually voracious alcoholic who is a figure of ridicule. The story is set in Alençon's prison, and the hero, Céladon (Blessebois), engages in a relationship with a beautiful female visitor, Dorimène, who is touched by his fate. She introduces him to her two sisters, and together with the jailer, Le Rocher, all engage in a debauched party that inevitably degenerates into erotic acts. In real life, the writer had made friends with Le Rocher, for which he enjoyed favorable treatment, including visits from women curious about the infamous inmate. In the novel, their special relationship comes to an end when Le Rocher discovers he is impotent and releases Céladon out of jealousy of his sexual performance. The newly liberated young man encounters a knight who is really Amarante disguised in male garb. The couple stop off at an inn and participate in an orgy with the innkeeper, Louis, and his wife. Following scenes depict Amarante persecuting Céladon because he will not marry her, and she has him imprisoned at For-l'Evêque, where his cellmate is the pederastic Baron de Samoi. The nobleman is infatuated with his new cellmate and this provokes Céladon to embrace Amarante when she comes to visit him. She is overjoyed, and believing the baron can assist her to persuade his cellmate to wed her, promises to refuse him nothing, whereupon the baron sodomizes her. At this point, Samoi's brother arrives, and is so pleased to see his brother engaging in heterosexual relations that he secures the release of the two captives. Finally, this brother, M. de La Graverie, marries Amarante. Together they run a school for the instruction of youth, where all the students end up contracting venereal diseases. Bougard judges this novel to be the only fundamentally erotic French novel of the seventeenth century.

He published several works at Leiden, including his first theatrical works. *Marthe Le Hayer, ou mademoiselle de Sçay* is an obscene comedy in three acts, also known as *Le bordel de Mlle de Sçay* [*Mademoiselle de Sçay's Brothel*] (1678) and other titles. This cynical comedy on love is another, more direct, criticism of his former fiancée. The play's central character, Clarice (who represents Marthe Le Hayer according to the preface), together with her maid, Génevote, wish to acquire Clérimont and his valet, Lubin, for lovers. The men demand that they be paid for their sexual services, and after a period of resistance, the women duly end up rewarding the male pair. Blessebois's last work, *Le zombi du Grand-Pérou* [*The Zombie of Grand-Pérou*] (1697), dramatizes the story of a spurned woman acquiring the power, through voodoo magic, to become invisible and being transformed into a zombie-like state at night in order to spy on the man she is obsessed with. Like all his writings, this is based on his experience—in this case, his efforts to help Félicité de Lespinay seduce Charles Dupont, the writer's master. This affair secured his notoriety in his place of exile and saw him condemned for magic in 1690, for which he was sentenced to be burnt in effigy and to make restitution to God.

Alexandrian labels Blessebois "the most curious erotic author of the seventeenth century," though the writer's influence on his contemporaries was minimal and most of his works were not widely disseminated or published during his lifetime, nor was he formally associated with other libertine writers. His achievement lies in his uncompromising and defiant attitude to censorship and authority. In particular, a leitmotiv running throughout his work is the belief that men are often the victims of the opposite sex's libidinous cunning. Toward the end of the seventeenth century, some physicians were adopting mechanistic theories of personality which supported the observation that men suffered from emotional phenomena similar to hysteria. It is interesting that Blessebois's work clearly resists such notions and highlights the medieval belief of women's disordered and voracious sexual temperament. When a presiding magistrate, interrogating him during one of his many brushes with the law, demanded to know whether the accused deserved his reputation of a corrupter of many women, the writer replied that he was instead a young man whom many wicked women had corrupted.

Biography

Born in Verneuil, Normandy, c. 1646 (possibly as late as 1650) to a recently ennobled bourgeois family. Moved to Alençon due to his widespread notoriety in his hometown as a proficient seducer of young women, 1668; the scandal caused by the circulation of a manuscript caused him to return home some months later. With younger brother Philippe, set fire to and destroyed official tax records in Verneuil, standing guard until the flames had destroyed all documentation, 1670. Captured at Montreuil-sur-Mer and began his first term of imprisonment at Alençon; banished permanently from France and goods requisitioned to the Crown, November 15, 1670. Granted special permission to leave prison due to a written offer of marriage made to Marthe Le Hayer, 1671. Enrolled in the army, 1672; arrested after his fiancée complained he had reneged on his marital promise, 1673. Escaped from prison at For-l'Evêque, 1674. Fled to the Netherlands and was a mercenary on one of 15 ships commanded by Admiral Tromp. Returned to France, imprisoned several times for violent acts; sent to Châtelet, 1678. Joined the French navy; condemned to the galleys for desertion, 1681. Deemed unfit to row and exiled to Guadeloupe, February 1686. Placed as a slave under the care of Charles Dupont, marquis du Grand-Pérou, 1686. Charged with sexual magic; condemned to make reparation in absentia, 1690. Died after 1697 and probably no later than 1700.

PAUL SCOTT

Selected Works

La corneille de Mademoiselle de Sçay. Edited by Frédéric Lachèvre. La Roche-sur-Yon: Imprimerie Centrale de l'Ouest, 1937.
Œuvres satiriques de P. Corneille Blessebois. Leiden: A. Doude and F. Lopez, 1676.
Le zombi du Grand-Pérou, ou La Comtesse de Cocagne. Brussels: A. Lacroix, 1697.

Further Reading

Alexandrian, Sabane. *Histoire de la littérature érotique.* Paris: Payot et Rivages, 1995.
Apollinaire, Guillaume ed. *L'Œuvre de Pierre-Corneille Blessebois.* Paris, Bibliothèque des Curieux, 1921.
Bougard, Roger G. *Érotisme et amour physique dans la littérature française du XVIIe siècle.* Paris: Lachurié, 1986.
Lachèvre, Frédéric. *Pierre-Corneille Blessebois, Norman (1646?–1700?).* Paris: Champion, 1927.
Pia, Pascal. *Les Livres de l'Enfer du XVIe siècle à nos jours.* 2 vols. Paris: Coulet et Faure, 1978.

BOCCACCIO, GIOVANNI

1313–1375
Italian poet and novelist

Giovanni Boccaccio, one of the most influential writers in European literature, is remembered primarily for his collection of one hundred tales, the *Decameron,* written in the aftermath of the Black Death which decimated Europe in 1348. The collection contains various different kinds of stories, and many of the tales are erotic or bawdy. The *Decameron* was the first vernacular literary work to have a truly international impact, and its audience was not restricted to any one social class. It was translated into Latin, Catalan, and French even before the advent of printing. Print spread it further still.

In his youth, Boccaccio wrote several narrative works, in both prose and verse, dealing with themes of courtly love. His poem *Filostrato*, c. 1335, told the popular medieval story of Troilus' betrayal by Cressida at the siege of Troy. His *Tesieda,* c. 1341, focused on the rivalry of two young knights over a beautiful maiden. Both were famously adapted by Chaucer and later dramatized by Shakespeare. Experimenting in a wide variety of genres, Boccaccio also wrote a lengthy and jumbled prose romance, *Filocolo,* c. 1336–1338; *Fiammetta,* a psychological prose narrative of a woman betrayed by her lover, c. 1343–1344; and several poems celebrating the beauty of nymphs and the sublimity of courtly love.

While many of these early works proved influential, they are all eclipsed by the *Decameron* [*The Ten Days*], 1348–1351, which consists of one hundred tales told by a group of aristocratic young women and men who have taken refuge in a Tuscan villa to escape the ravages of the Florentine plague. Written in simple, vigorous prose, the tales in the *Decameron* are realistic and domestic: they are about ordinary people, and are set in real places. While some tales are moralistic, they tend to be worldly and ironic. The erotic tales in the *Decameron* are characterized by their acceptance of the physical reality of sex and their criticism of clerical hypocrisy. While illicit sex is not necessarily approved of, neither is it castigated or punished.

About two thirds of the tales in the collection focus on sexual relations between men and women. Some stories are decorously romantic; others are bawdy and crude. Many of these tales deal with socially forbidden relations—young lovers confronting social obstacles, adulterous liaisons, lustful clerics, rape. There is little mention of homoeroticism or autoeroticism; in the

Decameron, sex is a matter between men and women to be discussed between men and women. While some of the sexually explicit tales have proved shocking to readers over the years, at no time is it suggested in the text itself that they are inappropriate for a group of young unsupervised, unmarried aristocrats. And on the seventh day the presumably virginal young women have no trouble coming up with tales of clever wives duping their foolish husbands. Still, most of the bawdiest tales are told by the three men in the group, including the story of Masetto (3.1), a cunning laborer who becomes the sexual servant of an entire convent full of nuns, and the tale of Alibech (3.10), a Muslim girl converted to Christianity by a hermit who teaches her how to put his "devil" in her "hell."

That the women in the group outnumber the men suggests the extent to which the *Decameron* was written with a primarily female audience in mind. While in later life Boccaccio stipulated that women should not read the book, in the text itself he always refers to his readers as "ladies." Boccaccio's portrayal of women in the *Decameron* is complex and multivalent. Women appear both as passive objects of desire and as lustful protagonists. Sometimes female sexuality is seen as a threat, sometimes it is celebrated. Although the tales do not always portray women in a flattering light, the group of storytellers creates an alternative society which is largely organized by women and in which women share power with men. The influence of women on the tales is represented symbolically by the feminine space of the enclosed garden in which the group meets, as well as by the hidden "Valley of Ladies," where the young women retire to bathe and the whole group gathers to tell the bawdy tales of the seventh day. Nonetheless, the fact that none of the tales deals with female friendship suggests that Boccaccio is interested in women primarily as they relate to men.

After the completion of the *Decameron,* Boccaccio devoted himself increasingly to humanist studies and to the compilation of encyclopedic works in Latin: *Genealogica deorum gentilium* [*The Genealogies of the Pagan Gods*], 1350–1371; *De casibus virorum illustrium* [*The Fates of Illustrious Men*], 1355–1360; and *De claris mulieribus* [*Concerning Famous Women*], c. 1361. Some have seen Boccaccio's shift from creative works in the vernacular to scholarly

works in Latin as the result of his friendship with Petrarch, whom he first met in 1350. Whatever the cause, it is clear that Boccaccio's later years were marked by increasing piety and asceticism. In the late 1350s, he took minor religious orders. By the 1370s there were rumors that he had become a monk.

The shift in Boccaccio's values is perhaps best demonstrated by his final fictional text, *Corbaccio* [*The Dirty Crow*], c. 1355, a misogynist rant in the form of a dream vision warning a young man not to marry. It is hard not to see this work as a repudiation of the amorous devotion to women and the playful celebration of earthly love which suffuse the *Decameron.* Besides the scholarly writings on Dante which occupied his later years, *Corbaccio* was Boccaccio's last work in the Italian prose which he had done so much to shape into a great literary language.

The influence of the *Decameron* on European literature is incalculable and enduring, not least as a model of erotic narrative. Its structure provided the model for the Marquis de Sade's *120 Days of Sodom;* and as recently as 1971 the Italian filmmaker and poet Pier Paolo Pasolini made a film version of the *Decameron,* focusing on several of the best-known erotic tales.

Biography

Born in the summer of 1313, probably in or near Florence—not in Paris, as long believed. Illegitimate son of a successful Florentine merchant. Joined his father in Naples as apprentice of the Bardi company of Florentine bankers, 1327. Studied canon law and Latin classics at the University of Naples, beginning 1330–31. Returned to Florence, winter 1340–41. In Ravenna and Forlì, 1346–47. In Florence at time of Black Death, 1348; father and stepmother died, leaving him head of family. First meeting with Petrarch, 1350. Traveled as Florentine ambassador to various Italian states, 1350–67. Organized military resistance to mercenary Fra Moriale, 1355. Took minor clerical orders, c. 1357. Birth legitimized by papal dispensation, 1360. Promoted teaching and study of Greek at the University of Florence after 1360. Left Florence and moved to his family's hometown of Certaldo for political reasons, 1361–65. In Naples, 1371–72. Lectured on Dante in Florence, 1373. Died at Certaldo, December 21, 1375.

IAN FREDERICK MOULTON

Selected Works

Il Filostrato (c. 1335). Translated with an introduction by Robert P. a Roberts and Anna Bruni Seldis, 1986.

Il Filocolo (c. 1336–1338). Translated by Donald Cheney and Thomas G. Bergin, 1985.

Teseida delle nozze d'Emilia (c. 1341), as *The Book of Theseus*. Translated by Bernadette Marie McCoy, 1974.

Elegia di Madonna Fiametta (c. 1343–1344), as *The Elegy of Lady Fiammetta*. Edited and translated by Mariangela Causa-Steindler and Thomas Mauch, with an introduction by Mariangela Causa-Steindler, 1990.

Decameron (1348–1351). Translated by G. H. McWilliams, 1972, and by Mark Musa and Peter Bondanella, 1982.

Il Corbaccio (c. 1355), as *The Corbaccio, or The Labyrinth of Love*. Translated and edited by Anthony K. Cassell, 1993.

De claris mulieribus (c. 1361), as *Famous Women*. Edited and translated by Virginia Brown, 2001.

Further Reading

Bergin, Thomas. *Boccaccio*. New York: Viking, 1981.

Hollander, Robert. *Boccaccio's Two Venuses*. New York: Columbia University Press, 1977.

Mazzotta, Giuseppe. *The World at Play in Boccaccio's Decameron*. Princeton, NJ: Princeton University Press, 1986.

Nelson, John Charles. "Love and Sex in the *Decameron*." In *Philosophy and Humanism: Renaissance Essays in Honor of Paul Oskar Kristeller*, 339–51. New York: Columbia University Press, 1976.

Tournoy, Gilbert, ed. *Boccaccio in Europe*. Louvain, Belgium: Leuven University Press, 1977.

BONAVENTURE DES PÉRIERS

c. 1510–1544
French humanist and poet

Little is known with certainty about the life of Bonaventure Des Périers, and the mystery that shrouds his life is equaled by the enigmatic nature of a number of his works or by their uncertain attribution. The earliest definitive reference to Des Périers links him to Robert Olivetan and Lefèvre d'Étaples in 1535, indicating that Des Périers assisted in the preparation of their vernacular (French) version of the Old and New Testaments. His religious leanings, while far from following Calvinist orthodoxy, were more in line with the Reformers than with the Catholics. Among his literary associations were many of the prominent French-speaking Calvinists, including Clement Marot, whom he defended against his detractors.

As secretary to Marguerite de Navarre, the sister of Francis I, king of France, Des Périers would have transcribed her works, including many of the tales that were later published in her *Heptameron*. Marguerite's powerful position at the court, her interest in the ideas of the Reformers, as well as her own literary pursuits made her an ideal employer for Des Périers. Her circle functioned as a forum for free thought, where the ideas expressed often ran counter to both Catholic and Calvinist sensibilities. Such ideas were found in the anonymous *Cymbalum mundi,* published both in Paris and Lyon (1537–38). The text came under the scrutiny of Francis I and the Parlement of Paris. Francis' direct intervention caused the Sorbonne to order the work burned and its publisher imprisoned. How Des Périers escaped punishment—if he had been identified as the author—is unclear. The most plausible explanation is that he benefited from Marguerite's protection. However, no unequivocal attribution of the *Cymbalum mundi* to Des Periers appeared until 1566 in Henri Estienne's *Apologie d'Herodote* [*Apologia of Herodotus*]. Now considered one of the major prose texts of the sixteenth century, it defies a transparent reading. The text presents a series of four prose dialogues modeled after Lucian and establishes a pre-libertine philosophical stance in the works of Des Périers. The dialogues themselves concern disparate events—from Mercury coming to earth in order to have the book of man's fate rebound, to Cupid's arrow propelling a recalcitrant woman into her would-be lover's arms, to a horse attempting to get permission from his owner to be able to go out on his own when mares are in season (the latter being the topic of discussion of two dogs). Concordant with many ideas of the Reformation, its critique of the split of the Reformers into various sects signals Des Périers's break with any established form of Protestantism. Indeed, the Sorbonne did not declare the text heretical; rather the condemnation rested on its being a "pernicious" book. Its dedication, "Thoaizas du Clévier (or Clénier) à son ami Pierre Tryocan," deciphered in the nineteenth century as an anagram for "Thomas l'Incrédule à son ami Pierre Croyant" [Doubting Thomas to his friend Peter the Believer] signals the skepticism that imbues the dialogues.

The volume *Recueil des oeuvres de feu Bonaventure des Périers* [*Collected Works of the Late Bonaventure des Périers*] appeared shortly after his death in 1544 in Lyon. It included his poems, a work modeled on Seneca, and a translation of the *Lysis* of Plato. The Platonic dialogue, in which the interlocutors are Socrates and a series of young boys, explores love in a homosexual context. One of the poems, addressed to Marguerite de Navarre, "Queste de l'amitié" [Search for Love/Friendship] restates the main points of the Platonic dialogue, although through its dedication, it places them in the mode of heterosexual Platonic love. Renaissance Neo-Platonism also informs another poem in the collection, the "Blason du nombril" [*Blazon of the Navel*] (see *Blason du corps* in this volume). The *blason*, poems in praise of the female body, had been revived by Marot and was particularly popular among the Lyon poets. While the majority of these poems eroticized a fragmented body (there were *blasons* of the eyebrow, the nose, the breast, etc.), Des Périers' poem retraces the myth of the androgyne. Thus, like the works of his patron Marguerite de Navarre, Des Périers' writings frequently reflect the broad scope of Neo-Platonism and Evangelism. It should be remembered that at the time of the publication of this collection, Des Périers was not yet directly associated with the *Cymbalum mundi*.

A second posthumous publication would radically change the literary standing of Des Périers. The *Nouvelles récréations et joyeux devis* [*Novel Pastimes and Merry Tales*] (1558) placed him in the context of another tradition, that of the short tale, and definitively established him as a master prose writer. Nonetheless, questions of authorship were raised about the collection. When it was reprinted in 1568, it had been augmented by some 39 tales. Critical consensus maintains Des Périers as the author for the first edition, but not for the appended tales.

Nouvelles récréations et joyeux devis

The *Novel Pastimes* as originally published contained 90 "nouvelles," although the first tale serves as a preamble to explain the author's intentions. It was published the same year as another posthumous collection of short tales, Marguerite de Navarre's *Heptameron*. Unlike that text, which, following in the tradition of Boccaccio, placed its tales in an elaborate frame structure, Des Périers's work is not set in a coherent, overarching structure, nor does it play different narrative voices against one another. Given that Des Périers was familiar with Marguerite's work and her desire to create a French Decameron, it is possible that Des Périers deliberately chose a different structure for his collection. A single narrative voice unites the tales, characterized in the main by their brevity. The order is not completely random: some tales in a series share a common character, others follow upon a similar theme, others have a similar geographic location. The tales themselves are models of simple, direct narration, demonstrating little interest in serious social satire or moralizing. The minimal development of characters, combined with ample dialogue, as well as narrative exposition, create fast-paced, easily accessible stories. The vast majority of the tales can be divided into three broad thematic categories: the Church, the Law, and sex, with protagonists from all social strata. These categories, which sometimes overlap, also recall the themes of the *fabliaux,* thus placing Des Périers's collection in the tradition of the short French comic tale.

Unlike the *fabliaux,* however, erotic subjects do not dominate the collection: horse thievery is as important as the "theft" of another man's wife. Further, however colored his other works may be by a Protestant morality and a Neo-Platonist love esthetic, love, when it appears in these tales, is a physical matter, better qualified as lust. The promiscuity of the clergy, adulterous relations, and sexual jokes form the core of the erotic tales in the collection. Typical plots include husbands who are cuckolded in spite of their efforts to preserve their honor; for example,

"De l'enfant de Paris nouvellement marie, et de Beaufort qui trouva moyen de jouir de sa femme, nonobstant la songeuse garde de dame Pernette" [Of the Newly Wed Parisian Youth, and Beaufort, Who Was Able to Have His Way with the Former's Wife, Despite the Careful Watch of Dame Pernette]. Others are frequently concerned with performance and ingenuity in matters of sexual relations; for example, "D'un jeune garson qui se nomma Thoinette pour ester receu a une religion de nonnains" (Of a Young Man Who Called Himself Thoinette So That He Could Enter a Convent"). Linguistic turns, as in "De Trois soeurs nouvelles épouses, qui répondirent chacune un bon mot à leur mari la première nuiét de leurs nopces" [Of Three Recently Married Sisters Who Each Answered Their Husbands by a Witticism on Their Wedding Night], three sisters must come up with a way to counter their husbands' discovery that they are not virgins. Their father offers two hundred écus to the one who has the best reply. The story ends in a series of puns, but the narrator does not say who wins, preferring to accord each one the sum. Overall, the ribald, bawdy nature of these tales and the unadorned language dealing with sex demonstrate Des Périers's ease with the "esprit gaulois" that amply colors the French short tale.

Biography

Born Arnay-le-Duc, c. 1510. Probably educated in Autun, at the abbey school of Saint Martin. Visited Lyon in 1533–34. Secretary to Marguerite de Navarre, 1536–41(?). Spent time in Paris in 1540s. Died, possibly a suicide, Lyon, c. 1544.

EDITH J. BENKOV

Selected Works

Le Cymbalum mundi en françoys, contenant quatre dialogues poetiques, fort antiques, joyeux et facetieux. Paris: Jehan Morin, 1537. Translated as *Cymbalum mundi: Four Very Ancient Joyous and Facetious Poetic Dialogues* by Bettina L. Knapp. New York: Bookman Associates, c. 1965.
Cymbalum mundi. Edited by Peter Hampshire Nurse, with a preface by Michael A. Screech. Geneva: Droz, 1983.
———. Edited by Max Gauna. Paris: Honoré Champion, 2000.
Nouvelles récréations et joyeux devis. Lyon: Robert Granjon, 1558. Translated as *Novel Pastimes and Merry Tales* by Raymond C. La Charité and Virginia A. La Charité, in *Studies in Romance Languages* 6. Lexington: University Press of Kentucky, 1972.
Nouvelles récréations et joyeux devis: I-XC. Edited by Krystyna Kasprzyk. Paris: H. Champion, 1980.

Further Reading

Hassell, James W. *Sources and Analogues of the* Nouvelles récréations et joyeux devis *of Bonaventure des Périers.* Athens: University of Georgia Press, 1970.
Sozzi, Leonello. *Les contes de Bonaventure Des Périers: Contribution à l'étude de la nouvelle française de la Renaissance.* Turin: Giapichelli, 1965.

BONNETAIN, PAUL

1858–1899
French novelist, journalist, and playwright

Major Work: *Charlot s'amuse*

On August 18, 1887, Bonnetain and four other disciples of the naturalist novelist Émile Zola (1840–1902) published an open letter accusing the Master of having perpetrated in his recent novel *La terre* [*Earth*] (1887) a gross attack on virtue. The irony is that Bonnetain himself had previously become known as a purveyor of filth and, because of the notoriety of his novel *Charlot s'amuse*, which took self-abuse as its theme, had earned himself the nickname "Bonnemain" ("Handy Andy"). As a naturalist writer, he, too, subscribed to a literary program in which scientific realism was used to construct a portrait of the underside of society and the degeneracy of individuals who inhabited it.

Charlot s'amuse [*Charlie Gives Himself a Helping Hand*] (1883) is a novel about a man who suffers from a deviation of the sexual drive (or "genital sense"), which in his case manifests itself as an irrepressible desire to masturbate. The teaching of the Swiss medical writer Samuel Auguste Tissot (1728–1797) was still generally accepted, and onanism was held to be responsible for softening the brain, destroying an individual's willpower, generating tuberculosis, and ensuring moral impotence. Bonnetain was prosecuted in December 1884 at the Assize Court in Paris and was acquitted. His Belgian publisher, Kistemaeckers, was similarly let off at the Brabant Assizes in December 1885. In both cases much was made of the literary quality of the work.

When *Charlot s'amuse* was next published, in 1888, it contained the text of the indictment together with a precise list of the 12 allegedly obscene passages selected as being "contrary to public decency." The reader could therefore more easily form his (or less probably her) own opinion as to whether the novel was pornographic or not. In addition, the book carried a supportive preface by a friend, Henri Céard (1851–1924), who was also a naturalist writer. Céard admitted that he had not "studied" the novel thoroughly, but he declared that he had been particularly touched by its "profound sadness," its "serene ferocity," the "quiet, sinister manner of its observations," and the "cruelty of life," as well as the "misery of passion" which it described. In addition, it showed "heredity in all its horrors" and "fate manifest in physiology." But, he contended, while it certainly attacked hypocrisy, the novel was above all artistically written. The choice of subject, he maintained, was not open to criticism, for masturbation already featured in the Bible and the *Confessions* of Jean-Jacques Rousseau: "*Charlot* provides a terrifying analysis of a penniless man promenading his vice across the whole of Paris but never being able to satisfy his dream, his erection yet more stimulated as he views photographs of nudes in gaslit windows, and so storing up his desires at each new step that no sexual contact will satisfy him—his only despairing recourse then being to his own hand." The details to which Céard alludes include the hero's drunken suicidal father and his nymphomaniac mother. Charlot's neurosis and vitiated sexual urge lead to epilepsy, anemia, and the general collapse of his personality. As a pretty child he is seduced and abused by several Catholic priests (the anticlerical tone of the work is in line with other contemporary novels on homosexual themes), and when he moves on to secondary school he forms an attachment with Lucien, a more "masculine" elder youth, who, after an initial sentimental affair, abandons him for women and the army. Charlot now learns to dissemble as he begins to masturbate more efficiently and to hide his vice.

He is filled with distaste for women, "which is, as it were, the punishment for self abuse." A visit to a prostitute does not cure him; and an affair with Fanny, another nymphomaniac, is successful only as long as they both continue to indulge their appetite for "ecstatic orgies of lust." Fanny abandons Charlot, leaving their baby son with him. He, having relapsed into his habit, learns from *Family Advice to Fathers* that "solitary abuse, when it does not lead to frightful diseases, inevitably results in madness or suicide." He therefore decides to preempt his destiny, and taking the child with him (for he fears that the boy will have inherited the family curse), he drowns them both in the nearby canal. While the novel may be read as a cautionary tale, there is no doubt that the lurid descriptive passages are quite powerful.

Biography

Born in Nîmes (Department of the Gard, southern France), 1858; died in Hong (Laos), 1899. Between the ages of 18 and 23, Bonnetain served in the French navy. Repatriated when he was suffering from malaria, which he contracted in French Guiana, he published his first novel, *Le tour du monde d'un troupier* [*A Trooper's Journey Around the World*] in 1882. He then embarked on a career in part-time journalism, which he supplemented by writing articles of literary criticism and further novels, among which two are considered his best: *Charlot s'amuse* (1883) and *L'Opium* [*Opium*] (1886). He also collaborated in the writing of several plays (e.g., *La Pelote* [*The Ball of Wool*] (1888), with Lucien Descaves, whose scandalous novel, *Sous-offs* [*Subalterns*] (1890), contains episodes describing sexual irregularities in the French army). He was colonial war correspondent for the newspaper *Le Figaro* and for a time its literary editor. He married Raymonde Ogé in 1888 after a brief but intense affair with Marie Colombier, then in her 40s, who was a celebrated literary scandalmonger. He allegedly helped Marie with her *Mémoires de Sarah Barnum* (1883), which was a satirical portrayal of the famous actress Sarah Bernhardt's recent tour of the United States. Publication of this book provoked a duel in which Bonnetain was slightly injured, and his honor remained intact. Marie has been thought to be the model for Fanny Legrand, the heroine of Alphonse Daudet's novel *Sapho* (1884), while the hero, Jean Gaussin, allegedly owes something to Bonnetain.

PATRICK POLLARD

Further Reading

Charlot s'amuse. Edited by Hubert Juin, with a preface by Henri Céard. Paris and Geneva: Slatkine Reprints, 1979.
Copley, A. *Sexual Moralities in France (1780–1980).* London: Routledge, 1989.
Stora-Lamarre, A. *L'Enfer de la IIIe République. Censeurs et pornographes (1881–1914).* Paris: Auzas Éditeurs Imago, 1990.

BOOK OF ODES [SHIH-CHING]

The *Shih-ching* [*Book of Odes or Book of Songs*] is one of the Five Classics of ancient Chinese literature. This collection consists of 305 songs, composed between c. 1000 and c. 600 BCE, grouped into four sections. The first section, the *Kuo-feng* [*Airs of the States*], includes 160 odes, arranged in 15 groups according to geographical area. All are folk songs from northern China, describing important events in the lives of ordinary people in ancient times. The second section, *Hsiao-ya* [*Lesser Elegant Odes*] contains 75 songs, some of which are folk songs, others were composed to celebrate banquets and feasts. The third section, *Ta-ya* [*Greater Elegant Odes*] includes 31 songs inspired by Chinese history and mythology. The final section, the *Sung* [*Hymns of Praise*] incorporates thirty songs for religious rites and feasts. These hymns were sung on ritual occasions in praise of the ancestors. Although the words of these songs are preserved in the *Shih-ching,* the music associated with them was lost in antiquity.

Traditionally the *Shih-ching* was said to have been compiled by Confucius (551–479 BCE), after he chose from among some 3,000 songs those that best conveyed his moral message. Although modern scholarship rejects this association, the *Shih-ching* was a key part of the Confucian canon. For many centuries, the songs were studied with a view to understanding the moral example that Confucius had found in them. As one of the Five Classics of Confucian learning, study of the *Shih-ching* received imperial sponsorship. Prior to the unification of China in 221 BCE there were a number of different versions of the *Shih-ching* in circulation, but only one survived the Han dynasty to be preserved to modern times. This version, the Mao, gave each ode a strong moral and political message, encapsulated in the short preface, or *hsü*. The Mao version also assigned a number to each ode, and this remains the most common form of identifying individual songs.

Approximately one third of the odes in the *Shih-ching* are on themes related to courtship, love, and marriage. Even the most erotic of these songs is assigned a moral, and many are associated with famous historical events. For example, the song *Ch'en-feng* [*Dawn Breeze*] (Mao 132), which describes the sexual frustration of a woman abandoned by her lover, was traditionally interpreted as a satire against Lord K'ang of Ch'in (r. 620–609 BCE), who neglected his wise ministers. Likewise, a song entitled *Chiang Ch'ung-tzu* [*I Beg You, Ch'ung-tzu*] (Mao 76) records a young woman telling her lover to leave the house silently, for fear of gossip. This ode was said to be a criticism of Lord Chuang of

Cheng (r. 743–701 BCE), who forgave his rebellious younger brother. Assigning a moral message to these songs seems to have been a very early development, and certainly predated the development of this book into one of the Confucian classics.

According to ancient Chinese historical works, the odes of the *Shih-ching* were already seen as conveying political and moral information in the Spring and Autumn period (771–475 BCE). At this time, these songs were regularly chanted or sung at diplomatic meetings and important conferences. These performances were not solely for entertainment; they were also intended to convey messages of loyalty and of criticism to particular members of the audience, and as such played a significant part in the ongoing negotiations. Even songs with a considerable erotic content were performed in this way. Sometimes only a single verse would be sung, due to the significance of the wording in the context of the discussions. Although people were aware of erotic elements found in many of these songs, this was not necessarily the most important aspect of the *Shih-ching*.

A number of the songs included in the *Shih-ching* deal with premarital sexual relations, and in particular with the festivals at which young people were encouraged to meet and develop relationships. These songs, which would form a particular challenge to later commentators, who were trained in Confucian gender roles, describe sexual relationships that take place outside of the control of the family and in which the women concerned have considerable freedom to choose their partners. It is clear from a number of odes that women played the lead role in the festivals at which young people met and chose their sexual partners. Some of these songs were composed for two choirs, one male and one female, singing alternate sections. The odes are often extremely frank in their portrayal of sexual desires and the ease with which they could be satisfied.

A number of songs in the *Shih-ching*, such as *Chiao-t'ung* [*Clever Boy*] (Mao 86), focus upon female sexuality. These odes usually describe pre- or extramarital sexual relationships, and in some cases detail the pain caused when a relationship sours. Among the songs describing extramarital relationships is *Nü yueh chi-ming* [*She Says the Cock Has Crowed*] (Mao 82), in which the wife orders her lover out of bed at cock-crow. Many of the themes of the songs in the *Shih-ching* were

later adapted for erotic verse by male poets, who took on a female persona in order to explore issues of sexuality, desire, and frustration.

No matter how apparently personal the subject matter of these songs, at no stage does the poet or singer attempt to create a subjective voice. The terms used to describe beautiful women and desirable men in these songs are highly generic, and no attempt has been made to individualize these figures. This marks an important distinction from later Chinese erotic verse, which often emphasizes the unique and personal nature of sexual relationships. In the twentieth century, the folk nature of many of the songs in the *Shih-ching* was reaffirmed. As traditional scholarship was rejected, and belief in the Confucian message of these odes declined, it was possible once again to explore the erotic nature of many of the songs incorporated in this ancient anthology.

OLIVIA MILBURN

Selected Works

Karlgren, Bernhard. *The Book of Odes*. Stockholm: Museum of Far Eastern Antiquities, 1950. This is a traditional translation, arranged according to the Mao commentary, with a transcription of the rhymes into reconstructed ancient Chinese.

K'ung Ying-ta. *Mao-shih cheng-yi*. Shanghai: Shanghai ku-chi ch'u-pan-she, 1990. This is a classic edition of this text. For a comprehensive list of editions, commentaries, and translations, see Michael Loewe, "Shih ching," in Michael Loewe, ed., *Early Chinese Texts: A Bibliographical Guide*, Berkeley: The Society for the Study of Early China, 1993.

Waley, Arthur. *The Book of Songs*. London: George Allen and Unwin, 1937. This translation is arranged by theme and pays particular attention to conveying the folk element of these songs.

Further Reading

Granet, Marcel. *Festivals and Songs of Ancient China*. Translated by E.D. Edwards. London: Routledge, 1932.

Hightower, James. *Han Shih Wai Chuan: Han Ying's Illustrations of the Didactic Application of the Classic of Songs*. Cambridge: Harvard University Press, 1952.

Nylan, Michael. *The Five 'Confucian' Classics*. New Haven, CT: Yale University Press, 2001.

Wang, C.H. *From Ritual to Allegory: Seven Essays in Early Chinese Poetry*. Hong Kong: The Chinese University Press, 1988.

———. *The Bell and the Drum: Shih-ching as Formulaic Poetry in an Oral Tradition*. Berkeley and Los Angeles: University of California Press, 1974.

Watson, Burton. *Early Chinese Literature*. New York: Columbia University Press, 1962.

BOREL, PÉTRUS

1809–1859
French fiction writer and poet

Although his name is little remembered today, in comparison with his contemporaries Théophile Gautier and Charles Nodier, Pétrus Borel was acknowledged as a literary innovator in his own lifetime. His distinctive prose writing, characterized by black humor, sadistic irony, narrative twists, and a mixture of styles and registers, made Borel's texts unique among the heavy hyperbole and lyricism of the Frenetic Romantic movement. Moreover, his self-stylization as "the Lycanthrope" (the werewolf) and his reputation as a passionate and promiscuous lover marked him as a colorful character of the nineteenth-century literary scene. It is a testimony both to Borel's writing and to his promotion of his self-image that he served as an acknowledged influence for the most important French poet of the nineteenth century, Charles Baudelaire, who shared Borel's pessimistic vision of "spleen et ennui." Elements of Borel's legacy can also be identified in the twentieth century, in the writings of the French Surrealists and the proponents of the Theatre of Cruelty, especially Antonin Artaud.

Borel's first major publication, a collection of poems entitled *Rhapsodies* (1831–32), offers little in the way of the sadistic aesthetic that would become his stock in trade. For the most part, it contains highly sentimentalized and conventional love poems. However, one poem, "Le Rendezvous," suggests perhaps the dark qualities that would come to characterize Borel's portrayal of eroticism. The poem recounts the anticipation of an anxious lover who is awaiting an encounter with his mistress. When finally she arrives, it is as a corpse, carried along in a casket. Overwhelmed with passion and sorrow, the lover immolates himself with a knife in order to join her in death.

Champavert, contes immoraux, published a year later, is regarded by critics as Borel's masterpiece. The collection comprises seven pieces of writing which, for want of a more accurate generic label, are named *contes* (short stories). In fact, they are hybrid texts, which place figures from history or folklore into fictional settings and situations. In the case of two of the *contes*, "Passerau, l'écolier" and "Champavert, le lycanthrope," the protagonists are recognizable as autobiographical constructions. Each *conte* gives an account of a central character who ends by raping, murdering, or dying as a result of his or her attempts to realize the impossible demands of passion, often in its adulterous or incestuous forms.

Despite the collection's subtitle, this work is not so much immoral as colored by a morbid sensibility and a heavy pessimism. The moral and sexual life of humankind is shown to be driven by an enjoyment of suffering, as in "Monsieur de l'Argentière, l'accusateur," which ends with a cameo description of an Englishman, who is an avid *amateur* of executions; or "Passereau," in which the eponymous hero begs the public executioner to kill him, in a darkly humorous passage of dialogue ("Je désire que vous me guillotinassiez" [I desire that you should guillotine me], Passereau declares at one point, revealing Borel's dual taste for masochistic sentiment and high-fallutin use of the French language, seen in his choice of the uncommon imperfect subjunctive).

Often the narratives take the form of a particularly grim illustration of "poetic justice." This is the case in one of the most effective tales in the collection, "Don Andréa Vésalius, l'anatomiste." In this story, a young bride neglects her elderly and impotent, but passionately attached, surgeon husband in favor of sexually attractive young men. One by one, these young men begin to disappear mysteriously. On her deathbed, the wife wishes to confess her infidelities to her husband. To her horror, he reveals that he has known of her affairs all along: indeed, it was he who killed her lovers in order to use their bodies in his anatomical experiments. At the story's close, the reader is invited to look through the window of Vésalius's laboratory, wherein he is dissecting the voluptuous corpse of a beautiful young woman, recognizable by her long, blond tresses as his wife. As is the case in all of the stories in *Champavert,* erotic appetite is ultimately punishable by death, but death itself is recuperated for erotic pleasure.

If *Champavert* marks the high point of Borel's writing, his novel *Madame Putiphar* (1839) is an altogether less accomplished work. The plot is convoluted and unwieldy and the novel too long. Having said this, it is probably the piece of writing for which Borel is best remembered, perhaps because it is more explicitly erotic and more obviously violent than the *contes,* in which shock operates on the psychological rather than the visceral level. (However, Borel's stated intention was to produce a political rather than an erotic work: the eponymous character is supposed to evoke Madame de Pompadour, and the character of the Pharaon is a satirical portrait of Louis XV.)

The most memorable erotic scenes in *Madame Putiphar* concern the kidnapping of the young heroine Deborah and her incarceration in the Pharaon's private brothel. Here she is trained as a courtesan for the King's bed, by a dominant lesbian Madame. In her biography of Borel and his circle (1954), Enid Starkie has pointed out the similarity in atmosphere and detail between these scenes and certain sections of Diderot's *La Religieuse.* The anticlerical sentiment of Diderot's work would doubtless have appealed to the cynical and anti-establishmentarian Lycanthrope.

The later chapters of *Madame Putiphar* also contain some extensive and gruesome descriptions of the physical torture meted out to the heroes Fitz-Whyte and Fitz-Harris during their incarceration in the state prisons of France. It is perhaps these descriptions that led Jules Janin, in his review of *Madame Putiphar,* to compare Borel to the Marquis de Sade. Janin condemned the novel's "charnal house" aesthetic, identifying it as symptomatic of the moral degeneracy of the 1830s. (It should be noted, however, that Janin had previously formed part of Borel's circle and was himself the author of works of Frenetic Romanticism.)

Contrary to Janin's claims, it must be stated that for the most part Borel's writing bares little resemblance to de Sade's. The description of sexual acts in Borel's text, for example, could never be described as pornographic. If the two writers can be said to have anything in common, it is rather the fact that both were individuals whose extreme sensibilities were exacerbated by periods of revolutionary bloodshed and civil unrest. Both writers chose to represent the violence of their *Zeitgeist* by displacing the cruelty they found there from the political level to the personal; from the battlefield into the bedroom. The lonely Lycanthrope Borel, in expounding Plautus's proverb "Homo Homini Lupus" [Man is a wolf to man], sought to demonstrate, like de Sade, that the finding of a certain piquant pleasure in the suffering of the other is an inevitable facet of the human condition.

Biography

Born in Lyons in 1809, the twelfth child of an ironmonger, Pétrus Borel was educated in Paris at the Petit Séminaire Sainte Elizabeth and the Petit Séminaire Saint Roch. Nicknamed "the Lycanthrope," he was the leader of the group of young, rebellious, republican poets known as the Petit Cénacle or the Bouzingos, who were involved in the July revolution of 1830 and developed the aesthetic school known as Frenetic Romanticism. In the late 1840s he worked as a colonial administrator in Algeria but was discharged from service in disgrace in 1855. Borel died July 17, 1859, in Algeria. According to his biographer, Claretie, his death was due to sunstroke, though other, more fanciful chroniclers claim that he expired owing to his overwhelming weariness with life.

Borel's best-known works are *Rhapsodies* (1831–32), *Champavert, contes immoraux* (1833) and *Madame Putiphar* (1839).

LISA DOWNING

Editions

Champavert, contes immoraux. Edited by Jane Strick. Preface by Jean-Luc Steinmetz. Paris: Phébus, 2002.
Madame Putiphar. Edited by Jane Strick. Preface by Jean-Luc Steinmetz. Paris: Phébus, 1999.

Selected Works

Rhapsodies. 1831–32
Champavert, contes immoraux. 1833
L'Obélisque de Louqsor. 1836
Robinson Crusoe (translation). 1836

Madame Putiphar. 1839
Le Trésor de la caverne d'Arcueil. 1927

Further Reading

Claretie, Jules. *Pétrus Borel, le lycanthrope*. Paris: Princebourde, 1865.
Gautier, Théophile. *Histoire du romantisme* [1872]. Paris: Jouaust, 1929.

————. *Les Jeunes France: Romans goguenards* [1833]. Paris: Flammarion, 1974.
Marie, Aristide. *Pétrus Borel le lycanthrope, sa vie et son œuvre*. Paris: La Force française, 1922.
Starkie, Enid. *Pétrus Borel en Algérie : sa carrière comme inspecteur de la colonialisation basés sur des lettres et documents inédits*. Oxford: Blackwell, 1950.
————. *Pétrus Borel, The Lycanthrope: His Life and Times*. London: Faber & Faber, 1954.

BOULLOSA, CARMEN

1954–
Mexican novelist, poet, and playwright

Son vacas, somos puercos

Carmen Boullosa writes poetry of great fluidity, craft, and beauty, and her considerable oeuvre includes essays, children's books, and plays. However, it is in the realms of her considerable novelistic oeuvre that eroticism is most clearly discerned and explored. In these, her primary concerns, despite the very different times and spaces depicted, are politics and the erotic.

Boullosa has observed that as a woman writer, she has been permitted to enter the spaces of the senses and the body, but not those of political ideas, nor has she been recognized as a particularly political writer. This is perhaps the next battle to be fought, but it would be misleading to give the impression that the body was always a site of access for women, and particularly Latin American women, writers. Marjorie Agosín, referring to such writers, talks of a tradition of modesty and claims that for them to speak out has required acts of daring and transgression. Here, Boullosa's fourth novel, *Son vacas, somos puercos*, a daring, inventive, and indeed political work, will be examined in the light of its treatment of both transgression and eroticism.

The novel, which portrays an almost exclusively male world, is set initially in 1666. It recounts the life of a young French boy by the incongruous name of Smeeks, presumably in allusion to Dickens' character in *Nicholas Nickleby* and to the misery there described, who attempts to escape a life of poverty and hardship by selling himself off for three years of slavery in the Caribbean. It is a curious tale which explores in some detail the cruel, often violent, but fascinating society in which he finds himself; a world populated by slave owners, slaves, both European and African, Native Americans, prostitutes, and pirates.

Smeeks, literate thanks to the tutelage of a priest in France, finds himself enslaved alongside an elderly African, Negro Miel, who teaches him many of the techniques he has learned as a healer, a process which is continued by his subsequent owner, a French surgeon, Pineau. On the death of the latter, Smeeks joins a group of pirates, working as a surgeon at sea, and the rest of the novel concentrates almost exclusively on his life amongst these pirates. It is a very masculine life—indeed, the island that he first lands on, Tortuga, is inhabited solely by men; nor do the pirates have any women amongst them. Women are generally viewed to be a problem; they cause fights between men and encourage them to settle down and to give up their lives of freedom. They would be disruptive of the strict codes of honor, which the pirates obey scrupulously.

Love appears when on the boat from France a boy reveals him/herself to Smeeks as a girl. Cross-dressing, with different readings in terms of identity and sexuality, is explored in greater depth in another of the writer's novels, *Duerme*.

Here the implication is that she dresses in this way to protect herself, and possible other interpretations are left hanging, but she shares her secret only with Smeeks, and puts his hand on her breast as proof. Smeeks becomes obsessed with her, referring to her as "She," the capital letter denoting her importance to him, but he never gets any opportunity to talk to her again. "She" becomes the unattainable, infinitely desirable and eroticized love object.

As a counter to this, the sexual act is treated in a particularly neutral and passionless way. Smeeks mentions almost casually that all three of his mentors—the French priest, Negro Miel, and Pineau—have had sexual relations with him, and at one point he opines that "if women serve to clean men of their seed, the body of another man could serve in the same way or even better" (p.62, my translation). He is taken to a brothel and eventually gets used to the notion of having sex with women, but has to overcome an initial repulsion to their smell. Sex in these cases is depicted as no more than a physical necessity.

Where sex is eroticized in the novel is in the case of rape. It is the pirates' prize and the culmination of their desire. The use of force and the humiliation involved render it infinitely preferable in their eyes to a visit to a prostitute. As is so often the case in novels, suspense and desire are interwoven, thus references are made to the siege of Maracaibo from early on, and finally, on reaching this place in the last section, the novel explodes in an orgy of rape and violence, both of which are depicted in erotic detail. Terrible scenes of torture are described, then of one pirate it is said that: "[H]e liked to kill the woman he was possessing, saying that the dying flesh tightened in such a way that there was no greater pleasure", something others try out of curiosity. Spanish women, who have internalized their own worth purely in terms of their virtue, are most powerfully represented by a beautiful woman from a wealthy family who with her adolescent daughter manages to hide from the conquering pirates, whose desire for them only increases with the passing of time. The scene of their discovery and multiple rape is described by Smeeks, who does not participate but narrates in almost loving, voyeuristic, detail: "[S]uch was the abuse that we left them (I saw it myself) slashed, lacerated; where they were not actually bleeding their flesh was raw, with wounds on their intimate parts and all around

them" (p.108). Their ultimate destruction is carried out by themselves when they somehow manage to find the strength to burn down the house they have been left in.

Such eroticization of violence is complex. Had the novel been written by a man, then accusations of misogyny would be difficult to counter, but the fact that it is by a woman sheds a different light on it. These things happened in times past and continue to happen, and to confront them in this way is instructive. For a woman to attempt to explore such issues from a male point of view is unusual and rather brave. Boullosa's work is notable for tackling these different and difficult topics, and its honest attempt in this case to confront the eroticization of violence is eye-opening and innovative.

Biography

Born in Mexico City, September 4, 1954, Boullosa attended the Universidad Iberoamericana and the Universidad Autónoma Nacional, both in Mexico City. She lived in Berlin as a writer in residence in 1995–6 and has taught at San Diego State and Georgetown Universities and La Sorbonne. Throughout 1994 she wrote a column for the Spanish newspaper *El País,* and she is a founder of the "Casa Citlaltepetl" with the International Parliament of Writers in Mexico City. She is separated from her partner of 20 years, and has two children. She has twice been awarded the Xavier Villaurrutia Prize, once for a poem, *La salvaja,* and the other time for her novel *Antes.*

LINDA CRAIG

Editions

Son vacas, somos puercos: Filibusteros del mar Caribe. México, D.F: Ediciones Era, 1991; as *They're Cows, We're Pigs,* translated by Leland Chambers, New York: Grove Press, 2001.

Selected Works

Poetry

El hilo olvida. 1978
La memoria vacia. 1978
Lealtad. 1981
La salvaja. 1988
Niebla: una poema. 1995
Salto de mantarraya. 2002, bilingual edition, translated by Psiche Hughes

Novels

Mejor desaparece. 1987
Antes. 1989
El médico de los piratas. 1992
La Milagrosa. 1993; as *The Miracle Worker.* Translated by Amanda Hopkinson, London: Jonathan Cape, 1994.
Duerme. 1994
Cielos de la tierra. 1997
Treinta años. 1999; as *Leaving Tabasco.* Translated by Geoff Hargreaves, London: Atlantic Books, 2001.
De un salto descabalga la reina, 2002

Plays

Cocinar hombres. 1985
Teatro herético. 1987
Papeles irresponsables. 1989
Quizá. 1995
Prosa rota. 2000

Further Reading

Croquer Pedrón, Eleonora. *El gesto de Antigona o la escritura como responsabilidad.* Santiago de Chile: Cuarto Propio, 2000.
De Beer, Gabriella. *Contemporary Mexican Women Writers, Five Voices.* Austin: University of Texas Press, 1997.
D'Lugo, Carol Clarke. *The Fragmented Novel in Mexico: The Politics of Form.* Austin: University of Texas Press, 1997.
Droscher, Bárbara, and Carlos Rincón, eds. *Conjugarse en infinitivo: La escritora Carmen Boullosa.* Berlin: Edición Tranvía, 1999.
Forne, Anna. *La piratería textual: Un estudio hypertextual de "Son vacas, somos puercos" y "El médico de los piratas" de Carmen Boullosa.* Lund, Sweden: Romanska Institutionen Solvegatan, 2001.
Ortega, Julio. *Arte de innovar (fabulaciones de Carmen Boullosa).* Mexico: UNAM/Ediciones de Equilibrista, 1994.

BOURGEADE, PIERRE

1927–
French writer, playwright, and poet

Eroticism and politics are interwoven in Bourgeade's work as two sides of a systematic exploration of the representations and phantasms of Western civilization. Bourgeade is as preoccupied with sex and death as de Sade or Bataille, who greatly inspired him. He shows a fascination for the minute description of rituals of pleasure and of humiliation and for violence and desecration. The eroticization of the prohibited takes the most diverse literary forms, from the "phallucination" poems (in *Ultimum moriens* [1984], dedicated to Philippe Sollers), to the short prose (*Les immortelles*), and de Sade–like theater (*Erzébet* [1998]), but creates a coherent body of work. Brevity is predominant. It leads sometimes to the incorporation of diary entries in novels such as *L'Aurore boréale,* defined, as much of Bourgeade's work could be, as an "ongoing movement between the 'imaginaire' and materiality." Apart from his later crime fiction, where rapidity is equally a distinctive feature, a significant part of Bourgeade's works consists of short stories that are linked together by an overall theme, whose various facets are highlighted. This is exemplified in *Les immortelles,* which may be considered as a collection either of short stories or of prose poems, and also applies to the stories of *L'Argent* (1998), as well as to the tales which make up *Eros mécanique,* which progress gradually toward the double meaning of the last tale, entitled "Le Trou," where Eros and Thanatos reunite. As such a title suggests, the largely archetypal vision of the female, almost invariably portrayed as available and disposable, is not only offensive, it is also threatening. The matrix metaphor is inverted into a symbol of destruction, as an abyss which serves as a representation of disappearance, leading to the voracity of death.

Although essentially realistic, the eroticism in Bourgeade's short prose draws upon a realm of fantasies, inherited from Surrealism, onanistic onirism, and visions of the bizarre. It often gives way to an emphasis on the pornographic, when it graphically depicts the openness, or the opening, of usually female bodies and when it deals with the revelation of the animality beyond the sophistication of social appearance and status. This aspect is reinforced by an overwhelming absence of feelings of love (as is indicated by the title of *No Love*, with Marie L., 2000), which is replaced by the portrayal of multiple fetishism and the fixation on infinite numbers of relentlessly substituted bodies.

An attempt toward a type of inventory or catalogue is visible in Bourgeade's prefaces, as in the collection *Lectures amoureuses* by J.J. Pauvert and also in his writings on scandalous artists or art forms, such as on the painter and photographer Pierre Molinier (1979) or the French icon of erotic cinema Brigitte Lahaie (1999). In the same fashion, an attempted mapping of perversions is presented metaphorically through the exploration of each of the 20 Parisian districts in *L'Autre face* (with Marie L., 1999). Similarly, the interest in new technologies, as seen in *Cybersex* or *Téléphone rose*, shows the willingness to discover unprecedented transgressions and, in doing so, to contribute to the understanding of a new humanity through its new sexuality. Special narrative attention is therefore paid to the most traumatic experiences, where the paroxysm of pleasure serves to highlight paroxystic fears, viewed as symbols and as symptoms of social conditions. This is linked with the exhumation of the violent unconscious of developed societies, as witnessed in works since *New-York Party,* where the materialism of desire leads to a commodification of murder. In this process, Bourgeade's writing of the erotic as an attempt to unveil a hidden truth demonstrates once again its intrinsically political dimension.

Biography

Born November 7, 1927, in Morianne, in the French Pyrénées, Bourgeade attended school in Orthez and Bayonne and studied law and politics in Bordeaux and Pau. He married in 1952 and became a solicitor at the Court of Appeal of Bordeaux (1952–54). He changed to a career in the administration, first as a director in the prefecture of the Department of Oise (1954–59), then in the prime minister's office, where he was in charge of relations with the headquarters of the army (1959–62) and vice general secretary

for youth affairs (1962–74). He was 38 when he published his first book, *Les Immortelles* (1966), a collection of short stories celebrating femininity and the female body, which was awarded the prix Hermès. His subsequent works, *La Rose rose* (1968), *New-York Party* (1969), *Le Violoncelle qui résiste* (1971), and *L'Aurore boréale* (1973), are characterized by the two recurring and increasingly interconnected themes of power and obscenity. He left the administration in 1974 in order to dedicate himself to writing. An extremely prolific writer, Bourgeade has published over 30 books to date. He earned praise for his political allegories, such as *L'Armoire* (1977) (which tells of the evasion from a form of totalitarianism to the fall into a form of servitude), *Une ville grise* (1977) (an account of the Prague Spring), and *Le Camp* (1979) (Nazi concentration camps), culminating in his stories on torture in Algeria, *Les Serpents* (1983), which was short-listed for the prix Goncourt and was awarded the prix Motta by the Académie française. These themes were continued on the stage, for which Bourgeade authored more than ten plays, including *Deutsches Requiem* (1973), *Orden* (1974), *Etoiles rouges* (1975), the award-winning *Palazzo Mentale* (1976), *L'autorisation* (1995), and *Le passeport* (1996). Power and obscenity also lie at the core of his acclaimed recent novel *Les âmes juives* (1998). The place of eroticism has become increasingly seminal in his most recent publications, such as *Sade, Sainte Thérèse* (1987), *Eros mécanique* (1995), and *Cybersex et autres nouvelles* (1997). It also permeates Bourgeade's exploration of the genre of the detective novel in works such as *Téléphone rose* (1999). He's been a member of the Conférence Sade since 2001, and collects erotic and surrealist objects.

DOMINIQUE JEANNEROD

Selected Works

Novels, short stories

Les Immortelles. Paris: Gallimard, 1966.
New-York Party. Paris: Gallimard, 1969.
L'Aurore boréale. Paris: Gallimard, 1973.
Sade, Sainte Thérèse. Paris: Gallimard, 1987.
L'Empire des livres. Paris: Gallimard, 1989.
La nature du roman. Paris: J. J. Pauvert, 1993.
Eros mécanique. Paris: Gallimard, 1995.
Cybersex et autres nouvelles. Paris: Éd. Blanche, 1997.
L'Argent. Paris: Gallimard, 1998.

Warum (1999). Paris: Pocket, 2001.
Téléphone rose. Paris: Gallimard, Série noire, 1999.
L'Autre face: Portrait de la face cachée de Paris (with Marie L.). Paris: Le Cercle poche, 2001 (Arléa, 1999).

Theater

Erzébet (with 3 gravures by Nathalie-Noëlle Rimlinger). Paris: Variable, 1998.

Other Texts

"A Noir corset velu." Original photographs by Henri Maccheroni. Paris: Les Mains libres, 1972.
Brigitte Lahaie. Photographs by Claude Alexandre. Paris: La Musardine, 1999.
Bourgeade, Pierre, Marie L., Paul Verguin, et al. *Contes érotiques de Noël.* Paris: La Musardine, 1998.

Ionesco, Irina. *Cent onze photographies érotiques.* Introduction by Pierre Bourgeade. Nyons: Borderie, 1980.
Marie L. *Confessée.* Preface by Pierre Bourgeade. Paris: La Musardine, 2000.
Molinier, Pierre. *Cent photographies érotiques.* Preface by Pierre Bourgeade. Nyons: Borderie, 1979.
Ultimum moriens. Gourdon: D. Bedou, 1984.

Further Reading

Bourgeade, Pierre. *L'Objet humain: Entretiens avec Sylvie Martigny et Jean-Hubert Gailliot.* Paris: Gallimard, 2003.
Peters, Renate. "Trompe l'oeil and Correspondences: Arcimboldo's Portraits and Pierre Bourgeade's *Une ville grise.*" *Dalhousie French Studies* 63 (Summer 2003): 135–46.

BOUSQUET, JOÉ

1897–1950
French writer

Le cahier noir

Like an obsessive primal scene, the basic motif of *Le cahier noir* is of a man narrating how he spanked a young woman, thereby experiencing an unexpected and incommensurable pleasure both sensual and spiritual. That motif is repeated every four or five pages, i.e., over 50 times in the book overall. That circularity would be very tedious if it were not for all the slight variations: the woman is usually spanked by hand, though occasionally the man uses a birch-rod or a whip; sometimes he also fingers her anus, sometimes he even sodomizes her, though the main variation concerns the relationship between the narrator and his victim. In the first part of the book, she tends to be his cousin, his girlfriend, his lover, his fiancée, or his wife; in the second part, she is also at times his teenage sister and at times his underage daughter. That combination of incest and pedophilia has made the book quite controversial; a conservative reader would readily find some of the scenes sickening and

unacceptable. Even in that second part, all scenes follow a regular pattern—for example, he is the older brother in his twenties coming back home after several years abroad, she sees him as a hero and just wants to be spanked by him like a little girl; or he is the father who has to punish his teenage daughter and spanks her, and they realize that they both really enjoy it. A recurrent and predictable element is the affected surprise of the two protagonists, who end up discovering an unsuspected yet immeasurable source of pleasure, promising themselves they would do it again and again.

Throughout this eulogy to spanking (which makes *Le cahier noir* a rather original text of erotic literature), the narrator is exclusively obsessed with young women's naked bottoms: other parts of the body (such as the breasts, legs, or face) are never mentioned, as anal sex (preferably with virgins) is undoubtedly his favorite sexual act. The few scenes of oral sex and vaginal sex are nothing compared with the sodomies which occasionally follow the spanking, usually with the man getting so fascinated with the woman's bottom (Bousquet uses the animal term *croupe*, rump) that he cannot resist and must penetrate it. Except on a couple of early

161

occasions written from the woman's viewpoint, women's perspectives are rarely mentioned: most women seem to appreciate the violence inflicted upon them; they even seem grateful to the man dominating them, which makes Bousquet a rather phallocentric if not misogynist author.

A particularity of *Le cahier noir* is its excessively lyrical style: scenes of spanking and sodomy are described in mystical terms, as experiences of spiritual communion and enlightenment, with reference to angels, light, and metaphysical revelations. The forbidden view of a woman's naked bottom and the "tender resistance" of her anus are presented as epiphanies with lengthy pseudo-philosophical, pseudo-poetical sentences which sometimes stop when the editor was not able to decipher Bousquet's handwriting anymore. Bousquet was often under the influence of drugs (mainly morphine, cocaine, and opium) when he wrote in his *Cahier,* and this is reflected in the text, the quality of which is sometimes dubious, both for the matter and manner. It is difficult to appreciate *Le cahier noir* as a linear literary work, probably because it was not meant to be read that way—published 39 years after the death of its author, it documents a man's fantasy world by recording numerous erotic scenes which keep intertwining the same key elements (spanking as a spiritual experience, women's *croupe*s as a vision of Heaven), occasionally integrating more disturbing components (the identity of the woman—sister, daughter). A possible key to understanding and analyzing the book is the title given by the author to one particular section (p. 69 in the 1997 edition from La Musardine), "Bases d'une érotologie," suggesting that as a literary project *Le cahier noir* aims to explore and explain an idiosyncratic aspect of eroticism (spanking) through a plethora of kaleidoscopic and complementary illustrations of it.

Biography

In May 1918, a 21-year-old lieutenant fighting in the north of France was hit in the spine by a German bullet which would forever paralyze his lower body. From then on, Joé Bousquet started writing and became a very prolific (albeit usually regarded as middle-of-the-road) author who cultivated friendships with writers such as Jean Paulhan, Louis Aragon, Paul Eluard, and Paul Valéry, as well as painters such as Jean Dubuffet and Hans Bellmer. Despite his disability, Bousquet was also a womanizer; many women wrote to him, several became close friends and came to visit him in Carcassonne, his city of origin in the south of France. He nicknamed one of them "Poisson d'Or," and in his *Lettres à poisson d'or* one can identify some key themes developed in *Le cahier noir*. There is no evidence that *Le cahier noir* was ever intended to be published: the manuscript was found in the form of two small notebooks and was published for the first time in 1989 by Albin Michel. The title was chosen by its editor, Christine Michel, based on anecdotes on the way Joé Bousquet allegedly referred to that text as the darker side of his writing. The collection of his *Oeuvre romanesque complète* was released by Albin Michel between 1979 and 1984 in four volumes; only a minor part of his correspondence has been published, notably by Gallimard in 1969.

LOYKIE LOÏC LOMINÉ

Further Reading

Blanchot, M. *Joé Bousquet*. Paris: Fata Morgana, 1987.
Gaudard, F.C. *Joé Bousquet et l'écriture*. Paris: L'Harmattan, 2000.
Nelli, R. *Joé Bousquet, sa vie, son œuvre*. Paris: Albin Michel, 1975.

BRANTÔME, PIERRE DE BOURDEILLE SEIGNEUR DE

c. 1539–1614
French memorist

Les dames galantes

Compiled in typically Renaissance fashion, *les dames galantes* [*The Lives of Gallant Ladies*] presents eight discourses with hundreds of anecdotes with titles like "Discourse on Women Who Make Love and Cuckold Their Husbands," "Another Discourse on the Beauty of a Beautiful Leg and Its Virtue," or "Discourse on Married Women, Widows and Girls, as to Which Are Warmer in Love than the Others," and the like.

As is the case with the essays of his contemporary Michel de Montaigne, Brantôme's discourses often seem to have little to do with such titles. Thus his discourse on cuckolding begins with an attack on cuckolded husbands who react by killing their wives and/or their wives' lovers. Brantôme—who never married himself—is naturally sympathetic to the latter. The same discourse finishes, more or less, with a digression on which season is best for lovemaking, and concludes airily that "all seasons are good, when you take them apropos." Similarly Brantôme says in his discourse on wives, widows, and girls: "In conclusion, vive the love of women!"

The very great interest of Brantôme's discourses resides, therefore, not in his digressions and strangely superficial conclusions, but in his anecdotes and the rather special attitude he takes toward his subject. He wrote more about sex than anyone in France before de Sade. He wrote more about feminine clothing, seemingly, than anyone before Marcel Proust. Interestingly enough, some of the ladies in the first collection (published as *Les dames illustres*) seem to be the same as the *dames galantes*, just part of life at the Valois court.

As the above may suggest, sex for Brantôme seems inseparable from court life. For Brantôme the court is not unlike a present-day American high school—a relatively small world full of little (but in Brantôme's anecdotes sometimes bloody) intrigues, where everybody is interested in everybody else's business. Brantôme himself declines to name any of his *dames galantes.* He includes disclaimers worthy of a stand-up comedian: "However, I don't want to accuse the great many honest and virtuous married women, who have behaved virtuously and constantly in the faith they have reverently promised their husbands... "

At the same time, though, Brantôme feels that it is something of a moral duty that love must be rewarded. Thus it is more or less required that "beautiful ladies must appear and show off their beauties." For Brantôme a love kept entirely secret is not a love really fulfilled. He quotes "[a]n opinion in love that I have seen defended by several, that a secret love is worthless, if it is not a little bit visible, if not to everyone, then at least to your closest friends."

In one of the most famous passages in Brantôme, he describes a cup belonging to his friend the Duke of Alençon, inside of which are engraved images of human couples and animal couples copulating. The idea is to tease female guests into drinking from the cup and to ask them what they see, as a means of bringing presumably private sexual thoughts into the public domain.

Meanwhile Brantôme's favorite sexual practice, apparently, is what he calls the "coup en robe" ("there's nothing like the coup en robe"). The *coup en robe* consists of having quick sex with a more or less fully dressed great lady in a closet, in an alcove, or some other semipublic place. Brantôme describes the pleasure "when you imagine that you defy, that you crush underfoot, that you press and have your way, and pull down and cast on the ground the cloth of gold, the drape of silver, the beading, the silk fabrics, with the pearls and precious stones, then your ardor, your contentment is greater."

Contrary to the accepted wisdom of the sixteenth-century physician Ambroise Paré, who recommended going slow, Brantôme quotes a great lady who condemns "the stupid women of the past who, wanting to be too delicate in their loves, shut themselves up in little rooms." She explains that "today, you have to seize your opportunities, and the quicker the better"—thus returning to Brantôme's persistent theme of how sexual, presumably private, things become part of the gossip and public life of the court.

Although everyone assumes that Brantôme's conquests were numerous, the author of the *Dames galantes* is anything but boastful. Time and time again in his discourses, he defers to his "good companions" and to the *dames galantes,* who, he says, know more than he does. He defers to our "authentic doctors of love," and even to the courtiers, who will "know better how to talk about this than I." He defers to "the natural philosophers... presenting many reasons; but I'm not a good enough philosopher to deduce them."

Brantôme never says just who these people are. Indeed there is no sixteenth-century French author who might qualify as more expert on sex than Brantôme himself. The inevitable conclusion is that this represents a narrative stance, a persona Brantôme adopts to speak humbly about his amazing subject, perhaps exemplifying his idea that to seduce women, one must adopt an "hardiesse modeste"—a modest daring. In the same way, Brantôme insists that his subject is untreatable—something which defies logical, rational classification. Brantôme writes:

> I know very well that I'm undertaking a big subject, and I would never be able to do it if I wanted to take it through to the end.... For all the paper in the Chambre des Comptes wouldn't be enough to write down half their stories, for of such people and such women I don't know any battle sergeant good enough to put them in rank and order.

Such is *Les dames galantes.* Writing the greatest French work of his time on sex, Brantôme adopts the stance of an ordinary guy—in Renaissance terms, a humble *serviteur* of court ladies. This man of some classical culture and reputation at court adopts (in spite of the seeming anachronism and the differences between the sixteenth century and our own time) something like the attitude of a reader of the *Daily News* or the *Daily Mail* or the like, coming across as an everyman eternally in awe of sex and the *dames galantes.* In another of his simple conclusions, he writes: "il n'y a pas de loi qu'un beau con ne renverse" [there is no law that cannot be overturned by a beautiful cunt], and elsewhere that "the [fair] sex always gets its way."

Biography

Born between 1539 and 1542, Brantôme divided his time between court life and military campaigns until 1584, when a fall from a horse left him incapacitated for many years—in all about 40 per cent of his life. He took up writing, beginning with biographies of military commanders and princesses of the court. His most famous work, however, which he titled *Second recueil des dames* [Second Collection on Women], is constantly reprinted under the title *Les Dames galantes.*

HERBERT DE LEY

Selected Works

Brantôme. *Lives of Fair and Gallant Ladies.* New York: Liveright, 1933.

Œuvres complètes. Edited by L. Lalanne, SHF [Société Honoraire de Français]. 11 vols. Paris: Renouard, 1864–82.

Recueil des Dames, poésies et tombeaux. Edited by E. Vaucherat. Paris: Pléiade/Gallimard, 1991.

Further Reading

Cocula-Vallières, Anne-Marie. *Brantôme. Amour et gloire au temps des Valois.* Paris: Albin Michel, 1986.

Cottrell, Robert D. "Montaigne, Brantôme et la courtisane Flora," *Bulletin de la Société des amis de Montaigne* Ser. 5(2, 1972): 33–37.

Daumas, Maurice. *Le système amoureux de Brantôme.* Paris: L'Harmattan, 1998.

De Ley, Herbert. *Brantôme or the Paradis d'amour.* Forthcoming.

Lazard, Madeleine. *Pierre de Bourdeille, seigneur de Brantôme.* Paris: Fayard, 1995.

BRAZIL

Almost two hundred years after the Portuguese arrived in Brazil, the Bahian poet Gregório de Matos (1636–96), influenced by the Spanish baroque, produced the country's first literary works of an explicitly erotic nature. Matos, known as Boca do Inferno (Mouth of Hell) for his mordant satire, also wrote lyrics in which ornate conceits couple religious mysticism with the boldly erotic. His most sensual verse apostrophizes the black and mulatto women of Bahia. In the century that followed Matos's death, baroque style went into decline and literature was not much concerned with the flesh. After independence (1822) the desire to forge a national literature was undertaken by subscribing, belatedly, to the tenets of the Romantic and Realist movements. Disregarding the shortcomings of such postcolonial endeavors, it is under the auspices of these movements, especially in the novels of the second half of the 19th century, that literary eroticism began to flourish in Brazil.

The leading proponent of Brazilian prose during the juncture between Romanticism and Realism is José de Alencar (1829–77). Alencar idealized the notion of the noble savage while celebrating the civilizing legacy of colonization. Even though social mores imposed a literary chastity of sorts, in his so-called urban novels describing bourgeois life in Rio de Janeiro, Alencar deals with themes such as prostitution and is indulgent and fetishistic in his description of women, notably in *Senhora* [*Madam*] (1875), where their feet are the object of sensual delight. Despite the greater predilection for verisimilitude and the development of characters' psychological profiles which ensued Alencar in the works of Realist authors, on the whole during this period sexuality was to remain unspeakable in literature, and eroticism was to be borne through suggestion rather than exposition. A case in point is the work of Joaquim Maria Machado de Assis (1839–1908)—celebrated as a master of Realism and often as Brazil's greatest author—where silence and ambiguity are deployed as the principal tropes of the erotic. His novels *Memórias Póstumas de Brás Cubas* [*Epitaph of a Small Winner*] (1881), *Quincas Borba* (1891), and *Dom Casmurro* (1900) deal with failed love and adultery; they are sensual in the extreme without resorting to language which might offend. Arguably, the height of erotic suggestiveness in Machado's oeuvre is the story "Missa do Galo" [Midnight Mass] (1894), where the narrator recalls one night as a youth waiting to attend midnight mass in the company of D. Conceição, who is married and whose husband is away. The story centers on their ambiguous silences and the wanton undertow which compels their coy exchange, making for the depiction of an implicitly illicit and highly seductive scene. Like Alencar before him, Machado conveys the sexual allure of his female characters through fetishistic use of synecdoche: he lavishes attention on women's arms, not just those of D. Conceição, but those of women throughout his narratives; he even wrote a story on this penchant, "Uns braços" [Arms] (1899).

With the advent of naturalism at the end of the 19th century, however, and the increasingly deterministic studies of human nature which came into vogue in the literature of the period, sexuality became a privileged theme. Moreover, Brazilian authors began taking liberties where their European counterparts bowed to decorum. Literature from the late 1880s to the turn of the century may be described in Foucauldian terms as having fostered diverse discourses aimed at explaining and ultimately controlling sexual behavior. In 1888, the year slavery was abolished, Raul Pompéia (1863–95) published *O ateneu* [*The Athenaeum*], a series of vignettes about life at a boys' boarding school. Sérgio, the protagonist, resents his internment, the boys who persecute him, and the director, and eventually sets fire to the school building. The novel has been described as a satire on the empire of Pedro II and its collapse, and as a message of hope for the nascent republic (1889). While at school Sérgio experiences both homosexual passion—a consequence of confinement—and heterosexual attachments which make aspects of his narrative lewd and unwholesome for the time, but Pompéia ostensibly attenuates prurient episodes by resorting to insinuation. The most infamous work of Brazilian naturalism, *Bom-crioulo* [*The Black Man and the Cabin Boy,* 1895] by Adolfo Caminha (1867–97), also broaches the subject of homosexuality in terms of pathology resulting from same-sex imprisonment. Amaro, known as Bom-crioulo [Good Black Man], is a fugitive slave working on board a merchant ship where he seduces the white cabin boy, Aleixo. When Amaro and Aleixo leave the ship, the latter is lured away by a Portuguese prostitute and is then murdered by the jealous Amaro. The story moves from the misery of the black population to the dishonorable nature of rakish Europeans and finally anticipates the demise of white Brazil in the death of Aleixo. Allegorical and pathological implications aside, Caminha's novel offers an open description of a homosexual relationship and is persuasive when emphasizing the dark homoeroticism of the sadistic world of sailors.

Lesbianism is given a comparable though less comprehensive treatment in Aluísio Azevedo's (1857–1913) novel *O cortiço* [*The Slum*] (1890), a story of social outcasts, promiscuity, and money, set in a tenement in Rio de Janeiro. Here women are seen to turn to other women out of dissatisfaction with men: Léonie, a French prostitute, seduces Pombinha, a simple girl living in the slum, because she is tired of men mistreating her. Lesbian liaisons, although comforting, are underpinned by the notion of deviance born of vice (prostitution); thereby, as with the above novels, moral judgement upholding the status quo sanitizes—and enables—a transgressive frisson. In each case the attempt to induce conformity is jeopardized by this frisson, which could incite further defiance of the endorsed norms.

In the years preceding the revolutionary Week of Modern Art (1922), the treatment of eroticism in poetry was dichotomous: poets such as Raimundo Correia (1859–1911) accrued eroticism to the celebration of longevity and the advances of science in tame exaltations of the sensuous perfection of nude statuary, whereas others like Augusto dos Anjos (1884–1914) and Alphonsus de Guimaraens (1870–1921),

despairing of such optimistic sentiment, wrote of the sensual coupling of self and otherness through death, cultivating a necrophile aesthetic. Prose manifestations of decadence during these years were fronted by João do Rio (pseudonym of Paulo Barreto, 1881–1921) a devout follower of Oscar Wilde, whose stories and novels aimed to chronicle the artifice, perversity, and sexual delinquency of the Brazilian belle époque. In his most famous story, "O bebê de tarlatana rosa" [*Rose Tarlatan Baby*] (1910), the narrator, Heitor de Alencar, desires an enigmatic woman wearing a pink baby costume during carnival; she accepts his advances on condition that he promise not to remove her mask, but in the throes of passion he tears it off and is horrified to find a face without a nose. The interchangeable intensities of attraction and revulsion, carnality and mutilation in this story again gesture toward the indivisibility of eroticism and death. Decadent literature of this sort constituted an important shift toward liberating sexuality from naturalism's scientific discourse of perversion; such dissonance was greatly exacerbated by the Modernist impetus.

The search for political and cultural innovation during the 1922 Week of Modern Art in São Paulo brought together nationalistic preoccupations with the avant-garde movements of European art, instigating years of intense literary production. Mário de Andrade (1893–1945), alias the "pope" of Brazilian Modernism, wrote *Macunaíma* (1928), a bawdy rhapsody of the ethnic and linguistic influences which shaped the Brazilian character. Another august figure of Modernism, Oswald de Andrade (1890–1954), published *Serafim Ponte Grande* [*Seraphim Grosse Pointe*] (1933), a satirical bricolage-cum-travelogue in which the protagonist stages an orgiastic revolt against bourgeois values. Of the poets associated with this generation, the prolific Manuel Bandeira (1886–1968) wrote love lyrics of erotic vigor, as did the illustrious Carlos Drummond de Andrade (1902–87) in *O amor natural* [*Natural Love*], which appeared only posthumously in 1992 because the poet had considered the collection too risqué.

In the wake of the initial phase of Modernism—coinciding with the Vargas dictatorship (1930–45)—came the neorealism of a regionalist fiction concerned with transition from agrarian to industrial society. One of the authors writing about the northeast, José Lins do Rego (1901–57), explored adolescent sexuality in works like *Menino de engenho* [*Plantation Boy*] (1932) and the autobiographical *Meus verdes anos* [*My Green Years*] (1956). In 1932 Jorge Amado (1912–2001) emerged as a misguided Marxist novelist idealizing the squalid lives of the Bahian lower classes, though by 1958, with *Gabriela, cravo e canela* [*Gabriela, Clove and Cinnamon*], his commitment to politics had been superseded by devotion to salacity. The regionalist tradition and the lessons of Modernism were subsumed by João Guimarães Rosa (1908–67) in his magnum opus, *Grande sertão: veredas* [*The Devil to Pay in the Backlands*] (1956), a strikingly neologistic epic of a *jagunço* (bandit) named Riobaldo and the hostile life of the *sertão* (backlands). Much of his monologue—a vehicle for reflection on meta-narrative concerns—relates to his desire for a fellow bandit, Diadorim. Although this dishonorable passion is seemingly redeemed by the fact that Diadorim turns out to be a woman—revealed only after she is killed—this does little to detract from the homoeroticism which prevails throughout the piece, or from the contention that desire is an undecidable force overriding biological instinct. The disruptive force of libido is also the subject of Lúcio Cardoso's (1913–68) *Crônica da casa assassinada* [*Chronicle of the Assassinated House*] (1959), where narrative play between concealment and restrained disclosure eroticizes the riving of the hegemonic family body by infidelity, incest, necrophilia, homosexuality, and transvestism. The erotic potential of the telling process itself is also explored in the work of Clarice Lispector (1925–77), which reflects on the violent pleasures inherent in the oppressive act of narration, as in *A hora da estrela* [*The Hour of the Star*] (1977). Her novels and stories arrest epiphanic moments at which femininity falters, negotiates the loss of domesticity, and is consumed by paroxysmal *horror vacui*. Diegetic eroticism in her work is tentative: nuances produced by poetic zeal subtending moments of introspection, never effects of debased dynamics of power and sexuality as found in the stories of *A via crucis do corpo* [*The Stations of the Body*] (1974), which have more in common with the sordid brutality of stories by Dalton Trevisan (1925–).

Censorship and repression during the military dictatorship (1964–85) caused many writers to go into exile; testimonial accounts of outcast existence flourished. During this period Rubem Fonseca's (1925–) discomfiting *Feliz ano novo* [*Happy New Year*] (1975) was banned because of its allegedly pornographic content, as were several plays by Nelson Rodrigues (1912–80). Rodrigues brought the scandal of deviant sexuality to the Brazilian stage. Although he subverts heterosexuality and the nuclear family in plays such as *Os sete gatinhos* [*Seven Kittens*] (1958), *Beijo no asfalto* [*Kiss on the Asphalt*] (1961), and *Toda nudez será casitgada* [*All Nudity Will Be Punished*] (1965), he binds transgression to public humiliation, instilling a sense of what should be deemed normative. In the aftermath of dictatorship and the experience of alienation, women and sexual minorities rose to literary prominence as part of the general drive to speak out against all forms of social injustice. Their discourses of gender and sexuality proved auspicious for the narrative expansion of eroticism, a trend which extends into the 21st century. Pioneering authors on the subject of female sexuality and the problematics of emancipation include Lygia Fagundes Telles (1923–), Hilda Hilst (1930–), Sônia Coutinho (1939–) and Márcia Denser (1949–). The most innovative narrative and poetic engagements with homoeroticism have come from Silviano Santiago (1936–), Edilberto Coutinho (1938–96), João Silvério Trevisan (1944–), Caio Fernando Abreu (1948–96), and Glauco Mattoso (pseudonym of Pedro da Silva, 1951–). Finally, also worthy of note are the fluidly sensual characters of João Gilberto Noll (1947–), the indefatigable pornography of João Ubaldo Ribeiro's (1941–) bestselling *A casa dos budas ditosos* [*The House of Blissful Buddhas*] (1999), and the maverick fusion of licentiousness and Judaic myth in Arnaldo Bloch's (1965–) inspired novella *Talk show* (2000), all of which augur a promising future for the erotic genre in Brazil.

KARL POSSO

Selected Works

Abreu, Caio Fernando. *Morangos mofados*. São Paulo: Companhia das Letras, 1995 [1982].

———. *Onde andará Dulce Veiga?* São Paulo: Companhia das Letras, 1990; as *Whatever Happened to Dulce Veiga?* translated by Adria Frizzi, Austin: University of Texas Press, 2000.

Alencar, José de. *Senhora*. Rio de Janeiro: Livros Técnicos e Científicos, 1979 [1875]

Amado, Jorge. *Gabriela, cravo e canela*. Rio de Janeiro: Record, 1995 [1958]; as *Gabriela, Clove and Cinnamon*, translated by J. L. Taylor and W. Grossman, New York: Bard Books, 1974.

Andrade, Carlos Drummond de. *O amor natural*. Rio de Janeiro: Record, 1992.

Andrade, Mário de. *Macunaíma*. São Paulo: Eugênio Cupolo, 1928; as *Macunaíma*, E. A. Goodland, London: Quartet, 1985.

Andrade, Oswald de. *Serafim Ponte Grande*. Rio de Janeiro: Ariel, 1933; as *Seraphim Grosse Pointe*, translated by Albert Bork and Kenneth D. Jackson, Austin: New Latin Quarter, 1979.

Anjos, Augusto dos. *Eu: outras poesias, poemas esquecidos*. Rio de Janeiro: Livraria São José, 1965 [1912].

Assis, Joaquim Maria Machado de. *Contos*. São Paulo: Ática, 1981 [1870–99]; as *The Psychiatrist and Other Stories*, translated by W. L. Grossman and Helen Caldwell, Berkeley and Los Angeles: University of California Press, 1963.

———. *Memórias póstumas de Brás Cubas*. Rio de Janeiro: Ediouro, 1980 [1881]; as *Epitaph of a Small Winner*, translated by W. L. Grossman, London: Vintage, 1991.

———. *Quincas Borba*. São Paulo: Moderna, 1995 [1891]; as *Quincas Borba: A novel*, translated by Gregory Rabassa, Oxford: Oxford University Press, 1999.

———. *Dom Casmurro*. Rio de Janeiro: Ediouro, 1996 [1900]; as *Dom Casmurro*, translated by John Gledson, Oxford: Oxford University Press, 1997.

Azevedo, Aluísio. *O cortiço*. São Paulo: Livraria Martins, 1973 [1890]; as *The Slum: A novel*, translated by David H. Rosenthal, Oxford: Oxford University Press, 2000.

Bandeira, Manuel. *Poesia completa e prosa*. Rio de Janeiro: Nova Aguilar, 1983.

Bloch, Arnaldo. *Talk show*. São Paulo: Companhia das Letras, 2000.

Caminha, Adolfo. *Bom-crioulo*. São Paulo: Ática, 1983 [1895]; as *The Black Man and the Cabin Boy*, translated by E. A. Lacey, San Francisco: Gay Sunshine Press, 1982.

Cardoso, Lúcio. *Crônica da casa assassinada*. Rio de Janeiro: José Olympio, 1959.

Correia, Raimundo. *Poesia completa e prosa*. Rio de Janeiro: Aguilar, 1961.

Coutinho, Edilberto (ed.), *Zero zero sexo: O erotismo no romance brasileiro contemporâneo*. Rio de Janeiro: Gráfica Record, 1967.

———. *Maracanã, Adeus*. Rio de Janeiro: Civilização Brasileira, 1980.

———. *O jogo terminado*. Rio de Janeiro: José Olympio, 1983.

Coutinho, Sônia. *Uma certa felicidade*. Rio de Janeiro: Francisco Alves, 1976.

Denser, Márcia. *Animal dos motéis*. Rio do Janeiro: Civilização Brasileira, 1981.

——— (ed.). *Muito prazer—contos eróticos femininos*. Rio de Janeiro: Record, 1982.

Fonseca, Rubem. *Feliz ano novo*. São Paulo: Companhia das Letras, 1989 [1975].

Guimaraens, Alphonsus de. *Obra completa*. Rio de Janeiro: Aguilar, 1960.

Hilst, Hilda. *A obscena Senhora D*. São Paulo: Massao Ohno, 1982.

Lispector, Clarice. *A via crucis do corpo*. Rio de Janeiro: Artenova, 1974; as *Soulstorm*, translated by Alexis Levitin, New York: New Directions, 1989.

———. *A hora da estrela*. Rio de Janeiro: Nova Fronteira, 1987 [1977]; as *The Hour of the Star*, translated by Giovanni Pontiero, Manchester: Carcanet, 1992.

Matos, Gregório de. *Poemas escolhidos*. São Paulo: Cultrix, 1976.

Mattoso, Glauco. *Línguas na papa: uma salada dos mais insípidos aos mais picantes—poemas*. São Paulo: Pindaíba, 1982.

———. *Memórias de um pueteiro: As melhores gozações de Glauco Mattoso—poesia*. 2nd ed. Rio de Janeiro: Edições Trote, 1982.

———. *Manual do pedólatra amador: Aventuras e leituras de um tarado por pés*. São Paulo: Expressão, 1986.

Noll, João Gilberto. *Romances e contos reunidos*. São Paulo: Companhia das Letras, 1997.

Pompéia, Raul. *O ateneu*. São Paulo: Martin Claret, 2000 [1888].

Rego, José Lins do. *Menino de engenho*. Rio de Janeiro: José Olympio, 1932; as *Plantation Boy*, translated by Emmi Baum, New York: Knopf, 1966.

———. *Meus verdes anos*. Rio de Janeiro: José Olympio, 1956.

Ribeiro, João Ubaldo. *A casa dos budas ditosos*. Rio de Janeiro: Objetiva, 1999.

Rio, João do. *Dentro da noite*. Rio de Janeiro: Instituto Estadual do Livro, 1978 [1910].

Rodrigues, Nelson. *Teatro completo*. Rio de Janeiro: Nova Fronteira, 1981.

Rosa, João Guimarães. *Grande sertão: Veredas*. Rio de Janeiro: José Olympio, 1956; as *The Devil to Pay in the Backlands*, translated by James L. Taylor and Harriet de Onis, New York: Knopf, 1963.

Santiago, Silviano. *Stella Manhattan*. Rio de Janeiro: Nova Fronteira, 1985; as *Stella Manhattan*, translated by George Yúdice, Durham, NC: Duke University Press, 1994.

———. *Keith Jarrett no Blue Note*. Rio de Janeiro: Rocco, 1996.

Telles, Lygia Fagundes. *Seminário dos ratos*. Rio de Janeiro: José Olympio, 1977; as *Tigrela and Other Stories*, translated by Margaret A. Neves, New York: Avon, 1986.

———. *Os melhores contos de Lygia Fagundes Telles*. São Paulo: Global, 1984.

Trevisan, Dalton. *O vampiro de Curitiba*. Rio de Janeiro: Civilização Brasileira, 1970 [1965]; as *The Vampire of Curitiba and Other Stories*, translated by Gregory Rabassa, New York: Knopf, 1972.

———. *Contos eróticos*. Rio de Janeiro: Record, 1984.

———. *A polaquinha*. Rio de Janeiro: Record, 1985.

Trevisan, João Silvério. *Testamento de Jônatas deixando a David*. São Paulo: Brasiliense, 1976.

———. *Em nome do desejo: Romance*. Rio de Janeiro: Codecri, 1983.

——— (ed.). *Amor com olhos de adeus: Antologia do conto gay brasileiro*. São Paulo: Transviatta, 1995.

———. *Troços e destroços: Contos*. Rio de Janeiro: Record, 1997.

Further Reading

Bosi, Alfredo. *História concisa da literatura brasileira*. 35th ed. São Paulo: Cultrix, 1994.

Coutinho, Afrânio (ed.). *A literatura no Brasil*. 3rd ed. 6 vols. Rio de Janeiro: José Olympio, 1986.

Echevarría, Roberto González, and Enrique Pupo-Walker (eds.). *The Cambridge History of Latin American Literature*. 3 vols. Cambridge: Cambridge University Press, 1996.

BREAST, THE

The female breast has been an erotic marker since it first emerged in pre-Christian texts. From the Hebrew Bible to contemporary erotica, it has sparked the male literary imagination. Most recently, however, it has been claimed by women authors as well, so as to present a feminine view of their most freighted body part.

Although the erotic breast appears as a literary trope in every age and place in the Western world, it follows the fads of its time: sometimes small breasts are in fashion, as in the Middle Ages and 1920s, more often the larger breast predominates, as in the Renaissance and 1950s. In erotic literature, the breast "peaked" during the Renaissance, the period to be considered primarily in this essay.

The only frankly erotic section of the Bible is found in the Song of Songs, a collection of love poems probably written by more than one author, including women. Female bodily delights are enumerated in a poetic inventory that became the model for untold imitations throughout the centuries to come:

> How fine
> You are, my love,
> Your eyes like doves'
> Behind your veil
> ....
> Your breasts
> Twin fawns
> In fields of flowers.

Breasts are also compared to "clusters of dates" and "clusters of grapes," the juice of which awakens desire "Like wine that entices / The lips of new lovers." Unlike any other part of the Bible, the Song of Songs is an unabashed paean to erotic pleasure, with breasts appearing as sensual symbols of reciprocal bliss.

While the Latin poets Catullus, Horace, Ovid, and Propertius celebrated the breast in their love poems, and French authors of medieval narratives sang the praises of little breasts (*les mamelettes*) that were commonly compared to apples and, less commonly, to round nuts (Garin le Loherain, Ogier le Danois, and Aucassin et Nicolette), it would take the consummate skill of Renaissance poets to turn the breast into an international fetish.

In France, the breast cult reached a verbal paroxysm between the 1530s and 1550s, launched by Clément Marot's *blason* entitled *Le Beau tétin* [*The Beautiful Breast*], written during the winter of 1535–36. A *blason* traditionally focused on the body parts of the female beloved: eyes, eyebrows, nose, ears, tongue, hair, chest, stomach, navel, buttocks, hand, thigh, knee, foot, as well as the breast (see the entry for *Blason du corps* in this volume). Marot playfully described the breast in the following manner:

> A little ball of ivory
> In the middle of which sits
> A strawberry or a cherry.
> ...
> When one sees you, many men feel
> The desire within their hands
> To touch you and to hold you.
> But one must satisfy oneself
> With being near you for my life!
> Or another desire will come.
> ...

For every reason, happy is he
Who will fill you with milk,
Turning the virgin's breast into
The breast of a beautiful, complete woman.

The poem narrates the effect produced by the sight of the breast on the male viewer. A beautiful breast is not only a stimulus to his desire, but also a source of masculine pride, since it is his seed that impregnates the female and transforms her into a milk-bearing creature. Such a breast allows the poet to spend himself in verbal ecstasy, and to act out a power fantasy of triggering the milk-production process.

The most famous French Renaissance poet, Pierre de Ronsard (1524–85), was also a breast man. In the long cycle of love poems dedicated to Cassandre, he refers over and over to her "beautiful breast," "virginal buds," "lawns of milk," "generous throat," "overly chaste breast," "hill of milk," "alabaster throat," "ivory breast," and so forth. He tells us that if he could only "grope around her breasts," he would consider his obscure fate more fortunate than that of kings. He envies the doctor who has the right to feel the breast of Ronsard's sweetheart at any time. Occasionally his hand will not take orders from his brain: "sometimes my hand, in spite of myself, / Transgresses the laws of chaste love / And searches at your breast that which inflames me." Yet even the pleasure of touching her bosom can cause regret: "I wish to God that I had never touched / My loved one's breast with so much mad desire." For now he has an admittedly greater need, which the beloved is not about to satisfy.

Ronsard's breast metaphors were sometimes borrowed from earlier Italian poets. In the tradition of Petrarch, he contemplated the joys of being transformed into a flea with the opportunity of biting the desired bosom. In the tradition of Ariosto, he imagined the female chest as an earthly paradise where "twin flows of milk" come and go like the ocean tide (Sonnet CLXXXVII). But we should not think that Ronsard's outpourings were merely literary conventions. Cassandre was a real person, the daughter of a Florentine banker in the service of the king of France, and the unrequited passion she inspired in him triggered his lubricious fantasies. On the frontispiece of *Les Amours*, written between 1546 and 1552, there are two medallions: one of Ronsard, the poet, crowned with a laurel leaf, and the other of a bare-breasted Cassandre at the age of twenty.

Compared with the marmoreal conceits of male poets, the few erotic texts that have come down to us from women tell a different story. Louise Labé (1524–65), a French poet from Lyon, described the turmoil in her chest she experienced in the absence of her former lover. She longed to be gathered up at his breast (Sonnet XIII) or to hold him once again at her own "tender breast" (Sonnet 9).

Since the first moment when cruel Love
Poisoned my bosom with his fire
I have burned from his divine fury,
No respite for my heart for even a day.

Breast and bosom betoken torment rather than titillation.

Similarly, a poem sent by a nun to her female lover reveals the mental ache associated with past pleasures. "When I recall the kisses you gave me, And how with tender words you caressed my little breasts, I want to die Because I cannot see you" (1986; Judith C. Brown). This kind of frank physicality is practically nonexistent in surviving premodern texts authored by women.

Following their continental counterparts, British male poets also employed the "blazon" as a showcase for the display of female body parts. Robert Greene's *Menaphon* (1589) provides a fairly standard example:

Her locks are plighted like the fleece of wool
...
Her lips are roses over-washed with dew
...
Her paps are like fair apples in the prime,
As round as orient pearls, as soft as down.

Michael Drayton (1563–1631) transformed his mistress's chest into a pastoral landscape replete with meadows and rivers: "Thy full and youthful breasts, which, in their meadowy pride / Are branch'd with rivery veines meander-like that glide." Thomas Lodge's *Rosalynde* (1590) offers the best mammary two-liner of the period: "Her paps are centers of delight / Her breasts are orbs of heavenly frame." Terms derived from nature, geography, and the cosmos, like "orbs," "globes," "worlds," and "hemispheres," vied with more common fruit and floral expressions, such as "buds," "strawberries," apples," and "cherrylets," to evoke the erotic enticements offered by a female bosom. Edmund Spenser (1552–99), equating female parts with different flowers, created an anatomical English garden in his Sonnet 64:

Her goodly bosom like a Strawberry bed;
Her neck like to a bunch of Columbines;
Her breast like lilies, ere their leaves be shed;
Her nipples like young-blossomed Jessamines.

His "Epithalamion" (a poem celebrating marriage) moves indoors to the kitchen, where the bride is offered up in oral terms, and breasts provide the pièce de resistance in a menu of edible delights:

Her cheeks like apples which the sun hath rudded,
Her lips like cherries charming men to bite,
Her breasts like a bowl of cream uncrudded,
Her paps like lilies budded.

Shakespeare, tiring of the blazon with its lily-white breasts, parodied that conventional form in his Sonnet 130:

My mistress' eyes are nothing like the sun;
Coral is far more red than her lips' red;
If snow be white, why then her breasts are dun.

By the time of his death in 1616, the blazon had petered out and paeans to the erotic breast were on the wane. John Donne (1571–1631), who brilliantly evoked genital activity in many of his erotic poems, paid scant attention to the female chest. A new, more domestic discourse was on the rise, with breasts the site of controversy over the practice of wet-nursing. In the seventeenth and eighteenth centuries the breast became politicized by such writers as Jacob Cats (1577–1660) in Holland, William Cadogan in England (see his influential 1748 *Essay upon Nursing*), Carolus Linnaeus in Sweden (1707–78), and especially Jean-Jacques Rousseau (1712–78) in France, all arguing for a return to maternal nursing.

But the erotic breast had not disappeared. It had simply gone underground for awhile. As Margaret Anne Doody points out in her *London Review of Books* article on my *History of the Breast* (1997), Samuel Richardson's novels offered both the eroticized and the maternal breast, the former in the sequel to *Pamela* (1740–41), the latter in *Clarissa* (1747–48). Lovelace in Clarissa gets carried away by the sight of the protagonist's bosom barely hidden under a white handkerchief: "And I saw, all the way we rode, the bounding heart (by its throbbing motions, I saw it!) dancing beneath the charming umbrage.... What a precious moment That! How near, how sweetly near, the throbbing partners." Clarissa, the possessor of the "throbbing partners" that so excite Lovelace, runs away with him under promise of marriage, but finds out to her sorrow that he intended only to seduce her. Her downward spiral into a house of ill repute, jail, and death is not so heavy on morality as to deaden its erotic tug. Lovelace, in the end, finds that he really loves Clarissa and offers her marriage, but it is too late. He dies, repentant, in a duel.

French eighteenth-century novelists were no less attracted by women's bosoms, most notably Jean-Jacques Rousseau (a breast man if there ever was one!) and Pierre Choderlos de Laclos in *Les Liaisons Dangereuses* [*Dangerous Liaisons*] (1782). In Laclos's masterpiece of erotic literature, the Vicomte de Valmont attempts the seduction of Mme. de Tourvel, a chaste judge's wife. He confesses to the Marquise de Merteuil, his accomplice in matters of seduction, that he is drawn to Mme. de Tourvel's "round supple figure" and specifically to her gorge (bosom) covered only by a single layer of chiffon. In the presence of her scarcely concealed breasts, Valmont admits: "My furtive but keen glances already spied out their enchanting shape." Slightly later he manages to feel their contours. In crossing a ditch, she is obliged to accept his help and he clasps her in his arms. "I held her breast against my own and, in that brief moment, I felt her heart beat faster." Laclos's depiction of the sexual games masterminded by two diabolical aristocrats caps a century of libertinage (libertine philosophy and debauchery) and points, in its own way, to the Revolution at hand.

The breast continued to surface in nineteenth- and twentieth-century erotic literature in poetry, novels, and memoirs, not to mention spectacle and film. European and American men continued to be aroused by the sight of a woman's bust, explicated by Freud as the source of a person's deepest emotions. He posited that sucking at the breast was not only the child's first activity, but also "the starting point of the whole of sexual life." Freud's case histories sometimes read like erotic literature, with breasts and penises appearing in every crevice of the human mind.

Conversely, writers influenced by Freud, that is, a significant number of twentieth-century authors, looked to the master of psychoanalysis for tacit approval of their own breast obsessions. From Ramón Gómez de la Serna's fanciful inventory of mammary delights titled *Senos [Breasts]* (1917) to Philip Roth's preposterous novella *The Breast* and Woody Allen's film *Everything You Always Wanted to Know About Sex* (both 1972), male authors have had license to eulogize, categorize, and ridicule what they deem to be women's defining appendages. Even if some of these works stretch the boundaries of the erotic into the comic and the absurd, they carry with them the aura of sexuality that is likely to excite a reader.

Gómez de la Serna treats breasts as if they had a life of their own. He represents them in a series of lyrical vignettes titled "The Best of Breasts," "The Inquisitor's Wife's Breasts," "The Breast Which Called Me from Behind," "A Duel over Breasts," "Breasts on the Beach," "The Breasts of the Woman with a Flat Nose," "False Breasts," "Circus Breasts," "Tatooed Breasts," "Stupid Breasts," "Breasts that Look at Themselves in the Mirror," and so forth. As an early proponent of surrealism (a literary and artistic movement born immediately after World War I), Gómez favored incongruous alliances: the breasts in his tales find themselves in surprising situations; for example, on a hermaphrodite's body or in a reliquary. They may be called upon to appear uncovered at night on a balcony, so that the author can see them from the window of his apartment. They may be presented to a "collector of breasts" so as to receive a certificate declaring that they are "delicate and opulent... luminous... pure and beautiful." As a fetish, to be sure, they represent a feminine essence that Gomez can never get enough of. Sacred, maternal, fundamentally erotic, breasts offer him "life preservers against death."

It is a long leap from male objectification of the female breast to texts written by women featuring their own breasts. Consider this exuberant 1996 poem by Alicia Ostriker on the acquisition of breasts:

All the years of girlhood we wait for them,
Impatient to catch up, to have power
. . .
When the lovers lick them
And bring us there, there, in the fragrant wet,
When the babies nuzzle like bees.

We hear the proud possessor of a burgeoning bosom and her pleasure in the exquisite sensations produced by a lover's mouth at the breast... or a baby's; for, as Ostriker tells us in another poem, mothers can become sexually aroused by the process of suckling.

Greedy baby
Sucking the sweet tit
....
when you suckle I am slowly moved
in my sensitive groove
you in your mouth are alive, I in my womb

Female erotica recognizes the breast as multifunctional. Throughout life it can play its role as a stimulus to desire, for both males and females; it also has a more primary role to play at that stage of life when one is breast-feeding an infant. Freud was right in positing a connection between suckling and sex, but, in the case of women, it may not have been exactly what he thought.

MARILYN YALOM

Further Reading

Bruillon, Viviane, and Marc Majesté (eds.). *Le Sein: Images Representations.* Paris: Editions l'Harmattan, 1996.

Falk, Marcia. *The Song of Songs, A New Translation.* San Francisco: HarperCollins, 1993.

Freud, Sigmund. *Complete Works.* Vols. 7 and 16. London: Hogarth Press, 1955.

Gent, Lucy, and Nigel Llewellyn (eds.). *Renaissance Bodies: The Human Figure in English Culture c. 1540–1660.* London: Reaktion Books, 1990.

Gros, Dominique. *Le Sein Dévoilé.* Paris: Stock/Laurence Pernoud, 1987.

Ostriker, Alicia. *The Crack in Everything.* Pittsburgh: University of Pittsburgh Press, 1996.

Prose, Francine, Karen Finley, Dario Fo, and Charles Simic. *Master Breasts: Objectified, Aestheticized, Fantasized, Eroticized, Feminized by Photography's Most Titillating Masters.* New York: Aperture, 1998.

Romi. *La Mythologie du Sein.* Paris: Pauvert, 1965.

Roth, Philip. *The Breast.* New York: Vintage Books, 1972.

Saunders, Alison. *The Sixteenth-Century Blason Poétique.* Bern, Frankfurt am Main, and Las Vegas: Peter Lang, 1981.

Serna, Ramón Gómez de la. *Seins.* Translated by Benito Pelegrin. Marseilles: André Dimanche Editeur, 1992.

Thornton, Louise, Jan Sturtevant, and Amber Sumrall, eds. *Touching Fire: Erotic Writings by Women.* New York: Carroll & Graf Publishers, 1989.

Yalom, Marilyn. *A History of the Breast.* New York: Knopf, 1997.

BRIGHT, SUSIE

1958–
American essayist, columnist, and anthologist

Susie Bright recorded her erotic fantasies in letters and poetry as a teenager and, in the early days of the feminist and sexual liberation movements, wrote about sexual issues for her peers in underground publications. In 1978, around the time of the assassination of gay city councilman Harvey Milk in San Francisco, Bright became fascinated by the sexual politics of the city's emerging gay community, and this dynamic cultural milieu became the focus of her academic studies at Santa Cruz. From 1981 to 1986, she worked at Good Vibrations, a sex toy boutique in San Francisco, first as a part-time salesperson, and later as manager. From 1984 to 1990, she wrote the mail-order catalog and created an extensive erotic video library for the store. During this period, she began reading her erotic poetry publicly in small storefront venues in San Francisco. Under the nom de plume of "Susie Sexpert," Bright wrote the first of many "Toys for Us" columns for the debut issue of the new lesbian sex magazine *On Our Backs* that she and others founded, and she soon became editor of the publication. Over time, the focus of the column expanded from consumer reviews and sex advice to commentary on pornography, sexual politics, and erotic adventurism. Many of the "Toys for Us" columns are collected in *Susie Sexpert's Lesbian Sex World.* Although these pieces were written for a lesbian audience, the book had significant crossover appeal for both female and male heterosexuals as well as for gay men. Bright soon began writing for a wider audience in such publications as *Playboy, Esquire, The Advocate, Hustler,* and the *Village Voice* and reviewed X-rated movies for the magazine *Penthouse Forum* from 1986 to 1989.

In the 1990s, Bright emerged as a prominent voice in the radical and often volatile discourse surrounding sexuality. She lectured widely, especially in universities, in community theaters, and at film festivals, and appeared at places as diverse as the Esalen Institute, the famous New Age retreat and study center located in California's Big Sur; the Modern Language Association; and the British Film Institute. Her lectures have frequently ignited controversy. She once received a death threat from a feminist antipornography group in Massachusetts, and her "Sexual State of the Union Address" delivered at Wellesley College near Boston in 1994 was nearly disrupted by a bomb threat. During this period, Bright published numerous articles and essays, and many of these early pieces are collected in *Susie Bright's Sexual Reality: A Virtual Sex World Reader,* and in *Susie Bright's Sexwise: America's Favorite X-rated Intellectual Does Dan Quayle, Catharine MacKinnon, Stephen King, Camille Paglia, Nicholson Baker, Madonna, the Black Panthers and the GOP....* She became a columnist for *Playboy Online,* the online sexzine *Labida,* and *Salon.com,* the most widely-read online journal of politics and popular culture. In 2001 she began her own Internet audio show, "In Bed with Susie Bright," on Audible.com. She also developed and taught two courses at Santa Cruz: "The Politics of Sexuality" and "The Politics of Sexual Repression." From time to time, she teaches "Reading, Writing, and Rethinking Erotica," and "How to Read/Write a Dirty Story," as online courses designed to help students understand, create, and publish literary erotic fiction.

Disappointed by the paucity of women's erotica and the marginalization of writers who did manage to publish their work, Bright conceptualized and edited *Herotica,* her first collection of erotic fiction by and for women, in 1988. The volume was so popular that she subsequently edited *Herotica II, Herotica III, Totally Herotica,* and the *10th Anniversary Edition of Herotica.* This series gave voice to such now well known writers as Pat Califia, Sarah Schulman, Lisa Palac, Carol Queen, and Joan Nestle, and introduced readers of erotica to emerging stars, as well to many nascent voices. From the first volume of the *Herotica* series, Bright consciously tracked and documented changing thematic and stylistic trends in short erotic fiction, and this practice continued in her next editing venture. In 1993, Mark Chimsky, an editor at Macmillan Publishers Ltd., invited Bright to edit a new series entitled *The Best American Erotica,* patterned after similar series of poetry and short stories. The idea proved a resounding success, with every collection achieving bestseller status. According to Bright's assessment, erotica of the 1980s was often autobiographical and heavily confessional, dominated by tales of youthful yearning, coming-of-age sagas, and coming-out stories. In the Introduction to the first volume, *The Best American Erotica, 1993,* Bright identifies a countertrend toward "porn noir," which eschewed confessional writing and focused on more imaginative work within a noirish milieu. She observes, however, that by the mid-1990s, the noir trend had waned and been largely supplanted by stories with more eclectic, visionary settings, which now included encounters with mysterious beings or strangers, as well as with more familiar character types. Many of these stories are notable too for the authors' adroit use of language for dramatic tension and erotic effect. In the 1994 collection, instead of discussing new trends in her Introduction, Bright offered readers and potential writers a primer on "How to Write a Best Erotic Story."

The 1995 edition marks the debut of excerpts from the work of some well-known writers that, according to Bright, qualify as erotica. The series would ultimately include excerpts from such best-selling authors as Nicholson Baker (from *Fermata*), Jane Smiley (from *Good Faith*), Marge Piercy (from *Three Women*), and Bret Easton Ellis (from *Glamorama*), as well as short stories by Robert Olen Butler, Celia Tan, Dorothy Allison, Mary Gaitskill, and the actor Alan Cumming. The 1996 volume reveals less emphasis on style and literary convention, formerly seen as necessary to distinguish "erotica" from "pornography," and an increasing interest in frank eroticism. In 1997, mythic themes from European fairy tales, the Old Testament, and Native American and Hindu traditions emerged. These stories also reflect gender-bending points of view, in which the gender and sexual orientation of authors no longer predict characterization, milieu, or action. This trend is independently confirmed by Carol Queen and Lawrence Schimel's collection, *Switch Hitters: Lesbians Write Gay Male Erotica... and Gay Men Write Lesbian Erotica.*

(There is no 1998 edition of *Best American Erotica.* That year, the publication date was moved forward from October 1998 to February 1999, to enable succeeding volumes to be published early in each calendar year.) In the Introduction to the 1999 volume, Bright cites the insoluble problem of pleasing everyone, and suggests that a story's appeal lies more in its ability to capture and hold the reader than in specific characters, setting, or specific sexual practices. As an example, she cites "The Hit," by Steven Saylor (writing as Aaron Travis), which readers ultimately voted as the top story of the series' first decade, although the characters and action lie well beyond the experience and interest of most readers. A number of stories in the 2000 edition mark a departure from glamour and the physical perfection of protagonists, and exhibit instead a lively interest in gross, misshapen, even puerile characters who are not, in the end, necessarily redeemed by sex. In the Introduction to the 2001 volume, Bright notes the explosion of erotica on the Internet, but reports that the quality is often superficial, predictable, and imminently forgettable. In contrast, her overarching goal in the *Best American Erotica* series is to offer the cream of short erotic fiction, in which the sex is psychologically compelling, exotic, and memorable. The 2002 edition continues the trend away from gender-centric points of view as authors plumb the depths of erotic experience from an unpredictable variety of gender perspectives.

In 2003, in addition to her selection of stories, Bright celebrated a decade of the series' publication by interviewing contributors about their lives, asking questions about education, jobs, interests, and awards, and about their experiences in writing erotica. This informal survey reveals that the interests and experiences of writers of erotica are as typical and unpredictable as those of the general population. This double volume also includes the results of an informal survey of readers regarding their favorite stories over the decade, a listing of the top 100 stories, with occasional commentary by the authors, and reprints of the top five stories. In the 2004 Introduction, Bright notes the appearance of two new mini-trends: tales featuring blood—vampires, cutting, or blood-sharing experiences—which she posits symbolize trust and sexual risk-taking in the age of AIDS; and male submission, which she suggests is a reaction to American military involvement in Afghanistan and Iraq. In 2005, rather than identifying new trends, Bright muses on the uses of pornography/erotica, and recommends sharing the stories with partners to enhance the erotics of sexual experiences.

Bright's work has won numerous awards, including the Firecracker Alternative Book Award for *Nothing but the Girl* in 1997, and *Susie Bright's Sexual State of the Union* in 2001; the Lambda Literary Award for *Nothing but the Girl in* 1997; and the Good Vibrations Venus Award, 1997. She was named "Best Sex Columnist of 1998" by the *New York Press* for her "Sexpert Opinion" column on Salon.com. In 1999 her documentary *Susie Bright: Sex Pest*, in which she argued for exploring sex beyond intercourse, won the Erotic Award for Best British TV documentary. In 2003, Bright was inducted into the X-Rated Hall of Fame, at the annual awards of the X-Rated Critics Organization. She has also garnered numerous accolades from popular publications: "the avatar of American erotica" (*New York Times*); "the X-rated intellectual" (*San Francisco Chronicle*); "America's ranking connoisseur of sex, porn, and freedom of physical expression" (*Book Magazine*); "the absolute bomb" (*Village Voice*); the "goddess of American erotica" (*Boston Phoenix*); "sexual Renaissance woman" (*Publishers Weekly*); "one of the leading thinkers and visionaries of our time" (*Utne Reader*); and a "national treasure, right up there with the Grand Canyon, the Okefenokee Swamp, and the Smithsonian's Nancy Reagan Memorial Dress Collection" (*The Millennium Whole Earth Catalog*). Regarding her willingness to tackle controversial topics and openly criticize pronouncements and policies that she sees as sexually repressive, *Rolling Stone* opined, "No one can accuse her of shutting up."

Since the late 1980s, Bright has been enormously influential in mainstreaming short erotic fiction and in enhancing its literary merit. She achieved her status as a significant figure in this movement because of her personal interest in sex and love of literature, and as a result of her desire to bring American erotica out of obscurity into the mainstream when no one else was interested in taking on the task.

Biography

Born Arlington, Virginia, March 25, 1958. Raised in California and Canada. BA,

Community Studies, University of California at Santa Cruz, 1981. One daughter, born 1990. Lives in Northern California.

REBECCA CHALKER

Selected Works

Author

Susie Sexpert's Lesbian Sex World. Pittsburgh and San Francisco: Cleis Press, 1990, 1999.
Susie Bright's Sexual Reality: A Virtual Sex World Reader. Pittsburgh and San Francisco: Cleis Press, 1992.
Susie Bright's Sexwise: America's favorite X-rated intellectual does Dan Quayle, Catharine MacKinnon, Stephen King, Camille Paglia, Nicholson Baker, Madonna, the Black Panthers and the GOP. . . . Pittsburgh and San Francisco: Cleis Press, 1995.
How To Write a Dirty Story: Reading, Writing, and Publishing Erotica. New York: Simon & Schuster, 2002.

Editor

Herotica. San Francisco: Down There Press, 1988, 1990, 1998.
Herotica II. With Joani Blank. San Francisco: Down There Press, 1992; New York: Penguin USA, 1992.
Herotica III. San Francisco: Down There Press, 1993; New York: Penguin USA, 1994.
Best American Erotica. New York: Simon and Schuster, 1993–2005.
Totally Herotica: A Collection of Women's Erotic Fiction. With Joani Blank. New York: Quality Paperback Book Club, 1995.
Nothing but the Girl: The Blatant Lesbian Image. With Jill Posener. Fountain Hills, CA: Freedom Editions.
Herotica, 10th Anniversary Edition with Afterword by the editor. San Francisco: Down There Press, 1998.
Three the Hard Way: Erotic Novellas by William Harrison, Greg Boyd, and Tsaurah Litzky. New York: Simon & Schuster, 2004.

Further Reading

Elias, James, Veronica Diehl Elias, Vern L. Bullough, Gwen Brewer, Jeffrey J. Douglas, and Will Jarvis, eds. *Porn 101: Eroticism, Pornography, and the First Amendment.* Amherst, NY: Prometheus Books, 1999.
London Guardian. "Faith, Hope, and Charity." October 20, 2001.
Moran, Jack. *The Erotic Mind.* New York: HarperCollins, 1995.
Murnighan, Jack. *The Naughty Bits: The Steamiest and Most Scandalous Sex Scenes from the World's Great Literature.* New York: Three Rivers Press, 2001.
New York Times. "Batman's Robin Shaves His Legs? Erotica as a Portrait of the Age." July 10, 1999.
Slaughter, Jane. "Susie Bright." *The Progressive.* December, 1999.

BUKOWSKI, CHARLES

1920–1994
American novelist and poet

Notes of a Dirty Old Man

Charles Bukowski's *Notes of a Dirty Old Man* is a collection of short stories and opinion pieces. It was first published by Essex House in 1969. City Lights Books has published it since 1973. The selections are from a column Bukowski wrote for the Los Angeles alternative paper *Open Press*. After *Open Press* folded in 1969, Bukowski's column was picked up by the *LA Free Press, Open City's* main competitor. The book represents a fourteen-month period of the late sixties when Bukowski's rising fame, due primarily to the *Open City* column and to *At Terror Street and Agony Way* (1968), led to problems with his superiors at the United States Post Office. John Martin (publisher of Black Sparrow Press) agreed to pay Bukowski one hundred dollars a month for life to write full-time. Resigning his position, he set about his first novel, *Post Office* (1971).

Notes of a Dirty Old Man is an important work in the Bukowski *oeuvre* because it represents a transitional period in his life and marks his return to prose, a genre he had abandoned for almost twenty years (although he did release short stories in chapbooks in the mid-sixties). The impetus came from *Open City's* founder, John Bryan. Although Bukowski had a disdain for journalism (he felt it was often "flat and careless" writing), he accepted Bryan's offer of a weekly column. Bryan's willingness to print anything Bukowski submitted gave Bukowski the freedom to experiment. In the introduction to the book, Bukowski acknowledged that it was the "absolute freedom to write anything you please" that improved his writing.

The pieces chosen for inclusion in the book vary greatly in style and topic. There are sociopolitical tirades and observations and straight fictional vignettes depicting the absurdity, irony, and hopelessness of the life of the downtrodden.

The bulk of the book, however, comprises works of autobiographical fiction. These describe Bukowski's troubled childhood, his travels through the United States, his growing fame as a writer, and his relations with women. The thread that holds this diverse amalgam of styles and topics together is the underlying theme of failure to attain lasting happiness. This is particularly evident in the manner in which Bukowski presents relations between men and women.

Notes of a Dirty Old Man offers a solely male, heterosexual, and misogynistic view of the physical relations between humans. The stories range from the sad to the comical, from violence to tenderness. Throughout the book Bukowski is consistent in presenting the view that the relationship between the male and the female is a disjointed one. The men in the stories are concerned with women in an almost solely sexual manner. When the female characters in the selections attach any emotional or nonphysical aspect to their sexual interactions, problematic situations arise; when they do not seek anything beyond the physical, the female characters are referred to as being "good women" by the males.

A typical "good woman" is Frankie's wife, the skirtless woman Bukowski comes across when walking home from a party. The woman remains nameless but can be read as the female representation of Bukowski: she just wants to have a few drinks and enjoy herself. However, her husband attaches restrictions upon her autonomy by hiding all her skirts and dresses. Bukowski feels some remorse after they have sex when he sees her leave in a ripped pair of his workman's trousers. However, when she does not attempt to wake him (he is only feigning sleep) or take any money from his wallet, he finds peace from this woman who "had given something to" (104) him without seeking anything besides the physical act of intercourse. The ending reinforces the note he had scribbled on a piece of paper during the party: "love is a way with some meaning; sex is meaning enough" (99).

This story ends with Bukowski falling asleep alone in his bed, the best indication of the presence of a "good woman." The story of the "300-Pound Whore" also ends with the male character falling asleep in bed, sexually satisfied and alone. After a comical love scene where Henry Chinaski (Bukowski's main fictional representation of himself) had to hang on to the sides of the bed in order to stay upon the bucking Ann, and which resulted in a broken bed, the male character felt sadness at the woman's departure. However, the story ends with a contentment similar to the story of "Frankie's Wife": Chinaski "naked between the new sheets of [his] new bed," with the woman gone without having accepted his offer of money, "slept, alone, gracious and touched by the miracle" (153).

Most of the erotic encounters in the book, however, are not portrayed as positively as the aforementioned episodes. Bukowski presents sex for the male as a necessity. The men see women as sexual objects, tolerated only because they provide sexual release. Masturbation is an option, but a depressing one. Thus, the men yearn for women, but wonder whether the emotional price attached to sex make it worthwhile. This notion is presented in the "Moss and Anderson" column. Although both characters admit that "the price is always too high" (53), they make a date with two women. The column ends with Moss telling Anderson that they have "an hour's freedom" left before they must pay the price of their autonomy in order to satisfy their need for sex.

In Bukowski's *Notes of a Dirty Old Man*, the erotic episodes are misogynistic, often presenting women as an unfortunate necessity of coitus. However, his portraits also offer keen insights into the male/female dichotomy. He draws a distinction between sex and love that challenges patriarchal society's positioning of woman as the seller of sex. Bukowski raises questions about the relationships between authority, personal freedom, and sexuality. He portrays what he has experienced: a culture that in its assignation of sexual roles has man as a fiend and woman as a whore. It is not surprising then that the erotic passages of the book, presented through Bukowski's wry wit, play like a tragicomedy where turmoil is rife and satisfaction rare.

Biography

Born Heinrich Karl Bukowski in Andernach, Germany, on August 16, 1920. Immigrated to the United States, first living in Baltimore, then moving on to California in 1923 with father, Henry, and mother, Katharina. Parents changed the child's name from Heinrich to Charles. Graduated from Los Angeles High School in 1939 and enrolled in Los Angeles City College, where he studied journalism, English, theater, and history. Dropped out of college in 1941. From 1942 to 1947 moved around the United States working menial jobs and writing stories. In 1947 returned to LA. Began working for the US Post Office, 1952, as a temporary mail carrier. Almost died from alcohol abuse, 1955, hospitalized in LA County Hospital and saved by blood transfusion from father. On September 7, 1964, Frances Smith (FrancEye) gave birth to Bukowski's daughter, Marina Louise. The FBI began investigating Bukowski, 1968, after being informed by the Post Office of his sexually explicit writings and unorthodox lifestyle. Resigned from the Postal Service in 1969 (he knew he was about to be fired for absenteeism) and began writing full-time. The movie *Barfly* released, 1987, staring Mickey Rourke and Faye Dunaway. Bukowski wrote the screenplay and had a small role as a patron in a bar. Diagnosed, 1993, with myelogenous leukemia. Bukowski died March 9, 1994.

MICHAEL KEARNEY

Editions

Notes of a Dirty Old Man. North Hollywood, CA: Essex House, 1969; San Francisco: City Lights, 1973.

Selected Works

Flower, Fist and Bestial Wail. 1960
Longshot Pomes for Broke Players. 1962
Run with the Hunted. 1962
It Catches My Heart in Its Hands. 1963
Crucifix in a Deathhand. 1965
Cold Dogs in the Courtyard. 1965
The Genius of the Crowd. 1966
2 Poems. 1967
The Curtains Are Waving and People Walk Through/The Afternoon/Here and in Berlin and in New York City and in Mexico. 1967
At Terror Street and Agony Way. 1968
Poems Written Before Jumping out of an 8-Story Window. 1968
A Bukowski Sampler. 1969

The Days Run Away Like Wild Horses Over the Hills. 1969
Post Office. 1971
Erections, Ejaculations, Exhibitions and General Tales of Ordinary Madness. 1972 (reissued as two separate books in 1983, *Tales of Ordinary Madness* and *The Most Beautiful Woman in Town*)
Mockingbird Wish Me Luck. 1972
South of No North. 1973
Burning in Water, Drowning in Flames: Poems 1955–1973. 1974
Factotum. 1975
Love Is a Dog from Hell: Poems 1974–1977. 1977
Women. 1978
Play the Piano Drunk/Like a Percussion Instrument/Until the Fingers Begin to Bleed a Bit. 1979
Dangling in the Tournefortia. 1981
Ham on Rye. 1982
Bring Me Your Love. 1983
Hot Water Music. 1983
The Bukowski/Purdy Letters: 1964–1974. 1983
There's No Business. 1984
Hostage (audio). 1985
You Get So Alone at Times That It Just Makes Sense. 1986
The Movie: Barfly. 1987
The Roominghouse Madrigals: Early Selected Poems 1946–1966. 1988
Hollywood. 1989
Septuagenarian Stew: Stories and Poems. 1990
The Last Night of the Earth Poems. 1992
Run with the Hunted: A Charles Bukowski Reader. 1993
Screams from the Balcony: Selected Letters 1960–1970. 1993
Pulp. 1994
Shakespeare Never Did This. 1995
Living on Luck: Selected Letters 1960s–1970s, Volume 2. 1995

Betting on the Muse: Poems and Stories. 1996
Bone Palace Ballet: New Poems. 1997
The Captain Is Out to Lunch and the Sailors Have Taken Over the Ship. 1998
What Matters Most Is How Well You Walk Through the Fire. 1999
Reach for the Sun: Selected Letters 1978–1994, Volume 3. 1999
Open All Night: New Poems. 2000
Charles Bukowski: Uncensored (audio). 2000
The Night Torn Mad with Footsteps: New Poems. 2001
Fly Like a Bat Out of Hell: The Letters of Harold Norse and Charles Bukowski. 2002

Further Reading

Brewer, Gay. *Charles Bukowski.* New York: Twayne, 1997.
Cherkovski, Neeli. *Bukowski: A Life.* South Royalton, VT: Steerforth Press, 1997.
———. *Whitman's Wild Children.* South Royalton, VT: Steerforth Press, 1999.
Christy, Jim. *The Buk Book.* Toronto: ECW Press, 1997.
Duval, Jean-Francois. *Bukowski and the Beats: A Commentary on the Beat Generation.* Nortville, MI: Sun Dog Press, 2002.
Harrison, Russell. *Against the American Dream: Essays on Charles Bukowski.* Santa Rosa, CA: Black Sparrow Press, 1998.
Locklin, Gerald. *Charles Bukowski: A Sure Bet.* Sudbury, MA: Water Row Press, 1996.
Richmond, Steve. *Spinning Off Bukowski.* Nortville, MI: Sun Dog Press, 1996.
Sounes, Howard. *Charles Bukowski: Locked in the Arms of a Crazy Life.* New York: Grove Press, 1998.
———. *Bukowski: In Pictures.* Edinburgh: Rebel, 2000.

BURROUGHS, WILLIAM S.

1914–1997
American novelist

Burroughs' distinctive contribution to a poetics of obscenity is manifest in his incisive empirical address to Western, particularly American, culture, in the cyber-tech perspective for his deconstruction of cultural habits, in the disciplined amoral ethos of his works, and in their ironic fusion of the heinous, the parodic, the ugly, and the hysterical to produce a complex grotesque vision of postmodern civilization. In his works, obscenity is imagistically and thematically conspicuous, pornography accordingly may be pertinent at any given moment, and eroticism, as such, is negligible (as for the distinction between pornography and eroticism, cf. "Pornography"). Burroughs' *Junky,* though pseudonymously published, established several of his fictive hallmarks. Most importantly, that work assumed Burroughs' characteristic documentary or quasi-documentary stance, which derives from its autobiographical narrative of drug addiction and ecology, as well as a couple of uncharacteristically decorous homosexual scenes. The narrative is conventionally chronological, but the narrator, Burroughs himself, is from the start disposed to living outside both convention and the law. Though Burroughs later called this outlaw stance a "romantic extravagance" of the time, it in fact became a staple of his subsequent work.

Naked Lunch elaborated the tension between conventional and "outlaw" cultures with a hyperbolical vengeance, not only imaging bourgeois institutions as analogues of criminal counterparts (narcotics agents and dealers, straights and gays, scientists and generalissimos, etc.), but dissecting the marketing strategy common to them all. Following the logic of capitalism, the cultural objective is to make consumers of the population. Addiction is the logical conclusion, and "the narcotics industry" is the paradigm. "Junk is the ideal product... the ultimate merchandise. No sales talk necessary. The client will crawl through a sewer and beg to buy.... The junk merchant does not sell his product to the consumer, he sells the consumer to his product. He does not improve and simplify his merchandise. He degrades and simplifies the client.... Junk yields a basic formula of 'evil' virus: *The Algebra of Need.*" Literally, junk is heroin; figuratively, it is the power of control to which all segments of society are addicted—domestic relations, sexual relations, political relations, public policy, etc. The greater the need, the greater the addiction, a straightforward calculus all the way to "total need."

Naked Lunch is conceived as a cultural alert that certain social habits indicate high levels of addiction. One such habit is capital punishment:

> Johnny is led in, hands tied.... Johnny sees the gallows and sags... his chin pulling down toward his cock, his legs bending at the knees. Sperm spurts, arching almost vertical in front of his face. Mark and Mary are suddenly Impatient and hot...Mark is adjusting the noose.
> "Well, here you go." Mark starts to push Johnny off the platform.
> Mary: "No, let me." She locks her hands behind Johnny's buttocks, puts her forehead against him, smiling into his eyes she moves back, pulling him off the platform into space.... His face swells with blood.... Mark reaches up with one lithe movement and snaps Johnny's neck... sound like a stick broken

in wet towels. A shudder runs down Johnny's body... Johnny's cock springs up and Mary guides it up her cunt, writhing against him in a fluid belly dance, groaning and shrieking with delight.

Burroughs says, "These sections are intended to reveal capital punishment as the obscene, barbaric, and disgusting anachronism that it is." In short, let advocates see their naked lunch. The "junk virus," Burroughs insisted, is "public health problem number one," and since *Naked Lunch* treats this problem, "it is necessarily brutal, obscene and disgusting."

Addictions proliferate, as one of the most pernicious masquerades under the banner of science. Dr. Benway is a kind of postmodern Joseph Mengele and is Burroughs' allegory of the consummate technocratic reduction of human being to the "soft machine." "I deplore brutality," says Benway, a control addict who prefers more subtle and efficient inducements of "anxiety" and feelings of "special guilt" that can be achieved with a disguised attack on the citizen's personal identity by an adroit "Interrogator." "Many subjects," says Benway, "are vulnerable to sexual humiliation," the procedures and effects of which he describes with insouciant obscenity: "I recall this one kid I condition to shit at the sight of me. Then I wash his ass and screw him. It was real tasty. And he was a lovely fellah too. And sometimes a subject will burst into boyish tears because he can't keep from ejaculating when you screw him. Well, as you can plainly see, the possibilities are endless like meandering paths in a great big beautiful garden."

Benway is just one of many agents of the "Nova Mob," like the *cosa nostra* nowhere and everywhere, and consequently "the black wind sock of death undulates over the land, feeling, smelling for the crime of separate life." The "cure" for separate life, of course, is addiction. This is the business of Benway's technology of the profane, creating and feeding the habit, whatever it may be. For the junky, as noted, is the perfectly self-contained consumer: "Probing for a vein in my dirty bare foot.... Junkies have no shame. . . They are impervious to the repugnance of others. . . The junky's shame disappears with his nonsexual sociability which is also dependent on libido. . . The addict regards his body impersonally as an instrument to absorb the medium in which he lives, evaluates his body with the hands of a horse trader. 'No use trying

BURROUGHS, WILLIAM S.

to hit here.' Dead fish eyes flick over a ravaged vein." The consequence is a culture of zombies completely absorbed with feeding their habits.

The Soft Machine, The Ticket that Exploded, and *Nova Express* all elaborate on these motifs, especially the technology of "Juxtaposition Formulae" whereby populations can be manipulated and subject to Nova control even unto the next millennium. Though *Queer* (1985) is a conventional narrative in the mode of *Junky,* and *The Third Mind* (1978) is an expository work addressed to methodology, Burroughs' later books continue the witty, incisive cyber-tech deconstruction of cultural obscenities that won him an international readership in the 1960s. He continued also to use the addiction trope to probe technocracy; as posed in *The Soft Machine* the question is, "Are these experiments really necessary?" Juxtaposition Formulae cultivate power addictions by creating and aggravating conflicts—between races, nations, genders, businesses, unions, etc., wherever it wants enmities pushed to "use of total weapons" in the face of "absolute need."

Burroughs' cold, ironic eye, his scientist perspective, and his existentially amoral grotesques, including a judicious obscenity, were instrumental in cultivating the rationalist, as distinct from sympathetic, poetics characteristic of postmodern literature. He and his works, especially *Naked Lunch,* became touchstones for a certain kind of cyber-punk hipness in both literature and pop culture. Moreover, though his theories of spontaneous composition and the cut-up method had been articulated and practiced by the cubists and surrealists, to say nothing of his friend Kerouac, they gained a new appeal by virtue of the perceptual vivacity that Burroughs' deadpan candor, wit, and grotesquerie imparted to the vulgar accuracy of his cultural critique.

Biography

William Seward Burroughs was born in 1914 in St. Louis, where his father owned and operated a lumber business. As a child he was subject to nightmares, and he later recalled "hearing a maid talk about opium and how smoking opium brings sweet dreams, and I said: 'I will smoke opium when I grow up.'" Though "neither brilliant nor backward in studies" in his progressive grammar and high schools, he did have an impressive reading habit that included Oscar

Wilde, Charles Baudelaire, and André Gide. At this time, too, he formed what he called "a romantic attachment for another boy" and a literary attachment to the autobiography of a minor outlaw. All of these things foreshadowed developments in his adult life and literary works. He graduated from Harvard University, where he studied English literature and discovered his growing sense of alienation from the middle-class sensibility of American life.

With a small trust fund following college, he traveled, dabbled in graduate studies of ethnology and archeology, and worked at various jobs from which experiences he drew on in later works, for example *Exterminator!* (1973). He met Allen Ginsberg and Jack Kerouac in 1944 and together they became the core figures of what would be called the Beat Movement. Burroughs, however, did not begin seriously writing until the early 1950s, and then largely at the insistence of Ginsberg. With Ginsberg's agency, Burroughs' first novel, *Junky,* was published under the pseudonym William Lee in 1953. Meanwhile, seeking what he called "kick... momentary freedom from the claims of aging, cautious, nagging, frightened flesh," Burroughs traveled in South America, North Africa, and Europe.

In 1958, excerpts from *Naked Lunch* had appeared in *The Chicago Review* and *Big Table* and the resulting obscenity charges gave the work notoriety. The full novel was published in 1959 by Olympia Press in Paris. Olympia Press also published *The Soft Machine* (1961) and *The Ticket that Exploded* (1962) in Paris. By 1964 Burroughs' readership and reputation were substantial, and Grove Press published *Nova Express* in New York in that year and *The Wild Boys* in 1971. He continued publishing through the '70s and by that point had long since become a counterculture icon. He lectured on the centerpieces of his distinctive poetics, spontaneous composition, and his "cut-up" collage method frequently in the 1970s and 1980s at Naropa Institute's Jack Kerouac School of Disembodied Poetics in Boulder, Colorado, founded and for many years directed by Allen Ginsberg. In the 1980s Burroughs settled in the university town of Lawrence, Kansas. *Queer* was published in 1985 and *The Western Lands* in 1987. His last known work, *Ghost of a Chance,* was published in a limited edition by the Whitney Museum, New York, in 1991. Several months after Allen Ginsberg's death, William Burroughs died at age

83 in Lawrence of a heart attack, August 2, 1997.

PETER MICHELSON

Selected Works

Naked Lunch. Paris: Olympia Press, 1959.
Nova Express. New York: Grove Press, 1964.
The Soft Machine. New York: Grove Press, 1966.
The Ticket that Exploded. New York: Grove Press, 1967.
Exterminator. New York: Viking, 1973.
The Job. New York: Grove Press, 1974.
The Adding Machine. New York: Seaver/H. Holt, 1986.
The Western Lands. New York: Penguin Books, 1987.

Further Reading

Goodman, Michael Barry. *Contemporary Literary Censorship: The Case History of Burroughs'* Naked Lunch. Metuchen, NJ: Scarecrow Press, 1981.
Finlayson, Iain. *Tangier: City of the Dream.* London: Flamingo Press, 1993.
Huncke, Herbert. *The Evening Sun Turned Crimson.* Cherry Valley, NY: Cherry Valley Editions, 1980.
Lydenberg, Robin. *Word Cultures: Theory and Practice in William S. Burroughs' Fiction.* Urbana: University of Illinois Press, 1987.
Miles, Barry. *William Burroughs: El Hombre Invisible.* New York: Hyperion, 1993.
Morgan, Ted. *Literary Outlaw: The Life and Times of William S. Burroughs.* New York: H. Holt, 1988.
Murphy, Timothy S. *Wising Up the Marks.* Berkeley and Los Angeles: University of California Press, 1998.
Skerl, Jennie. *William S. Burroughs.* Boston, Twayne, 1985.
Skerl, Jennie, and Robin Lydenburg. *William S. Burroughs at the Front: Critical Reception, 1959–1989.* Carbondale: Southern Illinois University Press, 1991.

BURTON, SIR RICHARD F.

1821–1890
British ethnographer, travel writer, translator

While Burton wrote over forty books, he is known primarily as a translator, especially of the works of Eastern eroticism that caused a sensation when they were circulated in 19th-century England. Burton could have faced prosecution under the Obscene Publications Act of 1857, although these works—namely the *Kama Sutra,* the *Perfumed Garden,* and the *Ananga Ranga*—are considered classics of erotic literature today. Burton's translations, and the extensive prefatory and explanatory material appended to them, constituted a major contribution to Victorian discourse on sexuality. As his biographer Fawn Brodie notes, "Burton's real passion was... for the hidden in man, for the unknowable, and inevitably the unthinkable. What his Victorian compatriots called unclean, bestial, or Satanic he regarded with almost clinical detachment" (p.16). Because of his detachment and fascination, Burton had a profound influence on the study and discourse of human

sexual behavior and was a forerunner of pioneering sexologists like Richard von Krafft-Ebing and Havelock Ellis.

Burton's entire career is marked by an interest in human sexual practices. His early writings—travel books, records of his explorations, and ethno-geographical studies—also include extensive notes about the sexual customs and social rituals of the native people he encountered. An avowed atheist, Burton nonetheless traveled to Utah in order to study the tenets of Mormonism—and the practice of polygamy. But his more sexually explicit observations about the practices he studied had to be relegated to footnotes and rendered in Latin to avoid censure and the censor. In his *Supplemental Nights,* Burton laments that he had "failed to free the Anthropological Society from the fetters of *mauvaise honte* and the mock-modesty which compels travelers and ethnological students to keep silence concerning one side of human nature" (VII, p.437). Burton saw his later career as a way to reverse this earlier failure. He translated and heavily annotated sexually themed texts: Eastern erotica, Latin poems by Catullus, several works of Italian literature, Brazilian poetry, and, most famously, the *Thousand Nights and a Night* and the *Kama Sutra*.

Burton hoped his translations would remedy the prudish reticence about sexuality that marked British culture. As he notes in the *Supplemental Nights*, "The England of our day would fain bring up both sexes and keep all ages in profound ignorance of sexual and intersexual relations" (VII). This, Burton claims, produces a culture that is actually more sexualized than the purportedly oversexed East. British women without an outlet for their physical needs and desires "relieve their pent-up feelings by what may be called mental prostitution" (*Supplemental Nights* VII): reading French novels. Burton's ideal world would free sexuality from shame and release both women and men from debilitating sexual repression. At the same time, Burton's project serves to extend his childhood tendency to resist authority, his adult desire to live outside the confines of British mores, and his longing literally and figuratively to find his own path. As Michel Foucault notes in *The History of Sexuality,* "What sustains our eagerness to speak of sex in terms of repression is doubtless this opportunity to speak out against the powers that be, to utter truths and promise bliss, to link together enlightenment, liberation, and manifold pleasures; to pronounce a discourse that combines the fervor of knowledge, the determination to change the laws, and the longing for the garden of earthly delights".

Despite his professed frankness in writing about sex, Burton often bowed to his culture's reticences. For instance, instead of the "Plain and Literal Translation" he promised for the "Arabian Nights Entertainment," his translation of the *Kama Sutra* substitutes the Sanskrit words *lingam* and *yoni* for "penis" and "vagina"—even though *yoni* never appears in the original Sanskrit and *lingam* only rarely. Moreover, Burton originated ideas of sexuality—particularly homosexuality—that reveal his priggishness. His "Terminal Essay" of the *Thousand Nights and a Night* proposes a "Sotadic Zone" where "the Vice is popular and endemic" (X), making the appearance of male homosexuality "geographical and climatic, not racial". While escaping the Victorian tendency to project the abject onto racial others, Burton nonetheless constitutes homosexuality as an alien "other." His treatment of pederasty is important in its frankness and lack of moral judgment, but it is also vexing in its desire to define male homosexuality as thoroughly "foreign" to British understanding.

Burton was equally intent on correcting what he saw as a commensurately serious shortcoming among his countrymen: their failure to understand "the East." Edward Said defines Orientalism as "the corporate institution for dealing with the Orient—dealing with it by making statements about it, authorizing views of it, describing it, by teaching it, settling it, ruling over it: in short, Orientalism as a Western style for dominating, restructuring, and having authority over the Orient". This is precisely how Burton characterized his work: "I consider my labors as a legacy bequeathed to my countrymen at a most critical time when England the puissantest [*sic*] of Moslem powers is called upon, without adequate knowledge of the Moslem's inner life, to administer Egypt as well as to rule India" (*Supplemental Nights* VII). Indeed, reviewers of the *Thousand Nights and a Night* presumed a connection between Burton's Orientalist knowledge and the proper administration of Empire. The *Home News* of 18 September 1885 suggests that Burton's aid may have saved General Gordon from his death in Khartoum, remarking that "it seems curious that his services could not have been utilized in the Soudan, when the want of competent Arabic scholars was so severely felt." (qtd. in *Supplemental Nights* VIII).

Burton, along with men like Forster Fitzgerald Arbuthnot, Leonard Smithers, Henry Ashbee, and Richard Monckton Milnes, circumvented the Obscene Publications Act of 1857 to publish works that Burton, at least, did not consider at all obscene. (The headnote to each volume of the *Thousand Nights and a Night* is an Arab proverb that may well summarize Burton's attitude: "To the pure all things are pure.") Burton and Arbuthnot founded an imaginary society, the Kama Shastra Society of London and Benares, which would print potentially actionable texts out of "Benares" or "Cosmopoli" (which were merely code for London) to get around laws governing books printed in England. Writing to John Payne about this project on January 15, 1883, Burton crows: "It will make the British public stare" (Wright II).

While he often seemed merely to want to shock "Mrs. Grundy," Burton clearly contributed to the gradual emergence of erotic candor in British cultural discourse. His translation of the *Thousand Nights and a Night*—which he claimed would be "a repertory of Eastern knowledge in its esoteric phase" (I)—was sold by subscription only, each volume costing one guinea. It made Burton a wealthy man. Isobel reports that Burton said, with sarcasm, "I struggled for forty-seven years.... I distinguished myself honorably in every way I possibly could. I translated a doubtful book in my old age, and immediately made sixteen thousand guineas. Now that I know the tastes of England, we need never be without money" (II). While Burton lived to gain acclaim for his *Arabian Nights* and his knowledge of the East, he died long before the British public was entirely convinced that discussion of sex was not, by definition, pornographic: the first publicly printed British edition of the *Kama Sutra* did not appear until 1963.

Biography

Born March 19, 1821, in Torquay, Devon. Family lived in France and Italy, returning to England only for brief visits. As a child, showed talent for languages; was fluent in Greek, Latin, Italian, and French before entering Trinity College, Oxford, in 1840. Expelled in 1842 for bad behavior. Sailed to India with a commission in the Bombay Army, a military branch of the East India Company. Spent seven years in Sind as a field surveyor and intelligence officer, often disguised as a Muslim merchant. Mastered Arabic, Hindi, and other Indian languages, while learning as much as he could about Indian culture. Wrote three books on Indian ethnography on his return, but became famous for his incursions into Medina and Mecca (1853)—Muslim cities forbidden to nonbelievers—made possible by his command of the language and disguise as an Afghani physician. Later traveled to Ethiopia and Somalia to the forbidden city of Harer, the citadel of Muslim learning. Took a tour of duty in the Crimean War. Afterward, traveled to Africa as an explorer. In 1857, along with John Speke, attempted to locate the source of the Nile. In 1860, traveled across the United States to Salt Lake City, Utah, to investigate Mormonism. In 1861, married Isobel Arundell and joined the British Foreign Office. Posted in 1865 to Santos, Brazil, but resigned in 1868 after deploring the conditions there. Landed a post in Damascus in 1869, but recalled in 1871 due to Turkish government's complaints about his conduct. Posted to Trieste, Italy, in 1872, in part due to influence exerted by Isobel's relatives. A desirable position, but too far from Muslim lands for Burton's tastes. Left him freedom and time, however, to write and to do the translating work that gained him entry into this encyclopedia. In 1886, knighted by Queen Victoria. Died October 20, 1890, in Trieste.

LeeAnne M. Richardson

Selected Works

Translations

The Kama Sutra of Vatsyayana. London: Hindoo Kama Shastra Society, 1883. Reprinted frequently; first publicly printed British edition: W. G. Archer (ed.), London: Allen and Unwin, 1963.

The Perfumed Garden of the Cheikh Nefzaoui: A Manual of Arabian Erotology. Cosmopoli: Kama Shastra Society of London and Benares, 1886.

A Plain and Literal Translation of the Arabian Nights' Entertainments, Now Entitled the Book of the Thousand Nights and a Night, With Introductory Explanatory Notes on the Manners and Customs of Moslem Men and a Terminal Essay upon the History of the Nights. 10 vols. Benares: Kama-shastra Society (for private subscribers only), 1885–8.

Supplemental Nights. 6 vols. Benares: Printed by the Kama-shastra Society (for private subscribers only), 1885–8. Both *Nights* were reprinted in full by The Burton Club and abridged in editions too numerous to list.

With F. F. Arbuthnot. *Ananga-Ranga (Stage of the Bodiless One) or, The Hindu Art of Love.* Cosmopoli: Kama Shastra Society of London and Benares (for private circulation only), 1885. Reprinted frequently, including as *The Ananga Ranga; or, the Hindu Art of Love,* New York: Putnam, 1964.

With Leonard Smithers. *The Carmina of Caius Valerius Catullus Now First Completely Englished into Verse and Prose.* London: Printed by the translators for private subscribers only, 1894.

———. *Priapeia or the Sportive Epigrams of Divers Poets on Priapus The Latin Text Now for the First Time Englished in Verse and Prose.* Cosmopoli: Printed by the tranlsators for private subscribers only, 1890.

The Erotic Traveller. Edited by Edward Leigh. New York: Putnam, 1967.

Love, War and Fancy: The Customs and Manners of the East from Writings on The Arabian Nights by Sir Richard Burton. Edited by Kenneth Walker. London: William Kimber, 1964.

Further Reading

Brodie, Fawn. *The Devil Drives: A Life of Sir Richard Burton*. New York: Norton; London: Eyre and Spottiswoode, 1967.

Burne, Glenn S. *Richard F. Burton*. Boston: Twayne, 1985.

Burton, Isobel. *The Life of Captain Sir Richard F. Burton, K.C.M.G., F.R.G.S.* 2 vols. London: Chapman and Hall, 1893.

Casada, James A. *Sir Richard F. Burton: A Biobibliographical Study*. Boston: G. K. Hall, 1990.

Colville, Jim. Introduction to *The Perfumed Garden of Sensual Delight*, by Muhammed ibn Muhammed al-Nafzawi, translated by Jim Colville. London: Kegan Paul, 1999.

Farwell, Byron. *Burton: A Biography of Sir Richard F. Burton*. New York: Holt, Rinehart, and Winston, 1963.

Foucault, Michel. *The History of Sexuality*. Translated by Robert Hurley. Vol. I: An Introduction. New York: Vintage, 1990.

Lovell, Mary S. *A Rage to Live: A Biography of Richard and Isobel Burton*. New York: Norton, 1998.

Nelson, James G. "Leonard Smithers and Captain Sir Richard Burton," *Journal of the Eighteen Nineties Society* 24 (1997): 3–12.

Phillips, Richard. "Writing Travel and Mapping Sexuality: Richard Burton's Sotadic Zone." In *Writes of Passage: Reading Travel Writing*, Edited by James Duncan and Derek Gregory, 70–91. London: Routledge, 1999.

Said, Edward. *Orientalism*. New York: Vintage, 1979.

Walton, Alan Hull. Introduction to *The Perfumed Garden of the Shaykh Nefzawi*, translated by Richard F. Burton. New York: Putnam, 1963.

Wright, Thomas. *The Life of Sir Richard Burton*. 2 vols. London: Everett and Company, 1906.

BYRD II, WILLIAM

1674–1744

Colonial American diarist

William Byrd II reflected in his diaries, prose works, and occasional verses the sexual values of an eighteenth-century English gentleman: frequently predatory and misogynistic, always insisting on chastity in one's wife but not expecting it in other men's wives, and often struggling with the conflict of passion and reason within himself.

Prose

Byrd is best known to students of early American literature as a diarist who, while not rivaling Pepys in style or incidents, meticulously documented the routines he employed in his gentlemanly self-fashioning. Although clearly not intended for an audience, the diaries reveal a man who recognized the unruliness of his libido and documented his flirtations, seductions, and whoring, as well as marital sexuality.

In addition to keeping the diaries, Byrd maintained a gentleman's commonplace book, a record of his reading and conversations during the eight years between his stormy first and his second marriage. As a result, several of its entries are hostile to women and suspicious of marriage, including citations of St. Basil, Plutarch, Petronius, Xenophon; several entries record erotic anecdotes about sexual voracity. Concerned about his own insatiable sexual desires, Byrd also transcribed relevant excerpts from Dr. Nicolas Venette's *De la génération de l'homme, ou tableau de l'amour conjugal* (of which Byrd owned two copies in French).

Byrd brought together many cynical and misogynistic commonplaces in the bawdy prose work "The Female Creed"—woman's confession of faith in men, in sentimentality, and in every possible superstition. It concludes, "I believe in my conscience, that tho' my Adorer loves Wine, and wenches, and gameing, more fondly than Pamperoni loves his Gut, yet my superior Prudence and attractions are sufficient to reclaim him, and to reform his wayward Inclinations into a loyal, confin'd, serious, harmless conjugal Love" (*Another Secret Diary* 475).

In letters and in "characters" (a popular Augustan literary form in which the foibles of character types or actual persons were satirized) circulated among friends, Byrd offered to a small audience an unsentimental view of love, female beauty, and lust. His self-portrait in the character "Inamorato l'oiseaux" is particularly revealing: "Love broke out upon him before his Beard, and he cou'd distinguish sex before he cou'd the difference betwixt Good & Evil. Tis well he had not a Twin-sister as Osyris had, for without doubt like him he wou'd have had an amourette with her in his mothers belly" (*Another Secret Diary* 276). In it he described the "Civil war between this Hero's Principles and his Inclinations" (276).

It is likely that Byrd collaborated with William Burnaby, a colleague in the Middle Temple, in the translation of Petronius' *Satyricon*, published in London in 1694, of which his notebooks translate the anecdote of "The Ephesian Matron" (*Another Secret Diary* 224–27). This faithfully grieving widow keeps vigil at her husband's tomb. Eventually a soldier guarding the nearby corpses of hanged men seduces her in the tomb, during which the family of one of the executed recovers his body. Faced with her lover's capital punishment for dereliction of duty, she replaces the missing body of the executed with that of her deceased husband.

In *The Secret History of the Line* (a novelistic rendition of the more straightforward *History of the Dividing Line betwixt Virginia and North Carolina Run in the Year of Our Lord* 1728) Byrd composed a humorous narrative that was circulated in manuscript form among a close circle of friends in Virginia and England. The picaresque *Secret History* depicts women as fair game for predatory males who are attentive to neither Christian sexual ethics nor gentlemanly hospitality when making advances on the wives or daughters of their various hosts along the surveying journey. Typical of the time, Byrd was not squeamish about interracial sexual liaisons between a gentleman and an inferior, but he also famously proposed in the *History* that miscegenation between European colonists and Native Americans would assimilate the latter into colonial society.

Verse

Like many 18th-century gentlemen, Byrd wrote occasional verses (published pseudonymously) characterized by wit, neoclassical allusions, and social commentary.

"Upon a Fart" is a parody of Anne, Countess of Winchelsea's "Upon a Sigh" and is alleged to have "cur'd that Lady of her Itch to Poetry" (*Another Secret Diary* 244). It employs the sentimental poem's characterizations of the sigh ("Gentlest," "Softest," "Shapeless") as ironic attributes of the fart. Farting entails gender differences as it is "rattled out by th' unbred swain, / But whisper'd by the Bashfull wench" (246). The poem ends with a description of what is perhaps the earliest record of the frat house prank of igniting farts, a diversion that Byrd attributes to "Maids at Court" who make visible the fart "burning blew" (246).

A visit to the spa at Tunbridge Wells in 1719 produced several poems that Byrd published under the name of "Mr. Burrard" in *Tunbrigalia: or, Tunbridge Miscellanies* (London, 1719). Dilettante "Water Poets" (as Richard Steele named them) wrote verses describing the habitués of resorts like Tunbridge Wells, Bath, Epsom, and Scarborough. Byrd's verses are conventional neoclassical encomia to beautiful and aristocratic women, all of whom were other men's wives.

William Byrd II employed conventional 18th-century literary forms to reflect aristocratic sensibilities about eroticism. At the same time, his diaries and commonplace book reflect his own struggles to rein in sexual passion with human reason.

Biography

Born in 1674 to William Byrd I, a Virginia planter and trader in frontier furs who was the son of an English goldsmith, and Mary Horsmanden. In 1681 his father sent him to be educated in England at the Felsted School; between 1690 and 1696, Byrd engaged in a merchant apprenticeship in the Netherlands and entered London's Middle Temple for law training, a situation that would also have provided his literary apprenticeship because it brought him into contact with the literary life of London. He became a protégé of Sir Robert Southwell, was inducted into the Royal Society for the Improving of Natural Knowledge, and was appointed an English agent for the Virginia Colonial House of Burgesses. An ambitious social climber, Byrd availed himself of the professional, political, social, and recreational opportunities that England offered the aspirant.

After the death of his first wife, he sought a socially advantageous second marriage but was thwarted in his first attempts at it. Eventually returning to Virginia, Byrd became an important leader in the colony's political and economic life. He accumulated a library of some 3,000 volumes, second in size only to the library of Cotton Mather, a Boston Puritan divine. His secret diaries, written in code, provide a window into colonial and English life. His leadership of a surveying party to define the border between Virginia and North Carolina resulted in his writing an account that combined the perspectives of an ethnographer and naturalist.

THOMAS L. LONG

Editions

Another Secret Diary of William Byrd of Westover, 1739–1714, with Letters and Literary Exercises, 1696–1726. Edited by Maude H. Woodfin. Richmond, VA: Dietz Press, 1942.

The Commonplace Book of William Byrd II of Westover. Edited by Kevin Berland, Jan Kirsten Gilliam, and Kenneth A. Lockridge. Chapel Hill: University of North Carolina Press, 2001.

The Prose Works of William Byrd of Westover: Narratives of a Colonial Virginian. Edited by Louis B. Wright. Cambridge, MA: Harvard University Press, 1966.

The Secret Diary of William Byrd of Westover, 1709–1712. Edited by Louis B. Wright and Marion Tinling. Richmond, VA: Dietz Press, 1941.

Further Reading

Dolmetsch, Carl. "William Byrd of Westover as an Augustan Poet." *Studies in the Literary Imagination* 9 (1976): 69–77.

Hayes, Kevin J. *The Library of William Byrd of Westover.* Madison, WI: Madison House, 1997.

Lockridge, Kenneth A. *The Diary, and Life, of William Byrd II of Virginia, 1674–1744.* Chapel Hill: University of North Carolina Press, 1987.

———. *On the Sources of Patriarchal Rage: The Commonplace Books of William Byrd and Thomas Jefferson and the Gendering of Power in the Eighteenth Century.* New York: New York University Press, 1992.

Marambaud, Pierre. *William Byrd of Westover, 1674–1744.* Charlottesville: University Press of Virginia, 1971.

Treckel, Paula A. "'The Empire of My Heart': The Marriage of William Byrd II and Lucy Parke Custis." *Virginia Magazine of History and Biography* 105 (1997): 125–56.

Wagner, Peter. "'The Female Creed': A New Reading of William Byrd's Ribald Parody." *Early American Literature* 19 (1984): 122–37.

C

CABINET SATYRIQUE, LE

Compilations of licentious poetry constitute a separate genre in the history of French literature, a genre that appears for only one quarter century, from 1600 to 1626. The action brought against Théophile de Viau for his participation in *Le Parnasse satyrique* [*The Satyric Parnassus*] (1622), and the conviction that followed, put an end to this prosperous age during which it was possible to publish bawdy works with the king's privilege. A similar genre had existed during the sixteenth century, a famous example being *Les blasons anatomiques du corps féminin* [*Anatomical Blazons of the Feminine Body*]. By the beginning of the seventeenth century, however, the genre had become more specific: editors tended to compile mainly satirical or openly sexual poems.

Le cabinet satyrique holds an eminent rank among the libertine collections and is one of the best representatives of the genre. This status derives in part from its ampleness: With 460 poems in the original edition of 1618, it is the most voluminous compilation of the time. Moreover, it had eleven reissues during the seventeenth century, a sign of its popularity. The work came out of the printing press of the Parisian editor Anthoine Estoc, who specialized in the publication of satirical collections. When *Le cabinet satyrique* appeared, Estoc had two other works of the same type in his catalogue, not to mention *Le Parnasse satyrique* that would be published four years later. Moreover, Anthoine Estoc exploited his own previous publications, as well as those of other printers, for two-thirds of *Le cabinet satyrique* are in fact previously edited poems. On the whole, half of the collection's poems are anonymous but, as the title proclaims, the rest belongs to "les plus signalez Poëtes de ce Siecle" (the most notorious Poets of this Century), that is the greatest satirists of the beginning of the seventeenth century: Mathurin Régnier, Pierre Berthelot, François Maynard, etc.

The foreword to the collection is distinguished by its length and ambition. First, along with the customary claims to novelty, one finds an attempt to build a genuine canon to which the work's content is presented as a continuation. Thus the illustrious predecessors of the previous century, like Pierre de Ronsard, as well as the Greek and Latin comic authors, are mentioned, and serve as guarantors of authority. Afterwards, the edifying purpose of the satirical genre is put forward as a subject of praise and glorification: Satirists are "des Philosophes deguisez" (disguised Philosophers) whose aim is to provoke a distaste for vice by depicting it without shame. Finally, the foreword's author presents *Le cabinet satyrique* as a harmonious, non-monstrous "corps de Livre" (body Book), that is a work carefully arranged with homogenous parts. This claim to order proves veracious: *Le cabinet satyrique*, besides a part made of miscellany, is composed of twenty-two sections more or less coherent, the latter comprising erotic testaments, epitaphs, and funerary poems.

Although the work in its entirety does not belong to the erotic genre, the first sections quickly emphasize sexual activity. The primary focus is on the genitals. The male organ is shown as tireless and monumental. Being always the woman's object of desire, it brings incomparable pleasure and is persistently exhibited as an enticing gift. As for the female organ, it is depicted using architectural metaphors (house, palace, inhabited cavern, etc.) that replace the floral comparisons of the previous century. It is especially blameworthy when too large. Such a preference explains itself by the fact that the *ars erotica* found in *Le Cabinet satyrique* is largely genitally bound. Although it can be conveyed by other gestures (touch, kiss), sensual pleasure is above all a result of coitus. Witness woman's desire for man's "liquor" presented as a new year's gift: "Margot, çà, je te veux donner / Un coup de V. pour t'estrener, / Afin que, toute ceste année, / Toi qui de sperme est affamée / Tu passe l'an joyeusement, / F..tant dés le commencement." (Margot, now then, I want to give you / A C*** blow as a gift / So that all this year / You who are thirsty for sperm / Might spend the year happily / F***ing from the beginning.) (t.1, p. 142, ed. Fleuret and Perceau), Witness also the condemnation of sodomy, supposedly leaving women unsatisfied and making men cowardly and odious to God.

Besides the strictly erotic inspiration, the satirical vein is also exploited. The poet's purpose is to show indignation when confronted by a certain character or situation. Satire thus becomes a pretext for depicting mores or human types, such as courtiers, to whom a long section is devoted. However, the misogynous inspiration predominates. Among other blemishes, the woman is blamed for her impudicity. For example, Sigognes describes in a poem a lascivious young woman who undresses as soon as she is asked to and whose bedroom is always encumbered with lovers even as others wait in the street. Among all feminine types, no one incurs insults as much as the old woman. Her late lubricity is laughed at, as well as her improper desire to imitate younger ones by giving herself up to love games. Also laughed at is the fact that she resorts to make-up in order to disguise—in vain—her ugliness. Satirists multiply baroque images to express the disgust with which this ugliness inspires them. Their style is principally based upon images of disease, darkness, stench, and upon sensations of flaccidity and ooze. Often associated with infernal deities, the old woman becomes mingled with the character of the witch flying on a broom and fornicating with the devil during Sabbath.

Cuckoldry has constituted a favorite theme in erotic texts since the Middle Age *fabliaux*, and an entire section of *Le Cabinet satyrique* is devoted to it. These poems bring out the wisdom and ethics of cuckoldry. Caused by women's lewdness, cuckoldry is thus bound to happen again and again, generating a kind of vicious circle where cuckolds cheat others in order to get even. An epigram by François de Maynard reveals the paradox of jealousy: To keep too close an eye on one's own wife induces her to break free and arouses envy among other men. The cuckold's jealousy is considered as an erroneous opinion: instead of worrying without reason, he should resign himself to enduring his fate, as great warriors do. Moreover, cuckoldry allows the husband to avoid the exertion of coitus thus prolonging his life.

Another section is dedicated to the Carnival spirit and celebrates "les jours gras" (meat days). The Saint-Germain fair is shown as the scene of true miracles, for there hunchbacks and one-eyed persons are adulated and given a thousand words of love. The Carnival brings back the golden age: it is a time during which fights are but games and during which men and women get drunk and "mettent cul bas" (put the ass down) together. Playing upon the etymology of the word, Pierre Motin shows that the carnival is the moment during which one enjoys flesh, be it banquet's meat or lovers' bodies.

DAVID DORAIS

Editions

Le cabinet satyrique ou recueil parfaict des vers piquans et gaillards de ce temps. Tiré des secrets cabinets des sieurs Sigognes, Regnier, Motin, Berthelot, Maynard, et autres des plus signalez poëtes de ce siecle. À Paris, chez Anthoine Estoc, au Palais en la galerie des Prisonniers pres la Chancellerie. M.D.C.XVIII (1618). Avec privilege du Roy. In-12.

Le cabinet satyrique enjoyed eleven other editions during the seventeenth century, from 1619 to 1700, mostly in Paris and Rouen.

Le cabinet satyrique [etc.]. Nouvelle édition complète, revue et corrigée. Avec glossaire, variantes, notices bibliographiques, etc. Gand: Duquesne, Paris: Claudin, 1859.

Le cabinet satyrique [etc.]. Nouvelle édition complète, revue sur les éditions de 1618 et de 1620 et sur celle dite du Mont-Parnasse, sans date. Bruxelles: Poulet-Malassis, 1864. The two latter editions were condemned to destruction by two French tribunals in 1865 and 1868.

Le cabinet satyrique. Première édition complète et critique d'après l'édition originale de 1618, augmentée des éditions suivantes, avec une notice, une bibliographie, un glossaire, des variantes et des notes par Fernand Fleuret et Louis Perceau. Texte orné de plusieurs reproductions. Paris: Librairie du bon vieux temps, Jean Fort, Collection des satiriques français, 1924.

Le cabinet satyrique. Illustrations de Pierre Leroy, gravées sur bois par Roger Boyer. Paris: Guillot, Collection du XVIIe siècle galant, 1952.

Further Reading

Few serious works have been written about French erotic poetry of the seventeenth century. The best reference is still the voluminous work of Frédéric Lachèvre.

Lachèvre, Frédéric, *Le libertinage au XVIIe siècle*, Genève: Slatkine Reprints, 1968 (Paris, 1909–1928), 15 vol.

The following two works deal directly with the subject but are of little interest.

Bougard, Roger G., *Érotisme et amour physique dans la littérature française du XVIIe siècle*, Paris: Gaston Lachurié, 1986.

Loude, Michel, *La littérature érotique et libertine au XVIIe siècle*, Lyon: Aléas, 1994.

These two articles are valuable for the background information they provide:

Houdard, Sophie, "Vie de scandale et écriture de l'obscène: hypothèses sur le libertinage de mœurs au XVIIe siècle," *Tangence*, 66 (2001): p.48–66.

Simonin, Michel, "Éros aux XVIe et XVIIe siècles" in *Eros in Francia nel Seicento*, Bari: Adriatica, Paris: Nizet, 1987, p.11–29.

CABRERA INFANTE, GUILLERMO

1929–2005
Cuban journalist and novelist

Guillermo Cabrera Infante was a key member of a group of Latin American activist intellectuals who brought about dramatic changes in Hispanic fiction by means of their radical innovations in narrative technique. Within this tradition of self-conscious intellectual outsiders, who write as if from exile but with a vivid flavor of their homeland, must be counted Pablo Neruda, Carlos Fuentes, Julio Cortázar, Octavio Paz, Gabriel García Márquez, and Mario Vargas Llosas.

Tres Tristes Tigres (1967, tr. *Three Trapped Tigers*, 1971) can hardly be considered a traditional novel; it lacks a plotline and there is no significant development of character or human relationships. It is, however, an extremely coherent book with a highly coherent internal structure that describes a world full of racial discrimination, social hypocrisy, and depicts a lost generation of youths in the throes of sexual frustration. The five main narrators share similar language, emotional and sexual experiences set against the background of Havana nightlife in the late 1950s. From the very outset, the announcement made by the club compere, "Tropicana, the most famous cabaret in the world" (which is written both in Spanish and in a deliberately poor English translation), the book is structured in such a way that the reader may easily become lost in a literary labyrinth of vignettes. The odd numbers deal with the traumatic story of this unhappy woman while the even numbers recount the physical consequences of her mental anguish, an anguish which has its origins in the traumas she underwent as an orphan (including abuse by her stepfather, a wretched childhood, marriage with a homosexual, and various other social and sexual dilemmas).

Probably the most autobiographical of his novels, *La Habana para un infante difunto* (1979, tr. *Infante's Inferno*, 1984), tells the story of a boy whose life changes dramatically when his parents moved to the Cuban capital, is brought up in a *solar* (a large residential house where entire families would squeeze into a single rented room with communal facilities), and exposed to a total lack of privacy. Readers are presented with an exquisite portrait of the main protagonist's journey of initiation as he is exposed to a sequence of comic adventures in his relentless search for love and happiness; ranging across the sexual, intellectual, and visual experiences that befall him as he familiarizes himself with the city that surrounds him: libraries, prostitutes, and, his greatest love of all, cinema.

Havana is, above all, a sensual city inviting erotic encounters. Once the anonymous youthful protagonist and his family have moved to the *solar*, the boy makes his first contact with a real prostitute, an adolescent girl living next door. As years go by our hero learns to exploit the lack of privacy of the *solar*, becoming an adept peeping tom. Neighbors provide him with plenty of platonic relationships. Relationships both erotic and chaste build among two of his favorite fellow-dwellers, a pair of sisters living upstairs, Esther, with whom he falls in love, and Fela, whom he desires and eventually manages to kiss.

Literature complements the visual experience providing a further source of pleasure. Disguised in the covers of "decent" books he begins to avidly consume erotic literature he borrows from friends. "Oral" sex, meaning reading aloud of "forbidden" romantic *folletines* (serial installments of novels), is a practice this adolescent also enjoys and exploits, mostly with his older female cousin.

Summer holidays suddenly bring a new meaning to his life as he spends some weeks in his hometown, led on by more experienced friends he starts exploring and eventually mastering the arts of masturbation. This will provide him with further difficulties once back in Havana as privacy is something not afforded in the *solar*.

A new road to pleasure is opened as our hero embarks upon the difficult task of losing his virginity. Social and religious habits in Havana make it even more difficult for men of his age to have sex with high school girls. His first trip to a brothel is arranged although, nervous and too traumatized by peer-group pressure, he fails to perform successfully: he will have to wait until he meets Julia, a married woman his own age, before he loses his virginity and inaugurates a long list of lovers. Later, the cinema becomes a major source of casual relationships promoted by elbow and leg rubbing, the closeness of the seats, and the anonymity of the darkness. It is there that he first witnessed a homosexual relationship: an old man jerking off a younger man in the toilet.

Cabrera Infante's passion for the big screen is evident. *Arcadia todas las noches* (1978, untranslated) is a collection of essays on Alfred Hitchcock, Howard Hawks, Orson Welles, and Vincent Minelli among others. Other works include *Holy Smoke* (1985), *Mi música extenuada* (1996, untranslated); *Mea Cuba* (1992). *Delito por bailar el chachacha* (1995) and *Ella cantaba boleros* (1996) share elements common to all his works: a persistent sense of humor, a passion for painting, photography, and music, particularly jazz, and the bolero craze. Cuban folklore is thoroughly and colorfully depicted, reflecting the strong influence of African culture. Women are invariably portrayed as sexually precocious, and the ease of erotic experience and sexual encounters with strangers in the lively nightlife of the capital city characterize the laissez faire sexual climate of the period.

Biography

Cabrera Infante was born in Gibara, Cuba, 1929. In 1947, he worked in Havana as a proofreader and edged his way into journalism by penning a few articles. He attended Journalism School (1950) but was expelled in 1952 after being fined and imprisoned for publishing the short story *English Profanities* which fell foul of Fulgencio Batista (head of the Cuban military regime) when published in the literary journal *Bohemia*.

Between 1950 and 1960, Cabrera Infante became an important member of the Cuban cultural elite; he wrote a weekly column for the magazine *Carteles* under the pseudonym G. Cain, many of which were later collected in

Un oficio del siglo XX (1973; tr. *A Twentieth Century Job*, 1991). Imitating Cinematéque Française, he founded Cinemateca Cuba while contributing to the Cuban Cinema Institute (closed in 1961 by the government) and the Writers' Association. He later edited *Lunes*, the literary supplement of the official Cuban newspaper *Revolución*.

In 1960, *Así en La Paz como en la guerra* (tr. *Writes of Passage*, 1993), a collection of short stories set in the 1950s (broadly speaking, the historical period in which Batista ruled the country), was published in France, Italy, and Poland, receiving the Prix International de Littérature in 1963.

In 1964, after Castro assumed power, he was sent to Belgium on a diplomatic mission. Subsequently he would never return to Cuba again, living first in Spain, and later, in London, where he resided until his death.

Vista del amanecer en el trópico (1974, tr. *View of Dawn in the Tropics*, 1978) won the Biblioteca Breve prize and in 1967, a second version, rewritten to circumvent Spanish censorship laws, was published under the title *Tres tristes tigres* (tr. *Three Trapped Tigers*, 1971) which further consolidated his international reputation.

CAROLINA MIRANDA

Editions

Tres tristes tigres, Barcelona: Seix Barral, 1967; as *Three Trapped Tigers*, tr. Donald Gardner and Suzanne Levine, New York: Harper & Row, 1971.

La Habana para un infante difunto, Barcelona: Seix Barral, 1979; as *Infante's Inferno*, tr. Suzanne Levine, London: Faber & Faber, 1984.

Selected Works

Así en La Paz como e la guerra. Barcelona: Seix Barral, 1971; as *Writes of Passage*, tr. John Brooksmith, Peggy Boyars, and the author, London: Faber & Faber, 1993.

Un oficio del siglo XX. Barcelona: Seix Barral, 1973; as *A Twentieth Century Job*, London: Faber & Faber, 1991.

Vista del amanecer en el trópico. Barcelona: Seix Barral, 1974; as *View of Dawn in the Tropics*, tr. Suzanne Levine, New York: Harper & Row, 1978.

Arcadia todas las noches. Barcelona: Seix Barral, 1978.

Holy Smoke, (originally written in English) New York: Harper & Row, 1985.

Mea Cuba, translated by Kenneth Hall and the author, New York: Farrar, Straus, Giroux, 1994.

Delito por bailar el Cha Cha Cha, Madrid: Alfaguara, 2000; as *Guilty of Dancing Cha Cha Cha*, tr. by the author, New York, U.S.A.: Welcome Rain Publishers, 2001.

Further Reading

Albarez-Borland, Isabel, *Discontinuidad y ruptura en Guillermo Cabrera Infante*, Gaithersburg, MD: Hispamerica, 1983.

Nelson, Ardis L., *Cabrera Infante in the Menippean Tradition*, DE: Juan de la Cuesta, 1983.

Macover, Jacobo, *El heraldo de las malas noticias: Guillermo Cabrera Infante (ensayo a dos voces)*, Miami, (FL, USA): Ediciones Universal, 1996.

Souza, R., *Guillermo Cabrera Infante*, USA: University of Texas Press, 1996.

CALAFERTE, LOUIS

1928–1994
French novelist, playwright, essayist, diarist and poet

Once described as a "Pasolinian character," Calaferte has often said that the usual interpretations of his multi-faceted work were biased by a profound misunderstanding. Indeed, not only is he the author of *Septentrion*, often described as a brilliant and powerful erotic novel, but also of twenty-odd respectable plays, autobiographic notebooks of reflections about his compulsive reading habits and his unwavering, unmediated faith in God, and even nursery rhymes. Yet behind this apparent heterogeneity, constantly driven by a throbbing sense of urgency, hides a unifying element. Indeed, Calaferte's writings are all haunted by the will to achieve an exhaustive self-portrait.

Even before *Requiem des innocents*, an account of his difficult early years, he felt the need to translate his experience into violent, uncensored verbal surges. He believed this sincerity to be the only way to attain literary truth, or accomplish a "vertical exploration," even a "drilling" of the self. Repeatedly declaring every novelist's fictional invention to be an imposture, he also claimed that all that he ever wrote was part of his life experience. Perhaps this is why the equation he often makes between eroticism, faith, and purity makes his voice so unique, especially in *Septentrion* and *La mécanique des femmes*.

During the exhausting, yet therapeutic final stages of writing *Septentrion* (1956–1962), Calaferte already thought of it as a "nodal point" in his life. First published in an out-trade edition (1963), the novel was immediately banned for obscenity by Gaullist censors, only to reappear in 1984. Although Calaferte always maintained that this interdiction was mainly aimed at the novel's feverish anarchical content, one cannot deny its gloomy, yet poignant atmosphere, filled with lurid eroticism and recurring pornographic episodes.

"In the beginning was Sex." By parodying the gospel according to John and quoting, undoubtedly by accident, Stanisław Przybyszewski's *Totenmesse* (1893), *Septentrion*'s incipit sets the entire novel's tone. One is immediately grabbed by the narrator's breathtaking stream-of-consciousness, a luxuriant combination of highly poetic lyricism and argotic imprecations against everyday conditions at the factory, as well as by the omnipresent erotic reveries and the unshakable will of writing a deflagrating book out of his misery. Along with the anonymous, often imaginary sex partners whom the narrator describes either as "tarts" or "whores" in the contempt-ridden inner monologues in which he engages every time he sees a skirt, he meets Nora Van Hoeck, a lascivious Dutch divorcée twice his age, and becomes her "sex object" out of pique. The first half of the novel narrates this year-long desperate, destructive relationship, whose only raison d'être is the humiliating stability brought by Nora's material comfort, which he ironically despises, and her insatiable, almost ghoulish sex drives. After unceremoniously dumping her and ungratefully stealing her money, he falls into even deeper poverty. Homeless, he realizes he has no real friend whom he could ask for help and, starving, he indulges in delirious erotic daydreaming.

Still, since *Septentrion* was intended to embrace the contradictory extremities of the self, darkness accordingly intermingles with beauty, hope, and the pure light of mysticism. For example, the title refers either to the seventh heaven, or to the seven stars of Ursa Major (aka the Plough, *septen triones* meaning 'seven oxen'). Moreover, not only is this brightness echoed by the novel's seven chapters, but also in its three parts, symbolically entitled "Genesis," "Omphalos," ('navel of the world'), and "Gamma" (Ursa Major's third star, but also the Greek letter γ, whose shape recalls the *mons veneris*). But most important, the miracle the narrator long hoped for occurs in the end, when a family he hardly knows takes him in, thus participating in his entry into creative writing: "Depths and summits, sex is death and resurrection. So saying, goodnight, I've said enough—*ite missa est*."

As for *La mécanique des femmes (The Way it Works With Women)*, conceived of as the "metaphysical" pendant of *Épisodes de la vie des mantes religieuses*, it is a collage of short tableaux, daily dramas, brief dialogues, and confessions of both female fantasies and disappointments. Almost each of them is constructed upon the brutal opposition between the banality of everyday situations and unexpected, yet relentless sex drives. Although these episodes are written from the perspective of either ordinary women or prostitutes, their narratee is always a man. Answering critics who accused him of simply projecting male fantasies of continuous sexual availability onto imaginary women, instead of really analyzing the 'female mechanics,' Calaferte again claimed there was no invention in the book, that is, nothing but the account of lived or recounted experiences. Moreover, since he thinks that all churches must accept responsibility for making a moral problem out of sex, he firmly believes that one never knows the other's secrets better as in eroticism. Perhaps this is why *La mécanique des femmes* insists, be it from a pseudo feminine perspective, on the motif of sex as an initiatory journey towards a "spiritual co-birth" of the self, or a mystical rite of passage. In fact, one of the book's *leitmotivs* could be summarized as follows: One must not deny, lower, nor soil beauty, but instead accept it with all its mysteries, like the idea of God.

"The inner adventure was surely worth exploring, but I don't have enough energy to go further," wrote Calaferte a few years after finishing *Septentrion*. However, one must acknowledge he never stopped questioning his understanding of desire.

Biography

Born in Turin, Italy, 14 July 1928. His family emigrated to France in the early 1930s, where he grew up in Lyons' poorest suburbs. Right after elementary school, during the German Occupation (1942), he began working as a warehouseman (in an electric battery factory, among others), spurred on by the sole obsession of becoming a writer. In 1946, dreaming of a career as a stage actor, he moved to Paris without the slightest resource. While doing some walk-on parts in theaters, he subsisted as a docker or by washing dishes. In 1953, after publishing two novels, he moved back to Lyons, settling in the nearby town of Mornant (1956–1969), and producing literary radio programs for the O.R.T.F. (1957–1974). Then, dedicating himself exclusively to writing, he created a gigantic oeuvre in various genres, receiving several prestigious awards: Prix Ibsen (1978), Prix de l'Académie française (1983), Grand Prix national des Lettres (1992), and Chevalier de l'ordre national du mérite (1993). Author of over a hundred titles, many published posthumously, he also illustrated some 5,000 graphic works. After a lifelong fight against illnesses, he died in Dijon on May 2, 1994.

SÉBASTIEN CÔTÉ

Selected Works

Requiem des innocents. 1952
Partage des vivants. 1953
Septentrion. 1963 (banned); 1984
No man's land. 1963
Satori. 1968
Rosa mystica. 1968
La vie parallèle. 1974

Épisodes de la vie des mantes religieuses. 1976
Le chemin de Sion. Carnets 1956–1967. 1980
Ébauche d'un autoportrait. 1983
Londoniennes. 1985
L'incarnation. 1987
Memento Mori. 1988
La mécanique des femmes. 1992; as *The Way it Works With Women*, translated by Sarah Harrison. 1998
Droit de cité. 1992
C'est la guerre. 1993; as *C'est la guerre*, translated by Austryn Wainhouse, 1999
Ton nom est sexe. 1994
L'aventure intérieure. Entretiens avec Jean-Pierre Pauty, Paris: Éditions Julliard, 1994; as *The Inner Adventure: Conversations with Louis Calaferte*. Translated by Willard Wood, 2003
Choses dites. Entretiens et choix de textes. Edited by Guillemette Calaferte, Ingrid Naour, and Pierre Drachline, 1997
Le sang violet de l'améthyste. 1998

Further Reading

Amine, Patrick. *Une vie, une déflagration. Entretiens avec Louis Calaferte.* Paris: Denoël, 1985.

Drachline, Pierre. "Louis Calaferte 1928–1994," *Encyclopædia Universalis* on-line, http://www.universalis-edu.com, accessed 21 April 2005.

Gordon, Donald E. *Expressionism: Art and Idea.* New Haven: Yale University Press, 1987.

Guichard, Jean-Paul. "'La Mariée mise à nu par...': Corps de femmes, regards de femmes dans la littérature au tournant du siècle," SITES: *The Journal of Twentieth Century Contemporary French Studies*, vol. 6, no. 1 (Spring 2002): 103–118.

Przybyszewski, Stanisław. "Das Geschlecht [Sex]," *Der Sturm*, vol. 1, no. 31–32 (29 September 1910; 6 October 1910): 243–244; [251]–252.

———. *Totenmesse*, http://gutenberg.spiegel.de/przybysz/totmesse/totmesse.htm, accessed 21 April 2005 (originally published in Berlin, 1893).

Roudiez, Leon S. "Review of *Septentrion, Lignes intérieures: Carnets 1974–1977*, and *Une vie, une déflagration*," *World Literature Today*, vol. 60, no. 1 (Winter 1986): 65–66.

Sanchez, Serge. "Calaferte sur le vif." *Magazine littéraire*, no. 343 (May 1996): 68–70.

Simon, Alfred. "L'œuvre de Louis Calaferte." *L'Avant-scène théâtre*, no. 725 (1 March 1983): 26–27.

Taylor, John. "From Darkness to Life (Louis Calaferte)." In *Paths to Contemporary French Literature*, New Brunswick, U.S.A., and London, U.K.: Transaction Publishers, 2004.

CALDWELL, ERSKINE

1903–1987
American novelist

Erskine Caldwell's first novels, *The Bastard* (1929) and *Poor Fool* (1930) were followed by a short story collection, *American Earth* (1931), which—although unpublished—he himself considered his first book. These stories lay the foundation for Caldwell's later recognizable style, namely a grimly deterministic perspective on human life in which the manipulation of power between men and women, whites and African-Americans, rich and poor disposed him towards a gothic preponderance for depictions of graphic violence and startlingly grotesque imagery.

Nevertheless, Caldwell did not receive any measure of success until the publication of *Tobacco Road* (1932) and *God's Little Acre* (1933). Both books were set amongst poor whites and featured a great deal of grotesque sexual behavior. In particular, the incestuous activities of the protagonists, which Caldwell presented as near inherent in the family pattern of the share-croppers, upset southerners and northerners alike, and culminated in a highly publicized obscenity trial in the wake of the publication of *God's Little Acre*. The publicity ensured the books status as a bestseller and the continued run of a theatrical adaptation of *Tobacco Road*, which ran on Broadway for over seven years.

The sexual content of Caldwell's work, his insistence on the grotesque absurdity of the deprived characters, and the animalistic nature of their psychological make-up, has thus often overshadowed Caldwell's reputation as a pro-proletarian writer of the period. In fact, Caldwell's perspective on sharecropping became sharpened as his political sympathies moved leftward during the Depression years. In both *God's Little Acre* and *Tobacco Road*, set in the brutalized countryside of the South, the characters remain oblivious to any notions of Southern gentility or nobility. Instead, Caldwell poignantly prefers to focus on the moral and physical destitution of a people described in starkly realist terms. In 1935, Caldwell published a collection of proletarian stories, *Kneel to the Rising Sun*, before moving on to a style of writing that leant itself more to his alleged objectivist style, namely documentary writing.

Some American People (1935) records Caldwell's journey through a Depression-torn America as does his later collaborations with the photographer Margaret Bourke White whom he married in 1939. As a couple they produced *You Have Seen Their Faces* (1937) on the plight of Southern sharecroppers, *North of the Danube* (1939) on Czechoslovakia, *Say, is this the USA?* (1941), and *Russia at War* (1942). Despite a tumultuous relationship and subsequent divorce in 1942, their collaborative efforts represent a unique combination of documentarist photography and Caldwell's quirky fictionalized accounts of the vernacular speech patterns of the people portrayed. In *You Have Seen Their Faces*, Caldwell dismisses any form of passive objectivity, instead choosing to polemically foreground the pathos of the sharecropper's plight.

Caldwell continued to write prolifically during the 40s. The subsequent decline in his critical status was abetted by a continued interest in the more lurid and commercial sale of paperback editions of *Tobacco Road* and *God's Little Acre*. These editions were more often than not published with paperback covers portraying an array of women with suggestively torn clothing and leering men in the background. After successive marriages Caldwell attempted to break away from this cycle by focusing on female protagonists. His 1950s novels: *Gretta* (1950), *Gulf Coast Stories* (1956), and *Certain Women* (1957) nevertheless all deal in various ways with the sexual behavior of unfulfilled women. Caldwell's reputation as one of America's most censored authors aided in the publication of these books at a time when Caldwell, in America, was considered a rather formulaic writer banking on earlier successes. As Caldwell moved on from his interest in the sexual behavior of women he began to deal more concertedly with issues of race and class in later work from the 1960s and 1970s: *Jenny by Nature* (1961) and *Close to Home* (1962) amongst others.

In total, Caldwell published well over 50 books of short stories, novels, and non-fiction but his work from the 1930s still stands as the foundation for his reputation as a writer engaged with the political and sexual spirit of his age. Despite the potential for his Southern fiction to be read as predominantly crass and sexually titillating, Caldwell's sociological sense and political sincerity combined to make him a crucial literary figure of his times.

Biography

The son of Ira Sylvester Caldwell, a minister, and Caroline Bell, a teacher, Caldwell was brought up in the deep South amidst the people and locations that would later inform his fiction and documentary writing. Caldwell's interest in the social, sexual, and race relationships of the South stems partly from his upbringing as a minister's son, as well as from his fascination with the oral storytelling traditions of his home region. Caldwell went to Erskine College in South Carolina and later the University of Virginia and Pennsylvania from 1920–1925. After graduating he worked as a newspaper reporter for the *Atlanta Journal* and as a book reviewer for the *Journal*, the *Houston Post*, and the *Observer* during which time he also

submitted scores of short stories, which were not published. In 1925, he married Helen Lannigan with whom he had two sons and one daughter. In 1984, he was elected to the American Academy of Arts and Letters. He remained prolific until his death in 1987.

CAROLINE BLINDER

Selected Works

Tobacco Road. 1932
God's Little Acre. 1933
Journeyman. 1935
You Have Seen Their Faces. 1937
Georgia Boy. 1943
Complete Short Stories. 1953
Close to Home. 1962

Further Reading

Arnold, T. Edwin, ed. *Erskine Caldwell Reconsidered*, Mississippi: University of Mississippi Press, 1990.
Arnold, T. Edwin, ed. *Conversations with Erskine Caldwell*, Mississippi: University of Mississippi Press, 1988.
Caldwell, Erskine. *Selected Letters*, 1929–1955. Virginia: McFarland and Co., 1999.
Cook, Sylvia J. *Erskine Caldwell and the Fiction of Poverty: The Flesh and the Spirit.* Louisiana: Louisiana State University Press, 1991.
McDonald, Robert L. *The Critical Response to Erskine Caldwell.* New York: Greenwood, 1997.
Macdonald, Scott, ed. *Critical Essays on Erskine Caldwell.* London: G. K. Hall and Co., 1981.

CALIFIA, PAT

1954–
American writer and poet

Macho Sluts

Macho Sluts is the most widely known of Pat Califia's works. The book is a loose collection of eight erotic stories, with an introduction and a final chapter on safe sex in the time of AIDS. Published in 1988 by Alyson Press, with one of

the stories having first appeared in *Advocate*, the book formed part of the range of lesbian erotica published in the late 1980s and early 1990s that challenged both Adrienne Rich's negation of variant lesbian sexuality within her concept of the 'lesbian continuum' which embraces all relationships between women, and Andrea Dworkin's anti-pornography claim that 'intercourse has nothing to do with lesbians or lesbian sexuality' (*Pornography: Men Possessing Women*, 1981).

Macho Sluts goes further than simply asserting the reality and validity of lesbian sexual desire in its detailed representation of a series of sado-masochistic scenarios within the leatherdyke community. Unapologetic and affirming in its tone, the book argues for an acknowledgment that passionate violence should not be seen in negative terms if it is the consensual choice of both/all partners.

The "Introduction" argues that sexual minorities have the right to pleasure themselves, and that for her the 'prospect of a human body being rendered helpless, put under slowly increasing stress, so that the maximum amount of sensation can run through skin, nerves, and muscles' is an erotic celebration of the body's stamina and grace. Stories such as *Jessie, Finishing School, The Calyx of Isis*, and *The Vampire* illustrate the sexual stimulation that comes from experiencing or receiving pain. The viewpoint of the stories keep switching so that the reader is implicated in both the sadist's and the masochist's roles and shares the pleasure of each. This serves to highlight the level of role-play and fantasy involved in the scenarios and to complicate the apparent power structures and symbolic frameworks of sexuality, since it is the "bottom" who controls the intensity of the transaction, in granting her consent, rather than the "top." This is even further complicated in *The Spoiler* where the master is a masochist who has made himself into a replica of his own desires.

Set in San Francisco dyke bathhouses, loft parties, and s/m gay bars, the stories celebrate a range of West Coast leatherdyke communities, as well as narrowing down onto the sexual couple or, in *The Calyx of Isis*, a whole group of dominatrices invited to play with one bottom. The stories argue for the presence and the visibility of a whole community of women choosing the pleasures of s/m, with their own etiquette and rituals, and their self-supporting structures.

A few of the stories are deliberately provocative, challenging social moralizers to rethink their positions. *The Hustler*, aimed at the anti-porn feminists, posits a world where the women's revolution has succeeded and s/m has been made illegal because it runs counter to a simplistic view of liberation and equal opportunities. The narrator finds herself hounded just as much by the censorious feminists as under contemporary society. *The Spoiler* is more surprising for the lesbian audience, since it is a narrative about gay s/m men. But as Califia argues, fantasy should be uncensored, and why shouldn't lesbians be free to fantasize about men? *The Surprise Party* has a lesbian apparently abducted by a group of policemen and subjected to a ritual of humiliation, beatings, and rape, an ostensible punishment for being a leatherdyke that, in the end, turns out to be a birthday present of her most intimate fantasy played out by gay friends. The level of role-play in fantasy, the levels of choice in the symbolic framework of gender and sexuality, the level of disciplined transformation necessary to play out the scenarios of s/m, all problematize the simple assumptions of the uninitiated reader and argue for a more informed tolerance of sexual radicals.

Most of Califia's work, fiction and non-fiction, has challenged social stigmatization of lesbian sado-masochism, and has sought to claim a space for them within feminist debates. From *Sapphistry*, her first book in 1980, through to *Sensuous Magic* in 1998, including her advice column for *Advocate*, collected into the *Advocate Adviser* in 1991, Califia has written explanations, suggestions, and advice for sexual radicals, focusing on broadening their enjoyment within a climate of safe sex. She is passionate in challenging social strictures. *Sex Changes* continues her support of sexual minorities in its support of transsexuals.

Alongside this non-fiction runs a strand of fictional writing, such as *Macho Sluts* and *Melting Point* where she uses the erotic tale or short story format to engage and arouse the reader. "My intention...was to use arousal as a gateway into the reader's heart and mind, a passage through which some new ideas or associations might enter...to use sexual energy to change the way people view themselves, their partners, and the world around them" (*Melting Point*, 1993). Although most known as a short story writer, Califia has also published one novel, *Doc and Fluff* (1990) and one book of poetry, *Diesel Fuel: Passionate Poetry* (1997), both on the same topic; the experiences of lesbian leatherwomen. *Doc and Fluff: The Dystopian Tale of a Girl and her Bike* is a science fiction novel where the villain is executed by a prophet of the Goddess as punishment for his series of rapes and murders, thereby contrasting his oppressive use of violence to the very different consensual and mutually erotic play of the lesbian s/m couple.

As Lisa Sigel argues, "Califia promotes lust in all its forms and her work contributes to the growing theoretical complexity about sexuality, both in relation to queer studies and to the pornography debates."

Biography

Born in Little Rock, Arizona, March 8, 1954. Attended the University of Utah where, at 17 she came out as a lesbian and changed her surname to that of a legendary Amazon queen. BA, San Francisco University, 1977. In 1978, she co-founded Samois (lesbian sado-masochist activists, see *Coming to Power*, 1981) and in 1979 began her advice column for the gay magazine, *Advocate*, becoming editor in 1990. Califia's essays and fiction focus on frank accounts of lesbian s/m desires. Her graphic accounts and her celebration of domination have lead to her being a central figure in the anti-censorship debates.

MERJA MAKINEN

Editions

Macho Sluts: Erotic Fiction. Boston: Alyson, 1988.

Selected Works

Sapphistry: The Book of Lesbian Sexuality. 1980
Caught Looking. 1986
Macho Sluts. 1988
Lesbian S/M Safety Manual. 1988 (edited)
Doc and Fluff: The Dystopian Tale of a Girl and her Bike. 1990

Advocate Adviser. 1991
Melting Point: Erotic Short Stories. 1993
Public Sex: The Culture of Radical Sex. 1994
Second Coming: A Leatherdyke Reader. 1996 (co-edited)
Diesel Fuel: Passionate Poetry. 1997
Sex Changes: The Politics of Transgenderism. 1997
Sensuous Magic: A Guide for Adventurous Couples. 1998

Further Reading

Barnard, P. C. "Macho Sluts: Genre-Fuck, S/M Fantasy, and the Reconfiguration of Political Action," *Genders*, 19 (1994).
Griffin, Gabriel. "Safe and Sexy: Lesbian erotica in the Age of AIDS," *Romance Revisited*, Lynne Pearce and Jackie Stacey (eds). London: Lawrence and Wishart, 1995.
Henderson, Lisa, Lesbian Pornography: Cultural Transgression and Sexual Demystification." *New Lesbian Criticism: Literary and Cultural Readings.* Edited by Sally Munt, Hemel Hempstead: Harvester, 1992.
Makinen, Merja, Embodying the Negated: Contemporary Images of the Female Erotic." *Image and Power: Women in Fiction in the Twentieth Century.* Edited by Sarah Sceats and Gail Cunningham, London: Longman, 1996.
Donna Mikowitz. "Pleasure Principles." *Women's Review of Books.* 12 (June 1995).
Sigel, Lisa. "Pat Califia." In *Significant Contemporary American Feminists.* Westport, Connecticut: Greenwood, 1999.
Watling, Clare. "Who Reads Macho Sluts?." *Textuality and Sexuality: Reading Theories and Practices.* Edited by Judith Still and Michael Worton, Manchester: Manchester University Press, 1993.

See also **Feminism; Lesbian literature; Sado-Masochism**

CALVINO, ITALO

1923–1985
Italian fiction writer and essayist

Gli Amori Difficili

Gli Amori Difficili [*Difficult Loves*], a collection of thirteen short stories, or "adventures," written between 1949 and 1967, is representative of Calvino's approach to the erotic: it is not just a fact of life like any other; it occupies a special place in human existence and, consequently, in literature. Eros is unutterable, suggests Calvino in his essay "Definitions of Territories: Eroticism" [The Uses of Literature]. That is why "even writers whose erotic imagination aspires to pass all bounds often use a language that starts off with the utmost clarity and then passes into a mysterious obscurity precisely at the moments of greatest tension, as if its end result could never be anything but inexpressible." Calvino, however, seems to have found his own way of expressing the inexpressible. As he acknowledges the intrinsic subjectivity of erotic experience, he describes it only from the point of view of one of the two involved characters. His protagonists are in love with their own erotic perceptions, which makes them appear narcissistic. Also, most of them become—for the first time—intensely aware of their own eros—the initiation, however different in each case, is always mesmerizing.

The narration of the earliest story "L'avventura di un soldato" [The Adventure of a Soldier] is so subjective that it is impossible to tell whether this is a sexual fantasy of a Private Tomagra stricken by desire for a corpulent widow with whom he happened to share a train compartment or the events are real and his advances are being silently appreciated. The soldier and the widow are asleep or pretend to be asleep. Tomagra's hand is exploring the widow's thigh; the muscles of his calf are sending impulses to her leg. Just one sense, touch, is involved in this game, and just one player, the soldier. The reader learns in detail what Tomagra's hand feels, but nothing beyond that. The ending of the story is ambivalent—maybe they make love, maybe not. The widow's silence remains impenetrable; it delineates the inexpressible dimension of the erotic. "L'avventura di un soldato" can be read as the invariant of all the other stories in the collection.

The traveler's adventure in "L'avventura di un viaggiatore" presents the night train as a vehicle of desire, and the traveling as a ritualized advance to the erotic object. In "L'avventura di una bagnante" [The Adventure of a Bather] Isolta, a respectable housewife, has lost her bathing suit while swimming far from the beach. The happy discovery of her own erotic relationship with water is replaced by a feeling of shame and helplessness. She spends the whole day in the sea until two men snorkeling around realize what the problem is and bring her a dress. The fact that the men have seen her naked makes Isolta feel pleasure—it has all happened under the water and through the water. At the same time the very idea of showing up naked outside the water is unbearable. Like Private Tomagra, she is daring only as long as blind touch is involved.

Sight, the principal sense of erotic attraction, is decisive in three of the "difficult loves." The nearsighted man of "L'avventura di un miope," unaware of his eye problem, believes that he has lost his savor of life because he has stopped noticing beautiful women in the street. The photographer of "L'avventura di un fotografo" becomes obsessed with making the camera see the world in the same erotic way he does. The poet of "L'avventura di un poeta," who has witnessed his lover's enchanting dance in the water in a sea grotto, for a short time believes that he would be able to turn this magical vision into poetry. But words come to his mind, "thick, woven one into another (...) until little by little they could no longer be distinguished; it was a tangle from which even the tiniest white spaces were vanishing and only the black remained, the most total black, impenetrable, desperate as a scream." The clerk in "L'avventura di un impiegato" has spent the night with an otherwise unapproachable beautiful lady. However, the impossibility to talk about his adventure makes him feel a painful tension, no different from the unfulfilled longing. Hence the potentiality of eros seems to be preferable to the speechlessness of the fulfilled desire. In "L'avventura di una moglie" [The Adventure of a Wife] recently married Stefania R. has spent the night with a young man, but has not slept with him. While remaining faithful to her husband, she has experienced the possibility of being unfaithful. This ambivalent situation gives her erotic pleasure and confidence as she replays it with other men in the neighborhood café.

"L'avventura di due sposi" [The Adventure of the Married Couple] is the only story in the collection which shows eros from the points of view of both characters. The man works during the night, the woman, during the day. They barely see each other, but it is precisely the absence of the other that makes their desires manifest. This story and "L'avventura di un lettore" [The Adventure of a Reader] introduce a conspicuous ironic note in Calvino's *Gli Amori Difficili*. Amedeo Oliva, the Reader, is divided between Proust's erotic narrative that he is devouring on a secluded beach, and an appealing woman whom he has just met there. After they make love, Amedeo is possessed again by his lust for reading. The eros of literature, unlike sexual desire, is insatiable.

In some of his later fictions Calvino tests another possibility of speaking about the inexpressible eros: going beyond the anthropomorphic boundaries. His narrators are simultaneously participants in a meta-erotic relationship with the worlds they describe and voyeurs of the erotic life of those worlds. Fantasies about the love affairs of the mollusks or unicellular organisms in *Le cosmicomiche* [*Cosmicomics*] or, for example, of the tortoises in *Palomar* [*Mr. Palomar*], as well as Marco Polo's poetic tales about fantastic cities of female names in *Le città invisibili* [*Invisible Cities*], demonstrate the erotic nature of human curiosity and imagination. *Se una notte d'inverno un viaggiatore* [*If on a Winter's Night a Traveler*], in turn, equates eros with reading.

Biography

Born October 15, 1923 in Santiago de las Vegas, Cuba; family moved to San Remo, Italy, 1925. Studied at the University of Turin, 1941–1947; degree in letters. Called to the draft by Mussolini's government, but went into hiding, 1943. Joined the Communist Resistance, 1944. Wrote for *L'Unità* [*Unity*], *La Nostra Lotta* [*Our Struggle*], *Il Garibaldino*, *Voce della Democrazia* [*Voice of Democracy*], *Contemporaneo*, *Città Aperta* [*Open City*], and *La Republica*, from 1945. Staff member, Einaudi publishers, Torino, 1948–1984. Married Esther Judith Singer, 1964; one daughter. Moved to Paris, 1967, and to Rome, 1980. Awards: *L'Unità* Prize, 1945; Viareggio Prize, 1957; Bagutta Prize, 1959; Veillion Prize, 1963; Feltrinelli Prize, 1972. Died of a cerebral hemorrhage in Siena, 19 September 1985.

KATIA MITOVA

Editions

Gli Amori Difficili. Torino: Einaudi, 1970, 1975, 1978, 1998; Milano: Mondadori, 1990, 1993 (most of the stories previously published in *Ultimo viene il corvo*, Torino: Einauldi, 1949, and *I racconti*, Torino: Einaudi, 1958); as *Difficult Loves*, translated by William Weaver, London: Martin Secker and Warburg, 1983; New York: Harcourt Brace, 1984; London: Pan Books, 1985; London: Minerva, 1993.

Selected Works

Il sentiero dei nidi di ragno. 1947; as *The Path to the Nest of Spiders*. Translated by Archibald Colquhoun, 1957; as *The Path to the Spiders' Nests*, translated by Archibald Colquhoun, revised by Martin McLaughlin, 1998.

Il visconte dimezzato. 1951, 1968; in *The Nonexistent Knight and The Cloven Viscount*, translated by Archibald Colquhoun, 1962, 1977.

Il barone rampante. 1957; as *The Baron in the Trees*, translated by Archibald Colquhoun. 1971, 1975.

I racconti. 1958; selections of these stories were published in *Adam, One Afternoon and Other Stories*. Translated by Archibald Colquhoun and Peggy Wright, 1957, 1983, and in *Difficult Loves*, 1984.

Smog and The Argentine Ant in *The Watcher and Other Stories*. Translated by William Weaver and Archibald Colquhoun, 1971, 1975.

Il cavaliere inesistente, in *The Nonexistent Knight and The Cloven Viscount*, translated by Archibald Colquhoun, 1962, 1977.

La giornata d'uno scrutatore, 1963; as *The Watcher* in *The Watcher and Other Stories*, translated by William Weaver and Archibald Colquhoun, 1971, 1975.

Marcovaldo, ovvero. Le staggioni in città. 1963, 1966; as *Marcovaldo*, or, *The seasons of the City*, translated by William Weaver, 1983.

Le cosmiciniche, 1965; as *Cosmicomics*, translated by William Weaver, 1968, 1977.

Ti con zero, 1967; as *t zero*, translated by William Weaver, 1969, 1976.

La memoria del mondo e altre storie cosmicomiche, 1968.

Il castello dei destini incrostati, 1969, 1973; as *The Castle of Crossed Destinies*, translated by William Weaver, 1976, 1977, 1979.

Le città invisibili, 1972; as *Invisible Cities*, translated by William Weaver, 1974, 1978.

Se una notte d'inverno un viaggiatore, 1979; as *If on a Winter's Night a Traveler*, translated by William Weaver, 1981, 1993.

Una Pietra Sopra. Discorsi di litteratura e società, 1980; as *The Uses of Literature: Essays*, translated by Patrick Creagh, 1986; as *The Literary Machine: Essays*, translated by Patrick Creagh, 1987.

Palomar, 1983; as *Mr. Palomar*, translated by William Weaver, 1985.

Sotto il sole giaguaro, 1986; as *Under the Jaguar Sun*, translated by William Weaver, 1988.

Lezioni americane. Sei proposte per il prossimo millenio, 1988; as *Six Memos for the Next Millenium*, translated by Patrick Creagh, 1988.

La strada di San Giovani, 1990; as *The Road to San Giovani*, translated by Tim Parks, 1993.

Romanzi e racconti (2 vols), edited by Mario Barenghi and Bruno Falcetto, 1991, 1993.

Perché leggere i classici, 1991; as *Why Read the Classics?*, translated by Martin McLaughlin, 1999.

Eremita a Parigi. Pagine autobiografiche, 1994.

Prima che tu dica "Pronto," 1993; as *Numbers in the Dark and Other Stories*, translated by Tim Parks, 1995.

Saggi. 1945–1985 (2 vols), edited by Mario Barenghi, 1995.

Further Reading

Ahern, John, "Out of Montale's Cave: A Reading of Calvino's Gli Amori Difficili." *Modern Language Studies* 12 (1982): 3–19.

Bloom, Harold (ed.) *Italo Calvino: Modern Critical Views*. Philadelphia: Chelsea House Publishers, 2001.

Gabriele, Tommasina. *Italo Calvino: Eros and Language*, London and Toronto: Associated University Presses, 1994.

Markey, Constance. *Italo Calvino: A Journey Toward Postmodernism*. Gainesville, FL: University Press of Florida, 1999.

McLaughlin, Martin. *Iatalo Calvino*, Edinburgh: Edinburgh University Press. 1998.

Ricci, Franco. *Difficult Games: A Reading of* I raconti *by Italo Calvino*. Waterloo, Ont.: Wilfred Laurier University Press, 1990.

Schneider, Marilyn. "Calvino's Erotic Metaphor and the Hermaphroditic Solution." *Stanford Italian Review* 2 (1981): 93–118.

CAO, XUEQIN

1715–1764
Chinese prose writer

Dream of the Red Chamber [*Hong Lou Meng*] (also known as *Shi Tou Ji* or *The Story of the Stone*)

Cao Xueqin's *Hong Lou Meng* is considered by many to be the best and most important work of fictional narrative ever written in China. First published in 1792, it circulated among family members and friends in various manuscript copies with commentary for something like fifty years. These copies eventually made their way to the marketplace, but growing numbers of readers were disappointed to find that the story broke off at Chapter 80. Gao E claimed to have found a fragmentary original ending and edited it to produce a complete 120-chapter version. Who actually authored the final forty chapters is a matter of great scholarly debate. Although no conclusive evidence has been found to support any particular claim, the vast majority of readers are familiar with the 120-chapter version.

There are so many matters of debate about this long novel (2,500 pages in English translation) that there are university departments, journals, and many monographs dedicated to *hongxue* or "redology"—comparable to Shakespeare studies in the West. To grasp the significance of the novel in China, according to Dore Levy, we would have to imagine a work with the popular appeal of Margaret Mitchell's *Gone With the Wind*, the critical acclaim of James Joyce's *Ulysses*, and that is twice the length of both combined.

Among the debates of "red studies" is what *Hong Lou Meng* is about. It has been read as a *bildungsroman*, a *roman à clef*, a Buddhist-Daoist allegory of disenchantment and enlightenment, a novel of manners, and a romance, among others. One way to explain the story is to follow the fates of two characters. The main character, Jia Baoyu, is the youngest and sole heir to the once vast Jia family wealth. Baoyu is surrounded by girl cousins and maids and frequently derides men and champions the inherent superiority of women. The family elders want to choose a primary wife for Baoyu and are essentially torn between two choices. The story follows Baoyu's relations with these two female cousins who are diametrically opposed—the frail and ill, Lin Daiyu, and her more robust, outgoing counterpart, Xue Baochai. Both young women are beautiful, intelligent, and talented at composing verse.

We first meet Baoyu in a previous incarnation. The Goddess Nüwa was repairing the sky with stones, and she had one left over when her project was complete. This stone had magical properties. It could move, speak, and feel. The Stone sat alone for a long time at the bottom of "Greensickness peak," when it grows attached to a beautiful Crimson Pearl Flower. He feeds it with dew drops, which confer upon it life. The Stone is then taken down into the world by an eccentric Daoist priest and Buddhist monk and is reborn as Jia Baoyu with a perfect piece of jade in his mouth. The Crimson Pearl Flower is reborn as Lin Daiyu who comes to live with the Jias after the death of her mother. There, she is fated to repay the stone for each drop of dew with a debt of tears.

Another major plot arch concerns the activities of Wang Xifeng, one of the daughters-in-law of the family Jia. Her involvement in the family finances and management gradually becomes one of control, and she oversees the moral and economic downfall of the once illustrious family. The contrast of Xifeng, the masculine woman who tends to the practical needs of the family and deals with the machinations of its members with Baoyu, the sensitive, feminine boy who lives his life primarily in the family garden with his girl cousins, writing poems and indulging their whims, exemplifies themes of crossing gender roles and crossing boundaries between pure, emotional interiority and the tainted, expressive worlds outside.

One of the major themes in *Hong Lou Meng* is the relation between appearance and reality. The world as it seems to be is "appearance" (*se*), and attachments are made to those appearances through "feeling" (*qing*). Appearances in *Hong Lou Meng* are seductive, and *se* also has the meaning of sex, or lust, and *qing* can also mean desire. In *Hong Lou Meng*, though, reality displayed in appearance is always empty, and attachment to it, *qing*, causes suffering. Thus, *Hong Lou Meng* in large part is about characters who (are fated to) suffer because of their desire, and the attainment or rejection of the truth that the only way to avoid suffering is to reject *se* by extinguishing *qing*.

Hong Lou Meng follows Jia Baoyu from his incarnation as a boy and the first arousal of his feelings, and first experiences with heterosexual and homosexual intercourse in the larger family mansions. He and his girl cousins then move into the family's enormous "Garden of Total Vision," built for the visit of the imperial concubine and complete with small houses enough for each of the girls and their personal maids. Baoyu is allowed to go live in the garden, as the only boy, where he regains his sexual innocence but begins to struggle with desire. The majority of his troubles and conflicts occur within the walls of the garden and those make up the majority of the novel from Chapter 18 to 99, when a wife is chosen for him. He then conceives a child, passes the civil service examinations, and then liberates

himself from feelings by abandoning the world. Wang Xifeng, who has a troubled marriage, is involved in a famous episode in which a distant "cousin" becomes infatuated with her as she intentionally frustrates his desires by making assignations with him and then causing calamities to befall him. He is so tortured by this behavior that he masturbates to death. In sum, the eros of *Hong Lou Meng*, lies primarily in the thwarting of desire and denial of its expression.

Biography

Cao Xueqin, author of *Hong Lou Meng*, is considered China's greatest novelist, although his only major work was not finished by him and little is known about his life. Cao was the grandson or grand-nephew of Cao Yin (1658–1712), who had a close relationship with the Kangxi Emperor. Cao Yin was appointed by the Emperor to the director of the Imperial Textile Factory in Nanjing in 1603 and because of his position, was extremely wealthy. After his death, the position was given to a couple of relatives, but because of mismanagement, was taken away by the Yongzheng Emperor in 1728. Many family positions and estates were confiscated and the remnants of the family moved to Beijing. Cao Xueqin was quite young at this time, and the downfall of the Jia family is often taken as a semi-autobiographical account of his own.

ANDREW SCHONEBAUM

Editions and Translations

The Story of the Stone. 5 vols; translated by David Hawkes and John Minford, London: Penguin, 1973–1986.
Hong Lou Meng Jiaozhu. Taipei: Liren Shuju, 2000.

Further Reading

Hsia, C.T. *The Classic Chinese Novel*, New York: Columbia University Press, 1968.
Levy, Dore. *Idea and Actual in* The Story of the Stone, New York: Columbia University Press, 1999.
Plaks, Andrew H. *Archetype and Allegory in the Dream of the Red Chamber.* Princeton: Princeton University Press, 1976.
Rolston, David L. *How to Read the Chinese Novel.* Princeton: Princeton University Press, 1990.

See also **Jin Ping Mei; Xiuta Yeshi; Zhulin Yeshi**

CAREW, THOMAS

c. 1594–1640
English poet

Thomas Carew's poetry forms part of that body of seventeenth-century verse generally termed "Cavalier Poetry," Like most other Cavalier poetry, the ideals Carew's verse expresses are those of the good life, often classical in nature and setting and providing the poet with a framework in which to explore issues of love and the erotic. Carew, like many other seventeenth-century poets, has a clear indebtedness to the Platonic ideas about love that were popular in the sixteenth century and to the more Petrarchan elements of Elizabethan love poetry. This means his poetry is concerned both with the erotic power of being scorned by a Petrarchan mistress and with the nature of sensuous erotic fulfillment.

As a poet in the Petrarchan line Carew is most at home when portraying the eroticized torments of unrequited love. In "The Spring," for example, the beauteous and bountiful nature of the summer is contrasted with the coldness displayed by his mistress: "all things keep / Time with the season, only she doth carry / June in her eyes, in her heart January." The trend of elaborately praising the mistress throughout the poem only for the scene to end in a final declaration of the speaker's tormented emotions is quite common in seventeenth-century verse, and Carew is one of the better poets writing in this style. Poems like "A Divine Mistress" exhibit Carew's dexterity within this form; the ability to frame the erotic within what is only hinted at, never directly alluded to. Like many others of this type, the poem does not deal at all with the specific details of the mistress (in fact the individual woman, if she existed at all, is irrelevant) but has as its sole purpose the speaker's reflection upon his own insatiable desire. Thus the woman is "divine" and without fault and these are both the factors that attract the speaker, but also leave him to conclude that her very divinity prevents the fulfillment of his lust: "She hath too much divinity for me / You Gods teach her some more humility." This tormented eroticism reaches its climax in Carew's song "Murdering Beauty" where the mistress' attractions prove too much for the speaker: "If she behold me with a pleasing eye / I surfeit with excess of joy, and die."

Carew does occasionally venture into the realm of the specific, as in the poem "Celia bleeding, to the Surgeon" where the speaker addresses the doctor who has drawn blood from Celia (in the seventeenth century a standard poetic name for the mistress) and declares to him "Thou struck her arm, but 'twas my heart / Shed all the blood, felt all the smart." Throughout the poem, blood is eroticised, flowing as it does through Celia's "azure veins." More erotic still in its use of the sensual is the poem "Upon a Mole in Celia's bosom" with its story of a bee who tried to build an "amorous spicy nest" upon the mistress' breast only to be overcome by the joy found in sucking "the Aromatic dew" from the breasts themselves.

It is really in Carew's non-Petrarchan poems, however, that we find the truly erotic descriptions that are more commonly associated with seventeenth-century verse. "To A.L., Persuasions to Love" functions with a similar intent as Marvell's "To his Coy Mistress" except where Marvell would later write an elaborate argument, brimming over with hyperbole and rather sinister in its intimations of death and the grave, Carew devotes far more of his poem to a much simpler argument—to give me pleasure, states the speaker, is also to discover pleasure for yourself. In Carew's words: "'twere a madness not to grant / That which affords (if you consent) / To you the giver, more content / Than me the beggar; Oh then be / Kind to yourself if not to me." Part of the attraction of Carew's poetry undoubtedly lies in the sheer simplicity of his language and rhetorical style. In "Lips and Eyes" Carew imagines a debate between the lips and the eyes as to which are more beautiful, with the eyes claiming the title on the grounds that they "pierce the hardest adamantine hearts," while the lips argue that from them "proceed those blisses / Which lovers reap by kind words and sweet kisses." This simplicity holds its own erotic appeal because it places desire and attraction with the physical world. The pleasures Carew describes are not of the metaphysical, spiritual, or emotional kind which often function to the detriment of physical sensations and physical satisfaction. The contrast between Carew's sensual eroticism and the reflective eroticism found in the poetry of Donne is quite clear in Carew's poem "The Rapture."

"The Rapture" could be read as a mere development from a poem like "To A.L., persuasions to love" but the intensely eroticized and sensual portrait of the woman in "The Rapture" makes it much more than this. From the opening couplet, the speaker places himself in the position of aroused lover, desperate for physical fulfillment, by no means ignoring the woman herself—"I will enjoy thee now my Celia, come / And fly with me to Love's Elysium." Instead of allowing the poem to turn into a piece solely about the male speaker's desire and pleasure, Carew makes the woman's body and her desires a central concern, and draws a highly erotic (and highly metaphorical) portrait of her body. Standard seventeenth-century tropes such as comparisons of parts of the woman's body with ivory or roses are present, but Carew's descriptions have a freshness and intensity not always to be found in verse of this kind. The woman's skin is "naked polished Ivory" and the speaker longs to penetrate the "rich Mine" of her "virgin-treasure." The gentleness of the opening descriptive passages soon moves on to an expression of the speaker's intense desires: "I'll seize the Rose-buds in their perfum'd bed / ... taste the ripened Cherry, / The warm firm Apple, tipped with coral berry." From this vision of "seizing" the speaker returns to the more lingering, caressing tone of the previous lines, narrating how he will "visit, with a wandering kiss, / The vale of Lilies, and the Bower of bliss." The emphasis throughout the poem lies with the need to acknowledge there is no shame in physical love; that sex should be free of "the hated name / Of husband, wife, lust modest, chaste, or shame" between lovers. Interestingly, considering the difference between this poem and Carew's other, more Petrarchan lyrics, it is in "A Rapture" that he cites the Italian poet: for, in the lovers' paradise described by the speaker: "Laura lies / In Petrarch's learned arms, drying

those eyes / That did in such sweet smooth-paced numbers flow / As made the world enamoured of his woe." Even Petrarch is seen to finally attain satisfaction for his desires in the Elysium Carew imagines. However, in the final fifty lines of the poem, the hyperbole reaches such heights because of the speaker's increasingly frustrated desire that it demystifies its ultimate purpose. "A Rapture" may contain more eroticized descriptions of the woman than some other seventeenth-century verse along similar lines, but the concluding message is the same. For all the speaker's high-flown talk of love and the absurdity of feeling shame for consummating desire, it is the need to satiate his own lust that proves the principle aim.

Biography

After a childhood in London, Carew matriculated from Merton College, Oxford in 1608, graduating B.A. in January of 1610 / 1611. Carew became secretary to the English ambassador to Venice in 1613, returning to England in 1615. Resuming his duties by accompanying the embassy to the Netherlands in 1616, Carew was dismissed as discretely as possible later that same year for "indiscretions" concerning the character of the ambassador. For the next two years Carew unsuccessfully sought employment, finally finding a position in 1619 accompanying Sir Edward Herbert's embassy to Paris. In the early 1620s, Carew became associated with Ben Jonson and the "Tribe of Ben" and was frequently seen at court. His first poem was published in 1622 amongst the commendatory verses prefixed to Thomas May's comedy The Heir. In 1630 he was appointed as a gentleman of the Privy Chamber ("Sewer in Ordinary to the King"), and his court masque, Coelum Britannicum, was performed in 1634. Carew also accompanied Charles I's expedition to Scotland in 1639. Thomas Carew died in 1640 and was buried in St. Dunstan's-in-the-West, Westminster on March 23 of that year. Poems appeared in 1640; a second edition was produced in 1642.

MARK LLEWELLYN

Editions

The Poems of Thomas Carew. Edited by Rhodes Dunlap, Oxford: Clarendon Press, 1949.

Further Reading

Bush, Douglas. *English Literature in the Earlier Seventeenth Century, 1600–1660*. Oxford: Clarendon Press, 1946.

Frontain, Raymond Jean. *"Discovering the Way to the New Elysium: Carew's 'A Rapture', the Renaissance Erotic Pastoral, and the Biblical Song of Solomon."* Publications of the Arkansas Philological Association, 21:1 (Spring 1995): 39–67.

Lyon, John. "Jonson and Carew on Donne: Censure into Praise," *Studies in English Literature, 1500–1900*. 37:1 (Winter 1997): 97–118.

Maclean, Hugh, ed. *Ben Jonson and the Cavalier Poets*, New York, London: W.W. Norton & Company, 1974.

Nixon, Scott. "Carew's Response to Jonson and Donne," *Studies in English Literature, 1500–1900*. 39: 1 (Winter 1999): 89–109.

Parfit, George. *English Poetry of the Seventeenth Century*. London: Longman, 1992 (second edition).

CARTER, ANGELA

1940–1992
British novelist, short story writer and journalist

Angela Carter wrote nine novels, numerous short stories, articles, and radio plays. Her writing is complex, erudite, and provocative, and marked by a persistent interest in sexuality and feminism. She possessed a keen wit and humor, and her comedy often found expression through darker forms of the Gothic, as well as through parody and the stylistic excesses of mannerism. Her 1979 essay, *The Sadeian Woman and the Ideology of Pornography*, articulates her approach to erotic writing, and, alongside her readings of Bataille, usefully places much of Carter's fictional work on sexuality. Carter works from a reading of Sade's writing to propose the notion of a "moral pornographer," one whose unflinching and honest attention to the materialist underpinnings of sexuality would unveil social inequalities and the mythologies of romance. For Carter, sexual relationships are the place where broader social and cultural relationships play out, and literature that directly approaches sex would be literature that illuminates gender relationships. The moral pornographer is in a unique position to serve as a "terrorist of the imagination," by linking pornography, a typically abstracted form, to the realities of everyday life.

Carter's fiction often unfolds in chaotic worlds that resemble Sade's. Novels like *The Infernal Desire Machines of Dr. Hoffman* (1972) and *Nights at the Circus* (1984) present picaresque tales of sexual adventures and depravities. In one scene in *Hoffman*, the main character, Desiderio, is subjected to serial rape while traveling with a carnival, enduring fierce but creative sodomy by the troupe known as the "Acrobats of Desire." Carter's interest in the possibilities and limitations of pornography are matched by her interest in the equally ambiguous uses of psychoanalytical theory. Her fiction explores alternatives to the Oedipal complex, as she engages and reworks Freud's theories within the modes of fiction and fantasy.

Carter also works within the genre of Gothic fiction as one strategy for interrupting narratives of romance, a mythology she deems more dangerous for women than pornography. Her early novels, especially *Shadow Dance* (1996) and *Love* (1971, rev. ed. 1987) explored the passivity of the female victim through relationships marked by triangulations, sado-masochism, and violent struggle. In *Shadow Dance*, Carter details the 'woman's suffering body through the character of Ghislaine, who is scarred at the hands of the sadistic Honeybuzzard. In *Love*, Annabel is likewise victimized by her boyfriend Lee and his brother Buzz. Both of these novels demonstrate Carter's intolerance for the victim prototype, and are unflinching in their refusal to romanticize or valorize female passivity.

Carter's 1977 novel, *The Passion of New Eve*, further debunks fictions of femininity. In this dystopian novel, the sadistic Englishman Evelyn journeys to an apocalyptic United States only to be captured by a radical woman's community where he is forcibly transformed from a man to a woman. Three of the main characters undergo sexual permutations: the narrator, Evelyn, is forcibly transformed through surgery into the pin-up girl Eve; the languorous masochist Leilah becomes the mythic warrior Lilith, while the glamorous actress-icon Tristessa, "Our Lady of Sorrows," is revealed to be a transvestite. Like her earlier novel, *Heroes and Villains* (1969), *The Passion of New Eve* unfolds in a post-apocalyptic future, a setting that allows Carter to explore human nature in the raw, separate from social niceties.

Carter's short stories continue her interest in demythologizing femininity, frequently accommodating this goal through her revisions of fairy and folk tales. "The Bloody Chamber," a version of the "Bluebeard" story, stands as one of Carter's best-known stories, and follows the misadventures of a young bride in the grasp of a ruthless voluptuary. Carter's interest in the werewolf motif finds expression through several short stories, as well as in her 1984 film collaboration with Neil Jordan, *The Company of Wolves*. Her later novels, like *Nights at the Circus* and *Wise Children*, demonstrate a shift away from the Gothic and an engagement with more readily recognizable comedic forms. But here as well, sexuality remains a focus. Her female protagonists in these last two novels actively claim their sexuality, as in the case of the octogenarian twins, the lively Chance sisters of *Wise Children*.

Carter's reputation as an erotic writer occurs through her feminism, specifically through her articulations of "moral pornography." Her fiction, while sexually explicit, retains a politically provocative edge. Eroticism in Carter is stripped of romance, and often brutally engaged with material realities. Her writing forestalls easy consumption, and instead invites thoughtful engagement with its comedic and sensual pleasures.

Biography

Born in South London, England, May 7, 1940. Early education in Balham, South London. Worked as reporter in Croydon and Surrey, 1958–1962. Attended University of Bristol, 1962–1965 (B.A. 1965 with specialty in Medieval Literature). Married Paul Carter 1960. Divorced 1972. Lived in Japan 1969–1972. Visiting professor of creative writing, Brown University, 1980–1981 (RI, USA), and Adelaide University, 1984 (South Australia). Contributor to *New Society*, *The Guardian*, and other journals. Taught creative writing, University of East Anglia, 1984–1987. Partner, Mark Pearce, from 1982. Son, Alexander, born 1983. Carter died February 16, 1992 of lung cancer.

LORENA RUSSELL

Selected Works

Burning Your Boats: The Collected Stories. The Collected Angela Carter. New York: Penguin, 1997.

The Curious Room: Plays, Film Scripts and an Opera. Edited by Mark Bell. The Collected Angela Carter. London: Chatto & Windus, 1996.

Heroes and Villains. New York: Penguin, 1969.

The Infernal Desire Machines of Doctor Hoffman: A Novel. London: Hart-Davis, 1972.

Love: A Novel. Rev. ed. London: Penguin, 1988.

The Magic Toyshop. London: Heinemann, 1967.

Nights at the Circus. New York: Penguin, 1984.

The Passion of New Eve. London: Virago, 1982.

The Sadeian Woman and the Ideology of Pornography. New York: Pantheon Books, 1978.

Shaking a Leg: Journalism and Writings. Ed. Jennifer S. Uglow. The Collected Angela Carter. London: Chatto & Windus, 1997.

Saints and Strangers. 1st American ed. New York, N.Y., U.S.A.: Viking, 1986.

Shadow Dance. New York: Penguin, 1996.

Wise Children. New York: Penguin, 1993.

Further Reading

Bristow, Joseph, and Trev Lynn Broughton. *The Infernal Desires of Angela Carter: Fiction, Femininity, Feminism*. Studies in Twentieth-Century Literature, London and New York: Longman, 1997.

Easton, Alison. *Angela Carter*. New Casebooks, New York: St. Martin's Press, 2000.

Gamble, Sarah. *Angela Carter: Writing From the Frontline*. Edinburgh: Edinburgh UP, 1997.

Lee, Alison. *Angela Carter*. Twayne's English Authors Series, New York and London: Twayne Pub.; Prentice Hall International, 1997.

Müller, Anja. *Angela Carter: Identity Constructed/Deconstructed*. Heidelberg: Universitätsverlag C. Winter, 1997.

Peach, Linden. *Angela Carter*. Modern Novelists. New York: St. Martin's Press, 1998.

Roemer, Danielle M. and Cristina Bacchilega. ed., *Angela Carter and the Fairy Tale*. Detroit: Wayne State University, 2001.

Sage, Lorna. *Angela Carter*. Plymouth, UK: Northcote House, 1994.

———. *Flesh and the Mirror*. London: Virago, 1994.

Tucker, Lindsey, ed. *Critical Essays on Angela Carter*. New York: G.K. Hall, 1998.

See also **Feminism**

CASANOVA, GIACOMO GIROLAMO

1725–1798
Venetian adventurer and autobiographer

History of My Life

Though Casanova was the author of a novel, several satires, plays, and various historical, etymological, and mathematical studies; his fame rests entirely on his *History of My Life*, first published in 1822. This libertine memoir differs radically in conception from traditional autobiographies, which in the eighteenth century were generally reconstructions of the public career of a man of letters (Gibbon, Goldoni) or, after Rousseau, descriptions of the author's psychological or "moral" development. Casanova instead recounts a private history that many of his contemporaries would have regarded as frivolous, immoral, or criminal, explaining in his preface that he is writing to re-experience in memory the pleasures he can no longer enjoy directly in his old age. Despite his title, Casanova's project is an erotic rather than a historical one: to recuperate, through narration, the sensual charge of past experience.

This intention to relive the pleasures of the past rather than analyze them may explain the sprawling, seemingly disorganized proliferation of erotic memories in *History of My Life*. Unlike other libertine writers (such as Duclos, whom he admired), Casanova does not tell the story of a young man's sexual and social education. Only his earliest, innocent crushes are presented as learning experiences. Casanova respects the virginity of Bettina, his tutor's sister, and of Lucia, the daughter of the manager of an estate where he is a guest, with disastrous consequences: the former marries a man who abuses and abandons her, while the latter is seduced by a local rake, then runs away from home and becomes a prostitute. He concludes that it is misguided to respect a woman's honor. After this initial, rudimentary lesson, his love affairs teach him nothing; the narrator claims to have been the "dupe" of women until he was sixty.

Casanova's subsequent relationships are marked by another departure from the libertine novel, where the hero often treats women as a form of prey to be manipulated and dominated. Scenes of domination are rare in *History of My Life*, and their tone is almost always jocular. For example, when a prudish newlywed disapproves of his flirtatious banter, sex provides a comic comeuppance. Alone with Casanova in an open carriage during a thunderstorm, she is paralyzed by her fear of the lightning. He seizes the opportunity to raise her skirts, sit her on his lap, and "carry off the most complete victory that ever a skillful swordsman won" (*History of My Life* 1: 153). The prude's false sense of modesty prevents her from objecting—if she protests, the carriage driver will turn and see everything—and in the end, she allows Casanova to have his way, admitting that he has taught her a strange lesson.

More often, the autobiographer stages his love affairs in ways that call his mastery into question, and that sometimes challenge even the fundamental distinction between male and female. In 1745, Casanova meets Bellino, a young castrato soprano. Fascinated by the castrato's mixture of masculine and feminine, and convinced that he is a woman, Casanova tries repeatedly to convince him/her to strip, and is driven nearly mad by Bellino's refusal. Casanova at last glimpses Bellino's body, and sees what he takes to be a penis, but this only increases his agitation. When the castrato comes to his bed, the narrator describes their climax before finally telling us that Bellino is indeed a woman—what he had seen was a false penis, worn so that the young singer could pass as a castrato in the Papal State, where women were not permitted on stage. According to François Roustang, Casanova's obsession with the indeterminacy of Bellino's gender suggests a basic trait of his personality: a simultaneous fear of and fascination with the loss of gender differentiation. Far from expressing a confident sense of male mastery, the libertinism of *History of My Life* may be rooted in Casanova's fear of being like a woman.

Just as Casanova's sexual fears are expressed in gender switching and indeterminacy, so his social anxieties come to the surface in episodes that blur and confuse categories of class. In Cesena, Casanova encounters the French adventuress Henriette, who has been traveling in Italy, disguised as a man. As in the case of Bellino, it is Henriette's initial indeterminacy of gender that sparks Casanova's interest (Roustang 98). When Henriette appears in women's clothes, however, she is transformed into the perfect image of a noblewoman. Now Casanova is fascinated by the indeterminacy of her social status rather than her gender: as a penniless adventuress, Henriette is an outcast, beyond the margins of society, yet at the same time she is a scintillating conversationalist, perfectly at home in aristocratic company, whose exquisite manners and social graces show all the marks of superior breeding. Her fascinating ambiguity is increased by her refusal to tell anyone her story or even her true name—that is, to define herself by an explicit avowal of her social position. Their romantic idyll comes to an end when she is recognized by a family acquaintance in Parma. She returns to France, leaving a message for Casanova, written with a diamond on the windowpane of his room at the inn: "You will forget Henriette, too."

In the story of Henriette, the erotic and the social are connected by the author's intention to problematize categories of both gender and class. In other episodes, Casanova links the erotic and the social through acts of homosocial bonding, a process in which a woman functions as a token of exchange in the formation of a relationship between two men. This can be seen at its simplest in Casanova's trip to Constantinople in 1745. There he meets a prominent Turkish official named Ismail, and becomes the object of his homosexual advances, which he initially rejects. However, when the Turk asks Casanova to join him in spying on his harem as they bathe, he becomes so aroused by the spectacle that he allows Ismail to masturbate him—after which he considers it his social duty to do the same for his host, despite his professed lack of homosexual attraction. The women in this episode never see or speak to Casanova; they function only as a means by which a bond is established between an older, socially superior man, and a younger man who is his social inferior. The same pattern is repeated many times in

History of My Life, most strikingly in the relationship between Casanova, his intended bride C.C., the nun M.M., and the French ambassador to Venice. In 1753, Casanova falls in love with C.C., a merchant's daughter, and asks for her hand in marriage. Her father responds by sending her to a convent on the island of Murano. Casanova attends the convent church every Sunday so that C.C. can see him from behind the grating where she is cloistered. He also catches the eye of M.M., who sends him a note inviting him to an assignation. Casanova later learns that C.C. and M.M. have become lesbian lovers and that M.M. is also the lover of François de Bernis, the French ambassador to Venice, and that de Bernis was watching through a peephole as he made love to the nun. De Bernis is impressed with both Casanova's physical prowess and his culture, and the three are soon established in a *ménage à trois*. Casanova is delighted to share the society of this leading member of the French ruling class, and after some initial hesitation he decides that he is socially obligated to reciprocate by allowing the ambassador to sleep with C.C. The advantages of this homosocial bond are both practical (the French peer's patronage is essential to Casanova's success in Paris after his escape from prison) and psychological: the exchange of women allows the son of an actress to see himself as in some sense the equal of de Bernis, whom he calls "the king of men."

The formation of a bond with a socially superior man is so important to Casanova that he twice repeats this strategy at the level of pure fantasy, telling us that he discovered and cultivated two young women who go on to become mistresses of Louis XV. Casanova does not literally share either of them with the king, nor is the king ever aware of Casanova's role in providing them, but the autobiographer nonetheless takes great satisfaction in this imaginary link. Louis XV's attraction to the women the adventurer has "given" him is transposed, in Casanova's mind, to an unwitting expression of esteem for the "giver." The beautiful O'Morphi and Mademoiselle Roman thus act less as objects of Casanova's desire than as a relay for an imaginary exchange of desire between king and commoner.

In the libidinal economy of *History of My Life*, the autobiographer's happiness and social well-being are guaranteed by this constant circulation of desire, either between men and women, between two women (Casanova is a spectator of numerous lesbian encounters), or between men, usually via homosocial bonding. Blocking this exchange leads to frustration, despair, and thoughts of death. This occurs during Casanova's trip to England, where he becomes obsessed with the courtesan Marianne Charpillon, who leads him on and bilks him of large sums of money. In Casanova's view, Charpillon is the epitome of the coquette, whose pleasure consists of stimulating desire while at the same time denying any trace of a corresponding desire in herself. For the first time in his life, Casanova is unable either to inspire passion in a woman or to reduce her to a sexual object: when he purchases Charpillon's favors for an evening, she positions herself in such a way that he cannot complete the act without forcibly raping her. Her impenetrable refusal of his desire reduces him to despair; he plans to commit suicide by throwing himself into the Thames, and is saved only by a chance meeting with a friend. Casanova regards his humiliation by Charpillon as the beginning of his life's decline, as if her refusal to keep his desire in circulation had irremediably weakened the foundations of his libertine system.

The remainder of *History of My Life* is in large part the story of a downward spiral of failure to find acceptable employment, of gambling losses, arrests, and expulsions from city after city. As unpleasant memories are increasingly mixed with the pleasant ones, it becomes more and more difficult for the aging Casanova to deny his precarious social position. The autobiographer compensates by again blurring the normal categories of sex and class in an episode of idyllic incest, articulated in two stages. In 1761, Casanova goes to Naples to visit his old acquaintance, the Duke of Matalona. Though the Duke is impotent, he preserves social appearances by keeping a mistress named Leonilda. Casanova falls in love with her, and they plan to marry, but just before the ceremony he is shocked to discover that she is his daughter by Donna Lucrezia, a middle-class lawyer's wife with whom he had had an affair seventeen years earlier. Casanova claims to be relieved that he had not slept with Leonilda before knowing her true identity, but he proceeds to commit what might be called incest at one remove: the three spend the night together, and Casanova

"quenches his fire" in Donna Lucrezia while gazing rapturously at their daughter, who in turn looks on enthralled. Desire again circulates and pleasure is shared in a parody of the bourgeois family that bends, but does not quite break, the incest taboo.

In the second, highly ambiguous part of his relationship with Leonilda, Casanova performs and at the same time disavows an act of subversion aimed at the familial structure of the aristocracy. In 1770, Casanova discovers that Leonilda is now the wife of the Marquis della C. . ., who married her in the hope of producing an heir, but whose age and infirmity make it difficult for him to carry out his conjugal duties. As a mason and a freethinker, the Marquis does not consider himself bound by the prejudices of society; according to Donna Lucrezia, he would have no objection if his heir were sired by another man. Like the Marquis, who apparently sees the prohibition against infidelity as a matter of social prejudice, Casanova views incest as socially taboo but perfectly normal in the state of nature: "She was my daughter, and nature, far from preventing me from having all the feelings of a lover toward her, forbade me to have only the inconsequential ones of father" (*History of My Life* 11: 307). This time, Casanova and Leonilda consummate the act—but they do so nearly unintentionally, without guilt or remorse, as the result of "an almost involuntary movement" that conveniently absolves them of responsibility.

Up to this point, Casanova has elaborated the episode within the terms of the broader eighteenth-century debate over nature and civilization. The continuation of the story focuses attention more narrowly on the aristocratic family. Revived by Casanova's engaging company, the Marquis declares his intention to "visit" his wife that evening, and Casanova wishes them "a fine boy to be delivered in nine months." Through Donna Lucrezia, the Marquis expresses gratitude to Casanova for the heir he is now sure he will have, but the autobiographer is deliberately ambiguous about the reason for the Marquis' thanks: is he grateful because he believes Casanova has sired his heir, as the narrator had previously hinted he would be? Or because he thinks Casanova has given him the strength to impregnate Leonilda himself? The question is not resolved, even when the narrator reports that the boy born nine months later resembled the Marquis.

Casanova's deliberate coyness about the parentage of Leonilda's child allows a double reading of this episode. If the baby's father is taken to be the Marquis, despite Casanova's hints to the contrary, then the autobiographer presents himself as the source of the elderly nobleman's new potency, symbolically superior to the flaccid aristocracy he has rejuvenated. But if the child is seen as Casanova's, despite the resemblance to the Marquis, then the autobiographer appears to go a step further, piercing the class barriers by which he had been excluded and leaving within them a son who, as a child of incest, is a highly overdetermined reproduction of himself: Casanova sired upon Casanova by Casanova.

The unruly proliferation of erotic memories in *History of My Life* is unified by an underlying philosophy of pleasure, perhaps loosely influenced by Condillac's popularization of the idea that human mental processes are based entirely on sensory perception. Casanova claims that he enjoys not only delicate sensations, but also "... high game on the very edge, and cheeses whose perfection is reached when the little creatures that inhabit them become visible. As for women, I have always found that the one I was in love with smelled good, and the more copious her sweat, the sweeter I found it" (*History of My Life* 1: 32). The wide range of his tastes, he insists, makes him capable of more pleasure than less open-minded men. Pleasure is just not a matter of solitary sensation, however; it must be given as well as taken. Casanova repeatedly underscores his ability to keep his sexual partners "swooning." His description of a seven-hour bout with M.M. is typical: "She was astonished to find herself capable of so much pleasure, for I had shown her many things which she thought were fictions. I did what she did not think she was entitled to ask me to do to her, and I taught her that the slightest constraint spoils the greatest pleasure" (*History of My Life* 4: 52). Nor is the sharing of pleasure limited to sex. In all social intercourse, pleasure given is the source of pleasure received, as Casanova suggests in a description of his dinner parties in Paris: "I matched well-chosen guests with exquisite suppers, at which my company saw that my pleasure depended on the pleasure I provided for them." (*History of My Life* 5: 230). It is precisely this joyous *exchange* of pleasure, both within the text and between text and reader, that distinguishes Casanova's *History of My Life* from the work of libertine thinkers such as Sade, and that constitutes the source of its enduring popularity.

Biography

Born in Venice, 2 April 1725, the son of an actor and an actress. Educated privately and at the University of Padua, 1734–1742. Unsuccessfully attempted a career in the Church, then in the military, 1743–1745. Unofficially adopted by Venetian senator Zuanne Bragadin, an enthusiast of the occult sciences, after Casanova convinced him that he possessed the secret of the *cabala*. Traveled in Italy and France, 1749–1753. Returned to Venice, joining a *ménage à trois* with the French ambassador and a nun. Imprisoned in 1755. Escaped in 1756, fled to Paris, participated in the foundation of the French state lottery and became wealthy. In 1757, met the Marquise d'Urfé, a student of alchemy and magic; swindled her repeatedly, claiming to have the power to regenerate her as a man. Invested in a silk-printing business; suspected of fraud in its bankruptcy and briefly imprisoned. Left France in 1759 to wander throughout Europe. Traveled to England in 1763; became obsessed with and was swindled by the courtesan Marianne Charpillon. Fled England to avoid prosecution for debt; sought employment at the royal courts of Prussia, Russia, and Poland, without success. Returned to Venice in 1774, but fled again in 1782, after a quarrel with a powerful nobleman. Accepted a position as librarian to Count Josef von Waldstein in 1785 and spent his last years at the Count's estate in Dux. Began his *History of My Life* circa 1790, telling the story of over a hundred love affairs; it remained unfinished at the time of his death on 4 June 1798.

TED EMERY

Editions

On his deathbed, Casanova entrusted the unfinished manuscript of *History of My Life* to his sister's son-in law, whose son sold it to the Brockhaus publishing firm in 1820. The first edition appeared in German translation from 1822 to 1828. The first version in the original French was published between 1826–1838, in an adaptation by Jean Laforgue, who altered Casanova's text significantly. All modern editions and translations were based on Laforgue until the publication of the Brockhaus-Plon edition of 1960–1962, which reproduced the text of the original manuscript. Of the French language editions currently in print, only Laffont reprints the text of Brockhaus-Plon; all others are based on Laforgue. At this writing, the only complete English translation based on Brockhaus-Plon is that of Willard Trask.

Casanova, Giacomo Girolamo. *Histoire de ma vie. Édition intégrale.* 12 vols. in 6. Wiesbaden and Paris: F.A. Brockhaus and Librairie Plon, 1960–1962.
———. *Histoire de ma vie; suivi de textes inédits.* Preface, Francis Lacassin. 12 vols. in 3. Paris: Laffont, 1993.
———. *History of My Life.* 12 vols. in 6. Trans. Willard R. Trask. New York: Harcourt, Brace, and World, 1966–1971. Rpt. 12 vols. in 3. Baltimore: Johns Hopkins University Press, 1997.

Further Reading

Caplan, Jay. "Drawing Kings: Casanova and Voltaire." In *In The King's Wake: Post-Absolutist Culture in France.* Chicago and London: Univ. of Chicago Press, 1999.
Childs, J. Rives. *Casanova: A New Perspective.* New York: Paragon House, 1988.
Craig, Cynthia C. "Gender, Genre, and Reading in the Texts of Giacomo Casanova." In *RLA: Romance Languages Annual* 7 (1995): 227–233.

Emery, Ted. "*Casanova Casanova*, the Novel, and the Woman as Desiring Subject: The Case of Bettina." *Studies in Eighteenth Century Culture*, 33. Baltimore and London: Johns Hopkins University Press, 2004. 277–292.
Flem, Lydia. *Casanova: The Man Who Really Loved Women.* translated by Catherine Temerson. New York: Farrar, Strauss, Giroux, 1997.
Kavanagh, Thomas M. "Casanova's Autobiography of Chance." In Thomas M. Kavanagh, ed. *Chance, Culture, and the Literary Text.* Michigan Romance Studies, 14. Ann Arbor: Univ. of Michigan, Dept. of Romance Languages, 1994. 151–172.
Luna, Marie Françoise. *Casanova mémorialiste.* Paris: Champion, 1998.
Roustang, François. *The Quadrille of Gender: Casanova's Memoirs.* translated by Anne Vila. Stanford, CA: Stanford Univ. Press, 1988.
Roy, Jeanne-Hélène. "Fashioning Identities: Casanova's Encounter with La Charpillon." *Intermédiaire des Casanovistes* 18 (2001): 1–9.
Thomas, Chantal. *Casanova: Un Voyage libertin.* Paris: De Noel, 1985.
———. "The Role of Female Homosexuality in Casanova's Memoirs." translated by Noah Guynn. *Yale French Studies* 94 (1998): 179–183.

CATALAN

The Middle Ages and the Baroque Period

The first examples of Catalan erotic literature are to be found in the Middle Ages, when the influence of the Occitan troubadours led several poets to imitate their style and themes. The best erotic poems are by Guillem de Berguedà (c. 1138–c. 1196) and Cerverí de Girona (XIII). In Cerverí's ironic 'Viadeyra,' for example, a woman is compelled by the poet to choose between her husband and her lover. In the fourteenth century, Bernat Metge (1340/1346–1413) adapted the second part of the poem *De vetula,* falsely attributed to Ovid, to Catalan prose. *Ovidi enamorat,* an ironic story about a poet who manages to be reunited with his lover twenty years after their first meeting, contains a detailed description of feminine beauty. Jaume Roig (?–1478) wrote the moralistic narration in verse, *Espill o el llibre de les dones* (1460), in order to advise young male lovers. In his misogynous work, Roig regrets women's attractiveness, which according to the author is used to control men. The satirical and anonymous poem of the fifteenth century, *Col·loqui de les dames,* also merits consideration. In it a married woman, a widow, and a devout woman, all of them apparently respectable, chat in a shameless tone about their sexual adventures and experiences. The poetic work by Francesc de la Via (c. 1380–c. 1445) is characterized by the sense of humor and the joy of life, often described with great sensuality. The best example of erotic literature of this period, however, is the chivalry novel *Tirant lo Blanc* by Joanot Martorell (1413–1465). After the Middle Ages, Catalan literature suffered a period of decadence that affected the sixteenth, seventeenth, and eighteenth centuries, and brought with it the lack of highbrow literary tradition. Until the end of the nineteenth century, then, eroticism could almost exclusively be found in the popular literature.

The Baroque period brought about a fusion of satire, eroticism, and scatology. The most representative author is the vicar Rector de Vallfogona, pseudonym of Francesc Vicent Garcia (1578/1579–1623). With poems like 'En apreci de estar enamorat,' extremely gross description of the physical appearance of a lady, he originated a school of authors called *vallfogonisme*. Albert Rossich published a selection of this kind of poetry, most of it anonymous, in *Poesia eròtica i pornogràfica catalana del segle XVII* (1989). The popular theater of the period also contains many sexual and scatological references; the most representative examples are the plays *Los amors de Melisendra* and *La infanta Tellina i el rei Matarot*, attributed to Francesc Mulet (1624–1675). Joaquim Martí edited some of these plays in *Col·loquis eròtico-burlescos del segle XVIII* (1996).

Eroticism and Scandal between 1850–1936

In the nineteenth century there is a cultural rebirth, and from this period onwards, popular and highbrow literature coexist, but only the popular one will allow elements of eroticism. The most famous plays of the period is *El Virgo de Vicenteta* (1845), by Josep Bernat i Baldoví (1809–1864). Far from the idealized woman portrayed by the Romantic Catalan authors, Vicenteta is very explicit in relation to her sexual needs, which she considers unattended by her husband. The success of this play originated a string of analogous works that have a similar structure and topic, with a husband cheated on by his wife. Pitarra, pseudonym of Frederic Soler (1839–1895), wrote *Don Jaume* in 1875, a parody that mocks Catalan history by means of sexual and lewd references. Because of its controversial content it achieved great success and had many imitators, such as Antoni Bulbena i Tosell (1854–1946) reported in *La bibliografia eròtico i priàpica catalano-valenciana* (1920), the first essay devoted to erotic literature in Catalan. At the end of the nineteenth century, playwrights from Barcelona developed a kind of popular theater which lacked explicitness owing to censorship and based its effectiveness on provocative language that exploited double meanings and the slang of prostitution. These plays

were performed in a district of Barcelona called El Paral·lel, soon to be known all over Europe as a very tolerant and dissolute area. It attracted, for example, the interest of Jean Genet (1910–1986), who described this underworld in *Journal du voleur* (1949). Some of the best known playwrights were Amichatis, pseudonym of Josep Amich (1888–1965) and Josep Montero (1869–1942).

At the beginning of the twentieth century, the social conservatism brought rise to several controversies around novels that mixed religion and sexuality. The cultural movement called *Modernisme* integrated eroticism into its program, because it was considered a crucial feature of the human being. In these novels, landscape, religion, and symbolism were loaded with erotic content; sex was presented as a negative force, uncontrollable and destructive. The biggest controversy was created by Bertrana's *Josafat* (1906), which tells the relationship of a prostitute with a bell ringer and takes place in the cathedral of Girona. Prudenci Bertrana (1867–1941) dealt with a similar topic in *Nàufrags* (1907), which narrates the frustrated love between a priest and his cousin. Another good example is *Solitud* (1905) by Víctor Català, pseudonym of Caterina Albert (1869–1966), with a female protagonist who is raped in the mountains.

During the 20s, the avant-garde movements and the development of the psychological novel lead to a new conception of sexuality. In relation to the avant-garde literature, *El poema de la rosa als llavis* (1923) by Joan Salvat Papasseit (1894–1924) features an uninhibited poet that guides a naïve young woman towards the erotic pleasures of life. This triumph of sensuality has been considered by critics the first and finest example of contemporary erotic poetry in Catalan. The Catalan psychological novel, with very few exceptions, is far from the explicitness of D.H. Lawrence. Carles Soldevila (1892–1967) explored the feminine psychology in *Fanny* (1929), *Eva* (1931), and *Valentina* (1933), which all take place in El Paral·lel. These novels were at the center of a heated controversy, since they depicted a new femininity through the portrayal of a rebellious woman that faces and frees herself from the social conventions of the bourgeois family. From a more humoristic point of view, in *Judita* (1930), Francesc Trabal (1898–1957) told the story of a passionate *amour fou* charged with sensuality. The biggest scandal, however, was provoked by Cèsar August Jordana (1893–1958) and his novel *Una altra mena d'amor* (1931). It narrates the relationship of a young man with a chorus girl of Paral·lel, from their initial desire to their final separation, and it reflects, in detail, the dissolute life of this district. This is also the topic of *Vida privada* (1932), a novel by Josep Maria de Sagarra (1894–1961) that portrays the decadence of Catalan aristocracy, corrupted by sex scandals, vices, and hypocrisy. The author depicts a cosmopolitan, two-sided Barcelona: during the day the characters live in the elegant district of l'Eixample; whereas by night they frequent the slum areas of the city.

The Arrival of Democracy and the Rise of Erotic Literature

The strict Catholicism of the Francoist dictatorship (1939–1975) established a harsh moral censorship. Moreover, it also banned the use of Catalan. As a response to the censorship endured during 36 years, the intellectual Joan Fuster claimed in 1978 that it was urgent to save the erotic patrimony of Catalan culture. During the late 70s, democracy allowed not only a more explicit eroticism, but forms of sexuality that had never been represented so far. Democracy also brought about the desire to normalize Catalan culture in all its aspects, including eroticism and sexuality. The peak of this normalization, which included the anthology *Antologia de la poesia eròtica catalana del segle XX* (1978) by Josep M. Sala-Valldaura, arrived when the group of writers known as Ofèlia Dracs won the Spanish erotic literature prize, Sonrisa Vertical, with the book of short stories *Deu pometes té el pomer* (1980). Manuel de Pedrolo (1918–1990), a very prolific author that cultivated all genres, published the novel *Els quaderns d'en Marc* (1984) anonymously, even after the end of Francoism and the lifting of censorship. Its secret authorship converted this jovial novel about a man who devotes his life to find and seduce the most beautiful Catalan women is a milestone of the Catalan erotic genre. *Obres púbiques*, his second erotic work, was published posthumously in 1991.

The poet Vicent Andrés Estellers (1924–1993) considered eroticism as one of the basic thrusts of life, and his poetry describes anonymous women that attracted the poet's desire. Sex is very present in all his work, with both a gentle and a bad side. Eroticism also goes in varied forms through the novels by Miquel Àngel Riera (1930–1996), such as *Panorama amb dona* (1983) or *Els déus inaccessibles* (1987). They present a carnal and sensual description of life, often linked with Majorcan landscape. Gabriel Ferrater in *Les dones i els dies* (1968) and Miquel Martí i Pol (1929–2003) in *Estimada Marta* (1978) also explored heterosexual desire in his poetry.

As for the new kinds of eroticism, in 1958 Blai Bonet (1926–1997) published *El mar*, a novel with strong homoerotic content, and Manuel de Pedrolo wrote in 1959 *Un amor fora ciutat*; it could only be published in 1970 and the author was prosecuted for public scandal. However, it was the end of the dictatorship that brought an important corpus of works with lesbian and gay eroticism. In relation to prose, the following authors must be mentioned: Carme Riera (1948-) with *Te deix, amor, el mar com a penyora* (1975), Biel Mesquida (1947–) with *L'adolescent de sal*, banned for two years and finally published in 1978, and Lluís Fernández (1945–) with *L'anarquista nu* (1978) opened new homoerotic grounds. The most prolific and controversial author was Terenci Moix (1943–2003), who wrote a number of novels and short stories with gay content, such as *La torre dels vicis capitals* (1968), *Món mascle* (1971), *La caiguda de l'imperi sodomita* (1976), *Lilí Barcelona i altres travestís* (1978), and *El dia que va morir Marilyn* (1978). The combination of Catalan identity, popular culture, and homosexuality was revulsive to the literary scene at the time. Blai Bonet (*El jove*, 1978), Biel Mesquida (*El bell país on els homes estimen els homes*, 1974), and Maria Mercè Marçal (*La germana, l'estrangera*, 1985) tackled same-sex relationships in poetry. After the explosion of the 70s, during the 80s, literature about gay and lesbian concerns was scarce, although it reappeared again in the 90s with novels such as *La passió segons Renée Vivien* by Maria Mercè Marçal (1952–1998) and *El joc del mentider* (1994) by Lluís Maria Todó (1950–).

Some of the more successful novels of the contemporary Catalan literature have an important erotic charge, which shows the importance of this topic during the first years of democracy. *La magnitud de la tragèdia* (1989) by Quim Monzó (1952–) portrays the life of a man with a permanent erection, and *Un negre amb un saxo* (1989) by Ferran Torrent (1951–) describes the atmosphere of prostitution and crime in

Valencia. *Temporada Baixa* (1990), by Maria Mercè Roca (1958–) and *Amorrada al piló* (1986) by Maria Jaén (1962–) became bestsellers thanks to their erotic content linked with new conceptions of femininity. *Temporada baixa* is a novel about jealousy and sex in which Roca contrasts a frustrated and obsessed man with his wife, a self-confident and determined woman. *Amorrada al piló*, whose popularity inspired a film version, is about a young radio announcer with a program about sexuality that avoids serious relationships and enjoys sex without complexes. The scarce essays devoted to Catalan eroticism have all been published in specialized journals with the exception of the dictionaries *Bocavulvari eròtic de la llengua catalana* by Pep Vila (1987) and *Diccionari eròtic i sexual* by Joan J. Vinyoles and Ramon Piqué (1989).

During the 80s and early 90s, important publishing houses such as La Magrana, Pòrtic, and El Llamp initiated collections of erotic literature that included novels by Catalan writers and translations of writers such as Henry Miller, Guillaume Apollinaire, the Marquis de Sade, and Pauline Réage. Pòrtic also created the prize La Piga, which was awarded to young authors such as Lluís-Anton Baulenas (1958–) and Rafael Vallbona (1960–). However, once the need to incorporate all genres in Catalan literature was fulfilled, during the mid 90s there was a decline and most of the specialized collections disappeared, arguably because eroticism had been included in mainstream literary production. Some of the short stories by Quim Monzó compiled in *Vuitanta-sis contes* (1999), for example, have to be considered among the finest examples of recent Catalan erotic literature.

The annual prize of erotic literature Vall d'Albaida created in 1993, however, shows that there is still interest in the genre.

JORDI CORNELLÀ-DETRELL

Selected Works

Martí Mestre, Joaquim, ed. *Col·loquis eròtico-burlescos del segle XVIII*, València: Alfons el Magnànim, 1996.
Rossich, Albert, ed. *Poesia eròtica i pornogràfica catalana del segle XVII*, Barcelona: Quaderns Crema, 1985.
Sala-Valldaura, J.M., ed. *Antologia de la poesia eròtica catalana del segle XX*, Barcelona: Proa, 1977.

Further Reading

Angelats, Francesc F. *L'amor i l'erotisme en la literatura catalana*, Barcelona: Barcanova, 1993.
Fernàndez, Josep-Anton. *Another Country: Sexuality and National Identity in Catalan Gay Fiction*, Leeds: Maneys for the Modern Humanities Research Association, 2000.
Fuster, Joan. "Salvem el patrimoni eròtic!" *Serra d'Or* 221 (February 1978): 35.
Renedo, Xavier. "De libidinosa amor los efectes." *L'Avenç* 123 (1989): 18–23.
Sala-Valldaura, Josep M. "Poesia catalana i erotisme." *L'Avenç* 123 (1989): 14–17.
Salvador, Vicent. "Eros i retòrica en la poesia d'Estellés." *L'Aiguadolç* 8 (1989): 35–44.
Soler i Marcet, Maria-Lourdes. "L'Amor com a deu vital o letal a la novel·la catalana moderna" In *Miscel·lània Jordi Carbonell* 6, Barcelona: Abadia de Montserrat, 1993.
Vila, Pep. "L'erotisme en l'escena catalana." *L'Avenç* 123 (1989): 24–27.
Castellanos, Jordi. "Narrativa catalana i erotisme, 1862–1936." *L'Avenç* 123 (1989): 28–33.

See also **Martorell, Joanot; Ferrater, Gabriel; Spanish Literature; Troubadours**

CATULLUS

c. 84–ca. 54 BCE
Roman poet

The best known of a circle of poets who styled themselves the *poetae novi*, Catullus left a short collection of verse in various styles—short lyrics, longer epic and narrative poems, and epigrams in the elegiac meter—altogether totaling fewer than 2300 lines. This collection of 113 poems, often audacious and fraught with sexual content, was all but completely lost at the end of antiquity and remained unknown until a single (now lost) manuscript was discovered in the thirteenth or early fourteenth century. The poems as we now have them are based on three copies of that damaged manuscript.

Apart from the obscenity and sexual insult that he frequently employed when attacking enemies, rivals, and others who displeased him, Catullus was the most erotic poet of the Roman world, rivaled in this respect only by Ovid. He worked in the tradition of Sappho, Archilochus, Anacreon, and other Greek lyricists of the seventh- to sixth-century BC who wrote in the first person singular about sexual experience. His chief erotic involvement was with a woman he calls Lesbia as a tribute to Sappho of Lesbos. This Lesbia is most often identified as Clodia Metelli, a married woman of aristocratic lineage who was some ten years older than Catullus. To judge from the 25 poems describing their relationship (13 of them mention her by name), the affair went on over a period of time, probably years, and was frequently interrupted by her infidelities and rejections of the poet. Catullus shows himself to be intense and demanding in all his relationships, sexual or not, and the poems of what is sometimes called the "Lesbia cycle," scattered through the collection, invite the inference that Lesbia was a woman of strongly independent, sexually adventurous ways who sometimes found the poet's importunities tedious if not annoying.

Like Homer presenting Helen of Troy, Catullus never describes Lesbia's appearance or the physical details of their encounters: he concentrates on the emotional effects of their turbulent affair. The couplet that best sums it up is poem 85, *Odi et amo*:

I hate and love. Why? You may ask but
It beats me. I feel it done to me, and ache.

(Ezra Pound)

One of Catullus' most striking accounts of love's betrayal and abandonment, possibly the best poetry ever written in Latin, is the lament of the legendary Cretan princess Ariadne, abandoned on a desert island by the Athenian hero Theseus after she has helped him kill the Minotaur and eloped with him. In these lines (132–201 of poem 64), Catullus seems to have projected his own experience with Lesbia into the voice of

a woman. One of the features of Catullus most valued by modern readers is his comparative freedom from the strongly masculine idiom of many classical authors. Some of this is the likely result of the poet's admiration for Sappho.

Catullus wrote other erotic poetry, ranging from a request for an afternoon of pleasure with the demimondaine Ipsitilla to a cycle of seven to nine poems about his affair with a boy named Juventius. This homosexual liaison is usually assumed to have been with a native of Verona living in Rome under the guardianship of the poet. Where the request to Ipsitilla is coarsely comical, the poems for Juventius are jealous of the boy's affection and protective of his feelings. There is also a love idyll describing a tête-à-tête between Septimius, a young Roman of the officer class, and his Greek sweetheart Acme.

The last of these reveals another aspect of Catullus' eroticism. He is an eager spectator of the sexual life of his friends. In poem 6 he demands the details of a torrid liaison in which his friend Flavius is engaged, tipped off by the noisy movements of the bed; in poem 10 he meets his friend Varus in the Forum and goes off with him to get a look at the new girl friend in her apartment; in poem 55 he wanders into the haunts of the "milky girls" to learn what new interest is keeping Camerius out of sight: "you can keep your mouth shut about this so long as I can be a participant in your *amor*." Vicarious eroticism is an important part of sexual pleasure for Catullus.

Though Catullus cannot reasonably be charged with writing pornographic poetry (as least no such poems have survived), he does defend the practice of writing sexually stimulating verse in poem 16:

A poet and his verse are different things:
He should be decent, but his poetry
Need not. His verses, if they're rather "soft"
Or shocking, and are able to excite
The readers' itchy parts, have wit and charm
Not for the little boys, but hairy men
Who don't know how to switch their tails ...

(Dorothea Wender)

The "itchy parts" in this translation are in the original *quod pruriat*, from which the modern "prurient" is derived.

Notwithstanding the raciness of his sexual language and the reckless ardor with which he pursues a disorderly and illicit affair, Catullus reveals a character that is in some respects conservative and conventional. For some readers he appears divided between the *dolce vita* of a Rome that was preoccupied with pleasure, scandal, and style and the straight-laced probity of his native Verona. Poem 17, set in a fictitious northern town named *Colonia*, suggests half-seriously that an older husband who is ignoring the wild ways of his young wife be thrown into the swamp as a sacrifice. Even in his affair with the notorious Lesbia, he more than once writes of his love as if she were a member of his family. Three of his seven long poems celebrate the institutions and ceremonies of marriage and are thoroughly traditional in the values they present.

More than a look into the life of Rome in the age of Caesar, Catullus' lyrics provide unguarded views into the complexity of a great poet under the influence of erotic forces beyond his control.

Biography

Gaius Valerius Catullus (c. 84–c. 54 BCE) was a native of Verona, Italy but spent most of his life as a poet in Rome. Little is known about Catullus except what he says about himself in his poems. The historian Suetonius says his father was a frequent host of Julius Caesar, but the poet himself was openly scornful of Caesar, accusing him (among other things) of sexually abusing young girls. None of this earned him the enmity of the future dictator, who remained an admirer. The date and circumstances of the poet's death are unknown.

DANIEL GARRISON

Editions

Fordyce, C.J. *Catullus.* Oxford 1961.
Garrison, D.H., ed. *The Student's Catullus.* 2nd. edition, University of Oklahoma Press, 1995.
Quinn, Kenneth. *Catullus. The Poems.* 2nd Edition. St. Martin's Press, 1973.
Thomson, D.F.S. *Catullus.* University of Toronto Press, 1997.

Selected Works

Haig Gasser, Julia, ed. *Catullus in English.* Penguin Books, 2001.
Goold, G.P. *Catullus.* Duckworth, 1983.
Lee, Guy. *The Poems of Catullus.* (Facing Latin and English), Oxford, 1990.

Further Reading

Martin, Charles. *Catullus.* Yale, 1992.
Quinn, Kenneth. *Approaches to Catullus.* Barnes & Noble, 1985.
Wiseman, T.P. *Catullus and His World.* Cambridge University Press, 1985.

CAVAFY, CONSTANTINE

1863–1933
Greek poet

Cavafy's eroticism often takes the form of a hesitant attraction to masculine beauty in the full bloom of a youth mythified by being viewed through the prism of an age-old Hellenism. Diffident in its expression, Cavafy's exploration of his erotic fascination only begins in earnest from 1911 onwards and comes to be identified as a major theme. Only one, short, erotic poem, "Epithimies" (1904, Desires), predates this period and anticipates frustrated desire and Hellenistic imagery as major features of Cavafy's subsequent eroticism which, as in this poem, frequently takes the form of a disillusioned meditation on the unbridgeable distance between an older poetic narrator and the ephemeral beauty of a youth he contemplates in the first-person while painfully aware of the proximity of death.

From 1911 onwards Cavafy's erotic poetry unassumingly evokes sensual moments of self-knowledge and desire in an autobiographical journey through a historically layered Alexandria, that might be said to begin with the dilemmas presented by his 1911 poem, "Ta Epikindina" [Risks]. There, a young Syrian student and fourth-century AD inhabitant of Alexandria, when faced with a choice between ascetic Christian abstinence and hedonistic pagan surrender, chooses a path of enlightenment through the pursuit of sensual pleasures, confident that his studies and willpower can afford him intellectual detachment. Two years later, the poet alludes to a night of sexual intoxication and release in "Epiga" [I Went]. Between 1913 and 1921, Cavafy writes 75 poems of which almost half are erotic, though he invariably avoids romantic lyricism in favor of restrained allusion that does, however, often promise voluptuousness. His 1917 poem "Idone" [To Pleasure] manages to celebrate the "Hara" [delight] and "Myro" [perfume] of pleasure in four lines that culminate in a pointed condemnation of "tin kathe apolafsin eroton tis rutinas" [every indulgence in habitual loves] that both views desire as a means of transcendence and rejects hackneyed poetic lyricism. Transcendence more often than not takes place in the mundane Alexandrian spaces Cavafy frequented, as in "Stou Kafeniou tin Eisodo" [1915, At The Café Entrance]. A routine setting is typically made transcendent by a classical association revealed by a frozen moment when the first-person narrator is stopped in his tracks by the entrance of an "oraio soma" [beautiful body], which he imagines must be the work of Eros at the height of his sculptural powers.

In 1918, Cavafy writes six erotic poems concerned with love's frustrations and the remembrance of past pleasures as the source of desire in the present: "Thimisou, Soma" [Body, Remember], "To Diplano Trapezi" [The Next Table], "Ap' Tes Ennia" [Since Nine O'Clock], "Kato Ap' to Spiti" [Under the House]. It is the retrospective view of these poems that also allow the first-person poetic voice to reach an acceptance of his outsider's position in relation to his inherited social class as, in "Noisis" [Understanding] he tenderly remembers his futile attempts as a guilt-ridden young man to mend his dissolute ways. With hindsight, he draws strength from the knowledge that the pleasures of his past are the source of his life as a poet, whose vocation it seems is to revive the feelings of the past, stretching back to antiquity in the case of "Aristoboulos" or a later poem such as "Technourgos Crateron" [1921, Silversmith].

His increasing temporal distance from those pleasures allows him to reflect on the ephemeral sensations of his past and on the relationship between mortality and beauty. Other such poems are "Makria [Far Away] (1914), "Griza" [Grey] (1917), "O Ilios tou Apoyevmatos" [The Afternoon Sun] (1919), "Tou Pliou" [On Board Ship] (1919), a group distinguished by taking the form of recollections of moments of sexual pleasure and adoration of the loved ones' now absent physical features.

Of the 51 poems Cavafy publishes in the last 11 years of his life, 23 are erotic works that, beyond developing the features I have discussed above, largely deal with the bitterness, separations, betrayals, and social degradation of homosexual love. Poems such as: "En Apognosi" [In Despair] (1923), "Prin Tous Allaxei o Chronos" [Before Time Should Change Them] (1924), "Sto Pliktiko Chorio" [In the Dreary Village] (1925), "To Eikosi Pempton Etos tou Biou Tou" [The Twenty-Fifth Year of his Life] (1925), "Mesa Sta Kapileia" [In the Tavernas] (1926), "Meres tou 1896" [Days of 1896] (1927), "Meres tou 1901" [Days of 1901] (1927), "Enas Neos, tis Technis tou Logou - sto Eikosi Pempton Etos tou" [A Young Poet in his Twenty-Fourth Year] (1928). Even among the shadows and twilight, imagery the poet favors, and the low dives and brothels he alludes to, the reader still catches glimmers in some of the pieces just mentioned and more fully in others such as "Dio Nei, 23 eos 24 Eton" [Two Young Men, 23 to 24 Years Old] (1927) and "O Kathreptis stin Eisodo" [The Mirror in the Front Hall] (1930) of the desire that makes Cavafy's poems so vital: the wish to continue basking in pleasure and beauty, if only in the memory, before even memory dies.

Biography

Born in Alexandria, Egypt, April 29, 1863, the youngest of nine children of a prosperous Greek merchant family. Probably educated at home until 1872, when his family moved to Liverpool, via Marseilles, Paris, and London, after his father's death in 1870, joining his two eldest brothers, who had left earlier to take over the offices of the family cotton business there and in London. In 1877, a downturn in the family's fortunes and the liquidation of the family business obliged most of the family to return to Egypt, after having spent a period of time in

London. Little known about this period, following the Egyptian financial crash of 1876, except that he undertook commercial studies at the Hermes Lyceum from 1881–1882. In 1882, after a period of civil unrest and the bombardment of Alexandria by the British fleet, the family was forced to leave for three financially difficult years in Constantinople, where Constantine, for the first time, explored his homosexuality in the city's brothels. In 1885, returned to Alexandria and settled there. He continued to study independently while working at the cotton exchange and writing for the *Telegrafos* [*Telegraph*] newspaper. In 1889, he entered the Ministry of Public Projects and worked there until his retirement in 1922. During this period made short visits to Paris, London, and in 1903, for the first time, to Athens. Increasingly, from 1912 onwards, withdrew from social life and devoted his time to poetry. Founded the literary review *Alexandrini Techni* [*Alexandrian Art*] in 1926. Died of throat cancer in Alexandria, 29 April 1933.

JOHN D. PERIVOLARIS

Selected Works

Poetry

Piimata. 2 vols, edited by G.P. Savidis. Athens: Ikaros, 1963.

Poems by C.P. Cavafy. Translated by John Mavrogordato. London, Chatto and Windus, 1951.
Présentation critique de C. Cavafy, 1863–1933 suivie d'une traducion intégrale des ses Poèmes. Translated by Marguerite Yourcenar and C. Dimaras, Paris: Gallimard, 1958.
The Complete Poems of Cavafy. Translated by Rae Dalven, New York and London: Harvest, 1961.
C.P. Cavafy: Anekdota Piimata, 1882–1923 [*C.P. Cavafy: Unpublished Poems, 1882–1923*]. Edited by George Savidis. Athens: Ikaros, 1968.
Passions and Ancient Days: Twenty One New Poems. Translated by Edmund Keeley and George Savidis, New York: The Dial Press, 1971; London: The Hogarth Press, 1972.
C.P. Cavafy: Collected Poems. Revised edition, edited by George Savidis, translated by Edmund Keeley and Philip Sherrard, Princeton, NJ: Princeton University Press, 1992.

Further Reading

Bien, Peter. *Constantine Cavafy*, New York: Columbia University Press, 1964.
Bowra, C.M. "Constantine Cavafy and the Greek Past." In *The Creative Experiment*. London: Macmillan, 1949.
Keeley, Edmund. *Cavafy's Alexandria*. Princeton, New Jersey: Princeton University Press, 1996.
Liddell, Robert. *Cavafy: A Biography*. 2nd edition, London: Duckworth, 2000.
Savidis, George, ed., *O Cavafis tou Seferi (Seferis's Cavafy)*. Athens: Hermes, 1984.
Sherrard, Philip. "Constantine Cavafy." In *The Marble Threshing Floor*. London: Vallentine, Mitchell, 1956.

CAYLUS, ANNE CLAUDE PHILIPPE DE

1692–1765
French playwright and novelist

Le Bordel ou le Jeanfoutre puni

A comedy in three acts, *Le bordel ou le jeanfoutre puni* [*The Brothel or the Punished Trickster*], is attributed to the Count of Caylus. From the start, the spectator (or reader) is warned: "The scene takes place in Paris, in a brothel." Valère, a debauched brawler, lusts after his cousin, the chaste Isabelle, who is in love with Clitandre. He sets up a rendezvous with her at Madame Bru, a famous Madam, by forging her lover's signature, whom he also invites to dine at the same place to compromise him. Thus appear Tonton, Desprez, Poirier, Fanchon, the ladies of the house. Valentin, Valère's servant, who is as debauched as his master, takes advantage of them. The plot fails. A police superintendent comes in with his archers to restore order: Valère is jailed in For-L'Evêque, some of the girls are released, the others taken to the General Hospital.

The play shows the great popularity of the private theaters in the eighteenth-century. Nobles, farmers general, and famous actresses stage, in their private mansions, obscene parades; licentious plays that are all erotic spectacles, whose more or less clandestine audience are the libertine society of the time. Some plays from the "ribald" repertoire are still known: *L'Art de foutre, ou Paris foutant* [*The Art of Fucking or Paris Fucking*] from Baculard Arnaud, *Le tempérament* [*The Disposition*] and *La nouvelle Messaline* [*The New Messalina*] from Grandval fils, *Vasta, reine de Bordélie* [*Vasta, Queen of Brothelia*] attributed to Piron, or *Le luxurieux* [*The Lecherous*] from Legrand, a member of the Comédie-Française.... For its part, the Théâtre de la Foire regularly parodies the new creations (without reaching the same licentiousness of course). Erotic theater rests on two principles, the obscenity of the language and the parody of the classical repertoire. In *La nouvelle Messaline*, Conine, Messaline's servant, says to Vitus: "She switches prick and despises yours./ Switch cunt, too and despise hers./ If you agree, I offer you mine."

In *Le bordel* [*The Brothel*], the characters only think about pleasure, prick in hand, the word fuck on the lips. It is about "calling things by their names." Valère says no to a girl "because she looks dainty when she says the word fuck." And one goes from *foutre* [fuck] to *fouteur* [fucker], *foutaise* [trifles], or *foutu* [fucked].

> Madame Dru: What is it that you want to do in this room you're asking me for?
> Valère: To fuck.
> Madame Dru: With whom?
> Valère: A cunt.

This three-act play ignores the rules of classical theater. The arrival of the superintendent at the end of the play is itself a play on theatrical denouement (as in Molière's *Tartuffe*, e.g.). It will not be until Sade that the one who maintains order will become a hardened criminal, whose entrance signifies added debauchery.

Caylus's play became a quick success. Voltaire wrote to one of his correspondents on February 18, 1740, "I hear that Gogo, Frétillon, the écosseuses, Prince Titi, the comedy of the brothel, the andouilles are being sold with great success. The foreigners never cease to admire the protection we grant to fine arts in France." (*Histoire de Gogo*, 1739, [*Story of Gogo*]; *Histoire de mademoiselle Cronel, dite Frétillon*, 1740, [*Story of Miss Cronel, also known as Frétillon*]; *Les ecosseuses, ou les oeufs de Pâques*, 1739, [*The Shellers or the Easter Eggs*]).

Histoire de Guillaume, cocher [Story of Guillaume, Coachman]

Every week, the count of Caylus invites to his home the members of the society of the Bout-du-banc, who also meet on Thursdays at the home of the count's mistress, the actress Miss Quinaut. Crébillon, Duclos, Voisenon, Collé, La Chaussée, Cahusac, Moncrif, and Mme de Graffigny attend these meetings. A writing-desk is set up on the table. Full of verve and wits stimulated by the competition, the members of this joyous literary society take turns to write a parody or licentious tale, a burlesque letter, a vulgar dialog written in the popular fashion, using the fishmongers of Les Halles's argot (it is in this style that Vadé publishes his *Lettres de la Grenouillère, entre M. Jérosme Dubois, pêcheur du Gros-Caillou et Melle Nanette Dubut, blanchisseuse de linge fin*, [*Letters from the Grenouillère, between Mr. Jérosme Dubois, fisherman from Gros-Caillou and Miss Nanette Dubut, washerwoman*]. Thus are also published *Les ecosseuses ou les oeufs de Pâques* (1739); *Les soirées du Bois de Boulogne* (1742) [*Evenings at the Bois de Boulogne*]; *Les etrennes de la Saint-Jean* (1742) [*Saint-Jean's Day's Gift*]; *Recueil de ces messieurs* (1745) [*These Gentlemen's Collection*]; *Quelques aventures des bals des bois* (1745) [*A Few Adventures from the Woods' Balls*]; *Les manteaux* (1746) [*The Coats*]; *Les fêtes roulantes* (1747) [*The Travelling Fêtes*]; *Mémoires de l'Académie des colporteurs* (1748) [*Memoirs from the Peddler's Academy*]; *Le pot-pourri* (1748) [*Medley*].

Although Caylus's part is essential and the *Histoire de Guillaume* is generally attributed to him, it is hard to determine exactly who wrote what in the creation of these unconstrained and rambling stories. These works can not be completely associated with erotic literature. The collections from the society of the Bout-du-banc, however, retain the satirical spirit, the naughtiness that shines through parodies, as well as the representation of the Parisian low bourgeoisie, workers, and artisans: penniless masters, coachmen, clerks, peddlers, milliners, shop girls, hairdressers, and street hawkers haunt bars and taverns in search of pleasure.

As a coachman, Guillaume is a witness to this boisterousness, to the excitement that accompanies thwarted love affairs, secret rendezvous, fights and insults, daily troubles, and money problems. The story of Guillaume is that of social climbing, not unlike the story of Jacob told by Marivaux in *Le paysan parvenu* [*The Fortunate Peasant*]. A cab driver (i.e., a public coachman), then a master's coachman, Guillaume ends up marrying a rich widow, Mme Allain, his employer. A whiff of vaudeville runs through the novel. Beyond the picturesque (of the language, the characters, and the situations), Guillaume relates the tumultuous ballet of love affairs and the effervescence of desire that drive the world.

Biography

Anne Claude Philippe de Tubières de Grimoard de Pestels de Levis, count of Caylus (1692–1765) became a great traveler and a lover of art and antiques, after a brilliant career as an officer. A member of the Académie des Beaux-Arts and of the Académie des Inscriptions et belles lettres, he wrote many texts on painting and archaeology. He led the society of the Bout-du-banc ("end of the bench"), writing fairy tales, libertine tales, love witticism, and comedies in the vulgar style.

PATRICK WALD LASOWSKI

Selected Works

Le bordel ou le jeanfoutre puni. S.l. n.d. (c. 1732).
Histoire de Guilleaume. S.l., n.d. (c. 1737).
Mémoires de l'académie des colporteurs, de l'imprimerie ordinaire de l'Académie. 1748.
Le pot-pourri, ouvrage nouveau de ces dames et de ces messieurs. Amsterdam, aux dépens de la compagnie. 1748.
Recueil de comédies et de quelques chansons gaillardes, Imprimé pour ce monde. 1775 (see also the numerous editions of the *Théâtre Gaillard*).

Further Readings

G. Capon and Y. Plessis. *Paris Galant au dix-huitième siècle: Les théâtres clandestins.* Paris, 1905.
Caylus, *Histoire de Guillaume, cocher.* Edited by P. Testud, Zulma, 1993.
Théâtre érotique français au XVIIIème siècle. Introduction by B. de Villeneuve (Raoul Vèze). Pauvert et Terrain vague, 1993.

CERVANTES SAAVEDRA, MIGUEL DE

1547–1616
Spanish novelist

Eroticism may seem to be in short supply in Cervantes's corpus. Don Quixote himself, for instance, is the courtly lover and eternal virgin. Sancho Panza apparently has a sexless and desexualized marriage of little importance. The pair's peregrinations involve many adventures, but no sexual ones, given Quixote's obsession with remaining chaste in the name of his lady Dulcinea (who never rewards his fidelity). The ageing knight may even be "saving himself," as per the medieval courtly love tradition, for a fictional and unattainable damsel in order to insulate himself from the terror of making sexual approaches to a real, unromanticized woman. Some scholars argue that don Quixote indeed wanted to consummate a sexual relationship with Dulcinea (pointing to the Cave of Montesinos episode as evidence); others (like John G. Weiger) believe he was impotent. The Quixote's quest is so profoundly anti-sexual (apart from some Freudian or Jungian scholarly readings that focus on biographic hints about Cervantes's "phallic mother") that it is difficult for the reader to perceive much sense of eros in the book. Indeed, except for occasional scatological insinuations or carnivalesque references to ample buttocks, the body and the bawdy initially seem not to be major concerns for Cervantes. However, careful scrutiny reveals many instances of gender play, transvestitism, voyeurism, and homoerotic tension in his works, as well as ample heterosexual desire.

Don Quixote, Parts I and II (published in 1605 and 1615, respectively) include numerous examples of transvestitism, which Cervantes himself perhaps encountered as the legacy of two literary conventions: the wandering cross-dressers of romance and the warrior women of epic. (Cervantes also wrote for the stage, where the device was not uncommon.) In an unusual and burlesque twist, in his episode of the "doleful duennas," men cross-dress as bearded ladies. In many cases, however, unstable gender identities in Cervantes were in part meant to provide a source of erotic titillation for the reader. Dorothea dresses as a boy to track down her seducer, don Fernando. There is an element of voyeurism as she washes her beautiful white bare feet, unaware of her onlookers. The children of Diego de la Llana take transvestitism a step further: a young woman captured by the patrols is brought to "Governor" Sancho in elaborate masculine dress. She insists she is thus attired to escape her feminine fate and see the world. She also reveals that her brother exchanged clothing with her, and the two experienced the pleasures of a night on the town having switched genders so successfully that he "look[ed] like a most beautiful damsel." Dulcinea herself (as the "real" peasant Aldonza Lorenzo) is suspiciously butch; described as having hair on her chest, her manly height and physical strength (and masculine odor) are emphasized. Ana Félix is also a cross-dressing woman—this time as an Islamic pirate. She frequently refers to the Turks as insatiable sodomites. Thus, believing her androgynously beautiful male Christian lover to be endangered when they are in exile in North Africa, she dresses him as a woman to save him from this threat.

In Cervantes's time, Spaniards severely punished male homosexuality in both secular and inquisitorial realms. Perhaps for this reason, sodomy was commonly attributed as a vice of the Turks and Moors, and Cervantes exploits this convention in his narratives. In the first Captive's tale in *Don Quixote*, the Spaniard speaks of a Venetian cabin boy captured by Uchalí, king of Algiers, who makes the lad his Ganymede. As we have seen, Don Gregorio's female lover dresses him as a woman to save him from the rapacious

appetites of the Great Turk. However, Cervantes also alludes to homosexuality among Christians and Spaniards. Homoerotic desire gives way to incestuous tension in the exemplary tale *Las dos doncellas* [*The Two Damsels*] which begins with yet another crossdressing woman, Teodosia, searching for the soldier who has seduced and abandoned her. Her own brother fails to recognize her in her male garb, and she is subjected first to his "eroticized scrutiny" as Barbara Fuchs calls it, then to a suspicion that he is restless with desire for her (as a woman) when he shares a room with her. In the exemplary novel *El amante liberal* [*The Generous Lover*], the beautiful and effeminate Cornelio is taunted by the virile Ricardo, who calls him a "Ganymede" and snarls at him, "Go, amuse yourself with your mother's maids; they will help you to set your hair and take care of your dainty hands that are better used to wind soft silk than to wield a sword." Overcome with "passion" (jealousy? Or something else?) Ricardo attacks Cornelio. The story also mentions gorgeous captive boys (clearly intended to be catamites) used to pay part of a ransom. In Cervantes' Byzantine romance, *Persiles and Sigismunda*, the cross-dressed heroine evokes homoerotic desire in an itinerant poet, who fantasizes about the beautiful "man" he sees, dressing him/her in his mind's eye in various stage costumes both male and female.

Cervantes also alludes to lesbianism in scenes such as the erotically charged meeting between the eponymous heroine of the pastoral romance *La Galatea* and her friend Florisa. When it comes to men, Galatea is "sexually exciting but not . . . sexually excited" as Edward Dudley terms her, perhaps because she prefers her own gender. Similarly, in the exemplary novel *Las tres doncellas*, Alicia Newberg points to a possible lesbian attraction between Nise and her maid Luisa.

Some recent scholars have speculated about Cervantes's own sexuality. It has been posited that during his five-year captivity in Algiers after the Battle of Lepanto, he had a sexual relationship (consensual or coerced) with his master, Hasan Pasha, given that Cervantes was accused of having committed "vices" in Algiers—a charge he went to great lengths to clear his name of. Yet, although Cervantes initiated four escape attempts, and helped other notable prisoners to escape, Hasan Pasha, who was renowned for his cruelty, never seriously punished him.

Of course there are also many examples of heterosexual desire in Cervantes's works. Besides the many beauteous women who appear and disappear from the winding narrative of *Don Quixote*—Dorotea, the fictional Dulcinea, Marcela, the Duchess, Camila, Lucinda, Zoraida—numerous Cervantine women turn the heads and melt the hearts of various fortunate and unfortunate suitors. Many are fairly conventional objects of male desire, exquisitely dressed and bejeweled, with teeth like pearls and hair rivaling the sun. But there are notable exceptions, such as the carnal and independent Halima (whose name means "one who has a lascivious dream"), who defies Islamic convention to pursue Ricardo lustfully in *The Generous Lover*; Leonora, who rejects the "jealous Extremeñan" who has married her; or Leonisa, the determined virgin who chooses her own husband. Even Maritornes, the ugly tavern-wench who ends up mistakenly in the arms of don Quixote in the darkness of the inn, selects her own man (the mule-driver), struggling against and punching anyone who gets in her way. (Does the fact that don Quixote embraces her, flatters her, and prevents her escape from his bed, while simultaneously verbally rejecting what he believes is her amorous pursuit of him, point to his sexual interest in women or to his rejection of them?)

Cervantes has been variously described as asexual, prissy about sex, guilty about sex, and obsessed with sex. It has been alleged that he feared women, hated his mother, had a repressed Oedipus complex, was a closet homosexual, wrote blatant sexual allegories, and feared the destructive nature of sexual desire. His writing has been described through the ages as coarse, anti-sexual, and rife with sexual symbolism, depending on which commentator one encounters. It remains the individual reader's delectable duty to decide who and what is right about Spain's greatest and most erotically elusive author.

Biography

Cervantes was born in 1547 in Alcalá de Henares, near Madrid, the son of a physician. In 1570, following his studies in Madrid, he became a soldier and in 1575 a ship he was on was captured by the Turks and Cervantes spent five years as a slave in Algiers. Upon his return to Madrid he held several temporary administrative posts and began his literary career. His first major work, *La Galatea*, appeared in 1588. In 1605, the first part of *Don Quixote* appeared, bringing him international recognition. Cervantes died in Madrid on April 23, 1616.

C.A. PRETTIMAN

Selected Works

The Portable Cervantes. translated by Samuel Putnam. New York: Penguin Books, 1976.
Exemplary Stories (Novelas Ejemplares). translated by C.A. Jones. New York: Penguin Books, 1986.
Eight Interludes (Ocho Entremeses). translated by Dawn Smith. New York: Everyman Paperback Classics, 1996.
La Galatea. Madrid: Ediciones Cátedra, S.A., 2000.
Obra Completa. Madrid: Centro de Estudios Cervantinos, n.d.

References and Further Reading

Armas, Frederick de. "Ekphrasis and Eros in Cervantes' *La Galatea*: The Case of the Blushing Nymphs." In *Cervantes for the 21st Century/Cervantes para el siglo XXI*. Studies in Honor of Edward Dudley. Francisco La Rubia Prado, ed. Newark: Juan de la Cuesta: 2000, 33–47.
Cascardi, Anthony J., ed. *The Cambridge Companion to Cervantes*. New York: Cambridge University Press, 2002.
Efron, Arthur. *Don Quixote and the Dulcineated World*. Austin TX: University of Texas Press, 1971.
El Saffar, Ruth Anthony, and Diana de Armas Wilson, eds. *Quixotic Desire: Psychoanalytic Perspectives on Cervantes*. Ithaca and London: Cornell University Press, 1993.
Garcés, María Antonia. *Cervantes in Algiers: A Captive's Tale*. Nashville: Vanderbilt University Press, 2002.
Johnson, Carroll B. *Madness and Lust: A Psychoanalytical Approach to Don Quixote*. Berkeley: University of California Press, 1983.
Nadeau, Carolyn A. *Women of the Prologue: Imitation, Myth, and Magic in Don Quixote*. Lewisburg: Bucknell University Press; London: Associated University Presses, 2002.
Newberg, Alicia. "The Love That Dares Not Speak its Name: A Lesbian Reading of Cervantes's *Las tres doncellas*." *Revista de Estudios Cervantinos de Terranova*, 1996.
Stoll, Anita K. and Dawn L. Smith, eds. *Gender, Identity, and Representation in Spain's Golden Age*. Lewisburg:

Bucknell University Press; London: Associated University Presses, 2000.

Thomas-Weightman, Sandi. "The Representation of Woman in *El amante liberal*: Goddess, Chattel and Peer." *Mester* 21, no. 1 (Spring 1992): 61–71.

Weiger, John G. *The Individuated Self: Cervantes and the Emergence of the Individual*. Ohio: Ohio University Press, 1979.

Weiger, John G., and Arthur Ephron. "Sex in the Cave: An Exchange on the Meanings of *Don Quixote*." *Paunch* 57–58 (January 1984): 201–210.

CHAMPSAUR, FÉLICIEN

1859–1934
French novelist

Dinah Samuel

Although he published more than thirty novels and collections of short stories over the course of a career which spanned half-a-century, Félicien Champsaur is remembered today, if at all, for his first work of prose fiction, published while still in his mid-twenties: *Dinah Samuel* (1882). The most straightforward way of approaching Champsaur's principle work of fiction is to consider it as one of a number of scandalous *romans-à-clef* prompted by rumors that the great French actress Sarah Bernhardt was planning to write her memoirs. Among the earliest of these were Edmond de Goncourt's *La faustin* (1882) and Marie Colombier's *Mémoires de Sarah Barnum* (1883). Both of these, like Champsaur's *Dinah Samuel*, emphasize the actress's Jewish extraction, rendering her not only vulgar and materialistic but also as alien and sexually threatening. But if Colombier's book is salacious and unpleasant, that of Champsaur is quasi-pornographic in its treatment of Bernhardt as a figure of fantasy and revulsion. Indeed, it might be claimed that *Dinah Samuel* is a study in sexual obsession.

Marie Colombier knew Bernhardt well (the two women had trained as actresses together), and many of the incidents in her fictional account, though distorted, are probably based on an element of truth. Whether Champsaur enjoyed a personal acquaintance with Bernhardt is not known. In any event, intimacy with its

subject was hardly necessary for the production of such a work since most of the stories concerning Bernhardt were already public property, the author's task being to take such elements as were required and to fit them into an alternative narrative of his own devising. One such story that did the rounds was that Bernhardt's mother, having been a prostitute herself, acted as a procuress with regard to her own daughters while they were still in their early teens. This story even found its way into the *Journal* of Jules and Edmond de Goncourt, who claim to have overheard it in a restaurant. In other versions, Bernhardt is said to have preferred elderly lovers since they alone had the means of supporting her lavish lifestyle.

Indeed, Champsaur's novel depends on such a view of Bernhardt's materialism since the plot, slight as it is, hinges on the fact that Dinah prefers a sixty-year-old Jewish banker of unprepossessing appearance to the charms of the much younger Patrice Montclar, the central male protagonist of the novel. Montclar, who clearly represents the author himself, is sexually fascinated with Bernhardt/Samuel from the outset of the novel, though this fascination is presented as highly fetishistic in nature. In the opening chapter, for example, Champsaur/Montclar attends a matinee performance at the Comédie Française during which the actress raises an arm to reveal that her armpit is unshaven, much to the delight of the voyeuristic spectator. (In defence of this passage, it should be noted that the armpit was treated in a similarly erotic manner by other French writers and artists of the same period.) During the course of the subsequent narrative, Montclar employs a number of stratagems to gain sexual satisfaction, including sleeping with the actress's double.

In addition to this fictionalized and sensationalist biography of Sarah Bernhardt, *Dinah Samuel* is also a sprawling discursive novel which includes (among much else) a literary manifesto in favor of the bohemian cultural life associated with the Montmartre of the late 1870s, a sequence of 45 sonnets purporting to be the work of Montclar, the complete text of a Pierrot play (also said to be by Montclar), and the prospectus for an advertising agency which claims to have harnessed natural star light for commercial purposes. Not surprisingly, much of this material is ephemeral in nature and has little relevance to the main plot of the novel. In subsequent versions of the novel, published in 1886, 1889, and 1905, Champsaur considerably abridged this extraneous material. Of equal significance, the 1889 version contained a new chapter ("La grande prostituée") in which Montclar, having finally seduced the actress, reduces her to the level of a prostitute. By the time of the 1905 edition, when Bernhardt would have been sixty, Champsaur was complaining of the "odour étrange de cimetière" (i.e., "peculiar mortuary odor") of her skin, so adding a suggestion of necrophilia to the book.

More than a hundred years after its initial publication, the focus of interest in the novel is the reverse of that which prevailed in 1882. Salacious gossip concerning the life of Sarah Bernhardt having little power to shock today, what is significant about *Dinah Samuel* is the manner in which the author reveals the extent of his own racist misogyny. The systematic devaluing of women who occupy a place in the public eye, especially by means of allegations of sexual misconduct, has been a common element in French writing since the late eighteenth century (one thinks, for example, of the pornographic pamphlets directed against Marie-Antoinette). Not surprisingly, allegations of lesbianism are also made against the actress. The level of resentment and hostility to Sarah Bernhardt displayed by Champsaur can only be seen as an indication of the actress's astonishing popularity, a popularity which extended from the early 1870s through to the eve of World War I. Champsaur's anti-Semitism, of course, was a product of the age in which he lived, though no

less reprehensible for that (significantly, the great tragic actress Rachel, who preceded Sarah Bernhardt as the star of the Comédie Française, would not seem to have been the subject of such attacks).

On a more positive note, the late 1870s and early 1880s were marked by the creation of a new type of entertainment space—combining elements of the theater, the literary café, and the beer-hall—which sought to appeal to a broad public seeking a taste of Bohemia. With its cheap cafés, rustic atmosphere, and low rents, Montmartre was the ideal setting for such ventures. Typical of such establishments were Emile Godeau's *Le club des hydropathes* and Rodolphe Salis's *Le chat noir*, both of which Champsaur frequented. In many respects, the highly charged erotic atmosphere of the cabarets (significantly, it would appear that Champsaur's novels were touted around *Le chat noir*) with their routines of comic sketches and popular songs was the very antithesis of the staid Comédie Française. Paradoxically, as general and academic interest in the Montmartre of the early *fin de siècle* has revived in recent years, the material Champsaur systematically expurgated from *Dinah Samuel* has assumed a fresh significance. More than fifty writers and artists active at the period make an appearance in the novel, the portrait of André Gill (Albert Max in the novel) being particularly noteworthy.

Biography

Born in 1859 in Turriers (near Digne) in southwest France. He had already made a modest name for himself in the Bohemian world of the cafés and cabarets of Montmartre by the time he was twenty. After his early participation in the production of small circulation newspapers and magazines, he became increasingly involved with the stage, devising several ballets and Pierrot plays among other works. Published more than thirty novels and collections of short stories. Died in Paris in 1934.

TERRY HALE

Editions

Dinah Samuel. Edited by Jean de Palacio, Paris: Séguier, 1999.

CHARRAS, PIERRE

1945–
French writer

Marthe jusqu'au soir (Marthe till the Evening)

Marthe is a middle-aged, well-educated, good-looking, Dior-wearing bourgeois woman whose husband Jean, a business lawyer by training, has just been appointed a government minister. Their social and professional success is complemented both by their solid and stable relationship and by the potential of their 20-year-old son Brice, currently studying at Princeton. One day at lunchtime, Marthe receives an allegedly urgent phone call from Lacombe, a nondescript secretary and speech writer working for her husband, who has openly praised his efficiency and intellectual qualities. Lacombe tells her they need to meet urgently and suggests a little restaurant nearby, not far from the church of La Madeleine. Once there, he gives her a black and white still from a videotape he also has in his briefcase. Albeit of poor quality, the photo distinctively shows Brice in college uniform fellating a man. Lacombe threatens to sell it to the press, which would lead to the ruin of Jean's career and put an end to all their ambitions for Brice. Marthe, initially believing Lacombe's blackmail to be financially motivated, promises to pay any amount of money—but Lacombe explains that he does not want any money: he wants her. He will give her the tape if she accepts to be his for the next five hours, that is if he can have Marthe till the evening, *Marthe jusqu'au soir*, hence the title of the book.

Incredulous at first, she rapidly realizes that she has no choice and must obey. The next five hours are worse than her worst nightmare, a descent into hell both for her body and soul alike, in a fine, upper-class brothel just behind the restaurant. With the help of a valet called Albert, Lacombe, who is as ugly as Marthe is elegant, gradually humiliates and degrades her. Albert notably makes her piss in a transparent jug by punching her abdomen and detachedly penetrates her using lots of greasy gel in order to lubricate her for Lacombe's much larger penis. Lacombe also obliges Marthe to slowly strip (Marthe hates being seen naked and who has only been naked in front of her husband), kisses her by force everywhere and eventually has sex twice with her on the bed. When she thinks it is over, he reveals to her the second part of the script he has been planning since he first met her and started fancying her: she is to spend the next three hours working as a prostitute in the brothel itself—and should she fail to attract any client, Albert will sodomize her. Lacombe's plan is precise and thoroughly thought-out: to stop seeing her as a highly desirable and ideal woman, he must make her literally become a whore. He will then have sex with her one last time in the late afternoon, but by then his feelings will hopefully have changed. She complies, calling herself Olga and having sex with three more men—though what exactly happens with them is not mentioned, not even hinted at, though Lacombe watches everything from behind a hidden mirror. In the event, Lacombe nonetheless fails to fall out of love with her: he tells her how even after seeing her pleasuring and serving other men, he still idealizes her. He is ready to let her go without even having sex with her one more time; a man of his word, he nonetheless gives her the videotape and decides to disappear from her life forever. He will either leave the country or kill himself, whatever she decides: he will call at ten in the evening to get his sentence, shortly before Jean arrives from his constituency. To stop Lacombe from committing suicide, she just has to pick up the phone when he calls. When he calls, at the agreed time, Marthe does not pick up the phone.

Marthe jusqu'au soir is an interesting novella in three main respects. Firstly, it uses sexual blackmail as a narrative cornerstone, whereas that topos of erotic literature is often just a secondary element as a pretext for sexual descriptions. Secondly, it offers a pleasantly written erotic illustration of hard concepts such as power, domination, and sacrifice. Thirdly, and most controversially, it succeeds in presenting both protagonists' viewpoints. Marthe may be the saintly victim of Lacombe's wicked plan, but Lacombe too is disturbingly presented as a victim—victim of his own ugliness and failure with women, victim of his impossible love for Marthe. His last words to her as he leaves the brothel room, '*Je vous aime,*' emphasize both the dramatic ending of the story and its human if not humane dimension. Yet he is so confused and deluded that the very fact that if he really loved her he would not treat her with such hatred does not seem to enter his psyche, and in a dodgy way the book almost seems to justify

why Lacombe designed his sophisticated method of rape.

Biography

Pierre Charras was born in Saint-Etienne in 1945. He originally trained as a teacher. He now lives and works in Paris.

LOYKIE LOÏC LOMINÉ

Selected Works

Marthe jusqu'au soir. Mercure de France. 1992.
Francis Bacon, le ring de la douleur. Ramsay. 1996.
Juste avant la nuit. Mercure de France. 1998.
La crise de foi(e). Arléa. 1999.
Comédien. Mercure de France. 2000.

CHAUCER, GEOFFREY

c.1345–1400
English poet

The Miller's Tale

A bawdy and licentious narrative, *The Miller's Tale* is told by a drunken and quarrelsome narrator. It tells the story of a clerk named Nicholas and the successful cuckolding of his master, an Oxford carpenter, and Nicholas's affair with the carpenter's much younger wife, Alisoun. The courteous Nicholas is in love with the wild and flirtatious 18 year-old Alisoun. In order for them to have time alone together, Nicholas tricks Alisoun's husband into believing that a second Biblical flood is about to take place. To save himself, the carpenter decides to sleep in a large tub that hangs suspended underneath the rafters of the house. This leaves Alisoun and Nicholas free to enjoy the sensual pleasures and secret love that Nicholas has long desired and to sleep in the marital bed together without fear of being disturbed. However, Alisoun has another admirer in the amorous parish clerk Absolon who desperately tries to

win her love. When Absolon comes to declare his love, Alisoun begs him to leave her alone. He promises to leave if she grants him a single kiss. Alisoun then promptly thrusts out her backside, which Absolon kisses in mistake for Alisoun's lips. Humiliated by this scene, Absolon determines to have his revenge on the laughing couple within and returns to beg another kiss. This time Nicholas offers his backside through the window, which Absolon brands with the red-hot iron he brought with him to enact his revenge. The subsequent noises from below (particularly the screams of agony from Nicholas and his calls for water) wake the carpenter in his rafter resting place and result in his assuming the floodwaters have begun to rise. He swiftly cuts the cords suspending his tub and plunges down from the attic into the scene below. Overall, the Tale alternates between the coarse and the light-hearted, but the early description of the young and beautiful Alisoun, in which she is said to be more beautiful to behold than an early-ripe pear ("She was ful moore blisful on to see / Than is the newe pere-jonette tree") reveals Chaucer's awareness of the importance of the erotic description, as he seductively introduces details about how Alisoun's apron ("A barmcloth as whit as morne milk") hangs around her loins, and his knowing reference to her "likerous ye," or flirtatious nature.

The Wife of Bath's Tale

The tale told by Alisoun, Wife of Bath, develops the idea of woman's mastery over her husband or lover that she promulgated in her Prologue, in which she also discussed and described in detail the varied relationships she had endured with her five husbands. The Wife of Bath is open and unabashed in providing her fellow pilgrims with stories of the "wo that is in marriage." She speaks openly of her luck in selecting five husbands rich in both their wealth and their more physical endowments: "I have picked out the beste / Bothe of hir nether purs and of hir cheste." While the Prologue focuses upon the overtly sexual, and often quite coarse nature of the Wife's own sexual experience (there are passages of great length on the genital differences between the sexes), her Tale focuses more upon the eroticism of sexual desire. Set in the realm of Arthurian legend, the tale concerns a lecherous knight who rapes a young maid: "maugree hir heed, / By verray force, he rafte hire maydenhed." Instead of being punished by King Arthur, the knight is handed over to the jurisdiction of the Queen and her court of ladies. The Queen sets the knight a challenge. He must discover within one year "what women love moost"—what it is that women most desire. After hearing many contradictory replies during his travels, the knight is about to return and confront his fate when he meets "a fouler wight ther may no man devise"—an ugly old hag. He asks her the same question that he has asked all the other women, promising to reward her for any instruction she might give. The old woman offers to tell him the answer only if he grants her the next thing she requests of him. He rashly agrees, whereupon the woman whispers the answer to him. Returning to court the knight declares that what women desire most is sovereignty over their husbands. He is granted a pardon, but the old woman immediately steps forward and demands that he marry her. The knight tries to break his word and implores the woman, "taak al my good, and lat my body go."

The knight is forced to keep his promise, and as the couple lie in bed after their marriage, the old woman asks what is troubling him. When he replies it is her ugliness, she states that this can soon be remedied and offers him a choice: either he can have her ugly and faithful or beautiful and faithless. Despairing at the impasse he is in, the knight flippantly offers her the choice, with the result that he is rewarded with a beautiful but faithless wife.

Troilus and Criseyde

Troilus and Criseyde is Chaucer's longest complete poem. It was probably written during the late 1380s, and was adapted from Boccaccio's *Il Filostrato* [*The Lovestricken*]. The story narrates a love affair set in Troy between Troilus, a young warrior, and Criseyde, widowed daughter of the astronomer Calchas. Troilus sees Criseyde, falls in love with her, and through the help of Criseyde's guardian, her uncle Pandarus, the couple begin a secret affair. Criseyde is subsequently returned to her father in exchange for a prisoner of war. Although she promised to return to Troilus, Criseyde is forced to take the Greek Diomede as her lover. Troilus, desolate and distraught at Criseyde's betrayal (which he sees in a dream) devotes himself to the ongoing battle and dies in glory, ascending to the seventh sphere from where he looks down upon the earth and realizes the vanity of human relationships. Chaucer's poem has been acclaimed for its depth of characterization (in sharp contrast to Boccaccio's original), but the poem is also interesting in its frank portrayal of the ideal of *fine amour*. As summarized by D.S. and L.E. Brewer, "*fine amour* may be said to be essentially (a) masculine, (b) sexual, (c) symbolic, (d) humble, (e) improving, and (f) private." The ideal allowed for an elevation of sex by moving the definition away from a purely biological and reproductive vision of physical love to an idealization of the sexual act as something to be enjoyed in its own right. Troilus's total absorption in Criseyde is thus both sexual and emotional. While Troilus desires erotic satisfaction, the poem stresses that the physical element of the relationship must be restrained in many ways in order for it to develop fully. Both promiscuity and marriage change relationships and stifle the possibility of fulfilling the aims of *fine amour*. The poem reflects the ambiguity between love in an earthly or natural sense and religious love, with both forms eroticized within the text. Troilus is perceived to be a better man through his love of Criseyde, but this is largely because he seeks to elevate natural love to the status of religious love and believes that his love of Criseyde is essentially holy. Troilus's use of language to explain and define his love is demonstrated in his prayer to Venus, which serves as a useful example of his attempt to combine the two seemingly contrary elements of emotional need and erotic desire. Ultimately, though, it is human or natural love that is seen to be fallible within the story, with Troilus's death suggesting the impossibility of combining the two ideals of religion and *fine amour*.

Biography

Chaucer was the son of the wealthy London vintner John Chaucer. He may have attended St. Paul's Cathedral School before he studied at the Inner Temple. During 1357 and 1358, Chaucer was a page to Elizabeth, Countess of Ulster. He was involved in the military campaigns in France (1359/1360) and returned to England after being ransomed in March 1360 (King Edward III contributing towards the ransom payment). In the late 1360s, Chaucer married Philippa, a relation of his patron John of Gaunt. Granted a pension by the king in 1367, Chaucer served as a diplomat throughout the 1370s and early 1380s and held many official positions during that period. His travels in Europe on behalf of the king brought Chaucer into contact with the European literature of the period and traces of these encounters can be found within his writings—the most obvious example being the influence of Boccaccio upon *The Canterbury Tales*. After 1386, with the absence of John of Gaunt, Chaucer fell upon harsher times and even after the granting of a pension by Richard II in 1394 his frequent supplications for advanced payments make clear his increasingly desperate financial state. Henry IV raised his pension in 1399 and so Chaucer's last months, after he returned to London to live in Westminster, were spent in relative comfort. Chaucer died in 1400 and was buried in the section of Westminster Abbey that since his death has been known as Poets' Corner.

MARK LLEWELLYN

Editions

The Riverside Chaucer. Oxford: Oxford University Press, 1987.

Further Reading

Brewer, D.S. and L.E., eds. *Troilus and Criseyde*, London: Routledge and Kegan Paul, 1971.

Dinshaw, Carolyn, *Chaucer's Sexual Poetics*, Madison: University of Wisconsin Press, 1989.

Knight, Stephen, *Geoffrey Chaucer*, Oxford: Basil Blackwell, 1986.

Leicester, H. Marshall, Jr. "'My bed was ful of verray blood': Subject, Dream, and Rape in the Wife of Bath's Prologue and Tale," In *Geoffrey Chaucer: The Wife of Bath*. Edited by Peter G. Beidler, Boston, New York: Bedford Books, 1996.

Mieszkowski, Gretchen, "Chaucer's Much Loved Criseyde." *The Chaucer Review* 26:2 (1991), 109–132.

Patterson, Lee. "'Experience woot well it is noght so': Marriage and the Pursuit of Happiness in the Wife of Bath's Prologue and Tale." In *Geoffrey Chaucer: The Wife of Bath*. Edited by Peter G. Beidler, Boston, New York: Bedford Books, 1996.

Sadlek, Gregory M. "Love, Labour, and Sloth in Chaucer's *Troilus and Criseyde*." In *The Chaucer Review* 26:4 (1992), 350–368.

Winny, James ed. *The Wife of Bath's Prologue and Tale*. Cambridge: Cambridge University Press, 1965.

———, ed. *The Miller's Prologue and Tale*. Cambridge: Cambridge University Press, 1971.

CHEKHOV, ANTON

1860–1904
Russian short-story writer and playwright

Anton Chekhov's "A Nervous Breakdown" ["Pripadok," also translated as "A Nervous Fit," "A Nervous Attack," "An Attack of Nerves," and "The Fit"] is an important part of the canon of nineteenth-century Russian literature devoted to the problem of prostitution. Written in 1888, it was published the following year in a collection of stories to honor the memory of the recently deceased writer Vsevolod Garshin, whose "An Occurrence" (1875) and "Nadezhda Nikolaevna" (1885) had developed the long-standing theme of the "fallen woman." Though a few of Chekhov's critics attacked the story for its subject matter, "A Nervous Breakdown" was not only well-received, but even met with little difficulty at the hands of the tsarist censors. The story was rejected only once, when it was to be reprinted in a collection called "For the Fallen" [Za padshikh"] in 1891. The entire collection was banned.

"A Nervous Breakdown" is the story of a law student named Vasil'ev, who, against his better judgment, is convinced to join his friends on a visit to a series of brothels on the notorious S___ Street (clearly modeled on Sobolev Street, a well-known red-light district in prerevolutionary Moscow). Prior to this excursion, Vasil'ev familiarity with "fallen women" was limited to books and newspapers, but he had already developed strong opinions on the matter: "He knew that there were such immoral women, who, under the pressure of fatal circumstances—their environment, a bad upbringing, necessity, etc.—were obliged to sell their honor for money." Vasil'ev's attitude clearly falls within the "progressive" side of late nineteenth-century Russia, since he assumes that prostitution is—at heart—a social problem. At the same time, his attitude is also based on romantic or religious concerns rather than on pure materialism: he is convinced that, despite their sins, prostitutes are still made in God's image, and can still hope for redemption. He agrees to join his friends not out of any

conscious sexual desire, but rather to become more knowledgeable about this moral problem.

Vasil'ev's disenchantment is almost immediate: first and foremost, he is appalled by the sheer vulgarity of his surroundings (the decor, the entertainment, the servants, the women's dresses and manners), and then by the mercantile basis of all brothel interactions: in the first house they visit, Vasil'ev naively spends his money buying drinks at a prostitute's request, unaware that the madam has instructed all her "girls" to get their clients to spend as much on food and drink as possible. After witnessing a scandalous scene where a client beats a drunken prostitute to the accompaniment of screams and tears, Vasil'ev refuses to continue his expedition and has a falling out with his friends. Upon returning home, Vasil'ev cannot stop thinking of the women and their fates, desperately trying to devise a solution to their plight. Eventually, his friends bring him to a psychiatrist. He asks the doctor if prostitution is evil, to which the psychiatrist responds: "My dear man, who could argue?" The psychiatrist gives him some medications, and soon Vasil'ev feels well enough to go back to the university.

Chekhov's approach to prostitution in "A Nervous Breakdown" is noteworthy for a number of reasons. Like most Russian prostitution narratives, it addresses the problem while remaining decidedly discreet in referring to sexual activity itself; Chekhov's story goes even further in that the protagonists visit several brothels without even having sex at all. "A Nervous Breakdown" maintains the high moral tone established for such stories by previous writers (especially Garshin), but it adds an element of self-consciousness that was previously absent. Vasil'ev has one advantage over the heroes of other tales of attempts at rescuing the "fallen woman": he has read their stories, and he knows how they usually end. In a clear reference to Nikolai Chernyshevsky's radical novel *What Is To Be Done?* [*Chto delat'?*] (1863), which established the pattern for Russian literature about prostitution for decades to come, he recalls cases in which men have liberated individual prostitutes from their madams and their pimps, set them up in their own apartments, and bought them "the inevitable sewing machine" to help them learn an honest trade. None of these attempts ends well, and all of them are a piecemeal solution to a wide-scale social problem. If prostitution stories are usually narratives of salvation (attempted or successful), Vasil'ev finds them unsatisfactory at least in part for their focus on the individual woman.

"A Nervous Breakdown" problematizes prostitution by placing it on the very cusp between the personal and the social: the story is about the lives of individuals, but the context is such that the main character can never be satisfied with an individual, small-scale answer. Indeed, Chekhov's brothel expedition can easily be interpreted as a microcosm for the entire Russian public sphere: besides Vasil'ev, a law student, the other two men on the S___ street tour are an artist and a medical student. Each of them represents the professions that, in theory, should be most concerned with this phenomenon, yet only Vasil'ev even considers it a problem. And none of them brings his expertise to bear when visiting the brothel: it is Vasil'ev, rather than the artist, who objects to his surroundings on aesthetic grounds, but Vasil'ev himself never considers prostitution from a legal point of view. This intersection between the established professions (such as medicine and law) and the "oldest profession" would be developed further in Alexander Kuprin's encyclopedic potboiler *The Pit* [*Iama*] (1908–1915).

Biography

Anton Pavlovich Chekhov was born January 17, 1860 in Taganrog, Russia. Completed medical school in 1884. Began his writing career in 1880, initially as the author of humorous short stories for popular newspapers and magazines, before moving on to longer narrative forms. His work in the theater in the 1890s and early 1900s established his reputation as one of the greatest playwrights of the modern era. After suffering from tuberculosis for twenty years, he died of the disease in 1904.

ELIOT BORENSTEIN

Selected Works

Chekhov, Anton. *Polnoe sobranie sochinenii i pisem.* 30 vols. Moscow, 1977.
Chekhov, Anton. "An Attack of Nerves." *The Portable Chekhov.* Edited by Avrahm Yarmolinksy. New York: Penguin, 1988.
Chekhov, Anton. "A Nervous Breakdown." *The Schoolmistress and Other Stories.* Translated by Constance Garnett. Ecco Press, 1986.

Further Reading

Borenstein, Eliot. *Men Without Women: Masculinity and Revolution in Russian Fiction, 1917–1929.* Durham: Duke, 2000.
Matich, Olga. "A Typology of Fallen Women in Nineteenth Century Russian Literature." *American Contributions to the Ninth International Congress of Slavists.* Vol. 2. Columbus, OH: Slavic Press, 1983. 325–343.
Meister, Charles W. *Chekhov Criticism: 1880 through 1986.* London: McFarland & Company. 1988.
Rayfield, Donald. *Chekhov: The Evolution of His Art.* London: Elek Books, 1975.
Siegel, George. "The Fallen Woman in Nineteenth Century Literature." *Harvard Slavic Studies* 5 (1970): 81–108.

CHEVRIER, FRANÇOIS ANTOINE

1721–1762
French satirist, political publicist, pamphleteer, and journalist.

A prolific writer, Chevrier tried many genres; in addition to several plays he published numerous writings based on private scandals, on the history and politics of several European countries, or a mixture of the two. There are sketches of social types in the manner of La Bruyère (*Les ridicules du siècle*), but really Chevrier was a scandalmonger; at best he aspires to be a sort of chronicler of the life of his times, like Restif de la Bretonne after him; and like Restif he seems to thrive on spying and reporting the gossip he has collected (*Almanach des gens d'esprit*), with, in his case, a particular fascination for, perhaps obsession with, the women of the Comédie Française and Opéra. A few writings in verse, like *Étrennes voluptueuses*, are similar to the playfully erotic poetry in the style of Dorat's *Fables or Baisers*, with the same sorts of pastoral themes and conventional motifs: for example, the five senses, the four parts of the day. All of Chevrier's work has been virtually forgotten; *Le colporteur* alone having been republished three or four times since the eighteenth century.

Le colporteur [*The Book Peddler*], which surfaced in France just months before Chevrier died, was a sort of clandestine bestseller. It is not a novel but a long dialogue in which the peddler, whose putative occupation is really just a cover for his role as rumor monger and police spy, relates all the scandalous gossip he has garnered from his rounds, which take him to all social circles and even to Versaille. The main subject is the sexual conduct and misconduct of numerous characters, some of whom are given their real names and some, like the promiscuous Belise, are not; many of the latter are all but impossible to decode today.

When Belise contracts syphilis from a capricious coupling in a carriage, the guilty party, the Marquis de Sarzanne, comes to her aid by using an actress to entrap her husband so he will believe it was he who, having gotten the disease from her, transmitted it to his wife, rather than the reverse; on this the narrator comments: "nothing about this should scandalize the austere reader: a husband, although the occurrence is remarkable, may sometimes sleep with his wife." Venereal disease (as the peddler says, "what was a horror when America was discovered has become in our time an accident to which the best people are subject") is the token of general circulation characterizing the mores in general. The detailing of the sources of Belise's case, like a similar passage in *Candide*, is a parody of generalized sexual dissoluteness:

> [Sarzanne] complained to Miss Deschamps of the Opera, who blamed the misfortune on a foreign minister, who in turn attributed it to the wife of a tax farmer; she imputed the cause of the indisposition to a standard-bearer of the Musketeers, who maintained it came from a neighborhood grocer's wife, who swore that for six months she had spoken with no one but a Capuchin brother who collected alms; the monk complained bitterly to Duchesse de ***, who protested she saw no one other than a Portuguese priest, who admitted he got it from a most tender conversation with Mademoiselle Brillant of the Comédie Française; the *actrice*, to exculpate herself, cast the blame on the Marquis de C***, but as this nobleman had been killed at Rosback, the research went no farther, and the genealogy of the disease that had just struck Belise remained imperfect.

The book is a long sequence of such gossip, dealing mostly with the nobility and their ties to the theater underworld. Chevrier does not lack wit, though it is cruel and vengeful.

As the quotation suggests, Chevrier had an anticlerical bent and pursued some specific priests with particular fury (*Vie du fameux Père Norbert*). The French police liaison in the Hague reported hearing that "some obscene works were found among his papers," but nothing that could merit that qualification is known to exist.

Biography

Chevrier was born in Nancy. He became a lawyer in 1743, but apparently practiced little if at all. He had little luck with his first publications in Paris. In 1746, he went to Italy and then to Corsica; was a member of the Corsican Academy (1749) and wrote a history of Corsica. He moved often, even among several cities—Paris, Nancy, Frankfort, Brussels—and made himself undesirable in most of them because of his political meddling and caustic writings. In 1758, he was sentenced in absentia to the galleys for writings offensive to religion and state, but persuaded the court to commute the sentence. Later, pursued by the French police for his political intriguing and expelled from the Austrian Netherlands, he moved to the Hague, and was about to be arrested at the request of the French crown in June 1762 when he traveled to Rotterdam where he died virtually penniless.

Philip Stewart

Selected Works

Recueil de ces dames. 1745.
Les Ridicules du siècle. 1752.
Étrennes voluptueuses. 1761.

Les Amusements des dames de B[ruxelles]. 1761.
Almanach des gens d'esprit. 1762.
Le Colporteur, histoire morale et critique. 1761; available in Romans libertins du XVIIIe siècle, Paris: Robert Laffont, 1993, pp. 755–884.
Vie du fameux Père Norbert. 1762.
Nouvelles Libertés de penser?

Further Reading

Trousson, Raymond, introduction to *Le Colporteur*, in *Romans libertins du XVIIIe siècle*, Paris: Robert Laffont, 1993, pp. 741–750.
Weil, Françoise. "Chevrier." In *Dictionnaire des journalistes, 1600–1789.* Oxford: Voltaire Foundation, 1999, pp. 225–228.

CHIKAMATSU MONZAEMON

1653–1725
Japanese kabuki and bunraku playwright

Chikamatsu Monzaemon sprang from warrior origins, but wrote about *chônin*, townsmen or plebeian inhabitants of *chô*, urban administrative districts in Japan's Edo period (1600–1868), who constituted a class, the upper members of which were wealthy merchants who had no part political issues and could do nothing but make money or look for various pleasures, art properties, silk arrays, *sharebon* or licentious books, ruinous sex adventures or love stories with prostitutes, courtesans or cute male actors, and so on.

The urban culture of the Genroku era (1688–1704) thrived in the Kamigata. The theaters, set near the pleasure quarters, offered representations of the *ukiyo*—floating world—a realm of appearence, where nothing, neither love nor fortune, could ever last. The erotic mood or overtone of the show was typical of such plays, in which a lover vainly tried to buy the prostitute he was in love with, but had no tricky slave to rely on as in Plautus' comedies. Not only *chônin* faced up to debts and money problems, but they sometimes were torn between *giri*, duty, and *ninjô*, human feelings.

Most of Chikamatsu's plays dealt with this difficult choice, as they offered "moving stories of ordinary people trapped by their situations—constrained by obligation (*giri*) and driven by affection (*ninjô*)—who finally asserted their dignity, refusing to abandon their love for another despite the cost of insistence" (C. Totman),

and the desperate lovers eventually committed a double suicide, *shinjû*. Although money was the main factor leading to death, the suicidal act for the sake of love was modelled upon death taken for one's feudal lords by warriors. The *chônin's* ethics competed with the *samurai's* one, also working as a warning against social injustice, and prostitutes often proved to be highly virtuous. The lovers died, but were saved by the Buddha. The *seppuku's* spectacular and heart-rending final scene was the proper way to salvation.

Although love was at the bottom of those prostitute-buying plays, and places or figures associated with prostitution—a road inn in Tanba Yosaku, a madam in Kasane izutsu, etc.—eroticism was a rather indirect motive or theme and definitely not the main issue of the plays. The latter display at least three kinds of erotic scenes: seduction; homoeroticism; and *shinjû*.

Chikamatsu's dramas are not devoid of scenes where women, wives, or prostitutes seduce men. In *Horikawa nami no tsuzumi*, Otane, a samurai's young wife, resists the advances of Yukaemon, another samurai, but Genemon hears them and thinks they have become lovers. Otane, frightened and drunk, tries to seduce Genemon to keep him silent about what he heard, traps him by making him exchange a fateful cup of *sake* with her, unlaces his belt, and they embrace and lie down with their heads on the same pillow.... Nothing very much different from the erotic passages in the works of Ihara Saikaku, except that the latter conceived love, *kôshoku*, as a means to connect people of different classes and celebrate life.

Homoerotic scenes are not rare in Chikamatsu's plays, but they are nothing but traditional and stereotyped, quite typical of the time's *nanshoku* or male love literature. *Shinjû mannengusa* takes place in mount Kôya, a monastery reputed for its *chigo* or pretty young pages the local monks often fell in love with and initiated to anal sex. One of the characters says: "A page in a monastery is the equivalent for a wife in the secular world," and male love shows through the whole first act. In *Shinjû yoigôshin*, the samurai Hanbei has to choose one male lover for his brother and opts for the one who will accept to disembowel himself. The anecdote demonstrates the hero has remained a true samurai. Lesbianism wasn't absent either from Chikamatsu's scenes. In *Satsuma uta*, Sangobei, dressed up as a woman to hide, is chatted up by the female servant Oshun who tells him: "Let's sleep as husband and wife. And as for tonight, would you like to be the woman, unless you'd prefer acting as the man?"

Shinjû means the heart's bottom and is translated as: double-love suicide. The word often recurs in the titles of the plays of Chikamatsu. It designates any behavior producing evidence of one's sincere feeling. It follows that death out of love is the highest expression of amorous sincerity. Killing the beloved or showing one's will to die for the sake of her before killing oneself is so to speak the ultimate sex or love act and goes along with a production of erotic effects. In *Sonezaki shinjû*, the courtesan Ohatsu must hide her lover Tokubei under the verandah and sits on the step. She then explains to Koheiji, Tokubei's unreliable friend, that Tokubei is in such a hopeless economic situation that he must die. She wonders aloud whether Tokubei is firmly resolved to die and asks the question to Tokubei by touching him with her naked foot. Her lover nods, takes her foot by the ankle and rubs it on his throat so as to signify he is going to kill himself. Eroticism is linked with death through Ohatsu's foot.

But nothing is more erotic than the dying female lover, for example in *Ikudama shinjû*, shaking as if she had an ultimate orgasm.

Biography

Not much is known for sure about the life of Chikamatsu Monzaemon: he descended from a *bushi* or samurai family from the province of Echizen; after his father quit his feudal service and moved to Kyoto, he was a page boy in the service of Ichijô Ekan, the local court's prince abbot, and became well-versed in Chinese, Japanese, sacred and profane literature, as well as in *jôruri*, a sort of epic recitative with dialogues, accompanied by *shamisen's* music and illustrated by a *ningyô* or puppet's play; his biography then consisted in the nomenclature of at least 150 dramas —he composed from 1673 on for *kabuki* and *bunraku*, oscillating between *jidaimono*, historical pieces, and *sewamono*, domestic ones.

GÉRARD SIARY

Editions

Nihon kotenbungaku zenshû. Tokyo: Shôgakkan. 1975, 2 volumes.

Selected Works

———. *Les tragédies bourgeoises*. Translated by René Sieffert, Paris: POF, 1991–1992, 4 volumes (24 plays).
———. *Major Plays of Chikamatsu*. Translated by Donald Keene. Columbia University Press, 1990.

References and Further Reading

Gerstle, C. Andrew. *Circles of Fantasy*. Convention in the Plays of Chikamatsu, Harvard University Press, 1986.

Leiter, L. Samuel. *Kabuki Encyclopedia*, London: Greenwood Press, 1979.

Pinguet, Maurice. *Voluntary Death in Japan*. Translated by fr. the Fr. by Rosemary Morris, Paris: Polity Press, 1993 (1984).

Totman, Conrad. *Early Modern Japan*. California University Press, 1995.

Walter, Alain. *Érotique du Japon classique*. Paris: Gallimard, 1994.

Yokota-Murakami, Takayuki. *Don Juan east/west—On the Problematics of Comparative Literature*. State University of New York Press, 1998.

CHILD-LOVE

The book commonly called *Child-Love* has on its title page "Private Letters from Phyllis to Marie on the Art of *Child-Love* or the Adventures and Experiences of a Little Girl/Showing how pretty little maidens indulge those secret passions, alone and with others, which but too often lead to their seduction at an early age/ London and Paris 1898."

It takes as its epigraph the rhyme

"When apples are ripe they are ready for plucking,
When girls are twelve they are ready for sucking,
At fourteen years they are ready for fucking."

The book is a form of seduction manual detailing all the sexual activities which can be performed with girls short of breaking the hymen. The narrator and ostensible writer is Phyllis Norroy who dedicates *Child-Love* to "Pretty Little Girls who while satisfying their own desires and those of their lovers, be they new women or children like themselves have retained their virginity and 'Never told tales out of school.'" Purporting to be twelve letters from Phyllis to her friend Marie, it follows the familiar pattern in erotica of a more experienced woman warning a less experienced one of sexual danger, while giving explicit descriptions.

The specific and reiterated danger is the loss of virginity in under-age girls, an event described in terms of grotesque horror. Phyllis sanctimoniously warns of how "my passions being aroused, I consented to my own seduction at the age of twelve years, and this, instead of adding to only destroyed the pleasure I had in the secret practices of childhood." The storyline describes how, over one summer on the South Coast of England, Phyllis goes through the gamut of sexual experience over the ages of twelve and thirteen.

Marie is in France producing nude photographs of little girls for sale. Phyllis encourages her in the first letter and gives advice on posing the children, as "there is no doubt a great and increasing desire among men to arouse and share their pleasures with little girls from ten to fifteen years of age."

In the second letter Phyllis tells how she was introduced to sex when she was twelve and was living with her aunt and uncle on the south coast. A wealthy Baronet, Sir Harry Norton, lives nearby and Phyllis finds that he has been watching her while she undresses to bathe in the sea. He leads her to a grassy bank where he kisses her, feels her vaginal lips and urges her to touch his penis but she is frightened and refuses. He smacks her on the behind and then brings himself to a climax by rubbing his penis on top of her vagina.

Letter three introduces Lady Norton who invites Phyllis to lunch and tells her story. She was orphaned as a child and found a playmate in Sir Harry who was also an orphan though ten years older than her. Her guardian, seeking to deny the future Lady Norton her inheritance, sought to corrupt her so that "she would have no further love for Sir Harry." He gave her sexually explicit books and pictures and encouraged her to masturbate while unsuccessfully attempting to seduce her. At fifteen she eloped to Paris under an alias with Sir Harry and "finding her lover bent on accomplishing his wishes, which was the climax of her own desires also, she gave him every help by bending her knees and keeping her legs apart...then came to her that indescribable sensation when a young girl's vagina is for the first time distended by the fully grown organ of a man many years older than herself."

The fourth letter describes how Lady Norton takes Phyllis into a secret chamber to the manor house and seduces her saying, "I want your child-love and to arouse and gratify your girlish desires." She ties up Phyllis' legs in a raised position and gives her cunnilingus then greases her anus and stimulates her manually.

Phyllis has a slightly younger friend called Helen who are playing among the sand dunes, letter five recounts, when they witness a young man raping a woman who is so overwhelmed by the experience that she surrenders to it and confesses love for him. They later find, as told in letter six, that this was an Earl's son and a Bishop's daughter.

In the seventh letter Phyllis is again with lady Norton who gives the girl an elaborate strap-on dildo with which to penetrate her and has the girl birch her until she climaxes and the dildo squirts milk. Lady Norton teaches Phyllis the technique of fellatio which "if properly carried out by a little girl, [is] the greatest protection to her virginity." The novel is now in full satiric flow: while supposedly protecting the virginity of girls, that staple of nineteenth-century sexuality, in fact its morality leads them to practice the most extreme acts of oral, anal, and flagellatory sex.

Lady Norton introduces Phyllis to her cousin Algy who buys her presents then fondles her vagina, greases her anus, and sodomizes her, "as I felt his cock entering my body I realised for the first time how different and how infinitely more delightful it was to submit to the real action of being buggered by a strong man than to the artificial means employed so often among girls alone...each warm jet of spunk that he had shot into me while he lay himself naked between my childish legs, had sealed a loving bond of union between us."

Letter nine has Algy and Phyllis having sex in the drawing room of her aunt's house on her thirteenth birthday while her relatives are conveniently away and she has sent the servants off with a gold coin each. She fellates Algy and, at the point of his orgasm, thrusts her finger up his anus. Now her friend Helen joins them in an orgy in which the girls stimulate each other orally and he sodomises Helen while Phyllis stimulates him anally.

The writer has no plot mechanism to take the story further, so the only complication which can be produced to create more material for the novel is the introduction of a new character in letter ten. Phyllis' pretty fifteen-year-old cousin Ethel, therefore, comes to stay. Phyllis encourages Sir Harry to watch unobserved while she, Helen, and Ethel undress. She procures Ethel for Sir Harry "for I thought it is a shame that so pretty and well developed a girl, who was nearly sixteen year so age, should any longer fret over the fact that she was still a virgin." Consequently Phyllis and Lady Norton tie up Ethel in a pose open for sex and she is penetrated vaginally by Sir Harry.

The last two letters give the climax in which, to add an erotic charge, for the first time Phyllis describes herself: 'My great mass of rich brown hair was falling about my face and shoulders down to my waist, my little breasts were just beginning to form, and my slit, without a trace of hair about it, stood out from between my rounded legs.'

She and Algy can restrain themselves no longer, and Phyllis is finally penetrated vaginally: "Oh that bursting pain was so awful that I never dreamt that such agony could be produced in the body of a child without its killing her, but nature came to my aid, and before a second pang I fainted." He is frightened at the physically debilitating effect of this sex on Phyllis and calls on Lady Norton, who organizes sal volatile, beef tea, and an ice pack, in a characteristic Victorian invalid scene.

The story ends with the traditional Victorian happy ending: Phyllis marries Algy who has come into a considerable fortune and become "one of the most promising officers in the Navy." Sir Harry becomes High Sheriff of the County and a Member of Parliament. Ethel is engaged to a younger brother of Sir Harry and Helen stays as Lady Norton's companion.

The book is obviously subversive of the division between child and adult sexuality but is also subversive of the aristocracy, the family, and of gender and generational roles in having girls penetrate men. By containing all these transgressions within the settings of the Victorian home and holiday it achieves a satirical edge which raises it above the mundane level of its prose. Phyllis writes, "Ah! Marie, it is a naughty world!"

JAD ADAMS

Editions

Supposedly published in aid of "The charitable organisation for the protection of pretty little girls," the book was most probably printed in Paris for Leonard Smithers and his French associate Duringe (his first name is unknown). A French translation, *Amours précoces: Scènes de la quinzième année* [Early loves: Fifteen-year-old Action] is in the British Library with a tentative date of 1900. Other English language editions were produced in Rotterdam (c. 1899–1900) by Bergé with the title *Love and Debauch* in Paris with a reprint in 1905. Another edition was printed in Paris in c. 1915–1920, and there was at least one U.S. reprint in New York, c. 1935.

Further Reading

Adams, Jad. *Madder Music, Stronger Wine: The Life of Ernest Dowson.* London: I.B. Tauris, 2000.

Kincaid, James R. *Child-Loving: The Erotic Child and Victorian Culture.* New York: Routledge, 1992.

CHOISEUL-MEUSE, FÉLICITÉ DE

c. 1770–c.1824
French novelist

Félicité de Choiseul-Meuse was a prolific novelist who mainly published respectable tales of love and adventure such as *Amour et gloire* [*Love and Glory*] (1817). She even wrote edifying stories of a morally undemanding kind, such as *L'Ecole des jeunes filles* [*School for Young Ladies*] (1822). But she also produced, in her earlier years, a series of more daring works: *Amélie de Saint-Far, ou la fatale erreur* [*Amélie de Saint-Far, or the Fatal Mistake*] (1802); *Julie, ou j'ai sauvé ma rose* [*Julie, or I Saved my Rose*] (1807?); and *Entre chien et loup* [*Twilight*] (1807). None of these three novels could be called pornographic, but they all deal with libertine themes, and all are concerned with women's sexual pleasure.

Amélie de Saint-Far is a story about feminine innocence. Amélie, a beautiful young girl on the verge of womanhood, is in the keeping of an unscrupulous guardian, Alexandrine, who is not virtuous herself, and is impatient at the sight of Amélie's flourishing virginity. Alexandrine has a lover, the impetuous Colonel Charles, who is powerfully attracted to Amélie, and one night forces Alexandrine to allow him into the young woman's room. But the sleeping virgin is so utterly charming that the would-be rapist lingers in contemplation of her beauty, enchanted by her sweet murmurings. He delays his attack for so long, in fact, that he eventually runs out of time, and Amélie remains intact. So powerful, so seductive is her innocence that it actually wins the aggressive male over to a gentler, more feminine form of sensuality. But Amélie's innocence does not guarantee her a passage through every erotic trial. The "fatal error" announced in the novel's title occurs later, when Amélie revives her

dear friend, the Duke de Nemours, who has almost drowned, by lying on him, and rubbing herself on him. First aid turns into copulation, but even this is not the end of Amélie's metaphorical virginity, because she is too innocent to know what she has been doing. Only when she yields to the duke a second time, having rather enjoyed the first, is she declared to have made the fatal error.

Julie, ou j'ai sauvé ma rose examines virginity in narrowly technical terms. The heroine, who recounts her own story from the point of view of successful maturity, tells how she elected to save her "rose" (her virginity), not by avoiding sexual contact, but by finding all sorts of ways to divert her male partners into other forms of pleasure, so that she would never be penetrated, and never risk pregnancy. This tactic is not presented in the novel as the height of virtue: it is just a sensible, yet pleasurable thing to do. Julie does not see herself as a tease, and does all that she can not to be a true erotic partner for her lovers, bringing them to satisfaction by practicing the most refined "caresses." At times, she doubts whether she has made the right choice, and on one occasion desires ardently to lose her cherished rose. But the man with whom she finds herself at that time is impotent. Julie's success depends on good fortune and on deceiving her partners. But her approach is presented as a viable set of tactics for women who wish, with safety, to make a career out of pleasure.

Entre chien et loup is about conjugal infidelity. A group of women are staying together in a country house during the hunting season. While the men are away on a hunting trip which lasts several days, the women take part in twilight sessions of intimate story-telling. Each tells how she deceived her husband in some way, usually by

235

not being a virgin at the time of marriage. They indulge and forgive each other's peccadillos, and moral complicity within the group extends to organizing financial support for the legal defence of one of their number. The story-telling is not a time of wildly licentious behavior: it is simply a period of permissiveness. Confessions are heard in the twilight, while male-centered rules are briefly suspended.

Around 1800, there tended in France to be a clear gender division in the production of stories about love and passion. Women novelists such as Adèle de Souza, Sophie Cottin, and Félicité de Genlis wrote sentimental stories in which young men and women died of unrequited love. On the other hand, male authors such as Mirabeau, Restif de la Bretonne, and Andréa de Nerciat were setting up the pattern of modern pornography, by writing forthright stories in which people took their sexual pleasure quickly and often. Choiseul-Meuse's erotic work, while self-consciously feminine, does not fit this gendered pattern. She focusses on women's pleasure and seductive tactics, attempting to make room for nuanced desires and gentle pleasures.

Choiseul-Meuse's later novels do not simply leave behind the earlier themes, although they focus less on feminine intimacy. Léonce, the hero of *Amour et gloire*, is a soldier, but not of the kind usually found in pornographic novels of that period, such as *Les Amours de garnison* [*Love-life in the Garrison*], where being a soldier is associated with straightforward sex, unencumbered by sentimentality or lengthy seduction. The expeditious use of women as sexual partners is very much the style of Léonce's fellow officer, the experienced Frédéric. But the focus of Choiseul-Meuse's novel is on Léonce, the young man in search of a pleasurably moral path which gives each woman the respect she deserves, but no more than that. The hero does in fact make one very bad error of judgment in this regard. He throws himself on the young, recently married, and pregnant Ursule. But Ursule goes cold and stiff—so cold, in fact, that her baby is said later to have died at that very moment. Despite Frédéric's observation that Léonce should not have been deterred by this "show" of reluctance, the hero comes to realize that Ursule's coldness is in fact a drastic symptom of genuine virtue. He thus learns to distinguish, in the course of his maturation, between women

like Ursule and those who, like the housekeeper Mariette, are available for seduction. It is fitting that, at the end, Léonce should marry a poised widow with whom he has been in love for some time. Mature love, in Choiseul-Meuse's work, seems to be beyond the moral agony that surrounds virginity. She certainly exploits the theme of virginity in narrative, as many libertine writers, including Sade, did before her. But she also seeks a way out of the confines of that theme, opening out into a world where feminine vice and feminine virtue are not so drastically opposed.

Biography

Nothing can be said with any authority about the life of Félicité de Choiseul-Meuse, not even the dates of her birth and death. She is believed to have been the mistress of the well-known cabaret singer, Gouffé. Her last published novel dates from 1824.

Peter Cryle

Selected Works

Amélie de Saint-Far, ou la fatale erreur. Hamburg and Paris: Chez tous les marchands de nouveautés, [1802?].
Julie, ou j'ai sauvé ma rose. Hamburg and Paris: Chez les marchands de nouveautés, 1807. [Translated into English as *Julie*, London: Odyssey Press, 1970.]
Entre chien et loup. Hamburg and Paris: Chez les marchands de nouveautés, 1809.

Further Reading

Cryle, Peter. *The Telling of the Act: Sexuality as Narrative in Eighteenth- and Nineteenth-Century France*. Newark, NJ: University of Delaware Press, 2001.
Cryle, Peter. "Making Room for Women in Pornographic Writing of the Early Nineteenth Century: *Entre chien et loup*, by Félicité de Choiseul-Meuse." In *Telling Performances*, edited by Rosemary Lloyd. Melbourne: Monash Romance Studies, 2000.
Glessner, Beth A. "The Censored Erotic Works of Félicité de Choiseul-Meuse." *Tulsa Studies in Women's Literature*, 16:1 (1997), 131–143.
Norberg, Kathryn. "Félicité de Choiseul-Meuse and the Salacious Novel" In *Going Public: Women and Publishing in Early Modern France*. Edited by Dena Goodman and Elizabeth Goldsmith, Ithaca: Cornell University Press, 1995.
Van Crugton- André, Valérie. "Félicité de Choiseul-Meuse: du libertinage dans l'ordre bourgeois." *Etudes sur le XVIIIe siècle*, 28 (2000), 109–115.

CHOISY, FRANÇOIS-TIMOLÉON, ABBÉ DE

1644–1724
French historian and memorialist

Although a prolific writer of works on religious thought and on ecclesiastical and royal history, the Abbé de Choisy is nowadays best known for his memorial writings, and in particular for the collection of autobiographical fragments known as the *Mémoires de l'abbé de Choisy habillé en femme* [*The Transvestite Memoirs of the Abbé de Choisy*]. Although written in the early Regency period at the request of the marquise de Lambert (1647–1733), Choisy's "transvestite memoirs" were published only posthumously and—initially, at least—in parts (in 1735 and 1839). They chronicle in a light and lively manner a number of relationships which Choisy claims to have conducted, while dressed as a woman, with a succession of young women from various backgrounds. Like Sidney's *Arcadia* and d'Urfé's *L'Astrée*, Choisy's memoirs thus offer variants of a popular early modern *topos* in which a male protagonist cross-dresses for purposes of seduction. Such works frequently aim to "reconcile eroticism and innocence" (Reynes, 1983) by blurring the boundaries between inter-female friendship and genuine heterosexual desire. The ease with which some such characters—and Choisy in particular—succeed in seducing women *while dressed as women* suggests the early modern period's relatively tolerant stance towards what would nowadays be called "lesbian" acts and desires. At the same time, Choisy's apparent skill at passing as a woman in even the most compromising of circumstances can certainly stretch credibility. Although his great-nephew, the marquis d'Argenson, vouches for the memoirs' authenticity, one cannot always tell whether Choisy might at certain points be embellishing the truth, seeking to bluff his reader, or being unwittingly duped by his own masquerades.

Whatever the case, cross-dressing is never simply a means to sexual conquest for Choisy. As the lavish descriptions of clothing throughout the memoirs illustrate, female attire can also have an erotic thrill of its own. Choisy attempts to justify the "bizarre" pleasure he derives from cross-dressing in two different ways; he attributes his transvestism both to his mother's idiosyncratic decision to have him brought up dressed as a girl and to a more general theory of mankind's self-love. Since love is born of beauty, which "is usually the lot of women," then it is only natural, he argues, that men who believe themselves beautiful will adopt feminine accoutrements. Choisy's personal vanity is considerable, yet also highly dependent on others. Indeed, although his sexual tastes are essentially heterosexual (he is particularly attracted to girls in their early teens), he enjoys and even requires the attention of male admirers as testimony to his feminine beauty.

Although the two principal sections of the memoirs are similar in structure and content, the nature of Choisy's transvestism differs in each. In one section, Choisy poses as a widow, the "comtesse des Barres," and moves to the country town of Bourges. Using his female persona as a disguise, he starts a secret liaison with a sixteen-year-old girl of noble stock, Mademoiselle de La Grise, who is apparently so innocent that she fails to recognize Choisy's true sex even during their sexual relationship. In a remarkable scene, Choisy has sexual intercourse with the girl in full view of a crowd of onlookers who, he claims, "increased the delight even more; it is sweet to deceive the eyes of the public." This remark is typical of Choisy's memoirs, throughout which the pleasures of theatrical and sexual performance are deeply intertwined. Choisy's second partner is an actress, Roselie, whom he dresses in male attire for his own pleasure. This "harmless amusement," however, stops

CHOISY, FRANÇOIS-TIMOLÉON, ABBÉ DE

once the young "man" starts to develop morning sickness.

In the other principal section, Choisy lives openly as a transvestite under the name of "Madame de Sancy." He starts a liaison with a young lady named Charlotte, whom, like Roselie, he also dresses in men's clothes; at one point, they stage a parodic marriage ceremony with both wearing the clothes of the opposite sex. Although public gossip about their activities prompts Choisy to abandon Charlotte, he is apparently happy for the sexual nature of his relationship with his next partner, Mademoiselle Dany, to become public knowledge. At one point, as in the other section of the memoirs, Choisy invites some dinner guests to watch him and his new partner in bed—even though this time he is fully recognizable as a man in women's clothing.

Choisy's memoirs suggest that the "Histoire de la Marquise-Marquis de Banneville" ("Story of the Marquise-Marquis de Banneville") is also his own work, although some attribute it to the pen of Charles Perrault. This curious tale of mistaken gender identity is clearly based on Choisy's own unconventional youth; it is, however, by his own admission an idealization of the truth: "The little Marquise could do many things which were forbidden to me, her superb beauty putting her under everyone's protection." Although the tale is not as sexually frank as the memoirs—no sexual activity takes place until the final page—its evocation of taboo sexuality is perhaps stronger. The tale's heroine is brought up unaware that "she" is in fact biologically male, and falls in love with a dashing young marquis who reciprocates "her" affection but is curiously unwilling to marry "her." When the marquise is finally told the truth of "her" own sex, "she" is appalled at "her" supposedly unnatural desires. However, physical pleasure takes over from reflection, and "her" initial shock is erased by her partner's caresses. Eventually, "she" persuades the marquis to marry, and only after their wedding is his reluctance explained: "he" is in fact a woman, and heterosexuality is restored. The conclusion to this tale is perhaps typical of Choisy's writings in that its ultimate assertion of heterosexuality cannot fully neutralize the eroticism that derives precisely from his playful, if at times a little insistent, troubling of gender boundaries.

Biography

Born in Paris, France, 16 August 1644. Studied theology at the Sorbonne, 1662–1666. Traveled to Italy, England, Siam. Accepted as member of the Académie Française, 1687. Died in Paris, France, 2 October 1724.

JOSEPH HARRIS

Editions

"Histoire de la Marquise-Marquis de Banneville." Mercure galant, dédié à Monseigneur le Dauphin (February 1695): 12–101.
"Histoire de la Marquise-Marquis de Banneville." Mercure galant, dedié à Monseigneur le Dauphin (August and September 1696): 171–238 and 85–185.
"Histoire de la Marquise-Marquis de Banneville." Paris: Anonymous, 1723.
Histoire de Madame la comtesse des Barres, à Madame la marquise de Lambert. Antwerp: Van der Hey, 1735.
Histoire de Madame de Sancy. In Mémoires de Choisy. Paris: Champollion-Figeac and Champollion fils, 1839.
Aventures de l'abbé de Choisy habillé en femme, preface by Paul Lacroix. Paris: Gay, 1862.
Mémoires de l'abbé de Choisy habillé en femme, edited by the chavelier de Percefleur [Fernand Fleuret and Louis Perceau], Paris: Bibliothèque des Curieux, 1920.
Mémoires de l'abbé de Choisy habillé en femme. Paris: Mercure de France, 2000.
Mémoires de l'abbé de Choisy habillé en femme. Toulouse: Ombres, 1995.
The Transvestite Memoirs of the Abbé de Choisy. Translated by R.H.F. Scott. London: Peter Owen, 1973 [also contains "The Story of the Marquise-Marquis de Banneville"].

Selected Works

Quatre dialogues [Four Dialogues], 1684 (with the abbé Dangeau).
Journal du Voyage de Siam fait en 1685 et 1686 [Journal of a Voyage to Siam Made in 1685 and 1686], 1687.
"Histoire de la Marquise-Marquis de Banneville" [The Story of the Marquise-Marquis de Banneville], 1695 (reprinted, each time with extensive additions, 1696 and 1723).
Mémoires pour servir à l'histoire de Louis XIV [Memoirs to Serve the History of Louis XIV], 1727.

Further Reading

Greenberg, Mitchell. "Absolutism and Androgyn: The Abbé de Choisy and the Erotics of Trompe l'Œil." In Repossessions: Psychoanalysis and the Phantasms of Early Modern Culture, edited by Timothy Murray and Alan K. Smith, Minneapolis and London: University of Minnesota Press, 1998.

Guild, Elizabeth. "Le moyen de faire de cela un grand homme": the Abbé de Choisy and the Unauthorized Body of Representation." *Romanic Review*, 85/2 (March 1994): 179–190.

Hammond, Nicholas. "All Dressed Up...: L'Abbé de Choisy and the Theatricality of Subversion." *Seventeenth-Century French Studies*, 21 (1999): 165–172.

Harris, Joseph. "Stealing Beauty: The Abbé de Choisy's Appropriation of the Feminine." In *Possessions*, edited by Julia Horn and Lynsey Russell-Watts, New York (and Frankfurt]: Peter Lang, 2002.

Parish, Richard. *The Abbé de Choisy (1644–1724).* A Historical and Critical Study, Oxford, 1974 (D. Phil. thesis).

Reynes, Geneviève. *L'Abbé de Choisy ou l'ingénu libertin*, Paris: Presses de la Renaissance, 1983.

Van der Cruysse, Dirk. *L'Abbé de Choisy, androgyne et mandarin.* Paris: Fayard, 1995.

CHOPIN, KATE

1850–1904
American novelist and short story writer

The Awakening

The Awakening was published to a deeply hostile reception in 1899, condemning its author to public ostracism, and subsequently fell into obscurity and then oblivion, from which it was not rescued until its reappearance in French translation in 1953. Its heroine's pursuit of sexual autonomy challenged Southern reactionary views of women which held maternal domesticity to be wholly adequate to their capacities and aspirations, and her liberation of an anarchic, promiscuous female sexuality undermined prevailing cultural myths which presented women as passive, passionless creatures characterized by an innate sexual apathy. A female-authored novel of adulterous passion, in which a wife deserts her husband, neglects her children, takes a lover, and commits suicide, was also a radical departure from the conventions of a genteel women's fiction devoted to historical romance and celebrations of marriage and motherhood.

The novel charts the newly awakened erotic yearnings of Edna Pontellier, a Kentuckian who has married unsatisfyingly into French Creole New Orleans society, during a long summer at the idyllic holiday retreat of Grand Isle in the Gulf of Mexico. As an outsider, Edna is confused by the Creoles' ambivalent sexuality, misled by a grossness which masks a real lack of sexual disturbance in their lives, and she is troubled equally by both. In their freedom from prudery and their uninhibited frankness of speech on the intimacies of sex and childbirth the Creoles appear to enjoy a guiltless, sophisticated sensuality which thrives in the lush ambience of the American tropic, but in reality this apparently open sexuality operates only within the closed conventions of marriage and is complemented by a fierce chastity and strict Catholic piety. In this chastely monogamous context, the devotions of her young admirer Robert Lebrun and his flirtations with other men's wives are merely conventional affectations, socially acceptable because they are unserious. Robert's unconsummated pinings are the aristocratic diversions of a latter-day courtly lover, a wholly pretend-affair which never poses any real danger to wifely chastity, and he mistakenly supposes Edna, as a woman of her class, to be familiar and complicit with the courtly code. When she, as an American, misconstrues both the code and his attentions, and his pretended feelings become real, Robert has to escape to Mexico to prevent the code (and the woman) from being violated, whereupon she starts an unfulfilling affair with a local philanderer, Alcée Arobin, who is willing, in the case of the non-Creole woman, to put the code aside.

For Edna, raised in a Presbyterian mistrust of sexuality, passion is not some bland property to be talked openly about and away, in Robert's fashion, but an obscure, suppressed force, a hidden thing that is secretly awakened and is mysteriously occasioned by the absence as much as by the presence of the lover. Her desire for Robert, aroused when he is away in Mexico, is primarily a fantasy eroticism, associated with her pubescent passion for a cavalry officer during her Kentucky girlhood, and the more distant the object of infatuation, the wilder and fiercer grow her yearnings. In Edna's consciousness, desire is habitually conceived in an imagery of unfathomable ocean currents and remote underground volcanoes, evoking "awe" and "delirium," and the passive narrative voice which has her lashed by every imaginable kind of wave—oceanic, musical, electrical—denotes a submissive longing to be engulfed and swept away by something uncontrollable. Her conformist businessman husband, the conventional rake Arobin, and the mannered effeminate Robert—all pallid, insipid creatures without any strong physical or sexual presence—are merely incidental to this "secret great passion." Thus the novel is, of necessity, a study in sexual solipsism, its erotic energy entirely a projection from its heroine's self-generated sexuality. Significantly, when Edna finally takes the sexual initiative with Robert, the only man for whom she shows any real desire, the phallic tropology is given to the woman while the man takes the female role. She bestows "a soft, cool, delicate kiss, whose voluptuous sting *penetrated* his whole being" and looks into his face "as if she would never *withdraw* her eyes more" (emphases added). Even before the rival claims of motherhood break symbolically into Edna's adulterous passion (she is summoned by her friend Adèle who is giving birth to another child), Robert's passive, squeamish response to her assault indicates that their love will not be consummated, abandoning her to the empty prospect of sterile liaisons with men like Arobin. Appropriately, even the sea, the site of her erotic adventure in which she learns spontaneously to swim "far out where no woman had ever swum before" and which appears at her death to enfold her in a sensuous, seductive embrace like a lover, is imaged as "an abyss of solitude" (the book's original title was *The Solitary Soul*). If Edna, as some mythopoeic critics have suggested, is archetypally reborn from her drowning into the mythic identity of Mermaid, Gulf Spirit, or Venus Aphrodite, goddess of sexual love, it is a lonely birth which takes place in an existential solitude far from the city world of men, and her final nakedness in the sea suggests, alongside her sexual awakening, a broader metaphysical communion

with the universe in which all social disguises are stripped away to reveal the radical aloneness of her essential, elemental being.

The Awakening is a masterpiece of condensed sensuous lyricism, abandoning chapter titles and employing surging oceanic imagery to maintain the impressionistic wave-like flow of Edna's reverie. Not surprisingly, given the novel's stylistic voluptuousness and its author's francophone background, elements of French *fin-de-siècle* writing—its hedonistic free-love mentality, erotic morbidity, and romantic fatalism—have been detected in Chopin's prose, while her theme of woman's victimization by her passions has been linked with the biological determinism of the American Naturalists (for Dr. Mandelet, love is merely Nature's decoy to secure mothers for the race). In Chopin's impromptu synthesis of styles, modes, and worldviews, European aesthetics and Mediterranean Creolism are drawn into the American cultural mainstream, resisting any definitive closure. At its climax, the novel, like its still-swimming heroine whose surname denotes a bridging agent, is left suspended in flux, in a process of becoming, and it can be read as a parable of Chopin's own literary awakening, demonstrating her openness to the many developing literary forms and influences that were fermenting as the new century dawned.

Biography

Born Katherine O'Flaherty in St. Louis, February 8, 1850 to an Irish immigrant father and Creole mother descended from French settlers. Educated at St. Louis Academy of the Sacred Heart, 1859–1868. Married Oscar Chopin, French Creole cotton trader, in 1870 and moved to New Orleans. Five sons and one daughter. Husband died of swamp fever, 1883. Published two novels, *At Fault* (1890) and *The Awakening* (1899), and two collections of short stories, *Bayou Folk* (1894) and *A Night in Arcadie* (1897). Died of a brain haemorrhage, 22 August 1904, while visiting the St. Louis World's Fair.

DEREK WRIGHT

Editions

The Awakening. Chicago and New York: Herbert S. Stone, 1899.
The Awakening: A Norton Critical Edition. edited by Margaret Culley, New York: Norton, 1976.

The Awakening. London: The Women's Press, 1978.

The Awakening. edited by Nina Baym, New York: Modern Library, 1981.

The Awakening and Selected Stories. edited by Sandra Gilbert, Harmondsworth: Penguin, 1984.

Selected Works

At Fault. 1890.
Bayou Folk. 1894.
A Night in Arcadie. 1897.

Further Reading

Bonner,Thomas ed., *The Kate Chopin Companion, with Chopin's Translations from French Fiction*, Westport, Connecticut: Greenwood Press, 1988.

Ewell, Barbara. *Kate Chopin*. New York: Frederick Ungar, 1986.

Koloski, Bernard, ed., *Approaches to Teaching Chopin's "The Awakening."* New York: Modern Language Association of America, 1988.

Koloski, Bernard. *Kate Chopin: A Study of the Short Fiction*. New York: Twayne, 1996.

Martin, Wendy ed*., New Essays on "The Awakening,"* Cambridge and New York: Cambridge University Press, 1988.

Rankin, Daniel S. *Kate Chopin and Her Creole Stories*. Philadelphia: University of Pennsylvania Press, 1932.

Seyersted, Per. *Kate Chopin: A Critical Biography*. Baton Rouge: Louisiana State University Press, 1969.

Seyersted, Per and Emily Toth ed., *A Kate Chopin Miscellany*. Natchitoches, LA: Northwestern State University Press, 1979.

Toth, Emily. *Kate Chopin: A Solitary Soul*. New York: Atheneum, 1989.

CHORIER, NICOLAS

c. 1609–1692
French lawyer, historian, erotic writer

L'Académie des dames

The many editions in Latin and French of *Aloysiae Sigea* (sometimes titled the *Meursius français*, etc., or, of course *L'Académie des dames*) were apparently widely read. This is because Chorier's book is the second publication in France to merit the name of sex manual—not just who might be having sex with whom, but in a practical way, how to do it. In terms of sexual possibilities, it goes much farther than Millot's *Ecole des filles* of 1655 (q.v.), into such areas as lesbianism and group sex, although the author was apparently not given any grief by the authorities.

Chorier's book, like Millot's *Ecole des filles* or Aretino's *Ragionamenti* (q.v.), is a dialogue between an experienced, (married) woman, Tullia, and an about-to-be married younger woman, Octavia. The book offers seven dialogues. The seventh is of questionable authenticity. The first finds Tullia and Octavia in bed together, as Octavia accepts Tullia's request that she place her fingers in Tullia's vagina and bring her to orgasm.

Things build up from there. Relations between Tullia and Octavia continue, and Tullia demands that Octavia recount in minute detail her wedding night, which is spied upon by her own mother, who puts her into bed with her heroically endowed new husband and then watches through the keyhole. Actually there is a lot of spying in *L'Académie des dames* and a lot of worrying about heroic members. Octavia learns that her mother, who enjoys a reputation of enviable virtue, is actually a dedicated libertine.

Things continue to develop. At the instigation of her mother, Sempronia, she, and Octavia are whipped by a priest. They find it exhilarating and ask for more. There are chastity belts, which mysteriously have extra keys.

Tullia explains how on a journey to the Rome region, and with the help of a middle-aged woman, Ursine, she spent an interesting afternoon with four merry men—a Frenchman, a German, and two Florentines. Starting with the Frenchman:

I obeyed him; but I had hardly moved my behind when I felt myself at the same time sprayed with a sweet liquid which sent me to seventh heaven. It was then that I shed all my modesty; I cared neither for honor, nor good manners (honnêteté); I lost even the memory of who I was and, among the confusion of all these pleasures, I came with extraordinary transports

The two Florentines, when their turn comes, practice what in French is called "le goût italien"—anal intercourse. There's more than one way to be deflowered, they declare, and proceed to *passer à l'acte*.

Eventually, Octavia finds herself with Tullia's friends Cléante and Médor. Octavia will have sex with Médor to return a favor owed by Cléante. Tullia directs the action, which is similar to the preceding. (The French surrealist writer Louis Aragon once remarked that while he had the greatest respect for those who believed that sex was forever different, he himself thought it was always pretty much the same.)

But now things take another turn. A recurring theme in Chorier is the unquestioning obedience women owe authority, their husbands, and the maintenance of wifely honor. Tullia explains that

It is permitted that a husband impose whatever laws he likes on his wife, and she must prudently observe them without objection. She's stupid if she imagines that there is something wrong with her obedience to him."

Before Tullia's marriage, her mother advises her that

You should consider Oronte . . . as a divinity on earth, you should cherish him and almost adore him and make yourself agreeable to all of his desires without imagining that they include anything dishonest in themselves. Those are, she continues, the prerogatives and the privileges of man; and here are the advantages of woman: She should believe if she is wise (sage), that since she was born for the pleasure of her husband, all the other men in the world are put there for nothing but her pleasure . . . .

Paradoxically, Tullia declares, "You have to believe that there is nothing that is not permitted to you, but that everything is forbidden." The general tone of the book suggests that this argument should perhaps be turned around the other way: everything forbidden and everything permitted.

Somebody might worry about so inconsistent a doctrine, but things take yet another turn. As it happens, Médor is late for the rendez-vous. The governor of the city likes to carouse with the young nobility. Cléante has managed to sneak out, but Médor has been retained. When Médor finally arrives and settles in, they are well on their way to realizing their goal of making love with Octavia ten times each, when there is a knock at the door. The two women's husbands are safely out of town. The call likely comes from the governor.

There follows what can only be described as an apology of hypocrisy. Tullia declares that:

Honesty consists only in appearances: *honestum est honestum viderei*. Men never get to the bottom of things; and since their mind is limited, they can see only what falls under their noses. We must put on the appearance of virtue in our actions, even the most criminal ones (speaking according to conventional mores); we will pass for honest even in the mind of the severest critics and the most austere censors of the pleasures of life. This, Octavia, is what we should work at, not imitating certain women who live without prudence, who cannot love without making known their passion, and who would find no pleasure in sex if they didn't tell everybody (contrast. Brantôme, infra).

Octavia responds that "It's a strange thing that we have to be so careful with actions which should be entirely free."

Tullia declares with conviction that "these are injust and rigorous laws, which these fake wise men have imposed upon us." We learn that the governor's messenger has indeed arrived and Tullia concludes that "You have to obey. The invitations of the great are so many commandments."

Elsewhere, in similar doctrinaire fashion, Tullia declares that notions of modesty and virtue are a "prejudice of our mind, which allows itself to be tyrannised by usage and custom." Octavia has remarked earlier that there is nothing rarer than "a wise [sage] and educated woman [a femme savante]" who stays within the limits of conventional conduct.

Actually, Tullia, her lover Cléante, and her husband Oronte formalize a contract in which, in exchange for some of Cléante's fortune, he gains free access to Tullia's body (improbable contracts are perhaps characteristic of classicist erotic literature; cf. La Fontaine, *Les troqueurs*].

Later on in the narrative, as Tullia goes to meet her four partners, Ursine dresses her in a white silk dress, so fine and so transparent that "I felt surrounded by a brilliant white cloud, rather than ordinary clothing . . . ."

Biography

Nicolas Chorier was a lawyer and polygraph in Vienne (France) and Grenoble in the seventeenth century. He wrote numerous "serious" books in Latin and French, including a *Histoire générale du Dauphiné*. He is remembered, however, for his erotic classic, printed and reprinted in Latin and French under various titles.

The publication history of Chorier's book is the result of elaborate subterfuge. The "serious" jurist apparently didn't want to be identified with his erotic book—or at least wanted to give the appearance of anonymity. The first edition was apparently published in Latin in Grenoble toward 1660. It was attributed to a learned Spanish lady of the sixteenth century, Luisa Sigea. The first title was *Aloisiae Sigea Toletana Satyra sotadica, de arcanis amoris, et Veneris*. The first edition was further attributed to a supposed Latin translator, one Joannes Meursius, a seventeenth-century Leyden scholar who died in 1653, before the first edition came out. The first French language edition was apparently published in 1680.

HERBERT DE LEY

Editions

L'Académie des dames, in Oeuvres Erotiques du XVIIe siècle. L'Enfer de la Bibliothèque Nationale. Paris: Fayard, 1988.
The Dialogues of Luisa Sigea. North Hollywood, CA: Brandon House, 1965.
Mémoires . . . . sur sa vie et ses affaires. Grenoble, 1868.

Further Reading

De Ley, Herbert. "Dans les reigles du plaisir. . . Transformation of Sexual Knowlege in Seventeenth-Century France." Edited by W. Leiner. *Onze Nouvelles Etudes sur l'image de la femme dans la littérature française du dix-septième siècle.* Tübingen: G. Narr, 1984.
Leibach-Ouvrard, Lise. "Pseudo-femino-centrisme et ordre (dis)simulé. La Satyre sotadica ...." *Papers in Seventeenth Century French Literature* (PFSCL) 1 (1992), 193–202.
———. "Sexe, simulacre, et 'libertinage honnête.' La Satyre sotadique ...." *Romanic Review* (RR) 83 (1992), 267–280.
Tobin, Ronald W. *Le Corps au XVIIe siècle.* Tübingen: Biblio 17 89, 1995.

CHRISTIAN, M.

1960–
American short story writer and novelist

After writing for nearly a decade with no publishing success, M. Christian took a class in erotica in 1992. The instructor, Lisa Palac, liked his story, "Intercore," so much that she published it in her magazine, *Future Sex*. From there, the story was selected for publication in *Best American Erotica 1993* and M. Christian's career as an erotica writer began.

Christian is often quoted as saying that the only thing he likes more than sex is writing. It is a statement easily borne out by his prolific and highly literate output since his first published story in 1992. He has crossed gender as well as sexual orientation lines in his work with chameleonic seamlessness, often leaving readers uncertain about who he is in real life. An intensely private person with an abundance of empathic emotion, he relishes the confusion he inspires and continues to write from perspectives he cannot experience but easily imagines.

With over 200 published stories, nearly two dozen anthologies, four collections, and two novels (one in the works) to his credit, Christian not only adores writing but has found a highly receptive audience for his work. Yet, it is not the sexual aspect of his writing that keeps him interested and busy—it is the process of storytelling. "I rarely write about things that turn me on," Christian says. "My biggest excitement is in the writing itself, the use of plot, characterization, description, etc."

Viewed widely throughout the genre as a master storyteller, Christian has been instrumental in helping to move erotica closer to mainstream fiction. His stories frequently deal with larger issues, such as moral ambiguity and crises of faith, within the context of a sexual situation. His emphasis is not so much on sexual acts as the motivations behind them. In many cases, sex is absent from his stories except as a means to an end for a character or as a backdrop to more universal, emotional dilemmas.

Proving himself even more versatile than simply writing from gay, lesbian, as well as straight viewpoints, Christian is also the author of some three dozen well-received horror and science fiction stories for such publications as *Space & Time, Talebones, Night Terrors*, and many anthologies and Web sites. He is also the co-editor (with Maxim Jakubowksi) of two mainstream anthologies, *The Mammoth Book of Future Cops*, and *The Mammoth Book of Tales of the Road*.

In *Dirty Words*, his first collection of gay erotica, the emotional landscape of his characters is revealed through the sexual situations in which they find themselves. The book was nominated by the Lambda Literary Foundation as the best collection of gay erotica in 2002, a rare distinction for a heterosexual writer.

His next book, *Speaking Parts*, was a collection of lesbian erotica that even *Curve* magazine, a magazine for and by lesbians, lauded. Because Christian never purports to be anything other than a heterosexual male, writing erotic fiction for certain orientations or genders, he is rarely condemned for writing outside his experience. On the contrary, his ability to capture the nuances of lesbian relationships in this collection was generally deemed extraordinary.

The Bachelor Machine echoed elements of Christian's first published story as well as his first anthology in its treatment of technology and science fiction. The stories are geared to a heterosexual and bisexual audience and take place in a future with surprising technological advances but timeless human quandaries. The book met with rave reviews from not only the erotica community but the professional science fiction world as well.

In his second collection of gay male erotica, *Filthy*, Christian's provocative, literary style is at its zenith. Through his signature style of eloquence and humor, he presents men at their best as well as their worst.

Over the years, Christian has been a respected columnist for a variety of publications and Web sites, including his celebrated "Confessions of a Literary Streetwalker" for the Erotica Readers and Writers Association (Web site). He has also authored various columns on everything from weird and unusual sex, to an analysis and celebration of movie villains ("They Only Wanted to Rule the World").

In addition, he is a Celebrity Author at Custom Erotica Source (www.customeroticasource.com), where he writes customized erotic fiction for individual clients. Beginning a new and exciting time in his professional life, he has also joined with the owner of Custom Erotica Source, Sage Vivant, in new writing projects, including the editing of five anthologies to date.

Christian's first novel, *Running Dry*, is not explicitly erotic but does deal with the power dynamic and love between two gay males amid a reinterpreted vampire ethos. More novels are in the works, both erotic and non-erotic.

Biography

Born in Whittier, California, 28 March 1960. Moved to San Francisco, 1988. Collection *Dirty Words* nominated for Lambda Literary Award, 2002.

JILL TERRY

Selected Works

Novels

Running Dry. 2006.

Collections

Dirty Words. Los Angeles: Alyson Books, 2001.
Speaking Parts. Los Angeles, 2002.
The Bachelor Machine. San Francisco: Green Candy Press, 2003.
Filthy. FL: Star Books, 2005.

Notable Anthologies (as editor)

Eros Ex Machina. Rhinoceros Publications, 1998.
The Burning Pen. Los Angeles: Alyson Books, 2001.
The Mammoth Book of Tales of the Road. New York, Carroll & Graf, 2002.
The Mammoth Book of Future Cops. New York, Carroll & Graf, 2003.
Confessions: Admissions of Sexual Guilt. Thunder's Mouth Press, 2005.

Further Reading

Christian, M. "Confessions of a Literary Streetwalker," monthly column available at http://www.erotica-readers.com (Erotica Readers and Writers Association).
Vivant, Sage and Christian, M. "Esoterica Erotica: The Road Less Traveled." *Moist* magazine, volume 1, issue 2, 2004.
Dean, William. "Inside The Bachelor Machine: An Interview with M. Christian." Clean Sheets (Web site): http://www.cleansheets.com/articles/interview_10.08.03.shtml. October, 2003.
Vivant, Sage. "News Flash: The best-seller writer of erotic lesbian fiction is ... a MAN!" *Brutarian*, Spring 2003.

CLARK, DAVID AARON

1960–
American novelist

One of the most mesmerizing themes in erotic fiction is obsession—think of Sir Stephen with O, Humbert Humbert with Lolita. In certain erotic novels, the narrator is haunted, by the object of his obsession. The narrator of David Aaron Clark's first novel, *Sister Radiance*, is haunted through the ages by a ghost lover named Luna.

Sister Radiance demonstrates that Clark knows obsession with an olfactory, tactile, kaleidoscopic familiarity.

Like William S. Burroughs—to whom he owes no small debt for the narrative freedom of *Sister Radiance*—Clark turns to post-modern science fiction as the most effective way to express his bleak, horrific vision of our times. His intensity keeps us with him on his trip through the lands of the dead even when the pace sometimes falters. *Sister Radiance* is a loosely structured series of stories, satires, scraps, even scenes from a film script, united by the narrator's search for the lost Luna—and by Clark's densely metaphoric language. This poetic approach to the eternal dance between Eros and Thanatos enables Clark to mystify, horrify, and intrigue the reader, while shuffling a dazzling deck of literary cards.

One of Luna's incarnations is a haughty and unapproachable redhead named Wanda. We meet her in a chapter entitled "Aphrodite in Ermine," the conceit of which is that the narrator has written a letter to the editor of *Penthouse Forum*. He tells of going up to Wanda/Luna's hotel room. Aware that she embodies his ideal woman, she tortures him, at first psychologically, and then physically—she drives a knife through his hand. He fights back and flees, but concludes his letter to *Penthouse Forum* with a declaration of undying love. The level of S/M play is matched with rhapsodies about murder and cozily domestic scenes of cannibalism. Drugs are used to flagellate the narrator's undeserving soul, and are an insufficient anodyne for his suffering. At the end of this long hallucination of a novel, he is living in a teepee, the last apparition of Luna before him, arrayed in bright colors and decked in gold and precious stones. With few specifically erotic passages, *Sister Radiance* reflects an ability to absorb and transmute a dizzying range of media and technology overload.

Clark's *The Wet Forever*, his second novel, features a doomed hero named Janus, an original creation seldom seen in erotic fiction: the Dostoyevskyan Underground Man with a sexual obsession. When Janus meets a dominatrix named Madchen, sparks fly—illuminating the dungeon environment of the novel, which moves as in an urban nightmare from New York to Berlin. (At the time of writing, Clark was playing in a punk rock band, The False Virgins, and living with his lover, who later committed suicide. He has said that the Janus and Madchen characters were to some extent taken from his own life.)

Sadomasochism is a dominant theme in all of Clark's work, which is why he was asked by the publisher Richard Kasak to write *The Marquis De Sade's Juliette: Vengeance on the Lord*. It is an epistolary novel, a la Bram Stoker, heavily influenced by the film directors Abel Ferara (and Freddie Francis, who made many of the classic Hammer horror films. Juliette, as envisioned by Clark, is the most destructively powerful domina ever to appear in New York. Clark deliberately sets out to rival Sade's *Juliette* in its horrific, hallucinatory presentation of nightmarish sadomasochism.

Clark's next novel, *Into the Black*, was commissioned by Maxim Jakubowski for his series, *Eros Plus*, and appeared in the United Kingdom in 1996. It is a horror novel in a way his previous fictions were not, with the supernatural in the forefront this time. Once again his protagonist is a professional dominatrix—Mary Ellen Masters—who has an encounter with a demonic force, an experience which deepens her perceptions of New York and the denizens of its sexual underground. Clark's dark vision is implacable and ferocious in *Into the Black*, and not for the squeamish.

Clark co-edited the anthology *Ritual Sex* with Tristan Taormino in 1996. Its theme is the many intersections of sex and religion, and includes contributions by Pat Califia, Samuel R. Delany, Alice Joanou, Thom Metzger, and Genesis P. Orridge.

True Blood, a collection of photographs by underground photographer Charles Gatewood, chronicles San Francisco's blood-play world. Clark contributed a poetic text that has a Rimbaudian intensity.

The unifying vision in Clark's world is spiritual. There is a God, and angels, but this makes no difference. Only the extremes of sadomasochism can express the horror of the damned souls he writes about, and the Sadean, subterranean worlds he creates.

Biography

Born in Camden, New Jersey in 1960. He graduated from Rutgers University with a major in journalism in 1985. He is the author of four novels, the editor of an anthology of erotic fiction, and has collaborated on books with photographers and comic artists. The first novel he wrote, *Sister Radiance*, was published second, in 1994, following the appearance of *The Wet Forever* in 1993. He has been a performance artist, musician, and magazine editor, and lives in Los Angeles, where he directs erotic videos.

MICHAEL PERKINS

Selected Works

The Wet Forever. 1993.
Sister Radiance. 1994.
The Marquis De Sade's Juliette. 1995.
Into The Black. 1995.
Ritual Sex (anthology, with Tristan Taormino). 1996.
True Blood. 1997.

CLELAND, JOHN

1710–1789
British novelist, playwright, and journalist

John Cleland is without doubt the most well-known of British writers of eighteenth-century, erotic literature. Whereas Eliza Haywood, Edmund Curll, or Matthew Lewis may also be familiar to the specialist, even students otherwise ignorant of the details of British literature are quick to remember John Cleland as the author of that infamous novel, *Memoirs of a Woman of Pleasure*, or, as it is more commonly known, *Fanny Hill*. Illegal in the United States until 1963 and in Great Britain until 1970, *Fanny Hill* is now frequently included in undergraduate surveys and is required reading for all serious students of the British novel. As well-known as the novel is, however, John Cleland has himself never emerged as a literary figure deserving more than "minor" status. His life—regardless of William Epstein's excellent 1974 biography—remains shrouded in mystery, and, with the exception of *Memoirs of a Woman of Pleasure*, his works are for the most part unread and out of print. Beginning in the 1990s, scholars have begun to make amends and realize the degree to which Cleland's life and work are both representative of the complexity of the eighteenth-century cultural marketplace and richly deserving of the renewed critical interest.

John Cleland was born in Kingston-on-Thames sometime during the late summer or early fall of 1710. Christened on September 24th at Kingston's All Saint's Parish church, he was the first child of William Cleland of Edinburgh and Lucy DuPass of Surrey. At the time of his son's birth, William Cleland was a struggling Army officer desperate to make ends meet. Although of respectable lineage—the Clelands were a well-known Scottish family—William had nevertheless grown up without the benefit of a family estate, which had been sold out of the family in 1640, and so had purchased a commission and served under Lord Mark Kerr at Almanza. When it became increasingly difficult

to support his family, William used his connections to acquire a position in the Civil Service. Appointed to the Commission of Customs in 1713, he was to remain employed throughout the most tumultuous years of the eighteenth century, a feat that offers eloquent testimony to his social and political skills. Indeed, he was well-known for his learning and conversation and evidently cultivated a wide circle of influential friends both in Edinburgh and London, among them Alexander Pope, Lord Orrery; Edward Harley, 2nd Earl of Oxford; and Richard Lumley, 2nd Earl of Scarborough. He was aided by his wife Lucy who, from contemporary reports, thoroughly enjoyed the circles in which her husband traveled.

In January 1721, at the age of ten, John Cleland entered the fourth form at the prestigious Westminster School, preparatory school for England's elite. For William Cleland, of gentle birth and moderate income, John's matriculation would have been quite an accomplishment, one that promised great things for son and father alike. The rigorous education and the easy transition to either Oxford or Cambridge were no less important than the invaluable social connections. School mates were the sons of the country's most powerful families, and many were destined to be England's leaders. John's tenure at Westminster, however, was to be brief. Although he distinguished himself in one short year and was chosen to be a King's Scholar—expenses paid by the crown and a berth at Oxford or Cambridge guaranteed—John left the school in 1723, two years after he had arrived and the same year that his younger brother Henry arrived. The reasons for John's departure remain unclear. Given his scholarship and his strong academic standing, financial difficulties or a poor performance seem less likely than some kind of embarrassing youthful indiscretion. Whatever the reason, John's circumstances changed abruptly, and by the age of seventeen, just about the same time he would have been off to the university, he had enrolled as a common foot soldier for the East

India Company and left London on board the schooner *Oakham* bound for Bombay.

The considerable difference between Westminster graduate and East India foot soldier suggests the possibility of some kind of breach between father and son. Either John Cleland was a strong-minded adventurer eager to throw his father's ambitions to the wind or an unlucky malcontent who was banished from the family circle. Either way it seems strange that the socially conscious Clelands should have supported a career that would take their eldest son so far from the elite circles of Edinburgh and London. On the other hand, the Clelands were certainly no strangers to military service, and the DuPass family did have considerable experience in India. Perhaps John Cleland sought the economic security promised by a career with the East India Company and was willing to risk the difficult and extended apprenticeship. In fact, Cleland moved rapidly up the ranks of the East India Company hierarchy. He moved first to the Bombay Island gun room and then to assistant, or "montross," to the gunners. He then switched into civil service, becoming an assistant secretary to the Mayor's Court and then Attorney. He applied for and received a promotion to "Writer" in the company's service in February 1731, and although this position was the lowest on the civil service ladder and paid a mere five pounds a year, and although Cleland was older than most of the other men at his rank, the promotion suggests that he was proceeding with long-term achievement in mind. He also had the full support of his father, who was required to secure the 500 pounds "security." A short three years later (the writer's standard apprenticeship is five years), Cleland advanced to "Factor," a promotion that both increased his salary to fifteen pounds a year and his responsibilities. This smooth advancement was, however, soon to hit a rough spot. In December 1734, Cleland was appointed attorney for one Lollaboy Soncurr, a Hindu, who had brought a suit against Henry Lowther. The latter was the Chief of the East India Company's Custom House at Surat, the former a merchant who asserted that Lowther had not paid his debt in full. The politically expedient course of action was obvious, but instead of towing the company line, Cleland countered with an unexpectedly impassioned defense: Lowther did not make a simple error but was consistently and irremediably incompetent, a disgraceful and unscrupulous embarrassment to the Company. The hearing quickly became the sensational event of the season, and when the Court ruled, Lowther was vindicated and Cleland disgraced. To add insult to injury, the Bombay Mayor's Court not only arranged for Cleland's banishment to parts unknown, but also for the event to be stricken from the records heading back to London. At the last moment, one of the Council, John Braddyll, changed his mind and insisted by way of his dissent that the entire hearing become public. The result was that Cleland's fate now hinged upon a verdict from London. He had to wait for more than a year, and in the ensuing months Lowther was dismissed for gross mismanagement, and the unthinkable became real: a low-level bureaucrat attacked a corrupt superior and emerged victorious. Several key promotions followed until in October 1737 Cleland attained the rank of Junior Merchant at thirty pounds a year. He was then appointed Secretary to the Council in January 1739, the same Council that only four years earlier was ready to end his career. Whether his success was largely attributable to skill or luck, John Cleland managed to overcome several obstacles and, against the odds, establish for himself a respectable position and a secure future with the East India Company.

Although there is no record of Cleland's intellectual pursuits during this period, one curious item now in the possession of the Bodleian Library at Oxford suggests that he was anything but idle. The book, a collection of miniature portraits of Indian rulers, was given to the library by Alexander Pope in 1737 and bears this inscription: "This Book, (containing one hundred & seventy eight Portraits of the Indian Rajahs, continued to Tamerlane & the Great Moguls his Successors as far as to Aureng-Zebe) Was procured at Surat by Mr. John Cleland, and given to the Bodley Library, as a token of Respect, by Alex. Pope." Working strenuously to resuscitate his career with the East India Company, Cleland also had time to collect books and pursue a correspondence with the most famous literary figure of his day.

No sooner was his career back on track than Cleland suddenly requested leave to return to London. On 5 September 1740, he informed the Council that "Certain Concerns of the utmost Importance to my private Fortune [require] my personal Attendance in England." A short two weeks later, Cleland boarded *Warwick* and sailed for England. After thirteen years in India, John Cleland was once again ready to seek his fortune back in his native land.

Cleland arrived home to disturbing news. His father, so successful for so many years, had finally been relieved of duty. Now sixty-six years old and in declining health, William Cleland was no longer useful to the Walpole administration. Neither his emotional remonstrance nor his more than twenty-six years of service proved effective: he lost his job in early June 1741. When his son arrived in August, he found his father dangerously ill from the kidney stones he suffered from for the last decade. After a brief reunion with his first child, William Cleland died on 21 September 1741. According to Pope, Cleland dutifully assisted his mother and sister, helping them move to a new house in St. James and generally supporting them through their painful loss. After this mention, however, details of Cleland's activities disappear. It is not until February 1747 that Cleland reappears in the historical record, when he was sued by one Thomas Cannon for 800 pounds and imprisoned in debtor's prison. Whether or not Cleland actually owed the money is not clear, but scholars agree that sometime during his imprisonment Cleland decided to write for money. Consequently, advertisements for Cleland's first by far most famous novel, *Memoirs of a Woman of Pleasure*, appeared while its author was still imprisoned in the Fleet.

The Memoirs of a Woman of Pleasure

Appropriately enough, given Cleland's imprisonment, *The Memoirs* is preoccupied with boundaries and their transgressions. Although, for example, the narrative follows the confessional model of Daniel Defoe's *Robinson Crusoe* (1719) and *Moll Flanders* (1722) and takes us quite deliberately from innocence to experience to perversion and then back to a "normal," middle-class marriage based on love and sexual compatibility, the boundary of most interest to Cleland is that between love and lust. Novels like Samuel Richardson's *Pamela* (1741)—one of the most important models for Cleland's fictional experiment—celebrate the former only by overpowering the latter. They begin with religious ideals—virtue, chastity, love—and work themselves grudgingly downward to the rather

embarrassing facts of the body. Cleland, on the other hand, begins with the material reality of the body, of pleasures that can't be denied, of desires that are inescapably and profoundly human. He then works his way up—quite satirically at times—to the emotional truths of human love.

Indebted as much to Hogarth's *A Harlot's Progress* (1732) as to Defoe's and Richardson' novels, Cleland begins with the orphaned, young Fanny leaving the peaceful countryside for the dangerous opportunities of London. Following its more respected predecessors, *Memoirs of a Woman of Pleasure* will focus upon the relationship between female identity and female virtue. Like *Pamela* and *Shamela* and *Moll Flanders* and *Roxana*, *Memoirs* wants to understand the mystery of womanhood. Unlike those predecessors, however, *Memoirs* refuses to make an ethical state (virtuous or corrupt) contingent upon a bodily condition (virginal or experienced). Fanny will engage in an amazing variety of "fallen" activities but will emerge virtuous (and married) in the end because virtue has been redefined as a state of the heart independent of sexual behavior. Love and lust, in other words, do not have to compromise each other because corporeal desire is an appetite like hunger whose appeasement is natural rather than sinful. Throughout the novel, Fanny will participate in sexual activity—sometimes for money, sometimes for love, sometimes for spite, sometimes to escape boredom, sometimes only because she wants to feel sexual pleasure—yet she is allowed to retain her character, her essential humanity, her innate and indissoluble "goodness" because—in the logic of the narrative—she is "real."

Fanny's reality results directly from her various and complex motivations, from her own conflicts and confusions, and from her willingness to assume the masquerades necessary to survive life in mid-eighteenth-century Britain. When her lover Charles is abducted and she is left at the mercy of an avaricious landlady, Fanny allows herself to be sold to Mr. H—. The scene of her surrender is crucial to the narrative because Fanny falls into a life of prostitution, into a world where her material survival is contingent upon sexual favors given and received. She also falls, with her attentive reader, into a narrative that justifies corporeal pleasure as inescapable from both human and literary experience.

As Fanny explains, she was (and presumably continues to be) "in love" with Charles and thus committed to traditionally romantic notions of sexual fidelity. But her "circumstances" overwhelm her "virtue": faced with unwanted intercourse, she faints dead away and awakens to find Mr. H— "buried in me." Fanny makes it clear that she was more acted upon than acting, that she was paralyzed by economic desperation and victimized by her lack of options. But she also makes clear that her fall, like Eve's before her, is a kind of awakening, a revelation bringing a certain kind of unanticipated knowledge. Although she awakens from her "trance" "passive and innocent of the least sensation of pleasure," thus proving to the reader her sincere love of Charles, the sexual body will not be denied for long. However much she would wish it otherwise, Fanny's body has a reality, a truth, that she can not control.

The passions of Fanny's body will of course retain center stage. She is, after all, a whore-in-training. As a result, we are not surprised when she loses her moral outrage and guilt and acquires a "grateful fondness" for Mr. H—. At the same time, she develops a thirst for "more society, more dissipation." When she discovers her "keeper" having his way with her maid—who is portrayed, by the way, as a false Pamela protecting a "*vartue*" she is all too willing to lose—Fanny revenges herself in kind with Mr. H—'s valet. This young, handsome, country lad is untutored in the ways of love but is equipped by nature with "such an over-sized machine" that even our experienced heroine is given pause. Fanny hardly profits—financially, that is—from the encounter. In fact, she herself pays the valet for his services. Why, then, does the narrative make so much of the event? And in what sense is Fanny now a "professional"? By way of an answer, consider an aside to Fanny's correspondent provided after another long account of intercourse with the valet:

> And here, Madam, I ought perhaps to make you an apology for this minute detail of things that dwelt so strongly upon my memory after so deep an impression. But, besides that this intrigue bred one great revolution in my life, which historical truth requires I should not sink upon you; may I not presume that so exalted a pleasure ought not be too ungratefully forgotten or suppressed by me, because I found it in a character in low life where, by the by, it is oftener met with, purer and more unsophisticated, than amongst the false ridiculous refinements with which the great suffer themselves to be so grossly cheated by their pride....

This interlude is crucial, Fanny tells us, because it marks her understanding of the highest pleasures of purely physical sex. Will, Mr. H—'s valet, is not her equal: he has no education, no experience, no feelings, no real "self" to speak of. He is merely an animal, a male body that needs to satisfy its desires, a prodigious penis animated with all the energies of youth. It is precisely because of his essential physicality and corresponding lack of "self" that Fanny is able to experience a sexual intensity unmarred by distractions of any sort. This event is "revolution[ary]" for our heroine because it introduces her to the highest pleasures the body can attain. She is a "professional," in other words, not because she has sex for money, which she doesn't, but because she has sex only to have sex, only to feel pleasure and satisfy her own desires. Like the book that bears her name, Fanny is now committed to passion.

Predictably, Fanny is soon caught in the act by a suspicious Mr. H—. She is given "fifty guineas," thrown out on the street, and forced to take up residence with Mrs. Cole, a good-natured Madame whose house of prostitution epitomizes "decency, modesty, and order." That these events bring Volume I to a close and that Volume II is almost exclusively preoccupied with Fanny's adventure as a "professional" in Mrs. Cole's residence should remind us that Cleland's exploration of the mystery of female sexuality, his celebration of the "mechanical" pleasures of the female body, is inextricable from Fanny's experiences as a "whore." Issues of female pleasure, in other words, are intimately tied to issues of female identity, and that identity is always already criminal in the sense that Fanny is by definition aberrant and perverse.

After a variety of minor adventures, the generous Mrs. Cole proposes a lucrative deception: the sale of Fanny's "fictitious maidenhead" to one "Mr. Norbert," a slightly dissipated young man of fertile imagination for whom female chastity is the Holy Grail of sexual fetishes. The price is 400 guineas, and the sale requires that Fanny play the part of the blushing maiden whose fear of defloration is such that no advantage be sacrificed without great struggle. The scene is farcical because Mr. Norbert is barely up for the job and because Fanny is contemptuous of his notions of female innocence but all too willing to play her part to the extreme:

> All my looks and gestures ever breathing nothing but that innocence which the men so ardently require in us, for no other end than to feast themselves with the pleasure of destroying it, and which they are so grievously, with all their skill, subject to mistakes in.

Norbert's fantasy is, according to Fanny, entirely solipsistic. His adoration of innocence has less to do with women than with his own need to be the conquering hero, the all powerful ravisher of virgins and other defenseless creatures. The long descriptions of Norbert's lame efforts thus work in conjunction with Fanny's editorializing to make clear that Cleland's real target was the idea of female chastity that made Samuel Richardson a famous man.

As comic as it is, however, the lengthy account of Fanny's supposed "defloration" by Mr. Norbert serves serious satiric ends. Cleland's target is Richardson's fetish: the male adulation of female chastity. Rewriting *Pamela*, Cleland returns to the scene where the predatory Mr. B— hesitates before the struggling virgin and the encouraging whore. The polar opposition so necessary to Richardson's fantasy (and Norbert's) collapses in on itself as Fanny finds it entirely possible to play both roles at once. Her story, of course, like both Pamela's and Shamela's before her, like Moll Flanders' and Roxana's as well, is itself a masquerade, a fictional account of female experience authored by a man eager to establish a new "realism." Cleland ups the epistemological ante, however, by tying the truth of his narrative to the truth of the female body. Those other stories, *Fanny Hill* suggests, are male fantasies as deluded as those of Mr. Norbert: first, because they omit graphic sexual descriptions; and second, because the pleasures they describe are exclusively male. *Fanny Hill*, on the other hand, speaks both the truth of human sexuality generally and of female sexuality in particular. *Fanny Hill* is real, Cleland would have us believe, because it describes and recreates for its readers the "reality" of women's pleasure.

Cleland's insistence on the reality of Fanny's pleasure stands in marked contrast to the inadequacies of its linguistic representation. Fanny apologizes repeatedly for her inability to represent the pleasure she feels, and the "subject" of her memoir is, regardless of its infinite variety, "eternally one and the same." That subject is of course sexual pleasure, and Fanny complains that words like "joys," "ardours," "transports," or "ecstasies" simply cannot represent the physical bliss of orgasm. To the author's unavoidably repetitive vocabulary, the reader must add her own "imagination" and "sensibility." Only then will the "pictures" of pleasure spring to "life."

Fanny's comments on the importance of the imagination to the fictional representation of physical pleasure are crucial to the narrative as a whole. Regardless of the inadequacies of language, for instance, Cleland goes to some trouble to emphasize the imaginative interplay between real sex and its fictional counterpart. Fanny, for example, plays the voyeur on numerous occasions, deriving real, physical pleasure from observing the erotic activities of others. At the very beginning of the novel, while under Phoebe's tutelage, she masturbates in a closet as she watches Mrs. Brown and her lover at play. Much later, during her first and only experience with group sex, her "imagination" becomes so "heated" by "all the moving sights of the night" that when she finally has intercourse the pleasure is almost unbearable. Then, at the very end of the novel, when Fanny describes her reunion with Charles, the imagination plays what at first appears to be a similarly important role:

> My thighs, now obedient to the intimations of love and nature, gladly disclose, and with a ready submission resign up the lost gateway to entrance at pleasure: I see! I feel! The delicious velvet tip!—he enters might and main with—oh!—my pen drops from me here in the ecstasy now present to my faithful memory! Description, too, deserts me and delivers over a task, above its strength of wing, to the imagination; but it must be an imagination exalted by such a flame as mine, that can do justice to that sweetest, noblest of all sensations....

With this scene the reader reaches the self-consciously humorous climax of *Fanny Hill*, a sexual experience with a pleasure so intense that its memory can conflate past and present, male and female, character and reader all into one moment of ecstatic union. We are to understand that with the reappearance of Charles, the "mechanical" pleasures of the body described earlier merge rather conveniently with the transcendent pleasures of true love. The result is a pleasure of theological import, of body and spirit together, that is accessible only through an "exalted" imagination. Seemingly more romantic than his nemesis Richardson—who, after all, ends *Pamela* with an obnoxiously practical marriage manual—Cleland insists all along on a powerful female sexuality, authentic and autonomous, but in the end he positions that sexuality within the reassuring confines of true love and the happily-ever-after of a middle-class, romantic marriage.

Memoirs of a Woman of Pleasure did not go unnoticed by the authorities. Early in November 1749, a Messenger of the Press knocked on Cleland's door and off he went to court. Letters were written; strings were pulled; fines were paid. And then, just when Cleland appeared to be in the clear, an unusual event occurred. On February 8, and then again exactly one month later on March 8, earthquake tremors rattled London complacency and reminded residents that it is never too late to repent. Exact reasons for the divine wrath were temporarily unclear, and, predictably, explanations varied, until, on March 16, the Bishop of London, Thomas Sherlock, set matters straight in a Pastoral Letter to his urban flock. The earthquakes, he explained, were sent to punish bawdy books and prints, in particular those "vile books" that relate the histories of whores. Just in case the Secretary of State, Thomas Pelham-Holles, First Duke of Newcastle, missed the subtlety of the Pastoral Letter, the good Bishop wrote directly to complain that *Fanny Hill* was "the Lewdest thing [he] ever saw" and that the Secretary should "give proper orders, to stop the progress of this vile Book, which is an open insult upon Religion and good manners, and a reproach to the Honour of the Government, and the Law of the Country." Unable or unwilling to argue with earthquakes, Newcastle issued a warrant the next day.

Once again, John Cleland appeared to be in serious trouble. But the Bishop of London could not bring about prosecution for a literary crime whose very status as crime was culturally undefined. Somehow or other, Cleland emerged unscathed. The Bishop of London continued to pressure the Duke of Newcastle; the Duke of Newcastle continued to pressure John Sharpe, the Attorney General; and Sharpe evidently endured the pressure manfully, but did little to pursue the case. Even if Cleland was eventually summoned before the Privy Council—and we are not sure that he was—the repercussions were negligible. The author of Fanny Hill was now securely in place at *The Monthly Review* where

he continued to churn out essays for his friend and co-conspirator, Ralph Griffins. Although no one could know it at the time, Cleland had officially embarked upon a literary career that had unfortunately already seen its zenith.

Memoirs of a Coxcomb

When circumstances forced Cleland to try his hand at the novel once again, the author of *Fanny Hill* was a sadder and wiser man. Beaten down by poverty and cowed by the courts, he resorted to formula: he rewrote his first novel from the male perspective. The passions of *Memoirs of a Coxcomb* (1751), however, are nothing like the passions of *Memoirs of a Woman of Pleasure*. Yes, William Delamore, the novel's hero, will, like Fanny before him, fall in love early on, experience a variety of sexual conquests, and then be happily reunited with his beloved at the novel's close. But William Delamore is more discreet than Fanny Hill. Although he confesses to having had sexual activity, the descriptions of his experiences are mild enough for Samuel Richardson or Jane Austen. Gone is the unbridled licentiousness; gone is the passionate storytelling; gone is the desire to arouse the reader. This new-found modesty, accompanied as it is by weak writing and unremarkable characterizations, has led numerous commentators to bemoan Cleland's sudden loss of talent. Where, they ask sadly, did the vitality of *Fanny Hill* go?

The answer seems clear enough: fear of prosecution, the burdens of poverty, and writing under deadline all conspired to produce mediocrity. But the real answer may be more complicated. Consider, for example, two remarkable and mutually illuminating passages from *Memoirs of a Coxcomb*. The first is a polemical aside offered by Delamore early in the novel:

I cannot here refrain from observing, that, not without reason, are the romance, and the novel writers in general, despised by persons of sense and taste, for their unnatural, and unaffecting descriptions of the love-passion. In vain do they endeavour to warm the head, with what never came from the heart. Those who have really been in love, who have themselves experienced the emotions, and symptoms of that passion, indignantly remark, that so far from exaggerating its power, and effects, those trifflers do not even do it justice. A forced cookery of imaginary beauties, a series of mighty marvellous facts, which spreading an air of fiction through the whole, all in course weaken that interest and regard never paid but to truth, or the appearances of truth; and are only fit to give a false and adulterated taste of a passion, in which a simple sentiment is superior to all their forced productions of artificial flowers. Their works in short give one the idea of a frigid withered eunuch, representing an Alexander making love to Statira.

This is a blistering critique of popular fiction for not being realistically passionate, and one would expect that the author of *Fanny Hill* would make good on his promise to deliver the "truth" of human desire. But now consider a scene at the beginning of the third volume, in which the hero visits a whorehouse, and, in what appears to be just a rewriting of a similar scene in *Fanny Hill*, the young prostitutes are asked, one after another, to tell their stories. In *Memoirs of a Woman of Pleasure*, the women are beautiful, and the stories they tell are of their sexual initiation. In *Memoirs of a Coxcomb*, the situation is the same, but the treatment is quite different. The women are as young and as pretty as those in *Fanny Hill*, but our narrator is not impressed. He notices that their dress is "tawdry," that it pretends a connection to "real high life" that their behavior belies. He notices too that their make-up is intended to conceal "the ill effects of their night vigils," but that it actually does the reverse: it establishes "the finished look of their trade." In short, both masquerades fail. Both reveal exactly that which they were intended to conceal. The same is true of the stories that are told. The first woman (they are all unnamed) claims to be "the daughter of a reverend clergyman" who was left "destitute" by his death and who was then "betrayed" into prostitution by a supposed friend of the family. Our hero's partner for the evening, who is by the way the least attractive of the group, scoffs at this recitation. She scoffs again at each of the other stories, as each relates "some tragical circumstance" and some rogue's "betrayal." When her turn finally comes, she speaks "very naturally":

> Gentlemen, if you have any curiosity concerning me, I hope you will be so good as to suspend it, 'till my story is *made* too; at present, I have not one ready, unless you will be contented with the plain truth, which is, that I am the daughter of an honest chairman, and as soon as I came of age to feel desires, having no education to awe, and instruct me of the danger of humoring them, I honestly gave way to their force, and was soon let into the great secret, by a young prentice in our neighbourhood, since which, after various adventures, I came at length to harbour here.

No manipulative fictions, no seductive fantasies, no self-serving masquerades. Indeed, she insists that there is no "story" at all—just "the plain truth." The latter is embarrassing, not to the men who listen, "they did not think a whit the worse of her for it," but to her fellow whores who are exposed and humiliated. Suddenly, the whore's story goes from a romantic tale of bad luck and betrayal, of good women losing out to bad men, to a devious and self-serving fiction. The moment is one of adjudication, of separating the good from the bad, the truthful from the deliberately deceptive. In that moment when a new "real" is trotted out, standards shift, measurements recalibrate, and prostitution and its stories are together brought up short.

When the unattractive, unnamed whore in *Memoirs of a Coxcomb* refuses to tell a story, she claims a "real" that exposes her fellow prostitutes as liars. Their stories, after all, are designed to absolve the tellers of all responsibility: whores are made, it would seem, only from bad luck and bad men. It is, she says, simply not so; whores are actually made from ignorance. Had she the "education to awe and instruct" her in the ways of desire, all would have been different. Cleland's unnamed whore also directly and powerfully challenges the novel of which she herself is a revision. The whores' stories in *Fanny Hill* are not about bad luck and betrayal, poverty and powerlessness; they are instead titillating, romantic, and without adversity of any kind. Their heroines fall into a sexual experience that is "natural" and loving, and they come to Mrs. Cole's establishment with no more regret than they would accept employment as barmaids or governesses. Thus with one short speech in an otherwise unremarkable novel, two separate fantasies about prostitution, about women and their criminal pleasures, are exposed as artificial claptrap. At the same time, as the earlier polemic suggests, Cleland issues a challenge to his fellow novelists: your stories, your whores, your pleasures are contrived, unreal, insubstantial; my story, my whore, and my pleasure are all real; listen and hear the truth.

Biography

Born in Kingston-on-Thames in 1710. First child of William Cleland and Lucy DuPass. Left Westminster School in 1722 after only two years of formal education. Served in Bombay first as a soldier and than as an administrator for the East India Company, 1728 to 1740. Returned to London, 1741. Imprisoned in Fleet Prison for debt, February 1748 to March 1749. First volume of *Memoirs of a Woman of Pleasure* published in November 1748; second volume appeared in February 1749. *Memoirs of Fanny Hill*, an expurgated abridgement of *A Woman of Pleasure*, is published in 1750, the same year as Cleland's first play, *The Oeconomy of a Winter's Day*. Followed by *The Case of Catherine Vizzani* and *Memoirs of a Coxcomb*, 1751; *Memoirs of the Present Age*, 1752; *The Dictionary of Love*, 1753; *Titus Vespasian*, 1755. Begins a thirty-year career as letter writer to the *Public Advertiser*, 1757. His second play, *Tombo-Chiqui*, appeared in 1758. Followed by *The Times*, a poem in two epistles, 1759 and 1760; *The Institutes of Health*, a medical treatise, 1761; *The Romance of a Night*, a collection of romances, 1762; *The Surprises of Love*, 1764; *Phisiological Reveries*, a medical treatise, 1765; *The Way to Things by Words and to Words by Things*, a linguistic treatise, 1766; *The Woman of Honor*, a novel, 1768. Dies in London, 1789.

BRADFORD MUDGE

Selected Works

The Ladies Subscription: A Dramatic Performance. London. 1755.
Memoirs of a Coxcomb. London, 1751; rpt. 1963.

Memoirs of a Woman of Pleasure. London, 1748–1749. Edited by Peter Wagner, 1985.
Memoirs of Fanny Hill. London, 1750.
"Reviews for the *Monthly Review*." London, 1749–1774.
The Surprises of Love. London, 1764.
Titus Vespasian: A Tragedy. London, 1755.
Tombo-Chiqui. London, 1755.
The Woman of Honour. London, 1768.

Further Reading

Braudy, Leo. "*Fanny Hill* and Materialism," *Eighteenth-Century Studies*, 4 (1970): 21–40.
Epstein, William H. *John Cleland: Images of a Life.* New York: Columbia University Press, 1974.
Foxon, David. *Libertine Literature in England, 1660–1745.* New York: University Books, 1965.
Graham, Rosemary. "The Prostitute in the Garden: Walt Whitman, *Fanny Hill*, and the Fantasy of Female Pleasure." *ELH*, 64 (1997): 569–597.
Gwilliam, Tassie. "Female Fraud: Counterfeit Maidenheads in the Eighteenth Century." *Journal of the History of Sexuality*, 6 (1996): 518–548.
Maccubbin, Robert ed. *'Tis Nature's Fault: Unauthorized Sexuality during the Enlightenment.* Cambridge: Cambridge University Press, 1987.
Moore, Lisa L. *Dangerous Intimacies: Toward a Sapphic History of the British Novel.* Durham: Duke University Press, 1997.
Moulton, Ian. *Before Pornography: Erotic Writing in Early Modern England.* New York: Oxford University Press, 2000.
Mudge, Bradford. *The Whore's Story: Women, Pornography, and the British Novel, 1680–1830.* New York: Oxford University Press, 2000.
Summers, Claude J. *Homosexuality in Renaissance and Enlightenment England.* New York: Haworth Press, 1992.
Wagner, Peter. *Eros Revived: Erotica of the Enlightenment in England and America,* London: Secker and Warburg, 1988.
Wagner, Peter ed. *Erotica and the Enlightenment.* New York: Peter Lang, 1991.

COCTEAU, JEAN

1889–1963
French artist, entrepreneur, filmmaker, socialite, and writer

Infused by a sense of the mystery of the universe and of the power of myth, much of Cocteau's artistic production—which included costume jewelry, mosaics, neckties, posters, pottery, tapestries, various objects he called "transformations," and work in the Chapels of Villefranche-sur-Mer et Milly-la-Forêt—was also fueled by an aesthetics of sensuality. As Milorad observes, sexuality drives his œuvre, permeating it like the invisible energy of a high-tension cable. Despite the eroticism of much of what Cocteau produced, spanning works as diverse as his drawings of naked sailors engaged in sexual activity with each other or his "Preparatory Notes on an Unknown Sexuality" for editions of Jean Genet's novels to his own cinema, which is deeply marked by a preoccupation with the male body as specular object and metaphorical source, Cocteau paradoxically shied away from openly admitting his own sexual identity. This prompts Robinson, for example, to observe that he reflected a deep-seated malaise, a form of self-rejection.

Escales

Light quatrains recounting episodes reminiscent of Cocteau's adolescent experiences in the port town of Marseilles, these rhymed legends evoking the licenciousness of sailors on shore leave were published in 1920 in a volume with illustrations by André Lhote. There was also a special private edition that contained a "secret museum" consisting of more overtly erotic poems and pictures than the rest: prostitutes Alice, Carmen, and Flora each engaged in sexual activities with their clients and Céline washing herself of the traces thereof as a ship leaves port.

L'ange heurtebise

In this deeply homoerotic poem purportedly written under the influence of opium, published in 1927 in the poetic collection *Opéra*, and inspired by Cocteau's love for Raymond Radiguet, who died of typhoid in 1923, a "brutal" and "bestial" angel swoops out of the sky to possess the poet. Whether read as an allegory of artistic genesis or fantasy of passive love and erotic surrender, at its essence it is a vision of the creative process: fertilization, possession, and fecundation, ultimately resulting in poetic birth. For Cocteau, the poem was as important in his œuvre as the *Demoiselles d'Avignon* was in Picasso's.

The White Paper

First published anonymously and in twenty-one copies in 1928 with the aid of Maurice Sachs, by its very title *Le livre blanc* [*The White Paper*]

suggests an official collection presenting a specific problem: in this case a plea for social acceptance of homosexuality. The short autobiographical novel was accompanied by an editor's note claiming that the literary talent contained within it outweighed by far its indecency and that the moral it contained disqualified it as a libertine work. It was republished—anonymously again—two years later but this time included provocative illustrations of young men. In the preface Cocteau writes: "I highly approve of the theory, that love begets respect, and that respect paralyzes desire, and that the erotic achieves best expression if none but the senses are allowed entry into the picture, the heart being left outside it." From the three episodes that ostensibly marked the narrator's love for the stronger sex forever and that begin this homosexual reverie—encounters with a naked farmboy on a horse, two undressed gypsies in a tree, and a hired waiter with a suggestive but out-of-reach bulge in his crotch—to the narrator's pseudo-conversion at the end, Cocteau juxtaposes erotic and compelling images of sexual joy and pain. He rehearses many of the literary and artistic themes he will explore elsewhere, including those of the man-horse, Pierre Dargelos, sailors, and religion. Moreover, Cocteau provides a key to his other works with their frequent translation of homosexuality into heterosexual symbols or codified images. As Robinson observes, he is nevertheless ultimately negative in his implications, for unhappiness is a constant undercurrent of the work and each episode ends in death or separation.

Erotiques

Difficult to date and—with the exception of "Dargelos en Athalie"—first published in 1981 in the edition of *The White Paper* edited by Milorad, the figures featured in the poems of this collection range from the sexually promiscuous Dargelos killing a chicken between his legs, demonstrating his self-pleasuring techniques, or displaying his anus and penis to a young, muscled cyclist masturbating against a wall. In addition, *Erotiques* includes the translation by Cocteau of a poem he believed to have been written by Peter Doyle for Walt Whitman.

Ils

This collection of drawings was edited by Annie Guédras and is divided into seven sections: "Eveil," "Marins," "Mythologie," "Etreintes," "Facéties," "Faunes," and "Innamorati." Included are erotic sketches of Greek figures, of naked bicyclists, of Dargelos engaged in solitary pleasure, and of wrestlers, fishermen, and cooks sharing in sexual pleasure. It also contains those scenes of brothel life and depicting the homosexual seduction of sailors that were included in the first edition of Jean Genet's *Querelle de Brest*.

The Blood of a Poet

Like the poem "L'ange Heurtebise," *Le sang d'un poète* [*The Blood of a Poet*] can also be considered an allegory for the origin of a poem. With its dreamy erotic images, its surrealism *avant la lettre*, this first film—of six directed by Cocteau—is a vehicle for and self-revelatory investigation behind the origins of creation as well as the prologue and prelude for the exploration by Cocteau of a new art form: the cinematic poem. With no technological knowledge of cinema, no direction, and restricted only by his million-franc budget, Cocteau conceived of the work as an animated cartoon, with faces and places chosen to correspond to the inventive freedom of a cartoonist and with the end result a cinematic celebration of the Orphic force and experience. Although some consider it a "glacial" work, others underline its disturbing, erotically charged images. For Williams, the view of the tight backside, the curve and slit of the young poet in the never-ending spiral that is *The Blood of a Poet* establishes the sexual economy, the general anal erotics of viewing that characterizes Coctelian cinema.

The "sodomitical" charge of the male gaze marking this sexual economy and anal erotics of viewing extends to Cocteau's other films too. In Cocteau's cinematic adaptation of the fairy story *La belle et la bête* [*Beauty and the Beast*], for example, both male and female homoerotic representations share in the symbolic construction of subjectivity, the recognition and love of sexual sameness. As Hayward notes, the homoerotic representation of the Beast is not the exclusive domain of Beauty and her male entourage. Similarly, in *Orphée*, which intensifies and extends the interval corresponding in the earlier play by the same name to Orpheus' descent into Hell and casts a lovely young princess as Death—echoing his earlier mimodrama *Le jeune homme et la mort*—, Cocteau uses mirrors to suggest the artist's need to escape convention via an erotic relationship with the self.

Biography

Born on 5 July 1889 at Maisons-Laffitte, near Paris. Attended Petit and Grand Condorcet and l'École Fénelon but never passed his baccalauréat exam. Although Cocteau is probably best known for his films, he only turned to the cinema in midlife, by which time he had already collaborated with such artists as Darius Milhaud, Vaslav Nijinsky, Pablo Picasso, Érik Satie, and Igor Stravinsky on libretti, oratorios, and ballets. Furthermore, he had produced and published a considerable number of often complex works of various genres and influences himself: criticism, drawings, journals, novels, plays, and poems—ranging from futurist and dada to cubist. Inspired by the public's rejection in 1919 of Stravinsky's *Rite of Spring*, whose premiere he attended, Cocteau was harshly criticized, even discounted for dilettanteism early in his career and admitted that since the age of fifteen, he had not stopped for a minute. Ultimately his multidimensionality, influence, flamboyance, and originality helped him garner wide respect and many honors including: election to Belgium's Académie royale de langue et de littérature française and immortal seat number thirty-one of France's Académie française, replacing Jérôme Tharaud; an honorary doctorate from Oxford University; honorary membership in the National Institute of Arts and Letters of New York; commandership in the Legion of Honor; and the title "Prince of Poets" in 1960. He died on 11 October in his château at Milly-la-Forêt, near Paris, an hour after learning of the death of his dear friend, singer Édith Piaf, that same day.

BRIAN GORDON KENNELLY

Selected Works

Lettre à Jacques Maritain. 1926.
Orphée. 1927, 1949.
Le livre blanc. 1928; as *The White Paper*. 1958.
Le sang d'un poète. 1930; as *The Blood of a Poet*. 1995.
L'éternel retour. 1944; as *Love Eternal*. 1966.

La belle et la bête. 1946; as *Beauty and the Beast.* 1991.
"Preparatory Notes on an Unknown Sexuality," 1955.
Le testament d'Orphée. 1960; as *The Testament of Orpheus.* 2000.
Le livre blanc, suivi de quatorze textes érotiques inédits et illustré de dix-huit dessins. 1981.
Ils: Dessins érotiques de Jean Cocteau. 1998.
Œuvres poétiques complètes. 1999.

Further Reading

Genet, Jean. *The Gutter in the Sky.* Philadelphia: André Lévy, 1955.
Genet, Jean. *Querelle de Brest.* Paris: Paul Morihien, 1947.
Genova, Pamela. Entry on "Cocteau, Jean," in *Reader's Guide to Lesbian and Gay Studies.* Edited by Timothy F. Murphy, Chicago and London: Fitzroy Dearborn, 2000.
Greene, Naomi. "Deadly Statues: Eros in the Films of Jean Cocteau." *The French Review,* 61.6 (1988): 890–898.
Hayward, S. "Gender Politics—Cocteau's Belle is not that Bête: Jean Cocteau's *La Belle et la Bête* (1946)" in *French Film: Texts and Contexts.* Edited by S. Hayward and G. Vincendeau, New York: Routledge, 1990.
Milorad. "Le livre blanc, document secret et chiffré." *Cahiers Jean Cocteau.* 8 (1979): 109–131.
Robinson, Christopher. *Scandal in the Ink: Male and Female Homosexuality in Twentieth-century French Literature.* London: Cassell, 1995.
Williams, James S. "For Our Eyes Only: Body and Sexuality in Reverse Motion in the Films of Jean Cocteau." In *Gender and French Cinema.* edited by Alex Hughes and James S. Williams, New York and Oxford: Berg, 2001.

COHEN, ALBERT

1895–1981
Greek francophone novelist and journalist

Cohen began writing in his mid-twenties, when he published a volume of poems (*Paroles juives*) and several short texts, in the Nouvelle revue française, notably (1922–1923). In 1927, he completed a one-act play, *Ezéchiel,* which would be performed at the Théâtre de l'Odéon (1931) and the Comédie Française (1933) but which would be published much later (1956). Early in his career, he settled upon the novel as the exclusive genre for his imaginative writing.

Soon after publishing his first novel, *Solal* (1930), he envisaged it as part of a three-volume cycle. He spent much of the 1930s working on this project and in 1938, under pressure from publisher Gaston Gallimard, extracted a discrete part of a lengthy manuscript in-progress to produce his second novel, *Mangeclous.* The dust jacket of *Mangeclous* announced as "imminent" the principal and concluding volume, to be entitled *Belle du seigneur,* but the project would be interrupted by the war. *Belle du seigneur* would not appear until 1968, thirty years after *Mangeclous.* Cohen's best-known work, *Belle du seigneur,* is both a monumental love story and a jeremiad against "passion-love," to borrow Stendhal's term *(De l'amour [On Love]).* Published when the author was seventy-three years old, it represents the philosophical and artistic culmination of his long activity as a writer. In 1969, a fourth novel, *Les Valeureux (The Valiant),* followed. The latter been contained in the manuscript of *Belle du seigneur* but appeared in a separate volume at the publisher's request.

Cohen's other published works are autobiographical. Originally published in installments in *La France libre* during the war, *Le Livre de ma mère* is a memoir, a work of mourning, and an essay on filial love. *Ô vous, frères humains* is an autobiographical essay devoted principally to the theme of love of neighbor, and *Carnets 1978* is a journal whose central themes are passion and filial love, friendship, the struggle for faith, and death.

Cohen's novelistic world is comprised of two realms. The first belongs to his protagonist Solal who, after leaving the Jewish ghetto of his native Cephalonia, rises to the heights of power in Paris and Geneva (Member of Parliament, Undersecretary General of the League of Nations) becomes immersed in a series of Western-style passionate romances. The other realm is of Solal's burlesque uncle and cousins, Saltiel "*Mangeclous*," Michaël, Mattathias, and Salomon—known as "les Valeureux"—comic characters who embody old-world Cephalonian Jewry in the Rabelaisian form Cohen gives it. For practical reasons Cohen gathered many of the adventures of the latter group in two separate volumes (*Mangeclous*, *Les valeureux*), whereas *Solal* and *Belle du seigneur* are chiefly concerned with the passions and pursuits of his Westernized hero. The two realms remain interwoven, however, and together comprise the author's fictional universe: Solal is constantly reminded of his origins, and "les Valeureux" are absorbed by his romantic and professional conquests.

The novelistic cycle begins, in *Solal*, with the title character's Bar Mitzvah on Cephalonia and his conquest of the wife of the French consul (around 1911). It concludes on the eve of World War II and the Shoah (1937). Influenced by Joyce and Proust, among early contemporaries, Cohen developed a unique voice and style in the late 1920s and 1930s. His fiction did not evolve in response to subsequent literary currents. *Belle du seigneur* and *Les Valeureux* improve upon and complete, but do not significantly reform, a project begun almost four decades earlier.

At the core of Cohen's writing is a dualistic conception of human nature. In the novels this view is principally expressed by Solal, who perceives individuals—women in particular—as animalistic creatures attracted by power and passion who are nonetheless capable of rising above these limitations to fulfill their higher potential as human beings. In his terms, people are subject to the laws of nature, which govern base instincts, including their sexuality and their worship of physical beauty and power. To this fallen state of humanity, he opposes the possibility of redemption inspired by the Laws of Moses and especially the Sixth Commandment interdiction against killing. Expressed by a character who engages in a profound but ultimately futile search for faith, this vision is humanistic rather than theological. The Sixth Commandment is evoked in the broadest sense, as calling on human beings not only to refrain from the act of killing, but also to transcend their animalistic nature, which is responsible for both enacted and implied aggression.

The theater for the conflict between animalistic tendencies and fully realized humanity is love. He—or she—who heeds the Sixth Commandment *desires* differently from lovers still bound by the natural laws. The latter are attracted to power and physicality—although they believe they are experiencing noble and exalted sentiments. "Redeemed" humans, in contrast, perceive and desire the gentle soul hidden behind the mask, seeking a love based on tenderness and free communication rather than tumultuous passion. This is the point of view of Solal who refers to sex as "the two-backed beast" (in Coward's fine translation) and declares: "I adore you but why must I always be straddling you like an animal to keep you happy[?]" (*Belle du seigneur* 883). This sort of redemption retains the status of an ideal, even a myth, however. Neither the implied author of Cohen's novels nor the autobiographical writer of the *Carnets* presents complete escape from the prison-house of the body as a viable possibility. For this reason, moreover, the elderly Cohen is unable to believe in an afterlife: "Is not sexuality the crude component of the human being and of what is called the soul?" (*Carnets* 98).

In Cohen's first novel, Solal follows a trajectory much like that of Julien Sorel in Stendhal's *Le Rouge et le noir* [*The Red and the Black*]. He seduces an older, respectable woman, and leaves his place of origin for Paris. There he becomes personal secretary to an important political figure, whose daughter he wins over and marries. As in the case of Stendhal's hero, a dazzling rise to power accompanies these amorous successes, followed by a precipitous fall to which his own internal passions greatly contribute. Many of the themes that dominate *Belle du seigneur* are already present in Solal. The young hero's father, rabbi and patriarch of Cephalonian Jewry, teaches his son to "disdain women and what is called beauty" (Solal 35). Solal will indeed scorn "females," and males, when, behaving as animals, they fail to realize their higher potential as human beings. Occasionally, the narrator is able to look upon the "glory of the beginnings" of passion love with tenderness and compassion. Addressing Solal and his second lover, Aude, he exhorts: "Play, friends, amuse yourselves, become drunk with love" (*Carnets* 31; Solal 74). Such moments are dependent on unstable conditions, however, and fleeting.

To a certain degree Cohen's representation of passion follows Stendhal's theory of crystallization. Stendhal describes how crystals form spontaneously on a twig which is introduced into a salt mine. For Stendhal, the lover acts like the mine, creating, through projection onto the bare frame of the beloved, a highly idealized object of love which when combined with requisite dynamics of doubt and jealousy gives birth to passion-love. Unlike Stendhal, however, who is content to celebrate the wonder of this creation, Cohen's Solal (and Mangeclous) constantly deflate the *élan* by recalling the unromanticized physicality of the twig. Solal regards kissing, for example, as "that soldering of two digestive tubes" (Solal 121). This tension between the joy of love and the painful awareness that it is ill-borne, of illusions and deceptions, advancing inexorably toward ruin, runs throughout Cohen's work. It is bound to an existential condition summed up by Solal in response to an ecstatic Aude: "He was disturbed by that pitiful enthusiasm and yet he was happy" (Solal 173).

Sometimes referred to as a novel of "anti-passion" whose intertexts in the broadest sense include the whole literature of adulterous love from the courtly romance to Leo Tolstoy's *Anna Karenina*, *Belle du seigneur* is organized around two seduction scenes. In the first, at the beginning of the novel, Solal arrives at Ariane's home on horseback, valet in tow, and breaks in through her bedroom window. He then disguises himself as an old Jew with a tattered greatcoat, fur hat, and blackened teeth. After he has had a chance to read Ariane's diaries and to listen to her musings from the bath, he confronts her: "'One evening at the Ritz, an evening decreed by Destiny, on the occasion of the Brazilian reception, I saw you for the very first time and loved you at once,' he said, and again he smiled his dark smile where two fangs gleamed" (*BS* 33). Claiming to have been present as a waiter at this high society function, and thus continuing to dissimulate his social and professional position as well as his physical beauty, Solal makes an impassioned speech, singing Ariane's glories, lyrically declaring his love for her, and begging her to receive the love of a feeble old man, with a white beard and just two teeth, but who promises to love and honor her as no other. In the style of the Hebrew Bible and liturgy, blended with Cohen's baroque turns of phrase, he goes on to declare her to be "she who redeemeth all women. Behold the first woman!" (*BS* 37). Then, the narrator relates: "He bent his knee before her, a gesture which made him look

quite ridiculous, then stood up and came towards her, towards their first kiss." Ariane, emitting a "yelp of fear and hate," hurls a glass at "that antique face." At this, Solal abandons his disguise, grins with all his teeth, stomps his boots and makes a second speech, in which he proclaims: "I shall leave now, but first, female of the species, hear me! Female thou art and as a female shalt be done by. Vilely shall I seduce you as you deserve and as you want" (*BS* 38).

Solal makes flawless preparations for the second seduction in his apartment at the Ritz Hotel. He shows favor to Ariane's crass husband, promotes him and arranges for him to go on an extended mission abroad. Inspired by the conquest of Anna Karenina by Count Vronsky, whose close-set teeth are continually evoked by Tolstoy's narrator, the seduction of Ariane is at once expository and performative. Surrounded by the trappings of wealth and power, blessed with his own thirty-two gleaming white teeth, the Undersecretary General seduces her with neither the libertine's promise nor the poet's encomium, but rather with an analytical exposition of the tactics essential to a successful seduction. Because it serves so effectively as a meta-discourse, thoroughly demystifying the very passion that it is instilling, and because the lovers' behavior so clearly confirms his message as they desperately seek to maintain the intensity of their initial passion by preserving its conditions of possibility, Solal's speech speaks a certain "truth." A constitutive element of this "truth" is his postulate of female heterosexual desire as tantamount to the worship of force.

In a brief but crucial scene mid-way through the novel, Solal makes a visit to Berlin where, again dressed as a traditional Jew, he is beaten unconscious on the street and taken in by the hunchbacked daughter of a wealthy Jewish antique dealer, now in hiding in a secret cellar. Peering from below out a small window, he takes in the sight of a column of marching German soldiers:

. . . mechanical and victorious, the young hopes of the German nation paraded, singing their joy at Jewish blood spilt, proud in their strength, proud in their strength in numbers, cheered by sweating girls with blonde plaits and arms inanely held high, gross sexual creatures excited by the spectacle of so much jackbooted manliness (*BS* 497).

This image of a group of girls aroused by the "jackbooted manliness" recalls Solal's own boots, which he stomps conspicuously in Ariane's bedroom and again at the Ritz. We know, however, that Solal's show of virility is the price he must pay in order to have that which he deeply needs: Ariane's love. It is not that he is any less driven by animalistic, sub-human drives than she. Indeed, on this point she has already taken him to task, asking why he does not simply declare his love to a humpbacked old hag. He responds:

> Because I am a miserable male! I accept that hairy men are carnivorous creatures! But not women! I cannot accept that of Woman, in whom I believe!...
>
> 'And as to admiring the beauty of women, who shall demur? For it is the promise of tenderness, a kind and loving heart, and motherhood. Those nice girls who want nothing more than to care for the sick and rush off to the front to be nurses when there's a war on warm the heart, and I am morally entitled to love their meat. But I cannot stomach the horrible attraction women feel for male beauty which signifies physical strength, courage and aggression, in other words animal virtues! That's what makes them unforgivable!'' (BS 338–339).

What, then, about Ariane? Is she not once more confirmed as a "female of the species," lusting after "male power," like these "gross sexual creatures"? And how is the reader to react to Solal's double standard? These questions raise an important question of their own—of the reliability of Solal's point of view.

Whatever authority Solal may gain from his shrewd demystification of passion love, his voice should not be mistaken for the point of view of the implied author or novel as a whole. Several signposts warn against a naive reading of Solal's discourse. First, Solal would have us believe that the fallen state of the love relationship, the fact that it had to take the perilous path of passion, results from a blindness on the part of Ariane, from her failure to see through his disguise to the inner beauty of the "old Jew of my heart." Yet this is of course a preposterous expectation, for the circumstances and disguise do not have the effect Solal attributes to them. He may appear old and ugly, but certainly not powerless. Standing with her alone in the bedroom, he naturally instills fear.

More important still, Solal's staging of this pure, redemptive love replicates passion love as

much as it defies or inverts it. The old Jew declares:

> And on that evening, decreed by Destiny at the Ritz, she appeared unto me, noble in the midst of the ignoble did she appear... Other men take weeks, months to fall in love, and love but little.... All I needed was the instant of one flutter of her eyelashes. Call me mad but believe me. A flutter of lashes . . . and suddenly I beheld the glory of spring and the sun and the warm sea and the transparency of water near the shore and my youth restored, and the world was born (BS 33–34).

The old Jew insists that Ariane fall in love instantly, as in courtly romances and as Solal has with her. What he fails to recognize, but which the novel as a whole makes clear, is that she becomes a sub-human woman, a "female," in his view, by refusing to participate in the very passion love that he later vehemently condemns.

In *Les valeureux*, Mangeclous pronounces himself rector of his own University, modeled after the Sorbonne, and located in the kitchen of his humble abode in the Jewish ghetto of Cephalonia. His first and only lesson—on seduction—serves as a farcical counter-point to the scene at the Ritz. If Solal's jeremiad was chilling, Mangeclous's is hilarious. Like Solal's, however, it provides a forceful point of view, and one must look beyond the discourse itself, to its narrative context, for further clues to the way in which the novel presents this discourse as mystified. In Mangeclous's own rendition of the image of the boots as a sign of virility and aggression, for example, he explains that the seducer "must shine his boots so that she will notice them and know that he is a vigorous knight, which will give her guilty thoughts, as she tells herself that he is muscular, capable of throwing punches, and endowed with a great power of copulation" (V 148). At this, one of Mangeclous's students exclaims ecstatically: "All that because of his boots!" Even in the Jewish ghetto, untainted by the world of western culture and literature, the performance of the anti-passion discourse arouses and seduces the listener. "Animal virtues" may appear no more noble as a result, but the image of the pure Old World as an alternative to the plight of Western lovers is demystified.

Ultimately, the *Solal* cycle invites us to have compassion for the sensitive, desperate protagonist who deflates powerful myths of passion according to which human beings lead their lives, but who also lives under the influence of other grand ideas. Shaped in large part by the prospect of fierce aggression beyond the realm of love, by the feeling of helplessness and dread before the emerging Nazi menace, Solal's cynical views of power and desire may be as illusory as the myths disseminated by what Mangeclous calls "all those European novelists who paint seductive pictures of passion and who, liars and poisoners, hide from our view the calls of nature, large and small, of the adulterous heroine and her accomplice!" (*V* 181).

Biography

Born on Corfu, 1895. Moved to Marseilles 1900. Educated in a Catholic elementary school and a public lycée. Studied law and literature in Geneva (1914–1919); obtained Swiss citizenship. Founded *La revue juive* (Editions N.R.F., 1925); Albert Einstein and Sigmund Freud on editorial board. Diplomatic Division, International Labor Bureau, 1926–1931. Representative of Chaim Weizmann, Paris 1939. In London during war, liaison for Jewish Agency for Palestine between governments in exile and Jews fleeing Nazism; wrote for Resistance press. Legal counsel to Inter-Governmental Committee for Refugees, 1944–1946; authored international agreement. Headed Protection Division, International Organization for Refugees, 1947–1948. International Labor Bureau, 1949–1951. Grand Prix du Roman de l'Académie française for *Belle du seigneur*, 1968. Officer of Legion of Honor, 1970. Controversial appearance in silk dressing gown on Bernard Pivot's *Apostrophes*, 1977. Died in Geneva, 1981.

L. Scott Lerner

*Translations of *Belle du seigneur* are from the Coward edition, with minor modifications. All other translations are my own.

Selected Works

Paroles juives. 1921.
Solal, 1930; as *Solal*. Translated by Wilfred Benson, 1933.
Mangeclous. 1938; as *Nailcruncher*, translated by V. Holland, 1940.
Le Livre de ma mère. 1954; as *Book of My Mother*. Translated by Bella Cohen, 1997.
Ezéchiel. 1956.
Belle du seigneur. 1968; edited by Bella Cohen and Christel Peyrefitte, (Pléiade) 1986; as *Belle du seigneur*, translated by David Coward, 1995.
Les Valeureux. 1969.
Ô vous, frères humains. 1972.
Carnets. 1978, 1979.
Oeuvres. Edited by Bella Cohen and Christel Peyrefitte, (Pléiade) 1993.

Further Reading

Auroy, Carole. *Albert Cohen. Une quête solaire*, Paris: Presses de la Sorbonne, 1996.
Cahiers Albert Cohen, n. 5, *L'Amour en ses figures et en ses marges*, 1995.
Goitein-Galpérin, Denise. *Visage de mon peuple. Essai sur Albert Cohen*. Paris: Nizet, 1982.
Lewy-Bertaut, Évelyne. *Albert Cohen mythobiographe*, Grenoble: ELLUG, 2001.
Paillet-Guth, Anne-Marie. *Ironie et paradoxe. Le discours amoureux romanesque*. Paris: Champion, 1999.
Schaffner, Alain. *Le goût de l'absolu. L'enjeu sacré de la littérature dans l'œuvre d'Albert Cohen*. Paris: Champion, 1999.

COHEN, LEONARD

1934–
Canadian poet, novelist, songwriter

The Favorite Game

This classic autobiographical novel (a *bildungsroman*) details Cohen's coming of sexual age. It weaves several threads of women variously pursued, bedded, lost, and rediscovered into a tapestry of tragicomic hedonism. Seeking love for sex's sake, and crafting art for love's sake, the erotic escapades of the relentless young poetic protagonist, Larry Breavman, earned Cohen the literary reputation of a Jewish-Canadian Henry Miller writing with the pen of a J.D. Salinger. "Breavman" connotes both "brave man" and "bereaved man." Breavman's bravery is manifest in his unabashed ardor and uninhibited lust, but his bereavement is more complex. He mourns not only loves unrequited, unattainable, and unforgettable, but also his father's premature death, his mother's gradual insanity, his tribe's impossible covenant, and his art's inevitable compromise. A more precise characterization of Cohen's maiden novel emanates from a purely Canadian literary perspective. From this vantage he is a successor of poet Irving Layton and novelist Mordecai Richler, and a spokesman for his generation of the Jewish experience in Montreal. But that experience also builds ineluctably on, and falls into the lacuna characterized by Canada's classic historical novel, namely Hugh MacLennan's *Two Solitudes*. While Canada's founding "families," the French and the English (or Scots) live unbridgeable peaks apart, Cohen introduces yet a *Third Solitude*: Canadian Jews, at once accepted and reviled by the *Two*, yet necessarily engaged with both in a complex cultural *ménage-à-trois*. This provides a backdrop for Cohen's insatiable erotic quest, defined in the mouth of Breavman:

> "What else is there? Conversation? I'm in the business and I have no faith in words whatever. Friendship? A friendship between man and a woman which is not based on sex is either hypocrisy or masochism. When I see a woman's face transformed by the orgasm we have reached together, then I know we've met. Anything else is fiction."

Beautiful Losers

This masterwork of the mature artist reveals Cohen's latent attraction to Taoist philosophy, in its balanced treatment of the sacred and the profane. The sacred thread of the plot recounts a fanciful history of Saint Catherine Tekakwitha, who flirted with her native Iroquois culture while resisting her scheming aunts' attempts to have her deflowered by young braves. Through experiments in asceticism tinged with female eroticism and masochism, Catherine transforms her sexual energy into spiritual radiance, and in so doing enthralls priests and performs miracles. The profane thread deals with a literal *ménage-à-trois*, a triangle involving the anonymous protagonist (Cohen's alter-ego), his wife Edith (an Indian descended from Catherine), and his best friend, F. Each pair in the triangle has sex of several different kinds, with exploratory kinkiness as a norm, and the realization of fantasy an expectation. Through his anonymous tormented writer, Cohen tells a tale of tormented characters engaging in tormented sex. Eros herself becomes transformed by the accompanying poetry, politics, and polemics. Cohen also resorts, albeit with moderation and reasonable taste, to abstract impressionistic episodes that lend the work distinctly Joycean overtones. He interleaves these threads with great dexterity, leading all the players except his leading character toward their various deaths by suicide, insanity, and asceticism—with Eros as a constant companion. In so doing, he recombines the clays and myths of his earlier novel, composed of English-, French-, and Jewish-Canadian elements, with that of the elemental indigenous Indian. The erotic glaze on this richer mixture is flecked with both miracles and misdeeds, and speckled with Cohen's wit.

> —You lousy fucker, how many times, five *or* six?
> —Ah, grief makes us precise!
> —Five or six, five or six, five or six?
> —Listen, my friend, the elevator is working again.
> —Listen, F., don't give me any of your mystical shit.
> —Seven.
> —Seven times with Edith?
> —Correct.

...Catherine Tekakwitha, I wanted to believe him. We talked until we exhausted ourselves, and we pulled each other off, as we did when we were boys in what is now downtown but what was once the woods.

Poems and Songs

Leonard Cohen is best-known and most admired for his poems and songs. These are not strictly separable, since many of his songs—most famously *Suzanne*—are poems set to music. Like his novels, Cohen's poetry is flush with the dialectic of love and the antics of sex. It also abounds with misplaced religious imagery, sado-masochistic allusion, and post-Holocaust defiance. Hence one encounters crucifixes without worship, razor blades without shaving, and *Flowers for Hitler* without condolences. Cohen has made his reputation first and last as a poet.

While his novels are centered in Montreal, and are arguably best-understood by Montrealers, his poems are universal in their desire for desire, love of love, and musings on the Muse.

Biography

Born in 1934 in Montreal, Quebec, to an affluent Jewish family. He was educated at McGill and Columbia. He has published two novels, eight volumes of poetry and songs, and has recorded ten albums of songs, or poems set to music. He declined a Governor General's Award in 1968, but accepted one in 1993.

LOU MARINOFF

Editions

The Favorite Game. Toronto: McClelland & Stewart, 1963; London: Secker & Warburg, 1963; Toronto: New Canadian Library, 1970.
Beautiful Losers. Toronto: McClelland & Stewart, 1966; New York: The Viking Press, 1966; New York: Vintage Books, 1993.

Selected Works

Let us Compare Mythologies. 1956.
The Spice-Box of Earth. 1961.
Flowers for Hitler. 1964.
Parasites of Heaven. 1966.
Selected Poems 1956–1968. 1968.
The Energy of Slaves. 1972.

Book of Mercy. 1984.
Stranger Music: Selected Poems and Songs. 1993.

Music

The Songs of Leonard Cohen. 1968.
Songs From a Room. 1969.
Live Songs. 1972.
New Skin for the Old Ceremony. 1974.
Best of Leonard Cohen. 1975.
Death of a Lady's Man. 1977.
Recent Songs. 1979.
Various Positions. 1984.
I'm Your Man. 1988.
The Future. 1992.
Cohen Live. 1994.
More Best Of. 1997.
Field Commander Cohen. 2001.
Ten New Songs. 2002.
The Essential Leonard Cohen. 2002.
Dear Heather. 2004.

Further Reading

Barrera, Paul. *Came So Far for Love.* Andover (UK): Agenda Limited, 1997.
Devlin, Jim. *In Every Style of Passion.* UK: Omnibus Press, 1996.
Dorman, Loranne & Rawlins, Clive. *Prophet of the Heart,* USA: Omnibus Press, 1990.
Graf, Christof. *So Long Leonard.* Heidelberg: Palmyra Verlag, 1990.
Nadel, Ira. *Various Positions: A Life of Leonard Cohen.* Toronto: Random House of Canada, 1996.
Scobie, Stephen. *Leonard Cohen.* Vancouver: Douglas & McIntyre, 1978.
Vassal, Jacques. *Leonard Cohen.* Paris: Albin Michel, 1974.

COLETTE, SIDONIE-GABRIELLE

1873–1954
French novelist, short-story writer, autobiographer, and dramatist.

Her earliest work consisted of a sequence of novels following the progress of an exuberant, and highly sexual, young woman from adolescence to adulthood: *Claudine à l'école* (1900), *Claudine à Paris* (1901), *Claudine en ménage* (1902), and *Claudine s'en va* (1903). Their mixture of engaging spontaneity with a playfully perverse sensuality ensured an immediate success. Her first husband, Henry Gauthier-Villars ("Willy") whom she married in 1893, exploited his wife's work (as he did all those who worked for him) by signing these works with his own pen-name until she left him in 1906.

Among her literary works from this period (she now signed herself Colette Willy) are *La Vagabonde* (1910) and its sequel, *L'Entrave*

(1913), both about music-hall life, which examine the situation of the divorced woman. Though Colette is often portrayed as the victim of Willy's salacious commercialism, there can be no doubt that she herself not only shared but also deliberately exploited the general fascination of the period with the erotic nature of human relationships. This is particularly true with regard to three novels, often considered among her best work, dating from this period: *Chéri* (1920), *La fin de Chéri* (1926), and *Le blé en herbe* (1923).

Colette's most sophisticated—and perplexing—works as far as the depiction of adult sexuality is concerned are *Chéri* and *La fin de Chéri*. Both concern a protracted love affair between an aging but wealthy courtesan, Léonie Vallon (Léa), and the adolescent son, Frédéric Peloux (Chéri), of one of her contemporaries. The age gap between this experienced woman of the world (she is in her mid-forties at the time the affair commences around 1909) and her teenage gigolo (he is only nineteen) should not be minimized: *Chéri* is by no means the straightforward story of the sexual initiation of a younger man. Peloux is not only exquisitely handsome but also intensely moody, vain, egoistical, and brutally insensitive. These psychological defects are partly explained by his illegitimacy, the lack of genuine affection that exists between himself and his mother, and social circumstance (not only does he lack a positive male role model but he also spends much of his time in the company of his mother's narrow circle of ageing, crotchety female friends and acquaintances). As the novel progresses, moreover, he becomes unhealthily emotionally dependent on Léa—so much so that even after his marriage to Edmée in 1913, the nineteen-year-old daughter of another of his mother's friends, he is unable to feel any great affection for her. Indeed, it is implied that neither finds the act of love-making satisfying. Shortly after the honeymoon, Peloux, in a highly enervated condition (betrayed by a spasmodic twitching of his jaw muscles), and still besotted with Léa, abandons his bride to racket around Paris in the company of a male friend.

Though Colette discreetly draws a veil over the actual act of sexual congress, in other respects *Chéri* is an extremely intimate novel which offers a wealth of detail concerning every aspect of how a wealthy mondaine such as Léa organizes her household from the breakfast menu to bathroom design. Of even more interest, however, is the probing of the psychological motivations of the main protagonists. It is particularly worth noting, for example, that Léa gains considerable sexual pleasure just from watching Peloux in a state of undress or semi-undress, even organizing open-air boxing lessons for her lover for this purpose. Peloux, who is extremely narcissistic by nature (he is continually looking at himself in the mirror), is only too willing to oblige her in this respect.

Though reviewing the entire five-year liaison between Léa and Peloux, *Chéri* is mainly set in the period just before World War I. It concludes with Peloux, after a final night of passion with Léa, finally abandoning his mistress, who suddenly looks very old (and undesirable) to him, to return to his wife. *La fin de Chéri* takes up the story five years later, Peloux having returned to Paris after an undistinguished (as befits his character) military career. In contrast with *Chéri*, which is undoubtedly an erotic classic, *La fin de Chéri* might almost be described an anti-erotic classic. Peloux, disgusted by his wife's pursuit of a career in hospital management (and her flirtatious relationship with a doctor) and his mother's new-found interest in share-dealing (this is the Paris of the Jazz Age), is progressively emasculated by all the women in his life. Even Léa, by now not only prodigiously overweight but also ill-kempt, has adopted a masculine persona, especially as she discusses in his presence their earlier affair with another elderly female. Discovering a secret cache of photographs of Léa in her prime, he tortures himself with wild imaginings about her previous lovers before shooting himself in the head. Not only is he is a victim of the nostalgia, listlessness, and disillusionment of his generation, he is also a late male victim of that catch-all *fin-de-siècle* malady: neurasthenia.

In comparison with the morbid sexuality and pessimism of *La fin de Chéri*, *Le blé en herbe* (1923; tr. *Ripening Seed*, 1955), which deals with awakening adolescent sexuality, is positively bucolic. *Ces plaisirs* (1932), on the other hand, is a jaundiced study of sexual depravity. Almost all of Colette's work has been translated into English, though some of the earlier translations are now extremely dated. Between 1951 and 1964, the British firm of Secker and Warburg undertook a 17-volume complete works. Only these translations have been retained below; many were later reprinted in paperback by Penguin in the United Kingdom and, with one exception, all were also published in the United States.

Biography

Born in Burgundy on 28 January, 1873 (her father, wounded at the battle of Magenta in 1859, was a local tax inspector), Colette's literary career initially evolved as a consequence of her relationship with the notorious writer and critic Henry Gauthier-Villars ("Willy") whom she married in 1893. The marriage was not a happy one, and Colette left Willy in 1906, earning a living as an actress and music-hall performer. In 1912, she married Baron Henry de Jouvenal (divorced 1925). Over the course of the next thirty years she published a variety of autobiographical writings, occasional adaptations and theatrical works, as well as producing a considerable body of journalism (it was only in 1923 that she began signing herself simply Colette). Her third marriage, to Maurice Goudeket, took place in 1935. *Gigi*, her final important work dealing with the politics of sexuality, was published in 1944.

TERRY HALE

Selected Works

Le Blé en herbe (1923). Translated by Roger Senhouse, *Ripening Seed*, London: Secker and Warburg, 1955; New York: Farrar Straus, 1956.
Ces Plaisirs (1932). Translated by Herma Briffault, *The Pure and the Impure*, London: Secker & Warburg, 1968; New York: Farrar Straus, 1967.
Claudine à l'école (1900), tr. Antonia White, *Claudine at School*, London: Secker and Warburg, 1956; New York: Farrar Straus, 1957.
Claudine à Paris (1901), tr. Antonia White, *Claudine in Paris*, London: Secker and Warburg, 1958; New York: Farrar Straus, 1958.
Claudine en ménage (1902), tr. Antonia White, *Claudine Married*, London: Secker and Warburg, 1960; New York: Farrar Straus, 1960.
Claudine s'en va (1903), tr. Antonia White, *Claudine and Annie*, London: Secker and Warburg, 1962; New York: Penguin, 1963.
Chéri (1920), tr. Roger Senhouse, *Chéri*, London: Secker and Warburg, 1951; with *The Last of Chéri*, New York: Farrar Straus, 1953.
La Fin de Chéri (1926), tr. Roger Senhouse, *The Last of Chéri*, London: Secker and Warburg, 1951; with *Chéri*, New York: Farrar Straus, 1953.
Gigi (1944), tr. Roger Stenhouse, *Gigi*, London: Secker and Warburg, 1953; with other works, New York: Farrar Straus, 1955.

Further Reading

Yvonne Mitchell. *Colette: A Taste for Life*. London: Weidenfeld and Nicolson, 1975.
Judith Thurman. *Secrets of the Flesh: A Life of Colette*. London: Bloomsbury, 1999.

COLLÉ, CHARLES

1709–1783
French playwright and songwriter

Chansons qui n'ont pu être imprimées et que mon censeur n'a point dû me passer

Collé's *Chansons qui n'ont pu être imprimées* (1784) is a classic example of the *grivois* or *graveleux* influence in eighteenth-century French songwriting. The epigram to the collection, *Sunt quædam bona, sunt mediocria, sunt mala multa*, attests to the mixed quality of the collection. The majority of the collection is comprised of *vaudevilles* (new lyrics written to existing and usually well-known melodies, identified by their title) or parodies of movements from eighteenth-century French operas (particularly Rameau's *Hyppolite et Aricie*, and *Les indes galantes*, both 1733); the remaining minority of works are short verse forms—Epigrammes, Couplets détachés, Sonnets, etc. Some of the original songs were themselves vulgar in origin, such as the air 'Lampons, lampons' which Collé uses several times—others were not. The structure of the collection has not been studied, but broadly speaking, Collé groups the vaudevilles in a first section (approximately pages 1 to 80), and keeps opera parodies together in the longer second section (pages 81 to end). Within this rough framework, however, the arrangement of the individual pieces is free.

The individual pieces are similar in their licentious and impertinent tone, where no theme is taboo. Some dominant themes are worth noting. The presence of the clergy is striking, from the opening strophic piece, 'La béquille perdue et retrouvée,' sung to the melody 'du Père Barnabas,' with its clear phallic metaphor, through 'Le bon catholique,' the 'Portrait de notre Abbesse,' and concluding with a *romance* sung to the melody 'Un jour le malheureux Lisandre,' alluding to the supposed homosexuality of the Jesuits, a theme which is developed in a number of songs in the collection. Female homosexuality is also described, as in 'On ne dispute point des goûts,' centerd on Socrates and Sappho.

The innuendo-laden 'Comment l'esprit vient aux filles' picks up a common *topos* of mid-eighteenth-century libertine writing, centered upon an innocent, young (usually peasant) girl and her progressive acquisition of *esprit*, designating not only intelligence but also practical sexual experience. Other songs are more direct, such as 'Sur une femme' which provides a lesson in female anatomy, concluding with the sexual organs: 'Le feu qui prend sa part vers le milieu, / Brûle le cul, & la place voisine.' Women are generally seen as licentious and dishonest, such as the narrative 'Chanson malhonnête,' where the *Je* decides to try to find 'une honnête femme / Qui ne fût pas trop putain,' but who is forced to conclude, at the end, that bourgeoise women are worse than the infamous dancers of the Opéra. The importance of social class is considerable; much of the humor of these songs comes at the expense of the nobility, such as 'L'éloge de Léandre,' who 'se dit Gentilhomme étant fils de putain, / Et voici le sujet où sa Noblesse il fonde: / Car sa mère foutant avecque tout le monde, / L'a bien pu faire noble aussitôt que vilain.' Mondain society is also frequently mocked, as in 'Sur le mariage de Mde. la Duchesse de Chaulnes avec Mr de Giac.'

Humor is also produced by the unexpected or the unrevealed, such as songs where the reader/singer must supply the missing or incomplete word which ends a verse line, as in the 'Vaudeville du mois de mai.' But much of the humor of the parodies is surely lost today, where readers are less familiar with the original opera from which a melody is borrowed. Whereas the contemporary public would have immediately grasped the distance between the new words and the old context from which the melody was borrowed, which with the serious *tragédies lyriques* of Rameau would have produced an effect of burlesque, such references today would need copious footnoting.

The theatrical aspect of this collection also deserves attention, because some of the pieces are not only derived from previous operas, but were also almost certainly written for inclusion in theater, as the title 'Vaudeville de Parade' indicates. The first of these is a strophic song where verses are taken successively by the characters of the *Commedia dell'arte* and the Fairs: Isabelle, Léandre, Cassandre, Gilles. Similarly, the inclusion of a Vaudeville de rentrée, or the 'Sur le théâtre italien,' suggests a level of borrowing between Collé's song collections and theatrical writing which would deserve further attention.

Biography

Born in 1709, Collé was the son of a *Procureur* at Châtelet, and intended for legal studies, which he never undertook. One of the first members of the Paris group of songwriters, the Société du Caveau, Collé's first works were songs, which were later to be published collectively; from these he started writing licentious *parades* and *comédies de société* (plays for private society theater). Protected by the Duc d'Orléans, his literary and material ambition grew, and he was also the author of libretti for *opéras-comiques* and plays performed at the Comédie-Française, including *Dupuis et Desronais* (1763), and *La partie de chasse de Henri IV* (first performed at the Comédie Française in 1774). On its publication in 1805, his *Journal* provoked reactions of shock, mixed with great curiosity for the material it includes on eighteenth-century cultural life.

MARK DARLOW

Editions

Chansons qui n'ont pu être imprimées et que mon censeur n'a point du me passer ([n.p.]: [n. pub], 1784).

Selected Works

Théâtre de société, ou Recueil de différentes pièces, tant en vers qu'en prose, qui peuvent se jouer sur un théâtre de société. 2 vols. (a Haye-Paris: Gueffier, 1768); Nouvelle édition, 3 vols. (Paris: Gueffier, 1777).
Chansons joyeuses mises au jour par un âne-onyme, onissime. Nouvelle édition, 2 vols. (Paris: [n. pub.], 1765).
Chansons nouvelles et gaillardes, sur les plus beaux airs de ce temps. Mises au jour rue de la Huchette, par un asne onime. Paris: Imprimerie de la veuve Oudot, 1753.

La Partie de chasse de Henri IV (comédie); Le Galant Escroc (comédie); La Vérité dans le vin, ou Les Désagréments de la galanterie (comédie); La Tête à Perruque ou le Bailli (petit conte dramatique). Four plays published in *Théâtre du XVIIIe siècle.* ed. by Jacques Truchet (Paris: Gallimard, 1974), vol. 2, pp. 599–727.
Journal et mémoires sur les hommes de lettres, les ouvrages dramatiques et les événements les plus mémorables du règne de Louis XV (1748–1772). 3 vols. (Paris: Didot, 1868).
Correspondance inédite. Edited by Honoré Bonhomme (Paris: [n. pub.], 1864).

Further Reading

Vladimir Bakum. *Charles Collé: the Man and his Work.* Ph.D. thesis. Columbia University, 1970.

COLLECTED WRITINGS OF FRAGRANT ELEGANCE

c. early twentieth century

Chinese Compendium

Such is the translation given by Robert van Gulik to *Xiangyan congshu*, a huge collection of writings on what culture added to nature to adorn life in the relationship between sexes. The collectanea are divided into 20 installments published between the years 1909 and 1911 totalling twenty volumes, or *ji* in Chinese. Dorothy Ko offered a slightly different translation for the title: *Collectanea of the fragrant and the beautiful.* She mentioned the year of publication as 1914 and referred to 20 volumes, instead of the 80 specified by van Gulik, a mystery easy to solve, for "volumes" may be translated two ways in Chinese: *ji* (20) and *juan* (80), the latter of which literally means a "roll," in fact a text of shorter size and perhaps better rendered as "chapter." As each *ji* is divided into four *juan* we get eighty volumes for the whole collection. The year 1914 refers perhaps to the second edition of the twenty installments put together. Whatever the case, the Taipei reproduction in 1969 of the movable-typed

edition is conveniently numbered on each of its 5868 pages, including some three to four hundred works in full or in lengthy extracts.

The compiler informs us at the end of his preface dated 1909 that he did not observe any chronological order or choose items for their surprising or enjoyable nature, not aiming at inciting any rapture of the senses. Little poetry is included. That need was met by a compendium published by Lei Jin in 1914, *Poems of Fragrant Elegance by Five Hundred Authors* [*Wubaijia xiangyan shi*], from which Georges Soulié de Morant selected the *Poèmes de lascivité parfumée* of his *Anthologie de l'amour chinois* (Mercure de France, Paris 1932, 247 p.).

Zhang T'ing-hua, our compiler, aware of the risks of hasty alterations, warns us that he abstained from any critical editing of the texts, culled from book collectors. They are quoted as he found them. Topical groupings, if any, are more or less haphazard. There is unfortunately no general table of contents for the twenty collections. Titles of books or other excerpts are simply at the head of each of the twenty installments. Authors are mentioned after the titles only when they reappear, followed by the texts. It can be rather cumbersome to find one's way, as no detailed indices are available, but the *General Catalogue of Chinese Collectanea*, published in Shanghai in 1959–1962, is a useful guide for the specialist. There the listing takes no account of the arbitrary division in four juan. Instead it informs of the number of chapters of the works copied in the collectanea, usually one, at most six. Unfortunately headings within the works copied are ignored. Authors are simply dated by vague dynastic slices which may cover one to three centuries. Still the *General Catalogue's* indices do work as a welcome, if rather coarse guide.

A Source Book of Chinese Sexual Life Through the Ages?

There is but one work possibly originating from before the Christian era and hardly more than two or three from writers who died in the Republican era starting in 1911. Some texts are rare items, others well-known and to be found in several earlier collections. Sorting out each item for different kinds of analytical classification would be required before making proper use of such a massive amount of material, the range of which may turn out to be both too large and too restricted. Medical or other technical books are discarded. Popular genres in colloquial language are ignored as well as jests or joke books. No material from this collectanea contributed to the rich harvest of Chinese sex jokes collected by Howard Levy. However, the wife-fearer as a favorite laughingstock is well represented in many kinds of literary pieces to be found in the *Collected Writings of Fragrant Elegance*. Of those translated, for example, in Levy's *Warm-soft Village*, one is in the seventh collection, the other in the first, the *Dulü* or *Rulings to Curb Jealousy*, attributed to Chen Yuanlong (1652–1736) by Yang Fuji (1747–1820); but it was already included in an earlier collection, *Chaodai congshu*. Parody of judicial sentences is a fairly early literary genre, a relaxing exercise better appreciated by scholars expected to join the higher bureaucracy empowered as judges. Feminine jealousy was rampant in the polygamous families of the well-off. It is no surprise to find the same work included in still another collected writing, *Qiuyu'an suibi* [*Notes from the refuge against autumnal rains*]. Of a similar parodic stance, *The Confession of a Wife-fearer* [*Junei gongzhuang*], in the seventh collection, probably belongs to a much later genre which may not be found anywhere else.

A Rare Item

On the other hand the piece immediately following the *Rulings* in the first *ji* is of a quite different order. Under the title, *Notes on The* Peony Pavilion *commented by three wives (Sanfu ping Mutan ting zaji)*, it is a long and moving piece of nearly twenty pages (211–230) signed by Wu Ren, a minor poet of Hangzhou who in 1694 published this annotated edition of the famous play of Tang Xianzu (1550–1616). It is the source document, directly or indirectly used by Dorothy Ko. An abridged version of her account (p. 70–71): "Chen Tong (ca. 1650–1665), like many other females of her times, was absorbed in the world of love evoked by *The Peony Pavilion*, an instant success upon its first publication in 1598. She became a devotee of the play, spending hours collating and correcting the different versions that book merchants purveyed. One day, she obtained a copy of the authentic edition. Unable to put it down, she starts writing comments on the margins of the pages. Even after felling ill, she stayed up all night reading. Her mother, worried about her health, seized and burned all her books. Chen's wet nurse, however, rescued volume one of her prized edition of *The Peony Pavilion*. Tucked away under a pillow, it was used to press dried flowers. Chen died not long before her wedding. The nurse then took the book to the home of Chen's betrothed, Wu Jen, together with a pair of shoes made by Chen for her future mother-in-law, and sold it to him for one ounce of silver. A drama aficionado himself, Wu Jen delighted in the tiny scribbling, full of Zen Buddhist insights, left by Chen Tong. Soon Wu Jen married another local girl, Tan Ze (ca. 1655–1675), who was as fond of the play as Chen Tong had been. Tan committed Chen's commentary to memory, completed the second half in Chen's spirit, and hand copied her comments and Chen's onto the margins of an original edition of the play that Wu had bought. She lent the copy to her niece, but reluctant to appear boastful about her talent, she pretended that the commentary was her husband's work. In 1675, three years after her marriage, Tan Ze also died. The ill-fated husband married a third time, more than a decade later, Qian Yi. She too, stayed up all night reading *The Peony Pavilion* and the comments by her two elder "sisters." She managed to convince her husband to reissue the play with commentary under the three women's names and sold her jewellery to finance the block-cutting and printing."

The Wife-Fearer

The fourteenth installment is almost entirely devoted to comments around the illustrious novel *The Story of the Stone*, while nearly half of the fourth collection deals with flowers and the art of arranging them. There, however, a Miss Hibiscus, in spite of her flowery name, is not dabbling with that sort of skill, but has drawn rulings issued from the inner apartments, pleasantly divided between six ministries as does the imperial government. Though the title, *Gui lü*, is translated by Howard Levy as *"How to Regulate the Bedroom"* (p. 52–61) it aims first of all at restricting the polygamous husband. To quote the first and the last penalties: "He is not allowed to meet girls from brothels whatever their beauty or skills. Transgression would be dealt as treacherous collusion with a foreign state. A hundred blows of heavy bamboo; hard labour outdoors." "Maids receive dresses, shoes, ornaments from their mistresses. Males are not allowed any secret donation. Transgression would be dealt with as abuse of power: sixty heavy blows, confiscation of the properties." For each of the thirty-one rules due penalties are tagged on.

Against Footbinding

Many a piece are far from being in a jocular tone. In the second installment, the great historian Zhang Xuecheng (1738–1801) pleaded for spreading learning among women in his essay negating the popular saying, *nüde wucai* (Feminine virtue is ignorance), *Fuxue* (p. 501–512), followed by the colophon of the same Yang Fuji (1747–1820) who picked it from the *Yihai zhuchen* [*Dust of Pearls from the Sea of Arts*] to include it in the earlier collection *Chaodai congshu*. The following piece, by the poet Yu Huai (1616–1696), *An Inquiry on Footbinding (Nüren xiewa kao*, p. 513–514), is perhaps even more famous, included in 1697 in the collectaned *Tanji congshu* (translated by Lin Yutang, *The*

Importance of Understanding, World Publishing, New York 1960, p. 221–224). The following discussion on footbinding, *Zhanzu tan,* of the illustrious poet Yuan Mei (1716–1798), refuting different theses for the antiquity of the custom, argues in the same vein, though he admits that women were reluctant to go barefoot in China and that men liked small feet already in early times. Other writings of Yuan Mei make his taste on the matter clearer: "If a woman has a three-inch bowed foot but short neck and thick waist, how can she ever give a light appearance when walking, as if she were skimming over the waves?" "What is the good of making a woman's feet so small because every generation is mad about this? I think that to maim your own daughter's limbs to make them prettier is like burning the bones of your parents in order to seek good fortune. How pitiful!" (see Howard Levy, *Chinese Footbinding*, p. 69 & 199). An even sharper pronouncement is to be found in our *Collected Writings of Fragrant Elegance*, seventh installment (p. 1880), among the extracts from the great essayist Xie Zhaozhe (1567–1624)'s *Wenhai pisha* [*Sands Culled from the Literary Sea*] published in 1609, more than a century previously, proving that women did not mind going barefoot in ancient times. He concludes, after negating any trace of footbinding half a millennium before his time: "But aren't feminine natural feet beautiful?" A bountiful harvest of footbinding-lore could be gathered, dispersed in the different collections, like, in the sixth one, the spicy ironical discourse on smelling small feet, *Xiaojiao wen* (1629–1630), by an obscure author, Guang Wangsheng. The same installment includes what looks like a newspaper report about women' associations approving a rejected project of the legislative chamber on prohibition of marrying concubines (p. 1695–1696), a step, claimed the concerned first wives, *dafu*, of a scope comparable to the abolition of slavery.

Fragrant Elegance of Times Past

The compiler lived in a time of changing values. His choice of materials was probably directed by some new trends of thought. It is no doubt significant that each of the later installments, from the twelfth one till nineteenth, are headed by the writings of the prominent westernizer Wang Tao (1828–1897), himself a pioneer in the discovery of minor genres of intimate writings like Mao Xiang (1611–1693)'s *Reminiscences of the Plum-Shadow Hermitage, Yingmei'an yiyu,* copied in the third installment (p. 585–614), at that time a text known only to a limited circle of connoisseurs. Still little-known is the long letter written by Yuan Zhongdao (1570–1624) for a young man living with a prostitute to beg the pardon of his elder brother (p. 1623–1627). The same may not be said nowadays about the extracts of Li Yu (1611–1680)'s writings in the last and twentieth installment (p. 5571–5628), *Casual Expressions of Idle Feeling, Xianqing ouji,* published in 1671. Is it by chance that Wolfram Eberhard (1909–1996) chose to translate nearly the same text, though the *Collected Writings of Fragrant Elegance* fail to include the last and fifth part, about the art of living with a woman and enjoying marriage? On the other hand Eberhard skipped entirely Yu Huai (1616–1696)'s discourse on footbinding which Li Yu quoted extensively (p. 1609–1611), with a number of unimportant variants, compared to the same text on p. 513 of the same *Collectanea.* Li Yu called Yu Huai his friend and assumed a rather unusual personal tone, like a fashion director confiding his tastes about "the perfect lady." The text here appears as a sort of treatise divided in four parts: (1) Opting for charm. (2) Embellishing the appearance. (3) Ordering the dresses. (4) Cultivating womens gifts for reading, writing, music, and dance. "Why shouldn't I buy one or two concubines, if I can afford them?" wrote Li Yu. The wife is compared to the fields of the landlord, their main asset; the concubines are his gardens, to be tended carefully. Even the best looking woman would still gain by embellishing herself, an art which starts with cleanliness, mouth-washing, and bathing. Physical appearance is but the basis for charm. Paramount is complexion: the fairer the better. Li Yu's explanation, in accordance with traditional Chinese medical ideas, is tied to the proportion of white male semen in combination with female blood at the time of conception. Second in importance are the eyes and the eyelashes, for, says Li Yu aptly, the face is the master of the whole body and eyes the master of the face. Finally come the hands, neglected by most people, though a good guide to the mind and the refinement of the girl. The desire for small feet brought on footbinding. It clashes with Li Yu's praise of naturalness. "What's the

good of feet so small that one can't walk? What difference with having suffered the penalty of hacked off feet?" "Somebody long ago told me that the Prime Minister Zhou of Yixing bought a beauty for a thousand pieces of gold. He named her Miss Carry. Her feet were so tiny that she could hardly move. She had to be carried; so her name. I replied: if such is the case, better buy for a few copper coins a beauty of baked mud. The Creator has endowed us with feet in order to let us walk!" For the final charm in women is their bearing, *taidu.* A girl who cannot walk without leaning on walls is a pitiable sight. "Charm is something which comes naturally to a person and directly grows out of her personality. It is not something which can be copied from others, for charm imitated is beauty spoiled." Lin Yutang goes on in his translation from Li Yu: "I was once in Yangchow, trying to pick a concubine for a certain official. There were rows of women in beautiful dresses and of different types. At first they stood all with their heads bent, but when they were ordered to hold their heads up, one of them just raised her head and looked blandly at me, and another was terribly shy and would not hold her head up until she had been bidden to do so several times. There was one, however, who would not look up at first but did so after some persuasion, and then she first cast a quick glance as if she was looking and yet not looking at me before she held her head up, and again she cast another glance before she bent her head again. This I call charm." (Lin Yutang, *The Importance of Understanding,* World Publishing, New York 1960, p.234). Li Yu, of course, concedes that there is charm acquired by training, but it is for performers on the stage, while natural charm is to be enjoyed at home.

Fragrant Memories of Brothel Life

High-class brothels were places where scholars and civil servants met, where courtesans practiced dance, music, and poetry. Many writings keep the memory of those places of enjoyment, of the cultural pastimes rather than of any sexual activities. In earlier times brothels were registered and required to offer public services. Biographies of the most glamorous courtesans take the larger part of that kind of work. Later those houses' prestige waned somewhat and they were called "green bowers," *qinglou.* There is in the collection one of the earliest and quite detailed description of a gay quarter of the Chinese capital, Ch'ang-an, between 789 and 881, the Northern quarter, *Beili zhi*, by Sun Qi (translated into French by Robert des Rotours, *Courtisanes chinoises à la fin des T'ang*, Paris: PUF 1968, 196 p.) is to be found in the fifth installment, where there is some attempt of grouping as it is followed by the *Jiaofang ji* (Record of the Entertainment Bureau, written after 762), Xia Tingshi (ca. 1316–after 1368)'s recollections from green bowers, *Qinglou ji*, a valuable document for the history of Chinese theater too, for there were no clear boundaries between these different kinds of entertainments. However, Yu Huai (1616–1696)'s no less famous reminiscences from those districts in the former Ming capital of Nanking, *Banqiao zaji*, are inserted in the thirteenth installment (translated under the title *A Feast of Mist and Flowers*, Yokohama 1967, by Howard Levy).

Though van Gulik wrote that the collectanea was "published in the years 1910–1911 when censorship became lax," it should be pointed out that it contains very little of an obscene or vulgar nature, true to its title of "Collected Writings of Fragrant Elegance." Any scorn it may have suffered was for its nature as a testimony of the leisure of an outlawed social group.

Biography

The compiler is using a pseudonym, Chong-tianzi, which is one used by Zhang T'ing–hua about whom nothing is known.

ANDRÉ LÉVY

Editions

Xiangyan congshu. Taipei: Ku-t'ing shu-wu. 1969.

Further Reading

Ko, Dorothy. *Teachers of the Inner Chambers: Women and Culture in Seventeenth-Century China*. Stanford University Press, 1994, p. 371.

Levy, Howard S. *Illusory Flame*. Tokyo: Kenkyusha 1962.

———. *Warm-Soft Village, Stories, Sketches and Essays*. Tokyo: Dai Nippon Insatsu, 1964.

———. *Chinese Sex Jokes in Traditional Times*. Asian Folklore and Social Life Monographs, vol. 58, Taipei: Orient Cultural Service, 1974, 361 p.

———. *Chinese Footbinding: The History of a Curious Erotic Custom*. London: Neville Spearman, 1975.

Li, Yü. *Die vollkommene Frau*. Übersetzt und eingeleitet von Wolfram Eberhard. Zürich: Die Waage, 1963, 136 p.

Lin, Yutang. *The Importance of Understanding*, New York: World Publishing, 1960.

COLLETON, JOHN (ROBERT WALTER MARKS)

1907–1993
American novelist, philosopher, and mathematician

The Novels

Colleton's first erotic novel, *The Trembling of a Leaf*, is a take-off on Somerset Maugham's 1921 novel of the same title, just as his fourth, *Replenishing Jennifer*, sends up Maxwell Bodenheim's *Replenishing Jessica* (1925). Erudition studs Colleton's fiction with references to Maeterlinck, Shakespeare, Hemingway, Stendhal, D'Annunzio, James, and Flaubert, with allusions to European history and mathematical formulae, and with urbane cultural and political commentary. His style succeeds through paradox: on the one hand, introspection and learning add elegance to narrative; on the other, they veneer a graphic sexuality whose impulses are demotic. *The Trembling of a Leaf*, told by a student besotted with his beautiful, blueblooded aunt Amy Dellmore, one-time "Charleston Woman of the Year," introduces one of Colleton's principal characters. Wealth, social station, and manners hide the outwardly demure Amy's hyperactive libido. A semi-public whipping releases her sexuality, which manifests itself in incest and exhibitionism; hidden triggers of desire are a recurrent Colleton motif. In subsequent novels, most of them narrated by Beauregard "Bill" Benton, a Georgia novelist and editor, Amy becomes one apex of a "southern" triangle formed by Benton and Cloris, Lady Cholmondeley, nee McGuire, herself a native of Chapel Hill, North Carolina. This fictional device may well have sexualized an eleven-year virtual ménage a trois involving Marks, his wife Hilde, and the novelist Carson McCullers.

Most of the novels revolve around the nymphomaniacal Cloris, who enjoys a marriage of convenience with a titled British entrepreneur with connections to the Mafia narcotics trade. A secret pederast, Lord Cholmondeley worries enough about appearances—he is also secretary of the Knights of Malta—occasionally to dispatch thugs in pursuit of Benton and Cloris, a circumstance that justifies their constant travel. When not soaking sheets together, Cloris and Benton collaborate on erotic art films (e.g., one based on *Oedipus Rex*); she directs the explicit screenplays that he writes, with results that her admirers compare to Buñuel and Pasolini. In each novel, Benton and Cloris seduce women who star in their films; these are modelled on actresses that Marks interviewed as a journalist: Audrey Hepburn, Sophia Loren, Gypsy Rose Lee, Jayne Mansfield, Kim Novak, and Mae West. Benton and Cloris continuously invent their sexual *personae* in a "Pirandello Game" (*Between Cloris and Amy*, 40) of talk: voicing fantasy and tracing branching implications lead inevitably to physical experimentation. Cinematic or literary, voyeurism is key to eroticism: Colleton's scenarios wed narcissism and lust through the dramatic agency of camera or observers. Benton will speculate on the visual angle best suited to represent lubricity, or on-lookers will critique an act of fellatio or sodomy, so that arousal can feed on arousal. "Sex is a reptile perpetually engaged in the pursuit of its own tail," says Benton (*The Pleasures of Cloris*, 49).

Benton deprecates his abilities as a writer, insisting that he lacks insight into character or motivation, at the same time that his fascination with erotic behavior underlines a conviction that the world is transparent to sex. Setting supplies verisimilitude. The appeal of a Colleton novel derives in part from Baedecker commentary on actual streets, restaurants, hotels, and monuments as characters pursue each other from South Carolina's Low Country to Italy's Amalfi Coast. More important, travel illustrates a Jamesian theme: the corruption of Americans as they learn from Continental aristocrats "a respect for the decadence of others" (*Up in Mamie's Diary*, 28).

Colleton renders decadence inventively. Aimee, Countess of Liechtenstein, gives each of her lovers a watch whose dial marks her menstrual cycle. The scholarly Contessa Borromini lectures on papal history and Umbrian architecture and can decipher Cretan Linear B, but chooses fashions that emphasize her lack of pubic hair. A soothsayer "reads" breasts and clitorises through "sciences" she calls mammaromanticism and clitoramancy. Lovers sneak through secret passageways or hide behind tapestries, but the most aristocratic setting, say a palatial marble bathroom, will be subverted by a leaky toilet. Appearance is all: polite Japanese tourists pretend that the naked couple they discover on an altar in a Doric temple are pieces of classic statuary. *The Naked Countess of Lichtenstein* (1976) comically anticipates later feminist views when the fictional La Concorrenza, a radical group of Italian women, proposes to liberate feminists from patriarchy through orgiastic sex, a way of attacking established political parties, including the communists, who are too masculine in their conservatism. Women in Colleton novels are invariably intellectually curious, sexually autonomous, and confident of their sensual power. In allowing them to stage manage their own pleasures, Colleton aims at a wide audience. The effect, both titillating and sophisticated, was the reason that his erotic novels sold more than a million copies in the United States (Gene Waddell, Archivist of the College of Charleston, to Joseph W. Slade, February 26, 2002 and March 5, 2002).

Biography

Born in Charleston, South Carolina, 1907. Marks flunked out of the College of Charleston and Yale University (1929), but after taking classes at the Sorbonne (1930) and Columbia University (1942), he received his B.A. (1951), M.A (1952), and Ph.D. (1953) from the New School for Social Research. A professional journalist, he wrote for *Esquire, Coronet, Popular Science*, and other magazines, often under pen names (Mark Ashley, John Charleston, Tradd Cooper, and Tycho Brahe), edited *Gentry* (1952–1954) and *Pocket* magazines (1954–1956), edited science texts for Bantam Books (1959–1967), and ghost-wrote Elsa Maxwell's syndicated society column (1960s). Marks popularized the work of Buckminster Fuller, wrote science and mathematics texts (under the name Bradford Smith), and published a novel on psychology (*The Horizontal Hour*, 1957). After teaching philosophy and cybernetics at the New School for Social Research in New York (1953–1970), he returned to Charleston, where he wrote erotic novels under the pseudonym John Colleton, the name of one of South Carolina's original "Lords Proprietor." Marks was married three times, to Sylvia (maiden name unknown), Hilde Russell, and Alice Barnette, but had no children of his own. He died of pneumonia in Charleston on August 8, 1993.

JOSEPH SLADE III

Selected Works

The Trembling of a Leaf. New York: Pocket Books, 1971.

The Enjoyment of Amy. New York: New York: Pocket Books, 1973.
The Pleasures of Cloris. New York: New American Library, 1974.
Replenishing Jennifer. New York: NAL, 1975.
Up in Mamie's Diary. New York: NAL, 1975.
Between Cloris and Amy. New York: NAL, 1976.
The Naked Countess of Lichtenstein. New York: Pocket Books, 1976.
On or About the First Day in June. New York: NAL, 1978.
Two Nymphs Named Melissa. New York: NAL, 1979.
The Seduction of Marianna. New York: NAL, 1980.
The Delights of Anna. New York: NAL, 1980.
Ring Twice to Enter. Under pseudonym Mark Ashley, New York: Popham Press/Charter (Grosset & Dunlap), 1980.
The Enticement of Cindy. New York: NAL, 1981.
Barefoot on Jill. New York: NAL, 1983; aka *Jill*. Amsterdam: Playboy Pikant, 1985.
Interjecting Valerie: Or Legs Across the Sea. New York: NAL, 1986.

Further Reading

Marks was an authority on twentieth-century photography, and left his collection of prints (e.g., Lewis Hine, Alfred Eisenstaedt, Margaret Bourke-White, Alfred Stieglitz) to the Gibbes Museum of Art (Charleston); his papers (51 boxes) are in the Library of the College of Charleston.

Carr, Virginia Spencer. *The Lonely Hunter: A Biography of Carson McCullers*. Garden City, NY: Doubleday and Co., 1975.
Cupp, Ruth. "Robert Marks: Charleston Writer As Exceptional As the City Characters He Praised." *Charleston Post and Courier*, 23 August 1993, Box 13, folder 25 of "Papers."
Greene, Karen. "Marks: Versatile Author." *Charleston Courier*, 19 October 1975, p. 2C.

CONFESSION AND GUILT

Augustine of Hippo elaborated the fundamental principle for much of Christian history: There is sexual intercourse only between a man and a woman, married to one another, and only for the purpose for procreation. All sexual behaviors, not meeting those conditions, were understood as immoral and sinful. A rigorous practice of confession provided a regulatory means for the development of Christian shame and guilt around sexuality.

Michel Foucault offers an intriguing hypothesis that Christian confession plays an important development of the notion of subjectivity and the discourse of sexuality. He traces the practice of confession to Greco-Roman philosophical obligation to know oneself. It became the cultural background for the development of the monastic practice of an examination of conscience, whereby a monastic was required to turn his thoughts completely to God and to confess to a spiritual mentor each of his thoughts not focused on God. Foucault observes that the examination of conscience was developed by John Cassian's *De Institiones Coenabiorum* and *Collectiones Patrum*. The monastic vigilantly ensured that he was chaste when no impure thoughts occurred. Foucault attaches great importance to the Fourth Lateran Council that made yearly confession obligatory in 1215. He sees confession as a rigorous examination of sexual thoughts and acts and as coercive technology of regulating behavior. The examination of sex through the lens of confessional speech led to the development of a western discourse on sexuality.

Private confession originated in sixth-century CE Irish monastic communities in the practice of spiritual direction whereby a monk would confess his faults to a superior or senior monk. The director would impose an appropriate penance upon the penitent monk. The practice of private confession was exported from Ireland to other European Christian regions or areas undergoing the spread of Christianity. The clerical confessor understood himself as a teacher; he used the opportunity of the confessional practice to correct and instruct penitents in the development of new inward disposition of remorse and directional change of life. The penitent was understood as a repenting sinner and was considered the lowest rank of Christian. The goal was to make Christians and newly converted Christian populations obey not only the Church but also its morality and laws. Newly converted European populations had a strong commitment to a more diversified and freer expression of sexuality than the Christians. Private confession became one of the principal means for censuring sexual behaviors outside the Christian norms of sexuality within marriage for only the purpose of procreation.

Confessional literature taught clergy interrogation techniques, passed on a developing theology of penance, and catalogued sins according to the severity of penance and confessional etiquette. It establishes the priest's authority and imparts knowledge that supports the priest's authority.

Private confession provided a regulatory practice to ensure clerical social control of Christian morality and in particular its moral teachings on sexuality. The priest was to investigate the sins of the penitent through interrogation, judge the guilt and remorse of the person confessing, and impose a penance. Sins were enumerated, examined, catalogued, and judged. If people sinned or did not fulfill their penance, they were supposed to feel guilty. The heart of confessional practice relied on the penitent's internal feelings of guilt and fear of damnation.

Pierre Payer (1985) is critical of Foucault for placing too much emphasis on the Fourth Lateran Council, the later penitential literature, and the sixteenth- and seventeenth-century Catholic moralists. He rejects the notion that practice of confession as form of social control of sexual expression. Payer points to the post-Lateran summas for confessors and manuals which abandon the bluntness of questions of earlier penitential literature; these manuals spend less time on sexual sins. One reason for such lax interrogation of sexual sins can be seen in Raymond de Penaforte's instructions to confessors to be very cautious with penitents and not to go into depth of special sins since they often fall into such sins after such pastoral interrogation. In other words, penitents might not have thought of such things, so do not give them any new erotic ideas. Another consideration Payer fails to consider is that during the thirteenth century, Christian moral teachings on sexuality are already refined and well embedded with various European countries and principalities.

Other medievalists such as Thomas Tentler (1977), Bryan Turner (1977), and A. J. Frantzen (1983) have understood along with Foucault the development of private confession as disciplinary practice or social system of guilt and expiation. Foucault's thesis can be found evidenced in the earlier penitential books, the emergence in post-Lateran summas for confessors, and moral theologies manuals. These are attempts to set up a rigorist sexual ethic, fundamentally outlined by Augustine's earlier position. Confessional literature instructs the priest in a disciplinary function of teaching Christians to feel guilt about sins and seek a cure for guilt from their sins.

Penitential literature became influential for moral theology that became dominant from the

Catholic Counter Reformation period into the twentieth century. The penitentials catalogue and rank sins according to the severity of penance assigned to the sin. The terminology for sexual sins is a problem. There is a lack of class nouns in Latin for illicit sexual sins, indicating an absence of abstraction for the varieties of sexual sins. The penitential books used verbal descriptions to articulate a particular sexual sin. A level of conceptualization and abstraction to produce a sexual vocabulary does not appear until the thirteenth-century summas for confessors. Sexual offenses constituted the largest single category of behaviors in the penitential books.

During the Catholic Counter Reformation, the summas were replaced in clerical education with manuals of moral theology. Alfonse Liguori (1696–1787), later declared a doctor of the Roman Catholic Church and founder of the Redemptorist order, wrote *Theologia Moralis* that examined rigorist and laxist interpretations of moral questions and a small guide for confessors, *Praxis Confessarii*. These became the basis of clerical education and preparation for Roman Catholic confessional practice well into the twentieth century. It became effective in the development of Catholic guilt around sexuality until Vatican II.

ROBERT E. GOSS

Further Reading

Brundage, James A. *Law, Sex, and Christian Society in Medieval Europe*, Chicago: University of Chicago Press, 1987.

Carrette, Jeremy R. (ed). *Religion and Culture: Michel Foucault*, New York, Routledge, 1999.

Foucault, Michel. *The History of Sexuality, Vol. I.* Translated by Robert Hurley, New York, Vintage Books, 1978.

Frantzen, A.J. *The Literature of Penance in Anglo-Saxon England*. New Brunswick, Rutgers University Press, 1983.

Payer, Pierre J. *Sex and the Penitentials: The Development of a Sexual Code.* Toronto. University of Toronto Press, 1984.

Payer, Pierre J. "Foucault on Penance and the Shaping of Sexuality." *Studies in Religion*, 14, 1985, 313–320.

Payer, Pierre J. "Confession and the Study of Sex in the Middle Ages," in *Handbook of Medieval Sexuality*. Edited by Vern L. Bullough & James A. Brundage. New York, Garland Publishing, 1996, 3–31.

Tentler, Thomas N. "The Summa for Confessors as an Instrument of Social Control," in *The Pursuit of Holiness in Late Medieval and Renaissance Religion*. Edited by Charles Trinkaus & Heiko A. Oberman. Leiden, E.J. Brill, 1974, 102–126.

Tentler, Thomas N. *Sin and Confession on the Eve of the Reformation*. Princeton: Princeton University Press, 1977.

Turner, Bryan S. "Confession and Social Structure," *The Annual Review of the Social Sciences of Religion.* vol. 1, 1977, 29–58.

COOPER, DENNIS

1953–
American poet, novelist, journalist, anthologist, magazine publisher, and art curator.

Dennis Cooper is among the most controversial of contemporary gay American writers. Cooper's creative corpus, totaling several collections of poetry, numerous essays and short stories, and six widely read and controversial novels, has been disturbing both gay and straight readers for some time with work that seems invested in celebrating anti-social and transgressive impulses, questioning "normality," disturbing conventional notions of the relationship between sociality and sexuality, and confronting readers with sexual violence and erotic perversion. Edmund White, in "Out of the Closet, On to the Bookshelf," says that Cooper is "[a]s obsessive as Sade and as far from ordinary morality as George Bataille" as he "meditates ceaselessly on violence and perversion." His work seems "dedicated to drugs, kink, and a fragile sense of beauty fashioned out of the detritus of American suburbs"—or, "the very stuff of Jesse Helms's worst nightmares." (282).

But Cooper's work is not without a tradition. In an article/interview in *The Advocate*, provocatively titled "Hannibal Lecture," Cooper claims affinity for the works of the Marquis de Sade, Rimbaud, Gide, Genet, and Burroughs, almost all of whom explored variations of queer transgression, of the tension between an "outlaw existence" versus the "prudent administration of desire" that many novels with gay content often explore. Elizabeth Young, in *Shopping in Space: Essays on America's Blank Generation Fiction*, says more specifically that "It is precisely at [the] point of sado-masochistic anal taboo that Dennis Cooper locates his work." Still, Young maintains that his work is "clear and aesthetically beautiful, and at the same time, dense, threatening and impacted with meaning" (236). Moreover, Young argues that Cooper's "fiction attempts to unravel a nightmarishly complex knot of predatory homosexual desire, murderous fantasy and perversion—shot through with shards of tenderness, vision and a fragmented, potent humanity" (66). His principle "muse type," the character that figures prominently in almost all of his work, is "the younger, troubled unhappy boy who turned to him for care and nurturance" (69).

To date, Cooper's principle literary contribution has consisted of a five-book cycle exploring themes of sexuality, violence, and murder, with a particular focus on the lives of his "muse type," late adolescent boys with homo-erotic interests. George Miles, a disturbed youngster, boyhood friend, and apparent inspiration for the five-book cycles, sometimes appears as a character, George, throughout the books, which include the novels *Closer, Frisk, Try, Guide,* and *Period* (Reitz). In a review of the last book in the series, *Period*, one critic claims that Cooper's novels "attempt to explain away his own childhood nightmares" (Shattuck B9).

The second novel, *Frisk*, has been perhaps the most controversial, particularly since it lures the reader into thinking that the narrator, provocatively called "Dennis," murders young men as a form of erotic fulfillment. In a way, *Frisk* is a strange coming out narrative in which the narrator traces the development of his fascination, since puberty, of seeing "snuff" pictures—several of which he saw as a young gay teen in a porn shop, perhaps inciting his desires and obsession. The result is a portrait of the artist as a young pervert. Increasingly, fantasies of violence and murder abound, and Dennis relates these in often chilling passages:

It wasn't that I didn't fantasize murdering hustlers. It's just that I tend to be too scared or shy the first few times I sleep with someone to do what I actually want. The worse that could, and did, happen was I'd get a little too rough. But the hustler would stop me, or I'd stop myself, before things became more than conventionally kinky, as far as he knew. (36)

Readers of Cooper's work will recognize this as familiar thematic territory: the conflict between imagining one's desires and the inability to realize them. According to Earl Jackson, Jr.'s essay, "Death Drives Across Pornotopia: Dennis Cooper on the Extremities of Being," which offers a psychoanalytical reading of some of Cooper's early novels and poems, the combination of eroticism and violence in Cooper's work offers us "an investigation into the interior of the body, a movement of objectification and obsessive violation of the body's contours, a peering inside the costume of the person to his real location" (143).

Indeed, part of Dennis' drive as a character in *Frisk* is a desire to collapse completely the boundary between self and other—quite literally: he says, "I can actually imagine myself inside the skins I admire. I'm pretty sure if I tore some guy open I'd know him as well as anyone could, because I'd have what he consists of right there in my hands, mouth, wherever" (51). Certainly, such "knowing" of another person results in—actually, originates in—turning the object of affection into an actual object. But such passages, as brutal as they are, also beg for our identification, even erotic understanding. Who doesn't bemoan the separation of self and other? Who hasn't tried drastic (if not murderous) ways to overcome the distance between desire and its beloved? We may resist complete identification, but there is a strong romantic, even erotically playful sentiment at work here: "I want to know everything about you. But to really do that, I'd have to kill you, as bizarre as that sounds" (67). At the same time, to countenance Dennis, the narrator's desires as "knowable," if not commendable, is to begin collapsing the boundary between Dennis the author and the reader's prurient interests. We are coming closer to understanding the hidden desires of the narrator as we continue reading the novel.

With such material, a question lingers: Is Cooper's work erotic? Cooper argues, in a way, that it is and it isn't. He maintains that *Frisk* "is about the difference between what is possible in one's fantasy life, and what is possible in one's real life... It tries, in various ways, to seduce the readers to believe a series of murders are real, then announces itself as a fiction, hopefully leaving readers responsible for whatever pleasure they took in believing the murders were real. [...] Murder is only erotic in the imagination, if at all" (reprinted in *Salon*). In a way, then, the novel serves as an opportunity to meditate on taking responsibility for our desires, on coming face to face with the often hidden, taboo, and perverse desires lurking beneath the surface of many lives. In an interview, Cooper maintains that "I present the actual act of evil so it's visible and give it a bunch of facets so that you can actually look at it and experience it. You're seduced into dealing with it. [...] So with *Frisk*, whatever pleasure you got out of making a picture in your mind based on ... those people being murdered, you take responsibility for it" (Laurence).

But Cooper's aims are not ultimately puritanical, suggesting the eradication of troubling or anti-social desires. Young says that, "For all the extremes and grotesqueries of his content, Cooper is a tender, lyrical and very romantic writer." Young also argues that, while Cooper's work isn't necessarily "pornographic," he has many "affinities with the French erotic tradition represented by...de Sade, Lautreamont and Bataille" (Shopping, 257). That is, like de Sade and the others in that erotic tradition, Cooper is invested in understanding what "extremes and grotesqueries" tell us about ourselves. In particular, he wants his readers to acknowledge the breadth—and depth—of desire as it draws us to other bodies in complex ways. Other critics, such as Kevin McCarron, disagree and they only see Cooper's work as "detachedly recording the death throes of a degenerate and rapidly decaying culture" (58).

Cooper, though, sees his work—and himself—very differently: "I thought people were seeing me as someone who jacked off to snuff videos. But it hasn't affected the way I write. I want my work to be very pure. It comes from a very pure space" (Canning, 309). More specifically, he maintains that "Ethics has been the center of all the books from the beginning" (Canning, 322). How so? A close reading of his work reveals that Cooper's narratives and characters are not just interested in transgressing societal norms as much as they are concerned

with understanding the value of their transgressive interests and fantasies—and how such fantasies impact and shape their social interactions with others. Indeed, it is the intersection between fantasy and reality, the life of the mind and the life of the social being, that becomes the core concern in Cooper's work: our fantasies of others, as disturbing as they may be, are part of what comprises our interest in others, and they should be acknowledged for the work they do in cultivating social relations, even if they remain only "fantasies." His novels, as challenging and anti-social as they seem on the surface, call for a fuller understanding and appreciation of desire, particularly transgressive desires, in the composition of social relations.

Biography

Dennis Cooper was born on January 10, 1953 in Pasadena, California. He attended Los Angeles county public schools until the 8th grade when he transferred to a private school from which he was expelled in the 11th grade. He attended Pasadena City College for two years, where he studied with poets Ronald Koertge and Jerene Hewitt and one year at Pitzer College in Claremont, California, where he studied with the poet Bert Meyers. In 1976, he founded *Little Caesar Magazine and Press*. From 1980 to 1983 he was Director of Programming for the Beyond Baroque Literary/Art Center in Venice, California. From 1983 to 1990, he moved between New York City and Amsterdam, Holland. He returned to Los Angeles in 1990.

JONATHAN ALEXANDER

Note: The Fales Library and Special Collections of New York University has an extensive archive of Cooper's papers and manuscripts: http://dlib.-nyu.edu:8083/servlet/SaxonServlet?source= / cooper.xml&style=/saxon01f2.xsl&part =body.

Selected Works

The Dream Police: Selected Poems 1969–1993 (Pub Group West, 1995; Grove Press, 1996; this volume collects the best of Cooper's poem from his previously published chapbooks and short volumes of poetry).
Closer. Grove: 1989.
Frisk. Grove: 1991.
Try. Grove: 1994.
Guide. Grove: 1997.

Period. Grove, 2000.

My Loose Thread. Cannongate Books, 2002.

Wrong. Atlantic Monthly Press, 1993.

Jerk. With Nayland Blake Artspace Books, 1993.

Horror Hospital Unplugged: A Graphic Novel. With Keith Mayerson. Juno Books, 1996.

All Ears: Cultural Criticism, Essays and Obituaries. Soft Skull Press, 1999.

Co-editor, with Amy Scholder and Jeanette Winterson, of *Essential Acker: The Selected Writings of Kathy Acker, an anthology* Grove, 2002.

Further Reading

Annesley, James. "Commodification, Violence and the Body: A Reading of Some Recent American Fictions." *American Bodies: Cultural Histories of the Physique.* Ed. by Tim Armstrong. New York: New York UP. 1996.

Bram, Christopher (with Dennis Cooper, Michael Cunningham, and others). "On Contemporary Gay Male Literature in the United States." *Queer Representations: Reading Lives, Reading Cultures.* Ed. by Martin Duberman. New York: New York UP. 1997.

Canning, Richard. "Dennis Cooper." *Gay Fiction Speaks: Conversations with Gay Novelists.* New York: Columbia UP, 2000.

Jackson, Earl, Jr. "Dennis Cooper". In *Contemporary Gay American Novelists.* Edited by Emmanuel S. Nelson. Westport, CT: Greenwood Press, 1993.

Jackson, Earl, Jr. "Death Drives Across Pornotopia: Dennis Cooper on the Extremities of Being." In

GLQ: A Journal of Lesbian and Gay Studies 1.2 (1994).

Laurence, Alexander. "An Interview with Dennis Cooper." *Free Williamsburg* 10 (2001). Available online at http://www.freewilliamsburg.com/still_fresh/january/dennis_cooper.html.

McCarron, Kevin. "'The Crack-House Flicker': The Scared and the Absurd in the Short Stories of Dennis Cooper, Dennis Johnson, and Thom Jones." *Yearbook of English Studies* 31(2001).

Reitz, Daniel. "Dennis Cooper." *Salon* (March 4, 2000). Available online at http://dir.salon.com/people/feature/2000/05/04/cooper/index.html.

Shattuck, Kathryn. "How Nightmarish Childhood Events Become a 5-Book Series, Now Finished." *The New York Times.* March 2, 2000.

White, Edmund. "Out of the Closet, Onto the Bookshelf." In *The Burning Library: Writings on Art, Politics, and Sexuality: 1969–1993.* Edited by David Bergman. London: Chatto & Windus, 1994.

Worton, Michael. "(Re)Writing Gay Identity: Fiction as Theory." *Canadian Review of Comparative Literature/Revue Canadienne de Littérature Comparée,* 21.1–2 Special issue: "Reading the Signs/Lecture des signes"; 1994.

Young, Elizabeth. *Pandora's Handbag: Adventures in the Book World.* London: Serpent's Tail, 2001.

Young, Elizabeth, and Graham Caveney. *Shopping in Space: Essays on America's Blank Generation Fiction.* New York: Atlantic Monthly Press, 1993.

CORNEILLE, PIERRE

1606–1684
French dramatist

L'Occasion perdue recouverte

Copies of *L'Occasion perdue recouverte* [*Lost Love Recovered*], composed of forty stances, were distributed secretly in Paris and were long attributed to Pierre Corneille before this claim was committed to print as part of a posthumous collection of the sayings and miscellanea of François Charpentier (1620–1702), a writer who had known Corneille. This work, *Carpenteriana*, which appeared in 1724, relates that,

while the poem was published anonymously, Pierre Ségurier, Chancellor and Keeper of the Seal, believed it to be the work of Corneille, and summoned the playwright for an audience to establish the truth of the matter. Ségurier was responsible for the legality of all publications appearing in France, and as early as 1647 had notified Parisian printers that the king was determined to stamp out books printed without official permission. The dramatist seemingly accepted the blame for the work, and allegedly undertook his translation of the *Imitation of Christ* as a penance imposed by Father Paulin of the capital's Nazareth Convent for having been responsible for such a licentious work.

This cleric was the chancellor's own confessor. Corneille's candidacy for authorship is reinforced by the fact that versification is elegant, and gratuitous vulgarisms are absent. Moreover, the manner in which the poem is set out and unfolds, lends itself to dramatic performance. The poem might not have survived if it had not been published in 1658 as part of an anthology, *Nouveau cabinet des Muses*, and later in 1661 by Benech de Cantenac. This court poet included it as part of his *Journal de Trévoux*, and he has also been proposed as the possible creator of the piece.

The poem contains bawdy and comic elements more commonly seen in contemporary comedy, such as the type of the cuckolded, jealous husband. Dorimant's honor is endangered by Cloris, his sexually voracious wife, who succumbs to the charms of Lisandre while her husband is absent. Cloris has fallen passionately in love with this young suitor and while, at first, she offers some resistance, finds herself so overwhelmed with passion that 'Lisandre pouvoit tout' (Lisandre could do anything'). She passes out soon afterwards, though she has clearly given consent before fainting. Lisandre's conquest is to prove short-lived, however, for he suddenly finds he is completely impotent at the moment of consummating their passion. He tries every available method to stimulate an erection, and hurriedly and furiously masturbates himself before Cloris comes round. When she does eventually regain her senses, she strokes his body, only to find no visible sign of reciprocation. As soon as she touches his penis, she moves her hand away, not, as the poet remarks, because of any distaste at the male member, but rather out of disgust at its flaccid state. At first, Cloris is understanding of his predicament, but this patience eventually wears thin and she dismisses her erstwhile lover, cruelly refusing to listen to his excuses. At this point, the couple overhears a noise downstairs, which turns out to be Dorimant who has returned announced, and the disappointed lover makes good his escape through the bedroom window. Lisandre spends a restless and sleepless night, anxious about his new sexual problem, and resolves to return to his mistress in order to resolve his condition one way or another. Lisandre returns to the house in the early hours of the morning, though in a somewhat dejected state, and enters the building when he observes Dorimant's departure. On reaching the bedchamber, he finds the object of his desire and

frustration sleeping naked on her bed. This unexpectedly stirs him and he rushes forward to wake her. He is in such an excited state that he ejaculates as soon as she awakens, and she is horrified to find herself covered in semen, and worse still, unsatisfied. The young man is still feeling in a sexual mood, and her anger turns to lust as he jumps on the bed to pleasure her.

The work directly refers to various sexual acts, and it is Cloris's expert masturbation of his partner that causes her to lose consciousness. Vulgar and popular expressions are rejected in favor of more poetic terminology for human genitalia: the male organ is coyly described as 'ce directeur de la nature' ['this leader of nature'], while the vagina is referred to as 'doux tyran de nostre raison' ['gentle tyrant of our reason'], as well as being euphemistically termed as 'un lieu qu'on ne nomme pas' ['a place that one does not mention by name']. More striking than the uncomplicated descriptions of sexual behavior are the constant allusions to lovemaking as being a natural and pleasurable act providing mutual satisfaction to both sexes. Both parties are equally eager to engage in intercourse, and the traditional depiction of a lascivious, unfaithful female, or alternatively, a predatory, forceful young male lover, are notably absent. Cloris may not be an altogether sympathetic creation, but she is an empowered woman in control of her sexuality. The poet describes her as being ashamed ['honteuse'] to find herself covered in ejaculatory fluid, but this sentiment is due to the fact that it has happened without her knowledge and has soiled the bed linen, rather than betraying any moral guilt. Lisandre does not impose himself on her, and she does not acquiesce to anything that she does not want to do. The poem presents her only apparent flaw as the fact that she has taken a lower-class lover. When she is awoken to find her lover has enjoyed an orgasm without her participation, she complains that men are free to have multiple sexual partners, while wives, particularly the younger spouses of older men, have to remain like captured birds imprisoned in cages. This critique of the double standards of society's attitudes towards adultery constitutes a forceful apologia for feminine emancipation within marriage, and the parity of the sexes. Lisandre's subversion primarily consists of her unambiguous possession of her body, rather than any transgression against codes of morality.

Biography

Pierre Corneille was born at Rouen on June 6, 1606 and is often cited as author of *L'Occasion perdue recouverte*, which was distributed privately in manuscript form, around 1650 and published as part of a poetry anthology in 1658.

PAUL SCOTT

Further Reading

François Charpentier. *Carpentariana, ou Recueil des pensées historiques, critiques, morales, et de bons mots de M. Charpentier*, ed. by Boscheron, Paris: Nicolas le Breton, 1724.

Nouveau Cabinet des Muses, ou l'Eslite des plus belles poésies de ce temps. Paris: Veuve Edme Pepingué, 1658.

L'Occasion perdue recouverte par Pierre Corneille. Paris: Gay, 1862.

Schoeller, Guy (ed.) *Dictionnaire des œuvres érotiques*. Paris: Laffont, 2001.

CORTÁZAR, JULIO

1914–1984
Argentinean novelist, short story writer, and essayist

Cortázar's works narrate a desire for an impossible plenitude beyond the binary oppositions and the hollow conventions which structure mundane bourgeois reality. His oeuvre, strongly influenced by the Surrealist movement, is committed to the blurring of boundaries between rationality and irrationality, to the ludic rupturing of the banal. This impetus to fracture the pedestrian continuum, however, often submits his characters to strategies of transgression which are oppositional, hence destined to the reiteration of binary structures and so to failure and self-obliteration. Within this perfidious and annihilative scheme, eroticism is often exploited as a vehicle for rebellion. From *Los reyes* [*The Kings*], his first published prose work, in which the incestuous passion binding Ariadne to the Minotaur vindicates the blending of beings beyond corporeal and spatio-temporal limitations as the non plus ultra of eroticism, Cortázar maintains a Bataillean discourse of the erotic as that which is inseparable from death and the notions of pure expenditure and non-regeneration. In other words, for Cortázar the erotic reneges productivity, the cornerstone of the social construct. As many of the stories in *Bestiario* [*Bestiary*], *Las armas secretas* [*Secret Weapons*] and *Final del juego* [*The End of the Game and Other Stories*] show, in his writing sexual acts constitute encounters with the other affording brief interludes of continuity between incomplete, discontinuous beings; a sense of continuity otherwise associated with voluptuous dissolution in death. Furthermore, the manifest dissociation of sexual practice from reproduction in these stories indicates the urge to transgress the edicts of social convention: Cortázar guards the erotic dissolution of being from acquiring a socially productive dimension. Nevertheless, although eroticism intimates deliverance from the pitiable state of individual separateness, the ensuing desire to rearticulate and fix being as an ineffable form of connectedness beyond life and death only begets anguish given the impossibility of the endeavour. Frustration born of this eroticized opposition to conventional existence exacerbates the horror of discontinuity, magnifies dissatisfaction with the empty routine and ritual of pedestrian life, and encourages dissipation through death. The suicidal denouements of stories such as "Manuscrito hallado en un bolsillo" [Manuscript Found in a Pocket] and "Lugar llamado Kindberg" [A Place Named Kindberg] in *Octaedro* [*A Change of Light and Other Stories*] strongly corroborate this reading, as does the orgiastic devastation of "Las ménades" [The Maenad] in *Final del juego* where the delirium of an audience drives them to ravish and devour musicians and lay waste to a theater, making explicit the dynamics of liberation and destruction at play in erotic abandon.

In Cortázar's most celebrated novel, *Rayuela* [*Hopscotch*], the Argentinean protagonist Oliveira—first in Paris, later in Buenos Aires—searches for a state of non-dualism, for a sense of authenticity or an origin untarnished by social machination. His adage, "en el principio fue la cópula" ("in the beginning was coition") emphasizes the importance of sex in relation to this coveted origin. As the novel goes on to show, sex here is mostly oral, masturbatory, and abusive; it is not creative in the reproductive sense. In *Rayuela* sex is only productive of a text—hence the interchangeable terms "the Word" and "coitus"—a text whose aim, paradoxically, is to undermine productivity and therefore social order itself. Oliveira's literary enterprise is to utilize eroticism as a means of breaking with social hegemony and returning to a point of unfettered creativity, of reaching his "kibbutz del deseo" ["kibbutz of desire"]. In Paris, Oliveira, the aloof intellectual, finds his antithesis in La Maga, a woman who represents infatuation and all that is ephemeral in life. La Maga executes a role often ascribed to women in Cortázar's fiction: the accessory enabling an eroticized (male) rite of passage. Oliveira experiments the transformative and disruptive powers of the erotic by rearticulating and defiling La Maga as Pasiphaë (Chapter 5). In such passages carnality is commensurate with fluidity, with an imaginative abandon of the objective world; particular significance is conferred upon the non-generative act of oral sex. Later, when Oliveira descends to the banks of the Seine (Chapter 36) and enters the idle—hence anti-social—world of the clochards, it is oral sex with the abject Emmanuèle that shores up the subversive barrenness of this act. Oliveira violates the taboo on filth by accepting the mouth of the foul vagabond who rouses visions of a desecrated goddess splattered with drunken soldiers' urine and semen; Emmanuèle's dirt is associated with death and decomposition, she is, however, seductive, stressing the sensuality of decay and dissolution. On that occasion a policeman arrives to interdict the public display of transgressive eroticism. In other instances, such as those involving La Maga—or her resurrection through Talita in Buenos Aires

(Chapter 54)—where the melding of her unruliness and Oliveira's intellect could offer a plenitude of sorts, the latter's preoccupation with his ego and with dialectics prevents or at least postpones such a redemptive union.

A decade later in the novel *Libro de Manuel* [*A Manual for Manuel*] where revolutionaries kidnap an official to secure the release of Latin American prisoners, Cortázar establishes an intimate relationship between political insurrection and sexual revolution: the progress of the protagonist Andrés is contingent upon transgression via sodomy. He forces Francine to have anal sex in a hotel overlooking a cemetery, hence emphasizing the association between this non-procreative sexual act and death. Similarly, Lonstein, who washes corpses in a morgue, develops an idiolect in reaction to the repression inherent in language and society (symbolic order) and declaims the need to liberate masturbation from its subaltern position vis-à-vis intercourse; he openly declares himself an onanist. The immediacy of death in these sexual exercises in sedition reasserts Cortázar's call for a breakdown in the equation of existence to perpetuation of the social regime (productivity). This idea finds its ultimate expression in Cortázar's most labyrinthine work, *62: Modelo para armar* [*62: A Model Kit*]. The eroticized breaching of individual egos in this novel undertakes a vampiric dimension which further problematizes the life/death distinction. Its protean continuum of characters negotiates libidinal and existential chaos, seduced by the undecidable nihilism/plenitude which defies articulation yet motivates, and inevitably frustrates, Cortázar's writing.

Biography

Cortázar was born of Argentinean parents in Brussels in 1914. He was taken to Banfield, Buenos Aires in 1918 where he was introduced to French and English literature. He later went on to teach and translate the work of Edgar Allan Poe, André Gide, and G.K. Chesterton among others. In 1951, partly because of dissatisfaction with the Peronist regime, he moved to Paris where he was to remain the rest of his life. There he produced most of his writing and worked as a translator for UNESCO. He became keenly interested in Latin American politics with the Cuban revolution of 1956–1959. His support of

Castro's administration was chequered but enduring, and he also backed the Sandinistas in Nicaragua. He died in 1984.

KARL POSSO

Selected Works

Novels

Divertimiento. Madrid: Alfaguara, 1988 [1949].
El examen. Buenos Aires: Sudamericana, 1986 [1950]; as *Final Exam*. translated by Alfred MacAdam, New York: New Directions, 2000.
Los premios. Madrid: Alfaguara, 1983 [1960]; as *The Winners*, translated by Elaine Kerrigan. New York: Pantheon, 1965.
Rayuela. Madrid: Cátedra, 1994 [1963]; as *Hopscotch*, translated by Gregory Rabassa, New York: Pantheon, 1966.
62: Modelo para armar. Madrid: Alfaguara, 1996 [1968]; as *62: A Model Kit*, translated by Gregory Rabassa, New York: Pantheon, 1972.
Libro de Manuel. Madrid: Alfaguara, 1997 [1973]; as *A Manual for Manuel*, translated by Gregory Rabassa, 1978.

Collections of Stories

Bestiario. Buenos Aires: Sudamericana, 1951; as *Bestiary*, translated by Alberto Manguel, London: Harvill, 1998.
Las armas secretas. Madrid: Cátedra, 1979 [1959].
Final del juego. Buenos Aires: Sudamericana, 1964; as *End of the Game and Other Stories*, translated by Paul Blackburn, New York: Pantheon, 1967.
Todos los fuegos el fuego. Buenos Aires: Sudamericana, 1966; as *All Fires the Fire and Other Stories*, translated by Suzanna Jill Levine, New York: Pantheon, 1973.
Octaedro. Buenos Aires: Sudamericana, 1974; as *A Change of Light and Other Stories*, translated by Gregory Rabassa, London: Harvill, 1984.
Alguien que anda por ahí y otros relatos. Madrid: Alfaguara, 1977.
Deshoras, Mexico: Nueva Imagen. 1983; as *Unreasonable Hours*, translated by Alberto Manguel, Toronto: Coach House, 1995.
Queremos tanto a Glenda. Mexico: Nueva Imagen, 1983; as *We Love Glenda So Much and Other Tales*, translated by Gregory Rabassa, London: Arena, 1985.

Other Writings

Los reyes. Madrid: Alfaguara, 1985 [1949].
Historias de cronopios y de famas. Buenos Aires: Minotauro, 1962; as *Cronopios and Famas*, translated by Paul Blackman, New York: Panethon, 1969.
La vuelta al día en ochenta mundos. Mexico: Siglo XXI, 1967; as *Around the Day in Eighty Worlds*, translated by Thomas Christensen, San Francisco: North Point, 1986.
Ultimo round. Mexico: Siglo XXI, 1969.
Viaje alrededor de una mesa. Buenos Aires: Rayuela, 1970.
Prosa del observatorio. Barcelona: Lumen, 1972.
Fantomas contra los vampiros multinacionales. Mexico: Excelsior, 1975.
Un tal Lucas, Madrid: Alfaguara. 1979; as *A Certain Lucas*, translated by Gregory Rabassa, New York: Knopf, 1984.
Los autonautas de la cosmopista. with Carol Dunlop, Barcelona: Muchnik, 1983.
Salvo el crepúsculo. Mexico: Nueva Imagen, 1984; as *Save Twilight*, translated by Stephen Kessler, San Francisco: City Lights, 1997.
Diario de Andrés Fava. Madrid: Alfaguara, 1995.

Further Reading

Alazraki, Jaime (editor). *Critical Essays on Julio Cortázar*. New York: G.K. Hall, 1999.
Alazraki, Jaime and Ivar Ivask (editors). *The Final Island: The Fiction of Julio Cortázar*. Norman: University of Oklahoma Press, 1978.
Alonso, Carlos J. (editor). *Julio Cortázar: New Readings*. Cambridge: Cambridge University Press, 1998.
Berriot, Karine. *Julio Cortázar l'enchanteur*. Paris: Renaissance, 1988.
Boldy, Steven. *The Novels of Julio Cortázar*. Cambridge: Cambridge University Press, 1980.
Garfield, Evelyn Picon. *Julio Cortázar*. New York: Ungar, 1975.
Hernández del Castillo. Ana. *Keats, Poe, and the Shaping of Cortázar's Mythopoesis*. Amsterdam: Benjamins, 1981.
Planells, Antonio. *Cortázar: Metafísica y erotismo*. Madrid: José Porrúa Turanzas, 1979.
Stavans, Ilan. *Julio Cortázar: A Study of the Short Fiction*. New York: Twayne, 1996.
Yovanovich, Gordana. *Julio Cortázar's Character Mosaic: Reading the Longer Fiction*. Toronto: University of Toronto Press, 1991.

COTTON, CHARLES

1630–1687
English linguist and essayist

Ερώτοττολις: *The Present State of Bettyland (1684)*

Agriculture and topography have been popular sources of sexual imagery from ancient times. According to Cotton, the world of antiquity was full of "great Husbandmen that kept their plows going day and night," their poets supplying appropriate metaphors of ploughing and sowing. The later manuring figure was established in English by the 1590s (Donne, "Sapho to Philaenis"). Sustained topographical imagery runs back to the Song of Solomon. Bettyland offers the *reductio ad absurdam* of Spenser's Garden of Adonis, with Lust trapped in a cave beneath the Mount of Venus; or his Bower of Bliss where the human topography of the garden gives special meaning to the fountain at its center. As allegory's credibility waned as an expression of universal truth, so it was used for fun: anarchic sex replacing divine order. Cotton burlesques the philosophical and imaginary voyage as well as the travel narrative catering for commercial interest or prospective emigrants—or indeed the armchair traveler, obvious counterpart to the reader of sex books. This vicarious dimension emerges through landscape painting; pictures of Bettyland making apt bedroom décor so that those without land will sometimes take shadow for substance and deface a picture with their "instruments of Agriculture."

Bettyland is divided into provinces, dominated by Rutland containing the capital Pego (p. 4). Others are "*Maldavia*, famous for the great City of *Lipsic*" (Mal or Moll is a common name for whores; while liberties taken with Leipzig evoke pox); "*Holland*, a mighty tract of land under the Command of Count *Horne*" (historically Horn associates with "*Guelderland*," but that province has unsuitable sexual connotations); and "the wide Province of *Will-shire*" (authorized by Shakespeare's "Wilt thou, whose

will is large and spacious"). Flora and fauna are described, flowers including "*Batchelors Buttons*" and "*Tickle me quickly*," while the animals, apart from "Hare and Coney," are limited to horned cattle. The most common birds are wagtails; though, since the land is low-lying, decoy ducks abound, the most celebrated being Circe (p. 30). Of water creatures there are few maids but a multitude of crabs and carps (pp. 12–13, 30). The most suitable crops and the best tracts of land are considered, some men paying a thousand or two "a year for a little spot in that Country, not so big as the palm of your hand" (p. 7; the vulvaic "spot" being a favored seventeenth-century usage). Legal aspects of tenure release a flood of popular puns on entailing, reversion, and enclosure.

Much of this is imitated and elaborated in Stretser's *New Description of Merryland* (1741), his Maryland quibble having been used 90 years before in *Mercurius Democritus* 5 (27 April 1652). Democritus's "*Floating Ark of pleasure*, bound for *Merry-land* man'd with female Mariners*," risks attack "about *Maidenhead* by the licentious Pr—roons" (obscenely punning on picaroons). The raciness is closer to Cotton than Stretser, comparison with whom is revealing about shifting sexual mores as well as a growing scientific discourse. Equally important is an aesthetic shift, Stretser tied to unity and consistency, whereas Cotton reminds that earlier imaginative prose often lumped a variety of forms happily together. Cotton not only innovates the erotic travel book but, when turning to the inhabitants of Bettyland, adumbrates that mode of spy literature associated particularly with Ned Ward. Like the bawd Quartilla, hoarse with pox, the two spies, Eucolpius and Eumolpus, who tour the London underworld, have names deriving from Petronius's *Satyricon*; the recovery in 1650 of a Petronius manuscript led to several editions in the 1660s, which left their mark on prose fiction. Visiting a brothel, the spies discover a table "furnished as if it had been for the supper of *Trimalcio* in *Petronius*"

283

(p. 102). But this merely distracts from the actual source, *Fifteen Real Comforts of Matrimony* (1683), p. 47, which identically portrays a "grave Father" with naked queans at supper, "while he as naked as they, crept under the Table,... snarling like a Dog" and snapping at their thighs while they threw him scraps. (But plagiarism is the norm in such books, and this in turn expands *Wandring Whore* 3 (1660) where several whores stand "stark naked round about a Table whilst [their client] lyes snarling underneath as if he would bite off their whibb-bobs.") The episode may explain Bettyland's province of Curland; though St Jerome's *caninas nuptias*, meaning the act of fornication, had its seventeenth-century cant equivalent. Another brothel scene lifted from *Fifteen Comforts* departs from the original in two respects. Firstly, the voyeurism is three-tiered: old man ogling whore; spies at their "peeping Crannies"; and of course the reader. Secondly, Bettyland is kept in view by way of fresh imagery, a whore exposing herself "as they draw the Curtain up from before the Scenes of a Theater": "she drew the Curtain gently up ... and showed the Prospect of a very fair Garden-plot of Maiden-hair, not green as in other Countries, but growing like a kind of black Fern" (pp. 98–99). The original plan is recalled, too, in the discussion of prevalent diseases. There is priapismus, a "Giant-like Distemper that lifts its head most stiffly against *Furor Uterinus*, as having a perfect Animosity against it" (p.154). "But the grand Senior Disease [with] as many Names and Titles, as the Great *Turk*," is pox; and one victim is hilariously pictured consoling himself "with *Hall's Meditations, Shakespeare, and Foxe's Book of Martyrs.*" Cotton regrets that Venus's wounded heroes are not hymned like those of Mars; though he, like Harington, was well enough read to know of books written "in honour of the Pox." He was also sophisticated enough to know that the very

voyages of discovery which produced the books he has parodied were contributing to a shift in sensibility, a new empiricism, which in turn necessitated that shift in expressive modes which he himself encapsulates in moving from pseudo-allegorical to a more direct kind of fictionalizing.

Biography

Charles Cotton, a Straffordshire wit grounded in the classical languages as well as French and Italian, published a translation of Montaigne's Essays and a continuation of Walton's *Compleat Angler* which first appeared in the fifth (1676) edition. He is remembered especially for the burlesque poem, *Scarronides: Or, Virgile Travestie* (1664, 1665). Ἐρώτοττολις published anonymously, is commonly ascribed to him; though Wing lists it under the title.

GORDON WILLIAMS

Further Reading

On the reprint, appearing in *The Potent Ally* (Jan. 1741) under the title *The Description of Bettyland*, see David Foxon, *Libertine Literature in England* 1660–1745 (1964), p. 17. Cotton's reputation for scurrility rests otherwise on verse burlesques, including a *Lucianic Burlesque Upon Burlesque, or The Scoffer Scoft* (1675), and *A Voyage to Ireland* (1670s), used by J. S. Farmer and W.E. Henley in compiling *Slang and its Analogues* (1890–1904), but no longer traceable. But the two most important items are *Scarronides* and *The Valiant Knight: or the Legend of Sr. Peregrine* (1663), whose relationship to Cervantes seems to come via Beaumont's *Knight of the Burning Pestle* since Peregrine's main battle is with pox. See Alvin Irwin Dust (ed.), Charles *Cotton's Works, 1663–1665:* critical editions of *The Valiant Knight* and *Scarronides* (New York/London: Garland, 1992). Roger Thompson, *Unfit For Modest Ears* (London: Macmillan, 1979) finds scant evidence in favor of Cotton's authorship of Ἐρώτοττολις.

CRÉBILLON, CLAUDE PROSPER JOLYOT DE

1707–1777
French novelist

Tanzaï et Néadarné

Tanzaï et Néadarné and *Ah, quel conte!* are largely broad social and political satires with a heavy coloration of oriental story and fairy tale: metamorphoses of people like a prince turned into a goose, fairies good and evil, ugly and fair, and so forth—all of whom, like the Greek gods, supernatural or not, are as sexually active as any human. This side of Crébillon gave him an early reputation as sole true heir of Hamilton's mantle as storyteller. Through the act of an unfriendly fairy, *Tanzaï* has his penis turned into an embarrassing, ludicrous chef's skimmer, and is forced to make love to a hideous witch before he can escape his dilemma. Néadarné, in turn, finds her vagina sealed up; she must surrender to the carresses of an ugly genie in order to be freed from the curse, and in the process feels shamed, shocked, and guilty over discovering the joys of sex. Happily for her, a charm restores her virginity before she has to confront her husband. Jean Sgard writes:

Crébillon's reputation is knowing how to say all the realities of sex while 'veiling' the obscenities. He does know how; but he also knows how to do the opposite, as here. In *Tanzaï*, the obscenity is avowed, it is enormous, Gallic, Rabelaisian; and all the realities of sexual life are displayed without false shame.

Obscenity, however, is a relative term and only in a very limited sense can it be applied to Crébillon, even the Crébillon of *Tanzaï*. In this case it is important all the same to distinguish between shaming and naming. The decency of language remains paramount in all his works; it is always proper, and highly stylized. There is a good deal about strategies of progression and possession—the way one little concession leads always to another, etc.—and Crébillon certainly alludes with unmistakable clarity to sensuous pleasures, even raptures, as he does to impotency; but that is about as far as he goes with respect to the technique or physiology of love.

Les égarements du coeur et de l'esprit

The worldly initiation of Meilcour at the age of seventeen is recounted by the protagonist himself, a form which allows for retrospective irony directed both at himself and at others in the story, particularly the women who propose to seduce him. The neophyte is necessarily incompetent: since nothing in his previous schooling prepares him for worldly ways, some formal orientation is required. A family friend, Madame de Lursay, determines that she should render him this service, which means familiarizing him with the routines of society, notably those of love. The possibility appeals to him as well.

But when it comes to communicating their mutual desires, Meilcour is so blocked by his respect for her—a term which she too insists on up to a point—that she has infinite difficulties overcoming it and inducing him to make some effort both to decode her own understated invitations and to assume some initiative of his own, without which her system will not function. Madame de Lursay understands Meilcour's awkwardness as well as he does, still she cannot fathom his failure to make some kind of overture, even after she has tried repeatedly to suggest to him that he construe certain ambiguities in more favorable ways.

His problem is always one of what to say, where "saying" becomes the metaphor for doing. Feigning contentment at his failure to appear one day, for instance, Madame de Lursay teases that had he come "we might have found ourselves all alone. What would we have found to say? Do you realize that a tête-à-tête is sometimes even more embarrassing than scandalous?" She knows, of course, that once he manages to utter

285

just some of the right sorts of things everything will work out, but he is so awed by her (thus fearing to offend her), and underconfident in himself (thus fearing failure), that he is unable to take advantage of the cues. "I have nothing more to say to you, and I even forbid you to guess what I am thinking," she once remarks. Since he fails to rise to such bait, the next time she tries reversing the terminology, and still bumps up against his dogged literalism: "I have nothing to say to you: guess what I am thinking, if you can, she said, looking me straight in the eyes. You forbade me to, I replied. Ah! she cried, I didn't think I had gone so far. But I will say no more." She cannot allow her language to be as brazen as her gaze; it is all he can do just to keep the "conversation" going. He later applies to himself the same metaphor: "A man with a hint of worldliness would have found any number of delicate things to say about what had just taken place, that help a woman out in such a situation; but I did not know any, and Madame de Lursay had to provide everything out of her own resources or resign herself never to speak to me." As he will concede afterward: "although basically I had triumphed only over obstacles I had put there myself, I nonetheless imagined that Madame de Lursay's resistence had been extreme."

Along the way, he falls head over heels for a marriageable girl, Hortense, and receives stern, cynical lessons on worldly conduct from Versac, who sees through everything, can identify every motive, even secret ones, and believes in the sincerity of no one. Versac is especially vicious toward Madame de Lursay, whom he describes as a consummate hypocrite and wholly indiscriminate in her sex life. Meanwhile, another mutual friend who is a bit older, Madame de Senanges, has the same idea as Lursay and tries to intervene on Meilcour's emotional calendar; Lursay's frustration is only heightened by her perfect awareness of what Senanges is up to. Much of the novel is composed of long dialogues, particularly between Meilcour and Versac on the one hand, and Meilcour and Madame de Lursay on the other.

As *Le sopha*, a sort of manual of specious arguments, will show, any conduct can be justified, even with the vocabulary of virtue and sentiment if skillfully manipulated. Meilcour has already made this discovery, as he dreams of his beloved Hortense while still in the arms of Madame de Lursay: had he been more advanced,

he says, "[i]n the very midst of the agitation into which Madame de Lursay had plunged me, I would have bemoaned the custom that does not allow us to resist a woman who takes a liking to us; I would have saved my heart from the disorder of my senses and, thanks to those delicate distinctions. . . I would have abandoned myself to all the charms of the occasion, without risking an infidelity."

Meilcour indicates at the outset that he is to become a rake in the mould of Versac before finally being redeemed by a worthy woman; but the novel was never completed.

Le sopha

This novel does without the fairies of the earlier "oriental" tales, but not without the transmogrification: the narrator, Amanzéi, is condemned to inhabit sofas (though he is allowed to move from one to another) until the day when two virgins will use him as the venue for their first sexual experience. Whence variations on a theme: Amanzéi reports on one episode after another where the protagonists' language persuade him he is about to be freed, only to discover that the most seemingly virtuous and pious are in fact not so inexperienced as they make it seem. Indeed, he learns that people talk themselves, and others, into sexual acts using a variety of pretexts, not excluding virtue and piety themselves: witness the couple (Almaïde and Moclès) who think it would be good for their understanding of chastity to experience what the temptation is that people must resist.

The novel spins out a repertory of kinds of women, and of ways of giving in. One woman seeks only pleasure and is little concerned by appearances; another accepts money but still insists on being mollified by words of sentiment. Despite the intrinsic interest of the scenes he necessarily witnesses (and which eventually come to bore him), Amanzéi really wants to be set free, and thus seeks out in preference the homes of timid or pious women, since it doesn't do him any good it they aren't virgins. But he discovers that nothing is more problematic than to detect that in advance. The most mordant satire concerns two pious souls just mentioned, who compensate as best they can for the privations of virtue by long conversations about vice; but this takes them far, so greatly do supposedly honest intentions tend irresistibly towards desire. Even virtue can serve as pretext, and this couple ends up just as do the others; but their ostensible lack of experience disappoints Amanzéi, for he finds himself still under the spell, meaning that at least one of them has lied. Then there is the very proper and virtuous Phénime, exasperated by the "respect" a young man persists in showing her (like Lursay and Meilcour in *Les égarements*): another false alarm; this woman was just as lascivious as any other.

Les heureux orphelins

The most unusual and original of Crébillon's novels from the standpoint of structure is *Les heureux orphelins*. It begins, like the English novel he was initially imitating, with a third-person narrative, the story of Lucie who, pursued by the unwanted desires of her adopted father Rutland, flees to London, works briefly in a milliner's shop, and ends up in Bristol as a sort of *dame de compagnie* of Madame de Suffolck, who is about to leave for Europe. In part two, the Madame de Suffolck later tells her the why of her trip and the story becomes an autobiographical narrative of her seducation and abandonment by a callous young noblemen, Lord Durham, who is schooled in the ways of France. She has realized that he too has arrived in Bristol, and Lucie learns that he is the same person as Chester, who more recently harassed her at the milliner's and would even have abducted her had she not fled. But he has been discovered and discredited by the seizure of his correspondence, which Queen Anne has turned over to Madame de Suffolck.

Half-way through, there is still nothing particularly libertine and certainly not very erotic about this novel, except for Madame de Suffolck's lyricism of passion. Then, however, everything changes. Parts three and four are constituted by the series of letters which Count Chester was writing to his French mentor, the Duc de ***, in which he relates his campaign to convert English high society to French morals, and more particularly the spectacular virtuosity of his simultaneous triple seduction of the admirable and passionate Madame de Suffolck, the Presbyterian prude Madame de Rindsey, and the coquettish but resistant Madame de Pembroock. Chester is the consummate libertine: a pupil of Versac's, one might say. When his friend Buttington challenges his intention to

seduce Madame de Rindsey by saying, "Do you flatter yourself you will ever find the expression of love in those large, pale, inert eyes?" Chester's answer is this: "That is her business; it is not her affections I need. Only vanity makes us insist on love; the reasonable man asks only for pleasures. Therefore I will forego her love, and answer you no less boldly that she will not leave me the worse off for it." At the end, Chester has not finished his story because, after his victory over Madame de Rindsey, he has barely taken up again the thread of his attack on Madame de Suffolck. We already know from her, of course, how that affair ended up; the novel's formal incompleteness is the result of the very seizure of correspondence that has made parts three and four possible.

La nuit et le moment

An essential element of Crébillon's two well-known dialogues, the basic premises of which are extremely straightforward, is the occasional narrative intervention, analogous to stage directions, which tell us at crucial points what the characters are doing alongside their (sometimes misleading) words.

The story of *La nuit et le moment* is as simple as can be: while in a country lodge with other friends, Clitandre wants to share some banter with Cidalise, in the latter's room, and sits at the foot of her bed. Soon, complaining of the cold, he gets in bed beside her so they can chat more comfortably. In short, only inches now separate them, but that is where the business of language comes in—for while the goal is in easy sight, the matter of proper consent must not be waived, and Cidalise is a decent woman, who will certainly not give in until the proper ritual has been accomplished.

In Crébillon there is a rather precise choreography, which this dialogue excellently illustrates, for improvising an amorous relationship on short notice, in other words, between two persons who up to that point never have professed any attraction to each other. It follows more or less fixed stages. As custom will have it, the male makes the opening advances, expressing his intentions, at first obliquely, by grammatical substitution: he might for example bring up some former lover of hers and say: in his stead, I would not have proven faithful, as he soon did. Progressively, he works his way around to an unambiguous declaration of love, preferably asserting that his sentiment is anything but new: I always wanted you, but since you did not seem to notice me, I lacked courage to speak up. As decency requires that the lady "resist," the remaining scenario consists of progressive concessions on her part. She avers that she hardly disliked him, on the contrary; in fact, any avoidance can be chalked up to prudence, that is, fear of proving only too susceptible. She does not deny being *sensitive*, and assures him of her friendship. By degrees friendship molts into love, and she will now say that she confesses her weakness but has no intention of going farther than that, which was already too far, at least on this occasion. Then, how weak indeed love does make a person!

Le hasard du coin du feu

The second of these dialogues presents a situation that is similar yet quite different in the premises of its form of fencing: the challenge this time is to get the couple to consummate their desires despite the total refusal of one of them to cooperate in the game, a stance which only exposes the ultimately pure sensuality of their behavior. The couple is manifestly set up: the Marquise, who is the Duc de Clerval's recognized mistress, all but tells him that she is leaving him alone with Célie so he can enjoy a little fun on the side, which she is committed in advance to forgive. And the Duc and Clélie certainly desire each other, a fact the Duc will refuse to varnish over with decorative but untrue words. Célie tries her best to get the Duc to utter some standard formula (even after the fact, for want of success beforehand), but the outcome proves she must be content with satisfying her senses and admitting as much. She won't even be able to enjoy the prestige of having had such a distinguished lover, since the Duc is publicly paired with another woman whom he has no desire to renounce.

Allusions to their previous affairs announce how this one will end: he says of one: "Ah, Madame, indecency on the one hand, and nature on the other, work things out so well and so promptly, that you both find yourselves of the same mind, although most often neither of you can say just how it came about." If the Duc is "indecent," it is a frank and proud indecency: he respects words enough not to abuse them; he

rejects hypocrisy (which is doubtless why the Marquise trusts him). He accepts the reality of the flesh and easily forgives its transgressions: "If we consider coolly how many things conspire against a woman's virtue, we would be more surprised at her ability to defend herself for a while, than we are generally scandalized at the rapidity with which she sometimes appears to concede defeat."

In the dialogues, as often elsewhere in Crébillon's work, we see couples groping not so much for clarity with regard to their own feelings or desires, but for acceptable formulas to cover with decency what they already know they would very much like to do.

The Languages of Love

From the start, Crébillon was always noted for his elegant but sometimes convoluted style and for his way of characterizing a certain type of society. As D'Alembert said, "in novels full of wit, and dictated by a deep understanding of all the shameful recesses of the human heart, he has traced with the most delicate and honest pen the refinements, nuances, and the very charms of our vices."

Though the emphasis is on rakes and coquettes, it should not be overlooked that there is much tenderness in a story like *Tanzaï and Néadarné*, and genuine love expressed in the cases of the eponymous Marquise de M*** and Duchesse de ***; witness the Marquise's cry: "If only our lives could begin anew, in some corner of the world, sufficient to ourselves, free of all cares, unknown to all, to be spent only in the pleasures of an eager, tender passion!" The first half of *Les Heureux Orphelins* too is a novel of love, with first Rutland's irrepressible passion for Lucie, later followed by Madame de Suffolck's memories of exultation: "No, nothing can depict the delight of those pleasures that confound the senses, and which the senses do not share. Ah, how true it is that for tender sensitive hearts, there is an ecstasy quite beyond anything they can make us feel!" Suffolck is a sort of reverse Princesse de Clèves, one who made the opposite decision and gave herself with abandon to her lover. And though Chester is a callous libertine, it is nonetheless important to take account of the strange beginning of his seventh letter in part four, in which he expresses at some length an astonishing degree of nostalgia for the days when he still knew the charms of naive fascination with a woman:

> When I recall, my dear Duke, what my first love affair meant to me when I was just entering society, what importance a woman had in my eyes, the delightful delirium into which I was plunged by the first tryst I obtained, and I compare that agreeable disorder with the cruel tranquillity in which I live today, I cannot help denouncing habit and experience, both of which, one by reflection and the other by practice, can only spoil our pleasures. What, indeed, do they put in the place of the lovely chimeras they take away, and what do we gain in seeing or imagining objects as they are? A lassitude which deprives them of their true merit in our eyes, or a diffidence that can never be anything but torment for us, since the constant fear of being deceived does not give us the means of escaping that fate.
>
> Precious credulity, to which I owed so much happiness, are you then forever lost to me?

Indeed to the jaded attitude of the consummate libertine, Versac, Chester, or Alcibiades there is never as such any attractiveness attached.

Between traditional passion (*amour-passion*) and capricious desire (*amour-goût*) the essential difference lies in the conception of the object of love, unique and irreplaceable in the first instance and functional and quite subject to substitution in the second. In few of Crébillon's novels do we encounter the notion that what the characters represent for each other is something absolute. Though love isn't necessarily disparaged, Crébillon sets about stripping sentiment of its prestige and proving that it is at bottom physiological. The oriental tales and novels differ in form but have much the same subject. The story of the liaison of Mazulhim and Zulica, which with its peripateia takes up a good portion of *Le sopha*, constantly plays on the ironic opposition between a publicly recognized liaison and a passing but irresistible amusement. The whole point of the game Crébillon forever portrays is that the language of love is so tainted with desire that, although it is constantly in use, it can never be taken as spiritually as it sounds: "Love had, in truth, rather little to do with it; but it took us a good while to notice it was wanting" (*La nuit et le moment*). If passions there be, they might at any time be overridden by the senses.

The "moment" of *La nuit et le moment*, also evoked in other works of Crébillon, is when one finds oneself more vulnerable than one would

have thought to the attraction of someone new, enough so to cheat on one's regular partner. The unexpected, whimsical or fleeting desire can give rise to subsequent shame, not because virtue has succumbed but because good judgment has. It is a matter of substitution: "One cannot be responsible for the moment," says the worldly-wise fairy Moustache to Néadarné; "sometimes nature acts alone, and you find yourself precisely in the situation of a dream which offers to your senses the things it wants to, and not the ones you would like." The only way a woman can be faithful to her lover, she goes on to say, is by complete avoidance of any situation in which infidelity is even possible: for were you to reach such a tempting pass, "nature would blow upon sentiment, and would not fail to put it out. It is true that when it flames up again, you are very surprised, but the thing is no less done" (*Tanzaï et Néadarné*). Nevertheless, in many cases the notion of unforeseen vulnerability is often just another pretext, as the narrator of the same tale asserts:

> It is rare for a woman of the world to find herself in a situation perilous to her without having wished it; her virtue is never done violence by the circumstances, and although more than one has said that when she made a certain assignation with her admirer during which she succumbed, she would not have done so had she not expected to keep her honor intact, one should always believe that she had no doubt about what would happen; and the proof of this is, that a man who has been given one of these innocent assignations has only to fail to take advantage of it, to provoke the almost irredeemable ire of the virtuous beauty who closed herself in with him.

Alcibiades remarks in *Lettres athéniennes*, "Despite the frequent examples we have, I have never been able to understand how it is that the boldness that often a woman neither desires nor expects from a man, can decide her in favor of a sentiment he does not inspire in her, or, to speak more accurately, serve momentarily as its substitute." Both of these quotations suggest that the woman's anticipation of the outcome may be only partly conscious; the point is that the language cannot resolve obscurity with respect to intentions, though the outcome always points to what at some level she really wanted.

There is a whole string of men, beginning with the hedonistic Sylph, and including not just Versac, Chester, and Alcibiades but also Mazulhim and Nassès in *Le sopha* and perhaps Clerval in

Le hasard du coin du feu, whose principal occupation is to create such "moments." Their key rule is to inspire love when they can but not fall in love themselves, in order to remain in control of all situations, which they manipulate in function of their own immediate goals, all of which generally tend toward establishing their own prestige in society at the cost of the women they have "conquered" and often undone. As Chester declares, the libertine is the lucid practitioner of a social science the model of which is purely mechanical:

> If all men could know as we do, my dear Duke, to what extent a genuine passion subjugates and abases them! There are so many things to which it subjects them but which, when they think like us, are under their own control, that there is not one who would not prefer to the always rather doubtful happiness of reigning in a heart through sentiment, the singular and flattering pleasure of making a soul behave as one wishes, determining it by one's own orders, making it experience the most contrary movements in succession; and from the haven of one's indifference, make it move like a machine, whose springs one directs, and which one commands at will to be still or active!

All the advantages are on the side of the manipulator; the women can do little more than undergo a process they can little understand. As the Sylph says to Madame R***:

> The sensuous woman gives in to the pleasure of the senses; the delicate woman, to the sweetness of feeling her heart is taken; the curious woman, to the desire for instruction; the indolent woman would find it too much trouble to refuse; the vain woman would suffer too great a loss if her charms went unnoticed, she wants to read in the fervor of her lover's desires the impression she can make on men; the miserly woman gives in to the base love of gifts; the ambitious woman, to illustrious conquests, and the coquette to the habit of giving in. (*Le Sylphe*)

It is an aspect of Alcibiades' masculine braggadocio, as it is of Chester's, to assert that he can methodically conquer any woman who thinks she can resist him.

Crébillon insists on the fact that the language spoken, difficult in a sense to analyze precisely because there is nothing specialized about it, functions as a special code. Everybody knows how to speak elegantly, but by just listening one would infer nothing reliable about conduct or character. Therefore, to shed light on the true meaning of words, there must be a double register which juxtaposes language and action. This is achieved either by the older perspective a first-person narrator now distanced from the person he or she was as protagonist, or by another voice observing but not participating in the advances. The actions have to be specified by such a narrator because, as Amanzéi says of Fatmé and a "Brahman": "They began a most tender conversation, but one in which love spoke a very strange language, in appearance one little suited for it. Were it not for their actions, I doubt I would ever have understood what they were saying." Not a whiff of sentiment here: Crébillon hardly denies it exists, but he observes that one cannot ascertain much about sentiment in a society where the language for negotiating love or momentary pleasure is strictly identical. Despite an element of nostalgia for unvarnished and natural truths, Crébillon's observations force him to an essentially cynical conclusion, which is that the apparent variety of the forms of love is merely that of its pretexts. However chaste the diction, everyone ends up in bed (or on an ottoman).

All of these fictions are premised on a certain social stratum where financial independence is a given and no one, especially the young, has any real occupation or vocation. "What can you do?" asks Clitandre:

> You are in society, you are bored, you see women who also are hardly enjoying themselves; you are young; vanity combines with idleness. If having a woman is not always a pleasure, at least it is always a sort of occupation. . . . I have sometimes been idle; I have found women who were perhaps not yet sure of the power of their charms, and so it is that, as you say, I have had some of them.

Meilcour too finds himself plunged as he enters adulthood into a society where the game of love is the only real business, and he describes it in its most representative aspect, which is its sexual activity.

More generally, much of Crébillon's dialogue is a satire on the conversational habits of elite society in general (it was sometimes said that Crébillon did not even invent them, but merely took notes on what he heard around him): "The arrangement, or rather the abuse of words, substitutes for thought," affirms Versac, who goes on to prescribe the rule to remember: "make your expressions refined and your ideas infantile; pronounce absurdities, maintain them, and start all over: such is the tone of the finest society." Given that Crébillon is constantly castigating hypocrisy, many of his characters, engaging though they may be by force of wit, are thoroughly unattractive and moreover are hardly convincing if they claim to be happy with themselves. The most original and least likable of all is probably Versac, the cold cynic who instructs Meilcour in the ways of unscrupulous self-advertisement and the pitiless exploitation of others, especially women.

Paradoxically, in most respects there is no substantial distinction between male and female characters; almost no one of either sex is genuinely seduced; in this world the subtle progressions of the true seducer are usually invoked only in jest. One can say of few of his female protagonists that they do not know what is happening to them, or have been caught with their guard down. Instead they are implicitly asking themselves: what are the minimal conditions for avoiding the shame, perhaps the scandal, of the utmost sexual abandon? Decorum is what is principally at issue; but even it is more or less a way of cheating with oneself, as the narrator of *Tanzaï* puts it:

On her own, a woman can avoid tarrying before images that might offend her modesty, but if a man she loves shows up, what is virtue to her then? If she still resists, it is not to save it; her loss would be too great. But one must give in with honor, and accompany one's weakness with grandeur: in a word, fall decently, and be able to excuse herself when she reflects on her disorder. Few women agree with this truth, but that does not keep it from being very much so.

Clitandre, relating his affair with Araminte, with whom he is in a situation parallel to his present one with Cidalise) touches on all these points:

We began to take some rather familiar liberties, and I was on the verge of having the ultimate obligation to her, when she was seized by a tender concern. She remembered I had not yet told her I loved her, and protested that unless I assured her she possessed my heart, however powerfully she felt drawn toward me, and even whatever evidence she had already given me of her susceptibility, she would unquestionably overcome it. I was quite aware that had she loved me, she would have had little reason to be pleased

with what I felt for her; but propriety, and my state at the time, only allowed me to deceive her, and I replied that I could not fathom how, with the indications I was then giving her of my feelings, she could persist in doubting them. Up till then she had appeared to yield to her tenderness only reservedly, but the certainty of being loved banished her scruples, and she became unbelievably tender, intense, and eager. (*La Nuit et le moment*)

His irony bears on the fact that although he disdained to invoke the word *love*, he made it possible for her to *infer* it, and she settled for that marginal concession. The differences are those prescribed by social custom and said to derive from nature, but in other respects the real category lines fall less between the sexes than between the urbane and the naive.

Biography

Claude Crébillon was born and educated in Paris, the son of Prosper Crébillon, a member of the Académie Française who was considered by many the greatest French tragedian since Racine. For much of his life he lived somewhat in the shadow of his father's fame, although their relations were not as hostile or even as strained as tradition has often suggested. Because of his father's status, he early enjoyed free entry at the Comédie Française, and about the same time (1726) formed a lifetime camaraderie with another aspiring writer, Charles Collé. Both wrote occasional pieces including parodies for the Théâtre Italien, and later collaborated on numerous plays and libretti. An amusing, lightly erotic tale entitled *Le Sylphe* in 1730 was already a sign of Crébillon's talent, which is fully declared in a romantic vein with *Lettres de la marquise de M*** au comte de R**** in 1732, and in a satiric vein with *Tanzaï et Néadarné, histoire japonais* in 1734.

While *Tanzaï* is a broad-ranging fantasy, in the pseudo-orientalist mode, of many things about French society, particularly its amorous mores, the target most immediately perceived was dispute over the papal bull Unigenitus (1713) which was still raging. One could not with impunity so skillfully heap derision on the Jesuits, not to mention the king and pope, and Crébillon was locked up in the Château de Vincennes for a few days to teach him a lesson.

In 1735, he published the first volume of *Les égarements du c'ur et de l'esprit* [*Aberrations of the Heart and Mind*], which was to be his most enduring success, even though he never completed it. Parts two and three were published in 1738, and his admirers asked him for years when the rest would be forthcoming; he claimed in 1743 that he had written three further sequels but never had time to polish them. Meanwhile, he was composing another racy, oriental tale called *Le Sopha*, which he finally published in 1742, only to be sent into exile (from April to July he had to stay at least thirty leagues, or 120 km, from Paris). He would not publish another novel for twelve years, unless he was indeed the author (likely but not proven) of *Les amours de Zéokinizul, roi des Kofirans*, which appeared in 1746. Another spoof on contemporary France (Zéokinizul is an anagram for Louis XV, Kofirans for the Français), this book bore the name *Krinebol*, itself an obvious anagram of Crébillon.

Sometime in 1744 he began a liaison with Henriette Marie Stafford, whose father had been secretary to Queen Mary of Modena, wife of King James II of Great Britain. Sister and aunt respectively of the second and third earls of Stafford, Henriette was born at the court in exile at Saint Germain en Laye in 1711, as was her godmother, Princess Louise Marie. Despite her standing, however (legal documents always preface her name with the honorific title *très haute et très puissante dame*), she had inherited little money and did not control it directly. Thus, soon after they married in April 1758, they entered a long period of financial constraint and even penury. Their only child, a son born in 1746, died in 1750, and later that year, unable to bear the cost of living in Paris, they moved to Sens. Crébillon continued to visit the capital frequently in search of literary opportunities, and for a while directed a journal called *La Bigarure*.

Finally, in 1753, a pension from the Duc d'Orléans along with an apartment in his Palais Royal enabled them to return to Paris, and the following year they had an apartment lent to them in Saint Germain. Meanwhile, a friend had sent to Henriette Eliza Haywood's *The Fortunate Foundlings*, of which Crébillon or perhaps the two of them together began a translation. It soon departed from the original, though Crébillon kept the title *Les heureux orphelins*, which he published in 1754. The critical reception was so harsh that he immediately abandoned it for *Ah, quel conte!*, another complex political and social satire, which was not received any better; both of these works were to be forgotten for over two centuries by literary history.

Such was not the case with his two famous dialogues, *La nuit et le moment* and *Le hasard du coin du feu* [*Fireside Fortunes*], which had been composed years earlier (between 1737 and 1745) but were published only in 1756 and 1763, respectively.

After Henriette died in 1755, Crébillon went through a lengthy process of sorting out his debts and assets, and moved back to Paris, where in 1758 he finally obtained a post for which he had long petitioned, that of royal censor. He led the life of a distinguished man of letters, writing two final novels, *Lettres de la duchesse de *** au duc de **** (1768) and *Lettres athéniennes* (1771). An edition of his collected works was published in 1772 and three others after his death, in 1777 and 1779. There were to be no more such editions for over two centuries, until the *Classiques Garnier* edition listed below.

PHILIP STEWART

Selected Works

Œuvres complètes, dir. Jean Sgard, Paris: *Classiques Garnier*, 4 vols., 1999–2002. There are many French editions of *Les Égarements du coeur et de l'esprit*, and several of the other titles are available in editions by Desjonquères (Paris).

Le sylphe, ou songe de Madame de R***, 1730.

Lettres de la marquise de M*** au comte de R***, 1732; translated in 1735 by Mr. Humphreys as *Letters from the Marchioness de M*** to the Count de ****.

Tanzaï et Néadarné, histoire japonaise, 1734; translated anonymously in 1735 as *The Skimmer*; or *The History of Tanzai et Neadarne*.

Les égarements du coeur et de l'esprit, 1735–1738; translated in 1751 Michael Clancy as *The Wanderings of the Heart and Mind* and in 1963 by Barbara Bray as *The Wayward Head and Heart* (London: Oxford University Press). It is included in *The Libertine Reader* edited by Michel Feher (NY: Zone, 1997).

Le sopha, conte moral, 1742; translated the same year as *The Sopha: a moral tale* and in 1927 by Martin Kamin as *The Divan* (NY, privately printed). Also included in *The Libertine Reader* (see previous entry).

Les heureux Orphelins, 1754.

Ah, quel conte! conte politique et astronomique, 1755.

La nuit et le moment, ou les matines de Cythère, 1756; translated in 1770 as *The Night and Moment* and in

1925 by Eric Sutton as *The Opportunities of a Night* (London: Chapman and Hall).
Le Hasard du coin du feu, dialogue moral, 1763.
Lettres de la duchesse de *** au duc de ***, 1768.
Lettres athéniennes extraites du portefeuille d'Alcibiade, 1771.

Further Reading

Conroy, Peter. *Crébillon fils: Techniques of the novel, Studies on Voltaire and the Eighteenth Century* 99, 1972.
Coulet, Henri. *Le Roman jusqu'à la Révolution,* Paris: Armand Colin, 1967, vol. I, p. 365–373.
Dornier, Carole. *Le Discours de maîtrise du libertin: étude sur l'uvre de Crébillons fils,* Paris; Klincksieck, 1994.
Fort, Bernadette. *Le language de l'ambiguïté dans l'oeuvre de Crébillon fils,* Paris: Klincksieck, 1976.
Funke, Hans-Günter. *Crébillon fils als Moralist und Gesellschaftskritiker,* Heidelberg: Carl Winter, 1972.
Giard, Anne. *Savoir et récit chez Crébillon fils,* Paris: Champion-Slatkine, 1986.
Sgard, Jean. *Crébillon: le libertin moraliste,* Paris : Desjonquères, 2002.
Siemek, Andrzej. *La recherche morale et esthétique dans les romans de Crébillon,* Oxford: Studies on Voltaire and the Eighteenth Century 200, 1981.
Siemek, Andrzej. "Crébillon précurseur de Laclos?," in René Pomeau et al., *Laclos et le libertinage,* Paris: Presses Universitaires de France, 1982, p. 47–61.
Stewart, Philip. *Le Masque et la parole: le langage de l'amour au XVIIIe siècle,* Paris: José Corti, 1973, pp. 148–184.
Stewart, Philip, and Miriam Ebel-Davenport. "Dossier Claude Crébillon—Henriette Marie Stafford," *Studies on Voltaire and the Eighteenth Century.* 2001:12, pp. 199–231.

CREVEL, RENÉ

1900–1935
French novelist and essayist

Les pieds dans le plat

Crevel had considerable difficulty finding a publisher for his last completed novel. Firstly, there was the problem of a masturbation scene set in Notre-Dame during the funeral of French President Paul Doumer (referred to anonymously as "the President of the Republic" in the definitive text). Secondly, some of Crevel's characters were thinly-veiled caricatures of well-known personalities: the Prince of Journalists was transparently based on Léon Bailby, proprietor of the Parisian daily *Le Jour,* and the female poet Synovie recalled the aristocratic author Anna de Noailles. The novel was finally published by Éditions du Sagittaire in 1933 with a frontispiece by Giacometti. It was not published again until 1974 when J.-J. Pauvert brought out an edition prefaced by Ezra Pound (Pound's original article dates from 1939).

This unconventional novel owes as much to the author's talents as a caustic pamphleteer as to his fictional imagination. The first six chapters introduce the thirteen characters who have gathered for lunch at the Provençal villa of Lady Primerose, the Marchioness of Sussex. The majority of these characters are members of the upper class whose activities influence the direction of European politics. Crevel's satire is directed particularly against Count Coudenhove-Kalergi's Paneuropean movement. Only two characters are spared Crevel's authorial scorn: the young American, Kate, whose child-like freshness recalls the heroine of Crevel's 1927 novel *Babylone* and the singer Krim, partly modelled on Mopsa Sternheim, Crevel's former lover and daughter of the German expressionist writer, Carl Sternheim. In the seventh (and longest) chapter, Crevel reveals himself as the luncheon's Fourteenth Guest and the final vestiges of novelistic plot and characterization give way to vehement denunciations of capitalism, colonialism, Catholicism, and sexual repression in a manner akin to Crevel's post-1930 non-fictional texts. The final eighth chapter summarizes what the future holds for each of the characters. However, the dismissive chapter heading ("Etc.,

etc."), allusions to Hitler's rise, and a concluding reference to "the next war" indicate that Crevel is far more concerned with contemporary socio-political issues than with the conventions of fiction.

Although the novel contains numerous references to sexual activity, Crevel is not in the least interested in offering titillation to his readers. He avoids direct descriptions of acts and body parts, preferring euphemism and periphrasis—rhetorical strategies that allow him to indulge his love of word play. More significantly, the novel's sexual material provides Crevel with a vehicle for exposing the myth of bourgeois respectability. Rich villa-owners (male and female) ogle the scantily clad adolescent builders who work on their properties. Crevel clearly delights in having the Prince of Journalists masturbate young Lord Sussex in a cathedral during the funeral service for the assassinated French President. The author's sacrilegious side also emerges in his presentation of Monsignor de Belle-Lurette de Troumoussu, the Bishop of Dakar who delights in the opportunities afforded by his office to indulge his twin passions: black men and sartorial extravagance. Two of Crevel's aristocratic female characters, Lady Primerose and the Duchess of Monte Putina, are former prostitutes. The third aristocratic woman, Archduchess Augusta, a Habsburg by marriage, derives sexual pleasure from sitting on a piano-stool cover depicting the profile of General Stéphanic, a Czech nationalist whose heroism she greatly admires. The furtive secrecy of bourgeois sexual behavior is contrasted with the straightforwardly robust desire of underprivileged groups: workers, blacks, and gypsies. In one incident, a gypsy lifesaver becomes stimulated while giving artificial respiration to a drowned virgin. Outraged, Archduchess Augusta strikes him in the crotch with the handle of her parasol—an ivory handle carved in the likeness of Emperor Franz-Joseph's head. The ivory head breaks into pieces against the gypsy's groin. The symbolic significance of the event is clear.

Often, the sexual practices mentioned in the novel are accompanied by a violence that complements the rage that animates the text's more polemical passages. The grandmother of the Prince of Journalists is sodomized by a stranger in the woods and later dies while attempting to swallow a large, black, obviously phallic candle (this family tragedy is presented as a symbol of France's defeat by Prussia in 1870). The Duchess of Monte Putina masochistically offers her breasts to the hot curling tongues of her hairdresser who proceeds to rape her after she has fainted. As a child, her son, Rub Dub Dub, also enjoys masochistic exercises on a climbing frame as the only form of release from a strictly regimented upbringing. After his mother has tricked him into a painful circumcision, he develops a fetish for menstrual blood. A pornographic film is described in which Augusta sodomizes herself with a three-dimensional representation of Italy before, literally, exploding. Finally, an eminent psychiatrist who subsequently commits suicide mutilates the body of his wife Synovie, a Catholic poetess, by cutting off her breasts to make cheese domes. Such violence is almost cartoon-like in its excess.

Sade was an important influence on Crevel in his later work and *Les pieds dans le plat* contains a lengthy quotation from *La philosophie dans le boudoir*. However, it is significant that the quotation should come from the Chevalier's attack on religion rather than from a sexually explicit part of the book. Ultimately, Crevel's work is more about revolution in the broad sense than about sexual revolution in particular.

Biography

Born in Paris in 1900. His first novel, *Détours*, was published in 1924. He wrote novels, essays, articles, and poems until his suicide in 1935. Throughout his career he struggled against tuberculosis. He was part of the Surrealist group around André Breton.

PAUL COOKE

Editions

Les pieds dans le plat, Paris: Pauvert, 1974; as *Putting My Foot in It*, translated by Thomas Buckley, Normal, Illinois: Dalkey Archive Press, 1992.

Selected Works

Détours. 1924.
Mon corps et moi. 1925.
La mort difficile. 1926; as *Difficult Death*, translated by David Rattray, 1986.
Babylone. 1927; as *Babylon*, translated by Kay Boyle, 1985.
Êtes-vous fous? 1929.

"L'Esprit contre la raison" et autres écrits surréalistes, 1986.
"Le roman cassé" et derniers écrits. 1989.
Lettres de désir et de souffrance. 1996.
Lettres a Mopsa. 1997.
Correspondance de René Crevel à Gertrude Stein. 2000.

Further Reading

Batache, Eddy. *La mysticité charnelle de René Crevel.* Paris: J.-M. Place, 1978.

Buot, François. *René Crevel.* Paris: Grasset, 1991.
Carassou, Michel, *René Crevel.* Paris: Fayard, 1989.
Chénieux-Gendron, Jacqueline. *Le surréalisme et le roman: 1922–1950.* Lausanne: L'Age d'homme. 1983.
Courtot, Claude. *René Crevel.* Paris: Seghers, 1969.
Devésa, Jean-Michel. *René Crevel et le roman.* Amsterdam: Rodopi, 1993.
Devésa, Jean-Michel, ed. *René Crevel; ou l'esprit contre la raison,* Lausanne. L'Age d'homme, 2002.
Rochester, Myrna Bell. *René Crevel: le pays des miroirs absolus.* Saratoga, CA: Anma Libri, 1978.

CRISP, QUENTIN

1908–1998
English writer

The Naked Civil Servant

Quentin Crisp wanted to call his autobiography *My Reign in Hell: a Reference to Lucifer's Refusal to Serve in Heaven (i.e., Respectable Society).* This title was rejected by his publishers in favor of *The Naked Civil Servant,* a reference to Crisp's years as an artist's model when he saw himself as ultimately employed by the Minister of Education.

The Naked Civil Servant only made Crisp a household-name when Thames Television turned it into an award-winning television film in 1976, with John Hurt as Crisp's 'representative on earth' (*How to Become a Virgin,* p. 71). The autobiography recounts Crisp's life into his mid-fifties and tells of living in relative obscurity as an effeminate homosexual in London, and of being tried, unsuccessfully for importuning. His later life as a celebrity is told in its sequel *How to Become a Virgin* and in his New York diaries *Resident Alien.*

Central to his autobiography is Crisp's belief that homosexuality could be seen as a disabling disfigurement which set him apart from the rest of humanity. Yet at the age of twenty-three, Crisp took the brave decision to make homosexuality a public issue by coming out, complete with make-up, long fingernails and hennaed hair, flamboyant clothes and high-heeled shoes. By his public display of effeminacy, Crisp aimed at confronting British prejudices and at demonstrating that 'effeminacy existed in people who were in all other respects just like home.' It was a crusade for integration that made Crisp the focus of anything from 'startled contempt to outraged hatred'—he was beaten unconscious for his appearance- and which isolated him from discreet homosexuals who wished to pass for straight in heterosexual society.

Crisp's autobiography, whilst giving a graphic account of the world of the homosexual, is written in a style of entertaining, witty aphorism combined with mordant humor. *The Naked Civil Servant* engages us with the world of his fellow male prostitutes during the inter-war years who frequented the Black Cat café in Soho and who made cups of tea last all night and tried each other's lipsticks. He also described games of cat and mouse with the police; being charged with soliciting and threatened with the laws of private indecency. Neighbors complained of what they could see through Crisp's open windows including, Crisp claims, 'a dismal affair' with a highly placed government official. Crisp guides the reader around queer clubs, dimly lit public toilets, and war-time London when the black-out turned the Capital into a homosexual playground for brief, romantic sexual encounters. Crisp describes being kissed by a man who emerged from the darkness and as suddenly melted back into it.

Crisp's accounts of his sexual experiences are archly anti-erotic as indeed are his descriptions of himself. He likened his own naked body to 'a plucked chicken that died of myxomatosis' and regarded squalor as his natural setting. The single room he occupied in Chelsea for forty years, made Sally Potter, the director of Orlando, weep with sadness at its filth, poverty, and dust (Paul Bailey, *The Stately Homo*). He viewed sex as 'the last refuge of the miserable' and preferred celibacy. From his first sexual experience with an Indian boy at school, through a succession of punters, chance encounters, long-term and live-in lovers like 'Barn Door' and 'the Czech,' Crisp 'did not expect any pleasure and there was none.' Recalling his affair with the seventy-year old Czech on day-release from a mental home, he remembered his lover reeking of cod-liver oil and bringing presents that included 'a suitcase full of fallen apples heavy with maggots that spent the afternoon crawling over the bed-cover.' Although erotic fulfillment eluded him in real life, Crisp harbored in youth 'erotic dreams the literature read to me in my childhood had coloured so romantically.' He dreamed of becoming the perfumed slave to some great man who was totally preoccupied by him alone. In reality, when he did become a slave, it was to Barn Door whose idea of lovemaking involved Neolithic lurches and with whom he took turns to sleep among the dust on the floor.

The sexual experiences he described were rarely the romantic ideal he sought but often brutal and above all loveless. A heterosexual partner told him that truly satisfactory sexual intercourse preserved the illusion of rape. This did not lead to erotic fantasy for Crisp, only monotony and 'the degrading effects of discomfort and exhaustion.' Whilst lovelessness might stem from Crisp's 'deep-seated indifference to the fate of others,' he believed that homosexual intercourse automatically robbed sex of its intrinsic function as a means of communication. 'Between two men [love],' argued Crisp, 'consists of each using the utmost force of his personality to gain access to the sexual organs of the other.' Thus, from his youth Crisp regarded sex as a weapon to subjugate and destroy the personalities of others. Ironically, the scrupulously polite Crisp felt that a lifetime of habitual acquiescence

honed him into 'a stockpile of rage' with 'a lust for tyranny.'

On one of the few occasions in which Crisp refers to the erotic, he argues that good homosexual sex is best achieved through masturbation, believing sexual intercourse a poor substitute for auto-eroticism. Eroticism for Crisp therefore, is the ultimate act of the egotist. Elsewhere eroticism is reduced to the commonplace, to bodily function. Commenting that human beings will respond to any erotic stimulus and that the anus is as capable of sexual excitement as the lips, Crisp relates this observation to a childhood memory of enjoying anal stimulus so much that he would rather have accidents than forgo the pleasure of retaining faeces until it was too late. As Paul Robinson confirms in *The Stately Homo*, any 'sense of erotic obsession.... is completely absent from the pages of *The Naked Civil Servant*.'

The American soldiers' occupation of wartime London when 'their bodies bulged through every straining khaki fibre towards our feverish hands' was pleasurable but the nearest Crisp came to a truly erotic experience was in Portsmouth. The evening was charged with erotic expectation and play as he flirted with a group of sailors. Whilst the night ended without sexual encounter, this was the only time Crisp 'ever sat in a crowd of people whose attention [he] really desired without once feeling that [he] was in danger.' This seemingly insignificant moment of erotic fulfillment with 'real men' lodged in Crisp's memory and is all the more poignant for its absence from the rest of his life.

Biography

Born Dennis Pratt in Sutton, Surrey on Christmas Day 1908. He attended boarding school in Derbyshire and afterwards London University but left without gaining a diploma in journalism. A flamboyant figure and effeminate homosexual, Crisp spent a lifetime fighting gay persecution. Moving to London in his early twenties, he worked briefly as a male prostitute, and in an assortment of jobs in art departments and as a tap dance teacher. He was also a nude artist's model for thirty-five years. He wrote numerous poems, plays, libretti, and stories but only books on window dressing and the Ministry of Labour were published before the first volume of his autobiography *The Naked Civil Servant* (1968) thrust him into the limelight. He undertook world tours with his show An Evening with Quentin Crisp, appeared in several films including *Orlando* when he played Queen Elizabeth I, and published further memoirs, diaries, and works on lifestyle. He also wrote film reviews for *Christopher Street* and *The New York Native*. He became a resident alien in the United States of America in 1981 and died in Manchester on 21st November 1999 on the eve of his one-man show.

BARBARA WHITE

Editions

The Naked Civil Servant. London: Flamingo, 1985.

Selected Works

Lettering for Brush and Pen, (with A.F. Stuart). 1936.
All This and Bevan Too. 1943.
How to Have a Life-Style. 1975.
How to Become a Virgin. 1981.
Manners from Heaven: A Divine Guide to Good Behavior. 1984.
How to Go to the Movies. 1988.
Resident Alien: The New York Diaries. 1996.

Further Reading

Bailey, Paul (ed). *The Stately Homo: A Celebration of the Life of Quentin Crisp*. London: Bantum, 2000.
Fountain, Tim. *Outlines: Quentin Crisp*. Bath: Absolute Press. 2002.
Ward, Phillip (ed). *Dusty Answers*. www.crisperanto.org. Consulted April 3, 2006.

CROS, CHARLES

1842–1888
French poet and inventor

L'album zutique

Numerous members of the Parisian bohemian movement contributed to *L'album zutique*: Cabaner, Antoine Cros, Charles Cros, Henri Cros, André Gill, J. Keck, Henri Mercier, Arthur Rimbaud, Léon Valade, and Paul Verlaine. Calling themselves the "zutistes," these artists met periodically at the Hôtel des Étrangers in late 1871 and early 1872 to socialize, experiment with alcohol (notably absinthe) and drugs, and to create satiric poems and illustrations mocking various styles and cultural figures of the day. The *Album zutique* contains original (and unpublished until 1936) works by Arthur Rimbaud, Paul Verlaine, and Charles Cros, and it is also a powerful and entertaining reminder of the biting satire which played a large role in the bohemian art and culture of the belle époque.

In 1936, the book collectors Auguste and Georges Blaizot advertised the *Album zutique* in a catologue of rare works to be sold on March 12 of that year. Until this point the manuscript had passed from collector to collector and had been held back from sale, probably due to the explicitly sexual content of its poems and illustrations. Publicists were also most likely reluctant to challenge existing copyrights of works by the already famous Rimbaud and Verlaine. References to the *Album zutique* did find their way into several studies however: André Fontaine in *Verlaine homme de lettres* (Delagrave, 1937), Yves-Gérard Le Dantec in the *Pléiade edition of Verlaine* (Gallimard, 1939), and Jules Mouquet in the *Pléiade edition of Rimbaud* (Gallimard, 1946). In 1961, Henri Matarasso and Pierre Petitfils wrote the study, "Rimbaud, Verlaine, Germain Nouveau et L'album zutique" in the *Mercure de France*. Finally, in 1964, Pascal Pia edited and wrote an introduction to a public edition of the *Album zutique*, which contains detailed notes on the works, as well as copies of the original manuscript, including illustrations. Although several of the poems from the *Album zutique* have been translated into English (in the complete works of *Rimbaud*, for example), no complete English translation of the Album has been published.

The *Album zutique* contains just over 120 poems dealing primarily with the themes of sexuality, politics, alcohol, drugs, and bohemian culture in general. The tone of the poems is decidedly sardonic, yet playful. The main objects of the various poets' railleries are the Parnassian poets renowned in their day, most particularly Auguste Creissels and François Coppée. Many of the poems are parodies or pastiches of existing poems twisted to contain more explicit material and decidedly more blunt descriptions of sexual acts. The ultimate goal of such mockery is to poke fun at anyone foolish enough to take his or her work (or self) too seriously. The poets of the *Album zutique* are particularly successful in achieving this goal in large part because they welcome the chance to make themselves the object of their own jokes. Valade's close friend Albert Mérat is the object of numerous jokes, for example. In irreverent bohemian fashion, the zutistes forge each other's signatures and the signatures of famous poets, often making it difficult to determine the authorship of a given poem. They also imitate styles and attribute various idiosyncrasies to one another. Cabaner, for example, is often described as having particularly eccentric sexual tastes. The *Album zutique* is full of charming and sexually explicit caricatures and sketches which have often been attributed to Rimbaud, but which are in all probability the work of numerous artists. It is indeed highly likely that the graphic nature of these drawings delayed publication of the *Album zutique* for quite some time.

The most famous poem in the *Album zutique* is the "Sonnet au trou du cul" ["Sonnet of the Asshole"]. A version of this poem was printed for the first time in 1903, in a private publication entitled *Hombres*. Its risqué subject matter aside, this sonnet is particularly famous because it is the only poem known to have been jointly composed by Rimbaud and Verlaine. It is an exuberant and hilarious parody inspired by the Parnassian poet Albert Mérat. Mérat had published a book of sonnets entitled *L'idole*, in which he dedicated poems to specific body parts of his mistress. There were however, several important parts he neglected to praise—an omission quickly rectified by Verlaine and Rimbaud. In addition to the "trou du cul," the zutistes would later compose a similar and equally explicit sonnet in honor of a mistress' tongue. Although the zutistes did not imitate Mérat's imagery or style, they did much to undercut his (or any) idealized vision of physical love. By insisting on the

traditionally taboo (anal sex) and at times humorous (flatulence) side of human physicality in a carefully crafted sonnet, Rimbaud and Verlaine deal a swift blow to idealism, both in love and in general.

In another striking poem written in Verlaine's hand, Baudelaire's famous sonnet "La mort des amants" ["The Death of the Lovers"] is rewritten as "La mort des cochons" ["The Death of the Pigs"]. "La mort des cochons" is a particularly obscene reworking of the original: Baudelaire's "soir fait de rose et de bleu mystique" ["night made of pink and mystical blue"] becomes "[u]n soir plein de foutre et de cosmétique" ["an evening full of fuck and cosmetics"]. This sonnet provides a concise example of the strategy to which the zutistes generally subjected the more traditional poets they parodied. Verlaine replaces the most highly romanticized references to romantic love with the most blunt and basely materialist descriptions of sexual organs and acts. In the final verse of "La mort des cochons" for example, Verlaine replaces Baudelaire's "[l]es miroirs ternis et les flammes mortes" ["the tarnished mirrors and dead flames"] with "[l]es spermes éteints et les régles mortes" ["the faded sperm and dead rules"]. While mimicking the structure and formal tone of the original piece, Verlaine adds a radical sexuality and a rebellious political stance. Such is the classic operation of parody, and as such it displays a deeper purpose than making the reader (or the poet) laugh. For all their bawdiness and blatant mimicry, the parodic poems of the Album zutique call for a genuine shattering of tradition and a re-evaluation of artistic, cultural, and sexual restriction.

Rimbaud's poem "Les remembrances du vieillard idiot" ["The Remembrances of the Idiotic Old Man"] represents another strain of poem prevalent in the Album. Contrary to its title, this poem deals with the subject of adolescent sexual urges and the confusion and social restriction which may accompany them. Rimbaud describes numerous family situations which instigate a sexual awakening. His mother, younger sister and father are each strongly eroticized, and a sense of guilt—not generally associated with Rimbaud—accompanies each incestuous reference. In the final stanza, the poet questions God, asking why sexuality must necessarily be coloured by misery and shame. Such blatant and shocking vulnerability reflects the more sombre and truly revolutionary side of the zutistes.

The *Album zutique* is a powerful example of the use of erotic themes and language by the bohemian poets to attack and undermine the formality of cultural and literary tradition. The parodies and pastiches, one-line witticisms, and frank discussions of sexuality are clearly very funny, but are also legitimate and forceful attacks on artistic and sexual repression, idealised physical love, and arrogance in all its forms.

Biography

Charles Cros was born on October 1, 1842 in Fabrezan, Southern France. He completed his baccelaureat in 1859, and studied medicine briefly. The infamous Nina de Villard was his mistress from 1867 to 1875, and in 1878 he married Mary Hjardemaal, with whom he had two sons: Guy-Charles (1879–1956), and René (1880–1898). Cros published several books of poetry: *L'artiste* (1869), *Coffret de Santal* (1873), and *Dixains réalistes* (1876). He collaborated with Théophile Gautier on Tombeau, was the editor of the *Revue du monde* (circa 1874–1876), and wrote monologues with the actor Coquelin. In 1879, he collaborated on several journals, notably *L'Hydropath* and *Le Molière*, and his re-edited *Coffret de Santal* earned him the prix Juglar. He continued to publish articles and monologues until his death in Paris on April 9, 1888. He was also an inventor whose experiments with the automatic telegraph and color photography are considered highly influential. Cros contributed to the *Album zutique* at the end of 1871, with his bohemian friends and colleagues.

PATRICIA BERNEY

Editions

Cros, Charles et al. *L'album zutique* (avec notes et une introduction par Pascal Pia). Paris: Jean-Jacques Pauvert, 1962.

Further Reading

Fontaine, André. *Verlaine homme de lettres*. Paris: Delagrave, 1937.
Forestier, Louis. "Sur l'Album zutique et le Calepin du mendiant Rimbaud, Verlaine, Nouveau et d'autres in Hay, Louis and Woesler, Winifried. Bern: Lang, 1979.
Le Dantec, Yves-Gérard. *Verlaine*. Paris: Pléiade, 1939.
Matarasso, Henri and Pierre Petitfils, "Rimbaud, Verlaine, Germain Nouveau et L'album zutique," *Mercure de France*, 1961.
Mouquet, Jules. *Rimbaud*. Paris: Pléiade, 1946.

CUISIN, P.

1777–c.1845
French short-story writer and essayist

A number of Cuisin's works are due for revaluation. *Clémentine, orpheline et androgyne, ou les Caprices de la nature et de la fortune* (1820), for example, is an early fictional study of a young woman attempting to come to terms with her own physical and mental bisexuality; *Les Ombres sanglantes* (1820) and *Les fantômes nocturnes; ou les terreurs coupables* (1821) announce the rise of the independent tradition of French horror writing that Charles Nodier labelled the "école frénétique" [frenetic school]; other works represent anecdotal descriptions of historical events or changes of political regime (e.g., *Les crimes secrets de Napoléon Buonoparte*, 1815). Cuisin's main area of interest, however, was concerned with prostitution and accounts of sexual conquest, though a number of these works have a satirical quality which precludes the simple label *erotica* or *pornography* being applied.

La galanterie sous la sauvegarde des lois

In the light of the shifting political sands of the period it is hardly surprising that many of

Cuisin's works, especially those dealing with prostitution or amorous adventures, should have fallen foul of the censor in the mid-1820s. In addition to *Clémentine, orpheline et androgyne*, the following were all banned at some point: *Les nymphs du Palais-Royal* (1815); *L'Amour au grand trot* (1820); *Les duels, suicides et amours du bois de boulogne* (1820); *La vie d'un garcon dans les hôtels garnis de la capitale* (1820); and *Les femmes entretenues dévoilées* (1821).

Typical of these works, and indeed of much of Cuisin's literary production, is *La galanterie sous la sauvegarde des lois* (1815), which might be described as a sequel to *Les nymphs du Palais-Royal* of the same year, in which the author is taken on a conducted tour of "one of the best conducted and most brilliant harems [i.e., brothels] of the Palais-Royal, perhaps the whole of Europe" by a Madame who is presumably anxious to procure some free publicity. The extent to which sexual mores and republican politics were fused in the literary imagination of the immediate post-Restauration is clearly revealed by this curious work. Among the nine "muses" who inhabit this "temple of Voluptuousness" are girls such as Rosalie, Josephine, Clarisse, and Adèle. However, it is not so much the lascivious descriptions of the girls themselves that is the main focus of attention as the increasingly peculiar nature of the apartments they occupy and the sexual services they provide.

Thus, Rosalie is portrayed in slightly anodyne fashion as entertaining a Swedish prince while awaiting the arrival of his British equivalent while Josephine, whom we are informed lost both her parents during the Emigration, would seem to be in a state of arrested childhood. With Clarisse, however, the sense of the bizarre begins to mount as she is shown rehearsing the part of Phèdre from Racine's 1777 play of the same title about an incestuous passion. This sense of the unusual and recherché reaches its apogee with the description of Adèle and her musical bed:

"Do not be deceived," whispered Madame L***, "the fascinating figure you see here in perfect harmony with Adèle [...] is supported by a rich voluptuary, the Marquis de Dersey, who is besotted with music [...]. This impetuous virtuoso is aroused only by vibrations and musical concerts; he can feel no pleasure except through the agency and organs of such instruments."

[And I remarked that] the very bed of the apartment was in the shape of a clavecin [and that] should one lie down on this singular musical couch and "make the slightest movement, then one would immediately experience, in strict time with the activity on the bed but by means of a device that was hidden out of sight, the sweetest harmony imaginable [...]"

"How original!" I thought. "What voluptuous bizarrerie! How could one possibly put into words here all the peculiarities of the human heart!" (pp. 81–82; my translation.)

In other words, not only is the Marquis de Dersey impotent with women but his only sexual pleasure is obtained by means of employing a proxy whose amorous exertions are transformed by some kind of artificial apparatus into music. This element of mechanical fantasy recalls, of course, the Enlightenment fascination with science and mathematics. Likewise, Clarisse's lover can only achieve sexual arousal by watching an actress in rehearsal, an activity which is compared with an old libertine's pleasure at being flagellated.

Given that commentators such as Chantal Thomas and Lynn Hunt have suggested that the political pornography of the *ancien régime* generally expressed a mounting anxiety about women invading the public sphere and sexual indifferentiation, often pictorially represented by an impotent Louis XVI watching on as Marie-Antoinette enjoys sexual congress with his own brother, it is difficult not to suggest that Cuisin's depiction of the luxurious brothel described in *La galanterie sous la sauvegarde des lois* belongs to the same tradition of "homosocial" Republican virtue. Such a view would seem to receive confirmation from the portraits of two later Muses, one of whom is described as a "savantasse" (e.g., a "female savant") and the other as a "bibliotheque-vivante" (e.g., a "walking library").

At the time that Cuisin was writing, the old wooden galleries of the Palais-Royal enjoyed a dubious reputation as a center for prostitution and gambling (not to mention, incidentally, the book trade). During the reign of Louis-Philippe, the area was extensively renovated such that, like the Republican discourse which permeates his work, Cuisin's descriptions of the area would have seemed anachronistic only a generation or so later. It is hardly surprising, therefore, that there have been very few reprints of his works, though there was an 1836 edition of *La galanterie sous la sauvegarde des lois* under a changed title. One or two other works were reissued by J.-J. Gay in the early 1880s though these, like all Cuisin's writing, have become scarce and collectible. None of his work would seem to have been translated into English.

Biography

Cuisin was a prolific minor novelist who flourished principally during the decade immediately after the Restoration of the French monarchy in 1814 and whose work sought to exploit, implicitly or explicitly, the intellectual confusion of the period whether with regard to medical science (especially with respect to sexual orientation), political history, or personal morality. Little is known about the author's life apart from information briefly noted in standard French nineteenth-century bibliographies: among other occupations, he claimed to have been variously a professional soldier, a man of letters, and the curator of a well-known anatomy cabinet.

TERRY HALE

Editions

La galanterie sous la sauvegarde des lois, Paris: *Chez tous les marchands de nouveautés*: 1815; as *Les Fastes, ruses et intrigues de la galanterie, Ou Tableaux de l'amour et du plaisir*, Paris: Terry, éditeur: 1836.

Further Reading

Hunt, Lynn (ed.) *Eroticism and the Body Politic*, Baltimore and London: Johns Hopkins University Press: 1991.
Thomas, Chantal. *La Reine scélérate, Marie-Antoinette dans les pamphlets*. Paris: Seuil: 1989.

CYRANO DE BERGERAC (SAVINIEN DE CYRANO)

1619–1655
French novelist and dramatist

L'Autre Monde

Savinien Cyrano de Bergerac's *L'Autre monde* [*The Other World*] is an unfinished burlesque novel, held by some to anticipate the modern genre of science fiction. In its two parts, the novel's hero finds ingenious ways to transport himself to the moon and the sun, respectively, and his various travels and encounters provide the author with scope to tackle a wide range of intellectual themes, from philosophy and religion to science and knowledge. Cyrano himself left his curious novel unpublished during his lifetime, no doubt aware of the controversial nature of the boldly irreverent attitudes it expresses. It was published only after his death, the first part in an expurgated edition of 1657 and the second in 1662. Only in the early twentieth century was the complete text of the novel published.

Although not explicitly an erotic work in itself, Cyrano's novel focuses on questions of sexuality in a manner atypical of most seventeenth-century French literature, and in many respects looks forward to the libertine, satirical, and philosophical fictions of the following century. Sex is a key philosophical concern for Cyrano because its role in procreation means that it is intimately bound up with ethical questions about life and existence more generally. Indeed, discussions of sex in the novel often raise the spectre of life's opposite, death, although the relationship between the two is complex and often unclear. In its procreative capacities, sex is held on both moon and sun as life-affirming. Bronze penises are sported by lunar aristocrats just as their earthly counterparts carry swords, and one of the moon-dwellers is appalled that in earthly society such symbols of generation are ignominious while those of destruction are honorable. Christianity is portrayed as unnatural in its emphasis on chastity, a worthless virtue whose honor is dismissed. If God had intended us to be chaste, explains one of the moon-dwellers, He would have made us self-propagating, like mushrooms. The "Kingdom of Lovers" on the sun also holds procreation as its goal. After a year's probation in the kingdom's noviciate of love, teenage boys are assessed on their sexual prowess and accorded between ten and forty young wives, depending on their capacities. Fecundity remains the focus: a husband may not sleep with a wife who is already pregnant, while sterile men, relegated to the status of servants, are condemned to mingle carnally only with equally barren women. (In allowing such acts, Cyrano thus shows himself to be more tolerant of sterile people's right to sexual pleasure than Denis Diderot would be in his Supplement to Bougainville's "*Voyage*" the following century). Characters twice argue that it is morally worse to abstain from sex and thus not to reproduce than it is to kill a child who has at least had the pleasure of living for some time. Sexual abstinence is figured as a double murder, since it prevents individuals from ever having existed as well as from continuing to exist in the present. Despite this focus on procreation, however, Cyrano is also keen to stress that giving rise to new life is often the last thing on one's mind when one is in the throes of sexual pleasure. Traditions that advocate respect for one's parents are, therefore, fundamentally misplaced, since one's own birth is little more than a side-effect of their unthinking licentiousness.

Alongside this emphasis on procreation, however, there are also numerous elements of homoeroticism in the novel, not least in the portrayal of occasional beautiful young boys who fascinate the hero. Perhaps surprisingly, though, even the novel's evocations of same-sex desire are often underpinned by a fascination with heterosexuality and procreation. Perhaps most striking is the ritual whereby the lunar philosophers choose to die. Tenderly embracing and kissing the friend whom he loves the most, the philosopher stabs himself in the heart; the beloved then presses his mouth against his until the philosopher dies, at which point the beloved drinks his fill of his blood and lets the others

present do the same. The friends spend the following three or four days in a cannibalistic orgy with a young woman, dining solely on their friend's corpse and hoping that he will be reborn from their embraces. In the second part of the novel, the dying embrace of the Greek heroes and lovers Orestes and Pylades gives rise to a pair of saplings whose fruit has aphrodisiac properties. Because of the heroes' love, anyone who eats an apple from one of these plants develops a sudden passion for anyone who has eaten the fruit of the other, a conceit which allows Cyrano to explain a series of transgressive passions, including incest, narcissism, bestiality, and sexual activity with plants. In this episode, love between men thus becomes the prototype of all true passion; even women who eat the fruit develop a vigorous love which betrays the virility of its source. On the other hand, the passion stoked up between any two men who eat the fruit is cast as "reciprocal friendship" (p. 176)—surprisingly coy terms after the more explicit description of Orestes and Pylades as "lovers." The work's combined fascination with homosexuality and concomitant anxieties about sterility are, however, treated in a quite different tone in another episode, where the moon-dwellers mistake the hero for a female and pair him up with another man, comically hoping that they will breed. Such juxtapositions of the comic and the serious, the Epicurean and the ethical, the grotesque and the utopian, are in many ways typical of the novel's unsettling and provocative stance towards all manner of issues.

Biography

Born Savinien de Cyrano in 1619 in Paris. Died in 1655 in Sannois, Paris.

A soldier and man of letters, he wrote a variety of works in different genres, including plays, satirical pamphlets, a fragment of a scientific treatise, and letters. He moved in various free-thinking circles, and was a friend of Gassendi, Tristan l'Hermite, Scarron, and Molière.

JOSEPH HARRIS

Editions

Histoire comique contenant les estats & empires de lalune. Paris: de Sercy, 1657; as *Voyages to the Moon and the Sun*, translated by Richard Aldington, London: Folio Society, 1991.

Voyage dans la Lune. Edited by Maurice Laugaa, Paris: Garnier-Flammarion, 1970.

L'Autre monde, in Libertins du XVIIe siècle, vol. 1. Edited by Jacques Prévot. Paris: Gallimard, 1998.

Les etats et empires du Soleil. Edited by Bérengère Parmentier. Paris: Garnier-Flammarion, 2003.

Further Reading

Alcover, Madeleine. *La pensée philosophique et scientifique de Cyrano de Bergerac*. Paris: Minard, 1970.

Carré, Rose-Marie. *Cyrano. Voyages imaginaires à la recherche de la vérité humaine*, Paris: Minard, 1977.

Mason, Haydn. *Cyrano de Bergerac, 'L'Autre Monde'*, London: Grand and Cutler, 1984.

Prévot, Jacques. *Cyrano de Bergerac romancier*. Paris: Belin, 1977.

Mourousy, Paul. *Cyrano de Bergerac: illustre mais inconnu*. Monaco: Rocher, 2000.

See also **Diderot, Denis; Libertinism; Science Fiction; 17th century French Literature**

CZECH

Although Casanova wrote his famous *Memoirs* during his stay at the Czech castle Duchcov and Prague was the city where Leopold von Sacher-Masoch studied. Erotic literature in the Czech language is quite rare, apart from a few periods of short-lived fertility. There are two reasons for this: First, Czech language books for common readership started to be published only since the beginning of the nineteenth century. Before the birth of the Czechoslovak Republic in 1918, Czech lands were part of German-speaking culture. Second, in the years 1938–1989, the Czech Republic was governed by Nazi and communist totalitarian regimes who banned publication of erotic books in general.

Prominent publisher and collector of erotic literature, Karel Jaroslav Obratil (1866–1945), sees two more reasons for this state. In his important study *Eroticke ex libris* [*Erotic ex libris*] (1928) he wrote: "The cause should be sought in the character of Czech nation which, by nature, is closer to the northern nations regarding its relation to sexuality. It never enjoyed the excesses typical for southern and western nations." Also, the lack of Czech higher aristocracy and relative freedom in the private sphere of citizens did not provoke Renaissance writers to write moralistic and political pamphlets which often used to contain erotic elements.

One of the rare exceptions is the work of Hynek z Podebrad (1452–1492), son of Czech king Jiri and an important politician and poet of his time. Podebrad was one of the few writers who composed his texts in the Czech language (rather than in Latin). Among the manuscripts which he wrote at the end of his life we can find the first Czech translations of several stories from Bocaccio's Dekameron (put into the Czech milieu) as well as some original poems. One of the poems is called Majovy sen ["A Dream in May"]. It tells about an erotic dream of the narrator in which he persuades his lady to make love with him. He almost succeeds but in the crucial moment the dream ends. Hynek also added one original story to the translations of Bocaccio in which he warns husbands not to ignore the needs of their wives. These texts remained in manuscript form until 1823 and 1840 when parts of them were published, but the erotic scenes were softened by the censors. Vaclav Flajshans, a 19th-century literary critic, called this text "the most obscene work of Czech literature." The complete edition of Hynek's manuscript appeared only in 1978 under the title *Spisovani slavneho frejire* [*Writings of a Famous Lady's Man*].

In the following centuries the erotic motifs proliferated mostly in folk songs and poems. Some of them were collected in the anthology *Erotika ceskeho obrozeni* 1780–1850 [*Erotica of Czech National Revival*, ed. by Jiri Hruby] (1928). Several of the included erotic and obscene poems were collected by Bozena Nemcova, the most important Czech writer of the early nineteenth century. Nemcova, a chaste woman, wrote the worst parts of poems in the Russian alphabet.

Strong erotic elements can be found in the diaries of Karel Hynek Macha (1810–1836), founder of modern Czech poetry. Parts of his diaries were written in a secret alphabet. However, it was soon deciphered by the literary historians of the late nineteenth century. They discovered that the poet made brief, but detailed notes about his sexual adventures with his female lovers, including the place and the type of the position. The content of the secret diaries was well known among students of literature, but remained taboo for publishers until the 1990's when they were finally printed.

According to Obratil, the first genuine erotic Czech book was an anonymously published collection of poetry *Sonata erotica* (1913). It was only in the 1920s when erotic books, both original and translated started to appear with some regularity. Any bibliography of erotic books in the Czech language has not been compiled yet, but it is estimated that some 500 erotic and pornographic books have been published there between 1920 and 1939. There were also several early attempts to establish an erotic magazine. They were either very innocent like the magazine *Amor* (at least 16 issues, since 1892) or they did not survive its premiere issue like *Rozmarna erotika* [*Frivolous Erotica*, 1913].

The borderline between erotic and pornographic books was unclear but there are some differences. Erotic novels were usually published without hiding the name of the author and publisher, often in some of the many specialized editions. Pornographic novels were often anonymous, they contained erotic illustrations, often more explicit than the literal content, and they were not distributed in the bookstores. The authors and publishers feared being accused of "moral corruption" so the books had been sent to subscribers only and published in limited series. Each of them contained a warning such as: "Issued in the limited number of 100 numbered prints intented for the close circle of friends. Each owner of this book agrees to store the book separately so that it will not fall into the hands of women, children, and mentally handicapped persons."

Advocates of erotic literature often stressed the difference between erotica and pornography. K.J. Obratil in the mentioned book *Eroticke ex*

libris writes of pornography: "Its language is crude and dumb, it lacks humor, it is low and raw, without any esthetic quality. Its intellectual content is empty of any idea."

Obratil, who was a teacher by profession and a publisher of textbooks for schoolchildren, was—together with Frantisek Trefny (?–?), Viktor Roubal (?–?), Stanislav Kostka Neumann (1875–1947)—the most important publisher and editor of erotic books.

Since the early years of the twentieth century specialized editions devoted to erotica flowered. They were, for example: *Zapovezene ovoce* [*Forbidden Fruits*], 1906–1908, 81 volumes, mostly by Czech authors; *Intimni knihovna* [*Intimate Library*], 1908–1911, 11 volumes, some anonymous; *Edice eroticka* (*Erotic Edition*, undated, 34 volumes including works by Giacomo Casanova, Catule Mendes, Guy de Maupassant), *Venusiny povidky* [*Venus Stories*], 1922–1924, 63 volumes of various quality, including Restif de la Bretonne, Octave Mirbeau, or Czech writer Stanislav Cerchovsky; *Zahrada Priapova* (1927–1929, [*Priap's Garden*], 4 volumes including *de la Bretonne or de Laclos' Dangerous Liaisons*, intended as a novelistic supplement to the nonfiction study *Dejiny lasky*, [*The History of Love*], *Knizky pro poteseni* [*Books For Your Pleasure*], 1928–1930, 22 volumes, including *Honore de Balzac, de Sade or Alfred de Musset*; *Horizont* 1932–1936, 21 mildly erotic or adventure volumes, including several books by Pitigrilli.

Most of these book lines contained rather subtle variants of erotic fiction or, many times, social and adventure stories with moral overtones. Maybe the most prolific publisher and writer of these books was Frantisek Trefny, who also owned a shop with erotic and hygienic goods. He wrote medical brochures as well as some 40 erotic novels. The longest of them was *Tajny klub maskovanych zen* [*The Secret Club of Masked Women*] (1933). In this adventure story men are kidnapped by a secret society of women, who turn the captives into their sexual slaves.

The single most famous Czech erotic text is a long poem *Rytir Smil* [*Knight called Shag*]. The author of the poem is unknown, the suspicion that it has been written by the great poet Jaroslav Vrchlicky has not been proven. It is even possible that the poem originated in some other country. The first known Czech edition comes from 1925. Since then, it has been republished many times. It also circulated in manuscript form when publishing erotic fiction was still forbidden and it almost became a part of modern Czech folklore. This vulgar, pornographic text tells a story about a knight who was a virgin until he was seduced by one of the castle's maids. In the meantime, her former lover mistook the maid in the dark for her grandmother.

Erotic content was not an exclusive theme of popular literature. Strong erotic elements were contained, for example, in the writings of Czech decadents. Most typical of them was Jiri Karasek ze Lvovic (1871–1951) whose poems from 1890's or his trilogy *Romany tri magu* [*Novels of Three Magicians*] contain homoerotic elements and caused some controversy when they were published. Eccentric writer and philosopher Ladislav Klima (1878–1928) also put some bizarre erotic elements into his stories. His dealing with necrophilic themes also intended to provoke a strong reaction among the petty-bourgeois audience.

Czech erotica reached its short Golden Age in the early 1930's in connection with the Czech surrealist movement. Surrealists, in their search for taboo and hidden aspects of the human psyche, were fascinated by sexuality. It is often used as a theme of surrealist paintings and collages, most notably by Jindrich Styrsky (1899–1942) and Toyen (pseudonym of Marie Cerminova, 1902–1980). Sex was often presented with irony and in connection with its antithesis—death.

Jindrich Styrsky edited the famous magazine *Eroticka revue* [*Erotic Revue*] (1930–1933). In the first year of its existence four issues were published in the course of the years 1930–1931. In the following years the magazine changed into an anthology and lasted two volumes only. *Eroticka revue* contained—like the older erotic magazines—a mixture of texts by Czech (mostly poems) and foreign authors decorated with pictures and drawings. However it differed from them in two ways: the erotic content was far more explicit, rather pornographic than just erotic, and the quality of both texts and pictures was very high. The translations were made mostly from French. Notable text is, for example, a poem "Balada o sisce" [A Ballad on the Cone] (1933) by Sirius Vokno. Under this pseudonym two important Czech playwrights Jiri Voskovec (1905—1981) and Jan Werich (1905—1980) were recognized. Its childish obscenity contrasted with other, more lyric poems in the volume. In addition to the stories and poems

Eroticka revue also contained such texts as "folk erotic dictionary" or a list of brothels in Paris. The magazine had a very limited print run, allegedly circa 200 copies of each issue. In 2001, the revue was published again in its first mass market edition.

Styrsky's activity did not end with *Eroticka revue*. At the same time he launched a limited erotic book line called Edition 69. In these volumes he maintained the highest quality of both content and form. In the promotion leaflet Styrsky wrote: "Edition 69 will include works of the highest literary values and graphic albums of perpetual artistic importance." He stressed that this edition will differ from pure, anonymous pornography: "Quality was my guide when I selected the titles. The names of poets, novelists, artists, and translators exclude any suspicion that I intend to distribute low and cheap pornography and anonymous private prints." Only six volumes were published in this series between 1931 and 1933. Three of them were written by Czech authors, the other three titles were books by the Marquis de Sade, P. Aretino, and a collection of Russian erotic folk tales.

The series was started by the novella *Sexualn nocturno—Pribeh demaskovane iluze* [*A Sexual Nocturno: A Story of Unmasked Illusion*] (1931) written by well known surrealist poet and activist Vitezslav Nezval. The text is clearly autobiographic and rather than being explicitly erotic it is an absolutely sincere personal account typical of surrealist writings. *Sexualni nocturno* consists of several interlinked evocations of the writer's early years in the town Trebic. It describes two formative experiences of the narrator/Nezval (the text is first-person narrative). First was a rather unpleasant memory in which the narrator writes an erotic mesage to his girl schoolfriend and is caught and punished by his landlord. The landlord is clearly a symbol of the petty-bourgeois mentality of small-town society. The core of the narrative describes in hypnotic details the narrator's first visit to a brothel and sex with a prostitute. This experience was so intense that for the narrator it is life-altering. Irrationality of the spontaneous sexual act led him to intellectual appreciation of unusual compositions and combinations, trying to "transfer the known into the unknown." Sexual initiation led him to the discovery of a special kind of vision which will later correspond with surrealism.

It is no surprise that for a would-be writer a large part of eroticism had a semantic nature. "Forbidden" words were being used by young Nezval as mantras—he repeated them over and over in his mind. The following paragraph from *Sexualni nocturno* is perhaps the most quoted piece of text in Czech erotic literature:

"The word fuck is diamond-like, hard, transparent, classic. As if it would fall off a precious alexandrine, like a jewel. It has a magic power, because it is forbidden. It is one of the cabbalist signs of erotic fluidum and I love it. I never say it loud in front of dirty women."

The third volume of the edition was a collection of verses *Thyrsos* (1932) written by acknowledged communist poet Frantisek Halas (1901–1949). The author is attracted by the innocent sexuality of youth to such an extent that some consider his poems to be on the border of pedophilic interest. They deal with such themes like lovemaking between brother and sister, young virgins discovering sexuality, or small children mimicking their parents in their sexual games. No other edition of this collection was allowed by the poet's family.

Nevertheless the collection was issued again without permission in the year 2000. The author's estate protested, forcing the publisher to recall the whole print run and destroy it.

The sixth, and last, volume of *Edition 69* was *Emilie prichazi ke mne ve snu* [*Emily Comes To Me In My Dreams*] (1933), a short lyrical text by Styrsky himself. In this sequence of memories, images and associations the writer remembers his imaginary girlfriend Emilie (who is, perhaps, Styrsky's own sister Marie). The text is heavy in symbols of age and loss as if written by an old man. In fact, Styrsky was 34 at the time of publication. The realization that memories and dreams may grow old and die is expressed by the deeply sad and nostalgic tone of the text. The text was accompanied by ten photo-collages by the author (12 in a few limited-edition prints). They depict couples making love in unusual contexts (like on the background of a starry sky) and contribute to the sardonic tone of the volume. The book was accompanied by an afterword of young psychoanalyst Bohuslav Brouk. The afterword, in contast to the text itself, is written enthusiastically, with almost revolutionary feeling. Brouk describes "pornophiles" almost in the terms of today's theoretics of popular culture. For him, the depiction of the beautiful human body is "the last argument" and "a weapon" of poor, oppressed, and socially marginalized people. Pornography, according to Brouk, is a democratic, revolutionary tool which dissolves boundaries between social classes. Emilie was republished in 2001, after being published in Germany in 1994 in translation.

Both *Eroticka revue* and *Edice 69* ended in the same year when a film, *Extase* [*Ecstasy*], by Gustav Machaty was been released. This Czech movie is perhaps the first film in the history of cinema which shows a naked woman's body.

In the course of World War II, and then during the strong communist regime of the 1950s, nothing even close to erotica could be published. After the first cultural warming in the 1960s, there was a wave of new writers who included erotic elements in their works. Their intention was to show human life in all its aspects, in contradiction to one-dimensional characters of socialist realism. Set in the time of the Nazi occupation of Czechoslovakia, Bohumil Hrabal's (1914–1997) short novel *Ostre sledovane vlaky* [*Closely Watched Train*] (1965) tells a story of a young man trying to find a woman who will end his virginity. Several examples of explicit scenes and language can be found in other Hrabal novels, like *Obsluhoval jsem anglickeho krale* [*I Was a Servant to the English King*], (exile edition 1980, regular Czech edition 1989). The melancholic and existential aspects of love are the motifs of Milan Kundera's (1929) short stories collected in *Smesne lasky* [*Laughable Loves*], (3 vols 1963–1968). Vladimir Paral (1932) portrayed the empty and mechanical life under the communist regime. In his works the sex degenerated into a simple fulfillment of need. Some of his late stories from the 1990s are more openly erotic.

Pure erotica was relatively rare in Czech poetry but it appeared in the works of such opposite writers as Jana Krejcarova (1928–1981), daughter of Franz Kafka's friend Milena Jesenska, an influential figure of the Czech literary and political underground, and communist poet Karel Sys (1946), later an editor of the erotic magazine *Sextant*. Little known were Krejcarova's poems Clarissa published as *samisdat* in 1951 and later as *Clarissa a jine texty* [*Clarissa and other Writings*] (1990). Many texts of Krejcarova show her passion to use explicit words for sexual activites and body parts, maybe under the influence of "total realism," a style coined by her lover, philosoper and writer Egon Bondy. The second edition also includes her letter to Bondy from c. 1962, which is maybe the most intimate and erotic piece of correspondence in Czech literature. Erotica took an important role also in the works of surrealist poet Karel Hynek (1925–1953) and, much later, underground poet J.H. Krchovsky (pen name of Jiri Hasek, 1960).

Because erotica was prohibited by the communist regime, it was sometimes used as a tool for literary expression by writers opposed to the regime. Jiri Grusa (1938), now a president of the International PEN Club, was accused of writing pornography by the communist state in the years 1969–1970. Under the pseudonym Samuel Lewis he serialized *Listy z Kalpadocie* [*Letters from Kalpadocia*] in the magazine *Sesity pro literaturu a diskusi* in 1969. Using the framework of a utopian novel, he depicted a dystopian society with a decadent obsession with sex and death. For all of these activities, Kalpadocians use their own language different from ours. Grusa shows that manipulaion of language can be used for the manipulation of the masses and that the use of "foreign" words can hide inhuman atrocities. The text was later published in *samisdat* as *Mimner aneb Hra o smrdocha* [*Mimner, or, the Stinker Game*, 1973]. A different version was published in German in 1986; the official Czech edition is from 1991.

The fall of the communist regime in 1989 has been followed by a boom of all prohibited literary forms, including erotica. The first pornorgaphic magazines appeared immediately, as well as numerous translations of erotic and pornographic novels. However, original Czech writings could not compete with translations. The newly opened area has been filled mostly by amateur writers fascinated by the possibility of writing about such topics. In the early 1990s some magazines like *Sextant* tried to raise erotica to an artistic and literary level but these attempts have proven to be commercially unsuccesful. Simple pornographic stories have been anonymously published in numerous booklets. The most prolific was the magazine *Cats* with its *Mini Cats* booklet line and bi-weekly magazine *NEI-Report* whose publisher issued many erotic and pornographic chapbooks. Some of them were bizzare crossovers like the anonymous *Diktatura sexu (Sex Dictatorship*, 1993) mixing elements of pornography, science fiction, and political satire.

Always considered as a dubious paraliterary genre, erotica has received minimal critical examination. As mentioned, the only Czech book dealing with erotic literature—and art—is still K.J. Obratil's *Eroticke ex libris* [*Erotic ex libris*] (1924). The books is an examination of erotic motifs on various ex libris drawings, a concise history of erotic literature in individual countries and also a passionate defence of erotic art in general. Obratil quotes Czech communist politician and poet Stanislav Kostka Neumann: "Erotic works illustrate not only morality, but the entire cultural history of mankind." Now, Obratil is known mostly for his magnificent collection of folk scatological and erotic humor and songs. His magnum opus is *Kryptadia* (limited print run 1938–1939, mass market edition 1999), three volumes of more than 1500 pages in sum. They represent one of the biggest collections of obscene and sexually explicit songs, poems, jokes, wall writings, and customs ever compiled. The songs are complete with music scores and a place where the song has been collected.

During the 1920s there was a broad discussion on the dangers of the lower levels of paraliterature like pornography and dime detective novels. Psychologists, school teachers, librarians, and politicians mostly agreed that this kind of literature is damaging the "nation's health" and, especially, its children. In 1927, there was a symposium organized by Masaryk's Institute of Public Education. Transcripts of the speeches were issued as the pamphlet *O pornografii a braku v literature* [*On Pornography and Trivialliteratur*] (1927). The conclusion of the meeting was that the best way to fight corrupt forms of literature is to promote the good ones. Much more careful and tolerant in his conclusions was the librarian Bohuslav Koutnik who, probably in reaction to the abovementioned transcript, published his own pamphlet *K psychologii literatury pornograficke a brakove* [*Towards the Psychology of Pornography and Trivialliteratur*] (1928). First he dealt with the slippery definiton of pornography. Koutnik saw how subjective the moral measures are, so he came out with a definition: "pornography is what it intends to be—pornography." He tried to calm down the sometimes hysterical "war with the pornography": "The harmfulness of it is generally overestimated and it is quite low in comparision to non-literary and non-artistic influences. Any negative defence by prohibition has small chance to be successful." More recent publication is *Male dejiny pornografie* [*Short History of Pornography*] (2001, ed. by Vaclav Span), an anthology of fragments from both foreign and Czech erotic and pornographic literature, selected mostly from old books and magazines like *Erotická revue*. The book lacks proper bio-bibliographic data and is far from being a critical edition useful for the study of this field.

IVAN ADAMOVIC

D

DACRE, CHARLOTTE

c. 1772–1825
English novelist and poet

Though all of Charlotte Dacre's Gothic novels would seem to have enjoyed reasonably good sales in their day (Byron even thought her a worthwhile target for mockery in his *English Bards and Scotch Reviewers* of 1809), her reputation today is largely based on a single work: *Zofloya; or, The Moor*. Though the work makes no real contribution to the development of the genre (the conventions of the Gothic novel were more or less fixed by 1800), the eroticism of the novel, especially in its portrayal of a heroine who is largely motivated by sexual desire, is undoubtedly more overt and sustained than in the majority of British productions. Indeed, it might even be argued that the novel seeks to subvert the established code of appropriate feminine behavior with its emphasis on piety, domesticity, and submissiveness.

Zofloya recounts the adventurous life of the young Victoria de Loredani in late fifteenth-century Italy. Born into a wealthy Venetian family, she is effectively orphaned when her mother, Laurina, allows herself to be seduced by the plausible but unscrupulous Count Ardolph, a high-ranking German. As a result of this liaison, Victoria's father is killed in a duel; Leonardo, her younger brother, flees the parental home vowing revenge; and Victoria is packed off to a gloomy castle—Il Bosco, near Treviso—where she is ill-treated by an elderly aunt, though it is unclear whether the latter is motivated by religious scruples or an innate sadistic streak.

The main interest of the novel, however, concerns Victoria's conduct after her escape from Il Bosco. Thus far, the reader has tended to sympathize with her as the unwitting victim of circumstances beyond her control. As the novel progresses, she increasingly takes control of events, moving from victim to aggressor in her own right. Returning to Venice, she becomes the mistress of the Conte Berenza, a "philosophical, delicate, and refined voluptuary" (70). Meanwhile, Victoria's brother also reappears, now in the guise of lover to Berenza's cast-off mistress, Megalena. Though the tone is erotically charged throughout (dealing with the careful grooming of a virgin by an older roué and the fascination of an adolescent boy for an older mistress), the language remains coy as to particulars:

The bland seductress Megalena possessed over [Leonardo] an unlimited power; she had caused a new world to open on his view; even yet he was not awakened from the dream of pleasure with which she had bewitched his soul; feelings and ideas, unknown before, swelled in his bosom, and his heart was rapidly becoming immersed in an infatuating sea of voluptuousness. (109)

As is often the case in Gothic fiction, the historical setting only serves to confuse matters. The attitudes and beliefs of Berenza clearly belong to the French Enlightenment of the eighteenth century while the language of the novel generally, which is couched in the terms of Romantic excess, could only be that of the period in which the work was written—this sense of Romantic excess increases as the novel progresses. Victoria, by now married to Berenza, tires quickly enough of him, transferring her affections to his brother, Henriquez. Her mind is also becoming increasingly unhinged. One night, the figure of a Moor, noble and majestic, clad in white robes and a turban bedecked with emeralds and pearls appears to her in a dream. This mysterious and awesome figure, who lends his name to the title of the novel, begins to materialize whenever she wishes, even providing her with a phial of poison. After first testing the poison on an old woman, Victoria embarks on a spree of murders, killing first her husband and then Henriquez's fiancée (who is thrown from a cliff). A further potion supplied by Zofloya allows her to bewitch Henriquez into spending a night of passion with her, though he commits suicide the following morning. Captured by brigands in the Apennines, Victoria watches her brother, the leader of the outlaws, hack Count Ardolph (who has also fallen into his clutches) to death before taking his own life. Victoria then concludes her pact with the devil, in which guise Zofloya now appears.

The fascination with revenge motifs probably ultimately derives from earlier Italian works such as Bandello's *Novelliere* (1554–1573) while the interest in poisons is perhaps inspired by various legends concerning the Borgias and French trial reports relating to the Affaire des Poisons (1672). But the principal model for *Zofloya* is M. G. Lewis's *The Monk* (1796), which likewise involves a pact with the devil. Indeed, the soubriquet Rosa Matilda presumably derives from one of the characters in Lewis's novel. In many respects, Victoria subsumes both the role of the virtuous sister and the corrupt sister, suggesting a familiarity with Sade's *Juliette ou les Prospérités du vice*

(1797). Though Victoria's criminal behavior is variously attributed to her mother's bad example and the heroine's own unbridled sexuality (or "the unrestrained passions of [her] soul,"," as Zofloya puts it (229), a modern feminist reading of the novel would conclude that the (female) reader's initial sympathy for the heroine is intended to lead to a complicity with her later aristocratic pursuit of physical gratification. At the very least, Dacre's representation of female sexuality marks a considerable advance on earlier fiction in the Gothic tradition.

Biography

Charlotte Dacre was probably born in 1772. Her father, a Jewish banker and a familiar figure in fashionable circles, called himself John (or Jonathan) King though his actual name was Jacob Rey. In 1779, he married Jane Rochfort Butler, daughter of the first Earl of Belvedere and widow of the second Earl of Lanesborough. Charlotte and her sister Sophia began writing in the late 1790s, publishing a collection of poems together, *Trifles of Helicon*, in 1798. Both sisters also enjoyed short careers as novelists in the early 1800s. As Rosa Matilda, Charlotte Dacre published four Gothic novels: *Confessions of the Nun of St. Omer* (1805); *Zofloya; or, The Moor: A Romance of the Fifteenth Century* (1806); *The Libertine* (1807); and *The Passions* (1811). Around 1804, Dacre began a liaison with Nicholas Byrne, the married editor of *The Morning Post*, whom she eventually married in 1815. The birth of two sons and a daughter between 1806 and 1809 perhaps implies that the author turned to authorship from financial necessity. She died in 1825, apparently following a long illness; her husband, who died in 1833, was stabbed by a masked man.

TERRY HALE

Selected Works

Rosa Matilda (Charlotte Dacre). *Zofloya; or, The Moor: A Romance of the Fifteenth Century*. 3 vols. London: Longman, Hurst, Rees, and Orms, 1806.

Further Reading

Hoeveler, Diane Long. *Gothic Feminism. The Professionalization of Gender from Charlotte Smith to the Brontës*. College Station, PA: Pennsylvania State University Press, 1998.
Michasiw, Kim Ian (ed.). *Charlotte Dacre: Zofloya; or, The Moor*. Oxford: Oxford University Press ("World Classics"), 1997.

DAIMLER, HARRIET (IRIS OWENS)

1933–
American novelist

The Novels

After writing *Darling*, Owens teamed with Marilyn Meeske on *The Pleasure Thieves*, an erotic reworking of a failed screenplay for a jewel thief caper movie written earlier by Meeske and Terry Southern. The plot of *The Pleasure Thieves* turns upon a merkin, a pubic wig designed to replace hair lost to diphtheria by the character Carol Stoddard; in the funniest scene, Stoddard masturbates with an arm from a plastic mannequin. For inspiration for her next novel, "Daimler" turned to Sade's *Philosophie dans le boudoir*. Owens's own favorite of her works, *The Organization,* self-referentially mimics Sade's dialogic structure so that characters modeled coyly on his can debate the nature of sado-masochism, and amuse themselves sexually in the name of the existentialism popular in Paris in the 1950s.

Daimler's reputation, however, derives from *Darling, Innocence,* and *The Woman Thing.* Taken together as a meditation on female sexuality at mid-twentieth century, they foreground women whose desire is linked with rage at gender inequity. *Darling* is a story of the symbolic death and resurrection of a painter. Gloria Hofstra, a 24-year-old virgin from Kansas City, is raped in her New York apartment house stairwell by a "dead-eyed" man with a knife. Excited by torment, she searches for rough lovers in the bars of Greenwich Village. She has intercourse at a marijuana party with Maurice, Jules, and Conrad; persuades two gay friends, Jack and Harry, to penetrate her simultaneously; and performs oral sex on a stranger in a cinema. Another stranger beats and sodomizes her, but his cruelty is thoughtless, not the single-minded, icy violence that will free her from the husk of a crushed self and liberate her as an artist. Gloria contrasts herself with Laura, long-suffering mistress of Christopher, a philandering sculptor. While Laura is merely a

victim, Gloria aspires to power, not domestic submission. Her recovery begins on Fire Island, where a teacher takes her forcefully but respectfully. At a beach orgy, she enjoys sex with another woman, finding in her lover's body healing reflections of her own. Returning to the city, she discovers her rapist, a trumpeter in a jazz club. Although the man does not remember her, and seems indifferent, she incites him to rape her again. Convinced that his "sperm will be [her] Eucharist" (1967, p. 72), she stabs him to death as she reaches orgasm. Restored to singularity by vengeance, she readies a story of self-defense for the police.

The gothic power struggles of *Innocence*, set in a vaguely American mansion, evolve from sickness, incest, and voyeurism as characters attempt to convert weakness to dominance. The narrator of the first half ("The Girl") is the ambiguously-gendered Adrian Ferdinard, a thirteen-year-old whose parents indulge her tyrannies because she suffers from flawed arteries. Corrupted by weakness, Adrian seduces her nurse, Rose, daily humiliates her, and forces her into an affair with Adrian's father, with whom the daughter identifies in her lust for control. The narrator of the second half ("The Boy") is André, Adrian's cousin, who spies on Adrian's manipulations; they are alter egos, both determined to dominate. Driven by resentment at having been disinherited as Adrian is by hatred of her "genetic" legacy, André trumps Adrian's sadism by sexually appropriating the nurse. When Adrian dies of her illness, however, Andre comes under the sway of Rose, who coolly parlays subservience into power.

While *Innocence* is a parable of claustrophobic sadomasochism, *The Woman Thing*, set in postwar Paris, explores the mind of an American expatriate writer beset with desire, anger, and confusion. The protagonist, Martha Heck, is locked in a destructive affair with MacDonald (based probably on Alexander Trocchi), a writer and heroin addict. Veteran of several abortions, convinced that marriage is a prison, Heck nonetheless wants to love and be loved, though MacDonald derides her belief that sex is a sacrament. Poverty and ethnic conflict—she is Brooklyn Jewish, he a Scot—scar a relationship more scabrous than erotic. Arguments over aesthetics, intercourse that resembles combat, and petty humiliations give meaning to their sex. MacDonald's cheapness and ugliness heighten her orgasms, while he calls her "an infection" (1967, p. 61), a metaphor she embraces, wanting to be the cause of his "disease and decay" (95). Conversations at the Deux Magots Cafe attack Americans as naive, inexperienced, and puritanical, characteristics personified by wealthy James Dykes, an American painter who copies the work of others. Partly because Dykes promises money, food, and a bath, and partly to make MacDonald jealous, Heck models for him. Dykes's lack of originality, he says, is a manifestation of the boredom that is his "strength" (1967, p. 87). When Dykes tells Heck that boredom has made him impotent, she fellates him, whereupon the deceiver promptly ejaculates. Because MacDonald seems indifferent, Heck seeks solace at Notre Dame, where an Austrian named "Adolf" first excites her by calling her a temptress, then dismisses her as a mere "healthy young American" (1967, p. 160). Deciding that "there are no interesting people in Paris" (1967, p. 158), Heck, a Daisy Miller at heart, dreams aimlessly of Spain or Greece. Girodias often cautioned Owens against making her "dirty books" too serious, but the combination of graphic, bruising sex, strong, unsentimental women characters, and perverse but robust intelligence endows them with considerable merit.

Biography

Born in Brooklyn in 1933 and educated, married, and divorced in New York, Iris Owens went to Paris because that "was where one began one's travels in the post-war period" (Iris Owens, conversation with Joseph W. Slade, 12 March 2003). There she met Christopher Logue, Patrick Bowles, Austryn Wainhouse, John Stevenson ("Marcus Van Heller"), and Alexander Trocchi, who supported their avant-garde magazine, *Merlin*, by writing "dirty books" for Maurice Girodias's Olympia Press. Into this circle of expatriates, said Terry Southern, Owens

brought "rapier wit and devastating logic" ("Flashing on Gid," p. 174). When a trip to Spain exhausted her finances, Girodias commissioned her to write several erotic novels, choosing "Harriet Daimler" as the pseudonym for her first, *Darling* (1956). Since returning to the United States, Owens has published two well-received mainstream novels, but nothing since 1984.

JOSEPH W. SLAOE

Selected Works

Darling. Paris: Olympia Press, 1956; North Hollywood, CA: Brandon House, 1967; New York: Grove Press, 1983; reissued as *Darling—Innocence: Two Novels*, New York: Masquerade Books, 1990.

The Pleasure Thieves. with "Henry Crannach" [Marilyn Meeske], Paris: Olympia Press, 1956; San Diego, CA: Greenleaf Classics, 1968.

Innocence. Paris: Olympia Press, 1956; Covina CA: Collectors Publications, 1967; New York: Olympia Press, 1968, 1970; New York: Grove Press, 1983; reissued as *Darling—Innocence: Two Novels*. New York: Masquerade Books, 1990.

The Organization. Paris: Olympia Press, 1957; reissued as *The New Organization*, Paris: Olympia Press, 1962; *The Organization*, San Diego, CA: Greenleaf Classics, 1967; New York: Olympia Press, 1968.

The Woman Thing. Paris: Olympia Press, 1958; reissued as *Woman*, Paris: Olympia Press, 1965; *The Woman Thing*, North Hollywood, CA; Brandon House, 1967; New York: Olympia Press, 1973; New York: Freeway Press, 1974; New York: Grove Press, 1984.

After Claude. New York: Farrar, Straus and Giroux, 1973; New York: Warner Paperback Library, 1973, 1974; London: Quartet, 1973, 1975.

Hope Diamond Refuses: A Novel. New York: Knopf, 1984.

Further Reading

De St. Jorre, John. *Venus Bound: The Erotic Voyage of the Olympia Press and Its Writers*, New York: Random House, 1996 (a.k.a *The Good Ship Venus*, London: Hutchinson, 1994.

Girodias, Maurice. *The Frog Prince*. New York: Crown, 1980.

Girodias, Maurice, ed. *The Olympia Reader*, New York: Grove Press, 1965.

Sawyer-Lausanno, Christopher. *The Continual Pilgrimage: American Writers in Paris, 1944–1960*. New York: Grove Press, 1992.

Southern, Terry. "Flashing on Gid." *Now Dig This: The Unspeakable Writings of Terry Southern, 1950–1995*. Ed. Nile Southern and Josh Alan Friedman. New York: Grove Press, 2001, pp. 168–175.

DAMOURS, LOUIS

French author
c. 1720–1788

Les lettres de Ninon de Lenclos au marquis de Sévigné (1751)

Celebrated courtesan, friend of intellectuals such as Saint-Evremond, Molière, La Rochefoucauld, and Scarron, and one of the most flamboyant women of the seventeenth century, Ninon de Lenclos (c. 1620–1705) had been dead forty-five years when, in 1751, Damours published a collection of fifty letters purporting to be by her. The *Lettres*—an anatomy of love—were addressed to Charles, Marquis de Sévigné (1648–1713), son of the illustrious marquise (1626–1696). Ninon's connection with the Sévigné family went back to 1650 when she enjoyed a brief amorous liaison with Henri (1623–1651), Charles's father. Twenty years later, the 50–year-old Ninon seduced Henri's 23-year-old son, tempting him from his mistress, la Champmeslé (1641–1698). Ninon's short and turbulent fling with Charles (March–April 1771) would have gone undocumented were it not for Charles's close relationship with his letter-writing mother. And though that affair bears no relationship to Damours' *Lettres*, its dénoue-ment is worth remembering. Exasperated and exhausted trying to serve two mistresses, torn between the two, and ultimately rejected by Ninon, Charles suffered a nervous breakdown replete with guilt-induced erotic hallucinations. His mother reported:

> 17 April 1671
>
> He told me last night that during Holy Week, he had gone in for such excess that he had developed a loathing for all that formerly used to make his heart leap; he was afraid to even think about it...and claimed he could see basketsful of breasts, and what-not! Breasts, thighs, kisses, basketsful of all manner of things, and in such abundance that his fancy was consumed with them all and still is.

Annoyed by such histrionics, Ninon lost patience with the young Marquis and after a month she gave him his marching orders—but not before putting it about that he had a soul like pap, a body resembling wet paper and the heart "d'une citrouille fricassée dans de la neige" (a pumpkin fried in snow).

Damours' *Letters* do not at all reflect the tone of the above-quoted anecdotes. Rather, in line with the canons of courtly love, this one-sided correspondence has the young man turn to an older, experienced woman for advice on how best to woo his beloved (an unnamed, widowed Countess). The older woman (the fictional Ninon) coyly acquiesces. She then proceeds to dispense advice in the course of her letters, conceived as responses to the young Marquis's queries and assumptions. Ninon's wit, her familiarity with aristocratic society, with the inner workings of the human heart, and the codes and conventions of *galanterie* make her a compelling confidante (though an insufferable name-dropper). The *Lettres* draw on well-known seventeenth-century antecedents, and describe the subtle progression of the Marquis's affection, from initial flirtation to the promise of an enduring union; every emotional response (and strategy) is recorded and analyzed: feigned indifference, suspicious rivalry, amorous restlessness, *marivaudage,* and so forth. At one point, Ninon even acts as a go-between, arousing both the jealousy of the Countess and the mistrust of the Marquis. Ninon's tone fluctuates between well-bred irony and hectoring exasperation, as she attempts to explain to the Marquis his own feelings and behavior; at the same time they offer a penetrating analysis of the female psyche. Throughout, her advice is constant. Love is physical: the need for love instinctive; it is an appetite dictated in part by vanity and it must be fed. The trick is to control the instinct, and not be controlled by it; hence, Ninon's repeated warnings against deifying the object of desire. In the aristocratic circles described, love-making was like a game of intrigue, a game spoiled by gossip, bad manners, brooding, and scenes. The important thing is to satisfy one's desire without undue or unnecessary suffering. To make a favorable impression, the best strategy is to put on a jovial, disengaged countenance. Old-fashioned ideals of honor and principle are antithetical to love—as is jealousy. In short, love should be a diversion, not a passion, for love-passion is unpredictable, dangerous, and short lived.

Informed by an epicurean sensibility, Damours' *credo* exemplifies a reaction against *préciosité*, and perhaps even against the *larmoyant* sentimental genre then in vogue. Notwithstanding, his ideas can be seen as part of a continuum in French literature which epitomizes love-as-*galanterie*, and whose expression extends from the *Romance of the Rose* to Proust and beyond. Hence, the traditional metaphors: love is to the heart what wind is to the ocean: it allows pleasant journeys but threatens destructive tempests; the lover is like a prospective client eying cloth in a boutique: he should never betray how much he wants the cloth; and most commonly, the lover's role is like that of a general attacking a fortified town: the best strategy is to find the wall's weakest point.

BIOGRAPHY

French lawyer, King's Counsel, Damours was born in Le Lude, a small town in northwest France. After the requisite studies, he was called to the bar and conducted a successful Parisian practice. Author of a number of highly specialized treatises on jurisprudence, economics, and politics, he also wrote two epistolary works under a female *nom de plume*. In 1751, Damours published the *Lettres de Ninon de Lenclos au marquis de Sévigné*. The deception was so well executed, and the letters so well received, that even after he confessed to having written them, an enthusiastic public was reluctant to believe that they were not the authentic work of Ninon de Lenclos, but entirely fictional. The same literary device is evident in Damours *Lettres de Miladi *** sur l'influence que les femmes pourroient avoir sur l'éducation des hommes* (1784), the difference being that the *Miladi* in question is not an historical personage.

E.M. LANGILLE

Editions

Eighteenth Century:

Les lettres de Ninon de Lenclos au marquis de Sévigné. Amsterdam, François Joly, 1750, 1752, 1754, 1757, 1758, 1761, 1767, 1768, 1770, 1772, 1775, 1776, 1779, 1782.

Modern:

Les lettres de Ninon de Lenclos au marquis de Sévigné. Paris, Garnier, 1870; 1879, pp. 327.
German translation, Leipzig, 1755; English translation, London, 1761; Dutch translation, The Hague, 1793.

Further Reading

Cohen, Edgar. *Mademoiselle Libertine*. London, 1970.
Debriffe, Martial. *Ninon de Lenclos: la belle insoumise.* Paris: 2002.

DANDURAND, ANNE, AND CLAIRE DÉ

1953-
French-Canadian writers

Twin sisters whose creative projects have always been complementary, Anne Dandurand and Claire Dé published their first book, *La louve garou*, in tandem in 1982. The she-werewolf of the title suggests the book's main motifs: (heterosexual) erotica and the feminine fantastic. Each story is signed by only one sister, though recurring themes and situations suggest that they read and reacted to each other's pieces during the writing process. Characters and motifs include ogres, witches, love potions, voyeurism, orgies, and fetishism. While some stories are humorous (in one of Dé's pieces, a vampire undergoes orthodontic treatments and makes it in Hollywood as a movie alien), most deal, through fantastic themes, with the life-and-death power of passion. Two lovers are shot at the moment of orgasm by the title she-werewolf observing them from outside (the female serial killer and detective motifs will recur in both women's writing), and their bodies merge for eternity; a woman who imagines her lover is unfaithful sets fire to them both, and they are once again bound together forever, in equal parts of agony and pleasure; a cannibal and an ogress devour one another and fall happily asleep. Though often fatal, love is the greatest good; images of violent death and merging suggest both a wild and lyrical, though ironic, romanticism (in one story, a poplar tree grows out of the heart of a jilted woman) and a fascination with aggressive impulses. Although the two sisters subsequently published separately, teasing references to each other's work continue to appear: in Dandurand's "Les étrennes," a teenager kills her rock star lover and cannot wait to tell her sister, Claire, about the deed; the young narrator of Dé's "L'amour éternel" says she is not a groupie like her sister Anne, then proceeds to murder her own lover.

In Dé's writing, desire is lyrically celebrated, but always as a prelude to loss: *Love as Natural Disaster* is the title of one of her short story collections. Many stories, as well as the novels *Soundless Loves* and *The Sparrow Has Cut the Day in Half* (written in haiku form) feature women who long for sex with their now-indifferent husbands and remember more ardent days. Love is literally these women's oxygen: when deprived of physical tenderness, they suffer devastating asthma attacks, and their choking sorrow is mirrored stylistically by syntaxical gaps and fragmented sentences. Sometimes, though, the roles are reversed and an abandoned man kills himself out of sorrow; love is a power game always lost by the one who loves more. But there are happy moments spent preparing for sex, dreaming of sex, enjoying a new lover, or simply remembering past bliss.

Dandurand's writing ranges from the poetic to the crude. Some stories feature feminist storm troopers out for revenge on callous men; for example, masturbating (and sometimes robbing) them on the subway. The short piece "Histoire de Q," published in 1985 in the now-defunct feminist magazine *La vie en rose*, created a storm of controversy. This parody of Pauline Réage's 1954 *Story of O* (the letter Q, in French, sounds like "cul," or ass; "histoire de cul" means a dirty joke) features a woman who, to take revenge on a lukewarm lover, has him kidnapped by a band of women and held in an isolated manor where he is violated and tortured. He enjoys the pain and discovers he cares for his lover after all; in the end, she appears and devours him. The story can be read as a feminist critique of traditional eroticism through role reversal, as a playful exploration of female aggression, or (Dandurand's explanation of how the story was written) as fantasized revenge on a real-life lover. The story shocked some editors and readers, who felt women's erotica should not be violent, vulgar, or confrontational.

This reaction underestimates the role of fantasy in Dandurand's writing as well as the variety of her approaches to sexuality. The short story collection *Voilà c'est moi: c'est rien j'angoisse*, which includes "Story of Q," also features tales of tender lovemaking in which passion is seen as the only antidote to violence, war, and death (a recurring theme). In "As Moist as Montreal," the narrator describes sex with a stranger in a dark alley, then, in the final paragraph, says she made it all up to keep things interesting between herself and her current lover. In a number of her books, including *Voilà c'est moi...* and the novel *Cracks*, Dandurand plays with the idea of an "imaginary diary," blurring the boundaries between reality and fiction and creating a safe space to explore and perhaps act on fantasies. In *The Waiting Room*, the narrator (who may be a succubus) imagines sex scenes involving herself, patients, and the doctor in various combinations. Though much of Dandurand's writing—often poetic, metaphorical, and lexically rich—joyfully celebrates sexual desire, her female characters suffer, like Dé's, at the hands of lukewarm or unfaithful men, though they are more likely to take violent revenge. For consolation, they return to their "imaginary diaries" to retell the story, to forget, to exorcise, or to change its ending. Men, though ardently desired, ultimately disappoint; writing never does.

Despite its insistent Gothic trappings and longing for happy endings, Dandurand's and Dé's writing is resolutely contemporary, pairing active, intense, sometimes aggressive women who "love too much"" and less-committed men. Often, the women are long-suffering victims (though even the wife in *Soundless Loves* ties up her husband, whips him, and excites him sexually before leaving him in a hotel room—but this may be a simple fantasy); they can be remorseless killers too. Critics have praised their boldness, their willingness to explore the dark side of sexuality, and their playful questioning of gender stereotypes. Both writers, working at the margins, take as their material violence, sadism, and emotional masochism as well as the delights of shared desire, offering extreme situations, a realistic portrait of human feelings and brief but intense erotic scenes.

Biography

Twin sisters born in 1953 in Montreal (Dé is the letter D, for Dandurand, made into a surname). They have been publishing together and separately since 1982. In 1987–1988, they co-wrote a TV series. Dandurand has been an actress, a union organizer, and a journalist; Dé has been involved in theater design and literary translation, and has written for the radio. Several of their books have been translated into English.

LORI SAINT-MARTIN

Selected Works

La louve garou. Montreal: Pleine lune, 1982.
Three By Three: Short Stories. Tr. Luise von Flotow, Montréal: Guernica, 1992.
Voilà, c'est moi: c'est rien, j'angoisse. Montréal: Triptyque, 1987.
L'assassin de l'intérieur/Diables d'espoir. Montréal, XYZ, 1988.

Deathly Delights. Tr. Luise von Flotow. Vehicule Press: 1991.
Un cœur qui craque. VLB: 1990. *Cracks*. Tr. Luise von Flotow, Stratford, Mercury Press, 1992.
Petites âmes sous ultimatum. XYZ: 1991; *Small Souls Under Siege*. Tr. Robert Majzels, Dunvegan, Ont.: Cormorant Books, 1991.
La salle d'attente. XYZ: 1994; *The Waiting Room*. Trans. Robert Majzels. Stratford: Mercury Press, 1999.
La marquise ensanglantée. Montréal, XYZ: 1996.
Les porteuses d'ombre. Montréal: Planète rebelle. 1999.
Le désir comme catastrophe naturelle. Montreal/Paris: L'étincelle, 1989; *Desire as Natural Disaster*. Tr. Lazer Lederhendler. Toronto: Exile Press, 1995.
Chiens divers (et autres faits écrasés). Montreal. XYZ, 1991.
Sentimental à l'os. Montreal: VLB, 1991.
Sourdes amours. Montréal: XYZ, 1993. *Soundless Loves: A Novella*. Tr. Lazer Lederhendler. Toronto: Exile Press, 1996.
Bonheur, oiseau rare. Roman pointilliste sous forme de haïku: Montréal, XYZ, 1996; *The Sparrow Has Cut the Day in Half*. Tr. Lazer Lederhendler. Toronto: Exile Press. 1998.

Further Reading

Gilbert, Paula Ruth, and Lorna Irvine. "Pre- and Post-Mortem: Regendering and Serial Killing in Rioux, Dandurand, Dé, and Atwood." *The American Review of Canadian Studies* (Spring 1999): 113–133.
Kellett-Betsos, Kathleen. "Anne Dandurand et le journal imaginaire." Lucie Joubert, ed. *Trajectoires au féminin dans la littérature québécoise (1960–1990)*. Québec: Éditions Nota bene, 2000: 35–48.
Saint-Martin, Lori. "Playing With Gender, Playing with Fire: Anne Dandurand's and Jeanne Le Roy's Feminist Parodies of *Histoire d'O*." *Nottingham French Studies*, 40.1 (Spring 2001): 31–40.
Von Flotow, Luise. "'Tenter l'érotique': Eroticism in Contemporary Women's Writing in Québec." *Québec Studies* 10 (Spring–Summer 1990): 91–97.
Von Flotow, Luise. "Women's Desiring Voices from Quebec: Nicole Brossard, Anne Dandurand, Claire Dé." Godon Collier, ed. *Us/Them: Translation, Transcription and Identity in Post-Colonial Literary Cultures*, Amsterdam/Atlanta: Rodopi, 1992: 109–119.

DEFOE, DANIEL

British novelist and journalist
1660–1731

Moll Flanders

Defoe's suggestively titled *Conjugal Lewdness: A Treatise Concerning the Use and Misuse of the Marriage-Bed* deals little with eroticism *per se,* except to condemn it outright as an end in itself. And, in spite of the inclusion on the frontispiece of *Moll Flanders* that his heroine was "Twelve Year a Whore" ("whore" meaning simply a woman who has sex outside of marriage) and "five times a Wife (whereof once to her own Brother)," Defoe's modern critics see the drive for economic survival as leaving little energy in his characters for sexual feeling. Moll's emotional life was formed at the very start when her mother was transported for felony. At three years old, the magistrates of Colchester place her in the care of a poor woman. When she is about fourteen years old, she is taken in by a wealthy family and seduced by the elder son. He offers her gold, but there is no doubt that she feels an overwhelming passion for him; after he discards her, she says "the agonies of my Mind [...] threw me into a high Feaver..." She is kept in bed by her illness for five weeks and afterwards is emotionally deadened towards men, who *then* become mostly objects of calculation to her. Yet sexual desire does not disappear. One married gentleman offers to sleep with her without any intercourse, but about this arrangement she was not "so wholly pleas'd ... as he thought I was," and, though she moralizes about it afterwards, is glad he finally has intercourse with her. But her strong passion is only reawakened later on by "Jemy," whom she calls her Lancashire husband. They must part, but her feelings for the child she has by him show her to be in no way heartless or cold. When she loses her looks she turns thief, but, after she has been arrested and is in danger of being hanged, she is stirred to make efforts for her survival only because she catches a glimpse of him in the same prison. She

succeeds in saving him and herself, and, transported to Virginia, grows rich with him and "died a penitent." Whatever moral Defoe intends, or pretends, in giving this account of Moll's life, the novel may well seem to be recommending strong sexual love as the really positive force in life.

Roxana

Though twentieth-century academic efforts have sought moral structure in *Roxana, The Fortunate Mistress*, readers may persist in regarding the novel as a series of adventures in the life of a courtesan. "At about Fifteen Years of Age, my father...married me to an Eminent Brewer," Roxana says, but he abandons her with five children and no money. She disengages herself from the children and begins a picaresque life with her servant, Amy, who feels a "violent Affection" for Roxana and sleeps in the same bed with her. Amy helps Roxana understand that, for a woman, unless she has money, life will be determined by the lust she arouses in men. Thus her kindly landlord, who later on is discovered to be a wealthy jeweller, soon reveals that he wants to make her his mistress, and succeeds. In spite of her moralistic protestations, Roxana enjoys her subsequent life as his mistress. And in spite of how she moralizes in the telling of it, presumably even her making Amy have sex with him doesn't qualify as any "interruption" in their happiness. Indeed, she enjoyed stripping off Amy's clothes and throwing her into bed with him. After they go to France together, however, her jeweller-lover is murdered in a robbery. Almost immediately she is aided by a Continental Prince. "Princes did not court like other Men," he says, tells her what he wants, what he can give her, and allows her one chance to accept or refuse. During this relationship, she learns that "Great Men...value not squandering away immense Wealth" because "they raise the Value of the Object which they pretended to pitch upon, by their Fancy." She gives him a child, and "it was something wonderful to me, to see this Person so exceedingly delighted at the

Birth of this Child, and so pleas'd with it..."
Her whole relationship with him lasts eight
years, and, though he had a wife and "two or
three Women, which he kept privately, he had
not in all that Time meddled with any of them."
Presumably male fidelity is the consequence of
powerful sexual desire for a particular woman,
but this happiness can be interrupted by the fits
of guilt to which men are prone. In this case, it is
brought on by the near death of the Prince's
wife, and he gives up Roxana. She must now
convey her fortune safely back to England.
Lust again comes to her aid with the Dutch
merchant, who, though married, commits himself so thoroughly to her cause that he will lose a
fortune and be driven out of Paris. When the
merchant appears in Rotterdam, he tells her his
wife is dead and begins to court her openly. "I
could not but smile however," she says, because
she has known the Prince and through his dir-
ectness the real motives of men. He finally has
intercourse with her and wants to marry her
afterwards, but Roxana refuses—in order to
keep control of her money and, pregnant,
returns to England. It is in London that the
famous episode of her dance in the Turkish
dress occurs—a dance that excites the King.
She amasses a great deal of money, but is beginning now to lose her looks. She takes up with a
Lord, who in his advanced age has "capricious
Humours," but he finally sickens her and she
gets rid of him. At fifty-odd years of age, she
sums up her adventures in these words:

> I may venture to say, that no Woman ever liv'd a Life
> like me, of six and twenty Years of Wickedness,
> without the least Signals of Remorse [...] I had so
> long habituated myself to a Life of Vice, that really
> it appear'd to be no Vice to me ...

Now she thinks of the five children she had to
leave years before. She does what she can for
them and re-encounters her Dutch merchant. In
his sharing of their wealth together she sees proof
of mutual trust. But Susan, her crazed daughter,
reappears, craving her mother, who cannot own
her as her daughter without destroying her relationship with her husband, and Amy, thinking
to please Roxana, murders Susan. The novel

concludes by declaring that "the Blast of Heaven
seem'd to follow the Injury done the poor Girl,
by us both," but, as in *Moll Flanders*, the moralistic pretensions of the novelist seem betrayed by
his power to portray human experience.

Biography

Born in 1660 in London, son of a tradesman.
Attended school of Rev. James Fisher and then
Rev. Charles Morton's Dissenting Academy. In
1883, a London hosiery merchant. Married in
1683. 1685 took part in Monmouth's rebellion.
Trade and travel the next seven years; in 1688
joined the march of William of Orange on
London. Bankruptcy in 1692. 1697: *Essay on
Projects*. 1697–1701: political agent for William
III. 1703: made to stand in pillory for *The Short-
est Way with the Dissenters*. 1703–1714: secret
agent for government. 1719: *Robinson Crusoe*.
1722: *Moll Flanders, Colonel Jack,* 1724: *Roxana*,
1727: *Conjugal Lewdness*. Died in London, April
1731.

GERALD J. BUTLER

Selected Works

Good Advice to Ladies. 1702
Moll Flanders. 1722
Colonel Jack. 1722
Roxana, The Fortunate Mistress. 1724
Conjugal Lewdness. 1727

Further Reading

Backscheider, Paula. "Defoe's Women: Snares and
Prey." *Studies in Eighteenth-Century Culture* 5
(1976): 103–120.
Birdsall, Virginia Ogden. *Defoe's Perpetual Seekers: A
Study of the Major Fiction*. Lewisburg: Bucknell
University Press. 1985.
Chandler, Frank. *The Literature of Roguery*. 2 vols.
Boston: Houghton Mifflin, 1907.
Dottin, Paul. *The Life and Strange and Surprising Ad-
ventures of Daniel De Foe*. Trans. Louis Ragan,
New York: Maculay, 1929.
Novak, Maxmillian E. *Realism, Myth, and History in
Defoe's Fiction*. Lincoln, NE: University of Nebraska
Press, 1983.
Woolf, Virginia. "Defoe." *The Common Reader*. New
York: Harcourt, Brace and Co. 1925.

DEFORGES, RÉGINE

1935–
French writer and publisher

While Deforges's own writing, located in the popular rather than the intellectual zone of the cultural spectrum, has not been accorded the serious critical attention increasingly given to other women writers of erotic fiction, she has nonetheless played an important role in various aspects of French cultural life in the second half of the twentieth century. She has been active in publishing, the cinema, and in writing. She played a significant part in the battles against literary censorship during the 1960s and 1970s in her capacity as publisher of erotic literature. She has written novels, both historical and loosely autobiographical, and erotic short stories as well as interviews and children's literature. As a writer she has made her own contribution to the growing body of erotic works written by women in French in the latter part of the century, helping to dispel the notion that erotic writing is predominantly male-authored. One of the books she read on a trip to Senegal in the late 1950s was Pauline Réage's novel *Story of O*. This work and its author were to have a particular influence on Deforges's developing career. Pauvert, who had originally published *Story of O*, and who had helped keep secret the identity of its author, arranged for Deforges to meet Réage for a series of interviews which were published as *O m'a dit: entretiens avec Pauline Réage* in 1975. The encounter with Réage was a very positive one for Deforges, who found that she had much in common with her interviewee, and their discussion proved vital in encouraging Deforges to begin writing herself.

Her earliest works were fictionalized autobiography, not erotic works in themselves, in the sense of works where erotic encounters drive forward the narrative. They were, however, works where sensuality and female pleasure play a significant role in character development. *Le Cahier volé* (1978) [*The Stolen Notebook*] is the work where these themes are most in the forefront.

The novel recounts the author's close physical relationship with a school friend, a relationship which in real life had led to her exclusion from school. There is a textual ambivalence about Deforges's presentation of lesbian sexuality which reflects a similar ambivalence in real life, for while her erotic encounters with the fictional Mélie are lovingly and sensually detailed, they are also explicitly identified by the narrator as a preparation for a more authentic male–female encounter.

Deforges has produced a range of other novels, mainly historical narratives, which foreground sensual female characters, but which are not erotic narratives. *La bicyclette bleue* [*The Blue Bicycle*] series is a case in point, tracing the central female character Léa Delmas, and her turbulent relationship with lover François Tavernier, through various key moments of France's recent historical past. Léa's exuberant sensuality finds expression not just in her enjoyment of sex, but also in her appreciation of food, nature, and the land.

While Deforges's novels invariably find a place for the celebration of female sensuality, it is in her short stories that she has concentrated exclusively on the exploration of female erotic experience. These works include three collections of short stories: *Contes pervers* [*Perverse Tales*] (1980), *Lola et quelques autres* [*Lola and Friends*] (1983), *Rencontres ferroviaires* [*Railway Encounters*] (1999) and *L'Orage, roman* [*The Storm, A Novel*] (1996), a work which, given its brevity, has more in common with Deforges's short stories than with her other novels, all of which are of substantial length.

Contes pervers and *L'Orage* contain the more transgressive subject matter, while *Lola et quelques autres* and *Rencontres ferroviaires* are more self-conscious, organized around themes and places. Unlike Deforges's other works, however, the focus of all four is female erotic experience. *Lola et quelques autres* contains a sequence of 13 stories, each of which takes its title from the name of its central character, in each case a woman whose name begins with the letter L. Each central character is identified with a particular area of Paris, described in the author's preface as 'la ville-femelle par excellence.' The stories recount sexual encounters in various parts of the city, in churches, outdoors, in libraries, featuring women old and young exploring and redefining the limits of their sexual experience, whether through multiple partners, encounters with strangers, female domination, or even the recognition that those deemed by polite society to be beyond the sexual pale, such as transvestites and older women, also have their right to erotic experience. *Rencontres ferroviaires* has a thematic link in that the stories are inspired by trains, stations, and railway journeys. Each of the six stories has in its title the name of a Paris mainline railway station. These stories are more self-conscious, with the author intervening to recount her own memories of trains, stations, even quoting at length from a story told elsewhere to provide a context for another set of erotic encounters, for the most part between unidentified strangers. The periodic use of the first person pronoun suggests, as does more explicitly some of the text, that the author has made use either of real events or of her own fantasies in the writing of the stories.

Contes pervers, as its title suggests, makes greater use of transgressive material, notably in its depiction of female characters who experience sexual pleasure in situations of submission, abjection, and violence, though in the penultimate story of the collection, the violence is experienced as an unwelcome form of aggression for its victims, a woman and her transvestite lover. *L'Orage, roman* recounts the grief of a young woman recently widowed, and who subjects herself to a sadomasochistic episode with the local village idiot, his father, brother, and dog, in order to fulfil a fantasy suggested by her dead spouse, a fantasy she had rejected when he was alive. The pain and abjection she suffers are depicted as a measure of her love for her husband, an offering to him, and in narrative terms act as the prelude to her suicide which will enable her to rejoin him in death.

Deforges poses some awkward questions, particularly for the female reader, by her tendency to cast women in submissive roles, by her depictions of sexual violence directed against women and her ambivalent attitude to lesbianism. There is little sense of a challenge to patriarchal values in her work. On the other hand, there is a more generous and liberating side to her erotic writing in its exploration of the variety and empowering nature of female erotic experience.

Biography

Born in Montmorillon, in the Poitou region of France on 15 August 1935. Excluded from school at the age of 15, after a complaint about her close relationship with another girl, her formal education was terminated early. Soon after, the family followed the father to Africa, where he was working in Guinea. Here, in the absence of a local *lycée* where she could continue her disrupted education, Deforges began work. She returned to France the following year and married her first husband Pierre Spengler in 1953, a marriage which was to last until 1964. She had a son by him, a daughter by Jean-Jacques Pauvert, and another daughter by her second husband Pierre Wiazemsky. In 1958, her long association with the world of publishing began when she started work in a bookshop. Through her work she met and began a long relationship with Jean-Jacques Pauvert the publisher. In 1965, they opened a bookshop together in which she had responsibility for the erotic books section. In 1968, she opened her own publishing house, L'Or du temps, which specialized in the publication of erotic literature. Deforges paid a high price for her interest in erotic literature, suffering regular legal actions brought against her as editor. Eventually, L'Or du temps went into liquidation in 1972. She began writing in the mid-1970s and continues to do so today. She is a member of the jury of the Prix Fémina.

ANGELA KIMYONGÜR

Selected Works

Interviews

O m'a dit: entretiens avec Pauline Réage. Paris: J-J Pauvert. 1975.
Les non-dits de Régine Deforges, entretiens, Lucie Wisperheim. Paris: Stock. 1997.
Entre Femmes, entretien, Jeanne Bourin. Paris: Blanche. 1999.

Fiction

Blanche et Lucie. Paris: Fayard, 1976.
Le cahier volé. Paris: Fayard, 1978.
Contes pervers, nouvelles. Paris: Fayard, 1980.

La révolte des nonnes. Paris: La Table Ronde, 1981.
Les enfants de Blanche. Paris: Fayard, 1982.
Lola et quelques autres. Paris: Fayard, 1983.
La bicyclette bleue.
La bicyclette bleue. Paris: Ramsay 1981.
101 Avenue Henri Martin. Paris: Ramsay, 1983.
Le diable en rit encore. Paris: Ramsay, 1985.
Noir tango. Paris: Fayard, 1991.
Rue de la Soie (1947–1949). Paris: Fayard, 1994.
La derniere colline (1950–1954). Paris: Fayard, 1996.
Cuba Libre! (1955–1959). Paris: Fayard, 1999.
Alger, ville blanche (1959–1969). Paris: Fayard, 2001.
Pour l'amour de Marie Salat. Paris: Albin Michel, 1986.
Sous le ciel de Novgorod. Paris: Fayard, 1988.
L'Orage, roman. Paris: Blanche, 1996.
Rencontres ferroviaires. Paris: Fayard, 1999.

Further Reading

Baronheid, Marc-Emile. *Régine Deforges. L'Inconduite,* Paris: Stock. 1995.
Brécourt-Villars, Claudine. *Ecrire d'amour: Anthologie des textes érotiques féminins 1799–1984.* Paris: Ramsay, 1985.
Frappier-Mazur, Lucienne. "Marginal Canons: Rewriting the Erotic," *Yale French Studies,* 'The Politics of Tradition: Placing Women in French Literature', no. 75, 1988, pp. 112–128.
Alex Hughes & Kate Ince (editors.) *French Erotic Fiction. Women's Desiring Writing, 1880–1990.* Oxford: Berg, 1996.
Richard, Anne. Entry on Régine Deforges *in Dictionnaire littéraire des femmes de langue française.* Paris: Karthala, 1996.

DEKOBRA, MAURICE

1885–1973
French popular novelist, travel writer, journalist

The name of Maurice Dekobra (1885–1973), derived from the 'deux cobras' that an African clairvoyant had used to read the Frenchman's destiny, was synonymous during his lifetime with globetrotting polyglot, ladies' man, and bestselling author. The most famous and successful of France's populist writers between the World Wars, Dekobra left an œuvre of around one hundred works. These consist mostly of novels, but also film scripts, plays, short stories, essays, and poetry, as well as translations (e.g., Defoe, Jack London), prefaces, anthologies, three autobiographies (including one in English) and countless newspaper articles. The pervasive mood of Dekobra's creative writing is erotic. His poetry—*Luxures* (1924) and pseudonymous erotica identified by Jean-Jacques Pauvert—mimics Symbolist decadence in its drug-addled suicidal spleen and seedy sexual underworld. His screenplays include adaptations of his own novels, as well as *The Siren of the Tropics,* written for Josephine Baker, the African-American cabaret celebrity and exotic sexual icon. It is in Dekobra's prose, however, that his erotic talent is fully developed, in a neo-Romantic style of exclamation marks, ellipses, literary ruminations, and extended punning imagery taken from popular science, philosophy, and history, as well as geometry:

> 'Woman is an obtuse angle that often changes its bisector.' (...) How many well-brought-up young women have we surprised in the complicitous penumbra of discreet boudoirs, who, for lack of a bisector, were studying the virtues of the isosceles triangle? (*Tu seras courtisane,* p. 26)

Dekobra's eroticism has two principal expressions. Bawdiness is usually reserved for humorous tales, such as *La Vénus à roulettes* (1925), played out by local laborers, prostitutes, petty thieves, and the odd foreigner in Paris bars and bedrooms. A more problematic version is found in his international works, especially the series of five exotic romances subtitled 'cosmopolitan novels' (1924–1928), which specialize in evasionism and a kind of primer of the planet's people and politics. *La Madone des sleepings* (1925), France's first bestseller and the epitome of Dekobra's œuvre, made him a contender for most-read French novelist worldwide. It also introduced his most notorious characters: Lady Diana Wynham, a beautiful wealthy widow, resolutely sexually active; and Irina Mouravieff, a sadistic Bolshevik fanatic.

Professional Acumen

As might be expected from a first-rate journalist, Dekobra was extremely skilled at exploiting contemporary phenomena, including the dramatic increase in female readership—at whom the publicity for his novels was exclusively aimed. A creator of memorable heroines, he was considered an expert on women, both as a gender and in their national differences. This was much utilized in his travel writings—where it supplied erotic thrills clandestinely, as pseudo-sociology and -ethnography—and in such works as *Le Geste de Phryné*, a collection of short stories divided into romances Scandinavian, Argentinean, Egyptian, etc. Dekobra also took advantage of fashionable settings: the bohemian gatherings of Montmartre, the frivolous and louche proto-Jet Set that was evolving from Europe's crumbling aristocracies and included international artists, scientists, diplomats, and American *nouveaux riches*. It is these men and women of the world who people his major novels, which allows him to recycle the literary tradition of *erotica per exotica*—mobile white man meets foreign woman in exotic location, sexual frisson ensues—in the context of contemporary socio-political upheavals. French literary exoticism, in sharp decline by the 1910s, was being revived by both the post-war publishing boom and the public's renewed fixation with all things foreign: mass tourism was establishing itself; reportage, particularly about the empire, was at its height; and cultural diversity at home was increasing because of the migrations of soldiers and refugees during and after the First World War. Dekobra responded with characters from and plots set in America, Europe, the Middle and Far East, and Africa, drawing on his own solo travels for documentation.

The Patriotism of Sex

There is, however, tension in Dekobra's exotic eroticism. The foreign heroine, while nominally independent both financially and emotionally, requires the (normally French) hero's help with various existential crises. This gives rise to sustained chemistry, but while Dekobra's heroines have largely jettisoned moral conventions, social considerations still intervene: the sudden restraints imposed by revolutions or economic downturns, his heroes' deliberate anachronistic chivalry. The resulting non-consummation causes frustration. It also permits regular cliff-hangers and discharges of libertine conversation.

Dekobra's raciness also depends on a backdrop of political violence and his version of psychoanalysis, a novelty in 1920s' France. His Parisian laborer workers treat sex as enjoyable but unremarkable, the members of his Smart Set as an emblem of the libertarian freedoms they blithely enjoy. Dekobra's Bolshevik characters, on the other hand, showcase their atavistic aggression by using sex as a commodity for barter and instrument of domination: lethal Irina Mouravieff is a pretty dominatrix, the 'Marquise de Sade of Red Russia'. Psychoanalysis is similarly associated with sexual control rather than therapy, resulting in a "bewitchment" akin to hypnotism or magnetism. In *Flammes de velours*, the sinister Dr Schomberg trains women in being *femmes fatales* at his hypnotic command. More light-heartedly, Lady Diana's analysis with Professor Siegfried Traurig consists of dream interpretation, sexual-history rehash, and an X-ray machine for 'the spectral analysis of your reactions during orgasm'. This orgasmometer reveals the patient's unconscious and allows Dekobra to treat sex in his habitually titillating manner, conceptually explicit and yet physically coy: the climax is brought about by a simple kiss.

That the two grand theories of communism and psychoanalysis are represented as perverse pansexualisms in their joylessness, functionalism, and stark gender disequilibrium has two implications. Dekobra polices the borders of the French psyche against the invasion of foreign carnal cultures and, by juxtaposition, promotes the French sexual tradition as the uncomplicated unpoliticized norm: male chivalry and "healthy" female willingness (especially from the widows, actresses, and 'spasm merchants' who constitute most of his minor characters). Many heroines, by contrast, are denied real happiness because of their emasculating sexual potency and "neurotic" promiscuity. Thrilling, but ultimately deniable, desires of total female emancipation and sexual self-control are thus safely acted out, and moralistically rejected, on behalf of Dekobra's women readers—from whom he received over 75,000 items of fan mail.

Under the banner of an urban(e) and patriotic erotic appeal, Dekobra skillfully combined exotic "perversions," traditional gender politics, current-affairs sensationalism, and demographic targeting to make his mark.

Biography

Born Ernest Maurice Tessier in Paris, 26 May 1885. Educated at Collège Rollin, Paris, 1895–1902. Moved to Germany 1902: factory work, French lessons, occasional Berlin correspondent for small French newspapers (arts criticism, society pages). From 1905 freelance London correspondent. Military service in Orléans, 1906–1908. From 1908 increasingly successful Paris journalist under new legal name of Maurice Dekobra, specializing in foreign reportage. Interpreter for Indian, British, and American Armies in First World War. As fulltime writer, traveled almost continuously in Europe, Africa, Middle East, 1921–1928; on Indian subcontinent, 1929; in United States and Far East, 1930–1934. Resided in New York and Hollywood, 1939–1946. Died of cardiac arrest in Paris, 2 June 1973.

TOM GENRICH

Selected Works

Luxures. Paris: Éditions d'art des Tablettes, 1924.
Tu seras courtisane. Paris: Éditions du Siècle, 1924.
Mon cœur au ralenti: roman cosmopolite. Paris: Baudinière, 1924. *Wings of Desire.* Trans. Neal Wainwright. London: Laurie, 1927.
La Vénus à roulettes. Paris: Éditions de La Nouvelle Revue critique, 1925. *Venus on Wheels.* Trans. Metcalfe Wood. London: Laurie, 1930.
La madone des sleepings: roman cosmopolite. Paris: Baudinière, 1925. *The Madonna of the Sleeping Cars.* Trans. Neal Wainwright. London: Laurie, 1927.
La gondole aux chimères: roman cosmopolite. Paris: Baudinière, 1926. *The Phantom Gondola.* Trans. Neal Wainwright. London: Laurie, 1928.
Flammes de velours: roman cosmopolite. Paris: Baudinière, 1927. *Flames of Velvet.* Trans. F.M. Atkinson. London: Laurie, 1929.
Sérénade au bourreau: roman cosmopolite. Paris: Baudinière, 1928. *Serenade to the Hangman.* Trans. Neal Wainwright. London: Laurie, 1929.
Le Geste de Phryné: amours exotiques. Paris: Éditions des Portiques, 1930. *Phryné, or, Love as a Fine Art.* Trans. Metcalfe Wood. London: Laurie, 1931.
Written with Lipstick. London: Hutchinson, [1938?].

Further Reading

Collas, Philippe. *Maurice Dekobra: gentleman entre deux mondes.* Paris: Séguier, 2002.
Davis, Robert Leslie. 'Maurice Dekobra: grand voyageur et romancier cosmopolite', unpublished doctoral thesis, Queen's University, Belfast, 1970.
d'Hariel, Jacqueline, and E. Gerber. *La Vie cosmopolite de Maurice Dekobra.* Paris: Éditions de la Nouvelle Librairie française, 1931.
Genrich, Tom. Chapter on Dekobra in *Authentic Fictions: Cosmopolitan Writing in the Troisième République, 1908–1940.* Oxford: Peter Lang, forthcoming.
Pauvert, Jean-Jacques. Entry on Dekobra in his *Anthologie historique des lectures érotiques*, 4 vols, Paris: Stock/Spengler, 1995.
Ripert, Pierre. "Le 'Best-seller' des wagons-lits." *Le Figaro,* 28 September 1974: 14.
Springer, Léon J. "Dekobra und Genossen." *Deutsch-französische Rundschau,* 1/6 (June 1928): 488–497.
Tonnet-Lacroix, Éliane. "Maurice Dekobra: romancier cosmopolite." In *Le Roman populaire en France au XXe siècle,* edited by Aleksander Ablamowicz. Katowice: University of Silesia, 1991.

DELANY, SAMUEL R.

1942–
American Novelist and Critic

Samuel R. Delany is a protean talent with a wide readership. Impatient with the traditional tropes of the science-fiction genre, his S-F novels are highly stylized, self-reflexive romances, stories that often seem constructed from fragments of colored glass. He has been equally impatient with the conventions of erotic writing. He finished *The Tides of Lust* in 1968, but it wasn't until its republication as *Equinox* in 1994 that critics and readers could see the true intentions of the work. There is an urgency to *Equinox* not found in Delany's speculative fiction. In it he has devils to exorcise, and means to persuade as of his intellectual seriousness. All the characters in *Equinox* seem but different aspects of one character, the author: the African-American Captain, on whose boat, *The Scorpion*, travel two children, Kirsten and Gunner, brought to India by the Captain for sexual service; an artist, Proctor; Catherine, a countess, mysterious, fatal; and Robby, a drifter who becomes the catalyst for the climactic scene of the novel.

The story is not complicated, although Delany's language is. It is the episodic narrative of a sexual voyage given added significance by Delany's technique of casting flashbacks in the form of reminiscences supposedly written by his characters. Incest, rape, masturbation, urolagnia, sodomy, necrophilia—every variety of sexual appetite is delineated with a corrosive savagery seldom seen in erotic writing. The role of the artist is a major theme. Delany is aware that he is the poet making myth out of his fantasies, but the sum of this artifice is a powerful novel in which sexual categories are rendered meaningless.

Hogg is a tour de force, a sacred monster. It stands almost alone in contemporary erotic writing, on a top shelf between Sade and Bataille, well out of the reach of even the most tolerant reader of sexual material. Written in 1969, finished days before the Stonewall riots, revised during the period when he was writing *Dahlgren*, *Hogg* resisted publication until 1995. It is the most politically incorrect, no holds barred, no sacred cow left unslaughtered, deliberately evil narrative most readers will ever encounter. Narrated by a mute eleven-year-old boy, it is a non-stop farrago of the forbidden, the cloacal, the assaultive, and transgressive. Utterly without redeeming social value, most would say, it is without question a literary masterpiece, a triumph of style over the violence of its content; so much so that it becomes what some critics have called "anti-pornography."

The first half of *Hogg* places us in Hell, a cellar with four rapists: the title character is a memorable beast, a sadistic misogynist, lord of this underworld articulate enough to voice some basic truths about racism, sexism, and violence. Hogg is Destruction embodied, just as the nameless boy narrator is Submission.

The situation only gets worse, as child molestation, murders, and rapes follow. The author, a black homosexual, expresses in Hogg a raging, transgressive hostility toward modern liberal shibboleths while at the same time analyzing sexism and racism with the ferocity of a brilliant child burning ants with a magnifying glass. *Hogg* is for the few and the select. (A year before her untimely death, the novelist Kathy Acker was most looking forward to reading *Hogg*).

First published in 1994, *The Mad Man* was reissued in 2002 in a heavily revised version. It is once again deliberately provocative in its celebration of promiscuous gay sex in the age of AIDS. Delany's protagonist is a graduate student named John Marr who is doing his thesis on Timothy Hasler, a philosopher murdered at a gay sex club years before. Marr becomes Hasler's biographer, and moves into his old building. As he uncovers Hasler's life, Marr becomes involved erotically with homeless men in his neighborhood. Two parallel story lines rife with sexual excess converge in a sprawling novel that is both mystery and love story. While the sexuality depicted in *The Mad Man* is as over the top as that in *Hogg*, here Delany's vision is more positive but equally as radical: he stands up for pleasure. Despite all the risky, raunchy sex he has, John Marr does not get AIDS.

Set in the time of the Emperor Hadrian, *Phallos* (2004) is a homoerotic novella which asks the question: How should gay men go about integrating pleasure with the ordinary vicissitudes of life? It is a tale within a tale, erudite and witty.

Delany's Speculative Fiction series *Return to Neveryon*, has the distinction of being the first novel from a major US publisher to deal with AIDS in the gay and straight communities.

In his erotic writing, Delany boldly asserts the primacy of pleasure. He demonstrates the possibilities for subversion in the genre.

Biography

Born Samuel Ray Delany in New York City, 1942. Educated at The Dalton School and the Bronx High School of Science. Attended City College of New York, 1960, 1962–1963. Ace Books published his first novel of speculative fiction, *The Jewels of Aptor*, in 1962. His first erotic novel, *The Tides of Lust*, was published by

Lancer in 1973. He is a prolific novelist and critic, and a major figure in the world of speculative fiction. He has held many distinguished academic posts, including appointments at SUNY Buffalo, University of Massachusetts at Amherst, and Temple University. His best known S-F work is *Dahlgren*, 1975. His most important erotic novel arguably is, *Hogg*, 1995.

Many volumes of criticism have been devoted to his work.

MICHAEL PERKINS

Selected Works

Equinox. 1994.
Hogg. 1995.
Phallos. 2004.

DELEUZE, GILLES AND FÉLIX GUATTARI

Deleuze, Gilles 1925–1995
Guattari, Félix 1930–1992
French philosopher and French analyst/social theorist

Deleuze and Guattari are not concerned with specific meanings or representations in literature; instead, they seek to engage with a text's potential for invention and transformation, what they refer to as its forces of "becoming" (*What is Philosophy?*). Literature for Deleuze and Guattari is vital when it plays with indirect discourse and infinitives, that is, subjectless or collective modes of speech which reveal the incorporeal lines of difference which enable such speech to take place and allow for the conception and ongoing transformation of different "minor" worlds (as opposed to the representation of fixed—"majoritarian"—identities or notions of the world). Theirs is an interest in literature as an assemblage of styles producing affects and precepts, intensities in language—impersonal rhythms and tones—which disclose and repeat the untimely power of difference to transform, disrupt, and create, to become other.

In much of their collaborative writing, Deleuze and Guattari focus on the issue of desire as the energy driving production and becoming. They are drawn to the philosophical potentialities of literary negotiations with the dynamics of desire, and so, as is often the case, to the erotic dimension of literary becomings. A very brief account of their construct of desire is necessary here.

For Deleuze and Guattari, the State constitutes a territoriality whose laws block the free flows of desire produced by bodies and the connections between them—the fragmented aggregates they term "desiring-machines"—the source of the libidinal energy behind all production. The State territoriality functions by assimilating deterritorialized desire-flows—desire as originally produced by said desiring-machines—into axiomatic codes which function in its service. Ironically, the State—the capitalist state in particular—liberates flows of desiring-production in the course of its expansion, but only with a view to the eventual re-inscription—reterritorialization—of such flows. For example, as "permissible" sexualities diversify, psychoanalytic codes multiply to reterritorialize all desiring-production around the Oedipal model in order to bind the reproductive family unit, ensuring State perpetuation. However, the reterritorialization process can never be entirely effective and this means that there is some room for deviation, for lines of change to unfold. For Deleuze and Guattari, great art, and in particular great literature, deterritorializes flows of desire—liberates life—into a state of becoming. So-called "Deleuzian" literature, therefore, deconstructs established boundaries by repeatedly scrambling—rendering inassimilable—the notion of a "majoritarian" meaning or text, thereby causing an "overflow or rupture [of] the sign's conditions of identity, and [...] books within 'the book' to flow and to disintegrate, entering into multiple configurations" (*Anti-Oedipus*, 243).

Kafka is celebrated by Deleuze and Guattari for translating everything—bureaucracy, politics, military forces—into assemblages of desire which flow between construction and dismantling. The figuration and collapse of planes of transcendence—law, reason, truth, being—into this immanence of desire makes Kafka's work erotic. Thus in *The Trial*: "where one believed there was the law, there is in fact desire and desire alone. Justice is desire and not law. [...] The whole of *The Trial* is overrun by a polyvocality of desire that gives it its erotic force" (*Kafka*, 49). The text—its transactions through fragments and segments—is the process of desire itself: "K realizes that he should not let himself be represented [...] that no one should come between him and his desire. He will find justice only by moving, by going from room to room, by following his desire" (*Kafka*, 50). According to Deleuze and Guattari, the dynamics of territorialization and deterritorialization of desire within its field of immanence in Kafka may also be seen to impel narratives such as Woolf's *The Waves*, where they enable "all kinds of becomings between ages, sexes, elements" (*A Thousand Plateaus*, 252), and Proust's *In Search of Lost Time*, where in relation to the beloved, they open up different worlds of affects and intensities, freeing multiple lines of becoming-other. Desire in these works proliferates endlessly, executing a transformational repetition of the creative process which constructs its plane of immanence. This delicate balance between repetition and transformation makes of such literary works erotic heterocosms not unlike those forged by the literature of courtly love or engineered by Sacher-Masoch in his narratives of suspended suffering and postponed gratification.

In the 1967 essay 'Coldness and Cruelty,' which prefaced the republication of Sacher-Masoch's novel *Venus in Furs* (1870) in the volume *Masochism*, Deleuze claims that 'sadomasochism' is an ill-considered composite of two 'perversions'—given that a masochist's pleasure would cancel out the sadistic ecstasy of victimization. Deleuze maintains that each of these 'perversions' must be examined individually in relation to the formal literary values of Sade's and Sacher-Masoch's writing, respectively. Sadean works direct and proselytize; their accelerating descriptions constitute an over-investment in the law (the father or superego) whose demonstrative function seeks to create a delirious world of violence and excess. Sade uses rational exposition to go beyond reason itself, and this results in excess stimulation which may be described as erotic ('Coldness and Cruelty', 37). Sacher-Masoch, in contrast, posits the pre-Oedipal mother and the possibility of rebirth as ideals: the masochist desires plenitude and a return to uterine oblivion (non-existence), a paradox which leads to the disavowal of reality and a postponement of pleasure. The masochist proceeds by drawing up contracts which enslave the (maternal) punisher and undermine the (paternal) law: castigation becomes the guarantee of pleasure, and the on-going anticipation of punishment and satisfaction suspends reality. The masochist thus fabricates a 'frozen' world of fantasy, an erotic heterocosm. Sacher-Masoch produces one such world of fixated fantasy through narratives which only progress via the restricted movement of differences generated by repetition, leaving the reader with "a strange and oppressive atmosphere, like a sickly perfume" ('Coldness and Cruelty', 34). Such erotic literary heterocosms are seen by Deleuze and Guattari as 'perverse' doubles of our mundane world which disrupt reality to enable "all of those becomings that are not produced only *in* art, and all of those active escapes that do not consist in fleeing *into* art" (*A Thousand Plateaus*, 187). In other words, these erotic heterocosms are vital because they propagate the desire to transform and innovate.

Biography

Deleuze is one of the most controversial philosophers of post-war France. His first works are revolutionary studies of major figures in the history of philosophy. He then went on to assemble his views on the philosophy of difference in two key volumes, *Difference and Repetition* (1968) and *The Logic of Sense* (1969). During this period Deleuze also wrote 'Coldness and Cruelty' (1967), an extended essay on the sexualizing effects of the play between difference and repetition in the writing of Leopold von Sacher-Masoch. Here Deleuze argues for the dissociation of masochism from sadism, which he maintains are structurally and philosophically incompatible. Following this, he began collaborating with Guattari, an analyst in the experimental La Borde clinic. Together they launched an infamous attack on Freud and Marx in the two-part study *Capitalism and Schizophrenia*—comprised of *Anti-Oedipus* (1972) and *A Thousand Plateaus* (1980). Their works aim to undo received notions of the subject, and explore the machinations of desire as a force which both produces and devastates social structure. Discussion in these tomes is often conducted in relation to literature, which they deem vital in the philosophical matter of inventing concepts.

KARL POSSO

Selected Works

Works by Gilles Deleuze

Proust et les signes. Paris: Presses Universitaires de France, 1977 [1964]; as *Proust and Signs*. Translated by Richard Howard. London: Athlone, 2000 [1972].
Présentation de Sacher-Masoch. Paris: Minuit, 1967; as *Masochism*. Translated by Jean McNeil. New York: Zone, 1989.
Différence et répétition. Paris: Presses Universitaires de France, 1968; as *Difference and Repetition*. Translated by Paul Patton. London: Athlone, 1994.
Critique et clinique. Paris: Minuit, 1993; as *Essays: Critical and Clinical*. Translated by Daniel W. Smith and Michael A. Greco. Minneapolis, MN: University of Minnesota Press, 1997.

Works by Gilles Deleuze and Félix Guattari

Capitalisme et schizophrénie tome 1: l'Anti-Oedipe. Paris: Minuit, 1972; as *Anti-Oedipus: Capitalism and Schizophrenia*. Translated by Robert Hurley, Mark Seem and Helen R. Lane. London: Athlone, 1984.
Kafka: Pour une littérature mineure. Paris: Minuit, 1975; as *Kafka: Toward a Minor Literature*. Translated by Dana Polan. Minneapolis: University of Minnesota Press, 1986.
Capitalisme et schizophrénie tome 2: Mille plateaux. Paris: Minuit, 1980; as *A Thousand Plateaus: Capitalism and Schizophrenia*. Translated by Brian Massumi. London: Athlone, 1988.
Qu'est-ce que la philosophie? Paris: Minuit, 1991; as *What is Philosophy?* Translated by Graham Burchell and Hugh Tomlinson. London: Verso, 1994.

Further Reading

Ansell Pearson, Keith, ed. *Deleuze and Philosophy: The Difference Engineer*. London/New York: Routledge, 1997.
Bogue, Ronald. *Deleuze and Guattari*. London/New York: Routledge, 1989.
Buchanan, Ian, and John Marks, eds. *Deleuze and Literature*. Edinburgh: Edinburgh University Press, 2001.
Goodchild, Philip. *Deleuze and Guattari: An Introduction to the Politics of Desire*. London: Sage, 1996.

DELICADO, FRANCISCO

c. 1480–c. 1535
Spanish writer

Retrato de La Lozana Andaluza

La Lozana Andaluza (1528), a proto-novel in dialogue, is the principal work for which Francisco Delicado, an obscure Spanish vicar, is known. The picaresque tale of a lusty Spanish prostitute who traverses the stewpots of Rome is certainly of great historical and linguistic value. But the work is mostly known for its obscenity, which has been variously interpreted as a device for censuring the libertinism of early sixteenth-century Rome, or as a carnivalesque and bawdy end in itself.

As far as the work's author is concerned, one of the few biographical bits of information we have is that Delicado himself suffered from venereal disease for twenty-three years before writing his novel (and wrote two medical treatises on it in 1525, "On Consoling the Infirm" and "On the Use of the West Indies' Wood"). The disease was probably incurred from his own trafficking with courtesans. Was *Lozana* perhaps intended to be a sort of literary revenge and cautionary tale? The author presents himself in the text as a sort of meta-character, one who interjects his own opinion presumably to justify Lozana's conduct. Are his seemingly apologetic comments actually sarcastic? The biographical evidence is contradictory. Delicado lived much of his adult life in Rome, possibly because he was driven out of Spain as a Jew after the Expulsion Edict of 1492. Thus, despite his venereal complaint, perhaps he felt genuine sympathy for his orphaned and sexually marginalized character because he himself knew exile.

La Lozana Andaluza is the story of a beautiful young Spaniard who is a "New Christian" (i.e., a Jewish convert). She inhabits a number of Mediterranean cities as the mistress of a variety of men after the death of her parents. Her birth name is Aldonza, but she changes it to "Lozana," which means *fresh* or *blooming*, also translated in English renderings as "lusty" or "exuberant." Her wanderings take her to Rome, where a Neapolitan boy named Rampín shows her the Eternal City's wonders. Lozana sets herself up as a courtesan shortly thereafter, with Rampín as her pimp and manservant. Predictably, she has sexual encounters with a number of men, whom she deceives and fleeces in various clever ways. When the author makes his "cameo" appearances as a character, she debates with him and gives him amorous advice. He ends up reluctantly concurring with her that in order to survive in this world one must resort to deception (although he takes her to task for doing so). Her picaresque and bawdy adventures continue as her lover Rampín spends a brief stint in jail and falls into a privy. Lozana gradually recognizes the necessarily precarious nature of life as a whore, and resorts to selling cosmetics, possibly because she, the most astute and pragmatic of women, has nevertheless found herself to be tricked and seduced by two swindlers. After turning a fine profit in the beauty business, she decides that she has seen the world and discovered, like Apuleius, that "all is vanity." At the story's end, she retires to the island of Lípari with her ill-gotten gains.

The character of the "Lozana" is a difficult one to interpret. As Bruno Damiani notes, she is both trickster and philosopher. Is she a "female rogue" or gamine? A lover, a whore, or a convert (given that Delicado's family was probably of Jewish origin, "convert" has a double meaning)? A syphilis-ridden wench who epitomizes the rottenness and moral corruption of Rome, and/or

of the age of the Hapsburg monarch Charles V? A scheming, *Corbacho*-style witch seeking to lure and entrap men, or the prototype of the self-willed, enterprising heroine? The message the reader derives from this book of "sketches" is largely based on one's visceral reaction to the protagonist, upon which hinges perceptions of authorial irony and intent.

If one reads the antiheroine as a razor-tongued, amoral, greedy *puta* who is supposed to repel and caution, then it is easy to agree with Gómez de la Serna that "the moral base of this book is principally to exhibit prostitutes stripped of their symbolic clothing, adding to [this laying bare], all the material and moral dangers that lie in wait for all who have dealings with them" (translation mine). However, if one interprets the protagonist only as a sort of Rabelaisian free spirit, excused from any sense of morality, corruption, or guilt, one can tip the balance too far the other way and decide with Wardropper that "Lozana is what she is because nature has generously endowed her [with charm and beauty], and because there are no scruples of any type that blunt the impulses of this child of Nature" (translation mine). In short, should the modern reader celebrate or condemn Lozana for her uninhibited sexual libertinism and philosophy of free love?

Although some nineteenth-century critics claimed that Delicado was unlearned, the novel is replete with classical references. Delicado compares Lozana to Demosthenes when praising her silver tongue. The Dedication makes reference to the Roman historical chronicler Juvenal, whose satirical sketches of classical Roman life served as a model for Delicado. Other classical influences on the author were Persius, Cicero, Apuleius, Seneca, and Aristotle (see Damiani). Significant too for Delicado were the Bible, medieval Spanish literature, and contemporary folklore, with which he was clearly familiar (the tale includes over 150 axioms of a homespun flavor which would have done Sancho Panza proud). *Lozana's* dialogue, structure, and subject matter also echo those of the great Spanish novel known to us as *La Celestina*—which presents a realistic portrait (a generation before *Lozana's* publication) of what Lozana might have been like in old age had she not abandoned her whorish ways.

Part diary, part travelogue, part didactic and moralizing essay, *La Lozana Andaluza* is now renowned as much for its brilliant language, sensual humor, folk aphorisms, and vivid place-descriptions as for its notorious "vulgarity." Whether it is truly a satire on the perils of immoral sexuality, or a celebration of an eloquent and skilful survivor, is up to the reader. That it is an artistic and realistic "memorandum" of the realities of Renaissance Rome, and a vitally important precursor to the picaresque novel genre, is indisputable.

Biography

Little is known about Francisco Delicado. He was born in Cordoba, Spain around 1480. His favorable portrait of Jews has led to speculation that he was himself a convert from Judaism. He lived most of his life in Rome, possibly having been expelled from Spain in 1492 along with other Jews and Muslims. After the sack of Rome, he went to Venice where he wrote *Retrato de La Lozana Andaluza*. He is known to have suffered from syphilis and possibly died from its effects around 1535.

C.A. PRETTIMAN

Selected Works

Portrait of Lozana: The Lusty Andalusian Woman. Potomac, MD: Scripta Humanistica, vol. 34. Translated by Bruno Damiani. 1987.
La lozana andaluza. Edición, introducción y notas de Bruno M. Damiani. Second edition. Madrid: Clásicos Castalia, 1982.

References and Further Reading

Beltran, Luis. "The Author's Author, Typography, and Sex: The Fourteenth Century Mamotreto of *La Lozana Andaluza*. In Giancarlo Maiorino ed., The *Picaresque: Tradition and Displacement*. Minneapolis, MN: University of Minnesota Press, 1996.
Brakhage, Pamela S. *The Theology of La Lozana Andaluza*. Potomac, MD: Scripta Humanistica, vol. 22.
Bubnova, Tatiana. "La lozana andaluza como lectura erótica." In Luce Lopez-Baralt, and Francisco Marquez-Villanueva, eds; *Erotismo en las letras hispánicas: aspectos, modos y fronteras*. Mexico City: Centro de Estudios Linguísticas y Literarias, Colegio de Mexico, 1995.
Damiani, Bruno M. *Francisco Delicado*. New York: Twayne Publishers 1974.
———. "*La lozana andaluza* as Precursor to the Spanish Picaresque." In *The Picaresque: A Symposium on the Rogue's Tale*, edited by Carmen Benito Vessels and Michael Zappala, 57–68. Newark: University of Delaware Press, 1994.
Deveny, Thomas. "*La lozana andaluza* entre los angloparlantes: *Portrait of Lozana, the Lusty Andalusian Woman*." *Cuadernos de Aldeeu* 4, no. 1 (April 1988): 91–96.
Dunn, Peter N. "A Postscript to *La lozana andaluza*: Life and Poetry." *Romanische Forschungen* 88 (1976): 355–360.
Fontes, Manuel da Costa. "The Art of 'Sailing' in *La lozana andaluza*." *Hispanic Review* 66, no. 4 (Autumn 1998): 433–445.
———. "Anti-Trinitarianism and the Virgin Birth in *La lozana andaluza*." *Hispania* 76, no. 2 (May 1993): 197–203.
Imperiale, Louis. *El contexto dramático de La lozana andaluza*. Potomac, MD: Scripta Humanistica, vol. 84. 1991.

DELTEIL, JOSEPH

1894–1978
French novelist and poet

Choléra

This Joseph Delteil novel is marked by traditional structure, but its style is perfectly surrealist: this split gives rise to the work's charm and interest.

The plot is conventional though it inverts the traditional pattern: a man is the object of female desire. The narrator (the one who says 'I' and whose autobiography opens the story) meets three innocent girls, and in turn becomes each one's lover. When they discover his trickery, the three friends decide to join a convent (*"none of us will have him!"*). Each of them writes to him however, in secret, the hope of possessing him. But each reunion is marked by a tragedy leading to the death of the beloved woman, and at the end of the novel, the rueful narrator can only affirm his misfortune: "Everything is over, er, er. Over."

The tale wouldn't be at all captivating if it weren't told in such a curious fashion. The young girls have foreign names (Choléra, Corne, and Alice), and troubling ways ("three pubescent virgin girls' games, chaste and limitless games, where six legs and thirty fingers relentlessly seek the truth"). The narrator claims to be the orphan son of a "great duke" and a "moujik," abandoned on the banks of the Marne, in Charentonneau. The Pampelune convent the three girls join is a product of pure imagination: all that matters is the burning road leading to it. The three friends perched on the back of a jackass, ride along this road ("there are mysterious connections between the donkey's body and the young girls' genitals"). It is the scene of a true epic which sees "all of nature become a jackass (or rather a jenny)," and the maids are followed by an amorous priest and a country policeman. Traveled by a narrator devoured by desire, the road leads to the most fanciful destinations and seems to cross the entire planet ("Now he was speaking out loud, and on the surface of the planet, millions of Hindus, Canadians, fellas and Cafras were listening to him, bare headed...").

The tale's apparent eroticism is that of surrealism: equally naïve and ribald, "innocent" though overtly scatological. It is, in fact, woven with a set of Rabelaisian images that are both joyful and healthy. There is no pornography ("sex, to my liking, should be a nocturnal instrument," says the narrator at one point), and love scenes are most often reduced to a simple suggestion ("Her left breast, with the movement of each breath, lifted a camellia: this made seventy-one camellias a minute. How could I dare love her, like everyone, on a sofa?")

The fact remains that the profound sensuality of Delteil's book comes, for the most part, from the passion it shows for writing: this is what establishes it as a reference work for the first half of the twentieth century. The reader will note that the narrator's most intense orgasms come when he is alone, during a truly pantheistic communion with nature, which needs no human presence: "I'm thirsty. I remove my jacket and toss it into a field. In shirt sleeves, I walk across a land of honey and genitals. With each step, my feet find carnal pleasure. [...] I feel the action of the muscles in my legs, the spasm of oxygen enjoying my lungs. The earth's exhilaration settles into my being...." This walk into the very heart of nature is a metaphor for the act of writing; the book then finds its justification in the constant questioning of what constitutes it and qualifies it as an object of desire, and a garden of pleasures. Thus the work is woven with insistent allusions to masters of literature, constituting a veritable metatext, the two major references pointing not only to Francis Jammes ("The complete poet: beard, books and life [...] Rimbaud's own brother"), but also and perhaps especially to Paul Valéry.

One of the esthetic keys to the book is given at the conclusion of the work, when Corne's body, in a faint, reminds her lover of the "sumptuous sonnet," 'La Dormeuse' (1922). Delteil's story is interrupted by the quotation, giving way to the poet from Sete's great lesson: poetry is a pure matter of "forms." Delteil restates this lesson in a less than academic way: "Oh syntaxe, oh synthesis, apogee, I wish I were a flaming heresiarch so I could violate you in a moonless city, on a night in the midst of an epidemic!"

Biography

Son of a modest family from the Cathare region, Joseph Delteil occupies a unique place in modern French literature. Associated early on with the surrealists (Jacob, Souplault, Aragon), his first two novels, *Sur le Fleuve Amour* (1922) and *Choléra* (1923) are wildly praised by André Breton, who makes him Radiguet's (the author of *Le Diable au Corps*) (1923) rival. But the publication of his *Jeanne d'Arc* (1925), followed by his scenario for Dreyer's film (*La Passion de Jeanne d'Arc*, 1928), and praise from Chagall and Claudel lead to his exclusion from the surrealist group.

Seriously ill from 1931 on, he definitively leaves Paris and begins to seriously question life ("I've reached an age when a bit of truth, a bit of humanity do a heart good"). He moves to la Tuilerie de Massane, near Montpellier, in 1937, to lead the life of a country writer with his American wife Catherine Dudley, creator of *La Revue Nègre*. La Tuilerie became a Mecca of "regional" culture, frequented by painters and poets, publishers and novelists, including his faithful and capricious friend, Henry Miller.

SERGE BOURJEA

Editions

Choléra. Editions du Sagittaire, chez Simon KRA, "collection de la revue européenne"" (Philippe Soupault, dr.), Paris, 1923.

Choléra. Les Hautes Plaines de Mane, éditions Robert Morel, collection blanche, 1970.

Choléra. Paris, Grasset, collection "Les Cahiers Rouges." 1983.

DENG XIXIAN

d. after 1594
Chinese sexual alchemy writer

Explanation of the Meaning of the Cultivation of Truth, by the Great Immortal of the Purple-gold Splendour

The title, *Zijin guangyai da xian xiuzhen yanyi*, translated by Robert van Gulik, as above, is rendered somewhat differently by Douglas Wile: *Exposition of Cultivating the True Essence by the Great Immortal of Purple Gold Splendour*. The book is known in joint editions, together with another work of Deng Xixian, his comments on *The True Classic of the Complete Union, by All-assisting Lord Ch'un-yang*, under a common title *Baizhan bi sheng* [*Victory Assured in Every Battle*]. The Chinese text is copied in van Gulik's *Erotic Prints* from a late-nineteenth-century Japanese print, checked with a Chinese one dated 1598.

The term *yanyi* (amplifying the meaning) was, since the sixteenth century, a rather common denomination for popular amplification turning history into romance. We may wonder whether the original edition was not a late Ming commercial venture caring for a larger public at a time when prohibition of licentious books was becoming lax. Should it be read as a pleasant pastiche of the battle of love rather than a serious guide to immortality? It is not likely. Van Gulik is rather inclined to associate it with several other Taoist works of sexual alchemy which disappeared from the Taoist Canon when it was reprinted in 1444–1447. But why has this particular work survived?

Whatever the case, the preface, claiming a hazy ancestry, clearly states the double aim of the author: how to beget children, male or female, how to gain health and long life. This latter quest is what is meant by "cultivation of Truth." The twenty chapters follow each other in logical sequence, with due regard for explicit pedagogy.

The double aim calls for apparently contradictory precepts. In Chapter 10, the beginner in the practice leading to long life should strive to eliminate lustful thoughts, but the last chapter underlines that perfect begetting can only be performed when both partners are euphoric: "When having intercourse it is necessary that both be aroused to obtain any result." Quite clear! The author is aware of the contradiction without solving it, for he pointed out at the very beginning of the same chapter: "Male and female by "absorbing" during their intercourse favour their longevity and lengthen their number of years, but ejaculating calm the womb and sow the grain." A lapse of the male point of view more consistently observed elsewhere? It goes with odd-numbers: the five rejections and five avoidances of Chapter one, nine times nine gentle intromission of Chapter 15, where due sequence is recommended for "absorbing" and "tempering," in order, when returning one's unshed semen, to "gain the most while injuring the least," a care for the female partner, which sounds late rather than early Ming (1368–1644).

In Chapter 18, rejuvenation through a female "crucible" is compared to grafting an old tree: the ideal girl should be above fifteen and less than thirty. Underlined in Chapter 4, the ideal requirements for "true crucibles" are women who have not yet given birth, who are clean and pure, and who are without bad breath or bad odor. However sexual vampirism is not without risks when man finds a truly lovable crucible. Chapter 11 deals briefly with the problem: when feeling about to ejaculate, quickly withdraw and apply the "locking" technique. According to van Gulik, the term means blocking the urethra with the fingers. For Douglas Wile, it implies the use of an age-old technique with the same result by contracting the sphincter without any help of the hand.

No doubt the author takes his task of explaining and listing recipes seriously. Chapter 13 entitled, "Great Pharmacopoeia of the Three Peaks," goes into minutiae about absorbing feminine secretions. Van Gulik pointed out that the text is quoted verbatim or referred to in several different works (*Sexual Life*, p.283). But couldn't it be the other way around?

Chapter 9, for example, about "Tempering the point and keeping it sharp" spares no details in explaining how to proceed in order to strengthen the male "jade stalk," for "during intercourse, if the male has big and long one, he will fill up completely the female vagina and she will be easily aroused." According to this handbook, massage, meditation, timing, and exercise could bring results without resorting to such a fantastical grafting as of a dog's penis described in the novel of Li Yu, *The Carnal Prayer Mat*.

On the whole the tone of mild vampirism and considerate care for the "crucible" points to a later period, why not a synthesis of sexual lore and Taoist practice of the sixteenth century?

Biography

Deng Xixian—Hoping for Sagehood—looks like a penname, Great Immortal of Purple-Gold Splendor being the title of Teng as disciple of Lû Dongbin, one of the eight immortals revered by Taoists. If we may ascribe to him the colophon referring to this and his other work, *True Classic of the Complete Union, by All-assisting Lord Ch'un-yang,* he was 95 in 1594, boasting of having had intercourse within sixty years with more than a hundred different women who bore him seventeen children.

ANDRÉ LÉVY

Editions

Gulik, Robert van. *Erotic Colours Prints of the Ming Period, with An Essay on Chinese Sex Life from the Han to the Ch'ing Dynasty, B.C. 206–A.D. 1644.* 3 vols. 210 + 243 + 50 p., privately published, Tokyo 1951, vol. II, p.97–117

Translations

Wile, Douglas. *Art of the Bedchamber, The Chinese Sexual Yoga Classics, including Women's Solo Meditation Texts.* State University of New York Press, Albany 1992,). "Exposition of Cultivating the True Essence by the Great Immortal of Purple Gold Splendour," p.136–146.

Further Reading

Gulik, Robert van. *Sexual Life in Ancient China, A preliminary survey of Chinese sex and society from ca. 1500 B.C. till 1644 A.D.,* Leiden: E.J. Brill 1961, p.280–285.

DENGCAO HESHANG ZHUAN [THE CANDLEWICK MONK]

There is little chance that this twelve-chapter-long erotic novel was the work of Gao Ming (who died in 1359), the Yuan dynasty (1279–1368) poet and playwright to whom it is generally attributed. Research on the pseudonyms which accompany it leads to other minor licentious works, but unfortunately to no attribution.

The banned-books list on which the novel appears for the first time nonetheless indicates that it circulated prior to 1810—and it did, indeed, survive proscription under various titles. It most likely dates back to the late Ming dynasty (1368–1644) or early Qing (1644–1911), and thus exemplifies the rich production of erotic fiction written in the vernacular language of mid-seventeenth-century China. *The Candlewick Monk* [*Dengcao heshang zhuan*], however, differs from the bulk of erotic novels of that time in its unusual combination of torrid eroticism, humor, and fantasy, which together display the author's unbridled imagination.

Yet this little novel is actually based on an earlier source written in classical Chinese and featured in the *Youyang zazu* [*Miscellaneous Morsels from Youyang*], a collection of anecdotes and tales recorded by the famous literati Duan Chengshi (ca. 803–863). In that collection, a short text entitled "Liu Jizhong" involves a small witch who springs out of a lamp to sow discord in the mansion of a respectable official. The same plot is later found in the repertoire of public storytellers of the tenth and eleventh centuries, who used it as a narrative under the title "Denghua popo" [Auntie Candle Flame]. It can also be found in the late-Ming rewriting of the novel *Pingyao zhuan* [*Suppressing the Demon's Revolt*] by Feng Menglong (1574–1646).

Never afraid of being provocative, the author of *The Candlewick Monk* appropriates this plot and adapts it in the erotic style. No longer is a single she-demon the source of problems, but an entire family of demons: mother, son (the Candlewick Monk), and his sisters, four succubae of astounding beauty who take over the house of Mandarin Yang. Once ushered in, the cunning little Monk who has sprung out of a candle flame, starts fulfilling the sexual wishes of Lady Wang, Mandarin Yang's neglected wife. The Monk not only varies his size in order to explore all the interstices of the female anatomy, he also feeds on the vaginal secretions of his partners, to whom he brings previously unsuspected pleasures. In order to save him from her husband's wrath, Lady Wang feels compelled to entrust the Monk to the care of her sixteen-year-old maidservant Jade, who quickly develops a passion for him as well. One day, while taking advantage of Jade, Mandarin Yang discovers the little Monk nestling between her breasts and beats him to death. The mother-demon and her daughters intervene, bringing the little Monk back to life so he can resume his lustful activities, while one of his sisters engages Mr. Yang in a tide of carnal debauchery spiced up with feats of erotic magic. The following day, the six demons vanish after promising to return

and conclude the union of the Monk with Changgu, the fifteen-year-old daughter of the house. To guard against it, Yang and his wife rush their daughter into a pre-arranged marriage with a young libertine, himself also very partial to matters of sex. It is however a clone of the bride that the groom actually weds, much to the chagrin of the young virgin Changgu, who must remain a mere spectator to her husband's expertise in the *ars erotica*. When the hoax is uncovered, the bridegroom is removed and Mr. Yang takes his place. The ensuing lovemaking plunges Mandarin Yang into such confusion that he finds himself close to raping his own daughter. The real daughter leaves her home to live with her in-laws. Lady Wang seizes the opportunity to call on the little Monk, who reappears blessed with even more handsome features and a larger sexual appetite. After the newlyweds return, the Monk seduces the young Ms. Yang, causing the cuckold to repudiate his wife, who soon passes away for having copulated too much. During the funeral, Mr. Yang, the father of the deceased, dies, leaving behind a widow and a maidservant (whom, in the meantime, has given him a son) longing for lovers. The two women eventually get their claws on a strong-limbed bonze whose services they share. The bonze ends up marrying Lady Wang, as predicted by the Candlewick Monk, but only after Wang's pilgrimage to the city of Hangzhou, where she has affairs with other bonzes. On the eve of her reunion with her soon-to-be new husband, the little Candlewick Monk makes one last appearance and reveals that the purpose of his original intervention in the story was to punish Mandarin Yang for an iniquitous sentence he had passed while in office, thus proving that each felony committed in this world is invariably rewarded in kind.

The complexity of the plot merely serves as a pretext to broach a wide variety of sex scenes displaying as many permutations as possible. However coarse and lewd are the story's sexual and verbal excesses, the claim for a total liberation of women from the yoke of a hypocritical Confucian society nonetheless rescues the novel. This intention runs through the whole story and marks it in such a clear way that one is left wondering whether the author of this remarkable novel is not actually a woman.

That mischievous Monk whose size grows according to women's will could well be the fruit of a frustrated spouse's daydreaming. Moreover, isn't this "now-big-now-small" motif a striking metaphor for the male sex organ? In Chinese culture, the glans of the penis is indeed very often compared precisely to the clean-shaven head of a bonze.

If, by chance, this novel turned out not to have been written by a woman, it was nevertheless clearly intended to be *read* by women. As such, it could, in short, be said to constitute some sort of literary dildo.

PIERRE KASER
Translated form the French by Victor Thibaut

Edition

Le Moine Mèche-de-lampe, roman érotique du XVIIᵉ siècle. Translated by Aloïs TATU. Arles : Editions Philippe Picquier, 1998.

DENON, VIVANT

1747–1825
French diplomat, art historian, and writer

In addition to a career in the arts which put his name on one wing of the Louvre, Vivant Denon is best known for one twenty-page prose work. *No Tomorrow* [*Point de lendemain*], first published in 1777, captures with concision and panache the spirit of *libertinage* so central to eighteenth-century French sociability. The story of a one-night sexual adventure, it stages a moment severed from past and future, a moment with no tomorrow. Epitomizing the libertine view of pleasure as dialectic between social convention and unexpected opportunity, it foregrounds chance as opening up new temporalities of experience, memory, and writing.

One evening, while waiting for his mistress at the Opera and suspecting he has been stood up, the narrator of this first-person memoir written many years after the events described is asked by his mistress's good friend, Madame de T, if he has plans for the evening. Deciding to take his chances, he leaves the Opera with her for a late-night ride that takes them to a château on the banks of the Seine belonging to Madame de T's estranged husband. On arriving there, the narrator realizes he has been chosen to be Madame de T's "companion" for the first evening she will spend with the husband from whom she has been separated for eight years. A second surprise comes the next morning, at the end of the story, when they are joined by the Marquis, Madame de T's current lover, whose status has been masked from the husband by the narrator's presence. His whole adventure, it turns out, was set up as a carefully constructed ruse to mislead the husband, to convince him, when the narrator returns to Paris that morning, that his wife has properly deferred to the spirit of their reconciliation.

But this is not how things worked out. With geography mirroring desire, the narrator's story is that of a movement from a public to a private space, from an open to a hidden and protected space. Madame de T and the narrator move from the public arena of the Paris Opera to a coach leaving the city, to a country château, to its garden, and to the grassy bank on which they exchange a kiss until Madame de T abruptly decides they must return to their separate rooms in the château. As they near the château, however, Madame de T changes her mind and leads the narrator down a darkened path toward a small pavillon for which Madame de T does not have the key—but which turns out to be open. This pavillon becomes a space beyond any plan establishing Madame de T as manipulator and the naïve young narrator as instrument. In the pavillon there reigns only the power of desire as a force born of chance to which both are equally subject. Carried beyond the categories of planner and duped, of active and passive, of taking and giving, of victory and defeat, they find themselves in a space where language's conventional oppositions hold no sway: "If, on the one hand, we wished to give what had been taken, on the other we wished to receive what had been stolen; and both of us hastened to obtain a second victory confirming our having been conquered."

This journey into desire's uncharted realm then continues from the garden to the château's most secret space: the hidden room Monsieur de T had built to fortify his languid sexuality at the time he and Madame were married. To enter this room is not so much to move from one point in space to another, but to step outside space, to lose all sense of continuity between here and there, between who I was and who I am, between past and present. A monument to desire, its indirect lighting and trompe l'oeil, its portico and temple consecrated to the goddess of love, compose the perfect replica of a classical grove complete with altar, chalice, garlands, grass underfoot, and the beckoning intimacy of a dark grotto. The room's walls are mirrors onto which erotic images have been carefully painted. This trip from the Opera to the secret room abolishes carefully laid plans and their deference to society's insistence on decorum and consequences. The mirrored room offers no breach through which society's objectifying gaze might watch and judge those who enter it. At liberty to continue or abolish their pure present of chance and the unexpected, the narrator and Madame de T discover there a pleasure uncontaminated by the rules and reciprocities of the social order.

The force of chance presiding over this brief affair takes its fiercest revenge against those who would define themselves as beyond its power, those who claim to manipulate it as only another instrument in the libertine's arsenal of deception. It may have been by design that Madame de T chose a companion for the evening, but it was by chance that her choice led to a movement of desire and pleasure initiating a quite unanticipated story, unwriteable by the narrator, of how that choice would affect her relation to her lover, the Marquis. The Marquis, too, is a would-be manipulator. Delighted that the coach trip has given the narrator an occasion to know and admire Madame de T, he cannot refrain from congratulating himself on being her lover: "Can you imagine that any man could make that woman settle down? It wasn't easy, but I have molded her character to the point where she may well be the one woman in Paris on whose fidelity one can count absolutely." No one, of course, is better able to appreciate the dubious value of that claim than the narrator. Swept up by his pride, the Marquis magisterially concedes that Madame de T does have one defect: "Between us, I have discovered only one failing in her. Nature, in granting her everything, refused her that divine flame which would crown all her blessings. She inspires everything, makes you feel everything, yet she feels nothing. She is a statue." The narrator, quite unaware of any such flaw—but hardly for the reasons the Marquis assumes—must fight his laughter as he replies: "But . . . you know her as though you were her husband!"

No Tomorrow is a tour de force of disabused analysis summarizing all the manipulations, illusions, and self-deceptions which were the essence of eighteenth-century libertinage. When the story ends, each character occupies a position different from what he or she had originally expected or connived at: Monsieur de T begins a reconciliation with his wife on terms decidedly different from those he had sought; Madame de T finds herself far more enchanted by her choice of an evening's companion than she had intended; and the Marquis as secret lover becomes the unwitting double of the cuckolded husband. As for the narrator, he can only observe that "I began to laugh at the role I was playing; and we became quite gay."

Biography

Born Vivant de Non in Givry, France, 4 January 1747, to a family of the minor nobility. Abandoned legal studies in Paris for the art world around the painter François Boucher. Distinguished for his elegance and strategic sexual liaisons, he wrote a three-act verse play for the Comédie-Française titled *Julie, ou le Bon Père* in 1769, the same year he became curator of the court collection of *pierres gravées* and was named *gentilhomme ordinaire du roi*. Began a diplomatic career in 1774 that took him to Saint Petersburg, Switzerland, and Naples. Published anonymously in June 1777 his short prose work, *No Tomorrow* [*Point de lendemain*]. Serving again as a diplomat in Italy at the outbreak of the Revolution, he was placed on the list of proscribed nobles. Protected by the painter Jacques-Louis David, he changed his name to Vivant Denon and returned to favor with the new regime. Frequented the salon of Joséphine de Beauharnais where he became close to

Napoleon who brought him on his expedition to Egypt in 1798. Published the first European study of Egyptian art in 1802. Named Director of the Louvre and supervised the forced acquisitions of art works in the territory conquered by Napoleon from 1802 to 1815. Retired from public life in protest against the restitution of the Louvre's acquisitions following Napoleon's defeat. Spent the last ten years of his life writing a monumental world history of painting which was published in 1829, four years after his death in Paris on 27 April 1825.

THOMAS M. KAVANAGH

Selected Works

Point de lendemain. Paris, 1777; Paris: Folio Classique, 1995; as *No Tomorrow*. Translated by Lydia Davis in *The Libertine Reader*, edited by Michel Feher. New York: Zone Books, 1997, pp. 732–747.

Further Reading

Chali, Ibrahim Arnin. *Vivant Denon ou la conquête du bonheur*. Cairo: Institut Français d'Archéologie Orientale du Caire, 1986.

Kavanagh, Thomas M. "Writing of No Consequence," in *Enlightenment and the Shadows of Chance*. Baltimore and London: Johns Hopkins University Press, 1993, pp. 185–197.

Kundera, Milan. *Slowness*. Translated by Linda Asher. New York: Harper Collins, 1996.

Lelièvre, Pierre. *Vivant Denon, Homme des Lumières, "Ministre des Arts" de Napoléon*. Paris: Picard, 1993.

Nowinski, Judith. *Baron Dominique Vivant Denon (1747–1825), Hedonist and Scholar in a Period of Transition*. Rutherford, NJ: Fairleigh Dickinson Press, 1970.

Sollers, Philippe. *Le cavalier du Louvre*. Paris: Plon, 1995.

Wells, Byron R. "Objet/volupté: Vivant Denon's *Point de lendemain*." In *Romance Notes*, 29(3), 1989, pp. 203–208.

DEPESTRE, RENÉ

1926—
Haitian and French poet, prose writer, essayist, and novelist

Depestre made an early sensational irruption onto the literary scene in 1945 with the publication of his first volume of poetry, *Étincelles* [*Sparks*] published at his own expense by the Imprimerie de l'État in Port-au-Prince. Later the same year, he cofounded a weekly newspaper, *La Ruche*, with fellow students, including Jacques Stephen Alexis who would later write the first Haitian novel with important erotic content, *L'Espace d'un cillement* [*In the Flicker of an Eyelid*] (1959). Since then Depestre continued to publish mostly poetry, but also numerous essays (in both French and Spanish-language journals), a number of which was collected in *Pour la poésie, pour la révolution* (1974), *Bonjour et adieu à la négritude* (1980), and *Le Métier à métisser* (1998). It was only late in life that he published his first fictions in Montreal *Alléluia pour une femme-jardin: récits d'amour solaire* (1973), which were the first Francophone Caribbean narratives that could be classified as forthrightly erotic. Those five short stories were received very badly, in particular by the Haitian intelligentsia who regarded them as "pornographic." Revised and expanded, a new volume published under the abbreviated title, *Alléluia pour une femme-jardin*, by Gallimard in Paris (1981), was awarded the Goncourt prize for short fiction, and enjoyed great success in bookstores. From that time on, Depestre's reputation as an erotic writer was firmly established, especially for his first novel, *Le mât de cocagne* [*The Festival of the Greasy Pole*] (1979) previously published in La Havana in 1975 (*El Palo ensabado*), contains an unforgettable erotic scene. Six pages in which the narrator describes a fantastic sensual massage of the protagonist, Henri Postel, by a young beauty, Élisa Valéry, which culminates in a coitus sublimely interrupted by the Mambo, Sor Cisa, possessed by the Goddess of Love, Erzuli. In 1988, Depestre published his second novel *Hadrianna dans tous mes rêves* in which *l'amour fou* [mad love] combining eroticism and marvellous vodou in the most surprising ways, and his second collection of short stories, *Éros dans un train chinois*, appeared in 1990. Although eroticism is omnipresent in Depestre's poetry, particularly in the volumes published before his Cuban exile and *Un arc-en-ciel pour l'occident chrétien* [A Rainbow for the Christian West] (1967) his great book of poetry about the mysteries of vodou and their irreverent bawdiness, only his fictions, in particular his two collections of short stories are truly erotic. For, with one exception, *Cantate d'octobre* [1969], Depestre's writings, whether poetic or fictional, are a broad mixture of eroticism and politics, but through their emphasis on either sexual pleasure or political struggle, we end up with different texts, engaged or erotic.

Alléluia pour une femme-jardin

The definitive edition comprises ten short stories; the first of which gives its title to the collection. This text recounts in four cantos the "two beautiful years" of an intense love relationship between an adolescent, Olivier, and his young aunt Isabella Ramonet, known as Zaza (which is also Elisa's nickname in *Le Mât*), a widow of "legendary beauty" who was the "star" of Jacmel. The last story, "Un retour à Jacmel," tells of the return to his native land of a young Haitian physician, Dr Hervé Braget (his name suggests the Haitian word for the male sex, "braguette"), which becomes the ladykiller of Jacmelian women of all ages and statuses. Between these two narratives which end on a more or less tragic note, Depestre makes his rather nomadic characters, always engaged in free love, wander from one continent to another. In contrast with Sade's exclusive and enclosed locations, their generally diverse and open locations stretch from racist America in Nashville, to Batista's corrupted Cuba, to the Cité Universitaire in Paris where Olivier Vermont in his "Mémoires du géolibertinage" remaps the world according to "the planet's erotic resources" as he discovers columns of young women (listed at length over two pages divided into three columns) with their own distinctive specificities. This multiplicity of imagined conquests recounted by Olivier demonstrates that Depestrian eroticism lies more in lyrical or ludic evocation of the "femmes-jardins" (those women who "freely assume their bodies' resources, give vent to the flowering of their sexuality, without pangs of guilt") than in the sexual act *per se*.

Éros dans un train chinois

This pre-eminence of the evocation of the sexual act over the act itself is pushed to the limit in *Éros dans un train chinois*. Depestre's linguistic prowess reaches its apogee at the end of the volume with a "GLOSSARY OF TERMS THAT DESIGNATE THE MALE AND FEMALE SEX IN THESE FICTIONS; CATALOGUE OF SOME GENERALLY ACCEPTED IDEAS ABOUT THE EXTRAORDINARY ADVENTURES OF SEXUAL ORGANS" which multiplies the intratextual cross-referencing from one definition to another as in any good dictionary. This nomenclature ranging from *Amande* [the female sex] to *Zoutil* [the male organ; also known as *Sa Majesté Tout-en-Un*] is the follow-up to the collection of "nine love stories and a sorcerer's tale" (as stated the subtitle) brought together according to an exemplary logic of unsatisfied desire (that of the Caribbean comrade shut up in the compartment of a Chinese train, trying in vain to convince his Maoist guide to share his bed) to unsatisfiable desire (that of a young Haitian with an "extra-ordinary" member that no woman is willing to enjoy until a cunning little girl, Josefina Finamour, offers him his first coitus which inaugurates nine days and nine nights of uninterrupted and shared pleasures). These two stories, "Faisane dorée" and "L'œillet ensorcelé," highlight how Depestre borrows from both learned and popular traditions, in particular from those of Haiti in order to weave his carnivalesque (in a Bakhtinian sense) erotic plots which are also political. For, beyond the demand for liberty, there is a manifest commitment to freedom itself, and a struggle against all "integrisms" (religious, social, political) which prevent the fulfilment and rapture of the free couple that man and woman form, without any domination by either sex. Indeed, this eroticism, which Depestre calls "solar," is very far from sadism and masochism, or any other "deviation."

Hadriana dans tous mes rêves

If sexual perversions or violence are marginal in Depestre's erotic short stories, it is quite different with his most known and praised novel, *Hadriana...* where some important characters are characterized by their sexual *deviations* or their sensual *outbursts*. On the one hand, Hadriana Siloé, in her journal, introduces herself as a bi-sexual who, in her coffin, dead-living, ardently would bite the breasts of Erzuli, the Haitian goddess of love, then in the same mood remembers her seven successive orgasms under the caresses of her best friend, Lolita, and her unappeased desires to make love with Patrick Altamont, the narrator, and her fiancé, Hector Danoze. On the other hand, the insatiable Germaine Villaret-Joyeuse, who killed her three husbands with her legendary *blow backs*, whom the story of her last extravagant will to take for a drive after her death in Jacmel opens the novel; or the *bòkò* (evil voodoo priest) Rosalvo Rosanfer who tried to make of Hadriana a zombi in order to subjugate her for his sexual fantasies.

Besides, as much as the voodoo is practically missing in the short stories, as much as it is omnipresent in *Hadriana...*, where it is intrinsically linked or associated to the sexual violence and the broad joke, which work out the narrative, but also to this outburst of senses, which makes of it a marvelous baroque and erotic text. Indeed, it is within the voodoo tradition that Depestre draws a series of metamorphoses allowing to this narrative, which opens on the death—that (real) of the widow Villaret-Joyeuse, then that (apparent) of her goddaughter, Hadriana, at the very moment where she accepts solemnly to marry Hector Danoze at Jacmel's cathedral—to lead to the very exuberant carnival and ribald memorable funeral watch of the white fairy of Jacmel on the Square of Arms.

Indeed, for the followers of this mostly festive and erotic religion, the death is not seen as a final step, but as a stage towards a beyond, *Nan Ginen*, Africa, always presents in the mind of the living as the paradisiac place before, *the middle passage*, the slave trade. Hence, death is not strictly lived as mourning, the funeral watch becomes a feast, at least a ceremonial to the memory of the deceased, where one must eat, drink, sing, dance up to the trance to serve (or appease) the *loa*, who express to the living by taking possession of their bodies and their heads, riding them, metamorphosing them into males or females, old men or pretty women, beasts or angels for their pleasures and festivities. Besides, the relationships between the human and their Gods mostly outline a very erotic ritual, which culminates with the mystical marriage, where the follower, the *sèvitè* must devote exclusively a room and a day to his or her loa at home; or the ultimate grade of the voodoo initiation, the "stay under the waters," rarely reached, for one must be chosen to live among the gods with his or her loa, in the country of Ife or the Simbi. Hence, Depestre could not find a better pretext than this story of zombie or living dead to explore with a profusion of versions the eroticism in all its states, the voodoo mythology being the site of expression of multiple metamorphoses and metaphors of erotic drives and the triumph of love beyond grave, which makes of *Hadriana...* the Depestre novel more rooted in Haitian traditions. But it is also the single one to be really erotic and the most involved in a dialogue with the Western erotic narrative tradion, mainly Georges Bataille's paradigm of eroticism and death, and Sade's rhetoric of overflowing the narrative by philosophical or sociological discourse or essay.

Biography

Depestre was born in Jacmel, on the southeastern coast of Haiti on 29 August 1926. He attended the Lycées Pinchat in Jacmel and Pétion in Port-au-Prince (1938–1944), then he went to France to study Political Science and Literature at Université de Paris-Sorbonne (1946–1950) with a scholarship from the Haitian government. Exiled or expelled several times from France, Czechoslovakia, Chili, Argentina, Brazil, and Cuba for his political activities, he returned briefly to Haiti in 1957, following a second exile in France where he was involved in political and literary movements through journals like *Présence africaine*, *Esprit*, *Les Lettres françaises*, and *Les Lettres nouvelles*. In this last journal, in the wake of "Krushchev's Secret Speech at the 20th Congress of the Communist Party of Soviet Union" (25 February, 1956), he published, in January 1957, his first criticism of the "real socialism" (*le socialisme réel*, as he called it). After almost one year of house arrest in Port-au-Prince, he fled to Cuba in March 1959 with his first wife, Edith Sorel, to join the Castrist Revolution. In Cuba he lived as "a Cuban among the Cubans" until his appointment as at the UNESCO's headquarters in

Paris in 1978. During his Cuban years, he was a commentator for Radio Havana, a collaborator of the prestigious journal and publishing house, *Casa de las Américas*, and taught at the Universidad de La Habana. He also translated several important Latin American poets into French: Nicolás Guillén, *Le grand zoo* (1965); Roberto Fernández Retamar, *Avec les mêmes mains* (1968); and Cesar Fernández Moreno, *Un catalogue de vieilles voitures* (1986). In the summer of 1986, he retired from UNESCO and left Paris to live with his second wife, Nelly Campano, and their two children (Paul-Alain and Stefan) in a small village in Southern France, Lézignan-Corbières, where he is still living as a French citizen which he became by naturalization in 1991. In 1988, he won the prestigious French literary award, the Prix Renaudot, and the Prix du Roman of the Belgian Académie Royale de Langue et Littérature Françaises for his second novel, *Hadriana dans tous mes rêves*. The Prix Apollinaire was awarded in 1993 for Depestre's *Anthologie personnelle*; and in 1994, the Italian award, Premio Grinzane Cavour, was awarded for the Italian translation of his first novel, *L'Albero della cuccagna, le mât de cocagne* (1979). In 1995, he received a John Simon Guggenheim Memorial Foundation fellowship, and in 1998, the Académie Française's Grand Prix de poésie for his entire poetic work.

JEAN JONASSAINT

Selected Works

Un Arc-en-ciel pour l'Occident chrétien. Paris: Présence Africaine, 1967 (*A Rainbow for the Christian West*, translated by Jack Hirschman. Fairfax, California: Red Hill Press, 1972; *A Rainbow for the Christian West*, edited and translated by Joan Dayan. Amherst: University of Massachusetts Press, 1977).
Alléluia pour une femme-jardin: récits d'amour solaire. Montréal: Leméac, 1973.
Alléluia pour une femme-jardin. Paris: Gallimard, 1981.
Hadriana dans tous mes rêves. Paris: Gallimard, 1988.
Éros dans un train chinois. Paris: Gallimard, 1990.

Le Mât de Cocagne. Paris: Gallimard, 1979 (*The Festival of the Greasy Pole*, edited and translated by Carrol F. Coates. Charlottesville: University Press of Virginia, 1990).
"Hallelujah for a Woman-Garden" (excerpt from *Alléluia pour une femme-jardin*, Alléluia pour une femme-jardin), translated by Erika Obey in *Rhythm & Revolt : Tales of the Antilles*, edited by Marcela Breton. New York: Plume, 1995.
"Rosena on the Mountain" (excerpt from *Alléluia pour une femme-jardin*, Roséna sur la montagne), translated by Carrol F. Coates, in *Ancestral House: the Black Short Story in the Americas and Europe*, edited by Charles H. Rowell. Boulder, Colo.: Westview Press, 1995; and *The Oxford Book of Caribbean Short Stories*, edited by Stewart Brown and John Wickham. Oxford and New York: Oxford University Press, 1999.
"A Return to Jacmel" (excerpt from *Alléluia pour une femme-jardin*, Un retour à Jacmel), translated by Carrol F. Coates, *Callaloo*, 24, 4 (2001): 983–988.

Further Reading

Carré Crosley, Bernadette. *Haïtianité et mythe de la femme dans Hadriana dans tous mes rêves de René Depestre.* Montréal: Éditions du CIDIHCA, 1993.
Couffon, Claude. *René Depestre.* Paris: Seghers, 1986.
Dayan, Joan. "*Hallelujah for a Garden-Woman*: The Caribbean Adam and His Pretext." *The French Review: Journal of the American Association of Teachers of French*, 59, 4 (1986): 581–595.
Dayan, Joan. "France Reads Haiti: An Interview with René Depestre." *Yale French Studies*, 83 (1993): 136–153.
Jonassaint, Jean. *Le Pouvoir des mots, les maux du pouvoir. Des romanciers haïtiens de l'exil.* Paris: Arcantère, and Montréal: Presses de l'Université de Montréal, 1986.
Kundera, Milan. "The Umbrella, the Night World, and the Lonely Moon." *The New York Review of Books*, 38, 21 (1991): 46–50 (Available online: http://www. nybooks.com/articles/3054).
Lapaire, Pierre-Guy. "L'Erotisme baroque, le *télédiol* et les femmes-jardins de René Depestre." *Essays in French Literature*, 27 (1990): 91–101.
Ste-Marie, Isabelle. *Représentations et fonctions du personnage féminin dans Alléluia pour une femme-jardin de René Depestre.* M. A. Études françaises, Université de Montréal, 2001.

DESFORGES

1746–1806
French dramatist and novelist

Desforges was known in eighteenth-century Paris as a witty playwright and actor. He achieved moderate success on stage and saw thirty of his plays staged. Late in his life, he wrote several libertine novels, most of them vaguely autobiographical, none of them very popular.

Legally the son of a wealthy Parisian porcelain dealer, Desforges was, in fact, the result of a liaison between Mme Desforges and the apparently famous Parisian doctor, "le docteur Petit." Most of the details of his life, particularly the more lurid ones, are known only through his autobiographical novel, *Le poète*. In it, he describes himself as precocious in every way, writing plays at age nine and engaging in sexual adventures at age six. His school years were marked by scandalous amorous adventures that often ended badly.

After his legal father's financial ruin and the death of Dr. Petit, Desforges was forced to relinquish his dilettantism to earn a living. After trying several different courses of study, he became an actor, first with the Comédie Italienne, then with a traveling theater troupe. By his own reports, the years between 1669 and 1775 were filled with amorous adventures in most of the major cities of France. He married an actress, whom he later divorced. He claims to have found true love late in life, in his second marriage. It was during his second marriage, at age 52, that he wrote his first erotic text—an autobiographical novel, *Le poète*. After its publication, he wrote several more mediocre, vaguely autobiographical libertine novels.

Le poète ou mémoires d'un homme de lettres

Desforges begins his memoirs by proclaiming himself an historian, not a novelist. Even if the tales of his youth might offend the morals of his readers, he would rather do so than offend what he calls the greater cause of historical truth. In spite of this authorial statement of complete accuracy, it is impossible to know how much of the book is an accurate chronicle of Desforges's own libertine adventures. His sexual initiation occurs at the age of six and a half, in the dormitory of his boarding school. After the young Desforges wakes abruptly from his first erotic dream, a twelve-year-old girl, Ursule, also a boarder at his school, encourages him to recount his dream in detail and then climbs under the covers and helps him reenact it. They continue as childhood lovers, sneaking around the school for about a year until Ursule falls for someone closer to her own age. Desforges's sexual life begins in earnest with Manon, who worked in his father's artificial flower shop. He describes their encounters in poetic detail, with a sort of rapturous joy:

> Another region is opened for me ... it's the sky; it's more than the sky, it's ... What double sighs! What unknown ardor! I burn, she burns with me ... with a fire!

She soon becomes pregnant, and is shuffled off by complicit family members. A liaison with the young Adélaïde also ends with her becoming pregnant. After becoming an actor, he travels through France, enjoying a succession of trysts. He seduces the young Gabrielle as well as her widowed aunt; Thérèse is seduced after meeting Desforges at mass; in Marseille a certain weakhearted Mlle Pezé drops dead *in flagrante delicto*. He paints himself as an amiable, earnest libertine, who genuinely loves each woman before something inevitably goes wrong. He often describes his sexual encounters with an overwrought mix of war and religious imagery:

> The celestial shelter is penetrated. The ecstasy of ravishing leads to the violence of irruption, and the priest and the worshiped one—both victims—momentarily leave life in the burning depths of love's sanctuary.

To summarize his four-volume account, he contends that each of his youthful liaisons led to some kind of disgrace or punishment. The final volume concludes with the names of each woman he seduced and the consequences of the liaison: disappointment, humiliation, prison, estrangement from children he fathered. He claims that his final punishment for seducing Angélique was marriage itself.

Les Mille et un souvenirs

In the author's preface, Desforges explains that just as he was deciding to embark on a career as a novelist, a friend presented him a manuscript that his father had found among a client's legal papers. Naturally, Desforges decides to publish the manuscript. In the frame of the novel, M. Mélincourt promises the widow Madame d'Arbel a libertine story every night in bed if she will agree to marry him. He provides her with a catalogue of titles which allows her to select each night's anecdote. They are adventurous tales of seduction, secret *rendez-vous*, cooperative valets, and watchful fathers. The details are more logistical—how to sneak into the beloved's bedroom—than erotic. Occasionally the *récit* is interrupted by the married couple who comment on the characters or stop the story for their own sexual pleasure.

Biography

Born Pierre-Jean-Baptiste Choudart-Desforges in Paris, September 15, 1746. Attended the *Collège Mazarin* and the *Collège de Beauvais* 1754–1763; studied medicine, then painting, but abandoned both; worked as a copyist and translator, 1765, began acting at the *Comédie Italienne*, 1769;

traveled throughout France with a troupe of actors beginning in 1769. Married an actress, Angélique Erlement, 1775; traveled with Angélique to Saint Petersburg to perform in Catherine II's court, 1779; all his manuscripts are stolen on his return trip from Russia, 1782; divorced Angélique, around 1786; published an account of his youthful libertinage, 1799. Died in Paris, August 13, 1806.

DIANE BERRETT BROWN

Selected Works

Theater

Richard et d'erlet. 1778.
Tom Jones à Londres. 1782.
La femme jalouse. 1785.
Le sourd, ou l'auberge pleine. 1790.
Les epoux divorcés. 1790.

Operas

Les promesses de mariage. 1787.
Joconde. 1790.
La liberté et l'egalité rendues à la terre. 1794.

Novels

Le poète, ou mémoires d'un homme de lettres. 1798.
Eugène et Eugénie, ou la surprise conjugale, histoire de deux enfants d'une nuit d'erreur de leurs parents. 1798.
Adelphine de Rostanges, ou la mère qui ne fut point épouse. 1799.
Edouard et Arabelle, ou l'élève de l'infortune et de l'amour. 1799.
Les mille et un souvenirs, ou les veillées conjugales. 1799.

DESNOS, ROBERT

1900–1945
French poet and prose writer

La liberté ou l'amour [Liberty or Love!] (1927).

Desnos's most significant book during his period of involvement with André Breton was undoubtedly *La liberté ou l'amour*, often seen as

the last great work of early Surrealism. The Surrealists had been experimenting with hypnosis as a means of liberating the subconscious since the autumn of 1922, and Desnos had proved a most responsive subject—so much so that he was soon able to enter a trance-like state almost at will. *La liberté ou l'amour*, he claimed, was a book written with "eyes wide shut." As might be imagined, a novel written under such conditions almost defies description. However, various themes do begin to emerge upon close reading. One of these is the narrator's search for the unique woman, a quest which involves unbridled eroticism (almost invariably of a highly fetishistic nature), the constant threat of violence, and the repeated evocation of the sea. The iterative structure of the work and the typically Surrealist use of startling metaphors and imagery are clearly visible in the following passage:

> How many times, in stormy weather or by the light of the moon, did I get up to contemplate by the gleam of a log-fire, or that of a match, or a glow-worm, those memories of women who had come to my bed, completely naked apart from stockings and high-heeled slippers retained out of respect for my desire, and more unaccountable than a parasol found floating in the middle of the Pacific by a steamship.
> (*Liberty or Love*)

La liberté ou l'amour may also be read as an adventure novel, though one darkly illuminated by the shades of three Surrealist heroes: the Marquis de Sade, Lautréamont, and Jack the Ripper. This aspect of the work is consistently emphasized during Sanglot the Corsair's obsessive pursuit of Louise Lame, which constitutes one of the central narrative strands of the work, and by means of a number of intensely blasphemous passages. Two episodes in particular would seem to have upset the authorities on the book's first publication: the first consists of Sanglot the Corsair's visit to the Sperm Drinkers' Club; the second concerns the description of the new Eucharist intended to celebrate the divinity of Bébé Cadum (a figure borrowed by Desnos from contemporary advertising hoardings promoting a brand of soap). Part of the latter ceremony involves a contraceptive sponge standing in for the traditional consecrated wafer. Nor would more conservative readers have appreciated a later execution scene in which the Marquis de Sade takes the place of Louis XVI. The consequence of the publisher's brush with the law was that *La Liberté ou l'amour* was only available initially in truncated form (subsequent editions, of course, have restored the offending passages).

Corps et biens

Desnos's novel (if it may be labelled as such) did not come into being in a vacuum. A number of early texts published in short-lived Surrealist periodicals (such as the childhood reminiscences, 'Confession d'un Enfant du siècle', published in *La révolution surréaliste* in 1926) or a personal credo entitled *De l'érotisme considéré dans ses manifestations écrites et du point de vue de l'esprit moderne* (written in 1953 but not published until 1953) are useful documents in charting the construction of the author's personal erotic agenda.

Biographical information also proves revealing. It is apparent, for example, that the mysterious unknown woman who haunts the author's imagination was, in fact, the chanteuse Yvonne George. The same singer similarly inspired a number of the poems in *Corps et biens* (note the continuing nautical imagery—the French expression 'perdu corps et biens' is best translated into English as 'lost with all hands'), especially a moving sequence of seven odes entitled 'A la mystériéuse'. These poems, despite their more traditional form and structure, enjoy a clear affinity with Desnos's Surrealist roots.

Generally speaking, the seeming paradox at the heart of *La liberté ou l'amour* and many of the later poems—how can love be both entirely pure and totally licentious—can only be resolved by close examination of the wider discussions on the subject that were engaged in by the Surrealist movement as a whole during the period in question. Although Desnos (who had recently been involved in an acrimonious rupture with Breton) does not feature in the discussions contained in *Recherches sur la sexualité, janvier 1928–août 1932* (edited by José Pierre in 1990), this work nonetheless represents the initial starting point for any wider inquiry.

Biography

Robert Desnos was born in Paris in 1900 and died of typhus at the Terezine (Theresiendstadt) concentration camp in June 1945, shortly after his liberation. An early member of the Surrealist group which formed around André Breton in the Paris of the 1920s, he was the author of a number of important prose works, often with a marked erotic interest, written while in a state of (self-induced) hypnotic trance. During the 1930s, following his rupture with Breton, his career focused on his work for radio and the newspapers. During his lifetime he published two major collections of poetry, *Corps et biens* (1930) and *Fortunes* (1942), generally seen as his major literary achievement. Indeed, Desnos is now considered one of the principal poetic voices of the twentieth century. Remaining in Paris after the outbreak of the Second World War, he was soon involved in Resistance activity; he was arrested by the Gestapo in February 1944.

TERRY HALE

Selected Works

Corps et biens. Paris: Gallimard, 1930; in *Desnos: Oeuvres,* ed. Marie-Claire Dumas. Paris: Gallimard, 1999.

De l'érotisme considéré dans ses manifestations écrites et du point de vue de l'esprit moderne. In *Robert Desnos:*

Nouvelles Hébrides et autres texts, 1922–1930, ed. Marie-Claire-Dumas. Paris: Gallimard, 1978.

La Liberté ou l'amour. Paris: Editions du Sagittaire, 1927; in *Desnos: Oeuvres,* ed. Marie-Claire Dumas. Paris: Gallimard, 1999; tr. Terry Hale, *Liberty or Love!.* London: Atlas Press, 1993.

Further Reading

Caws, Mary Ann. *The Surrealist Voice of Robert Desnos.* Massachusetts: University of Massachusetts Press. 1977.

Dumas, Marie-Claire. *Robert Desnos ou l'exploration des limites.* Paris: Klincksieck, 1980.

Pierre, José. *Recherches sur la sexualité, janvier 1928– août 1932.* Paris: Gallimard, 1990; as *Investigating Sex: Surrealist Discussions, 1928–1932,* translated by Malcolm Imrie. London: Verso, 1992.

DI GIORGIÒ, MAROSA

1932-
Uruguayan poet

Misales

Since the beginning of her literary career in the early 1950s, di Giorgio forged her own poetic path away from the Nativist movement who seek to reproduce the rural landscape and further still from the socially committed poetry that was embraced by other Uruguayan writers of her time. Her lyrical texts transport the readers to a rural, yet supernatural, and sensual world eternally lightened by the moonlight. The plots are minimal and the intense metaphorical images create a rare and original emotional space. At their center is a young girl (not unlike the protagonist from *Alice in Wonderland* by Lewis Carroll, whom di Giorgio has recognized among her "literary parents") who finds solace away from her dominant mother and her numerous relatives in a garden, a protective and dreamlike place where she can freely interact with animals, plants, and other natural beings. Over the years, di Giorgio's fictional world has

remained practically intact, a fact that she has acknowledged by comparing it to a forest in which she has been planting more trees.

With the publication *Misales* [*Missals*], with its subtitle "erotic stories," di Giorgio's magical and sensual world became openly erotic. The book is a collection of thirty-five short compositions, most of them containing the word "missal" or "mass" in the titles, thus suggesting from the start the strong presence of the sacred in everyday life. Indeed, God and the Roman Catholic rites are a recurring theme throughout the book: the young girl who carries a doll in one hand and a missal book in the other, the female who is crucified by the young and virile lover, who announces: "Mi nombre es Dios. No me reconociste" (My name is God. You didn't recognize me).

Right from the book's opening words: "Salió un perro-zorro y vino al ruedo. Tenía el hocico largo, trotó un poco y robó un huevo" [A dog-fox left and approached the hedge. He had a long snout, he trotted a little and stole an egg], the reader is drawn into a mysterious space, reminiscent of the Biblical paradise or fairy tale scenarios inhabited by virgins with such symbolic names as Mrs. Desirée, Mrs. Saint Elizabeth, and Mrs. One, who cross the prairies all dressed in black habits and have a "trenza que las partía por la mitad desde la nuca al ano" (a braid that parted them in two from the nape to the anus), robust young horseriders, lovers who fornicate in the forest, dogs, butterflies and other natural creatures -including many species of animals native to di Giorgio's birth region. These characters interact with each other without restrictions and participate in the stages associated with the lovemaking process: the mate selection, the seduction, and finally the "coito deslumbante y terrífico" (dazzling and terrific coitus). The masculine being is usually the predator who approaches the female (either a virgin or one who had a husband for a long time) in order to announce that her bridal night has arrived. The phallus is described as a dagger, a tongue or a "robusto, afelpado., en cuya punta se formaba algo, empezaba a salir una cosa, como con trabajo, como una rosa del Cabo, una clara preciosa, que ella quiso tocar y beber" (robust and plush, at the end of which something was forming, something was beginning to come out, as if struggling, like a rose or a gardenia, a precious egg white, that she wanted to touch and drink), while the female organs are "una gran enagua sexual, todo de clitoris ... como pimpollos de rosas rojas en hilera"—a big sexual petticoat, all made of ovaries ...like rows of rosebuds). The female fertility is endless and the menstrual period is a "drop of crystalline water" or a "circular and red cherry." After the copulation, the female becomes pregnant and gives birth to a variety of things, such as eggs, rabbits, lizards, and mushrooms. At the same time, female gestation is intimately connected to food and the protagonists feed each other or end up devouring their own offspring, thus suggesting even further the regenerative life cycles and the strong link that exist between people, animals and nature.

Biography

Marosa di Giorgio was born in the northwestern region of Salto where her parents and maternal grandparents, Italian peasants from near Florence who immigrated to Uruguay, owned two small farms. Her childhood and adolescence in the countryside among her extended family profoundly impacted her life and intimately inspired her literary work. Since the early eighties, she resides in the city of Montevideo.

RENÉE SCOTT

Selected Works

Los papeles salvajes. 2 vols. Montevideo: Arca, 1989–1991. They include the previously published books: *Poemas* 1954, *Humo* 1955, *Druida* 1959, *Historial de las violetas* 1965, *Magnolia* 1965, *La guerra de los huertos* 1971, *Está en llamas el jardín natal* 1971, *Gladiolos de luz y luna* 1974, *Clavel y tenebrario* 1979, *La liebre de marzo* 1981, *Mesa de esmeralda* 1985, *La falena* 1987, *Membrillo de Lusana* 1991, *Misales (relatos eróticos)* 1993; *Misales (relatos eróticos).* Santiago: LOM, 2001.
Camino de las pedrerías. Montevideo: Planeta, 1997.
Reina Amelia. Buenos Aires: Adriana Hidalgo, 1999.
Los papeles salvajes, Buenos Aires: Adriana Hidalgo, 2000. It includes *Los papeles salvajes* and *Díamelas a Clementina Médicis.*

Further Reading

Echavarren, Roberto. "Marosa di Giorgio, última poeta del Uruguay." *Revista Iberoamericana.* Special issue dedicated to Uruguay. 160–161 (1992): 1103–1115.
Pallares, Ricardo. "Marosa di Giorgio: Liebre de marzo en febrero." *Tres mundos de la lírica uruguaya actual.* Montevideo: Ediciones de la Banda Oriental, 1992. 45.
Porzecanski, Teresa. "Marosa di Giorgio: Uruguay's Sacred Poet of the Garden." *A Dream of Light and Shadow.* Ed. Marjorie Agosín. Albuquerque. University of New Mexico Press, 1995. 303–314, 327–328.
Scott, Renée. "Entrevista con Marosa di Giorgio." *Discurso literario.* 3.2 (1985): 271–273.

DI NOTA, DAVID

1968–
French novelist

Apologie du plaisir absolu

David di Nota's *Apologie du plaisir absolu*, dedicated to a Maria Cristina Franco Ferraz, is a first-person novel relating the narrator's quest for a dress for his wife Vitalie. The narrator's name remains unknown, but various similarities with the author's life (both are former danseurs, both wrote a novel) suggest that David di Nota modeled the narrator, at least in part, after himself.

Two explicit sexual episodes aside, both of which involve the author and Vitalie, the novel contains few explicit sexual references. The entire novel, starting as Vitalie is about to wake up and ending with the characters' return from their Saturday afternoon shopping trip, takes place in a single day. Relatively brief, involving a mere two characters, and following a simple storyline, it could qualify, notwithstanding its description as a novel in the title page, as a short story.

The title's reference to "absolute pleasure" alludes not only to the few erotic episodes, but also to the narrator's optimistic belief in man's capacity to be happy on Earth. This is expressed in the lengthy descriptions of minute details that fill the narrator with contentment, most of them pertaining to Vitalie's body, clothes she tries on, or beauty products he applies to her face.

The author's attention to tiny details, very similar stylistically to Yukio Mishima's in novels such as *The Temple of the Golden Pavilion* (1956), translates into a frugal, at times meager, plot. The narrator successively observes young women in a neighboring park while Vitalie is still asleep; forages through her lingerie and beauty products; waits impatiently in the toilets as she talks to her mother on the phone; makes love with Vitalie; enters into a dispute when she refuses to go out to buy a dress, as promised; eats his breakfast; reads a magazine; makes love with Vitalie again; takes a bath with, washes, and applies make-up to Vitalie; spends hours with her trying on dresses in various fashionable Parisian clothing stores; eats a late lunch; then finally buys an evening pant suit for her and heads back home as the day draws to an end.

The two, relatively brief, erotic scenes both take place in the morning. Shortly after Vitalie wakes up, she and the narrator have sex on the carpet. An hour or so later, they repeat the performance in the living room. In keeping with the unostentatious storyline, the love scenes have little to do with the main fare of much popular pornographic writing—tales of indefatigable vaginas, enormous penises, and odd sexual techniques—and remain, cunnilingus aside, of the man-and-woman, man-on-top variety. Even though the narrator is attracted to Vitalie's lingerie, he stops short of fetishism. He briefly mentions his intention to give Vitalie a spanking (*fessée*), but decides against it. For most of *Apologie du plaisir absolu*, eroticism is a subtext, rather than an explicit component, of the novel. As the narrator takes a bath with Vitalie and washes her, regularly points out her beauty and sexual appeal, and eyes her as she changes clothes in clothing stores, his attention to small details of her anatomy—breasts, legs, skin, in particular—more than the characters' actual involvement in sexual intercourse, conveys a sense of continued, jubilant sexual desire.

Homosexuality and the reversal of traditional gender roles are two major sub-themes. Even though the narrator professes his aversion for a gay clothing salesman, he displays all the characteristics associated with male homosexuality in the popular psyche: professional danseur, attracted by fashion, women's clothes and make-up, sophisticated, and garrulous. Vitalie, on the other hand, matches the description of the stereotypical male: less talkative, in charge of all important decisions, she quickly finds shopping tiresome, and dresses in men's apparel. These cross-gender roles do not play a significant role in the erotic scenes.

The novel's briefness (148 pp.), fractured nature, short sentences, many of them with no verbs, the use of the first person and of the present tense, and the time limitation to a single day's span all help carry the impression that the narrator is jotting down sensations and ideas in real time, as he is experiencing them, even during the two erotic scenes. Small events, such as the noise of a spoon in the breakfast bowl or the sight of soap scum on Vitalie's breasts, trigger long soliloquies on the shape of the bowl or on the chemical characteristics of beauty products. Many of these remarks are well thought out and make good use of tasteful puns, well-placed adjectives, and the French language in general. As they become constant and not always significant, some of these digressions, particularly regarding the role of *haute couture* and the feel and appearance of every single dress in a half-dozen stores, can become tiresome. They also abruptly interrupt the narrative, as does a paragraph on Coco Chanel's hatred for the color purple that is somehow inserted half-way through the first love scene. The use of unusual French words and of specialized knowledge borrowed from fields ranging from medicine to chemistry and literature has the same effect: when put to good use, it is witty and intriguing; when abused, the author comes across as verbose and pedantic and the story loses its focus.

Biography

Born on December 27, 1968, David di Nota started as a dancer in the prestigious Opéra de Paris. Resenting other dancers' dullness and competitive drive, he abandoned his dancing career in the early 1990s and started a literary career. Now living in London, he is the author of several short novels in French, including *Festivité locale* (1991), *Apologie du plaisir absolu* (1993), *Quelque chose de très simple* (1995), and *Traité des élégances, I* (1999), all of them published by Gallimard, in the *L'infini* collection edited by Philippe Sollers.

PHILIPPE R. GIRARD

Editions

Apologie du plaisir absolu. Paris: Gallimard, 1993.

Selected Works

Festivité locale. 1991.
Apologie du plaisir absolu. 1993.
Quelque chose de très simple. 1995.
Traité des elegances I. 1999.

Further Reading

Kirkup, James. "Low-Life International," *Times Literary Supplement* no. 4637 (14 February 1992): 15.
Philipps, John. *Forbidden Fictions.* London: Pluto Press, 1999.
Rosario, Vernon A. *The Erotic Imagination: French Histories of Perversity.* Oxford: Oxford University Press, 1997.
Savigneau, Josyane. "Au fil des lectures: un coup pour rien." *Le Monde* (19 November 1993).

DI PRIMA, DIANE

1934–
United States poet and novelist

Memoirs of a Beatnik

Diane Di Prima's *Memoirs of a Beatnik* is fictionalized autobiography, a mixture of memoir and erotic fiction chronicling di Prima's early years as a poet and bohemian in New York City in the early 1950s. It was published in 1969 by Olympia Press—The Traveler's Companion, Inc., reissued in 1988 by Last Gap Press, and reprinted in 1998 by Penguin Books.

Memoirs of a Beatnik, which has sold more than any of di Prima's books, is loosely structured upon the organic drift of the seasons from 1953 through 1956, relying upon the cinematic technique of montage to present sets of inter-connected ideas regarding di Prima's identity as Beat poet and sexual adventurer.

As Beat history, *Memoirs* records valuable insights about Greenwich Village and the place of the woman artist in the burgeoning art world following World War II. Di Prima writes convincingly of the bar scene in the Village, the pads inhabited by painters and writers, and the "Rule of Cool" governing subterranean behavior for women. One catches glimpses of what life must have been like for di Prima as she honed her talents as a poet: her study habits and reading lists; her relationship with the poet Ezra Pound, with whom she corresponded when he was at St. Elizabeth's Hospital in Washington, DC; her first reading of Allen Ginsberg's "Howl," which jolted her into realizing that she wasn't the only one writing poetry to represent the marginalized and abject; and the composition of her first book of poems.

More often, di Prima relies on fiction to explore sexual practices and mores. She herself experimented widely with sex, believed in free love, and had several children out of wedlock, but she states in the afterword to the 1988 edition of *Memoir* that most of the sex scenes are fabrications written to placate her publisher, Olympia Press's Maurice Giodias.

As erotica, the book takes its cue from the word "Beatnik," a term coined by San Francisco journalism Herb Caen in the late fifties. "Beatnik" is a trivializing pejorative that through the suffix "nik" transformed "Beat," defined in the popular media as sex crazed and anti-establishment, into the evil "pinko commie" of the Cold War, while simultaneously converting the demon Beat of free sex into the childish and comic, effectively nullifying the cultural threat posed by Beat. *Memoirs*, then, plays with the notion of Beat sexual practice as paradoxically degenerate/dangerous and infantile/inconsequential.

Di Prima's fantasies rely rather clumsily on flashbacks and dreamscapes to introduce sex scenes. Strings of characters are presented in a minimal story line frequently interrupted by long scenes of explicit sex. The language resists subtlety and titillation to embrace vulgarity. "Cocks," "cum," and "fuck" are used repeatedly. Lesbian and heterosexual sex is featured, including group sex, the most illustrative being an orgy with Beat heroes Jack Kerouac, Allen

Ginsberg, and Peter Orlovsky. Rape and incest narratives appear as well.

By writing for hire, di Prima created a self that exists as sex object and male fantasy. The lesbian scenes function much as they do in male-focused erotica, as a salacious trigger of male sexuality. The rape and incest scenes are modeled on a form of a masculine fantasy: the taking of the female body for male sexual gratification is accepted as the woman gives herself up to the power of the male body, even at times persuading herself that she enjoys the violation.

But *Memoirs* presents a complicated process of undermining its own textuality. The sex stories, many of which ratify male power, also suggest that women need to shape and assert their sexual identity in ways that defy male power. Di Prima's heroine strives to reject the cultural mandate that a woman is defined in her relationship to a man. For instance, most of the males in the book are known only by their first names, stripped of patriarchal heritage and thus individuality and power. The narrator leaves them when she wants to, and both the Beat and Beatnik narratives end when she realizes she is pregnant, a scene which is described as entirely woman-centered: her lover has left for the day, and she serenely packs her books, ready to take off without him into the unknown.

All erotic fantasy in *Memoirs* is eventually subverted to some degree by the juxtaposition of non-fiction prose forms, such as a diatribe against contraception and an interactive passage in which the narrator tells readers to use a blank space provided to list their favorite kisses. The most dramatic anti-erotic device is the use of two subchapters that break the erotic template, making explicit the relationship between fabula and audience. The first describes a mid-November evening during which the narrator and her friends have an orgy; the sex is explicit and hot. The fallacy of the Beatnik myth is exposed in the next subchapter, in which reality is presented as indifference, boredom, a cold apartment, and no sex.

In its play with narrative construction, its embracing and rejection of its erotic content, *Memoirs of a Beatnik* has emerged as an important example of the experimental drive characterizing both Beat literature and the women's movement, suggesting that the erotic, while it has a place in both myth and reality, is not the primary substance by which "Beat" or "woman" is defined.

Biography

Born in 1934 in Brooklyn, New York. Di Prima is the one female writer most readily identified with the American Beat literary movement. She attended Hunter High School in New York and then Swarthmore College from 1951 to 1953. She co-founded the New York Poets Theater and the Poets Press; and co-edited with poet and activist Amiri Baraka (LeRoi Jones) *The Floating Bear* (1961–1969), one of the most important avant garde publications from that period. Her first book of poems, *This Kind of Bird Flies Backwards*, was published in 1958.

DiPrima has authored over a dozen volumes of poetry and two memoirs, taught poetry at Naropa University in Boulder, Colorado, and was awarded National Endowment for the Arts grants in 1966 and 1973.

NANCY M. GRACE

Editions

Memoirs of a Beatnik. New York: Olympia Press, 1969; San Francisco, CA: Last Gasp of San Francisco, 1988; rpt. New York: Penguin Books, 1998.

Selected Works

This Kind of Bird Flies Backwards. 1958.
Dinners and Nightmares, 1961. Expanded ed. 1998.
The New Handbook of Heaven. 1965.
Seven Love Poems from the Middle Latin. 1965.
Haiku. 1966.
Hotel Albert: Poems. 1968.
L.A. Odyssey. 1969.

Kerhonkson Journal. 1971.
Revolutionary Letters. 1971.
The Calculus of Variation. 1972.
The Floating Bear: a Newsletter. 1973.
Freddie Poems. 1974.
Selected Poems. 1956–1975. 1975.
Loba: Parts I–VIII, 1978. 1998; *Parts 1–16, Books I & II*, 1998.
Pieces of a Song: Selected Poems. 1990.
Seminary Poems. 1991.
Recollections of My Life as a Woman: The New York Years. 2001.

Further Reading

Butterick, George. "Diane Di Prima" *Dictionary of Literary Biography* 16, The Beats, ed. Ann Charters. Detroit: Gale Research, 1983, 149–160.

Friedman, Amy L. "'I say my new name': Women Writers of the Beat Generation," *The Beat Generation Writers*, ed. A. Robert Lee. London, Connecticut: Pluto, 1996: 200–216.

Grace, Nancy M. "Snapshots, Sandpaintings, and Celluloid: Life Writing of Women of the Beat Generation," in *Girls Who Wore Black: Women Writing the Beat Generation*. New Jersey: Rutgers UP, 2002.

Kirschenbaum, Blossom S. "Diane di Prima: Extending La Famiglia," MELUS 14: 3–4 (Fall/Winter 1987), 53–67.

McNeil, Helen. "The Archaeology of Gender in the Beat Movement," *The Beat Generation Writers*. Ed. A. Robert Lee. London, CT: Pluto, 1996), 178–199.

Libby, Anthony, "Diane Di Prima: 'Nothing Is Lost; It Shines In Our Eyes'." In *Girls Who Wore Black: Women Writing the Beat Generation*. Ronna C Johnson and Nancy M. Grace, eds. NJ: Rutgers UP, 2002.

Waldman, Anne. "An Interview with Diane Di Prima." *The Beat Road*. Ed. Arthur and Kit Knight. California, PA: 1984, 27–33.

DISKI, JENNY

1947–
British novelist and essayist

Three themes pervade all of Jenny Diski's stories: a troubled search for religion (which will not be addressed here), a fascination with mentally distressed characters, and a strong presence of eroticism and desire. It is, indeed, the specific combination of sex and madness that characterizes Diski's work. Erotic encounters feature in Diski's fiction both as a means of escaping the drab reality of everyday life and as catalytic events which help the characters transgress the constricting rules of society. Sexual ecstasy is employed by Diski in its original sense of ex-stasis, that is, of being outside oneself. Orgasmic experiences, along with dreams during sleep, become a means of transcending reality and entering a different realm. This escapist theme is reinforced in her writings by a tendency to portray characters who seem to linger permanently on the verge of a nervous breakdown, often shunning family responsibilities or simply fleeing from intolerable social and personal circumstances. The distrust of—and resistance to—the outside world carry with them further implications for Diski's characters. Repeatedly they seem to prefer auto-eroticism and masturbation over sexual contact with other people, further precluding the outside world. Even where sex occurs with partners, a lack of intimacy persists. The often isolating experience of mental trauma further adds to the feeling that Diski's characters are constricted by their melancholic individualism and incapacity to share emotions. The ecstatic, escapist theme also resurfaces in Diski's autobiographic essay *Skating to Antarctica*, where she describes her favorite space as an all-white room, devoid of any visual stimulus. It is her longing for this rare environment that causes Diski to take a trip to the Antarctic.

Diski's first novel, *Nothing Natural*, is at the same time her most explicitly erotic and most excessive text. Told from the perspective of Rachel, a single mother in her early thirties, the novel traces her unusual relationship with Joshua. Starting from a chance meeting at a mutual friend's, Rachel soon develops an obsessive longing for the elusive and secretive Joshua, which grows even stronger once she realizes that his aggressive and even physically violent lovemaking awakens in her a sado-masochistic penchant of which she was unaware until then.

Mo, the protagonist in *Rainforest*, is a young researcher who plans a trip to the jungle in order to collect scientific data. There, she realizes both that her ivory-tower view of the orderly structure of nature does not hold up against the chaotic reality of the actual environment and that her own repressed sexuality, once it is released during a brief visit by one of her colleagues, proves that she has a physical body as well. She abandons her academic career and turns to cleaning houses, preferring to re-establish order in a universe that no longer provides her with clear answers.

Some of the minor characters from *Rainforest* reappear in *Happily Ever After*, a novel that follows the lives of the inhabitants of a small house in London. Liam, a former colleague of Mo and now the owner of the apartment building, has been left by his second wife, his former student Grace, and now lives in a semi-permanent alcoholic stupor, which is interrupted only by visits from Daphne, an elderly woman and former novelist who lives in the attic. Even though Liam is obsessed with youthful beauty—he left his first wife and family in order to enjoy Grace's breasts freely—he finally succumbs to Daphne, whose shriveled old body seems to fade from his perception once he has learned to love her for who she is. Even after she leaves him, he is content with his life, finding happiness in country walks and conversations at the local store. All through the novel, his earlier, immature sexuality metamorphosizes into mature eroticism, and he increasingly focuses on the life of the mind. True to its title, *Happily Ever After* ends on a very optimistic note, which is rare for Diski's texts. Even though the novel includes its share of grim moments, including a desperate case of infanticide, it leaves Liam in a contentedly a-libidinous state, and Daphne at ease with her crazed view of life.

While experimentations with narrative point of view occur in a number of Diski's texts, no narrator is more peculiar than Nony in *Like Mother*, the anencephalic baby of Frances, whose story makes up the bulk of this novel. Frances grows up in postwar London, rebelling against the phony values and empty façade of her parents' lives by quietly chanting swear words and by using her prepubescent body to create and then control desire in Stuart, who will much later father Nony. She withdraws into ballet dancing, shunning all emotional involvement with her surroundings. When she gives birth to her brainless child, she rejoices in the fact that Nony will never feel or know pain.

Some of the short stories in *The Vanishing Princess* also deal overtly with erotic themes. "Leaper," which takes its title from a woman's suicide, examines desire for physical love as it arises in the vicinity of death. Diane, the lesbian partner of the dead woman, is seeking sexual solace from a woman she met immediately after her lover's death. Their brief but passionate encounter comes to an abrupt end when Diane reveals her involvement with the suicide victim.

"Bath Time" revolves around the sensual longing for uninterrupted time spent by oneself, and the impossibility of combining intimacy and privacy. "Shit and Gold" is a modern retelling of the classic fairy tale of the miller's daughter and Rumpelstiltskin. However, the task of finding the vindictive dwarf's name is replaced by the heroine's proposal to make him forget his name during three nights in which she uses all her sexual experience to delete his memory.

With *Only Human: A Comedy*, Diski returns to her initial theme of obsessive desire. While her early novels relied extensively on the physical longings and ecstasies of her characters, in this book she concentrates more on the psychology of eroticism. The narrative is a retelling of the biblical story of Abraham and Sarah, told in part from the perspective of God, who, to make things worse, grows increasingly jealous of the love and passion his human creatures invent. The novel also expands on Diski's fascination with the divine, the obsessive, and the erotic.

Biography

Born in London, England; repeatedly spent time in mental institutions, first when she was 14; subsequently lived with the novelist Doris Lessing; attended University College, London; worked as a teacher; studied anthropology; married, one daughter; regular contributor to the *London Review of Books* and the *Observer*.

GERD BAYER

Selected Works

Nothing Natural. 1986.
Rainforest. 1987.
Like Mother. 1988.
Then Again. 1990.
Happily Ever After. 1991.
Monkey's Uncle. 1994.
The Vanishing Princess. 1995.
The Dream Mistress. 1996.
Skating to Antarctica. 1997.
Don't. 1998.
Only Human: A Comedy. 2000.

Further Reading

Bayer, Gerd. "'A sterile promontory:' Jane Rogers's and Jenny Diski's Views of the Future." *Arachne*, 6/1 (1999): 79–92.

Bizzini, Silvia Caporale. "Language and Power in Jenny Diski's *Rainforest*" in *Theme Parks, Rainforests and Sprouting Wastelands: European Essays on Theory and Performance in Contemporary British Fiction.* Edited by Richard Todd and Luisa Flora. Amsterdam: Rodopi, 2000.

Nordius, Janina. "Molds of Telling: Metafictional Sliding in Jenny Diski's *Like Mother*." *English Studies: A Journal of English Language and Literature*, 72/5 (1991): 442–53.

Rosner, Victoria. "Gender Degree Zero: Memoirs of Frozen Time in Antarctica." *A/B: Auto/Biography Studies*, 14/1 (1999): 5–22.

Werner, Hans C. *Literary Texts as Nonlinear Patterns: A Chaotics Reading of* Rainforest, Transparent Things, Travesty, *and* Tristram Shandy. Göteborg, Sweden: Acta Universitatis Gothoburgensis, 1999.

DJEBAR, ASSIA

1936–
Algerian novelist

Described by Kenneth Harrow as the dominant voice in Maghrebian fiction, she is above all known for her ability to express women's revindications within a context of Islamic faith, rewriting Algerian history, and theorizing identity. Indeed, one element of her own biography often discussed in her fiction is the fact that French schooling cut her off from a gynecea, the warmth of female companionship otherwise taken for granted by women of her culture, as well as cutting her off from Berber and Arabic-language culture. Yet with all this, there is still a notable erotic element to her fiction. Studies published by Clerc and Timmerman show that her works, and in particular two novels in the

Algerian Quartet, are not without a troubling sexual tension, particularly in the case of an adulteress in *Vaste est la prison* and of a political prisoner in *La femme sans sépulture*. In the absence of consummated desire, it is especially as visual or scopic desire that the erotic element is expressed. Yet an earlier novel, *L'Amour, la fantasia* is also revealing of this element. When a French soldier views a group of unveiled women, they react indifferently, saying that his gaze is not the same as that of an Algerian man. They wonder whether he has a gaze at all. A hedge separates them from him, yet it is not this physical element that makes them feel safe, but the look itself. The women feel at liberty, since there is no perceived threat of seduction. By contrast, the Algerian man's gaze is considered almost tactile. Clerc interprets this gaze based on Freud's concept of the incest taboo: the unveiled woman, regardless of her relation to the male viewer, is a possible object of desire.

Vaste est la prison recounts the estrangement of a married couple from the perspective of Isma, the wife, who is a musicologist, university lecturer, and filmmaker. Indeed, the film she is making can safely be assumed to be *La Nouba des femmes du Mont Chenoua*, Djebar's 1979 film, yet the identity of author, narrator, and protagonist do not meld. This fluid identity of the actants, especially since the intimate history in the narrative present alternates with twentieth-century Algerian history, has been theorized as giving formal expression to the sisterhood the author aspires to. The passage of greatest erotic tension in *Vaste est la prison* is perhaps the one in which the adulterous protagonist dances in front of her beloved. She had long resisted being "touched by a man," or dancing as a couple. Her objective was the autonomous body. Yet on this fateful summer night she loses herself completely in the delirium of dance, and afterwards, looking back, realizes that she has been "seen" by the beloved. When her marriage disintegrates, and Isma confesses to her husband, he becomes violent, repeatedly attempting to strike her in the eyes and blind her, thereby underscoring the importance of the gaze to desire.

La femme sans sépulture is about the heroic Zoulikha, a woman who fought in the Algerian resistance, died, and whose whereabouts are unknown. Her family is therefore unable to grieve properly. The paradoxes in this novel are poignant. It is the repeated and intensified interrogation by the French police commissioner that pushes Zoulikha to choose a life as a guerilla in the mountains, a fact for which she is grateful. As for the interrogations, they are not without a palpable sexual tension felt by both parties, troubling in light of their ideological differences, the power imbalance between them, and the context itself. The narration also confuses the violence contained within such desire, hinting that this rape would not be entirely unwanted. But just as the text suggests taboo sexuality of colonizer and colonized, it reflects upon some marital unions among Algerians as exploitive. This is the case with a girl fourteen being married to a man of more than seventy, as well as with one of Zoulikha's husbands, who was quickly depleting her inheritance.

Vaste est la prison and *La femme sans sépulture* are novels in which marriage is represented as neither happy nor lasting. Yet the protagonists find the resolve to start anew. Perhaps it is their female networks, the certain solidarity of grandmothers, mothers, sisters, and even in-laws that gives them the courage to do so. Eroticism is therefore but one aspect of love, which is most importantly sororal. Despite a few cases of cowardice, the lasting impression of *La femme sans sépulture* is of a feminine support group on which Zoulikha can fall back.

Another work that is interesting from the perspective of erotic literature is *Nuits de Strasbourg*, which discusses sexuality more explicitly than these novels set in Algeria. Yet perhaps because of this, it seems less representative of Djebar's fiction. In another way, it is representative, however, because it situates sexuality within a context of power, of struggle, including the specter of violence.

Biography

Assia Djebar is the pseudonym of the Algerian writer, playwright, and filmmaker Fatima-Zohra Imayalen, born on 4 August 1936 in Cherchell, Algeria. She attended French schools as a young girl and studied history at ENS Sèvres (1955) as the first Algerian woman to be accepted there. She taught history at the University of Algeria (1962–1965), and French literature and cinema (1974–1980). In 1958 she married resistance member Ahmed Ould-Rouïs, whom she divorced. In 1980 she married the poet Malek Alloula. From 1983–1989, member of a French ministry advisory group dedicated to Algerian emigrants and their representation on television. Founding member, in 1993, of the International Parliament of Authors. Distinguished Professor and Director of the Louisiana State University French and Francophone Studies Centre, the largest of its kind in the United States, since 1997. Since Fall 2001 she has been Silver Chair Professor of French at New York University. Among her numerous distinctions are the 1996 Neustadt Prize for Contributions to World Literature, the 1997 Yourcenar Prize, and the *2000 Friedenspreis des Deutschen Buchhandels*. She is a member of the Belgian *Académie Royale de Langue Française* and on June 16, 2005, she was elected to the *Académie Française*. Djebar has been mentioned as a candidate for the Nobel Prize in Literature.

FRANK RUNCIE

Selected Works

La Nouba des femmes du Mont Chenoua, 1979 (film).
Les Femmes d'Alger dans leur appartement, 1980–*Women of Algiers in Their Apartment*. Charlottesville, VA: University of Virginia Press, 1992.

L'Amour, la fantasia, 1985—*Fantasia: An Algerian Cavalcade*. London: Quartet, 1989 New York: Heineman, 1992.
Vaste est la prison, 1995—*So Vast the Prison*. New York: Seven Stories, 1999.
Les nuits de Strasbourg. Arles: Actes Sud, 1997.
La Femme sans sépulture. Paris: Albin Michel, 2002.

References and Further Reading

Calle-Gruber, Mireille. *Assia Djebar ou la résistance de l'écriture. Regards d'un écrivain d'Algérie*. Paris: Maisonneuve et Larose, 2001.
Clerc, Jeanne-Marie. *Écrire, Transgresser, Résister*. Paris and Montreal: L'Harmattan, classiques pour demain, 1997.
Harrow, Kenneth, ed. *The Marabout and the Muse. New Approaches to Islam in African Literature*. Studies in African Literature. Portsmouth, NH and London: Heinemann and James Curry, 1996.
Mortimer, Mildred P. "Reappropriating the Gaze in Assia Djebar's Fiction and Film." *World Literature Today* (Autumn 1996): 859-66.
Timmerman, Sophie. "Obsession et frustration: dépasser l'érotique dans *Vaste est la prison* et *La femme sans sépulture*," in Donachie, Sarah F. and Harrison, Kim (eds). *Love and Sexuality. New Approaches in French Studies*. Modern French Identities vol 32. Oxford: Peter Lang, 2005.

DON JUAN

The Myth from Tirso de Molina to Molière and Byron

Don Juan's name has become synonymous with seduction and serial sex, and the term 'don Juan' can be applied to any man who is sexually successful with numerous women. But despite the strong emphasis on sex indicated by the don Juan figure, comparatively few of the hundreds of works dedicated to the character and theme are clearly erotic (although in the case of the many dramatic versions this would be affected by staging and performance). While before Romanticism the tale did facilitate male fantasies about women's sexual desires, it also had overtly moral purposes about death and judgement. The earliest known version, *El burlador de Sevilla* [*The Trickster of Seville*], popularly attributed to Spanish playwright Tirso de Molina and thought to date any time between 1616 and 1625, brings don Juan's career to an end with the statue of an angry father of one female victim, a man who don Juan killed in a duel over her honor: the statue drags don Juan to Hell for failing to repent of his sins. The original don Juan shows few erotic sensibilities, and his true purpose lies in ruining women's reputations and tricking them into sex. The pleasure lies in conquest rather than the satisfaction of sexual desire. Subsequent versions, including Molière's *Dom Juan* (1665) and Mozart and da Ponte's opera *Don Giovanni* (1787), kept the same emphasis on the flouting of social conventions and on female conquest in preference to overt displays of eroticism. In these two works don Juan fails to carry out a successful seduction—his fame as a seducer resting on his reputation—so that flirtatious foreplay rather than the sexual act itself becomes the primary vehicle for suggestions of sexual desire. In contrast, an excess of actual sexual encounters bordering on rape, in Shadwell's *The Libertine* (1675), directly countered any sense of eroticism. Molière did, however, allow *his* don Juan to feel that to be faithful to one woman was to be unjust to all the rest, implying that for don Juan indiscriminate sexual activity was simply a kindness to women—a justification that would subsequently become more overt with Kierkegaard.

With the advent of Romanticism, the emphasis shifted from judgement for sins to the male individual quest for fulfilment, which would often take the form of a search for the perfect woman who, of course, could never be found. Byron's poem *Don Juan* (1819–1824) includes a virginal don Juan's initiation into sex by an older woman as well as the sex slave of a harem of Turkish women and the plaything of the Russian Empress Catherine, in each case suggesting a fantasy of the passive male as a sex toy for women—an element that would reappear in twentieth-century versions. Possibly the most significant work about don Juan in this era was not any work of literature, but philosophy, Søren Kierkegaard's *Either/Or*, which included two essays on Mozart's *Don Giovanni*. Kierkegaard takes up Molière's earlier notion of don Giovanni's serial fornication as a kindness to women by presenting him as the epitome of female erotic desire. Later in the same work Kierkegaard offers us a voyeuristic portrait of Mozart's donna Elvira, whose hysteria at the loss of don Giovanni leaves her running about in a revealing dishevelled state, a motif of erotic display also found in relation to donna Anna in E.T.A. Hoffmann's short story 'Don Juan' (1813), a reinterpretation and critique of Mozart's and da Ponte's character. Hoffmann also asserted that, despite her avowals to the contrary in the opera, Anna succumbed to don Juan's sexual persuasions—generally a more pleasurable notion for the male reader than her avowed commitment to her virtue. Also significant in respect of eroticism is the most popular Spanish version, Zorrilla's *Don Juan Tenorio* (1844)—performed annually in Spain and better known there than the Tirso

original. In this version, don Juan finds his good woman, Inés, and intends to reform her: her death sends him back on his old course, but her ghost returns to redeem him as he dies. This overly sentimental play nonetheless provides a focus of eroticism in the character Inés: an innocent novice, she describes in detail her awakening sexuality, while elsewhere don Juan himself comments that he will open her up like a flower to the dew.

In the same year, 1844, the protagonist of Nikolas Lenau's poem *Don Juan* seduces women until he becomes sated, and throws away his life in a duel through sheer boredom. Lenau's motif of satiety introduced a note of weariness with the life of seduction and the endless pursuit of sex that would become more commonplace as don Juan left Romanticism behind and began a search for utopias beyond women. Twentieth-century versions of don Juan move his quest on to a search for higher entities than the perfect woman. Many of these don Juans, indeed, shun the company of women, who nonetheless chase after them as a result of their insatiable desire—the male fantasy made manifest. Shaw's drawing-room comedy version, *Man and Superman* (1901–1903), contains much about the search of John Tanner (don Juan) for the Nietzschean Life Force, and his flight from the predatory Ann Whitefield, who succeeds in capturing him at the end. Their final exchange is suggestive of a sexual climax, as they talk more urgently and Ann breathes harder and faster. For Shaw's women, however, sexuality is a means to an end, subordinate to the drive to reproduce. Max Frisch's *Don Juan oder die Liebe zur Geometrie* (Don Juan or the Love of Geometry: 1952, revised 1961) works a similar vein. This don Juan wishes to devote his time to the abstract study of geometry, but the insatiable demands of women drag him in a mire of drinking and bad temper. Shaw's and Frisch notion of don Juan as the victim of female desire occurred earlier with Edmond de Rostand's *La dernière nuit de don Juan* (1914), where don Juan functions as a plaything for women. Thus although don Juan himself popularly symbolizes endless sexual pleasure, don Juan's history comes in the end to mean the degeneration and staleness of such pleasure, suggesting that its erotic possibilities will sooner or later be exhausted—a sort of literary detumescence.

ANN DAVIES

Editions

Versions of the Don Juan story are numerous. Those listed below are only a selection:

Byron, Lord George Gordon. *Don Juan*, ed. by T. G. Steffan, E. Steffan and W. W. Pratt. London: Penguin, 1973.

Frisch, Max. *Gesammelte Werke in zeitlicher Folge*, III, 95–175, ed. by Hans Mayer. Frankfurt: Suhrkamp, 1976.

———, *Don Juan oder die Liebe zur Geometrie*. Ed. by D.G. and S.M. Matthews. London: Methuen, 1979.

Hoffmann, E.T.A. 'Don Juan: eine fabelhafte Begenbenheit, die sich mit einem reisenden Enthusiasten zugetragen.' *Fantasie- und Nachtstücke*. Munich: Winkler, 1960, 67–78.

Kierkegaard, Søren. *Either/Or: a Fragment of Life*. Trans. by Alastair Hannay. Harmondsworth: Penguin, 1990.

Lenau, Nikolaus. 'Don Juan: dramatische Szenen,' In *Sämtliche Werke*. Ed. by E. Castle Leipzig: Hesse und Becker Verlag, 1900.

Molière, [J.-B.P. de.]. 'Dom Juan, ou le festin de pierre', *Œuvres complètes*. Ed. by Georges Couton, vol. II, Paris: Gallimard. 1971.

Mozart, Wolfgang Amadeus. *Il dissoluto punito ossia il don Giovanni*. Neue Ausgabe sämtlicher Werke Serie II, Bühnenwerke Werkgruppe 5, Band 17, Basle: Bärenreiter Kassel, 1968.

Rostand, Edmond. *La dernière nuit de Don Juan*. Paris: Charpentier and Fasquelle, 1921.

Shadwell, Thomas. 'The Libertine' in *Libertine Plays of the Restoration*. Ed. by Gillian Manning. London: Dent, 2001.

Shaw, Bernard. *Man and Superman: a Comedy and a Philosophy*. London: Constable, 1931.

Tirso de Molina. 'Tan largo me lo fiáis,' *Obras dramáticas completas*. Ed. by Blanca de los Ríos, vol. II., Madrid: Aguilar, 1952.

———. *The Trickster of Seville and the Stone Guest (El burlador de Sevilla y el convidado de piedra)*. Ed. by Gwynne Edwards. Warminster: Aris and Phillips, 1986.

———. attrib. *El burlador de Sevilla*. Ed. by Alfredo Rodríguez López Vázquez, 6th edn, Madrid: Cátedra, 1994.

Zorrilla, José. *Don Juan Tenorio*. Ed. by David T. Gies. Madrid: Castalia, 1994.

Further Reading

Davies, Ann. *The Metamorphoses of Don Juan's Women: Early Modern Parity to Late Modern Pathology*. Lewiston: Edwin Mellen Press, 2004.

Feal, Carlos. *En nombre de Don Juan: estructura de un mito literario*. Amsterdam: John Benjamins, 1984.

Felman, Shoshana. *The Literary Speech Act: Don Juan with J.L. Austin, or Seduction in Two Languages*. Trans. by Catherine Porter. Ithaca: Cornell University Press, 1983.

Ginger, Andrew John Hobbs and Huw Lewis (editors). *Selected Interdisciplinary Essays on the Representation of the Don Juan Archetype in Myth and Culture*. Lewiston: Edwin Mellen Press. 2000.

Mandrell, James. *Don Juan and the Point of Honor: Seduction, Patriarchal Society, and Literary Tradition*. University Park, PA: University of Pennsylvania Press, 1992.

Smeed, J. W. *Don Juan: Variations on a Theme*. London: Routledge, 1990.

Weinstein, Leo. *The Metamorphoses of Don Juan*. Stanford, CA: Stanford University Press, 1959.

DONNE, JOHN

1572–1631
English Poet and Cleric

John Donne (1572–1631) was the first and greatest of the Metaphysical Poets: a term coined by Dryden to describe their characteristic exploitation of unpredictable imagery; their forceful juxtapositions of abstract with concrete and of colloquial with learned allusion. Donne's poetry falls like his own life into two distinct categories: secular and sacred. The second of these, like his magnificent sermons and his prose works generally, makes only slight and conventional use of erotic reference, as in the conclusion to *Holy Sonnet* 10 (XIV):

...for I
Except you'enthrall mee, never shall be free,
Nor ever chast, except you ravish mee.

The use of erotic material, description, and anecdote in his secular poetry however is pervasive, in registers that range from brash self display in certain of the *Elegies* through occasional, Juvenalian detachment in the *Satyres*, ritualistic sensuality in the *Epithalamia* and wit, light-hearted or cruel; mischief and exquisite tenderness in the *Songs and Sonnets*. The first and last of these groups are considered here in more detail.

The Elegies

Only a very few of his public poems were printed in Donne's lifetime. It is likely that the *Elegies* were among his earliest work, written while he was at the Inns of Court, and intended for circulation among his fellow students: a specific, intellectual, all-male readership, and one very self-conscious at this time of its culturally avant-garde status. The Roman poets, especially Ovid, Martial, and Juvenal, are obvious influences. In these poems, sexual and erotic reference is exploited in a number of ways. *The Comparison* is simply structured by ingenious, epigramatic pairing of the attributes of a Blazon of Beauty with its repulsive opposite:

> Is not your last act harsh, and violent,
> As when a Plough the stony ground doth rent?
> So kisse good Turtles, so devoutly nice
> Are Priests in handling reverent sacrifice,
> And such in searching wounds the Surgeon is
> As wee, when wee embrace, or touch, or kisse.
> (ll.47–1151)

The disturbingly multivalent image of priestly sacrifice recurs in the formal context of Donne's *Epithalamion* for the marriage of the Earl of Somerset, December 1613:

> So, shee...
> ...at the Bridegroome's wish'd approach doth lye,
> Like an appointed lambe, when tenderly
> The priest comes on his knees t'embowell her;
> (ll. 87–90)

Images transposed in this way so as to heighten the different registers in which they occur are typical of Donne's erotic discourse generally, most subtly in the *Songs and Sonnets*.

The two *Elegies* most famous for their inventive and energetic display of erotic wit are *To his Mistris Going to Bed* and *Loves Progress*. The former is a dramatic monologue, a form Donne uses frequently. The colloquial invocation, with which it opens is characteristic:

> Come, Madame, come, all rest my powers defie,
> Until I labour, I in labour lye. (ll.1–2)

The uninhibited celebration of sensual delights that follows is likely to be more wishful thinking than autobiography. The splendid clothes and ornaments the lady is commanded to cast aside are those either of a rich, even a noble lady, or of a very expensive courtesan, neither a likely sexual partner for a student of average means. The lovers' situation is in any case a dramatic context for passion and its verbal analysis:

> Licence my roving hands, and let them goe
> Behind, before, above, between, below.
> Oh my America, my new found lande... (ll.25–27)

Loves Progress is a debate-variation on the common motif of the woman's body as a landscape to be explored. The lover's goal being 'the Centrique part' or vagina, he may approach it from the head, traveling downwards as Shakespeare's Venus indicates to Adonis (*V and A*, ll.229234) or from the feet, as does Nashe in his *Choise of Valentines* (ll.100 ft), where the lady is a prostitute. Donne's pragmatic conclusion and the puns on financial dealing which express it suggest that in this instance so is his:

> Rich Nature hath in woman wisely made
> Two purses, and their mouths aversely laid;
> They then which to the lower tribute owe
> That way which that exchequer lookes must goe.
> (ll. 91–94)

The Songs and Sonnets

These are now generally recognized as falling into two groups. In the first are poems that center primarily on a conceit, and sometimes a situation, most often erotic. Ovid, and his Renaissance followers are direct influences. *The Indifferent*, for instance, is a replay of *Amores* II iv, and *The Flea* exploits the Seduction Poem format to take to new and brilliantly funny extremes the common trope of the lover's comments on the intimacy a flea enjoys with his mistress:

> Marke but this flea, and marke in this,
> How little that which thou deniest me is:
> Mee it suck'd first, and now sucks thee,
> And in this flea, our two bloods mingled bee...
>
> Oh stay, three lives in one flea spare,
> Where wee almost, nay more than maryed are:
> This flea is you and I, and this
> Our mariage bed and mariage temple is;
>
> Though parents grudge, and you, w'are met,
> And cloystered in thiese living walls of Jet.

The lady kills the flea, and points out that neither of them seems the worse for it:

'Tis true, then learne how false feares bee;
Just so much honor, when thou yeeld'st to mee,
Will wast, as this flea's death tooke life from thee.

In the second group are poems of mutual or unrequited passion, and some, possibly influenced by Neoplatonic concepts, which deal with the union of true lovers as a kind of transcendence:

Thou sunne....
Shine here to us, and thou art everywhere;
This bed thy center is, these walls, thy sphere.
(*The Sunne Rising,* 11. 25–30).

Among these extraordinary philosophical and intellectual explorations of physical passion, *The Dreame* takes the situation of Ovid's *Amores* I. v., where Corinna wakes the poet from his siesta to make love until both are exhausted, recasting it with subtlety and tenderness:

Thou art so true, that thoughts of thee suffice,
To make dreames truth; and fables histories;
Enter these arms, for since thou thought it best
Not to dreame all my dreame, let's do the rest.

The Extasie is the most difficult of these poems, and also the most revealing. It presents a rare experience, of spiritual union, and its analysis through Donne's very precise perception of the relation of such a state, once achieved, to physical consumation. The interdependence of erotic and intellectual passion is taken to the highest reach of human potential:

To'our bodies turn wee then, that so
men on love revealed may looke;

mysteries in soules do grow,
yet the body is his booke.

Biography

Born in London in 1572. Brought up as a Catholic: studied at the Inns of Court from 1591; saw military service abroad 1596–1597; secretary to Sir Thomas Egerton 1598; MP for Brackley, Northants. 1601. His elopement with his employer's neice, Ann More, in the same year, effectually ended his hopes of further advancement. After years of poverty alleviated by occasional patronage he converted to Anglicanism, and was ordained a priest in 1615. His clerical career was highly distinguished. He was elected Dean of St Paul's, 1621, a post he held until his death ten years later.

ELIZABETH WATSON PORGES

Editions

The Elegies and the Songs and Sonnets. Ed. Helen Gardner. Oxford University Press, 1963.
The Satires, Epigrams and Verse Letters. Ed. W. Milgate, Oxford University Press. 1969.
The Epithalamions, Anniversaries and Epicedes. Ed. W. Milgate. Oxford University Press, 1978.

Further Reading

Smith A.J. (ed.). *John Donne: The Critical Heritage.* London, 1975.
Carey J. *John Donne: Life, Mind and Art.* London 1981.
Docherty T. *John Donne, Undone.* London, 1986
Marotti A.F. *John Donne, Coterie Poet.* University of Wisconsin Press, 1986.

DORAT, CLAUDE-JOSEPH

(1734–1780)
French poet, novelist, dramatist

(attributed) *Les Egarements de Julie*

A novel in three parts first published in 1755. Controversy exists regarding its authorship. Barbier's *Dictionnaire des œuvres anonymes* (3rd edition, 1874, vol. 2, p.38) attributes the novel to J.A.R. Perrin (died 1813), as does the Brancart edition of 1883, whereas others cite Dorat as the author, including Georges Albert-Roulhac and Magdy Gabriel Badir.

The 1755 edition by Hochereau l'aîné in Amsterdam is rare. Better known editions followed in Amsterdam in 1756 and in London in 1776. As its title would suggest, the novel is a late manifestation of the libertine novel for which Crébillon fils is famous. The work's style is galant and its content is suggestive rather than obscene, but in spite of this the work was forbidden during the Restoration, added to the Index in 1825, and officially condemned by order of the Cour Royale de Paris on 5 August 1828.

Narrated in the first person, *Les egarements de Julie* follows the heroine from her humble origins in a series of adventures around France, focusing on her sexual development and her social ascent. From the early age of 13, Julie decides to make the most of her physical charms in order to improve her material situation. In insisting upon the theme of *égarement* (in the sense of the principal character being led astray), the work retains the plotline of the libertine novel (Cp. Crébillon fils's better known *Les egarements du cœur et de l'esprit*, 1736–1738), whilst containing a moralizing strand, which sees the heroine reconciled with bourgeois moral values at the close of the work. In accordance with this dual influence, perhaps, the early stages of the novel contain interspersed retrospective comments of regret which suggest that Julie was obliged to act as she did according to her libertine temperament and her penchant for vice:

> Qu'êtes-vous devenus, bouillants transports, appétits déréglés, auxquels je ne savais rien refuser? Temps orageux d'une jeunesse inconsidérée, je vous ai employés à courir follement après un bonheur dont je ne saisissais jamais que l'ombre (1776 edition, vol. 3, pp. 99-100).

The explanation which passages such as this give for her early actions is a combination of age, natural temperament, and education ('Qui put jamais résister au vice, après avoir eu le malheur d'y être instruit? nous ne fûmes jamais que ce qu'on nous fit', vol. 1), but in contrast with the older Julie's retrospective judgements as narrator, the young character seems at the time to lack any concern for the future, or any moral conscience relative to her actions. Julie seems quite at home with the rules of society, one of the guiding principles of which is women's power over men.

The first section charts Julie's early sexual experiences and the origins of her social ambition.

The style is restrained, which means that the sexual episodes in the novel are alluded to clearly but never described in detail. Julie's first contact with sexuality comes from spying on a childhood friend (Sophie) and her lover; setting up one important strand of the work as a whole; namely, that sexual pleasure can be voyeuristic as well as physical, and one of the reasons for the work's anonymous publication was almost certainly these early pages, where a lesbian scene between Julie and Sophie is alluded to. Julie's first lover, Sieur Valérie, is also introduced, but is pitted against the older but rich financier M. Poupard, described throughout as physically repulsive and morally ridiculous but who is intended for Julie in an arranged marriage by her aunt. Encouraged by Poupard's advances, Julie soon learns that she can easily flatter him enough to be showered with presents, without committing herself physically.

After having been tricked out of her new-found fortune by a third man, the Marquis de Bellegrade, the second part sees the newly impoverished Julie enter into a relationship with the merchant Démery, very much along the lines of her previous liaison with Poupard. More importantly, she also meets a young serving girl, Cécile, leading to a second apparently lesbian scene in the book, until it turns out that Cecile is actually a young man (Vépry) in disguise and Julie and he become clandestine lovers. The second section is notable for the rocambolesque elements which it uses: unfortunate turns of the plot, such as when Démery dies of an attack of apoplexy which obliges Julie and Vépry to leave Bordeaux for Marseille, chance meetings, such as the following episode in Marseille when Julie meets her childhood friend, Sophie, and surprise events, such as when Sophie's new fiancé turns out to be the same Marquis de Bellegrade from part one.

In the third part, Julie plans her revenge on Bellegrade by ruining his relationship with Sophie, yet the result is that the situation turns against her and Vépry leaves her. Despite the 1970 edition's claim that '[l]a dernière partie n'ajoute rien aux succès comme aux déboires de la ravissante Julie', the final section inflects the plot to a significant extent: Julie falls into a serious illness, only to be saved by an unattractive but modest philosophical man, Gerbo, who lives on the floor above. Though a seemingly

357

unlikely candidate for her affections, Gerbo's tale of previous misfortunes at the hands of people less virtuous than him, his care for Julie, and his virtuous and modest nature touch Julie to the extent that she will settle with him, and as narrator, finish her tale by deploring her licentious nature.

Les malheurs de l'inconstance

An epistolary novel in two parts first published in 1772, and including a preface by the author. The plot is centred upon the Duc de ***, who has failed to seduce Mme de Syrcé. In order to get his revenge, he encourages his young nephew cousin the Count de Mirbelle to seduce her and then ruin her reputation; the Duke also plans to win Mirbelle's current lover, the English widow Lady Sidley, for himself. Mirbelle is originally hesitant, yet is spurred on by the Duke's mockery, seduces Mme de Syrcé but then falls genuinely in love with her. Sidley learns of the new liaison by an anonymous letter and, heartbroken, retires from society, whereas Mme de Syrcé, when she has learned everything from Mirbelle himself, miscarries their child and dies. The now ruined Mirbelle kills the Duke in a duel.

The Duke, upon whom the plot is centered, may be taken as one of the models for Laclos's comte de Valmont, despite differences in style and skill between the two authors (Trousson, p. 894). If Lady Sidley is a self-styled habituée in misfortune ('Le ciel semble m'avoir fait naître pour les chagrins les plus sensibles; &, s'il me donna le courage, ce fut pour l'exercer par l'infortune' [part 1, letter 1]), who eschews social convention and proudly follows her heart, Mme de Syrcé fights her feelings for Mirbelle until the end of part one. In the final letter, Mirbelle, having secretly followed her flight to the country to avoid him, comes across her in a garden and she gives in to him.

Despite the 'frivolity' and superficiality with which much of his work was charged by contemporaries, Dorat's novel, ten years before *Les liaisons dangereuses*, creates a genuinely tragic ending, borne of the breakdown of moral order in a society characterized by dissipation. In posing, in filigree, the problem of the interrelation of nature and society, the novel also asks the fundamental question of whether man is morally good or bad (1983 edition, p. ix–x).

Biography

The younger son of a noble family, Dorat served briefly in the military before resigning his post to take up writing. His literary output, spanning the 1760s and 1770s, is abundant and varied, yet widely considered by contemporaries and later critics as superficial; only recently has the importance of some of his works been recognized. An author of *Héroïdes*, six tragedies, a text on theater (*La déclamation théâtrale*), and novels (six are attributed to him, yet only three with certainty), Dorat's narrative work is in line with contemporary developments in the genre which link sensibility and virtue, with some echoes of Rousseauism, even though contemporaries were scornful of such writers' mingling of philosophy and libertinage ('des espèces de Socrate de toilette qui ont affublé la philosophie et la morale de toutes les franfreluches de la frivolité', Baron Grimm, *Correspondance littéraire*, quoted by Trousson, p.891). Laurent Versini has recognized the importance of Dorat's *Les Malheurs de l'inconstance* for some of the characters and situations in Laclos's *Les liaisons dangereuses* (1782). His output also contains libertine poetry, notably *Les baisers* (1770), an imitation of the work of the same title (*Basia*) by the neo-Latin poet Joannis Secundus (Fr. Jean Second) (B. The Hague, 1511 – D. Tournai, 1536).

Mark Darlow

Editions during Dorat's lifetime

[Anon.] *Les egaremens de Julie* (Amsterdam: Hochereau, 1755). 3 parts in 1 volume. Various later editions, including (Amsterdam: 1756); (London: 1776); (London: 1782).

[Anon.] *Les malheurs de l'inconstance, ou lettres de la marquise de Syrcé et du comte de Mirbelle* (Amsterdam, et se trouve à Paris: Delalain, 1772). 2 parts.

[Translation] *The Fatal Effects of Inconstancy; or, Letters of the Marchioness de Syrce, the Count de Mirbeele [sic] and others* (London: J. Bew, 1774). 2 vols.

Les Baisers, précédés du Mois de mai (La Haye/Paris: Delalain, 1770).

Modern Editions

Perrin. *Les egaremens de Julie*, texte collationné d'après l'édition princeps de 1756, revu sur l'édition de 1782. Paris: Editions Eryx, 1950.

Perrin. *Les egarements de Julie*. Conte moral. Réimpression textuelle sur la rarissime édition de 1776. Bruxelles: A Brancart, 1883.

Dorat, Claude-Joseph. *Les egarements de Julie*. Préface par Georges Albert-Roulhac. Paris: C. Bertrand, 1970.

Dorat, Claude-Joseph. *Les Malheurs de l'Inconstance*, préface de Alain Clerval. Paris: Desjonquères, 1983.

Les Malheurs de l'Inconstance is also republished in *Romans libertins du XVIIIe siècle*, ed. Raymond Trousson. Paris: Robert Laffont/Bouquins, 1993, p. 885–1047.

Further Reading

Versini, Laurent. *Laclos et la tradition. Essai sur les sources et la technique des 'Liaisons dangereuses'.* Paris: Klincksieck, 1968 (on Dorat, see esp. p.145)

Gabriel Badir, Magdy. 'L'ascension sociale de la courtisane au dix-huitième siècle dans *Les Egarements de Julie* et *Fanny Hill'*, *Studies on Voltaire and the Eighteenth Century*, 305 (1992), 1435–1438.

Merlo, Paul Yves. 'Claude-Joseph Dorat, ou l'évolution du poète de l'inconstance au romancier du danger des liaisons', Ph.D. diss. University of California, Santa Barbara, 1972.

DOSTOEVSKY, FEDOR

1821–1881
Novelist, short-story writer, journalist

The Russian 20th-century philosopher Nikolai Berdiaev wrote that Fedor Mikhailovich Dostoevsky "laid bare the sensual element in the complex Russian nature and his plots are worked out in the stormy atmosphere of passion: there is nothing like it in any other Russian writer," which earned him the epithet "the Russian Sade." Sexual desire plays an important role in his works and "the plots of Dostoevsky's great novels of the period 1866 to 1880 are moved by sexual secrets and scandals" (Fusso 2002–2003, 47). His works are considered erotic not because they arouse sexual desire, but because they present eroticism as a philosophical problem with ethical, psychological, and social implications. Structurally, the author presents the problem of eroticism through a complex doubling of plot lines and characters, typically contrasting tender, maternal affection to destructive and stormy sexual passion. Synthesis of the two is achieved not in the establishment of a traditional family, as in Tolstoi's *War and Peace*, for example, but in the subordination of sensuality to compassion. There are, in fact, few happy couples in Dostoevskii's work.

His first published work, the epistolary novel *Bednye liudi* [*Poor Folk*] (1846), exhibits the strong influence of the Naturalist writer Nikolai Gogol, whose most famous characters—lowly civil servants—are characterized by deeply repressed sexual desires and, in some cases, a morbid fear of women and marriage. The hero of *Poor Folk*, Makar Devushkin, is a humble clerk whose surname derives from the Russian word *devushka* (young lady). The novel is structured around his epistolary attempts to court Varvara, a sentimenal woman with a past reminiscent of Rousseau's Julie. Devushkin hopes to woo her with his literary style, but she is violently seduced and carried off by Bykov, whose name is taken from the Russian word for bull. In what would become a recurring motif in Dostoevsky's work, a gentle, somewhat feminine hero loses the girl to a strong and violent male who inhabits a more traditional masculine identity.

The fallen woman appears again in "Zapiski iz podpol'ia" [Notes from the Underground] (1864) in the character of Liza, a young prostitute who longs to be loved and to escape the life of the brothel. The underground man, combining the violent passion of Bykov and the sentimental tenderness of Devushkin, is both moved to comfort Liza and to dominate her. In a moment of sentimental tenderness, he is sexually aroused and possesses her—illustrated in the text by an ellipsis—after which he seeks to humiliate her by placing money in her hand. Liza's refusal of the money demonstrates her pride and dignity in the most degrading circumstances. The tyranny of men is also the theme of "Krotkaia" [The Gentle Creature] (1876), a desperate first person narrative by a pawnbroker, similar in character to the underground man, whose wife leaps from a window clutching an icon in order to escape his sadistic treatment.

The prostitute Liza is clearly a prototype for Sonia in *Prestuplenie i nakazanie* [*Crime and Punishment*] (1866), the first of Dostoevsky's great novels written after his Siberian exile. Driven to prostitution to support her half-siblings, the meek Sonia exhibits great moral strength. Raskolnikov, the hero of the novel, who kills an old pawnbroker to prove that he is above the law, learns humility from Sonia and eventually does what she commands, confessing his crime in Haymarket Square and kissing the earth that he defiled. Raskolnikov's double in the novel is Svidrigailov who has also committed a crime. Rumors circulate that he corrupted a young girl who later, on the eve of his suicide, haunts his dreams, staring at him with an impudent, adult smile on her face. In the expurgated chapter from *Besy* [*The Demons*] (1872), entitled "U Tikhona" [At Tikhon's], the radical Stavrogin also confesses to the rape of a young girl, thus exposing a violent will to power at the heart of his utopian politics. So central is this motif to Dostoevsky's portayal of sexual desire and the power relations between men and women that it has been rumored since the late 19th century that the author himself committed such a crime. Ieronim Iasinsky made it the subject of a short story entitled "Ispoved'" [Confession] (1888), in which Dostoevskii confesses to his literary nemesis, Ivan Turgenev, that he raped a young girl.

Dostoevsky's novel *Idiot* [*The Idiot*] (1868) explores the psychology of the gentle male as embodied in the Christ-like Prince Myshkin, whose name is formed from the Russian word for mouse. Myshkin is torn between his love for the socially acceptable and progressive Aglaia and Nastasia Filipovna, a passionate woman with a past. Inspired, it appears, less by passion than by a desire to save Nastasia, Myshkin pledges to marry her, but Nastasia is ultimately unable to accept his offer and runs to the violent Rogozhin who eventually murders her. Having failed to save Nastasia or to find love for himself, Myshkin returns to Switzerland at the novel's close, his health destroyed. His fate is not unlike that of Aleksei, the hero of *Igrok* [*The Gambler*] (1867), whose passion for the emancipated Polina appears to both mirror and feed a growing addiction to gambling,

which leaves him a physical and emotional wreck.

Erotic passion is also central to *Brat'ia Karamazovy* [*The Brothers Karamazov*] (1880), a novel organized around the crime of parricide. Violent tyranny is associated with unbridled sensuality in the character of the father, Fedor Karamazov. Each of the three brothers, Dmitrii, Ivan, and Alesha has a particular relationship to the erotic. Dmitrii, or Mitia, the eldest brother, is a traditional member of the upper class who indulges his sensual tastes and appetites, while Ivan, a modern intellectual, subordinates his erotic desires to his radical philosophical and political ideals. Alesha, a character in the tradition of Prince Myshkin, is a gentle young man who, at the beginning of the novel, is studying under Father Zosima to become a monk. Smerdiakov, who may be the illegitimate child of Fedor, is an utterly corrupted individual. The main female characters are Grushenka, another woman with a past who uses her sensuality to tempt Fedor Karamazov and his sons, and Katerina Ivanovna, who combines elements of aristocratic pride with the seriousness of purpose of that century's "new woman." Although Katerina Ivanovna punishes Dmitrii by delivering damning and spiteful testimony against him, she reveals what is for Dostoevsky the feminine virtue of self-sacrifice in her desire to save Ivan from his nihilism.

Dostoevsky's most damning portrait of unbridled sensuality is perhaps the one contained in the short story "Bobok," which appeared in the author's column *Dnevnik Pisatel'* [*Diary of a Writer*] in 1873. In it, Dostoevsky presents the posthumous sexual confessions of decaying corpses in a graveyard. The title, "Bobok," which means *seed*, is a reference to the New Testament parable of the mustard seed. In contemporary Russian society, it would seem, there is no fertile soil for the seed of spiritual insight to take root.

Dostoevsky's presentation of eroticism as a struggle between compassion and passion, which is closely connected to political and philosophical issues of power, earned him a central place in Russian writings on the philosophy of love in the fin-de-siecle. Strongly influenced by Neo-Platonism, various writers and thinkers of the late nineteenth and early twentieth century saw in Dostoevsky's work the confrontation of fundamental philosophical principles—masculine and feminine, body and spirit, the dionysian and the apollonian. Vladimir Solov'ev saw the resolution of such antinomies in Sophia, the feminine principle of holy wisdom, Viacheslav Ivanov in the androgyne, and Vasilii Rozanov in the sexual union of a man and a woman.

Biography

Born in Moscow, 30 October 1821, the son of a doctor; attended the Military Engineering School in St. Petersburg,1837–1843; then served the minimum term in the military. Published his first work of fiction, *Bednye liudi* [*Poor Folk*], 1846. Sentenced to death for involvement with the radical Petroshevsky Circle but reprieved at the last moment; sentence commuted to time in a prison labor camp in Siberia, 1850–1854, followed by internal exile, 1854–1859. First wife died of tuberculosis on 15 April 1864; his brother, Mikhail, died on 10 July 1864. Had disastrous affair with Apollonaria Suslova (nicknamed Polina) and developed gambling addiction. Married his stenographer, Anna Grigorievna Snitkina in 1867; had four children; one died in infancy, another at age three. In addition to fiction writing, was active as an editor and a journalist; wrote a column of social commentary and fiction, *Dnevnik pisatelia* [*Diary of a Writer*], at irregular intervals between 1871–1881. Died of a hemorrhage in his throat on 29 January 1881.

BRIAN JAMES BAER

Editions

Polnoe sobranie sochinenii v tridtsati tomakh. Edited by G.M. Fridlender. *et. al.* 1972–.

Selected Works

Bednye liudi. 1846, as *Poor People.* Translated by Hugh Aplin, 2002.
Besy. 1872, as *The Possessed.* Translated by Constance Garnett, 1963.

"Bobok." 1873, as "Bobok," translated by Jessie Coulson, 1968.
Brat'ia Karamazovy. 1880, as *The Brothers Karamazov,* translated by Richard Pevear and Larissa Volokhonsky, 1990.
Idiot. 1868, as *The Idiot,* translated by Richard Pevear and Larissa Volokhonsky, 2002.
Igrok. 1867, as *The Gambler,* translated by Constance Garnett, 2003.
Podrostok. 1875, as *The Adolescent,* translated by Richard Pevear and Larissa Volokhonsky, 1003.
Prestuplenie i nakazanie. 1866, as *Crime and Punishment,* translated by Sydney Monas.
Zapiski iz podpol'ia. 1864, as "Notes from Underground," translated by Mirra Ginsburg, 1974.

Further Reading

Berdyaev, Nicholas. *Dostoevsky.* Translated by Donald Attwater. Cleveland and New York: World Publishing, 1969.
Breger, Louis. *Dostoevsky: The Author as Psychoanalyst.* New York: New York University Press, 1989.
Fusso, Suzanne. "Dostoevsky's Comely Boy: Homoerotic Desire and Aesthetic Strategies in *A Raw Youth.*" *Russian Review* 59:4, 2000: 577–596.
———. "'Secrets of Art' and 'Secrets of Kissing': Towards a Poetics of Sexuality in Dostoevsky," *The Dostoevsky Journal: An Independent Review* 3–4, 2002–2003: 47–58.
Jackson, Robert Louis. "Dostoevsky and the Marquis de Sade," in *Dialogues with Dostoevsky. The Overwhelming Questions.* Stanford: Stanford University Press, 1993: 144–161.
Murav, Harriet. "Dora and the Underground Man," in *Russian Literature and Psychoanalysis.* Edited by Daniel Rancour-Laferriere. Amsterdam/Philadelphia: John Benjamins, 1989: 418–430.
Shestakov, V.P. (editor). *Russkii eros, ili, Filosofiia liubvi v Rossii.* Moscow: Progess, 1991.
Slonim, Marc. *Three Loves of Dostoevsky.* New York: Rinehard, 1955.
Strauss, Nina Pelican. *Dostoevsky and the Woman Question: Rereadings at the End of the Century.* New York: St Martin's Press, 1994.
Zohrab, Irene. "'Mann-mannliche' Love in Dostoevsky's Fiction (An Approach to *The Possessed.*" In *The Dostoevsky Journal: An Independent Review* 3–4, 2002–2003: 113–126.

DOUGLAS, NORMAN

1868–1952
Travel writer, novelist and essayist

Some Limericks

Gershon Legman claims that the limerick in its modern form was accidentally created when Edward Lear's 1846 *Book of Nonsense* (a volume of "very tepidly humorous limericks") was reprinted in London in 1863. Seized upon almost immediately by publishers and magazine editors in Britain and North America, the limerick fad was launched under such innocuous rubrics as "nonsense rhymes" or "nursery rhymes." The obscene or scatological limerick, which circulated primarily by word of mouth, would likewise seem to have become rapidly very popular.

Since the limerick is not generally familiar outside English-speaking countries, it is as well to provide an example here. Attention is particularly drawn to the rhyme scheme (*aabba*), the fact that the opening line almost invariably contains a geographic reference, and the fact that the limerick in its 'adult' form is generally associated with exclusively male gatherings. Significantly, this particular example was published in *The Pearl. A monthly journal or facetiae and voluptuous reading* (1879–1880) under the heading "nursery rhymes":

> There was a young man of Peru,
> Who was hard up for something to do.
> So he took out his carrot,
> And buggered his parrot,
> And sent the results to the zoo.

If Legman's suppositions are correct, the birth, apogee, and decline of the limerick largely coincide with Norman Douglas's own life span. Though modest by later standards (Legman's 1964 collection contains more than 1700 examples), the sixty or so specimens that Douglas provides represent an important contribution to the study and popularity of the form—as is suggested both by the numerous pirate editions of *Some Limericks* which have been put into circulation (Legman lists six, and there has been several more subsequently) and the fact that several later compilations (such as Count Palmiro Vicarion's *Book of Limericks*, 1955) were clearly written in imitation of Douglas.

The interest of *Some Limericks*, however, is not restricted only to the nature of the "lyrics" (to employ Douglas's term) themselves but also includes the mock-scholarly introduction and detailed footnotes and indexes which accompany them. Cyril Connolly claimed in 1965 that *South Wind* survives as a novel "because it pleases, because Douglas's cackle is still infectious." The same might be said of *Some Limericks*, with its wry annotations, listing of variant lines, and spurious references. In a sense, the limericks themselves (and it is not known how many, if any, Douglas wrote himself—the one cited above from *The Pearl* is certainly included) are of less importance than the modernist games that the author is intent on playing with them.

This is, of course, to locate *Some Limericks* as more central to Douglas's *oeuvre* than is usually assumed to be the case. Interestingly, about the same time he started collecting material (circa 1917), he must also have begun to compile that list of "abusive, vituperative or profane expletives" (i.e., the swear words of Florentine cab drivers) which he mentions in a footnote to *Alone* (1921) but which, in fact, had been cut from the manuscript on the advice of his friend John Mavrogordato. Indeed, the use Douglas threatens to make of these Tuscan blasphemies is close in spirit to the later limerick collection since the project would not only entail the "scientific" recording" of data but also "an elaborate commentary" which might also be described as a "study in folklore." (*Alone*, p. 176) Equally significant, Douglas's autobiography (*Looking Back*, 1933) also involves a complex game between a seemingly inconsequential corpora (namely, the visiting cards that various callers have left behind) and the author's own memoirs of the individuals in question.

That being said, Douglas himself was renown for his earthly sense of humor and there can be no doubt that the material contained in *Some Limericks* held a particular appeal for him, not least as an antidote to the hypocrisy and stuffiness which he considered pervaded British sexual morality. (Psychologically, the limerick is, of course, an indication of sexual anxiety.) He probably also rejoiced in the fact that the original edition of *Some Limericks* was printed by Orioli (a close friend and traveling companion) in Florence the same year that the same publisher brought out the first edition of D.H. Lawrence's *Lady Chatterley's Lover*. Given the intense rivalry which existed between the two men, it is not altogether impossible that Douglas delighted in bringing out a work which far surpassed Lawrence as far as four-letter words were concerned. He would no doubt be delighted to learn that today, since it was published in a limited edition of only 110 copies, *Some Limericks* is an extremely scarce and collectable work.

Biography

George Norman Douglas was born in 1868 at Falkenhorst, near Thüringen in Austria, of mixed Scottish and German descent. In 1893, he sat the examinations for the British Diplomatic Service and was quickly posted to St Peterburg where, within two years of his arrival, a minor sexual indiscretion (the first of many to follow) effectively put paid to any hope of further advancement. Retreating to Italy, he bought a villa overlooking the Bay of Naples with money inherited from his father and set about writing the studies of the area and travelogues of trips further afield for which he is still justly acclaimed: *Siren Land* (1911), *Fountains in the Sand* (1912), *Old Calabria* (1915), *Alone* (1921), *Together* (1923), and *Capri. Materials*

for a Description of the Island (1930). His first novel, *South Wind* (1917), later listed by Cyril Connolly as one of the key 100 books of the Modern Movement, became an international best-seller. Meanwhile, Douglas's eclectic range of interests gave rise to a collection of *London Street Games* (1916), a bawdy and occasionally scatological compilation of limericks (*Some Limericks*, 1928), and two intriguing books on aphrodisiacs (*Paneros: Some Words on Aphrodisiacs and the Like*, 1930; *Venus in the Kitchen*, 1952). He died in Capri in 1952.

TERRY HALE

Editions

Some Limericks: Collected for the use of Students & ensplendour'd with Introduction, Geographical Index, and with Notes explanatory and critical, Privately Printed [Florence: G. Orioli], 1928; New York: Printed by Guy d'Isère for David Moss, 1928; [Philadelphia, 1931]; [Paris?] 1929; Privately Printed [Paris: Obelisk Press], 1939; Boston: Nicholson and Whitney, 1942 [Paris: Obelisk Press? C. 1950]; as *From Bed to Verse. An unabashed anthology*, [Wiesbaden] Germany: Very privately printed, 1945; New York: Grove Press, n.d. [1967]; Industry, CA: Collector's Publications, 1968; as *The Norman Douglas Limerick Book*, London: Anthony Blond, 1969.

Further Reading

Connolly, Cyril. *The Modern Movement. 100 Key Books from England, France and America, 1880–1950*. London: André Deutsch and Hamish Hamilton, 1965.

Douglas, Norman. *Alone*. London: Chapman & Hall, 1921.

Douglas, Norman. *Looking Back*. 2 vols. London: Chatto & Windus, 1933.

Holloway, Mark. *Norman Douglas: A Biography*, London: Secker and Warburg, 1976

Legman, Gershon (editor). *The Limerick: 1700 examples, with notes, variants and index*. New York: Bell, 1969

Vicarion, Count Palmiro [i.e., Christopher Logue]. *Book of Limericks*. Paris: Olympia Press, 1955.

DRAMA

From the dawn of Western drama with the Greeks, theater has been intimately connected to eroticism, since dramatic action invariably centers on conflict arising from the correlation between, and incompatibility of, power, duty, and desire. Indeed, tragedy evolved in part from fertility rites associated with Dionysus. Primitive cultures often enacted rituals focusing on the violation of sexual laws, and the acting out of forbidden desires on stage, notably in Sophocles's *Oedipus* trilogy (c. 428 BCE), can be read as a further extension of this cathartic process. It is striking that over 2500 years later, Sigmund Freud would refer to such types in Greek tragedy as manifestations of deep-seated human sexuality. Euripides's *Hippolytus* (428 BCE) and Sophocles's *Phaedra* deal with the passion of a stepmother for her husband's son, Hippolytus, seeing in him an idealized, and younger, version of her spouse. The same story has inspired many other dramatic works throughout the centuries, including versions by Seneca the Younger (54 CE), Jean Racine (1677), Per Olov Enquist (1980), and Sarah Kane (1996). Structuralists have interpreted this myth as constituting an inverted form of the Oedipus tale.

The phallic ceremonies and ribaldry of pagan rites passed over into comedy, which often ventured into erotic topics. Cratinus's *The Bottle* (423 BCE) deals with a man's wife and mistress battling for his affections. The central element of Aristophanes's *Lysistrata* (411 BCE) is the power of sex within a community. An Athenian woman, the comedy's protagonist, is exasperated at the war against Sparta dragging on without resolution, and comes up with a novel method of forcing the Greek soldiers to sue for peace: depriving them of sexual relations. This and other comedies by Aristophanes (448–380 BCE) are characterized by an underlying bawdiness, and plays such as *Wasps*, *Birds*, and *Frogs* combine social satire and humor with obscenity. The reception and commercial success of these sexual comedies influenced the course of later writers, such as Menander (c. 342–292 BCE) who retained sensuality as an integral feature of his works, and it may be argued that this ultimately altered the development of comedy to include the obscene as a usual component. Bawdy and obscene mime and farce was the standard fare of the theaters throughout the Roman Empire. The comedies of Plautus (c. 254–184 BCE) take up Greek stock types; in *Pseudolus* (191 BCE), the protagonist is in love with a prostitute, and mixes with pimps, other harlots, and indulges in revels as part of his journey to marry her. Prostitutes, pimps, and sexually excited youths are standard in Plautine drama. Roman comedy and mime took on negative connotations for the Christians, and this affiliation with sexual excess would later arouse the censure of the Church. Even though the Council of Illiberis (305 CE) mandated that the acting profession was incompatible with the Christian faith, the indecent pose and dress of female mime artists of the Byzantine theater would be condemned by ecclesiastics as late as the tenth century.

Theatrical performance on the Indian subcontinent dates back around five thousand years, and evolved largely independent of Western influence, with the exception of some Hellenistic elements introduced during Alexander the Great's invasion. The concept of the tragic, in its traditional Western sense, was absent from Indian theater, resulting in a predominance of romantic tragi-comedy, stemming from both Hindu and Buddhist traditions. *Mriccha Katika* [*The Little Clay Cart*] (c. 2nd century BCE) probably by Shudrakaone, is of the earliest known Sanskrit plays, and sets out the love of a young man named Charudatta for a rich courtesan, Vasantasena. The romance is complicated by the attraction of a rival courtier for the same young woman. The play was made into a movie, *Utsav*, directed by Girish Karnad in 1984. In a similar vein, Kalidsa's *Malavika and Agnimitra* (c. 3–4th centuries CE) dramatizes a king falling in love with a princess disguised as a maid, and overcoming his principal wife's jealousy in order to wed her. The stock commonplaces of later Western comedy are here: disguised identity, romantic intrigue, supported by an undercurrent of sensuality. As with many Hindu religious stories, there is very little explicit erotic portrayal, although dramatizations of the Shaiva and the Vaishnava myths centered on the union of the lord and his consort, a divine couple of lovers joined harmoniously. While this lacks the incestuous or deceitful desire integral to the Greek or Roman stage, it does give expression to the idealistic coupling of male and female principles of love. Sanskrit literature would also produce one of the earliest and most celebrated treatises on love and sexuality, Vatsyayana's *Kama Sutra* (1st–6th centuries CE).

Chinese drama similarly centered on romantic tragi-comedy, though in a much more stylized form. In Wang Shih-fu's *His hsiang chi* [*Romance of the Western Chamber*] (c. 13th century), the heroine, Hai-t'ang, becomes a second wife, only to find this happiness destroyed when her new spouse's first wife has him poisoned, since she wishes to be free to be with her new lover. In one scene, Hai-t'ang comments on her luck in finding a husband, and details the vices prevalent in her society, with mistresses, orgies, and promiscuity being the order of the day. Traditional Chinese drama was never in the vernacular nor without music until the early twentieth century, following the 1907 revolution. One of Confucius's precepts laid down that actors' bodies be covered as much as possible. As a result, female characters developed a "sleeve language," using their robes in graceful and sometimes sensual movements. Like Chinese drama, Japanese drama is underpinned by conventions, and is, in many respects, close to the Western operatic tradition. The roles in the two main strands of theater, *kabuki* or popular drama and the *Nōh* plays, were traditionally played by men, though the replacement of women during the early stages of *kabuki* (c. 1603–1652) was a drastic attempt to subdue eroticism. However, a different kind of erotic potential was created with the use of male adolescent prostitute performers known as *wakashu* who perfected the role of *onnagata*, or carefully stylized women. Chikamatsu Monzaemon (1653–1724) wrote a series of brutal plays involving failed love and suicide, the *Buuraku*. The zenith of *kabuki* was during the eighteenth century, and erotic subjects

were among the most popular plays, together with dramas dealing with the exploits of outlaws. In more recent times, Mishima Yukio (1925–1970) wrote some twentieth-century adaptations of the traditional *kabuki* genre. His *Madame de Sade* (1965) caused a scandal due to its subject matter; one of the characters, the Countess de Saint-Fond, represented carnal desires. Shuji Terayama (1935–1983) has produced several plays dealing with the scenario of the seduction of young men by mature women, tormenting them and driving them to violence or insanity in the process. The development of Korean drama dates back to religious and folk rituals, and traditional plays depict corrupt officials committing adultery, or sexually active Buddhist monks, among other themes. These were usually performed in village squares and lacked the elevated style and status of classical Chinese and Japanese theater.

As with Greek drama, European drama began as an expression of religious narratives from the tenth century onwards. By the thirteenth century, the staging of these liturgically based events rapidly moved from the church to public squares, and such performances became major episodes in the life of the local community and environs, lasting several days and attracting a large number of participants and spectators; it is estimated that as many as 16,000 people gathered at an eight-day Passion Play performed in Reims in 1490. Inevitably, the plays developed a reputation for rowdiness and general debauchery, which led to the Paris Parliament banning them from the capital in 1548. By this time, theater, while still confined to religious topics, was firmly out of clerical control and with a central emphasis on the suffering body, with the obvious erotic potential of the interaction of female and male actors within a relatively confined local environment. This is particularly true in the dramatization of the legends of virgin martyrs such as Agnes or Catherine whose refusal to submit to the sexual demands of an oppressive tyrant led to torture and execution. As Passion plays faced interdiction throughout Europe during the course of the sixteenth century, whether from censorious Catholic or Protestant ecclesiastics objecting to the non-biblical content, troupes and theaters increasingly began to experiment with staging works on non-religious topics. In Coventry, the last religious cycle of Passion and Corpus Christi plays was staged in

1580, in Shakespeare's youth, and the setting up of professional acting companies and commercial theaters followed in the wake of the mysteries' demise.

The standard plot of the *commedia dell'arte*, which arose in Italy during the sixteenth century and whose influence and stock characterizations spread across Europe, usually involved a pair of young lovers overcoming obstacles in order to marry—and thus legitimately satisfy their desire—and bawdy farce was a mainspring of this genre, which has been passed on to comedy until this day. Jean-Baptiste Poquelin Molière's comedies leave much room for visual gestures related to sexual references, and suggestive wordplay is an essential ingredient. One of the most celebrated examples occurs in *L'Ecole des femmes* (1662; *The School for Women*), where the innocent pupil Agnès declares to her master, Arnolphe, who has brought her up in ignorance in order to marry her himself, that a young male intruder has taken something from her, and stops mid-sentence. This conjures up, in the mind of Arnolphe and the spectator, images of her virginity or various bodily parts having been appropriated by her new suitor, only to discover that it is her glove that the young man has carried off with him (even though this seemingly innocuous gesture suggests a fetishized object). Elizabethan drama differed from its religious antecedents, and indeed from its Continental equivalents in one substantial respect: female roles were usually played by boys. While this precluded a criticism often levelled against European theater, that actresses demeaned the status of their gender and deliberately aroused lascivious feelings in their predominantly male audience, the cross-dressing dynamic raises the question of homoeroticism. Anti-theater commentators such as John Rainoldes concentrate on the danger of watching beautiful boys wearing women's clothing. One of the first plays openly to deal with a homosexual subject was Christopher Marlowe's *Edward II* (c. 1592). Theatrical costumes for actresses became freer and decorsetted in the early part of the nineteenth century in Europe and North America, and later on *décolleté* gowns became normative, leading to accusations of lewdness that were essentially unchanged from those levelled against actresses two centuries earlier.

Renaissance comedies of love are inherently both erotic and chaste. There is rarely any direct portrayal of sexual activity; eroticism is projected to offstage behavior and to descriptive passages, or confined to more indirect allusions to sexuality such as innuendo. One reason why heterosexual interaction is unseen is evidently related to the fact that, in England at least, sexual play would appear unconvincing to contemporary audiences given that the heroine was played by a boy actor. Cross-dressing by males was a comic device; in women it was designed to be alluring. In early modern drama, the most common occurrence of the sexual act tends to be violent. Sexual assault is depicted as an effect of extreme male desire imposed on a beautiful female. The violation of women is essentially tied to male power structures, and the motif of sexual violence is portrayed in relation to homosocial ties. Such tragedies are an evolved form of the traditional saint's play where a female martyr successfully resists the lecherous advances of a persecutor. The Roman legends of Lucretia and Virginia, in which the protagonist commits suicide, is a common topos in early modern theater, prominent examples being Thomas Heywood's *The Rape of Lucrece* (1608) and John Webster's *Appius and Virginia* (c. 1608). Such verbal testimony is designed to titillate as well as inform the audience, the sexual content inviting the voyeuristic complicity of the male spectator. Thomas Middleton's *Women Beware Women* (c. 1622) contains the "seduction" scene of Bianca by the Duke while her mother-in-law plays chess (II, 2). The young woman is lured away from the game and shown naked pictures, evidently in order to arouse her sexual appetite. Consensual, though offstage, sex is portrayed in Middleton's *A Mad World, My Masters* (c. 1605), which concerns an adulterous meeting. Similarly, a reported sexual act is at the crux of *Othello*. Desire is the prelude to marriage, and the fact that a substantial proportion of early modern drama deals with couples who have not consummated their union contributes to the creation of an erotically charged and expectant atmosphere. Shakespeare's *Romeo and Juliet* (c. 1594) allows the pair to have conjugal relations (in III, 5, Romeo leaves after his wedding night), creating a love that is unashamedly both romantic and sexual.

English comedies written between 1590 and 1640 generally adhere to a tenet maintaining that marriageable young women should be modest in speech. In Shakespeare's *Much Ado About*

Nothing, Hero's maid, Margaret, tries to cheer up a heavy-hearted bride by joking she will 'be heavier soon by the weight of man', and Hero scolds her immodesty. Very few comic heroines express physical desire in explicit or vulgar terms, and eroticism is most often expressed through lewd dialogue and erotic puns, a typical example being John Fletcher's *Wild Goose Chase* (1621). The Whitefriars Theatre opened in 1607 and specialized in the contemporary public taste for suggestive comedies. Notable examples of plays staged at the theater include Ben Johnson's *Volpone* (1606) which contains 97 bawdy jests, Lording Barry's *Ram Alley* (1608) which has a total of 153 lewd jokes. John Day's *Humour out of Breath* (1608) was a romantic comedy about two dukes and their respective families engaged in a feud; in the women's wishes for their match, they engage in strong conversation that contravenes early modern propriety that demanded that a young women know and say nothing of the male body. In Ben Johnson's *Bartholomew Fair* (1614), a woman's need for a chamber-pot leads to her initiation into prostitution. Jacobean drama often implies a morbid eroticism in connection with women, and plays' sexual language, such as Middleton, is frequently more explicit than Shakespeare's. These features, briefly extinguished under the Puritan Commonwealth in England, were continued with the Restoration comedy of manners and endured until the early part of the eighteenth century.

In more modern times, the history of eroticism in the theater is closely linked to the rise of censorship. This became an increasing phenomenon during the eighteenth century in Europe, and was linked with both changing demographical trends in society as well as the growth of libertine attitudes connected with Enlightenment ideas. The interplay of master–servant relationships of European comedies did not exclude sexually and socially subversive readings, even if the status quo was left intact at the dénouement. The Licensing Act of 1737 gave powers of censorship of the stage to the Lord Chamberlain's Office; the Examiner of Plays had to approve all texts of plays in British theaters until the abolition of the office in 1968. Towards the end of the eighteenth century, however, some plays began to attack codes of aristocratic and bourgeois morality in increasingly open ways. Leandro Fernández de Moratín's *El Viejo y la niña* [*The Old Man and the Young Girl*] (1786) typifies this new wave of socially informed comedies, and explicitly undermines the notion of arranged marriages. Romantic liaisons were therefore held up as a personal choice, and this may be seen as a burgeoning expression of sexual liberation.

Towards the end of the nineteenth century, and throughout the twentieth, theater became associated with the avant-garde movement. The French playwright Georges de Porto-Riche published several plays on the eternal triangle of a man torn between his wife and his mistress, for example *Amoureuse* [*A Loving Wife*] (1891) and *Le Viel homme* [*The Old Man*] (1911), as well as producing a modern version of *Lysistrata* (1893). The plays of Henrik Ibsen (1828–1906) feature a strong vein of sexual tension, typified in *A Doll's House* (1879), which caused controversy over its iconoclastic depiction of marriage. Oscar Wilde's social satires can also be read as transgressive in their challenge to widely accepted social conventions and morality in plays such as *The Importance of Being Earnest* (1895). Somerset Maugham and Noël Coward both wrote comedies about the new sexual freedom experienced in the 1920s onwards in Britain. In Maugham's *The Constant Wife* (1926), the protagonist, Constance, gains economic independence through working and also sexual freedom when she embarks on holiday with a lover for six weeks. Federico Garcia Lorca's (1898–1936) dramatic output is characterized by surrealist elements and a sexual frankness that disturbed Spanish audiences of the 1930s. Terence Rattigan and Tennessee Williams managed to disguise their homosexuality through presenting their viewpoint as women. Rattigan's *Deep Blue Sea* (1949) was written after the suicide of the author's partner. Rattigan had intended this to be a gay love story, but modified this idea to a heterosexual plot since a homosexual theme would not have been approved by the Lord Chamberlain and would have damaged his reputation. In the same year, Williams's *A Streetcar Named Desire* deals with the sexually active Blanche Dubois and her impotent husband, whose sexual problems, so it is hinted but not explicitly spelled out, stem from his latent homosexuality. Gay and lesbian drama assumed increasing significance in the late twentieth century, coinciding with the decriminalization of homosexual acts in many parts of the world since the 1960s, and the shift in attitudes this engendered. Jo Orton's farces, such as *Entertaining Mr Sloane* (1964), and *What the Butler Saw* (1969), are emblematic of these new sexually licentious works of the decade. Martin Sherman's *Bent* (1979), a gay love-story against the backdrop of a concentration camp, and Tony Kushner's *Angels in America* (1990), about AIDS, represent how far once taboo issues have penetrated mainstream drama. These trends, together with the growth of feminist theater since the 1970s, demonstrates the progressive nature of theater to reflect society's questioning of conventional notions of sexual and gender roles.

PAUL SCOTT

Further Reading

Bamford, Karen. *Sexual Violence on the Jacobean Stage.* Basingstoke: Macmillan, 2000.

Bly, Mary. *Queer Virgins and Virgin Queans on the Early Modern Stage.* Oxford: Oxford University Press, 2000.

Daileader, Celia R. *Eroticism on the Renaissance Stage: Transcendence, Desire and the Limits of the Visible.* Cambridge: Cambridge University Press, 1998.

Fischer-Lichte, Erika. *History of European Drama and Theatre.* Trans. by Jo Riley London and New York: Routledge, 2002.

Hartnoll, Phyllis. *The Theatre: A Concise History.* 3rd edn. Rev. by Enoch Brater London: Thames and Hudson, 1998.

McCabe, Richard A. *Incest, Drama and Nature's Law, 1550–1700* (Cambridge: Cambridge University Press, 1993).

Nicoll, Allardyce. *World Drama from Æschylus to Anouilh,* 2nd rev. ed (London: Harrap, 1976).

O'Connor, Sean. *Straight Acting: Popular Gay Drama from Wilde to Rattigan* London and Washington: Cassel, 1998.

Paster, Gail Kern. *The Body Embarrassed: Drama and the Disciplines of Shame in Early Modern England.* Ithaca: Cornell University Press, 1993.

Watson, Jack and Grant McKernie. *A Cultural History of Theatre.* New York and London: Longman, 1993.

DU BELLAY, JOACHIM

c. 1522–1560
French poet

L'antérotique de la vieille et de la jeune amye (1549)

Published only once in his lifetime, this short narrative poem is a piece of juvenilia. It was printed alongside the first edition of *L'Olive*, Du Bellay's collection of 50 sonnets, but was omitted when that work was published in an expanded edition in 1550. There is, however, only scant thematic connection between the two works. *L'Olive* commemorates the poet's chaste and mystical love for an unnamed lady and is a conscious demonstration of the literary theory set forth in *La deffence*. *L'antérotique de la vieille*, on the other, hand, is a declamatory invective which represents the negation of Du Bellay's poetic *credo* both in form—rhymed decasyllabic verse—and inspiration—libertine realism.

Described by several critics as being of dubious taste, *L'antérotique de la vieille* is an account first of the world's ugliest, and then, of the world's most beautiful woman. The title of the poem is somewhat baffling for *anterotique* derives, not from the classical Greek "anterot," signifying "requited love," but, rather, from the sixteenth century neologism Αντέρως, or "anti-love," which Huguet took to mean *contr'amour*, or "antithesis of the subject of love." The contrast between the old hag and the young maiden corresponds to a traditional poetic idea—the celebration of womanly beauty tempered by thoughts of its inevitable decay and destruction. However, the grotesque realism of the first portrait precedes the second. And the old crone's ugliness occupies more space than the idealized beauty of the maiden and the love she inspires— 95 compared with 74 lines. The poet's conclusions regarding the vaunting and transforming power of love occupies the remaining 46 lines of the poem.

Du Bellay's portrait of the elderly duenna and his description of her as protector of the young virgin (*Vieille peste des jeunes filles* v. 48), draws on well-worn classical models from Horace, Sextus Propertius, and Ovide. Du Bellay may also have been influenced by both Guillaume de Lorris and Jean de Meun(g) who were temporally and geographically closer to him. They too give grotesque descriptions of the ravages of age, similar to those in the *Anterotique*. Du Bellay's Old Woman is all but bald, and has only three blackened stumps for teeth. Her eyes are bloodshot and her wrinkled face is covered with grime. In fact, so ugly is she that the sun hides itself in her presence and her putrid breath reminds the poet of the sulphurous gates of Hell. And she is an intolerable troublemaker who has done more harm in this world than the "*fatale Pandore.*"

The description of the young maiden stands in sharp contrast to this and instead of looking back seems to anticipate the formal perfectionism expressed three centuries later by such poets as Gautier (*Émaux et camées*) or Oscar Wilde (*Salomé*). *La jeune amye* is an allegorical figure for virginal feminine beauty. She arouses both erotic desire and poetic inspiration. Nevertheless, Du Bellay rarely rises above the hackneyed in his imagery: the maiden's golden hair is a diadem, her rosy complexion recalls early dawn, her skin is now polished ivory, now shimmering alabaster. So thrilling is her beauty that she is comparable to all the treasures of the East, and so on. What does come as a surprise is the absence in the poem's conclusion of any obvious moral lesson. Du Bellay does not, for example, imply that the beautiful girl will, if she lives to old age, join the ranks of the decrepit. Instead he insists on the renewing power of love "Quel est (ô Amour) ton pouvoir." (V. 203), and he even has the old woman, in the role of voyeur, respond to sexual arousal, for having espied the poet and his maiden, she attempts to seduce the startled poet. The poet does not return the compliment. Rather he concludes that the power of love is such that it can "warm the bones" of someone as unlikely as the hideous *Vieille*.

Certes vanter tu [amou] peux bien
Qu'en ciel & terre n'y a rien
Qui plus fort que ton feu se treuve.

(You [love] can certainly boast that
In heaven and earth there is no fire hotter than yours)
V204–206

Du Bellay wrote another poem on a similar theme, *Contre une vieille*, published in 1558 in the collection of verse entitled *Les Jeux Rustiques*.

Biography

1522?–1560, French poet of the Pléiade whose manifesto, *La deffence et illustration de la langue francoyse* (1549), urges the study and of the classics and the use of French as a literary language. Du Bellay's poetry is imitative of Latin and Italian models and includes a collection of Petrarchan sonnets, *L'Olive* (1549) as well as *Divers jeux rustiques* (1558). He served in Rome for four years as secretary to his cousin, Cardinal Du Bellay. Two further volumes of verse, *Les Regrets* (1558) and *Les antiquités de Rome* (1558) blend Du Bellay's impressions of Rome with nostalgia for his native Anjou. They contain some of his best known poems. The *Antiquités* was translated by Edmund Spenser (*Complaints*: 1591).

E.M. LANGILLE

Editions

L'Antérotique de la vieille & de la jeune amye [à la suite de *l'Olive*]. Paris, Arnoul l'Angelier, 1549, in-8°.
L'Antérotique de la vieille & de la jeune amye, 3rd part of collected verses published by Charles Langelier, 1561 and 1562, in-4°.
L'Antérotique de la vieille & de la jeune amye, in the collection entitled *l'Olive et autres œuvres poëtiques...* Paris, Federic Morel, 1561, in-4°.
Recueil d'Aubert, 7th part, ff. 50 r°-53v°. Paris, Federic Morel, 1568 and 1569, in-8°.
Joachim Du Bellay, *Œuvres poétiques*, critical edition by Henri Chamard, Vol., 1. Paris, Cornély et Cie, 1908.

Further Reading

Cameron, K. *Concordance des œuvres poétiques de Joachim Du Bellay*. Geneva, Droz. 1988.
Chamard, H. *Joachim du Bellay, 1522–1560*. Travaux et mémoires de l'université, III, 24 Lille : 1900. Reprinted Geneva; Slatline, 1969.
Gadoffre. *Du Bellay et le sacré*. Paris: Gallimard, 1978.
Gray, F. *La Poétique de Du Bellay*. Paris, Nizet, 1978.
Keating, L.C. *Joachim Du Bellay*. Twaynes's World Authors. New York: 1971.
Saulnier, V.L. *Du Bellay, l'homme et l'œuvre*. Connaissance des lettres, 32. Paris Hattier, 1963.

DU CAMP, MAXIME

1822–1894
French novelist, poet and essayist

A 'man of letters'—travel-writer, journalist, novelist, poet, art critic, social historian, biographer, and pioneer photographer—Maxime Du Camp is nonetheless chiefly remembered for his friendships with the writers Gustave Flaubert and Théophile Gautier, his *Souvenirs littéraires* (1882–1883) and early experiments in photography. He was editor of the *Revue des deux mondes* where Flaubert's *Madame Bovary* was first published in serial form (1856–1857) and famously suggested cuts to his friend's novel. A 1996 biography describes Du Camp as a 'spectateur engagé' on the nineteenth-century French literary scene and this is perhaps an apt description. A friend of great writers rather than a great writer himself, he is also the dedicatee of the final poem of Baudelaire's *Les fleurs du mal* (1857), 'Le Voyage'.

The orphan son of a famous surgeon, Du Camp was financially independent and thus free to sample a variety of occupations. He met Flaubert in Paris in 1843. Flaubert was a reluctant student of law, Du Camp was a dandy, man-about-town, and occasional journalist. It was an intense attachment. During a trip to Rome in 1844, Du Camp carved his and Flaubert's names on a pillar in the Temple of Fortune and wrote to his friend that it was 'like a silent prayer to the goddess that she never separate us'. Realizing an adolescent dream, in his early twenties Du Camp had traveled alone to Asia Minor, Italy, and Algeria and published an account as *Souvenirs et paysages d'orient* (1848). It was he who encouraged the more sedentary-by-nature Flaubert to travel. The friends first took a walking tour through Brittany in 1847, an account of which they set down in *Par les champs et par les grèves*, each contributing alternate chapters. The travelogue was not published in complete form until the early 1970s.

Their next journey was more ambitious. Du Camp had taken up the new art of photography in 1849. The same year, he secured an official assignment from the French government to travel to the Near East to photograph sites of archaeological interest. Flaubert was to accompany him, charged with the task of information collection by the Ministry of Agriculture and Commerce. In the autumn of 1849, Du Camp and Flaubert set off on a tour which was to take eighteen months and which would encompass Egypt, Palestine, Syria, Asia Minor, Greece, and Italy. After their return, Flaubert began work on *Madame Bovary*, while Du Camp concentrated on photography and journalism. He had returned from the East with several hundred paper negatives mostly of the antiquities, including the first photographs of the Sphinx and the temple at Abu Simbel. The resulting book, *Egypte, Nubie, Palestine et Syrie. Dessins photographiques recueillis pendant les années 1849, 1850 et 1851* (1852), was the first book of photographs to be published in France. Each copy contained one hundred and twenty-five original photographs. *Le Nil, Egypte et Nubie* (1854) contained a further two hundred and twenty.

The two books were popular successes, and their author was made an Officier of the Légion d'Honneur (he had already been made a Chevalier for his role in the 1848 revolution) and celebrated as a 'voyageur'. Both Flaubert and Du Camp had set out with an expectation of the Orient informed by the writings of Romantics such as Hugo and Chateaubriand and the paintings of Eugène Delacroix, as a fantasy space into which assorted desires—erotic and imperialist—could be imaginatively projected. Although Du Camp's written and photographic records of their travels are, for the most part, factual and journalistic in style, they would be instrumental in reinforcing the continuing nineteenth-century fascination with romantic antiquity and an imaginary Orient. Certainly Du Camp's carefully edited version of their travels, with the obligatory smattering of exotic local 'color', is entertainingly complemented by the alternative account afforded by Flaubert's travel notes and letters home to their mutual friend, Louis Bouilhet, which abound with tales of visits to prostitutes and bath-houses (see *Flaubert in Egypt: A Sensibility on Tour*). For example, Flaubert observed Du Camp's state of polymorphous erotic agitation in the Orient: 'we had scarcely set foot on shore when Max, the old lecher, got excited over a negress who was drawing water at a fountain. He is just as excited by little negro boys. By whom is he *not* excited? Or, rather, by *what*?' Flaubert found his friend's published accounts of their travels 'insignificant' and 'flat beyond words'.

A glimpse of the other Du Camp is also to be found in an amusement he undertook with Flaubert and Bouilhet in 1846–1847. 'Jenner, ou la Découverte de la vaccine', a burlesque parody of a classical five-act tragedy, exists only as one act and outline notes. The piece is a scatological exercise in periphrasis, never intended for publication but revelatory of a particular kind of nineteenth-century repressed.

Du Camp's first novel, *Le livre posthume, Mémoires d'un suicidé* (1853) was a manifesto of Saint-Simonian anti-romanticism portraying art as an undertaking with a moral, even humanitarian, aim. The hero, 'eaten up by the devouring anxieties of impossible dreams', is eventually driven to suicide. *Les forces perdues* (1867), usually considered Du Camp's best novel, covers similar territory to Flaubert's *Education sentimentale* (1869), in its depiction of a young man's affair with an older woman and ultimate disillusionment. As in *Le livre posthume*, the hero cannot bear to continue living in the world and the novel ends with his death.

Du Camp also published plentiful art criticism, a volume of poems, *Les chants modernes* (1855), social histories of Paris and veritable mines of information about nineteenth-century French literary culture and personalities, the *Souvenirs littéraires* and *Souvenirs d'un demi-siècle* (the latter not until 1949, fifty years after his death). The only works to be translated into English are the *Souvenirs littéraires*, his 1890 biography of Gautier and a short fable, *The Three Flies*, published in 1902.

Biography

Born in Paris, February 8, 1822. Educated at the Lycées Louis-le-Grand and Charlemagne, Paris.

Traveled alone in Asia Minor, Italy and Algeria in 1844–1845, then with Gustave Flaubert in the Near East in, 1849–18451. Served as an officer in the revolution of 1848. With Théophile Gautier and Louis de Cormenin, founded the *Revue de Paris* in 1851. Following its suppression in 1859, moved on to the *Revue des deux mondes*, then to the *Journal des débats*, 1864–1894. Made a Chevalier of the Légion d'Honneur in 1848 and became an Officier in 1852. Elected to the Académie Française in 1880 and subsequently became its director. Died in Baden-Baden, 8 February 1894.

NOLA MERCKEL

Selected Works

With Gustave Flaubert and Louis Bouilhet. 'Jenner, ou la Découverte de la vaccine.' In Flaubert, *Oeuvres complètes*, vol. 7, Paris: Club de l'Honnête Homme, 1971–1976.

With Gustave Flaubert. *Par les champs et par les grèves* in Flaubert, *Oeuvres complètes*, vol. 10, Paris: Club de l'Honnête Homme, 1971–1976.

Souvenirs et paysages d'Orient. 1848.

Egypte, Nubie, Palestine et Syrie. Dessins photographiques recueillis pendant les années 1849, 1850 et 1851, accompagnés d'un texte explictif et précédés d'une introduction. 1852.

Le livre posthume, Memoires d'un suicidé. 1852. Ed. by Rodolphe Fouano. Paris: Editions de Septembre, 1991.

Les chants modernes. 1855.

Le Nil, Egypte et Nubie. 1860.

Les forces perdues. 1867.

Paris, ses organes, ses fonctions, sa vie. 6 vols. 1869–1875.

Souvenirs de l'année 1848. 1876.

Les convulsions de Paris. 1878–1879.

Lettres inédites à Gustave Flaubert. Messina: Edas, 1978.

Théophile Gautier. 1890, trans. by J.E. Gordon. Port Washington & London: Kennikat Press, 1972.

Souvenirs littéraires. 1882–1883, as *Souvenirs littéraires: Flaubert, Fromentin:, Gautier, Musset, Nerval, Sand*, preface by Michel Chaillou, Brussels: Editions complexe, 2002. Translated as *Maxime Du Camp's Literary Recollections*, 2 vols, London & Sydney: Remington & Co, 1893.

Souvenirs d'un demi-siècle. 1949.

References and Further Reading

Finot, André. *Maxime du Camp*. 1949.

Senneville, Gérard de. *Maxime Du Camp: Un Spectateur engagé du XIXéme siècle*. Paris: Stock, 1996.

Steegmuller, Francis. Trans. and ed. *Flaubert in Egypt: A Sensibility on Tour*. Harmondsworth: Penguin, 1972.

See also **Flaubert, Gustave, Gautier, Théophile, Orientalism**

DU FAIL, NOËL

c. 1520–1591
French author of rustic tales

Propos rustiques (1547); *Balivernes ou contes nouveau d'Eutrapel* (1548); *Contes et discours d'Eutrapel* (1585)

A series of 13 village tales in dialogue form, Du Fail's *Propos rustiques* was a popular work that ran to 8 editions from 1547 to 1580. The *Propos* was intended to glorify rural life, by comparing an idealized tranquil past with a decadent and noisy turbulent present. The tales are set in two imaginary hamlets: Flameaux, which shows no trace of outside or modern influences, and Vindelles, the epitome of "modern decadence." The three narrators Ansèlme, Huguet, and Roger, assembled for an open air banquet, recount the successive tales whose fluid structure is perfectly suited to digressions, interjections, and lively discussion. Du Fail's denunciation of modern life attacks the abandonment of traditional values and the wickedness he observed especially in young people. Like Plautus, Virgil, Pliny, and, closer in time to the author, Rabelais, the socially conservative Du Fail makes the case that country folk should be made to realize how well off they are, and that, further, they should not try to better themselves by abandoning traditional patterns of life. We are told, for example, in tale 6—*La difference du coucher de ce temps et du passé, et du gouvernement de l'amour de village*—that the intrusion of foreign (Italian) manners has encouraged the village youth to squander their time in vain, unclean pursuits. Young "gallants" haunt the village tavern. They are idle, dandified coxcombs, who flirt shamelessly, but display no loyalty towards their amorous conquests. And for their part, the young women, according to the misogynist lawyer Huguet, may make an ostentatious show of affection and even kiss a man on the mouth, but they love only money and material gain. In sharp contrast to the present, the villagers of the past lived in prelapsarian innocence. Whole families might sleep in the same bed without fear of outrage; a man might even see a woman completely naked without displaying signs of arousal. In fact, so innocent were the people of these times that it was not uncommon for a grown man to know nothing of sex, save masturbation. "Now," in contrast, boys of 15 are not only sexually experienced, they routinely catch venereal infections, including the dreaded syphilitic pox, called alternately "*le chancre des Pollains*" or the "*mal Italien.*" In this portrait of the decline of rural life, change has come through contact with noxious outside influences, typified by the new-fangled Italian manners much in evidence at the Valois court. The confrontation between past and present is an "epic" battle between the inhabitants of the two villages, Flameaux and Vindelles, a fight in which women folk take a leading and symbolic role.

A similar tendency toward social conservatism is evident in *Les Balivernes* as well as in the *Contes et discours d'Eutrapel*. Three men, Eutrapel, Polygame, and Lupolde discuss various aspects of life in the village. Eurtapel, is a rustic gentleman and confirmed bachelor whose name derives from the Greek Σντραπελοζ signifying jocose or jocular. Polygamy, on the other hand, means married more than once, or, a remarried widower. Not surprisingly, the three men talk a good deal about women, and the advantages and perils of marriage. Eutrapel wants to find a wife, preferably an ugly one, on the grounds that she would be less likely to cuckold him. This claim gives rise to a lively discussion, the conclusion of which is a composite portrait of the ideal wife who, according to Lupolde, would have an English face, Norman breasts, a Flemish body, and most importantly, a "cul de Paris." He then affirms that infidelity in women is the result of a husband's brutish tyranny, or is a response to his jealousy and possessiveness. To maintain a wife's affection, the best strategy, he claims, is to grant her an "honest Christian" freedom. Adultery in men is also condemned, and once again the dangers of promiscuity, especially venereal infection, are invoked. Finally, the argument against the desirability of marriage appears all but unassailable when Eutrapel introduces a cuckold who bemoans how he has become "his wife's son, her little sausage, her spindle," and so forth. His despondency provides Eutrapel with the perfect excuse never to marry.

Du Fail is a fascinating chronicler of the profound changes afoot in sixteenth-century rural life. His attitudes are even more compelling when one considers that, highly educated and clearly receptive to the ideas of the Reformation; he nevertheless portrayed the Catholic peasantry of his native Brittany as a model of human happiness.

Biography

Lord of la Hérissaye, magistrate, and author of three books of country tales, Noël Du Fail was born into the rural aristocracy of Brittany c. 1520 (Château Letard, in Saint Erblon [Ille-et-Vilaine]). His biography is sketchy. We do know that he studied under the celebrated Hellenist and professor of rhetoric Turnèbe (1512–1565) at Sainte Barbe College in Paris, and that, although a gifted student, he led a rowdy and turbulent existence. Unlucky at cards, and unable to pay his debts, he joined the army to avoid creditors (1543–1544). In 1553, he became a counselor to the Lower Court of Justice at Rennes, and occupied that post until 1571, at which point he took a seat as a High Court judge (Parlement de Bretagne) in the same city. Excluded from the High Court in 1572 because of his Protestant sympathies, he was re-admitted in 1576, and retained his position until 1586. Du Fail's career in the law inspired a work on the decrees of the Parlement de Bretagne (*Mémoires*

recueillis et extraits des plus notables et solennels Arrests du Parlement de Bretagne [1579]), which became a standard reference work for over two centuries. Du Fail is now remembered, however, for his literary vignettes of rural life drawn from the point of view of a sixteenth-century country judge. Inspired in part by Rabelais, whose wit and earthy sense of fun he shares, Du Fail published two collections of *contes* in 1547–1548, *Les Propos rustiques*, and *Les Balivernes, ou contes nouveaux d'Eutrapel*. A third collection of tales published in 1585 and entitled *Contes et discours d'Eutrapel*, is a continuation of *Les Balivernes*.

E.M. LANGILLE

Editions

Propos rustiques ; *Les Balivernes, ou contes nouveaux d'Eutrapel*, éd., P. Jourda, Conteurs français du XVIe siècle, Gallimard, Bibliothèque de la Pléiade, Paris, 1971.
Les propos rustiques. texte original de 1547, interpolation et variantes de 1548, 1549, 1573, ed., Arthur de la Borderie, Slatkine reprints, 1970.
Propos rustiques, texte établi d'après l'édition de 1549, éd., Gabriel-André Pérouse et Roger Dubuis, Droz, Gevève, 1994.
Contes et discours d'Eutrapel, éd., D. Jouast. Paris, 1875.

Reference and Further Reading

Philipot, E. *La vie et l'œuvre de Noël du Fail*, gentilhomme breton, Champion, Paris, 1914.
——— *Essai sur le style et la langue de Noël du Fail.* Champion, Paris, 1914.
L'Histoire de la France rurale. T. II., sous la direction de E. Le Roy Ladurie, Seuil, Paris, 1975.
Noël du Fail, écrivain, Actes et articles. Sous la direction de C. Magnien Simonin. Vrin, Paris 1991.

DU LAURENS, HENRI-JOSEPH

1719–1793
French novelist

Dulaurens wrote disguised under a number of pseudonyms including d'Henriville, Laurent d'Henriville, abbé de Saint Albin, Brises-Crosses,

Modeste-Tranquille, and Xang-Xung. The ethical freedom of the individual was the central concern of this defrocked priest, journalist, pamphleteer, philosopher, and novelist, whose bold ideas on pleasure were viewed as so much impertinence in the eyes of the clergy.

Work

The work of Dulaurens echoes the concerns of the Enlightenment. Following in the steps of the *philosophes*, the writer attacked society's framework of sexual and moral prohibitions while defending a view of man as the slave of prejudices, institutions, and churches that were in opposition to his nature: "In all actions of life, the only voice to heed is the voice of nature, while ensuring that one does not succumb to another form of slavery, that one remains one's own master and not the slave of oneself and of one's ideas." Man can attain happiness only by discovering and following his natural instincts, because moral or religious laws are merely the masks of authority and power. By using two characteristics of eighteenth-century philosophy—irony and the idea of utopia—Dulaurens criticized all conventions opposed to nature and preached the discovery of the experience of pleasure, the fulfilment of the body through which man discovers his true nature, his self-awareness and, ultimately his freedom.

In *L'Arrétin moderne* [*The Modern Arrétin*] an essay first published in 1763 under the title *Arrétin ou la débauche de l'esprit en fait de bon sens* [*Arrétin or the Debauchery of the Mind as a Matter of Good Sense*], the tribulations of Xang-Xung serve as a pretext for a wealth of anecdotes and reflections. In the midst of discussions on topics as varied as agriculture, beards, and the usefulness of vice, one comes upon the *Histoire merveilleuse & édifiante de Godemiché* [*The Marvellous and Edifying Story of Godemiché*] whose incipit is worth citing: "Godemiché was born in year one of the creation of the monastic wishes of young fifteen-year-old girls forbidden by law from disposing of their birthright." The story relates the experience of Sister Conception, who has become pregnant by the Father Superior. In an effort to change the outcome of events, the latter consults a sorceress and follows every one of her prescriptions without scruple. The young nun must be fed mandrakes and black pudding in order that the oracle pronounced by an aged Sybil in chapter 23 of *La bonne foi du Diable* [*The Devil's Good Will*] may come to pass: ."..a virgin will bear Godemiché. This child, the picture of virility, will be the comfort of young girls and make the miseries of convent life easier to bear." The plan succeeds; once in the bosom of the young abbess, Godemiché quickens with life and reaches puberty.

> "The first use he made of his existence was to slide from the abbess's bodice to a place that modesty forbids me to name [...] The abbess immediately fell into throes of ecstasy: "[...] a delicious spasm shot voluptuously through her at each thrust from Godemiché and she cried out: ah!...ah! I'm dying...my sweet Jesus, is it possible that goodness has made your creatures susceptible to such rapturous bliss? Scarcely had Godemiché filled the mother abbess with his unction than he flew [...] under the skirt of a young novice [then] flitted from nun to nun, filling them with pleasure."

Similar emotional outbursts are also found in *Imirce ou la fille de la nature* [*Imirce or The Daughter of Nature*] (1765). In this experimental novel, Dulaurens intends to show that human nature is first and foremost animal, and that human specificity frees itself of this animality little by little. We assist at the artificial creation of two naive characters and at the spontaneous development of their intellectual, moral, and metaphysical notions. Ariste, a philosopher, decides to perform an experiment by placing two children, Imirce and Émilior, in a cave. Sex comes into play very early: Lying beside Imirce, Émilior "caresses her budding breasts." At the end of the twenty-two years of the experiment, Imirce leaves the cave, discovers the world and recounts her impressions, ever in harmony with the goodness of nature: "Our hearts, pure as day, and our innocent hands found nothing wrong in these natural caresses [...] This instinct is without doubt a natural one [...] Modesty is a virtue of education." In the character of Imirce, sentiment gives way to instinct and an inconstancy seen as quite natural is thus legitimized: "I was naked, [Ariste] kissed my breasts with rapture, smothered me with caresses. I looked beneath his clothes, to see if he had the same object with which my lover gave me so much pleasure; he understood what I was thinking and intoxicated me with the sweet delights of love. Novelty, change, are pleasant to women and made my pleasure all the more intense; and from that moment, poor Émilior was forgotten."

The anti-religious rehabilitation of pleasure, a leitmotif in the works of Dulaurens, is the theme of *La Chandelle d'Arras* [*The Candle of Arras*] (1765). In this mock-heroic epic of eighteen cantos, composed in less than two weeks, the writer attacks prejudice by reworking an old legend, which holds that in 1105 the Virgin bestowed upon the Bishop of Arras a miraculous candle capable of curing that city's inhabitants. The story relates the grotesque adventures of Jerome Nulsifrote and Jean la Terreur, two violinists of Arras. Jean la Terreur visits Purgatory and Hell and holds a number of conversations with Adam, Moses, and Joseph. Then, suspended high above the abbey of Avennes on Saint Dunstan's bow, he decides to let go: "Suddenly the holy king grabbed hold of his machine; at the same moment the bow grazing his body sliced off his instrument." Jean la Terreur's "sad machine" falls into the budding bosom of a young sister in tears: "...on this white breast Priapus quickens with life and, sliding from the bodice to underneath the shift, proceeds to lose himself, we don't quite know where [...] suddenly, Godemiché springs from her shift and flies off to fill Mother Cornichon with his unction." At the end of a long journey, Jean la Terreur receives a candle from the Virgin. But Dulaurens's audacious pen has this object of fervor perform miracles quite different from those for which it was intended, as testified by the experience of a young virgin come to venerate it: "Holy lamp! You burn me up, what charms you have! Divine pastor! Keep going, push the candle in more, if you can..."

Biography

Born in Douai on May 27, 1719, Henri-Joseph Laurens (also Dulaurens or Du Laurens) waged a lifelong battle with authority. Dulaurens already had a reputation for being a troublesome, though brilliant, student during his days at the Jesuit College in Anchin. The publication in the same book of his first works, *Discours sur la beauté* [*Discourse on Beauty*] and *La vraie origine du géant de Douai* [*The Real Origin of the Giant of Douai*] (1743), earned him a forced exit when his lampooning of a number of people was viewed as slanderous. Subsequently judged responsible for the subversive writings of others, notably Jean Meslier, Voltaire and Holbach, he was obliged to flee the country to escape imprisonment. Ordained a priest in 1744, Dulaurens soon rebelled against clerical discipline; he published a collection of satire against the Jesuits, *Les Jésuitiques,* the same year he left the priesthood (1761). He next appears at the center of

various scandals including an escapade with a nun from the convent of Saint Julien of Douai, who stole a purse containing around 20,000 *livres* (pounds of silver) before running off with him. Allusions to his poverty are many. Dulaurens writes *"pour avoir du pain"* [to buy bread]; even more urgently, *"la faim l'oblige d'aller vite"* [hunger obliges him to move quickly]. After a period of wanderings and illicit writings, he was arrested. He publicly renounced his errors on June 19, 1767 and on August 31 was condemned to life imprisonment. Dulaurens spent 21 years in the prison in Mayenne, then was transferred to the convent-prison in Marienborn where he died insane on August 17, 1793.

DOMINIQUE PÉLOQUIN

Selected Works

La vraie origine du Géan de Douai en vers françois, suivie d'un discours sur la beauté où l'on fait mention des belles de cette ville. Douai, 1743.

Les Jésuitiques, enrichies de notes curieuses pour servir à l'intelligence de cet ouvrage. Rome [Paris], 1761.

Le Balai, poème héroï-comique en XVIII chants. Constantinople, 1761. La Haye, 1763.

L'Arrétin ou la Débauche de l'esprit en fait de bon sens. Rome, 1763.

Irmice, ou la fille de la nature. Berlin, 1765.

La Chandelle d'Arras, poème héroï-comique en XVIII chants. Berne, 1765.

Le compère Mathieu, ou les Bigarrures de l'esprit humain. Londres. 1766.

Je suis pucelle, histoire véritable. La Haye, 1767.

L'Antipapisme révélé ou les Rêves de l'antipapisme. Genève, 1767.

Further Reading

Collectif, *Dictionnaire des œuvres érotiques, domaine français*, préface de Pascal Pia, Paris, Éd. Robert Laffont, coll. "Bouquins", 2001 [Mercure de France, 1971].

Collectif. *Éros philosophe. Discours libertins des Lumières*, Études rassemblées par F. Moureau et Alain-Marc Rieu, Paris, Honoré Champion, 1984.

Ehrard, J. *L'Idée de nature en France dans la première moitié du XVIIIe siècle.* Paris, Albin Michel, 1994.

Fellows, O. et A. Green. "Diderot and the abbé Du Laurens", *Diderot Studies*, I (1949), pp. 27–50.

Goncourt, E. et J. de. *Portraits intimes du XVIIIe siècle.* Paris, 1924.

Groubentall de Linière, M.F. *Notice sur la vie et les ouvrages de l'auteur*, en tête de l'édition *de La Chandelle d'Arras*, Paris, 1809.

Nabarra, A. article *Dulaurens*, in *Dictionnaire des Journalistes, 1600–1789*, éd. J. Sgard. Oxford, Voltaire Foundation, 1999 [Grenoble, 1976], pp. 354–357.

Racault, J. "Le motif de de l'"Enfant de la Nature." Dans la littérature du XVIIIe siècle ou la recréation expérimentale de l'origine" *Primitivisme et mythe des origines dans la France des Lumières, 1680–1820*, Paris, 1989, pp.101–117.

Rivara, Annie, "Préface" *Imirce ou la Fille de la Nature*, Publications de l'Université de Saint-Étienne, coll. "Lire le Dix-huitième Siècle." 1993.

Vernière, P. *L'enfant de la nature, d'"Imirce" à Gaspard Hauser"." Lumières ou clair-obscur*. Paris, Presses Universitaires de France, 1987.

DUBÉ, JEAN-PIERRE

1954–
Canadian novelist

La grotte

La grotte is like a grenade lobbed at a formerly church-dominated society and its surviving vestiges. Although it is not a Sadean novel, Dubé, like Sade, uses transgression as an important tool. The explicit depiction of homosexuality, especially in the clergy, is among the elements that would have been unthinkable until recently. This novel is full of madness and anger arising, in part, out of stern moral condemnation of all but church-approved manifestations of sexuality.

Because *La grotte* is recounted in fragments which are not in chronological sequence, the story emerges only slowly. A tortured and psychologically unstable priest is attracted to a young boy in a residential school and initiates a sexual relationship with him. One night, he encounters the young adolescent walking with a girl near a religious grotto and, in a jealous rage, strikes out at him with a plaster statue of the Virgin, killing him. The stories of other characters affected by that murder are told in various parts of the novel. Finally, the girl, now a young woman, recognizes him. He is sentenced to a long period of incarceration during which he is visited by a counsellor who reveals that he was the victim's best friend. The friendship that develops between them evolves into love. This time the homoerotic element emerges as a positive factor. A process of healing and liberation takes place for both men. The eroticism of these passages is sensual, tender, and healing. Its depiction can perhaps be read as a sign that a revolution has occurred in the Franco-Manitoban community. However, this redemption is not available to the woman who witnessed the death of her friend. Her trauma goes back even further, to the grief and loneliness of her widowed father who took her into his bed to console him for his loss. It was less the incest itself that has broken her, than the brutal rejection by her father when he discovered she was pregnant. For her there is no going back, no finding of healing through erotic love.

The role of eroticism in this novel clearly goes beyond psychological factors to the political, social, and institutional factors that contribute to them. This novel emerges from a very specific milieu. Like the large French majority in Quebec, the francophone population of Manitoba had historically been almost uniformly Roman Catholic. A small minority in an overwhelmingly English-speaking province, it relied on the Church for its social structures and its way of life, from its origins at least until the 1960s. After 1970, the change to reliance on more secular language-based organizations came swiftly. Nevertheless, the embrace of the austere version of Catholicism (the term *jansénisme* is used in Canada) that typified the Quebec-based francophone Catholic clergy was not relaxed all at once. The intensity of this carefully constructed novel arises, in part, from the stifling moral atmosphere that resulted and, in part, from the enclosed, embattled situation of the French-language society within a mainly anglophone province.

Ma cousine Germaine

This novel of adolescent love and sex is dominated, for two-thirds of its length, by the exploration of their sexuality by two adolescents, both aged sixteen. Although Germaine plays a major role in it, to a large extent *Ma cousine Germaine* is an exploration of masculinity. The title is a play on the French term for *first cousin* which, in the feminine, is *cousine germaine*. Germaine is a first cousin of Jean-Paul, the narrator and principal protagonist of the story. Because they are first cousins, their love and sexual passion has an ambiguous status, on the border between acceptable and incestuous. Aware of this, they take care not to show undue signs of affection in public. The result is a very secret affair in which their intimacy flourishes. Its growth is described in numerous explicit and highly erotic passages of sexual experimentation as they discover their sexuality and the various ways that their bodies and their imagination can provide pleasure. The last third of the novel marks a sharp reversal after their affair is discovered by Germaine's mother. Jean-Paul and Germaine have another cousin, Marc, who is a tough, violent, a bully. Marc kidnaps Jean-Paul and, while raining blows on him, demands to be told Germaine's most intimate secrets. Jean-Paul fears for his life and, in his attempt to escape, accidentally causes Marc's death. The remaining part of the novel recounts Jean-Paul's flight in Marc's car across the American border and his new life as he assumes Marc's identity, thus, in a sense, becoming his own cousin. He meets a woman whom he later marries. His greatest sexual discovery, however, arises out of his relationship with Bill, his employer, who reveals to him sources of sexual pleasure of an intensity that he had never imagined. They form a deep friendship and the sexual attachment is as gentle as it is intense.

Ma cousine Germaine takes place in a more or less contemporary setting in which the church is, at most, a background presence. Although a social evolution has occurred since the period depicted in *La Grotte*, the individual is still subjected to strong social pressures arising out of prejudices, gender stereotypes, and intolerance. In this highly erotic novel, certainly one of the most explicitly sexual ever written and published in French in Manitoba, heterosexuality and homosexuality alike are both celebrated passionately and condemned harshly. When Jean-Paul's mother discovers her son and her niece together in his bedroom, she reacts with understanding and wisdom. When Germaine's mother discovers them, she reacts with outrage and condemnation and makes their behavior a matter of public knowledge. Soon words like incest and perversion are being used by Marc who had always taunted Jean-Paul with homophobic barbs, merely because he had given up playing hockey to play a less rough version, called *ringuette*, on a mixed team.

Ma cousine Germaine is, in part, a protest against phobic, mindless sexual prejudice. It is also a work of erotic literature that is a milestone in the social and artistic maturation of French-language literature of western Canada.

Biography

Jean-Pierre Dubé was born in 1954 in La Broquerie, a village in the southeast of the Canadian province of Manitoba. Dubé pursued university studies in philosophy at the Collège Universitaire de Saint-Boniface (affiliated with the University of Manitoba) and at the Université Laval, Quebec City. A journalist by profession, he was for a number of years editor-in-chief of the Manitoba francophone weekly *La Liberté*. He has since worked as an educational policy advisor. Among his works are two plays, two novels, and two scenarios for musical stage productions, all in French. It is his novels, *La Grotte* and *Ma cousine Germaine*, that contain an important erotic element.

ERIC ANNANDALE

Selected Works

La grotte. St. Boniface, Manitoba: Les Éditons du Blé, 1994.
Ma cousine Germaine. St. Boniface, Manitoba: Les Éditions du Blé, 2000.

References and Further Reading

Bélanger, Georges, review article. "Ma cousine Germaine" in *Francophonies d'Amérique* 13 (2003): 221–223.
Finney, James de, review article. "La Grotte" in *Francophonies d'Amérique* 6 (1996): 85–87.
Kasper, Louise Renée, review article. "La Grotte" in *Cahiers franco-canadiens de l'Ouest* 6:2 (1995): 341–342.
MacDonell, Alan. review article. "Ma cousine Germaine" in *Cahiers franco-canadiens de l'Ouest* 13:2 (2001): 205–207.

DUCHAMP, MARCEL

1887–1968
French-American artist and prose writer

Modern art historians regard Marcel Duchamp as one of the most influential artists of the 20th and 21st centuries. Yet most of his life he rebelled against art, even against his own famous cubist-futurist canvas "Nude Descending a Staircase"—and created pieces of "anti-art" which he refused to commercialize. These works, plus his life style of contented semi-poverty, of reading and playing chess, constituted nothing less than an attempt at deconstructing the whole enterprise of Western art, which he considered "washed up." In addition, he was one of the most literate of modern artists, well-versed in mathematics and science and greatly influenced by French symbolist writers, from Rimbaud and Laforgue to Mallarmé and Jarry. His major works rely to a great extent upon his literary notes and titles, writings which are full of erotic word play and creative puns. He once stated that art's only legitimate "ism" was eroticism, as against movements like Cubism or Surrealism.

Brought up a Catholic, he became an atheist at an early age, earned money in Paris by drawing risqué cartoons, and experimented in the radical new movements of Fauvism and Cubism. After 1912, he began creating works that substituted satire, literature, erotic humor, and pataphysics (Alfred Jarry's imaginary science) for Classical, Romantic, and Modernist art. From the middle of the twentieth century to this day, artists in the Pop, Minimalist, Primitive, Cognitive, Post-Modernist, Performance, and other art movements have been strongly influenced by his anti-artistic, anti-social, anti-capitalist, and anti-religious iconoclasm.

The best-known examples of Duchamp's conceptual, literary anti-art pieces are what he called his "readymades." These are ordinary items purchased in flea markets or hardware stores and given the status of unaesthetic sculpture merely by the chance selection of the indifferent artist and his casual attachment of a title to them. By far his most significant readymade was a urinal he bought in a plumbing store in New York in 1917 and entitled "Fountain." He rotated the fixture 90 degrees so that the drain holes would spout urine if it were used; and of course the title reflects back on the male user. But the urinal also suggests a number of puns from French slang. Duchamp had recently arrived in New York and enjoyed bilingual humor, also bisexual humor. Common slang terms in the French of the time for a prostitute were latrine and pissotière [public urinal], and the French word fontaine, in the feminine gender, had been popularly in use for "vulva" since the Middle Ages. Indeed, the urinal has the shape of a vulva, which makes it both yonic and phallic. In his notes there is the comment, "One has for female only the public urinal and one lives by it" (*Salt Seller*, p. 23). Further bisexuality along with religious satire were added to "Fountain" by the nicknames he and his friends gave to it which were based on its iconic, religious appearance when placed on its back: the Madonna of the Bathroom and the Buddha of the Bathroom. Finally, Duchamp signed the work "R. Mutt" which is a play on the manufacturer's name, J.L. Mott, and motte, the French word for "pubis, pussy." It also includes the French pronunciation of art (the "R"). Elsewhere Duchamp used the R-art reference in an invented word "arrhe" and in the double R of his female name for himself, Rrose Sélavy. The name is pronounced "Rose, c'est la vie," with the added slang meaning of "Rose (the vulva) is life."

All this word play and erotic humor had a serious purpose, to mock the social importance of the traditional bourgeois art object and to establish erotic shock as an aesthetic method. Later he created a phallus out of plaster and called it "Objet-Dard," "Object-Prick," a play on objet d'art. When he reproduced these works in miniature collections to give to friends, he made sure that each one contained sixty-nine pieces.

Many of Duchamp's erotic works involved machinery. He had always wanted to be a mathematician or a scientist, and his writings and sketches are full of fantastic scientific inventions. An important influence was his friend Francis Picabia's paintings of machines making love. But his own most powerful machine, a machine célibataire [bachelor machine] entitled "The Large Glass" or "The Bride Stripped Bare by Her Bachelors, Even," comes closest to Jarry's electrical-magnetic "Machine-to-inspire-love" from his science-fiction novel *The Superman* (1902).

In Jarry's work, the love-machine is attached to the Superman, falls in love with him, overheats, explodes, and immolates him in a kind of orgasmic love-death. Duchamp's machine is less violent but equally masturbatory. It consists of two superimposed plates of cracked glass nine feet tall divided into two rectangles, upper and lower. The top one contains the Bride enclosed by the two plates, her body and various organs vaguely resembling automobile parts, with a "love cylinder" and a "reservoir of love gasoline." The lower rectangle has nine malic ("male-ish") molds representing nine uniformed Bachelors which are attached to other sexual machines. The auto-eroticism is coded into the French title, "La Mariée mise à nue par ces celibataires, même." MARiée and CÉLibataires include the name of the artist MARCEL, and même, "even," is a pun on "m'aime," "loves me." The title thus contains both "Marcel loves me" and "the Bride loves me." The virgin Bride also represents the Virgin MARIE in Mariée. The puns transmit the message of the glass, that art like profane and sacred love is a humorous, see-through fiction of desire (Duchamp called it "hilarious").

Lodged permanently at the Philadelphia Museum of Art, "The Large Glass" also consists of 93 documents of enigmatic notes dealing with the machine's operation. This operation is mostly mental since (1) the parts do not move; and (2) Duchamp got tired of working on the piece after eight years and left the rest of it up to the spectator's imagination. Conceptually, the documents reveal that the Bride strips herself bare while masturbating and gives a signal to the Bachelors to become aroused and assist her in her stripping and in her (potential) orgasm by their ejaculation.

The last twenty years of Duchamp's life from 1948–1968 were spent on a complementary project, "Étant donné," another large work installed in the Philadelphia Museum. Here the Bride is again stripped bare and is spied upon by spectator-voyeurs through a peephole in a door. This time she is realistically portrayed as a mannequin lying nude and faceless on her back, her sex gaping, her left hand holding a phallic gas light. In the distance there is a yonic waterfall (cf. "Fountain") activated by a motor. She has just had an orgasm; and her body is modeled on that of Duchamp's great love of the 1940s, Maria Martins. The "Étant donné" of the title is usually translated "Given" or "Given that." The artist was given his love, Maria, given that she was his desire.

Thus the Bachelor-Artist along with his bachelor machines can only aspire; and like Ixion he makes love to a mental fiction in the shape of a goddess, a dea ex machina, from whose imaginary union the work of anti-art is born—and dies. Both Brides are a secular travesty of desire, of the vulva, the Fountain, the Rose, the Madonna of the Bathroom, the Virgin Mary. Duchamp's work and life demonstrate that humans are virtual games-people, and that "art," "arrhe," is an absurd erotic pun, a crazy coition of the word and the world. Biological desire is life, the spectator's life and the life of the artist-non-artist Marcel Duchamp, aka Rrose Sélavy. Rrose, c'est la vie.

Biography

Born at Blainville-Chevon, Normandy, France, 28 July 1887. Educated at the École Bossuet,

Rouen, 1897–1904; studied painting at the Académie Julian in Paris and worked as an apprentice printer in Rouen, 1904–1905. Military service, 1905–1906. Cartoonist in Paris, 1906–1910, painted Fauvist and Cubist works. Exhibited controversial painting "Nude Descending a Staircase" at New York Armory Show, February 1913. Turned down for war service in 1914 because of heart murmur, moved to New York in 1915. Period of readymades, 1913–1917. Executed "The Large Glass," 1915–1923, worked with members of the New York Dada movement. Moved back to Paris, 1923, lived there until 1942, became chess expert, married Lydie Sarazin-Levassor in 1927, divorced seven months later. Collaborated with French Surrealists, 1934–1942, moved back to New York, love affair with Maria Martins, 1946. Married Alexina (Teeny) Sattler in 1954, became naturalized American citizen in 1955. Worked secretly on last major piece "Given: 1. The Waterfall, 2. The Illuminating Gas," from 1946 until his death from cancer on 2 October 1968.

Selected Works

The Bride Stripped Bare by Her Bachelors, Even: A Typographic Version. Richard Hamilton of Marcel Duchamp's Green Box, translated by George Heard Hamilton, New York: George Wittenborn, 1960.

A l'infinitif (The White Box). Translated by Marcel Duchamp and Cleve Gray, New York: Cordier & Ekstrom, 1966.

Notes and Projects for the Large Glass. Edited by Arturo Schwarz, translated by George Heard Hamilton, Cleve Gray, and Arturo Schwarz. London: Thames and Hudson, 1969.

Salt Seller: The Writings of Marcel Duchamp (Marchand du sel). Edited by Michel Sanouillet and Elmer Peterson. New York: Oxford University Press, 1973. Reprinted as *The Writings of Marcel Duchamp*, New York: Da Capo Press, 1989.

Marcel Duchamp: Notes. Edited and translated by Paul Matisse. Boston: G. K. Hall, 1983.

Manual of Instructions for "Étant Donnés 1. la chute d'eau. 2. Le gaz d'éclairage...." Philadelphia: Philadelphia Museum of Art, 1987.

Further Reading

Ades, Dawn, Neil Cox, and David Hopkins. *Marcel Duchamp.* London: Thames and Hudson, 1999.

Belting, Hans. *The Invisible Masterpiece.* Translated by Helen Atkins. Chicago: Chicago University Press, 2001.

Cabanne, Pierre. *Dialogues with Marcel Duchamp.* Translated by Ron Padgett. New York: Da Capo Press, 1987.

Camfield, William. *Marcel Duchamp: Fountain. Houston:* Houston Fine Arts Press. 1989.

Carrouges, Michel. *Les Machines célibataires.* Paris: du Chêne, 1976.

d'Harnancourt, Anne, and Kynaston McShine (editors). *Marcel Duchamp.* New York: Museum of Modern Art, 1973.

Duve, Thierry de. *Kant after Duchamp.* Cambridge: MIT Press, 1996.

Golding, John. Marcel *Duchamp: The Bride Stripped Bare by Her Bachelors, Even.* London, Penguin, 1973.

Henderson, Linda Dalrymple. *Duchamp in Context, Science and Technology in "The Large Glass" and Related Works.* Princeton: Princeton University Press, 1998.

Jones, Amelia. *Postmodernism and the En-Gendering of Marcel Duchamp.* Cambridge: Cambridge University Press, 1994.

Joselit, David. *Infinite Regress, Marcel Duchamp 1910–1941.* Cambridge: MIT Press, 1998.

Kuenzli, Rukdolf E. and Francis M. Naumann. *Marcel Duchamp Artist of the Century.* Cambridge: MIT Press, 1989.

Lebel, Robert, *Marcel Duchamp.* Translated by George H. Hamilton. New York: Grove Press, 1959.

Paz, Octavio. *Marcel Duchamp, Appearance Stripped Bare.* Translated by R. Phillips and D. Gardner. New York: Seaver Books/Viking Press, 1978.

Schwartz, Arturo. *The Complete Works of Marcel Duchamp.* 3rd revised edition, 2 vols, New York: Delano Greenridge, 1997.

Siegel, Jerrold. *The Private Worlds of Marcel Duchamp. Desire, Liberation, and the Self in Modern Culture.* Berkeley and Los Angeles: University of California Press, 1995.

Tomkins, Calvin. *Duchamp. A Biography. New York:* Henry Holt and Company, 1996.

DURAS, MARGUERITE

1914–1996
French novelist

Marguerite Duras's creative corpus includes an unknown quantity of dimestore fiction published during the Occupation and more than ninety novels, stories, plays, and films. The great majority of those texts address issues of sexuality and desire. Duras returns insistently to the scene of desire, studying it close up, slowing it down, repeating and transforming its details, its lighting, its rhythm, and the sequence of its unfolding. She textualizes incest in *La vie tranquille*, *Un barrage contre le Pacifique*, *Navire night*, *La pluie d'été*, *Agatha*, *L'Amant*, *L'Amant de la Chine du nord* and lesbian desire in works such as *Un barrage contre le Pacifique*, "Théodora," *Le ravissement de Lol V. Stein*, *India Song*, *La femme du Gange*, *L'Amant*, and "Dialogue avec une Carmélite." If she subtly infers unarticulated male homoerotic desire in 1970s texts with redoubled male figures (such as *Détuire dit-elle*), as James C. Williams contends (18), she explicitly addresses male homosexuality in *La maladie de la mort* and *Yeux bleus cheveux noirs*. But throughout her career, Duras remained primarily concerned with relations *between* the sexes and most especially with female characters and feminine desire. She valorized female characters, increasingly brought them to the textual fore, and examined their erotic relations and the unsatisfied longings, impossible communication, and unbridgeable separations she associated with those relations. Duras's preference for heterosexual relations at their most extreme provoked one critic to recall her use of the term "impossible" love (Frost, 131) and another to conclude that in her work "the most sexually desirable of other bodies is that very body with which, for reasons of cultural custom, social, or personal circumstances, or even sexual orientation, no relationship is possible" (Hill, 139). Many forms of difference separate Duras's characters from one another, including those related to gender, class, race, and ethnicity (*Un barrage contre*

le Pacifique, *Moderato cantabile*, *L'Amant*, *L'Amant de la Chine du Nord*), national identity, colonial divisions, and political allegiances (*Hiroshima mon amour*, *L'Amant*, *L'Amant de la Chine du Nord*, *La Douleur*'s "Ter le milicien" and "Albert des Capitales"), mental states, and sexual orientation.

In 1940s–1950s texts such as *La vie tranquille*, *Les impudents*, "Le Boa," and *Un barrage contre le Pacifique*, Duras presents adolescent heroines approaching heterosexual initiation with a 'cautionary' erotic scene revealing the inequalities and violence of normative bourgeois patriarchal heterosexual relations. Theses scenes are commonly placed outside the reader's direct gaze by means of figural or allusive rendering or, more commonly, by their placement before or after the time of the main narrative. In "Le Boa," Duras give the cautionary erotic scene a humorous and ironic spin by figuring it in the barely veiled form of violent weekly relations between an emphatically phallic boa and its ever-expanding roster of sacrificial chicks. Every Sunday, colonial zoo keepers bring a live chick to the boa's cage, where it regularly finishes ingesting its chick before the girl arrives for her weekly outing. She sees only the aftermath of the murder, in which the boa sits, ensconced in the chick's tepid down, still trembling with pleasure and digesting its meal. Duras's narrator categorizes this murder as an "impeccable crime," for it leaves no trace, no blood, no sign of remorse.

Duras further unveils the violence and power relations structuring bourgeois heteroerotic relations in *Un barrage contre le Pacifique*, whose young heroine is so enthralled in a filmic scene of heterosexual love that she continues to watch, as if past the end of the film, as the erotic scene devolves into violent destruction:

Their mouths approached one another, with the slowness of a nightmare. Once they are close enough to touch, their bodies are cut off. Then, in their decapitated heads, you see what you wouldn't know how to see, their lips face-to-face, open halfway, open still more, their jaws fall apart like in death and in a brusque and fatal relaxation of their heads, their lips join like octopuses, crush each other, try in the deliriousness of the starving, to eat, to make each other disappear in a reciprocal absorption (189).

This scene permits the girl to recognize that equality in heterosexual relations is an "impossible and absurd ideal to which the structure of the organs clearly does not lend itself" (189), and that, given current relations of power, it is this film's beautiful courtesan who will be consumed.

In so far as they effect revelation and cast change as possible, this early writing articulates an optimistic outlook on heterosexual erotic relations. They offer young females the possibility of recognizing the violence of heterosexual relations and of defining their roles in them differently. In contrast to Beauvoir's contemporaneous claim that women have no organ suitable for use as an alter ego and thus cannot achieve full sexual subjectivity, Duras's young heroines discover viable alter egos in their breasts, which she portrays as symbols of autonomy, transcendence, and power into which they project themselves and in relation to which they define their sexual identities. "Le Boa"'s heroine declares that "outside of the house, there was the boa, here, there were my breasts" (107), while *Un Barrage*'s female protagonist rides colonial city streets in a black limousine defining herself in relation to the "erection of her breasts, higher than everything standing in that city, over which they would prevail" (226). She goes on to orchestrate her own heterosexual initiation, choosing the man, the place, the time, and the dress. Rather that emerge as victim of this scene, she derives an ethical lesson from the blood and bodily fluids it commingles: "That in love, differences could abolish themselves to such an extent, she would never forget" (343).

From the late 1950s–1970s, Duras shifted her focus to slightly older women, the bourgeois fiancées, wives, and mothers she contends suffer the most of brutal patriarchal oppressions: "Damned and scorned" since the bourgeois revolution, they have been constrained to live "chez elles, imprisoned, satiated, in a concentration camp universe [and] a state of "infernal idleness [...] I don't know anything worse than that, even in misery. Women living in misery are happier than bourgeois women. Its an agent [facteur] of suicide" (Marguerite Duras à Montréal, 75). Her writing of this period is often considered her most political, as it articulates themes proximate to those being debated in feminist and psychoanalytic research. Throughout her career, Duras set erotic relations in relation to social, cultural, institutional, and historical contexts. In this period, she experiments with ways in which disturbing or dislocating normative erotic relations might deconstruct normative gender relations and social structures.

To that end, Duras captures bourgeois women as they are awakening from their infernal torpor and beginning to stir. She finds *Moderato Cantabile*'s Anne Desbaresdes as her son's piano lesson (and her own state of torpor) is interrupted by a woman's piercing scream. Desbaresdes rushes to a nearby café only to see, in its dimly lit recess, a woman lying dead on the floor with a man sprawled out on top of her. His face, expressionless except for the indelible mark of desire, is covered with blood from the dead woman's mouth. As this scene closes, his mouth glues itself, once again, to hers. This violent scene mesmerizes Desbaresdes, as it does one of her husband's employees, Chauvin, who also happened to witness it. The rest of this narrative traces their attempt to reconstruct this scene in dialogue, each of them playing the role of one of its protagonists. The novel and their efforts end on an allusive and ambiguous note, with the narrativization of the café murder: "I would wish you were dead," he says, to which she responds, "It is done."

Duras similarly captures the heroine of *Le ravissement of Lol V. Stein* as she begins to stir—but for the second time. Her first movement had occurred a decade earlier, at the S. Thala ball, where she was to announce her engagement to Michael Richardson. Before that announcement could be made, however, an older woman, Anne-Marie Stretter entered the room with an erotic charge of such magnitude that it wrenched desire out of normative bourgeois circuits. Captivated, Richardson moved with Stretter onto the dance floor as Lol V. Stein receded with her friend Tatiana Karl to assume a spectatorial position in to this erotic scene. Lesbian desire also circulated, as Karl caressed Stein's hand, and Stein spoke of her need to invite Stretter to dance. For the remainder of the night, as desire circulated freely, Lol escaped and forgot the strictures of bourgeois desire, attaining as she did "the wisdom of the ages." When at daybreak desire reintegrated normative erotic and social structures, Lol re-entered her previous trance-like state. Ten years later, married with children, she had just remembered and re-found Tatiana and is beginning her attempt to remember the S. Thala ball and its erotic dynamics so as retrieve and extend its gains. To that end, she persuades Tatiana and her lover to continue their weekly trysts at a hotel as she watches from a rye field. She later takes Tatiana's lover to S. Thala, visits the ballroom, recalls the ball's events to him, accompanies him to a hotel room for sex, and, in its course, briefly re-accesses the state achieved at the S. Thala ball. *Le ravissement* articulates a diminishing faith in the revolutionary potential of sexuality and desire, or, perhaps, a recognition that any such gains are necessarily individual and ephemeral. Provoked spontaneously and accidentally, the S. Thala ball's intense erotics yields the most dramatic and sustained disruption of bourgeois heteroerotic relations. Lol's subsequent endeavor yields a short-lived leap outside, but also the possibility of continuing her attempt, uninterrupted. As this novel's trio returns to its position in the hotel room and the rye field, Duras links their ongoing efforts to the *longue durée* of "God knows how many affairs like Lol V. Stein's, affairs nipped in the bud, trampled upon, and . . . massacres, oh! you've no idea how many there are, how many blood-stained unrealised attempts are strewn along the horizon, piled up there."

Duras took a break from writing in the 1970s, but her films of that decade address similar concerns. *Nathalie Granger*'s heroine embodies the purely negative politics of refusal that distinguish Duras's political views from the feminist political agendas of that era, for instance, while *India Song* studies the erotic relations of one woman and two men in an explicitly colonial context and endows its heroine with the passivity Duras associated with women's historical situation and political potential. In her 1970s interview with Xavière Gauthier, *Les parleuses* Duras clarified her views on numerous subjects crucial to understanding her textual erotics, including women and bourgeois patriarchy, feminine desire, homoerotic desire, and the relation of writing and politics.

By her 1980 return to prose writing, Duras had entered the period of her greatest political despair. She was convinced that Western

hegemony was at its end, but that it had succeeded in installing so great a chasm between the West and the East that only a catastrophe could equalize things. Her writing of this era distinguishes itself from her pre-1980 work by its increased distance between protagonists, its invigorated attention to sadomasochism, and the increased explicitness, brutality, and violence in its erotic depictions, which combine with an increasingly minimalist style to propel scenes of dark and disturbing erotic relations directly center stage. The hope implicit in the 1940s–1950s work and the revolutionary or transformative aims implicit in the 1960s and 1970s now give way to hopelessness, despair, and an ultimately conservative stance on erotic relations. The transformative hope she once placed in women and homosexuals, based on their shared marginalization under bourgeois patriarchy and the complicity and revolutionary advantages she believed derive from such exclusion (see *Les parleuses*) now cede the place to negative assessments like the *Les yeux verts* piece on "Femmes et homosexualités," which dismisses both militant feminism and homosexuality, or *Outside*'s "Dialogue avec une Carmélite," which permits self-flagellation to replace lesbian desire as a means of sexual release.

The problems Duras now identifies with homosexuality are of a piece with her enthusiastic embrace of women as the only desiring sex and of heterosexuality as the only site structured by difference and thus the only place in which desire can arise ("Pour moi, le désir ne peut avoir lieu qu'entre le masculin et le féminin, entre des sexes différents" [*Monde extérieur*]). On this view, lesbian eroticism lacks the difference required for desire and male homosexuals, unable to enter into erotic relations with women, are equally exiled from desire, caught up in narcissistic, masturbatory, and sterile relations. Duras develops this account in her explicit writings with male homosexuality, in *La maladie de la mort* and its 1986 rewrite, *Les yeux bleus cheveux noirs*, which portray the contractual relations of a heterosexual woman with a man, readers are invited to recognize as gay and, in the later text, with two men, one straight and one homosexual. Both texts associate females with desire and life and gay men with bodily ignorance and death, and both establish heterosexual relations as the inevitable endgame of all erotic relations. They thus perform, as James Williams finds all of Duras' experiments in erotic pleasure do, "a sublimatory, rhetorical appropriation of the Other as a defence against the threat of homosexual indifferentiation" (Williams, 158).

Despite Duras' enthusiasm for heteroerotics, they scarcely fare better in this phase of her writing, associated as they are with violence, death, unachieved communication, and negative outcomes. She examines sadomasochism, as she had previously, but now she diverges more sharply from the western erotic tradition to examine the woman's relation to that dynamic. In her scenario for Alain Resnais' *Hiroshima mon amour* she had explored heterosexual eroticism in relation to the social and historical contexts of the previous decade—fascism, collaboration, Franco-German relations, and the purges. Then, she had left the sexual relations between the Nazi soldier and the girl from Nevers off scene, showing instead him shot and dying as his love lay grieving across his body. Returning in the 1980s, the erotics of fascism, she eroticizes violence itself, including the violence of torture, and portrays a French woman's libidinal attraction to a fascist male body in *La Douleur's* "Ter le milicien" and "Albert des Capitales.

Similarly, while *L'Homme assis dans le couloir*, *Les yeux bleus cheveux noirs*, and *La maladie de la mort* all establish Duras as a writer of erotic fiction, one of them, *L'Homme assis dans le couloir* also forced the issue of her relation to pornography.

To briefly recall, this short text is entirely composed of a violent sex scene rendered without emotion, personalization, or temporal or spatial precisions. It features three characters—a detached narrator (who is perhaps female and who Duras elsewhere suggests may be herself), a man seated in a shadowy corridor, and a woman lying before him, on the ground, across a path, in the sun. She spreads her legs open to his gaze, then spreads open her labia as well. She cries out. Standing above her, he urinates on her body, beginning with her mouth and proceeding down to her vagina. He presses his foot on her body and uses it to roll her around in the dirt. He presses down harder still. As he retreats to the shadowy corridor, she continues crying out. She goes to kneel before him, performing oral sex until his pleasure turns to pain, and then licking his anal region. Turning her over, he

penetrates her and articulates his desire to kill her. She says that she wants to be beaten; "qu'elle voudrait mourir." [33]). Amid the ensuing cries, insults, and beatings, she says "oui, que c'est ca, oui" (thus reminding readers of *Hiroshima mon amour's* famous refrain "Tu me tues, tu me fais du bien"). He continues insulting and beating her until, finally, her head flops about on her neck, her face becomes a "chose morte" (35), and the scene falls silent. He lies down on her body (in the manner of so many previous characters, including the boa, *Hiroshima mon amour's* female lover, and the male in *Moderato cantabile's* opening scene). Motionless, she is dead, or merely asleep.

Due to the international success of its film version, Duras is perhaps best known to many spectators as the author of *L'Amant* and, to many readers, as the author of its 1991 reworking, *L'Amant de la Chine du Nord.* These novels examine erotic relations with a long history in Duras's corpus, including the lesbian desire of the young (semi-autobiographical) heroine for her classmate, Hélène Lagonelle, which receives an explicit and more violent retelling, as Hélène's breasts elicit not only the girl's erotic desire, but desire to kill. Both novels address her relations with her younger brother, which *L'Amant de la Chine du Nord* trace in detail and reveal as having been consummated. But most importantly, these novels also return to the erotic events Duras considers the origin of her writing: her erotic relationship with a man here revealed as radically separated from her by differences of class, race, age, and ethnicity. Here as elsewhere in her late writing, the fact that she is white and he is of Chinese origin, that she is from the lowest *colon* class and he from a well-placed Chinese family, that she is poor and he rich, that he is in his late twenties and she is in her mid-teens, that his religious and ethnic traditions foreclose the possibility of marriage, all of these *differences* augment their erotic desire and diminish the chance of communicating or of overcoming their multileveled separations, rendering their love both productive and "impossible."

Biography

Born Marguerite Donnadieu, 4 April 1914 in Gia Dinh, Indochina (Vietnam). Attended Lycée

Chasseloup-Laubat, Saigon. Moved to France, 1933. Faculté de droit; *licence,* mathematics and political science; Ecole libre des sciences politiques. Colonial Ministry, 1937–1940. Marries Robert Antelme, 1939. First child deceased at birth, 1942. Younger brother deceased, 1942. Member, Resistance group, Mouvement National des Prisonniers de Guerre et des Déportés September 1943. Antelme arrested and deported, June 1944–June 1945. Divorced, 1946. Son with Dionys Mascolo, 1947. Member, French Communist Party, 1944-1950. Anticolonial activism, 1950s–1962. Helped found Comité d'Action Etudiants-Ecrivains, May '68. Protests deaths of immigrant workers living in Foyer Franco-Africain, 1970. Relationship with young homosexual man, 1980–1996. Two alcoholic cures and a six-month coma, 1980s. Died Paris on March 3, 1996.

JANE WINSTON

Selected Works

Agatha. Paris, Editions de Minuit, 1981.
L'Amant. Paris, Editions de Minuit, 1984.
L'Amant de la Chine du Nord. Paris, Gallimard, 1991.
L'Amour. Paris, Gallimard, 1971.
Aurélia Steiner, in *Le navire night.* Paris, Mercure de France, 1979.
A Ernesto. Boissy St Léger, François Ruy-Vidal et Harlin Quist, 1971.
Un barrage contre le Pacifique. Paris, Gallimard, 1950; folio 1992.
"Le Boa," reprinted in *Des Journées dans les arbres.* Paris, Gallimard, 1954.
C'est tout. Paris, P.O.L., 1995.
Dix heures et demie du soir en été. Paris, Gallimard, 1960.
La douleur. Paris, P.O.L., 1985.
L'Homme assis dans le couloir. Revised, Paris, Minuit, 1980.
Les impudents. Paris, Plon, 1943; Gallimard, folio, 1992.
India Song. Paris, Gallimard, 1973.
La maladie de la mort. Paris, Minuit, 1982.
Marguerite Duras à Montréal. eds., Suzanne Lamy and André Roy, Montréal, Spirale, 1981.
Moderato Cantabile. Paris, Minuit, 1958.
Navire Night. Paris, Mercure de France, 1979.
Le marin de Gibraltar. Paris, Gallimard, 1952.
Le monde extérieur. Paris, P.O.L., 1993.
La pute de la côte normande. Paris, Minuit, 1986.
La pluie d'été. Paris, P.O.L., 1990; Gallimard, folio, 1994.

Le ravissement de Lol V. Stein. Paris, Gallimard, 1964.
La vie tranquille. Paris, Gallimard, 1944; Gallimard, 1950; folio, 1992.
Les yeux bleus cheveux noirs. Paris, Minuit, 1986.
Les yeux verts. Nouvelle édition augmentée, Paris, Chaiers du cinéma, 1987.
Yann Andrea Steiner. Paris, P.O.L., 1992.
With Xavière Gauthier, *Les Parleuses.* Paris, Minuit, 1974.

Further Reading

Andrea, Yann. *Cet amour-là.* Paris: Pauvret, 1999.
———, *M.D..* Paris, Minuit, 1983.
Antelme, Robert. *L'Espèce humaine.* Paris, La Cité universelle, 1947.
Blanchot, Maurice. *La Communauté inavouable.* Paris, Minuit, 1983.
Blot-Labarrère, Christiane. *Marguerite Duras.* Paris, Seuil, 1992.
Borgomano, Madeleine. *Duras. Une lecture des fantasmes,* Brussels, Cistre, 1985.
Cesari, Claire, *Marguerite Duras: de Lahore à Auschwitz.* Paris, Geneva, Champion-Slatkine, 1993.
Cohen, Susan D. *Women and Discourse in the Fiction of Marguerite Duras. Love, Legends, Language.* Oxford, Macmillan, 1993.
Crowley, Martin. *Duras, Writing and the Ethical: Making the Broken Whole.* Oxford, Clarendon, 2000.
Frost, Laura. *Sex Drives: Fantasies of Fascism in Literary Modernism.* Ithaca, London, Cornell, 2002.
Guers-Villate, Yvonne. *Continuité/Discontinuité dans l'œuvre durassienne.* Brussels, Editions de l'Université de Bruxelles, 1985.
Hill, Leslie. *Marguerite Duras: Apocalyptic Desires.* New York. London, Routledge, 1993.
Ince, Kate. "L'Amour la Mort: The Eroticism of Marguerite Duras." PPs. 147–173, in Alex Hughes and Kate Ince, eds., *French Erotic Fiction: Women's Desiring Writing, 1880-1990.* Oxford, Berg, 1996.
Mascolo, Dionys. *Autour d'un effort de mémoire. Sur une lettre de Robert Antelme.* Paris, Maurice Nadeau, 1987.
———. *Le Communisme.* Paris, Editions Gallimard, 1953.
Marini, Marcelle. *Territories du féminin. Avec Marguerite Duras.* Paris, Minuit, 1977.
Williams, James S. *The Erotics of Passage: Pleasure, Politics, and Form in the Later Work of Marguerite Duras.* Liverpool, Liverpool University Press, 1997.
Willis, Sharon. *Writing on the Body.* Urbana, Chicago: University of Illinois Press, 1986.
Winston, Jane Bradley. *Postcolonial Duras: Cultural Memory in Postwar France.* New York, Palgrave, 2001.

DUSTAN, GUILLAUME

1965–2005
French writer

"Autopornobiographies"

Dans ma chambre (1996) is an "autofiction" charting the sexual activities and relationships of the narrator as he fucks and is fucked by a series of lovers including Quentin, Terrier, Sté-phane, and Serge. Initially, Dustan's style seems a disconcertingly simple, even simplistic, re-hearsal of different sexual encounters based around the Paris "gay ghetto" in the Marais. However, the dead-pan oral tone, interlaced with hip slang and English-American express-sions, effectively conveys the repetitiveness, the superficial chic, and also the readily available pleasures of a lifestyle based on sex, drugs, and "le look." Not unlike Renaud Camus's *Tricks* (1988) and Hervé Guibert's *À l'ami qui ne m'a pas sauvé la vie* (1990), the first of Dustan's fiction is an interesting combination of self-ab-sorption and detachment, narcissism and self-deprecation. The detachment can also be seen as a way of dealing with the ritualized or non-ritualized violence of some of the relationships, the constant presence of AIDS—all of Dustan's friends are HIV positive—and the claustropho-bia of a strangely closeted if flamboyantly sex-centered world. At the end of the text he does, however, decide to leave Paris for a distant over-seas job, at the very time his sex with his main partner, Stéphane, seems to be turning into love.

In his second novel, *Je sors ce soir* (1997), Dustan is back in Paris. Despite the death of a close friend and the increasing threat of AIDS, he is happy to be back in the clubs with "his ghetto brothers," where he can look at men with pleasure and without fear. There follows a diary-like description of pick-up rituals—timing, posi-tioning, body-styles and dress-codes—conscious as he is that he needs to work out to follow the increasingly Americanized fashion for muscle-men. Will he or won't he score? He lingers and loiters in hope, alternating dancing, shitting,

taking ecstasy, and removing and replacing his carefully chosen t-shirt, according to the time and the activity. As the drug takes effect, the text itself becomes more disjointed, ending with his going home alone, masturbating, and going to sleep. Whether modestly or self-promotionally, the book ends with some two hundred credits to other writers, musicians, film-stars, and friends.

Dustan's next work, *Plus fort que moi* (1998), opens with a brief biography—his father's de-parture and the murder/suicide of a family of friends—before charting his own sexual history from teenage park encounters and backroom initiations to the publication of this volume. The text does, therefore, offer an account of the making of a particular kind of a modern, urban, French gay man, defined in terms of the Paris scene and, within that, scrupulously deli-neated sexual preferences and positions: the au-thor cruises not just the clubs and the streets but, increasingly, the Minitel, in search of compatible partners with an arsenal of sexual acrobatics, sex-toys, and role-plays. Now himself HIV posi-tive, his desire for strong sensations is gratified by ever more men and ever harder sex—fisting, dildos and bondage—as, with unprotected sex, he risks and even invites inevitable death: his sexual journey has become a kind of imitation or even parody of Céline's *Voyage au bout de la nuit* or O'Neill's *Long Day's Journey into Night*. Both he and his increasingly indiscriminately chosen partners are all pleasurably abjected "sluts." The text ends with the previously men-tioned escape from Paris, but not before he dreams of an encounter with an ape...

Other texts

Having done for the French gay male what wri-ters and film-makers such as Catherine Millet and Catherine Breillat are doing for the sexual life of the French heterosexual woman—except that Dustan is perhaps even more famous for his support of "barebacking" — he then publishes a rather different text, *Nicolas Pages* (1999).

This is a "real-time" diary account of Dustan's various activities and *amours* between 1995 and 1998, framed by his affair with fellow-author, the eponymous Pages, whom he met when they were invited to appear on the Belgian media. Here the literary model seems to be less Camus, Guibert, Céline, or O'Neill than, perhaps, Bret Easton Ellis, though for the fame rather than for the violence: both Dustan and Pages are, no doubt mistakenly, thought to represent "the new gay dandyism," with *Nicolas Pages* offering both a hymn to gay sex and an exposure of the stigma suffered by gay men in straight society, but in a mode which is constantly playful, picaresque, and parodic. Dustan's next novels, also published in his own series by Balland, remain in this playful mode, with *Génie Divin* (2001) comprising a patchwork of short essays, jottings, and interviews (including one with Bret Easton Ellis) and with *LXiR ou Dédramatison La Vi Cotidièn* (2002) even more disjointed and "cool." Here gayness is an aspect of style: the one-night stand has become the flip one-liner; serial sex has become the disjointed paragraph; violence can be read in a set of capitals or exclamation marks. Representing or debunking the discourses of the new millennium, *LXiR* turns every *que* (*that*) into *queue* (*prick*): the fun of sex is still omnipresent, but textualized in parody, punctuation, and pun.

Biography

Born William Baranès in 1965. Took the pseudonym Guillaume Dustan in 1995. Achieved celebrity with his first novel *Dans ma chambre*, published by P.O.L. in 1996. Has since published a regular series of novels with P.O.L. and with Balland where he currently edits their "Le Rayon" collection, formerly "Le Rayon Gay." He has also produced a number of short films including *Nous* and *Back*.

OWEN HEATHCOTE

Selected Works

Dans ma chambre. 1996.
Je sors ce soir. 1997.
Plus fort que moi. 1998.
Nicolas Pages. 1999.
Génie Divin. 2001.
LXiR ou Dédramatison La Vi Cotidièn. 2002.

Further Reading

Authier, Christian. *Le Nouvel ordre sexuel.* Paris: Bartillat, 2002.
Salducci, Pierre (editor). *Écrire gai.* Montreal: Alain Stanké, 1999 (includes article by Dustan entitled "Un désir bien naturel").
Bourcier, Marie-Hélène. *Queer Zones. Politiques des identités sexuelles, des représentations et des savoirs.* Paris: Balland, 2001.
Heathcote, Owen. "S(h)aming the Other: Repetition, Abjection and the Culture of Redemption in Vincent Borel's *Un ruban noir*, Guillaume Dustan's *Dans ma chambre* and Éric Jourdan's *Sexuellement incorrect*," forthcoming in Lucille Cairns (editor). *Gay Cultures in France.* Bern: Peter Lang.
Schehr, Larry. "Writing Bareback." *Sites*, 6/1 (2002): 181–202

DUTCH

The history of Dutch erotic literature is better described through the history of the book trade than through literary history. Although, from the seventeenth century on, the Dutch have been industriously supplying the European erotica market, the country has produced but few writers of erotica of its own whose works have been able to stand the test of time due to their inherent quality and/or the extent of the scandal they caused. Much of Dutch erotica was written and published anonymously and has remained anonymous. Publishers rather published translations than originals. It is therefore no coincidence that one of the few well-known twentieth-century erotic Dutch novels is set in the antiquarian world and was originally written in English: in 1970, W. Schors published, under the pen name of Armand Coppens, *The Memoirs of an Erotic Bookseller,* of which a Dutch version appeared in the same year. Even more significantly, Schors's protagonist, a bookseller whose search for pornography entangles him in various sexual adventures, shows no interest in pornography from the Netherlands: he is solely interested in the French, German, and English classics.

This lack of interest in homegrown erotica is also reflected in the state of (academic) research: the studies and articles about the subject are quickly summed up, there is still no bibliography of Dutch or Dutch-language erotica, much of the original works have not yet been republished and Dutch anthologies of erotica, such as the *Lusthof*-series by Leonard de Vries, from the sixties, or the recent compilation of masturbation poetry by Rob Schouten, are filled with translations. The few studies treating Dutch so-called pornography and erotica hardly ever consider it in it's own right, but compare it to explicit French and English books, to conclude that the Dutch books are less: less erotic, less philosophic, less libertine, less literary.

It is therefore rather difficult to give a survey of Dutch erotic literature. The genre is mostly determined by its readership, by censors, and other critics. And this framework is totally absent in the Netherlands. Although very early on (since 1669), Dutch law made 'obscenity' a separate censorship category, the list of early modern titles actually censored on this ground is rather short, and consists mostly of French erotica or translations from the French. A general prohibition was in force, but in daily practice it was often impossible to implement it: what was banned in one town was published in the next. This pragmatic tolerance raised expectations and set the standard for later times. In 1770, when the States of Holland tried to increase censorship measures against books and pictures *'which by their obscene content could insult good virtue and pervert youth'* some Dutch publishers reacted with a long request, in which they stated that obscenity was a subjective concept, that the authorities had no constitutional right to keep people from 'poisoning' their own virtue, and which concluded with a practical objection: sales were not stopped by prohibition. On the contrary: the small booksellers, the ambulant booksellers, canvassers, and wandering Jews made good money from it.

Golden Age of Dutch Erotica

Because there was little censorship, a Grub Street canon of scandalous titles was never established. This does not mean that no erotica was published: from the seventeenth century on, the Netherlands at certain intervals functioned as the sex shop of Europe. Around 1660, the Elzeviers started to publish the erotic works of Pietro Aretino and Niccolò Franco. Soon, others followed suit with publications of the French classics *L'Academie des dames* and *L'École des filles,* after which a flow of *chroniques scandaleuses* and monastery erotica was either channelled abroad in French form or translated into Dutch to serve the domestic market. The history of erotic literature in the Netherlands is characterized by these kinds of peaks of several decades, in which the surge of export and translation kindled the Dutch authors' interest in erotica. The second half of the seventeenth century is a first key moment. In this period, the first Dutch erotica specialist arises: Timotheus ten Hoorn of Amsterdam. He seems to have had a hand in nearly every erotic novel published during this period. He and his associates translated French pornography, *chroniques scandaleuses,* and erotic love stories. He was probably the first European publisher to establish an *officiel*—an 'official' catalogue consisting of semi-erotic, medico-sexologic, and gallant books—indicating to potentially interested readers where to obtain erotica. After thus testing the waters, he started publishing sexually explicit Dutch novels. He was intensely involved with his product. His authors write that their publisher stimulated, pushed, and pressured them to make them write faster, write more, write better, write a second part. It was even rumored that he had written one or more of the novels himself, although there is no proof for this.

Whereas up to that point erotica consisted mainly of dialogues between an older and a younger woman, set in court circles or in the monastery, Dutch writers chose the form of the picaresque novel for their erotic stories. Their novels are urban, mercantile and anti-idealistic in every respect. The hard truths and pragmatic rules of the city life prevail. The protagonists are students, merchants, craftsmen, thieves, lawyers, and whores. The protagonist and narrator of *D'Openhertige juffrouw*—an Amsterdam whore—is proud of her status as an ambitious business woman, and is not ashamed of making a living in prostitution: 'the fists are made of the same flesh as the arse'. She is a city woman, self-made, self-sufficient, independent, and proud. She wants to be accepted by society, not, like Moll Flanders, by striving for the virtuous position of 'wife' but through recognition of her position of whore. Money is as vital to these new city ethics as lust. To the *juffrouw*, a happy affair is an affair that brings in both sexual and financial satisfaction. When her husband refuses to pay her, she denies him sex, when he does not satisfy her sexually, she finds her satisfaction elsewhere. The *juffrouw*'s outlook is systematically materialistic: she is of the opinion that human behavior is determined by physical factors. Money and economic relations determine the make-up of society at large. Social practice is not determined by moral philosophy, but moral philosophy should be founded in social practice.

D'Openhertige Juffrouw is the first known example of the whore autobiography as a literary form. Not only did this give a new unity and logic to the anecdotes told, it also gave the writer the possibility to convincingly attack contemporary morals and literary practices. By revealing her own secrets and the secrets of her trade, the *juffrouw* acquires the right to demand the same openness from everybody. It is not surprising that the whore autobiography would be used by many of the famous French and English erotic novels of the eighteenth century.

Novels like *De Leidsche straatschender of de roekeloze student* (The Leiden Rogue or the Reckless Student, 1679), *De Haagsche lichtmis* (The The Hague Rogue, 1679), *D'Openhertige juffrouw* (The Outspoken Mistress, 1680), *'T Amsterdamsch Hoerdom* (The Amsterdam Whoredom, 1681), *De doorluchtige daden van Jan Stront* (The Illustrious Deeds of John Shit, 1684) remained popular for a long time: all through the eighteenth century reprints of these novels were published. The novels were also translated into German, French, and English. The interest in the English translation of *D'Openhertige juffrouw*, *The London Jilt*, even went as far as America: at the end of 1683,

John Usher, a Boston bookseller, ordered two copies of this book with the London bookseller Chiswell. In 1684, he wanted to order more copies, but this time Chiswell had to disappoint him: 'The London Jilt is out of print and not to be had'. Usher did not have to wait too long: in 1684, a year after the first edition, the 'second edition corrected' appeared.

Eighteenth and Nineteenth Centuries

After the death of Timotheus ten Hoorn, in 1710, it would take until the nineteenth century for a new erotica expert to arise. Due to competition from France, Germany, and England, in the eighteenth century the Dutch book trade limited itself more and more to the domestic market: the majority of French and English erotic texts —*Fanny Hill*, Sade, Mirabeau—was not even translated. Attention shifted to erotic poetry. This genre had already been practiced in the seventeenth century, by among others Willem Godschalk van Focquenbroch and Matthijs van der Merwede van Clootwijk, who after the publication of his erotic-libertine collection *Uytheemsen oorlog ofte Roomsche mintriomphen* (1651) was forced to public penance before he could enter the officialdom of The Hague. In the eighteenth century, this burlesque-erotic tradition was continued, in among others the anonymously published poetry collections *Het reukwerk van Venus* (1750) and *Galante dichtluimen* (1780). There is some speculation that the latter could have been written by the famous author Willem Bilderdijk, or by poet and translator Hendrik Riemsnijder. Poet, translator, and playwright Pieter Boddaert (1776–1805) posthumously became famous as an erotic poet, when in 1805, his friend, the popular publisher Hendrik Moolenijzer sr., published two books: *Levensgeschiedenis (...)* and *Poëtische en prosaische portefeuille van mr. Pieter Boddaert, verzameld en uitgegeven door eenigen zijner vrienden*. Both these books became big successes. During the whole of the nineteenth century, other erotic writings would surface, supposedly from his estate.

In the second half of the nineteenth century, the publication and export of erotica became big business again. Sexually explicit magazines were known as 'articles d'Amsterdam'. The extremely liberal attitude towards explicit writings prevalent in the Netherlands until 1911 was attractive to foreign erotica publishers and sellers. Via Brussels, especially French publishers, such as Gay and Brancard, supplied the north. Specialised Dutch publishing companies also profited from the 'open' legislation.

As early as 1860, the obscure Amsterdam publisher 'Mulder II' had begun to publish erotic works: erotic poetry and anonymous erotic-satiric prose, such as *Het minnespel* [*Courting*, erotic stories based on Biblical stories] and *De ontuchtigheden van het tweede keizerrijk* [*The Lasciviousness of the Second Empire: 'Scenes of worst bestial depravity, derived from secret memoirs from the Empire'*] The torch was taken over by the 'Artistiek Bureau', a pseudonym of Rotterdam publisher Bergé. Bergé and his heirs build up a considerable list of 'titillating' books, both in English and in Dutch. The example of the bureau was quickly followed by other Dutch publishers; German publishers also aimed at the Dutch market. The periodical was discovered as medium for erotica: *Pst Pst* and *De zwarte kat*, for instance, explored and crossed the boundaries of morality.

1880–1940

From the end of the nineteenth century, the rise of the so-called pornography trade is reflected in other texts. The *Dictionary of the Dutch Language* mentions occurrences of the word 'pornography' or derivatives thereof only from 1900. As of 1900, a lively legal discussion was entertained about the definition of pornography and the measure in which production, distribution, and publication of sexually explicit writings should be punished. In 1910, the study *Distribution of Offensive Writings* by Voorink appeared, in 1920 *The Pornography Trade* by Van Waes. From the thirties on, the 'State Bureau Concerning the Trade in Women and Children and the Trade in Lascivious Publications' issued lists of titles 'which are to be considered offensive to virtue', in which several Dutch authors were mentioned, most of whom have since sunk in oblivion.

But by that time, there were quite a few well-known writers working in erotica. Naturalism, in trying to paint a faithful picture of reality, could lead to explicit attention to sexuality. The famous thirteenth chapter from *Een liefde* [*A Love*] (1888) by Lodewijk van Deijssel caused quite a stir with a masturbation scene of the female protagonist Mathilde. It made his fellow-author and friend Frederik van Eeden cry out: 'The book is irksome, annoying, revolting—shocking!—just shocking! that's the word'.

The erotic threat was extended by a new phenomenon—gay erotica. The best-known gay novel is *Pijpelijntjes* [*Scenes from the Amsterdam Pijp*] (1904) by Jacob Israel de Haan. The uproar caused by this outspoken novel cost De Haan his job at the newspaper and his friendship with Aletrino, who recognized himself in one of the protagonists of the book. Aletrino and De Haan's fiancée tried to buy all copies of the first print and shortly after that, a new print appeared in which the characters were less easily recognizable. The dedication to Aletrino was replaced by a motto from Catullus: 'I will fornicate with you from the front and the rear, you who—because my poems are a bit lascivious—think that I myself am not too modest either'. In the twenties, the poet, novelist, and critic E. du Perron published several collections of obscene poetry under the pen names Cesar Bombay and W.C. Kloot van Neukema (W.C. Nut to Fuckinhurst).

After the Second World War

After the Second World War, the literary world was rudely awakened by the raw and realistic novels of Gerard Reve, Willem Frederik Hermans, Anna Blaman, and Jan Wolkers, followed by the beat generation, of which the rogue novel *I Jan Cremer* caused the biggest stir. Prosecution was rare. One of the few examples is the trial against Johan van Keulen, who between 1955 and 1968 wrote the very popular *Bob and Daphne* series under the pen name Han B. Aalberse. He was eventually sentenced, the offensive character of the books was deemed 'dangerous for public health'. The third part of the series was then republished in a bowdlerized version. The series was undoubtedly inspired by *Lolita*, of which Johan van Keulen made the first translation in the world, published in 1957 by publisher Oisterwijk.

The sixties gave new momentum to Dutch erotica. This decade initiated mass production, at first only with a torrent of translations: apart from *Lolita* also many books by Sade. The Dutch series of Olympia Press was exclusively occupied with the publication of translations. Dutch hopefuls were always turned down by editor Gerrit Komrij: 'they are really *nothing*. Shabby mud, as limp as a rag, and very, very Dutch'. One of the few books of Dutch origin published by the Olympia Press appeared only in an English and German version: *House of Pain*: the memoirs of SM queen Monique von Cleef. The author of this book was Willem van den Hout (1915–1985), who under the pen names Willem W. Waterman and Joke Riviera wrote erotic novels and stories for the well-known explicit Dutch magazines *Candy* and *Cash*. Although Van den Hout claimed to have written a Dutch version (*De griezelwereld van Monique van Cleef*) the manuscript has never been retrieved.

Dutch erotica sells best when it is as un-Dutch as possible. That could be the reason why the English-written *Happy Hooker* (1971) by Xaviera Hollander is the most famous 'Dutch' erotic work. This also goes for Flemish literature: the most productive erotica publisher of Flanders, the Dageraadpers, initiated its 'white series' with *De belevenissen van een gouvernante*, according to the title page a translation of *Adventures of a Governess* by South-African writer James B. Richardson Jr., in reality an erotic novel by J.D. Burton, written in crude Flemish. After that, the same publisher undertook Sade translations, done by famous Flemish authors like Gust Gils, Claude Krijgelmans, Freddy de Vree. The last two clearly caught the bug: under pen names such as 'Jug me Bash' and 'Jan Vlaming', they wrote several erotic stories, through which the Dutch language was enriched with pleasantly hilarious erotic expressions. This series reached its peak with the novels by Heere Heeresma aka 'Johannes de Back', whose brother Faber Heeresma translated erotica for De Dageraad. In his novels such as *Gelukkige paren* (1968), Heeresma, who since 1954 had some fame as a writer of satirical novels, offered a 'funny look behind the curtains of the decent citizen (and his wife)', whose sexual taboos were violated, as was to be expected in the sixties. Heeresma also ridiculed the hypocrisy of erotica, by ironically interjecting in this stories with 'Hey, you. Getting wet down there?' His stories balance serious excitement and playful absurdity.

The rigid poise of the Belgian authorities, who tried to restrict the distribution of magazines like *Playboy* and *Sextant* and the establishment of new so-called porn magazines, only inspired resistance. The problems Jef Geeraerts encountered on publication of his *Gangreen I. Black Venus* just made things worse: in 1972, he published *De fotograaf* under the pen name of Claus Trum, a book that would have made the Black Venus blush, and on the cover of which publisher Walter Soethoudt wrote: 'this book is the end; after this, no other books will ever be written'. In the same year, Louis Paul Boon published *Mieke Maaike's obscene jeugd*, according to Boon himself written to scare off the Catholic fans he had acquired with the success of *Daens* (1971). In this story about the precocious nymphomaniac Mieke Maaike, Boon dispenses with conventional sexual morality. He gives his erotic fantasies free reign, taunts the public at large, insults marital virtue, and upsets moralists and prigs. Of this cult novel, tens of thousands of copies have been sold. Also in 1972, *De Geisha* appeared, a novel by Theo Kars about a man living with two women. The novel, originally offered to the Olympia Press, appeared with the more conventional Arbeiderspers and was an immediate success: within 20 years, it was reprinted 17 times.

From the eighties on, erotica, the description of sex, and the use of so-called pornographic slang have become integrated in literature at large. Hugo Claus, Herman Brusselmans, Tom Lannoye, Joost Zwagerman, Roland Giphart, Adriaan Morriën, Hans Warren, Bertus Aafjes, Lydia Rood: these are but a few names from among the many authors writing erotic poetry and stories. Apart from a firm foundation of sexually explicit magazines, there is a constant production of collections about love and sex, erotic series, and theme issues on pornography of magazines. In a country and a time where sex and erotica are so integrated in public space, it no longer seems useful to isolate 'erotic literature' as a separate category.

INGER LEEMANS

Selected Works

[Anonymous]. *De Amsterdamsche lichtmis, of Zoldaat van fortuin* [*The Amsterdam Rogue, or Soldier of Fortune*] (1731). Edited by B. Pol. Muiderberg: Coutinho, 1983. (Populaire teksten uit de late Republiek, 1).

[Anonymous]. *De belydenis van een lichtmis* [*The Confession of a Rogue*], Edited by A.N.W. van der Plank. Deventer: Sub Rosa, 1982. (Series: Populair proza uit de 17e en 18e eeuw, 1).

Anonymous, [Elzevier, Pieter?]. *De doorluchtige daden van Jan Stront: Opgedragen aan het kakhuis : bestaande in een uitgelezen gezelschap, zo van heren als juffers. Tweede deel gedrukt voor de liefhebbers*] (1696) [*The Illustrious Deeds of John Shit, Dedicated to the Shit House: In Excellent Company, Consisting of Both Gentlemen and Ladies. Second Part, Printed for the Lovers*]. Edited by Inger Leemans. Utrecht: IJzer, 2000.

Anonymous. *D'Openhertige Juffrouw, of D'Ontdekte Geveinsdheid (1680).* [*The Outspoken Mistress, or Hypocrisy Revealed*] Edited by J. Kloek & I. Leemans & W. Mijnhardt. Leiden: Astrea, 1998. (Duivelshoekreeks 10).

Boddaert, Pieter. *Poëtische en prosaïsche portefeuille van mr. Pieter Boddaert [...].* [*The Poetry and Prose Portfolio of Mr. Pieter Boddaert*] Amsterdam: Hendrik Moolenijzer, 1805.

Cleef, Monique von & Wiliam Waterman. *House of Pain: The Strange World of Monique von Cleef The Queen of Humiliation: An Autobiography and a Message to All Human Slaves.* New York: Lyle Stuart, Inc., 1974.

'Coppens, A.' [W. Schors]. *The Memoirs of an Erotic Bookseller.* London: Luxor Press, 1969.

Focquenbroch, W.G. *Bloemlezing uit de gedichten en brieven van Willem Godschalck van Focquenbroch,* [*Anthology of the Poems and Letters by Willem Godschalck van Focquenbroch*] Edited by C.J. Kuik. Zutphen: W.J. Thieme & Cie. See also: http://www.focquenbroch.nl/

Haan, Jacob Israël de. *Pijpelijntjes* [*Schenes from the Amsterdam Pijp*], Den Haag: Kruseman's Uitgeversmaatschappij, 1974.

Hollander, Xaviera. *The Happy Hooker.* New York: Regan Books, 2002.

Kars, Theo. *De Geisha* [*The Geisha*]. Amsterdam: Arbeiderspers, 1972.

Merwede van Clootwijck, Matthijs van der. *Gedichten: een keuze uit 'Uytheemsen oorlog, ofte Roomse mintriomfen'* [*Poems: a Selection from 'Foreign Wars, or Roman Love Triumphs'*], edited by Paul Dijstelberge. Amsterdam: ADL, 1992.

Perron, E. du. *Verzamelde erotische gedichten* [*Collected erotic poems*], Edited by K. Lekkerkerker. Zandvoort: Eliance Pers, 1980. 4 volumes. Reeks: Erotisch Panopticum.

Further reading

Beekman, K.D. "Paul de Kock, een veel geciteerd eroticus" ["Paul de Kock, a Frequently Quoted Eroticist"], *Literatuur* 10 (1993), 83–87.

Beekman, K.D. "L. van Deyssel's *Een Liefde* en de kritiek" ["L. van Deyssel's *A Love* and the Critics"], *Spektator* 1 (1971-1972) 5, 246–258.

Buijnsters, P.J. "Libertijnse literatuur in Nederland gedurende de 18de eeuw?" ["Libertine Literature in the Netherlands in the Eighteenth Century?"], in Idem, *Nederlandse literatuur van de achttiende eeuw: Veertien verkenningen.* Utrecht: HES publishers, 1984, 99–113.

Haks, Donals. "Libertinisme en Nederlands verhalend proza, 1650–1700" ["Libertinism and Dutch Narrative Prose"] in G. Hekma & H. Roodenburg (ed.), *Soete minne en helsche boosheit: Seksuele voorstellingen in Nederland, 1300–1850.* Nijmegen: Sun, 1988, 85–105.

Keyser, Marja. "Frederik Muller over erotica" ["Frederik Muller on Erotica"], in Idem & J.F. Heijbroek & I. Verheul (ed.), *Frederik Muller (1817–1881): Leven en werken.* Zutphen: Walburg Pers, 1996, 184–189, 313–314.

Komrij, Gerrit. *Verzonken boeken* [*Sunken Books*], Amsterdam: Arbeiderspers, 1986.

Knuttel, W.P.C. *Verboden boeken in de Republiek der Vereenigde Nederlanden* [*Forbidden Books in the Dutch Republic*]. Den Haag, Nijhoff, 1914. (Bijdragen tot de geschiedenis van den Nederlandschen boekhandel 11).

Leemans, Inger. "Het pornografisch offensief. De korte bloeiperiode van de Nederlandstalige pornografische roman, 1965–1975" ("The Pornographic Offensive. The Short Halcyon Days of the Dutch Pornographic Novel, 1965–1975"), *Yang* 37 (2001).

Leemans, Inger. *Het woord is aan de onderkant. Radicale ideeën in Nederlandse pornografische romans 1670–1700* (*Bottom Takes the Floor. Radical Ideas in Dutch Pornographic Novels 1670–1700*), Nijmegen: Vantilt, 2002.

Sanders, Wim. "Een jonge meester in het huis van de pijn: Girodias, Komrij en de Olympia Press Nederland" [A Young Master in the House of Pain: Girodias, Komrij and the Olympia Press Holland], *Parelduiker* 2004 (2), 2–21.

Schalken, Tom. *Pornografie en strafrecht: Beschouwingen over het pornografiebegrip en zijn juridische hanteerbaarheid* [*Pornography and Criminal Law: Reflections on the Definition of Pornography and its Juridical Viability*], Arnhem: Gouda Quint/Brouwer, 1972.

Schenkeveld-van der Dussen, M. A. "De poetica van een libertijnse zelf-voyeur" [The Poetics of a Libertine Self-Voyeur], *De nieuwe taalgids* 82 (1989), 2–15.

Schenkeveld-van der Dussen, M. A. "De geestelijke (?) minnevlammen van Matthijs van der Merwede van Clootwijk" ["The Spiritual (?) Love Flames of Matthijs van der Merwede van Clootwijk"], *De nieuwe taalgids* 85 (1992), 14–25.

Steur, A.G. van der. "Pieter Boddaert jr. (1766–1805): raadsels rond een 'vermaard dichter'" [Pieter Boddaert jr. (1766–1805): Enigma's Surrounding a 'Famous Poet'], in A. de Haas (ed.), *Achter slot en grendel: Schrijvers in Nederlandse gevangenschap 1700–1800.* Zutphen: Walburg Pers, 2002, 200–206.

Vermeersch, Peter. *Het slijk der zinnen. Pornografie in België* [*The Mud of the Senses. Pornograpohy in Belgium*], Leuven: Kritak 1987.

Waterschoot, J. "De vieze boekjes van uitgever Mulder II (1822-1865): Scabreuze poëzie en bijtende satire" ["The Dirty Books of Publisher Mulder II (1822–1865): Bawdy Verse and Ruthless Satire"], *Boekblad* 157 (1990) 26, 16–17.

Anthologies

Brederode, Désanne van (e.a.). *Zin. Niet-correcte erotische verhalen van vrouwen* [*In the Mood. Non-correct erotic stories by women*], Amsterdam, Muntinga, 2001.

Chamuleau, Rody. *Jantje zag een pruikje hangen: Nederlandse priapeeën door de eeuwen heen* [*Johnnie Saw a Wig: Dutch Priapics through the Ages*], Rotterdam: Ad Donker, 1991.

Rood, Lydia. *Louter lust* [*Sheer Lust*]. Amsterdam, Prometheus Groep, 2002.

Schouten, Rob. *Met de hand: Bevredigende gedichten* [*By Hand, Satisfying Poems*], Amsterdam: Arbeiderspers, 1992.

Straten, Hans van. *Razernij der liefde: Ontuchtige poëzie in de Nederlanden van Middeleeuwen tot Franse tijd* [*The Rage of Love: Bawdy Poetry in the Netherlands from the Middle Ages until the French Period*], Amsterdam: Arbeiderspers 1992.

L. de Vries. *Spiegel der vrijerij en minnekunst : vertonende allerhande taferelen van de liefde en wellust... dit alles ten dienste van vrijers en vrijsters en allen die minnen uit het rijk van Venus en Cupido* [*Mirror of Courting and the Art of Love: Showing All Kinds of Scenes of Love and Lust... to Serve Both Male and Female Lovers and All Those Who Love from the Realm of Venus and Cupid*]. Four volumes (Lusthof der sexen, Liefdes lusthof, Eros' lusthof, Venus' Lusthof), Amsterdam: Meulenhoff, 1964–1968.

DUVERT, TONY

1945–
French novelist and essayist

One of the most polemic and aggressively positive, but also one of the most private and elusive of French sexual minorities, Duvert defends the right of people to live their lives according their own needs and values. He promotes guilt-free sexual expression, including pornography, sadomasochism, and transvestitism. A prerequisite for and symbol of social liberation, sexual freedom for Duvert requires the dismantling of "heterocratic" stereotypes, the rejection of the constraining categories of contemporary social values, the undoing of the repressive socio-economic order which underpins capitalism and stifles positive, natural sexual curiosity and erotic sensitivity. In place of homosexual identity, for example, Duvert privileges a more generalized and unproblematized fusion of the homosocial and homoerotic.

Récidive

Like much of his fiction, Duvert's first novel rehearses many of the techniques of the French New Novel; it is self-conscious, self-contradictory, self-questioning, self-referential, and self-mutilatory. As a series of scenes, some unfinished, a "homotextuality," as Phillips sees it, that questions the various versions of and hypotheses for a quest for sexual experience and identity by a "chorus of subjectivities" led by, and/or leading astray, a fifteen-year-old runaway who is crossing France and recounting adventures, *Récidive* is also unconventional and non-linear. It unveils the mechanics of narration, while it undermines psychological reality and the possibility for a fixed or grounded homosexual essence. Narrator-voyeurs, perspectives, and narration shift are confused: between a teenaged boy and an older (?) writer; between lovers passed en route and objects of desire, forester, sailor, recluse, youths; and between first- and third-person. Duvert foregrounds the highly mobile and sometimes violent nature of an often-marginalized, shifting sexuality. As social contexts change, so do the fragments and recombinations of memory and fantasy. As the boundaries between childhood, adolescence, and adulthood, between reader and narrator-voyeurs are blurred and/or transgressed, the binary structures of heterosexuality and textuality as exclusivities are undermined, and moral responsibility is evaded. He rewrote and republished this novel less than a decade after it first came out by shortening it and changing episodes. The newer version still privileges circularity, repetition, dislocation, and fragmentation, however. Indeed, it further

393

exemplifies the trangressive repetition announced by its title and staged within it.

Other creative works by Duvert are equally as inventive and unconventional. They include (but are not limited to): a cutting and subversive dictionary (*Abécédaire malveillant*); a pornography which exposes and deconstructs its own fascinations (*Journal d'un innocent*); an indictment of the parents of male children (*L'île atlantique*); a satire of science, religion, psychiatry, the police, and high society (*Un anneau d'argent à l'oreille*); a series of darkly suggestive vignettes, scenes of town life that expose the sordid and surreal (*District*); and an extravagant, Rabelaisian composite of imagined professions from the past involving scatology, sexual initiation, and murder (*Les petits métiers*).

Le bon sexe illustré

Duvert's first book of essays targets conventional sex education material, the five-volume *Encyclopédie de la vie sexuelle de la physiologie à la psychologie* with its misinformed opinions, repressions, fears, taboos, and abuses, written for five distinct age groups: children from ages seven to nine and ten to thirteen; teenagers from ages fourteen to sixteen and seventeen to eighteen; and adults. This sexual encyclopedia is attacked as a mountain of heterocratic, divisive, birth-centric, antisexual propaganda. Duvert argues that its glorification of family, marriage, babies, and parental power, its indoctrination, censorship, and sanitization of information primarily brainwashes. In its artificial imposition of gender roles and morally correct behavior, it upholds an overarching, unhealthy, and crippling sexual order. In the ideology governing tolerated pleasures, the possibility for childhood eroticism is never entertained and thereby pathologized, if not erased. It represents the repression of socio-economic order and exposes the control of a profit-and-loss-oriented society. Duvert urges that the eroticism of minors, children, and adolescents, those representing the present and future of society, be recognized and that their rights to make love, and not only listen to their parents speaking of it, be defended. To recognize and appreciate the distinctive eroticism of the young would be to diminish their social conditioning, to free them from the grips of the family, and to acknowledge

their autonomy as desiring subjects. As a result of such sexual liberation, the two fundamental pillars of the sexual order, the duty to procreate like one's parents and the right parents have claimed to "own" their offspring or "products," would be dismantled and the processes of reproduction of power halted.

L'enfant au masculin

In his second book of essays, Duvert extends the arguments against heterocracy introduced in *Le Bon sexe illustré*. He focuses on and defends adolescent homosexuality in chapters with titles as different and far-reaching as "The Art of Loving" and "The Family and its Homo," "Maternity" and Misogyny," "Neo-Puritanism" and "The Seven Deadly Sins." Society purportedly tolerates, integrates homosexuality. However, only one-fifth of French parents admit that they would accept the homosexuality of one of their children. In France, the right to be homosexual is only recognized after an adolescent turns eighteen. Furthermore, the more rights and freedoms one wins as an adult, the more minors are marginalized. Homosexual relations between adults and minors are seen as abnormal and criminal. At the root of the heterocratic domination and injustice exposed by Duvert is a totalitarian sexual culture that is neither class- nor sex-related but supported both by males and females, mothers and fathers, conservatives and liberals. It is taught in school, cherished in the family, and exemplified in the media. Until the right of heterosexuals to "reproduce" themselves and their ideologies in their children is abolished, and with it heterocracy itself, Duvert insists that true freedom of life and lifestyle, the language and means by which to address, articulate, and live out the full spectrum of erotic nature, can never be possible.

Biography

Born in 1945 in Villeneuve-le-Roi in the French Val-de-Marne. His works span three decades and range in importance and recognition: from crossword puzzles in the now-defunct *Gai Pied* magazine to essays; from criticism in the literary journal *Critique* and often-cruel vignettes to ludic and subversive novels that confuse genres and narrative points of view, satirize, indict, intertextualize, and interrogate. He was awarded the Prix Médicis in 1973 for *Paysage de fantaisie (Strange landscape)*, his fifth novel. Since 1989, Duvert has ceased publishing. There has been speculation — but no proof — that he and the writer Renaud Camus are one and the same.

BRIAN GORDON KENNELLY

Selected Works

Récidive. 1967, 1976.
Interdit de séjour. 1969.
Portrait d'homme couteau. 1969.
Le voyageur. 1970.
Paysage de fantaisie. 1973; as *Strange landscape*, translated by Sam Flores, 1976.
Le bon sexe illustré. 1974.
Journal d'un innocent. 1976.
District. 1978.
Les petits métiers. 1978.
Quand mourut Jonathan. 1978; as *When Jonathan died*, translated by D.R. Roberts, 1991.
L'île atlantique. 1979.
L'enfant au masculin. Essais, livre premier. 1980.
Un anneau d'argent à l'oreille. 1982.
Abécédaire malveillant. 1989.

Further Reading

Heathcote, Owen. "Jobs for the Boys? Or: What's New About the Male Hunter in Duvert, Guibert and Jourdan?" in *Gay Signatures: Gay and Lesbian Theory, Fiction and Film in France, 1945-1995.* Edited by Owen Heathcote, Alex Hughes and James S. Williams. New York and Oxford: Berg, 1998.

Phillips, John. *Forbidden Fictions: Pornography and Censorship in Twentieth-Century French Literature.* London: Pluto Press, 1999.

Pinon, Laurent. "Tony Duvert: La persistance du lieu," *La Parole vaine,* 7 (1995): http://www.atol.fr/lldemars2/lestextes/pinon/pinduvert.htm

Robinson, Christopher. *Scandal in the Ink: Male and Female Homosexuality in Twentieth-Century French Literature.* London: Cassell, 1995.

Schehr, Lawrence R. *The Shock of Men : Homosexual Hermeneutics in French Writing.* Stanford: Stanford University Press, 1995.

Smith, Steven. "Toward a Literature of Utopia" in *Homosexualities and French Literature: Cultural Contexts / Critical Texts.* Edited by George Stambolian and Elaine Marks. Ithaca: Cornell University Press, 1970.

Verdoux, C. et al. *Encyclopédie de la vie sexuelle: de la physiologie à la psychologie.* 5 vols, Paris: Hachette, 1973.

E

E.D.

Nineteenth-century French novelist

Under these initials from 1888 to 1894, a remarkable French author clandestinely published in Paris sixteen erotic novels that had a keen success among the fans. Afterward he disappeared without a trace, and nobody succeeded in piercing his anonymity. Who really was E.D.? In 1930, Louis Perceau, on the basis of information from specialized booksellers, speculated that E.D. was "a Faculty teacher in Montpellier" named Edouard Desjardins. However, when Pascal Pia wrote *Les livres de l'enfer* [*Books of the "Enfer,"* or publicly forbidden section, of the Bibliothèque Nationale], he examined the archives of the university of Montpellier and found no Edouard Desjardins on the schoolteacher list. He supposed that E.D. could have been a civil servant of Gironde, Edmond Dumoulin, of which they know absolutely nothing. As well, as yet there has been no thorough study on E.D., who seems a ghost of the French erotic literature of the Belle Epoque.

Nevertheless, by the quality of his style (which was why he was taken as a teacher of arts) and the variety of his intrigues, E.D. well deserves his reputation. His first book, *Mes amours avec Victoire* [*My Love with Victoria*] (1888), described as a "small novel of extragallant love," had a new edition the next year, revised, corrected, and augmented. The narrator tells how, immediately after having met the Baroness Victoria, they gave each other all the possible pleasures. His second book, *Le marbre animé* [*The Lively Marble*], "by E.D., author of *Mes amours avec Victoire,* Brussels, 1889"—the indication of Brussels or London as a location of provenance was a way for the French publishers to avoid censorship—was the tale of the initiation into sexual pleasures of a frigid princess. Afterward, E.D. published a *Théatre naturaliste* [*Naturalistic Theater*] (under the imprint "London, Collection of the French Erotic of the XIX century, published by the Society of Cosmopolitan Bibliophiles"), containing seven one-act plays, which were also separately published: *En cabinet particulier* [*In Private Cabinet*], *La discipline* [*The Discipline*], *Après le bal* [*After the Ball*], *La vengence est le plaisir des dieux* [*The Vengeance and the Pleasure of Gods*], *Entre-deux*

[*Intervening Period*], *La raison du plus fort est toujours la meilleure* [*The Strongest Reason Is Always the Best*], *Il ne faut pas jouer avec le feu* [*Do Not Play with Fire*]. These plays could be performed, in dishabille and behind closed door, by volunteer actors, for as a catalogue says, "The author provides explanations as much stunning as precise."

In two years, E.D. published so many books that it is probable that he had written them some time ago and put them aside. He published three novels on sapphism, *La comtesse de Lesbos, ou la nouvelle Gamiani* [*The Countess of Lesbos, or the New Gamiani*] (1889), *Lèvres de velours* [*Velvet Lips*] (1889), and *Lesbia maîtresse d'école* [*Lesbian Schoolmistress*] (1890). In the foreword to the first, the author warns that his Countess of Lesbos, unlike Musset's Countess Gamiani, is "the personification of gentleness." Affairs of pure voluptuousness are interwoven with tender affection, which indeed is what the Countess is searching with her girlfriends. The continuation of her adventures, *Lèvres de velours,* begins in Seville, where she has surrounded herself with lesbian dancers, led by the naughty Miss Pirouett, who executes with her "a ballet like they don't dance at the Opera," that is, a choreographic orgy, whose lascivious figures seem to be doing waltz steps. These lesbian dancers, who have "bizarre and charming practices," sometimes accept men in their intimacy. With regard to *Lesbia maîtresse d'école,* this novel was inspired by a case in the news, in which the headmistress of a girls boarding school in the provinces was arrested for allowing the schoolgirls to caress each other at will. E.D. imagined what could happen in this boarding school with such humor and goodwill that he invited the reader to exonerate these crazy virgins.

When two famous English novels of "le vice anglais," *Curiosities of Flagellation* and *The Birchen Bouquet,* were translated into French, E.D. wanted to show that he was capable of treating the subject. The first part of *Jupes troussées* [*Trussed Skirts*] (1889) is "La Discipline au couvent [The Discipline at the Monastery]," adapted from the souvenirs of the chaplain of the abbey of Thétieu. The second part, "Une séance au Club des Flagellantes" [A Session at the Flagellant's Club], is preceded by this advice: "This story is the translation of a letter of my young friend, Sir John Seller, who assisted,

disguised as a woman, in the session that he describes for me upon my request." *Les Callipyges, ou les délices de la verge* [*The Calypicians, or the Delights of the Stick*] (1889) is presented as a series of conferences on the different manners of whipping, pronounced by woman educators in London boarding schools or in "five o'clocks" at Lady Finefleece's or Lady Splendidorbs'. Another novel by E.D. on flagellation is *Défilé de fesses nues* [*Naked Buttock Parade*] (1890), a collection of anecdotal letters.

In the erotic fairy tale genre, E.D.'s novel *L'Odyssée d'un pantalon* [*Odyssey of a Pair of Pants*] (1890), relating the adventures of a man transformed in woman's panties (that is, at that time lacework and rustle pants) which assist in the intimate acts of their owner, was of great originality. The two-volume *Mes etapes amoureuses* [*My Loving Stages*] (1890) had as its subtitle "By E.D., author of *L'Odyssée d'un pantalon.*" In the foreword to the first volume, E.D. explains that it was the success of *Mes amours avec Victoire* that induced him to write *Mes étapes,* in which the lover of Baroness Victoria relates all the adventures he had before meeting her. After the novel *Les exploits d'un galant précoce* [*The Exploits of a Precocious Gallant*] (1890), the hero of which is a cherub beginning his feminine conquests at the age of fourteen, E.D. published his best novel, *Odor di femina* [*Womanly Odor*] (1891), a history of a Parisian who, weary of women of the world, takes refuge in the countryside and gives himself up to frantic lovemaking with all kind of peasant women.

Although the novelist ended his career at the end of the nineteenth century, in 1904 a publisher put the E.D. initials to *Mémoires d'une danseuse russe* [*Memoirs of a Russian Dancer*], a second-rate book which had previously appeared without an author's name, in order to take advantage of E.D.'s repute. E.D. also must have been a libertine poet, for various catalogues cite a book of his called *Rondeaux et sonnets galants* [*Gallant Rondeaux and Sonnets*], which has been unobtainable.

Such was the itinerary of this masked writer, of whom we do not know whether he was married or single, a man of trade or a rich dilettante—and whose erotic writings are among the most curious of the Third Republic.

SARANE ALEXANDRIAN

Bibliography

Alexandrian, Sarane. *Histoire de la littérature érotique* [History of Erotic Literature]. Paris: Seghers, 1989; pocket edition, Paris: Payot et Rivages, 1995.

Apollinaire, Guillaume, Fernand Fleuret, and Louis Perceau. *L'Enfer de la Bibliothéque Nationale*. Paris: Mercure de France, 1913. (The "Enfer" was a section of the National Library containing books forbidden to the public.)

Perceau, Louis. *Bibliographie du roman érotique au XIXe siècle* [Bibliograpy of the Erotic Novel of the Nineteenth Century]. Vols. 1 and 2. Paris: Georges Fourdrinier, 1930.

Pia, Pascal. *Les Livres de l'Enfer* [Books of the "Enfer"]. Vols. 1 and 2. Paris: C. Coulet et A. Faure, 1978.

EGYPTIAN LOVE POETRY, ANCIENT

Ancient Egyptian love poems have survived antiquity in the form of four papyrus collections, a number of small fragments, and one large ostracon. Though all of these materials hail from the period 1300–1150 BCE, the language employed in them reflects a more archaic stage of development, suggesting that the poems might be copies or later editions of earlier love lyric traditions.

Native terms applied to these materials include "songs" ('sw), "utterances" (r'w), and "sayings" (tsw). A number of poems also open with the words "the beginning of the song of entertainment" ('>t-> m 's sΔmΔ-ib). This title appears also in a few tombs in conjunction with banquet and dancing imagery, suggesting that at least some of the love poems served as diversions at festive occasions.

Though the poems themselves do not appear to have been used in ritual contexts, in a few cases, cultic settings provide literary contexts for the lyrics. Thus, the lovers who speak and are described in the poems are sometimes said to be en route to a cultic festival or center. Some of the poems also employ language elsewhere associated with deities, especially Hathor, the goddess of love. In one poem, Hathor is even invoked by a lover for her help in securing her beloved's perpetual affection.

Egyptian love lyrics are well known for their sophisticated language and emotive contents. Each of the extant poems records the innermost desires of male and female lovers who laud their love for each other, albeit indirectly, in the first person and in alternating stanzas. Periodically, the poet also makes his voice known. Though the lovers frequently address each other as "sister" and "brother," as well as by a few royal epithets, no incestual relationship is implied. Typically the poems express premarital desires (only one of the poems references marriage explicitly) and often characterize love as a state of mutual bliss and perpetual sensual desire.

A number of topics and themes pervade the love poems, many of which reflect the rich Nile landscape, with its serene and reliable waters and fertile flora and fauna. Thus in Papyrus (P.) Chester Beatty I, we find the female voice describing her lover as "a gazelle prancing over the desert." Elsewhere the beloved is likened to heavenly bodies. The male voice in the aforementioned poem, for example, describes his beloved as "more lovely than all women, look, she is like the Sothis star rising, signaling a happy year!"

Often the lovers describe each other by listing their most alluring bodily features, sometimes equating them with flowers and the attributes of animals. P. Chester Beatty I, for example, portrays the woman as saying, "He offered me the delights of his body; his height is greater than his width!" P. Harris 500 employs agricultural language: "I am yours like an acre planted with flowers for me, and with every kind of sweet-smelling herb."

In one poem, pomegranate and fig trees do the speaking and eventually offer the lovers shade. Throughout, the lovers' innermost desires are expressed self-consciously, even insecurely. They are love-sick for each other, and yet often their attempts at secret trysts are frustrated. In one poem, P. Harris 500, the male lover even feigns illness to get the woman's attention: "I'll lie down inside, then I will fake sickness, then my neighbors will come in to visit, then (my) 'sister' will come along with them. She will put the doctors to shame, because she knows what really ails me!" The love-sick state of the lovers sometimes provides the poet with an opportunity to describe the lover as a medicine. Thus, in P. Chester Beatty I, we: "Greater is she to me than the compendium. My *wd3* is her entering from the outside. Seeing her, then, is health—she opens my eyes, rejuvenating my body." This verse also demonstrates the literary sophistication that one finds in these poems. Here, the Egyptian word *wd3* is used for its polysemous nature. On the one hand, it refers to the Eye of Horus, a magical amulet used by Egyptian doctors and embalmers for resuscitating life; and on the other, the pictorial dimensions of the script suggest "seeing" (the word is written with the image of an eye). The poet underscores these associations by saturating the poem with references to seeing, medicine, doctors, diagnoses, and rejuvenation. Such puns are common in the Egyptian love poems.

Metaphorical language abounds, and much of it is shared among the collections. One hears, for example, frequent references to locked doors, morning's first light, and love as an intoxicating liquor. Egyptian love poetry offers a veritable feast for the senses. Taste, sight, touch, smell are all referenced. Thus, in P. Harris 500, we find: "[T]he scent of your nostrils, only you, is what revives my heart!" A great many features, including some of the aforementioned themes and metaphors, appear also in the biblical Song of Songs, which has led some scholars to see Egyptian influence in the biblical poem.

Unlike the erotic elements in Mesopotamian love poetry, the erotic aspects of Egyptian love poetry are rarely explicit, but are instead often expressed by way of euphemisms, innuendos, and double entendres. In P. Chester Beatty I,

we read: "You will have your desire with her door-bolt, and the porticoes will shake. The sky descends with a breath of its wind, so that it brings you her perfume." In P. Harris 500, we find: "My sister's mansion, her door is in the midst of her home. Her doors are open, the bolt is unlocked.... Oh that I were made the door-keeper!" Sometimes, metaphors are chosen for their sexual charge, like the aphrodisiacs mentioned in P. Harris 500: "Sister is a lotus bud, her breasts are mandrakes." Such subtlety goes in the face of a number of Egyptian artistic representations (as well as mythological texts) that do not shy from graphically portraying sexual activity. Be that as it may, rich metaphors and the tight structural patterns of the oscillating monologues are sufficient to evoke erotic tensions and lend to the poems' exquisite beauty.

SCOTT B. NOEGEL

Editions

Foster, J.L. *Love Songs of the New Kingdom*. Austin, TX: University of Texas Press, 1969–1974.

Fowler, B.H. *Love Lyrics of Ancient Egypt*. Chapel Hill: University of North Carolina Press, 1994.

Fox, Michael V. *The Song of Songs and the Ancient Egyptian Love Songs*. Madison: University of Wisconsin Press, 1985.

Lichtheim, M. *Ancient Egyptian Literature*. Vol. 2. Berkeley and Los Angeles: University of California Press, 1976, pp. 182–93.

Simpson, W.K., ed. *The Literature of Ancient Egypt: An Anthology of Stories, Instructions, and Poetry*. New Haven, CT: Yale University Press, 1976, pp. 315–25.

Further Reading

Fox, Michael V. "Love, Passion, and Perception in Israelite and Egyptian Love Poetry." *Journal of Biblical Literature* 102 (1983), 219–28.

Manniche, Lise. *Sexual Life in Ancient Egypt*. London: Kegan Paul Foundation, 1997.

White, J. B. *A Study of the Language of Love in the Song of Songs & Ancient Egyptian Love Poetry*. SBL Dissertation Series, 38. Missoula, MT: Scholars Press, 1978.

ELIADE, MIRCEA

1907–1986
Romanian novelist, short story writer, and historian
of religions

Maitreyi

Maitreyi is the fictional representation of an
episode from the author's biography. Upon his
return from India, Mircea Eliade wrote this
novel, which won the Techirghiol-Eforie Prize
offered by the Cultura Nationala Publishing
Press in 1933. The book was an instantaneous
best seller. In 1988 *Maitreyi* (under the title
La Nuit Bengali) also became a successful
movie with Hugh Grant and Supriya Pathak.
In 1974 the female prototype of the novel, the
real Maitreyi Devi (1914–1990), daughter of the
Indian philosopher Surendranath Dasgupta,
responded to Mircea Eliade, offering her own
version of the story in her book *Ne hanya te*
[*It Does Not Die*]. It is one of the very few cases
in world literature when two writers and protagonists of the same events give each their own
perspective of it, and surely potmodernism
influenced Maitreyi Devi's voicing of the margin.

In *Maitreyi,* Allan, a young engineer, has
come to India imbued with all the colonial prejudice about his whiteness and alleged superiority. For two years, Allan has no interest in seeing
real Bengali life. He lives among Indian English
friends (English people either born or having
lived for a long time in India) and enjoys the
pleasures of sex with white girls. His only interest is in finding new sensual experiences. The
first meeting with Maitreyi means nothing to
Allan. She seems dirty and uninteresting, one
of those "black" girls.

But all of this changes when he is invited to
tea in the home of his boss, engineer Narendra
Sen, Maitreyi's father. This is the moment when
a very special gaze exchanged by the two young
people creates an enormously particular and intimate communion between them. Unaware of
the spiritual intimacy that has already sparkled
between his elder daughter and Allan, Narendra

Sen makes a fateful invitation. In agreement
with his wife, he invites Allan to stay with
them. Their intention is to adopt Allan culturally, that is, to help him understand the real India,
the profound India. But this "profound" India
will prove to be their own daughter. The young
girl's body will become the territory of exploration and appropriation for the young white male
who has felt attracted by the mystery of the
Indian land from the very beginning of his sojourn in this exotic country. The body of the
beloved will become a metonymy for the Indian
land. But his colonial position hides a painful
ambiguity. On the one hand, Allan is tempted by
the new life that is being offered to him; he wants
to know this life and dominate it by knowing it,
penetrating it. On the other hand, he feels that
this new life might change him, disempower him,
and make him abandon his old self. Significantly
for this cultural conflict, Maitreyi's first gift
to Allan is Lafcadio Hearn's *Out of the East,* a
book by an expatriate who yielded to the charm
of another Asian country, Japan, and finally
almost completely assimilated. In the first part
of the novel, cultural and racial issues play a
very important role. Maitreyi herself is not bereft of colonial prejudice. She confesses proudly
that she is whiter than her sister, Chabu, and
consequently Chabu will have more difficulty in
finding a suitor, and her dowry must be higher.

The knowledge and love game between Allan
and Maitreyi will develop slowly but as precisely
as the traditional Indian dance. Allan, although
having gone through several sexual experiences,
is still virginal in mind and spirit. On the contrary, Maitreyi, a virgin from the physical point
of view, has already had love experiences of
amazing intensity. She has been in love with a
tree and with Rabindranath Tagore, her guru.
Maitreyi's voluptuous but spiritual communion
with these partners is an enormous challenge for
Allan. It is at this moment of the novel that both
protagonists get rid of the prejudice and stereotypes that are brought about by the colonial
situation they are in. They become the eternal

man and woman in love. Maitreyi's ardent, violent, almost physical thirst for purity creates an oxymoronic space for Allan, who is accustomed to the idea that love can find its accomplishment only in bed. Delicate but highly sensuous intimacy grows gradually. The protagonists' bodily communication through the furtive touch of their legs and feet creates an extremely high tension that goes beyond sexuality. After a symbolic Indian engagement ceremony which consists of Maitreyi offering Allan a jasmine wreath, the two lovers accomplish the ultimate rites of love. For Maitreyi this union must result in fertility and children in order to avoid sin. For both lovers this amorous experience is beyond the carnal. It is a contact with the spiritual, with the supranatural through the touch of flesh, of eyes and lips. It is absolute possession. But as in all love stories, the lovers are finally discovered and Allan is thrown out of the house because he has broken the sacred bond of hospitality. The Sens can judge this situation only through their cultural criteria.

Maitreyi is cruelly beaten by her father, but she tries to keep in touch with her lover. On the other hand, Allan tries to cure himself of his amorous intoxication through abstinence and spiritual recollection in the Himalayas or through other sexual experiences. But everything fails. In a tragic symmetry, Allan is now regarded by the Indians with the same racial prejudice that he himself had at the beginning of his Indian love story. Finally, Allan gets a new job in Singapore and leaves India. There, he finds out that Maitreyi has tried to become a pariah in order to be able to join him. She has given herself to the vegetable seller and has become pregnant. Allan will forever long to look into Maitreyi's eyes once again.

Evolving according to the pattern of the great love stories of the world, which always unite protagonists from opposed families or milieus, Maitreyi and Allan's story is a sophisticated and passionate erotic novel in which the flesh becomes the way to reach the spiritual. Colonial and cultural connotations nuance a love story that takes place in an exceptionally delineated exotic milieu.

Biography

Born in Bucharest, died in Chicago. Eliade made his debut, while a high school student, with a

fantasy, *Cum am descoperit piatra filosofala* [*How I Discovered the Philosopher's Stone*]. He studied philosophy at the University of Bucharest in the 1920s. The period 1928–1932, when he studied at the University of Calcutta, which awarded him a Ph.D. in philosophy, was a decisive intellectual experience for him. Between 1933 and 1939 he was a lecturer on the faculty of letters and philosophy at the University of Bucharest. In 1940 he became a diplomat. Five years later Eliade settled down in Paris and started teaching at the Ecole de Hautes Etudes. In 1956 he was invited to the University of Chicago as a visiting professor, and eventually got tenure as professor there. Eliade published novels, stories, and numerous philosophical essays. The great synthesis of his studies on religions and myths is *Histoire des croyances et des idées religieuses,* which appeared between 1976 and 1978.

MICHAELA MUDURE

Editions

Maitreyi. Bucuresti: Editura Cultura nationala, 1933; Bucuresti: Editura "Cugetarea" – P. C. Georgescu Delafras, 1946; Bucuresti: Minerva, 1986; as *Bengali Nights,* translated by Catherine Spencer, Chicago: University of Chicago Press, 1994.

Selected Works

Huliganii, 2 vols. 1935
Domnisoara Cristina. 1936
Nunta in cer. 1938
Secretul doctorului Honigberger. 1940
Traité d'histoire des religions. 1949
Aspects du mythe. 1963
Pe strada Mantuleasa. 1968
La tiganci si alte povestiri. 1969
De Zamolxis a Gengis-Khan. 1970
Histoire des croyances et des idées religieuses. 1976–78
Memoires I (1907–1937).
Les promesses de l'équinoxe. 1980

Further Reading

Calinescu, George. *Istoria literaturii romane de la origin pina in prezent.* Bucuresti: Fundatia regala pentru literatura si arta, 1941.
Craia, Sultana. *Ingeri, demoni si muieri: o istorie a personajului feminin in literatura romana.* Bucuresti: Univers, 1999.
Glodeanu, Gheorghe. *Poetica romanului romanesc interbelic: O posibila tipologie a romanului.* Bucuresti: Libra, 1998.

Handoca, Mircea. *Viata lui Mircea Eliade*. Cluj-Napoca: Dacia, 2000.

Lovinescu, Eugen. *Istoria literaturii romane contemporane*. Bucuresti: Editura Librariei Socec, 1937.

Micu, Dumitru. *Istoria literaturii romane: De la creatia populara la postmodernism*. Bucuresti: Saeculum, 2000.

Parvulescu, Ioana. *Alfabetul doamnelor. De la doamna B. la doamna T*. Bucuresti: Crater, 1999.

ELTIT, DIAMELA

1949–

Chilean novelist

The narrative work of Diamela Eltit offers multiple interpretative possibilities and is marked by its transgression of norms of identity and meaning. Her fiction inscribes an erotic female subject that actively desires and surrenders to her bodily pleasures, in a context of relentless violence and surveillance. It is through the female body, portrayed in marginalized and fragmented terms, that Eltit explores the erotic component. The female body in her novels is held together by the minute interaction between different corporeal parts, which are frequently on the verge of collapse, precluding the construction of a whole corporeal image or stable gendered identity. The importance of corporeal experience and sexual desire in the constitution of a female subject is stressed, and gender difference is posited in terms of fluidity and openness, shattering the notion of binary opposites and normative cultural categories of gender and sex.

It is important to note the relationship between body and language in Eltit's fiction, since language supports the erotic function of her novels. Language is portrayed as flowing from the somaticized maternal body, which is the origin of a mother tongue. Julia Kristeva's concept of the maternal semiotic, the "repressed, instinctual maternal element," is embedded in the flow of Eltit's poetic language, which makes palpable a prohibited return to the pulsating and intimate pleasure of the infant–mother relationship, thus challenging the phallocentric structure of desire.

Also of importance in Eltit's narrative is the link between the textual and the physiological body. The rupture of language and syntax in her novels is linked to the corporeal images of female wounds and mutilation. Nelly Richard has also noted how the self-reflective nature of Eltit's writing, which frequently performs a cyclical whirl of auto-citation, mirrors the auto-eroticism of the female body in her narrative.

No synopsis can be given of Eltit's narrative, since there is no plot in the traditional sense. Her fiction demands the collaboration and participation of the reader. Eltit published three novels in Chile during the Pinochet dictatorship (1973–90). The most immediate impact of her first two novels, *Lumpérica* (also known as *E. Luminata*) (1983) and *Por la patria* [*For the Fatherland*] (1986), lies in their experimental character, which provoked within critics a response that Eugenia Brito has described as one of "fascination" and "horror." The estrangement induced in the reader by the narrative strategies employed in these novels, which include the fragmentation of language, shifting time frames, and the absence of an authorial narrative voice, reflects the disorientation of postcoup Chilean society. While Eltit is publicly uncompromising with regard to her challenging style of writing, the publication of her third novel, *El cuarto mundo* [*The Fourth World*] (1988), has led critics to comment upon the increasing linearity and accessibility of her novels from this point on, a shift possibly influenced by the end of military rule in 1989. Although Eltit's texts post-1988 are undoubtedly more accessible in linguistic and structural terms, they retain their complexity and audacity on semantic and thematic levels and actively resist the prevalence of neo-liberal market forces in Chile.

Much of the erotic imagery and language of Eltit's fiction stem from her first novel,

Lumpérica. This novel stages a scenario that hinges on one character (L. Iluminada—viz., "la illuminada," the illuminated one), one space (a public square), an illuminated neon sign ("El luminoso"), and a defined length of time. The novel unfolds into a brittle, nightmarish world of marginality in which the body of L. Iluminada is violently penetrated and marked by the beam of light emanating from the male "luminoso"; an apparatus stripped of any human attributes. This novel posits a defiant, feminine sexuality and consciousness struggling to gain linguistic and corporeal expression in a context of extreme repression. The erotically charged gestures and poses of L. Iluminada are juxtaposed to religious discourse; the boundaries between binary opposites, such as mind/body and torture/pleasure, are blurred throughout; and the incessant rubbing of L. Iluminada and the "pale people" who shadow her suggests a form of nonphallic eroticism.

Coya is the female protagonist of *Por la patria*, who challenges the usual tropes of nationhood by ousting the young male "hero" (Juan) and positing a ferocious and active female presence and sexuality. Set against the backdrop of a shantytown overrun by a military raid and a female prison, this novel juxtaposes cultured Spanish language to the Chilean oral vernacular known as *coa*, in a performance that Eltit describes as linguistic "incest": an intermingling of disparate discourses and genres. Carnal incest is also depicted in the relationship between Coya and her parents. The escalating linguistic chaos that surrounds Coya's corporeal intimacy with her mother dominates the first section of the novel, transgressing the established symbolic order of language and desire.

The transgression of the incest taboo is once again explored in *El cuarto mundo* and in Eltit's sixth novel, *Los trabajadores de la muerte* [*The Workers of Death*] (1998). The latter is structured as a triptych, which stages the incestuous relationship between a young man and his half-sister. While drawing closely on Greek tragedy, the novel's epilogue and prologue place it firmly within the context of contemporary Chilean society. *El cuarto mundo* is narrated by fraternal twins (one male and one female), whose narrative emerges from the suffocating spaces of their mother's womb and the family home. Embedded in dysfunctional family affiliations, this novel centers on the twins' conception, gestation,

and subsequent "fraternal" incest. Allusions to voyeurism, guilt, confession, castration, and corporeal disintegration pepper the narrative. The second section of the novel, narrated by the female twin, is dominated by the pulsating sexual desire that marks her relationship with her brother, and ends with the birth of the twins' baby: the novel itself.

In *Vaca sagrada* [*Sacred Cow*] (1991), menstrual blood is introduced into the sphere of erotic pleasure and violence, breaking the cultural taboo that marks this female bodily fluid as shameful and repulsive. As the title of this novel suggests, the perception of the female body in society is ambiguous and double-edged. Eltit's fiction urgently demands that attention be drawn to the violence inflicted on the female body through the existing male-oriented social, political, and linguistic structures, which prevent women's self-representation and oppressively regulate their desire.

Biography

Born in Santiago de Chile, August 24, 1949. Eltit studied to become a Spanish teacher at the Universidad Católica in Santiago and subsequently obtained a degree in literature from the Universidad de Chile. She is a professor of literature at the Universidad Tecnológica Metropolitana in Santiago, where she currently teaches. Eltit has also taught as a visiting fellow at UCLA–Berkeley and at Stanford, Columbia, and John Hopkins, among other universities. She remained in Chile during the Pinochet dictatorship (1973–90), during which time she began her literary career, defying the harsh censorship laws and the restriction on the circulation of books. Eltit was one of the four founding members of CADA (Colectivo de Acciones de Arte), an artistic and political collective founded in 1979 in opposition to the military regime and dissolved in 1985. This collective formed part of the artistic and cultural movement labeled the "Escena de avanzada" ("avant-garde" movement) by the Chilean cultural critic Nelly Richard. Eltit also produced her own performance and video art during the dictatorial period, and has collaborated closely with video artist and fellow founder of CADA Lotty Rosenfeld for many years. To date, Eltit has published seven novels, the transcript of the testimony of a vagrant in Santiago, a collaborative photoessay, and a collection of essays. She has also written film scripts and is a frequent contributor to the Chilean journal *Revista de crítica cultural* [Journal of Cultural Criticism]. Essays by Eltit have also been published in the Chilean press and in national and international journals. In 1985 she was awarded a Guggenheim fellowship in recognition of her literary work, and in 1995 she was awarded the José Nuez Martín prize, awarded annually to the best novel published in Chile, for her fifth novel, *Los vigilantes*. From 1990 to 1994, with the reestablishment of democracy in Chile, Eltit acted as the cultural attaché of the Chilean embassy in Mexico City.

MARY GREEN

Selected Works

Novels

Lumpérica. Santiago: Ornitorrinco, 1983; Santiago: Planeta, 1991; Santiago: Seix Barral, 1998; as *E. Luminata*, translated and with an introduction by Ronald Christ, Santa Fe: Lumen, 1997; as *Lumpérica*, translated by Florence Olivier and Anne de Waele, Paris: Des Femmes, 1993.
Por la patria. Santiago: Ornitorrinco, 1986; Santiago: Cuarto Propio, 1995.
El cuarto mundo. Santiago: Seix Barral, 1988, 1996; as *The Fourth World*, translated by Dick Gerdes, Lincoln: University of Nebraska Press, 1995; as *Quart-Monde*, translated by Alexandra Carrasco, Paris: Christian Bourgois, 1992.
Vaca sagrada. Buenos Aires: Planeta, 1991; as *Sacred Cow*, translated by Amanda Hopkinson, London and New York: Serpent's Tail, 1995.
Los vigilantes. Santiago: Sudamericana, 1994.
Los trabajadores de la muerte. Santiago: Planeta, 1998; Buenos Aires: Norma, 2001.
Mano de obra. Santiago: Seix Barral, 2002.

Nonfiction

El padre mío. Santiago: Francisco Zegers, 1989.
El infarto del alma. With Paz Errázuriz. Santiago: Francisco Zegers, 1994.
Emergencias: Escritos sobre literatura, arte y política. Edited and with an introduction by Leonidas T. Morales. Santiago: Planeta/Ariel, 2000.

Further Reading

Avelar, Idelber. *The Untimely Present: Postdictatorial Latin American Fiction and the Task of Mourning*. Durham and London: Duke University Press, 1999.
Brito, Eugenia. *Campos minados: Literatura post-golpe en Chile*. Santiago: Cuarto Propio, 1990.
Kadir, Djelal. *The Other Writing: Postcolonial Essays in Latin America's Writing Culture*. W. Lafayette, IN: Purdue University Press, 1993.
Labanyi, Jo. "Topologies of Catastrophe: Horror and Abjection in Diamela Eltit's *Vaca Sagrada*." In *Latin American Women's Writing*. Edited by Anny Brooksbank Jones and Catherine Davies. Oxford: Clarendon Press, 1996.
Lértora, Juan Carlos, ed. *Una poética de literatura menor: La narrativa de Diamela Eltit*. Santiago: Cuarto Propio, 1993.
Morales, Leonidas T. *Conversaciones con Diamela Eltit*. Santiago: Cuarto Propio, 1998.
Norat, Gisela. *Marginalities: Diamela Eltit and the Subversion of Mainstream Literature in Chile*. Newark: University of Delaware Press; London: Associated University Presses, 2002.
Olea, Raquel. *Lengua víbora. Producciones de lo femenino en la escritura de mujeres chilenas*. Santiago: Editorial Cuarto Propio, 1998.
Richard, Nelly. *Margins and Institutions: Art in Chile since 1973*. Edited by Paul Foss and Paul Taylor. Melbourne: Art and Text, 1986.
Tierney-Tello, Mary Beth. *Allegories of Transgression and Transformation: Experimental Fiction by Women Writing Under Dictatorship*. Albany: State University of New York Press, 1996.

ELUARD, PAUL

1895–1952
French poet

Like Charles Baudelaire before him (truly the first French poet to mirror modernity, to

struggle with the crisis inherent in portraying its always ready obsolescence), then Rimbaud and Lautréamont among the more prominent to follow in his footsteps, Paul Eluard was committed to the pursuit of freedom. Whether as a soldier witnessing firsthand the absurdity of World War I at the beginning of the twentieth century, as a Dadaist and Surrealist poet of the 1920s breaking or (re)making prosodic vessels to escape the tired constraints of convention, as a political activist flirting with and eventually embracing Communism in 1942 as a way to overcome the tyranny and terror of social injustice, or finally, as the lover of three of the more important companions in his life (Gala, Nusch, and Dominique, seeking to reposition woman at the center of an erotic cosmogony), he sang his song of liberty. Indeed, if Paul Eluard were to be remembered for no other reason, it would have to be for his lifelong commitment to *liberté*.

But early on he found that to liberate—to find a language to say something new in poetry not bound by tradition or rational thought, or by the smug rhetoric and *idées reçues* of the bourgeoisie—was a particularly difficult road to travel in the modern era. When, not long after the publication of his *Poèmes pour la paix* [*Poems For Peace*] (1918) and his discharge from the military, Eluard became a member of the Parisian literati (a Dadaist, a colleague of Tristan Tzara, Louis Aragon, André Breton, and Philippe Soupault, among others), he willingly and knowingly joined the ranks of an artistic cabal bent upon repudiating everything, even at the risk of denying or destroying itself. All too quickly Dadaism became a conformity of nonconformity and ran amok of its own derisive, contradictory logic. Spearheaded on the whole by a small contingent who discerned this impasse, Surrealism emerged from the confusion with Breton reconfiguring it in *Le premier manifeste du surréalisme* [*The First Manifesto of Surrealism*] (1924), promoting, in the words of Wallace Fowlie, "total liberty in all human activities, including the activity of love" (*Age of Surrealism*, 144). It would seem, then, that Surrealism sought to sanction all forms of sexual experimentation, including perversion—not only as behaviors within the grasp of every human being but as generative sources of art. While this hardly proved to be the case for Eluard either literally (his relationships throughout his life tended to be traditional) or aesthetically (throughout his career, he treated love and its thematic congeners discreetly or indirectly, often associating them with "nature"), the possibility of creating a rift in timeworn taboos in order to access a superior reality—to liberate a

surreality in which contradictions would cease to exist, in which lovers would exist as one— was more than enough to compel him to cast his lot with the Surrealist cause. He became one of its tireless workers, contributing extensively to the movement's flagship review, *La révolution surréaliste,* as well as *Une vague de rêves,* its first collected publication. Likewise, he was a coauthor with Benjamin Péret of *152 Proverbes mis au goût du jour* [*152 Proverbs Adapted to the Taste of the Day*] (1925); with Breton and René Char of *Ralentir, travaux* [*Slow, Under Construction*] (1930); and with Breton again of *L'Immaculée conception* [*The Immaculate Conception*] (1930).

Paul Eluard found his true poetic voice in *Au défaut du silence* [*For Lack of Silence*] (1925), the collection *Capitale de la douleur* [*Capital of Pain*] (1919–1926), *Les dessous d'une vie, ou la pyramide humaine* [*The Underpinnings of a Life, or The Human Pyramid*] (1926), and *L'Amour et la poésie* [*Love and Poetry*] (1929). While drawing upon the subversive energy at the heart of Surrealism to craft what Fowlie has deemed "a new erotology" (146), an unwavering belief in the regenerative, destructively creative capacity of love, he began a slow, almost imperceptible stepping away from Breton and his poetics. (The final break occurred in 1938, when Breton insisted upon separating political activism, that is, an alignment with the French Communist Party and its hope for advancing humanitarian goals, from the revolutionary but isolationist nature of his concept of Surrealism.)

Through a series of short, prose-poem pieces devoid of any traditional prosody, *Capitale de la Douleur* conveys a general angst with respect to inhabiting a poorly made world besieged by perpetual war and degradation—a new form of what the Romantics in the nineteenth century called the *mal du siècle.* But in the long run, *Capitale* extols our fundamental need to love as well as be loved, to celebrate "the mystery wherein love creates and delivers" ("Celle de toujours, toute" [She of all times, all]).

Love in its largest meaning, in its emergence and immediacy, in its disruptively creative potential for opening out to the new, free, and unfettered, would be more than enough to convince Paul Eluard to pursue it in his literary and political endeavors until the very day he died— with an oeuvre exemplified by *La vie immédiate* [*Immediate Life*] (1932), *Facile* [*Easy*] (1935), *Les yeux fertiles* [*Fertile Eyes*] (1936, illustrated by

Pablo Picasso), *Chanson complète* [*Complete Song*] (1939), *Donner à voir* [*Offering up Something to See*] (1939), *Poésie ininterrompue* [*Uninterrupted Poetry*] (1946), *Corps mémorable* [*Memorable Body*] (1947), and *Le Phénix* [*The Phoenix*] (1951).

In *Derniers poèmes d'amour* [*Last Love Poems*] (published posthumously in 1962), he has left us the following extraordinarily simple yet utterly profound summation of his lifelong voyage toward love and freedom: "Tu es venue la solitude était vaincue /... / J'allais vers toi j'allais sans fin vers la lumière / La vie avait un corps l'espoir tendait sa voile" [You came, the solitude was vanquished /. . . / I went toward you, ceaselessly toward the light / Life was palpable, hope unfurled its sail].

Biography

Born Paul-Eugène Grindel, in Saint-Denis, north of Paris on December 14, 1895. Only child of an accountant and a seamstress. After four years of study in Paris, entered a Swiss sanatorium in 1912 to treat a tubercular condition that would plague him for the rest of his life; at the same time met Helena Diakonova (Gala), whom he would marry in 1917 despite his mother's misgivings. Served in the army during World War I as a corpsman and an infantryman. Was gassed. After publishing *Poèmes pour la paix* in 1918 under the name of Eluard, surname of his maternal grandmother, he attracted positive critical attention from various members of the Parisian literati. Discharged in 1919, he became one of them, associating more often than not on a daily basis with Breton, Tzara, Aragon, Soupault, Picasso, Man Ray, Paul Klee, and Salvador Dalí, among others. In the next several years, he was an active contributor to Dadaism and Surrealism, with individual poems as well as collaborations. Of particular note is *Répétitions* (1922) with Max Ernst.

After publishing *Mourir de ne pas mourir* [*Dying from Not Dying*] in 1924, which he felt would be his last work, Eluard began a ménage à trois with his wife and Ernst. This arrangement brought on the wrath of his father, who was still supporting him at that stage in his life. Eluard ran away and traveled the world, only to meet up with Gala in Singapore seven months later.

He published *Capitale de la douleur* in 1926, considered a major contribution to his commitment to poetry and the role that love was to play in it. Joined the French Communist Party. When his father died in 1927, Eluard enjoyed a brief inheritance that was squandered in slightly less than four years. Divorced Gala in 1930, after which she quickly became Dalí's muse and companion until her death in 1982. In that same year in which his divorce was finalized, he met a young and beautiful Maria Benz (Nusch) and fell head over heels in love, as detailed in *La Vie immédiate* [*Immediate Life*] (1932) and *Comme deux gouttes d'eau* [*Like Two Drops of Water*] (1933). Married her in 1934, but not before being expelled from the French Communist Party in 1933. Even though excluded from this movement, he continued to support what he felt was its potential for furthering the common good. At the outbreak of the Spanish Civil War in 1936, he tried to reconnect with the Communists through support for the Loyalists as the only viable means of countering the spread of fascism. With similar concern and activism, he joined the underground forces in Vichy France, resisting the Nazis at every opportunity through his poetry, pamphlets, and leaflets. He renewed his Communist ties finally in 1942. Then, after the liberation of France, he traveled extensively from 1944 on as its postwar cultural ambassador. Devastated by the sudden death of his beloved Nusch in 1946, he published in her memory *Le temps déborde* [*Time Overflows*], then *Corps mémorable* [*Memorable Body*] in 1947. At a conference for the World Peace Council held in Mexico in 1949, Eluard happened to meet Dominique Laure, who would become his third wife some two years later. He celebrated their love, its emergence and renewal, in one of the last books published during his lifetime, *Le phénix*. Struck down by a heart attack in September 1952, Paul Eluard died of heart failure two months later on November 18.

MARIE-AGNÉS SOURIEAU

Selected Works

Les malheurs des immortels. With Max Ernst. Paris: Librairie Six, 1922; translated as *Misfortunes of the Immortals* by Hugh Chisholm, New York: Black Sun Press, 1943.

Capitale de la douleur. Paris: Editions de la Nouvelle Revue Française, 1926; revised, 1946; translated as

Capital of Pain by Richard M. Weisman, New York: Grossman, 1973.

Ralentir travaux. With André Breton and René Char. Paris: Editions Surréalistes, 1930; translated as *Slow, Under Construction* by Keith Waldrop, Cambridge, Mass.: Exact Change, 1990.

L'Immaculée conception. With Breton. Paris: José Corti, 1930; translated as *The Immaculate Conception* by Jon Graham, introduction by Antony Melville, London: Atlas, 1990.

Poésie et vérité / Poetry and Truth. Translated by Roland Penrose and E. L. T. Mesens. London: Gallery Editions, 1942/1944.

A Pablo Picasso. Les Grands peintres par leurs amis, no. 1. Geneva: Editions des Trois Collines, 1944; Paris and Geneva: Editions des Trois Collines, 1945; translated as *Pablo Picasso* by Joseph T. Shipley, New York: Philosophical Library, 1947.

Le Dur désir de durer [The Dour Desire to Endure]. With 25 original drawings and a frontispiece by Marc Chagall. Paris: Editions Arnold-Bordas, 1946; bilingual edition translated by Stephen Spender and Frances Cornford, Philadelphia: Grey Falcon Press, London: Trianon Press, 1950.

Poésie ininterrompue, II. Paris: Gallimard, 1953; translated as *Unbroken Poetry II* by Gilbert Bowen, introduction by Jill Lewis, Newcastle-upon-Tyne: Bloodaxe, 1996.

The Penguin Book of French Verse. Vol. 4. Edited by Anthony Hartley. London: Penguin, 1959; expanded edition, 1966; revised edition incorporating all four volumes, 1975.

French Poetry, 1820–1950, with Prose Translations. Edited and translated by William Rees. Harmondsworth and New York: Penguin, 1990.

Editions and Selections

Paul Eluard: Selected Writings. Translated by Lloyd Alexander, with introductory notes by Louis Aragon, Louis Parrot, and Claude Roy. New York: New Directions, 1951; London: Routledge & Kegan Paul, 1952; republished as *Uninterrupted Poetry: Selected Writings of Paul Eluard*, Westport, Conn.: Greenwood Press, 1977.

Derniers poèmes d'amour de Paul Eluard. Preface by Lucien Scheler. Paris: Club des Libraires de France, 1962, including *Le Dur désir de durer, Le Temps déborde, Corps mémorable,* and *Le Phénix*; bilingual edition, published as *Last Love Poems of Paul Eluard*, translated with an introduction by Marilyn Kallet, Baton Rouge: Louisiana State University Press, 1980.

Selected Poems: Paul Eluard. Bilingual edition, edited and translated by Gilbert Bowen, introduction by Max Adereth. London: Calder/New York: Riverrun Press, 1988.

Ombres et soleil / Shadows and Sun: Selected Writings of 1913–1952. Translated by Lloyd Alexander and Cicely Buckley. Durham, NH: Oyster River Press, 1995.

References and Further Reading

Balakian, Anna. "Post-Surrealism of Aragon and Eluard." In *Surrealism: The Road to the Absolute.* New York: Noonday Press, 1959.

Barthes, Roland. *Le Plaisir du texte.* Paris: Editions du Seuil, 1973; translated as *The Pleasure of the Text* by Richard Miller, New York: Hill and Wang, 1975.

Bogan, Louise. "The Poetry of Paul Eluard." In *Selected Criticism: Prose and Poetry.* New York: Noonday Press, 1955.

Carmody, Francis J. "Eluard's Rupture with Surrealism." *PMLA* 86 (September 1961): 436–46.

Caucci, Frank. *Les voix d'Eros: La poésie amoureuse de Paul Eluard et de Pablo Neruda.* New York: Peter Lang, 1989.

Caws, Mary Ann. "Paul Eluard." In *The Poetry of Dada and Surrealism: Aragon, Breton, Tzara, Eluard and Desnos.* Princeton, NJ: Princeton University Press, 1970.

Fowlie, Wallace. "Eluard: the Doctrine of Love." In *Age of Surrealism.* Denver: Swallow Press / New York: Morrow, 1940.

———, ed. "Paul Eluard." In *Mid-Century French Poets: Selections, Translations, and Critical Notices.* New York: Grove Press, 1955.

Griffin, Susan. *The Eros of Everyday Life: Essays on Ecology, Gender and Society.* New York: Bantam Doubleday Dell, 1995.

Meadwell, Kenneth W. "Paul Eluard." In the *Dictionary of Literary Biography: Modern French Poets.* Vol. 258, 189–209. London: Bruccoli Clark Layman, 2002.

Nadeau, Maurice. *Histoire du surréalisme, suivie de Documents surréalistes.* Paris: Editions du Seuil, 1964; as *The History of Surrealism* by Richard Howard, introduction by Roger Shattuck. New York: Macmillan, 1965.

Nugent, Robert. *Paul Eluard,* New York: Twayne, 1974.

Paglia, Camille. *Sexual Personae: Art and Decadence from Nefertiti to Emily Dickinson.* New Haven, Conn.: Yale University Press, 1991.

Paul, Pamela. *Pornified: How Pornography Is Transforming Our Lives, Our Relationships, and Our Families.* New York: Times Books, 2005.

Raymond, Marcel. *De Baudelaire au surréalisme.* Revised edition. Paris: José Corti, 1940; translated as *From Baudelaire to Surrealism.* New York: Wittenborn, Schultz, 1950; London: Owen, 1957.

Rickett, Paul. "Paul Eluard 1895–1952." In the *Encyclopedia of Literary Translation into English.* Vol. 1, 930–32. London: Fitzroy Dearborn Publishers, 2000.

Whitting, Charles. "Eluard's Poems for Gala." *French Review* 41 (1968).

EMINESCU, MIHAI

1850–1889
Romanian poet, fiction writer and journalist

Poems

Eminescu's best erotic poems were actually inspired by his relationship with the poet Veronica Micle, one of the most elegant and beautiful women of the time, the wife of a university professor from Iasi. Their relationship, with its ups and downs, has given Romanian literature both an impressive epistolary and a beautiful and passionate chapter of literary history. The biographical circumstances were mediated by the poet's successful processing of Romantic motifs from European poetry: the lake, the blue flower, and the solitary genius. In Eminescu's erotic poems the male principle is a positive force, whereas the feminine principle is negative or (if the woman is very young) potentially negative. Woman is a privileged form of *coincidentia oppositorum,* a coincidence of opposites. The search for the perfection embodied in a female form must be abandoned. As there is no perfect woman, the Eros is both pain and joy.

Eminescu's perspective of the couple goes back to the Platonic model. He is sensuous, lucid, polemical, but also reflexive and detached. Very often his portrait is derived from a character from Romanian mythology (the Flyer), symbol of the young girls' nascent sexuality: "dauntless, dark-curled fairy prince" (*Calin, Pages from a Tale,* 133) (citations throughout are from Popescu, *Poems*). She is usually blond, fair-skinned, blued-eyed. Her cheeks have the color of the apple skin. With Eminescu, love is either retrospective (memory), as in *Down Where the Lonely Poplars Grow, When Memory*, and *So Delicate,* or prospective (hope for the future) as in *Desire* and *The Lake.* The natural milieu plays a very important role in Eminescu's erotic poetry. The deep forest is symbolic of the mysteries of sex; the lake, the spring, the river stand in for the biological juices of sexuality; the lime tree ensures the aromas of the amorous encounter; the moon and the stars create a cosmic mirror for the lovers' earthly desire; and the flowers, and particularly the blue flower, are associated with the female, with her beauty and fertility. Love creates one of Eminescu's compensatory universes. Dissatisfied with the shallow exigencies of his contemporaries, the poet hopes that love will help him surpass the straitjacket of the contingent. Unfortunately, he is to be disappointed. Bitter irony and cynicism make him transform his beloved from the icon of his youth poems into the frivolous puppet of his last poems. The poet bitterly remarks that people take all too seriously an instinct, "one of nature's needs" (*Satire IV*, 173) and do not realize that the great puppeteer of all times is will, the force that is behind everything that exists.

Eminescu constructs woman in oppositional images and through constraining idealization. She is angel or demon, Venus or Madonna, icon or puppet. But in spite of his awareness of woman's dual nature, the poet cannot help loving the woman: "I adore this demon saint with big blue eyes and golden hair" (*Venus and Madonna*, 57). The spiteful compensation that the poet offers himself and his reader is the idealization of woman. Be it a hypernegative or hyperpositive idealization, Eminescu's woman is always a construction of man. Within the couple, the relation between the partners is that between the Demiurges and his creature. With very few exceptions, it is always man who initiates the sexual game, and desire is overwhelming. The sexual union is extremely rare, as the poet prefers daydreaming and shivering expectancy to the brutal and undeniable fulfillment of sexual desire.

Blue Flower is one of the few poems by Eminescu in which the woman takes the initiative. The first part of the poem is conversational. The young woman invites the man in the midst of superb, glimmering, mating-inspiring nature: "Come where cool crystal brooks complain / Their fleeting fate midst forest greens, / And where the hanging cliff out leans / As though the thunder on the plain" (84). Frolicking, sensual games are to be played by the two partners: "[M]y long golden hair undone / Around your neck in coils you'll wind." Body language signals desire. This conversational part contrasts with the last stanza, where the poet regrets his commitment to pure intellectual pursuits and mourns his lost blue flower.

Calin: Pages from a Tale is an erotic story placed in a mythic" lonely castle" amidst an "ancient forest" (131). Calin (the Flyer) climbs up the steep walls of the castle and enters the bedchamber of the emperor's daughter. *Calin* is one of the few poems by Eminescu in which mating follows courting. The two lovers are "clasped in close embrace" and drink the "lover's joy their fill" (135). A child is born out of their embrace and the emperor angrily drives his daughter away. But the remorseful Calin searches for his beloved and a superb wedding follows. It is significant that Eminescu succeeds in uniting his lovers through the holy and comforting bond of matrimony only in a mythic environment as in *Calin.* The human wedding is humorously parallelled and mirrored by that of the gallant butterfly and "a timid violet moth" (140).

Eminescu's best-known poem, translated as *Lucifer* by Popescu and as *Hyperion* by Levitchi and Bantas, is an erotic story which proves the poet's capacity to make eros mediate between the ontological levels of the universe. The poem is a mythic story about the love between the beautiful young daughter of an emperor and the Evening Star. The astral suitor is invoked twice by the emperor's daughter from her palace situated on the shore of the sea, a privileged space and a threshold between liquid and nonliquid mirrors. The two apparitions of the lover from the beyond are two cosmic births: from the sky and the sea the first time, from the sun and the night the second time. The Evening Star is asked by the emperor's daughter to give up immortality because it looks like death to her. From this point in the plot the ways of the two characters diverge. The astral suitor goes back to the place where the world has originated in order to renounce his immortality, but Demiurges can offer him only the following options: hero of the spirit or hero of the deed. Hyperion cannot give up his immortal status as a genius. At the same time, in a corner of the palace (notice the limitations of the space as compared with the cosmic

lodge of Hyperion), Catalin, "a page boy of that house," will teach Catalina the gestures of love. The princess and the genius will be forever locked into their respective statuses. The longing for evening stars of the princess and the longing for death through love of the eternal genius cannot change the Law. *Lucifer/Hyperion* is an exquisite poem in which eros gets philosophical and cosmic values. It is a poem about the contradiction between the earthly and the beyond that attract each other, as in an amorous game, and then must separate. The illusion of communion is only a supreme coronation of eros and not its permanent status.

Biography

Born in Botosani, died in Bucharest. He studied at Chernovtsy (now in Ukraine), Vienna, and Berlin without taking a degree. He made his debut with a poem in *Familia* in 1866. Iosif Vulcan, the editor-in-chief and an important Romanian cultural militant, changed the young poet's name from Eminovici into Eminescu. The poet was a member of "Junimea," an extremely influential literary society of the time. In 1870–71 he published several poems in *Convorbiri literare,* the literary magazine of Junimea. These poems define a new direction in the evolution of Romanian poetry. In 1877 Eminescu settled down in Bucharest. For six years he worked as a journalist at *Timpul,* a conservative newspaper of the time. The mentor of Junimea, Titu Maiorescu, edited the first collection of Eminescu's poems in 1883–1884. In 1884, Eminescu fell seriously ill, and in the six remaining years of his life he alternated between periods of lucidity and of serious mental disorder.

MICHAELA MUDURE

Editions

Poesii. Bucuresti: Socec, 1884; *Poezii*; Iasi: Editura scoalelor, 1896; Bucuresti: Editura "Nationala" S. Ciornei, 1928; Bucuresti: Cugetarea-Georgescu Delafras, 1940; Bucuresti: Editura de stat pentru literatura si arta, 1956; Bucuresti: Editura pentru literatura, 1961; Bucuresti: Eminescu, 1971; Bucuresti: Minerva, 1987; Bucuresti: Editura Academiei Republicii Socialiste Romania, 1989; Bucuresti: Fundatia Culturala Romana, 1991; Bucuresti: Prometeu, 1997; Chisinau: Cartier, 1998; as *Poems,* translated by Peter Grimm, Cluj: Cartea romaneasca, 1938; as *Poems,* translated by Corneliu M. Popescu, Bucharest: Eminescu, 1978; as *Poems,* translated by Roy MacGregor-Hastie, Cluj-Napoca: Dacia, 1989; as *Poems,* translated by

Leon Levitchi and Andrei Bantas, Bucuresti: Teora, 1999.

Selected Works

Poesii. 1884.
Opere complete. 1902.
Scrieri politice si literare. 1905.
Articole politice. 1910.
Opere. vols. I–XVI. 1939–1989.
Basme. 1977.
Cugetari. 1979.
Literatura populara. 1979.
Teatru. 1984.

Opera esentiala. 1992.
Geniu pustiu: proza literara. 1997.
Chestiunea evreiasca. 1998.

Further Reading

Calinescu, George. *Opera lui Mihai Eminescu.* Bucuresti: Minerva, 1985.
Muresanu Ionescu, Mariana. *Eminescu si intertextul romantic*, Iasi: Junimea, 1990.
Papu, Edgar. *Poezia lui Eminescu. Elemente structurale.* Bucuresti: Minerva, 1971.
Petrescu, Ioana Em. *Cursul Eminescu.* Cluj-Napoca: Universitatea Babes-Bolyai, 1993.

ENGLISH: UNITED KINGDOM, SEVENTEENTH CENTURY

The study of historical erotic literature must be carried out both within its context as well as in terms of current critical theory. Most modern academic discussions have tended to focus on what is described as the sexually explicit, obscene nature of early modern "pornographic" writing. There is much debate, however, as to whether the use of the word *pornography,* which was coined in the 19th century, actually applies to this period. Historians such as Ian Frederick Moulton and Lynn Hunt argue that the forms of erotic representation that we now ascribe to this term are meaningless in the context of 17th-century erotica.

In order to study erotic literature in this period, the significant role that politics, society, and culture played in the formation of sexual beliefs and practices must be acknowledged. 17th-century erotic writing was in fact a mirror of the times in which it was written. This was a period of dramatic political, social, and cultural changes, all of which affected the types of materials that were published. Erotic literature, in particular, was particularly evident at times of political stress and during the Restoration.

It was also a time of major growth in literacy among both men and women. By the end of the Stuart period, the English had achieved a level of literacy unknown in the past and unmatched elsewhere in early modern Europe. In parallel with the nation's growing ability to read was the surge in commercial culture—the extension of regional and national markets in commodities and consumer items—thanks to better communications and to newspapers.

Despite periodical censorship, a great number of poems, plays, books, and ephemeral publications that either related to or attempted to rouse sexual desire appeared in print. The gulf between sexuality/gender as illustrated in the modern media and the individual lives of real people is similar to the mismatch in early modern society between idealized images of conduct and daily experience. Rather than mirroring actual behavior, much erotic literature was designed to shock as much as to arouse. Almost all sexual literature was written by males and was often highly misogynistic, showing cynicism about women, love, and marriage.

The greatest profusion is referred to as "libertine" writing, produced during the Restoration. However, large amounts of erotica in the form of manuscripts, as well as printed works, were produced and consumed throughout the entire century. Donne's elegies, Shakespeare's sonnets, and Thomas Nashe's "filthy rhymes," for example, tended to circulate amongst readers in manuscript form. The London theater industry, which had developed rapidly and successfully from the 1560s, offered what many people considered to be godless, immoral and subversive plays. In the early part of the century, these included scripts by Ben Jonson, such as *Volpone* (1605), which explored the relationship between discourses of eroticism and the erotic performance.

There were numerous other types of publications, including ballads; broadsheets; pamphlets; chapbooks, or "penny merriments"; almanacs; and books which addressed sexual issues. A great number of erotic works were imported from the Continent and sold in London. Domestically printed publications were published either anonymously or under a false name to avoid prosecution. Many printers also tried to conceal their identities, oftentimes using a false name and/or imprint for the place of printing. The printed works themselves were also often sold "privately" by booksellers rather than showing them "publickly, with the Title Page lying open upon the Stall as other books do, when they are newly out."

At the beginning of the century, both the nation and the political system had been crippled by years of bad harvests, the high costs of warfare, popular unrest, and rising crime rates. For many workers in the printing industries, the beginning of the reign of James I signaled further hardships. In 1603 the new king passed on the monopolistic rights that had formerly belonged to the late Watkins and Roberts to the Stationers' Company. This included exclusive right to produce and wholesale the highly lucrative "English stock," which included private prayers, prymers, psalters, and psalmes in English or Latin, as well as a range of popular and/or ephemeral literature.

As the reign of James I, one of the most criticized monarchs in English history, ended, Charles I came to the throne of a country plagued by a troubled parliament and the beginning of the Thirty Years' War in 1618. The Stationers' Company had a tight hold on the printing industry, allowing only around 50 printing presses to operate in London. The company regularly attempted to prosecute offenders, often unsuccessfully. Charles aided their efforts by establishing the most repressive system of press censorship since the reign of Elizabeth I.

Many of the works that were considered to be "lascivious" in the early part of the century, however, were later seen as relatively harmless. These included translations of the elegists Ovid, Catullus, Tibullus, and Propertius, as well as the novelists Petronius and Apuleius. More contemporary works, such as Donne's Ovidian Elegies in 1633 and two bawdy parodies of Chaucer in 1639, were actually censored by the Licenser of the Press.

During the 1640s, however, revolutionary events resulted in an absence of censorship and legal controls, which enabled independent printers to operate in London. This new freedom resulted in the production of massive numbers of new books, pamphlets, and other ephemeral literature. It has been estimated that more books and pamphlets were printed between 1640 and 1660 than in the entire rest of the century.

Many of these addressed topics that would previously have been deemed treasonable, seditious, or scandalous to appear in print. These included political issues, religious topics, and matters of a sexual nature. In fact, sexual freedom and release from the constraints of marriage were tremendously popular topics in books and pamphlets written during the 1640s and 1650s. Anti-Puritan satire, especially dealing with their sexual shortcomings, were also extremely common. Sir Francis Fane's *Iter Occidentale, or The Wonders of Warm Waters,* for example, tells of a Quaker woman who lures "a well Hung Proselyte into the water and so begins an aquatic orgy."

The portrayal of women with voracious sexual appetites was a common feature in contemporary writings. In the *Art of Courtship,* a new bride says, "[N]ow I find such solid bliss, that I'd not be a virgin now." Cuckoldry was another prevailing theme, as was masculine impotence or at least inadequacy. The chapbook *Nine Times a Night* claimed:

Nine times a night is too much for a man,
I can't do it myself, but my sister Nan can.

John Fletcher's play *The Custom of the Country,* first performed in 1619 and later revived during the Restoration period, carries this theme further. It features Rutillio, "the lustiest fellow" in the play, who labors under the sexual demands placed upon him by the brothel. In one scene, Rutillo bemoans his physical state, ruined by the requirements of servicing up to fourteen women a day:

> Now I do look as if I were Crow-trodden
> Fy how my hams shrinke under me; o me,
> I am broken-winded too; Is this a life?
> Is this the recreation I have aimd at?
> I had a body once, a handsome body,
> And wholesome too. Now I appeare like a rascall
> That had been hung a yeare or two in gibbets.

According to a chapbook called *Fumblers-Hall, kept and holden in Feeble-Court, at the sign of the Labour-in-vain, in Doe-little-lane*, married women also put excessive sexual demands upon their husbands, whose abilities were demeaningly referred to "as a straw in the Nostrils of a Cow, a very slug, a meer fible" or "a meer Gut, a Chittlering, a Fiddle-string that will make no musick to a Womans Instrument."

Most publications of this sort appeared under anonymous names, often without identifying the publisher and with false imprints. For example, the first known surviving English edition of *La puttana errant, overo dialogo di Madalena e Giulia*, appeared in 1650. Although this claimed to have been written by Aretino, it was clearly a fake which originated with Ferrante Pallavicino in 1641. Published under the pretext of being a text-book of rhetoric, it was in fact a satirical work on rhetoric, the Jesuits, religion, and sex. It took the form of a dialogue between Madalena and her fellow whores in a brothel, describing their way of life and the arts of persuasion they needed to learn.

The English version, *The Whores Rhetorick*, first published around 1660, took a slightly different form. It is based on the exquisite whore Julietta, who had just arrived in London from Venice. Much of the book is based on the successful efforts to defraud clients through the efforts of the crafty bawd Magdalena and Gusman the pimping hector. Intervening sections discuss sexual techniques and aids, such as the "strummulo" and the "merkin," which were forms of false pubic hair for whores worn bald through overwork. It also related current sexual scandals, such as the Dutch whore who had Rhenish wine poured into more than one orifice, and a drunken whore with a candle stuck in her "commodity" which had to be extinguished by a "codpiece engine." Samuel Pepys mentioned

being tantalized, yet horrified by this book in a diary entry from 1668. Although he used the work as a masturbatory aid, he later destroyed the book by burning it.

La puttana errant was only one of a number of erotic works imported from the Continent and translated into English. *L'Ecole des filles*, or *The School of Venus*, also proved to be very popular, after first appearing in 1655 under the false imprint of Leyden. As with other contemporary examples, this takes the form of two dialogues. The major characters are Robinet, who has fallen in love with sixteen-year-old Fanchon, and her older and far more experienced cousin Susanne. The first part of the book consists of a conversation between Fanchon and Susanne. It begins with some basic anatomical and linguistic sexual facts, including a fairly clinical description of orgasm.

> The boy thrusts to and fro with his rump to insert the yard, while the girl clings to him, feeling the friction and movement of his organ inside her.... [T]he excitement which is provoked by the gentle irritation and rubbing along the length of their passages... overwhelms them to such an extent that you see them almost swoon with ecstasy giving little thrusts towards each other as they discharge the substance which has excited them so much.

Fanchon follows Susanne's advice, and in the second half of the book relates her sexual activities with Fanchon in great detail. Susanne praises her student for learning so well and proclaims that she is truly "a mistress in the fine art of love." Evidence suggests that many readers felt that this was a depraved and corrupting work. Samuel Pepys' diary commented that it was "the most bawdy, lewd book that I ever saw."

Such works continued to appear in print, however, despite periodical attempts at censorship. Booksellers who stocked foreign imports could be fined and shut down, while publishers in England were often prosecuted by the authorities. In 1662 parliament passed a detailed licensing bill that heralded the beginning of a new period of censorship:

> An Act for preventing the frequent Abuses in printing seditious, treasonable, and unlicensed Books and Pamphlets, and for regulating of Printing and printing Presses... [due to] the general licentiousness of the late times, many evil disposed persons have been encouraged to print and sell heretical, schismatical, blasphemous, seditious and treasonable books, pamphlets and papers.

Possibly the best-known author of erotic writings during this period was John Wilmot, the second earl of Rochester (1647–1680). Wilmot was one of the rowdiest rakes in the court of Charles II, where he wrote a range of highly misogynistic and aggressive satirical and erotic works, such as "The Wish":

Oh! That I could by some new Chymick Art
Convert to Sperm my Vital and my Heart;
And, at one Thrust, my very soul translate
Into her— and be degenerate.
There steep'd in Lust nine Months I would remain,
Then boldly fuck my Passage back again.

Rochester was also the author of *Sodom, or the Quintessence of Debauchery*, a play which was written and presented for Charles II and his courtiers. Peopled by characters named after the genitals and various sexual acts, the script covers topics ranging from pederasty through the various uses of dildos. Such writing was particularly popular with Charles II, who enjoyed the sexual guiltlessness and experimentation lauded in court verses written by men such as Buckingham, Butler, Dorset, and Roscommon. Many of these celebrated the virtues of the male organ, such as this poem by Lord Charles Buckhurst, Earl of Dorset and Middlesex:

Dreaming last night of Mistris Harley
My Prick was up this morning Earley
And I was fain without my gowne
To rise i'th' Cold to gett him downe.{i}

Many translations of Continental works of erotic literature made their first appearances in England during the Restoration. One popular example was *Aloisiæ Sigeæ Toletanæ Satyra sotadica de arcanis Amoris et Veneris* [*The Sotadic Satire on Secret Loves and Lusts*], which was attributed to the Spanish writer Luisa Sigée of Toledo. The work was not, in fact, written by this daughter of an expatriate Frenchman who lived in Toledo from around 1530 to 1560. Although actual authorship cannot be proved, it seems likely that Nicolas Chorier translated the first version of the Latin work sometime in the mid-17th century. The earliest surviving French edition, *L'Académie des dames*, dates from around 1680. Two English versions quickly followed, although it is not known whether they were translated from the Latin or the French text. The first, called *Tullia and Octavia*, appeared by or in 1684, followed by *A Dialogue Between a Married Lady and a Maid* in 1688.

Tullia and Octavia is based on a conversation between the nineteen-year-old Tullia, who is married and sexually experienced, and her fifteen-year-old cousin Octavia, who is about to be married. Their seven dialogues are divided into two parts, beginning with a discussion of petting, followed by a demonstration by the older girl. In the third and fourth episodes, Tullia describes her husband's penis and how he pleasured her on their wedding night. By this time Octavia has been married to Pamphilius, and the final episodes cover a range of topics from flagellation, sodomy, and incest through to group sex.

Another contemporary Continental work which dates from around 1672 was *Vénus dans le cloître, ou la religieuse en chemise. Entretiens curieux...par l'abbé du Prat* [Venus in the Cloyster, or the Nun in Her Smock. Curious Interviews by Father Prat], usually attributed to Jean Barrin. The original text consists of three dialogues about sex, taking place in a convent between the nineteen-year-old Sister Angelique and the sixteen-year-old Sister Agnès. Although actual sexual encounters are glossed over, the book infers that many different types of sexual pleasure were allowable, provided that certain conditions were followed. In the earliest known English edition, from 1683, Sister Angelica and Agnes conduct five dialogues about sex, interspersed with passionate lesbian lovemaking. The two young nuns also indulge in reading dirty books brought in by confessors and coupling with priest, monks, friars, and gardeners.

The Whores Rhetorick was another English translation that first appeared in 1683, claiming to be based on the previously mentioned *La puttana errant* of Ferrante Pallavicino. An anonymous author referred to as "Philo-Puttanus" produced this edition in London for English readers. This version focuses on Dorothea, the daughter of a once-prosperous but now ruined cavalier. Advised by the old bawd Mother Creswell to become a prostitute to relieve her poverty, the text contains two dialogues between the two women. These consist mainly of instructions about the whore's arts of lovemaking, combined with general rules on treating customers. Philo-Puttanus also used his work to broadcast his anti-Puritan views, attacking conventicles and the self-righteous lechery of many of its members.

Another well-known Continental work, by Nicolas Venette, was *Tableau de l'amour conjugal,* originally written in French but translated into several languages. The English version of 1681 claimed to be a handbook of sexual advice, although it actually contained a range of material, from bawdiness through to explicit sexual practices. It also contained a mixture of folk wisdom about sexual behavior, recipes for herbal aphrodisiacs and prophylactics, and remedies for sexually linked diseases.

The production of such works undoubtedly fulfilled a variety of purposes for contemporaries. As in any period, English society and culture had an enormous impact on 17th-century erotic literature. It appears that the purpose of many works was to cause erotic excitement and gratification, regardless of the realities of life and art. On the other hand, others were clearly used as vehicles for political, religious, and social discourses. If erotic literature does offer an escape from the harsh realities of life, then it is easy to see why it emerged as a major force during this period.

LOUISE HILL CURTH

Selected Works

All of the primary works are available in digital form to subscribing institutions on the Proquest database *Early English Books Online.* Those that can be found in hard-copy format are listed below.

Donne, John. *The Elegies.* Bloomington: Indiana University Press, 2000.

Fletcher, John. *The Custom of the Country.* London: Nick Hern, 1998.

Jonson, Ben. *Volpone.* Edited by Robert N. Watson. 2nd ed. London: A & C Black, 2003.

Marlowe, Christopher. *All Ovid's Elegies.* In *The Complete Works of Christopher Marlowe.* Edited by Roma Gill. Vol. 1. Oxford: Clarendon Press, 1987.

Rochester, John Wilmot. *The Complete Works.* Edited by Frank H. Ellis. London: Penguin, 1994.

Venette, Nicolas. *Conjugal Love, or, The Pleasures of the Marriage Bed.* New York: Garland, 1984.

Further Reading

Bloch, Ivan. *Sexual Life in England Past and Present.* London: Oracle, 1996.

Crawford, Patricia. "Sexual Knowledge in England, 1500–1750." In *Sexual Knowledge, Sexual Science: The History of Attitudes to Sexuality,* Edited by R. Porter and M. Tiech, 82–106. Cambridge: Cambridge University Press, 1994.

Foxon, David. *Libertine Literature in England, 1660–1745.* New York: University Books, 1965.

Hunt, Lynn, ed. *On Pornography: Obscenity and the Origins of Modernity, 1500–1800.* New York: Zone Books, 1993.

Johns, Adrian. *The Nature of the Book: Print and Knowledge in the Making.* Chicago: University of Chicago Press, 1999.

Moulton, Ian Frederick. *Before Pornography: Erotic Writing in Early Modern England.* Oxford: Oxford University Press, 2000.

Porter, Roy. "The Literature of Sexual Advice Before 1800." In Porter and Tiech, *Sexual Knowledge, Sexual Science,* 134–57.

Porter, Roy, and Lesley Hall. *The Facts of Life: The Creation of Sexual Knowledge in Britain, 1650–1950.* London: Yale University Press, 1995.

Tang, Isabel. *Pornography: The Secret History of Civilisation.* London: Macmillan, 1999.

Thompson, Roger. *Unfit for Modest Ears: A Study of Pornography, Obscene and Bawdy Works Written or Published in England in the Second Half of the Seventeenth Century.* London: Macmillan, 1979.

Wagner, Peter. *Eros Revived: Erotic of the Enlightenment in England and America.* London: Secker and Warburg, 1988.

ENGLISH: UNITED KINGDOM, EIGHTEENTH CENTURY

The English 18th century provides an especially fertile field for the study of the development of erotic literature. Beginning as it does with "libertine literature," ending with the emergence of "pornography" proper, and fueled in between by the meteoric rise of the novel, erotica disentangled itself from its many generic tributaries and assumed its modern identity as the more artistically inclined category of sexually explicit representation.

Libertine literature at the end of the 17th century appeared in England as "whore dialogues," as various other kinds of irreverent and anti-ecclesiastical satire, and as scandal fiction. Although they can be very different in tone and subject matter, whore dialogues feature dramatic conversations between an older, experienced woman and a younger, inexperienced maid. Direct descendants of Pietro Aretino's *Ragionamenti* (1536), these dialogues were imported into England by way of France. Chief among them were Michel Millot's *L'Ecole des filles* (1655), Nicolas Chorier's *Satyra sotadica* (1660), and Jean Barrin's *Vénus dans le cloître* (1683). The first became *The School of Venus* (1680), the second *A Married Lady and a Maid* (1740), and the third *Venus in the Cloister* (1725). England's foremost libertine poet at the end of the 17th century was John Wilmot, second earl of Rochester (1647–80). His poetic invectives employed sexual obscenity in the service of social and political satire. Circulated at court in manuscript form, Rochester's poetry was first published after his death and went on to become a staple of the 18th-century "curious" book trade. Less obscene, more erotic, and much better known was Aphra Behn's scandal fiction. *Love-Letters Between a Nobleman and His Sister* (1684), for example, like scandal fiction generally, retold a well-known political scandal of the day. Written as a series of letters, it experimented with language's ability to re-create sexual passion. It too, along with Behn's plays and short fiction, was readily available in early-18th-century England.

During the first decades of the century, however, neither Rochester's poetry nor Behn's fiction dominated the market: they took their places alongside bawdy street ballads, sensational medical manuals, obscene travelogues, trial proceedings, and criminal biographies—as well as the infamous and often reprinted whore dialogues. Libertine literature, in other words, assumed myriad forms. Satirical, rationalist, anti-ecclesiastical, it delighted in the ease with which the indisputable realities of the body could be used to mock the pious ideals of church and state.

After the novel moved to center stage, however, which coincided with the unprecedented popularity of Samuel Richardson's *Pamela* (1740), libertine literature gradually receded from the cultural marketplace. Its educated irreverence and quick wit gave way before the novel's ability to create sexual passion for character and reader alike. John Cleland's *Memoirs of a Woman of Pleasure* (1749), or *Fanny Hill*, as it is better known, provides the case in point and a watershed moment for English erotica. Before *Fanny Hill*, erotic and/or obscene literature was intermixed and intermingled with other genres and subgenres. Whore dialogues combined lascivious passages with sex education, anti-ecclesiastical diatribes, and radical philosophy. Medical treatises vacillated between sound advice about sexual disorders and lurid tales from pseudo-science. Travelogues figured distant lands as female genitalia and punned their way shamelessly through the allegory. Trial proceedings re-created the sensational events of notorious criminals and captured all of the unspeakable details from high-profile divorces. Bawdy poetry kept the seventeenth-century ballad alive and well. After *Fanny Hill*, the novel slowly pushed aside its competitors and assumed its place as the genre of choice.

The undisputed champion of unscrupulous booksellers in early-18th-century London was Edmund Curll, and for almost half a century—from roughly 1705 to 1745—he dominated the "curious book" trade. Alongside his more legitimate offerings, one could have found an impressive selection of bawdy works—Rochester's poetry and Behn's fiction certainly. John Marten, who wrote *Gonosologium novum* (1709), a salacious treatise on venereal disease, was in Curll's employ. So was Robert Samber, who translated the infamous whore dialogue *Venus in the Cloister* (1725). Thomas Stretzer, who wrote the obscene travelogue *A New Description of Merryland* (1741), produced that and numerous other books for Curll's shop. In the literary world of the early 18th century, before *Fanny Hill* and pornography proper, in a world where all sorts of very different books experimented with the representation of human sexuality, Edmund Curll was a central figure, and his bookshop serves as an apt emblem for a terrain vastly different from the literary landscape of today.

Street ballads were a common feature of 18th-century London, and many dealt with risqué subjects. *The Pleasures of a Single Life* (1701), *The Fifteen Comforts of Cuckoldom* (1706), and *The Fifteen Plagues of a Maiden-Head*

(1707) are typical of the genre. *The Pleasures of a Single Life* enjoyed a short-lived popularity and spawned numerous imitations. It relates how one man's imprudent marriage destroys the peace and tranquillity of his solitary life. After the joys of bachelor paradise are enumerated, the villain is introduced, and it is obvious that her adulterous behavior is not long to follow:

> But the curs'd Fiend from Hell's dire Regions sent,
> Ranging the World to Man's destruction bent,
> Who with an Envious Pride beholding me,
> Advanc'd by Vertue to felicitie,
> Resolv'd his own Eternal wretched State
> Should be in part reveng'd by my sad Fate;
> And to at once my happy Life betray,
> Flung Woman, faithless Woman, in my Way:
> Beauty she had, a seeming modest Mein,
> All Charms without, but Devil all within,
> Which did not yet appear, but lurk'd, alas, unseen.

In *The Fifteen Plagues of a Maiden-Head* (1707), a woman laments her continued virginity and complains of what the early 18th century termed "green sickness":

> Of late I wonder what's with me the Matter,
> For I look like Death, and am as weak as Water,
> For several Days I loath the sight of Meat,
> And every Night I chew the upper Sheet;
> I've such Obstructions, that I'm almost moap'd,
> And breath as if my Vitals all were stop'd.
> I told a Friend how strange with me it was,
> She, an experienc'd Bawd, soon grop'd the Cause,
> Saying, *for this Disease, take what you can,*
> *You'll ne'er be well, till you have taken Man.*

Cheaply produced and cheaply consumed, poems like these were most likely read aloud in pubs and coffeehouses.

Medical manuals were also an important source of sexual information, alternatively objective and scientific and prurient. John Marten's medical treatise *Gonosologium novum, or a New System of the Secret Infirmities and Diseases, Natural, Accidental, and Venereal in Men and Women* was prosecuted for obscenity in 1709. It was the first time that the author—rather than the printer or publisher—was named in the case; and it was also the first time that a medical treatise was charged with an offense against civic morals. Published as an appendix to the sixth edition of Marten's *A Treatise of all the Degrees and Symptoms of the Venereal Disease* (1708), the *Gonosologium novum* represents a long line of medical works that combine some knowledge of anatomy with folklore, fable, and prurient curiosity. Other popular works of the period include *Aristotle's Master-piece* (1690), which was not by Aristotle, and *Onania, or, The Heinous Sin of Self-Pollution, and All its Frightful Consequences in Both Sexes* (1708). Both went through numerous editions throughout the course of the century. Marten's prose is typical of the genre:

> *Platerus* tells us he saw a *Clitoris* once in a Woman, as big and as long as the neck of a Goose. Indeed the *Clitoris* in a Woman is very like a Man's *Yard*, its end is like the *Glans* or *Nut* of a Man's, and erects and falls as a Man's does, and as in Men the seat of the greatest Pleasure is in the *Glans* or *Nut*, so is this in Women, for therein is the rage and fury of Love, and there has Nature plac'd the peculiar seat of Pleasure and Lust, from whence 'tis call'd *Amoris Dulcedo* and *Aestrum Veneris*; for the Man's *Yard* rubbing in Copulation against the Womans *Clitoris*, causes those excessive Ticklings, delightful Itchings, and transporting Pleasures to both Sexes; and the more of that Serous Matter (before spoken of) the Woman sheds in the Act, the greater still is the Pleasure in both, for as the Man's *Yard*, and principally the *Nut* of it, fills with Spirits in the Actions of Love, so also does the Womans *Clitoris* at the same time, which conjunctly together, gives that charming Delight to those Parts, and the whole Animal Functions, which, as to relate is inexpressible, so in the Act sometimes it is almost unbearable, especially where both Parties meet with equal Desire and Freedom; for if we love Persons whose Inclinations are answerable to ours, and whole Parts are proportionable, our Flame is happy, and nothing but Pleasure, Delight, and Tenderness, is the consequence of our lawful Love; for the Enjoyments which attend the Actions for the continuance of our kind, are the highest gratifications of our Senses that can be.

Marten enthusiastically supports the physical pleasures of procreation, but unlike the street ballads—which seem resolutely misogynistic—*Gononsologium novum* is careful to make men and women equal partners in the experience.

Venus in the Cloister (1725) was the most important whore dialogue of the early 18th century. translated by Robert Samber, *Venus* was published by Edmund Curll and, like *Gonosologium novum*, incurred prosecution. Expanded from the original three dialogues into five, the 1725 edition included strongly worded anti-ecclesiastical sentiments and several graphic scenes involving flagellation. The story of Curll's trial was told first by Ralph Straus in *The Unspeakable Curll* (1927)

417

and then repeated by David Foxon in 1965, only to be revised recently by Alexander Pettit. Curll's trial is important first because the bookseller was the foremost purveyor of libertine literature in the early 18th century, and second because the prosecution set the standard for English obscene libel law for the next two hundred years.

Another important subgenre of libertine literature was the obscene travelogue. *A New Description of Merryland* (1741) figures female genitalia as a distant and exotic land. *Merryland* traces its roots to Charles Cotton's *Erotopolis. The Present State of Betty-land* (1684). Thomas Stretzer, the author of *A New Description,* was also responsible for both *The Natural History of the Arbor Vitae, or Tree of Life* (1732), which combines botany and erotica in an effort to satirize the scientific enthusiasms of the day, and *Merryland Display'd: or plagiarism, ignorance, and impudence, detected. Being observations, on a pamphlet intitled A new description of Merryland* (1741), which purports to refute the earlier work. Edmund Curll, in a characteristic attempt to corner the market, was responsible for printing both *A New Description* and *Merryland Display'd.* The former went through seven editions in 1741 alone. Similar titles of the same type include *The Natural History of the Frutex Vulvaria or the Flowering Shrub* (1732) and *Teague-root Display'd: Being Some Useful and Important Discoveries Tending to Illustrate the Doctrine of Electricity, in a Letter from Paddy Strong-Cock to W– W————N* (1746).

Also popular throughout the 18th century, and readily available in Curll's bookshop, was criminal literature: biographies of famous rapists, murderers, and thieves, or sensational accounts of their trials. Even so respectable an author as Henry Fielding (1707–54) tried his hand. In 1746 he published *The Female Husband: or, The Surprising History of Mrs. Mary, alias Mr. George Hamilton,* a cross-dressing Methodist lesbian who seduced unsuspecting women for financial gain. Related in kind to the *Old Bailey Session Papers* and the *Accounts from Tyburn,* Fielding in *The Female Husband* is at once horrified by and fascinated with lesbian transgressions. Particularly interesting is his association of lesbian lust with Methodist "enthusiasm."

After Cleland's *Memoirs of a Woman of Pleasure* appeared in 1749, Edmund Curll's world of obscene travelogues and pseudo-medical manuals slowly disappeared. The confusing genre mishmash sorted itself out according to rules more acceptable to a modern audience. Medical treatises would continue their preoccupation with venereal disease and masturbation but would eventually learn to stick with fact and leave the longer imaginative flights to the novelists. Bawdy poetry and obscene travelogue writing would move into periodicals, where prose fiction would slowly gain the upper hand. Criminal accounts and trial proceedings would remain popular, but with less pressure on writers to re-create the crime with fictionalized immediacy. After *Memoirs of a Woman of Pleasure,* in other words, the novel becomes the genre of choice for those wishing to arouse an audience. Curll's deceptions and depravities—his bawdy poetry, his books on flogging and venereal disease, his treatises on hermaphrodites, his extended parodies of contemporary botany, his editions of Behn and Rochester, his trial accounts and proceedings—would all lose their appeal, and in hindsight appear a bit silly, adolescent even. By 1789, the year the Bastille fell, sexual obscenity and the novel were joined at the hip.

The novel, of course, played a crucial role in the cultural life of the 18th century, and scholars have made much of its unique influence upon the modern state. The industrial revolution moved people into cities, increased available goods and services, and expanded the middle classes. With more leisure time and increasing literacy, more and more people turned to novels for entertainment.

Interestingly, the novel began the century in disgrace: it was an illegitimate, subliterary form dominated by both women writers and women readers. Delarivier Manley (1663–1724) and Eliza Haywood (1693–1756) were two early novelists who, along with Aphra Behn (1640–89), borrowed freely from restoration drama and were unembarrassed to foreground sexual intrigue in their fiction. Popular and impassioned, these novels captured the attention of critics, who deplored what they saw as their cheap sensationalism and pleaded for the refined pleasures of high literature. Before long, male authors, attracted by profit and aware of other options for prose fiction, sought to reform the genre. Samuel Richardson (1689–1761), among others, made the case for the novel as a didactic form capable of educating young readers. *Pamela* (1740) took London by storm and replaced the scheming viragos of Behn, Manley, and Haywood with a virginal heroine capable of pushing all depraved souls to the moral high ground. Cynics, like Henry Fielding and John Cleland (1709–89), found Richardson's sanctimonious preaching hard to take and responded in kind, Fielding with *Shamela* (1741) and *Joseph Andrews* (1742) and Cleland—arguably—with *Memoirs of a Woman of Pleasure*. Cleland offered readers a novelistic "realism," in which characters actively pursued a "real" sexual pleasure that was in turn vicariously accessible.

Following Cleland's lead, British erotica at the end of the 18th century flourished in cheap serials like *The Bon Ton* (1791–95) and *The Bacchanalian Magazine* (1793), in novels like Matthew Lewis's gothic fantasy *The Monk* (1796), and in French imports like the Marquis de Sade's *Justine* (1791) and *Juliette* (1799).

Lewis's revision of Ann Radcliffe's gothic formula retained the mysterious landscapes of an unspecified past but exchanged the virginal heroine ever-anxious about sexual violation for a libidinous monk eager to pursue newfound pleasures. Whereas the former creeps around castles and graveyards perplexed by men whose status as hero or villain is never entirely clear, the latter yields to one temptation after another until he has raped and murdered his way to an unfortunate end. Radcliffe's denouements, in which supernatural events are given rational explanations, yield to Lewis's finale, in which the Devil appears in all his satanic splendor. Throughout *The Monk,* Lewis's erotic imagination teases readers with titillating glimpses of forbidden pleasures.

The 18th century began with libertine literature—not only with the obscene poetry of Rochester and the scandal novels of Aphra Behn, but also with bawdy poetry, sensational medical manuals, whore dialogues, criminal literature, and obscene travelogues. Erotica as we know it hardly existed. It appeared briefly whenever authors found themselves describing a seduction or a conquest, only to disappear when the larger purpose—e.g., satiric, historical, medical—intervened. By the end of the century, however, both serious authors like Lewis and Radcliffe and unprincipled hacks who wanted to earn a few shillings had realized how beautifully the novel could represent sexual passion—for the enjoyment of character and reader alike. Although the modern pornography industry was still decades away, the erotic imagination was alive and well.

BRADFORD K. MUDGE

Selected Works

Anon. *The Fifteen Comforts of Cuckoldom*, 1706
———. *The Fifteen Plagues of a Maiden-Head*, 1707
———. *The Natural History of the Frutex Vulvaria or the Flowering Shrub*, 1732
———. *The Pleasures of a Single Life*, 1701
———. *Teague-root Display'd*, 1746
Barrin, Jean. *Venus in the Cloister*, 1725
Behn, Aphra. *Love-Letters Between a Nobleman and His Sister*, 1684
Chorier, Nicolas. *A Married Lady and a Maid*, 1740
Cleland, John. *Memoirs of a Woman of Pleasure*, 1749
Cotton, Charles. *Erotopolis. The Present State of Bettyland*, 1684
Fielding, Henry. *The Female Husband*, 1746
Lewis, Matthew. *The Monk*, 1796
Marten, John. *Gonosolgium novum*, 1709
———. *A Treatise of all the Degrees and Symptoms of Venereal Disease*, 1708
Millot, Michel. *The School of Venus*, 1680
Strezer, Thomas. *The Natural History of the Arbor Vitae, or Tree of Life*, 1732
———. *A New Description of Merryland*, 1741
———. *Merryland Display'd*, 1741

Further Reading

Ballaster, Rosalind. *Seductive Forms: Women's Amatory Fiction, 1684–1740.* New York: Oxford University Press, 1992.
Bold, Alan, ed. *The Sexual Dimension in Literature.* New York: Barnes & Noble, 1982.
Bouce, Paul-Gabriel, ed. *Sexuality in eighteenth-century Britain.* Manchester: Manchester University Press, 1982.
Brewer, John. *The Pleasures of the Imagination: English Culture in the Eighteenth Century.* New York: Farrar Straus Giroux, 1997.
Castle, Terry. *Masquerade and Civilization: The Carnivalesque in Eighteenth-Century English Culture and Fiction.* Stanford, CA: Stanford University Press, 1986.
———. *The Female Thermometer: Eighteenth-Century Culture and the Invention of the Uncanny.* New York: Oxford University Press, 1995.
Foucault, Michel. *The History of Sexuality: An Introduction.* New York: Vintage, 1980.
Foxon, David. *Libertine Literature in England, 1660–1745.* New York: University Books, 1965.
Gallagher, Catherine. *Nobody's Story: The Vanishing Acts of Women Writers in the Marketplace, 1670–1820.* Berkeley and Los Angeles: University of California Press, 1994.
Gilbert, Ruth. *Early Modern Hermaphrodites: Sex and Other Stories.* New York: Palgrave Press, 2002.
Hitchcock, Tim. *English Sexualities, 1700–1800.* New York: St. Martin's, 1997.

Hunt, Lynn, ed. *Eroticism and the Body Politic*. Baltimore: Johns Hopkins University Press, 1991.

———. The Invention of Pornography: Obscenity and the Origins of Modernity, 1500–1800. New York: Zone Books, 1996.

Jordanova, Ludmilla. *Sexual Visions: Images of Gender in Science and Medicine Between the Eighteenth and Twentieth Centuries*. Madison: University of Wisconsin Press, 1989.

Kendrick, Walter. *The Secret Museum: Pornography in Modern Culture*. New York: Penguin, 1987.

Laqueur, Thomas. *Making Sex: Body and Gender from the Greeks to Freud*. Cambridge: Harvard University Press, 1990.

Loth, David. *The Erotic in Literature*. New York: Dorset Press, 1961.

McCalman, Ian. *Radical Underworld: Prophets, Revolutionaries, and Pornographers in London, 1795–1840*. Cambridge: Cambridge University Press, 1988.

Moulton, Ian. *Before Pornography: Erotic Writing in Early Modern England*. New York: Oxford University Press, 2000.

Mudge, Bradford K. The Whore's Story: Women, Pornography, and the British Novel, 1684–1830. New York: Oxford University Press, 2000.

——— Sex and Sexuality. Parts Three and Four. Erotica, 1650–1900, from the Private Case Collection at the British Library, London. London: Adam Matthew, 2003.

Paulson, Ronald. *Popular and Polite Art in the Age of Hogarth and Fielding*. Notre Dame, IN: University of Notre Dame Press, 1979.

Pettit, Alexander, and Patrick Spedding, eds. *Eighteenth-Century British Erotica*. 5 Vols. London: Pickering & Chatto, 2002.

Phillips, Kim, and Barry Reay, eds. *Sexualities in History: A Reader*. New York: Routledge, 2002.

Porter, Dorothy, and Roy Porter. *Patient's Progress: Doctors and Doctoring in Eighteenth Century England*. Stanford, CA: Stanford University Press, 1989.

Porter, Roy, and Robert Mulvey, eds. *Pleasure in the Eighteenth Century*. New York: New York University Press, 1996.

Shattuck, Roger. *Forbidden Knowledge: From Prometheus to Pornography*. New York: St. Martin's Press, 1996.

Stanton, Domna. *Discourses of Sexuality: From Aristotle to AIDS*. Ann Arbor: University of Michigan Press, 1992.

Stevens, Walter. *Demon Lovers: Witchcraft, Sex, and the Crisis of Belief*. Chicago: University of Chicago Press, 2002.

Straus, Ralph. The Unspeakable Curll, being some account of Edmund Curll, bookseller; to which is added a full list of his books. London: Chapman and Hall, 1927.

Wagner, Peter. *Eros Revived: Erotica of the Enlightenment in England and America*. London: Secker & Warburg, 1988.

Warner, William. *Licensing Entertainment: The Elevation of Novel Reading in Britain, 1684–1750*. Berkeley and Los Angeles: University of California Press, 1998.

See also **Cleland, Cotton.**

EPIGRAMS AND JESTS

Poggio Bracciolini's boast that his *Facetiae* flooded all of Europe was not an idle one (see the entry on Poggio). Variants of his jests appear in collections throughout Europe from 1450 onward; indeed, collections of jests and of epigrams, the other major form employed for rendering the bawdy or comic aspect of sexuality in a terse mode, were a staple in early modern Europe from the beginning of printing onward. G. Legman sees Poggio as the father of the modern dirty joke, and anyone interested in pursuing the modern joke, as it developed from the jest, would be well served to read through the two hefty tomes of Legman's *Rationale of the Dirty Joke*. The jest vogue in England was

particularly long-lived, dating from the appearance of several of Poggio's tales at the end of Caxton's edition of Aesop's *Fables* (instructive in and of itself in terms of transmission of texts from the German collector and translator Heinrich Steinhowel in the 1470s to the French translation by Julien Macho in 1480 and so on to Caxton in 1484) and *A C. Mery Talys* in 1525 well into the 17th century and beyond. It should be noted that the collections of Poggio and many others were essentially the work of humanists, so that while the material has always been of interest to folklorists and more recently scholars engaged in cultural studies, these works are hardly representative of folk culture or "lower class" literature. Riddles and paradoxical encomia are even more learned modes in which bawdy humor plays a significant part. Jests are continuously recycled in these collections, often without attribution, whether in detached collections or in collections that purport to be about a single figure (e.g., Scoggin or Tarlton). While many of the jests included in these collections have nothing to do with matters sexual (they often are nothing more than the supposed witty remark of a particular personage or a very short tale with a moral appended), a goodly number are what we (and readers at the time) would term bawdy. The humor in this material is particularly revealing with regard to societal norms and values, as Keith Thomas has pointed out in his commentary on the early modern jest. If the jest often turns on witty verbal ripostes or comments, the players and narrative actions are stock and formulaic. Thus shrews and scolds, wives who will not be controlled, are held up to ridicule, but so are foreigners, members of the clergy, peasants, and the most despised and comic figure of all, the impotent, stupid cuckold. Wives who deceive deserving cuckolds or braggart husbands are rarely ridiculed, but rather are admired. Thus the husband who brags to his wife about having had sexual relations before marriage with another woman who was then foolish enough to confess her sin gets his comeuppance when his wife allows that she did the same, and with the family servant, for years before marriage and never said a word. Lubricious clergymen are proverbial from Poggio on, of course, and venal papist clerics are given new life in England's most ardently protestant collections. Farts are let in the most public of places (and foisted on others in ways that prove doubly embarrassing to the perpetrator). Doctors are quacks who make wildly inappropriate diagnoses that sometimes actually work because sexual intercourse is touted as the best remedy for all female disorders.

Jest material also found its way into another form in English literature in the early modern period, the epigram. From John Heywood's collection of epigrams (numbering 600 in the 1562 edition) on into the 17th century, the art of the epigram was practiced by such notables as Sir John Davies, John Donne, Everard Guilpin, Sir John Harington, and Ben Jonson, as well as such lesser lights as Henry Parrot and Samuel Pick. As Guilpin noted in one of his epigrams

addressed to the reader, it is expected that an epigram will be bawdy; readers should not "some wanton words to blame, / They are the language of an Epigramme." The players in these verses are many of the same who hold the scene in jests; witty wives, clever courtesans, sycophantic courtiers, sexually voracious widows, and stupid cuckolds are the stock figures. Often the epigrammatists work from classical models (Martial being the favorite, of course); bawdy puns are critical to the humor of many of these poems, as well as a traditional use of metaphors from the musical and military realms. Two examples should suffice, the first from Everard Guilpin (1598):

> The world finds fault with *Gellia*, for she loues
> A skip-iack fidler, I hold her excus'd,
> For louing him, sith she her selfe so proues:
> What, she a fidler? Tut she is abus'd?
> No in good faith; what fidle hath she vs'd?
> The *Viole Digambo* is her best content,
> For twixt her legs she holds her instrument.

The second example comes from Henry Parrot (1613):

> A Souldier once a Widdow would haue woo'd,
> But being poore and loath to be deni'd,
> Durst not impart how he affected stood,
> Which she as soone thus censur'd as espi'd:
> *You may be valiant (sir) but seeme vnlusty,*
> *That either haue no weapon, or tis rusty.*

Even more than the jests, the epigrams depend upon the economical setting of the scene, an understanding of stock figures (with regard to sexuality, social standing, and intelligence), and language that is manipulated in a witty fashion.

Taken together, jests and epigrams give an especially good picture of the humor in matters sexual in the early modern period and help us understand the movement to the dirty joke.

DAVID O. FRANTZ

Selected Works

Bracciolini, Poggio. *The Facetiae of Giovanni Poggio Bracciolini*. translated by Bernhardt J. Hurwood. New York: Award Books, 1968.

Davies, Sir John. *The Poems of Sir John Davies*. Edited by Robert Krueger. Oxford: Clarendon Press, 1975.

Guilpin, Everard. *Skialetheia*. Edited by D. Allen Carroll. Chapel Hill: U of North Carolina P, 1974.

Harington, Sir John. *The Letters and Epigrams of Sir John Harington*. Edited by Norman E. McClure. Philadelphia: U of Pennsylvania P, 1930.

Hazlitt, W. C., ed. *Shakespeare Jest-Books*. 3 vols. 1864. Reprint, New York: Burt Franklin, 1964.

Parrot, Henry. *Laquei ridiculosi: or Springes for Woodcocks*. London: 1613.

Pick, Samuel. *Festum voluptatis, or the Banquet of Pleasure*. London: 1639.

Further Reading

Frantz, David. *Festum voluptatis: A Study of Renaissance Erotica*. Columbus: Ohio State UP, 1989.

Hudson, H. H. *The Epigram in the English Renaissance*. 1947. Reprint, New York: Octagon Books, 1966.

Legman, Gershon. *The Rationale of the Dirty Joke*. 2 vols. New York Grove Press, 1968. Vol. 2 published as *No Laughing Matter*, New York: Breaking Point Inc, 1975.

Thomas, Keith. "The Place of Laughter in Tudor and Stuart England," *TLS* 3906 (26 Jan. 1977): 77–81.

Thompson, Roger. *Unfit for Modest Ears*. London: Macmillan, 1979.

Wilson, F. P., "English Jestbooks in the Sixteenth and Early Seventeenth Centuries." *Huntington Library Quarterly* 2 (1938–39): 121-58.

ERNAUX, ANNIE

1940–
French writer

Although Annie Ernaux cannot be classified as a writer of erotic literature, sexuality, particularly in relation to social class, gender, and writing, is an important theme in several of her texts. In the early works *Les armoires vides* (1974) and *Ce qu'ils disent ou rien* (1977), the narrative traces the female protagonist's adolescent discovery of sexual pleasure. These texts contain strikingly vivid descriptions of an active desiring female subject and of the intense physical pleasure she experiences in her first sexual encounters. In *Les armoires vides*, this capacity for physical pleasure pre-dates adolescence, and the narrator describes a childhood delight in the pleasures of all of the senses: "But the world was mine, made up of a thousand pieces to hunger after, to thirst after, to touch and to tear" (*Les armoires vides*, trans., 31). There is a clear connection between these depictions and the representation of adolescent sexual pleasure, which is marked by a generalized sensuality. Despite strong social and religious constraints and controls, Ernaux's young heroines pursue their pleasures with determination and even recklessness: "My body is alive in a thousand places and I know that they have not all yet been revealed" (*Les armoires vides*, trans., 94).

In *Passion simple* (1992), Ernaux turns to the depiction of adult desire. In an overtly autobiographical text, Ernaux describes a liaison with a Soviet diplomat. The book opens with the evocation of images from a pornographic film, which are scarcely visible because Ernaux does not own a decoder for the encrypted channel. After this point, although the physical nature of the relationship is made clear, the details are mostly absent from the text—the images of the opening in some ways standing in for this absence. Almost ten years later, in 2001, Ernaux published the *journal intime* she had kept during the period of this relationship, under the title *Se perdre*. The title implies total abandonment to desire, loss of self in the experience of passion. In this text, sexual pleasure is depicted more overtly, and the narrator, unlike her adolescent predecessor, is sexually experienced and dominant. The Russian lover undergoes a kind of sexual apprenticeship and is transformed, becoming a flexible and responsive lover, physically if not emotionally: "A thought: in Leningrad he was very clumsy (shyness? or relative inexperience?). He is becoming less awkward, so am I a kind of initiator? I am delighted with this role, but it is fragile, ambiguous. There is no promise that the relationship will last (he might reject me as a whore)" (*Se perdre*, 28).

As this quotation suggests, the narrator's sexual dominance is undermined by emotional insecurity. In *Passion simple* and *Se perdre,* the narrator is at the same time dominant in terms of sexual savoir faire, fame, and beauty, and is subjugated to her desire. The strength of her passion is such that it dominates her thoughts, and as we learn from the dreams recounted in *Se perdre,* even her unconscious. Although the lover is passionately involved on a physical level, there is no sense of an equivalent obsession. Furthermore, with less time and leisure to devote to the liaison, he dictates the terms of when and how often the lovers will meet. However, this is not merely a sado-masochistic game designed to increase erotic pleasure. The lover thus takes on the power of the mother who determines when the infant will be nurtured, and in his absence, the female narrator becomes an abandoned child, suffering a form of terror in this abandonment. In both texts, but particularly in the *journal intime,* Ernaux constantly underlines her own association of passion with death, grief, and mourning. In a characteristic moment of self-analysis, she herself points to the parallels between her relationship with her lover and the mother–daughter fusion which is a theme of *Une femme* and *"Je ne suis pas sortie de ma nuit"*: "I read in a psychoanalytical article that the 'terror beyond words'—how I love that phrase—experienced by babies, the terror of separation from the mother, is gradually overcome. A crucial stage is achieved when the child is able to retain an image of the mother in her absence" (*Se perdre,* 224). My analysis, which is presented in Thomas 1999 and 2005, and broadly based on object relations theory, is that Ernaux's narrators, like the other mainly white Western women discussed by the object relations theorists, never fully reach that stage of development. In this sense, total abandonment of self to the Other and resulting feelings of terror and panic, a kind of emotional freefall, are a feature of certain occidental femininities. From this perspective, erotic passion is inevitably linked to emotional suffering. For Ernaux, writing provides the only way out of this impasse and is sometimes seen as having the potential of filling a profound emotional void.

However, there is another side of the coin in Ernaux's writing. In a short text entitled "Fragments autour de Philippe V.," the narrator seems able to retain both the image of her lover and her sense of her own power. It is she who initiates the sexual relationship: "I kept going back to this gesture, my hand in his hair, without which nothing else would have happened. The memory of this gesture, more than anything else, filled me with intense, almost orgasmic pleasure. It occurred to me that it was of the same nature

as the act of writing the opening sentence of a book" (Ernaux in Thomas 1999, 178). The lovers also literally preserve the moment of their sexual encounter. They make love lying on a piece of paper and keep the image created by the mix of sperm and menstrual blood which results: "We did the same thing in the following two or three months. It had become an added pleasure. The impression that the orgasm was not the end of everything, that a trace of it would remain" (ibid.). Here we perhaps find the realization of Ernaux's tentative indications of the potential of writing in *Passion simple* and *Se perdre.* We also find an evocation of Barthesian *jouissance* and a clear association of the domains of writing and of the erotic.

In *L'Usage de la photo,* jointly written with Marc Marie and published in 2005, Ernaux returns to the association of passion with loss and death. The text includes fourteen photographs of "landscapes after love"—the lovers' clothes, abandoned while making love. As Ernaux and Marie wrote their texts separately and in relation to these images, an intertwining narrative of the relationship develops. However, alongside the love story is "'the other scene,'" the scene of the battle which was being played out in my body—a blind, stupefying—is this really happening to *me*?—struggle between life and death," for during the relationship and the writing, Ernaux was being treated for breast cancer (*L'Usage de la photo,* 12). In this text, the struggle to "preserve a trace of our moments of passion," through the photographs and the writing, is constantly accompanied by the presence of the threat of death and a sense of the transience of human relationships. Nonetheless, here, as in "Philippe V.," Ernaux transgresses a number of taboos—she depicts the male body as object of her desire, she is both vulnerable and powerful, and perhaps most tellingly of all, she seems to escape from the cycle of physical pleasure followed by emotional pain. The lover is present in the text both as writing subject and object of desire, and illness and treatment become the sites for eroticism and emotional intimacy: "My stay at the Curie Institute for my operation was the sweetest of times. The tumour and ganglions had been removed. The analysis of the tissues would tell us whether a complete mastectomy would be necessary. M. spent hours in my embrace. The smiles of the nurses and auxiliaries indicated their approval" (*L'Usage de la photo,* 12). This writing of the female body in illness as actively desiring and desirable fully justifies the claim that Ernaux's writing of the erotic is profoundly feminist.

Biography

Born in Lillebonne in 1940, Annie Ernaux grew up in Yvetot and studied literature at the University of Rouen. She taught in secondary schools in Annecy and Cergy-Pontoise (Paris region), where she still lives. Subsequently, and until her retirement in 2000, she prepared students for the CAPES teaching qualification by distance education. She is the author of fourteen books published by Gallimard and one work on writing authored jointly with Frédéric-Yves Jeannet and published by Editions Stock. Her first three works are autobiographical novels, whereas in all the other works, which incude diaries, Ernaux refuses the novel as form and makes a clear autobiographical pact with the reader.

LYN THOMAS

Selected Works

Les Armoires vides. Paris: Gallimard, 1974; translated by Carol Sanders, *Cleaned Out,* Illinois: Dalkey Archive Press, 1990.

Ce qu'ils disent ou rien [*What They Say Goes*]. Paris: Gallimard, 1977.
Une femme. Paris: Gallimard, 1988; translated by Tanya Leslie, *A Woman's Story,* London: Quartet Books, and New York: Seven Stories Press, 1990.
Passion simple. Paris: Gallimard, 1992; translated by Tanya Leslie, *Passion Perfect,* London: Quartet Books, and *Simple Passion,* New York: Seven Stories Press, 1993.
"Je ne suis pas sortie de ma nuit". Paris: Gallimard, 1997.
Se perdre. Paris: Gallimard, 2001.
L'Écriture comme un couteau. Entretien avec avec Frédéric-Yves Jeannet. Paris: Stock, 2003.
L'Usage de la photo. With Marc Marie, 2005.
"Fragments autour de Philippe V." In *L'Infini* 56 (Winter 1996): 25–6; translated in appendix 1, Thomas 1999, 177–79.

Further Reading

Day, L. "Class, Sexuality and Subjectivity in Annie Ernaux's *Les armoires vides.* In *Contemporary French Fiction by Women: Feminist Perspectives,* edited by M. Atack and P. Powrie. Manchester and New York: Manchester University Press, 1990.
McIlvanney, S. *Annie Ernaux: The Return to Origins.* Liverpool: Liverpool University Press, 2001.
Thomas, L. *Annie Ernaux: An Introduction to the Writer and her Audience.* Oxford and New York: Berg, 1999.
———. *Annie Ernaux, à la première personne.* Paris: Editions Stock, 2005.
Thumerel, F., ed. *Annie Ernaux: Une oeuvre de l'entre-deux.* Arras: Université d'Artois- Presses, 2004.

EROS

In the ancient Greek tradition, the word *érōs* expressed and paradoxically unified the psychosomatic and metaphysical modes of human desire. The former can be satisfied, though temporarily; the latter is insatiable.

In the Homeric epics (8th century BCE), which provide examples of satisfiable desire, eros commonly denotes a craving for food and drink. Eros as sexual desire is controlled by the goddess Aphrodite. After she has saved Paris from the sword of Menelaus, Aphrodite relieves his stress by causing him to desire Helen more than when he first saw her and snatched her from Sparta (3.442). The goddess forces Helen, whose passion has now cooled, to satisfy Paris' burning eros (3.414–417). Similarly, with the help of Aphrodite's magical girdle that can fulfill any sexual wish (14.223), Hera makes Zeus feel a stronger eros for her than he has ever felt for another woman, even for Hera herself (14.294, 315). Covered by a golden cloud, they make love on Mount Ida, from which the battlefield can be seen. Exhausted, Zeus falls sound asleep, while one of the fiercest battles of the Trojan War, involving men and gods, is taking place. These two scenes show that sexual gratification defines

Aphrodite's patronage. In the *Odyssey,* in turn, the goddess Athena controls eros by leaving it unfulfilled. She awakens young Nausicaa's sexuality and uses her strong attraction to Odysseus to help him earn the Phaeacians' sympathy, which is crucial for his survival (6, 1–245). She inflames the hearts of Penelope's suitors with eros (18.212–13) without any intention of satisfying it. On the contrary, Athena's goal is to weaken the suitors and justify their punishment. Thus, in the story of the *Odyssey,* almost entirely directed by the virginal goddess of wisdom, war, and handicraft, Athena, the power of eros is for the first time redirected toward goals beyond the sexual or even against it. In Virgil's *Aeneid* (1st century BCE), Aphrodite/Venus, who plays Athena's guiding role in Aeneas' journey, uses the power of eros, now personified as her son, Cupid, to kindle erotic passion in Queen Dido and assure a warm reception for Aeneas at Carthage (1.907–940). True to her nature, however, and risking the anger of the marriage goddess, Juno, Venus makes sure that Dido's sexual desire for Aeneas is fulfilled, at the price of Dido's suicide later, when Aeneas abandons her.

Hesiod's *Theogony* (late 8 century BCE) introduces two personifications of desire. As a creative and procreative principle, Eros is a primeval cosmic deity, a limb-melter, who overpowers the mind of gods and humans (120–1). As Aphrodite's aspect, Eros appears, without a genealogy, on the day of the goddess's birth and becomes her attendant (221).

A fragment by Parmenides (5th century BCE), "she devised Eros first of all the gods," suggests that desire as a cosmic principle occupied the minds of some pre-Socratic philosophers. The Orphic religious movement, which took shape in the 6th century BCE, personified eros as Phanes, who, being both "female and father," initiates all creation (Guthrie, 80, 100–102). In an Orphic account of the beginning, given by Aristophanes (5th century BCE) in his comedy *Birds,* Eros hatches from a "wind-sown" egg, born by Night. He mingles all things together, from which Heaven, Ocean, Earth, and the gods are born. In all accounts, the origin of the cosmic eros as a principle of creation remains obscure, but it is omnipresent. Consequently, any epistemic interest in the universe must involve eros. Thus the metaphysical concept of eros is conceived.

The physical eros, in its turn, personified as Aphrodite's attendant in the *Theogony,* gradually becomes a fully developed, multifaceted mythological character. Greek lyric poetry gives a strong impact to this development by capturing eros's paradoxical character. Sappho (7th century BCE) expresses eros oxymoronically: sweet–bitter, pleasure–pain, love–hate. Initially represented as a young man, Eros progressively rejuvenates to become a mischievous winged baby-boy with a bow and arrows, the Roman Cupid, and is said to be a son of Venus by Mercury or Mars, or of Iris by Zephyr. In Ovid's *Metamorphoses* (early 1st century CE), a work about desire as a creative force, Cupid's dark side is shown. He makes the god Apollo burn with passion for Daphne but hits her with an arrow that causes hate. After a long chase, Daphne turns into a laurel tree, thus leaving Apollo's desire forever unsatisfied (1.452–567). For the first time, sexual gratification is withdrawn by Cupid himself, and at that from a god as powerful and desirable as Apollo. Ovid's Cupid also assists in the abduction and rape of Prosepine by Pluto, the god of the underworld (5.346–571). Although he denies it, Cupid probably caused the incestuous love of Myrrha for her father (10.298–502).

On the whole, Greek lyric poetry and Ovid's *Metamorphoses* demonstrate how sexual desire, though in principle satisfiable, can be a source of uncertainty and torment for both humans and gods. It is irrational and unpredictable, like baby Cupid's behavior. Along with the Orphic vision of eros as a universal principle, the awareness of the inherent complexity of eros's psychosomatic mode prepared the grounds for a merger with its metaphysical mode. It first occurred in Plato's dialogue *Symposium* (385–378 BCE).

In the *Symposium,* several prominent Athenians, gathered at a male drinking party, deliver speeches in praise of the god Eros. By ethical, religious, scientific, mythological, and aesthetic arguments, employed in accordance with the speaker's particular occupation, each eulogy justifies pederasty. Gratification of his lover's sexual desire will make the beloved boy a better citizen, the speakers imply. To Socrates, however, desire is insatiable by nature. His eulogy, relating the teaching of Diotima, a priestess who instructed young Socrates in the art of eros, shows erotic experience as climbing from one form of partial fulfillment of desire for the beautiful to another. Sexual desire for a particular youth is only the first step in one's eros-driven journey toward the "absolute, pure, unpolluted by human flesh" (211e) metaphysical idea of the Beautiful. Sigmund Freud, who insisted that "the enlarged sexuality of psycho-analysis coincides with Eros in the divine Plato" (*Three Essays on the Theory of Sexuality,* 1920), would have qualified Socrates' eulogy as a praise of the successful sublimation of sexual desire into desire for other forms of creativity, with education and absolute knowledge at the top. As the speech of the uninvited guest Alcibiades at the end of the *Symposium* reveals, however, Plato must have realized that redirecting physical eros toward a metaphysical object could work for Socrates and a handful of virtuous philosophers, but not for everyone. Years ago, the older and unattractive Socrates had rejected the sexual advances of the famously handsome young Alcibiades but was willing to share with him his eros for knowledge. Now a prominent politician and a general, Alcibiades still feels wounded by the unsatisfied physical desire of his youth. He loves and hates Socrates, who, like Eros, is able to kindle uncontrollable desire in others but appears to be in full control of his own desire. In his *Confessions* (397–400), St. Augustine tells about his ordeal of climbing the ladder of eros.

Apuleius (2nd century CE) shows the ambivalence of the Platonic understanding of eros in the tale of Cupid and Psyche, inserted in his novel *Golden Ass.* The tale can be read as an allegory of the soul's disastrous desire to know the physical eros instead of just experiencing it in the darkness. Knowing eros means losing it. After much hardship, the two lovers marry in heaven. Psyche becomes immortal and gives birth to a daughter, Pleasure. Only in the abstract realm of eternity could the curious, reflective soul truly unite with eros's immediacy. This changes after courtly love is invented and glorified by the French troubadours in the 11th–13th centuries and after the term "platonic love" (coined in the 15th century by Marsilio Ficino to describe Socrates' relationship with his followers) begins to be applied to an intimate, affectionate relationship without sex. The impossibility of satisfying sexual desire is converted into a source of poetic inspiration. Dante's *Divine Comedy* (early 14th century) is perhaps the most fascinating example of unfulfilled, sublimated physical eros.

Modern romantic love seems to be a continuation of the ancient non-Platonic eros, exemplified in Aristophanes' speech in Plato's *Symposium.* Aristophanes explains the origin of sexual desire and its insatiability by telling a myth according to which Zeus cut humans into two halves as a punishment for their hubris. Consequently, everyone is longing for his or her other half, although after the first generation of those divided creatures, such a "half" simply does not exist. Hence eros is a longing for physical completeness that can never be fully satisfied. Since the ideal physical union is not possible, romantic lovers are looking for "soul mates." Thus, romantic love endorses the earthly marriage of Cupid and Psyche, or of physical and spiritual desire. This combination of immediacy and reflectivity makes for an inexhaustible literary theme.

Pure physical eros, however, has found its own niche in literature. The best examples of Western erotic literature explore the tension between the psychosomatic and the metaphysical modes of desire and tend to engage in the centuries-long dialogue on the ambivalent, paradoxical nature of eros. For example, Thomas Mann's novella *Death in Venice* (1912) epitomizes the Platonic chase of eros's meaning: its protagonist frantically pursues a beautiful young boy, described as the god Eros himself. In *Ulysses* (1922), through Molly Bloom's character, James Joyce gives voice to what may be heard as repressed sexual desire in Homer's Penelope. Vladimir Nabokov, in *Lolita* (1955), creates the concept of the nymphet, symbolic of the immediacy and transience of eros. The namesake character of the novel is both realistic and, through numerous literary allusions (from Plato and Ovid to Proust and Poe), symbolic of the writer's enchantment with eros.

KATIA MITOVA

Further Reading

Barthes, Roland. *A Lover's Discourse. Fragments.* Translated by Richard Howard. New York: Noonday, 1993.

Bartsch, Shadi, and Thomas Bartscherer, eds. *Erotikon: Essays on Eros, Ancient and Modern.* Chicago: University of Chicago Press, 2005.

Carson, Anne. *Eros the Bittersweet.* Princeton, NJ: Princeton University Press, 1986.

Guthrie, W. K. C. *Orpheus and Greek Religion.* Princeton, NJ: Princeton University Press, 1993.

Korn, Irene. *Eros: The God of Love in Legend and Art.* New York: Todtri, 1999.

Lewis, C. S. *The Four Loves.* New York: Harcourt Brace, 1960.

Loraux, Nicole. *The Experiences of Tiresias: The Feminine and the Greek Man.* Translated by Paula Wissing. Princeton, NJ: Princeton University Press, 1995.

Mills, Jane, ed. *Bloomsbury Guide to Erotic Literature.* London: Bloomsbury Publishing, 1993.

Paz, Octavio. *The Double Flame: Love and Eroticism.* San Diego: Harcourt Brace, 1995.

Rougemont, Denis de. *Love in the Western World.* Translated by Montgomery Belgion. New York and London: HarperCollins, 1974.

EROTIC ASPHYXIATION

The term *erotic asphyxiation* describes sexual practices in which pleasure is gained by depriving the brain of oxygen, resulting in temporary euphoria. This can be achieved by means of strangulation, suffocation, or hanging. It is most usually practiced by men as an accompaniment to masturbation. Depriving the brain of oxygen prolongs the erection and intensifies orgasm. When practiced alone, as part of onanism, it is termed auto-erotic asphyxiation. Recreational asphyxia can also occur between sexual partners as an accompaniment to intercourse, and is a frequent feature of (particularly gay male) pornography and sadomasochistic sexual iconography.

Contemporary detective narratives and erotic thrillers, on both page and screen, are the most popular representational loci of this sexual practice. Erotic asphyxiation allows for a handy twist in the traditional epistemology of detective fiction. The conventional understanding of motive is turned on its head, as the burden of blame and guilt is taken off the perpetrator and placed instead on the victim, who literally died of pleasure. A highly misogynistic example of this conceit is seen in Michael Crichton's political thriller *Rising Sun* (1992). The frequency of this motif in works of popular culture is attested to ironically in Thomas Harris's thriller *The Silence of the Lambs* (1988), when Dr. Hannibal Lecter tells Clarice Starling that a patient who boasted of murdering his lover was more likely to have killed him accidentally during "some banal erotic asphyxia transaction."

The somewhat bizarre nature of this practice means that it provides a source of dark humor in some high-culture literary texts. In his poem "Bohème de chic" in the collection *Les Amours jaunes* (1873), the proto-Symbolist French poet Tristan Corbière uses the simile "roide comme un pendu" [stiff as a hanged man], in a pun which plays on the associations of rigor mortis and erection, drawing ribald attention to the effect of hanging on the male physiognomy. Similarly, in Samuel Beckett's *Waiting for Godot* (1948), when considering suicide, Vladimir and Estragon joke pruriently about the beneficial side effects of being hanged.

Owing to its erection-enhancing properties, erotic asphyxiation is usually associated with male sexuality. However, a favored trope of eighteenth- and nineteenth-century novels is the eroticized constriction of the female form by the wearing of corsets. The archetypal figure of the swooning woman, overcome by desire and shortness of breath combined, is embodied in eponymous heroines Moll Flanders (Daniel Defoe, 1722), Clarissa (Samuel Richardson, 1747–48), and Madame Bovary (Gustave Flaubert, 1857). Thus, a disguised form of erotic asphyxiation is linked, by means of heavily codified cultural-historical stereotypes and practices of femininity, to women's sexuality.

One rare example of erotic asphyxiation featured in female-authored erotic writing as a conscious and explicit part of female sexual fantasy is found in the French novella *Le Boucher* [The Butcher] (1988) by Alina Reyes. *The Butcher* contains a short description of what appears to be a mild form of erotic asphyxiation, where the protagonist's lover applies pressure to her neck during a session of lovemaking: "[T]u t'asseyais sur moi, mettais tes mains autour de mon cou,

427

doucement tu serrais, et le plafond tournait" [You sat on top of me, put your hands around my neck, softly you squeezed and the ceiling swam before my eyes]. Here, the act is described in terms that reflect its heady and sensuous effects. However, the neutral, detached tone that characterizes the narrative means that the significance of this episode is hard to interpret and the narrator's pleasure is not described in any detail.

The flip-side of the desire to be deprived of oxygen for sexual pleasure would be the desire to strangle the other in the interests of inflicting simultaneous torture and arousal. The constriction of the throat during sexual intercourse also causes the vagina or anus to tighten, heightening the pleasure for the penetrator. In de Sade's *Justine* (1787, 1791, and 1797/1799), one of the many sadistic libertines into whose hands Justine falls has a particular penchant for deathly games. The cellars of Roland's chateau contain the paraphernalia of the gothic aesthetic: skeletons, severed heads and bones, as well as a wax effigy of a naked woman and a collection of coffins. It is in this atmospheric chamber that Roland will play with Justine's mortality—buggering and strangling her and then forcing her to stand on a stool while a noose is placed around her neck. If she is to evade death, she must cut the cord in the nick of time when the masturbating libertine kicks the stool from under her feet. Erotic asphyxiation here shades into the necrophilic imagination, as Roland's thrill is achieved by engineering an encounter between life and death. In *Juliette* (1797), the giant Minski takes the erotic conceit a step further, when he strangles a young girl to death while raping her.

These tableaux from de Sade doubtless influenced many scenes in English Gothic and French Decadent writing, nineteenth-century aesthetic schools which privilege the most extreme and morbid features of the human imagination. One good example is Joris-Karl Huysmans's Decadent masterpiece of Satanism, sadism, and madness, *Là-Bas* (1891), which dwells on lurid descriptions of Gilles de Rais's habit of half-hanging victims before cutting their throats.

Probably the most striking literary example of this phenomenon is found in Georges Bataille's celebrated pornographic novel *Histoire de l'oeil* [*The Story of the Eye*] (1928). In one episode involving blasphemy and torture, the female protagonist Simone strangles an aging priest until his penis is erect. She then straddles his erection and continues to squeeze his throat while having intercourse with him. On the point of death, he ejaculates into her, uniting *la mort* and *la petite mort* in the most literal way. Bataille's philosophical writing on pornography holds that sexuality is inevitably equated with death in the human imaginary. This is because sex effects the psychological trangression and dissolution of the boundaries between self and other, doing violence to our sense of integrity and separateness. This phenomenon is referred to by psychoanalysts as "ego annihilation." In light of Bataille's philosophy of sexuality, erotic asphyxiation (alongside vampirism, bloodletting, and sadomasochistic torture) becomes a privileged trope with which to express literally the liminal nature of sexual experience, the collusion of Eros and Thanatos.

LISA DOWNING

Further Reading

Aaron, Michele, ed. *The Body's Perilous Pleasures: Dangerous Desires and Contemporary Culture*. Edinburgh: Edinburgh University Press, 1999.

Bataille, Georges. *Erotism: Death and Sensuality*. Translated by Mary Dalwood. San Fransisco: City Light Books, 1986.

———. *The Accursed Share*. Translated by Robert Hurley. 3 vols. New York: Zone, 1991–98.

Dollimore, Jonathan. *Death, Desire and Loss in Western Culture*. Harmondsworth: Penguin, 1998.

Downing, Lisa, and Dany Nobus. "The Iconography of Asphyxiophilia: From Fantasmatic Fetish to Forensic Fact." *Paragraph: A Journal of Modern Critical Theory* 27 (2004): 1–15.

Kunzle, David. *Fashion and Fetishism: A Social History of the Corset, Tight-Lacing and Other Forms of Body-Sculpture in the West*. Harmondsworth: Penguin, 2002.

Nobus, Dany. "Une jouissance à couper le souffle: à propos d'un cas d'asphyxie auto-érotique." *La cause freudienne: Revue de psychanalyse* 31 (1995): 117–23.

Nobus, Dany, Julien Quackelbeen, and Karin Temmerman. "Auto-Erotic Asphyxiation: A Sexual Practice in Neurosis and Perversion." *Clinical Studies: International Journal of Psychoanalysis* 3 (1997), 31–54.

Quackelbeen, Julien, and Karin Temmerman. "Auto-Erotic Asphyxia from Phenomenology to Psychoanalysis." *The Letter: Lacanian Perspectives on Psychoanalysis* 8 (1996): 42–60.

ESQUIVEL, LAURA

1950–
Mexican novelist, screenwriter

Laura Esquivel is the author of novels, short stories, film scripts, children's books, and journal articles. Esquivel's writings are infused with eroticism and carry a message of love, harmony, and the satisfaction of sexual desire in female–male relationships. In her novels—*Like Water for Chocolate, The Law of Love, Swift as Desire*—Esquivel expresses her refusal to categorize masculinity and femininity. Instead, she unifies them in one sphere of masculine-feminine understanding, sensuality, and pleasure which is reached through the wisdom of erotic energies connected by external elements such as food or music. In her works, Esquivel also explores the existence of true love based on strong emotions and erotic electricity. A flow of positive energy and high sexual desire is established between twin souls. Their extreme voluptuousness translates into the deepest orgasms and such an intense level of mental and physical unity that twin souls blend seamlessly into one being.

Esquivel uses parody and humor to deconstruct the traditional values of patriarchal society, in which powerful and corrupted subjects, either sexually repressed or sexually abusive, exercise their power over other people's lives. Her works represent the demystification of obedience and passive sexuality in women, dismissing these notions as mere social constructions. She overturns Latin American feminine subordination, creating female characters that make their own decisions and are open to erotic experimentation. Esquivel's heroines enjoy masturbation, premarital sex, lustful thoughts, and casual sex—aspects of sexuality previously reserved for Latin American men and absolutely condemnable in women.

Like Water for Chocolate

In her first novel, *Like Water for Chocolate* (1989), Esquivel blends highbrow as well as popular cultural values and narrative forms. In this parodic novel the author subverts the principles of "feminine literature" (*folletín, culebrón,* magazines for women, cookbooks, etc.), rewriting and revalorizing them. Esquivel mixes a tragicomic love story with traditional culinary recipes from her own family. The novel illustrates the close relationship between cooking and loving, food and sex. Both the kitchen and the bedroom have traditionally been considered spheres of repression and prohibition for women. Esquivel states that these places are absolutely essential, redefining kitchen and bedroom as spheres of freedom, where gastronomic and sexual pleasure are activated thanks to feminine activeness and knowledge.

The story in *Like Water for Chocolate* is about the life of Tita De La Garza, who lives in northern Mexico during the early 1900s, a time of revolution. Being the youngest daughter, she is required by family tradition to remain single and to care for her tyrannical mother. When Tita is forbidden to marry Pedro, her true love, Pedro marries Rosaura, Tita's sister. Unlike Tita, Rosaura represents the sexually repressed and morally alienated woman. Her rotten body symbolizes her inability to enjoy both delicious food and voluptuous sex.

Tita has the magical power of expressing her desires and emotions through the food she prepares, provoking high sensual experiences in some and terrible digestive problems in others. Tita's quail in rose-petal sauce prompts such a powerful sexual ardor in Gertrudis, Tita's oldest sister, that Gertrudis is able to satisfy her impetuous internal desire only after working in a brothel for months. The connection between the culinary and the erotic is also established by the frequent comparisons between cooking food over a fire and Tita's body burning with passion. The intensity of Tita and Pedro's unsatisfied sexual desire is sublimated in voluptuous glances and the unbearable fire of passion that burns them alive. Forced to respect social conventions for many years, during their first and only uninhibited sexual encounter, Tita and

Pedro's all-consuming sexual power ignites every corner of the ranch.

In Esquivel's *Like Water for Chocolate,* social and sexual feminine stereotypes are broken down, reasserting the notion that cooking and sex are realms that belong to a revaluated feminine culture.

The Law of Love

Esquivel's *The Law of Love* (1995), parodies science fiction, soap operas, and adventure novels. Although highly satirical, it can also be read as a romantic novel about the power of true love and the interconnection between mind, body, and soul. Breaking with literary conventions, the novel contains illustrations and comes with a CD.

In the 16th century, Cortés' Captain Rodrigo profanes the Pyramid of Love, thus opening a period of unrestrained lust, violent passions, unsatisfied love triangles, and crimes. Set in 23rd-century Mexico City, the mission of Azucena, the heroine of the novel, is to reinstate the law of love on Earth. She is a young Mexican "astroanalyst" who uses music to encourage her patients to regress to their previous lives in order to heal the damage they have endured. Azucena tries to find her twin soul Rodrigo, who disappeared after only one night of voluptuous lovemaking. Advanced future technology makes it possible to retain one's Self (soul) and transfer it into another body "container," thereby enabling one to change his or her gender, race, and age. Esquivel uses such liberation of the body's characteristics to humorously exemplify the sexual power of stereotypical blondes in Mexican society, the rejuvenating effects of sexual activity in elderly people, and the possibility of abused women seeking revenge against their rapists.

The ability to inhabit another gender's body reaffirms the author's rejection of the feminine/masculine dichotomy. This idea is also illustrated in the passages where twin souls engage in sexual intercourse, reaching a complete fusion of mind, body, and soul. Regardless of the body's gender, every single atom penetrates and is penetrated, while dancing in harmony and experiencing an intense and continuous orgasm.

Swift as Desire

Published in 2001, Esquivel wrote this novel as a tribute to her father, who worked as a telegraph operator. Unlike her previous novels, the main character is a man. Júbilo is a telegraph operator gifted with the power of "hearing" other people's emotions. The waves of sensuality flowing between Júbilo and his wife Lucha allow Esquivel to establish a comparison between the telegraph and erotic pleasure. Júbilo's fingers transmit electrical impulses through Lucha's body. He sends her messages in Morse code using her clitoris. The contact of her vagina with his penis recharges their sexual batteries. The exchange of energies and thoughts during their lovemaking is similar to the transmission of electrical currents in telegraphic messages. As in her other novels, Esquivel represents an ideal of harmonious and reciprocal erotic desire that grows between true lovers, while rejecting the cult of violence and sexual aggressions inflicted on women as characterized by the hated figure of don Pedro and his rape of Lolita.

In her novels Esquivel subverts social and literary conventions in an attempt to liberate women from social and sexual repression. Nevertheless, her liberation of the feminine body takes place within the limits of "regulated" heterosexual relationships, and she does not go further by creating any erotic fantasies or sexual excesses that transgress these limits.

Biography

Laura Esquivel was born in Mexico City, where she attended Escuela Normal de Maestros and worked as a teacher for eight years. She married and later divorced Mexican actor and film director Alfonso Arau, with whom she has a daughter, Sandra, then married Javier Valdés. Esquivel's success rests on her acclaimed first novel, *Like Water for Chocolate* (1989), which quickly became a best seller, then a movie, for which Esquivel wrote the script and which won numerous Ariel Academy Awards in Mexico in 1992. Esquivel was named 1992 Woman of the Year in Mexico and received the 1994 ABBY award from the American Booksellers Association of the United States, a first for a foreign writer.

CRISTINA RUIZ SERRANO

Selected Works

Como agua para chocolate: Novela de entregas mensuales con recetas, amores y remedies caseros. Edited by

430

Editorial Planeta Mexicana, 1989; as *Like Water for Chocolate: A Novel in Monthly Installments, with Recipes, Romances, and Home Remedies,* translated by Carol Christensen and Thomas Christensen, 1992.

La ley del amor. Edited by Plaza and Janés, 1995; as *The Law of Love,* translated by Margaret Sayers Peden, 1996.

Tan veloz como el deseo. Edited by Plaza and Janés, 2001; as *Swift as Desire,* translated by Stephen Lytle, 2001.

Further Readings

Alemany Valdez, Herminia M. "Entre olores y sabores: El erotismo en tres narradoras hispanoamericanas: Castellanos, Esquivel y Buitrago." *Cuervo* 19 (1998): 3–11.

Cammarata, Joan F. "*Como agua para chocolate*: Gastronomía erótica, mágicorrealismo culinario." *Explicación de Textos Literarios* 25 (1996): 87–103.

Carrera, Liduvina. *La metaficción virtual.* Caracas: Unversidad Católica Andrés Bello, 2001.

Gant-Britton, Lisbeth. "Mexican Women and Chicanas Enter Futuristic Fiction." In *Future Females, The Next Generation,* Edited by Marleen S. Barr. Lanham, MD: Rowman and Littlefield, 2000.

Glenn, Katleen M. "Postmodern Parody and Culinary-Narrative Art in Laura Esquivel's *Como agua para chocolate.*" *Chasqui: Revista de Literatura Latinoamericana* 23 (1994): 39–47.

Saltz, Joanne. "Laura Esquivel's *Como agua para chocolate:* The Questioning of Literary and Social Limits." *Chasqui: Revista de Literatura Latinoamericana* 24 (1995): 30–37.

Vital, Alberto. "Erotismo, feminismo y postfeminismo." *Texto Crítico* 4 (1998): 25–34.

Whittingham, Georgina J., and Lourdes Silva. "El erotismo ¿fruto prohibido para la mujer? En *Como agua para chocolate* de Laura Esquivel y *Del amor y otros demonios* de Gabriel García Márquez." *Texto Crítico* 4 (1998): 57–67.

ESSAYS: NONFICTION

Essays have played an important part in the history of erotic writing, not least as it was in this format that many of the important new ideas about sexuality were first expressed. It should, however, be remembered that these essays followed on from earlier erotic nonfiction writing, viz., the nonfictional autobiography and the religious confession. One of the first places to look for erotic nonfiction is the autobiographies of the Roman Catholic saints, such as St. Augustine, who candidly wrote about masturbation, and St. Teresa of Avila, in whose *Life* is included a subtle discussion of lesbianism in her early life. Such religious *memoires,* while fruitful up to a point, should also be read conjunction with secular *memoires,* such as those by Jacques Cassanova and Jean-Jacques Rousseau. These sources often became the bases of later essays on erotic topics, as did the writings of the Marquis de Sade and others who described their sexual theories through the medium of fiction.

The essay is more closely related to the medical writing about sexuality that appeared more and more frequently. Medical works began to problematize sexuality in a different but comparable way as had the former religious tracts: by challenging commonsense approaches to sexual issues based on ideas about health and illness. An important text in this sense was Samuel Tissot's (1728–1797) *On Onania: or a Treatise upon the Disorders Produced by Masturbation* (1760), which reformulated the way that doctors addressed masturbation until the late nineteenth century. Tissot's impact on writing about masturbation was extreme. French author François Lallemand picked up on Tissot's proscription of masturbation and included many case histories about the problems associated with it, including a detailed description of the consequent illness, spermatorrhoea. The same could be said of the many other doctors who wrote about masturbation and the associated medical problems, such as William Acton (1814–1875). Acton and others also wrote about other aspects of sexuality, including venereal disease and male sexual development. Some doctors even went so far as to write about birth control, although this topic was not considered appropriate until the early twentieth century, and even then was suspect.

Erotic essays were not always associated with the medicalization of sexuality. The essay was a form utilized by Karl Heinrich Ulrichs, the German homosexual law reformer, who wrote numerous works which justified the existence of homosexuality, influenced important thinkers with his theory of homosexuality (i.e., a female soul in a male body, and vice versa), and attempted to repeal the notorious Paragraph 175 from the Prussian legal code, which criminalized homosexual behaviors. Ulrichs' impact was major. Homosexuals supported his attempts to repeal the anti-homosexual laws, and sexologists such as Richard von Krafft-Ebing adopted some of his thought on the topic. Ulrichs' writing had the effect of stimulating many other works on homosexuality.

Other responses to sexuality and the law also came in the form of essays. In the summer of 1885, the British journalist W.T. Stead wrote a series of articles for the *Pall Mall Gazette* about the white slave trade, entitled "The Maiden Tribute to Modern Babylon." These pieces decried the state of prostitution, and in particular childhood prostitution. He provided the reader with descriptions of the screams of virgins when being deflowered, and also explained how he had procured a young girl for the low sum of £5. The effect of Stead's campaign was to raise the age of consent from 13 to 16 and to further criminalize homosexuality to not only include sodomy, but also extend to "indecent acts" committed in public or private. This was realized by the 1885 Law Amendment Act, proposed by Henry Labouchere. It should be added that Stead's unscrupulous journalistic techniques landed him in prison for child abduction.

The discipline of sexology is an important one to consider in connection with erotic essays. It developed after the 1870s as a response to the lack of understanding about sexuality, not only in the forensic sciences, where explanations were sought by medical jurists for specific sex acts, but as a response to some of the significant developments in psychiatric theory, including the somaticism championed by Wilhelm Griesinger and others, and the psychological turn brought about by those interested in hypnotism. Attempts were made by sexologists to explain sexual perversions and normal sexual desires in terms of these theories.

An important early sexologist was the aforementioned Richard von Krafft-Ebing, who is most famous for his book *Psychopathia Sexualis*, first published in 1886. In this text, Krafft-Ebing categorized many different sexual "perversions" under the basic categories of homosexuality, sadism and masochism, and the fetishes. The book was itself a best seller, going through many updated editions. One of the reasons for its success was the vast number of case histories within the text which depicted so-called perverse sexual acts. These were read not only by doctors and lawyers, but also by the general public, some of whom enthusiastically wrote their own cases down for Krafft-Ebing and sent them in for his benefit.

The Berlin psychiatrist Albert Moll also made significant contributions to writing about sex. Apart from Moll's further investigations into homosexuality and child sexuality, he contributed a model of sexual desire that involved a general description of the two phases of (1) being aroused and (2) achieving orgasm. For Moll, these two phases were able to explain all individual sexual responses, regardless of the specificities of the arousal and the methods of attaining orgasm.

Other contributors of erotic essays included the English classicist John Addington Symonds, who emphasized the historical practices of homosexuality in two privately printed pamphlets in order to argue that it was not a perverse activity but a normal and natural phenomenon that had existed in some of the noblest cultures in the world, such as ancient Greece. Likewise Edward Carpenter, the sandal-wearing feminist vegetarian from Sheffield who advocated homosexual rights, used ethnological and historical evidence to argue that homosexuality was not perverse and that it should be acceptable to society at large.

The premier English sexologist, Havelock Ellis (1859–1939), contributed significantly to debates about sexuality in his vast *Studies in the Psychology of Sex* (1897–1928), in which Ellis gathers together as much historical, literary, and scientific evidence as possible to explain different sexual behaviors and to push a political agenda that involved sexual liberation and wider understanding of the sexuality of women and other sexual minorities. In this he was rather like his German counterpart, Magnus Hirschfeld. Both Ellis and Hirschfeld were interested in changing the world with regard to sexuality. In this they were a part of the longer sexological tradition of liberation.

There was significant contribution toward aspects of this sexual liberation by feminists in England, such as Stella Browne and Marie Stopes, both of whom utilized the findings of sexual science in their arguments for birth control and women's rights in sexual pleasure. Browne, Stopes, and the American Margaret Sanger thought that women should be erotically satisfied and that they should not live in fear of unwanted childbirth. Some of the feminist aspirations of other writers will be examined below.

The vision of sexuality that most captured the modern world was the psychoanalysis of Sigmund Freud (1856–1939). Although Freud adopted many ideas from sexology, he also contributed to the wider acceptance of ideas about childhood sexuality and about people's individual sexual development. Central to Freud's work was the concept of the libido as a pleasure-seeking drive that serves as the basis for dreams, desires, and actions. Freud has been criticized, however, for the attitudes toward female sexuality that he promulgated. In this respect, the work of some later psychoanalysts, such as Karen Horney and Clara Thompson, has been useful in treating women more like individuals and challenging some of Freud's more sexist assumptions. Other psychoanalytical work that should be mentioned has involved more detailed attention to the young child, which has in some instances been corrected, challenged, or elaborated by Melanie Klein, Anna Freud, Wilfred Bion, and others. Sexuality has played a varied role in the theories of these different analysts.

Apart from the diaspora of sexologists and analysts caused by World War II, including Otto Rank, Wilhelm Reich, and Max Marcuse, which led to a greater volume of work about sexuality and a wider readership interest, there were local interests in writing about sexuality that should be taken into account. As the majority of sexological texts were written in German, it is useful to address some of the other European traditions. One country that has often been associated with erotic writing has been France, although this is far more because of the reputation of French fiction throughout the nineteenth century. Apart from significant contributions to

psychoanalytic theory, by Jacques Lacan and others, there has been a philosophical tradition that has written about the erotic. Georges Bataille, author of the erotic fiction classic *Histoire de l'oeil* [*The Story of the Eye*] (1928), argued in a series of essays that sexual union causes a momentary indistinguishability between otherwise distinct objects, particularly love and death. These two themes of erotism and death were the major ones with which Bataille engaged, showing how they blend around agony and ecstasy. Bataille's approach was a development of some of the later writings of Sigmund Freud on Eros and Thanatos, the sex and death instincts, as well as engaging with de Sade's conception of pleasure.

In *The Double Flame: Love and Eroticism* (1993), Mexican Octavio Paz furthers Bataille's (and de Sade's) elucidation of the erotic by demonstrating how it surpasses the functional goal of sex. The erotic is treated by Paz as an integral fact of being human. But rather than taking the reader toward the violence through which both death and the erotic are welded together (for Bataille and de Sade), Paz emphasizes the outcome of this eroticism: love, which for Paz was considered a reason to exist.

Other French authors explored the violent aspects of eroticism through the writings of the Marquis de Sade. Important contributions to the reevaluation of de Sade's writing came from Pierre Klossowski, Simone de Beauvoir, and Roland Barthes, all of whom treated him as the point from which new thinking about sexual and social possibilities might be started. Not all of this attention was directed toward de Sade, however. A part of de Beauvoir's rethinking about the erotic was contained in her essay on the actress Brigitte Bardot, in which she considers the gender and erotic possibilities of films such as *And God Created Woman*.

Attention was also directed toward the erotic by the famed writer of erotica Anaïs Nin. In her essay "Eroticism in Women," Nin distinguishes between erotica and pornography: Pornography "bestializes sexuality" by bringing it "back to the animal level." Eroticism, on the other hand, "arouses sensuality without this need to animalize it." (*In Praise of the Sensitive Man*, 8). This eroticism is also seen in Roland Barthes, *Lover's Discourse*, which celebrates the erotic by focusing on desire from a semiotic perspective without addressing sexual impulses, giving us a text very different to earlier erotic essays about sex.

In America, the sexological tradition had been well established in the late nineteenth century, with authors like William Hammond, James Kiernan, and Harold Moyer contributing essays about sex to psychiatric journals. Beyond this early sexology which focused on the perversions, as had that of Europe, there was a push in American sexology to establish a normative sexual desire, meaning heterosexuality. This was done in the studies by Robert Latou Dickinson (1861–1950), Clelia Mosher (1863–1940), and Katherine Bement Davis (1860–1935). The most important example of such in the first part of the twentieth century came from Alfred Kinsey (1894–1956) and his coworkers, who published *Sexual Behavior in the Human Male* (1948) and *Sexual Behavior in the Human Female* (1953). Both of these texts were detailed descriptions of the sexual practices of Americans, and put forward images about them as far more sexually active—in many different, nonheterosexual ways—than had previously been thought. Needless to say, the "Kinsey Reports" were best sellers, regardless of the rather dry tone and detailed statistics (which failed to satisfy statisticians, however).

The next best-selling American sexological work was William Masters and Virginia Johnson's *Human Sexual Behavior* (1966), which concentrated on the physiological aspects of sex, rather than the social or psychological aspects (although these were touched on as well). The most important contribution of Masters and Johnson was their work on the female orgasm, which did much to challenge Freud's conception of the clitoral orgasm being an immature precursor to the "proper" or sexually mature vaginal orgasm. Masters and Johnson claimed that there were no physiological differences between the two.

Not all American erotic essays were sexological. Important essays were written in the 1950s and 60s which embodied the new spirit of postwar American sexual liberation, such as Norman Mailer's famous "The White Negro: Superficial Reflections on the Hipster." Mailer argued that the "hipster," the young white male who listened to jazz, embodied by Jack Kerouac and others, approached sex with a "negro" sensibility: that is, a brashness that Mailer did not see in white culture. A different response to

American sexuality was presented by Norman O. Brown, in *Loves Body* (1966). In this text, Brown explores what he saw as the human condition after the "fall from grace," based on the writings of Freud, Friedrich Nietzsche, D. H. Lawrence and others, through the use of aphorisms which had a certain resonance with his mid-sixties audience after a spiritualized sexuality.

Another significant resonance that was felt throughout America and the rest of the world in the 1960s was feminism. Not only was there interest in Betty Friedan's *The Feminine Mystique* and Germaine Greer's *The Female Eunuch,* but also widely published were texts which explored sexual and erotic possibilities from a feminist standpoint, such as Helen Gurley Brown's *Sex and the Single Girl* (1962) and *Sex and the Office* (1964). Not only did Brown in these two texts cause a sensation—celebrating female sexuality outside of marriage—but she also began writing a newspaper column, *Woman Alone.* In 1965 she became editor of *Cosmopolitan* magazine, which she redesigned as *the* publication for young women, by focusing on female sexuality. The circulation of *Cosmo* skyrocketed as a result, and Brown remained editor of the magazine until 1996.

Less subtle responses to the new sexual attitudes of the 1960s, and specifically to the erotic industry, came from the magazine *Suck,* a British publication that subverted male-focused erotic magazines such as *Screw, Mayfair,* and *Playboy.* The chief intellectual contributor to this magazine was Australian feminist Germaine Greer, who first published her justifiably famous essay "Lady Love Your Cunt" in *Suck* in 1971. This essay called for the acceptance of the female body by women and challenged the male-centered eroticization of the vagina apparent in male-focused erotica.

The body became both a site for feminist struggle and a site of eroticism in some of the more sophisticated feminist texts. Monique Wittig's *The Lesbian Body* (1973) insisted that a reinvented language was needed to better understand the experiences of women. She describes in graphic detail the bonding of two women lovers, their viscera entwining and disentangling as their relationship ebbs and flows between them. This new, embodied language was not necessary for many of the women contributing their fantasies to Nancy Friday's huge-selling discussion of female sexual desires and fantasies, *My Secret Garden* (1973). Friday's text is an analysis of different women's sexual dreams, which lends itself to erotic reading in the same way as does the sexological texts of the nineteenth century: through personalized accounts from real individuals, rather than heady prescriptions from theoretically savvy authors. Further feminist attention to sexuality, which also sold very well, came from Shere Hite, whose *The Hite Report on Female Sexuality* (1976) and *The Hite Report on Male Sexuality* (1981) both describe what men and women want in bed, how they are sexually satisfied, and what they communicate to their partners about their desires.

In her article "This Sex Which Is Not One," French psychoanalyst and philosopher Luce Irigaray questioned the assumption that female sexuality was dependent upon male sexuality, as is assumed in the Freudian canon. Employing a revised version of psychoanalysis that extended the implications of Karen Horney's work, Irigaray asked, "Where is female sexuality located if it always refers back to the penis? Where does female pleasure reside?" Underlying these questions is the criticism of Freud's insistence that the penis is the only true sex organ. Further, Irigaray posited female pleasure as auto-erotic, because a female is always touching herself:

> A women "touches herself" constantly without anyone being able to forbid her to do so, for her sex is composed of two lips which embrace continually. Thus, with herself she is already two—but not divisible into ones—which stimulate each other. (100)

Other feminist reformulations of female sexuality are myriad. They stretch from Gayle Rubin's feminist reappropriation of BDSM (bondage-discipline-sadomasochism) sexuality to the hardly erotic reactionary works of Sheila Jeffreys and other anti-sensualist feminists who oppose these feminist reworkings of the erotic with comments relating feminist reappropriations of desire to buying into male-centric fantasies about child pornography and universal rape.

To say that essays themselves are erotic is somewhat strange. They are, however, one of the key sites for the multiple engagements with eroticism, from sexological prescription to feminist resistance. People have read these essays for multiple reasons: as erotic stimulation, as information about sex, as political criticisms of sexual issues, and as documents by practitioners within specific fields of discourse about sex (such as sexologists). This survey has illustrated the breadth of discussion of eroticism within the essay form, although it is by its very nature a difficult task to give such an overview. What people take from the essays they read is always personal.

IVAN CROZIER

Further Reading

Barthes, Roland. *A Lover's Discourse: Fragments.* Translated by Richard Howard. New York: Hill and Wang, 1978.

Beauvoir, Simone de. "Brigitte Bardot and the Lolita Syndrome." Translated by Bernard Frechtman. *Esquire*, August 1959, 2–38. Reprinted as *Brigitte Bardot and the Lolita Syndrome*, New York, Reynal Press, 1960.

Greer, Germaine. "Lady Love Your Cunt." *Suck*, 1971. Reprinted in *The Mad Woman's Underclothes: Essays and Occasional Writings*. London: Pan Books, 1986. Reprinted without permission at http://www.f-word.org/essays

Hite, Shere. *The Hite Report on Female Sexuality*. New York: Macmillan and Bertelsmann, 1976.

———. *The Hite Report on Male Sexuality*. New York: Alfred Knopf and Bertelsmann, 1981.

Irigaray, Luce. *The Sex Which is Not One*, trans. Catherine Porter, Cornell UP, Ithaca, 1985.

Mailer, Norman. "The White Negro: Superficial Reflections on the Hipster." *Dissent* 4:3 (Summer 1957): XXX.

Masters, W.H., and V.E. Johnson. *Human Sexual Response*. Boston, MA: Little, Brown & Co 1966.

Nin, Anaïs. "Eroticism in Women." In *In Favor of the Sensitive Man, and Other Essays*. New York: Harcourt, Brace & Co., 1976.

Oosterhuis, Harry. *Stepchildren of Nature: Krafft-Ebing, Psychiatry and the Making of Sexual Identity*. Chicago, IL: University of Chicago Press, 2000.

Wittig, Monique. *The Lesbian Body*. Translated by David LeVay. Boston, MA: Becon Press, 1973.

ÉTIEMBLE, RENÉ

1909–2002
French essayist and novelist

René Étiemble wrote only one overtly erotic novel, *Blason d'un corps* (1961), which was published as a *récit*. Eroticism however, is a constant theme throughout the diverse domains of his oeuvre. His first novel, *L'Enfant de chœur* (1937), deals with the sexual education of a young boy and was deemed by critics as being outrageously erotic. His work as an editor, translator, and writer of prefaces made him an important purveyor of Eastern eroticism in France, the masterpieces of which he edited amongst nonerotic works in his collection *Connaissance de l'Orient*. In a later essay, *L'Érotisme et l'amour* (1987), he explained his position on eroticism as a school of tolerance and as a manner of opposing tyrannies, emphasizing eroticism's essential difference from pornography. The encyclopedist Étiemble, who authored the entry on "Littérature érotique" in the *Encyclopaedia Universalis*, advocated the humanism of eroticism. Eroticism is the proof that "man everywhere is the same in the flesh" and that provided that religion does not oppress his delights, "he can invent similar ingenious pleasures everywhere."

Both of the novels *L'Enfant de chœur* and *Blason d'un corps* are characterized by the fastidious observation of the flesh, in particular of physical scents and secretions. Disease and the desire of the sick body play an important part in both stories, haunted by the specter of syphilis in the first and tuberculosis in the second. Scientific precision in the description of the body is common to both novels. This links them to the rest of Étiemble's work, which is conceived as a pedagogical enterprise of demystification. In *L'Enfant de chœur*, situated in a puritan Catholic western province of France, the main character, the young André Steindel, fatherless, like the author himself, describes in intimate detail his relationship to his mother, whose naked and diseased body haunts him and whose stench "hypnotizes" him. After experimenting with "the necessary homosexuality of boarding schools," but "lacking a vocation" and encountering a schoolgirl aged only thirteen, he completes his sexual apprenticeship with a visit to a brothel, which ends not in satisfaction, but in shame and distress. The novel tells of the disarray in discovering the body, and the boy's visit is an introduction not so much to pleasure as to the suffering induced by the loss of innocence.

Written more than twenty years later, *Blason d'un corps* is, as the title suggests, a seemingly more pacified vision of the sexualized body. It deals with an eroticism of remembrance, since it is a posthumous elegy to shared pleasure in the form of a letter a man writes to his recently deceased lover. Eroticism appears not simply as a therapy for the body, but as a quest for otherness, as well as an instrument of knowledge. Yet it is at the same time damaging, as the now isolated narrative voice remembers, through its counting of the numerous wounds inflicted, awaited, and received. It is also associated with an attempted suicide, and the last wound it leaves in the void created by the disappearance of the lover is unhealable.

As an Orientalist editor, Étiemble's role in diffusing a refined eroticism, as opposed to "an Occidental sexual barbary," in France was on the one hand the result of a humanist concern with transcending cultural specificities (culminating even in the idea of an anti-religion of eroticism as a means of accessing the cosmic order), and on the other hand a view of Sinology as a way of purifying eroticism through a renewal of its overfreighted lexicon, leading to the project of constituting a universal treasure of the fundamental images of love.

Defining eroticism as the physical act of love, Étiemble recommends reading texts such as the *Kama Sutra* in order to free eroticism from the pornographic industry. Refusing at the same time "the metaphysical obscenity of Georges Bataille," he shows that his views on eroticism are not immune to moralism, castigating transgressions as deviances and perversions aimed at "satisfying strange and sad errors in human behavior: incest, bestiality and sadism."

Biography

René Étiemble was born January 26, 1909, in Mayenne, France, and obtained his baccalaureate degree at the Lycée de Laval before attending the Lycée Louis-le-Grand and later L'École Normale Supérieure (1929–32) in Paris. After completing his Agrégation in grammar (1932), he studied Chinese at the School of Eastern Languages, where he founded an association in support of Mao Zedong (1934) and joined the Thiers Foundation (1933–36), where he took part in the movements of writers against fascism. Invited to the Writer's Congress in Moscow, 1934, he met Yassu Gauclère, who was to become his first wife.

L'Enfant de chœur, his first novel, was published in 1937 by Gallimard. The same year, he was invited to teach at the University of Chicago, where he lectured until 1943 before joining the Office of War Information in New York. He then taught in Egypt at the University of Alexandria, where he founded the literary review *Valeurs* in 1945. Back in France in 1948, he continued publishing articles of literary criticism in the *Nouvelle Revue Francaise* and also in *Les Temps Modernes*. He received the Prix Sainte-Beuve in 1952. The same year, he had a disagreement with Sartre and also presented his doctoral thesis on *The Myth of Rimbaud*. He was elected professor of comparative literature at the Sorbonne in 1955, a post he would occupy until 1978. He published an anthology of the French novelists of the eighteenth century in the series *La Pléiade* and founded in 1956 (also through Gallimard) the collection *Connaissance de l'Orient*, which was supported by UNESCO and devoted to the promotion of non-European cultures.

His novel *Blason d'un corps* (1961) met with some scandal, whereas his essay on the decline of the French language, *Parlez-vous franglais?* (1964) earned him fame. He married Jeannine Kohn in 1963. Amongst his many and varied fields of interest, Chinese civilization was one of the most enduring, alongside his struggles against prejudice and racism and his major contribution to comparative literature. He died in Vigny (Eure-et-Loir) on January 7, 2002.

DOMINIQUE JEANNEROD

Selected Works

Novels

L'Enfant de chœur. Paris: Gallimard, 1937.
Peaux de couleuvre. Paris: Gallimard, 1948.
Blason d'un corps. Paris: Gallimard, 1961.

Short Stories

Trois femmes de race. Paris: Gallimard, 1981.

Essays

Hygiène des lettres, II, Littérature dégagée, 1942–1953. Paris: Gallimard, 1955.
Le Mythe de Rimbaud, II, Structure du mythe. 2nd ed. Paris: Gallimard, 1961.
Le sonnet des voyelles: De l'audition colorée à la vision érotique. Paris: Gallimard, 1968.
"Jeou P'ou-Touan ou Jou Pu-Tan." *Nouvelle Revue Française* (January 1963): 108–13.
Yun yu: Essai sur l'érotisme et l'amour dans la Chine ancienne. Geneva: Nagel ("Trésors inconnus"), 1969.
Parlez-vous franglais? Paris: Gallimard, 1973.
Mes contre-poisons. Paris: Gallimard, 1974.
Naissance à la littérature ou le Meurtre du père. Paris: Arléa, 1987.
L'érotisme et l'amour. Paris: Arléa, 1987.
Nouveaux essais de littérature universelle. Paris: Gallimard, 1992.

Editions and Prefaces

Crébillon, Claude-Prosper Jolyot de. *Les Égarements du cœur et de l'esprit*. Edited and annotated by Étiemble. Paris: Gallimard, 1977.
Jin Ping Mei. *Fleur en Fiole d'Or*. Preface by Étiemble. Paris: Gallimard/Bibliothèque de la Pléiade, 1985.
Li, Yu(1611–1680?). *Jeou-Pou-Touan ou la Chair comme tapis de prière*. Preface by Étiemble. Paris: Club français du livre, 1980.
Mori, Ogai. *Vita sexualis ou l'Apprentissage amoureux du professeur Kanai Shizuka*. Preface by Étiemble. Paris: Gallimard, 1981.
Romanciers du XVIIIe siècle. Preface by Étiemble. Paris: Gallimard, Bibliothèque de la Pléiade, 1965.
Senancour, Étienne de. *De l'Amour, selon les lois premières et selon les convenances des sociétés modernes*. Preface by Étiemble. Paris: Club français du livre, 1955.
Verlaine, Paul. *Oeuvres libres, les amies, femmes, hombres*. Preface by Étiemble. Paris: Cercle du livre précieux, Le Cabinet rose et noir, 1961.
For a complete bibiliography of Etiemble, see Levi and Kohn, *Étiemble, Le Mythe d'Étiemble*, 333–64.

Further Reading

Hornsby, David. "Patriotism and Linguistic Purism in France: Deux dialogues dans le nouveau langage françois and *Parlez-vous Franglais?*" *Journal of European Studies* (December 1998): 331–54.

Marino, Adrian. *Etiemble ou le comparatisme militant.* Paris: Gallimard, 1982.

Martin, Paul, ed. *Pour Etiemble.* Arles: P. Picquier, 1993.

Lévi, Angélique, and Jeannine Kohn-Étiemble. *Le Mythe d'Étiemble: Hommages, études et recherches.* Paris: Didier Erudition, 1979.

Peschel, Enid-R. "Étiemble: The Novelist as Healer." *USF-Language-Quarterly* 12 (1973): 35–42.

EXETER BOOK RIDDLES, THE

The author(s) and compilers of the Exeter Book will never be definitively known, but it is possible to hazard opinions about the nature and period of its composition. The manuscript was donated to the library of Exeter Cathedral (where it still remains) by Leofric, the first Bishop of Exeter, who died in 1072. Most scholars are generally agreed that some of the poetry and riddles could date back to the eighth century, although most of the work contained in the Exeter Book suggests a composition date of around 975. The Exeter Book comprises some of the most important poems written in Anglo-Saxon that survive from the period: "Christ," "The Seafarer," "The Wanderer," "Deor," "Juliana," "The Phoenix," "Widsith," "The Whale," "Wulf and Eadwager," "The Husband's Message," and "The Wife's Complaint," together with a collection of Anglo-Saxon riddles. It is these riddles, particularly those classified as "obscene" by some editors, that prove most interesting in terms of the erotic.

It could be argued that riddles by their very nature are erotic works of literature. Constantly offering readers, by definition, alternative and unsettled answers, riddles flirtatiously defer their own meanings, leaving the imagination to propose its own solution. The small number of so-called obscene riddles to be found in the manuscript are far from subtle in their use of double entendres, but the fact remains that many editors of the Exeter Book are at pains to reproduce more salubrious meanings or answers to them. The Exeter Book does pose problems for the modern reader not only because of the general difficulties of reading the original Anglo-Saxon, but also because of the specific and precise nature of the language in which the riddles were composed. No modern translation can offer readers the same suggestiveness, the same clues to the riddles' answers in an identical manner to those offered in the original. The difficulties are greatly increased by the need to make the riddles both soluble and enigmatic, something that cannot always be achieved. Any translator of Riddle 77 (answers: churn / a woman / sexual intercourse) must face the difficulty of making the riddle suggestive enough to allow its secondary meaning to be apparent while acknowledging that "churn" in Anglo-Saxon is *cyren*, a feminine noun. The translator therefore has to face the difficulty that "she" is too obvious, and "it" is so misleading it might leave the answer far too obscured.

In an attempt to defer some of the more eroticized elements of these riddles, some editors have even gone so far as to suggest that the solution of the riddle is not even the chief purpose of the genre. Riddle 74, for example, has the answers "onion" and "penis," depending on how prudish the reader might or might not be. The fact that both of these answers can be argued points to the presence of a subtler humor in Anglo-Saxon literature than some might suppose. The riddle that produces such diverse answers is able to do so only through the cleverly ambiguous nature of its phraseology. With the opening words "I am a wonderful thing, a joy to women," and references to "I stand up high and steep over the bed," "She seizes me, red, plunders my head," and a conclusion that is translatable as "Wet is that eye," the answer "penis" might appear fairly sure, but in frustrating the reader's certainty over the solution, the riddle itself acts as an eroticized form.

Like all riddles, those found in the Exeter Book function upon the principle of metaphor and resemblance. Part of the process of reading them depends upon a certain willingness to be open to the "calculated deception" of the form. This "deception" is evident in the continual plausibility of the alternative sexual meaning that works in parallel to the more acceptable answer. Riddle 79, for example, reads:

> I am hard and sharp, strong in entering,
> bold in coming out, good and true to my lord.
> I go in underneath and myself open up
> the proper way. The warrior is in haste
> who pushes me from behind a hero with his dress.
> Sometimes he draws me out, hot from the hole.
> Sometimes I go back in the narrow place—
> I know not where. A southern man
> drives me hard. Say what my name is.

The tame answer is a gimlet or poker; the obscene answer is obvious. As a riddle, however, the piece functions on three levels. First, it is a description of the functional object it claims to have as its answer—the poker. On a secondary level it is also simultaneously the description of the penis that provides its alternative answer. Thirdly, and perhaps most importantly, it is a piece that reflects back upon the reader something of his or her own assumptions about the description. In other words, part of the interest within these riddles must depend upon which of the two answers one reaches first. In this respect the riddles that deal with sex or the genitals are not innocent at all because the meaning is often all too clear from very early on. Riddle 75 supposedly offers the possibility of "key" as one answer, but the answer of penis or cock is apparent from the opening few words, "splendidly it hangs by a man's thigh." These pieces, in which the sexual imagery is crude and the riddle's only purpose is to be indecent, fail because

they deny the erotic possibilities that riddles and riddle solving can offer. The more successful riddles sustain the erotic element that is intrinsic to the form.

MARK LLEWELLYN

Editions

The numbers used in this entry correspond to the edition of the riddles Edited by Paull F. Baum.

The Riddles of the Exeter Book. Edited by Frederick Tupper, Jr. Boston: Ginn and Company, 1910.

The Exeter Book Part II: Poems IX–XXXII. Edited by W. S. Mackie. London: Early English Text Society, 1934.

The Exeter Book. Edited by George Philip Krapp and Elliott Kirk Dobbie. London: George Routledge and Sons Limited, 1936.

Anglo Saxon Riddles of The Exeter Book. Translated by Paull F. Baum. Durham, NC: Duke Univeristy Press, 1963.

The Exeter Book Riddles. Translated and edited by Kevin Crossley-Holland. Harmondsworth: Penguin Books, 1979.

Further Reading

Gameson, Richard. "The Origin of the Exeter Book of Old English Poetry." Anglo-Saxon England 25 (1996): 135–85.

Nelson, Marie. "Four Social Functions of the Exeter Book Riddles." Neophilologu 75:3 (July 1991): 445–50.

Rulon-Miller, Nina. "Sexual Humor and Fettered Desire in Exeter Book Riddle 12." In Wilcox, ed., Humour in Anglo-Saxon Literature.

Smith, D. K. "Humor in Hiding: Laughter between the Sheets in the Exeter Book Riddles." In Wilcox, ed., Humour in Anglo-Saxon Literature.

Tigges, Wim. "Snakes and Ladders: Ambiguity and Coherence in the Exeter Book Riddles and Maxims." In Companion to Old English Poetry, edited by Henk Aertsen and Rolf H. Bremmer. Amsterdam: Vrije UP, 1994.

Wilcox, Jonathan, ed. Humour in Anglo-Saxon Literature. Woodbridge, England: Brewer, 2000.

EXOTICISM

The near homophony of *exoticism* and *eroticism* has often led to a conflation of the two terms, with this purported synonymy fueled by the nineteenth-century idea, popularized by Sigmund Freud, that sexuality itself is somehow "exotic." Moreover, there is a tendency to classify certain erotic practices (regardless of the geographical location in which they take place or from which they originate) as "exotic," a categorization epitomized by the adoption of the French adjective *Exotique* for the title of a well-known 1950s American fetish magazine. Etymologically, however, the words remain entirely distinct. Exoticism is a highly complex term, describing processes that range from the domestication of radical difference (geographical, cultural, sexual, or otherwise) to the attempted perpetuation of this difference in contrast to the context in which it is represented or into which it is received (see Célestin 1996, Forsdick 2001, Moura 1998). The principal commentator on the exotic, the early-twentieth-century French traveler and author Victor Segalen, describes "sexual exoticism" in his *Essay on Exoticism* (1904–18) but uses this phrase to highlight the differences between the sexes and to avoid the overt eroticization of the exotic implicit in the work of his contemporaries, such as Pierre Loti and Pierre Loüys. Segalen's own novels, in particular *Les Immémoriaux* (1907, set in Tahiti) and *René Leys* (1922, set in Beijing), point nevertheless to the central role played by exoticism in erotic literature: i.e., the imaginary potential of "elsewhere"—and its often stereotyped inhabitants—to provide an outlet for a range of sexual desires, fears, and fantasies repressed or carefully policed at home (see Gay 1984).

Any exploration of this close kinship of the exotic and the erotic fully begins with a consideration of travel and colonial expansion, two practices whose often sexual motives are regularly occluded (see Gill 1995, Hyam 1990, Littlewood 2001, Stewart 2000). Travel to cultures deemed exotic takes individuals from their everyday surroundings, allowing escape not only from the social and moral codes of home, but also from its moral absolutes. Moreover, the practical circumstances of travel often provide a context and opportunity for sexual encounters—the hermetic environment of various means of transport provides a common frame for works of erotic literature (e.g., *Pleasure Bound: Afloat and Ashore*, 1908, 1909), just as detached encounters with a series of strangers allow sequential, varied, and instructive contact with a range of sexual partners and practices (e.g., the *Emmanuelle* series).

Exotico-erotic literature, relating a range of different journeys and experiences abroad, took a variety of forms: conventional novels and travel narratives were supplemented by alternative tourist guide books (e.g., *The Pretty Women of Paris, Being a Complete Directory or Guide to Pleasure for Visitors to the Gay City*, 1883) and a number of foreign sex manuals, as well as other translated texts that disseminated common perceptions of the inherent eroticism of the East (e.g. Sheikh Nefzaoui's *The Perfumed Garden*, Li Yu's *The Carnal Prayer Mat*, and the *Kama Sutra*). By the late nineteenth century, translation of Eastern erotica had also become a major contribution to the genre, especially in Britain and France, where fake translations of exotic works, provided with the trappings of scholarly authenticity, were common and very popular.

In erotic literature, an exotic decor is often seen as little more than a scene-setting device to permit the display of sexual activity (see Marcus 1966)—e.g., the anonymous *Pleasures of Cruelty* (c. 1880) is set in Turkey, but contains no Turkish characters and very few references to the country in which its action takes place. However, it must be recognized that the use of radically different cultures in erotic literature is often part of wider, preestablished processes of representation, appropriation, and domestication of hazily defined geographical areas such as the

Orient (see Said 1979; Schick 1999). Spaces such as the harem, public baths, and the slave market, characters such as the eunuch or concubine, or practices such as polygamy and bestiality are more than tropes or themes of erotic literature: they are aspects central to any exploration of the ways in which Europe has understood, represented, and controlled other cultures. Elsewhere is customarily sexualized as much as sex itself is exoticized. Regions viewed by Western readers as both exotic and marginal are presented as deregulated spaces in which travelers can behave, often in active sex tourism, in ways that would be deemed inappropriate at home (e.g., *Venus in India, or Love Adventures in Hindustan*, 1889). Consequently, it is frequently difficult to distinguish between fictional erotic literature and travel writing, as Western travelers have tended actively to identify other geographical areas in terms of their inhabitants' sexual behavior (see *Flaubert in Egypt*, 1972). Male travelers, for instance, experience the extraordinary sexual techniques of Oriental women, but exotic locales also allow women and gay travelers an erotic license that would be prohibited at home (e.g., *The Adventures of Lady Harpur*, 1894).

Such association of exoticism and eroticism creates an ethno-erotic literature of passive voyeurism in which the geographical margin serves not only as a space where the indigenous population behaves in a way that would be deemed grotesque at home (accordingly marking off the accepted borders of civility), but also where (often naive) women travelers are subjected to the attentions of lascivious indigenous males (e.g. *The Lustful Turk*, 1828, a clear illustration of the fantasies of "white slavery"). Accordingly, fear is complemented by both fantasy and vicarious pleasure, as sexual practices undesirable at home are projected onto the inhabitants of other countries. Islam, for instance, characterized by polygamy and divorce, is commonly presented as a sensual religion, with its male adherents granted unbounded sexual license, while its women are portrayed as both submissive and yet sexually ravenous.

The geographical evolution of erotic literature's exotic themes reflects to some extent travel literature's interest in shifting tropological zones. Seventeenth-century interest in the Ottoman seraglio gave way to an Enlightenment focus on Polynesia (see Porter 1990); and the nineteenth-century interest in what was perceived as Parisian permissiveness has been replaced, as global diversity (and with it exoticism) is seen to decline, by sexual encounters with aliens (see Heldreth 1986). There remain, however, recurrent locations with privileged status, principal of which is the harem (see Grosrichard 1979, Huart and Tazi 1980, Pucci 1990). For example, *A Night in a Moorish Harem* (c. 1902) describes a night spent in a Moroccan harem by the shipwrecked protagonist with nine concubines of different nationalities. The harem becomes an erotic utopia whose international inhabitants possess exaggerated sexual desires and where sexual encounters are both plural and sequential, seemingly always different yet in reality always the same. In tending to repeat these exotic motifs and stereotypes, such literature becomes a self-sufficient and self-referential archive that ultimately says much more about the European erotic imagination than the countries it purports to represent.

References and Further Reading

Célestin, Roger. *From Cannibals to Radicals: Figures and Limits of Exoticism*. Minneapolis and London: University of Minnesota Press, 1996.

Flaubert, Gustave. *Flaubert in Egypt: A Sensibility on Tour*. Translated and Edited by Francis Steegmuller. London: Bodley Head, 1972.

Forsdick, Charles. "Travelling Concepts: Postcolonial Approaches to Exoticism." *Paragraph*, 24.3 (2001): 12–29.

Gay, Peter. *Education of the Senses: The Bourgeois Experience from Victoria to Freud*. Vol. 1. Oxford and New York: Oxford University Press, 1984.

Gill, Anton. *Ruling Passions: Sex, Race and Empire*. London: BBC Books, 1995.

Grosrichard, Alain. *Structure du sérail: La fiction du despotisme asiatique dans l'Occident classique*. Paris: Seuil, 1979.

Heldreth, Leonard G. "Close Encounters of the Carnal Kind: Sex with Aliens in Science Fiction." In *Erotic Universe: Sexuality and Fantastic Literature*. Edited by Donald Palumbo. New York: Greenwood, 1986.

Huart, Annabelle d', and Nadia Tazi. *Harems*, Paris: Chêne; Hachette, 1980.

Hyam, Ronald. *Empire and Sexuality: The British Experience*. Manchester and New York: Manchester University, 1990.

Littlewood, Ian. *Sultry Climates: Travel and Sex*. London: John Murray, 2001.

Marcus, Steven. *The Other Victorians: a Study of Sexuality and Pornography in Mid-Nineteenth-Century Britain*. London: Corgi, 1966.

Moura, Jean-Marc. *La Littérature des lointains. Histoire de l'exotisme européen au XXe siècle*. Paris: Champion, 1998.

Porter, Roy. "The Exotic as Erotic: Captain Cook at Tahiti." In *Exoticism in the Enlightenment*, edited by Roy Porter and G. S. Rousseau. Manchester and New York: Manchester University Press, 1990.

Pucci, Suzanne Rodin. "The Discrete Charms of the Exotic: Fictions of the Harem in Eighteenth-Century France." In *Exoticism in the Enlightenment*, edited by Roy Porter and G. S. Rousseau. Manchester and New York: Manchester University Press, 1990.

Said, Edward W. *Orientalism*. New York: Vintage, 1979.

Schick, Irvin C. *The Erotic Margin: Sexuality and Spatiality in Alteritist Discourse*. London and New York: Verso, 1999.

Stewart, Lucretia, ed. *Erogenous Zones: An Anthology of Sex Abroad*. New York: Modern Library, 2000.

F

FABERT, GUILLAUME

c. 1940–
French author

Autoportrait en érection

Contrary to what is stated in its subtitle, *Autoportrait en érection* [*An Erectile Self-Portrait*] (1989) is not really a novel. Of course, the way Fabert Guillaume (a pseudonym) narrates his various sexual adventures produces a coherent whole, but the work's genre leans more toward a peculiar form of thematic autobiography or that of the practical handbook. Gifted with a tongue-in-cheek humor and well served by a style both ornamented and precise, yet never stilted or vulgar, Fabert addresses in more or less chronological order each and every element that constitutes the spectrum of his past and present sexuality.

Having drawn up in a pseudo-objective tone the "specification sheet" of his penis (length, shape, peculiarities, pros and cons, etc.) in the first chapter ("On Vanity"), Fabert then describes his sexual awakening, the first wet dream he had at the age of fourteen, as well as the education he received from his mother, who was a relatively liberated woman for her time. Although she had but good intentions regarding sexuality, she also passed down two deep-rooted prejudices: the penis is repulsive, while the female body is beautiful in all its parts (which includes the genitals, adds Fabert). He then writes that his experience proved both to be inaccurate. Hence, from the age of eighteen, he considers his penis to be a genuine object of beauty, while he must admit he first thought the whole artistic tradition, including Praxiteles and Ronsard, had lied about the ambiguous charms of female genitals. Fortunately, he writes, he has come to appreciate a number of nuances over the years.

To ensure an efficient coverage of the multifaceted sexual life he shared with exactly 20 female partners, among whom 6 were profoundly loved and cherished, Fabert proceeds to a thematic classification. Thus, every brief chapter of the book either gives an account of a specific sexual practice or position (whether he fancies it or not), addresses more abstract emotional concepts directly related to the sexual act, or narrates a unique moment of his early experience with sex ("On Juvenile Flirting").

Although he began his exploration of the female body with the mouth ("On Kissing"), he soon discovered that neither hard work nor virtuosity would change the fact that kissing alone rarely causes overwhelming sensations. But since a passionate kiss often announces something far more fulfilling, he always complies with this compulsory ritual. In the chapter entitled "On Gymnastics," Fabert passes in review various key positions, some comfortable, some precarious, reminding the reader that Casanova claimed he once did it through the grating of a convent parlor. First, in spite of all disadvantages of the "missionary" position (an "archaic curiosity"), he must admit that this basic position cannot be totally dismissed. Fortunately, thanks to innovative partners, he gradually discovered some creative variations, one of them involving a solid table and the woman's legs pointing upward. Of course, he says, this position prevents any embrace, which is unfortunate for the emotional reasons. Fabert also likes the "Amazon" position, especially when he feels like letting his partner do most of the work, and the "69," as long as it remains but an "hors-d'œuvre." Yet, the position he describes with the most details and wit, thus clearly showing his preference for the female buttocks, is the "dorsal-ventral," commonly known as "doggy-style," along with its almost infinite variations, including sodomy, which he discovered by accident during a passionate teenage relationship. Finally, he provides a handbook for those interested in achieving an all-too-seldom perfect fellatio, and later confesses his penchant for onanism, which he practices solely out of pleasure, never as a substitute.

In other chapters Fabert instead focuses on emotional "side effects" of sexuality. For example, he evokes with humor the frustration he suffered as a young man desperately trying to become a lover without any theoretical knowledge, normally gained by reading erotic literature, or imagination. In order to prevent the mutual disappointment inevitably caused by such ignorance, he coyly concludes by saying that "one never reads enough." He also addresses the complex notion of desire, which can fade away as fast as it grows for reasons sometimes unrelated to physical attraction, as well as the importance of natural lubrication,

which indicates the partner's pleasure level, and the power of the female orgasm. Regarding the male climax, Fabert makes a clear distinction between ejaculation and orgasm (*jouissance*). While far too many ejaculations fail to fulfill one's expectations, he claims the orgasm is the exception everybody longs for. Accordingly, the most powerful orgasm he ever experienced remained a unique moment, yet still very vivid in his memory. Fabert does not, however, consider himself to be a Don Juan, whose goal is to collect sex affairs in a catalogue of female conquests. On the contrary, he rather sees himself as a gourmet lover who finds pleasure in a patiently elaborated sex ritual, in which gentleness, spontaneity, complicity, and authoritarianism are tightly intermingled.

Autoportrait en érection is a witty and enjoyable account of the sexual experiences of a middle-aged male heterosexual from the Parisian bourgeois class, fully aware of his (constructed) macho attitude. Perhaps that is why Fabert concludes his self-portrait with an apology to all women, especially his former partners, reminding them that he is only human.

Biography

Given that *Autoportrait en érection* was written under a pseudonym, there is little to say about Guillaume Fabert or, at least, about the person who hid behind this name. But since he thinks that every autobiography, even a fictive one, must begin with a portrait of the hero, Fabert dedicates a paragraph to a factual, almost medical depiction of his anatomy. In this straightforward presentation, whose apparent sincerity might recall the opening pages of Michel Leiris's *L'âge d'homme* [*Manhood*], one learns that the book is the story of a forty-four-year-old European man who is 1.80 meters tall (5′11″) and weighs 83 kilos (183 pounds). Fabert also tells of the banality of his face, the heaviness of his jaw, and the catastrophic look of his teeth, all of which do not prevent him from being perceived as virile by women. But as the book's title suggests, the only thing that really matters to him in *Autoportrait en érection* is his penis: "My penis constitutes, without any doubt, the most magnificent part of my anatomy."

SÉBASTIEN CÔTÉ

Editions

Autoportrait en érection. Paris: Régine Deforges, 1989; Paris: Presses Pocket, 1990; Paris: Éditions Blanche,

1997; as *Selbstporträt eines Aufrechten. Erotische Bekenntnisse*, German translation by Alexandra von Reinhardt, Munich: Heyne, 1990.

FABLIAUX

Fabliaux (pronounced "fabli-ōz") are short comic narratives composed between the late twelfth and mid-fourteenth centuries. Although related to the fable (*fabulellum* ["little narrative"], diminutive of the Latin *fabula*), the fabliau (singular, pronounced "fabli-ō") also owes much to other narrative forms—the exemplum, the lay, the *dit,* and even romance. Some fabliaux are known in English (e.g., *Dame Sirith,* a number of Chaucer's *Canterbury Tales*), and others influenced later writers such as Boccacio; but this is principally a northern French tradition. Authors of certain fabliaux are well-known figures of French medieval literature—Jean Bodel, Rutebeuf, Jean de Condé—but for most we have just a name or an alias (Garin, Courtebarbe, Haiseau), or not even that. Equally, it is rarely possible to assign a precise date to a particular fabliau. The authors of fabliaux took much subject matter from the oral culture dominant in early medieval Europe, and they would have expected their stories to be reworked, performed, and/or read aloud. It could be argued that it is the centrality of this oral culture to the fabliau tradition that makes these texts so lively. Fabliaux tend to be short, usually comprising just a few hundred lines. Although there are a number of texts which lack any great literary merit, others are surprisingly sophisticated, subtly developing their theme and tone. But all share a common goal: to make the audience laugh.

It is generally acknowledged today that these tales—of which there are about 150 conserved in some 40 manuscripts—were destined for the same audience which enjoyed courtly literature. Composed in the vernacular and in octosyllabic rhyming couplets, these often bawdy tales are the product of an increasingly important urban society and frequently contain what first appears to be a moral teaching. However, this, as does every other aspect of the genre, needs to be taken with a huge pinch of salt, for the fabliaux subvert reality and depict, often hilariously, the world turned upside-down. So, the "moral" or "example" at the end of a fabliau is almost always ironic, cynical, or irreverent. The *dramatis personae* is fairly broad: townsfolk, clerks, widows, peasants, priests, monks, farmers, thugs, rich and poor middle classes, wandering knights, thieves. In addition to this, the down-to-earth situations (gambling, begging, buying and selling, the conjugal and extraconjugal bed, solving disputes, practical jokes) and the variety of locales (farms, shops, streets, mills, towns and villages, taverns) have led some scholars to see in the fabliaux a reflection of the real world; but however tempting this may be, it is vital to bear in mind that a mirror distorts and that all is not as it first appears in the fabliau world.

The classic fabliau scenario is that of the duper duped. There is always a victim—frequently a priest or a peasant or a cuckolded husband—and the plots often depend on misunderstandings and lively dialogue. The language can be coarse and the action vulgar, cruel, and tasteless. Grotesque sexual intrigue abounds, but it could be argued that there is little that is truly "erotic" here if the term is understood to mean "titillating": the reader encounters often obscene descriptions of sexuality, but these are almost always designed to stimulate laughter, not arousal. In defying the linguistic etiquette of courtly literature, and in their regular and explicit descriptions of sexual desire, the fabliaux both parody and subvert courtly conventions. In particular, the devious, nagging, and lecherous women of the fabliaux offer a vivid contrast to their idealized portrayal in courtly texts. The role of fabliaux women has given rise to much scholarly debate on the anitfeminism of the genre; nevertheless, it must be noted that female characters, although physically abused and depicted as unscrupulous and sexually voracious, often end up on top (both metaphorically and physically). What is more, the pure and idealized ladies of courtly texts and the lustful women of the fabliaux are just two sides of the same coin: both portraits—the "realistic" and the "idealized"—reveal to some degree an obsession with eroticism.

The eroticism of the fabliaux is generally hedonistic and uncomplicated. Fabliau sex has almost always been viewed by scholars as "normal," excluding practices such as sodomy, incest, fellatio, and homosexuality. Indeed, R. Howard Bloch, in the "postface" to Rossi's *Fabliaux érotiques*, notes that even the sexual positions of the fabliaux comply with the rules imposed by the Church (any position other than the missionary being proscribed). However, this view has recently been challenged by Brian J. Levy ("Le Dernier tabou?"), who identifies a number of descriptions of sexual activity which is clearly *contra naturam*. Furthermore, although descriptions of genitals, libido, and desire can be extremely detailed, the sex act itself tends to be passed over quickly, often in a matter of only a line or two. There are, of course, exceptions (such as *L'Esquiriel*, see below); but in general, sexual intrigue is more important to authors of fabliaux than detailed descriptions of coitus. This has led Philippe Ménard (*Fabliaux français*, p. 69) to question to what extent the fabliaux can be labeled "erotic" at all: "If the sexual pleasure of the lovers seems so 'normal' that it defies prolonged description, where is the eroticism to be found?"

The best way to get a flavor of the fabliaux is to read one or two of the stories they tell. *Les quatre souhais saint Martin* [*Saint Martin's Four Wishes*] is the story of a peasant who is granted four wishes by Saint Martin. The peasant's overbearing wife manages to persuade him to grant her the first wish, and she wishes for the peasant's body to be covered in penises, for his small member has never been able fully to satisfy her. Taken aback to find himself covered in genitals, he uses the second wish to return the compliment, and so his wife finds her body covered with vaginas. Realizing that they have wasted two wishes, the couple agree to wish for all of these genitals to disappear, intending to use the fourth wish to make themselves rich. However, removing all of the genitals in the third wish caused even the original genitals to vanish—so, the fourth wish simply restores them to their former state. The moral is not to trust your wife.

In *La borgoise d'Orliens* [*The Wife of Orleans*], a husband, suspecting his wife of adultery with an itinerant clerk-entertainer, hatches a plot to catch her *in flagrante delicto*. He pretends that he has to travel away on business and then takes the place of the lover at the couple's nocturnal rendezvous; but his wife recognizes him and plans to deceive him. Calling him "my lover," she locks him in a room, promising to release him and take him into her bed when the household is asleep. She then returns to the rendezvous point and meets her real lover. After having sex with the clerk, she signals to the household that she has managed to lock "that clerk who keeps bothering me" in a room, and offers a reward to those who will teach him a lesson. And so the husband, mistaken for the wife's lover, is badly beaten with clubs and bludgeons and is thrown out of the house. His wife enjoys a night with her lover, and the husband returns the following day in a pitiful state but happy, having been duped into believing that he has a faithful wife.

In *La saineresse* [*The Leech-Woman*], a husband who boasts that he can never be cuckolded is taught a lesson by his wife: she has herself bled in private by her lover disguised as a woman. Once alone they waste no time in having passionate sex, and she then recounts all, in detailed but flowery euphemisms, to her stupid husband; the latter believes that her words—"I have been bent over this way and that," "I have been treated by a delicious ointment which the healer kept in a small sack and applied with a tube"—describe a medical treatment.

La damoisele qui ne pooit oïr parler de foutre [*The Girl Who Could Not Bear to Hear About Fucking*] tells of a girl who is duped into having sex with a man who pretends to be equally prudish and to have the same linguistic qualms as she. Using metaphors to describe their genitals, the man succeeds in "watering his colt at the fountain." Similarly, in *L'Esquiriel* [*The Squirrel*], a half-witted girl is told by her mother never to say the name of the thing men have between their legs. A man who overhears this presents the girl with his erect penis, calling it a squirrel which has just laid two eggs. It is hungry and, luckily, the girl has just eaten a handful of nuts: by inserting it into her vagina the squirrel can feed on the nuts in her stomach.

Le Prestre ki abevete [*The Priest Who Spied*] tells of a peasant whose beautiful wife has a priest for her lover. One day the priest decides to pay her a visit but finds the peasant sitting at dinner with his wife. The priest spies through a hole in the locked door and yells: "What are you good people doing?" When the peasant replies, "We are eating," the priest calls him a liar: "It seems to me that you are fucking!" The peasant swaps places with the priest, suspecting a trick: he wants to see for himself. Once inside the house, the priest locks the door and immediately begins having sex with the peasant's wife. The peasant peeks through the hole in the door and accuses the priest of screwing his wife; but the priest insists that he is eating, and the peasant believes him. The moral is that one hole satisfies many fools.

Not all fabliaux deal with sex, but a mere glance at some of the titles shows how popular the subject is for their authors: *Le chevalier qui fist parler les cons* [*The Knight Who Made Cunts Speak*], *Cele qui se fist foutre sur la fosse de son mari* [*The Woman Who Was Fucked on Her Husband's Grave*], *Cele qui fu foutue et desfoutue* [*The Woman Who Was Fucked and Unfucked*]; *La Coille noire* [*The Black Bollock*]; *Les putains et les lecheors* [*The Whores and the Perverts*], *L'Evesque qui beneï le con* [*The Priest Who Blessed the Cunt*], *L'Anel qui faisoit les vis grans et roides* [*The Ring That Made Pricks Big and Stiff*], etc. However, it must be reiterated that these stories are not really meant to arouse, but rather to provoke laughter: the medieval titles seem to make this quite plain. Sex is a fruitful theme for authors wanting to shock, to depict a reverse image of what is acceptable, or to mock contemporary attitudes of various parts of society.

A number of fabliaux give brilliant vignettes offering ironic and sophisticated commentary on some aspect of contemporary life; others are little more than extended (and not universally subtle or successful) puns. Black humor abounds: there is violence, sex, adultery, scatology, illness, death, unjust punishment, and humiliation. The general coarseness and "low" style of the fabliaux led early scholars, in particular Joseph Bédier, to believe that these texts were intended for the lower, urban classes. But in manuscripts, the fabliaux are found copied alongside poems of courtly love; and indeed, the literary tradition of *fin'amor* can be considered a faithful reflection of the coarse fabliaux, if once again it is remembered that reflections distort. Most scholars today follow Per Nykrog, to some degree at least, in viewing the fabliaux as another string in the minstrel's bow and a testament to the (naturally) varied tastes of an audience of nobles and/or middle-class townsfolk. It is also generally agreed that along with the smutty and not always very funny extended jokes, the corpus of fabliaux offers some of the very best examples of storytelling in Old French literature.

ADRIAN TUDOR

Editions

Recueil général et complet des fabliaux des XIIIe et XIVe siècles. Edited by Anatole de Montaiglon and Gaston Raynaud. 6 vols. Paris: 1872–1890.

Selected Fabliaux. Edited from B.N. Fonds Français 837, Fonds Français 1952 and Berlin Hamilton 257. Edited by Brian J. Levy with notes by Cedric E. Pickford. Hull: Hull University French Texts, 1978.

Nouveau recueil complet de fabliaux [NRCF]. Edited by Willem Noomen and Nico Van den Boogaard. 10 vols. Assen: Van Gorcum, 1983–1988.

Eighteen Anglo-Norman fabliaux. Edited by Ian Short and Roy Pearcy. London: Anglo-Norman Text Society, 2000.

Translations into English

Benson, Larry D., and Theodore Andersson. *The Literary Context of Chaucer's Fabliaux.* Indianapolis: Bobbs-Merrill, 1971.

DuVal, John, and Raymond Eichmann. *Cuckolds, Clerics and Countrymen: Medieval French Fabliaux.* Fayetteville: University of Arkansas Press, 1982.

———. *The French Fabliaux B.N. MS 837.* 2 vols. New York and London: Garland, 1985 (parallel Old French and English text).

Harrison, Robert. *Gallic Salt: Eighteen Fabliaux Translated from the Old French.* Berkeley and Los Angeles: University of California Press, 1974.

Hellman, Robert, and Richard O'Gorman. *Ribald Tales from the Old French.* New York: Crowell, 1965.

Translations into Modern French

Brusegan, Rosanna. *Fabliaux.* Paris: Union Générale d' Editions, 1994.

Dufournet, Jean. *Fabliaux du moyen âge.* Paris: Garnier-Flammarion, 1998.

Leclanche, Jean-Luc. *Chevalerie et grivoiserie: Fabliaux de chevalerie.* Paris: Champion, 2001.

Ménard, Philippe. *Fabliaux français du moyen âge.* Genève: Droz, 1979.

Rossi, Luciano, and Richard Straub. *Fabliaux érotiques, textes de jongleurs des XIIe et XIIIe siecles.* Paris: Livre de Poche (Collection Lettres Gothiques), 1992.

CD Recording

Vice and Virtue: Old French Fabliaux and Pious Tales. Read by Brian J. Levy and Adrian P. Tudor. Provo, UT: The Chaucer Studio, 2003.

Further Reading

Bédier, Joseph. *Les Fabliaux. Etudes de littérature populaire et d'histoire littéraire du moyen âge.* Paris: Bouillon, 1893.

Bloch, R. Howard. *The Scandal of the Fabliaux.* Chicago: Chicago University Press, 1986.

Dufournet, Jean. "Les Relations de l'homme et de la femme dans les fabliaux: un double discours." In *Femmes – Mariages – Lignages, XIIe – XIVe siècles. Mélanges offerts à Georges Duby,* edited by Jean Dufournet et al. Brussels: De Boeck-Wesmael, 1992.

Cooke, Thomas D., and Benjamin L. Honeycutt, eds. *The Humor of the Fabliaux: A Collection of Critical Essays.* Columbia: University of Missouri Press, 1974.

Lacy, Norris J. *Reading Fabliaux.* New York: Garland, 1993.

———. "Sex and Love in the Fabliaux." In *Sex, Love and Marriage in Medieval Literature and Reality,* edited by Danielle Buschinger and Wolfgang Spiewok. Greifswald, Germany: Reineke, 1996.

Levy, Brian J. *The Comic Text: Patterns and Images in the Old French Fabliaux.* Amsterdam and Atlanta: Rodopi, 2000.

———. "Le Dernier tabou? Les Fabliaux et la perversion sexuelle." In *Sexuelle Perversionen im Mittelalter,* edited by Danielle Buschinger and Wolfgang Spiewok. Greifswald, Germany: Reineke, 1994.

Lorcin, Marie-Thérèse. *Façons de sentir et de penser: Les Fabliaux français.* Paris: Champion, 1979.

———. "Le Personnage du cocu dans les fabliaux français." In *Der Hahnrei im Mittelalter / Le Cocu au moyen age. Actes du Colloque du C.E.M. de l'Université de Picardie Jules Verne,* edited by Danielle Buschinger and Wolfgang Spiewok. Greifswald, Germany: Reineke, 1994.

Ménard, Philippe. *Les Fabliaux. Contes à rire du moyen âge.* Paris: PUF, 1983.

Muscatine, Charles. *The Old French Fabliaux.* New Haven, CT: Yale University Press, 1986.

Nykrog, Per. *Les Fabliaux: Étude d'histoire littéraire et de stylistique médiévale.* Copenhagen: Munksgaard, 1957.

Ribard, Jacques. "Et si les fabliaux n'étaient pas des 'contes à rire.'" *Reinardus* 2 (1989): 134–43.

Rychner, Jean. *Contribution à l'étude des fabliaux: Variantes, remaniements, dégradations.* 2 vols. Neuchâtel: Faculte des Lettres, 1960.

Stearns Schenck, Mary Jane. *The Fabliaux: Tales of Wit and Deception.* Amsterdam and Philadelphia: Benjamins, 1987.

Tudor, Adrian. "Concevoir et accoucher dans les fabliaux, les miracles et les contes pieux." *Reinardus* 13 (2000): 195–213.

FÁBULAS FUTROSÓFICAS, O LA FILOSOFÍA DE VENUS EN FÁBULAS

Fábulas futrosóficas, o la filosofía de Venus en fábulas is the title of a collection of anonymous poems published by an unnamed compiler and printed, according to the title page, in London in 1821. Whereas the date has not been questioned, it is commonly supposed that the original slim volume of 40 poems was printed in the south of France, possibly in Bordeaux, though no detailed typographical analysis has been carried out to support this claim. A subsequent edition, dated 1824, adds a sonnet and an "Oda a Príapo" to the original 40 fables. The date of composition could be as early as the 1780s–90s to judge by references in the footnotes and the preliminary listing of moral lessons. The original compiler implies they are by a single poet, and the editors of the 1984 limited edition (*Dos árcades futrosóficos y un libertino a la violeta*) propose the authorship of Leandro Fernández de Moratín, though adducing no stylistic or ideological support for their claim, and Moratín scholars have not supported his authorship. The attribution to Moratín had previously been proposed by Camilo José Cela in 1974, dismissing the manuscript attribution to the more credible Bartolomé José Gallardo added to his copy of the 1821 edition. Moratín's authorship is acquiesced in by Cerezo, while admitting the absence of hard evidence.

As was common with nearly all Spanish texts of an erotic nature in the period up to the mid-nineteenth century, the volume was condemned by the Church; an edict of the Cardinal Archbishop of Toledo prohibited the work in 1827, and it was included in Carbonero's subsequent *Índice de libros prohibidos* (1873), even though the Spanish Inquisition had been officially abolished in 1834. Because of the rarity of copies of the original editions and the limited circulation of the 1984 printing, the poems have not attracted the attention of literary critics, in spite of their interest for the history of ideas and in particular late-eighteenth and early-nineteenth-century views of sexuality.

The 40 compositions in the 1821 edition (to which all subsequent references will be made) form a curious grouping. Like many eighteenth-century fable series, most of the poems concern animals, though 6 mix animals and humans, and 9 deal with humans alone. More curious is the fact that one composition features two satyrs, another animals and Priapus, and the two most curious poems contain, respectively, dialogues between the male and female sexual organs, and between "sarna" (scurvy) and "gálico" (sexually transmitted disease). The array of animal protagonists is wide (numbers in parentheses indicate the number of the poem): cats (2 and 16), monkeys (3, 19, and 29), foxes (4 and 22), dogs (5, 8, 14, 21, and 23), lions (5, 10, and 16), hares (6), sparrows (11), donkeys (13, 16, and 25), mice (15), horses (17), chickens (18), wolves (20), deer (26), pigs (28), flies (32), and cows (40). Sometimes the reasons for choosing the particular animal seem to correspond to popular characterizations of their behavior, usually from a sexual perspective. In some poems the portrayal of the animals suggests they are merely humans in disguise, while in others the comparison between human and animal behavior is consistently suggested. One poem (5) might be interpreted as portraying animals as representatives of ecclesiastical figures, in an obvious

suggestion of satire. However, the author is adept at creating ambiguity in this respect.

The sense of the poems forming a collection is not easy to determine. The first poem invokes Venus and seems prefatory in intent, yet though the label of "fables" is given the collection as a whole, some compositions (e.g., 24) do not emphasize a moralizing or didactic purpose, and some concerning humans relate to the other poems only because of the prevailing exploration of sexuality. Yet, notwithstanding the predominant sexual themes, the poems are not erotically provocative. They explore sexuality, pointing at hypocrisy or anomalies of behavior, but the aim seems not to arouse, and the assertion of a *philosophical* standpoint, underlined in the title, is uppermost. One notable incongruency derives from the preliminary listing of moral lessons, ostensibly illustrated by the individual poems. Some hardly seem to relate to the composition indicated, suggesting that they might have been added by another hand, possibly the anonymous editor's. This is especially striking when the poem itself ends with an explicit moral that diverges somewhat from the one stated earlier.

If the preliminary list of moral points provides one, albeit dubious, framing device, another derives from footnotes to individual poems, which sometimes take the form of editorial clarifications of intellectual points. So the first poem refers to the Spanish Academy Dictionary's inclusions and exclusions of sexual vocabulary. Another (12) provides the Latin original of an allusion to Martial. A note to poem 19 claims that a reference to what might be a clitoris or penis in a monkey refers to a recent scientific finding. Another (20), underlining the scientific context of many of the poems, refers, somewhat oddly, to articles in the defunct periodical *El corresponsal del censor* (1786–8), which dealt with the consumption of fish and the influence of the physical on the moral realms. Yet another (38) touches on the varied explanations of the geographical origins of sexually transmitted diseases.

As to poetic forms, 22 of the compositions prefer rhyme, with assonance for the remainder. Long (hendecasyllabic) lines are used in 14 poems, the usual alternative heptasyllabic form in 10, a mixture of both in another 6, while the remainder comprise octosyllables (8 poems) and hexasyllables (3 poems). The choices are characteristic of Spanish eighteenth-century neoclassical poetry. After making a point concerning the avoidance of earthy language in the first poem, the remainder show no reticence about vulgar terminology for sexual descriptions; yet *joder* (to fuck) appears in only 9 poems, and *carajo* (prick) in 11. As is usual in works that adopt a contemporary popular style, a range of figurative phrases for sexual behavior, often euphemistic, is employed, introducing changes of register and thus variety and interest. Language is direct and clear, avoiding obscurity of metaphor, as is customary in neoclassical poetic expression in Spain.

In contrast to the sexually related fables of Félix María Samaniego, the author of the *Fábulas futrosóficas* shows less concern to entertain as storyteller. The story element, which forms the focus of each poem, is not conveyed with the concision and refined feeling for suspense or structure which Samaniego exhibits; the author prefers instead to provoke in the reader a questioning of moral positions or links between biological and material phenomena, or sometimes the relation between the moral and the physical. And though the initial list of moral points sometimes seems to be assertive and dogmatic, the poems themselves frequently leave issues in the air and even explicitly ask the reader to draw conclusions.

The range of thematic concerns is wide: the human wish to regulate sexual behavior contrasted with the apparent anarchy of natural impulses; the contrast between male and female attitudes to sex, both in its physical aspects (impotence, uncertainty as to parenthood) and in its moral ones (possessiveness, jealousy); differences between animal and human perspectives (sexual availability); the material, physical component of desire and the contribution of mental and cultural conditioning; the role of prejudice ("the prohibited attracts") in sexual behavior; the irrational in sexual relationships; varieties of sexual practice (masturbation, castration); aspects of the sexual organs (size, anomalies); techniques of seduction; and female devices used to deceive men. When ecclesiastics figure in the poems, they are invariably portrayed as officially wishing to repress sexual behavior while negating their own advice in practice. While some of the concerns illustrated—for instance, ecclesiastical repression and social privilege—seem characteristic of the moment of composition, other issues seem modern, prefiguring subsequent debates on the differences between the sexes, inherited and learned characteristics, and the nature of the relation between the mental and the physical.

PHILIP DEACON

Editions

Fábulas futrosóficas o la filosofía de Venus en fábulas. London: n. p., 1821. *Fábulas Futrosoficas, ó La filosofia de Venus en Fabulas.* London: n. p., 1824. *Fábulas Futrosóficas o La Filosofía de Venus en Fábulas.* Madrid: El Crotalón, 1984.

Further Reading

Cela, Camilo José. *Enciclopedia del erotismo.* In *Obra completa.* Books 14–17. Barcelona: Destino, 1982–1986.

Cerezo, José Antonio. "Leandro Fernández de Moratín." In *Literatura erótica en España: Repertorio de obras 1519–1936.* Madrid: Ollero y Ramos, 2001.

FAIRY TALES AND EROTICISM

At first sight, the association of fairy tales with eroticism might seem surprising and somewhat puzzling. As a genre, fairy tales are considered to be aimed mostly at children, while eroticism in general, and erotic literature in particular, would be more appropriately characterized as a typically adult genre. Yet, because of their formulaic nature and of the stereotypes they convey, fairy tales have been constantly rewritten, in different modes and registers, for adults and for children, in naive (or pseudo-naive), or erotic texts.

Many literary fairy tale rewritings in the erotic mode can be characterized by two complementary tendencies. Some erotic fairy tales aim at denouncing the naively simplistic world of the fairy tale by reinscribing sexuality within the fairy tale genre (see, for example, Jean-Pierre Enard's *Contes à faire rougir les petits chaperons* [*Tales to Make Little Red Riding Hoods Blush*], 1987). Other recent fairy tale rewritings aim not only at denouncing the stereotypically asexual and artificially cleansed world of traditional fairy tales, but also at critiquing their (implicit) sexual and (explicit) gender ideology. In this instance, the presence of sexual motifs serves as a subversion of conventional marital closures and their consequent compulsory felicity, and of the double principle on which such an ideology is based: female passivity and male agency. These erotic fairy tales thus rephrase the mandatory inscription of sexual practices in fixed and predictable gender roles by refusing to abide by the exclusive recognition of heterosexuality as the sole ideological and narrative contract.

In erotic rewritings, some fairy tales and heroines have led to a more vibrant, and erotically charged, corpus than others. Among the most popular heroines, one who is famous for her 100-year sleep has struck the imagination of many writers. Denounced as the very negation of female agency by many critics (including Simone de Beauvoir), Sleeping Beauty was finally brought back to life in a famous trilogy: *The Claiming of Sleeping Beauty*, *Beauty's Punishment*, and *Beauty's Release* (1983–1985, reprinted 1990). First presented as having been written by an unknown "A.N. Roquelaure," the trilogy was then revealed to be the work of popular novelist Anne Rice. As the editorial paratext suggests, this trilogy, written as a "hypnotic and seductive adult fairy tale" beckons the reader "into a sensuous world of forbidden dreams and dark-edged desires." The *Beauty* trilogy thus expands the wanderings of the formerly passive heroine, taking her, and the reader, into an erotic underworld. Acting as a foil to sugary renditions of fairy tales cleansed of all desire other than that of being overtly romantic, the trilogy aims at giving an explicit account of various impulses (dominance and submission), as well as sexual orientation and practices.

Edited collections of erotic fairy tales prefer to rewrite not one but various stories from our childhood and to allow popular heroes and heroines to enter a new world of erotic adventures. Acknowledging that "everywhere we turn in fairyland, the libido is running rampant," Michael Ford asked male writers to rewrite old stories in his collection of erotic fairy tales, *Happily Ever After: Erotic Fairy Tales for Men* (1996, p. 2). In this edited volume, 28 fairy tales are revisited within the context of sexual orientation, gay identity, and queer politics—among others, *Pinocchio* (Bruce Benderson), *The Three Bears* (Michael Lassell), and *Jack and the Beanstalk* (William J. Mann), as well as the inevitable *Beauty and the Beast* (Thomas Roche).

While the practice of erotic rewritings of fairy tales as a critique of ideological and literary practices (as opposed to the mere presence of sexual motifs in earlier versions) seems to be a rather contemporary phenomenon, such a practice in fact goes back to the very origin of the literary fairy tale, and to an important ideological turning point, a time when religious, philosophical, and literary practices came under heavy attack: the Enlightenment. Following the translation of erotically charged oriental tales, *The Arabian Nights*, into French by Antoine Galland (*Les Mille et une nuits*, 12 vols, 1704–1717), many writers used the fairy tale to criticize various forms of authority in libertine and erotic fairy tales. Among those many writers, one in particular is remembered today for his libertine novels and tales set in a highly encoded (and whimsical) Orient, which allows him both to describe erotically charged stories about an erotic "other" and to criticize the French legal, literary, and religious establishment: Claude Crébillon (known as Crébillon *fils,* 1707–1777). One of his oriental fairy tales, *L'Écumoire* [*The Skimming Ladle*] (1734), features among others an enchantment of a rather dubious nature. Instead of a penis, a Prince is endowed with a skimming ladle (hence the title) because he refuses to wait until he is 20 before marrying, and because he fails to have an old woman and a venerable priest swallow the handle of the ladle (which incidentally was immediately interpreted as featuring the *Bulle Unigenitus*, an important religious document).

The erotic and iconoclastic nature of this sexual tale attacking religion caused its author's temporary exile. Crébillon's later production was as erotically charged, though not as polemic. His *Le Sopha* [*The Sofa*] (1742) is the story of a sofa that could enter many boudoirs and later tell erotic tales of failed and successful love stories. Such an invisibility employed to titillate voyeuristic readers is also at the center of another marvelous tale, Diderot's *Bijoux indiscrets* [*Indiscreet Jewels*] (1748), in which a bored and curious sultan is given a magical ring which allows him to extract confessions from every woman's "jewel," as "every woman toward whom [he turns] the stone will recount her intrigues in a loud, clear, and intelligible voice. But do not imagine that they shall speak through their mouths" (354). As Michel Foucault was later to postulate in the first volume of his *History of Sexuality* (especially Part IV), Western modern sexuality and its desire less to repress than to know begins with this erotic tale of "enforced confession" and could be considered as a transcription of Diderot's novel and its emblem of the "talking sex" (p. 101). Ironically, this erotic tale of, and by, "Indiscreet Jewels" acts as a foil to so many other universally known and loved traditional fairy tales which, of course, enforce less a desire to know and say than to hide and silence erotic practices.

JEAN MAINIL

Further Reading

A.N. Roquelaure [Ann Rice]. *The Claiming of Sleeping Beauty*, *Beauty's Punishment*, and *Beauty's Release*. New York: Penguin, 1983–1985; reprinted, New York: Plume, 1990.

The Arabian Nights: Tales from a Thousand and One Nights. Translated and edited by Richard F. Burton, introduction by A.S. Byatt. New York: Modern Library Classics, 2001.

Crébillon *fils*. "The Sofa." Translated by Bonamy Dobrée. In *The Libertine Reader: Eroticism and Enlightenment in Eighteenth-Century France*, edited by Michel Feher. New York: Zone Books, 1997.

Diderot, Denis. "The Indiscreet Jewels." Translated by Sophie Hawkes. In *The Libertine Reader: Eroticism and Enlightenment in Eighteenth-Century France*. Edited by Michel Feher. New York: Zone Books, 1997.

Enard, Jean-Pierre. *Contes à faire rougir les petits chaperons*. Paris: Ramsay, 1987.

Ford, Michael, ed. *Happily Ever After: Erotic Fairy Tales for Men*. New York: Richard Kasak, 1996.

Foucault, Michel. *Histoire de la sexualité*. Vol. 1, *La Volonté de savoir*. Paris: Gallimard, 1976; as *The History of Sexuality: An Introduction*, New York: Vintage, 1990.

FAULKNER, WILLIAM

1897–1962
American novelist

Between 1868 and 1933, the legal standard for obscenity changed in the United States: the 1868 standard, taken from the British case *Queen v. Hicklin,* was "whether the tendency of the matter charged as obscenity is to deprave and corrupt those whose minds are open to such immoral influences." The 1933 *Ulysses* case, *U.S. v. One Book called "Ulysses",* redefined this standard, establishing instead that a text would be obscene if it might "arouse" a "person of average sex instincts." The move from *Hicklin* to *One Book* was the legal expression of a broader cultural sense that the Victorian standards regarding the representation of sexuality

were prudish. During roughly the same period, American literary modernists, like their contemporaries in other parts of the globe, began to write about explicitly sexual topics. In the first few decades of the twentieth century, these authors faced an acute conflict: how might they represent sexuality without also inviting the legal charge of obscenity? William Faulkner, the infamously rude Mississippi modernist, explored the cultural meanings of this problem perhaps more thoroughly than any of his American contemporaries.

Faulkner was interested in illicit forms of sexuality in particular, and indeed, Jean-Paul Sartre described Faulkner's 1925 masterpiece *The Sound and the Fury* as obscene: the action of the novel, he observed, is "under each word, like an obscene and obstructing presence" (79). Although Faulkner is best known for his literary contribution to American letters, Sartre's comments about this social aspect of *The Sound and the Fury* might be applied of Faulkner's work more generally. As even a glancing review of his major novels attests, Faulkner also examined the new freedom to represent sexual themes explicitly. His representations of sexuality, moreover, flirt with the outrageous: for him, it was rape and incest, for example, that most directly conveyed the historical problems in the American South.

Obscenity, it seems, provided Faulkner with a neat figure for the reconsideration of several familiar American tropes in the context of modernism. In his hands, tamer nineteenth-century representations of relations between young white girls and slaves, for example, gave way to explicit accounts of the illicit acts that lead to mixed blood—"miscegenation." For Faulkner, that is, the representation of obscenity entails a look at the pervasive and paralyzing fear of interracial sex. Over the course of *Absalom, Absalom!* (1936), to take the most obvious example of this, it is gradually revealed that the alluring and enigmatic Charles Bon is both part black and part Sutpen. His black, Sutpen blood renders the fact that Bon has been courting Judith Sutpen, his half-sister—doubly transgressive, since he seeks to commit both incest and miscegenation. Bon makes this frequently cited declaration to Judith's brother Henry: "I'm the nigger that's going to sleep with your sister." Henry, whose own ties to Judith are erotically charged, would rather the problem be that Bon and Judith are related. As several critics have argued, the possibility that his sister might engage in interracial sex is more disturbing to Henry than the potential incest, and indeed it is this that leads Henry to shoot Bon. This instance of fratricide emerges in the novel as a futile gesture. Whether or not Judith and Charles consummate their erotic tie, miscegenation—clearly obscene—has already, in the broad historical context of Southern history, transpired. Here as elsewhere in Faulkner, obscenity comes to signify an inevitable deterioration of social life itself. Where social life rests upon clear racial stratification, miscegenation is, as Faulkner's novel portrays it, devastating.

Although Faulkner is clearly concerned with social issues like miscegenation, he is certainly as interested in formal experimentation. His representation of obscenity, accordingly, examines both its thematic and formal elements. *The Sound and the Fury* is a case in point. That quintessentially modernist novel depicts the censure of Caddy Compson, a promiscuous young girl who has become pregnant. As punishment for contributing to the ruin of her family's name, she is banished from the Compson household. In particular, her mother forbids her name from being spoken in the house, and Caddy is also, quite literally, *ob-scene* in *The Sound and the Fury*. That is, she is blocked from the scene—offstage as it were—a dominating character, but one whose force seems to come from the very fact of her absence. Her status outside of narration seems to hinge on her status outside of the social world within the novel, and the empty center she does not quite occupy defines the formal structure of the novel. This structural absence, the novel suggests, is a formal expression of Caddy's thematic ties with the obscene.

This overlapping of obscene themes with formal structure emerges again and again in Faulkner's work. All of Faulkner's representations of sexual young women are marked by an absence that resembles Caddy's. In *Sanctuary* (1931), for example, Temple Drake is raped with a corn cob. Although this gruesome act is quite clearly at the center of *Sanctuary*'s action, it is also conspicuously absent from the narrative, depicted only obscurely in a moment when "sound and silence" have become "inverted." Like Caddy, Temple too seems to be an "obscene and obstructing presence." Lena Grove in *Light in August* (1932) becomes pregnant out of wedlock, and her journey to find the father, who has fled, provides the basis for the story. But the illicit nature of Lena's seminal act is elided: she speaks only according to the dictates of a respectability she has already conspicuously violated. Miss Rosa in *Absalom, Absalom!*, repetitively blocked by doors throughout the novel, seems a perfect figure for Faulkner's reader: aware of pervasive illicit activity but not quite able to see it. In Faulkner, then, violations of the social order are shown to entail exclusions.

It should be observed that although Faulkner made frequent use of the concept of obscenity in his work, none of his novels was ever actually deemed obscene by any U.S. court. This might at first seem surprising, given that several tamer novels—James Joyce's *Ulysses* most famously—were in fact considered legally obscene during Faulkner's career. But censorship in general is contingent on somewhat random circumstances, including, most obviously, whether or not anyone brings an illicit text to the attention of a court. What this suggests is that a text might well be illicit without being illegal. *Sanctuary,* for example, is indisputably Faulkner's most outrageous novel, and it is arguably one of the more outrageous novels written by anyone in his era. But it was never under the ban. Almost 20 years after the novel was published, it was cited in *Commonwealth v. Gordon* (1949), a Pennsylvania obscenity case. But the charge did not stick, and it was determined that *Sanctuary,* along with a number of novels, including Faulkner's *Wild Palms* (1939) and Erskine Caldwell's *God's Little Acre* (1933), were not obscene.

Faulkner's examination of obscenity is not, therefore, a result of any direct experience with the law. His contributions to American letters, however, must be understood in terms of his explication of prevailing cultural views toward illicit expression. His publisher is reputed to have responded to his first reading of *Sanctuary* by saying, "Good God, I can't publish this. We'd both be in jail." Surely this came as no surprise to Faulkner: after all, he wrote his most acclaimed novels in the midst of the most widely publicized debates about obscenity in the history of the United States. The author himself claimed that with *Sanctuary,* he had written "the most horrific tale" he could "imagine." Whether or not Faulkner experienced censorship directly, then, his work needs to be understood in relation to the obscene. His novels suggest, in particular, that the loosening of obscenity standards brought with it an anxiety about the loss of previously protected cultural mores. Faulkner seems to suggest that the loss of these protections posed a threat to American cultural identity. This is a somewhat surprising conclusion for a renegade author like Faulkner to draw. This Faulknerian discrepancy regarding censorship speaks volumes, it seems, about American letters, obscenity, and modernism more generally.

Biography

Born William *Falkner* in New Albany, Mississippi, on September 25, the eldest child of Maud and Murray Falkner. Just before Faulkner turned five, the family moved to Oxford,

Mississippi. Faulkner lived in Canada, New Orleans, Hollywood, and Virginia, but spent most of his life in Oxford. Because his work is so clearly rooted in this region of Mississippi, acclaimed biographer David Minter describes Faulkner as "our great provincial." Joined the British Royal Air Force in Canada because he did not meet U.S. Army physical requirements, but World War I ended before he served. Sherwood Anderson helped him publish his first novel, *Soldier's Pay* (1926). Won the Nobel Prize in Literature in 1949. Won the Pulitzer Prize in 1954 for *A Fable,* and again in 1962 for *The Reivers,* published just before his death. Faulkner died near Oxford on July 6, 1962.

FLORENCE DORE

Selected Works

Soldier's Pay. 1962
Sartoris. 1929
The Sound and the Fury. 1929
As I Lay Dying. 1930
Sanctuary. 1931
Light in August. 1932
Absalom, Absalom! 1936
A Fable. 1954
The Town. 1957
The Mansion. 1960
The Reivers. 1962

Further Reading

Bleikasten, André. *The Ink of Melancholy: Faulkner's Novels, from The Sound and the Fury to Light in August.* Bloomington: Indiana University Press, 1990.

Boyer, Paul. *Purity in Print: The Vice-Society Movement and Book Censorship in America.* New York: Charles Scribner's Sons, 1968.

Davis, Thadious. *Faulkner's "Negro": Art and the Southern Context.* Baton Rouge: Louisiana State University Press, 1983.

Irwin, John T. *Doubling and Incest/ Repetition and Revenge: A Speculative Reading of Faulkner.* Baltimore: Johns Hopkins University Press, 1975.

Kartiganer, Donald M. *The Fragile Thread: The Meaning of Form in Faulkner's Novels.* Amherst: University of Massachusetts Press, 1979.

Magowan, Kimberly. "Strange Bedfellows: Incest and Miscegenation in Thomas Dixon, William Faulkner, Ralph Ellison, and John Sayles." Diss., University of California, Berkeley, 1999.

Matthews, John T. "The Elliptical Nature of *Sanctuary.*" *Novel: A Forum on Fiction* 17.3 (Spring 1984): 246–65.

Minter, David. *William Faulkner: His Life and Work.* Baltimore: Johns Hopkins University Press, 1980.

Sartre, Jean-Paul. "On *The Sound and the Fury:* Time in the Work of William Faulkner." In *Literary and Philosophical Essays*, trans. Annette Michelson. London: Rider, 1955.

Schauer, Frederick. *The Law of Obscenity*. Washington, DC: Bureau of National Affairs, Inc., 1976.

Weinstein, Philip. *Faulkner's Subject: A Cosmos No One Owns*. Cambridge and New York: Cambridge University Press, 1992.

Legal Cases

Commonwealth v. Gordon. 66 Pa. D. and C. 101 (1949).
Queen v. Hicklin. LR 3 QB 360, 371 (1868).
U.S. v. One Book Called "Ulysses." 5 Fed. Supp. 182 (1933).

FEMINISM: ANTI-PORN MOVEMENT AND PRO-PORN MOVEMENT

Few questions have divided feminist thinkers and activists more sharply than the pornography issue. This article attempts to chart opposing feminist views on pornography and their implications for women's lives and writing rather than chronicle the history of pro- and anti-pornography feminist activism, though it is impossible to entirely separate the two. The question is relevant for this book because the feminist debate around pornography (and also around classics of literary erotica) has led many women artists to develop new forms of sexual self-expression, thereby changing the face of erotic literature. At stake here are complex issues of sex, power, gender relations, speech and representation, bound up as well with questions of race, sexual orientation, and social class.

In fact, there are three camps involved in the feminist pornography debate (the expression "sex wars" is often used to describe the way questions of sexuality polarized feminists in the 1980s): anti-pornography feminists, anti-censorship feminists, and pro-pornography feminists. The latter two categories partially overlap, but there is an important distinction: many anti-censorship feminists condemn pornography but suggest other ways to fight it besides suppression, while pro-pornography feminists defend their right to consume and/or make it. (In addition, a number of academic feminists have applied literary, psychoanalytic, political, and cultural-studies approaches to the study of pornography.)

Pornography and Anger

The feminist anti-pornography movement came to prominence in the mid- to late 1970s in the context of the so-called sexual revolution (one consequence of which was an explosion of pornographic magazines and films) and of rising feminist activism. An influential anthology, *Take Back the Night: Women on Pornography* (1980), gave previously published articles wider exposure. In this book and elsewhere, pornography came under fire not because it was sexually explicit, immoral, or anti-marriage, as conservatives—from whom most anti-pornography feminists are careful to distance themselves—had long objected, but because, by portraying women as mindless sex objects and willing victims, it promoted misogyny and eroticized violence. In this view, pornography is vicious anti-female propaganda, even a form of "sexual terrorism" (Kathleen Barry). "Pornography is about slavery," says Adrienne Rich.

Many anti-pornography feminists, including Susan Brownmiller in her 1975 book about rape, blame pornography for sharply rising rape and domestic-violence rates. According to this argument, pornography "teaches" that women long to be raped, abused, and even killed; many men learn the lesson all too well, moving from spec- tatorship to enactment. Some feminists, like Diana E. H. Russell, argue that even nonviolent pornography encourages men to rape. In Robin Morgan's often-quoted phrase, "Pornography is the theory and rape the practice." Pornography is also harmful, these feminists argue, because by depriving women of their full humanity, it allows men to deny them political equality and exploit them sexually and economically, while under- mining their sense of self-worth and making them less likely to fight back.

Pornography, anti-pornography activists claim, is a lie told by men about all women. In addition, lesbian women and women of color, among others, have taken pornography to task for its homophobia (for example, portraying les- bian sex as a pale copy of heterosexual sex or "using" it to stimulate male voyeurs) and racism (treating women of color as monsters, animals, etc.). Finally, anti-pornography feminists have drawn attention to the abuse, intimidation, and coercion experienced by some women in the the multibillion-dollar porn industry. (In this view, women who say they enjoy doing porn films are victims or sell-outs). Because it is pro- foundly anti-woman, pornography, many acti- vists argue, is a form of hate speech and should be banned as such. In response to opponents of censorship, these feminists say that freedom of speech is simply a diversionary tactic: only men—and the huge companies that produce pornography—have freedom of speech today; women have already been silenced. From this perspective, pornography censors women rather than the other way around, preventing them from attaining their full potential; in fact, endangering their very existence.

In *Only Words* and elsewhere, Catharine A. MacKinnon argues that rather than a form of speech worthy of First Amendment protection, pornography is an act of violence against women, both the real woman in the picture and others who might later be harmed because of it; legal action is the best way to defend victims of sex discrimination. Working with Andrea Dworkin, MacKinnon proposed a definition which reads, in part: "Pornography is the sexual- ly explicit subordination of women, graphically depicted, whether in pictures or in words"; a list of unacceptable types of representations follows. Dworkin and MacKinnon fought to have ordinances (which would have allowed

women harmed by pornography to sue produ- cers) enacted in several American cities, but these ordinances were subsequently declared unconstitutional.

While concentrating on mainstream pornog- raphy, anti-pornography feminism also tackled canonical erotic literature. As early as 1969, Kate Millett denounced D.H. Lawrence, Henry Miller, and Norman Mailer as advocates of male supremacy. Given that during the 1970s, French erotic literature acquired a kind of world- wide chic, it is not surprising to find it being attacked from without—in her 1974 *Woman Hat- ing*, Andrea Dworkin devotes chapters to Pauline Réage's *Histoire d'O* and to Jean de Berg's *L'image*—as well as from within. *Les châteaux d'Éros*, by Anne-Marie Dardigna, takes on de Sade, Bataille, Pierre Klossowski, and other dar- lings of the French literary establishment. Far from being the harbingers of a new and radical sexuality, Dardigna says, these authors simply rehash the traditional vision of male domination and female inferiority. Nancy Huston arrived at similar conclusions in her *Mosaïque de la porno- graphie*, as had Xavière Gauthier in her earlier book on literary surrealism. Condemning both literary erotica and mainstream pornography, which they say deliver the same sexist messages, these writers call for women to develop their own erotic imaginations, but consider the task to be almost impossible given their patriarchal conditioning.

Censorship Under Attack

The anti-censorship camp emerged mainly in reaction to anti-pornography feminists' work, criticizing not only their calls for censorship but also their view of women and of hetero- sexual sex. Many Canadian feminists in this camp articulated their views in the 1985 work *Women Against Censorship*. According to these writers and others, anti-pornography feminism attracted many women because it offered a clear target (pornography) and promised a quick fix (censorship). Anti-censorship feminists criti- cized some anti-pornography activists for por- traying women as helpless but pure creatures in need of protection (Andrea Dworkin also says that all intercourse is akin to rape), a point which connects their views to those of the Chris- tian right despite obvious differences (indeed, conservative leaders fought alongside Dworkin and MacKinnon in some states to pass anti-pornography legislation, a point made much of by anti-censorship feminists). Gayle Rubin compares what she calls feminism's increasing preoccupation with moral—rather than political or economic—issues to the politically disastrous shift in 19th-century feminism from a radical critique of women's role and status to a defense of women based on their alleged moral superiority. From this perspective, anti-pornography feminism prevents women from embracing their sexuality, flooding them with guilt, fear, and shame.

Anti-pornography activists see pornography as the root cause of women's oppression, or at least its clearest expression; in the view of anti-censorship feminists, however, it is merely a symptom. Marcia Pally points out that male domination long predated mass pornography and reigns supreme in many modern societies where pornography is outlawed; countries like Japan and Denmark have legal pornography industries without marked increases in sexual crimes. (Anti-censorship feminists also point out that only about 6% of pornography, according to most estimates, is violent.) Following extensive literature reviews, a number of observers have independently concluded that there is no credible evidence demonstrating a causal link between consumption of pornography and violent behavior. Those who feel it is important to discuss, critique, and, if necessary, condemn sexual representations (without censoring them) generally locate pornography within a continuum which includes sexist advertising, films, and music videos, among others, all of which may be equally harmful, if only because they circulate more widely.

Anti-censorship feminists also point out that the distinction between (unacceptable) pornography and (acceptable) eroticism varies widely from one person to the next: for conservatives, any sexually explicit material, such as a sex education textbook, would be pornographic. Conversely, since to outlaw certain productions one must clearly define them, anti-pornography feminists tend to claim that the distinction is easily made. Yet even within feminism, many competing definitions exist. One difficulty is intentionality: if representations of violent sexuality were outlawed, for example, what would be the status of a feminist documentary denouncing rape? What about consensual lesbian or gay

sadomasochistic (S/M) sex? And how can the ambiguities, the ironies, the subtleties of art be weighed and judged?

Censorship is a double-edged sword, these feminists warn: our male-dominated court system is far more likely to target lesbian and gay erotica (generally published by small presses unable to afford legal fees) and feminist explorations than it is to ban *Playboy* or *Penthouse*. In fact, as often noted, most 1990s attacks on the National Endowment for the Arts (NEA) were aimed at explicit sexual images created by gay men or feminist women; under anti-pornography laws, Canadian customs officers have refused to allow books by Kathy Acker, Oscar Wilde, and Marguerite Duras, among others, into the country, and lesbian bookstores have been charged and convicted for selling magazines such as *Bad Attitude*.

More generally, anti-censorship feminists argue, censorship curtails women's freedom while claiming to protect them: censorship is an attempt to dictate what sexual behavior is acceptable, an attempt to control women themselves. Many fear that censorship will silence and disempower women interested in exploring the complexities of their sexual lives. Nadine Strossen sums up the classic First Amendment position: "Big Sister is as unwelcome in our lives as Big Brother" (15).

What then, if anything, should be done about pornography? Anti-censorship feminists who also oppose pornography have advocated or practiced other courses of action, including consumer boycotts, "Take Back the Night" marches, targeting the distribution chain, restricting public display of pornographic materials, working for better salaries for women so they are not tempted to do sex work, improving sex education in the schools, etc. But the best solution, some say, is woman-centered alternatives to standard pornography.

During the 1980s and 1990s, many feminists shifted the focus of debate toward the benefits for women of sexually explicit material. Women who practiced socially stigmatized sexuality, including lesbians, proclaimed their right to explore their sexuality from within the feminist movement. The editors of an early collective work, *Coming to Power: Writings and Graphics on Lesbian S/M* (first edition 1981), insist that writing about their S/M sexuality—against claims that all lesbian relationships are inherently tender and free from power dynamics—is a form of feminist inquiry. The book is a mixture of erotic fiction, political analysis, definitions, and safety tips; its authors, often under pseudonyms, speak of lesbian S/M sex as creative, spiritual, playful, loving, and empowering. This book is only one example of women redefining sexuality as a source of feminist energy and a positive self-image.

Coming to Power, with its punning double focus on pleasure and empowerment, captures the spirit of exploration and consensuality behind most pro-pornography writing. The focus is on reclaiming sexuality for women, thereby violating age-old taboos (symptomatic titles include *Whores and Other Feminists*, *Bad Girls and Dirty Pictures*, and *Talk Dirty to Me*). Much of this writing is by women directly involved in the sex industry, most of whom say they enjoy their work and chose it freely. Carol Queen and others have chided anti-pornography feminists for being anti-sex and anti-desire, inviting feminists to listen to sex-trade workers on issues like the body, sex, and female agency, as well as supporting them in their struggle to improve their working conditions.

Celebrating Pornography

While anti-pornography feminists have emphasized the links between pornography and real-life violence, pro-pornography feminists counter that pornography is fantasy and not reality. (For a nuanced view of pornography as both reality and fantasy, see Jane Ussher's *Fantasies of Femininity*; Drucilla Cornell's anthology *Feminism and Pornography* brings together a variety of feminist responses). Marcia Pally writes that fantasy provides catharsis, allowing desires and fears to play out harmlessly in words and images: "The idea that what happens in fantasy happens in life is neither science nor feminism but voodoo." Laura Kipnis defends various types of pornography—from images using obese people to *Hustler*—as both subversions of the reigning political order and defiant explorations of fantasies with deep personal and cultural resonance; pornography is about pleasure and freedom rather than violence and hatred, she says. Sallie Tisdale, in *Talk Dirty to Me*, attempts to destigmatize both sex and the act of watching it. Wendy McElroy calls pornography and

feminism natural allies because both challenge institutions such as the family and traditional assumptions about sexuality. Many observers list ways in which pornography benefits women as well as men: on a personal level, in addition to providing entertainment and sexual release, it destigmatizes, educates, and serves as sexual therapy; on a political level, it pushes back the borders of acceptable thought, speech, and behavior, therefore providing more freedom for everyone.

Anti-pornography feminists often claim that women are not interested in pornography or that they are forced by their mates to consume it. But clearly, pornography is no longer a male-only preserve. By 1990, in the United States, close to half of all adult videotapes were rented by women in couples or women alone. In *At Home with Pornography: Women, Sex, and Everyday Life*, Jane Juffner focuses on women's consumption of pornography and erotica, including literary anthologies, cyberporn, and adult cable channels, resources which sometimes challenge and sometimes reinforce traditional values.

If women are dissatisfied with traditional pornography, some feminists say, they should make their own. And many have done just that. Whatever their sexual orientation and preferences, these women share the desire to reconcile their feminism and their sexuality while refusing to practice "politically correct" sex or downplay the sexual dimension of their lives. Before the 1960s, few women wrote erotica, although many, from Sappho to Gertrude Stein and Colette, included descriptions of desire and physical pleasure in their writing. One of the first works of female erotica, *Histoire d'O* (1954), published by the French woman Dominique Aury under the pseudonym Pauline Réage, was an international best seller and inspired a feature film. The tragic story of O, a career woman turned into a sexual slave, also aroused widespread feminist ire.

Since the 1980s, as taboos around women's and alternative sexualities have weakened (political backlash notwithstanding), many more women have begun producing erotica/pornography. Although the focus of this article is on written work, the women's erotic film industry deserves mention: for instance, 1984 saw the creation of Femme Productions (founded by Candida Royalle) and Fatale Video (launched by Debi Sundahl), nonsexist adult video production companies. That same year, Debi Sundahl and Susie Bright created *On Our Backs,* a lesbian sex magazine whose title is an irreverent response to *off our backs,* a feminist anti-porn newspaper. Susie Bright has also been involved with literary anthologies such as *Herotica* and the annual *Best American Erotica.* Specialized collections like the Britsh "Black Lace" series are also widely read.

Capitalizing on the success of earlier works such as Nancy Friday's *My Secret Garden,* while filling in the gaps in them, many specialized anthologies have appeared: collections of heterosexual, lesbian, and bisexual erotica, as well as African American, Latina, and Asian American erotic collections are all available in mass-market editions. Whether they feature established writers (as do the *Penguin Book of Erotic Stories by Women* and *Pleasure in the Word: Erotic Writing by Latin American Women*) or "ordinary" women, anthologies of literary erotica have provided a safe space for many women to explore sexual desires, realities, and fantasies. According to some observers, distinctions between men's and women's erotic writing do exist: women writers develop plots and characters more fully and tend to locate sexual practices within real-life situations such as work and relationships. However, women's erotica is not limited to gentle "vanilla" sex: violence, S/M, and aggressive impulses are all frequent themes. Pornogothic, for example, relies on bondage, vampire imagery, black magic, fetishism, leather and latex, dungeons, and body modifications. Many texts, especially lesbian short fiction published in magazines and fanzines, play with the borders between genders, featuring consensual bondage, sex with gay men, strap-on dildoes, etc. A number of magazines, including *Lezzie Smut, Lickerish,* and *Quim,* to mention only a few, explore various facets of lesbian sexuality. As Judith Butler has shown, lesbian sexual power games (butch/femme, whips, leather) parody heterosexual practices and expose traditional male/female roles as cultural masquerade.

Throughout the Western world at least, women's erotic writing is thriving. A very partial list of contemporary women's erotic and/or sexually explicit writing, literary or not—much of which, like Andrea Dworkin's graphic *Mercy,* deals with women's sexual ills rather than attempting to arouse the reader—would have to include Angela Carter, Joan Nestle, Ann Oakley, and Jeannette Winterson (U.K.), Christine

Angot, Catherine Breillat, Viriginie Despentes, Annie Ernaux, Claire Legenre, Alina Reyes, and Françoise Rey (France), Joanna Russ, Pat Califia, Kathryn Harrison, and Anne Rice (United States), Isabel Allende, Laura Esquivel, Cristina Peri Rossi, and Silvana Ocampo (Latin America), Nelly Arcan, Dionne Brand, Nicole Brossard, Anne Dandurand, Claire Dé, Lili Gulliver, Evelyn Lau, and Daphne Marlatt (Québec/Canada), Elfriede Jelinek (Austria), and many others. In fact, in some countries, more women than men are writing about sex, a situation few would have predicted 20 years ago. Themes and approaches vary widely: some writers celebrate sex, others explore painful topics such as incest, rape, violence, and sexual rivalry. Stereotypes of women as naturally modest, gentle, and asexual have been widely challenged; explicit sex and violence, like crude language, are no longer a male preserve. While not all of this material is innovative or challenging, and some women's writing reinforces the sexual status quo rather than questioning it, its sheer abundance is a sign of change. Despite taboos and censure, women's explorations of sexuality would seem to be here to stay.

LORI SAINT-MARTIN

Further Reading

Anthologies

Barbach, Lonnie, ed. *Pleasures: Women Write Erotica.* New York: Doubleday, 1984.

Bell, Roseann P., Reginald Martin, and Miriam DeCosta-Willis, eds. *Erotique Noire / Black Erotica.* New York: Doubleday, 1992.

Bright, Susie, ed. *Herotica: A Collection of Women's Erotic Fiction.* San Francisco: Down There Press, 1988.

———. *Herotica 3: A Collection of Women's Erotic Fiction.* New York: Plume, 1994.

Bright, Susie, and Joani Blank, eds. *Herotica 2: A Collection of Women's Erotic Fiction.* New York: Plume, 1992.

Fernandez Olmos, Margarite, and Lizabeth Paravisini-Gebert, eds. *Pleasure in the Word: Erotic Writing by Latin American Women.* New York: Plume, 1993.

Gonzalez, Ray, ed. *Under the Pomegranate Tree: The Best New Latino Erotica.* New York: Simon and Schuster, 1996.

Kensington Ladies' Erotica Society. *Ladies' Own Erotica: Tales, Recipes, and Other Mischiefs by Older Women.* Berkeley, CA: Ten Speed Press, 1984.

Kukada, Geraldine, ed. *On a Bed of Rice: An Asian-American Erotic Feast.* New York: Doubleday, 1995.

Morris, Kathleen, ed. *Speaking in Whispers: Lesbian African-American Erotica.* Chicago: Third Side Press, 1996.

Sheba Collective, eds. *Serious Pleasure: Lesbian Erotic Stories and Poetry*. Pittsburgh: Cleis, 1991.

Sheiner, Marcy, ed. *Herotica 4: A New Collection of Erotic Writing by Women*. New York: Plume, 1996.

Slung, Michele, ed. *Slow Hand: Women Writing Erotica*. New York: HarperCollins, 1992.

Taormino, Tristan, ed. *The Best Lesbian Erotica, 1997*. San Francisco: Cleis, 1997.

Critical Studies

Assiter, Alison, and Carol Avedon, eds. *Bad Girls and Dirty Pictures: The Challenge to Reclaim Feminism*. London: Pluto Press, 1993.

Brownmiller, Susan. *Against Our Will: Men, Women and Rape*. New York: Bantam, 1975.

Burstyn, Varda, ed. *Women Against Censorship*. Vancouver: Douglas and McIntyre, 1985.

Butler, Judith. *Gender Trouble: Feminism and the Subversion of Identity*. New York: Routledge, 1990.

Coming to Power: Writings and Graphics on Lesbian S/M. Boston: Alyson Publications, 1981, 1987.

Cornell, Drucilla, ed. *Feminism and Pornography*. Oxford: Oxford University Press, 2000.

Dardigna, Anne-Marie. *Les châteaux d'Éros ou les infortunes des sexes des femmes*. Paris: Maspero, 1981.

Dworkin, Andrea. *Woman Hating*. New York: E. P. Dutton & Co., 1974.

———. *Pornography: Men Possessing Women*. New York: Perigee, 1981.

Huston, Nancy. *Mosaïque de la pornographie*. Paris: Denoel-Gonthier, 1982.

Jones, Richard Glyn, and A. Susan Williams, eds. *The Penguin Book of Erotic Stories by Women*. London: Penguin, 1996.

Juffner, Jane. *At Home with Pornography: Women, Sex, and Everyday Life*. New York: NYU Press, 1998.

Kipnis, Laura. *Bound and Gagged: Pornography and the Politics of Fantasy in America*. Durham, NC: Duke University Press, 1996.

Lederer, Laura, ed. *Take Back the Night: Women on Pornography*. New York: Bantam, 1980.

Wendy McElroy. *XXX: A Woman's Right to Pornography*. New York: St. Martin's Press, 1995.

MacKinnon, Catharine. *Only Words*. Cambridge, MA: Harvard University Press, 1993.

Millett, Kate. *Sexual Politics*. New York: Ballantine, 1969.

Nagle, Jill, ed. *Whores and Other Feminists*. New York: Routledge, 1997.

Pally, Marcia. *Sex and Sensibility: Reflections on Forbidden Mirrors and The Will to Censor*. Hopewell, NJ: Ecco Press, 1994.

Segal, Lynn, and Mary McIntosh, eds. *Sex Exposed: Sexuality and the Pornography Debate*. New Brunswick, NJ: Rutgers University Press, 1993.

Stossen, Nadine. *Defending Pornography: Free Speech, Sex, and the Fight for Women's Rights*. New York: Scribner, 1995.

Tisdale, Sallie. *Talk Dirty to Me: An Intimate Philosophy of Sex*. New York: Doubleday, 1994.

Ussher, Jane. *Fantasies of Femininity: Reframing the Boundaries of Sex*. London: Penguin, 1997.

Williams, Linda. *Hard Core: Power, Pleasure, and the "Frenzy of the Visible"*. Berkeley and Los Angeles: University of California Press, 1989.

See also **Women's Writing in French; Women's Writing in Spanish; Women's Writing in English; Réage, Pauline**

FERRATER, GABRIEL

1922–1972
Spanish poet

In the mid-1950s, Gabriel Ferrater made the acquaintance of important Spanish and Catalan poets such as Jaime Gil de Biedma, Carlos Barral, and Joan Vinyoli. As a result of this friendship he also started to write poetry, although only for a few years, until 1963. Ferrater published only three books of poetry: *Da nuces pueris* (1960), *Menja't una cama* (1962), and *Teoria dels cossos* (1966). In 1968 he collected all his 114 poems in the volume *Les dones i els dies* [*Women and Days*] and decided to stop writing poetry. His work was quite different from Catalan poetry of the time, so it was some time before it gained recognition. However, after his death many contemporary Catalan poets have declared him a master, and now he has a pivotal position in contemporary Catalan literature.

Les dones i els dies, written over a short span of five years, contains all of his poems. It is not, however, a mere collection of his previous books, since Ferrater corrected and reorganized his poetry. The result, then, is a new work that conveys Ferrater's collected concerns. The title already shows the interests of the poet: the flow of time and his relationships with women. These are the axis of his work, which is very unitary. In Ferrater's poetry there are three main thematic groups: poems dealing with literature, poems devoted to describing the social situation of the time, and poems about his personal experience, which can be divided into two groups: those that focus on the flow of time and those that narrate erotic experiences. Ferrater's poetry is generally based on the moral reflection of a specific experience, but with a chronological detachment that allows the poet to analyze the lived experience. For Ferrater, moral life consists of exploring the space between the lived experience and the subsequent reflection in which this experience takes form. Furthermore, in his poetry the notion of passion acts as a central force. The energy produced by this force is interpreted by the poet as capable of taking man beyond love, morality, social observation, or sentimental frustration.

The poet often idealizes a teenager full of life who is aware and makes use of her body. Since Ferrater describes this young person when he is already a mature man, poetry also becomes a way to relive and explain adolescence.

In many of his poems, such as "Temps enrere," "Dits," "Ídols," and "Cambra de la tardor," Ferrater reflects in the present time about a past erotic experience by describing the place where it took place, usually a room with a view. The experience usually involved sexual intercourse, and the poet provides a brief and subtle description of his lover. Sometimes the poems also contain erotic moments without sexual intercourse, such as "El distret," where the poet, on a roof, observes a young woman who is combing her hair, or "Jocs," where the poet watches the sensual movements of a woman playing basketball. In many compositions, such as "Oci" and "Xifra," the poet observes and depicts his young lover when she is sleeping next to him. Other poems, such as "Joc," offer a direct, rejoicing, and jovial view of pleasure. Ferrater proposes an egoistical pursuit of the small pleasures of life as the only way to reach happiness. Ferrater's erotic descriptions are usually subtle. The poet is attracted to certain parts of the female

body: thighs, feet, knees, and bellies. These are central to the poet's exploration of eroticism and sexual desire, and they often appear in his discourse. On a few occasions, however, he explicitly refers to the crotch area of his lover, such as in "Mädchen" and "Cançó idiota." There are even more explicit poems such as "Úter," a tribute to the uterus, in which the poet describes himself embracing the crotch of his lover, and "Mudances," in which the female lover is touching the erected penis of her partner.

The various topics that appear in Ferrater's poems reflect, in general, the incidence of time in his relationships. He feels especially attracted to youth, and in his poems it is easy to find feelings such as posession, unfaithfulness, and love. Ferrater's suicide at the age of 50 has been interpreted by Montserrat Roser as an answer to the physical decadence that menaced the way of existence explored in his poems. The sense of death is intrinsically linked to eroticism, because in life the only possible source of pleasure, the body, is being progressively destroyed. The poet has only the short relief of the sporadic erotic experiences.

It is also important to take into account the moral concerns of contemporary Catalan society, which are evoked in Ferrater's social poems. In the "Poema inacabat," for instance, the poet claims that he is not the perverse. Clearly he is referring to the Franco dictatorship, which promoted a sinful view of sexual relationships.

In *Les dones i els dies* the poet tries to reconstruct his identity through feelings. For Ferrater, this experience becomes inextricably linked with hedonism and eroticism, so he advocates a down-to-earth approach to poetry, and his own poems display a fairly comprehensive description of erotic encounters. In spite of the complexity of his work, his poems are easy to understand, because they offer a realistic portrayal of everyday life written in a more colloquial language.

Biography

Born in Reus, Spain. In 1954 he started to read in mathematics but did not finish this degree. Later on he obtained a degree in romance philology. Ferrater was a poet, art and literary critic, translator, linguist, and lecturer at the Universitat Autònoma of Barcelona. A man of vast culture and many interests, he translated works from German, English, Polish, and Swedish. Ferrater died in Sant Cugat del Vallès, Spain.

JORDI CORNELLÀ-DETRELL

Selected Works

Ferrater, Gabriel. *Les dones i els dies*. Barcelona: Edicions 62, 2002.
———. *Women and Days*. Translated by Arthur Terry. Todmorden, UK: Arc Publications, 2004.

Further Reading

Macià, Xavier, and Núria Perpinyà. *La Poesia de Gabriel Ferrater*. Barcelona: Edicions 62, 1986.
Perpinyà, Núria. *Teoria dels cossos de Gabriel Ferrater*. Barcelona: Empúries, 1991.
———. *Gabriel Ferrater: Recepció i contradicció*. Barcelona: Empúries, 1997.
Roser i Puig, Montserrat. "Eroticism in the poetry of Gabriel Ferrater." *Journal of Catalan Studies*, 2000. http://www.uoc.es/jocs/3/articles/ferrata2 (accessed February 27, 2006).

See also **Catalan Literature**

FERRÉ, ROSARIO

1938–
Puerto Rican novelist, essayist, poet, and short story writer

Rosario Ferré is known for her literary and political essays and poetry, but her greatest renown is as a writer of fiction. Since the publication of her first book of short stories in 1976, she has achieved fame as a keen observer of the history and culture of her native Puerto Rico. Her work centers on the balances and imbalances of power that are in conflict in all relationships, be they political, sexual, romantic, or familial.

Ferré was born into an established and influential Puerto Rican family. Her father, Luis Ferré, was a pro-statehood governor of Puerto Rico (1968–1972). Ferré's fiction often centers on the fading aristocracy of Puerto Rico and the divisive legacies of the plantation system. Though her own position is one of privilege, she is openly critical of the class system and racial discrimination in Puerto Rican society, and works like *The Youngest Doll* and *Sweet Diamond Dust* clearly portray the hypocrisy of the island's aristocracy.

Ferré's first collection of stories, *Papeles de Pandora* [*The Youngest Doll*], was published in 1976 and laid the foundation for many of the themes of her later works: the connection of the personal (and specifically, the sexual) with the political, the demystification of sexuality and

eroticism, and the inherent power imbalances of most heterosexual couplings. In terms of erotic content, the most discussed story of the collection is "When Women Love Men," which employs one of Ferré's preferred literary devices, the double, or doppelganger, to highlight the virgin/whore dichotomy imposed on women in Latin culture. Two women, one the wife and the other the lover of a dead man, meet years after the death of the man who linked them. Both women are named Isabel, and though their external differences are emphasized (one is black, the other white; one a prostitute, the other a society wife), as they take turns narrating each other's story, it becomes clear that they are two sides of the same coin, or two halves of a whole: "[E]very lady hides a prostitute under her skin, This is obvious from the way a lady slowly crosses her legs, rubbing the insides of her thighs against each other.... A prostitute, on the other hand, will go to similar extremes to hide the lady under her skin" (134). Isabel Luberza's life as a comfortable, asexual wife is made possible only through the heightened sexuality of Isabel la Negra, who satisfies the husband's sexual needs but also serves as a symbol of the physicality denied to "good" women. As Ferré makes clear, through the denial of women's sexuality, both the virgin and the whore have been "shortchanged both sexually and economically."

The publication of *Papeles de Pandora*, and particularly of "When Women Love Men," led to Ferré's work being labeled "pornographic" due to her frank use of sexual terminology. In "The Writer's Kitchen," an essay included in *Sitio a Eros* (1980), Ferré herself responds to such a categorization, stating that language considered sexually obscene has for too long been the exclusive domain of male writers and that women have both the right and the obligation to reclaim such language. She laments the absence of discussion of obscenity in women's literature and feminist literary criticism, and lays claim to the sexual insult as a tool to be hurled back in the face of the oppressors.

Other pieces in *Sitio a Eros* examine the role of eros in women's writing and lives. Ferré draws on Simone de Beauvoir in calling for an active, transcendental love that would free women from the constraints of passivity and dependence. She analyzes the works of women writers that she admires for their expression of this sort of self-assertive eros, such as Virginia Woolf, Mary Shelley, Julia de Burgos, and Alexandra Kollontai. In Ferré's view, these writers challenged the patriarchal system through their expressions of active feminine love. She calls for other women to allow their subjective, irrational, and distinctly feminine passion to come forth in their writing.

Ferré's later fictional and critical works continue to explore the topics laid out in *Papeles de Pandora* and *Sitio a Eros*. The collection of stories *Maldito amor* [*Sweet Diamond Dust*], published in 1987, again investigates the ties between political power, sexual and romantic relations, and Puerto Rican identity. Perhaps the most erotic language of the collection is reserved for the island itself, as she describes its almost orgasmic profusion of smells, tastes, and colors: "the honeyed yam and the thick-lipped one that leaves you monstruck if you eat it at night, the mysteriously aphrodisiac gingerroot, with emerald swords unsheathed and blooming lips pursed in blood, which afforded us a profitable smuggling trade all through the nineteenth century; the golden ripe plantain and the green one with silver tips, quivering on the branches of Mafofo and Malango trees" (5). Rather than portray Puerto Rico as an untainted Eden, she draws attention to the political realities behind the sensual "paradise"—the exploitation of African slaves and the native Taíno Indians at the hands of first the Spanish, and later the Creole landowners. The human relations in the stories mirror this exploitive dynamic, as complex networks of victimization and power supersede the possibility of romantic love.

Ferré made the somewhat politically controversial decision to begin writing in English in 1995, with the publication of *The House on the Lagoon*. This book, and her subsequent novel in English, *Eccentric Neighborhoods*, continue to explore the erotic in the context of multigenerational family sagas, but the broad historical sweep of the novels somewhat diminishes the focus on the erotic. Nevertheless, in these novels, as in her earlier works, sexuality is frequently presented as a tool too often employed in service of avarice, dominance, and betrayal.

Biography

Born in Ponce, Puerto Rico in 1938. Earned a Bachelor of Arts degree from Manhattanville College (1960), New York, a master's degree from the University of Puerto Rico, Río Piedras (1985), and a Ph.D. in Latin American literature from the University of Maryland, College Park (1987). Editor and publisher of *Zona de Carga y Descarga*, a journal of Puerto Rican literature. Taught Latin American literature at the University of California, Berkeley; Rutgers University; Harvard University; Johns Hopkins University; and the University of Puerto Rico, Río Piedras. Finalist for the National Book Award in 1995, for *House on the Lagoon*. Resides in Puerto Rico.

ALEXANDRA FITTS

Selected Works

Papeles de Pandora. 1976; translated as *The Youngest Doll*, 1991 *Sitio a Eros*, 1980
Maldito amor. 1987; translated by the author as *Sweet Diamond Dust*. 1988
El coloquio de las perras. 1990
La batalla de las vírgenes. 1993
The House on the Lagoon. 1995
Eccentric Neighborhoods. 1998
Flight of the Swan. 2001
A la sombra de tu nombre. 2001

Further Reading

Castillo, Debra A. "Surfacing: Rosario Ferré and Julieta Campos, with Rosario Castellanos." In *Talking Back: Toward a Latin American Feminist Literary Criticism*, edited by Debra A. Castillo. Ithaca, NY: Cornell University Press, 1992.

Castro-Klarén, Sara. "Unpacking Her Library: Rosario Ferré on Love and Women." *Review: Latin American Literature and Arts* 48 (1994): 33–5.

Fernández Olmos, Margarite. "From a Woman's Perspective: The Short Stories of Rosario Ferré and Ana Lydia Vega." In *Contemporary Women Authors of Latin America: Introductory Essays*, edited by Doris Meyer and Margarite Fernández Olmos. Brooklyn, NY: Brooklyn College Press, 1983.

Gascon Vera, Elena. "Sitio a Eros: The Liberated Eros of Rosario Ferré." In *Reinterpreting the Spanish American Essay: Women Writers of the 19th and 20th Centuries*, edited by Doris Meyer. Austin: University of Texas Press, 1995.

Guerra Cunningham, Lucía. "Sitio a Eros." *Letras Femeninas* 9 (1983): 57–9.

Hintz, Suzanne S. *Rosario Ferré: A Search for Identity*. New York: Peter Lang, 1995.

Jaffe, Janice. "Translation and Prostitution: Rosario Ferré's Maldito amor and Sweet Diamond Dust." *Latin American Literary Review* 23 (1995): 66–82.

Umpierre, Luz María. "Un manifiesto literario: Papeles de Pandora de Rosario Ferré." *The Bilingual Review* 9 (1982): 120–26.

Urrea, Beatriz. "El cuerpo femenino: Identidad(es) problemitizada(s) en dos cuentos de Rosario Ferré." *Revista de crítica literaria latinoamericana* 22 (1996): 279–300.

Vega Carney, Carmen. "Sexo y texto en Rosario Ferré." *Confluencia* 4 (1988): 119–27.

FIELD, MICHEL

1956–
French writer and journalist

Impasse de la Nuit

Divided into 12 chapters, organized as a journey through the night, from "Dusk" (Chapter 2) to "Dawn" (Chapter 12), *Impasse de la Nuit* is structured in an elaborate and dynamic way. The *impasse* of the title is both a literal one-way cul-de-sac as a typical setting for casual sex encounters and the metaphorical realization that the Night (occasionally personalized) is an alternative universe not compatible with mainstream life, heteronormative sexuality, and conventional relationships. *Impasse de la Nuit* is set in a busy, urban, labyrinthic, decadent Paris, whose topology of erotic landmarks revolves mainly around places with strong sexual connotations (such as the Rue Saint Denis, its sex shops, its seedy night clubs with lesbian peepshows, and its cafés where prostitutes meet and relax between clients) and places where people have sex in public (Bois de Boulogne, car parks, porn movie theatres, and men's public toilets).

The narrator is a writer working on a book about the night, with a special interest in some of those "night people" who tend to become sexually active then: voyeurs, exhibitionists, prostitutes, and transvestites, all people who would otherwise be labeled as perverts or deviants. Doing research for his book, the narrator reflects on his surroundings and on his past experiences and adventures, and explores parts of his sexuality restrained so far. Such are the two dimensions of *Impasse de la Nuit*: the intellectual, if not philosophical, dimension, which makes the book a reflective essay on erotic literature, or at least a poetic treatise on voyeurism, and the embodied dimension, with the erotic narration of sexual scenarios, situations, and encounters.

Whereas the main part of the book appears as a journal in which the narrator records erotic stories (with limited linear narrative and no sense of chronology) and their analysis (like a flowing stream of consciousness), three chapters ("Correspondence I," "Correspondence II," and "Correspondence III") consist of extracts of letters exchanged between the narrator and a past female lover. These letters are directly reminiscent of *Les Liaisons dangereuses*, both because of the literary technique itself, not uncommon in erotic literature, and because of the sophisticated quality of the language and style, which could easily be read as a pastiche of Choderlos de

Laclos. The letters powerfully relate some of their staged erotic adventures, all taking place at night, which is presented as the liberating factor, typically with her stripping and masturbating in public places such as car parks, watched by several men who also masturbate, whilst her lover stands anonymously amongst them.

A leitmotiv of *Impasse de la Nuit*, voyeurism is illustrated in numerous ways: there is, for example, the enigmatic café in the Bois de Boulogne where regular patrons only go to see exhibitionist couples touching each other up under the tables, with the approval of the old, seemingly bigoted landlady, as long as there are no children around; there is the episode of the narrator observing his half-naked female neighbor through the window whilst his girlfriend goes down on him and asks him to describe the scene until he comes; there is also the story of a couple straightforwardly having sex in a car whilst other men stand around and masturbate, creating a sort of complicity, if not bonding, between all the men present. Yet voyeurism is not just illustrated but also conceptualized, if not justified, both culturally and philosophically. With due reference to history and literature, voyeurism is explained as a socially constructed male privilege; the voyeur is defined as the best theoretician of desire, whose playful gaze, innocently perverted, bridges a gap between men and women. Albeit possibly sexist and arguable, this analysis nevertheless gives the book its intellectual edge and original quality, differentiating it from a mere pornographic novel, a process reminiscent of de Sade developing philosophical issues and arguments even in his most sexually explicit texts. This is certainly due to Michel Field's background as a philosophy teacher (if not as a philosopher), which comes to the surface here, as in all the passages where the text suddenly shifts from graphic erotic evocations to metaphysical evaluations of pleasure, gender identity, or sexual desire. A related characteristic of the author is his love of the French language, coupled with remarkable stylistic skills: his prose is highly poetic, and several passages are pure

plays with puns, alliterations, and homonyms, exemplified in the first words of Chapter 2: "Nuitamment. Nuit, amant" [Nightly. Night, lover], which makes the translation of the book extremely difficult.

Eventually, it is worth noting that *Impasse de la Nuit* lends itself very well to queer reading and queer analysis, for three main reasons. Firstly, it presents and represents a vast array of culturally marginal forms of sexuality (such as leather fetishism and cross-dressing, exhibitionism, prostitution, casual homosexual and bisexual sex encounters), which perfectly fall under the umbrella term of "queer" as defined by queer theory. Secondly, the sexual scenes depicted and the accompanying comments repeatedly blur the male/female and straight/gay boundaries, a key tenet of queer theory with evident echoes of postmodernism. Thirdly, it problematizes notions of gender/sex/sexual identity, as in the last chapters, where the narrator (who used to wear leather clothes and flaunt his heterosexuality over gay men he would only have passive oral sex with) starts to dress up as a woman, carefully choosing female silk underwear ("Silk, my feminine identity.... Silk, my feminine double"), wearing a suspender belt, heavy makeup, high-heel shoes, and a sexy dress before courageously going out to sell his/her transvestite body to the night—the Night being again the liberating factor and the only way to gain a new identity, to achieve a metaphorical and metaphysical ascesis in an *impasse* from which it will not be possible to return.

Biography

Michel Field is a well-known journalist and cultural commentator on French radio and television, yet in the 1980s he also wrote three novels: *Le Passeur de Lesbos* (1984), *Impasse de la Nuit* (1986), and *L'Homme aux Pâtes* (1989). Originally released by Bernard Barrault, they have been republished by Editions Robert Laffont.

Loykie Loïc Lominé

FIELDING, HENRY

1707–1754
British playwright and novelist

Works

The sexual content of Fielding's works was evident in his own time, when he was excoriated for his "lowness" by Richardson, Johnson, and Hawkins, who said that Fielding's virtue "was that of a dog or a horse." His works are not erotic in the sense that *Fanny Hill* is, but they give sexual realities their force, generally with comic effect, against moral hypocrisy, especially in women.

His burlesque and farce plays depended on sexual humor as much as on political satire, and *Shamela*, his travesty of *Pamela*, focuses on the sexuality of Richardson's servant-girl heroine to portray her as a hypocrite working on the sexual responses of a gentleman so he will marry her for her profit and that of her lover. In *Joseph Andrews*, he portrays in Lady Booby, her servant Slipslop, and Betty the Chambermaid all the energy of female lust, directed at the young and handsome Joseph. A careful reading reveals even in the "pure" Fanny, who is in love with him, the same powerful drives at work. Indeed, Fanny is first introduced in a verbal picture that stresses her sexual attractiveness according to eighteenth-century criteria:

> *Fanny* was now in the nineteenth Year of her Age; she was tall and delicately shaped; but not one of those slender young Women, who seem rather intended to hang up in the Hall of an Anatomist, than for any other Purpose. On the contrary, she was so plump that she seemed bursting through her tight Stays, especially in that Part which confined her swelling breasts. Nor did her Hips want the Assistance of a Hoop to extend them.

The long paragraph continues listing her physical delights. Throughout the subsequent adventures, only the continual presence of Parson Adams is what prevents Joseph and Fanny from consummating their desire for one another.

In *Tom Jones* the handsome hero does not remain even technically "pure." Women will not let him. Jones is first seduced by the sexually aggressive Molly Segrim, but then falls in love with Sophia Western, a beautiful young virgin who is the daughter of the owner of the estate adjoining the one on which he—a foundling— lives under the protection of Squire Allworthy. But the young Blifil, presumed heir to the estate and a cold sadist, hopes to marry Sophia himself, in spite of her detestation of him:

> Now the Agonies which affected the Mind of *Sophia* rather augmented than impaired her Beauty; for her Tears added Brightness to her Eyes, and her Breasts rose higher with her Sighs.... *Blifil* therefore looked on this human Ortalan with greater desire than when he viewed her last; nor was his Desire at all lessened by the Aversion which he discovered in her to himself. On the contrary, this served rather to heighten the Pleasure he proposed in rifling her Charms, as it added Triumph to Lust; he had some further Views, from obtaining the absolute Possession of her Person, which we detest too much even to mention...

Jones, after Blifil has tricked Allworthy into expelling him, affirms his love for Sophia but nevertheless, after exciting himself thinking of her charms, goes off on a chance encounter with Molly into "the thickest Part of the Grove." Fielding tries to maintain that Jones's "imprudence" with women causes him all his subsequent troubles (and modern literary criticism, especially in the United States, has generally sided with Fielding's argument), but the circumstances in which Jones finds himself are always such that only a young man not homosexual—unless he is as cold as Blifil—could resist seduction. When she precedes him at an inn, even the "pure" Sophia gives Jones a trail to her by leaving a muff that has sexual significance for both of them. On his way to London, however, he is seduced by the naked breasts of Mrs. Waters, and in London is seduced by Lady Bellaston. But, out of desire for him, Sophia forgives him everything, and in the end the villainies of Blifil are exposed, Jones is to be Allworthy's heir, and

Sophia marries him. Then transpires "that happy Hour which... surrendered the charming *Sophia* to the eager Arms of her enraptured *Jones*." The sexual feelings of the men and women in the novel are usually revealed to the reader, for they function as the novel's sure index of their characterization. Indeed, *Tom Jones* can be seen as a penetrating study of people in a society where the power and significance of sexual motivation is not acknowledged.

Fielding's last novel, *Amelia*, lacks the comic gusto of *Joseph Andrews* and *Tom Jones*, because the London world he portrays is so grim that the good-natured, sexually warm man and woman are barely saved from destruction. Captain Booth is a Tom Jones after marriage. The novel opens with him in a debtor's prison, where, though he adores his wife, Amelia (modeled as was Sophia on Fielding's beloved Charlotte), he nonetheless is seduced by a former lover whom he encounters there. He tries to hide this lapse from Amelia and does not realize till the end that she knew of it and long ago forgave him. Very interesting are the quiet but powerful erotic feelings of Amelia herself, most often overlooked by readers. Certainly she gratifies Booth. "Here ended all that is Material of their Discourse," we are told at one point, "and a little Time afterwards they both fell asleep in each other's Arms; from which time Booth had no more Restlessness, nor any further Perturbation of his Dreams." And another time, after his jealous fears have been allayed, he "caught her in his Arms and tenderly embraced her. After which the Reconciliation soon became complete; and Booth in the Contemplation of his Happiness entirely buried all his jealous Thoughts." But also she is gratified by him. She says that as long as she has "such a Husband to make life Delicious" she can easily accept poverty: "'Am I of a superior Rank of being to the Wife of an honest Laborer? Am I not one of common Nature with her?'" Thus, she affirms her sexual nature in common with all women, and it is just this kind of affirmation which is truly at the center of Fielding's novels.

Biography

Born April 22 at Sharpham Park, Somersetshire. Studied at Eton, 1719–1724. His first publication and first play appeared, 1728. Enrolled as student of letters, 1728, University of Leiden; ceased studies in 1729. Began career as dramatist, 1730. Marriage to Charlotte Cradock, 1734. Dramatic career ended by Licensing Act, 1737, brought on by his farces against Prime Minister Walpole. Edited the anti-Walpole *The Champion,* 1739. Called to bar, 1740. Death of Charlotte, 1744. Married Mary Daniel, 1747. Traveled to Lisbon, 1754, in hopes of restoring health. Died October 8 in Junqueria, near Lisbon.

GERALD J. BUTLER

Selected Works

Shamela. 1741
Joseph Andrews. 1742
Tom Jones. 1749
Amelia. 1751

Further Reading

Battestin, Martin C. *Henry Fielding: A Life*. London and New York: Routledge, 1989.

Butler, Gerald J. *Fielding's Unruly Novels*. Lewiston, NY: E. Mellen, 1995.

Cross, Wilbur L. *The History of Henry Fielding*. 3 vols. New Haven, CT: Yale University Press, 1918.

Digeon, Aurélien. *The Novels of Fielding* [1925]. New York: Russell and Russell, 1962.

Paulson, Ronald, ed. *Henry Fielding: The Critical Heritage*. London: Routledge and Keagan Paul, 1969.

Rawson, C.J. *Henry Fielding and the Augustan Ideal Under Stress*. London and Boston: Routledge and Keagan Paul, 1972.

Sherbo, Arthur. *Studies in the Eighteenth Century English Novel*. East Lansing: Michigan State University Press, 1969.

Smallwood, Angela J. *Fielding and the Woman Question: Theory and Practice from Fielding to Freud*. Tallahassee: Florida State University Press, 1985.

Varey, Simon. *Henry Fielding*. Cambridge: Cambridge University Press, 1986.

Wagner, Peter. *Eros Revived: Erotica of the Enlightenment in England and America*. London: Secker and Warburg, 1988.

FLAUBERT, GUSTAVE

1821–1880
French novelist

Precociously exposed to the sight of his surgeon-father dissecting a fresh young female corpse, Flaubert's erotic life was always deliriously complicated: a procession of the delicate and the brutal, a roaringly farcical quarrel between the romantic idealist and the cynical connoisseur of prostitution. An incident from the author's 25th year will serve to illustrate the achieved pattern of his imagination.

It was the summer of 1846 and Flaubert was walking across Brittany when he came upon an ancient fragment of Eros: "A few miles from the little village, hiding in the middle of a beechwood, there stands a granite statue, six feet high, a naked woman, with her hands over her breasts. Seen in profile, with her fat thighs, her plump buttocks, her knees bent, she has a sensuality which is both barbaric and refined. At the foot of the pedestal there is a large basin, carved from the same granite, and it can hold sixteen barrels of water. The Breton peasants used to worship her as an idol: women who had just given birth came to bathe in the basin at her feet, and young people eager to marry would dive into the water. Then, under the eyes of the goddess, they would engage in the solitary entertainment available to the melancholy lover" (Wall 2002, 136–7). Flaubert was delighted with his peasant Venus. She was, he wrote, "the invigorating, exciting, healing idol, the incarnation of health, of the flesh, the very symbol of desire, the manifestation of that eternal religion rooted in the very bowels of man" (Wall 2002, 137). A century before surrealism, Flaubert had already understood, in the figure of this rough goddess, the secret harmony of the sexual and the sacred.

This would become the darkest and most potent theme of his work as a novelist. And Flaubert's refusal to sift the pure from the impure would soon land him in trouble. When *Madame Bovary* was prosecuted for offending against religious morality, it was specifically because "voluptuous images are mixed up with things sacred," because Emma "murmurs to God the adulterous caresses she has given to her lover," because the book would fall into the hands of "young girls and married women" (Wall, 234). Answering his accusers, Flaubert offered a defense judiciously adjusted to the spirit of the age. He declared that his work was eminently moral because it was written for educated men, not young girls. "Sincere books may sometimes have a certain salutary pungency. Personally I deplore rather those sugary confections which readers swallow without realizing that they are quietly poisoning themselves.... Readers in search of lascivious material, readers who may take harm, will never progress beyond the third page of what I have written. The serious tone will not be to their taste. People do not go to watch surgical operations in a spirit of lubricity" (Wall 2002, 349).

The psychosexual subject of Flaubert's next novel, *Salammbô*, was even more perilously explicit. Only the exoticism of the setting, Carthage in the third century BCE, would preserve it from the official censors of the French Second Empire. Flaubert's artistic purpose was clear. Privately, he explained that "the most furious material appetites are expressed unknowingly by flights of idealism, just as the most sordidly extravagant sexual acts are engendered by a pure desire for the impossible, an ethereal aspiration after sovereign joy. I do not know (nobody knows) the meaning of the words *body* and *soul,* where the one ends and the other begins. We feel the play of energy and that is all" (Wall 2002, 249).

In the real world, the free play of psychic energy was, of course, subject to the cramping effects of censorship, actual or merely anticipated. Having been found not guilty in his trial for *Madame Bovary,* Flaubert did not relish the possibility of another prosecution. At the center of *Salammbô* he placed a scene of sumptuously perverse fancy-dress eroticism in which the naked priestess of the moon becomes entwined with a large serpent. This image was remarkably congenial to the educated taste of the 1860s, raised on a rich diet of grand opera and history painting. Indeed, *Salammbô* resonated down through the collective fantasy life of a whole generation, producing a short-lived school of paintings and statues portraying women with snakes, still to be found in provincial museums and galleries (Dijkstra, 272).

In his next novel, *L'Éducation sentimentale*, Flaubert returned to his own day. This was to be a love story, but it was modern love, blighted, like the modern world, by a selfish, nervous habit of calculation. The hero is driven by an exalted, poetical, adolescent passion for an unattainable older woman. His sexual history is a tissue of perplexity, frustration, and betrayal. There is no climax, no release, no satisfaction: only a lingering finale of self-estrangement, intellectual exhaustion, emotional sterility, and a lugubriously ironic memory of a schoolboy escapade in a brothel. The chastened, greying protagonists agree emphatically that it was "the best time we ever had."

Ingeniously constrained in his fiction, Flaubert is gloriously unbuttoned in his letters. Here we catch the artist at play, turning the adventures of the flesh into words. Flaubert's surviving letters, their genitalia snipped away by a pious executor but restored by his twentieth-century editors, are exceptionally rich in the epistolary-erotic. Writing from Egypt to his stay-at-home friend Louis Bouilhet, Flaubert teased him with lingeringly detailed accounts of his experiments in the bathhouses and brothels of the East. "Out here it's quite the thing. People confess to their sodomy and talk about it over the dinner-table in the hotel. Sometimes you deny it mildly, then everyone gives you a rollicking and eventually you own up. Travelling for my own edification and entrusted with a government mission, we have considered it our duty to engage in this mode of ejaculation" (*Selected Letters,* 137).

Writing to his newfound mistress Louise Colet in the late summer of 1846 Flaubert combines amorous ingenuity, psychological refinement, and a murky ambivalence. The mix is typically both distressing and exciting. He stages the scene of his midnight rereading of her letters. In Flaubert's hands this becomes a comic-erotic ritual of great imaginative intensity, designed to stir the memory and quicken the pulse of writer and reader alike. When the house is asleep he unlocks the drawer of the cabinet where he hides his treasures. On the writing table, he arranges his collection: a miniature portrait, a lock of blonde hair, and a handkerchief, evocatively stained. Folded in an embroidered bag, here are his letters from Louise, the pages faintly scented with musk. And here is the most precious relic of all, a pair of her slippers. He gazes at them and his hand trembles as he reaches out to touch them. He inhales their bouquet of verbena. He imagines the warm feel of her foot inside them. Endearingly ridiculous, he eventually confesses to her, "I think I love them as much as I love you" (Wall 2002, 104).

Biography

Born in Rouen, France, December 12. Son of Achille Cleophas Flaubert, a wealthy surgeon and professor of medicine. Attended the Collège Royal, Rouen, 1831–1839; the École de Droit, Paris, 1841–1845. Abandoned legal studies because of ill health, 1845. Lived on private income. Traveled to Italy, 1845; Egypt, Palestine, and Greece, 1849–1851; Algeria and Tunisia, 1858. Maintained a sporadic relationship with the poet Louise Colet, 1846–1855. Published six novels, including *Madame Bovary* (1856), *Salammbô* (1862), *L'Éducation sentimentale* (1869), and *Trois contes* (1877). Died of a stroke at Croisset, near Rouen, May 8, 1880.

GEOFFREY WALL

Further Reading

There are no exclusively erotic works by this author, but the two following items are recommended.

Flaubert, Gustave. *Flaubert in Egypt: A Sensibility on Tour*. Edited by Francis Steegmuller. London: Penguin Books, 1996.

Selected Letters. Selected and translated by Geoffrey Wall. London: Penguin Books, 1997.

Secondary Reading

Bernheimer, Charles. *Figures of Ill Repute: Representing Prostitution in Nineteenth Century France*. London: Harvard University Press, 1989.

Brombert, Victor. "*L'Éducation sentimentale*: Profanation and the Permanence of Dreams." In *The Novels of Flaubert: A Study of Themes and Techniques*. Princeton, NJ: Princeton University Press, 1966.

Dijkstra, Bram. *Idols of Perversity: Fantasies of Feminine Evil in Fin-de-Siecle Culture*. New York: Oxford University Press, 1986.

Heath, Stephen. *Flaubert: Madame Bovary*. Cambridge, Cambridge University Press, 1992.

Orr, Mary. *Flaubert: Writing the Masculine*. Oxford, UK: Oxford University Press, 2000.

Tooke, Adrianne. *Flaubert and the Pictorial Arts: From Image to Text*. Oxford, UK: Oxford University Press, 2000.

Wall, Geoffrey. *Flaubert: A Life*. London: Faber, 2002.

FOUGERET DE MONBRON, LOUIS CHARLES

1706–1760
French novelist, essayist, and satiric poet

Le canapé couleur de feu

Very quickly, after his arrival in Paris, Fougeret de Monbron patronizes the backstage of the Comédie-Italienne, the whorehouses, and the cafés. With his satirical mind, he likes the company of the girls and of the "bad subjects." He is also seen joining the Bout-du-Banc society (see Caylus). It is here, no doubt, that he becomes acquainted with Crébillon's novel, *Le Sopha*, which circulates under the form of manuscript copies. Fougeret was thus inspired to write his *Canapé*, which was published in 1741, one year before crébillon's novel.

Le canapé (which would afterward take the title *Le canapé couleur de feu*) is presented at first as a burlesque parody of fashionable fairy tales. For not having responded to the lubricious desires of the fairy Crapaudine, the knight Commode is transformed into a couch. Condemned to be the witness of the pleasures that will be taken on him, he will only be disenchanted when a lover will fail with his partner. Thus the novel opens, after the failure of a ridiculous new husband to satisfy his young wife. His failure causes the couch to transform itself into the young knight Commode, who then begins the narrative of his misadventures.

It can be seen that to the elegance of Crébillon's language, and the refined environment *Le sopha* offers, Fougeret opposes the rudeness and the immediate vigor of the satire, as a challenge. The writer multiplies scenes ridiculing the nobility and revealing the vices of the clergy: the couch thus passes from one universe to another, in a comic rhapsody. Here, a "pious vagrant" deflowers a girl; there, a religious dressed up as a little boy who does not know his catechism is being whipped by a prostitute and then whips her in his turn; four monks have a rendezvous to meet the famed Fillon at her whorehouse; a pious bourgeois and her confessor are enema fans, leaving ill-smelling traces. Fougeret in *Le Canapé* denounces the hypocrisy of all religions, and in his depiction of the French Jansenists, the Convulsionaries appear as many "jesters," skillful in misleading the world.

At the end of his adventures as a couch, after having suffered a thousand jogs and thrusts during sex between the lovers lying on him and celebrated his disenchantment with the young wife, Commode will be appointed by the fairy as Great Sarbacanier of the Crown.

Margot la ravaudeuse

In *Margot la ravaudeuse: Histoire d'une prostituée*, Fougeret de Monbron goes on stripping away the layers of dubious respectability concealing the vices of his time. Margot, a girl of the streets, is the illegitimate fruit of the union of a soldier and a seamstress. Through her own work as a mender of torn stockings, her little hand discovers the vanities and lies behind the lustrous garments. Then she herself is drawn into the world of pleasures. Very quickly, in the novel, the bodies tumble in fighting or in being carried away in pleasure. The beds cracking under the vigor of sexual intercourse and the screaming and whimpering of pleasure assure us that sex is a noisy and rowdy thing, which beautiful speeches seek to cover up in vain and which sets in motion the vast uproar of the world. Mender, prostitute, Opera dancer, maintained woman—thus does Margot tell of her tribulations.

The story of Margot's adventures fits in with the many novels giving the "girls of the world" (the expression dates from the Regency) the right to speak: *La belle allemande* by Antoine Bret (1745), *Panfiche* by Gimat de Bonneval (1748), *Histoire de Mlle Brion* (1754), and *Les egarements de Julie* by Jacques Perrin (1755). And all of these worldly belles share the same lucid and vigilant perspective on eighteenth-century European society—here and there the same temper flare-ups, the same taste for pleasure; the same reflections, bitter or violent, on social prejudice, on the miseries of the job; the same fear of the police and venereal disease; the same series of relocations; all marking the ups and downs of an existence submitted to the desire of men.

Fougeret (who translated *Fanny Hill* by Cleland) gives Margot a disillusionment in men, a sentiment he shares with her. However, his heroine is full of a conquering energy. Margot enjoys pleasure. She tears down facades. She launches a challenge to the world through her outspokenness. She is a woman who speaks and who does not allow herself to be duped. Hence, laughter runs throughout the novel. The overwhelming power of the "histoires comiques" that *Margot la ravaudeuse* tells makes the reader recall that laughter has its part in pleasure, that the comic is always sexual.

Biography

Fougeret de Monbron was born in Péronne on December 19. He arrives in Paris at the age of twenty. He sells back his office of a valet of the king's chamber, abandons all functions, and multiplies his trips across Europe, to Turkey, and to Russia. Watched by the police, imprisoned for his writings and satirical outspokenness, he appears to his contemporaries as a cynical and misanthropic writer. He dies in Paris on September 16.

PATRICK WALD LASOWSKI

Editions

Le Canape, par M. de.... La Haye: Papi, s.d [1741].
Le Canape couleur de feu, par M. de.... Amsterdam: Campagnie des libraires, 1741.
Margot la ravaudeuse. Hamburg: n.p., 1800 [1750]

Selected Works

La henriade travestie en vers burlesques. Berlin, 1745.

Further Readings

Benabou, E.M. *La prostitution et la police des moeurs au XVIIIeme siecle*. Paris: Fayard, 1987.
Cortey, M. *L'Invention de la courtisane au XVIIIeme siécle*. Paris: Editions Arguments, 2001
Lasowski, P. Wald, ed. *Romanciers libertins du XVIIIeme siecle*. Paris: Gallimard, "La Pleide, 2000.

FOWLES, JOHN

1926–
English novelist, short story writer, and nonfiction writer

John Fowles's fiction consists of erotic quest romances in which sensitive, independent, and enigmatic women are pursued and captured, lost and recovered, betrayed and deserted, defiled and even destroyed by intellectually inferior, emotionally insulated, and sexually inept men. These men desire absolute power and control and possession of what they cannot fully understand, but they are also hypocritically self-punishing creatures who masochistically seek feminine correction of their masculine selfishness and ignorance. Their sibylline mistresses, whom they learn *from* but not *of*, set harsh tests from which some benefit nothing while the more discerning are given glimpses by their female *anima* of a superior intimacy of intelligence and desire, unfathomable by their own sex. The quest is never fulfilled, but the questors, freed from dependence on the objects of their passion, are educated into a difficult but more authentic freedom, learning from their losses and defeats about the mysterious nature of love, the impossibility of absolute knowledge, and the limitations of a left-lobe logic that categorizes and imprisons experience, whether in a locked cellar or on a pedestal.

In Fowles's England the Victorian age ends with the Second World War. The libidinal hang-ups of his questing anti-heroes are really hang-*overs* from the sexual manners and myths of an earlier, more repressed age and are exemplified in the narcissistic protagonist of *The Magus,* who rejects his nubile Australian girlfriend for an Edwardian wraith conjured from a magician's phantasmagoric masque. It is the secret wish and fear of the Fowlesian male, and of the surrogate author quarreling with his erotic muse in *Mantissa*, that his women should be simultaneously demure and provocative, virginal and promiscuous, tender and unforgiving. The conflicting pressures raging within the protagonal male psyche foist upon the female characters a mythic contradictoriness and unpredictability or, alternatively, polarize them into princesses and wantons, icons of magical unattainability debased by sexual access into seductresses and whores. Among these paired opposites are Charles's prim conventional fiancée Ernestina and the mysterious, dangerous Sarah in *The French Lieutenant's Woman*; the sensual and spiritual sisters Nell and Jane, and their alter egos Miriam and Marjory, with whom the hero of *Daniel Martin* enjoys parallel sexual relations; and, in the title story of *The Ebony Tower*, the septuagenarian painter's two young female acolytes, the mystic "Mouse" and the vampish "Freak," who arouse harem fantasies in the mind of a visiting art critic.

This pernicious sexual idealism is given its crudest form in Frederick Clegg, the lowly government clerk of *The Collector* who spends his lottery winnings kidnapping an upper-class art student. For the obsequious, depraved Clegg there are two kinds of women—those you respect and those you abuse—and Miranda, the captive object of his fixation, descends in his eyes from one to "the other sort" in the sadomasochistic drama of power and abasement, class guilt, and revenge which is played out in his secret cellar. When Miranda's failure to communicate with her captor drives her, in desperation, to sexual advances that reveal his impotence, he pruriently punishes her forfeiture of his "respect" by roping her naked to the bed and taking obscene photographs, to which he then masturbates, "taking" the woman in the only way he knows—through a camera lens. A butterfly collector, Clegg stalks, captures, chloroforms, photographically exhibits, and finally kills Miranda as if she were one of his specimens.

Nicholas Urfe, the hapless victim of an occult theatrical extravaganza, or "godgame," staged by the island mage Conchis in *The Magus*, is a more sophisticated, educated Clegg. An ogler of photographed female breasts, Nicholas also prefers the onanistic fantasy to the real thing (the actress who acts out whatever he wants the mysterious Edwardian Lily to be tells him, "The real me's a lot less exciting than the imaginary one"), and, as with Clegg, his self-abasement has its obverse side. When, during the degrading and humiliating ordeals of his "disintoxication," the virginal "Lily" metamorphoses into actress, schizophrenic god-daughter, and sadistic psychiatrist, Nicholas's darker desires—to flog her, to watch her perform in a pornographic film and copulate with a black lover—are brought into play and meta-theatrically enacted in the psychodrama of the masque.

In *The French Lieutenant's Woman* this schizophrenic sexual psychopathology is traced to its origins in the Victorian era, an age of sanctified womanhood and child prostitutes, bowdlerized literature and massive pornography, which was neurotically in "two minds" about women and sex. Mirroring the crisis of his age, Charles Smithson by turns douses and fuels the flames of his forbidden passion for Sarah Woodruff, the self-styled "scarlet woman of Lyme." When she offers him her love at the Undercliff and then herself at an Exeter hotel, he seizes both and then runs away (respectively, to his angelic betrothed and the nearest church). Sarah's story of her seduction by the French man Varguennes is a deliberate lie intended to seduce Charles, first vicariously, by making him a voyeur of the event who identifies with her seducer, and later in person, when she concocts a sprained ankle to set up the book's single, explosive sexual encounter in the hotel. A "pure" woman acting the role of a fallen one, Sarah, with knowing irony, fulfills the contradictory male desire for a virginal seductress (only at the moment when she ceases to be a virgin is she revealed, for the first time, to have been one). The trick is played so that Charles may remain, Victorianly, in two minds, unable to decide or even distinguish between his two figmentary Sarahs—the "innocent victim" and "wild abandoned woman," the *femme fatale* and melancholic hysteric—and he is kept in his confusion by the alternative endings which counterweight reconciliation with mutual rejection and abandonment.

The novel's narrator is also caught in two minds, waxing nostalgic for an age when sexual pleasure was sharpened by denial and recognizing fiction's complicity with repression. Mystery, says Fowles in *The Aristos*, energizes desire and fuels imagination; frustration nourishes fantasy, and this is equally true for writer, reader, and character. Fowles, who as French graduate, ex–naval lieutenant, and amateur naturalist combines features of Sarah's two lovers, has confessed to being ignorantly in love with and seduced by his heroine, and, as in *The Magus*, he places both the reader and himself in the position of the bewildered protagonist. Conchis, whom Fowles originally conceived as a woman, and the unknowable Sarah perform a conjuring striptease in which layer after layer of illusion is whisked away to reveal only another disguise; gratification is delayed, and denouements are deferred and dissolved to give the reader an unconsummated pleasure of the text. Even in *A Maggot*, where it is transcended by celestial history, the erotic plot is a powerful engine of narrative suspense and intrigue, driven by the prostitute's titillating tales of satanic orgies and her lord's voyeuristic threesomes (similar fantasies keep imagination alive in the dessicated Hollywood of *Daniel Martin*).

In *The Ebony Tower* the erotic origins of composition are indicated by the painter's nickname for his amanuensis, "Mouse," formed by inserting an O-shaped vulva into the word "Muse," but in the metafictional *Mantissa* the writer's muse is a figmentary creature of *his* will, not he of hers, so her costume-changes from sex therapist and punk dominatrix to pert nymph and geisha occur auto-erotically, in the grey cells of his brain, making this both the most explicitly erotic and aridly cerebral of Fowles's works.

Biography

Born John Robert Fowles in Leigh-on-Sea, Essex, March 31. Educated at Bedford School, 1940–44; Edinburgh University, 1944; New College, Oxford University, 1947–50: B.A. (honors) French, 1950. Lieutenant in Royal Marines, 1945–46; *Lecteur* in English, University of Poitiers, France, 1950–51; English teacher at Anargyrios College, Spetsai, Greece, 1951–52; various teaching posts in London, 1953–63, including Head of English, St. Godric's College, Hampstead. Married Elizabeth Whitton 1956 (died 1990). Received Silver Pen Award, 1969, and W. H. Smith Literary Award, 1970, for *The French Lieutenant's Woman* and Christopher Award, 1981.

DEREK WRIGHT

Selected Works

The Collector. 1963
The Aristos: A Self-Portrait in Ideas. 1964; revised edition, 1968
The Magus. 1965; revised edition, 1977
The French Lieutenant's Woman. 1969
The Ebony Tower. 1974
Daniel Martin. 1977
Mantissa. 1982
A Maggot. 1985
Wormholes: Essays and Occasional Writings. 1999

Further Reading

Conradi, Peter. *John Fowles*. London: Methuen, 1982.
Fawkner, H.W. *The Timescapes of John Fowles*. Rutherford, NJ: Fairleigh Dickinson University Press, 1983.
Huffaker, Robert. *John Fowles*. Boston: Twayne, 1980.
Loveday, Simon. *The Romances of John Fowles*. London: Macmillan, 1985.
Olshen, Barry N. *John Fowles*. New York: Ungar, 1978.
Palmer, William J. *The Fiction of John Fowles: Tradition, Art, and the Loneliness of Selfhood*. Columbia, MO: University of Missouri Press, 1974.

Salarmi, Mahmoud. *John Fowles's Fiction and the Politics of Postmodernism.* Rutherford, NJ: Fairleigh Dickinson Press, 1992.

Tarbox, Katherine. *The Art of John Fowles.* Athens: University of Georgia Press, 1988.

Wolfe, Peter. *John Fowles: Magus and Moralist.* Lewisburg, PA: Bucknell University Press, 1976; revised edition, 1979.

Woodcock, Bruce. *Male Mythologies: John Fowles and Masculinity.* Brighton, UK: Harvester Press, 1984.

FRANKLIN, BENJAMIN

1706–1790
American essayist, journalist, and memoirist

"Letter of Advice to a Young Man on Choosing a Mistress"

Written in 1745, a period that biographer Carl Van Doren calls Franklin's "salty year," "Letter of Advice to a Young Man on Choosing a Mistress"—published during its interesting history under a variety of titles, including "Old Mistresses' Apologue"—may initially shock readers familiar primarily with the sage, staid voice the author employed in other writings. After it languished in obscurity for many years, several people who could have effected its publication in the 19th century saw it as too frank and indecorous for public consumption. In the 1880s, when Franklin's papers were owned by the United States government, Secretary of State Thomas Bayard denied a request by John Bigelow to include it in a collection of Franklin's papers. In 1895, Franklin scholar John Back McMaster, who deemed the piece "too indecent to print," could not bring himself even to mention its name, but did offer this allusion: "Nothing in his whole career is more to be lamented than that a man of parts so great should, long after he had passed middle life, continue to write pieces so filthy that no editor has ever had the hardihood to print them" (Granger, 266, 278).

Even as "Choosing a Mistress" was judged too prurient for publication, however, it was surreptitiously printed and circulated among a small group of gentlemen. Secretary of State Bayard evidently shared it with a friend, and soon after several copies were produced and distributed via a private printing press owned by Paul Leicester Ford. Apparently, for a time in the late 19th century Franklin's bagatelle was a guilty pleasure for the elite to enjoy out of earshot of decent society. By the time it was finally published in unexpurgated form in the 1920s and 1930s, the pleasure was no longer a secret. In 1938, Franklin enthusiast Abraham Rosenbach displayed it as part of his Free Library of Philadelphia exhibit "The All-Embracing Doctor Franklin." His judgment of "Choosing a Mistress" as "[t]he most famous and the wittiest essay ever written by Franklin" indicates the degree to which standards of public taste had changed.

Perhaps the piece became more acceptable because, in addition to being less squeamish about matters of sex and the body, 20th-century readers had a greater appreciation for the complexity of Franklin's satire. Addressed to an unnamed, unknown youth who has previously admitted to the writer "violent natural Inclinations" regarding the female sex, the letter recommends "Marriage [as] the proper Remedy." Without a wife, a man "resembles the odd Half of a Pair of Scissars" (*sic*). Presuming that this advice will not satisfy his lustful associate, Franklin's persona grudgingly offers an alternative: "But if you will not take this Counsel, and persist in thinking a Commerce with the Sex inevitable, then I repeat my former Advice, that in all your Amours you should *prefer old Women to young ones.*" He supports his position with eight reasons that, taken together, suggest a man of long experience in love, a utilitarian, and a unique kind of male chauvinist.

The older woman's deep well of experience, claims the epistler, makes her a more capable conversationalist. As her beauty fades, she will work harder to be useful. She will maintain more discretion in her liaisons than a girl, and even "if the Affair should happen to be known, considerate people might be rather inclin'd to excuse an old Woman who would kindly take care of a young Man." A bachelor need not worry about illegitimate pregnancy or the ruinous "debauching [of] a Virgin." An older woman will not be embittered by a tryst, but will, whatever the outcome, be "*so grateful*!!" These claims subtly belittle the fairer sex by suggesting that on the one hand, young women have nothing to recommend them except beauty and sex appeal, and on the other that older women may "have more Knowledge of the World," but it is a positive attribute only insofar as it is employed in the service of a man.

The portion of the argument that likely accounted for the letter's earlier scandalous reputation, however, emerges in an ironic version of the *blason du corps feminin*. A man should bed an older woman

> Because in every Animal that walks upright, the Deficiency of the Fluids that fill the Muscles appears first in the highest Part: The Face first grows lank and wrinkled; then the Neck; then the Breast and Arms; the lower Parts continuing to the last as plump as ever: So that covering all above with a Basket, and regarding only what is below the Girdle, it is impossible of two Women to know an old from a young one. And as in the dark all Cats are grey, the Pleasure of corporal Enjoyment with an old Woman is at least equal, and frequently superior, every Knack being by Practice capable of Improvement.

While the bagatelle's comic climax is certainly unflattering to women on a very literal level, it also satirizes both the letter's writer and its addressee. The embarrassing scenario should serve to chasten the youth's shallow sexual desires, against which his older friend has already warned. Moreover, the reader is almost certainly meant to cackle at the elderly male paramour's exaggerated practicality in matters of love, reflected in his laughably clinical description of the body, his matter-of-fact solution to the problem of confronting a wrinkled face in coitus, and his use of the word "Improvement"—which suggests Franklin parodying his own well-known literary personae.

Biography

One of the most legendary figures in American history, Benjamin Franklin was born January 17 in Boston, Massachusetts. A renowned publisher, scientist, inventor, philosopher, diplomat, and civil servant, Franklin was also a prolific writer who demonstrated a fascination with human potential for self-improvement. His most famous works include his *Autobiography*, a series of *New England Courant* editorials produced under the pseudonym Silence Dogood, and the aphorisms and literary selections attributed to the fictional Richard Saunders in *Poor Richard's Almanack*. Franklin also penned a variety of short, miscellaneous works, some of which he called "bagatelles," trifles to amuse his friends. These bagatelles sometimes remind readers of the human foibles that balance the virtues Franklin is so revered for espousing. He died on April 17.

MARK S. GRAYBILL

Selected Works

Benjamin Franklin's Autobiography. New York: Norton, 1986.
The Papers of Benjamin Franklin. New Haven, CT: Yale UP, 1954–.

Further Reading

Granger, Bruce I. *Benjamin Franklin, an American Man of Letters*. Ithaca, NY: Cornell UP, 1964.
Huang, Nian-Sheng. *Benjamin Franklin in American Thought and Culture, 1790–1990*. Philadelphia, PA: American Philosophical Society, 1994.
Middlekauff, Robert. *Benjamin Franklin and His Enemies*. Berkeley and Los Angeles: U of California P, c. 1996.
Tise, Larry E., ed. *Benjamin Franklin and Women*. State College, PA: Pennsylvania State UP, c. 2000.
Van Doren, Carl. *Benjamin Franklin*. New York: Viking Press, 1938.

FRENCH: SEVENTEENTH CENTURY

The impact of political developments in France during the seventeenth century on literary output can be likened to a rein encircling artistic expression. The assassination of Henri IV in 1610 resurrected widespread fears that the now unified nation could once again descend into the discord of the religious wars that had devastated late-sixteenth-century France. Largely as a precautionary measure to safeguard central stability, the delegates of the Estates-General of 1614–15, traditionally a body that forced royal compromise, effectively abandoned France to absolutism: this was the last gathering of the Estates until 1789. The growth of absolutism during the century is seen in the trend toward gathering artists, scientists, and writers under official patronage, as well as in the founding of official institutes to oversee and codify artistic endeavor. Cardinal Richelieu founded the Académie Française in 1635 in order to regulate and preserve the purity of the French language. It is no accident that its first official pronouncement was a judgment on Pierre Corneille's *Le Cid* (1636), demonstrating that policing the arts had become government business and that literary production was henceforward expected to conform to carefully determined guidelines.

With the backdrop of the Counter-Reformation and resultant burgeoning spiritual movements, together with the foundation of religious orders by notable figures such as François de Sales and Vincent de Paul, an identifiable group of writers, known by the disparaging term "libertines," made their mark on the literary establishment. Libertinism during the seventeenth century is somewhat different from the notion of it during the Enlightenment, when it would be understood as much more of an organized, intellectual movement. During this period, libertinism was an all-enveloping concept covering a wide range of people, from freethinkers to atheists; in other words, the heterodox. Flushed with the success of officialdom turning a blind eye to their excesses—which included the public heckling of clerics preaching in the pulpit—due in part to the sympathy of Louis XIII (whose same-sex tendencies were an open secret), the libertines' situation was transformed as a result of the successful prosecution of Théophile de Viau. The poet, part of a group of libertines notable for works glorifying homoeroticism, narrowly escaped the death penalty, and his trial was conducted by secular authorities, marking the transition to state, rather than ecclesiastical, control of censorship.

Moralists, such as Samuel Chappuzeau, opined that certain subjects were to be excluded from the stage, and emphasized the function of theatre as moral instruction. By stressing the ethical dimension of drama, authors went on the counterattack. The appearance of the anonymous poetry collection *Le Parnasse des poëtes satyriques* (1622), attributed to Viau, marked the beginning of the censorship battle in France, as this work was published without the *privilège du Roi*, or official permission. The licentious poems in this work include vivid descriptions and terminology for genitalia and the sexual act, using vulgar as well as more poetic euphemisms for sexual activity, including sodomy. This method is shared by Claude d'Esternod, who dedicates a poem, *Le parfact macquereau suivant la cour* [*The Perfect Pimp Following the Court*] (1619), to the beautiful Magdelaine, exhorting her to give away her favors for free, as she used to, instead of insisting on a high fee. This appeared in a collection published in 1619 as *L'Espadon satyrique*.

One of most celebrated anthologies of erotic verse during this period is *Le cabinet satyrique* [*The Satirical Cabinet*] (1618), with contributions from poets such as Régnier. This anthology presents sexual freedom in a positive light: contributions deal with lesbianism, nymphomania, prostitution, and masturbation, in addition to a discussion of the speed of erection and ejaculation. The *Nouveau cabinet des muses* [*New Cabinet of Muses*] (1658) contains *L'Occasion perdue recouverte*, a sexually explicit poem probably written by Pierre Corneille around 1650. Jean de La Fontaine's *Contes et nouvelles en vers* (1665–74) detail lustful peasants, predatory clergy, and unfaithful wives, though the content is muted in comparison with earlier poetry collections (and it is for this reason that the work was granted a *privilège du Roy*), and the style is more bawdy than explicit. *Le dortoir*, for example, deals with a pregnant nun who is admonished by her abbess for having committed a sin. The transgression in question does not turn out to be fornication, but rather not having cried for help when the unfortunate nun was ravished in the convent grounds; this she did so as not to break the order's rule of silence. Clément's *Relation du Voyage de Copenhague à Brême* [*Account of a Voyage from Copenhagen to Bremen*] (1676) subverts travel writing with a verse account of a peculiar trip featuring morally dubious characters encountered in inns along the way.

While the seventeenth century is characterized by the flourishing of all branches of the theatre, both in tragedy and in comedy, this was accompanied by vehement disapproval from certain ecclesiastical quarters, culminating in open condemnation of the theatre. Suspicion of the stage often focused on actresses who were held to arouse libidinous feelings in their largely male audience. Unlike in England, where female roles were ordinarily played by boys, women played female roles in France, with the exception of older characters, whom actresses customarily refused to play. This meant that plots involving seduction or relations between the genders and love intrigues were afforded a realism that would have been impossible with an entirely male cast. Cross-dressing was a common motif in French theatre, invariably involving romantic intrigue and the "male" figure being courted by another male. Examples include Charles de Beys's *L'Hôpital des fous* [*The Madhouse*] (1636) and Jean-Baptiste Poquelin (Molière's) *Le dépit amoureux* [*The Lovers' Quarrel*] (1656). In the latter, the comedy's central character, Dorothée, engages in amorous talk with another man while disguised in male garb. Although subsequently unveiled as a woman, this does not exclude a homosexual reading. So prevalent was this leitmotiv in public theatre that it even filtered into religious drama (for example, Montgaudier's *Natalie* [1654]).

Works dealing with a homosexual theme, outside of moral treatises and confessors' manuals, are generally circumspect during the seventeenth century, though there are exceptions. A notable example is the treatment of Henri III's alleged sexual preferences and favorites, to interest of historians and public alike throughout the seventeenth century. Thomas Artus's *Les hermaphrodites* (1605) is a satire on Henri III's alleged transvestism, and although the monarch was assassinated in 1589, the work was published only in 1605, with a frontispiece of the king wearing a feminine dress complemented by makeup and jewelry. Several poems composed by Faucherand de Montgaillard, published posthumously in 1606 as *Gaillardises du Sieur de Mont-Gaillard*, satirize the licentious activities of courtiers and favorites at the late monarch's court. These works demonstrate an unintentional consequence of these late-sixteenth-century libels: a growing awareness of same-sex love. The topic is not entirely absent from drama: Michael Hawcroft has argued that Pierre Corneille's *Clitandre* (1632) portrays "a kind [of] love that prefaces, dictionaries, and other dramatists did not explicitly mention or depict."

While swiftly and meticulously repressed and destroyed, libels on the sexual peccadiloes of powerful figures continued to appear throughout the seventeenth century. Cardinal Mazarin was the namesake of the "Mazarinades," pamphlets published from small presses during the turbulent years of the Fronde (1648–1652) which escaped official scrutiny. Some attacked the cardinal for an addiction to sodomy, while others accused him of sexual relations with the queen mother and regent, Anne of Austria. A seven-page Mazarinade entitled *La custode de la reyne qui dit tout* [*An Account of the Queen Which Tells Everything*] (1649) is a bitter, explicit account of the queen's alleged affairs, and though the author was caught distributing the pamphlet on the same day he had printed it, a menacing crowd prevented his execution. Similarly, *Les amours d'Anne d'Autriche* [*Anne of Austria's Loves*] (1692, though originally published around 1649), probably written by Eustache Le Noble, presents Anne as having fathered Louis XIV by a long-term lover, Count Rantzou. A later work in this tradition, *Amours de Louis le Grand et de Mademoiselle du Tron* [*Loves of Louis the Great and Mademoiselle du Tron*] (1697), sets out the purported circumstances of a love affair between the aging Sun King and a voluptuous young noblewoman, in which their passionate meetings are arranged by the complicity of a priest. This is a thinly veiled satire on Louis XIV and Madame de Maintenon. Such sexually charged polemics would persist to the period leading up to the French Revolution.

Writers entertaining heterodox opinions in matters of religion and philosophy faced a hostile and repressive climate, in which they were frozen out of the artistic mainstream. This resulted in an unusually steadfast sense of fraternity among figures who were ostracized or who identified themselves as libertines. A play that typified the tensions between moralists and libertine writers was Molière's *Tartuffe*. This comedy about an unscrupulous fraudster worming his way into a family by masquerading as a devout Catholic and playing to the head of the household's pious sensibilities was rightly viewed by the *dévots* (a secretive and powerful group of prominent Catholics) as a thinly veiled attack on their movement and its influence in contemporary society. The work was officially prohibited in 1664, a revised version suffered the same fate in 1667, and the text we possess now, the edition of 1669, is a watered-down version of the original. As with much satirical literature, Molière uses sexuality as the protagonist's downfall, in this case his lust for the wife of the head of household, Orgon. The fact that the dramatist persisted in rewriting the play into a version that eventually escaped censure, reveals that sexually charged drama was commercially successful. The link between political and sexual subversion is tantalizingly hinted at by the dramatist in the final act when Orgon is compromised through keeping some documents for a friend banished after the civil war of the Fronde. By the 1660s, trends in public taste had evolved, influenced by religious and cultural movements, resulting in the almost complete elimination of comedy relying on sexual (mis)behavior and bodily functions, though Molière relies on innuendo, double entendres, and older husbands obsessed with preserving their young wives' fidelity as his comic ammunition.

The execution of the libertine poet Claude Le Petit in 1662 for obscene and blasphemous writing was a reminder of the potential consequences of falling foul of the limits of what the authorities would accept. In Molière's *Dom Juan* (1665), at face value a play dealing with the comeuppance of a religiously and sexually deviant protagonist, the dramatist subtly undermines the moral implications of the last scene where Dom Juan is dragged down to Hell as divine retribution for his sinful ways; Sganerelle, his faithful servant, is affronted at not having been paid and shouts after his master: "Ah mes gages! mes gages!" [What about my wages?] (V, 6). The depiction of sexuality in the tragedies of Pierre Corneille and Jean Racine is on a more subtle level. It is interesting that Corneille sets his martyr-play *Polyeucte* (1643) only two weeks following the marriage of the protagonist rather than the gap of several years specified in the original legend, firmly emphasizing that the central couple operate on the level of a sexual rather than domestic relationship. Similarly, in Racine's *Phèdre* (1677), Hypolite is not presented as the youth vowed to celibacy in the legend, but is in love with a princess. However, both Corneille's *Polyeucte* and Racine's *Britannicus* (1669) neutralize homoerotic elements that may be detected in source accounts (Metaphrates and Tacitus).

Roger de Bussy-Rabutin's *Histoire amoureuse des Gaules* [*Amorous History of the Gauls*] (1665) records the romantic adventures of various ladies of Louis XIV's court, and was published without the author's knowledge after his mistress lent the manuscript to one of her friends. The published work, altered in places by Madame de La Baume, cost the author over a year in the Bastille, and a frosty welcome when he attempted to return to court life, ensuring a lifelong exile from Versailles. While it details the relative promiscuity of some courtly women, the work concentrates more on the political intrigue of such liaisons rather than offering any apologia for sexual liberty. This case mirrors French society's attitudes to sexuality; while adulterous behavior was not uncommon among the ruling classes, this was firmly a taboo subject. Ostracism, not execution, was how the establishment dealt with its own. Rabutin's narrative derives from the genre stylized by Pierre de Brantôme (1540?–1614); the first seventeenth-century edition of his *Recueil de dames galantes* [*Collection of Gallant Ladies*] was published at Leiden in 1665 as part of his memoirs.

The distribution of such works, with the ensuing scandal they produced, typifies the relative ease with which works could appear without the necessary official permissions. Another method of bypassing the censors, employed by dissenters in philosophy and religion as well as sexual free-thinkers, was to have their monographs printed in the Netherlands (sometimes a false title-page was provided to give the appearance of a foreign imprint). Another alternative was to disguise a work's erotic content and present the imprint under the guise of an instructional manual.

Joan DeJean criticizes the common trend of categorizing nearly all seventeenth-century erotica as libertine writing. Charles Sorel's *L'Histoire comique de Francion* [*Comic Story of Francion*] (1623) may contain some erotic scenes, but this follows on, in style and content, from the *Decameron,* on which it is modeled. Exemplifying a tradition inherited from Rabelais, François Béroalde de Verville's *Le moyen de parvenir* [*The Means of Succeeding*] (1610) is essentially a sexual comedy which deals with virginity, chastity, and clerical celibacy in a bawdy and inventive novel, focusing on various sexual issues, such as a husband having to use a fork in order to break his new wife's hymen. The depiction of such incidents can be read as supportive of a greater degree of sexual education. The anonymous *Les quinze marques approuvées pour cognoistre les faux cons d'avec le légitimes* [*The Fifteen Approved Methods for Recognizing False and True Cunts*] (1620) is a narrative detailing how midwives determine, after a careful examination of the genitalia, whether a young rape victim's account of her ordeal is true. Nicolas Venette's *Tableau de l'amour conjugal* [*Representation of Conjugal Love*] (1686) similarly deals with the problem of a young man trying to decide the most suitable age to marry, and sets out the advice of various sages, including theologians, atheists, and men living in debauchery. However, the book contains outmoded medical opinions for curing sexually transmitting diseases, and a discussion of intercourse between a married couple is followed by a treatise extolling virginity.

The genre of the fairy tale, which flourished in France between 1690 and 1715, rarely portrays love in physical terms, though there is often a strong undercurrent of sexual suggestion. In Charles Perrault's "La Belle au bois dormant" [Sleeping Beauty], it is mentioned that the princess does not need to sleep much after she has met her prince. "Le Petit chaperon rouge" [Little Red Riding Hood] feels the wolf's naked body when she joins her "grandmother" in bed and is much amazed, though also curious, at the hairy figure. The author warns, in a moral at the end of this tale, that women need to be most wary of wolves that are not to be found in the forest, which highlights the sexual metaphor running through the story. Sexual aggression also defines many tales. Marie Catherine D'Aulnoy's "Vert et Bleu" is erotically charged: the amorous Prince Vert gazes at Bleu bathing naked. The tale contains muted eroticism in that hope for marriage is also desire for physical union. There is a concentration on male voyeurism, but D'Aulnoy presents independent heroines who need compatible partners to satisfy their lives; in "La Belle aux cheveux d'or" [Beauty with the Golden Hair], the protagonist rescues the king's favorite (explicitly called "mignon" by the unmarried monarch) from the control of his master and ends up marrying him when her husband inadvertently poisons himself. Free from the possessive machinations of his king, D'Aulnoy notes the couple is not only happy but also "satisfied," thus completing the heterosexualization of Avenant ("Comely").

However, the fairy tales' unapologetic presentation of romantic love accepts the dominant discourse of sexuality, with its implicit exaltation of patriarchy. The invariable elements are that of women needing to find a husband in order to become contented and whole, whereas men must discover or affirm their masculinity through daring exploits. Nevertheless, as with the novel, this form of fiction allowed writers to express liberal attitudes to sexual matters, albeit in a heavily disguised form reliant on tropes.

The seventeenth century saw the publication of a number of erotic libertine works, and the growing commercial popularity of the novel saw this literary genre used as an experimental vehicle by some writers wishing to test the limits of what the public would buy and, moreover, what the ever-vigilant authorities would tolerate. Three of the most notable, if not notorious, novels are Michel Millot's *L'Escole des filles* [*The Girls' School*] (1655), Nicolas Chorier's *Le Mersius français ou l'académie des dames* [*The French Mersius, or the Ladies' Academy*] (1680, originally published in Latin in 1660), and François Chavigny de la Bretonnière's *Vénus dans le cloître ou la religieuse en chemise* [*Venus in the Cloister, or the Nun in Her Smock*] (1683). The publication and subsequent international popularity of these books marks a shift from Italy to France as the most significant center of libertine activity. The first two of these works deal with the sexual education of an innocent teenaged girl

479

by a more experienced woman of the world. These follow on from an earlier tradition exemplified by the anonymous *Les secrettes ruses d'amour* [*Love's Secret Schemes*] (1610), which discussed, from a male perspective, the seduction of women and concluded that widows made the best lovers, as they combined experience with independence. Millot's work (whose publication he paid for together with Jean L'Ange, though the authorship remains uncertain) is generally considered to be the first widely available pornographic literary text. Nicolas Foucquet, Louis XIV's disgraced finance minister, was found to have a copy preciously stored in a secret room in one of his mistress's houses.

The pornographic genre had been created, and James Turner has described such works as "erotic-didactic fantasy organized around the fiction of the speaking agent." While Millot's work is relatively tame by libertine standards—it contains no blasphemous references or overt political subversion—it is marked by sexual explicitness, and official emphasis was laid on eliminating the work rather than those responsible for its publication, who were handed strikingly lenient sentences. It is possible to view the work as resisting the demands of a newly victorious absolutist establishment following the end of the recent civil war, and its obscenity as a defiant pose struck against the expectation for artists to render appropriate homage to the government. The title of Molière's *Ecole des femmes* [*School for Wives/Women*] (1662), a comedy about the romantic and sexual awakening of an innocent young girl, echoes that of Millot, which illustrates how far this work had permeated popular culture.

Chorier's *Académie* goes further than Millot in including lesbian acts and orgiastic scenes. Chorier is attributed with the authorship of *Le putanisme d'Amsterdam* [*Whoredom in Amsterdam*] (1681), a curious study of this city's prostitutes detailing their common ruses, makeup techniques, and way of life. The work takes the form of a mystical, nocturnal visitation to the red-light district led by a supernatural spirit, though the level of detail and familiarity suggests that the author was well acquainted with the world he was describing. This provides an unusual and incisive survey of seventeenth-century prostitution, together with an earlier work, *Infortune des filles de joie* [*Misfortune of Goodtime Girls*] (1624), attributed to Adrien de Montluc. As well as a glimpse into prostitutes' methods, and some moral reflections on the trade (which castigates clients as well as the women), the work concludes with a reflection on the attraction, and revulsion, attached to thin women.

Chavigny's *Vénus* is a work composed of dialogue between characters, in this case three conversations between two young nuns, Angélique and Agnès, who justify sexual activity as a natural gift from the Creator, and the pair view their relationship with young clerics as fulfilling normal desires. As well as presenting an apologia for free love, the work concludes with the pair initiating intimacy with each other. Through satire of established religion and its representatives, in particular through focusing on hypocrisy and sexual excess, writers gave new life to a long-standing criticism of Catholicism. In their struggle for liberty of artistic expression against the constraints of standards of decency set by Church and State, the endeavors of such libertine writers sowed the seeds of the Enlightenment.

PAUL SCOTT

Further Reading

Bougard, Roger G. *Érotisme et amour physique dans la littérature française du XVIIe siècle*. Paris: Lachurié, 1986.

DeJean, Joan. *Libertine Strategies: Freedom and the Novel in Seventeenth-Century France*. Columbus: Ohio State University Press, 1981.

Hawcroft, Michael. "Homosexual Love in Corneille's *Clitandre* (1632)." *Seventeenth-Century French Studies* 15 (1993): 135–44.

Lever, Maurice. *Les Bûchers de Sodome: Histoires des "infâmes"*. Paris: Fayard, 1985.

Phillips, Henry. *The Theatre and Its Critics in Seventeenth-Century France*. Oxford: Oxford University Press, 1980.

Schoeller, Guy, ed. *Dictionnaire des œuvres érotiques*. Paris: Laffont, 2001.

Seifart, Lewis C. *Fairy Tales, Sexuality, and Gender in France, 1690–1715: Nostalgic Utopias*. Cambridge: Cambridge University Press, 1996.

Turner, James Grantham. *Schooling Sex: Libertine Literature and Erotic Education in Italy, France, and England, 1534–1685*. Oxford: Oxford University Press, 2003.

FRENCH: EIGHTEENTH CENTURY

Erotic literature flourished in 18th-century France, particularly after 1740, when a resurgence in explicitly pornographic writing was inaugurated with the publication of the best-selling novel *Histoire de D[om Bougre], Portier des Chartreux [History of D(om Bougre), Porter of the Carthusian Monks]* by Gervaise de Latouche. In fact, the flowering of French Enlightenment philosophy that took place toward the middle of the century corresponded with a renewed interest on the part of writers and publishers in the production of a wide variety of erotic works. Between 1747 and 1748 alone, the materialist La Mettrie put out his radically mechanist philosophical treatise *Machine Man;* Montesquieu finished *The Spirit of the Laws;* the most famous pornographic work of the century, *Thérèse philosophe [The Philosophical Thérèse]* (attributed to Boyer d'Argens), appeared in print; and Diderot published the erotic orientalist tale *Les bijoux indiscrets [The Indiscreet Jewels]*.

Erotic and obscene writing played an important role within the culture of the French Enlightenment, both as a form of literate entertainment and as a vehicle for the development and diffusion of new modes of thought. Literary scholars and historians (including Robert Darnton, Jean M. Goulemot, Lynn Hunt, and Jean Mainil) have emphasized the close ties linking ancien régime erotic writing to the more canonically philosophical texts for which the period remains known. Not only did several of the most prominent *philosophes* produce erotic, obscene, or libertine writings, but the expression "livres philosophiques," used by booksellers of the period to designate illicit texts, referred to obscene novels such as *Margot la ravaudause [Margot the Darner]* (1750), as well as to works of philosophy.

The corpus of 18th-century French erotic literature includes salacious poems (notably *Ode à Priape [Ode to Priapus]* by Alexis Piron, 1710), dialogues, short stories, and *libelles* or *chroniques scandaleuses* (the "libels" or "scandalous chronicles" of the activities of aristocrats and

public figures). Of all these forms, erotic and obscene poetry has perhaps been the most neglected in treatments of the 18th century, even though the tradition is an impressively varied one which embraces verse from the mildly scabrous (Voltaire's *La pucelle d'Orléans [The Maid of Orleans]*, 1755) to the openly indecent (*La foutromanie [Fuckmania]*, attributed to Sénac de Meilhan, 1778). Eighteenth-century erotic poetry was read and appreciated for its ability to arouse and delight its readers. For intsance, in his essay *La volupté [Sensuousness]* (1745?), La Mettrie discusses what he calls the "double happiness" of simultaneously perusing erotic poetry and frolicking in the "fresh, tufted" grass with his mistress. Erotic verse could be openly obscene and philosophical (as was the case with *La foutromanie*) or written in a more stylized idiom, like the *Poésies érotiques [Erotic Poems]* (1778) of Évariste Désiré de Forges, vicomte de Parny.

Despite the interest erotic poetry held for 18th-century readers, it is the erotic novel that represents at once one of the most popular and one of the most innovative genres of the period. While the designation "libertine novel" has been used to include everything from the allusive fiction of the abbé Prévost to the joyful bawdiness characteristic of Andréa de Nerciat, discussions of Enlightenment literary eroticism have traditionally distinguished between the libertine novel of worldliness and seduction (the *roman mondain*), on the one hand, and the obscene or pornographic novel on the other. Critics have historically been reluctant to associate the frank obscenity of the latter with the elegant suggestiveness of the former, even though the two genres share an Epicurean focus on sensual and sensorial pleasure as a *summum bonum* or greatest good.

The most representative examples of the libertine novel, whose practitioners include Claude-Prosper Jolyot de Crébillon, Charles Pinot Duclos, Claude-Henri Fuzée de Voisenon, and Claude-Joseph Dorat, highlight reiterated scenes of seduction, elegantly and sometimes elliptically narrated, which take place in the opulent, idle, and highly stylized world of the most privileged classes of ancien régime France. The aesthetic that these novels promote (or in some cases, subtly call into question) is based on the valorization of an ethos of frivolity, ephemerality, and superficiality as the source not only of sensual gratification but of an aristocratic mastery of both self and other. This mastery comes about through the close study and careful imitation of social conventions, so that the libertine may more expertly manipulate those who are governed by them. The ritualized seduction of one libertine by another—or the equally ritualized education of a young man into the ways and means of this type of seduction by an older woman—expresses, in the *roman mondain*, an erotic hedonism that is also an understanding of the social world as malleable and transformable according to the disciplined will of the aristocratic individual. The rites of love, in libertine novels, are also rites of subjugation. Or, as the libertine Versac remarks to the young Meilcour in Crébillon *fils*'s *Les égarements du cœur et de l'esprit* [*The Wayward Head and Heart*] (1736–38), "It is only by appearing to submit to all that [women] ask of us that we succeed in dominating them." The best-known exemplar of the worldly libertine novel is probably *Les liaisons dangereuses* [*Dangerous Liaisons*] (1782), by Choderlos de Laclos, remarkable for its detailed and insightful portrayal of a libertine woman, the marquise de Merteuil, who describes the practice of seduction as a form of individual emancipation from the constraints placed by society on feminine sexual desire. Unlike many other libertine works, however, *Dangerous Liaisons* seems to conclude with an adherence to a sentimental moral perspective, in that the libertine protagonists end up either dead (the vicomte de Valmont) or disfigured and disgraced (Merteuil).

Libertine writings typically depict an aristocratic milieu in which the careful manipulation of strict social codes serves both to mask sexual desire and to facilitate seduction. Libertine ladies know that they must feign innocence with each new lover they take, while their male counterparts are obliged to show the signs of "authentic" passion even as they undertake their second or third sexual conquest of the day. Through the portrayal of a social environment in which appearance is valued above all else—a world in which even the most apparently sincere outpouring of sentiment is liable to serve only the instrumental function of accumulating sexual triumphs—libertine novels call into question the idea that words, expressions, or gestures can possess one true or essential meaning. The universe of *libertinage* is one of masks, disguises, and double entendres, in which the moral relativism of the libertines is heightened by the necessity of conforming to social norms themselves in constant flux. In the words of Crébillon *fils*'s arch-libertine Versac, "Is it not necessary to have a lively, varied intelligence in order to take on unfailingly the roles that each moment demands you play... to be passionate without having feelings, to cry without being moved, to seem tormented without being jealous?" The ideal of polite hypocrisy that is expressed in this passage—and elsewhere in libertine literature—perversely includes strong elements of social criticism. The absolute insincerity of the consummate libertine mirrors the pervasive bad faith of a society in which discourses of moral and religious piety often appear to be used to conceal rabid self-interest. This strain of ideological critique is perhaps most visible in the work of the marquis de Sade, an author who seems to deny the very possibility of an ethics that is not simultaneously a practice of domination.

The oriental tale—in which exoticism serves to heighten the narrative's erotic effects—is an important and highly successful variant on the libertine novel of seduction. These texts participated in the wave of fashionable orientalism initiated, in France, by the translation of the *Les mille et une nuits* by Antoine Galland [*The Arabian Nights*] (begun in 1704). They include Diderot's famous *Indiscreet Jewels* (set in a fantastical Congo), as well as Crébillon *fils*'s erotic social satire *Tanzaï et Néadarné, histoire japonaise* [*The Skimmer, or The History of Tanzaï and Néadarné*] (1734) and his ribald *Le sopha* [*The Sofa: A Moral Tale*] (1742), Voisenon's *Le Sultan Misapouf* [*The Sultan Misapouf*] (1746), and Jacques Rochette de La Morlière's *Angola* [*Angola: An Eastern Tale*] (1746). The image of the "oriental" harem—which, for French authors, tended to evoke fevered visions of lesbianism and despotic patriarchal privilege—also figured prominently in novels whose primary focus was not always explicitly erotic. The latter include Montesquieu's *Lettres persanes* [*The Persian Letters*] (1721) and Prévost's *Histoire d'une grecque moderne* [*The Story of a Modern Greek Woman*] (1740).

Oriental tales usually (although not always) profit from the change of scenery they introduce to add elements of political and social critique to the serial depiction of libertine adventures. For instance, the *Indiscreet Jewels*, in which women's "jewels" are made to talk by way of a magic ring, is not only an investigation of what has been presented by writers from Diderot to Freud as the enigma of female sexuality; it is also a timely and satirical account of the morals, fashions, and rituals of the court of Louis XV (1710–1774). In the *Jewels*, Diderot uses the bawdy conceit of the talking jewel—the vagina as origin of both secrets and knowledge—to investigate an enlightened fascination with the search for rational, empirically verifiable truth in domains ranging from metaphysics to court politics. Diderot's dual strategy—partly frolicsome, partly analytical—is typical of a genre whose most playful aspects could serve as counterpoint to (and flimsy concealment of) critical accounts of the repressiveness of ancien régime orthodoxy. In the widely read *Mémoires turcs* [*Turkish Memoirs*] (1743) attributed to Claude Godard d'Aucour, the author produces a bracing critique of occidental prejudice and moral hypocrisy in the midst of a portrayal of an entirely fantastical (and often ridiculous) Orient populated by whirling dervishes, sacred prostitutes, and sexy slave girls.

The rise of the oriental tale, a widespread phenomenon in which the *Indiscreet Jewels* and the *Turkish Memoirs* played significant parts, gave evidence of a growing French fascination with the nature and cultural order of non-European societies. The popularity of the *conte oriental* persisted throughout the first half of the century and well into the second. In the most sophisticated versions of the genre, the eroticism of a fantastic Orient functions simultaneously as a reflection of what was perceived as the growing decadence of the French aristocracy and as a foil allowing for the construction of a vision of European society as characterized by rationality, orderliness, and a commitment to social progress.

The emphasis of libertine novels—worldly and orientalist—is on the witty manipulation of language and the playful evocation of an atmosphere of sophisticated and self-conscious sensualism. The obscene novel, traditionally considered somewhat beyond the pale by scholars of the period, is more explicit—both sexually and philosophically. In obscene works, sexual exploration combines with more or less daring intellectual experimentation. For instance, *Thérèse philosophe* is both a raunchy coming-of-age tale and a materialist tract, while La Morlière's *Les Lauriers ecclésiastiques* [*Ecclesiastical Laurels*] (1748) includes a scathing critique of clerical bigotry, as does *History of D.* Similarly, Pierre Nougaret's *Lucette ou les progrès du libertinage* [*Lucette, or A Libertine's Progress*] (1765–66), although its ending is grim and punitive, contains hints of a potentially transgressive moral relativism. Somewhat later, in the years around the French Revolution, Gabriel-Honoré Riquetti, comte de Mirabeau, produced a series of obscene works combining a Voltairean skepticism, a critique of oppressive ancien régime traditions (such as that of the *lettre de cachet*), and lively depictions of sexual practices, including male prostitution (in *Ma conversion ou le libertin de qualité* [*My Conversion, or the Libertine of Quality*], 1783), masturbation, bestiality, nymphomania, lesbianism (in the essay *Erotika biblion*, 1783), sodomy, group sex, and male homosexuality (in the short story *Hic et haec*, 1798). The marquis de Sade, also writing toward the end of the century, is well known (and increasingly canonized) for his pornographic texts which are intended to provoke the reader physically *and* intellectually.

While contemporary scholars have tended to see philosophy and pornography as fundamentally separate endeavors, 18th-century novelists (de Sade included) use the technique of obscene depiction as both empirical demonstration and persuasive rhetorical device. The reader is swayed by the obscene narrative to lend credence to the philosophical arguments of the text, thus proving conclusively the naturalness, forcefulness, and ubiquity of sexual desire. In many obscene novels (as in the work of the marquis de Sade), obscene passages are therefore interspersed with philosophical argument. The goal of the obscene novel is not only the arousal of the reader, but enlightenment in a broad sense: the reader, in ridding him/herself of prejudice and what was often perceived as the "veil" of superstition, emerges from the novel with a newly clarified understanding of the importance of the senses in the development of knowledge about the world, the naturalness of sexual impulses, and the hypocrisy of churchly condemnations of the free expression of sexual desire. In this sense, the pedagogical aims of the obscene novel are at one with those of the French Enlightenment as it has been traditionally characterized, and include a commitment to empiricism, the promulgation of limited individual freedoms, and the development of a moral law based in an understanding of natural processes. As Monsieur T*** remarks to Thérèse in the beginning of The Philosophical Thérèse, "these excessive ticklings that you feel in that part which rubbed against the column of your bed... are urges as natural as those of hunger and of thirst." Obscene novels take an interest in sexuality as a natural "mechanism" of the human organism.

Because the sexual practices depicted in Enlightenment obscene writings (as well as in libertine novels) are often quite diverse, the delimitation of the domain of the "natural," far from functioning consistently as a way of restricting the expression of sexual desire, reveals itself to be subject to almost infinite expansion. Both men and women are characterized, in obscene literature from the middle of the century in particular, as actively sexual and capable of experiencing a wide range of erotic pleasures. In The Philosophical Thérèse, the heroine's mentor wholeheartedly recommends masturbation as a way for women to assuage sexual impulses without running the risks of penetrative heterosexual intercourse (including pregnancy, the loss of reputation, and disease). Women are described as having "the needs that men do; they are molded from the same clay, even though they cannot make use of the same resources."

This egalitarian perspective on sexual desire is not unique to The Philosophical Thérèse. In La Mettrie's philosophical essay L'Art de jouir [The Art of Pleasure] (1751), for instance, long passages are devoted to the joys of both male and female orgasm. Moreover, La Mettrie ends the essay with a discussion of the pleasure to be taken in acts of male homosexuality (although he condemns lesbianism as unnatural). "Believe me, my love," he writes, "love makes of every beloved a woman; the empire of love recognizes no limits other than pleasure!" There is some evidence that the libertine ethos, as expressed in both ancien régime literature and aristocratic social life, included at least a limited acceptance of homosexual desire as a part of sophisticated sexual practice. In the La véritable vie privée du maréchal de Richelieu [The Authentic Private Life

of the Maréchal de Richelieu] (1790), attributed to Jean-Benjamin de la Borde and Louis-François Faur, the maréchal, who was, along with Casanova, one of the most famous libertine figures of the century, is shown with relative equanimity on the part of the author(s) to have appreciated the charms of male and female lovers over the course of his many travels.

Lesbianism, on the other hand, was at once the object of a certain amount of fascination and—in theory, at least—entirely nonexistent as a sexual practice at the origin of a specific sexual identity or type. The libertine marquise de Merteuil, in Dangerous Liaisons, describes engaging in lesbian sexual relations with her naive pupil, Cécile, as a test of the girl's sensual aptitude. In Diderot's erotically inflected novel La religieuse [The Nun] (1796), the seduction of the heroine by another nun is depicted at length and in highly sensual terms, although Diderot ultimately portrays lesbian desire as a perverse consequence of the unjust and unnatural imprisonment of women in convents. In obscene novels, implicit or explicit lesbianism generally functions to heighten the erotic effect of voyeurism.

Obscene writing became progressively more political in the years leading up to the French Revolution, as pornographic critiques of despotism proliferated in the form of chroniques scandaleuses and libelles. In the 1770s and 80s, libelles were widely distributed throughout France by means of clandestine publishing networks. These writings portrayed the "private lives" of kings and courtiers as well as the amorous adventures of women of the court (from queens to royal mistresses) and included, as the century wore on, increasingly scabrous and explicitly anti-royalist components. One milder example, the Anecdotes sur Mme la comtesse du Barry [Anecdotes About Madame du Barry], probably by Matthieu-François Pidansat de Mairobert, focused on the infidelities of Louis XV's mistress and portrayed the king as a cuckold periodically blinded by his own lecherous desires. The heedless libertinage characteristic of Louis XV's regime in fact provided fodder for booksellers long after the king's death, and Robert Darnton has pointed out that the defamation of Louis XV played a key role in the fall of Louis XVI in the Revolution. In the last decades of the century, the transfer of power from an absolutist monarch to a republican political order was accompanied by and narrated in vivid descriptions of the impotence of the king and the "depraved" promiscuity of Marie-Antoinette, as Lynn Hunt, Jean Mainil, and others have discussed. The revolutionary period witnessed an explosion in the production of obscene pamphlets and images portraying the pornographically debauched habits of the most privileged classes; in these works, the critique of the ancien régime is undertaken through the politicized description of sexualized bodies—from the decaying, syphilitic visages of aristocratic women to the virile nudity of the new citizens of the Republic.

Libertine and obscene novels, pornographic *libelles*, and bawdy tales continued to be written and circulated throughout the last decade of the 18th century. Nicolas-Edmé Restif de la Bretonne published his *Anti-Justine*, promoting a kinder, gentler eroticism in response to what the author deemed the "horrors" of the marquis de Sade, in 1798. Andréa de Nerciat, whose vivid and inventive prose references early forms of libertine eroticism with its insouciant epicureanism, was particularly active during the revolutionary period and beyond. Vivant Denon, author of the quintessentially libertine tale *Point de lendemain* [*No Tomorrow*] (1777), published a revised edition of this celebrated work as late as 1812. Denon's story of a one-night affair between a cultivated older woman and a younger man manifests a characteristically libertine fascination with the ephemeral pleasures of the body, the fantastical trappings of great wealth, and the subtle manipulation of stylized language for seductive effect. Nonetheless, despite their extraordinarily refined tastes, the lovers of Denon's tale act out a fundamental truth of sublunary human existence. "We are such *machines*," declaims the hero. Although *Point de lendemain* is in one sense the tale of a young man's passage into sophisticated adulthood, the lesson that the hero learns from his more experienced lover is simply that moral certitudes ring hollow in the face of pleasure. "I looked hard for the moral of this adventure," he affirms, "and I found none."

Notably, the beginning of the 19th century coincides with the publication of the first series of libertine novels known to have been written by a woman, the comtesse Félicité de Choiseul-Meuse. Her *Julie, ou J'ai sauvé ma rose* [*Julie, or I Have Saved My Rose*] (1807) contains explicitly erotic descriptions of many different varieties of feminine sexual experience, although the female protagonist is careful always to resist penetration (not unlike her predecessor, the philosophical Thérèse). As Julie explains, "To refuse the ultimate favor is to know how to experience true pleasure." Yet the first decades of the 19th century also witnessed the intensification of a climate of political and intellectual repression. Just as the aristocratic tradition of libertine eroticism did not survive the demise of the monarchy, the era of "enlightened" pornography eventually came to an end with the transformation of obscene writing into an illicit private pleasure with seemingly little connection to public life.

Thematically, French erotic writing of the 18th century demonstrates specific interest in and curiosity about the minds and bodies of women in particular. In this sense, erotic literature of the Enlightenment shares the preoccupations of the 18th-century French novel more generally, since both genres are intimately concerned with feminine experiences, sentiments, and social roles of women. This concern is especially visible in the obscene novel—with its reliance on female narrators and scenes of voyeurism centered around women's bodies—but is also salient for discussions of the libertine novel, in which what contemporaries increasingly saw as a debauched "feminization" of tone and focus was reflected in a precious prose style and a fascination with the study of female psychology. Twentieth-century feminist critics have nonetheless remarked on the fact that the explicit portraits of feminine sexuality that appear in what is commonly understood as the corpus of 18th-century erotic literature were exclusively produced by men. Women writers, on the other hand, tended to excel in a genre which has not always been included in discussions of eroticism: the *roman sentimental*, or the sentimental novel.

While the erotic aspects of the sentimental novel did not necessarily appear consequential to literary critics of later periods, 18th-century commentators showed a strong awareness of and anxiety about the effects of precisely this type of novel on feminine sexuality. The erotically stimulating (and indeed potentially dangerous) elements of the form were highlighted again and again. For instance, Jean-Jacques Rousseau famously remarked, "No chaste girl has ever read novels." This comment targeted not obscene literature, as modern readers might expect, but precisely the kind of sentimental novel epitomized in Rousseau's own *Julie, ou la Nouvelle Héloïse* [*Julie, or the New Heloise*] (1761). It was feared that women, thought to be highly responsive to sensation and less amenable to the influence of reason, would be seduced by novels into cultivating a heightened state of sensibility that would leave them at the very least vulnerable to seduction, if it did not spur them to seek out the means to satisfy an increased desire for feeling of all kinds. The image of the woman reader, ubiquitous in the art and literature of the period, was itself a suggestive one, since the woman who read was seen as implicitly in a state of distraction and reverie (not unlike that presumed by 18th-century doctors to be brought on by masturbation). Rousseau writes, in the last book of his *Émile* (1762), of a woman who has fallen in love with a character from a novel and is thus unable to play her proper role as wife and mother. Similarly, the doctor D. T. de Bienville, in his famous treatise on *La nymphomanie ou traité sur la fureur utérine* [*Nymphomania, or Dissertation on the Furor Uterinus*] (1771), affirms the close relationship between excessive reading of novels and the development of uncontrollable sexual urges in women. In his discussion of the most dangerous kinds of novel, Bienville cites the "tender novel" (*roman tendre*) alongside the "lascivious" and the "voluptuous" types. In these and many other sources, it is clear that 18th-century critics and readers understood the sentimental novel to have significant effects on the stimulation of sexual desire; in other words, the novel of sensibility was thought to be *as* "erotic" as libertine and obscene texts. The similarities between the two genres may help to explain in part why the famously obscene marquis de Sade, who was himself the author of sentimental novels, did not hesitate to describe Rousseau's *Julie* as a literary chef d'oeuvre.

The vision of erotic pleasure outlined in sentimental novels is nevertheless distinct from that typical of libertine and obscene texts. While the latter tend to focus on sexual mastery and sexual knowledge, respectively, the eroticism of the sentimental novel inheres in the portrayal of feelings—particularly feelings of sympathy, longing, and unfulfilled (yet all-encompassing) desire. In Françoise de Graffigny's *Lettres d'une Péruvienne* [*Letters from a Peruvian Woman*] (1747), the female protagonist is wracked by love for her absent betrothed. In Marie-Jeanne Riccoboni's *Lettres de Milady Juliette Catesby* [*Letters from Lady Juliet Catesby*] (1759), the heroine describes her struggle to resist her desire for a man she believes to be a rake; both her resistance and her erotic yearning are portrayed in evocative and voluptuous terms. In the sentimental novel, unlike its obscene and libertine counterparts, not only the gratification of desire but the endless deferral of it could incite eroticized feelings of sympathetic identification in readers. The masochistic pleasure to be taken in unfulfilled longing functioned as the feminine counterpart to the sadistic delight of sexual conquest. The differences between the sentimental and the libertine aesthetic are most neatly encapsulated in the marquis de Sade's twin masterworks, *La nouvelle Justine* [*The New Justine*] (1797) and *L'Histoire de Juliette* [*The Story of Juliette*] (1798–1801). In the former, the exaggeratedly sentimental Justine is repeatedly subjected to the most horrific of sexual tortures, while the latter depicts at length the sadistic delight taken by the libertine Juliette, Justine's sister and alter ego, in the misery of others. In these novels, de Sade parodically reveals the mechanisms by which the sentimental heroine gives erotic pleasure to readers through her masochistic resignation to suffering, while the libertine whore derives erotic joy from the sexual subjugation of her victims.

Over the course of the century, authors of literary, scientific, and legal texts became more preoccupied with what was coming to be seen as the fundamental distinctiveness of women's sexuality, which was often described as more enigmatic and disorderly than that of men. Twenty-five years after the publication of the adventures of the salacious and highly sexed Thérèse, Diderot explained in his article *Sur les femmes* [*On Women*] (1772) that women rarely experience orgasm, and are unlikely to feel the pleasure that men do even in the arms of a lover. Diderot writes of women, "Organized entirely differently from us, the mechanism that evokes voluptuous pleasure in them is so delicate and so difficult to reach, that it is not surprising that it should not work properly." The mechanistic and libidinous universe delineated by the obscene philosophical novel was giving way to a social domain marked by sexual difference as an explanatory principle. Women's mysterious sexual "organization" served in part to explain their social subordination, since, for both men and women, sexuality was emerging as a crucial component of behavior—a key that might unlock the secrets of human nature.

The most famous literary instance of the developing interest in the explanatory power of sexual desire is probably the autobiography of Jean-Jacques Rousseau, *Les confessions* [*Confessions*] (1782–1788). Here Rousseau describes in great detail the genesis and development of his sexual predilections. He discovers early on that he takes great pleasure in being beaten, particularly by older women. Rousseau writes, "Who would have thought that this childhood punishment, received at the age of eight at the hand of a girl of thirty, would have marked my tastes, my desires, my passions, my self for the rest of my existence?" Interestingly, Rousseau depicts his sexual and sensual life as essentially psychological: "I have possessed very few women, but I have nonetheless experienced much pleasure in my own way, that is to say, in my imagination." This interiorization of sexuality—as an index of individual personality or identity—is a modern phenomenon (and one that is quite foreign to the libertine tradition, for instance). Rousseau goes on to recount other formative incidents in his erotic experience—an experience that later eras would characterize as perverse—including episodes of exhibitionism and prolonged masturbation. Even though Rousseau's stated intention is not to arouse his readers, his work represents an important development in the literary portrayal of eroticism, since the extraordinary attention which Rousseau devotes to the presentation of his sexuality is a sign of a new interest in sexual desire as a crucial part of individuality.

The erotic literature of the French 18th century, in all its diversity, reflects the atmosphere of social transformation (and, ultimately, upheaval) in which it was produced. Libertines and their ilk functioned as the mouthpieces of a new Lockean empiricism *and* as the representatives of the most joyously superficial of aristocratic aesthetics, depending on the contexts in which they found themselves; the focus of the erotic novel may be subversively materialist (as in *The Philosophical Thérèse*) or apparently frivolous (as in Crébillon's *The Sofa*). Protagonists range from sexually emancipated prostitutes (*The Story of Juliette*) to beautiful aristocratic ladies (*The Wayward Head and Heart*) to a talking bidet (Antoine Bret's *Le *****, histoire bavarde* [*The Bidet, a Talkative Tale*] (1749);

characters in Enlightenment erotic writing may be depicted as literal sex machines (driven to copulate by predetermined natural forces) or as sexual aesthetes (hypersophisticated masters of the cultivation of erotic sensation).

On the other hand, not all 18th-century eroticism includes explicitly transgressive or critical elements. While the libertine or obscene novel often flirts with the more or less obvious violation of the codes governing virtuous behavior, the sentimental novel deals with the difficulties (and pleasures) inherent in the perfect obedience to these same codes. What does unify these extraordinarily wide ranging genres, however—and what is perhaps also their most characteristic sign—is a belief in the close connection of the erotic life of individuals to modes of thought that appear to modern readers as philosophical and political. For 18th-century writers of all stripes, the portrayal of erotic desire is never innocent. During this period, even the most explicit description of sexual congress was understood to make a point about what was considered (or *should* have been considered) natural human behavior as well as about the justness of the social order in which this behavior took place. While the link between the political, the philosophical, and the erotic has appeared less inevitable in later periods, in 18th-century France it was the heightened awareness of this tie that gave erotic literature its critical bite—and gives it, ultimately, its continued relevance.

NATANIA MEEKER

Further Reading

Cryle, Peter. *Geometry in the Boudoir: Configurations of French Erotic Narrative*. Ithaca, NY: Cornell University Press, 1994.

Cusset, Catherine, ed. *Libertinage and Modernity*. New Haven, CT: Yale University Press, 1998.

Darnton, Robert. *The Forbidden Bestsellers of Pre-Revolutionary France*. New York and London: Norton, 1995.

Delon, Michel. *Le savoir-vivre libertin*. Paris: Hachette, 2000.

Feher, Michel, ed. *The Libertine Reader: Eroticism and Enlightenment in 18th-Century France*. New York: Zone Readers, 1997.

Goodden, Angelica. *The Complete Lover: Eros, Nature, and Artifice in the Eighteenth-Century French Novel*. Oxford: Clarendon Press, and New York: Oxford University Press, 1989.

Goulemot, Jean-Marie. *Forbidden Texts: Erotic Literature and Its Readers in Eighteenth-Century France*. Cambridge: Polity Press, and Philadelphia: University of Pennsylvania Press, 1994.

Hunt, Lynn, ed. *The Invention of Pornography: Obscenity and the Origins of Modernity, 1500-1800.* New York: Zone Books, 1993.

Jaquier, Claire. *L'Erreur des désirs: Romans sensibles au XVIIIe siècle.* Lausanne: Payot, 1998.

Mainil, Jean. *Dans les règles du plaisir. . . Théorie de la différence dans le discours obscène, romanesque et médical de l'Ancien Régime.* Paris: Kimé, 1996.

Mauzi, Robert. *L'Idée du bonheur dans la littérature et la pensée françaises au XVIIIeme siècle.* Paris: Armand Colin, 1960.

Miller, Nancy. *French Dressing: Women, Men and Ancien Régime Fiction.* London and New York: Routledge, 1995.

Nagy, Péter. *Libertinage et révolution.* Paris: Gallimard, 1975.

Reichler, Claude. *L'Age libertin.* Paris: Minuit, 1987.

Stewart, Philip. *Engraven Desire: Eros, Image, and Text in the French Eighteenth Century.* Durham, NC: Duke University Press, 1992.

Trousson, Raymond, ed. *Romans libertins du XVIIIe siècle.* Paris: Laffont, 1993.

FRENCH: NINETEENTH CENTURY

Although Nineteenth century France was content to retain the anodyne but usefully Protean term *amour,* French life and culture in the new bourgeois age was saturated with an unprecedented concern with sexuality that manifested itself in every sphere of existence, assuming, on the part of moralists and hedonists alike, the status of a veritable obsession. In much French writing of the period, this obsession was intertwined with fundamental social and political concerns, though with the flourishing Decadent aesthetic of the fin-de-siècle, sexuality would increasingly become a specialized domain savored for its own sake and distinguished only with difficulty from the pornography in which the same authors sometimes engaged. From early in the century, the ever more widespread disregard for conventional restraints on sexual behavior encouraged by the new economic order, and the increasing readiness to depict it in words or in the visual arts, went hand in hand with both a more general loosening of literary constraints and the promotion of greater specificity and explicitness in the descriptions of the external world to be found in the related realms of journalism and "realist" fiction. These latter developments frequently led to the juxtaposition, within the same composition, of high and low genres and a mingling of language both elevated and crude, mundane and exotic, that not only permitted a representation of the tensions underlying the new social reality, but challenged taboos the roots of which went much deeper than the perspectives of either literature or polite society. Of equal consequence was the establishment of a new literary marketplace, in which the consumer's desires were indulged more or less subtly and with greater or lesser good grace, depending on the author's commitment to other aesthetic, philosophical, or moral imperatives.

Such examples of apparent restraint as existed in the literary treatment of love were rarely unrelated to this obsession with the sexual. As Roland Barthes observed of Eugène Fromentin's seemingly chaste "personal novel," *Dominique* (1863), if the explicit sexual dimension is erased, it nonetheless makes itself felt elsewhere in the writing, starting with bisexual name of the title character. Likewise, whereas the love poetry of Lamartine might seem to characterize the canonical image of French Romanticism, its wider historical significance derives from its representing one of the two extremes of erotic discourse, with the literal absence of the opposite extreme constituting an implied presence that both defines and questions it. The readiness with which "Le Lac" was felt to invite parody is noteworthy in this respect: an erotic version (complete with the French equivalent of four-letter words and an inevitable sexual play on the verb *jouir*) appeared in 1845, while Flaubert, in *Madame Bovary* (1857), has his Rouen boatman (an ironic counterpart of the Venetian gondolier of the Romantic stereotype) sing verses from the selfsame poem as he rows the adulterous couple who are his passengers. In the case of

Alfred de Musset, the Romantic poet himself becomes an (anonymous) pornographer as the author of *Gamiani ou deux nuits d'excès* [*Gamiani, or Two Nights of Excess*] (1833). The phenomenon to be studied, therefore, is not merely the explicit manifestation of sexuality, but the more or less total eroticization of 19th-century French society, its interactions, and its relationships of power. That the eroticization of modern life and culture was identified by contemporaries as a specifically French phenomenon is illustrated by the way Victorian England was ready to demonize contemporary French literary production, though this attribution to France of the role of forbidden Other alerts us to the presence of mythmaking, an activity which also is unlikely to be absent from the ways in which French society constructed images of itself. In 1888, the English translation of Zola's novel *La Terre* (1887) earned its publisher, Henry Vizetelly, a prison sentence. The depravation of Oscar Wilde's Dorian Gray was attributed by his creator to his reading of French literature, while the same author's erotic drama *Salomé* was produced in Paris (in French) rather than London. Unsurprisingly, few of the most influential or widely read French novels of the period escaped the papal Index (though the latter seems to have been compiled in accordance with a rhythm of fits and starts that now seems quaintly quixotic). Yet it was not the case that the French authorities sanctioned sexual license. In different ways, according to the hue of the particular political regime, they remained largely committed to censorship. Though somewhat less so than stage productions or the press, books were regarded as potentially dangerous. In the later years of the Restoration, for example, amid justifiable fears of political insurrection, the owners of *cabinets de lecture* were ordered to destroy all titles that had been placed on the Index for being immoral or irreligious, categories that overlapped considerably in the mind of the censor.

Censorship was pursued with impunity, notwithstanding its nature as a double-edged sword. From the point of view of literary fame, it mattered little whether the authors of *Madame Bovary* (1857) and *Les fleurs du mal* [*The Flowers of Evil*] (1857) were acquitted on charges of obscenity. (Flaubert, who wielded the twin advantages of an aesthetic of indirect statement and a cultivated moral ambiguity, was;

Baudelaire, whose poetry appeared more obviously inflammatory of the senses, was not.) In both cases, the work received unprecedented exposure, though Baudelaire was obliged to expunge some dozen poems whose erotic nature had given particular offense. As for the trial of Antony Méray, author of *La part des femmes* [*The Woman's Share*] (a novel serialized in a Fourierist newspaper in 1847), it was immortalized by the mention it received in Flaubert's *L'Education sentimentale* (1869). Censorship was, moreover, always ready to make an ass of itself. As Théophile Gautier recorded in his preface to *Mademoiselle de Maupin* (1835), the vicomte Sosthène de La Rochefoucauld attracted derision, in the closing years of the Restoration, for ordering the Opera dancers to wear longer skirts and for imposing a plaster fig leaf on every public statue. In *Madame Bovary*, Flaubert brilliantly catches the hypocrisy of much censorship: the outraged Homais, caught between his sense of propriety as the bourgeois *père de famille* and his self-congratulatory pose as a freethinker, castigates his young assistant Justin for reading a manual of conjugal love before informing the assembled company that in the right hands, the volume (the copy is presumably his) of course has a legitimate educational purpose.

Nonetheless the pursuit of indecency on the part of the authorities was invariably a response to an imagined political threat rather than an expression of general puritanism or prudery. A number of the political *chansons* Béranger wrote during the Restoration, and which led to his imprisonment, showed the censor to have been right to sense an ulterior motive behind obscenity. The Revolution of 1789, with the pornographic writings of Mirabeau and his imitators, the obscenities that peppered Hébert's newspaper *Le Père Duchesne*, and, above all, the crude pornographic satires depicting Marie-Antoinette engaging in incest, lesbianism, masturbation, and insatiable nymphomania, had provided some sulphurous examples. If the sexual scenes in Zola's early novel *La confession de Claude* (1865) attracted the attention of the censors of the Second Empire, the decision not to prosecute was due to their (correct) conclusion that the work was not politically subversive. One can, nevertheless, only conjecture how the same author's Rougon-Macquart cycle would have fared had the less repressive Third Republic not intervened.

The erotic obsession marking out 19th-century French literature was closely linked to the new prominence accorded women in post-Revolutionary France and heralded in symbolic fashion by the way the cultural philosopher and writer Madame de Staël was considered by Napoleon an enemy of some consequence. Whether as an increasingly complex, not to say perverse, object of desire or as the embodiment of her own sexual desires, Woman, as her often superior vitality (or individuality) as a literary fictional character revealed, came to possess a significance that both conferred on her the potentiality of embodying multiple "novelistic" intrigues (in a society where dramatic changes in fortune were the hallmark of the new socioeconomic reality). This posited her as a threat to what was still a world in which men—however inadequate (or "feminized") Stendhal, Balzac, Flaubert, and Zola might show them to be—remained the dominant force.

The 19th-century French male was nonetheless at risk from the new status of women. His increasingly ludicrous formal attire, completed by phallic top hat and cane, was a gift for caricaturists and became viewed as a theatrical garb that connoted standing and respectability but which, especially in depictions of the demimonde, was at odds with the moral and physical grubbiness it concealed. Its function as the uniform of the dandy, who, according to a Baudelaire or a Barbey d'Aurevilly, represented a cultivated superiority that went beyond the realm of costume, nonetheless reinforced the sense of an uneasy relationship with the female sex. The threat represented by women in the 19th-century French imagination was all the greater in that Utopian thinkers such as Saint-Simon and Fourier explicitly advocated the emancipation of women, while their female counterparts, notably Flora Tristan, readily adopted a feminist agenda and terminology. The more extreme facets of these imaginary societies might justify the luxury of ridicule, but no such belittlement, nor the adoption of an age-old misogynistic discourse, could seriously dent the fixation of the age upon the figure of Woman, nor palliate the dread that patriarchal structures would prove as flimsy as those quarters of Paris reduced to rubble by the grandiose schemes of that other Utopian, Baron Haussmann. It is only with slight exaggeration for humorous effect that Balzac, writing in 1848, looked back to "the great female emancipation of 1830." The new prominence of Woman would duly find further expression in Villiers de l'Isle-Adam's novel *L'Eve future* [*The Future Eve*] (1886), which featured a beautiful android indistinguishable from a real woman.

This did not mean that the course of historical inevitability ran as smoothly as reformers would have wished. It is significant that Zola, in *Germinal* (1885), has the body of the female mineworker clothed by the same overalls as the male miner's, thereby rendering her sexless, while in *L'Assommoir* (1877), Gervaise's descent into alcoholism reenacts a topos previously considered masculine. It is striking, too, that whereas novel writing in the first decades of the century was virtually the exclusive province of women, the reverse became true after 1830. Margaret Cohen has argued that the significance and value of "sentimental" writing by women have been obscured by the prestige of subsequent male-authored works of "realism." Yet initially such works of realism represented a hijacking by male writers of the novel's specifically feminine concerns. Rather than eliding the female perspective, or relocating it in an unproblematic past, Stendhal and Balzac offer the female reader the delight of a bolder feminine individuality, with the added (if doubtless insidious) prestige of being revealed by a male gaze and therefore accorded a proof of its origin outside the cocoon within which female writer and reader enclose themselves. Yet Mathilde de la Mole's Romantic self-image in Stendhal's *Le rouge et le noir* [*The Red and the Black*] (1830), while it possesses the realist status that might appear to sanction that of an emancipated woman, is subtly subordinated, by virtue of constituting an extra layer of heroic imitation, to the depiction of Julien Sorel and his overweening ambition. It was Balzac who was regarded by his contemporaries as having, in Jules Janin's mocking words, "invented women." The vast interlocking fictions of the *Comédie humaine* contain the most remarkable diversity of female personages, separated not only by individual temperament and circumstances, but by age, class, marital status, and sexual orientation and united only through the fascination they arouse as a result of the novelty of their exposure and the ways in which they use (or disdain to use) their sexuality for their advancement. As if dissatisfied with existing categories, Balzac created others, some of which, notably the hitherto unacknowledged "woman in her thirties" (*la femme de trente ans*), were gratefully received by the appropriate section of his readership. It was as if the novelist had usurped the privilege of access to the secrets of the woman's bedroom accorded usually only to priest or physician. To judge by his fan mail, his female readers more generally felt gratitude for the extraordinary empathy he showed with regard to their desires and emotions. The fate of the liaisons he depicted was nonetheless shown to depend, disconcertingly or reassuringly according to one's standpoint, on the prevailing social forces rather than on conventional morality.

The changing attitudes and behavior of women in a politically unstable world brought an unfamiliar compulsion to understand and redefine relations between the sexes, as may be seen in the way, for example, the century is marked out by such works as Stendhal's *De l'Amour* (1822), the historian Jules Michelet's *L'Amour* (1858) and *La Femme* (1859), and Paul Bourget's *Physiologie de l'amour moderne* (1891). (Bourget's writings were lampooned for their social exclusivity by Octave Mirbeau in *Le Journal d'une femme de chambre* [*Diary of a Chambermaid*], 1900.) At the key turning point in his career, Balzac published his humorous but insightful *Physiologie du mariage* (1829), a work he never repudiated and a topic to which he frequently returned. Its overtly sexual perspective serves as an appropriate introduction to the anarchy that had ensued from the way marriage had evolved. As Patricia Mainardi has shown, the combination of arranged marriages (often between partners of disproportionately different ages) and the lack of even limited divorce laws in France until 1884 inevitably led not only to adultery but also to a whole sexual subeconomy (involving married women and girls of easy virtue alike) catering to the young man denied more legitimate outlets. The unique figure of the accommodating *grisette* beloved by the Parisian Latin Quarter population, anatomized by Janin, nostalgically recalled by Théodore de Banville in his poem "L'Amour à Paris," and lovingly drawn (along with her counterpart, the *lorette*) by Gavarni, was the uncomplicated response of the marketplace. Yet the obsessive desire for a mistress, recorded in the first part of *Mademoiselle de Maupin*, is also the cause of the hero's downfall in Gustave Drouineau's proto-Balzacian novel *Ernest, ou le travers du siècle* [*Ernest, or the Distance of a Century*] (1829). More fundamentally disruptive of established order, the liaison between a young man and an older married woman, based on reciprocal sexual attraction, establishes itself as a topos susceptible of some telling variations, notably in *Le rouge et le noir* and *L'Education sentimentale*. Such instances cannot be dismissed as copycat examples of a young male's fantasy. They are, still more, the product of profound tensions within the way French bourgeois society ordered its sexual economy. Small wonder that the 19th-century French novel and the novel of adultery appear almost synonymous.

If it is easy for each new age to appear to be the first to discover sex, the erotic obsessions of the French 19th century contrasted strikingly with those of the ancien régime, albeit with certain strands of continuity that must be considered first. That the *roman libertin* of the previous century exerted a formative influence on the writers of Balzac's generation cannot be denied. As for the Marquis de Sade, he was read both more and less often than he was mentioned. The existence of an ambiguous dividing line between the erotic and the pornographic explained the similar attraction of the "gay [happy] novels" (*romans gais*) of Pigault-Lebrun, though these, together with the novels of his much maligned but also much read "successor," Paul de Kock, also tapped into a much older tradition of Gallic, anticlerical humor. In early-nineteenth-century France, as Balzac's *Physiologie du mariage* confirms, both Rabelais and Sterne were immensely popular and were taken to license narratives that contained a certain elevated or learned smuttiness (*grivoiserie*). It is to this tradition that Balzac's *Contes drolatiques* [*Droll Tales*] (1832–37), written in pseudo-Rabelaisian French, belong, as does Maupassant's story "Mes vingt-cinq jours," [My Twenty-five Days], which links a magnificent walnut forest to an ingenious penance imposed by the village priest on his female parishioners who "fall."

Yet 18th-century concepts of the erotic, outside the realm of pornography, remain distinct from those of the century that followed. If poets such as Gautier and Gérard de Nerval (and to a certain extent Verlaine) looked back nostalgically to the 18th century, it was to an age when a largely visual representation of erotic activity emphasized a notion of "la vie galante" that stressed wit, sensual yet tasteful pleasures, and intelligent, self-conscious idealization. The physical activity of sex was not expunged but alluded to by witty innuendo which, while sometimes obscene, nonetheless addressed itself to the reader's intelligence with a *clin d'oeil,* a wink. It was the opposite of the explicit—the representation had to be "read" for it to reveal more than its picturesque exterior. As in the case of the *roman libertin,* the emphasis on intelligence was a mark of its aristocratic nature. The history of eros in 19th-century France is, in contrast, one of *embourgeoisement,* "bourgeoisification." Nowhere is this more apparent than when Balzac, in *La Cousine Bette* (1846), dubs Valérie Marneffe a "Madame de Merteuil bourgeoise."

As the bourgeois age progresses, there is an ever-increasing emphasis on the body and its secrets, as is shown by Balzac's comic portrait of Mademoiselle Cormon in *La vieille fille* [*The Old Woman*] (which makes much play with 18th-century *grivoiserie*), a temporarily uxorious spinster of advancing years who has to be cut out of her corset after fainting. The same fixation with the female body will later appear in certain of Mallarmé's poems, though in an infinitely more refined manner, with corporeal forms evoked suggestively as absences, thereby embodying the essence of "pure poetry." Meanwhile, the progression of the nude from the polished classical and academic perfections of Ingres and Gérôme to Courbet's obese bathers (whom Barbey d'Aurevilly accused of "polluting the stream in which they bathe") showed a development that responded to a call for greater realism, which in the eyes of some equated with ugliness. Yet nudity on its own achieved only a limited effect. A greater degree of erotic realism was achieved by that most "literary" of painters, Manet, when, in *Le déjeuner sur l'herbe* (1863), he surrounds his female nude with male picnickers who are fully clothed, or when, in his *Olympia* (1863), he has the courtesan (a forerunner of Zola's Nana) clothed by her nudity and her sexuality alluded to by a phallic cat who would make a reappearance in Zola's novel *Thérèse Raquin* (1867). Works by Balzac (*Le chef-d'oeuvre inconnu* [*The Unknown Masterpiece*], 1831) and Zola (*L'Oeuvre* [*The Work*], 1886) took the reader into the studio to see the very real (reluctant) nudity of the amateur model. The convention by which the beloved is little more than a name is left well behind as Baudelaire embraces with all his senses (but also his mind) those erogenous features of his mistress's body to which he finds himself obsessively drawn.

The *femme fatale,* that dramatic and exotic form of the newly "realist" fantasy of the dominant female (for example, Mérimée's Carmen, 1847; Rachilde's *La Marquise de Sade,* 1886; or Mirbeau's Clara in *Le jardin des supplices* [*The Garden of Torments*], 1898–99), was required to have a highly developed physical allure. The Bible and antiquity, coupled with a personal experience of exotic sexual tourism, provided Gautier and Flaubert with the inspiration for further awe-inspiring examples of female physicality, such as Cleopatra, the fictional Salammbô, and the Queen of Sheba (in Flaubert's *La tentation de Saint-Antoine,* 1874), just as other writers were drawn to Judith and Delilah. Joris-Karl Huysmans's exploitation, in *À rebours* [*Backward*] (1884), of the biblical story of Salomé, which he took over from the painter Gustave Moreau, led to his exploiting, in a decadent (and highly cerebral) manner, the use the character makes of her body to impose absolute power on the patriarch who engendered her. Female nudity is fundamental to the more accessible libertinism of Pierre Louÿs, in such popular works as *Aphrodite* (1896), the story of a courtesan in 1st-century Egypt.

It is nonetheless the explicit emphasis on physical sexual activity that most surely characterizes the 19th-century French novel. Mérimée in *La double méprise* [*The Double Mistake*] (1833) and Flaubert in *Madame Bovary* were ready to scandalize (and delight) the bourgeois public with the unmistakeable evidence of sexual coupling behind the blinds of a moving coach. More generally, Flaubert, Maupassant, and Zola gave a new centrality to the sexual act itself and depicted both the preliminaries and the locations in which it took place with a new level of detail. The film directors Visconti and Godard were later able to find suggestive erotic scenarios amongst Maupassant's short stories, while Buñuel found inspiration in *Le journal d'une femme de chambre* (first published in *La Revue bleue* in a bowdlerized version) and Louÿs's *La femme et le pantin* [*The Woman and the Puppet*] (1898).

It is, arguably, the relentlessly erotic character of Zola's Rougon-Macquart novels that offers the most wide-ranging reflection of the frenzied eroticism of the age. Sex for Zola was not so much a subject as a vast metaphor for a society in the throes of autodestruction, though he was not unaware of the subject's allure. Even the evocations of the vegetables in *Le ventre de Paris* [*The Belly of Paris*] (1873) or the department-store window display in *Au bonheur des dames* [*On the Happiness of Ladies*] (1883) connote sexuality. The apparently regulated social order of the apartment block in *Pot-Bouille* [*Pot-Face*] is exploded by the unmasking of the building as the locus of illicit sexual desire, whether satisfied or frustrated. More generally, the living and working conditions of the modern city, in which the increasing encouragement of consumerist behavior, coupled with a new emphasis on the provision of entertainment, heightens expectations with regard to the satisfaction of appetites of every kind, bringing strangers into a new physical proximity that stimulates both sexual promiscuity and voyeurism. If scenes of undisguised voyeurism are frequent in Zola's novels, it is as if the Parisian environment makes voyeurs of us all, author and reader included. Yet, it was the anonymity of the city, and the stimulus of the chance encounter, that had been at the heart of Baudelaire's eroticization of the city. If his activity as *flâneur* was that of a dandy, aesthete, and refined connoisseur, subsequent writers and artists came to view the boulevards of Haussmann's Paris as locations in which individuals eyed each other up with a brazenness previously associated only with the world of prostitution. As the streets became the location for an ever-growing section of the population, there was a corresponding need for popular forms of leisure to be organized and controlled, as Huysmans shows in depictions of young working-class men and women both in the workplace and in places of entertainment such as the fairground (*Les soeurs Vatard* [*The Sisters Vatard*], 1879; *En ménage* [*Some Housework*], 1881).

Most indicative of the *embourgeoisement* of erotic activity in 19th-century France, however, is the intimate relationship between sex and money. Throughout the century, prostitution was the obsessive concern of the authorities and literary practitioners alike. Parent-Duchâtelet's report on prostitution in Paris (1836), published early in the July Monarchy, was widely read. Far from being a matter for automatic condemnation, prostitution was the subject of debate. Given the nature of marriage in 19th-century France, it is not surprising that it had its

defenders. So central was it to the period's thinking that Fourier, in keeping with his practice of rehabilitating negative concepts through the simple tactic of overturning their marginal status, placed universal prostitution at the heart of his blueprint for relationships between the sexes. In the literary realm, with no such intention on the part of the authors concerned, the prostitute similarly progressed from being a minor to a major figure. It is scarcely an exaggeration to say that she became the premier female literary character of the age, and certainly satisfied its appetite for superficial variety. The widespread curiosity about the courtesan's superior expertise finds tangible expression in the scene in *La Cousine Bette* in which the naive and virtuous wife, Adeline Hulot, is stunned by the opulent domestic surroundings of her rival, Josépha. From deluxe *objet d'art* to the bargain-basement streetwalker, from those who exploited their position to gain wealth and influence to those who maintained a conscience and a capacity to love or those who set an example of repentance, the species spawned a rich set of subspecies. Balzac's Coralie, his Florine, or his Esther Gobseck, Flaubert's Marie (in his early story "Novembre") or his Rosanette (in *L'Education sentimentale*), Janin's Henriette (in *L'Âne mort et la femme guillotinée* [*The Dead Ass and the Guillotined Woman*], 1829), Hugo's Marion de Lorme, Sand's Lélia, the *lorette* Suzanne in Méray's *La Part des femmes*, Dumas *fils*'s Marguerite Gautier (his "Lady of the Camellias"), Maupassant's Boule de suif, Huysmans's Marthe, the Goncourt brothers' Elisa, Zola's Nana, the list could easily be prolonged. The high-fashion locales of Parisian prostitution, the Palais-Royal and the Opéra, as well as the more humble red-light district that forms the backdrop for *Gambara*, are given due prominence by Balzac, while both the Goncourts and Maupassant took their readers inside a *maison close*, a "closed house." In both literature and the visual arts, the brothel was all but indistinguishable from the theatre in what was a vast spectacularization of life in the French capital. Balzac's totalizing vision, moreover, makes prostitution the dominant metaphor of the *Comédie humaine*, and one that incorporates rather than excludes literary production.

Sex was also ensured prominence by the employment of more empirical forms of scientific inquiry, especially in the realm of medicine. Yet medical attention continued to focus on masturbation in the wake of Dr. Tissot's celebrated 18th-century treatise on onanism. The portrait of a teenage boy in Balzac's *Le médecin de campagne* [*Country Medicine*] alludes to a need for him to be cured of the practice; while Mallarmé's evocation of poetic sterility and the dramatization of "disappearing vision" in "L'après-midi d'un faune" [*Afternoon of a Fawn*] and "Victorieusement fui le suicide beau" [*Victoriously Fled the Beautiful Suicide*] have been interpreted as an acknowledged punishment for adolescent masturbation. Balzac's theory of a limited vital fluid, together with the overtly sexual context of his tale of the wild ass's skin that shrinks with each satisfaction of a desire (*La peau de chagrin* [*The Skin of Sorrow*], 1831), may be regarded as forming part of a similar sexual pathology. The frustrating debate over the nature of female sexuality (and sexual pleasure) inevitably spilled over into nonmedical spheres. Flaubert's Emma Bovary, the Goncourts' Germinie (*Germinie lacerteux*, 1864), whose life was based on the inclination of their own maid to debauchery, Zola's Renée (his attempt at a modern Phaedra in *La curée* [*The Quarry*], 1872), to say nothing of Mirabeau's chambermaid, would have been inconceivable without the emergence of new views of female physiology. These views, and their fictional repercussions, indeed presented a challenge to what had previously prevailed as truth (*vraisemblable*).

The perception of an explosion of sexual activity was intertwined with questions of public hygiene as much as with those of morality (though the imaginary newspaper article included by Zola in *Nana* [1880] indicates how easily the same language could be made to do double service). In the 1830s morgue literature of Janin and Petrus Borel and his Romantic circle, as well as in other contemporary "social novels" (*romans de moeurs*), the prostitute's inevitable removal to the "hospital" was taken to indicate the venereal ward. If Dumas *fils* has the Lady of the Camellias die of consumption, this demands to be seen as a euphemistic allusion to a sexually transmitted disease, as must surely be the exotic infection passed on to Valérie Marneffe by her Brazilian lover, and, for all its superior realism, Nana's death from smallpox caught from her infant son. The plaster statue of a priest in *Madame Bovary* peels in giveaway fashion. But such cases are of minor importance alongside the way in which sex in 19th-century France was associated with disease and death through the fear and reality of syphilis, of which Flaubert laconically observed in his *Dictionnaire des idées reçues* [*Dictionary of Generally Accepted Ideas*]: "[M]ore or less everyone is affected by it." (In 1900, some 15 percent of all deaths were considered to be from the disease.) Literary syphilitics included Baudelaire, Flaubert, Maupassant, Alphonse Daudet, and Jules de Goncourt, with the disease being pronounced responsible for any evidence of a pessimistic outlook on life, also associated with the influence of Schopenhauer. Initially not always mentioned by name, it is plainly the cause of the husband's death in Balzac's *Le lys dans la vallée* [*The Lily of the Valley*] (1836). Chapter 8 of *À rebours* recounts Des Esseintes's nightmare vision of the disease. Daudet's posthumous *Aux pays de la douleur* [*In the Land of Suffering*] is an autobiographical account of a man in the painful tertiary stage of the disease. Less direct illustrations of a self-aware syphilitic imagination may be found in some of Baudelaire's imagery.

The morbidity of the closely related Naturalist and fin-de-siècle aesthetics likewise drew on scientific thinking that stressed the animalistic in man. In Zola's *La Terre*, the peasant is shown to display a quasi-sexual obsession with the soil, but there is nothing indirect about the author's choice of language to depict it. If sexual incontinence, including that of an (admittedly amnesiac) priest in *La faute de l'abbé Mouret* [*The Sin of Father Mouret*] (1875), a novel which reworks the Garden of Eden motif, is a constant presence in the Rougon-Macquart cycle, it is, in contrast to the case of the cynical journalist Georges Duroy in Maupassant's novel *Bel-Ami* (1885), rarely controlled; the sexual adventurer Octave Mouret (see *Pot-Bouille* and *Au bonheur des dames*) may be counted an exception. Yet there is a still more general association in Zola's fiction between sex and death. It is the emphasis on the proximity of the sexual urge and the desire to kill that takes Zola's fiction beyond a more mundane association of sex and violence. The desire for illicit sexual congress forms the background to the husband's murder in *Thérèse Raquin*, but it is in *La bête humaine* [*The Human Animal*] (1890) that the principal character's homicidal response to exposed female flesh, which is presented as the product of a tainted heredity, unites the two in a more modern perspective. His sexual relationship with his victim is moreover indissociable from the fact that she is urging him to murder her husband, just as she confesses to having, under duress, abetted the latter in the murder of an older man who had taken sexual advantage of her before she was married.

The fact remains that it is the sheer variety of sexual subjects that marks out 19th-century French literature, with those subjects that had previously invited ribaldry now becoming a matter of sexual pathology. In addition to the voyeurism and prostitution already highlighted, these included:

- Incest (the sibling example of Chateaubriand's *René,* 1802; the uncle and niece in Zola's *Le Docteur Pascal,* 1893)
- Undisclosed sexual secrets (Stendhal's *Armance,* 1827)
- Impotence (Mme de Duras's *Olivier ou le secret,* 1826; Balzac's *La peau de chagrin* and *La Vieille fille*)
- Sexual fiascos (the celebrated chapter in the 1853 edition of Stendhal's *De l'Amour*)
- Homosexuality (Custine's *Aloys*; Hugo's *Claude Gueux*; Balzac's *Vautrin*)
- Lesbianism (Balzac's *La fille aux yeux d'or* [The Girl with the Golden Eyes], 1834–5; Joséphin Péladan; Baudelaire's "Lesbos" and the two poems entitled "Femmes damnées"; the title originally envisaged for *Les Fleurs du mal* was *Les Lesbiennes*)
- Hermaphroditism/androgyny (updating the old fictional stratagem of cross-dressing and frequently associated with lesbianism and/or male homosexuality) (Latouche's *Fragoletta,* 1829; Balzac's *Sarrasine,* 1831, and *Séraphita,* 1835, and his George Sand–type character, Félicité des Touches; Gautier's *Mademoiselle de Maupin* and his poem "Contralto" in *Emaux et camées,* 1852; Péladan; Rachilde's *Monsieur Vénus,* 1884; Jean Lorrain's *Monsieur de Phocas,* 1901)
- Castration (*Sarrasine; La peau de chagrin;* Balzac's semi-autobiographical *Louis Lambert,* 1835)
- Bestiality (a female panther's infatuation with a soldier in Balzac's arguably jocular story *Une passion dans le désert*)
- Prolonged virginity (Balzac's old maids)
- Nymphomania (albeit with all due discretion, Emma Bovary)

- Frigidity (*La peau de chagrin,* which also incorporates hints of lesbianism and hermaphroditism)
- Fetishism (clothes and footware in *Madame Bovary;* and the more literal (and fatal) case of boot fetishism in *Le journal d'une femme de chambre*).

Pornography as an entity, to which 19th-century literary eroticism inevitably relates, represents a special case, given its status as the "already written," and features as a thematically legitimized presence rather than as a properly constituted subject. A familar topos, shared with pornographic fictions themselves, consists of the collection of curiosa locked away in the owner's library or with the pages (and, above all the plates) hidden behind rich bindings, the object themselves of fetishistic desire. An example may be found in the flagellation addict's library in Edmond de Goncourt's *La Faustin* (1881–2), with its "curious bindings stamped with phallic emblems." In a degraded version of such decadence, Mirbeau's chambermaid is exposed to obscene engravings by various predatory employers, male and female alike. (The same novel also contains the hilarious discovery by a customs official of a dildo in one of her mistress's jewel cases.) Such evocations of pornography partake of the tantalizing play of the hidden and the revealed and may, to an extent, be seen as emblematic of the period's conception of the book in general. More generally, the relationship between "nobler" forms of French 19th-century writing and the pornography with which its authors were so familiar remains to be studied, starting most fruitfully perhaps with the particular attraction exerted by Flaubert's representations of the "real."

As Mario Praz demonstrated with unprecedented erudition in *The Romantic Irony,* the predominant obsession within 19th-century French representations of sexual desire was with the sadomasochistic. The prevailing erotic sensibility was duly traced by him to the influence, both specific and general, of the Marquis de Sade. As early as 1824, a French Academician alluded to the latter's nefarious influence. This was further promoted by Janin's article of 1834 (duly read by Flaubert later in the decade). By 1843, the critic Sainte-Beuve felt authorized to claim that de Sade and Byron were the two principal influences on modern literature. In 1851 a conservative critic (Horace de Viel-Castel) produced a long list of those marked by de Sade's influence, including George Sand, Musset, Eugène Sue, and Dumas *père*. Depending on the specificity of one's criteria, the list was either too long or not long enough. A more exclusive survey would highlight Petrus Borel's "Sadification" of the stereotypes of the English gothic novel and the ambiguities of pain and pleasure that permeate the poetry of Baudelaire ("I am the wound and the knife," he writes in "L'Héautontimoroumenos"). The Goncourt brothers recorded Flaubert's obsessive delight in de Sade, whom he evidently regarded as a "dark comic genius" and whose presence is unmistakable in Flaubert's juvenilia as well as in *La tentation de Saint-Antoine* and *Salammbô*. Sadistic torture and flagellation are featured in Péladan's *La vertu suprême* (1900), Paul-Jean Toulet's *Monsieur du Paur* (1898), and Mirbeau's *Le jardin des supplices*. De Sade's name is never mentioned as such in *Comédie humaine*, but traces of Balzac's awareness of his writings are evident.

The examples given would appear to constitute a veritable (and largely complete) compendium of sexual particularities evoked for their own sake, a response to the compulsion to embrace the universal through an exhaustive compilation of diverse particularities, though one that was fated more often than not to remain stuck in a contemplation of diversity and fragmentation. (Thus the "Notice" to *À rebours* rehearses the different types of woman possessed by Des Esseintes but is obliged to recognize that the character fails to transcend a feeling of jadedness.) The obsession with categorization and differentiation permeates even the illicit, as may be seen in the attempts to distinguish between *grisettes*, *lorettes*, and *insoumises*, which, as in the case of the narrative discourse of Balzac's *Comédie humaine*, constitutes a response to the panic felt in the face of both the amorphous and the multiple difference. In 1842, Dumas *père* wrote a piece entitled "Filles, lorettes et courtisanes." The proliferation of *codes* and *physiologies* (there was a *Physiologie de la lorette*) showed the long reach of the Napoleonic legal and administrative example, while Fourier's sexual Utopia was ordered, almost parodically, by categories and numbers.

Sexual inquiry in imaginative literature was, in other ways too, generally synonymous with the fundamental epistemological inquiry underlying much of the literary writing of the age. It represented a means of pursuing inquiry beyond the familiar and beneath the surface, and was a means of entry rather the end of the quest in itself. The exclusiveness of the sexual reference varied considerably, and the latter was by no means necessarily the foremost referent. The texts listed from the gerontocratic Restoration, for example, especially those involving scenarios of impotence, invite just as readily a reading in terms of political allegory (as does the shrinking of the skin in *La Peau de chagrin*, written in the wake of the July Revolution), while hermaphrodite and androgyne fictions may be regarded essentially as allegories of the divided Romantic artist. Yet the movement toward an ever more specialized form of sexual inquiry is undeniable. The Symbolist fin-de-siècle, with its fascination with the occult, spiritualism, and the Wagnerian, pursued a cult of the rarefied, the perverse, and the artificial for their own sakes rather than as part of the post-Rousseau dialectic that had formed the starting point of a Baudelaire. The focus on marginal sexual tastes nonetheless represented a continuation of the dandy's ambition to be the member of an elite.

In the final analysis, the erotic universe that has been surveyed, for all the prominence it gave to the nature and role of women, remained predominantly a male world, one in which Aurore Dudevant was led to dress in male costume and take the *nom de plume* George Sand. Not only were the vast majority of the authors men, they wrote mainly from outside the approved institution of marriage. Balzac teasingly attributed the authorship of his *Physiologie du mariage* to "a young bachelor" and remained a bachelor for virtually his entire life. If Zola sought to reduplicate his married life and surroundings in his additional life with his mistress, the many other bachelors included Sainte-Beuve, Stendhal, Mérimée, Baudelaire, Nerval, Flaubert, the Goncourt brothers, Maupassant, Arthur Rimbaud, and Jean Lorrain. The poet Paul Verlaine was hardly a model husband. Of these, few were exclusively homosexual, but the literary world they constituted was largely misogynistic and homosocial. Mérimée wrote letters of an explicitly sexual nature to Stendhal, whose own correspondence and personal writings did not want for a similar explicitness. The sexually scabrous exerted a strong attraction on Flaubert and still more so on the deeply misogynistic Goncourts.

A pornographic product of Musset's pen has already been noted. Maupassant had a justifiable reputation as an erotomaniac and, like Fourier, professed an attraction to lesbians (see, for example, his story "La Femme de Paul," 1881). He wrote some 40 risqué tales of varying complexion, mainly for the newspaper *Gil Blas*, together with pornographic poems and a light-hearted pornographic play entitled *A la feuille de rose, maison turque* [*With the Sheet of Pink, Turkish House*] (1875), privately performed with Flaubert in the audience and with fellow writers such as Mirbeau taking part. A whole section of Lorrain's work (he was a flamboyant dandy, homosexual, and ether addict) was pornographic, while his press pieces devoted to Parisian women took readers into the shadowy realities of the demimonde. Louÿs developed an expertise in French pornographic and libertine bibliography. Verlaine wrote two collections of obscene verse, *Femmes* and *Hommes*, published pseudonymously and posthumously, respectively, which celebrated sexual activity with both sexes. Certain of Rimbaud's prose poems have been decoded (controversially) to reveal obscene meanings.

Baudelaire recorded his misogynist views in *Mon coeur mis à nu* [*My Heart Exposed*]. Woman was presented by the poet as horrendous because she embodied the natural. In "Les Bijoux," one of his poems condemned in 1857, the attraction of the naked woman comes not from her unclothed body but from the artificial jewels decorating it. Barbey d'Aurevilly refused to be taken in by Baudelaire's evocation of the erotic charms of woman and dubbed him the "virgin poet." As for Michel Butor, writing a century later, he was led to suppose that the poet had discovered that although he was attracted to women, he was not able to perform as a man. Balzac's sexual orientation was for a time the subject of speculation by his contemporaries. Whether or not one accepts the claim that women sensed Flaubert to be a "feminine type," his writings support the view of him as a masochist. As for the seemingly pro-feminist *Madame Bovary*, Baudelaire claimed that Emma had the makeup of a man, and the novel can be read just as convincingly as the expression of a pervasive male fantasy as it can as a detached psychosociological study of female sexuality. It is this ambiguity that makes it the exemplary text with

regard to the French 19th-century incarnation of the erotic.

Yet the particularities of many of the authors in question should not be allowed to undermine the significance of the obsession with sexuality in 19th-century France. This obsession intersected with all the other major discourses through which the period sought to confront the problem of knowledge in a world that was changing at an unprecedentedly rapid rate. If the location of sexual desire in the body was acknowledged unashamedly, it was the recognition of its twin location in the mind that ensured that 19th-century French writers probed its more profound dimensions. The changing face of sex provided a privileged indicator of a new socioeconomic reality, in which the creation and satisfaction of desire was paramount. Still more importantly, the dismantling of conventional boundaries rendered the sexual sphere an incomparable area for experimentation and discovery, as well as allowing it to present a powerful challenge to institutions wielding power. Reading itself, newly commercialized and increasingly a mass activity, became intertwined with the pervasive subject of prostitution through the conjoining of money and pleasure. And if desire was predominant at the level of subject, so the literary representation itself became an object of desire, thereby blurring provocatively the distinction between writing that was pornographic and writing that allegedly was not.

MICHAEL TILBY

Further Reading

Angenot, Marc. *Le Cru et le faisandé: Sexe, discours et littérature à la Belle Epoque*. Brussels: Labor, 1986.

Barthes, Roland. *Sade, Fourier, Loyola*. Paris: Seuil, 1973.

Bernheimer, Charles. *Figures of Ill-Repute: Representing Prostitution in Nineteenth-Century France*. Cambridge, MA: Harvard University Press, 1979.

Birkett, Jennifer. *The Sins of the Fathers: Decadence in France and Europe, 1870–1914*. London: Quarter Books, 1986.

Bolster, Richard. *Stendhal, Balzac et le féminisme romantique*. Paris: Minard, 1970.

Brooks, Peter. *Body Work: Objects of Desire in Modern Literature*. Cambridge, MA: Havard University Press, 1993.

Busst, A.J.L. "The Image of the Androgyne in the Nineteenth Century." In *Romantic Mythologies*, edited by Ian Fletcher. London: Routledge & Kegan Paul, 1967.

Clayson, Hollis. *Painted Love: Prostitution in French Art of the Impressionist Era*. New Haven and London: Yale University Press, 1991.

Cohen, Margaret. *The Sentimental Education of the Novel*. Princeton, NJ: Princeton University Press, 1999.

Corbin, Alain. *Les Filles de noce: Misère sexuelle et prostitution (19e et 20e siècles)*. Paris: Aubier Montaigne, 1978. In English as *Women for Hire: Prostitution and Sexuality in France after 1850*, translated by Alan Sheridan. Cambridge, MA: Harvard University Press, 1990.

Duchet, Claude. "L'Image de Sade à l'époque romantique." In *Le Marquis de Sade*. Paris: Armand Colin, 1971.

Felman, Shoshana. "Rereading femininity." *Yale French Studies* 62 (1981): 19–44.

Foucault, Michel. *Histoire de la sexualité, I : La Volonté de savoir*. Paris: Gallimard, 1976. In English as *The History of Sexuality*. Vol. 1: *An Introduction*, translated by Robert Hurley. New York: Pantheon, 1978; London: Allen Lane, 1979.

Jacob, Paul L., bibliophile [i.e. Paul Lacroix]. "La Vérité sur les deux procès criminels du marquis de Sade." *Revue de Paris* 38 (February 1837): 134-44.

Janin, Jules. "Le Marquis de Sade." *Revue de Paris* 11 (November 1834): 321-60.

Kelly, Dorothy. *Fictional Genders: Role and Representation in Nineteenth-Century French Narrative*. Lincoln: University of Nebraska Press, 1989.

LaCapra, Dominick. *'Madame Bovary' on Trial*. Ithaca and London: Cornell University Press, 1982.

Laforgue, Pierre. *L'Eros romantique. Représentations de l'amour en 1830*. Paris: Presses universitaires de France, 1998.

Mainardi, Patricia. *Husbands, Wives, and Lovers: Marriage and its Discontents in Nineteenth-Century France*. New Haven and London: Yale University Press, 2003.

Matlock, Jann. *Scenes of Seduction: Prostitution, Hysteria, and Reading Difference in Nineteenth-Century France*. New York: Columbia University Press, 1994.

Overton, Bill. *Fictions of Female Adultery, 1684–1890*. Basingstoke: Palgrave-Macmillan, 2002.

———. *The Novel of Female Adultery: Love and Gender in Continental European Fiction, 1830–1900*. Basingstoke: Macmillan, 1996.

Parent-Du Châtelet, Alexandre. *La Prostitution à Paris au XIXe siècle*. edited by Alain Corbin. Paris: Seuil, 1981. First published in Paris, 1836, as *De la prostitution dans la ville de Paris*.

Perceau, Louis. *Bibliographie du roman érotique au XIXe siècle*. 2 vols. Paris: Foudrinier, 1930.

Praz, Mario. *The Romantic Agony*. London: Collins, 1960 (first English edition, 1933).

Rousset, Jean. *Leurs yeux se rencontrèrent*. Paris: Corti, 1981.

Schor, Naomi. *Breaking the Chain: Women, Theory and French Realist Fiction*. New York: Columbia University Press, 1985.

Segal, Naomi. *The Adulteress's Child: Authorship and Desire in the Nineteenth-Century Novel*. Cambridge: Polity Press, 1992.

Tanner, Tony. *Adultery in the Novel: Contract and Transgression*. Baltimore: Johns Hopkins University Press, 1979.

Viallaneix, Paul, and Jean Ehrard, eds. *Aimer en France 1760–1860*. Proceedings of an international symposium at Clermont-Ferrand. 2 vols. Clermont-Ferrand: Publications de la Faculté des Lettres et Sciences humaines, 1980.

Waller, Margaret. *The Male Malady*. New Brunswick, NJ: Rutgers University Press, 1993.

White, Nicholas. *The Family in Crisis in Late Nineteenth-Century French Fiction*. Cambridge: Cambridge University Press, 1999.

Williams, Roger L. *The Horror of Life*. London: Weidenfeld and Nicolson, 1980.

FRENCH CANADIAN

There is neither a Marquis de Sade nor an Andréa de Nerciat in the literature of Québec for a specific reason: "Our literature will be solemn, meditative, spiritual, religious and evangelistic." This attitude, imposed by Mgr Henri-Raymond Casgrain as early as 1866 in the *Le Foyer Canadien,* served as a guide to all Québécois writers. One can easily understand that this advice did nothing to promote the emergence of eroticism in Québec's literature. For nearly a hundred years, several generations of literary critics, themselves loyal Catholics, continued to control and forbid eroticism in fiction. In this severe ideological context, a strong censorship inevitably came down hard on any novel containing erotic themes. For example, *La Scouine* (1918) by Albert Laberge was denounced by Monsignor Bruchési as "vile pornography,"

498

primarily for a scene depicting sexual content, masturbation, and bestiality.

Despite this climate of moral control, eroticism still found its way into Québec literature at the turn of the 20th century under the guise of realism. Already discredited by Catholic ideology, which viewed sexuality solely as a means of procreation, the erotic theme was first represented as a trivial act. Henceforth, every pretext became justifiable for nudity: the genitalia of the virtuous heroines are exposed publicly by unexpected falls in Rodolphe Girard's *Marie Calumet* (1904) and Arsène Bessette's *Le débutant* (1914); other female protagonists voluntarily exhibit their naked bodies to excite their partners, an act which was unthinkable in novels during the 19th century; prostitution in Montreal is described in great detail in *Le débutant;* morally forbidden sexual behaviors, like masturbation, fantasy ("evil thoughts"), adultery, and homosexuality, are described in such a manner that they appear as subtle and ironic commentaries on religious doctrine.

Another constant in Québec eroticism at the beginning of the 20th century was its fairly sadistic nature. The scenes of rape and brutal violence are numerous. Claude-Henri Grignon's *Un homme et son péché* (1933) is a good example of this phenomenon. Séraphin Poudrier, the protagonist, sexually tortures his wife, Donalda: "Once, just once, Séraphin took her brutally." Donalda is very similar to O, the heroine of the *The Story of O*, considered among the most sadistic French novels of the 20th century. "Completely frustrated in both body and soul, by her desire for love and maternity, Donalda embodies a submission so absolute that her story is essentially a Catholic and French-Canadian version of *The story of O*" (Smart, *Écrire*). Lemont, another character in the same novel, repeatedly rapes a number of young peasant women. Rather than being filled with remorse, the memory of these aggressions contributes to the novel's erotic ambience: "He [Lemont] remembered the scene with sensual thoughts. His imagination enveloped him with pleasurable sensations. These bewitching and speedy moments sparked in him a most violent desire!" Several other novels portray the same type of realistic and violent sexual behavior. In Gabrielle Roy's classic *Bonheur d'occassion* [*Luck of the Occasion*] (1945), Jean Lévesque rapes Florentine Lacasse, and in André Giroux's *Au-delà des visages*

[*Beyond Visages*] (1948) the rape and murder of a young woman is followed by a somber post-coital mood. In fact, it is as if although paradoxical, "this realistic literature also agrees with the essentials of moral discourse: yes, sex is violent, perverse, ridiculous, vile or pathological" (Angenot, *Le cru*).

In examining the French Canadian literature of the period from 1900 to 1960, it is important to discuss a reoccurring and more positive erotic figure: the stranger. In the Catholic world of guilt and secrecy, the characters who come from elsewhere are the only ones who can bring the liberating power of eroticism. In Louis Hémon's *Maria Chapdelaine* (1916), a young fur trader, François Paradis, appears out of nowhere in the close-knit village of Péribonka, where he captivates and seduces the young virgin Maria. Overwhelmed by her desires, she attempts to imagine "the first gestures of love that would unite them." In *Le survenant* by Germaine Guèvremont (1945), the eponymous character arrives in Chenal du Moine, where he literally irradiates his erotic energy: "Everything was happening as if Le Survenant, Eros incarnate, did nothing but awaken the sensuality and the latent eroticism of the villagers like the wild forces of their universe" (Major, p. 203). Finally, in Adrienne Choquette's *La coupe vide* [*The Empty Cup*] (1948), it is Patricia, an American woman in her prime, who arrives and seduces a group of four young college students who hover around her with excitement: "She offered her hands, coquettishly, so that they might help her stand up. Patricia quivered: stealthy lips brushed her wrist. Resolutely, the woman took the lead and decided to ignore the young man who had stolen her scent." These erotic games are possible only in the presence of the strangers, because they are not influenced by Catholic doctrine.

In the 1960s, this literary trend adapted itself to the sweeping winds of liberal change, known as the Quiet Revolution, which blew over Québec society. The representation of eroticism became much more openly disobedient. Here we find scenes of necrophilia and sadism in Marcel Godin's *La cruauté des faibles* [*The Cruelty of the Weak*] (1961); lesbianism in Louise Maheux-Forcier's *Amadou* (1963); incest, rape, and pedophilia in Marie-Claire Blais's *Une saison dans la vie d'Emmanuel* [*A Season in the Life of Emmanuel*] (1965); consummate and guiltless adultery in Roger Fournier's *Le journal d'un jeune marié* [*Diary of a Newlywed*] (1967); multiple rape scenes in Hubert Aquin's *L'Antiphonaire* (1969); homosexuality in Blais's *Le Loup* [*The Wolf*] (1973); bloody and sadistic murders in Victor-Lévy Beaulieu's *Un rêve québécois* [*A Québécois Dream*] (1972).

All of these novels, and many others, voluntarily exceed the dogma of normative sexuality and explore a variety of unusual sexual practices. Here, the sacred mingles with the profane but no longer in a hierarchical relation, but rather in an interrelationship which generates desire and erotic pleasure. Transgression also arises, obviously, but without the guilt traditionally associated with the censure of the Catholic Church toward any representation of carnal/erotic pleasure. Eroticism separates itself simultaneously from the can(n)ons of literary aesthetics and religious ideology.

The Quiet Revolution, along with the sexual revolution, offers a new type of first-person narrator, who exhibits a liberated eroticism and aggressively demands a larger place in Quebecois fiction. However, it would be naive to narrow our discussion to a celebration of the liberating aspects of eroticism, which relies primarily on sexual punishment imposed on the weak—usually women and children who feed the erotic transgressive excitement. In the revolutionary eroticism of the 1960s, the ancestral fear of feminine erotic strength—which came directly from the Christian mentality—was still alive: "[B]ecause of her power to awaken masculine desire and therefore upset the order of male domination of the world, the female body must then be—following masculine logic—subdued, dismembered, mutilated" (Smart, *Écrire*). Whether it be rape, adultery, murder, or necrophilia, the sexual cruelties of revolutionary eroticism are inevitably perpetrated on women's bodies, which, as Anne-Marie Dardigna (1981) states, "serve as the best target for sexual aggression."

In the early 1970s, eroticism distanced itself from the world of politics. Yves Thériault's *Oeuvres de chair* [*Works of the Flesh*] (1975) was the first text in Québec that overtly displayed its erotic content by featuring the subtitle "Erotic Tales" on its cover. The collection is composed of 16 erotic short stories whose inventive titles rely on double entendres that play on both culinary and sexual themes: "The Prepubescent Partridge," "The Seductive Steak au Poivre," "The Nubile Quail Terrine," "The

Adulterous Ham," etc. Most of these stories take place during the Middle Ages in an abbey or monastery where the religious characters prepare elaborate feasts that often transform into orgies. Transgression serves again to create an erotic climate in the texts, although in Thériault's stories it imbues joy and pleasure rather than destruction and guilt. Other tales may have more contemporary settings, but they all combine culinary and sexual sensuality. The meals, like the sexual acts, are meticulously detailed to highlight the pleasurable effect that each bestows on the protagonists. In *Oeuvres de chair*, it is thus the abounding details of the narration which create the collection's erotic climate.

The same phenomenon of excess in erotic writing is apparent in *Les cornes sacrées* [*The Sacred Horns*] by Roger Fournier (1977). Since the publication of his first novel, *À nous deux* (1963), eroticism has held a major role in Fournier's works. In *Les cornes sacrées*, the thematic takes on a magnitude previously unequaled. Both a tale of sexual initiation and a mythological allegory, *Les cornes sacrées* follows the adolescence of Nobert, who leaves the lower St. Lawrence River Valley with his young bull, Pigeon. Along their journey, each experiences his first sexual encounter. The apotheosis occurs in Greece as an orgy erupts including all of the villagers. A river of sperm literally flows into the fields from the collective sexual encounter. Everything is in superlative form in Fournier's text; eroticism is spread excessively. The characters' genitalia are enormous; the sexual positions, Olympian (having intercourse on the back of a bull); and the entire world is united in orgasm: "The cry is a caress that will cause the entire world to have an erection." Eroticism intensifies to the point that it becomes what Gaëtan Brulotte (*Œuvres de chair*) calls a commonplace of the genre: "In erotic literature, excess is a common theme and sexual prowess is beyond the reach of normal mankind. Excessive genitalia size, overstimulated characters, complex or often impossible coital positions, and abundant sexual energy all greatly exaggerate the human reality." In fact, with this type of novel, eroticism essentially exceeds all forms of realism and thus becomes its own particular genre of literature.

Continuing throughout the 1970s, the feminist movement and a new generation of female writers greatly contributed to the creation of a new form of eroticism. In *French Kiss* (1975),

Nicole Brossard associates the pleasure of language with that of sexuality. Erotic play is interwoven with linguistic play, in this case, alliteration: "Encore qui vient à suivre dans le texte ainsi que sur la langue, des substituts érotiques, encore que l'on sent basculer dans l'ombre des joues, des jouissances mouvementées comme je jouis dans le jus" [What follows in the text as well as on the tongue are erotic substitutes to such a degree that one feels thrown into the shade of cheeks, turbulent pleasures, like when I have an orgasm in my juices]. More than ten years later, the narrator in Dandurand's *Un coeur qui craque* [*A Heart That Breaks*] (1990) explains the effects that composing erotic literature has on her: "[W]riting, in the scorching heat of summer, stories like the one in the previous chapter, still wet with fresh ink, make me moisten and drip all over, too!... Sad madwoman that I am, lock me up and give me a straitjacket to keep me from masturbating." Like conjoined twins, writing and erotic experience are fused together, making both from the creation of pleasure, which is exactly what the female narrator in Harvey's *Un homme est une valse* [*A Man Is a Waltz*] (1992) means when she describes this particular phenomenon to her readers: "Writing while performing fellatio is difficult, but possible."

Within the erotic texts penned by, usually postmodern, women, the female narrators are themselves authors who write about their own erotic adventures. Shoshana Felman (1981) explains the intimate relationship between text and sex: "That which is erotic is always linguistic.... The sexual act always connotes an act of language.... The sexual act of the narrator can be nothing but a linguistic exercise." In the particular case of erotic literature, the sexual encounter is inevitably an act of language; these narrators are quite conscious of this, and for that reason they create a form of sexual excitation in their texts and vice versa.

Another discovery in the female version of eroticism in Québec was the male body! Eroticism had previously been the domain of the masculine perspective on the woman's body—but along came a feminine vision which describes men. In this literature there is often a great deal of commotion at the discovery of the phallus:

It's round! It's long! It's firm! It's like marbled steel! This is what they call a charming cock! This is what is meant by an erection! And the head! Red and shiny, dotted with stars, of liquid diamonds. The foreskin is pulled taut by the force of erection. The phallus is placed on a pedestal, decorated with bushy hair; his hot and heavy testicles, tucked into their pouch of brownish skin, dangle like ripe figs. (Boisjoli, *Jacinthe,* 1992)

As the sex point of view changes, the male body becomes lasciviously desirable and is therefore described, objectified, and broken down into its constituent parts. Abdomen, skin, hair, chin, butt, hips, hands, pubic hair, testicles, butt crack, neck, shoulders, arms—all of the male anatomy participates in the erotic encounter. The five senses are also included: the sight of the naked male body; the countless sounds of orgasmic delight that resonate in a partner's ears; the smells of men evoked by every imaginable metaphor from the woods to tobacco; the taste of a lover's salty skin and of almond-like or peppery sperm; and finally, the touch of every caress, lengthened in meticulous detail.

Since the 1980s, a new erotic perspective has emerged in which a heroine like Pauline Harvey's in *Un homme est une valse* (1992) is not afraid to demonstrate her desire for her companion or her own sexual pleasure: "A man is a tool for reaching orgasm, if there are lovers, they shall be called pleasure, sexuality. A man is a waltz." Because of the dynamics of movement between partners, dance is the best metaphor to illustrate a style of eroticism most commonly found in feminine writings. The greatest joy in the realization of an erotic ballet is the opening and abandonment of oneself. This time, however, it is the male that is opened: "He wants the belly, he wants the vagina, to open himself inside," and the woman's body is inhabited by a new presence. With nipples and clitorises erect, flowing vulvas and vaginas, flesh and bottoms caressed or tortured with delight, a new world is offered to discover: "She teaches me the geography of the land of Women" (Boisjoli, *Jacinthe*), a world which spins on the axis of pleasure.

Here, the notion of sexual fulfillment is not directly oriented to a single and final orgasm; the dynamics of "the waltz," of a dance, would not permit it. One must be careful, however, not to limit this point of view to an erotic otherworldliness where women participate uniquely in relationships based on love, stormy or insipid, but always romantic. Feminine eroticism is quite similar to the masculine with regard to its practice. The major difference is that it appears under the aegis of values considered exclusively feminine, such as love and sharing. As with the masculine model, transgression always serves as an impetus of desire—without, however, also being tragic.

Examples of transgression joyously gleaned from erotic works of several Québécoise writers include: the title character in *Jacinthe* corrupting her young 15-year-old neighbor and destroying everything traditionally viewed as authority—a nun, a pastor, a bishop, a professor, a psychologist—while confessing a fondness for sodomy; the heroine of *Un coeur qui craque* performing fellatio on a handicapped person while in a restaurant; and the protagonist in *Un homme est une valse* fantasizing about the adulterous acts she could perform with all of the men in her life. There is nothing to fear in the transgression in these texts because it is not performed in a context of guilt or fear; it has only one goal: pleasure beyond the norm, be it accepted or forbidden.

Amidst the explosion of erotic texts plumed by female authors in Québec during the 1990s, one in particular would stand out from the pack and help erotic literature gain acceptance from the literary establishment of Québec as a genre in its own right. The "sexplorer" Lili Gulliver, created by Diane Boissoneault, travels to the four corners of the Earth searching for sexual adventures in the tetralogy titled *Gulliver's Universe*. The first novel of the series, *Paris* (1990) tells of her vacation in the City of Lights, where she successively has sexual relations with Gérard, a psychiatrist; Francis, a wine steward in a restaurant; and Carl, an escort. Nothing is off-limits to her because she is on a mission to catalog the performance of her lovers and to create the *Gulliver Guide to International Intercourse*. Her ultimate goal is to find the world's greatest lover, or at least to provide a list of suggestions to her girlfriends.

In the second volume, *Greece* (1991), Lili finds herself in a place she lovingly refers to as the Land of Cocks, where she, among other activities, takes advantage of the local resources to create a cheerful description of the male genitalia: "Among the cocks I have known, there have been big ones, enormous ones, small ones, and tiny ones, malleable ones, soft ones, round ones, those that were bent like a boomerang, erect ones and limp ones, etc." The third book

in the series is *Bangkok, Hot and Humid* (1993), which deals with the "sexploits" of Lili in Asia. Her tales overflow with clichés of small penises and the carefree sexuality of the Taiwanese. Lili eventually falls in love with Richard, an American.

In the fourth volume, *Australia Topsy-Turvy* (1996), Lili finally meets the world's greatest lover, Tarzano Rambo, a composite of the love-hate aspects of the ideal man. With her mission accomplished, Lili returns to Québec but refuses to abandon her erotic activities and international projects: "I can do it under any circumstance and in every position. I allow myself to be taken everywhere and come what may! I no longer try to make sense to myself; I abandon myself to pleasure. Always make me come and let it never end, *Please!* That will be my Australian vacation, after which we'll see.... Who knows, Lili in Africa?"

During the second half of the twentieth century, eroticism had its unveiling in Québec's literature. After a rough start of being ostracized by religious literary authorities, several courageous or naive authors were able to bypass these restrictions by using guilt or a moral when portraying the thematic. It was not until the 1960s, along with the liberating trend in Québec society, that eroticism became a common and accepted literary theme. Later, in the 1970s, fueled by the feminist movement, with its entourage of women writers, eroticism became a true literary genre. The erotic texts written by women brought with them a new dimension on a thematic often viewed with a guilt that was the fruit of the Judeo-Christian tradition which had had such a hold on the imagination of the Québec people. At the end of the millennium, Lili Gulliver appears in Québec's literature like a sexual adventurer who travels around the world seeking pleasure for herself and for the benefit of all the women of Québec. From that point on, eroticism has been rightfully recognized by several institutions in Québec: sections in libraries have been dedicated to eroticism, publishers have printed collections of erotic works, and many newspaper articles have been devoted to erotic themes. From the limits of Catholicism and censorship, eroticism in Québec has become, throughout the years, feminine and joyous. Who can complain?

ÉLISE SALAÜN

Selected Works

Aquin, Hubert. *L'Antiphonaire*. Montréal: Le Cercle du Livre de France, 1969; as *The Antiphonary*, translated by Alan Brown. Toronto: Anansi, 1973.

Beaulieu, Victor-Lévy. *Un rêve québécois*. Montréal: Éditions du Jour, 1972; as *A Québécois Dream*, translated by Ray Chamberlain. Toronto, Exile Editions, 1978.

Bessette, Arsène. *Le débutant. Roman de mœurs du journalisme politique dans la province de Québec*. Saint-Jean, Québec: Le Canada français, 1914; Montréal: Éditions HMH, 1976.

Blais, Marie-Claire. *Une saison dans la vie d'Emmanuel*. Montréal: Les Éditions du Jour, 1965; Paris: Grasset éditeur, 1966; as *A Season in the Life of Emmanuel*, translated by Edmund Wilson, New York: Farrar, Strauss and Giroux, 1966.

———. *Le Loup*. Montréal: Éditions du Jour, 1973; Paris: Éditions Robert Laffont, 1973; as *The Wolf*, translated by Sheila Fishman, Toronto: McClelland and Stewart Limited, 1974.

Boisjoli, Charlotte. *Jacinthe*. Montréal: Éditions de l'Hexagone, 1990.

Brossard, Nicole. *French Kiss*. Montréal: Éditions du Jour, 1974; as *French Kiss or a Pang's Progress*, translated by Patricia Claxton, Toronto: Coach House Quebec Translations, 1986.

Choquette, Adrienne. *La coupe vide*. Montréal: Éditions Fernand Pilon, 1948.

Dandurand, Anne. *Un Coeur qui craque. Journal imaginaire*. Montréal: VLB éditeur / Messidor, 1990.

Fournier, Roger. *À nous deux*. Montréal: Le Cercle du Livre de France, 1963.

———. *Journal d'un jeune marié*. Montréal: Le Cercle du Livre de France, 1967.

———. *Les cornes sacrées*. Paris: Albin Michel, 1977.

Girard, Rodolphe. *Marie Calumet*. Montréal: n.p., 1904; Montréal: Serge Brousseau, 1946.

Giroux, André. *Au-delà des visages*. Montréal: Les Éditions Variétés, 1948; Montréal: Éditions Fides, 1966.

Godin, Marcel. *La cruauté des faibles*. Montréal: Éditions du Jour, 1961.

Grignon, Claude-Henri. *Un homme et son péché*. Montréal: Éditions du Totem, 1933; Montréal: Éditions du Vieux Chêne, 1935.

Guèvremont, Germaine. *Le Survenant*. Montréal: Éditions Beauchemin, 1945; Paris, Librairie Plon, 1946.

Gulliver, Lili. *Paris*. Montréal: VLB éditeur, 1990.

———. *La Grèce*. Montréal: VLB éditeur, 1991.

———. *Bangkok, chaud et humide*. Montréal: VLB éditeur, 1993.

———. *L'Australie sans dessous dessus*. Montréal: VLB éditeur, 1996.

Harvey, Pauline. *Un homme est une valse*. Montréal: Les Herbes rouges, 1992.

Hémon, Louis. *Maria Chapdelaine. Récit du Canada-français*. Original illustrations by Suzor Côté. Montréal: J.-A. Lefebvre, 1916; Paris: Librairie Delagrave, 1916.

Laberge, Albert. *La Scouine*. Montréal: Privately printed by Imprimerie Modèle, 1918.

Maheu-Forcier, Louise. *Amadou*. Montréal: Le Cercle du Livre de France, 1963.

Roy, Gabrielle. *Bonheur d'occasion*. 2 vols. Montréal: Société des Éditions Pascal, 1945; Montréal: Éditions Beauchemin, 1947; Paris: Flammarion, 1947.

Thériault, Yves. *Œuvres de chair*. Montréal: Stanké, 1975; Montréal: VLB éditeur, 1982; as *Ways of Flesh*, translated by Jean David, Agringourt, Ontario: Gage Publishing, 1977.

Further Reading

Angenot, Marc. *Le cru et le faisandé : sexe, discours social et littérature à la Belle-Époque*. Brussels: Éditions Labor, 1986.

Brisson, Marcelle. *Éros au pluriel*. Montréal: Hurtubise-HMH, 1984.

Brulotte, Gaëtan. *Œuvres de chair : figures du discours érotique*. Paris, L'Harmattan, 1998.

Collective. "De l'Erotisme." *Liberté* 9 (November-December 1967).

Dardigna, Anne-Marie. *Les châteaux d'Éros ou les infortunes des sexes des femmes*. Paris: Maspero, 1981.

Hamel, Réginald. "L'Erotisme dans les romans, contes et nouvelles entre 1900 et 1940." *Parti Pris* 1, nos. 9, 10, 11 (1964).

———. *La littérature et l'érotisme suivi d'un cours essai bibliographique*. Montréal: Institut de Réhabilitation de Montréal, 1968.

Major, André. "'Le Survenant' et la Figure d'Éros dans l œuvre de Germain Guèvremont." Voix et Images, Vol. II, no. 2, (1976), 195–208.

Paterson, Janet. *Moments postmodernes dans le roman québécois*. Ottawa: Les presses de l'Université d'Ottawa, 1990.

Pelletier, Jacques. "Une exploration de l'enfer québécois." *Voix et images* 3 (December 1977).

Saint-Martin, Lori. "Mise à mort de la femme et 'libération' de l'homme : Godbout, Aquin, Beaulieu." *Voix et images* 10 (1984): 107–17. Reprinted in Lori Saint-Martin, *Contre-voix : essai de critique au féminin*, Québec: Nuit blanche éditeur, 1997.

Salaün, Élise. *La Chair triomphante : discours religieux, juridique et critique sur l'érotisme dans le roman québécois (1940–1960)*. Sherbrooke, Québec: Université de Sherbrooke, 1995.

———. "La passion selon elles." In *Lectures du genre*, edited by d'Isabelle Boisclair. Montréal: Éditions du Remue-Ménage, 2002.

Smart, Patricia. *Écrire dans la maison du Père*. Montréal: Éditions Boréal, 1990.

Von Flotow, Louise. "Tenter l'érotique : Anne Dandurand et l'érotisme hétérosexuel dans l'écriture au féminin contemporaine." In *L'autre lecture, la critique au féminin et les textes québécois*, edited by Lori Saint-Martin. Vol. 2. Montréal: XYZ éditeur, "Documents" collection, 1994.

FRENCH (UP TO THE RENAISSANCE, INCLUDING THE MIDDLE AGES)

Despite the dominant moral influence of the Catholic Church in medieval France, the literature of the period, ranging roughly from the 10th through the late 15th centuries, foregrounds erotic relationships in a wide variety of genres. That France was not a united country, politically or linguistically, explains the existence of two distinct, yet interrelated literary traditions—one written in the various dialects of *langue d'oc* (Provençal), the linguistic group of southern France, the other in *langue d'oil,* the group of dialects ranging across northern France and into what is now England. The earliest manifestation of a literature explicitly concerned with sexual pursuits appeared in the southern dialects. By the 10th century, the langue d'oc gave birth to the *troubadours,* whose erotic poetry would spread both north and south. As the troubadours' works became better known in the north, partially as a result of political alliances, erotic themes found their way into the works of the northern French poets, the *trouvères.* Celtic literature and Arthurian legends also play a significant role in northern French literature, finding their greatest expression in lays and romances. By the late 11th century, the adulterous erotic triangle was commonplace. The themes articulated in the poetry of the troubadours and trouvères and composers of lays and romances dominate nearly all French medieval texts, although some specific variants developed. In contrast, the epic neglects most references to the erotic. As a parallel to these serious genres, the comic literature of medieval France, first in the *fabliau,* then in the *nouvelle* and the farce, treat these same themes in an irreverent fashion.

Whether serious or comic, attitudes toward sexual relations in medieval French literary texts were heavily influenced by the notions of gender and sexuality that society held. At the same time, those texts contributed to the construction of those same notions. One of the most pertinent questions revolved around the ideal of female chastity and the implications for those women who did not remain chaste. Should a lady, whatever her social status, engage in a sexual relationship before marriage? What are the consequences for her? Further, what are the consequences of an adulterous relationship? A second aspect of this literature also merits attention. The vast majority of these texts deal only with heterosexual erotic relationships. Nonetheless, same-sex relations, primarily male, haunt many of the most representative erotic relationships and also are hinted at in the epic.

Troubadour poetry developed in and around the affluent courts of the southern French nobles. Partially because of trade, partially because of favorable geographic situation, and partially through the greater romaniziation of the area during the Roman Empire, the courts of southern France displayed a refinement in the late 10th and early 11th centuries that was not as evident as their northern counterparts. It was in this setting that a new genre of love poetry flourished, the *canso.* The poets themselves were frequently members of the nobility. The lyric poems of such early troubadours as Bernard de Ventadour and Jaufré Rudel posit an idealized love between a humble lover and a lady who is distant either emotionally or geographically to the point of being unobtainable. Frequently, she is married. Although frustrated in his efforts to approach her, the humble lover remains faithful and maintains a cloak of secrecy to protect his beloved's reputation. The troubadours created an erotic discourse of *fin' amors* (refined/"good" love) that continued into the 16th century. Its poetics are those of desire and deferral.

Alain's Chartier's "Belle Dame sans mercy" (c. 1424) captures the essence of the troubadour lyric, taking it to the logical conclusion of the rejected lover's death. (Indeed, some 400 years later, Yeats would take Chartier's title as his own for one of his greatest poems). Yet, there are counterpoints to the cruel lady. Christine de Pizan's *Cent balades d'amant et de dame* [*100 Ballads Between a Lover and a Lady*] (c. 1409–10) creates a dialogue and traces the evolution of the relationship. Refusal leads to acquiescence and abandonment, and it is the lady who faces death, betrayed by her lover. Between these two extremes lies the *alba,* or "erotic dawn song." Troubadour poets created a feminine voice, and the conceit continued on in northern lyrics as well. The coming of the dawn signals the end of the night that the lady has spent with her lover and a moment of separation. The genre subverts both social structures and the stereotypical cruel lady, creating a thematic that is at once transgressive and erotic. Typically, a watchman alerts the couple of the impending dawn and possible discovery of the adulterous affair. The male lover and his lady bid farewell, consoled in anticipation of another night together.

Early northern poets, trouvères such as Gace Brulé, Conon de Béthune, and Adam de la Halle, retained love as a theme; but it is in the romance and the lays that the clearest shift from the *canso* occurs, and *fin'amors* changes into *amour courtois,* or courtly love. Where the troubadour's *canso* sings nearly exclusively of unconsummated desire, northern texts focus on a passionate, all-consuming love, which may lead to exile or death. While not all relationships in the literature are adulterous, through the legends of Tristan and Iseut and of Lancelot and Guinevere the erotic triangle of husband/wife/lover becomes the model for romantic love. The locating of desire and love outside of the marriage bond reflects the social structures of the period. Marriage was most often a business transaction in which women served as a type of currency. And although no single complete text of *Tristan and Iseut* has survived in Old French, the fragmentary versions from the late 12th century clearly establish the conflict between love and marriage in the Western literary tradition. In spite of her betrothal to Tristan's uncle Marc, Iseut falls passionately in love with Tristan and he with her. The lovers struggle: on the one hand they try to resist their desire; on the other hand, they attempt to overcome the obstacles that separate them. This struggle eventually leads to their deaths, inextricably linking the notions of love, death, and the lovers' willingness to die for their love.

Chrétien de Troyes (d. 1185), one of the most influential courtly writers, composed verse romances firmly locating the Knights of the Round Table in the French literary canon. His *chevalier de la charette* [*The Knight of the Cart*] (c. 1180) recounts the story of Lancelot, Guinevere, and Arthur. Like Tristan and Iseut, the adulterous lovers struggle, unsuccessfully, to curb their desire and to break off the relationship. The tale of Lancelot and Guinevere, like that of Tristan and Iseut, would be written and rewritten throughout the medieval period, beginning with the anonymous prose *Lancelot* in the early 13th century. Yet, not all of Chrétien's romances focus on the adulterous liaisons of the protagonists. In *Yvain, ou le chevalier au lion* [*Yvain, or the Knight of the Lion*] (c. 1178), he poses the problem of how to reconcile erotic desire with social duties. The beginning of the romance hints that Arthur is a weakened king because of his excessive desire for Guinevere. The hero of the tale, Yvain, marries and, after losing himself in physical pleasure with his wife, begins a series of adventures, eventually leading him back to a balance between the erotic and the social. Chrétien also condemns marital infidelity (on the part of the husband) and rape in his brutal tale of *Philomela* (c. 1165). An integration of erotic desire also motivates the protagonists in his *Erec et Enide* (c. 1165) and *Cligès* (c. 1176), the latter proclaiming itself to be an anti-*Tristan.* Thus, while working within the courtly tradition, Chrétien expands its limits and attempts to deal with the more problematic nature of sexual relationships in a highly structured society.

Adulterous triangles and illicit sexual encounters infuse nearly all examples of courtly literature. The *Lais* (c. 1170) of Marie de France, a collection of twelve short verse tales, exploit this theme in varied ways. As in Chrétien's works, the Celtic and Breton legends that inspired many of these tales bring with them a supernatural element. That a lover turns himself into a bird so that he might spend the night with his beloved, as in *Yonec,* or that a wife learns that her husband is a werewolf, as in *Le bisclavret,* heightens the erotic tension in the tales. *Le chèvrefeuille* [*The Honeysuckle*] relates an episode of *Tristan and Iseut,* using the metaphor of the two entwined as the honeysuckle is around the tree to symbolize their desire, blurring the metaphor of love and death.

One important subgenre of the medieval lyric poem, the *pastourelle*, complicates the thematic of the suppliant lover by reversing many of its conventions. In a typical scenario, a knight recounts his encounter with a shepherdess. Invariably he asks for her favors, mimicking the discourse of the trouvères, and frequently she acquiesces; the poem thus relates a successful seduction. In a number of *pastourelles,* the shepherdess refuses the knight's advances, but unlike the idealized lady who receives respect for her refusal, thus generating another series of poems, sexual desire dominates and the shepherdess is taken by force. These poems of rape often reflect class relationships. Whereas in the courtly model the lover and object of his affection are of similar social status and the lady herself is frequently revered and feared for the erotic power she exerts over her lover, a shepherdess suffers by her inferior position. Nonetheless, in some instances a shepherd is the sexual aggressor. Thus the *pastourelle* articulates conflicts along class and gender lines, hinting at the tensions around the eroticism in the genre.

At the opposite end of the erotic spectrum are the *fabliaux,* a genre that flourished from the 12th to the 14th century. The corpus consists of some 170 short comic tales in verse, the majority of which are anonymous. As examples of bawdy humor—the "esprit gaulois"—the storylines regularly echo the courtly erotic triangle, although the characters that populate these texts are normally members of the bourgeoisie or clergy or are peasants, with occasional appearances by nobles. Yet, as in "La Bourgeoise d'Orléans," the resolution often leads to possibilities of continued infidelity as the wife outmaneuvers her jealous husband. Jean Bodel, one of the first authors of fabliaux, establishes the lubricity of the clergy in his "Gombert et les deux clercs" [Gombert and the Two Clerks] (c. 1190). Satire of the clergy's sexual mores is a major theme of the genre, one that continues on into the 14th- and 15th-century short tales in prose—"nouvelles"—and on into the Renaissance. Language also furnishes a theme for sexual comedy in the fabliaux, which sometimes are elaborated around a sexual metaphor, based on the renaming of sexual organs. A young man attempting to trick a girl into a sexual relationship relies on a metaphor of an animal and food, as in "L'Escuiruel" [The Squirrel] or "La dame qui abevra le polain" [The Lady Who Watered the Horse]. Similar sexual metaphors figure in fabliaux such as "Porcelet" [Piglet] and "La dame qui aveine demandoit pour Morel" [The Lady Who Asked for Wheat for Morel], but here they function as linguistic games to initiate sex in a married couple.

To a certain extent, the prose *nouvelle* (short story) and the farce, two genres which grew in popularity in the 14th and 15th centuries, carried on the sexual themes of the fabliaux. *Les cent nouvelles nouvelles [The Hundred New Tales]* (c. 1460) took inspiration in length from Boccaccio's *Decameron,* albeit eschewing its complex structure. The 45th nouvelle offers a typical example of the use of Italian sources: it relates the story of a young man who disguises himself as an itinerant washerwoman in order to gain access to the ladies of the house. As in an anecdote, these tales create an erotic scenario that is usually played out with little detail or development. What the nouvelle supplied to a population that was slowly becoming literate, the farce staged in the public square. A farce such as the 15th-century "Le ramoneur de cheminées' [The Chimney Sweep] plays out the double entendre of the work of the chimney sweep as he visits the houses of townswomen while their husbands are away. In "La confession Margot" [Margot's Confession], the eponymous heroine whose name indicated a loose woman recounts her sexual adventures to a priest who revels in the account. Overall, as in the fabliaux and the nouvelles, the farces rely primarily on stereotypes and stock situations, with little nuance.

Perhaps the most unique text of the period is the 22,000-line *Roman de la Rose,* begun in the 1130s by Guillaume de Lorris and then completed some 40 years later by Jean de Meung. In it, the courtly tradition collides with a rationalist, realist approach to relations between the sexes which focuses on reproduction. This highly controversial and popular text is read through the filter of either courtly love (for Part 1) or Christine de Pizan's late-14th-century literary debate over its misogyny and vulgarity (Part 2). Guillaume de Lorris' beginning (only a bit over 4,000 lines) articulates the central trope of the Lover trying to obtain his goal, the Rose, who is enclosed in a garden. Allegorical figures such as False Friend or Fair Welcoming people the garden and help or hinder the lover on his way to his goal. Taking up Lorris' unfinished work, Jean de Meung expanded the dialogues to a more philosophical discourse, highlighting

Reason and Justice as important figures. Where Guillaume de Lorris' lover might have been content to gaze from afar, Jean de Meung's lover determines to pluck the Rose, encapsulating the conflict between idealized woman on the pedestal and the carnal nature of desire.

While heteroerotic relationships dominate the literature of this period, an underlying tension, suggesting the possibility of the homoerotic, pervades many of the most "heterosexual" of the texts. Few examples in medieval French literature deal explicitly with homosexual relationships. A single poem from the 13th century by Beiris de Romans, a *trobaritz* (female troubadour), addressed to Lady Maria, "her source of all happiness," uses the same language and imagery as her male counterparts to express longing and desire. Sexual ambiguity appears in a number of romances, in which a cross-dressed woman develops an erotic relation with a woman and may marry her. Cross-dressing in these tales does not originate from lesbian desire. For example, in Heldris de Cournualle's *Roman de Silence*, the daughter is raised as a boy for purposes of ensuring her inheritance. In *Huon de Bordeaux,* the Virgin Mary intervenes and changes the crossed-dressed woman into a man at the moment of her marriage. The 14th-century *Roman d' Yde et Olive* presents a more complex set of variables. Yde dresses as a man to flee from her father's incestuous affections. As a man, she marries, and her wife must navigate the erotically ambiguous marriage without revealing her husband's gender. In terms of medieval society, it could be suggested that a female same-sex relationship may well have been less threatening than incest.

Male homoaffective relationships often appear to coexist with the suggestion of a possible homosexual one. The *chanson de gestes* (epic poems) depict the world of knights and soldiers, downplaying the role of female characters. One of the earliest examples is *Ami et Amile* (c. 1200), in which the eponymous heroes form an idealized couple. Even though they each marry a woman, at the close of the poem it is Ami and Amile who share a tomb, as they had earlier shared a bed. Queer readings of courtly literature point up the closeness between Tristan and Marc (who had remained unmarried), the ties between Yvain and Gauvain, between Lancelot and Galehaut or Lancelot and Arthur. The world of companion knights leads to strong homoaffective ties that may have been a literary equivalent of the closet. These types of relationships (like their adulterous heterosexual counterparts) most frequently end in separation, exile, or death. Even the *Roman de la Rose* does not resist a queer reading. Fair Welcoming, a male figure, attracts the Lover nearly as much as does the Rose, and rosebud itself is described in phallic terms. A number of Marie de France's lays present characters of suspect sexuality. Lanval is accused by Guinevere of preferring young men to women. The lay offers a heteronormative conclusion, with Lanval having a lover, although it is she who appears to have the active role in the partnership. "Le Bisclavret" [The Werewolf] offers the most provocative conclusion: the werewolf who had been kept like a beloved dog by the king who found him receives loving kisses from that same king when he is again transformed into a man. The homosocial bonds that were the fabric of medieval French society offer possible glimpes into a homoerotic subculture.

The themes found in French medieval literature are consonant with many of the overarching social structures. Marriage appears frequently in these texts, but it functions as an obstacle to love, or at least to sexual pleasure. Erotic relationships within marriage can be as threatening as extramarital ones, for they may cause the husband to neglect his social duties. As woman's access to power was, in the main, limited in medieval French society, so is her role in many of these texts. Exercising choice in her sexual relationships usually leads to condemnation. Where she does succeed, it is most often as a negative example, a warning. Same-sex eroticism appears to exist primarily in the margins. While male homoaffective relationships develop in many of the texts, they are never fully articulated as erotic. Thus, the overwhelming effect of this literature is to reinforce normative gender roles and to manage erotic desire within a markedly limited range of possibilities.

EDITH J. BENKOV

Further Reading

Allen, Peter L. *The Art of Love: Amatory Fiction from Ovid to the Romance of the Rose.* Middle Ages Series, edited by Edward Peters. Philadelphia: University of Pennsylvania Press, 1992.

Ariès, Philippe, and Andr Bjin, eds. *Western Sexuality: Practice and Precepts in Past and Present.* Oxford: Blackwell, 1985.

Baldwin, John W. *The Language of Sex: Five Voices from Northern France around 1200*. Chicago and London: University of Chicago Press, 1994.

Bloch, Howard R. *Medieval Misogyny and the Invention of Western Romantic Love*. Chicago and London: University of Chicago Press, 1991.

Boswell, John. *Christianity, Social Tolerance and Homosexuality: Gay People in Western Europe from the Beginning of the Christian Era to the Fourteenth Century*. Chicago: Chicago University Press, 1980.

Brundage, James A. *Law, Sex, and Christian Society in Medieval Europe*. Chicago and London: University of Chicago Press, 1987.

Burgwinkle, William. *Sodomy, Masculinity, and Law in Medieval Literature: France and England, 1050–1230*. Cambridge: Cambridge University Press, 2004.

Duby, Georges. *Love and Marriage in the Middle Ages*. Translated by J. Dunnett. Chicago and London: University of Chicago Press, 1994.

Furber, Donald, and Anne Callahan. *Erotic Love in Literature: From Medieval Legend to Romantic Illusion*. Troy, NY: Whitston Publishing Company, 1982.

Gravdal, Kathryn. *Ravishing Maidens: Writing Rape in Medieval French Literature and Law*. Philadelphia: University of Philadelphia Press, 1991.

Lochrie, Karma, Peggy McCracken, and James Schulz, eds. *Constructing Medieval Sexuality*. Minneapolis and London: University of Minnesota Press, 1997.

Murray, Jacqueline, and Konrad Eisenbichler, eds. *Desire and Discipline: Sex and Sexuality in the Premodern West*. Toronto, Buffalo, and London: University of Toronto Press, 1996.

Paden, William D. *The Voice of the Trobairitz*. Philadelphia: University of Pennsylvania Press, 1989.

Payer, Pierre. *The Bridling of Desire: Views of Sex in the Latter Middle Ages*. Toronto: University of Toronto Press, 1984.

Sautman, Francesca, and Pamela Sheingorn, eds. *Same Sex Love and Desire among Women in the Middle Ages*. New York and London: Palgrave, 2000.

Sigal, Gale. *Erotic Dawn-Songs of the Middle Ages: Voicing the Lyric Lady*. Gainesville: University Press of Florida, 1996.

Taylor, Karen J., ed. *Gender Transgressions: Crossing the Normative Barrier in Old French Literature*. New York and London: Garland, 1998.

FRIDAY, NANCY

1937–
American novelist

My Secret Garden

In the first chapter of *My Secret Garden*, Nancy Friday argues that the inception for the book came from two rejections of the idea that women have sexual fantasies, both by men—the first private the second public. When she told a lover a fantasy, he put on his trousers and left. When she made a heroine of a potential novel have a fantasy, the editor rejected it as making her a freak. In many ways, *My Secret Garden: Women's Sexual Fantasies* was compiled to prove these men wrong: to show that most women do have a rich fantasy life. Published in 1973, at the beginning of the Women's Liberation Movement in America, it was joined by Shere Hite's *Hite Report: A Nationwide Study of Female Sexuality* (1976) as part of the attempt to establish what women's sexuality was actually like, as opposed to what a phallocentric society inferred it should be. Compiled from interviews and questionnaires publicized through the newspapers, *My Secret Garden* seeks to give voice to an area of femininity silenced by cultural expectations. Consisting of a series of transcribed fantasies, identified only by the women's first names, the book is divided into six chapters which are introduced by the author, as she seeks to explain why women fantasize, the childhood source of these, and the female guilt around male anxiety that often accompanies such fantasies when they are not accepted. The main strength and interest of the book lies in the fantasies themselves. Sex with an anonymous stranger or in front of an audience, rape fantasies, and the thrill of the forbidden top the favorite ones reported. As Friday is keen to stress, the irrational world of sexual fantasy is very different from the actuality of sexual practice, and the fact that so many women report the thrill of being forced to enjoy sex has more to say about their guilt over the cultural prescription of feminine decorum and frigidity in the early 1970s than about a real desire to be raped. Black men, young boys, dogs, and other women were favored partners for white women. Friday, who rejected a college education because of her desire to be closer to her audience as a writer, has no real model of how to analyze the fantasies she presents, though she does articulate a superficial Freudianism, but her refusal to pathologize is one of the book's strengths. Coming at the time of white middle-class women's banding together in sisterhood, the book, with its first name terms, as Jane Gallop argues, "brings women together as confidantes and sisters" to help create a climate where it is safe for women to confess to having a rich and lush fantasy life.

My Secret Garden was a best seller, and soon gave rise to a sequel, *Forbidden Flowers: More Women's Sexual Fantasies,* in 1975. Less groundbreaking, it followed the same format and compared the sexual fantasies of a younger generation, those who grew up in an era of sexual expression, with the Beatles and Elvis Presley, to see if they carried the same guilt factor translated into being "forced" to enjoy their sexuality. Again the fantasies themselves are the interest, interleaved with Friday's encouraging comments about how they show not that the women are neurotic but that they are enjoying their bodies. The fantasies range from being initiated into sex in church, as a religious ritual, to incestuous relationships involving dogs. Again, Friday refuses to pathologize or analyze, taking them all at face value, though her Freudian model now posits the disapproving mother as inhibiting women's sexuality.

In 1980, Friday varied the format by turning her attention to male fantasies, *Men in Love: Men's Sexual Fantasies—The Triumph of Love over Rage.* Arguing that men's sexual excitement, "his secret garden," formulates itself in ways that women may not recognize as love and may at times find disturbing in its aggression, Friday posits a scenario where men are independent and their need for love forces them to abandon this security and bind themselves to women, in settling down. The conflation of love and sex in this work and the

normative view of marriage make this the most conservative of Friday's work, as she explains to women that they need to realize how much men "worship women's beauty" and long for women who will share responsibility for sex. The most favored fantasy was a voyeuristic watching of a woman masturbating.

Friday's final compilation to date, *Women on Top,* was issued in 1991. It situates the early 1990s as a much more somber sexual climate, due to AIDS, abortions, and unwanted pregnancies, than was the heady sexual curiosity of the 1960s and 70s. But the younger generation of women accept fantasies as a natural part of their sexuality. Female fantasies in this new society, "wallpapered with sex," focus less on guilt and anxiety at being in control (i.e., rape fantasies) and more on women in control, women with women, and women as sexually insatiable. Young women now take masturbation as a normal part of their sexuality, and part 2 of the book, "Separating Sex from Love," is in praise of masturbation, for allowing women to become more sexual and orgasmic and to distinguish sex from love and thus, like men, separate from the mother. Friday's continuing to place all blame for sexual inhibitions on the child's early relationship with the mother is a pop Freudianism which fails to see mothers as also inflected by social prescriptions, and equally vulnerable. Asserting that while women are changing and are now more in control of their sexuality, men are not and are being frightened by women's assertiveness, she claims that this is "women's responsibility, having started the sexual revolution, to finish the job."

Where Friday's first book, *My Secret Garden,* helped give voice to the burgeoning feminist demands for rethinking cultural prescriptions of femininity, her stance has become increasingly questioning of feminism. Many of her assumptions, models, and conclusions lack a sophistication that in the climate of the 1990s is more problematic than it had been in the 1970s. Women's fantasies about having sex with other women are linked to a "nostalgia for the mother's breast" that obscures and silences a whole range of erotic desires. As Andrea Stuart argues, her lack of cultural specificity and her bland assumption that she speaks for every woman, of whatever age, ethnicity, or sexual orientation, makes the project prescriptive in its own way: "Yes she

509

has put women's erotic lives on the map; but I suspect that by enshrining women's sexuality in this particular way, Friday may have helped to cut us off from the possibility of creating our own erotic language." But where the explanations unwittingly censor, the fantasies themselves continue to demonstrate the wild diversity and complexity of real women's sexual fantasies, and in documenting and publishing them, Friday has helped to change the climate of opinion on women's sexuality and their erotic desires.

Biography

Born in Pittsburgh, Pennsylvania, August 27, she attended Wellesley College. She began as a reporter and magazine editor in the early 1960s, before becoming a freelance writer. She is most well known as a compiler of best-selling books of women's emotional and sexual experiences, from the 1970s through to the 1990s. She has been married twice, to W.H. Manville (October 1967) and Norman Pearlstine (July 1988).

MERJA MAKINEN

Editions

My Secret Garden: Women's Sexual Fantasies. New York: Trident, 1973; London: Virago in association with Quartet, 1975; 25th anniversary issue, Pocket Books, 1998

Selected Works

My *Secret Garden: Women's Sexual Fantasies*. 1973
Forbidden Flowers: More Women's Sexual Fantasies. 1975
My Mother/My Self: The Daughter's Search for Identity. 1979
Men in Love: The Triumph of Love over Rage. 1980
Jealousy. 1985
Women on Top: How Real Life Has Changed Women's Sexual Fantasies. 1991
The Power of Beauty. 1996

Further Reading

Bright, Susie. "Rape Scenes." In *Sexual Reality: A Virtual Sex World Reader*. Pittsburgh, PA: Cleis, 1992.
Gammell, N.F. "My Secret Garden." *English Studies in Canada* 25 (March 1999).
Gallop, Jane. "Snatches of Conversation." In *Women and Language in Literature and Society*, edited by Sally McConnell-Ginet et al. New York: Praeger, 1980.
Stuart, Andrea. *New Statesman and Society* 4, December 6, 1991.

FRITSCHER, JACK

1939–
American novelist and editor

Jack Fritscher has been many things: tenured university professor, novelist, writer of short stories, biographer, magazine editor, maker of more than 200 erotic videos, photographer, chronicler, and critic of American pop culture. His writing links all these activities into an exploration of eroticism, which is, for Fritscher, an arena of masculine-identified sexuality. His approach is twofold. On the one hand he is the formally trained critic and ethnologist, curious about all aspects of human behavior, as demonstrated in his nonfiction titles *Popular Witchcraft: Straight from the Witch's Mouth* and

Mapplethorpe: Assault with a Deadly Camera. On the other, he is the writer-artist dramatizing a personal vision—expressed, for example, in his ambitious signature novel, *Some Dance to Remember*. There, as well as in all of his writing and photography, his focus is on what he calls "homomasculinity"—less the act of sex itself, more a complete state of being.

He sees in the very males who attract him—bodybuilders, cowboys, cops, men in sports gear and uniform—ritualized totems of the potent American Dream, taken from his own dream visions, as well as from the dreams of the intense cult following whose tastes he has recorded and reflected for many years on page and screen. He believes, as the author of the award-winning

510

novel *The Geography of Women*, that just as women now investigate gender, similarly many men have become increasingly curious about their own gender identification. In his view, true homomasculinity, far from canceling out the female principle, offers the valid gender balance of male animus that the female anima demands and deserves. His writing dramatizes the fact that there is in male-to-male sex an underlying current of violence—that sexual relationships between grown-up men, the bulls and bears of the herd, often veer toward displays of brute strength, and even beyond this to episodes of action-adventure that outsiders might view as violence. As an American erotic writer, he also perceives that these outbursts of physical competition are intrinsic to the nature of American life. Usually quite cinematic, his style is often as challenging as his content. So naturally does he fit eros into revelations of what it is to lead a sexual human life that he refers to his literary erotica as "men's adventure stories." In *Burning Pen: Sex Writers on Sex Writing*, Fritscher, distancing himself from autobiography, explained his gonzo journalistic approach to reflexive erotica in his essay "Porno Ergo Sum": "I inhale experience. I exhale fiction."

In another gay-studies essay, "Erotic Writing Manifesto," he added: "The gay erotic writer is to gay non-erotic writers what Ginger Rogers was to Fred Astaire: gay erotic literature does everything gay literature does, but does it backwards and in high heels adding to its Olympic degree of difficulty and pleasure."

"One hopes," he writes, "when one works in erotic literature to constantly redefine what we consider to be erotic. I often develop fetish-based stories, perhaps foreign at first to the reader who ultimately gets seduced by this strange alternative-angle approach to orgasm. This freshens the surprise and delight of the genre with both beauty and terror—and for many readers, terror is their only hard-on."

Fritscher mixes his first-person verisimilitude with character development, screenplay-like story arcs, and dialog typified by stories such as "Wild Blue Yonder," "How Buddy Left Me," "Daddy's Big Shave," and "Foreskin Prison Blues." Stylistically, he creates erotic rhythms through word choice and precise punctuation, as in the comic erotica of the 3,000-word short story "Three Bears in a Tub (A One-Sentence Romance)" in *Best American Erotica,* 2003. His

images of sex comment on human life: eroticism is means toward humanism.

As San Francisco editor-in-chief of *Drummer*, Jack Fritscher developed, and in some cases brought to print for the first time, themes that have since become staples of gay literature: the concept of "gay pop culture" itself; the gender identity of homomasculinity; the fetish analysis of bondage, cigars, rubber, bears, and edge play. His writing of erotic interviews and feature articles balances his erotic fiction.

As he wrote, in his role as founding adviser to the Erotic Writers Association, 2002: "Erotica is the essential writing of lesbigay culture the way that blues and rap are essential to African-American culture. No one successfully dares censor blues or rap. Yet both the puritan 'straight mainstream' of publishing, as well as the exclusionism of the self-anointed 'gay literary establishment' have too long censored lesbigay erotic writing by denying both its cultural essence and its literary nature. Historically, everything has been rigged against erotica—agents, publishers, printers, distributors, bookstores, reviews, and awards. Yet erotica is a quintessential form of human expression, because it is the subtext of life, as much as erotica is always the avant garde of art." His Catholic-school education—as well as his longtime career commitment to the Catholic priesthood—may explain how, though Fritscher's erotica may seem Freudian, it is really more Jungian and basically Platonic in its ejaculatory ideal. "My S&M erotica," he has written, "spins out of the central image and the main archetype of Western culture: the handsome, muscular, masculine, nearly naked Christus, bound, whipped, and crucified."

Biography

Jack Fritscher was born in Jacksonville, Illinois, June 20. Educated for the Catholic priesthood at the Vatican's Pontifical College Josephinum, 1953–1963; first published, 1958; received doctorate in philosophy, Loyola University, Chicago, 1968, having written his thesis on *Love and Death in Tennessee Williams*; founding member, American Popular Culture Association, 1968; wrote novel, *I Am Curious (Leather)*, 1969, published 1972, and republished as *Leather Blues*, 1984; wrote *Popular Witchcraft: Straight from the Witch's Mouth*, 1973; university professor, teaching American literature and cinema, 1967–1976; founding editor-in-chief of San Francisco–based *Drummer* magazine, 1977; wrote signature novel *Some Dance to Remember* using his own erotic journals, 1970–1982; created and edited with Mark Hemry first 'zine of the eighties, *Man2Man Quarterly*, 1980–1982; from 1977 onward, wrote short stories, features, poems, plays, and screenplays later anthologized in six volumes, including the canonical *Corporal in Charge of Taking Care of Captain O'Malley*, 1978; in addition wrote transgender erotica, "Aqua-Nymph," 1981, and lesbian novel, *The Geography of Women,* 1998, as well as cross-cultural Celtic fiction, "Chasing Danny Boy," 1999; wrote erotic memoir *Mapplethorpe: Assault with a Deadly Camera,* 1994; wrote benchmark essay on erotic theory, "Porno Ergo Sum," 2001; since 1969, has been an erotic photographer shooting covers and centerfolds; created Palm Drive Video, 1982, writing and directing more than 200 erotic feature and gay documentary videos; founding member advisory board, Erotic Authors Association, 2002; Story Teller of the Year Award, 2002, for priest sex-abuse novel, *What They Did to the Kid: Confessions of an Altar Boy*; wrote erotic pop-culture history of *Drummer* magazine in the documentary anthology *Eyewitness Drummer: A Memoir of the Gay History, Pop Culture, and Literary Roots of the Best of* Drummer *Magazine,* 2003. His books have sold more than 110,000 copies, and his erotic videos more than 250,000 copies. Two of his videos, including *Dureau in Studio,* produced by Mark Hemry, profiling the erotic painter-photographer George Dureau, New Orleans, are in the permanent collection of the Maison Europeene de la Photographie, Paris.

EDWARD LUCIE-SMITH

Selected Works

"Love and Death in Tennessee Williams." Ph.D. dissertation, Loyola University of Chicago, 1968. Available at http://jackfritscher.com

I Am Curious (Leather): A Novel. New York: Target Studio, 1971; as *Leather Blues: A Novel,* San Francisco: Gay Sunshine Press, 1984.

Popular Witchcraft: Straight from the Witch's Mouth. Bowling Green, OH: Bowling Green University Popular Press, 1972; as *Popular Witchcraft,* Secaucus, NJ: Citadel/Lyle Stuart Inc., 1973; as *Popular Witchcraft* (revised second edition), Madison: University of Wisconsin Press/Popular Press, 2005.

Corporal in Charge of Taking Care of Captain O'Malley and Other Stories. San Francisco: Gay Sunshine Press, 1984; as *Corporal in Charge and Other Stories,* London: Prowler Press, 1998; San Francisco: Palm Drive Publishing, 2000.

Stand by Your Man and Other Stories. San Francisco: Leyland Publications, 1987; as *Stand by Your Man,* San Francisco: Palm Drive Publishing, 1999.

Some Dance to Remember, Stamford, CT: Knights Press, 1990; as *Some Dance to Remember: A Memoir-Novel of San Francisco 1970–1982.* New York, London, Oxford: Haworth Press, 2005.

Mapplethorpe: Assault with a Deadly Camera. Mamaroneck, NY: Hastings House, 1994; as *El fotographo del escandelo,* translated by J.A. Bravo, Barcelona: Ediciones Martinez Roca, 1995.

Jack Fritscher's American Men. Photography selected and introduction by Edward Lucie-Smith. London: Gay Men's Press, 1995.

Rainbow County and Other Stories. San Francisco: Palm Drive Publishing, 1997.

The Geography of Women: A Novel. San Francisco: Palm Drive Publishing, 1998; as *Geographia Gynaikon,* translated by Andreas Pikakes, Athens: Periplous Publishing, 2000.

Titanic: Forbidden Stories Hollywood Forgot. San Francisco: Palm Drive Publishing, 1999.

What They Did to the Kid: Confessions of an Altar Boy. San Francisco: Palm Drive Publishing, 2001.

Jacked: The Best of Jack Fritscher. Collected and edited by Jesse Grant. Los Angeles: Alyson Books, 2002.

Eyewitness Drummer: *A Queer Studies Memoir of the Gay History, Pop Culture, and Literary Roots of* Drummer *Magazine,* 2005. Available at http://jackfritscher.com

"Corporal in Charge: The One-Act Play." In *Gay Roots: Twenty Years of Gay Sunshine: An Anthology of Gay History, Sex, Politics, and Culture.* edited by Winston Leyland. San Francisco: Gay Sunshine Press, 1991.

"Erotic Artist Chuck Arnett: His Life/Our Times." In *Leatherfolk: Radical Sex, People, Politics, and Practice,* edited by Mark Thompson. Los Angeles: Alyson Publishing, 1991.

"Chasing Danny Boy." In *Chasing Danny Boy: Powerful Stories of Celtic Eros,* edited by Mark Hemry. San Francisco: Palm Drive Publishing, 1999.

"Introduction." In *The Leatherman's Handbook: Silver Jubilee Edition,* edited by Larry Townsend. Los Angeles: LT Publications, 2000.

"Mapplethorpe." In *Censorship: An International Encyclopedia,* edited by Derek Jones. London: Fitzroy Dearborn Publishers, 2001.

"Porno Ergo Sum" and "Wild Blue Yonder." In *The Burning Pen: Sex Writers on Sex Writing,* edited by M. Christian. Los Angeles: Alyson Publications, 2001.

"Three Bears in a Tub." In *Best American Erotica 2003,* edited by Susie Bright. New York: Touchstone/Simon & Schuster, 2003.

"Homomasculinity: Framing Erotic Keywords of Queer Popular Culture." Queer Keyword Conference, April 15, 2005, at University College Dublin, Ireland. Available at http://jackfritscher.com

Further Reading

Denoyelles, Bill. "Gay Art, Robert Mapplethorpe and the Titanic 70s: An Interview with Jack Fritscher." In

The Archive No. 9. New York: Leslie-Lohman Gay Art Foundation, Winter 2002.

Lucie-Smith, Edward. "Introduction." In *Jack Fritscher's American Men*. London: Gay Men's Press, 1995.

Thomas, Claude. "Afterword: Gay American Literature." In *Rainbow County and Other Stories*. San Francisco: Palm Drive Publishing, 1999.

FURNITURE

It might be thought, on the basis of modern stories, that erotic literature tells about people doing things in bed, but the bed is not usually the main focus of interest in stories written before 1850. The most common piece of furniture in classical boudoirs, as described in French libertine literature, is the sofa, or divan. When paintings and engravings of the time show people making love, and when literature describes them doing so, they are not usually "in" bed, as in modern stories, but sometimes leaning on or spread across a divan or some other piece of furniture, using it as support. Even where a bed is present, the characters are likely to have one foot on the floor.

Furniture is often described in seventeenth- and eighteenth-century stories as providing, so to speak, a ready-made shape, waiting to be adopted. Women are said in French to be "curved" on sofas, turned into seductive shapes by aligning themselves with the contours of the furniture. If it is remembered that another vital element of boudoir decor was the mirror, one can begin to understand that classical libertines were quite deliberate and self-conscious about the poses they were adopting. Literature, engravings, and paintings on the walls showed how it was done; the furniture provided material support; and mirrors allowed people to see that they were doing it properly.

In the latter half of the eighteenth century, erotic stories began to tell more and more of furniture that broke during the action. Instead of the classical stability that allowed poses to be

taken up like tableaux and enjoyed for themselves, one finds incidents in which the furniture cracks and falls apart. It may be just a chair, or perhaps some kind of light bed made of webbing, but the furniture now appears quite unstable. And lest this might appear simply as a comical turn of events, deflating erotic tension, readers are continually told that the resulting collapse is a good thing. Rather than pulling the lovers apart, disturbing their erotic poise, it actually throws them together. As they fall, the man penetrates more deeply, the woman yields more completely; it is in fact the happiest of accidents. The point of this rather new kind of story, which flourishes in French around 1790–1800, seems to be that true, natural pleasure does not need to follow ready-made boudoir shapes. But the breaking bed or the chair that comes crashing down is in its own way a model for using furniture erotically, suggesting that the best positions are not the ones that lovers adopt with care, but the ones they fall into.

The historical change in erotic furniture described in stories has a technical dimension. Instead of the firmness and stability associated with classical sofas, the furniture described around 1790–1800 is noteworthy for its resilience. Beds are often sprung and made for bouncing on. Making love in coaches also comes into vogue in stories of that time, and it was sometimes said then that coaches were better than boudoirs, precisely because of their continual movement.

Late-nineteenth-century stories in French describe a different kind of boudoir from the

513

classical one, which had clean lines, pastel hues, and plenty of mirrors. Fin-de-siècle boudoirs are generally dark places, with walls of deep pink or red, heavy drapes, and soft, deeply capacious furniture. This is the time when erotic stories are filled with atmosphere, in the quite literal sense of the word. The sensations of the outside world hardly penetrate at all, and the air is thick with perfume, if not with ether or opium. Around 1880–1900, the bed becomes the archetypal centerpiece, the surrounding decor being barely visible, and therefore, in the proper sense, hardly a decor at all. In libertine stories of 1750, and even as late as de Sade's novels, around 1800, boudoirs are well-lit places in which the characters perform erotic routines with theatrical overtones. But at the end of the nineteenth century, the action usually takes place deep inside the bed, with the rest of the room lost in a haze. What matters most is no longer the shape of the furniture, but its rich material qualities.

Quite a lot of erotic stories actually feature items of furniture as central characters. *Le sopha* (1740), by Crébillon, and *Le canapé couleur de feu* [*The Fire-Colored Sofa*] (1741), by Fougeret de Montbron, are stories typical of their time. Crébillon's novel, which continues to be widely read, tells the story of a man whose soul is imprisoned in sofas by a magic spell. He can gain release only if a virginal woman gives herself to a man for the first time on a sofa in which the hero is currently residing. In the kind of libertine world described by Crébillon, there is a shortage of virgins, and it seems as if the hero will never find release, try as he might to find the right sofa, the right house, and the right woman. But he eventually does so, and the story is able to end. There is no mention in Crébillon's novel of sweat or strain, or wet patches: the sofa is simply a support for lovemaking, and a perfect vantage point from which a "soul" can tell erotic stories.

It was still possible for a piece of furniture to be the narrator-hero in a fin-de-siècle novel, but the thematic role became quite different. *Les Mémoires d'une chaise longue* (1903), by Victorien Du Saussay, focuses on the rivalry between a chaise lounge and a bed. They stand side by side in the apartment of a promiscuous bachelor, and each can be used for seduction. The chaise lounge, which tells the story, sees itself as the proper place for libertine dalliance, and regards the bed as a vast, unthinking place of sleep and death. The chaise lounge tells proudly of its own erotic sensitivity, of its capacity to vibrate in sympathy with any who might make love on it. So sensitive is the sofa, indeed, that it suffers from the kind of nervous disorder which is widespread in literature of the time, and acutely present in erotic stories. The chaise lounge admits to being hysterical. Its springs are its nerves, and they are so hypersensitive that the chaise lounge's condition eventually degenerates into neurasthenia. It also develops a drinking problem. Such erotic pathos would have made no sense to eighteenth-century libertines. It represents the most extreme development of sympathetic, atmospheric furniture. In the fin-de-siècle, eros crosses over into sickness, and the furniture is caught up in the epidemic: the chaise lounge itself is sick with desire and pleasure. As the dominant notions of pleasure changed over time, so did the furniture.

PETER CRYLE

Further Reading

Brulotte, Gaëtan. *Œuvres de chair: Figures du discours érotique.* Quebec: L'Harmattan, Les Presses de l'Université Laval, 1998, pp. 361–64.

Cryle, Peter. "Breaking the Furniture in Erotic Narrative: Towards a History of Desire." *French Studies* 52 (October 1998): 409–24.

Delon, Michel. "Luxe et luxure: Réflexions à partir de Sade." *Nottingham French Studies* 37 (1998): 17–25.

———. *Le Savoir-Vivre libertin.* Paris: Hachette Littératures, 2000.

Renard, Jean-Claude, and François Zabaleta. *Le Mobilier amoureux ou la volupté de l'accessoire.* Briare: Chimères, 1991.

G

GARCÍA LORCA, FEDERICO

1898–1936
Spanish poet and dramatist

The most popular poet in Spain at the time of his death, Lorca's successful literary career lasted only eighteen years. His juvenilia, much of it prose, reveals his early preoccupation with the vicissitudes of love and desire, and his letter correspondence often expresses the voice of a subject who struggled with the social implications of sexuality. His relationships with Salvador Dalí, Emilio Aladrén, and Rafael Rodríguez Rapún, as well as with Phillip Cummings while he was in New York, reflect Lorca's poignant and frustrated sense of love as expressed in his poetry and plays. The principal characteristic of Lorca's concept of eros is frustration: love and desire, heterosexual and homosexual, are at best, unrequited, at worst, fatal. Although it is now commonly accepted that Lorca was gay, until the 1990s, literary critics generally silenced his homosexuality, either by ignoring it altogether or suppressing it in favor of a more "universal" interpretation of his concept of eros.

In his poetry Lorca adopted both traditional and avant-garde techniques, drawing on predecessors such as Shakespeare and Góngora, employing forms such as the ballad and the sonnet, yet also seeking innovation by turning to free verse and surrealism. In *Romancero gitano* (1928), Lorca engages in a poeticization of the mythic figure of the gypsy, infusing the traditional form of the romance with his profound passion for Andalusia. Lorca transforms the popular traditions of Andalusian culture and the figure of the gypsy into a poetic expression of eros as anguished and violent, producing a collection suffused with sexual desire, violence, and death. Desire appears as a masculine "wind" wielding a heated sword, and sexual relations are characterized by deception, adultery, and incest; in "Thamar y Amnon," for example, Lorca draws on the Biblical theme of incestuous love in which Amnon violently rapes his sister and flees. In *Poeta de Nueva York*, written in New York between 1929 and 1930, Lorca eschews the traditional form of the ballad for free verse and surrealist symbolism, exchanging Andalusia for the urban space of New York. He leaves behind the narrative quality of the ballads and strives for a personal yet highly hermetic expression of his tragic, anguished vision of eros; the gritty urban space of New York reflects his sense of alienation. Several of the poems convey the poet's struggle with his own homosexuality, juxtaposing the happiness of his childhood and former friendships in contrast with his present emotional state. Yet it is the famous "Ode to Walt Whitman" that offers the most explicit engagement with homosexuality as a source of frustration and alienation: Lorca extols the virile, masculine image of Walt Whitman from *Leaves of Grass* and rejects the depraved, promiscuous urban homosexual. Between 1935 and 1936, Lorca worked on a collection of sonnets that has come to be known as *Sonetos del amor oscuro*. The lyrical voice speaks to an absent beloved, expressing the anguish and frustration provoked by the beloved's absence; the gender of the poem's addressee is not specific but in many instances suggests a male recipient. Love oscillates between corporeality and spirituality, between a desire for physical contact that is rarely achieved and a vision of love as a spiritual connection that extends beyond the body. In *Diván del Tamarit* (1933–1934), the poet, influenced by Emilio García Gómez's anthology *Poemas arabigoandaluces*, draws creative inspiration from the traditional forms of the *ghazal* and the *qasida* to extol the virtues of homoerotic passion. In spite of formal and thematic differences in his poetry collections, Lorca's works in verse consistently employ nature imagery (rivers, barren trees, the moon) as symbols of human desire.

Lorca's dramatic works share the same vision of love and desire as his poetry: Homosexual and heterosexual love suffers from frustration, social opprobrium, and fatal destinies. *El público* (1930), an avant-garde theatrical work influenced by surrealism, is Lorca's most explicit treatment of homoeroticism as various male characters ask each other what would happen if they were to declare their love for one another. As a metatheatrical work, it dramatizes the possible phobic reactions of the public to the theatrical representation of homosexuality. *La zapatera prodigiosa* (1930) and *Amor de don Perlimplín con Belisa en su jardín* (1933) take inspiration from the traditional narrative of the "old cuckold" whose youthful wife seeks amorous and erotic attention from virile paramours. While comedic in tone, the plays nevertheless announce Lorca's profound engagement with the asymmetry of erotic relations in which the subject's desires are

stronger and thus remain unrequited by the emotionally vacant other. *Así que pasen cinco años* (1931) portrays the fatality of a desire in a surrealist guise as the central protagonist; a young man must wait five years before being reunited with his beloved, who in turn scorns him. In a card game at the drama's denouement, he is forced to play his Ace of Hearts (symbolic of love) and dies. Similarly, in *Bodas de sangre* (1932), the female protagonist's marriage plans end in death as her former lover and future husband kill each other in a violent, jealousy-driven battle. In *La casa de Bernarda Alba* (1936), the youngest of the five Alba sisters, Adela, maintains a passionate affair with her sibling Angustias's suitor, Pepe the Roman. At the end, Adela, believing that her mother, Bernarda, has shot and killed Pepe, commits suicide. Desire is also linked to sterility in Lorca's dramas, his plays populated by female characters who lament the absence of men and the failure to bear offspring. In *Yerma* (1934), the eponymous protagonist anguishes over the failure to bear offspring and ultimately kills her husband, Juan. In *Doña Rosita la soltera* (1936), the titular character vainly waits for her cousin to return from America to marry her, only to discover after her youth has passed that he is engaged to another woman. Lorca's poetic and dramatic works thus strike a consistent chord: love is a wound, a transient source of happiness whose rapid passing leads to pain and despondence, and at its most tragic, to destruction and death.

Biography

Federico García Lorca was born on June 5, 1898, in Fuentevaqueros, near Granada. Lorca originally wanted to study music but followed his father's wishes and initiated his studies in law and humanities at the University of Granada in 1914. In 1918, Lorca published his first book, *Impresiones y paisajes*, a work of prose that was followed by his first poetry collection, *Libro de poemas*, in 1921. An uninspired student, Lorca moved to the Residencia de Estudiantes in Madrid in 1919, enjoying the greater freedom that Madrid offered and completing his law degree in 1923. In 1924, he wrote the highly successful *Romancero gitano*, published in 1928. A dramatic shift occurred in 1929 when Lorca undertook a year-long trip to New York, prompted in large part by his struggles with homosexuality. Enrolled at Columbia University, he composed the surrealist-inspired *Poeta en Nueva York* and worked on the dramas *Así que pasen cinco años* and *El público*; he also composed a first version of *Yerma*, later revised and staged in December 1934 in Madrid. Upon his return in 1931, Lorca collaborated with the university theater group La Barraca, representing plays of the Spanish Golden Age around the country. Focused more on theater than on poetry, Lorca wrote *Bodas de sangre* in 1932, first performed in 1933 in Madrid, and *Doña Rosita la soltera* in 1935, which premiered the same year in Barcelona. In 1935, he also worked on a collection of sonnets, commonly known as *Los sonetos del amor oscuro*. In 1936, Lorca composed his last play, *La casa de Bernarda Alba* (not staged until 1950 in Madrid), and continued working on the sonnets. In the midst of increasing political turmoil Lorca returned to Granada in July 1936, against the advice of friends who urged him to leave Spain. On August 19, just days after the outbreak of civil war, Lorca was assassinated by members of the right-wing Falange. The motives for his murder—whether punishment for his left-wing political leanings or his homosexuality—remain a matter of historical debate.

PATRICK PAUL GARLINGER

Selected Works

Romancero gitano [*Gypsy Ballads*]. 1924, published 1928.
Poeta en Nueva York [*Poet in New York*].1929–1930, published 1940.
La zapatera prodigiosa. [*The Shoemaker's Prodigious Wife*]. 1926.
Amor de don Perlimplín con Belisa en su jardín [*Love of Don Perlimplín with Belisa in the Garden*]. 1925.
El público [*The Public*] (1930).
Así que pasen cinco años [*Thus Five Years Pass*] (1931).
Bodas de sangre [*Blood Wedding*] (1932).
Yerma (1934).
Doña Rosita la soltera [*Doña Rosita the Spinster*] (1936).

Sonetos del amor oscuro [*Sonnets of Dark Love*] (1984).
La casa de Bernarda Alba [*The House of Bernarda Alba*] (1936).
Diván del Tamarit [*Divan of Tamarit*] (1933–1934, published 1940).

Further Reading

Anderson, Andrew A. *Lorca's Late Poetry: A Critical Study*. Leeds: Francis Cairns, 1990.
Degoy, Susana. *Lo más oscuro del pozo: figura y rol de la mujer en el teatro de García Lorca*. Granada: Ediciones Miguel Sánchez, 1999.
Eisenberg, Daniel. "Federico García Lorca," in *Spanish Writers on Gay and Lesbian Themes: A Bio-Critical Sourcebook*. Edited by David William Foster, Westport, Connecticut: Greenwood, 1999.
Garlinger, Patrick Paul. "Voicing (Untold) Desires: Silence and Sexuality in Federico García Lorca's *Sonetos del amor oscuro*." *Bulletin of Spanish Studies*. 79 (2002): 709–730.
Gibson, Ian. *Federico García Lorca: A Life*. New York: Pantheon, 1990.
Gibson, Ian. *Lorca-Dalí: El amor que no pudo ser*. Barcelona: Plaza & Janés, 1999.
Herrero, Javier. "The War of the Stars and the Birth of the Moon: Homosexual Poetics in the Early Lorca." *Bulletin of Hispanic Studies* 77 (2000): 571–583.
Morris, C.B. *Andalusian Son: The Lyrical Landscapes of Federico García Lorca*. Nashville: Vanderbilt University Press, 1997.
Newton, Candelas. "Los paisajes del amor: Iconos centrales en los *Sonetos* de Lorca." *Anales de la literatura española contemporánea* 21.1–2 (1986): 143–159.
Sahuquillo, Angel. *Federico García Lorca y la cultura de la homosexualidad masculina: Lorca, Dalí, Cernuda, Gil-Albert, Prados y la voz silenciada del amor homosexual*. Alicante: Instituto de la Cultura Juan Gil-Albert, 1991.
Smith, Paul Julian. *The Theatre of García Lorca: Text, Performance, and Psychoanalysis*. Cambridge: Cambridge University Press, 1998.
Soufas, C. Christopher. *Audience and Authority in the Modernist Theater of Federico García Lorca*. Tuscaloosa: University of Alabama Press, 1996.
Walsh, John K. "A Logic to Lorca's *Ode to Walt Whitman*." In *¿Entiendes? Queer Readings, Hispanic Writings*. Edited by Emilie L. Bergmann and Paul Julian Smith. Durham: Duke University Press, 1995.

GARCÍA MÁRQUEZ, GABRIEL

1928–
Colombian journalist and novelist. Nobel Prize in Literature (1982).

Cien años de soledad [*One Hundred Years of Solitude*], García Márquez's most successful book, was written within a framework of social crisis, censorship, repression, and the tyranny of successive Right-wing governments, all necessary elements for this new stylistic literary mode. Magic realism allowed writers to, apparently, "depoliticize" their work and create magical and marvelous worlds which invite the suspension of disbelief.

One Hundred Years embraces a range of universal themes encompassed in this novel: solitude, love, sex and desire, and the circularity. These themes are encompassed within the story of the decline and fall of a family who have founded a new town 100 years before.

"Many years later, as he faced the firing squad, Colonel Aureliano Buendía was to remember that distant afternoon when his father took him to discover ice." With that opening sentence an omniscient narrator evokes the end of a vital cycle from the very outset. This chronological confusion, the present seen from the perspective of the past, will continue throughout the main recurrent episodes of the novel.

One of García Márquez's recurrent themes is the failure of collective memory and the lack of accountability for actions taken in the past. Yet, the most outstanding theme is incest. The story begins with Úrsula and José Arcadio's incestuous marriage (they are direct cousins). The family dynasty is not only founded in incest; the physical consummation will occur at least once in each of the seven generations. Driven by irresistible physical urge brothers, sisters, cousins, aunts, and nephews intermarry and procreate. Aureliano José will marry Pilar Ternera. Yet he is in love with Amaranta, his aunt, who in turn is madly jealous of his wife. José Arcadio will marry Rebeca, who was adopted by his parents and brought up with the rest of the siblings as a blood sister. Amaranta, although she dies still a virgin, can only experience sexual arousal while playing with her nephews. Finally, as he faces the firing squad, Colonel Aureliano will try to evoke the memory of his wife but feels ashamed when he can only recall the smell of his mother.

Sexual relations are rarely simple and straightforward between members of the clan. Choice of sexual partner is frustrated by various taboos such that sexual intercourse rarely goes hand in hand with love. It takes Ursula and José Arcadio more than a year to consummate their marriage, haunted as she is by the fear of giving birth to a baby with a pig's tail —a curse which has already manifested itself once before in the family. Colonel Buendía seeks physical solace with Pilar Ternera because of lack of interest by Remedios. Aureliano consoles himself with Rigromanta before he turns to Amaranta Úrsula. Indeed, Amaranta Úrsula and Aureliano are the only couple that are in love and manage to physically consummate that love. Ironically, Amaranta gives birth to the last Buendía, the one who bears a pig's tail, and whose story closes the cycle of the family and the town of Macondo.

El amor en los tiempos del cólera [*Love in the Times of Cholera*], the story of a love triangle, is perhaps the most autobiographical of García Márquez's books. Florentino Ariza must wait fifty years before finally marrying the love of his life, Fermina Daza, who rejected him in favor of a better match. But Florentino Ariza, after having spent a lifetime securing his economic success, seizes his opportunity when her husband dies. They set out on Florentino's ship and he puts up the flag indicating cholera so that nobody will bother them in their renascent lives and long-awaited sexual reunion.

Florentino Ariza, however, is essentially an erotomaniac. The principal way in which it manifests itself is with regards to his ability to compose love letters, not just on his own behalf, but for others as well. Although he had dedicated his heart to one person, he abandons himself physically to some 622 (García Márquez is quite precise about the number) passionate and sometimes long-standing love affairs, devoting himself to this amorous antiquarianism with the same intensity as the passion he professes for Fermina. Given that Florentino Ariza is an excellent letter writer, logorrhea plays an important role in his long courtship process. In fact, Florentino Ariza might best be likened to Cyrano de Bergerac, who it might be remembered composed poetry on behalf of star-crossed lovers. Indeed, he brings so many couples together that he soon finds himself composing replies to his own love letters.

García Márquez is also concerned with the depiction of social imposture. He is particularly mocking of Fermina's husband Juvenal Urbino. Urbino is an educated and well-traveled man who knows how to treat women. He is especially patient with their first lovemaking experience, as realizeshis wife is terrified of physical intimacy.

Although most of García Márquez's stories are set within a fictional time and place, they can be read as ironic and humorous but also tragic epics that reflect, often negatively, and denounce Latin American and particularly Colombian social and political reality. Other works include the novella and various collections of short stories *No One Writes to the Colonel, The Stories of Big Mama's Funeral, Innocent Erendida and Other Stories* and the recent *Memorias de mis putas tristes*. In this short novel, García Márquez's first after ten years, an elderly journalist decides to celebrate his 90 years in a grand way; an expensive treat only his long-time friend Rosa Cabarcas, who runs the most prestigious brothel in town, could arrange for him. His life changes radically, however, when he sees the young woman lying in bed, completely naked, and he finally meets himself, close to dying, not of old age but of love.

Biography

Born in 1928 in Aracataca, in the province of La Guajira, Colombia, his career commenced in journalism. Between 1947 and 1955 he published regularly in various Colombian newspapers such as *El Espectador, Crónica,* and *El Heraldo*. In Spain, he contributed to *El Pais*. In 1955, he published his first book *La Hojarasca*, followed in 1958 by *El Coronel no tiene quien le escriba*. He founded the magazine *Alternativa* in 1974 and the short lived *El otro* [*The Other*] in 1982

(closed for political reasons) and was editor of the *Semanario Crónica* in 1950.

The 1940s, 1950s, and 1960s witnessed a wave of innovative, young Latin American writers who, influenced by modernists such as Proust, Joyce, Woolf, and Faulkner, became known as "el boom." Miguel Angel Asturias was considered the precursor of this group; other members included Agustín Yanes, Alejo Carpentier, Juan Rulfo, Carlos Fuentes, Julio Cortázar, Mario Vargas Llosas, Guillermo Cabrera Infante, and Manuel Puig.

García Márquez's relatively low profile career as a journalist ended in 1982 when he won the Nobel Prize for *Cien años de soledad* which, by its twentieth anniversary in 1987, had sold 30 million copies and had been translated into 36 languages. During the intervening years, with an international spotlight firmly fixed on South American literature, García Márquez continued to write steadily.

Editions

Cien años de soledad. Buenos Aires: Sudamericana, 1967; as *One Hundred Years of Solitude,* translated by Gregory Rabassa. New York: Harper & Row, 1970.

El amor en los tiempos de cólera. Bogotá: La Oveja Negra, 1985; as *Love in the Time of Cholera,* translated by David Campbell, 1997.

Selected Works

La hojarasca. Bogotá: Ediciones S.L.B., 1955; as *Leaf Storm and Other Stories,* tr. Gregory Rabassa. New York: Harper & Row, 1972.

El Colonel no tiene quien le escriba. Medellín, Colombia: Aguirre Edit, 1961; as *No One Writes to the Colonel* (contains *No One Writes to the Colonel* and T*he Stories of Big Mama's Funeral*). Tr. J.S. Bernstein. New York: Harper & Row, 1968.

La mala hora. México: Ediciones Era, 1966 as *In Evil Hour,* tr. Gregory Rabassa. New York: Harper & Row, 1979.

El otonio del patriarca. Barcelona: Seix Barral, 1975; as *The Autumn of the Patriarch.* Tr. Gregory Rabassa. New York: Harper & Row, 1976.

La triste historia de cándida Eréndira y su abuela desalmada. Buenos Aires: Sudamericana, 1972; as *Innocent Erendida and Other Stories.* Tr. Gregory Rabassa. New York: Harper & Row, 1979.

Crónica de una muerte anunciada. Bogotá: La Oveja Negra, 1981; as *Chronicle of a Death Foretold.* Tr. Gregory Rabassa. New York: Knopf. 1983.

Collected Stories. Tr. Gregory Rabassa. New York: Harper & Row, 1984.

Memorias de mis putas tristes. New York: Vintage Español, Random House, 2004.

Further Reading

Bollettino, Vicenzo. *Breve estudio de la novelística de García Máarquez*. Madrid: Playor, 1973.

Ludmer, Josefina. *Cien años de soledad de G.García Márquez: una interpretación*. Buenos Aires: Tiempo Contemporáneo, 1972.

Méndez José Luis. *Cómo leer a García Márquez: una interpretación sociológica*. Puerto Rico: Editorial de la Universidad de Puerto Rico, 1989.

Murray, G.R., ed. *Critical Essays on Gabriel García Márquez*. Boston, MA.: G. K. Hall, 1987.

Oyarzun, K. and Megenney, W.W. (ed). *Essays on Gabriel García Márquez*. Riverside, CA.: University of California, Latin America Studies Program, 1984.

GAUCLÈRE, YASSU

1907–1962
French essayist and novelist

Gauclère's literary career suffered many misfortunes which delayed its reception (*L'Orange bleue* was only republished once, almost twenty-five years after it was written), as did her untimely death which limited her work and its influence. She wrote only three novels, the first two of which are dominated by erotic themes. Eroticism in Gauclère's work serves as a counterpoint to a perverted innocence, marked by a questioning of abjection, secrets, suffering, and guilt. It appears within the narrative as a figure of sin (in *L'Orange bleue*) or as the tyranny of the flesh (in *La clé*), creating in Gauclère's *œuvre*, an eroticism of anti-eroticism. In the same way as Jean Paulhan remarked the surprising respectability of *Histoire d'O* by Pauline Reage, Gauclère's eroticism could be branded as pitilessly respectable. Her mastery of form both exposes and contains the exhibition of the intimate.

The cover of *L'Orange bleue*, carries the word 'Récit..' Written between 1933 and 1939, the novel, in a manner reminiscent of André Gide's autobiographical *Si le grain ne meurt* (1926), tells the first person account of the gradual sexualization of the subject. In Gauclère, however, this process is one of an objectification, even a reification of the body. The narrative depicts the very young boarding school girl, innocently falling prey to several practices and abuses, with an increasing sense of estrangement. The main theme of the novel is the displacement of the fatherless girl, who moves from one place to another and often from hands to hands. Barely eleven years old, she is presented with a succession of abusive substitute fathers, who despicably introduce themselves as 'petit papa' or 'Uncle Joseph' and try to take advantage of her. Interestingly, the attempt to pervert her involves making her read erotic books, namely the series of *Claudine* by Colette, since 'a little girl who reads *Claudine* can see everything..' The young girl converts to Catholicism, and later experiments with the repressive order of several religious institutions, where she tries to escape the sin of the flesh through mysticism. She also hopes to redeem her Jewish father, and yearning for the vocation of celibacy, prays that if she ever is to get married, the marriage will remain white.

The quasi-sacrificial interiorization of values imposed upon her is also undermined by the sensitive portrayal of the unavowed eroticism of the meticulous school rituals, such as the nuns' curiosity, the discipline, the common stripping of the boarders, and the everyday humiliations. Predating Foucault, Gauclère demonstrates the erotic potential existing in the inscription of power relationships on the girls' bodies. The teaching of feminine behavior by the nuns, the corporal punishment, and prohibitions such as not crossing one's legs, prove to be an instruction into temptation and an incitation to representations of impurity. This awareness helps to transform a victimized eroticism into an eroticism of conquest, and to regain freedom from the infinite casuistic of religion. Yet such conquest leads

GAUCLÈRE, YASSU

her only to be rejected into a world dominated by the aggression of desiring and objectifying looks: 'Then I was able to understand the world which had been depicted as being so dangerous. I'd had no money, no books, no friends and I'd meet disgusting gentlemen, who'd call me doll..'

An even more tragic form of eroticism is at the core of her novel *La Clé*, dedicated to Etiemble. As the title suggests, the novel, set in Paris and in Mexico, deals with closure. The failure of a metaphoric key to open the prison built around the main female character, in her desire to be untouchable, is rendered in the opening chapter by the discovery of her putrescent body two months after her suicide. Once an object of unwanted desires, she has been reduced to a stanching corpse. Dominated by this figure of decomposition, physical love in the novel finds a parallel with a process of corruption, degradation, and physical pain. The recurrence of animals involved in or as inspiration for sexual acts (a parrot, a bull, a man disguised for sexual rituals as a cock, another as a horse), suggests an identity between copulation and bestiality she cannot accept: 'Love was male and female blinded by the species.' However, the only real escape is death.

The diversity of erotic themes interwoven in Gauclère's novels, their rich psychoanalytical content, and the quality of her style makes her *œuvre* particularly original. Its neglect by critics appears completely undeserved and calls for a systematical rediscovery.

Biography

Léonie (aka Yassu) Gauclère, was born on the 10th of January 1907 in Paris. She studied Philosophy at the Faculté des lettres de Bordeaux and obtained the Agrégation de Philosophie in 1931, in the same year as Ferdinand Alquié, Claude Lévi-Strauss, Robert Derathé, and Simone Weil. She taught Philosophy in several high schools, including Lycée de Moulins in 1931, Lycée de Toulouse, (1932–1936) and Lycée de Sèvres (1936–1938). She met her future husband, Etiemble (*), at the Moscow International Writers' Congress, in 1934 with whom she wrote a remarkable biography of Rimbaud in 1936. Etiemble's scandalous debut novel *L'Enfant de choeur* (1937), which tells of the

sexual education of a young boy, is dedicated to her, while Gauclère's first novel, *L'orange bleue,* deals with the sexual apprenticeship of a young girl. Published in June 1940, during the French exodus before the arrival of the Nazi armies, copies of the book could reach neither the public, nor the critics. Fearing for her life because of her Jewish background, she left France for America where Etiemble was teaching. She taught in Hamilton College until 1943. After leaving teaching, she worked as a civil servant, as an attaché in the Government Press service, in Alger and Paris (1944), and at the French Embassy, in Cairo (1945–1947). She divorced Etiemble and became a civil servant for UNESCO in Paris, continuing to write and was awarded the Prix Sainte-Beuve in 1951 for her second novel, *La Clé*, dedicated to Etiemble. *L'orange bleue* was republished in 1961. She died young on the 22nd of September, 1962.

DOMINIQUE JEANNEROD

Selected Works

Novels

L'Orange bleue. Paris: Gallimard, 1940 (Nouvelle édition, Gallimard 1961).
Sauve qui peut. Paris: Gallimard, 1955.
La clé. Paris, Gallimard: 1951.

Other Works

Étiemble, René and Yassu Gauclère. *Rimbaud*, Paris: Gallimard, 1936.
'Une petite fille et Dieu.' *Lettres françaises*. n.3, janvier 1942. Buenos Aires: *SUR*, 1942.
Lawrence, Thomas Edward. *Lettres de T. E. Lawrence.* Translated by René Etiemble and Yassu Gauclère. Paris: Gallimard, 1948.

Further Reading

Pia, Pascal. *Dictionnaire des œuvres érotiques*. Paris: Robert Laffont, Bouquins, 2001.
Who's Who in France. Paris: J. Lafitte, 1951.
Temerson, H. *Biographie des principales personnalités, décédées en 1961*. Paris: H. Temerson, 1962.
Nourissier, François. 'Portrait de l'aventurier.' *La chronique littéraire*. Le Figaro, 29 octobre 2004.
Philipponnat, Olivier and Patrick Roger Lienhardt. *Stéphane: enquête sur l'aventurier*. Paris: Grasset, 2004.
Wattel, Béatrice and Michel Wattel. *Qui était qui, XXe siècle: dictionnaire biographique des Français disparus ayant marqué le XXe siècle*. 2e éd., Levallois-Perret: J. Lafitte, 2005.

GAUTIER, THÉOPHILE

1811–1872
French poet, novelist, and journalist.

Though *Mademoiselle de Maupin* must be considered Gautier's most important discussion of eroticism, the subject, often in a highly veiled manner, is omnipresent in his work. A number of the *contes fantastiques* [fantasy tales] of the 1830s and 1840s consist of opium-induced reveries which seem to be leading to imaginary (and, invariably, frustrated) erotic encounters. 'Omphale' (1834) and 'Clarimonde' (1836) are best described as erotic ghost stories. The erotic is, in fact, also the theme of Gautier's 1835 novel: D'Albert, a young poet, finds the embodiment of his ideals of love and physical beauty in Théodore, a charming young squire (who is, of course, the Mademoiselle de Maupin of the title). D'Albert's choice of an androgyne as love-object, however, gives rise to all manner of aesthetic, intellectual, and psychological paradoxes which Gautier explores with relish in his diffuse and complex novel. While *Mademoiselle de Maupin* was shunned by the general public, its influence on French Romanticism and the decadent movement (especially Sainte-Beuve, Baudelaire, and Swinburne) was considerable.

Gautier's most overtly erotic (or offensive) work, however, was a long communication which he sent from Rome in October 1850 to Apollonie Sabatier, an enchanting *demi-mondaine* who was maintained by a rich banker. She also numbered Baudelaire and Flaubert among her devoted admirers. Surprisingly, given its Rabelaisian content, hand-written copies of this letter would seem to have circulated more or less freely in the Parisian literary milieu for a number of years (a version was read to the Goncourts in December 1857, for example). Though it did not make its way into print during the lifetime of either the author or the recipient, Augustus Brancart, the celebrated clandestine bookseller who had recently moved his center of operations from Brussels to Amsterdam, issued it as *Lettre à la Présidente* in 1890. ('La Présidente,' perhaps in

honor of her capacity as a hostess, was Gautier's own affectionate nickname for Mme. Sabatier). Later editions (now as *Lettres à la Présidente*) are often augmented by a further seventy or so short notes by Gautier to Mme Sabatier, mainly dealing with matters such as tickets for the opera, together with the handful of erotic poems that the author had been wary of publishing under his own name during his lifetime.

Given the capital importance of the *Lettre à la Présidente*, it is surprising that literary critics and biographers still tend to make little or no reference to it. Nowhere else, however, does Gautier reveal himself so unreservedly. This is especially important with regard to an author such as Gautier who, though his work is dedicated to the cult of beauty and amorous encounter, was apparently not only incapable of commitment (except perhaps to women who were unattainable) but also haunted by images of disease, physical deformity, scatological excess, and the frustration of desire. In many respects, the *Lettre à la Présidente* represents the very antithesis of *Mademoiselle de Maupin*.

The letter itself begins by recounting one of the nocturnal fantasies ("fantasmagories nocturnes") that Gautier experienced in Geneva involving the use of a wire pulley (of the kind employed by acrobats on the stage) for the purpose of coition. A few days later, in the countryside, he is fantasizing about a woman with three nipples. More alarmingly, a picture of a military battle that he notices in an auberge at the Simplon Pass metamorphoses before his eyes into a pornographic image: "The cannons were transformed into ejaculating penises, the wheels became testicles, the barrels erections, and the smoke simulated the frothy cream of spurting semen" (my translation). At Domo d'Ossola, the glimpse of a bottle of olive oil gives rise to some speculative remarks on its possible employment in the hands of aristocratic pederasts, a vice he seems to identify with English travelers. This is followed by a bewildering kaleidoscope of images: an erotic marionette theater; animals copulating in the street; and a description of a nine-hour coach journey during which time he is continually aroused by the rubbing of the upholstery (the vehicle's suspension, apparently, is to blame). In Venice, he employs a pimp to take him and his traveling companion (Louis de Cormenin, though he is never formally identified) on a tour of the back streets, where a heavily-pregnant woman offers herself. Though only 22, she has already given birth to six children. Mercifully, the offer is declined: "Be as enterprising as you like, you can hardly ram a foetus back into it's mother's belly; and it's no fun to feel some brat treating the end of your penis as a trampoline" (my translation). Florence, Rome, and Naples offer a similar variety of exotic experiences.

Why did Gautier send this curious missive to his friend in Paris? Internal evidence would seem to suggest that Gautier had never made love with Mme. Sabatier (or "trinqué du nombril," i.e., rubbed navels, in Gautier's curiously childish expression), so one suggestion must be that the *Lettre à la Présidente* was merely an exercise in masculine bravado. The recipient, however, would not seem to have been in the least scandalized by the letter. This implies, perhaps, that such matters were talked about fairly freely in front of her. More generally, Gautier's fascination with such images is clearly part of a broader phenomenon: the nineteenth-century bourgeois male fascination with dirt and prostitution.

There are a number of late nineteenth-century and early twentieth-century translations of *Mademoiselle de Maupin* into English, but readers should be aware that many of these will not be very reliable. *Lettre à la Présidente* remains untranslated.

Biography

Gautier was born in Gascony in 1811 but spent most of his childhood in Paris. Along with writers such as the temperamental Pétrus Borel and the nomadic Gérard de Nerval, he belonged to the young Romantic school of the early 1830s (Le Petit Cénacle) whose members looked to Victor Hugo as their spiritual leader while actively seeking to surpass him on the strength of their own macabre or aesthetic excesses. Gautier's first book, a collection of poetry, passed almost unnoticed in 1830; *Albertus*, a bizarre fantasy about a young poet who sells his soul to the devil for love, suffered a similar fate two years later; while *Les Jeunes-France, romans goguenard* (1833), essentially a collection of sketches satirizing the aesthetic pretensions of his Parisian literary friends, was too narrow in its appeal to attract a wide audience. The same might be said of his most important literary work of this early period, *Mademoiselle de Maupin* (1835). Though Gautier's preface is now considered one of the principal manifestoes of Art for Art's Sake, the licentious subject matter of the novel (which deals with the myth of the androgyne) caused the book to be shunned by middle-class readers. The commercial failure of this novel may have pushed Gautier towards developing a career as journalist, critic, and travel writer. Though he continued to publish fiction throughout his life (including *Le Capitaine Fracasse*, 1863, an engaging picaresque novel), French readers in the mid-nineteenth century would have been equally aware of his work as a theater reviewer and art critic. He died in 1872.

TERRY HALE

Selected Works

Lettres à la Présidente. Preface by Pascal Pia, in Jean-Jacques Pauvert (ed.), *L'Erotisme Second Empire*, Paris: Carrere, 1985.
Mademoiselle de Maupin, (ed.) Geneviève van den Bogaert. Paris: Garnier-Flammarion, 1966.

Further Reading

Richardson, Joanna. *Théophile Gautier: His Life and Times*. London: Max Reinhardt,1958.
Barsoum, Marlene. *Théophile Gautier's Mademoiselle de Maupin: Towards a Definition of the "Androgynous Discourse."* New York: Peter Lang, 2001.

GAY (MALE) WRITING

Although gay erotic writing undoubtedly shares many of the characteristics of straight writing, the marking of homosexuality in terms of object choice gives any gay eroticization of the male body a different political, social, and ethical edge. By putting the sex (back) into homosexuality, gay erotic writing makes a statement about itself and about sexual identity which arguably has more in common with women's erotic writing than with much straight male writing about women. Such eroticization is, however, a two-edged weapon. On the one hand, it foregrounds a sexuality which has been traditionally subject to censorship, self-censorship, and stigma. On the other hand, it can give the impression that male gays are at least as phallocratic as heterosexuals. Gay male erotic writing can, therefore, be seen to be treading a fine line between, on the one hand, using "men are beautiful" (or at least, sexy) to show that "gay is beautiful" and, on the other, making it look as if gays are unreconstructedly phallocentric. In many cases the writing discussed here will not simply fall into one of these categories and be either hegemonic or counter-hegemonic but be rather, in a variety of ways, both: by combining modes of identification and distance, much of the writing charted here will combine pleasuring the male body with an awareness, analysis, and even alienation of that pleasure. Erotic fantasies will be constructed as they are demystified, demystified as they are constructed and, as a result, the simplistic assimilation of sex(uality) and identity will be simultaneously asserted and questioned. Even some gay pornography—and this is doubtless one of the reasons for its interest for literary and cultural critics—can be seen as operating at these different levels and giving its readers and viewers opportunities for the demystification of its (and their) seemingly most visceral fantasies.

One way of simultaneously asserting and demystifying the assimilation of sexuality and identity is to allow gayness to be submerged into a generalized, universalized homoeroticism.

Although, for instance, Grant Foster's collection of short stories, *Long Slow Burn* (2001), is trailed as "masterful gay erotica," gayness as such recedes before "a tidal wave of testosterone" where each man has a "piece" with "a life of its own" and, with wives and families at least temporarily removed, can surrender to the "beast trapped within [him]": boys will be boys and locker-room horseplay leads to irresistible sex between inexperienced narrators and a series of muscled sportsmen, truckers, and bodyguards. This emphasis on immediate physical and emotional connection between men is, in William J. Mann's short story, *By the Numbers*, attributed to "the libidinous network that makes up the queer nation" (Lawrence Schimel, *The Mamoth Book of Gay Erotica*, 1997). With their "gaydar" and "secret scent" all gay men are linked "dick to dick" across the United States and, according to Steven Saylor writing as Aaron Travis, also across the centuries: the homoeroticism of Roman statuary is repeated in the equally accessible sculpted beauty of present-day Italians (*Do as the Romans Do*, ibid., pp. 58–66). If, in Neil Bartlett's acclaimed *Ready to Catch Him Should He Fall* (1990), the young protagonist, Boy, immediately connects with the older but equally beautiful O(ther), this is also seen as part of the feverish—some would say promiscuous—homoeroticism of The Bar where they meet, which gaybashers seek, in vain, to eradicate. Even in this quintessentially gay novel, the sexual aura of the symbolically named Boy and O extends, as in the previous texts, over time, space, and specific identities: here again, boy(s) will be boy(s) and gay sex(uality) merges with a universalized male-to-male eroticism, presided over by a similarly generalized "Mother."

At the same time as implicitly turning the Boy into an archetypal Cupid or Eros himself, gay narratives also deconstruct the tautology that "boys will be boys," notably in childhood or adolescent (auto-)fictions such as Edmund White's celebrated *A Boy's Own Story* (1982). Whereas "real" boys are characterized by their "reedy, sinewy, scruffy maleness" (p. 119), the physically retiring narrator combines the alienation of precociously internalized stigma with the self-distancing of coruscating adult prose: however pleasurably he "cornholes" with fellow youngsters and experiments with local hustlers, the narrator wants to be and remain heterosexual. Struggling to distinguish sincerity from insincerity, real identity from fantasized romances, the narrator finally becomes himself through a gratuitous act of betrayal—thus echoing the links between homosexuality and deviance/deviousness suggested by Gide's youthful "counterfeiters" (*Les Faux-monnayeurs* [1926]) and Genet's young criminals (*Notre-Dame-des-fleurs* [1944]). Relatedly, *A Boy's Own Story* recalls a whole series of schoolboy narratives by authors as different as Emmanuel Carrère, Jean Cocteau, Éric Jourdan, Håkan Lindquist, Yukio Mishima, Henri de Montherlant, Alain Peyrefitte, and Michel Tournier, where self-questionings combine with erotic awakenings, and also texts where a mature narrator seduces compliant Arab boys, from Gide's *L'Immoraliste* (1902) to Tony Duvert's *Journal d'un innocent* (1976), or where he simply admires one from afar as in Thomas Mann's *Tod in Venedig* (1912). By charting the conflict between the beauty of the boy and "the world's spleen and deceit" (White) such texts ask: Where is the homosexual? On the side of beauty or on the side of deceit?

Although such adolescent self-questionings can be discarded when the boy becomes a man, homoerotic hedonism is still problematized in "adult" fictions—for example, by other forms of (self-)destructiveness, by the implications of promiscuity, and by AIDS. In James Baldwin's *Giovanni's Room* (1957), for example, a combination of Giovanni's murder of his employer and the narrator's eventual preference for a relationship with a woman, Hella—who still rejects him—results in the execution of Giovanni and the isolation of the other protagonists: the gorgeous Giovanni is seen by Hella as "a sordid little gangster" and the narrator is left alone. While ostensibly very different in period and in tone, gay men's *penchant* for a handsome "bit of rough" also leads to betrayal, unfulfilment, and even prison in Alan Hollinghurst's *The Swimming-Pool Library* (1988). Even if youth, beauty, money, and connections give the narrator-hero, Will, access to repeated good sex,

that sex concentrates on a relatively underprivileged, well-honed waiter, who betrays him, and on a homeless, sensuous Black, who is, like Giovanni, also drawn into murder. If, at the same time, other characters' minor misdemeanours lead to arrest or imprisonment, then gay sex is shown to be either semi-innocently exploitative or unjustly persecuted, by gay-bashing in the streets or in the courts. Since, moreover, homoeroticism crosses time—from the images in Lord Nantwich's Roman pavement to The Shaft—and space—from 1930s Egypt to contemporary London—and indeed class—from Wormwood Scrubs to the gentleman's club — homosexual desire is shown to be constantly linked not just to arbitrary, hypocritical, social oppression but, even more dangerously, to elegant, hedonistic self-oppression. Equally ambivalent is the fiction dealing with ageing and AIDS—often taken together as in Pier Vittorio Tondelli's *Camere separate* (1989) and Andrew Holleran's *The Beauty of Men* (1996). On the one hand, Holleran's mid-fifty-year-old protagonist, Lark, agonizes over the deaths of his friends and over fellow gays' continued emphasis on youth, beauty, and the appropriate body parts. On the other hand, writers such as Ramon Fernandez in *La gloire du paria* (1987) celebrate the dignity and loyalty of AIDS-affected couples and others, such as Hervé Guibert, even see AIDS as a "marvellous disease," giving AIDS an aestheticized, eroticized aura. Whether AIDS is seen as unalloyedly calamitous or strangely empowering, it is, in both cases, eroticized: if only because of the very nature of AIDS, the AIDS patient's combination of self-analysis, self-contemplation, and self-withdrawal is, like the gay adolescent's self-questioning and the gay adult's (self-)oppression, a constant reminder of the link between eros and gay identity.

As can be seen from the presence of young if often unpremeditated gay killers in *The Swimming-Pool Library*, *Giovanni's Room*, Tõnu Õnnepalu's *Piiririik* (1993) and Fernando Vallejo's *La Virgen de los Sicarios* (1994), and from the related, recurring appeal of "rough trade," gay eroticism can be more than tinged with a suggestion of violence, whether in the choice of partner (compliant boy initiated by older man), in the sexual act itself (active/passive and accompanying dress codes), or in the socio-cultural-historical context of the relationship: internalized oppression, AIDS, or war. Internalized stigma, as in Mishima (where hypermasculinity is close to ultra-nationalism), and in Fernandez, is often accompanied by references to the archetypal "gay" martyr, Saint Sebastian, and, from the earliest known epic, *Gilgamesh*, to Pierre Guyotat's *Tombeau pour cinq cent mille soldats* (1967), male-to-male bonding is often accompanied by warfare and death. Although gay violence sometimes seems to figure in the writer's life as much as in his art—Gilles de Rais, Sade, Genet, Mishima—and although some gay serial killers have themselves generated more publications than many actual authors—Jeffrey Dahmer, John Wayne Gacy, Dennis Nilsen—it is the carefully coded, ritualized forms of what might be broadly called sado-masochism which have prompted most fictional representations, from the prolific output of John Preston (*Mr. Benson*, 1992) to the parodic but deeply disturbing fictions of Dennis Cooper (*Frisk*, 1991). While the latter exposes the inseparability of desire and violence and of representation and pornography, the former is an apologia of ritualized S/M between the narrator-slave and the master-Mr. Benson, in contrast with "real" sadists represented by a vicious German, Hans. By associating gay bonding with violence—whether the supposedly instinctual violence of the untamed boy as in Éric Jourdan's *Les Mauvais Anges* (1984) or the cultivated violence of the older man as in Joël Hespey's letter-novel *S.M. Roman* (1994)—the male homosexual is shown to be more, rather than less, masculine than his heterosexual equivalent. Thus Hespey's older Sylvain repeatedly urges his trainee, Marc, to "take it like a man": submissiveness and pain give unprecedented access to a physical and psychological virility which Marc can then pass on to future trainees in an unending transfer of male empowerment. This enhanced masculinity is, moreover, achieved through an inseparable combination of violence and writing: Marc is instructed to write his own S/M novel and he literally "gets off" on a sheet of paper he sends to Sylvain with every letter on which their relationship depends. Hespey's text thus demonstrates the inseparability of violence, male-to-male sex, and representation. Put differently, the real or symbolic tear shed by the "submissive" male reinforces the "money-shot" of gay fiction.

Despite this enhancement of masculinity—and corresponding elimination of any suggestion of the effeminized gay—much gay fiction still blurs or questions the compartmentalization of sexual difference (Guy Hocquenghem's *Ève* (1987)), gender roles (the novels and plays of Jean Genet), and homosexuality and heterosexuality. In Cyril Collard's *Les Nuits fauves* (1992), for example, the presumably bisexual hero, Jean, is sexually active with Laura, Samy, and a host of other men, and in Hespey's *S.M.*, Marc identifies neither as homosexual or heterosexual, but as, simultaneously, Sylvain's slave and heterosexual lover of Nicole. Indeed, part of the excitement of such fiction is to lure the supposedly heterosexual man into a more erotically fulfilling gay affair—witness Grant Foster's "The Wedding Thief" in *Long Slow Burn* and the gay tryst of the handsome, married Beauchamp in Armistead Maupin's *Tales of the City* (1972). What seems to matter here is less the relevance of precise sexual categories than a general increase in erotic activity amidst an equally general "gaying" of sexuality and thereby a general "queering" of the community, society, and even the world. If gay men have been oppressed, then liberation means global gay sex—not just for self-identified gays, but for all. In this welcome reversal of conventional sexual hierarchies it is the straight who joins the gay out of the closet of sexual hypocrisy and inhibition.

OWEN HEATHCOTE

Further Reading

Aldrich, Robert. *The Seduction of the Mediterranean: Writing, Art and Homosexual Fantasy*. London: Routledge, 1993.

Griffin, Gabriele. *Who's Who in Lesbian and Gay Writing*. London. Routledge, 2002.

Haggerty, George E. (editor). *Gay Histories and Cultures: An Encyclopedia*. New York: Garland, 2000.

Heathcote, Owen, Alex Hughes and James S. Williams, (editors). *Gay Signatures: Gay and Lesbian Theory, Fiction and Film in France, 1945–1995*. Oxford: Berg, 1998.

Hines, Derrek. *Gilgamesh*. London: Chatto & Windus, 2002. *Inverses. Littératures, Arts, Homosexualités*. 1, 2001.

Larrière, Michel. *Pour tout l'amour des hommes: Anthologie de l'homosexualité dans la littérature*. Paris: Delétraz, 1998.

Lilly, Mark. *Gay Men's Literature in the Twentieth Century*. Basingstoke: Macmillan, 1993.

Malinowski, Sharon (editor). *Gay and Lesbian Literature*. Detroit, MI: St James Press, 1994.

Murray, Stephen O. and Will Roscoe. *Islamic Homosexualities: Culture, History, and Literature*. New York: New York University Press, 1997.

Phillips, John. *Forbidden Fictions: Pornography and Censorship in Twentieth-Century French Literature.* London: Pluto, 1999.

Plummer, Ken. *Telling Sexual Stories: Power, Change and Social Worlds.* London: Routledge, 1995.

Robinson, Christopher. *Scandal in the Ink: Male and Female Homosexuality in Twentieth-century French Literature.* London: Cassell, 1995.

Woods, Greg. *A History of Gay Literature: The Male Tradition.* New Haven, CT: Yale University Press, 1998.

GE HONG

283–343
Chinese poet

Baopuzi

Ge Hong is a famous Taoist writer of the Jin dynasty. His works are plentiful, and many of them, such as his writings on poetry and strategy, have long disappeared. But fortunately the two books for which he is known, *Baopuzi neipian* and *Baopuzi waipian*, have come down to us. The *Baopuzi neipian* [*The Inner Chapters of the Master Who Embraces Simplicity*] is certainly the most interesting of the two. This book, which is well known in Taoist circles, remained hidden for many centuries, but has become the object of close studies during the last hundred years or so, in China, Japan, and in the West. It is nothing less than an immortality handbook in twenty chapters, and deals with all possible aspects of the subject: technical, moral, philosophical, etc.

About half of the book concerns the techniques one has to master in order to become immortal. As Ge Hong himself puts it (Chapter 8), "He who seeks immortality only has to acquire the essential, that is treasuring your essence, circulation of breath, and absorption of one great medicine. This is enough, there is no need for more." The three arts Ge Hong mentions here have occupied the minds of Taoists during at least two millennia. Put into plain words, they make reference to Taoist sexual techniques, the Chinese yoga known today as *qigong*, and alchemy. If the last of these is seemingly no longer studied in China, the first two are still practiced by many Chinese, especially *qigong*.

The art we are interested in here is that of the bedchamber (*fangzhong shu*), which is essential, according to Taoist belief, to attaining immortality, but also in avoiding diseases and enjoying a long life. Ge Hong remains very discreet about the details of Taoist sexual techniques, but does give us a few hints, which we shall examine here. First of all, he reaffirms, as the famous Confucian philosopher Mencius (or Mengzi) did many centuries before him, that eating and having sex are part of human nature: "Mankind's way wants you to eat exquisite food, to wear light and soft clothes, to unite yin and yang, to gain a position in society (...). To abandon wife and children, to live alone in the mountains and swamps, to remain hidden and cut off with human nature, to be lonely, having nothing but trees and stones as neighbors, all this is unworthy" (Chapter 3). But more than a hedonist activity, sex, just like *qigong* and alchemy, is a therapy against old age, if practiced properly. For both abstinence and debauchery cause damage to a man's health: "Man should not abstain completely from yin and yang. If he does so, he will soon develop obstructive diseases. Those who live reclusively and in celibacy often suffer from illness and do not live to old age. On the other hand, to abandon oneself to a life of pleasure is a danger to one's life. He alone who knows the balance between economy and waste can avoid damages" (Chapter 8).

As to the right way of having sex, it is simple in theory, though somewhat disconcerting for a twenty-first-century westerner. The idea, which one finds throughout Chinese sex history, is for the man to retain his semen, and send it through his spine up to his brain. Sperm has very little chance, we know, of running up one's spine to one's brain, but there are various ways of retaining it, "As for the arts of the bed-chamber, there are more than ten schools. One uses them to compensate for loss and to cure illness. If one can collect yin [positive energy] to fortify his yang [negative energy], he will prolong his life. The gist of it consists of one thing: returning your essence to reinforce your brain. True Men (Taoist immortals) pass on their methods mouth to ear but never write them down." Fortunately, others beside Ge Hong have written down some of these secret methods, making it possible for all to learn and practice them.

Ge Hong incidentally mentions a rather simple way of extending one's life span: "Zhang Cang, minister under the Han dynasty, discovered by chance a very simple method: he used to suck his wife's milk, and thus lived up to a hundred and eighty years" (Chapter 5). (*Book of Han* [*Han shu*], written in the 1st century CE). However, the author exaggerated the effect of this particular practice, for the *Book of Han* talks about it being 'only' a hundred and twenty years.

The longest and perhaps most interesting passage about sex in Ge Hong's work is a kind of poem, willingly obscure but full of imagery. Just like many ancient Taoist texts, one needs a number of clues to understand its exact meaning, but most of them have long disappeared, and we can only call upon our imagination in order to appreciate this pure piece of erotic poetry:

"He chews and sips the precious flower,
In the infinite sky purifies his mind,
Outside himself meditates on the five lights,
Inside himself preserves his nine essences;
He reinforces the jade lock into the gate of life,
Links the pole star to the yellow court,
And brings the three lights into his clear room.
The breath of the origin flies to him and purifies his body,
On his golden beam he collects the divine liquor,
Repudiating the white forever and retaining the black,
He freezes his limpid fountain into his cinnabar field,
And leads his submerged pearls to the five cities.

The alabaster cauldron comes down onto the furnace,
The adorned bird raises its head and cries;
The jasper flower raises its ear,
The heavenly deer spits out jade.
He keeps the primal laws in his scarlet palace,
Conceals the nine lights in the darkness of his cave,
The cloud loft increases and joins heaven,
The long valley fills itself and the fabrics are mixed.
(...)
He sits down, then lies in his purple chamber,
Chews and sucks the golden flower,
Shining autumn mushroom,
Rosy flower and emerald stalk,
Precious ointment clear and pure,
Quiet overflowing and continuous rain from the clouds.
He appeases his hunger, quenches his thirst,
Travels to the heart of things,
Nourishes himself with peace and harmony,
And retains *hun* and *po* souls.
Filled are his bones, light his body,
He can whip wind and clouds to fly up to the sky,
And ride the chariot of chaos and live eternally."
(Chapter 5)

Biography

Ge Hong was born in Jurong in 283 to an influential family. He became a minor southern official during the Jin dynasty but often retreated for years at a time to Mount Luofu where he did most of his writing. He died there in 343.

PHILIPPE CHE

Further Reading

Che, Philippe. *La Voie des Divins, Immortels, les chapitres discursifs du Baopuzi neipian*. Gallimard, Paris, 1999.
Needham, Joseph. *Science and Civilisation in China*. vol. 5/3, Cambridge, 1976.
Saley, Jay. *The Master who Embraces Simplicity: A Study of the philosopher Ko Hung, A.D. 283–343*, Chinese Materials Center, San Francisco, 1978.
W, James. *Alchemy, Medicine and Religion in the China of A.D. 320, the Nei p'ien of Ko Hung*. Cambridge, MA:MIT Press, 1966; New York, 1981.
Van Gulik, Robert. *Sexual life in ancient China*. E.J. Brill, Leiden, 1961.

GENDER

Gender Roles in Erotica

From ancient erotica to modern-day erotica, male and female sexuality takes a wide variety of guises. Whores are to be found in brothels; virgins wait in family homes to be seduced by libertines; gullible virtuous nuns find their introduction into libidinous abandonment through secular paramours or villainous priests; female flagellants are found in parlours, boarding-schools, and vice dens disciplining their charges; while morally unencumbered rustic peasants occupy the Arcadian landscapes free from guilt. All of these images present complex views about gender and male/female sexuality.

Gender disparities are distinctly evident in the treatment of the sexual roles of men and women. Women were, and continue to be, portrayed alternately as passive/submissive, wild/passionate, Madonna/Whore in ancient and modern depictions. In erotica, frequently, women are seen as being overpowered by men, a line which followed the sexual attitude dominant in society throughout the ages. However, as well as indulging in the conquered virgin themes (see *Virginity*), erotica frequently transgresses these traditional submissive roles, depicting women as sexually assertive or as unbridled nymphomaniacs. More recently, from seventeenth-century erotica onwards, both qualities are combined in anti-religious erotica, as seen in the nun's character in *Venus in the Cloister* (French original, 1683; English reprint, 1692). The innocent female *religieuse* is initially portrayed as submissive, gullible, and a victim. Once introduced to sex, she becomes as lascivious as the other female characters, their sexual downfall being blamed on the men. The male religious characters are invariably cast in a poor light, as tyrannical debauchers of young innocent girls. This was a reflection of seventeenth- and eighteenth-century anti-Catholic sentiment which fired the production of images of sexually depraved priests.

The notion of an essential female lasciviousness is routinely expressed throughout erotica.

Women have long been believed to be connected to nature and, as such, have been portrayed seen as unrestrained and sexual wanton. For example, the landscaped female (a concept influenced by the ancients such as Ovid) was updated in the eighteenth century. In *A New Description of Merryland* (1741) the land is depicted as wild, unpredictable, and unruly, echoing the uncontrollable force of the Hippocratic humoral female body. The female flagellant as seen in *Exhibition of Female Flagellants* (1777; J.C. Hotten reprint, 1872) is dominant, elegant, and refined whilst gradually unleashing her passions. In twentieth-century erotica, the female dominatrix clad in leather wielding a whip has overshadowed the more refined version of the eighteenth-century flagellant.

The most prominent image of masculinity was, and still is, one of self-possession and control, the polar opposite of its female counterpart. The male body is often depicted as the principal force for reproduction, as in *Arbor Vitae, Or the Natural History of the Tree of Life* (1732); conversely in some erotic satire, men are made completely redundant, as in John Hill's *Lucina Sine Concubita* (1750), in which women reproduce independently via parthenogenesis, echoing men's concern over female sexual autonomy. Although men are frequently depicted as aggressors, despite their control and power within the sexual hierarchy, they are often seen as less energetic sexually and easier to weaken physically. Erotica through the centuries has contained subtle warnings to men to be restrained or women would sap their strength.

By the nineteenth century, erotica was becoming increasingly aggressive. Rape themes became more common and included violent scenes which placed women in a subordinate role. A further change over the last two hundred years can be seen in flagellation fantasies. In the eighteenth century, women were the most likely victims of the female dominatrix character but during the Victorian era, men were also being depicted in roles of both victim and aggressor.

Homosexuality is rarely mentioned in seventeenth- and eighteenth-century erotica, except disparagingly. By the nineteenth century, explorations of homosexual love are being made in works such as *Teleny, or the Reverse of the Medal* (1893), a work by a number of authors, one of whom is sometimes said to have been Oscar Wilde; and *Priapeia* (1889).

Gender and Readership

It is generally assumed that erotica was traditionally written and read by men. It is generally well-known that in eighteenth-century England, groups of libertines such as Sir Francis Dashwood, Paul Whitehead, John Wilkes, and the members of a notorious "hell-fire" club kept an extensive library of erotica. However, there is plenty of evidence to suggest that women both wrote and read erotica.

Seventeenth and eighteenth-century erotica frequently targeted women in their prefaces with an "address to the ladies" indicating that the writers of erotica either aimed their material at a female readership or wished to create the allusion of one in order to add another layer of fantasy for male readers. Female characters in *Venus in the Cloister*, Thérèse Philosophe (1748) and *Memoirs of a Woman of Pleasure* (1749) are depicted as enjoying pornographic books. Mainstream books also portrayed women as reading erotica, as in Fielding's fictional *Shamela* (1741) who favored *Venus in the Cloister*.

Although the creation of a female persona who read about sex was a literary device in order to establish the sexual nature of a character, evidence exists that some women were writers and readers of erotica. Sarah Lennox liked to read anything she regarded as "wicked," such as Voltaire's *Candide* (1759) or the pornographic *le Canapé* (1741) of which she exclaimed, "Tis the filthiest most disagreeable book I have ever read." Women gave and received pornographic books and particularly appreciated fine copies. Women read about sexual intrigues in women's magazines which occasionally carried risqué trial reports, racy poems, and sexual satires. Francis Place noted that *The Ladies Magazine*: or, *The Universal Entertainer* (1749–1753) carried all three, including Hill's *Lucina Sine Concubitu*. The anonymous late seventeenth-century sex guide, *Aristotle's Master-Piece*, was thought decent enough to give as a present to engaged couples despite the fact that young apprentices masturbated over it.

Women also played a role in its publication. Paula McDowell has traced the activity of women in Grub Street between 1678–1730 whence erotica emanated. During the 1980s, the debate about reading erotica became a complicated feminist debate with dispute over the opinions of Dworkin and McKinnon who posited the view that pornography is a violence against women and should be banned. This ignores the notion that some women want to continue enjoying reading it. By the turn of the twentieth century, it was clear that many women wrote and read pornography and female fantasies were more likely to be included in erotica for the enjoyment of women.

Transvestism itself has a long history (see *Transvestism*) but transexuality has become a more prominent issue in the west towards the end of the twentieth century, although 'Lady Boys' have a much longer standing history in the east in places such as Thailand and India. With the advent of the Internet, pictures and scenes of transsexuals within an erotica content have become common-place and add to a distinctly more diversified understanding of gender, in which gender is no longer a bipolarized state but is made up of many layers of self-identification.

JULIE PEAKMAN

Further Reading

Butler, Judith. *Gender Trouble. Feminism and the Subversion of Identity*. London: Routledge, 1990.
Corfield, Penelope. "History and the Challenge of Gender History." In *Rethinking History*, Vol. 1, No. 3 (1997), pp. 241–258.
Darnton, Robert. *The Forbidden Best-Sellers of Pre-Revolutionary France*. London: HarperCollins, 1997.
Dworkin Andrea. *Pornography: Men Possessing Women*. London: Women's Press, 1981.
Foxon, David. *Libertine Literature in England 1660–1745*. New York: University Books, 1965.
Goulemot, Jean Marie. *Forbidden Texts. Erotic Literature and its Readers in Eighteenth-Century France*. Cambridge: Polity Press, 1994.
Kendrick, Walter. *The Secret Museum: Pornography in Modern Culture*. New York: Penguin, 1987.
Kraakman, Dorelies. "A Historical History of Sexual Knowledge for Girls in French Erotic Fiction, 1750–1840." *Journal of the History of Sexuality*, Vol. 4, No. 4, 1994.
Laqueur, Thomas. *Making Sex. Body and Gender from the Greeks to Freud*. Cambridge, MA: Harvard University Press, 1992.

MacKinnon, Catherine A. *Only Words.* Cambridge: Cambridge University Press, 1993.

Marcus, Steven. *The Other Victorians: A Study of Sexuality and Pornography in Mid-Nineteenth Century England.* New York: Basic 1964.

Moulton, Ian Frederick. *Before Pornography: Erotic Writings in Early Modern England.* Oxford: Oxford University Press, 2000.

Porter, Roy and Lesley Hall. *Facts of Life. The Creation of Sexual Knowledge in Britain, 1650–1950.* New Haven and London: Yale University Press, 1995.

McDowell, Paula, *The Women of Grub Street. Press, Politics and Gender in the London Literary Marketplace 1678–1730.* Oxford: Oxford University Press, 1998.

Norberg, Kathryn. "The Libertine Whore: Prostitution in French Pornography from Margot to Juliette" in Lynn Hunt (editor). *The Invention of Pornography: Obscenity and the Origins of Modernity, 1500–1800,* New York: Zone Books, 1993.

Peakman, Julie. *Mighty Lewd Books: The Development of Pornography in 18th Century England.* London, Palgrave, 2003.

Peakman, Julie. *Lascivious Bodies: A Sexual History of the Eighteenth Century.* London, Atlantic, 2004.

Sigel, Lisa Z. "Name Your Pleasure: The Transformation of Sexual Language in Nineteenth-Century Pornography." *Journal of the History of Sexuality*, Vol. 9. No. 4, October 2000.

Tillyard, Stella. *Aristocrats: Caroline, Emily, Louisa and Sarah Lennox 1740–1832.* London: Vintage, 1995.

Trumbach, Randolph. *Sex and the Gender Revolution. Heterosexuality and the Third Gender in Enlightenment London.* Chicago and London: University of Chicago Press, 1998.

GENET, JEAN

1910–1986
French novelist and dramatist

Genet's work is remarkable for the incendiary tone which characterizes plays, novels, and rhetorical essays alike. Although Genet shocks through the explicit depiction of gay sex, sexuality is always accompanied in his work by the shadow of criminality: the *Journal du voleur* tells the story of a homosexual thief and prostitute who wanders across Europe in a state of unremitting poverty and extreme solitude. Because of the correspondence of the narrative to the myth surrounding Genet in the post-war years, and in part due to Jean-Paul Sartre's account of Genet's life and work, the book has frequently been considered as an autobiography. While the links between Genet's own lived experience and the events of the *Journal* are more problematic than at first appears, the *Journal* is central to Genet's concerns in its juxtaposition of criminality and homosexual identity.

Notre-Dame-des-Fleurs (1948) is set in gay Montmartre, and is concerned, like most of Genet's fiction, with relationships of power as well as with sexuality. The relations of the drag queens and their lovers and pimps operate according to a rigid social framework. Here, as in Genet's prison fiction (notably *Miracle de la rose* (1946)), passive homosexuals occupy the lowest position in the hierarchy. In the homosexual *milieu* of the prison or the penal colony, social hierarchies are reproduced: the prisoners adopt a strict, self-imposed pecking order in which specific roles are adhered to. Prisoners are categorized according to active or passive roles in sex, the despised "cloche" becoming a chattel borne proudly by the dominant "marle." In *Notre-Dame-des-Fleurs*, passive partners and queens are *not* simply promoted to the most powerful roles in an effort to reverse preconceptions regarding their status. Much of the subtlety and power of Genet's work lies instead in the insidious confusion wrought in power relations by those who are apparently most marginalized by them. In a Montmartre café, Divine, the queen upon whom the narrative centers, is gushing with camp eloquence when her false teeth fall out. Placing them upon her head, she reverses the humiliation of the situation, announcing "je serai reine quand même." The humiliating stigmatization of gay characters paradoxically becomes the means by which their identity is most powerfully asserted.

Genet's most famous works, the plays *Les bonnes, Le balcon,* and *Les nègres,* go still further in questioning the social categorization of sexual behavior. In *Le balcon,* sexual role-play consists of assuming the trappings of the different representatives of social authority who pass through Madam Irma's brothel, including the General, the Chief of Police, and the Bishop. While the "real" action (including a muted revolution) is happening elsewhere, the main players in that action periodically return to the brothel. Each is crucially dependent on the baroque fantasy realm which it creates: when the General rides into a fantasized battle on the back of one of the prostitutes, sex has become simply the means of assuming identities, of projecting images. The radical sidelining of the "real" produces the uncomfortable suspicion that the real is forged precisely *within* the deluded role-play of the brothel scenes. The array of appearances and uniforms denoting social authority exactly mirrors those in the brothel, and their bearers' identities can only be maintained through the theatrical performances which the brothel permits. The sexual becomes the domain in which the inherent theatricality of power structures is exposed.

Elsewhere, meanwhile, sexuality is an aberrant field in which power is no longer functional. For most of the *Journal du voleur,* power relations seem to have been abandoned entirely: it seems that everything that Genet's character "Jean" does will, instead of redeeming him, drag him further into social and sexual humiliation. The scandalous war-time novel *Pompes funèbres* (1947), meanwhile, contains Genet's most graphic and complex treatment of sex, including ludicrous vignettes of Hitler engaged in a variety of sexual acts. Homosexuality is an essential part of Genet's universe and yet it is betrayal, more than solidarity, that characterizes the relationships of his gay characters. In *Pompes funèbres,* the narrator-protagonist is trying to come to terms with the death of his lover, Jean Decarnin, killed by the Nazi militia. His extraordinary solution is the fantastic creation of Riton, the militia man whom he imagines to have killed Jean, and who becomes the subject of extended sexual fantasies; in order to take control of his grief at the death of Jean, the narrator perversely exacerbates it, striving to make of his imaginary betrayal of Jean the site of an ironic pleasure. The narrator's ruminations on Riton's sexual relationships are imbued with a powerful charge which hovers between eroticism and violence. Although *Pompes Funèbres* is perhaps Genet's most explicit and barbed book, it resonates with his other novels in its exploration of sexuality as an arena in which power relations may be played out, tested, and ironised. The quasi-erotic betrayal of Jean is a means of mastering the fact of Jean's death, and therefore of reversing the condition of disempowerment which it entails.

Biography

Born Paris, 1910. Given up to the *Assistance Publique* by his mother; raised by a foster family in the Morvan region; primary school education. Abortive apprenticeships; runs away and is sent to the children's penal colony Mettray (Tours region), 1926; Signs up for the army, 1929; Postings in Syria and Morocco; deserts, 1936. Series of journeys through Europe, including Italy, Albania, Yugoslavia, Austria, Czechoslovakia, Poland, and Germany. Returns to France and is imprisoned, 1938. Dates the beginning of his writing from this period. Meets Cocteau and Sartre, 1943–1944. Publication and premier of Genet's play *Les bonnes,* 1947. Publication of novels *Miracle de la rose* (1946), *Pompes funèbres* (1947), and *Notre-Dame-des-Fleurs* (1948). Publication of *Journal du voleur,* in part based on wanderings in the thirties, 1949. Directs *Un Chant d'amour,* the only film which he will both write and bring to fruition, 1950. Publication of Jean-Paul Sartre's *Saint Genet: comédien et martyr,* Sartre's "existentialist biography" of Genet, announced as the first volume of Genet's *Œuvres complètes,* 1952. Publication of the plays *Le Balcon* (1956) and *Les nègres* (1958). First Paris performance of *Les paravents,* at the Odéon, accompanied by violent protests due to its portrayal of the French military and of the Algerian War, 1966. Genet's first major political writings, 1968. Involvement with the Black Panthers and with the Palestinian cause, 1970. Publication of *Quatre heures à Chatila,* one of Genet's most important political pieces, concerning the massacre of Palestinians at Chatila refugee camp, 1983. Death (Paris), 15th April 1986. Posthumous publication of *Un captif amoureux,* 1986.

DAVID HOUSTON JONES

Selected Works

Miracle de la Rose (Paris: Marc Barbezat-L'Arbalète, 1946); as *Miracle of the Rose,* translated by Bernard Frechtman (London: Faber, 1973).

Les Bonnes (Paris: Marc Barbezat-L'Arbalète, 1947); as *The Maids,* translated by Bernard Frechtman (London: Faber, 1953).

Pompes Funèbres (Paris: Gallimard, L'Imaginaire, 1947); as *Funeral Rites,* translated by Bernard Frechtman (London: Faber, 1969).

Notre-Dame-des-Fleurs (Paris: Marc Barbezat-L'Arbalète, 1948); as *Our Lady of the Flowers,* translated by Bernard Frechtman (London: Paladin, 1963).

Journal du voleur (Paris: Gallimard, 1949); as *The Thief's Journal,* translated by Bernard Frechtman (London: Faber, 1965).

Les Paravents (Paris: Marc Barbezat-L'Arbalète, 1961); as *The Screens,* translated by Bernard Frechtman (London: Faber, 1963).

Querelle de Brest (Paris: Gallimard, L'Imaginaire, 1953); as *Querelle of Brest,* translated by Gregory Streatham (London: Blond, 1966).

Oeuvres Complètes 6 vols. (Paris: Gallimard, 1952–1991).

Further Reading

Bersani, Leo. *Homos*. Cambridge, MA: Harvard University Press, 1995.

Bickel, Gisèle A. *Jean Genet: Criminalité et transcendance*. Saratoga: Anima Libri, 1987.

Bougon, Patrice. 'Le travail des mots et la décomposition narrative dans *Pompes Funèbres.*' *Roman 20/50,* 20 1995.

——— 'Le cliché, la métaphore et la digression dans *Pompes Funèbres* et *Un Captif amoureux.*' *L'Esprit créateur*, 35, no. 1, 1995.

Bradby, David. *Modern French Drama 1940–1990*. Cambridge: Cambridge University Press, 1990.

Coe, Richard N. *The Vision of Jean Genet* London: Peter Owen, 1968.

Creech, James. 'Outing Jean Genet.' *Yale French Studies*, special issue, *Genet: In the Language of the Enemy*, ed. Scott Durham. 91, 1997.

Davis, Colin. 'Genet's *Journal du Voleur* and the Ethics of Reading.' *French Studies,* XLVIII, no. 1 (January 1994), 50–62.

Davis, Colin. *Ethical Issues in Twentieth-Century French Fiction: Killing the Other*. Basingstoke: Macmillan, 2000.

Dichy, Albert and Pascal Fouché. *Jean Genet: Essai de chronologie 1910–1944*. Paris: Bibliothèque de littérature française contemporaine de l'université de Paris VII, 1988.

Durham, Scott (ed.) *Yale French Studies*, special issue, *Genet: in the Language of the Enemy,* 91, 1997.

Fredette, Nathalie. 'Jean Genet: les Pouvoirs de l'Imposture.' *Etudes Françaises*, 31/3 (1995–1996), 87–101.

Gaitet, Pascale. 'The Politics of Camp in Jean Genet's *Our Lady of the Flowers*' in Bougon (ed.) *L'Esprit créateur,* numéro spécial, *Jean Genet: Littérature et Politique,* 35, no. 1 (1995), 40–49.

Jones, David Houston. *The Body Abject: Self and Text in Jean Genet and Samuel Beckett*. Oxford: Lang, 2000.

Knapp, Bettina L. *Jean Genet*. Boston: Twayne, 1989.

Lucey, Michael. 'Genet's *Notre-Dame-des-fleurs*: Fantasy and Sexual Identity.' *Yale French Studies,* special issue, *Genet: In the Language of the Enemy*, ed. Scott Durham. 91 (1997), 80–102.

Magedera, Ian. '*Seing* Genet: a propos *Glas* by Jacques Derrida.' *Paragraph,* 21, no. 1 (March 1998), 28–44.

Magazine Littéraire, numéro spécial, *Jean Genet,* no. 313 (septembre 1993).

Meitinger, Serge. 'L'Irréel de jouissance dans le *Journal du Voleur* de Genet.' *Littérature,* no. 62 (mai 1986), pp. 65–74.

Millot, Cathérine. *Gide, Genet, Mishima: Intelligence de la perversion*. Paris: Gallimard, 1996.

Oswald, Laura. *Jean Genet and the Semiotics of Performance*. Bloomington, IN: Indiana University Press, 1989.

Read, Barbara (ed.). with Ian Birchall. *Flowers and Revolution: A Collection of Writings on Jean Genet*. London: Middlesex University Press, 1997.

Robinson, Christopher. *Scandal in the Ink: Male and Female Homosexuality in Twentieth-Century French Literature*. London: Cassell, 1995.

Roman 20/50. numéro spécial, *Jean Genet,* no. 20 (décembre 1995).

Running-Johnson, Cynthia. 'Genet's "Excessive" Double: Reading "Les Bonnes" through Irigaray and Cixous.' *French Review,* 63, no. 6 (1990), 959–966.

Sheringham, Michael. 'Narration and Experience in Genet's *Journal du Voleur*' in Robert Gibson (ed.) *Studies in French Fiction in Honour of Vivienne Mylne*. London: Grant and Cutler, 1988.

Stewart, Harry E., and Rob Roy McGregor. *Jean Genet: A Biography of Deceit 1910–1951*. New York: Peter Lang, 1989.

Thody, Philip. *Jean Genet: A Study of His Novels and Plays*. London: Hamish Hamilton, 1968.

Watts, Philip. 'Political Discourse and Poetic Register in Jean Genet's *Pompes Funèbres.*' *French Forum,* 17, no. 2 (May 1992), 191–203.

White, Edmund. *Genet*. London: Picador, 1994.

GEORGE, STEFAN

1868–1933
German poet

From his earliest verses, written when he was still a schoolboy, to his last collection, published in 1928, Stefan George's poetry bears witness to his same-sex inclinations. Although the nascent homosexual rights movement claimed him as one of their own as early as 1914, for decades later critics preferred to overlook this pervasive aspect of George's poetry. In 1987, Marita Keilson-Lauritz corrected these decades of homophobia in her work *Von der Liebe, die Freundschaft heißt: zur Homoerotik im Werk Stefan Georges* [*On the love called friendship: the homoerotic in Stefan George's work*]. As Keilson-Lauritz mentions in *A Companion to the Works of Stefan George*, "there is no doubt that the concept of love in the texts of Stefan George is a homoerotic one. That is to say, even if George never would have called himself a 'homosexual,' the main subject of his texts is love of men and boys."

George's earlier work is symbolist, having been strongly influenced by Mallarmé and his circle. The collections *Hymnen* [*Hymns*], (1890), *Pilgerfahrten* [*Pilgrimages*], (1891), *Algabal* (1892), and *Die Bücher der Hirten-und Preisgedichte* [*The Book of Eclogues and Eulogies*], (1894) reflect this influence of symbolism, an influence which ends with the publication of *Das Jahr der Seele* [*The Year of the Soul*], (1897) and *Der Teppich des Lebens* [*The Tapestry of Life*], (1900). In this earlier period many poems dealing with queer desire and identity do so in a decadentist and medievalist context. This picture changed in 1902 when George met the precocious 14-year-old Maximilian Kronberger, who died of meningitis two years after. George deified the youth as "Maximin" in *Der siebente Ring* [*The Seventh Ring*], (1907) and in subsequent collections, *Der Stern des Bundes* [*The Star of the Covenant*], (1914) and *Das neue Reich* [*The New Empire*], (1928). Here George expressed queer sexuality often in more religious language representing an increasing vatic and pedagogical vocation in his late work.

Queer sexuality in all of his poetry is, however, strategically disguised. George dubbed this "übergeschlechtliche Liebe" [supersexual love], encompassing homosexual love, platonic love, friendship, and love transcending sex, gender, and age, all frequently connected to "lust und pein" [lust and pain]. As Keilson-Lauritz notes, one of George's strategic disguises lies in the use of the gender-neutral second person singular. The poet also played with ambiguous metaphors and allegory. Far beyond simply creating ornamental and ultimately substitutable lexical deviance, George's use of metaphor helps to blur the boundaries of gender and desire. His poetry grapples with the tension between the heterosexist reality of Wilhelmine Germany and a repressed same-sex sensitivity.

These strategies both mask and signal a profound social conflict. Since George lived in a period of extreme social, political, and economic change, this is particularly significant. His times saw strong challenges to conventional concepts of sex, gender, and sexuality fueled by the emergence of the sexology of Tardieu, Ulrichs, Westphal, Tamassia, Charcot, Magnan, Havelock Ellis, Krafft-Ebing, Raffalovich, and others. The growth of psychoanalysis added further to this competition of ideas. Magnus Hirschfeld's *Jahrbuch für sexuelle Zwischenstufen* [*Yearbook for Intermediary Sexual Stages*] appeared at roughly the same time as George's *Blätter*, 1899 to 1923, and Freud published his *Drei Abhandlungen zur Sexualtheorie* [*Three Essays on the Theory of Sexuality*] in 1905, only two years before George's *Der siebente Ring*.

As homosexual acts were still outlawed in Germany, however, the fear of being singled out makes George's preference for metaphor and more oblique forms of presentation understandable as self-protection. George's oblique expression contrasts sharply with the direct autobiographical articulation championed by his contemporaries. This allowed George to deal with a variety of queer subjects such as pederasty (in poems like "Sieh mein Kind ich gehe" [See my child, I leave] and "Mein kind kam heim" [My child came home]), hermaphroditism (So sprach ich nur in meinen schwersten tagen [These words were said when living was a loss], "Der du uns aus der qual der zweiheit löstest" [You took away the pain of inner schism], "Ist dies der knabe längster sage" [Is this the boy of oldest legend], and "Ich bin der Eine und bin Beide" [I am the One, I am the Two]), and sadomasochism ("So werd ich immer harren und verschmachten" [And must I always thirst and wait], "Lobgesang" [Encomium], "Empfängnis" [Conception]). While accepting same-sex sexuality and other queer phenomena as neither pathological nor sinful and reviving Greek models of platonic love and love of boys, the range of queer *performativity* and the complexity of the queer strategies at work nonetheless betray an internalization of late nineteenth- and early twentieth-century European scientific and religious discourses on sexuality.

This multifaceted treatment of same-sex eroticism, which found its real-life corollary in the ambiguous cultural politics of the male-bonded George-*Kreis*, makes George a *moderne à contrecœur*. His work, despite its general antimodernist position, fits into the larger picture of queer modernist poetry by Verlaine, Rimbaud, Cavafy, Kuzmin, Lorca, Crane, Saba, Cernuda, and the like. The elitist forms of *Männerphantasien* inherent in George's eroticism, torn between utter devotion and self-preservation, also place him in the aesthetic and moral vicinity of Jean Genet, who might at first glance appear to be an antipode.

In the still topical controversy surrounding George that resulted from the Nazi appropriation of his work, it is a *vérité inavouable* for certain apologists that his work has a protofascist character and that his treatment of same-sex eroticism relates to this character. Other critics who consider George an ideological precursor of Nazism have usually done so from a heterosexist perspective. However, the link between George's notion of a "Secret Germany" and his understanding of sexuality must be avowed. Thus a queer—not gay hagiographic—approach to George's output and its wider political ramifications becomes all the more necessary.

Biography

Born into a Catholic family of wine merchants of partly French heritage in the village of Büdesheim near Bingen, Germany, 12 July 1868. Attended Gymnasium in Darmstadt (1882–1888), becoming proficient in Greek and Latin while continuing courses in French and English, and teaching himself Norwegian and Italian. Upon graduating, traveled throughout Europe. In Paris (1889) met Albert Saint-Paul, Paul Verlaine, Stéphane Mallarmé, and other symbolist poets. Subsequently studied Romance literature for three semesters at Friedrich-Wilhelm University in Berlin (1889–1891). While in Berlin, cofounded the *Blätter für die Kunst* [Pages for Art], which was to become a prominent literary journal in the years between 1892 and 1919. In 1891, met Hugo von Hofmannsthal in Vienna, starting an intensive friendship lasting until 1906. All through the rest of his life remained a wanderer, continually on the move mainly between Heidelberg, Munich, Berlin, and Switzerland. In 1927, received the Goethe Prize of the city of Frankfurt am Main. In 1933, declined the Nazis's offer of membership in the Preussische Dichterakademie, reflecting a complex antipathy and sympathy for German National Socialism. Died near Locarno, Switzerland, on December 4, 1933.

MAX D. KRAMER

Selected Works

The Works of Stefan George. Translated by Olga Marx and Ernst Morwitz. New York: AMS Press, 1966 (first edition 1949).
Poems. Bilingual edition translated by Carol North Valhope and Ernst Morwitz. New York: Schocken, 1967 (first edition 1943).

Further Reading

Aarts, Jan. "Alfred Schuler, Stefan George and Their Different Grounds in the Debate on Homosexuality at the Turn of the Century in Germany." *Among Men, Among Women,* (editors: Mattias Duyves et al.). Amsterdam: Sociologisch Instituut, 1983.
David, Claude. *Stefan George, son œuvre poétique.* Lyon: IAC, 1952; as *Stefan George. Sein dichterisches Werk,* translated into German by Alexa Remmen and Karl Thiemer. Munich: Carl Hanser, 1967.
Hamecher, Peter. "Der männliche Eros im Werke Stefan Georges." *Jahrbuch für sexuelle Zwischenstufen,* 14 (1914).

Keilson-Lauritz, Marita. *Von der Liebe, die Freundschaft heißt: zur Homoerotik im Werk Stefan Georges.* Berlin: Rosa Winkel, 1987.

Kiefer, Otto. "Der Eros bei Stefan George." *Geschlecht und Gesellschaft*, 14 (1926/1927).

Norton, Robert E. *Secret Germany: Stefan George and His Circle.* Ithaca, NY: Cornell University Press, 2002.

Rieckmann, Jens (editor). *A Companion to the Works of Stefan George.* Rochester, NY: Camden House, 2005.

Travers, Martin. "Fascism and Aesthetic Self-Fashioning: Politics and the Ritualised Body in the Poetry of Stefan George." *Renaissance and Modern Studies*, 42 (1999).

GERMAN: TWENTIETH AND TWENTY-FIRST CENTURIES

Erotic literature is defined here as a genre with three progressively explicit types of text: the erotic, the sexual, and the pornographic imaginary in its linguistic expressions and versions; progressively explicit is understood as the representations of the erotic imaginary from the implicit (i.e., erotic) to the more explicit (i.e., sexual) to the most explicit (i.e., pornographic) in content and form. The designation of erotic literature is thus employed as an umbrella term and is understood by the levels of linguistic explicitness of the imaginary from the erotic to the sexual to the pornographic. It is in this context that our focus in describing German-language erotic literature in the twentieth- and the first years of the twenty-first century is to be understood.

While there are many examples of the erotic text in twentieth-century German-language literature, for example passages about Madame Chauchat in Thomas Mann's *Magic Mountain* or in Robert Musil's descriptions of youthful confusions and experiences of sexuality in his novel *Törless* or his allusions to incest in *The Man without Qualities* or in Frank Wedekind's *Pandora's Box*, our focus is on texts where the imaginary, the thematics, and their descriptions are linguistically and in the imaginary explicit from erotic to sexual to pornographic in form and content. It should be mentioned, however, that perhaps the best example of the low-key sensual-erotic belletristic text par excellence in German is Arthur Schnitzler's (1862–1931) *Traumnovelle* (1925) [*Dream Story*, trans. Otto P. Schninnerer, 1927] — the short novel adapted to the film *Eyes Wide Shut* by Stanley Kubrick (1999).

In German-language literature of any period erotic texts as defined here are a minor genre in form, content, and numbers published. For example, while at the end of the eighteenth century German erotic texts acquired the themes and forms of the *roman libertine*, they did not achieve the aesthetic and linguistic elegance of the French texts and that with regard to the nineteenth century — and perhaps even to date — it can be argued that only one author's work, Leopold von Sacher-Masoch's (1836–1895) *Venus im Pelz* [*Venus in Furs*] (1870) has acquired world-wide renown while the memoirs of opera singer Wilhelmine Schröder-Devrient (1804–1869), *Memoiren einer Sängerin* [*Memoirs of an Opera Singer*] (1862), are in some sources noted as the most famous text of German-language erotic literature (although the authorship of *Memoiren einer Sängerin* by Schröder-Devrient is contested). The memoir shows the influence of the Marquis de Sade's *Justine* with numerous descriptions of sadomasochism.

Twentieth-century German-language erotic literature (including the first few years of the new millennium) can be described by the following characteristics: 1) the translation of foreign texts of erotic literature dominates while original German-language texts are scarce; 2) although German-language erotic texts are frequent before World War I, the most active period where erotic texts and the publishing of such occur is in the period of post-World War I to 1933 when the Nazi government is installed, 3) most texts are published in private editions and the criticism that these texts are of popular literary quality when compared with high-brow/canonical texts — as argued by Englisch already in 1927 (see below) — remains a characteristic of the genre up to several decades after World War II, and 4) with the arrival of new media in the 1990s, in online material where text and visuals represent a type of *Gesammtkunstwerk*, an innovative period is in the making whose developments are yet to be seen.

In twentieth-century German literature the most prominent erotic text is *Josefine Mutzenbacher. Lebensgeschichte einer wienerischen Dirne, von ihr selbst erzählt* [*Josephine Mutzenbacher: The Life Story of a Viennese Prostitute, as Told by Herself*] published in 1906 and attributed to the novelist and theater critic Felix Salten (pseudonym of Siegmund Salzmann, 1869–1945). Heavily influenced by Cleland's *Fanny Hill* (1749), the text is written in Viennese dialect with sexual and pornographic descriptions about the heroine's life who by her thirteenth year had already had more than two dozen lovers. A sequel entitled *Josefine Mutzenbacher und ihre 365 Liebhaber* was published in 1925, with similar descriptions of pornographic content. Another text of some renown of the period is C.W. Stern's 1909 collection of thirty tales taken from the fairy tales of the Brothers Grimm where the tales in the collection are re-written in sexualized language. Also interesting is the four-volume translation of the *1001 Arabian Nights* entitled *Tausend und eine Nacht. Arabische Erzählungen* (1913, trans. Gustav Weils, ed. V. Ludwig Fulda, and illustrated by Fernand Schulz-Wettel) where the erotic content is not the text itself but the illustrations. There are also B. Stern's (no relation to C.W. Stern mentioned above) 1908 *Illustrierte Geschichte der erotischen Literatur aller Zeiten und Völker* [*Illustrated History of Erotic Literature of all Times and Peoples*], a compendium with excerpts of texts and with much German-language material and Fritz Foregger's novel published in 1913, *Die Liebespredigt* [*Sermon of Love*] with love poems about oral sex, masochism, homoeroticism, necrophilia, aphrodisiacs, etc.

Since the mid- to late-nineteenth century, when in literature the urban environment and urbanity became dominant themes and the main locus of literature, also in erotic literature it has been city life that has become the most frequent setting and theme. In particular, Berlin and Vienna, the two largest German-speaking cities of Europe, have become both the location of the stories in the texts as well as the location of the publication of the texts. Here are the most prominent examples of this genre of erotic literature: the loves and sexual exploits of the Berlin prostitute are the theme of Richard Werther (pseudonym of Ernst Klein) who has published since 1907 novels such as *Freudenmädchen* [*Women of Pleasure*], *Tagebuch einer Bordelldirne, Lore* [*Diary of a Woman of Pleasure, Lore*], *Durchtollte Nächte, durchjubelte Tage* [*Crazy Nights, Wild Days*], and *Der lüsterne Detektiv* [*The Horny Detective*]. The usual plot is about the exploits of prostitutes in city night life, with the sexual and pornographic description of stereotypical excesses. Another popular novel of the period before World War I, also attributed to Richard Werther, is *Memoiren eines Arztes* [*Memoirs of a Physician*]. Loosely connected descriptions written in a retrospective mode, the story is about a physician whose sexual interest is in under-aged girls and who oversees a sanatorium for women where he enjoys life as a peeping tom. A further example of urbanity and sexuality in literature from the period before World War I is the novel *James Grunert. Ein Roman aus Berlin W* [*James Grunert: A Novel from Berlin West*] (1908) not the least because of the biography of its author, Werner von Bleichröder, who was the son of Bismarck's banker Gerson von Bleichröder (1822–1893), the first Jew who was ennobled without having to convert. Werner von Bleichröder describes in first-person narrative his life as the son of a banker named James Grunert. The novel's setting located in Berlin's high society and aristocracy, James begins his sexual life when as a ten-year-old he is seduced by the mother of one his school friends. Attracted to women with power, Bleichröder's alter ego Grunert's stories are about wild sexual lust in Berlin's affluent upper class including many a coming-of-age young woman. The at times unflattering description of the upper-class teenage women and their sexual promiscuity suggests the author's intention to criticize the Berlin society he obviously knew well as the son of a wealthy banker who in turn has had several kept mistresses.

As mentioned previously, German-language erotic literature of the twentieth century has been dominated by translations: the genre begins with the publication of Pietro Aretino's *I Ragionamenti* [*The Dialogues*] about the life of the courtesan, translated by Heinrich Conrad, published in 1903. Conrad also published the German translation of the prototype of the *roman libertin*, Nicolas Chorier's *Académie de dames*, and Casanova's memoirs. By the 1920s, following the liberalization of society in the Germany of post-World War I including the abolition of censorship in 1918, many French and Italian texts of the Renaissance were published in translation in private editions but also regular publishers took advantage of the new interest of the reading public in erotic literature. For example, the *Decameron* was published in 1924 by the Berlin publisher Neufeld and Henius (translated by Klabund).

A prominent author as translator of classics of erotic literature is Franz Blei (1871–1942; Blei used the pseudonyms Medardus and Dr. Peregrinus Steinhövel) — known today as a supporter of Franz Kafka, Robert Musil, and Hermann Broch, and their literary legacies. During his life, however, Blei was decried as a "pornographer." Blei's translations include Lucian, Laclos's *Liaisons dangereuses*, Vivant Denon's *Point de lendemain*, Antoine de la Salle's *Quinze joyes de marriage*, the amorous poems of Johannes Secundus, etc. In several anthologies, he published mainly French classics of erotic literature but authored erotic comedies himself, wrote commentaries about Franz von Bayros's erotic-sexual drawings, and published various other erotic material in *Ametyst* and *Opale*, magazines he founded. Examples of his own writing of erotic literature include *Lesebuch der Marquise* [*The Reader of the Marquise*] and *Von amourösen Frauen* [*About Women in Love*]. In his autobiography, *Erzählung eines Lebens* [*The Story of a Life*] (1930) he describes his first love with a Viennese girl in sexual detail.

Of importance is that for Blei erotic literature is framed within a social context and in his autobiography he discusses the meanings and functions of social mores in philosophical excursions where one of his arguments is the negation of the moral necessity of monogamy altogether. Further, in a scholarly context, in his *Formen der Liebe* [*Shapes of Love*] (1930), Blei presents in essays his thoughts on the meaning and history of eroticism. Further examples of translations in the period include translations such as the anonymous *Roman de mon alcôve* (1869) translated as *Die Geheimnisse meines Alkovens* (trans. Fred Marr, 1910).

Arguably, the most significant German-language contribution to erotic literature is scholarship and not fiction per se, namely Paul Englisch's 1927 *Geschichte der erotischen Literatur* [*History of Erotic Literature*], a work that to date is considered the largest and most reliable source of the topic. Little is known about the author and the name is likely a pseudonym: he was born in 1887, studied law and accumulated wealth in the retail business, a cultivated man who acquired a large private library. In his history of erotic literature, he defines the genre as "the description of sexually charged feelings of love — owing to the excitation of the nervous system and as a result of the stimulation of sensual desires — to one's self, to one's own gender, or to the opposite sex" (3, trans. Totosy). The book contains shorter chapters about Greek and Roman antiquity, French erotic literature is described in no less than twenty-one chapters whereby the most detailed description is devoted to the eighteenth century, six chapters are devoted to Italian material, and three chapters to English erotic literature while the periods of German erotic literature are detailed up to the 1920s. Non-European erotic literature is discussed in an appendix of the book. In addition to an overwhelming amount of information and detail, Englisch shows no prejudice and mixes descriptions of content with his critical remarks and his observations about historical contexts. Further, in 1932 Englisch published an anthology of erotic short stories, *Anthologie der erotischen Literatur aus vielen Jahrhunderten* [*Anthology of Erotic Literature*], with a preface by Franz Blei, in Vienna (private edition; rpt. in 1966). Blei's preface is of interest because he not only reiterates his objection to monogamy but discusses pornography and argues that owing to its fictional representation of sexual acts, pornography as mere "virtual reality" ought to be understood as a kind of "idealistic romanticism." Although the texts in the anthology are from a wide array of sources and cultural geographies, the selections are mostly tame and even from *Josefine Mutzenbacher*, the selected text is the most unerotic possible.

In German language scholarship about erotic culture, it is of note that for the first two decades of the twentieth century, the best source of primary as well as secondary literature is Hugo Hayn and Alfred N. Gotendorf's eight-volume *Bibliotheca Germanorum erotica et curiosa* (1912–1929). Another scholar whose work is internationally renown is Eduard Fuchs (1870–1940) who published the six-volume *Illustrierte Sittengeschichte vom Mittelalter bis zur Gegenwart* [*An Illustrated History of Morals from the Middle Ages to Contemporary Times*] (1909–1912) and *Geschichte der erotischen Kunst* [*History of Erotic Art*] in 1920. What makes the classification of these works of scholarship erotic literature is the visual representation of sexuality in the books which at the time would have had considerable impact. Although Fuchs's depictions in categories such as "Prostitution in the Renaissance," "The Business of the Brothel," or "The Lust of Monks and Nuns" indicate an intention to polemicize, the pictures would have had undoubtedly an erotic impact on readers and viewers of the time.

In his *History of Erotic Literature*, Englisch credits Fritz Thurn (the pseudonym of either Adolf Gruss or Fritz Foregger) as the best author of erotic literature of 1920s Germany. Thurn's *Weisheiten der Aspasia* [*Aspasia's Wisdom*] (1923) suggest an author with a classical education while at the same time his text attests to his knowledge of the genre aimed at the "Erregung sinnlicher Begierde" [awakening of erotic/sexual desire]. The locus of the novel is ancient Athens and we are in the palace of antiquity's most famous courtesan, Aspasia, later the wife of Pericles. The text is a quasi-historical novel whereby focus is on the description of sexual exploits and pornographic imagery. With Aspasia, the main character is Alcibiades who is invited by Aspasia to partake in her activities as a matron to virgins whom she educates in the art of love, in theory and in practice. Alcibiades participates in Aspasia's lessons by a string of sexual acts such as the defloration of a Spartan prisoner of war and similar exploits and he responds to Aspasia's flirtations with his ability to withhold his orgasm until his lover and himself arrive at the highest levels of pleasure and satisfaction. What is interesting in the narrative is that Thurn's language is elegant and that he uses no common or coarse vocabulary when describing body parts or sexual acts. In the next chapters of the book, Alcibiades is allowed to partake in the lessons Aspasia offers to her young virgins and in eight lessons we read about body hygiene, particularities of the sexual organs, positions of lovemaking, the "auxiliary arts of Aphrodite" (fellatio, the relationship of desire and pain,

etc.), and about the various duties and prescriptions for the behavior of a courtesan. While these descriptions are highly entertaining, the text also includes various stories of sexual escapades, dispersed throughout the narrative and the author's intention is to present auto-reflective responses to his narrative. Perhaps of ironic dimensions is the description of the final scene of an orgy where participants include Aristophanes and Euripides. Aspasia is a complete hostess who satisfies all artistic and life desires of the event which includes members of the Spartan envoy to Athens. Instigated by Pericles, the hosts' objective is to subvert the resolve of the Spartans by engaging them in sexual pleasures in order to have them sign the Athenians' demands for a truce scheduled for the day after. Thus, the text connects the art of love and excesses of desire with politics and art to the common good versus war. The message is, of course, "make love not war," in 1923, an example of the ideas of the 1960s flower generation, here located in antiquity.

Other examples of the erotic novel in the inter-war period include Heinrich Wandt's *Erotik und Spionage in der Etappe Gent* [*Erotica and Espionage in the Headquarters at Gent*] (1929), a novel about the sexual escapades of a group of military officers. A novel of aesthetic quality as well as social and historical value is the autobiographical novel of Erica Fischer, *Aimee und Jaguar. Eine Frauenliebe* [*Aimee and Jaguar: A Women's Love Story*] (1943; rpt. 1994), a novel about lesbian love during World War II in Germany (the novel was adapted to film, directed by Max Farberbock [1999]). A prominent example of fetishist literature is Hanns von Leydenegg's 1932 *Der gestiefelte Eros. Lebensbeichte eines Schuhfetischisten* [*Eros with Boots: Confessions of A Shoefetishist*], illustrated by Paul Kamm, a text about transvestitism, flagellation, etc.

In the history of sexuality in general, the work of Magnus Hirschfeld (1868–1935) is of great importance. An early scholar of sexuality, Hirschfeld has published—primarily for scholarly as well as educational purposes— much work in the field, for example his *Die Homosexualität des Mannes und des Weibes* [*Male and Female Homosexuality*] (1914), the annual of scholarship *Jahrbuch für sexuelle Zwischenstufen* (1899–1923), the learned journal *Zeitschrift für Sexualwissenschaft* [*Journal of Scholarship about Sexuality*] (1908–1913) as well as, with Maria

Krische, the educational magazine *Die Aufklär-ung* [*Enlightenment*; with the parallel meaning of sexual education] (1929–1930), and his principal work, *Die Geschlechtskunde* [*Study of the Sexes*] (1926). Further, Hirschfeld cooperated in the making of Richard Oswald's 1919 film about homosexuality, *Anders als die Anderen* [*Different from the Others*] and founded the world's first institute of research into sexuality, the Berlin Institute for Sexual Science (Institut für Sexual-wissenschaft), 1919–1933. Hirschfeld frequented the avant-garde group of the "Friedrichshagener Dichterkreis" in the 1890s where many other writers, intellectuals, and artists congregated, such as Lou Andreas-Salomé, Max Baginski, Leo Berg, Max Dauthendey, Gerhart Haupt-mann, August Strindberg, Rudolf Steiner, or Frank Wedekind for example, and many of whom have published various genres of texts with erotic or sexual content. In 1931, Hirschfeld went on an American lecture tour and at the time he was hailed as the leading expert of the field. A practicing homosexual, Hirschfeld sup-ported the theory that hormones may be a source of homosexuality and his notions led other researchers to attempt to cure homosexu-ality with hormone injections. Hirschfeld died in exile in France and his Institute was destroyed by the Nazis. Among numerous other publica-tions by Hirschfeld and his collaborators, the educational and scientific journal *Die Ehe* [*Mar-riage*], edited by Ludwig Levy-Lenz 1929–1932 is of note (the journal contained a large amount of nude photography. Founded in 1982, Hirsch-feld's legacy is continued with the Magnus-Hirschfeld-Gesellschaft in Berlin. In a similar way, in the intersections of culture and erotic literature, the efforts and successes of feminist and pacifist Helene Stöcker (1869–1943) are to be mentioned because of her work in women's rights and women's sexuality: Stöcker's autobio-graphical novel *Liebe* [*Love*] (1922) contains many of her ideas about women's sexuality, for example. With the arrival of the Nazi govern-ment in 1933, all eroticism and of course sexual-ity and pornography, literary or other, have been banned and destroyed.

After World War II, the work of 1999 Nobel Prize recipient Günter Grass (1927–) — for ex-ample, *Die Blechtrommel* (1959) [*The Tin Drum*, trans. Ralph Manheim] (1962), *Der Butt* (1977), [*The Flounder*, trans. Ralph Manheim] (1985), etc. — are of relevance of the first order as they contain numerous sexual and pornographic descriptions.

In the context of the sexual revolution it was, in particular, the business activities of one woman, Beate Uhse (1919–2001), who contribu-ted much towards the acceptance of erotic culture in Germany, first via a mail-order company and later in sex shops, in cities throughout the coun-try, where books and now, of course, videos and magazines of pornographic content are sold. The quality of printed material sold in the Beate Uhse shops is mostly in the category of popular/vulgar pornography. The Beate Uhse Erotic Museum in Berlin exhibits excellent material from the pop-ular to the highly artistic: for instance, the museum's first catalogue *Sodom Berlin* (2002) is interesting as it contains an essay, "*Sodom Berlin*: Berlin as a Place of Eroticism and Erotic Art" by Hans Jürgen Döpp, and a series of reproductions of sexual and pornographic drawings by artists such as Charlotte Berend-Corinth (1880–1967), Michel Fingesten (1884–1943), George Grosz (1893–1959), Rudolf Schlichter (1890–1955), Erich Goldmann (1899–?), Otto Schoff (1884–1938), Hans Bellmer (1902–1975), and draw-ings by artists whose biographies are to date as yet unknown such as "Ernst Gerhard" and "Hildebrandt."

In the genre of popularizing knowledge about sexuality is the work of Oswald Kolle, who in the 1960s and 1970s published popular books and appeared in films where he attempted to explain the mysteries of relationships and sexu-ality (Kolle, in his '70s, lives in Amsterdam today). In the 1970s, the sexual prose about lesbian sadomasochism by Marlene Stenten (1935–) found a following with her novel *Albina. Monotonie um eine Weggegangene* [*Albina: Mo-notony about One Gone Away*] (1986) and in the 1980s Elfriede Jelinek's (1946–) novel *Lust* [*Lust*] (1989) and Brigitte Blobel's (1942–) col-lection of erotic short stories in *Venusmuschel* (1982) received acclaim as well as created debate and controversy. Of interest are also texts by Dorothea Zeemann (a.k.a Dora Holzinger, 1909–1993), theater critic, novelist, journalist, nurse, and author of two autobiographies *Einü-bung in Katastrophen* [*Practice in Catastrophe*] (1979) and *Jungfrau und Reptil* [*Virgin and Reptile*] (1982) where she describes in sexual detail her affair with the novelist Heimito von Dodererand author of the trilogy *Das heim-liche Fest* [*The Secret Celebration*] (1986), *Eine*

Liebhaberin [*The Lover*] (1989), and *Reise mit Ernst* [*Travels with Ernest*] (1991), all with sections of sexual descriptions.

Visual texts of eroticism and sexuality published in the 1980s include Robert Lebeck's (ed.) *Playgirls von damals. 77 alte Postkarten* [*Playgirls of Past: Seventy-Seven Postcards*] (1987), Uwe Scheid's multi-volume book about nudes in photography, *Das erotische Imago* [*The Erotic Imagination*] (1986, 1991).

In the 1990s, Doris Lerche (1945–) who published the volume *21 Gründe, warum eine Frau mit einem Mann schläft* [*Twenty-One Reasons Why a Woman Beds a Man*] (1993) and Doris Dörrie's (1955–) collection of short stories *Bin ich schön?* [*Am I Beautiful?*] (1994; adapted to film in 1997) achieved some renown where a women's point of view and voice are stressed although sexual or pornographic descriptions are not to be found in her text; rather, it is the reference to such domains of life that make the text of interest. Dörrie has also achieved renown with her films and her interest in erotic and sexual matters in Germany with texts such as *Liebe in Duetshland: Deutsche Paare im Gespräch mit Doris Dörrie* [*Love in Germany: German Couples in Intervied by Doris Dörrie*] (1995). Other examples of erotic prose of the 1990s include Ulla Hahn's *Ein Mann im Haus* [*Man in the House*] (1991), Marlene Streeruwitz's *Frauenjahre* [*Women's Years*] 1996), and Karin Rick's collection of short stories *Sex, Sehnsucht und Sirenen* [*Sex, Desire, and Sirens*] (1991) and Regine Nössler's collection of short stories *Wie Elvira ihre Sexkrise verlor* [*How Elvira Got Rid of Her Crisis of Sex*] (1996). Increasing acclaim is accorded to the erotic texts of Sophie Andresky who focuses on the female voice such as in her novel *Feucht. Erotische Verführungen* [*Moist: Erotic Seductions*] (2000) and in her collections of short stories *In der Höhle der Löwin* [*In the Cave of the Lioness*] (1998) and *Das Lächeln der Pauline* [*Pauline's Smile*] (1997).

As mentioned previously, it is translated texts that dominate German-language erotic literature of the period after World War II and up to the 1980s. At times, however, the translation of a canonical erotic text results in exceptional quality and in literary historical advance. For example, the Chinese classic, Chin Ping Mei's *The Adventurous History of Hsi Men and His Six Wives* (in mainland China only recently taken off the list of censured books), was published in

an unexpurgated German translation in 1967 (*Djin Ping Meh. Schlehenblüten in goldener Vase*, trans. Otto Kibat and Artur Kibat, rept. 1987) at a time when the novel's English translation did not include the text's pornographic sections. Or, already in the 1960s, translations appeared also of such texts as Guillaume Apollinaire's pornographic novel *Les Onze mille verges ou les amours d'un hospodar* [*Die elftausend Ruten*, trans. Rudolf Wittkopf] (1970).

Texts of erotic literature were available for readers in communist East Germany to a much lesser extent than to readers in West Germany of course. An exception was the monthly *Magazin für Lebenskunst* [*Magazine of the Art of Living*] (founded in 1924, after 1945 published in East Berlin) that published photography, articles, and short stories of rather tame eroticism. However, nude photography, for example, otherwise hardly available in East Germany, appeared in this publication and thus its existence is of some importance in the history of East German literature and culture and represents an exception to the rule. A few writers, despite censorship, were able to write and publish texts with erotic and sexual content and language. Examples include Irmtraud Morgner's (1933–1990) feminist novels *Hochzeit in Konstantinopel* [*Wedding in Constantinople*] (1968), the trilogy *Leben und Abenteuer der Trobadora Beatriz nach Zeugnissen ihrer Spielfrau Laura* [*The Life and Adventures of Troubadura Beatriz According to her Ioculatrix Laura*] (1974, 1983; one critic calls the trilogy "socialist magical realism"), and *Amanda. Ein Hexenroman* [*Amanda: A Witchnovel*] (1983) and Gabriele Stötzer (1953–) who in her novels with a feminist outlook mixes German dialect, the lower-case writing of nouns, and sensual–sexual language when describing love and lovemaking.

Just before the collapse of communism, the East German government allowed, in 1988, the publication of translations of erotic classics such as by Octave Henri Marie Mirbeau and Andréa de Nerciat as well as *Josefine Mutzenbacher* and August Maurer's 1799 novel *Leipzig im Taumel. Nach Originalbriefen eines reisenden Edelmanns* [*Leipzig in Swing: The Correspondence of a Traveling Nobleman*], a text with sexual and pornographic descriptions.

In the 1980s and 1990s, anthologies represent efforts by diverse publishers to market erotic literature. For instance, between 1986 and 1996 several editions were published of *Die klassische Sau. Das Handbuch der literarischen Erotik* [*The Classic Sow: A Manual of Erotic Literature*] and its sequel *Die neue klassische Sau* [*The New Classic Sow*], edited by Eva Zutzel and Adam Zausel (pseudonyms). Texts in these volumes are not arranged by historical periods but thematically with selections from antiquity (Catullus, Ovidius), the Renaissance (Aretino), the eighteenth century (Cleland, Diderot, Restif de la Bretonne, de Sade), and, in volume two, focus is on contemporary literature where also some German authors such as Gottfried Benn, Robert Gernhardt, Eckhard Henscheid, Elfriede Jelinek, Eugen Neter, Peter Rühmkorf, Cora Stephan, and Kurt Tucholsky are included. Material selected in these anthologies at times also include erotic texts from canonical literature such as by Flaubert, Joyce, Proust, and Musil. Other anthologies of interest include Hansjürgen Blinn's *ich will dich. Die hundert schönsten erotischen Gedichte* [*I Want You: One Hundred of the Most Beautiful Erotic Poems*] (2001).

The 1991 anthology put out by the publisher Haffmans, *Komm. Zieh dich aus. Das Handbuch der lyrischen Hocherotik deutscher Zunge* [*Come, Take Your Clothes Off: The Manual of German Erotic Lyrics*], contains texts of some interest (the volume appeared previously in a shorter form in 1970, entitled *Dein Leib ist mein Gedicht* [*Your Body is My Poem*]. It contains material from the Middle Ages (these are actually of lesser pornographic content and are more in the vein of the *Carmina Burana*) and selections of poems by Conrad Celtis, Johannes Secundus, Paul Fleming, and Hoffmann von Hoffmanswaldau. In the second volume where the focus is on the twentieth century, we find the erotic poetry of canonical authors such as Dehmel, Brecht, George, Rilke, Wedekind, Lasker-Schüler, Benn, etc., and examples of sexual word games by Arno Holz. However, these examples of German erotic poetry are either very low key or coarse rather than sexual or pornographic: a line in one of Berthold Brecht's poems illustrates this best: "Am besten fickt man erst und badet dann / [Best is to fuck first and bathe later] ("Sauna und Beischlaf"). An exception are the more sexual poems about lovemaking of Karl Krolow (1915–1999) although despite his light and popularizing style his poetry is with a serious tone.

An important role in the publishing of erotic literature is Claudia Gehrke's publishing house Konkursbuch, founded in 1979. Based on principles of feminism and on the commitment to support new ways and forms of literature, Gehrke's support of erotic literature includes lesbian writing such as Cornelia Saxe's *ClitClip* (1994). The book is engaging aesthetically with photographs by Mayanne Könst. Similarly, the 1993 volume of verse by the Japanese-German author Yoko Tawada, *Das Bad* [*The Bath*] (1989), contains drawings of nudes of exceptional quality and her novel *Opium für Ovid. Ein Kopfkissenbuch von 22 Frauen* [*Opium for Ovidius: A Pillow of Twenty-Two Women*] (2000) is about female eroticism and sexuality, or, the novel about sadomasochism and love among lesbians by Regina Nössler, *Strafe muss sein* [*Punishment is a Necessity*] (1994) contains color photography of high aesthetic standards. Gehrke also publishes, first in 1982 and annually since 1988, *Mein heimliches Auge. Das Jahrbuch der Erotik* [*My Secret Eye: The Annual of Eroticism*]. The volumes contain uncensored texts of many types, prose, lyrics, essays, photographs, pictures of paintings, and drawings by renown and lesser-known authors. Aesthetically, the books are of high quality and of importance is that the books are a forum for new authors. For example, it is in these annuals that work by Alissa Walser, Dagmar Fedderke, and Sybille Szymanski first appeared. Fedderke has published several novels and collections of short stories with Konkursbuch such as *Pissing in Paris. Eine Reiseführer* [*Pissing in Paris: A Travelbook*] (1994) and *Die Geschichte mit A.* [*The Story with A.*] (1993), a novel also taking place in Paris and a take on Pauline Reage's *The Story of O.* In Fedderke's novel, too, the story is about a woman's slavery to a man but here the events occur in every-day life rather than in privileged and secluded settings. The description of the protagonist's angst when participating in group sex, in a public establishment, or the ridicule of some male participants' bath robes are parts of the text as well as the description of the orgy itself. Of interest is that Fedderke employs the narrative strategy where she Germanizes the original French terms she has introduced at the beginning of the novel.

In twenty-first-century German-language erotic literature, instead of the description of sexual acts or that of erotic imagery, sexual desire is the dominant theme whereby it often appears as the focus of anthologies and so-called "erotische

Lesebücher" (a reader of erotic stories). An example of this genre is Susanne Rehlein's collection *Bitte streicheln Sie hier!* [*Would You Please Fondle Hier!*] (2000) of twenty-two short stories. The young authors of this type of erotic literature attempt to show that eroticism takes place in one's imagination rather than in physical and raw sex while at the same time the imagination is capable of exploding in the wildest fantasies. For example, Katrin Röggla, in her short story "Bettgeschichten" ["Bedtime Stories," in Rehlein's collection] uses few explicitly sexual or pornographic words with the effect that her descriptions appear analytical rather than erotic and certainly not pornographic. Thomas Hettche—who rendered Aretino's *Sonetti lussuriosi* in German—presents in his novel *Nox* (1995) a text where he describes the orgies of his protagonists in such a way that the textual characteristics of the narrative, together with the protagonists, attain a surreal and virtual quality. Thus, dissimilar to the consciously organized breaking of taoos in current French-language erotic literature (e.g., Michel Houllebeque, Christine Angot, Catherine Millet, or Philippe Djian), in contemporary German erotic literature attention appears to be on the aestheticization of narrating the sexual act and its surrounding imaginary, whereby the said aestheticization occurs mainly on linguistic levels. This is particularly evident in Thomas Lehr's *Nabokovs Katze* [*Nabokov's Cat*] (1999) or in Ulrike Draesner's *Mitgift* [*The Dowry*] (2002), for example. This turn to the aesthetics of the word is perhaps best exemplified in Norbert Kron's *Autopilot* (2002), where the narrative is distanced and analytical in the extreme in descriptions such as the protagonist's lovemaking with his girlfriend. Of note are Detlev Meyer (1950–1999) who wrote homoerotic texts such as the trilogy *Im Dampfbad greift nach mir ein Engel* [*An Angel Grabs Me in the Sauna*] (1985), *David steigt aufs Riesenrad* [*David Climbs the Ferris Wheel*] (1987), and *Ein letzter Dank den Leichtathleten* [*Last Thanks to Athletes*] (1989), and a volume of poetry, *Stern in Sicht* [*Star in View*] (1998) and Ralf König (1960–) who writes homoerotic comic strips, several of which were adapted to film. The trend in contemporary German-langage literature to narrate sexuality continues and, for example, at the 2003 Frankfurt Book Fair, texts with descriptions of sexual and pornographic detail appeared in abundance

(e.g., Michael Lentz, *Liebeserklärung*, Alban Nikolai Herbst, *Meere*, Hans-Josef Ortheil, *Die grosse Liebe*).

A sub-genre of erotic literature is erotic science fiction and in German there are some examples of such as presented and discussed in Jürgen vom Scheidt's (ed.) *Sex im All* [*Sex in Space*] (1987).

As everywhere, also in German-speaking countries, the Internet is a medium where erotic material including pornography—visual as well as text— has exploded since the 1990s. It is thus not surprising that Web sites abound with erotic writing. New media technology allows for the presentation of text and visuals and thus there are many online sites where text is presented with paintings, photography, pictures of sculpture, and drawings. Similarly, the multi-media situation encourages the presentation of erotic texts with film and sound and while there are few such available as of yet, it is an obvious development yet to come. Also, Web sites include the presentation of the reading of texts similar to tapes or CDs with prose read by authors or actors. Web sites of interest where erotic literature, mostly short stories, can be found in German include *Das Literatur-Café. Erotische Literatur. Kurzgeschichten und Gedichte* (2002): <http://www.literaturcafe.de/>, *Erotische Literatur für Frauen* (2002): <http://www.fraue-nerotik.de/literatur.html>, *Erotisches zur Nacht. Die Erotik-Vorleseshow in Berlin* (2002): <http://www.erozuna.de>, *Erotik für Frauen* (2002): <http://www.arte-erotica.de>, *Erotische Literatur Seiten* (2002): <http://www.erotische-literatur-seiten.de/>, *Erosa. Das Online-Magazin für erotische Literatur* (2002): <http://www.erosa.de>, *Erotische Geschichten.de* (2002): <http://www.erotische-geschichten.de>, or *Aranitas erotische Geschichten* (2002): <http://www.aranita.de/>.

CAROLIN FISCHER and
STEVEN TOTOSY DE ZEPETNEK

Further Reading

Aresin, Lykke, and Kurt Starke. *Lexikon der Erotik.* München: Knaur, 1996.

Barrantay, Alexander. *Lieben, aber wie? Das Liebes-, Lehr- und Lesebuch für schwache Stunden.* München: Schmitz, 1957.

Bolen, Carl von: *Geschichte der Erotik.* St.Gallen: Allgemeiner Verlag, 1952.

Borneman, Ernest. *Ullstein-Enzyklopädie der Sexualität.* 1969. Berlin: Ullstein, 1990.

Borneman, Ernest. *Sex im Volksmund. Die sexuelle Umgangssprache des deutschen Volkes.* Reinbek bei Hamburg: Rowohlt, 1971.

Broggi Beckmann, Giuliana, ed. *Das große Lesebuch der Erotik.* München: Wilhelm Goldmann, 1994.

Busch, Marion, and Gerhard Müller. "Dekadente Erotik in Hermann Bahrs Roman *Die gute Schule.*" *Dekadenz in Deutschland.* Ed. Dieter Kafitz. Frankfurt: Peter Lang, 1987. 51–71.

Duca, Lo. *Das moderne Lexikon der Erotik von A–Z. Eine reich illustrierte aktuelle Enzyklopädie in zehn Bänden.* München: Desch, 1969.

Eder, Franz, and Sabine *Frühstück, eds. Querschnitte 3. Neue Geschichten der Sexuali*tät. Wien: Turia + Kant, 1999.

Fischer, Carolin. *Gärten der Lust. Eine Geschichte erregender Lektüren.* Stuttgart: Metzler, 1997.

Flotow, Luise von. "Translating Women of the Eighties: Eroticism, Anger, Ethnicity." *Culture in Transit: Translating the Literature of Québec.* Ed. Sherry Simon. Montréal: Véhicule, 1995. 31–46.

Freibeuter. Special issue 21 *Geilheit.* Berlin: Klaus Wagenbach, 1984.

Gorsen, Peter. *Sexualästhetik. Grenzformen der Sinnlichkeit im 20. Jahrhundert.* Reinbek bei Hamburg: Rowohlt, 1987.

Graeff, Max Christian, ed. *Der verbotene Eros. Unstatthafte Lektüren. Ein Lesebuch.* München: Deutscher Taschenbuch, 2000.

Jauch, Ursula Pia. "Jenseits der Puderquaste. Franz Blei, Literat mit vielen Eigenschaften." *Neue Zürcher Zeitung* (22 June 2002).

Lederer, Rosemarie: *Grenzgänger Ich. Psychosoziale Analysen zur Geschlechtsidentität in der Gegenwartsliteratur.* Wien: Passagen, 1998.

Linklater, Beth V. "Erotic Provocations: Gabriele Stötzer-Kachold's Reclaiming of the Female Body?" *Feminist Studies in German Literature & Culture* 13 (1997): 151–170.

Palmer, Craig Bernard: *The Significance of Homosexual Desire in Modern Literature.* Ph.D. Dissertation. Seattle: Washington University, 1997.

Riess, Curt. *Erotica! Erotica! Das Buch der verbotenen Bücher.* Hamburg: Hoffmann und Campe, 1968.

Risholm, Ellen, and Erin Crawley. "*Lust* and Jelinek: Violating the Commonsensical." *High and Low Cultures: German Attempts at Mediation.* Ed. Reinhold Grimm and Jost Hermand. Madison: University of Wisconsin Press, 1994. 107–113.

Strack, Friedrich. "'Aber das Fleisch ist stark!': Zur erotischen Lyrik des Expressionismus." *Annäherungsversuche. Zur Geschichte und Ästhetik des Erotischen in der Literatur.* Ed. Horst Albert Glaser. Bern: Haupt, 1993. 279–300.

Vesela, Gabriela. "E.E. Kisch und der deutschsprachige Prager erotische Roman." *Philologica Pragensia* 28.4 (1985): 202–215.

GERVAISE DE LATOUCHE, JEAN CHARLES

1716–1782
French novelist

The only positive attribution of *Histoire de Dom Bougre, portier des Chartreux* [*The Story of Friar Bugger, Porter of a Charterhouse*] to Jean Charles Gervaise de Latouche comes from the *Mémoires secrets*, often well-informed, for November 1782: "Monsieur Gervaise, author of the *Portier des Chartreux*, that famous book that caused him such trouble, has died." Whoever the author was, he had very good reason for trying to keep his identity a secret. As for

another book attributed to Gervaise in some reference works, *Mémoires de Mlle de Bonneval* (1738), all that can be said is that there is no known evidence for this.

The *Histoire de Dom Bougre* is perhaps, the most famous and infamous of all erotic novels of the eighteenth century. The first known edition was printed probably in December 1740. The name Bougre, a near-homonym of the English *bugger* or sodomite, was thinly veiled as B¼ or B*** in the first editions; nineteen other editions have been listed in the eighteenth century, some under the variant titles *Mémoires de Saturnin, Le*

Portier des Chartreux, and *Histoire de Gouber-dom*. It became paradigmatic for pornography in general; allusions to it are found everywhere, and there appears to have been an early English translation. Not the least scandalous aspect of the *Histoire de Dom B**** was the eighteen illustrations made for the first edition, two of them fold-outs; others followed in 1748 and later for subsequent editions.

Like *L'École des filles*, an anonymous work of 1655, and the sixteenth-century *Ragionamenti* of Aretino, the story of Dom Bougre takes the form of a process of sexual initiation, The narrator, Saturnin, is a monk and son of a monk whose awakening is first provoked when he accidentally witnesses, through a convenient hole in the partition, a monk joyously copulating with Toinette, the woman he believes to be his own mother, while her husband is off in the fields. So inspired, Saturnin undertakes to educate his putative sister, Suzon; she in turn relates her own introduction to many things sexual, while a pupil in a convent, by Monique, in the process quoting the latter's own story. Among Monique's discoveries during her unhappy convent days is the use of dildos, not to mention priestly lovers, among the nuns.

Although he never gets Suzon, all the other women Saturnin encounters in the first half of the book lust actively after him. The first is Toinette herself: "and so it was that my very first time, I cuckolded my putative father, but so what?" Toinette thinks it wise to pack him off to a monastery, and thus ends Part One: but not before he cavorts with Madame Dinville, Suzon's godmother, as well as the parish priest's mistress and governess Françoise, and their daughter Nicole. Others he can enjoy vicariously through masturbation: "Your imagination plays, skips about among all those who have charmed your eyes: the brunette, the blonde, the petite, the tall one: with a turn of the wrist you fuck anyone you want: your desires know no social barriers; you can go all the way to the throne, and the proudest beauties, forced to yield, give you whatever you ask."

The book does not want for style, most evident in portraits of apparently pious churchmen; but when it comes to sex everything is not only highly explicit but vulgarly blunt. Where some erotic novels resort to sometimes playful euphemisms, here it is just cunt, prick, fuck:

always the crude word; even the women say "Let's fuck" rather than something more delicate or roundabout. There are just enough mock-heroic metaphors to suggest a tongue-in-cheek approach to it all, such as the moment when Saturnin is caught with Nicole behind a locked door:

> I said to Nicole that, since we had been discovered, there was no reason to hesitate. She approved this courageous resolution by her silence and, herself giving me an initial thrust of her loins and putting her tongue back into my mouth, challenged me to rise to the occasion. And like proud warriors who in the line of fire, defying deadly artillery aimed at them on a rampart, calmly continue their work and laugh at the harmless sound of the canon fire roaring overhead, we labored intrepidly to the sound of Françoise pounding against the partition.

Eight years later, in Part Two, when he has finished his training and is about to be ordained, Saturnin is initiated into the orgiastic rituals of his Benedictine monastery. Despite his name, Bougre is not attracted to men, though he delivers a limited apology of buggery: "everyone takes his pleasure where he finds it; mine is to empale a woman when I see one; but if a handsome lad appears, should I give him a foot in the butt? No, simpleton: a dick in the butt." Still, the only bugger explicitly mentioned is Father Casimir, of whom it is said that when he saw a handsome lad he "went into rut and whinnied." Saturnin learns that there are not one but two circles of debachery in the monastery, supplied with their own pool of women, not to mention plenty of fine food and wine. One, who invites him to mount her, admits to being his very own and still active mother, but he will not go that far. He is also the beneficiary of disculpatory speeches not only about Biblical precedents for incest, but more generally the desirability of providing ample sexual opportunities within the monastery, the better to maintain an edifying appearance austerity without.

Ultimately, Saturnin becomes so sated that he is unable to perform even when surrounded by lewd women. It is then that the elderly Father Simeon tells him of the joys of seducing sweet, pious women from his privileged position in the confessional. Indeed he quickly identifies a target, a most devout young woman who absolutely throws herself at him: she turns out to be Monique. But just as, having taken his private pleasures with her, he is about to add her to the monastic harem, he is discovered, and expelled. In Paris, he is picked up by a prostitute who turns out to be Suzon; from her he contracts syphilis, during the treatment for which she dies and he is castrated. In this sorry state he appeals to a Charterhouse which takes him in and makes him its porter, whence the book's title.

Although inherently anticlerical or at least antimonastic, with its numerous unrepentant stagings of orgies in convents (Saturnin refers to monks as "sacred hogs, abundantly fed by the piety of the faithful"), the book has no ostensible religious or philosophical posture. Its single driving argument is for the naturalness and joy of orgasm and everything conducive to or associated with it. This motivation is equal among men and women, who live for virtually nothing else, without the slightest sentimental overlay. As Monique says: "when they say 'Monsieur is in love with Madame,' it's exactly as if they had said 'Monsieur saw Madame; the sight of her aroused desire in his heart, and he can't wait to stick his prick in her cunt.' That is the true meaning of the phrase: but since as decorum would have it, such things not be said, the custom is to say 'Monsieur is in love.'"

Biography

The only three things we know about Gervaise de Latouche—that he was born in Amiens in 1716, that he was a secretary of the barrister Lambotte, and that he was one of the prime suspects for authorship of the *Histoire de Dom Bougre, portier des Chartreux*—all come from police files. He was not among the dozen colporteurs or possible authors who were sent to the Bastille for some weeks or months in 1741 as the police tried to track down the culprits and quash the book, perhaps because he had a discreet and powerful protector.

PHILIP STEWART

Editions

Histoire de Dom B*** portier des chartreux, écrite par lui-même. Montréal, Quintal Associés. 1969.
Histoire de Dom Bougre, portier des chartreux. Paris: Fayard. "L'Enfer de la Bibliothèque Nationale," t. III, 1985.
Romanciers libertins du XVIIIe siècle. Dir. Patrick Wald Lasowski. Paris, Bibliothèque de la Pléiade, 2000, t. I.
Le Portier des Chartreux. Arles: Actes Sud, 1993.

Translations

Patrick Kearney (*The Private Case*, London: Jay Landesman, 1981, p. 193) lists a translation entitled *The History of Don B*. and dated 1743, of which there is no known copy; also *The Life and Adventures of Silal Shovewell*, London, 1801 and 1907. An abridged translation by Howard Nelson was published in 1967 under the title *The Adventures of Father Silas (Le Portier des Chartreux) by Beauregard de Farniente* (!) (Los Angeles: Holloway House), and later under the title *The Lascivious Monk* (London: W. H. Allen, 1970).

Further Reading

Clerval, Alain. notices in the Pléiade edition listed above, pp. 1104–1120.

GHAZALI, MEHEMMED

Turkish poet
c. 1460–1535

Ghazali was the pen name of a certain Mehemmed, who was also known as Deli Birader [Crazy Brother] among the Turkish learned circles of the early sixteenth-century Ottoman Empire. There is little information about this Ottoman poet's youth but he was probably born around 1465 in Bursa, in the northwest of what is today Turkey. He was educated in religion in Istanbul, the educational center of the time. He taught in several Anatolian institutions of higher education, and he later attended the court of Sultan Bayezid II's son, the crown prince Korkud (1467–1513), in the provincial town of Manisa in western Anatolia. There he composed two works commissioned by Korkud's courtier Piyale Bey. When Prince Korkud was executed on the orders of his brother Selim I, Ghazali was assigned to a dervish lodge in his birthplace, Bursa, though he left this post to return to teaching. Upon retirement, he organized a fund-raising campaign in which he wrote panegyric poems for different patrons, using the money to found a mosque, a dervish lodge, a garden, and a bathhouse in Beshiktash, a small suburban district of Istanbul. Ghazali's bathhouse was most probably designed to serve sailors, since the Empire's naval forces were anchored on the shores of this neighborhood.

During the peak of his fame, Ghazali enjoyed the patronage of the state elite, among them the Grand Vizier Makbul Ibrahim Pasha and the bureaucrat Iskender Çelebi. In his later years, the gatherings in his bathhouse created an uproar in Istanbul, and eventually gossip about Ghazali and Memi Shah, a male attendant in the bathhouse, forced Ghazali to move to Mecca in 1531. Once in Mecca, using money he had raised through a second 'poetry campaign,' Ghazali founded a mescid and a garden. Not long after, Ghazali died in the Holy City circa 1535, when he was approximately 70 years old.

Ghazali authored the first Ottoman Turkish literary composition on sexuality. Publicly suppressed and privately reproduced for centuries, this prose composition, embellished with several passages in verse, was presented to the aforementioned Piyale Bey. The work, titled *Dâfi'ü'l-gumûm ve râfi'ü'l-humûm* [*Repeller of sorrows and remover of anxiety*], is a mock sex manual. It classifies several illicit sexual practices grouped in seven chapters, the titles of which read as follows: (1) The benefits of marriage and sexual intercourse; (2) The war between the pederasts and the fornicators; (3) How to enjoy the company of boys; (4) How to enjoy the company of girls; (5) Masturbation, nocturnal emissions and bestiality; (6) The passive homosexuals; and (7) The pimps.

Dâfi'ü'l-gumûm ve râfi'ü'l-humûm was intended for the all-male learned circles of the sixteenth-century Ottoman Empire. Throughout the work, constant reminders of the illicit

character of the sexual practices described are balanced with Ghazali's inclination to tickle the sexual passion of its readers. The titillating character of the work becomes apparent in the detailed depictions of sexual organs in the form of longish odes; the painstaking directions on how to seduce boys or girls; descriptions of the sexual positions, which yield maximum pleasure; and other such subjects. The alternation of funny stories and poems of mockery adds to the playfulness of this sexually impulsive work. In *Dâfi'ü'l-gumûm ve râfi'ü'l-humûm*, the conspicuous misogyny underpins the general pederastic discourse prevalent among the learned men in the Ottoman Empire. In this work, boys figure as the most prominent objects of sexual desire, primarily for reasons of accessibility—while women were excluded from the exclusively masculine public space of the sixteenth-century Ottoman Empire, boys moved freely in this public sphere. Short anecdotes, poems, and stories exploring pederasty all focus on sexual pleasure, and on ways of tricking unassuming boys into sexual acts, whereas the sections on adultery bear messages of caution, highlighting the discourse of 'the wiles of women.'

Here is an example of an erotic verse from the *Dâfi'ü'l-gumûm ve râfi'ü'l-humûm*:

With a glance the beloved roasted the bird of heart
    you won't even eat it, the poor pigeon
Seeing the beloved it tumbles up to the sky
    So that he would be attracted to the pigeon
O Gazali, the fire of your words burned its wings
    It can't carry the message to the beloved, the
    pigeon

In this three-verse lyric poem, the pigeon symbolizes the lover's heart, his sexual organ, and a messenger between the lover and the beloved respectively. However, the straightforward nature of the following selection that contains a comparision of vagina and anus from the same work is in stark contrast to the playfulness of the preceding one:

True, the pussy vomits blood once a month
    But the anus always shits from its mouth
True, the pussy widens when it delivers
    But any boy's anus with shit shivers.

While *Dâfi'ü'l-gumûm* refers to and relies on works in Arabic, Persian, and Turkish, and is referred to and quoted by subsequent Ottoman Turkish works, there is nothing comparable to it in the Ottoman Turkish literary tradition.

Of course, this apparent uniqueness may reflect the reductive modernist reconstruction of the Ottoman literary canon, which suppresses works of this character.

Apart from this forgotten text, Ghazali composed a religious treatise in verse. In a letter written while in Mecca to friends in Istanbul, Ghazali addresses them one by one, and mocks them jokingly, using sexual metaphors. This unruly Ottoman poet stands out among his contemporaries with his command of Ottoman Turkish prose and poetry, and his composition of a work, *Dâfi'ü'l-gumûm*, that gives expression to the suppressed erotic voice in this particular early modern tradition (see Turkish Literature).

Biography

Born in Bursa, Turkey, c. 1460. Educated as a religious scholar in Istanbul. Taught in various Anatolian educational institutions and attended the court of the crown prince Korkud, [1510s?]. Upon retirement, moved to Istanbul and constructed a mosque, a bathhouse, and a dervish lodge; relocated to Mecca in 1531 upon rumors of impropriety; died there in 1535.

SELIM S. KURU

GIDE, ANDRÉ

1869–1951
French novelist. Nobel Prize in Literature (1948)

André Pul Guillaume Gide described himself as being simultaneously like a young boy having fun and a disapproving Protestant minister. This duality is found in many of his individual works (e.g., *Les nourritures terrestres* [*Fruits of the Earth*], 1897, expressing the symbiosis of sensuality and asceticism in lyrical prose) and in his literary output as a whole. In *Si le grain ne meurt...* [*If It Die...*] (1920) he records, among other details of his early life, his idealized love for his cousin Madeleine Rondeaux.. He declared that she was the heavenly pole of his life, the antithesis to which was his own erotic Hell. This conflict informs the background to *L'Immoraliste* [*The Immoralist*] (1902), paired with *La porte étroite* [*Straight is the Gate*] (1909). Furthermore, *Si le grain ne meurt...* contains a description of his sexual liberation in North Africa, recording an encounter with an Arab youth in the dunes (1894) and visits with Oscar Wilde and Lord Alfred Douglas to a sordid male brothel (1895). This autobiography, which stops short at his marriage, is designed as a 'private' confession to run parallel to the public argument in defence of pederasty put forth in *Corydon* (first, incomplete and limited edition, 1911; first full public edition, 1924). In *Corydon*, a series of four 'Socratic' dialogues, a homosexual doctor argues from the biological, ethical, and historical (mainly ancient Greek) standpoints that same-sex love, here restricted to male adult and adolescent, is not only natural but is in fact desirable. When it is controlled and does not entail excess, it is respectful of the masculine selfhood of each participant, reveres women, and, in the case of the youth, leads to successful marriage. The book denies that there is any truth in the then current medical model of 'moral disease,' takes issue with the feminization of the homosexual allegedly portrayed in Proust's *À la recherche du temps perdu*, and challenges the widespread hypocrisy and cowardice Gide saw among his contemporaries. Doubtless from his awareness of his own sexual nonconformity Gide developed a parallel interest in criminality and moral anarchy. These elements are also frequently present in his works, being used to orchestrate the irresoluable conflict between desire and self control, Nature and Culture, duty to the self and duty to society, freedom and repression. Seldom far removed from the theme of sexuality is the closely associated idea of education, this being again an element inherited from the tradition of pederastic Greek love. An allusive example of this occurs in the play *Philoctète* (1899). Here the young Néoptolème is being taught the virtue of self reliance by the hero Philoctète, and, although there is nothing sexually explicit, there was enough to encourage Gide's friend Paul Valéry to half expect the youth would in due course be seduced. There are noteworthy homosexual elements in another of his plays of this period (*Saül*, 1903), but the case for including *Le roi Candaule* (1899) is problematic. *L'Immoraliste* tells in confessional form the story of Michel who follows the path from sickness to health, from constraint to freedom, from sexual repression to the acknowledgement of desire. The book contains the portrait of an Outsider, Ménalque, who has been ostracized by society and who was modeled partly on Oscar Wilde and partly on a close friend, Eugène Rouart. But more significantly Gide makes the link between nonconformity in general and healthy self knowledge. Michel is attracted to Arab youths, and the description of them is suggestive: indeed the text ends by expressing the thought that even after an affair with a local girl he finds her brother more attractive. The 'drama' of Michel's life is exacerbated by the love he bears his wife which is in conflict with his half-expressed desires and hope for freedom. As a contribution to the novels of the time with more or less overt homosexual themes *L'Immoraliste*, with its Nietzschean title, is among the best, allowing the moral issues it raises to transcend the particular nature of the hero's sexuality. More obviously subversive and outrageous are certain elements in *Les caves du Vatican* [*The Vatican Cellars*] (1914), where the youthful Lafcadio appears naked (in a photo), and receives an education from various uncles (friends of his mother's), some of whose attentions are ambiguous and 'comradely,' to borrow Walt Whitman's term. Lafcadio is urged by the arch-criminal Protos to use his good looks to blackmail his male admirers. The book contains innuendoes on a priest's liking for boys, which so offended the Catholic writer Paul Claudel that he broke off his friendship with Gide. On the whole, however, this is a burlesque story where suggestiveness forms only one strand of a complex web of anarchy. *Les faux monnayeurs* [*The Coiners*] (1926), originally conceived as a sequel to *Les caves du Vatican*, expresses a more mature and comprehensive treatment of sexual relationships than its

antecedent. The hero of the book, the novelist Édouard, is in love with Olivier, the close school friend of Bernard. A range of emotional situations is presented, and the feelings of both boy and adult are explored from subjective points of view. Apprehensive uncertainty that one's feelings may not be reciprocated is followed by episodes where Olivier deserts Édouard for Passavant (a rival, rather camp, author), and Bernard replaces him momentarily. The reconciliation and mutual declaration of Édouard's and Olivier's love is effected after the young man's suicide attempt on the brink of happiness (a Dostoievskian motif). Gide's achievement here is not to have written a gay novel, but to have explicitly presented a major homosexual subject in an innovative work about society, its complexity, and its open-ended eventfulness. A lesbian theme appears in *Geneviève* (1936), a novella forming part of the trilogy *L'École des femmes* [*The School for Wives*]. Taking the form of a schoolgirl's infatuation, the episode in question bears witness to Gide's intention to explore a woman's point of view under the influence of a group of feminist English friends who included Dorothy Bussy, author of the novel *Olivia* (sent to Gide in manuscript in 1933, but only published in 1948), which develops a similar story. In 1946, *Thésée*, a burlesque prose narrative, appeared, describing in a mythological and symbolic form the course of Gide's life. Although the hero Thésée declares himself to be uniquely interested in women, including the famous Phaedra, and Ariadne who is shown here as a nymphomaniac, the book includes a description of Cretan homosexual customs which are worked into the plot structure. Gide asserted that an understanding of his pederasty held the key to many of his writings. Overall, his treatment of erotic episodes and themes is suggestive, rather than explicit (the recent French editions of his *Journal* and *Si le grain ne meurt* have nevertheless published previously omitted material). He is careful to relate sexuality to more general issues of behavior, although this does not prevent him from often celebrating in various forms the joys and delights of same-sex relationships between adult and adolescent.

Biography

Born 22 November 1869 in Paris. 1877, enrolled briefly at the École Alsacienne (Paris), but was expelled for 'bad habits.' His education was thenceforward disrupted. He returned to the École Alsacienne in 1887 (Rhétorique). 1880 (28 October), death of father. 1888, Lycée Henri IV (Philosophie). 1891 (January), first substantial publication: *Les cahiers d'André Walter*, and (December) first met Oscar Wilde in Paris. 1892, rejected for military service on grounds of health (tuberculosis). 1895, death of mother and marriage to his cousin Madeleine Rondeaux. 1916, significant religious crisis (*Numquid et tu... ?*), the beginning of his love for Marc Allégret, the son of a Protestant minister, close friend of the family. 1918, traveled to Cambridge with Marc, finding on his return that his wife had burned all his letters to her. 1923 (18 April), birth of Catherine, daughter of Gide and Elisabeth van Rysselberghe (adopted after the death of Madeleine Gide). 1932, Gide became increasingly involved in Communist activity, culminating in his visit to the USSR (1936). He published his travelogue (*Retour de l'URSS*, 1936) and further criticisms (*Retouches...*, 1937). 1938 (7 April), death of his wife. 1947 (5 June), was awarded an honorary doctorate at Oxford University, and (13 November) the Nobel Prize for Literature. 1951 (19 February), died in Paris. Buried at Cuverville (Normandy), his friends objecting that a Protestant minister had conducted a religious service over him. 1952 (24 May), his complete works were placed on the *Index librorum prohibitorum* by the Catholic Church.

PATRICK POLLARD

Selected Works

Essais critiques. Edited by P. Masson. Paris: Bibliothèque de la Pléiade, 1999.
Journal 1887–1950. Edited by E. Marty and M. Sagaert. Paris: Bibliothèque de la Pléiade, 1996–1997.
Romans, Récits et Soties. Œuvres lyriques. Edited by Y. Davet and J.J. Thierry. Paris: Bibliothèque de la Pléiade, 1961.
Souvenirs et Voyages. Edited by Pierrre Masson. Paris: Bibliothèque de la Pléiade, 2001.
(1897 *Les Nourritures terrestres*). *Fruits of the Earth*. translated by Dorothy Bussy (1949).
(1902 *L'Immoraliste*). *The Immoralist*. Translated by Dorothy Bussy (1930).
(1903 *Prétextes*). *Pretexts. Reflections on Literature and Morality...* selected by Justin O'Brien. (1949).
(1909 *La Porte Étroite*). *Straight is the Gate*. Translated by Dorothy Bussy (1924).
(1914 *Les Caves du Vatican*). *The Vatican Swindle* [aka *The Vatican Cellars*]. Translated by Dorothy Bussy (1927).
(1919 *La Symphonie Pastorale*). *Two Symphonies...* Translated by Dorothy Bussy (1931).
(1920–1921 *Si le grain ne meurt...*). *If it dies...* Translated by Dorothy Bussy (1935).
(1923 *Dostoïevski*). *Dostoievsky*. Translated [anon.] (1925).
(1924 *Corydon*). *Corydon*. Translated by Richard Howard (1983).
(1926 *Les Faux-Monnayeurs*). *The Counterfeiters* [aka *The Coiners*]. Translated by Dorothy Bussy (1927).
(1927 *Voyage au Congo*). *Travels in the Congo*. translated by Dorothy Bussy (1929).
(1931 *Œdipe* and 1946 *Thésée*). *Two Legends, Theseus and Oedipus*. Translated by John Russell (1950).
(1932–1954 *Journal*). *The Journals*. Translated by Justin O'Brien (1947–1951).
(1936 *Retour de l'URSS*). *Back from the USSR*. Translated by Dorothy Bussy (1937).
(1952 *Ainsi soit-il ou les jeux sont faits*). *So Be It; or, The Chips are Down*. Translated by Justin O'Brien (1960).

Further Reading

Brée, G. *André Gide, l'insaisissable Protée*. Paris: Les Belles Lettres, 1953.
Copley, A. *Sexual Moralities in France (1780–1980)*. London: Routledge, 1989.
Delay, J. *La Jeunesse d'André Gide (1869–1895)*. Paris: Gallimard, 1956–1957.
Goulet, A. *Fiction et vie sociale dans l'œuvre d'André Gide*. Paris: Minard, 1986.
Martin, C. *André Gide ou la vocation du bonheur (1869–1911)*. Paris: Fayard, 1998.
Pollard, P. *André Gide: Homosexual Moralist*. New Haven: 1991.
Robinson, C. *Scandal in the Ink*. London: Cassell, 1995.
Savage, C. *André Gide. L'Évolution de sa pensée religieuse*. Paris: Nizet, 1962.
Sheridan, A. *André Gide. A Life in the Present*. London: Hamish Hamilton, 1998.
Stambolian, G. and Marks, E. *Homosexualities and French Literature*. Ithaca, NY: Cornell University Press, 1979.
Walker, D. *André Gide*. London: Macmillan, 1990.
Martin, C. *Bibliographie des livres consacrés à André Gide 1918–1995*. Lyon: Centre d'Études gidiennes, 1995.
Savage-Brosman, C. *An Annotated Bibliography of Criticism on André Gide 1973–1988*. New York: Garland, 1990.

GILGAMESH

The longest and best known work in Mesopotamian literature was based on oral and written narratives concerning Gilgamesh, the king of Uruk. The standard version of the epic was discovered in the library at Nineveh (eighth–seventh centuries BCE). It incorporates some but not all known Sumerian Gilgamesh stories, episodes from the Old Babylonian version from the early second millennium, and completely new material. The colophon mentions the authorship of a scribe called Sin-leqqe-unini, a scholar who lived during the Kassite period, around 1500 BCE. The work is not primarily an erotic novel. The main theme is the problem of death and dying and the quest for immortality. It deals with heroism and kingship and the values of Mesopotamia's urban civilization. However, episodes describing sexual encounters and the ambiguous love between Gilgamesh and Enkidu raise fundamental and subtle questions about eroticism and human relationships. There is now a vast secondary literature about the epic, and numerous translations in different modern languages have appeared. The following summary inevitably reveals my own subjective understanding of the original text which is fragmentary in many places and thus still poses many unresolved difficulties of interpretation. Gilgamesh as introduced in prologue, is two-thirds divine (his mother is the goddess Ninsun) and one-third mortal. His vitality is likened to that of a rampant bull who gives no rest to the young men and women of Uruk. The gods answer the complaints of the people by specially creating a being that will match his ardour. This is Enkidu, shaggy-haired and wild, who lives far from the cultivated plains in the semi-desert. He eats and drinks like the beasts and destroys the traps of the hunter. He is thus described as the antithesis to Gilgamesh, who as king of the ancient city of Uruk, represents the values of urban civilization. The king hears about Enkidu and rather than sending a group of young warriors he dispatches Shamhat, the voluptuos one, a courtesan, to meet the beast-like creature. She lies down uncovered, opens her legs and is encouraged take wind of him, to do for him, the primitive man, as women do. Their love-making lasts for six days and seven nights and thereafter the wild animals turn away from Enkidu and he has lost the power of his legs to run as before. He realizes that he has been transformed and the courtisan takes him to the city, where Gilgamesh is perfect in strength which arouses Enkidu's desire to challenge him. Shamhat tries to modify his aggression towards Gilgamesh by revealing to him two dreams which Gilgamesh recounted to his mother who interpreted their meaning for him. Both dreams involve an object falling from the sky which he is unable to lift but which he loves as a wife and treats as equal. In both cases the word for the object can be construed as a pun referring to male and to certain cult personnel attached to Ishtar who may have had connotations with ambiguous sexuality. Shamhat reiterates Ninsun's interpretation that Gilgamesh is about to gain a male friend and advisor, a companion in strength, and that they will love one another. Enkidu completes his transformation by drinking beer and eating bread for the first time, having his hair cut and donning clothes. When he finally meets Gilgamesh, barring his way to father-in-law's house (where presumably Gilgamesh intends to claim his *droit de seigneur*), he bars his way and they wrestle in the public square until the doorframe quake. The text becomes broken here and when it resumes the two protagonists acknowledge each other's strength and qualities and seal their friendship with an embrace. Enkidu weeps, and again a gap on the tablet obscures why. The text then describes their first adventure, to cut down cedar trees in a forest sacred to the god Ellil. They succeed, having killed the guardian spirit monster Huwawa, and return triumphant to Uruk. The next episode concerns Gilgamesh and his relationship with the city-goddess Ishtar, who in Sumerian literature was described as the one whose love legitimized and blessed the ruler of the city. In the epic Ishtar's proposal of marriage is rudely rejected by Gilgamesh who recounts the miserable fate of her human and animal ex-lovers and expresses his fear that he would be treated in the same way. The goddess vows revenge but Gilgamsh and Enkidu kill the Bull of Heaven sent to destroy them. The heroes return to the palace where they lie down to sleep. Enkidu dreams that the gods had decided to punish him for the slaying of their creatures and that he will die. The dying Enkidu curses the huntsman and courtesan for bringing him to Uruk. She shall suffer deprivation and humiliation, to be slapped by drunkards and suffer homelessness. But he relents when he remembers that she had brought him to Gilgamesh and he blesses her instead, that she should grow wealthy and prominent in society, with husbands leaving their wives for her sake. Enkidu dies and the grief-stricken Gilgamesh leaves his city and begins his quest for Utnapishtim, the survivor of the great flood, to ask him how he obtained eternal life. The story then unfolds, incorporating numerous adventures as well as the flood-narrative. Gilgamesh realizes that human destiny is death and returns to his city, where he inspects the ramparts and orders his story to be written on copper tablets, thus securing another kind of immortality.

The erotic content of *Gilgamesh*, apart from the initial seduction of Enkidu, is marked by ambivalence. The homo-erotic tenor of Gilgamesh[1]s love for Enkidu as communicated by the dreams and is more complex if one considers that Gilgamesh takes on the role traditionally held by female personages who marry the outsider or steppe dweller. The eroticized notion of the Other is here projected onto Enkidu, but their own identities undergo a profound transformation in the process. In the Sumerian narratives, the female representative of urban civilization brings about the assimilation of the outsider. Here, the value system of the steppe clashes with that of urbanism—Gilgamesh rejects Ishtar and turns himself into a creature of the wilderness in his quest for knowledge.

His failure to find the answer opens up the possibility of return to Uruk where he will complete his destiny on earth.

GWENDOLYN LEICK

Editions

Parpola, Simo, with the assistance of Mikko Luukko and Kalle Fabritius. *The Standard Babylonian Epic of Gilgamesh: Cuneiform Text, Transliteration, Glossary, Indices and Sign List*, Helsinki: Neo-Assyrian Text Corpus Project, 1997.

George, Andrew. *The Epic of Gilgamesh*. Harmondsworth: Penguin Classics, 2003.

George, Andrew. Kalle Fabritius *The Babylonian Gilgamesh Epic: Introduction, Critical Edition and Cuneiform Texts*. 2 vols. Oxford: Oxford University Press, 2003.

Translations

Bottéro, Jean. *L'épopée de Gilgames: le grand homme qui ne voulait pas mourir*. Paris: Gallimard, 1992.

Dalley, Stephanie. *Myths from Mesopotamia*. Oxford, New York: Oxford University Press, 1989.

Ferry, David. *Gilgamesh: A New Rendering in English Verse*. Newcastle upon Tyne: Bloodaxe Books, 1993.

Foster, Benjamin. *The Epic of Gilgamesh: A New Translation, Analogues, Criticism*. New York: Norton, 2001.

George, Andrew. *The Epic of Gilgamesh. The Babylonian Epic Poem and Other Texts in Akkadian and Sumerian*. Harmondsworth: Allen Lane, 1999.

Kovacs, Maureen Gallery. *The Epic of Gilgamesh*. Stanford, CA: Stanford University Press, 1989.

Jackson, Danny P. *The Epic of Gilgamesh*. Verse rendition (Introduction by Robert D. Biggs). Wauconda, IL: Bolchazy-Carducci Publishers, 1992.

Further Reading

Harris, Rivkah. *Gender and Aging in Mesopotamia: The Gilgamesh Epic and Other Ancient Literature*. Norman, OK: University of Oklahoma Press, 2000.

Leick, Gwendolyn. *Sex and Eroticism in Mesopotamian Literature*. London and New York: Routledge, 1994.

Maier, John. *Gilgamesh: A Reader*. Wauconda, IL: Bolchazy-Carducci, 1997.

Tigay, Jeffrey H. *The Evolution of the Gilgamesh Epic*. Philadelphia, PA: University of Pennsylvania Press, 1982.

GIMFERRER, PEDRO

1945–
Spanish poet, novelist, essayist

The underlying poetics to all of Pedro Gimferrer's writings is the centrality given to language. For Gimferrer, literature is primarily an act of language, something that is created solely by language; consequently its only reality is linguistic. Contextual approaches to literature fail if they dismiss the importance of language. Thus the reader can understand his preference for writers whose devotion towards language is paramount, as well as his interest in literary movements that ascribe a central role to language, like Surrealism, or authors such as Lautréamont, Arthur Rimbaud, or Stéphane Mallarmé. Gimferrer's poetry is marked by the mentioned writers and movement, while at the same time shows its concern for decadent scenarios as can be read in *Arde el mar* [*Sea Burning*] (1966) or for the cinema in *La muerte en Beverly Hills* [*Death in Beverly Hills*] (1968). It can be perceived that his is an attempt to create a reality independent from everyday reality, based on an artistic past or on cinema. That is the reason why his journal, *Dietari*, does not contain any reference to himself but to the books he kept reading during those years.

Eroticism in Gimferrer's writings is present as a central theme and also as subordinate or suplementary. Sometimes it pervades the atmosphere that the poem creates, but in others it plays an active part. There are two different approaches to eroticism. In poems of an early period of his career, decadence rules over ambience, characters, and actions. Thus, it is a soft eroticism that is present as for example in "Oda a Venecia ante el mar de los teatros" [Ode to Venice before the sea of the theaters], it is easy to perceive that the ambient is charged of decadence and that the mention to the naked or dead body in line 19 intends to be part of the decorative setting of a poem in which the main subject matter is that of the remembrance and the loss of youth. "Cuchillos en abril" [Knives in April] also presents some features of a very soft and delicate eroticism in which the poet declares his hatred by adolescents because of the physical distance between them. The loss of youth means also the loss of passion and the physical decay that the poet feels and makes him grow angry against young people.

Later on, in *La muerte en Beverly Hills,* there is a slight change and decadence is not that of *fin-de-siècle*, but the golden age of American cinema already vanished by the 1960s. Eroticism is present fragmentarily. It is desire that moves the narrator and creates a series of hallucinated images, some of them erotic, as I have said, with no relation to reality. There can be found female bodies stripped of their psychological features, since only physical indications are to be read in the poems. These bodily characteristics reinforce the impression of *femme fatales*, as were imagined when seen in films (see poem II). Eroticism in the book is linked to the loss of a paradise, that of adolescence, as can be seen in poem IV, and that of cinema, since for Gimferrer and other writers of his generation, cinema was so important that during some years they thought of the prevalence of cinema over literature.

Nonetheless, these are lesser examples of his erotic poetry. The other erotic current present in his poetry has to do with unceonventional sex. In 1976, Gimferrer publishes *L'espai desert* [*Desert Space*] in which sexuality is present in unconventional forms. He acknowledges the subtle and indirect importance of Wiliam Butler Yeats's poem "Crazy Jane Talks with the Bishop": "But love has pitched his mansion in / the place of excrement." Soft eroticism has turned into something less exquisite. Desire has left its place to unconscious impulses of death. In *Mascarada* [Masquerade], section 37, Gimferrer describes an act of coprophilia. He is describing a teenager's buttocks. There is a gap between the vulgar action and its exquisite description. *El callejón de la guardia prusiana* [*The Backstreet of the Prussian Guard*] is no doubt his best erotic text. It is a short novel written in 1969 but not published until 2001. The novella is a catalogue of unconventional sexual practices such as coprophilia in the first chapter or masochism (Chapter 4), plus homosexuality (Chapter 6) during an uncertain early twentieth century in Middle Europe.

In general, eroticism is bound on the unconventional, as is Gimferrer's peotics and life. His clear preference for Surrealism, both in literature and life, makes him explore the dark side of sexuality. He moves from decadent eroticism towards hard porn, though always described by means of a literary language that can lessen its disgusting facets. The dissociation that the poet perceives between his self and society, and its consequent rebellion, is not expressed in political terms, but in terms of social costumes. Thus, the prevalence of unconventional sexual practices is the reflection of the poet's rebellion, different from the Romantics, though inspired by them and by the ideas of the early twentieth century, that is, by Surrealism and Sigmund Freud's essays on culture and sex.

Biography

Born in 1945 in Barcelona, Pedro Gimferrer stands as the most gifted and important poet of the generation of 1970s, and the one who brought new life to Spanish poetry in the late 1960s. In 1969, he quit writing in Spanish in favor of his native Catalan. His activity as a reviewer, editor, and poet marked the path that Spanish poetry was to follow in the 1970s. Besides, he has written articles for journals, collected in *Dietari 1979–1980* (1981), [*Accounts book*], two novels, *Fortuny* (1983) and *El callejón de la guardia prusiana* (1999) [*The Backstreet of the Prussian Guard*] and a number of essays, *La poesía de J.V. Foix* [*J.V. Foix's poetry*] (1974), *Radicalidades* [*Radicalities*] (1978), *Lecturas de Octavio Paz* [*Readings on Octavio Paz*] (1980), *Perfil de Vicente Alexandre* [*Profile of Vicente Aleixandre*] (1985), *Cine y literatura* [*Cinema and literature*] (1985), among them. Nonetheless he is better known for his poetry.

Santiago Rodríguez Guerrero-Strachan

Selected Works

Arde el mar [*Sea burning*]. 1966.
La muerte en Beverly Hills [*Death in Beverly Hills*]. 1968.
Poemas 1963–1969 [*Poems 1963–1969*]. 1969.
Els miralls [*Mirrors*]. 1970.
Hora foscant [*Dark hour*]. 1972.
Foc cec [*Blind fire*]. 1973.
L'espai desert [*Desert space*]. 1977.
El vendaval [*Gale*]. 1988.
La llum [*The Light*]. 1990.
Mascarada [*Masquerade*]. 1998.

Further Reading

Amorós, Amparo. "La retórica del silencio," *Los cuadernos del norte*. 16 (1982): 18–27.
Barella, Julia. "Pedro Gimferrer: poesía en catalán." *Peña Labra*, 39 (1981): 17–22.
Barella, Julia. "La reacción veneciana: poesía española en la década de los setenta." *Estudios Humanísticos*, 5 (1983): 69–76.
———. "Un paseo por el amor en venecia y por *La muerte en Beverly Hills*." *Anthropos*, 140 (1993): 50–54.
Beltrán Pepió, Vicente. "Poética y estadística: nuevos y novísimos poetas españoles." *Revista de literatura*, 88 (1982): 123–141.
Bou, Enric. "P.G. día a día: del escritor a la escritura." *Anthropos*, 140 (1993): 41–44.
Busoño, Carlos. "Estudio preliminar a Guillermo Carnero." *Ensayo de una teoría de la visión. Poesía 1966–1977*. Madrid: Hiperión, 1983: 11–68.
Carnero, Guillermo. "Culturalism and 'New' Poetry. A poem by Pedro Gimferrer: 'Cascabeles' from *Arde el mar*." in Andrew P. Debicki, (ed.) *Quaderni di Letterature Iberiche e Iberoamericane* 11–12 (1992): 19–36.
Castellet, Josè M. (ed.) *Nueve Novísimos*. Barcelona: Barral Editores, 1970.
Castellet, Josè M. "Pere Gimferrer." *Els escenaries de la memòria*. Barcelona: Ediciò 62, 1988: 249–262.
Debicki, Andrew P. "Una poesía española de la postmodernidad: los novísimos." *Anales de literatura española contemporánea*, 14 (1989): 33–50.
Debicki, Andrew P., ed. *Studies in 20th Century Literature. Contemporary Spanish Poetry: 1939–1990*. 16 (1992).
Debicki, Andrew P. "*Arde el mar* como índice y ejemplo de una nueva época poética." *Anthropos*, 140 (1993): 46–49.
García de la Concha Víctor. "Primera etapa de un noísimo: Pedro Gimferrer, *Arde el mar*." *Papeles de Son Armadans*, 190 (1972): 45–61.
Gracia, Jordi. "Introducción." in Pedro Gimferrer, *Arde el mar*. Madrid: Cátedra, 1997: 11–98.
Jiménez, José Olivio. "Redescubrimiento de la poesía: Arde el mar de Pedro Gimferrer." in *Diez años de poesía española 1960–1970*. Madrid: Ínsula, 1972: 364–374.
Lázaro Carreter, Fernando. "De *Arde el mar* a *Exili*." En *Creació i crítica en la literatura catalana*. Barcelona: Publicacions de la UB, 1993: 123–128.
López, Ignacio Javier. "El olvido del habla: una reflexión sobre la escritura de la metapoesía." *Ínsula*, 505 (1989): 17–18.
Martínez Torrón, Diego. "La poesía de Pere Gimferrer (1963–1982)." in *Estudios de literatura española*. Barcelona: Anthropos, 1987: 451–474.
Moral, Concepción G. y Pereda R.M., eds. *Joven poesía española*. Madrid: Cátedra, 1987.
Peña Labra, 62 (1986–1987).

Pritchett, Kay. ed. *Four Postmodern Poets of Spain. A Critical Introduction with Translations of the Poems.* Fayetteville: The University of Arkansas Press, 1991.

Provencio, Pedro. *Poéticas españolas contemporáneas. La generación del 70.* Madrid: Hiperión, 1988.

Siles, Jaime. "Ultimísima poesía española escrita en castellano: rasgos distintivos de un discurso en proceso y ensayo de una posible sistematización." *Iberoromania*, 34 (1991): 8–31.

Talens, Jenaro. "Reflexiones en torno a la poesía última de Pedro Gimferrer." *Ínsula*, 304 (1972): 15.

GINSBERG, ALLEN

1926–1997
American poet

Allen Ginsberg's many talents induced him to assume a variety of cultural roles in his lifetime, arguably more such roles than any other writer in the history of American literature. He was a social critic and scholar, a professor, a polemicist, an activist for both general and sexual politics, a religious and cultural guru, a literary critic, promoter, and publicist, a photographer, a counterculture icon, a blues-pop-rock singer, a prosodist, and, of course, a poet. He began his career as a poet, and the other roles followed. His celebrity was such, however, that it rivaled and at times eclipsed his poetic achievements. This was in large part because his critical posture was not just insistently Left and anti-establishment, but also self-consciously transgressive. This synthesis informed his poetry and poetic theories, and frequently his poetry was the voice of his critique. In general, his stances were liberally to the Left of social norms, as they were in his satirizing polite "queer society' ("In Society," 1947), his lyricizing drugs and drug culture ("Paterson," 1949), his jeremiad against American materialism (*Howl*, 1955–1956), his parody of America's Red-scare, Cold War, homophobic, racist xenophobia ("America," 1956), his critique of the Vietnam War ("Wichita Vortex Sutra," 1966), his exorcism of nuclear reactors and waste ("Plutonian Ode," 1978), to say nothing of his paeans to bisexuality ("Love Poem on Theme by Whitman," 1954), homosexuality ("Love Comes," 1981) and various other "unnatural acts" over the years.

Ginsberg's transgressive stance persistently raised an interrogation of the individual's relation to the social order. Whether his theme was war, pollution, CIA drug dealing, governmental malfeasance, censorship, sex, history, or love, his address was essentially to the individual and collective state of being. This was articulated succinctly in his early poem, "Metaphysics": "This is the one and only / firmament; therefore / it is the absolute world. / The circle is complete. / I am living in Eternity. / The ways of this world / are the ways of heaven." Notwithstanding the occasional patina of Buddhist or transcendental mysticism, Ginsberg's vision is anchored in this dialectic of the ways heaven reflects this world, rather than the other way around. And the ways of this world are often down and dirty. Accordingly, a near systemic use of obscenity is one, perhaps the most pervasive, function of transgression in Ginsberg's work. In "Wichita Vortex Sutra," for example, a poem of high seriousness indicting the Vietnam War, the prologue declaims the need that a new "Man of America, be born," with "No more fear of tenderness" as manifest in an image of bisexual eroticism, which is abruptly emphasized by varying an old epithet, "How big is the prick of the President?" And two lines later he further satirizes one of the most conspicuously vigorous American chauvinists, J. Edgar Hoover, with a punning version of a phallic joke, "How little the prince of the FBI, unmarried all these years!" A few pages later in that same volume, *The Fall of America*, he proposes resolutions to the Vietnam War, environmental abuses, and racism not so much via obscenity as meticulously calculated vulgarity in four precise lines under the title "Kiss Ass," "Kissass is the Part of Peace / America will have to Kissass Mother Earth / Whites have to Kissass Blacks, for Peace and Pleasure, / Only Pathway to Peace, Kissass." His inclusion of *pleasure* in so unlikely a venue is vintage Ginsberg, a satyric indication that even such noble causes as racial justice should not be all work and no play.

One aspect of Ginsberg's *jouissance*, then, is the tactical deployment of more obscenity or less to vivify the appeal of his social critique, which often simultaneously functions as a validation of homosexuality. "America" is a paramount instance. In this raucous send-up Ginsberg brilliantly satirizes the paranoia of cold war chauvinism and concludes, "It's true I don't want to join the army or turn lathes in...factories, I'm nearsighted and psychopathic anyway. / America I'm putting my queer shoulder to the wheel." In its adroit deconstruction by parody of normative assumptions about "perversity" and the good order of political economy this image is characteristic Ginsberg. Even where critique is not an object there is the frequent implication that celebrating hedonism is a political validation of it. In his 1974 song "Hardon Blues," for example, he gets right in the reader's face with his first line, "Blues is like a hardon comes right in your mouth," winds on that motif for several choruses and concludes by widening his focus to include geriatrics, "If I don't get it off right now, someday it'll all be gone." In *Howl*, madness and self destruction victimize a whole generation, caused by the cultural materialism symbolized in "Moloch." Moloch's dominance is countered by Neal Cassady, who has so "sweetened the snatches of a million girls trembling in the sunset" that the poem is essentially a tribute "to the memory of his innumerable lays of girls." Be that as it may, the appeal of Moloch and madness is potent, so Ginsberg trains the tactical weapon of obscenity on both sexual politics and its cultural context.

For all of Ginsberg's self conscious transgression of poetic and social norms, however, his work also has a distinctly erotic dimension, that is, one focused more on love than on obscenity. While *Kaddish*, his great lament for the death of his mother Naomi, is not erotic as such, it does imply via the degenerative state of his mother's life a motif of cultural desexualization. Naomi's madness subsumes her vitality, the sexual aspect of which is suggested by her youthful sensuous spontaneity, subsequently lost in her alienation from her husband. The motif of psychic confusion and sexual dysfunction is at once substantiated and dispatched in the poet's brief moment of Oedipal temptation when in the hospital Naomi's gown slips upward revealing her vagina. This image is obliquely erotic and contextualized by what is in general a tender elegiac tone. This stance is in fact characteristic of Ginsberg's erotic works although it is also informed by sexual longing or activity. "The weight of the world," Ginsberg observed early on, "is love." After an invocation of this "burden" and its "solitude," in which he evokes images of sex where "the hand moves / to the center / of the flesh... and the soul comes / joyful to the eye, " he concludes "yes, yes, / that's what / I wanted, / I always wanted... / to return / to the body / where I was born." Love, for Ginsberg, is indeed, as the saint says, on the arm. "Love Poem on Theme by Whitman" is an explicitly sexual poem evoking bisexual eroticism, and "Many Loves" is yet more elaborately explicit a reminiscence of Ginsberg's initial seduction by and of Neal Cassady, a passion he sustained and declaimed for a lifetime. Other poems describe Ginsberg's sexual relations with various, usually young men, and some similarly address his relations to his longtime lover Peter Orlovsky, and one, "This Form of Life Needs Sex" (1961), is an idiosyncratic apologia for his homosexuality. Perhaps his most famous erotic poem, "Please Master" (1968), is simultaneously an elegiac love poem to Cassady and a celebration of masochistic submission. As so often with Ginsberg, it accordingly confers a double legitimacy on "perverse" pleasure with its implicit wink at the straight world and its interrogation of "normal" pleasures.

Biography

Allen Ginsberg was born in Newark, New Jersey, the son of Louis—teacher and poet—and Naomi—a radical Russian emigree—Ginsberg, and both parents were to figure prominently in his work, especially his mother. The elder Ginsberg took the young Allen to neighboring Paterson and introduced him to William Carlos Williams, whose advice to leave off imitations of Renaissance poets and attend to the cadences of his own voice and ear became a touchstone for Ginsberg's verse composition. Similarly, his early exposure to socialist thought and causes, which permeated his extended family, profoundly impressed him and became the intellectual foundation of his life and work. While still in primary school his mother's mental health began to deteriorate, and much of the trauma of her agonistic relation to capitalist culture is evoked in his epic poem, *Kaddish*, published in 1961. He matriculated to Columbia University in 1944, the same year he met William Burroughs and Jack Kerouac. He was expelled briefly from Columbia in 1945 for drawing obscene graffiti, a pertinent foreshadowing of later years. He returned to graduate in 1948. He had a good academic record, but perhaps obtained his most vital literary instruction from Burroughs, who introduced him to such writers as Kafka, Celine, Rimbaud, and Kerouac, who encouraged him further along the lines of the spontaneous composition Williams had earlier recommended.

There followed a period of odd jobs and drifting, during which he was a merchant seaman, a dishwasher, and welder among other things. He went to San Francisco in 1953 and was for a time a market researcher, at which he had some success. By 1954, he had again met up with Kerouac and Burroughs there and had in addition met Kenneth Rexroth, Robert Duncan, Gregory Corso, Gary Snyder, Michael McLure, and Lawrence Ferlinghetti. This group of friends and acquaintances became the core of the "San Francisco Renaissance," the "Beat Generation," and its writers. His public reading of *Howl* in San Francisco in 1955 at once inaugurated the Beat movement and stamped Ginsberg as its foremost figure. When *Howl and Other Poems* was published in 1956, it was sufficiently popular to warrant Ferlinghetti's City Lights Books' publication of a second edition, which was indicted for obscenity. The trial exonerated the poem, its author, and its publisher, but in its course made all three icons of the Beat Generation and the "counterculture" it reflected.

With the publication of *Kaddish and Other Poems* in 1961, Ginsberg had added two of the most important poems of the post-war or postmodern period to the canon of American literature. Acknowledgment was by no means uniform, as the taint of obscenity clung to his works and was enforced for many by the flamboyance of his personality (e.g., removing his

trousers at a public reading of his works), his self–proclaimed homosexuality, his public apologias for hallucinogens, and his radical, confrontational style of politics. In addition to the two major works, by the end of the sixties Ginsberg had published *Empty Mirror* (1961), *Reality Sandwiches* (1963), and *Planet News* (1967), the latter two only slightly less popular than *Howl* and *Kaddish*. As the Vietnam war continued through the decade Ginsberg was a vocal critic and conspicuous protestor against it, most famously in Chicago during the 1968 Democratic convention.

By 1970, Ginsberg was an international celebrity and an index of countercultural potency. *The Fall of America, Poems of these States* was published in 1972, *Allen Verbatim*, interviews and conversations about poetics, politics, and such cultural institutions as the CIA's involvement in drug trafficking' in 1974, and *Mind Breaths, Poems*, 1977. After the United States withdrew from Vietnam in 1974, Ginsberg devoted considerable time and energy to the Jack Kerouac School of Disembodied Poetics that he had founded in conjunction with the Buddhist Naropa Institute in Colorado. He was its director for many years, and under his aegis many of his old Beat comrades—including Burroughs, Corso, Snyder, Ferlinghetti, and others—came to teach there on occasion. His *Collected Poems* were published in 1984, and subsequent poems appeared in *White Shroud*, 1986, and *Cosmopolitan Greetings*, 1994. He died April 5, 1997 in New York City at the age of 70. A National Day of Remembrance was held in 25 cities across the United States and around the world on April 13, 1997.

PETER MICHELSON

Selected Works

Collected Poems, 1947–1980. New York, 1984.
Selected Poems, 1947–1995. New York, 1996.

Further Reading

Breslin, James E. *From Modern to Contemporary.* Chicago, 1984.
Howard, Richard. "Allen Ginsberg." *Alone with America.* New York, 1980.
Hyde, Lewis, ed. *On the Poetry of Allen Ginsberg.* Ann Arbor, MI: 1984.

Kramer, Jane. *Allen Ginsberg in America*. New York, 1969.

Merrill, Thomas F. *Allen Ginsberg*. Revised edition. Boston, 1988.

Miles, Barry. *Ginsberg: A Biography*. New York, 1989.

Mottram, Eric. *Allen Ginsberg in the Sixties*. Brighton, England: Unicorn Bookshop, 1972.

Pearloff, Marjorie. *Poetic License*. Evanston, IL, 1990.

Portugese, Paul Cornel. *The Visionary Poetics of Allen Ginsberg*. Santa Barbara, CA, 1978.

Schumacher, Michael. *Dharmation: A Biograph of Allen Ginsberg*. New York, 1992.

GODARD D'AUCOUR, CLAUDE

1716–1795
French novelist, satirist, playwright, and financier.

There is no known echo of *Lettres au chevalier Danteuil et de Mademoiselle de Thelis* (1742), or of d'Aucour's other early works. His *Mémoires turcs* of 1743, on the other hand, enjoyed some notoriety to which numerous subsequent editions testify. This novel is in some ways an imitation of Montesquieu's *Lettres persanes* (and of its imitations such as Poullain de Saint-Foix's *Lettres d'une Turque à Paris*), but clearly his model is even more Claude Crébillon, whose *Le Sopha* had appeared just the previous year. Composed in the form of a diptych (first the adventures of Dely, then the letters of Achmet), the novel features Muslim initiations into the loose sexual mores of Parisians, and other kinds of contrasts between amorous and religious ways of the Turks, Persians, and French. It is thus largely a piece of social satire, much of it directed at the Church and the clergy, none of which is particularly scintillating compared with d'Aucour's distinguished predecessors.

His only work that is at all remembered today is *Thémidore*, which was published clandestinely—that is, without authorization of the book police—in 1744. It is a fairly short novel, the witty story of a few months in the gamboling life of a handsome libertine magistrate (*conseiller au Parlement*) of twenty-four, and rife with allusions to contemporary Parisian life. Thémidore enjoys all the insolent privileges of rank, including that of having his enemies locked up when needed. The protagonist's dissolute behavior appeared on several counts to reflect that of the real Alexis Dubois d'Anisy, also a *conseiller au Parlement*, whose father, a powerful judge, had the police seize the book and send the bookseller, named Mérigot, off to a fortnight in prison.

These adventures (mainly amorous), which make no claim other than to entertain, are described at the outset as being written with discretion: in other words, crude language is always avoided in favor of metaphorical suggestion; but nevertheless "sometimes risqué and apt to provoke coquettish thoughts." Nevertheless, "love" in this book never refers to anything other than sexual desire, and denotation of sexual activity is more explicit than anything one would find in Crébillon or Duclos. The emphasis is not on seduction but on variety and performative prowess; one variation on the lovers' virtuosity is to copulate through the grill of a convent parlor where Thémidore's father has had Rozette confined.

Less laden with hedonistic philosophizing than many other erotic novels, this one is notable for its unusually frank lyricism about sexual pleasure: "How often, amidst these delights one can only feel, did I wish to be consumed in what I was feeling! Why has nature limited our strength, while extending our desires so far? Or rather, why do they not come in equal proportion?" The protagonist has no principles, but also no doctrine.

There is, however, a sort of mechanistic theory at work. "You can make men do what you wish, once you have discovered the art of setting in motion certain springs that power their whole machine." Like other literary libertines in the wake of Versac (in Crébillon's *Égarements du cœur et de l'esprit*), Thémidore claims perfect knowledge of women and can therefore explain specific events through general rules: "Tears are contagious: if one woman weeps, another will too, as well as any others who happen along, ad infinitum." Even the pious have their particular sensual vulnerabilities (echoes of Marivaux's *Le paysan parvenu* and Crébillon's *Le sopha*); indeed Thémidore recommends devout women to any friend who is "sensual, delicate, and refined in his pleasures."

The text is rich in metaphors so graphic that they are almost not metaphorical at all: "She frolics with pleasure, but she holds it back as long as she can from its true destination: what an unusual taste, to prefer caressing a good fruit to squeezing out its juice!" Watching Laura play the flute, Rozette protests the "indecent" way it is done: "she objected to the tonguing, and insisted that a woman should never touch a flute in company." Indeed much of the book's humor, and good humor, lies in its frankly joyful metaphors: "We had promised each other to wait until that night; but unmindful of that, we borrowed against the future. She led me from one pleasure to another, and strewed with flowers the avenue to the palace, where I was received with full honors." One could almost call it a comic novel, such is the levity and gaiety that temper its licence.

Another notable feature of the work is the expectation of expertise on the woman's part. Rozette is technically accomplished and knows how to modulate her roles to maximize pleasure: "Rozette knew the map of my journey; she had seen me point to the spot where I intended to go, and had decided to provide me some entertainment along the way." It may be that some of her delaying tactics hint at the art of awaiting moments of infertility so as to limit her own exposure to risks of pregnancy. An original aspect of this skill is the erotic function of decor: the mirrors and violet sopha, not to mention the lace Rozette wears and the heady perfume filling her boudoir and, are integral parts of the sensual

atmosphere, in this way foreshadowing Vivant Denon's *Point de lendemain.*

Biography

Claude Godard was the son of a cloth merchant and civic leader in Langres; he took the name d'Aucour from Jean Barbier d'Aucour, perhaps his uncle, a member of the Académie Française who had died in 1694. In his youth, determined to succeed as a writer, he produced a flurry of works in several genres, particularly plays and satires; but he did not pursue. In 1747 he made a rich marriage to Claire Poisson (distant cousin of Madame de Pompadour) and became a highly successful financier, trading at first in foodstuffs and military supply, and finally a Fermier Général (partner in the national tax franchise) in 1754. He was ennobled in 1756, and acquired the title of Marquis de Plancy in 1764. He joined a Masonic lodge in Paris called "Les Amis Réunis" in 1776 and managed somehow to survive the Revolution.

PHILIP STEWART

Selected Works

Mémoires turcs, avec l'histoire galante de leur séjour en France, 1743. *Thémidore*, 1744.

Editions

The original text of *Thémidore* is included in two anthologies: *Romanciers libertins du XVIIIe siècle*, edited by Raymond Trousson (Paris: Robert Laffont, 1993), and vol. I of the Pléiade edition by the same name, directed by Patrick Wald Lasowaki (Paris: Gallimard, 2000). The former, like a separate edition of 1980 (Paris: Lattès), bears a dubious subtitle, *Mon histoire et celle de ma maîtresse*, which is not found in editions prior to 1781.

Further Reading

Trousson, Raymond. introduction to *Thémidore* in *Romans libertins du XVIIIe siècle*. Paris: Robert Laffont, 1993.
Dictionnaire de biographie française. T. XVI (1985).
Dufrenoy, Marie-Louise. *L'Orient romanesque en France 1704–1789*. Montréal: Beauchemin, 1946.

GOMBROWICZ, WITOLD

1904–1969
Polish novelist and playwright

Pornografia

Gombrowicz's third novel, *Pornografia* [*Pornography*], was written in 1958 and published in 1960 by Kultura, Paris. It is representative of the intense eroticism without sex which permeates Gombrowicz's writing. In his preface to *Pornografia*, the author describes it as a "noble," "classical," "sensually metaphysical novel" (9). "Man, as we know, aims at the absolute. At fulfillment. At truth, at God, at total maturity (...) [In *Pornografia*] another of man's aims appears, a more secret one, undoubtedly, one which is in some way illegal: his need for the unfinished... for imperfection... for inferiority... for youth..." (5). This peculiar twist on Socrates' understanding of eros in Plato's *Symposium* is dressed in an absurdist plot and poetic imagery.

The action of *Pornografia* takes place in Poland, during World War II. Fryderyk and Witold, who before the war were men of theater and letters, are visiting acquaintances at a country estate. There they become fascinated with the teenagers Karol and Henia and, in particular, with the undeveloped potential for a sexual attraction between the two youths. Starving for creation, but deprived of their normal creative means, the two guests immediately recognize in the young people perfect material for molding and fall into a passionate fictionalizing of reality. They make the teenagers perform a series of symbolic acts that are supposed to rouse the latent erotic urge between them: from Henia's turning up Karol's trousers to performing an erotic pantomime designed for a single voyeur, Henia's official fiancee Waclaw, to committing a murder together.

The four characters form a quadrangle of half-admitted, half-suppressed erotic magnetism: Henia and Karol are attracted to each other only in so far as they are watched and dominated by the two directors of the performance. They are obedient and at the same time playfully aware of their erotic power over Fryderyk and Witold: "(...) if the Older is submitted to the Younger—what darkness! What perversity and shame! How many traps! And yet Youth, biologically superior, physically more beautiful, has no trouble in charming and conquering the adult, already poisoned by death" (Preface, 9). The two elderly men are embarassed to communicate directly about this, and exchange secret letters to compare notes on recent events and design their plot. From the very beginning of the novel, there is a sense of suppressed homoerotic attraction between them that is vented through their shared watching of the young couple.

The voyeurism in the novel is described by Witold as "żerująca pornografia"—pornography that feasts on the object of desire. The exact object of desire remains, however, obscure. Nothing really happens between the two young people. It is precisely the potential relationship between Henia and Karol, and between themselves, that keeps Fryderyk and Witold aflame. A painful and sweet sense of blockage escalates toward a series of absurd deaths in the end of the novel.

Lady Amelia, Henia's would-be-mother-in-law, is the first to die. The last pillar of propriety in the novel, under Fryderyk's influence she loses her decorum and fights with a farmboy caught in the pantry. Fatally wounded by him with a kitchen knife, she dies, indifferent to the crucifix, with her eyes fixed on Fryderyk. Three more homicides follow with no tragic significance whatsoever. According to Witold, killing is "no less sensual, no less guilty, no less ardent than love" (188). In the eroticized world of the novel, the murders have the relieving function of orgasms. This pattern—essentially a parody of tragic death in drama—can be observed also in Gombrowicz's plays *Iwona, Ksiezniczka Burgunda* [*Ivona, Princess of Burgundia*], *Ślub* [*The Marriage*], and *Operetka* [*Operetta*].

"I do not believe in a nonerotic philosophy. I do not trust any desexualized idea," the author confesses in his *Diary*. In *Pornografia*, as well as in his other novels, Gombrowicz explores erotic desire as a creative force. Pairs of creator figures similar to that of Fryderyk and Witold, and linked by a relationship of erotic attraction and uncertainty, appear in *Trans-Atlantyk* [*Trans-Atlantic*] and *Kosmos* [*Cosmos*]. This model can be traced back to Gombrowicz's first novel, *Ferdydurke*, in which the grotesque relationship between the teacher and his thirty-year-old student has sadomasochistic overtones. In *Trans-Atlantyk*, Witold, a fresh exile in Argentina, observes Gonzalo's game of seduction. Its object is a simple-minded adolescent Polish boy. The act of observation and Witold's role as a narrator, however, gradually lead to a symbolic collaboration with Gonzalo whose first aim is to liberate the boy from the authority of his father and fatherland. The foreign and the strange are presented as a source of irresistible erotic appeal. The relationship between Fryderyk and Witold in *Pornografia* is less asymmetrical, but the creative initiative remains in Fryderyk's hands. In *Kosmos*, Witold takes over. He both generates the plot and narrates it, while his partner and roommate Fuks, is a passive, but needed witness. Significantly, in this novel Witold tends to divide himself into an acting and narrating consciousness, none of which is fully aware of the causes and meaning of the events (for example, he himself hangs a cat and afterwards wonders who of the other characters could have done this). As the story progresses, the narrating voyeur Witold becomes more and more fascinated with the acting Witold's erotic perception of the world. Witold falls in love with himself—a kind of narcissism both admitted and parodied in the *Diary*. Thus, paradoxically, the mechanism of the novel's creation is exhibited to the reader, but appears to be a mystery to its creator. By undressing the devices of his own literary imagination, in *Pornografia* and *Kosmos*, Gombrowicz seduces the audience into a voyeuristic participation in his creative process.

Biography

Born August 4 1904 in Małoszyce, Poland. Studied at Warsaw University, 1922–1927; law degree, 1927. Studied philosophy and economics at the Institut des Hautes Études Internationales, Paris, 1927. Contributed to Warsaw newspapers, from 1933. In 1939, visited Argentina and remained there until 1963. Wrote for Buenos Aires newspapers, from 1940. Secretary, Polish Bank, Buenos Aires, 1947–1953. In 1963, moved to Berlin, then to Vence, France, 1964–1969. Married Marie-Rita Labrosse, 1969. Awards: Kultura Prize, 1961; International Literary Prize, 1967. Died in Vence, 25 July 1969. Author of five novels, short stories, four plays, and a *Diary* (1953–1966).

KATIA MITOVA

Editions

Pornografia. Paris: Kultura, 1960; edited by Jan Błoński, Kraków: Wydawnictwo Literackie, 1986; as *Pornografia* translated from the French by Alaistar Hamilton. New York: Grove Press, 1966; republished in *Cosmos and Pornografia*, New York: Grove Press, 1985.

Selected Works

Pamiętnik z okresu dojrzewania. 1933; new extended edition under the title *Bakakaj*, 1957, 1986.
Ferdydurke, 1937, 1957, 1986; as *Ferdydurke*. translated by Eric Mosbacher. New York: Grove Press, 1961; translated by Danuta Borchardt. 2000.
Iwona, księżniczka Burgunda. 1938 (in *Skamander*); as a book, 1958, 1986; as *Ivona, Princess of Burgundia*, translated by Krystyna Griffith-Jones and Catherine Robins. 1969.
Trans-Atlantyk. 1953, 1957, 1986; as *Trans-Atlantyk*, translated by Carolyn French and Nina Karsov. 1994.
Ślub. 1953, 1986; as *The Marriage*, translated by Louis Iribarne. 1969.
Kosmos. 1965, 1986; as *Cosmos*, translated by Eric Mosbacher. 1985.
Operetka. 1966, 1986; as *Operetta*, translated by Louis Iribarne. 1971.
Dziennik 1953–1966. In *Kultura*, Paris, 3 vols, 1969, 1986; as *Diary*, edited by Jan Kott. translated by Lillian Vallee. 3 vols, 1988—1993.
Entreitiens avec Dominique de Roux (in French). 1968, 1969; as *A Kind of Testament*, translated by Alastair Hamilton. 1973.
Przewodnik po filozofii w szesc godin i kwadrans. 1971.
Wspomnienia polskie. Wedrowki po Argentynie. 1977.
Gombrowicz filozof. 1991.
Dziela zebrane. 15 vols. In progress, 1986—
Aforyzmy, refleksie, mysli i sentencje. 1994.

Further Reading

Boyers, Robert. "Aspects of the Perverse in Gombrowicz's *Pornografia*." *Salmagundi* 17 (1971): 19–46.
Dedieu, Jean-Claude. *Witold Gombrowicz*. Paris: Marval, 1993.

Głowiński, Michał. "Parodia konstruktywna (O 'Pornografii' Gombrowicza)" in *Gombrowicz i krytycy*, edited by Zdzisław Łapiński. Cracow: Wydawnictwo literackie, 1984: 365–383.

Gomori, George. "The Antinomies of Gombrowicz." *Modern Language Review* 73 (1978): 119–129.

Hultberg, Peer. "Pornografia i alchemia: prolegomena do analizy *Pornografii* Gombrowicza." *Pamiętnik literacki* 64 (1973):179–188.

Jarzębski, Jerzy. *Gra w Gombrowicza*. Warszawa: Panstwowy Instytut Wydawniczy, 1982.

Jeleński, Constanty and Dominique de Roux (editors). *Gombrowicz*. Paris: l'Herne, 1971.

Łęgierski, Mihał. *Modernizm Witolda Gombrowicza: Wybrane zagadnienia*. Stockholm: Almqvist & Wiskel, 1996.

Pawłowski, Janusz. "Erotyka Gombrowicza" in *Gombrowicz i krytycy*, edited by Zdzisław Łapiński. Cracow: Wydawnictwo literackie, 1984, pp. 531–560.

Thompson, Ewa. *Witold Gombrowicz*. Boston: Twayne, 1979.

GOVARDHANA

Twelfth–Thirteenth century
Sanskrit poet

Govardhana composed one work that we know of, the *Āryāsaptaati* (The Collection of Seven Hundred Verses in the *Āryā* Meter). Apart from this we have only a handful of stray verses in the anthologies. The anthology the *Saduktikaramata* [*The Ear-Nectar of Good Verse*] compiled at the court of his patron contains the majority of these, but verses are also to be found in an anthology from the Cåhamåna court, the *Çår gadharapaddhati* (c. fourteenth-century Rajasthan) as well as Ropa Gosvåm's *Padyåvali* (c. seventeenth-century Bengal).

The third verse of Jayadeva's *Gotagovinda* lists and praises the prominent poets of the literary salon of Lakßmaᵃasena's court. While Jayadeva says of himself "only Jayadeva knows the perfection of verbal arrangement," he remarks that Govardhana "has no rival for his crafting of true subjects of supreme erotic sentiment." *Āryåsaptaat* verse 39 is a panegyric to Lakma'asena. Thus we have positively conclusive evidence for placing these poets together. Verses of all the Sena court poets abound in the *Saduktikarᵃåmata*. This is one of a handful of such conclusively documented literary salons in the history of Sanskrit letters, and the poets bore in common a commitment to intense and finely crafted eroticism.

Govardhana's poetry is well known for its explicit, even risqué description of sexuality. The sex scenes of his poetry are embedded in ironic vignettes of rustic life.

Govardhana is an exquisite commentator on the contradiction between rural and urban modes of comportment. He mocks the context-sensitivity and potential absurdity of Sanskrit ideals of feminine allure in a sardonic verse:

> Straighten your gait. Leave off, girlfriend, all your urban ways. Here, thinking you a witch, the village-head will beat you just for casting crooked glances.
>
> (140)

The sidelong glances so basic to erotic communication in Sanskrit poetry, lose their eroticism in the village; they are deprived of their august universality, and revealed to be *någara* "urban." In the wrong locale, a woman could be identified as a witch, when she is simply trying to seduce—a hilarious sequence of events.

The precedent for this style of rustic erotic description was originally set in the third century by the Prakrit poet and Såtavåhana king Håla who composed his *Sattasa* in Mahårår Prakrit. Håla's collection contains seven hundred some odd verses, and the sections, arranged alphabetically, are called *Vrajyå*-s. These are elements Govardhana adapted to his Sanskrit composition. He himself comments on his Prakrit antecedents:

> Speech whose flavor is suited to Prakrit has been forcefully drawn into Sanskrit, as if the Yamunå, whose waters naturally flow downward, were drawn forcibly to the firmament of the sky.
>
> (I.52)

What Govardhana had dragged into Sanskrit from below was also a frank and bawdy mode of depicting sexuality, verging on the vulgar (what in Sanskrit literary theory is referred to as "*gråmya*" 'of the village'). He is fond of puns and this punning verse even verges on the pornographic:

> Pressed to her ample thigh, your hand making the shape of an elephant with extended trunk; like an elephant butting against a riverbank, *gåra*[eroticism/red decoration made on elephants' bodies] adorns you.
>
> (505)

In the introductory and closing portions of his poem, Govardhana reflects on his art, characterizing his poetic departure; at one point valorizing a poetic nakedness:

> Naked for the erotic style, like a beloved naked for lovemaking, is pure language full of aesthetic emotion conducive to pleasure. Language without aesthetic emotion, but replete with rhetorical figures, is unpleasant like a lifeless, ornamented doll.
>
> (I.54)

Govardhana's poetry often conforms very much to what he has to tell us about it. His pithy and realistic descriptions abandon the often-stereotyped character of classical Sanskrit poetry and he is at pains to define the matter of poetry as unalloyed worldly experience:

> A *sotra* is composed by the crooked glance of a young girl. The corner of a wanton lady's eye composes a commentary thereon. Poet-boys study the sense from the sub-commentary strung together by her messenger-girl.
>
> (I.50)

He goes as far as to advocate a hands-on approach for poets:

> Only of a poet who has tasted the nectar of a beloved's lips are the verses sweet. A cuckoo does not sing a sweet tone without tasting the mango blossom.
>
> (I.49)

He likewise defends the relevance and practical importance of his worldly poetry:

> Those proud-minded men who lack respect for this *Åryåsaptaat*, like men who lack a female go-between, they do not enter the heart of a lover-girl.
>
> (I.53)

Lakma'asena's kingdom was invaded in 1204/5 by the Turkish conquistador Muhammud Bakhtiyar Khalji, ushering in a new era in Bengal and South Asia as a whole. The Delhi Sultanate was founded in 1206, eclipsing the sovereignty of the regional states of the medieval period. A new era had likewise begun in the Sanskrit poetry of this period. At the Sena court an unprecedented poetic experimentation took place, characterized by a mixing of the high and the low, courtly and rustic varieties of eroticism. Govardhana was the practitioner and commentator *par excellence* on this new variety of erotic verse and that he was among the cleverest Sanskrit poets of the tradition is attested by his title "*åcårya*" master. Some of the greatest scholars of a later period of Indian intellectual history were to compose commentaries on his work, including such luminaries as the grammarian Någeabhaa and the scholar of law and custom [*dharmaåstra*] Anantapa[a]∂ita.

That Govardhana was widely read in the wake of his lifetime is attested by the broad diffusion of manuscripts of his work. There have been some works modeled on the *Åryåsaptaat*, including Bihår Lål's Hind Sattasa (c. seventeenth century) and Viçvevara's Sanskrit *Åryåsaptaat* (c. eighteenth century).

Biography

Flourished in the latter half of the twelfth century CE at the court of king Laksma[a]asenaof Bengal (present India/Bangladesh).

JESSE ROSS KNUTSON

Further Reading:

Chowdury, Abdul Momin. *Dynastic History of Bengal c. 750–1200 A.D.* Dacca: Asiatic Society of Pakistan, 1967.

De, Sushil Kumar. "Bengal's Contribution to Sanskrit Literature and Studies in Bengal Vaisnavism." Indian Studies Past and Present, Calcutta, 1960.

Ingalls, Daniel H. "A Sanskrit Poetry of Village and Field: Yogeçvara and his Fellow Poets." Journal of the American Oriental Society, vol. 74 no.3, 1954.

———— *An Anthology of Sanskrit Court Poetry: Vidyåkara's Subhåßitaratnakoßa.* Harvard Oriental Series 44, Harvard University Press, Cambridge, 1965.

Lienhard, Siegfried. *A History of Classical Poetry: Sanskrit—Pali—Prakrit.* Vol. 3 fasc. Of *History of Indian Literature* ed. Jan Gonda. Wiesbaden: Harrassowitz, 1983.

GRAINVILLE, PATRICK

1947–
French novelist

Les Flamboyants

From his early "mythical biography," Patrick Grainville has drawn attention to the luxuriance of his vocabulary, and to the wealth of his metaphors. His novel *Les Flamboyants* reveals a use of sensuous images, particularly vivacious when the king Tokor and his mistress Helen are describing men or women. Helen is portrayed through Tokor's desire, her legs are compared to "sweet whips." At this moment, his style becomes vigorous like Claudel's verve. Provocative women form the bulk of the splendours of Tindjili Palace: they are compared to water flowing from one room to another; they become like "fetishes" with manes of hair, tufts, bush, and perfumes. Some are "tall," "carnal," or compared to mermaids, daurades, or fleshy fruits. Tokor, the "king of women," wants to be named "the great Analogist," and his words are lush and fertile: Helen is a female Python, a "pythonne," and "La Méza" is "the great Cantharid." Helen decides to cast a refined and gourmet eye on reality, and it is the principle in which the whole novel has been written.

The location of the novel, an African and equatorial country, enables the author to draw the main outlines of an erotic, violent, and lively society. The novel begins with a hurricane, like a kind of Nature's climax above the capital of Mandouka. Its people are at the same time animated and voluptuous, with a huge, muddy, and stinky shantytown. Most of the novel is located in the "completely naked Hourla, fur-lined with massive green," and hypnotized characters leave the capital to penetrate the "flesh of the Yali country." Tokor dreams about the bush as if it was a hairy female body. African nature seems to be ruled by animal forces and sexual impulses, like the night violated by sudden yells. Tokor dreams of a "phallocratic Arcadia" on the riverside of Maloumbé. In the Toura villages, a

sexual ritual initiation between teenagers is described in a visual and ethnographic way.

An intense excitement, linked to animality, lifts up the story, with wild imagination fired by the tropical aspects of nature and by the strange behavior of king Tokor.

He is well known for his "pansexualism," his passion for rape, and frolicsome games, like swallowing hummingbirds and expelling them through his anus, half alive. Tokor is much like an animal, unlike his guest, William, compared to an angel. The king of Yali loves lying in the mud of Maloumbé, being licked and tramped by wild animals who come to drink at night. He loses consciouness and is assaulted by carnal and humoral sensations. Just like what used to happen when he was alive, King Soloa dies covered by thousand of butterflies. Nicknames enable the metamorphosis of some characters into animals: Lucy is called "dragonfly" and Moanda the "serpent-eater." The "female forces" of the shantytown are compared to "antilopes," and the Méza is an "animal queen" with an exciting fur. The countryside is often compared to animals, like the savannah crossed by fugitive furs. Exotic animals suggest sexual images, like girafes, compared to "telluric necks," or to "golden phallus."

One reason for the omnipresence of nature and animality in this novel is that eroticism is regarded as sacred in a dionysian sense. The Yali country, a carnal abyss, is often compared to flesh. The five hundred special guards are virile and naked: in order to prepare for war they are kept prisoners of the fleshy and soft embrace of flowers for two days. A woman called "la Bouboubou" is compared to a volcano, and a lake turns into a real volcano which Tokor enters, like "the rapist of the Prometheous fire." The king introduces himself as "the great Concupiscent of the kingdom." When he desires to sleep with Helen, he does so "tellurically," and everybody around him goes into raptures over his telluric ecstasy. The Yali country is considered as sacred, and even the teenagers of the slum dream of lying naked in the dust, in a sort of intercourse with Earth. King Tokor is so excited that he strokes the impalas and sits among them as if he were on a sofa. He then, of embracing the stellar heaven mass, pierced by stellar splinters after having shared saucy stories with his officers. The dionysiac eroticism culminates with the Diorles, a tribe hidden in the equatorial forest.

They are seen bathing, naked, clasped in each other's arms, before they are massacred by the "yulmatian bestiality." They glitter with golden mud; men hold their genitalia in a small purse, whereas females exhibit shared vaginas with an artificially erected and painted clitoris. More astounding are the Ludies met by William at the end of the novel: they have thin thighs, fair skin, and only exhibit pure emotions. Androgynous, they have a clitoris that can be used as a penis, and practice all manner of sexual, oral, anal, and incestuous relations, until they die at the age of eighteen. They do what they want with their bodies and symbolize a longing for a lost Eden, located in the Hourla. This place is at the same time real and part of a fairy-tale. Tokor is perhaps too crude to see them, but he is pointed out as "the king of the Hourla and of the Diorles," or as the "uncounscious" of the Yali country. Therefore, his dead body is cut into different pieces put in various points of the Hourla, to be eaten and swallowed by wild beasts.

The lost paradise represented in this novel can be found in the forest with the young Diorles, and with the licentious creatures called Ludies, but the ultimate and extreme love of Tokor for Helen is part of it too. Their love is compared to "a vast fireplace of eternal embers."

Biography

Born in 1947, at Villers (Calvados), he is a certified art teacher. He published his mythical biography in three volumes. Received the Prix Goncourt for *Les Flamboyants* (1976).

Selected Works

La Toison. Gallimard, Paris, 1972.
La Lisière. Gallimard, Paris, 1973.
L'Abîme. Gallimard, Paris, 1974.
Images du désir. Playboy/Filipacchi, Paris, 1978.
L'orgie, la neige. Seuil, Paris, 1990.
L'Ombre de la bête. Balland, Paris, 1993.

Further Reading

Radioscopie with Jacques Chancel. 1977.
Hutton, M.A. "Cultural Metissage: Victor Hugo, Egon Schiel and the Egyptian in Patrick Grainville's *Les Anges et les faucons*." Texte/Image, Durham, University of Durham, 1999.

GRANDES, ALMUDENA

1960 –
Spanish journalist, novelist, and short-story writer.

Grandes' literary career was launched in 1989, while still working at a publishing house when her first book won the XI *La Sonrisa Vertical* prize for *Las edades de Lulú* [*The Ages of Lulu*] (1989). Powerfully written, Grande's debut novel had immediate impact: it has not only been translated into 21 languages but also adapted for film by Spanish director Bigas Luna that same year. In 2002, Grandes won three prizes for her *Los aires difíciles*; the XI Premio Arzobispo San Clemente, the Premio Salambó and the IV Premio Julián Besteiro de las Artes y de las Letras. *Los aires difíciles* debuted at the top of the Spanish bestseller lists when it was published in February 2002, and remained on the lists until June. Since then, translations have been published in Italy, France, Germany, Israel, and the Netherlands.

Grandes is known for her journalistic work; she frequently writes for the Sunday magazine of

El País newspaper, but her greatest renown comes from her fiction. Grandes mainly concentrates socially and geographically in Madrid—the city background often becomes an essential part of the story— painting a colorful picture of the life of the bourgeois family, particularly the sexual, romantic, and familial relationships. At times, the characters and the atmospheres Grandes writes about could be compared to the Spanish social novel of the 1960s, although Grandes avoids moralistic comment or judgment. Grandes' main characters are usually women, whom she often presents as almost asexual. These protagonists tend to tackle the constant allusions to their somewhat unfavorable physical aspect with a positive attitude, acceptance of personal appearance, sense of humor, and irony which usually pays off, as they never fail to find sexual and sensual balance.

Las edades de Lulú [*The Ages of Lulú*] is an intensely erotic novel chronicling the sexual awakening and subsequent sexual adventures of María Luisa Ruiz-Póveda y García de la Casa. Brought up in a middle class family in Madrid, Lulú, her family nickname, foreshadows her precocious sexual awakenings. Deprived of her mother's love and affection, Lulú turns to her older brother Marcelo who would never be without his best friend Pablo, the person who would trigger Lulú's obsession, longing, and relentless search for validation and acceptance.

It is Pablo, who is 12 years older than 15-year-old Lulú, who inspires Lulú to explore her own sexual fantasies so deeply that by the end of the book she will reach unfathomable depths.

Pablo decided not to take her back home after a concert. Instead, he leads her to his apartment and then prepares her in a way he finds suited to her age. Pablo disappears and when he comes back he is "bearing a bowl of lather on which a mirror and a razor lay crossed." Palo's obsession with a lack of pubic hair, school uniforms, and the look of innocence will become a trademark: "...He took off my knickers, pulled me abruptly towards him, [...] 'Why are you doing this?' 'Because you don't have a little girl's cunt. And I like little girl's cunts, especially when I am about to debauch them.'"

The book begins with an explicit description of a gay porn video Lulú is watching at home. A series of flashbacks reveal the protagonist's torrid sexual adventures. Led by the hand of sexual mentor Pablo, first boyfriend, then husband and father of her only daughter, Lulú's darkest desires are fostered by him who enjoys and promotes the ludic sexual hunting that depicts Madrid's most obscure night life: their cruising includes gay bars, pick up joints, and illegal brothels.

Pablo would be her corruptor and eventually her savior; Lulú's thirst for sexual discovery takes them through voyeurism, homoeroticism, and the power-plays of incest and degradation. As years go by, Lulú becomes more perverse, becoming addicted to sodomy not only dominated by Pablo but also by other men including a threesome: Pablo induces the blindfolded protagonist to her own brother Marcelo. Other heterosexual partners become her usual exercise, more often than not preferring homosexuals and transvestites which become Lulú's fascination.

Lulú's obsession with gay multi-partner sex continues even after their marriage with Pablo has collapsed: she sets out on her own in an even darker, at times frightening, quest to satisfy her insatiable desires. Lulú, now cruising solo, takes part in all sorts of orgies introducing the reader to a most peculiar S/M Madrid community. Her new friends, a bunch of transvestites, gigolos, and taxi boys offer her to take part in "little parties" they would hold. At the beginning these would be just for the sake of having some fun for free: Lulú's financial situation was beginning to decline as a result of her expensive sexual practices as she would hire two or three people at a time.

Yet, this last time, Lulú is invited to take part in a mega party that would be sponsored by an unanimous, perverse, rich gentleman—an invitation she cannot turn down but which will almost kill her.

At the time *The Ages of Lulú* was published, Grandes was already working on her second novel *Te llamaré Viernes* (1991) followed by *Malena es un nombre de tango* (1994) and a short story compilation *Modelos de mujer* (1996) representative of Spanish postmodernism about seven women that give an overview about the way in which different generations of Spanish women act and interact in a society that witnessed historical changes. *Atlas de geografía humana* (1998) and *Los aires difíciles* (2002) came out next. Her most recent work is *Castillos de cartón* (2004).

Other stories by Grandes have also been taken to the cinema: *Malena*, a film based on her *Malena es un nombre de tango* (1996, dir. Gerardo Herreo) and *Aunque tú no lo sepas* (2000, dir. Juan Vicente Córdoba) based on "El vocabulario de los balcones" were produced.

In March 2002, Grandes was awarded the IV Julián Besteiros literary prize in recognition for her work as a writer and journalist.

Biography

Almudena Grandes Hernández was born in 1960 in Madrid, Spain. Grandes studied History and Geography at the Universidad Complutense in Madrid. A "daughter of Franco," as women of her own generation who were brought up under Franco's regime are usually called, Grandes was reborn after the *Generalisimo's* death, in 1975, when Spain awoke to a radical change in uses and customs.

CAROLINA MIRANDA

Editions

Las edades de Luhí, Barcelona: Tusquets, 1989; as The Ages of Lulu (Lurid & compelling story of the sexual awakening of Maria Luisa Ruiz-Poveda y Garcia de la Casa)tr. Sonia Soto. New York: Grove Press, 1989.

Selected Works

Te llamaré viernes. Barcelona: Tusquets, 1991.
Malena es un nombre de tango. Barcelona: Tusquets, 1994.
Modelos de mujer. Barcelona: Tusquets, 1996.
Atlas de geografía humana. Barcelona: Tusquets, 1990.
Los aires difíciles. Barcelona: Tusquets, 2002.
Castillos de cartón. Barcelona: Tusquets, 2004.

Further Reading

Carballo Abengózar, Mercedes. "Almudena Grandes: sexo, hambre, amor y literatura." in *Mujeres novelistas*, edited by Redondo Goicoechea, Alicia. Madrid: Narcea, 2003.

GRANDVAL, FRANÇOIS-CHARLES RACOT DE

1710–1784
French actor and dramatist

In 1752, Grandval acquired a property in the rue Blanche and had it joined to the house that his mistress, Mlle Dumesnil, a tragedienne at the Comédie-Française, had purchased some time previously. It was in this place, designated the *Barrière Blanche*, that the two actors founded a private theater where, it is widely held, several of Grandval's erotic pieces were staged or otherwise recited. Because of the clandestine nature of Grandval's works, questions surrounding their origin persist to the present day. There are, however, eight pieces of which he is the undisputed author.

The originality of Grandval's dramatic work stems in large part from the spirit of burlesque that informs each of his plays. A pervasive, strictly sexual eroticism together with a raunchiness of dialogue sometimes bordering on the scatological are used to parody seventeenth-century writers and, in particular, the great tradition of French classical tragedy. Grandval's theatrical experience had given him a throrough knowledge of drama, enabling him to rewrite famous scenes and celebrated tirades in an erotic and parodic context. Based on a borrowing of some of the best-known verses of the classical tradition, this poetics of ironic and playful imitation reveals a wish to discredit the prestige of the tragic genre, and indeed of tradition in general. Accordingly,

Grandval's erotic plays are unforgiving in their criticism of all forms of authority, a theme at the core of Enlightenment thought. This point of view is particularly conspicuous in four of his most important pieces.

Les Deux Biscuits (*The Two Cookies*), a one-act tragedy in verse, takes the audience to the kingdom of Astracan and into the palace of Abusef. We first learn that Dilazal, son of the late king of Astracan, is hiding under the bed of the princess Abusef. Gaspariboul, a usurper who has cuckolded all the husbands in the kingdom, is courting the princess without knowing that Dilazal, her lover, is still alive. The play opens with the princess awaking from sleep as Dilazal leaves his hiding place, irritated with his mistress for having showered Gaspariboul with her favors the previous evening. But the princess defends herself well. Yes, she had organized a supper with Gaspariboul; Dilazal had, despite himself heard everything from his hiding place. However the pastry-cook, Rissole, had prepared two cookies for the occasion: "L'un était composé de mouches cantharides / Qui redonnent la force aux amants invalides, / Dans l'autre dominait l'opium et le pavot" [One was made of Spanish flies / Which return strength to impotent lovers / In the other were mainly opium and poppy seeds]. Abusef had simply eaten the wrong cookie. Satisfied, Dilazal asks the princess to organize another meeting with Gaspariboul in a tone that calls to mind Act II, Scene III of Racine's *Britannicus:* "À travers ce rideau je verrai votre foi / Madame, en lui parlant, songez que je vous voi." [Through this curtain I will see how true you are / Madame, while you speak to him, remember that I am watching.] Gaspariboul is deceived, and the lovers then decide to emasculate him as punishment for his career as a cuckold. A critical element underscores the association with this extract from Racine's play. Finally, the acrostic formed by the names on the list of actors removes any doubt as to authorship by allowing Grandval to sign his work with brio.

For Grandval, the main function of eroticism was its use as a tool for spoofing—and so further subverting—seventeenth-century values. This is clearly the case in *La Nouvelle Messaline*, a one-act burlesque tragedy in verse. The play features a heroine so debauched that her lovers are incapable of satisfying her sexually. Disappointed, she feigns a call to the religious life in order, she affirms, to "*tâter du moine*" [try out the monks] in a Carmelite convent. Before proceeding with her plan, however, the lady curses the inadequacy of her lovers by crying out in fury: "Ô rage ! ô désespoir ! ô Vénus ennemie !/ Étais-je réservée à cette ignominie ?/ N'ai-je donc encensé ton temple et tes autels/ Que pour être l'objet du faible des mortels ?" [O fury! O despair! O hostile Venus! / Have I then been destined for this ignominious fate? / Have I worshipped at your temple and your altars / Only to end up an object of mortals' feebleness?] This borrowing from Corneille's *Cid* (1636) and, notably, from the monologue of Don Diego, one of the most celebrated tirades in classical drama, highlights the function of eroticism in Grandval's works: the erotic element adds to the parody and so helps overturn and criticize the authority enjoyed by the tragic genre a century earlier. This "*ô rage! ô désespoir!*" also appears in *La Médecine de Cythère*, a two-act vaudeville show.

Corneille's *Cid* is again a target for parody in *La comtesse d'Olonne*. Inspired by an episode concerning the countess in the *Histoire amoureuse des Gaules* (1665) by Bussy-Rabutin, this short piece falls within the same subversive vein. The sleeping Madame d'Olonne (Argénie) dreams she sees the ghost of the Duke of Candale, her first lover. Upset at having been deceived so many times, he announces that "un chancre confondra [s]on con avec [s]on cul."[a canker will confuse her cunt with her arsehole."] In the following scene, we learn that the countess is in love with the Count de Guiche (Bigdore) but is in doubt as to his sexual orientation. She asks advice of the Countess de Fiesque (Gélonide) who knows him well and is told that the Count "par inclination,[...] est un branleur de pique." [The Count "...has a liking [...]for jerking off dicks."] Nevertheless, Madame d'Olonne is determined to offer herself to him. Scene III is a parody of Act II, Scene II of the *Cid*. Here, certain famous passages from the *Cid* are caricatured as follows: "Je suis jeune, il est vrai,/ À peine ai-je vingt ans, mais aux couilles bien nées,/ La valeur n'attend pas le nombre des années." [I'm young, it's true, / Not yet twenty, but to well-born balls, / Value's not measured by the count of years.] Unfortunately for Argénie, the count remains impotent. In the last scene, however, he returns and acquits himself successfully: "Je fais des cons aux culs beaucoup de différence, / Et si jusqu'à présent j'ai mieux aimé les culs, / Reine, c'est que les cons ne m'étaient pas connus." [I definitely distinguish between an arsehole and a cunt, / And if until now I have preferred arseholes,/ Majesty, it's because cunts were unknown to me.] Here again, eroticism is used in the service of parody to overturn the Cornelian heroic ethic.

Biography

François-Charles Racot de Grandval was born in Paris on October 23, 1710, the son of Marie Macé and Nicolas Racot de Grandval, a harpsichordist and dramatist. The younger Grandval first made a name for himself as an actor. His career began on November 19, 1729 when, under the name Duval, he performed the title role in the tragedy *Andronic* by Campistron. On December 31st of the same year, he was admitted to the Comédie-Française, where he remained until 1762. As an actor, Grandval excelled in the role of *petit-maître*; he was so good that his work served as a model for interpreting this type of character. He returned to the stage on February 6, 1764 to play Alceste in *The Misanthrope* but left for good in 1768, apparently because of the "dégoût que son grasseyement inspirait au public, dont il avaitété l'idole" [the disgust his throaty manner of pronouncing the "r" inspired in the public, which had at one time idolized him"] (Mlle Clairon). He died in the rue Blanche, Paris, on September 24, 1784.

MARC ANDRÉ BERNIER

Selected Works

La comtesse d'Olonne. Comédie en un acte, en vers. 1738.
L'Eunuque ou la fidèle infidélité. Parade en vaudevilles, mêlée de prose et de vers, Montmartre, 1750. [Brenner: Représentée chez Mlle Dumesnil, 1749]
Sirop-au-cul ou l'heureuse délivrance. Tragédie héroï-merdifique, 3 actes en vers. Au Temple du Goût, 1751.
Les deux biscuits. Tragédie traduite de la langue que l'on parloit jadis au royaume d'Astracan, et mise depuis peu en vers françois, 1 acte, se vend à Astracan, chez un Libraire, 1752 [Brenner: Représentée chez Mlle Dumesnil, 1749]
La nouvelle Messaline. Tragédie, 1 acte, en vers (par Pyron dit Prepucius). À Ancone, chez Clitoris, librairie rue du Sperme, vis-à-vis la Fontaine de la Semence, à la Verge d'Or, 1773 [1752].
Léandre-Nanette ou le double qui-pro-quo. Parade en un acte, en vers et en vaudevilles, achevée en 1755. À Charlotte de Montmartre, Clignancourt, 1756.
La médecine de Cythère. Parade, 2 actes en vaudeville, tirée des fastes de Syrie. Clignancourt, 1756.
Le tempérament, tragi-parade, traduite de l'Egyptien en vers français et réduite en un acte. À Charlotte de Montmartre, en octobre 1770. Au Grand Caire. [Brenner: en octobre 1755. Au Grand Caire, 1756].

Further Reading

Alexandrian, Sarane. *Histoire de la littérature érotique.* Paris: Seghers, 1989.
Alméras, Henri d' et Paul d'Estrée. *Les théâtres libertins au XVIIIe siècle.* Paris: H. Daragon Éditeur, coll. "Bibliothèque du vieux Paris," 1905.
Brenner, Clarence D. *A Bibliographical List of Plays in the French Language, 1700–1789.* California: Berkeley, 1947.
Capon, G. et R. Yve-Plessis. *Les théâtres clandestins.* Paris: Plessis Libraire, coll. "Paris galant au dix-huitième siècle," 1905.
Clairon, Hippolyte. *Mémoires.* Genève: Slatkine Reprints [réimpression de l'édition de Paris: Ponthieu Libraire au Palais-Royal, 1822], 1968.
Dictionnaire des œuvres érotiques, domaine français. Préface de Pascal Pia, Paris: Éd. Robert Laffont, coll. "Bouquins," 2001 [Mercure de France, 1971].
L'intermédiaire des chercheurs et curieux: correspondance littéraire, "notes and queries "français, questions et réponses, communications diverses à l'usage de tous, littérateurs et gens du monde, artistes, bibliophiles, archéologues, généalogistes, etc. Paris: Vve B. Duprat [puis] Libraire de la Suisse romande [puis] Sandoz et Fischbacher, 1864–1940. [XVIIe année, 25 mai 1884].
Grente, Georges, dir. *Dictionnaire des lettres françaises. Le XVIIIe siècle*, édition revue et mise à jour sous la direction de François Moureau, Paris: Fayard, coll. "La Pochothèque," 1995 [1960].
Pauvert, Jean-Jacques, éd. *Théâtre érotique français au XVIIIe siècle*, Paris: Terrain Vague, 1993.
Weller, Émile. *Dictionnaire des ouvrages français portant de fausses indications des lieux d'impression et des imprimeurs depuis le XVIe siècle jusqu'aux temps modernes*, Hildesheim/New York: Georg Olms Verlag, 1970.

GRASS, GÜNTER

1927[-]
German novelist, dramatist, poet, essayist, and artist

One of Germany's most prolific and political authors, Günter Grass is perhaps best known for the Danzig trilogy of *The Tin Drum*, 1959, *Cat and Mouse* [*Katz und Mouse*], 1961, and *Dog Years* [*Hundejahre*], 1963. *The Tin Drum*, while certainly controversial, is the least erotic of these works, focusing on a self-proclaimed savant named Oskar who purposefully stunts his growth at the age of three so that he can avoid entering the world of adults. The work has achieved its greatest notoriety through Schlöndorff's Oscar-winning 1979 film, which purportedly shows a pre-teen male performing oral sex on a teen girl. On the basis of this scene, an Oklahoma County district judge ruled in 1997 that the film constituted child pornography (a decision that was overturned in the following year). In the latter two works, erotic imagery is explored more directly through male characters caught in the transition from adolescence to adulthood, and from peace to war, each embodying the extremes of virility, violence, and impotence. An extraordinarily political author, Grass uses these characters metaphorically to examine Germany's own right of passage from the beginning of World War II through its conclusion.

Like *The Tin Drum*, both *Cat and Mouse* and *Dog Years* are presented through the eyes of unreliable narrators. Grass creates polarized male friendships in each of these works, with one figure being especially virile and the other largely impotent. The narrator of *Cat and Mouse*, Pilenz, comes to idolize his best friend, Mahlke, when the latter transforms from a sickly youth who is unable to swim or ride a bike into the strongest diver (and overall athlete) of their group. In the work's most erotic, and homoerotic, scene, Pilenz and Mahlke join their male friends in group masturbation on an abandoned minesweeper. At first Mahlke does not take part in the ritual, but he is spurred on by Tulla, a young girl who is also present (and who reappears as a sexually promiscuous adult in *Dog Years*). The other adolescents, and Pilenz in particular, are awed by both Mahlke's pronounced physical endowment and the strength of his orgasm. It is noteworthy that Mahlke remains, according to the untrustworthy narrator, uncomfortable around females and dedicated to one unattainable female figure: the Virgin Mary. This brief, defining scene of male masturbation later contrasts Pilenz's admittedly unsuccessful attempts at love-making, and magnifies his own hero-worship of the reportedly chaste Mahlke. Indeed, Pilenz's impotence is attributed to his having been the sexual object of a priest, which intensifies his interpretation of Mahlke as a religious but sexually potent figure.

Few critics have considered the relationship of Pilenz and Mahlke from a primarily homoerotic perspective, perhaps in part because it can be difficult to reconcile this interpretation with the heterosexual Grass's tendency to construct characters based upon his personal and political background. This aspect of their relationship is best symbolized by the abandoned minesweeper, an image that frames the story and signifies the suppression of those potentially explosive emotions that should not be detonated. Of particular note, the minesweeper is partially submerged and contains a radio room that is above water-level, but only accessible through a prolonged and dangerous dive. Mahlke is the only one of the adolescents capable of making this dive. As a sexual metaphor, he is therefore the only one who can enter this otherwise forbidden area, and, once inside, radio contact-emotional, verbal communication-are no longer possible.

Just as the two friends began their emotional journey on the minesweeper, they are brought back to it for the conclusion. They are separated when Mahlke steals a soldier's medal and is transferred to another school by the principal, Dr. Klohse. A few years later, Mahlke returns as a successful soldier with his own medal, but Klohse will not allow him to speak at his former school. Mahlke slaps him across the face, and chooses not to return from his military leave. At the urging of his childhood friend, Mahlke agrees to go briefly into hiding, returning to the scene of their group masturbation and Mahlke's earlier diving triumphs. Mahlke and Pilenz are once again on the minesweeper, but this time Pilenz seems to be the one in control. He encourages Mahlke to dive again into the radio room, and he gives him provisions so that he can stay submerged for a long period of time. The story ends ambiguously, however, and Pilenz reports that Mahlke never resurfaces. In the mind of Pilenz, Mahlke is completely consumed within the minesweeper, much as Pilenz is consumed by telling the story of the great Mahlke.

In *Dog Years*, Grass moves beyond the stunted childhood of *The Tin Drum* and the pained adolescence of *Cat and Mouse* into the adulthood of post-War Germany. Themes of guilt, trust, and retribution are explored through the long, complex friendship of Eddi Amsel and Walter Matern. Their relationship spans several decades and is characterized by a subtler current of homoeroticism than that which connected Pilenz to Mahlke, with Grass focusing here on the balance of the introspective, creative male artist (Amsel) and the hyper-masculine, destructive soldier (Matern).

Although they begin as literal blood brothers, the two are consistently brought into conflict by the ideologies around them. Matern alternately protects and bullies Amsel, who is half-Jewish, at one point leading a Nazi gang in beating his friend so severely that all of his teeth must be replaced. Yet his volatility is tied explicitly to his virility: at the conclusion of the war, Matern seeks vengeance against all ex-Nazis (except himself) largely by sleeping with their daughters, wives, and girlfriends. In contrast, Amsel's sexuality seems suppressed into the creation of terrifying sculptures and scarecrows. The name "Matern" appears naturally and ironically tied to "maternal," but it is Amsel who evokes the image of a mother, giving birth to his art. It is significant that their aspect of the narrative concludes with a ceremonial bath that cannot cleanse them from the past.

Much literary criticism centers on Grass's political statements and artistic struggles. However, he also infuses a number of his works with an erotic (and often homoerotic) undercurrent that is inextricably tied to the violent and sexualized masculinity that defined much of Nazi Germany. The dangerous and forbidden male friendships of Pilenz/Mahlke and Amsel/Matern, in particular, should also be analysed within this erotic context.

Biography

Born in Danzig, October 16, 1927. Attended elementary school (*Volksschule*) and high school (*Gymnasium*) in Danzig, 1933[-]1944. Member of the Hitler Youth (*Hitlerjugend*), 1937[-]1941. Served as anti-aircraft gunner and soldier in World War II and visited Dachau concentration camp [*Konzentrationslage*], 1944[-]1945. Studied sculpture at Düsseldorf Academy of the Arts, 1948[-]1951. Traveled to Italy and France, 1951 [-]1952. Continued study of sculpture at Berlin Academy of the Arts, 1953. Married Swiss ballet dancer Anna Schwarz, 1954 (divorced 1978); three sons and two daughters. Befriended Willy Brandt and supported the Social Democratic Party (*Sozialdemokratische Partei Deutschlands*), 1961; officially joined the Social Democratic Party, 1983. Elected to the American Academy of Arts and Sciences, 1970. Controversial film version of Grass's first novel, *The Tin Drum* [*Die Blechtrommel*], directed by Volker Schlöndorff premiered, 1979. Married German organist Ute Grunert, 1979; no children. Elected president of the Berlin Academy of the Arts. Major awards and honors: Berlin Critics' Prize, 1960; Berlin Fontane Prize, 1968; honorary doctorate from Harvard, 1976; honorary doctorate from the University of Poznań, 1990; honorary doctorate from the University of Gdańsk (formerly Danzig) and honorary Polish citizenship, 1993; Literature Prize of Bavarian Academy of Fine Arts, 1994; the Nobel Prize for Literature, 1999.

WALTER RANKIN

Selected Works

Die Blechtrommel. 1959; as *The Tin Drum*, translated by Ralph Manheim, 1961.
Katz und Maus. 1961; as *Cat and Mouse*, translated by Ralph Manheim, 1963.
Hundejahre. 1963; as *Dog Years*, translated by Ralph Manheim, 1965.
Hochwasse. 1963; as *Flood* in *Four Plays*, translated by Ralph Manheim and A. Leslie Willson, 1967.
Örtlich betäubt. 1969; as *Local Anaesthetic*, translated by Ralph Manheim, 1969.

Further Reading

Arnold, Heinz Ludwig editor. *Blech getrommelt: Günter Grass in der Kritik*, Göttingen: Steidl, 1997.

Cunliffe, Gordon W. *Günter Grass.* New York: Twayne, 1969.

Keele, Alan Frank. *Understanding Günter Grass.* Columbia, SC: University of South Carolina Press, 1988.

O'Neill, Patrick. *Günter Grass Revisited.* New York: Twayne, 1999.

Preece, Julian. *The Life and Work of Günter Grass: Literature, History, Politics.* New York: St. Martin Press, 2001.

Reddick, John. *The "Danzig Trilogy" of Günter Grass: A Study of The Tin Drum, Cat and Mouse, and Dog Years.* New York: Harcourt Brace Jovanovich, 1974.

GRAY, ALASDAIR

1934–
Scottish novelist

Sexuality is a recurring theme of Gray's fiction. Two of his novels, *1982 Janine* and *Something Leather*, are especially erotic.

1982 Janine

1982 Janine consists of the sexual fantasies and reminiscences of Jock MacLeish which take place during a night he spends at a hotel in Greenock, a small town outside Glasgow. Jock is an alcoholic with a failed marriage who has not been with a woman for many years. In order to beat chronic insomnia and sexual frustration, he resorts to masturbation.

The first ten chapters of the book present Jock's fantasies. These involve various plots. In the first fantasy plot Janine has a job interview at an exclusive millionaires' club in Scotland. She is dressed in revealing clothing. During the interview, one of the members of the club makes sexual advances towards her, but the fantasy has an anticlimactic ending which brings no satisfaction to Jock.

The same premature ending characterizes the second fantasy plot, set somewhere in America. Superb intends to meet her lover. But her all-powerful policeman husband has her arrested and brought to a police station, where she is tortured and raped by Big Momma. The two fantasy plots are combined in a third one. Here, Helga is a director of erotic films in which the other women of Jock's fantasies appear.

The unresolved fantasies and the depressing recollections drive Jock to a suicide attempt. But an inner voice, referred to as God, helps him pull through. After this turning point, Jock reviews his formative years and by dawn he is a new man, determined to quit his job and seek out Denny, his first love.

It is also Gray's most overtly political novel. The date *1982* of the title points to the specificity of Jock's experience. The night that the novel unfolds is set around the time of the Falklands war. Jock has a vested interest in voting for Thatcher, yet he hides the fact because of his uneasy moral conscience. He justifies his crypto-conservatism by adopting the winner-versus-loser dialectic which also underlies his sexual fantasies. Gray does not so much parody Jock, as sympathize with his struggle to escape the vicious circle of the domination logic which is manifest in masturbatory fantasizing and in Thatcherite politics. At the end, Jock is transformed into a new man.

Something Leather

Something Leather is written from the points of view of women. In the first chapter, June is shopping for a leather outfit. She comes across a specialist shop "The Hideout." In a photograph album of patterns, June sees provocative pictures of a woman which excite her. Later, Donalda, an employee of "The Hideout," delivers June's order and seduces and handcuffs her. Donalda summons her accomplices Senga and

Harry to June's apartment. The chapter ends at the point "where the reader was likely to be most intrigued."

Gray provides flashbacks to the stories of the four women whose lives have converged. Harry's aristocratic mother neglected her. When a Scottish nanny was found smacking Harry, the mother sent her to boarding school. Harry viewed the smacking as the only act which took her into account, so she tried to have someone whip her again. When this failed, she devoted all her energy into art, particularly her "bum garden" project. Eventually she became a famous artist.

June is a clever and attractive woman who was always entangled with self-promoting, egotistical men. Her marriage collapsed when she realized that her husband was intent only upon his own satisfaction. Donalda and Senga came from poor families in Glasgow. They both have had failed marriages. Donalda was forced to prostitute herself. They both ended up distrusting men and eventually team up in "The Hideout" business.

Harry came to Glasgow in order to prepare an exhibition as part of the European Cultural Capital shows—an event which really took place in 1990. The Glasgow accent reminded her of her nanny and the spanking experience. So, Harry hired Senga to fulfil her fantasies. It was Senga who organized the capture of June in order to satisfy Harry.

Chapter 12 continues the story from the end of chapter 1: Harry, Senga, and Donalda sexually torture June—they hang her from a swing, cane her, shave her hair, and Harry tattoos bees on June's back and face. But June is not really hurt because all of the women show her affection. When June wakes up alone and is longing to meet them again, she realizes that she feels gratified. She is now a new June, converted to new erotic practices and excited to start a relationship with Harry.

Gray's juxtaposition of Queen's English and the Glaswegian accent is witty and entertaining. *Something Leather* can be read as a satire of the Englishness of the remodeled Glasgow as "Europe's Culture Capital." But below the surface humor, there is Gray's pessimistic denial of any real progress or change. Thus, the revamped Glasgow is only a temporary makeover which hides the squalor, repression, and desperation of its citizens. And, like Glasgow, June's conversion to S&M and homophilia, does not signal a deeper transformation: June is attracted to Harry, who, like June's old husband, is self-centerd and quick to use people to further her ends.

Gray does not outright condemn his characters. He is happy *for* June, because she has found individual satisfaction in her niche of erotic pleasures. And, at the same time, Gray is unhappy *with* June's individualism and un-self-awareness. *Something Leather*'s open end relies on this ambivalence, which engenders the unresolved opposition of private versus public satisfaction.

Biography

Born in Glasgow, December 28, 1934. His first novel, *Lanark*, was published in 1981. He graduated from the Glasgow School of Art in 1957. He has written novels, poetry, plays, short stories, an historical–political book, and has edited a collection of prefaces. All are illustrated by himself. He was awarded the Whitbread Novel Award and the Guardian Fiction Prize for *Poor Things* in 1992. The University of Glasgow appointed him Professor of Creative Writing in 2001.

DIMITRIOS VARDOULAKIS

Selected Works

Lanark. 1981.
1982 Janine. 1984.
Something Leather. 1990.
Poor Things. 1992.

Further Reading

Axelrod, Mark, editor. *The Review of Contemporary Fiction*, special issue, 15/2 (1995).
Bernstein, Stephen. *Alasdair Gray*. Lewisburg, PA: Bucknell University Press, 1999.
Craig, Cairns. *The Modern Scottish Novel: Narrative and National Imagination*. Edinburgh: Edinburgh University Press, 1999.
Crawford, Robert and Thom Nairn, editors. *The Arts of Alasdair Gray*. Edinburgh: Edinburgh University Press, 1991.
Jansen, Carola M. "Die Welten und Mikrokosmen des Alasdair Gray." Scottish Studies vol. 31, Frankfurt am Main: Peter Lang, 2000.
Loyns, Paddy and John Coyle, editors. *The Glasgow Review: Alasdair Gray and Other Stories*. Special issue, 3 (1995).
Whiteford, Eilidh. "Engendered Subjects: Subjectivity and National Identity in Alasdair Gray's *1982, Janine*." *Scotlands*, 2 (1994): 66–82.
Witschi, Beat. Glasgow Urban Writing and Postmodernism: A Study of Alasdair Gray's Fiction. *Scottish Studies* vol. 12, Frankfurt am Main: Peter Lang, 1991.

GREEK ANTHOLOGY

The *Greek Anthology* ('bouquet') is a collection of some 4000 epigrams written between the second century BCE and about 900 CE. The history of the transmission of the texts is complex: the *Anthology*, as we now have it, is composed of the 'Garland' of Meleager of Gadara (Syria), who died on the island of Cos in about 100 BCE, together with the 'Garland' of Philip (collected in the reign of Nero in the first century CE) and other groups of poems composed by Asclepiades (about 300–270 BCE), Strato (third century CE), Paulus Silentiarius and Agathias (both sixth century CE), and a number attributed to Anacreon (sixth century BCE) but written in the second century CE. In about 900 CE, Constantine Cephalas, a Byzantine, made a major collection of the foregoing material to which he added more. Another, enlarged, version of his edition was put together shortly afterwards, and it is this which is known as the *Palatine Anthology*. But in 1301 a Byzantine scholar, Maximus Planudes, produced a reduced version, probably based partly on previous abridgements, which omitted some heterosexual erotic items as well as the pederastic poems which constitute book XII of the Palatine collection. Planudes's *Anthology* was first printed in 1494 and was the standard text for the Renaissance. The full *Palatine Anthology* was not rediscovered until 1606 and was only completely published early in the nineteenth century (selections from Strato's 'Pederastic Muse' were first published separately in 1764 and 1774). Although there are some differences in the sequences of poems according to the variations in the manuscript tradition, the contents of the *Anthology* are divided into fifteen books: Christian epigrams (I), descriptions of statues (II), temple inscriptions (III), the prefaces of Meleager, Philip and Agathias (IV), curses (VI), epitaphs (VII and VIII), oracles, riddles and problems (XIV), and miscellaneous topics (IX, X, XIII, and XV). Book XI, which contains a number of erotic subjects, is composed of two parts: sympotic (1–64) and satirical (65–442) epigrams, while book V is devoted to mainly heterosexual erotic epigrams and book XII contains poems uniquely relating to the love of boys and youths. In the latter, some 94 epigrams in two substantial sections can be attributed to Strato, the rest belonging to Asclepiades, Melager, and others, making a total of 258. They are presented in no particular order or grouping. 'Some of the epigrams of Strato are elegant and clever,' wrote Philip Smith in a widely used handbook of Greek biography and literature in the nineteenth century, 'but nothing can redeem the disgrace attaching to the moral character of his compilation.' These pederastic epigrams cover a variety of situations, but they do not idealize their subject matter or give it a spiritual or philosophical disguise reminiscent of Plato or Socrates. The object of one poet's passion is an adolescent (12–18 years old), whose loss of attractiveness is confirmed by the sprouting of a beard (e.g., epigrams XII.24 to 27: Polemo's lover had promised to make a sacrifice if his beloved boy should return safely from his travels, but when he comes back bearded the lover retracts his vow. XII.30: Nicander is told his legs are getting hairy, and if his backside does likewise he will have fewer lovers). Some boys play hard to get, some ask for payment, some are only too happy to agree immediately. Youths are considered to bring more pleasure than women, for, in addition to being more natural in their behavior and appearance, they are vigorous, candid, straightforward, and smell honestly of the gymnasium. This does not mean that they can be relied on to be faithful, however, and the poets often complain about their fickleness. Praise and blame of this sort was, in fact, a commonplace in the Alexandrian period (third century BCE to second century CE) in debates on the relative merits of the love of women or boys. The poems celebrate the boys' bodies: lips, smooth buttocks (XII.37, 38), Diocles's cock seen at the baths (XII.207), or Alcimus's—once like a little pink finger, it now resembles an enormous arm (XII.242). Eyes dart flames (XII.110), or flash like stars (XII.196). Boys are dangerous tempters (XII.139), and dishes worthy of the gods

(XII.68). The rapacity of the beloved is such that he can only be caught by a well-baited hook (XII.42), or perhaps he acts as if arse means gold (XII.6). The love of boys is fleeting, and fades like roses in the heat (XII.195). The lovers are jealous, become impatient, are enslaved, fall regretfully out of love. They engage in combat with the beloved, enjoy his kisses, and during drinking and feasting (the 'symposia' and the 'comoi') they celebrate him with wine and song. Several epigrams in books XI and XII are aimed sarcastically (and perhaps sometimes rather enviously) at teachers who take advantage of their pupils (XII.34, 219, 222). Others are more simply scurrilous (XI.225—three men on a bed make four if you count the middle one twice; XI.272—on passive males). The love of boys is described as fire, tempest, and wounding in battle, while the pursuit of them is variously compared with hunting and snaring. Among a certain amount of conventional imagery, the pederastic poems of the *Anthology* often convey their message with realism, wit, and pointed plays on words. The situations they describe may now seem to us daring, but this adds to their vigorous charm. The 310 erotic poems of book V are, with few exceptions, heterosexual and are addressed to women who may be the poet's beloved, his adored sexual object, his difficult mistress, his unattainable ideal beauty. The occasions tend to be described more conventionally than in book XII, and there is less room given to naturalistic elements. The reason for this may well be that the poets are imitating models of sophisticated dalliance and sensual love, so that we may often doubt whether particular poems are expressions of real feelings rather than exercises in rhetoric. There are certain similarities with the gallant poetry of seventeenth and eighteenth-century England and France. The names of the beloved women are often conventional, and so,

too, is the range of imagery used: night, moon, shipwrecks, arrows of desire, the dawn arriving all too soon, and so on. So we read that Doris has chained the poet with a strand of golden hair (V.230), and that Asclepias's eyes are blue like the sea and invite him to sail on waves of love (V.156). Despite this, many poems avoid banality, while, together with several epigrams in the satirical section of book XI, some are frankly obscene: Lydia says she can satisfy three men simultaneously (V.49); Conon's wife is taller than him, so in bed where are his lips when their feet are level? (XI.108); on cunnilinctus (XI.329); the poet advises sodomy if the beloved is pregnant (V.54). With its wide range of subjects and variations in tone and style, the *Greek Anthology* can justly be ranked among the great books of Western literature.

PATRICK POLLARD

Further Reading

The Greek Anthology. With an English Translation by W.R. Paton. London and Cambridge (MA): Loeb Library, 1916 (reprinted and revised 1979).

Anthologie grecque. Texte établi et traduit par Pierre Waltz [et Robert Aubreton] en collaboration avec Jean Guillon [Félix Buffière et Jean Irigoin]. Paris: Les Belles Lettres (Collection Budé): vol.II (livre V) revu et corrigé 1990; vol.X (livre XI) 1972; vol.XII (livre XI) 1994.

The Greek Anthology and other ancient Greek epigrams. A selection in modern verse translations, edited with an introduction by P.Jay [Revised edition]. Harmondsworth: Penguin Books, 1981.

Buffière, F. *Eros adolescent. La Pédérastie dans la Grèce antique*. Paris: Les Belles Lettres, 1980.

Cameron, A. *The Greek Anthology from Meleager to Planudes*. Oxford: Clarendon Press, 1993.

Symonds, J.A. *Studies of the Greek Poets. Third edition*. London: A. and C. Black, 1920 (1893).

Tarán, S.L. *The Art of Variation in the Hellenistic Epigram*. Leiden: Brill, 1979.

GREEK: MODERN

For a long time Modern Greek writers faced the difficult task of incorporating in their works the heritage of ancient Greece with that of Byzantium, which has decisively shaped post-classical Greek experiences. To a certain degree this struggle, especially when done consciously, dominated and often suppressed the free expression of erotic feeling. Inextricably intertwined with Greek history, Modern Greek literature often chose to channel eroticism through reflection on national issues. Lyric and gentle tones of tender desire, allusions, and youthful memories often suffice in order to relate the erotic experiences of a nation preoccupied with preserving its identity. The yearning for the beloved is often compared with the desire for freedom; explicit sexual descriptions, especially in works relating the foreign occupations suffered by the Greeks, tend to carry negative connotations, often associated with lack of modesty or crimes that fuel the anger of the enslaved people. On the contrary, sanctioned relationships undergo consummation amid passionate descriptions of feelings; explicit references are limited to the physical changes that the enamoured witness on their bodies. In addition, during the few carefree moments that the Greeks celebrated in their recent history, they gave precedence to a humorous approach of love, which allowed the writers to become slightly more descriptive and even obscene. In addition, in all their literary history Greek writers, almost unanimously, praise youthful love and the first erotic experience, perhaps because reality and social pressures were soon to impose their pace on the erotic mood of the individuals. It could be said that by way of continuing the Hesiodic notion of Eros, Modern Greek writers still classified love, romantic or more sensual, as the unwanted affliction that tortures the body and the mind with reminders of a short-lived youth and social issues that often remain unresolved.

Nevertheless, in more recent years, eroticism found more substantial expression in Greek literature and indeed produced some excellent descriptions of sensual fulfilment. In particular the feminine erotic experience found its voice in the works of Freddy Germanos' (1934–1999) such as his *Tereza* of 1997, in Mara Meimaridi's *Magisses tis Smirnis* (2001) and in Kostas Karakasis' *Athina* (2000). These novels, among numerous others, focus on the exceptional stories of unusually strong women that succeeded in a masculine world of different social norms. The heroines' search for love and pleasure becomes the mirror for the customs of their epoch which they set to overcome. In the following pages the history of Modern Greek Erotic Literature is reviewed chronologically with emphasis given on the more recent centuries.

The Byzantine Heritage

The fall of Constantinople in 1453 arguably signifies the start of Modern Greek literature, sealed with the epic of *Digenis Akritas* and the chivalric romances of the fourteenth century. This tradition is believed to continue unbroken until 1669 when Crete fell to the Turks.

Digenis Akritas, published in 1875 from a manuscript at Trepizond (K.N. Sathas and E. Legrand), survived in five more versions: two from Andros, from Grottaferrata near Rome, from Oxford and Escorial. The middle of the eleventh century is a *firm terminus ante quem* for the original text. The main hero is Vasilis Digenis Akritas: the first three books talk about his origin; the other five relate his adventures and his love story, an elopement, with the girl's cooperation. In book six (Grottaferrata ms.) or seven (the other mss.) Digenis narrates his duel with the Amazon Maximo with erotic overtones. Sexual references are frequent and explicit in a celebration of youthful virility and passionate bravery.

From 1204 to 1261, Constantinople was occupied by Frankish Crusaders. Despite their short stay, they exercised a strong influence in literature from the thirteenth to the fifteenth century. Under the influence of the *Chronicle of the*

Morea, a series of Romances of Love and Chivalry were produced: they typically depict the separation of two lovers, who suffer trials and adventures until they are happily united. Unlike the *Epic of Digenis*, the romances represent a more romantic orientation in Modern Greek reminiscent of the French roman courtois and the ballads of the Arthurian cycle. The erotic element is dominant, with its melancholy and oppression, but also with its sensual fulfilment. The love of adventure and the fairytale motifs, employed profusely, indicate a strong eastern influence. The writers also knew the romances of the Second Sophistic from which they borrow their long and detailed descriptions (ecphrasis). In some romances we find *katalogia*, apparently independent demotic songs of the time. Five romances came down to us: *Libistros and Rodamne*, probably written in the fourteenth century in demotic Greek; *Kallimachos and Chrysorrhoe* by Andronicus Palaeologus with its abundant legendary elements dates between 1310 and 1340; and *Belanthros and Chrysantza*, with its sensual tone, distinguished for its demotic language. The two other romances are adaptations of popular western originals of the twelfth century: *Imperios and Margarona*, a version of the French *Pierre de Provence et la belle Maguelone*, and *Fiorios and Platziaflora*, a recension of the French romance *Floire et Blanchefleur*. The Greek adapter, who wrote just before the middle of the fifteenth century, drew directly on a metrical Tuscan version of the early fourteenth century, *Il cantare di Florio e Biancifiore*. His focus on youthful love and the spiritual affinity between the couple seems to herald a new spirit. These romances introduced the Greek public to then contemporary European notions of love, although the endless and often unnecessary adventures of the couple, tend to be tiring for the reader. Once more, love gradually falls into the background as the incentive that fuels the tenacity of the enamoured couple, often leaving essential issues of sexual maturation and compatibility unanswered. In a way, these works carry back to Greek speaking audiences the spirit of Menander, mostly evident, in cases of lost children who are finally recognized and have their social status reinstated.

Krumbacher also referred to 'romances with a national subject' such as the *Life of Alexander*, a metrical version of the well-known Hellenistic romance of Pseudo-Callisthenes dated in 1388.

The *Tale of Achilles* or *the Achilleid* of the fifteenth century is a love romance about the mythical hero Achilles. Despite their intentions, these romances fail to persuade the reader in the emotional depth of the passions they describe.

In the places which remained in Frankish domination after 1453 (mainly on the coasts and islands) literary production was little affected by the great disaster. There in the second half of the fifteen century, Byzantine tales gradually gave way to erotic lyric songs, both demotic and more artistic. The earliest (ca 1450) and most remarkable collection, the *Erotopaignia*, survives in a British Museum manuscript and paves the way for the poetry of the second half of the fifteenthfifteenth century. It may be a collection of entirely demotic lines or, possibly, the original works of a learned poet.

The autobiographical poems of S. Sachlikis date in the late fifteenth and early sixteenth century and draw on his rather prodigal life. *Kastro or Chandax* (nowadays Heraclion) features his quarrels with courtesan Koutagiotaina, while his *Strange Story* satirizes the courtesans. His lines revive the underground life of this great harbor, a then colony of Venice. Interestingly, his exaggerated images are more convincing, perhaps because he focuses on realistic figures rather than dainty daughters of the nobility. Marinos Falieros wrote two similar poems distinguished for their original erotic imagery and their allegorical mood: the poet sees in his dreams (one of the poems is entitled *History and Dream*] his beloved together with Destiny and Pothoula (personification of love). An important, yet anonymous, erotic composition appears to have been *The Rimada of the Girl and the Youth* (which Legrand called *La séduction de la jouvencelle*), a lyric work distinguished for its narrative skill and genuine demotic expression. Its sensual realism, full of freshness and grace, shows close affinity with demotic love songs.

At the same period in Cyprus, a series of exceptional lyric love-poems was produced under the spell of Petrarchism. The poems were written in the Cypriot idiom, the Italian hendecasyllable (instead of conventional decapentesyllable) and in a variety of Renaissance forms: sonnets, octaves, terzinas, even canzones, sestinas, ballades, barzelettas etc. The Italian influence on these poems is marked; some are direct imitations of Petrarch and his followers (J. Sannazaro and P. Bembo); others full of the spirit of Petrarchism. The love-poems of Cyprus are one of the highest points of Renaissance literature in Greece, but had no sequel after 1571 when Cyprus fell to the Turks.

In 1570, almost the only Greek lands left under Venetian domination were Crete and the Ionian islands. Both were to play an important role in literature, Crete at once, the Ionian islands later. Cretan literature of the late sixteenth and of the seventeenth centuries is a Golden period in the history of Modern Greek literature. The writers of this period elevated the demotic idiom to pure literary language. Theater, which returned to Europe only under the free spirit of the Renaissance, was introduced in Crete by George Chortatsis, a near contemporary of Shakespeare. His earliest work, *Gyparis or Panoria* (c.1585–1590), was a pastoral play modeled on *La Calisto* of Luigi Grotto (Venice, 1583), a typical Italian *tragicommedia pastorale*, with the exception that the plot involves two pairs of enamoured shepherds: Gyparis loves Panoria and Alexis, Athousa. The shepherdesses scorn their love and prefer to live hunting in the woods. Chortatsis' *Erofili* (c. 1585–1600) was based on the Italian Classical *Orbecche* of Giambattista Giraldi (1547), which he handled with complete originality: the secret marriage of Erofili and Panaretos is tragically brought to an end when her father, king Philogonos, kills the groom and serves his limbs to Erofili, who commits suicide. The chorus of girls kills the king. Between the acts four intermezzi dramatized the episode of Rinaldo and Armida from the *Gerusalemme Liberata* of Torquato Tasso. In Chortatsis' works love becomes the incentive for extraordinary adventures and amazing turns of fortunes that can transform with its magic the dull lives of his young protagonists. In addition, in correspondence with literary movements in the west, love becomes the tool for exploring novel literary forms. His two other tragedies that survived are later than Erofili and inferior in poetic worth. *King Rodolinos* by Joannes Andreas Troilos of Rethymno, printed in Venice in 1647, drew on the late dramatic work of Tasso, *Il Re Torrismondo* (1587), which relates the conflict between love and friendship. Chortatsis also engaged with erotic themes in his most popular comedy *Katzourbos* (c.1595–1600) which originates in the Italian *comedia erudita* of the sixteenthsixteenth century. *Fortounatos* of Markos Antonios Foskolos is clearly indebted to *Katzourbos*. *Stathis*, an anonymous play written before 1648, is akin to Shakespeare's *A Midsummer's Night Dream* and revolves around the erotic adventures of two couples.

All the works of this period are dramatic, apart from the early *Voskopoula* and the more mature *Erotokritos*. *Voskopoula*, first printed in 1627, was popular despite its naïve treatment of pastoral love. *Erotokritos* by Vitsentzos Kornaros has been characterized as a love poem but Politis insists on calling it, a verse–romance. In his introduction the poet states his subjects as 'power of love' and the 'troubles of arms.' The poem relates in five parts and 10,000 lines the love of Erotokritos and Aretousa, their toils and troubles until the final happy ending. The tale could be seen as the most successful epilogue to the romances of the early Byzantine period, now fully adjusted to the Cretan reality of the seventeenthseventeenth century; long descriptions convey the yearning of the two lovers and their unbreakable devotion to each other in almost lyric tones. *Erotokritos*, written c. 1640–1660 at Sitia and Kastro, takes its theme from a medieval French romance of chivalry by Pierre de la Cypède, *Paris et Vienne*. The Turkish occupation of 1669 begins a decline in poetry for a century and a half. After 1669, the tradition of Cretan literature was preserved in the Ionian Islands, but it was not continued. The 150 years between 1669 and 1821 (Greek Revolution) may be divided in two main periods, the division coming c. 1770–1780. In 1774, the Russo-Turkish treaty of Kutchuk Kainardji gave special privileges to the Greeks in the Turkish Empire, thus ensuring the rise of a new, prosperous urban class. During the next fifty years, a new energy was manifested in all fields and of course, in erotic composition. Greek Enlightenment entered into its peak in the last decades of the eighteenth century.

All along these centuries, the demotic song that defies chronological classification was continuously popular. It flourished for the last time just before the War of Independence, chiefly in mainland Greece. The demotic *paraloges*, songs more artistically accomplished, often treated the themes of love and marriage. The marriage songs are closely connected with the wedding ritual, but the love songs are distinguished for their lyricism and grace. They are often confined to distichs, lianotragouda or amanedes, patinades or mantinades, but many are longer ballads.

In most songs the erotic element appears suppressed by the war-like environment of the heroes; yet the widespread ballad of *Chartzianis* or the *Sun-born maiden* introduces erotic themes along with transvestism. Baud-Bovy places it in the Dodecanese in the twelfth century. Here and more generally in the islands of the Aegean, a whole series of love songs had its origin. They belong to the time of the Frankish occupation, from the thirteenth to the fifteenth century, the age of the romances of love and chivalry, among which we find many *katalogia*. The Frankish influence is strong; their lyrical tone is reminiscent of the *Erotopaignia*. Among the love-songs, Baud-Bovy distinguishes a group evolving around the unconventional figure of the mistress or the unfaithful wife. These songs bring to mind the poems of Sachlikis; their origin must be Crete, from the thirteenth and fourteenth centuries (the earliest songs) to the sixteenth. Demotic songs will continue to be written and reproduced throughout the seventeenth and eighteenth century favoring detailed physical descriptions in order to convey eroticism: the eyes, the way she walks or dances, her elaborate clothing, the beloved's beauty spots, all excite the pain and impatience of the lover in a pastoral environment that exhibits pathetic fallacy for his suffering.

The Nineteenth Century

The last decade of the eighteenth century and the first two of the nineteenth were most critical for modern Hellenism. The Greek nation was slowly but surely approaching a new unity and was nearing the final liberation. Rigas Velestinlis or Pheraios, born c. 1757 in the Thessalian village of Velestino, published in Vienna after his arrival in 1790–1791. Rigas was devoted to the national cause and became, after his murder in 1798, the first martyr of Greek liberty; however, his first work, *The School for Delicate Lovers* (Vienna, 1790), was a collection of six short love-stories, the first in modern Greek literature. A translation, apparently, from Restif de la Bretonne, a less known French author, it had considerable success. In 1792, also in Vienna, an unknown writer published a similar work, *The Results of Love*, three original tales that drew more on the Greek social life of Constantinople and Wallachia, where flirting was fashionable among the youths of the elite. A new class of wealthy traders enjoyed for the first time the luxury of playful, feminine company in an ambience of almost Parisian eroticism. The unknown writer inserted in his stories short popular poems which combine eastern melancholy with a premature and confused romanticism.

Athanasios Christopoulos, born in 1772 at Kastoria, published his *Lyric* in 1811, thus inaugurating a new period in Modern Greek poetry. At first glance, his 'Erotic' and 'Bacchic' songs (his own division) belong to the realm of contemporary European classicism. The 'Bacchic' songs, for which his contemporaries called him the 'new Anacreon,' were imitations of the numerous post-classical anacreontics. He sings of love and wine, and represents himself as continuously lovesick; his love is never a grand passion, but rather a sport or amusement. His poems, full of mythological details, lack passion, as critics often pointed out. Yiannis Vilaras, born in 1771 at Ioannina, published in 1814 the *Romaic Language* which included erotic verse. Dionysios Solomos was born in 1798. He had an Italian education, but upon his return to Greece in 1818 at the age of twenty, he taught himself to compose poetry in Greek. His themes are full of the revolution of the Greeks against the Turks and he wrote the National Anthem. In 1834, a large part of his poem *Lambros* was published in the Ionian Anthology: Lambros, a minor Don Juan, who seduces young Maria, is wicked in conduct but great in soul. At the time of composition, Solomos was tormented with romantic visions, but the piece was later reworked. Solomos' poetry remained fragmentary and never reached completion. We have a sketch of *La Donna Velata*, his one real love-poem. Generally the Heptanesian School initiated with Andreas Kalvos (born in Zakynthos in 1792) was far too preoccupied with national and social problems to produce erotic verse. Antonios Matesis (1794–1875), a friend of Solomos, wrote a drama called *The Basil Plant* (1830) commenting on social contrasts at the beginning of the eighteenth century: a young man from the second-best families loves a girl from the best. Julius Typaldos in his *Divers Poems* (1856) also produced some erotic verses. Aristotelis Valaoritis from Leucas (1824–1879), a politician and poet, was inspired by the romanticism of Victor Hugo.

After the establishment of the Greek state, intense intellectual and literary activity was developing side by side with political life. Romanticism dominated French and soon Greek literature around 1830–1840. Greek Romantic poets opted to compose in the Katharevousa. Their erotic visions like their language often seems restrained and lacks sincere passion and vivacity. Panagiotis Soutsos (1806–1868) wrote lyric, erotic poems in the manner of Christopoulos. In 1827, he wrote the *Traveller in Greece*, published in 1831. The two protagonists, the Traveller and Ralou, meet again, fail to recognize each other, faint, suffer delusion, commit suicide, exchanging with their last breath the most heart-rending words of love. In 1835, he published the poetic collection *Guitar* including love-poems. Alexandros Rizos Rangavis (1809–1892) was of a noble Phanariot and a cousin of Soutsos. Among his work that amount to 19 volumes, *Dimos and Eleni* (1831) combined Byron's Romantic structure with an overlay of Greek culture. George Zalokostas (1805–1858) from Epirus wrote some erotic poems. Demetrios Vernadakis (1834–1907) and Spyridon Vasiliadis (1845–1874) wrote romantic plays in classical speech forms. Achilles Paraschos (1838–1895) represents the end of Romanticism in Greece. In his love poems, the *Myrtles*, included in his Complete Works (1881) romanticism almost collapses into a parody of itself.

In the nineteenth century, important writers of fiction like Emmanuel Roidis (1836–1904) with his *Pope Joan* (1865), Alexandros Papadiamantis (1851–1911) with his *Fonissa* (1903), and Georgios Vizyinos (1849–1896) with *My Mother's Sin* touch upon issues of gender and social oppression. Here again sexuality and procreation are depicted as harshly imposed by social norms that the individuals never questioned; mute suffering and self-inflicted guilt do not allow for any romantic escape from a miserable, disorientated life. Only tragic highlights signify the rotten side of sexual occurrences. Other writers of the period include Ioannes Papadiamantopoulos, a symbolist writing under the name Jean Moréas. He influenced several writers such as Konstantinos Hadzopoulos (1868–1920) and the poet Miltiades Malakasses (1869–1943). The eroticism of their works is often reduced to an exploration of feelings, while sensual innuendos linger in the misty weather as painful memories. Georgios Souris (1853–1919) was a political satirist in the tradition of Aristophanes but also wrote humorous, obscene rhymes.

The Twentieth Century

Until the middle of the twentieth century Greek literature was preoccupied with social issues; hence, Andreas Karkavitas (1866–1922), known for his sea tales, published only two erotic stories, the *Lygeri* (1890) and the *Old Loves* (1900). Argyris Eftaliotis (1849–1923), influenced by Shakespeare, wrote his *Words of Love*, a series of sonnets addressed to his wife. In his verses love and conjugal affection overcome sexual passion. The novelist Gr. Xenopoulos (1867–1951) recognized as his masters, realists Balzac and Zola, along naturalists Dickens and Daudet. Some of his novels were: *Margarita Stefa* (1893), *Laura* (1915), *Anadyomeni* (1923), and *Teresa Varma Dakosta* (1925). From all his works, *The Secrets of Countess Valeraina* (1904) and *Stella Violanti* (1909) were most influential. At the end of his life, using demotic for the first time, he wrote the lyrical novel *First Love* (1920) drawing on his early memories of Crete. Yiannis Vlachogiannis (1867–1945) wrote in demotic prose erotic stories such as *The Cock* (1914), distinguished for its psychological nuances. On stage, for about ten years from 1888 a new kind of play, the Comidyll, became a popular vehicle of eroticism; it was a kind of comedy with songs introduced, which hoped to escape Romanticism. The first real such musical is the very popular *Fortune of Maroula* by D. Koromilas (1850–1898). The erotic element functions almost complementarily in a play that evolves around a central erotic theme, indeed the paradox of most of Greek literature. On stage as in literature, love is chosen to exemplify and ridicule oppressive social norms. In 1891, Koromilas wrote a dramatic idyll, the *Lover of the Shepherdess*, in bombastic decapentesyllables, offering a beautified picture of pastoral life in the mountains.

Kostas Krystallis (1868–1894) published two collections, *Poems of the Fields* (1890) and the *Singer of the Village and the Pasture* (1892) attesting his strong influence from the demotic songs. After his death sonnets became particularly popular, under the sway of Parnassianism. Lorentzos Mavilis of Corfu (1860–1912) wrote his most successful sonnets around 1895–1900. Ioannis Gryparis (1870–1942) also made a triumphant appearance in Modern Greek poetry with a series of sonnets, under the title *Scarabs*. The influence of Heredia or Theophile Gautier (they belong to Parnassianism) is evident both on his *Scarabs* and the *Terracottas*. But in *Intermedia* (1899–1901) he favored the technique of symbolism. One of the most popular lyric poets in the early part of the twentieth century was Georgios Drosines (1859–1951). His work includes the poetic volumes *Photera skotadia* (1903–1914) and *Klista Vlephara* (1914–1917). The poet Maria Polydouri (1902–1930) also gained renown for her intense, love lyrics. The eroticism of her verses is a fresh breath of uninhibited sexual gratification.

Palamas (1859–1943), born in Patras, is one of the best known Greek poets of the twentieth century. His death in 1943 during the German occupation was attended by thousands. He published *The Songs of My Fatherland* in 1886 and his *Lambs and Anapaests* in 1897. His best poetry is contained in *Asalephti Zoi* (1904). His long poem *Phloyera tou Vasilia* (1910) presents a pageant of Byzantine history; his epic masterpiece *The Twelve Words of the Gypsy* (1907) relates the aspirations of Modern Greeks. His poetry is full of subtle eroticism associated with a classical concept of beauty. While Palamas was at his zenith in Athens, Konstantinos Kavafis (Cafavy) (1863–1933), who succeeded him in importance, was working at Alexandria, an isolated area of Hellenism. His first publications in katharevousa begin in 1886; their romantic and pessimistic tone is close to the poetry of Dimitrios Paparrigopoulos (1843–1873), with clear influences by Hugo and Musset. In 1891, Kavafis published in a pamphlet the *Builders* and in 1896 he wrote the *Walls*, poems synonymous with his unique style. The corpus of his acknowledged poems amounts to 154 given that he disowned much of his work. His poems divided in philosophical, historical, and erotic, are short and were often circulated in small pamphlets. Much has been written about his homosexuality and the role it played in the composition of his poems, but later criticism drew attention on other elements of his work. His purely erotic poems are few, although the figure of a beautiful youth, or most typically his memory, is omnipresent in his poetry. Fundamentally Kavafis is preoccupied with transmuting his erotic sentiment into poetry. Dinos Christianopoulos (1931–) found in Cavafis a model of homosexual expression. Angelos Sikelianos from Leucas sprang from the tradition of the Heptanesian School. His early works, influenced by late Parnassianism and Symbolism, were omitted from his Collected Works, the *Lyric Life* (1946). His first real poem, *The Light-Shadowed* of 1907, was published in 1909. Sikelianos' obsession evolved around the identification of the poet with nature, a theme anticipated in his early *Hymn of the Great Return* and his long composition, *Prologue to Life*. In 1915–1917 he published four parts, each entitled Consciousness —of the earth, of race, of woman, and of faith (the fifth, the consciousness of personal creativity, was published much later). Sikelianos conceived in his poetry a universal vision of a world evolving around love. He wished the erotic element to claim its place in the universe and allow for an 'erotic,' a cosmic union between the poet and divine creation. In his *Study of Death* (1936–1939) he appears as searching for the primal essence of the feminine and for an identification of body and soul, which could eventually conquer mortality. He also wrote a series of lyric poems called *Orphic* (1927–1942), the *Sacred Way* (1935) and the *Attic* (1942). Sikelianos' search for the primordial feminine element is a recurrent theme in Greek literature, typically associated with classical nuances of fertility and motherhood.

Nikos Kazantzakis (1883–1957), a contemporary of Sikelianos, reflected in his numerous works on social immorality and the hypocrisy of the clergy. Love and lust, described with vivid detail, are seen as covered with the guilt society attached to them. Kazantzakis always envisioned the liberation of man through his own humanity and sensual love is for him a most powerful expression of our mortal boundaries. Among his most popular novels, are *Zorba the Greek* (1943), *The Greek Passion* (1948), and *The Last Temptation of Christ* (1951). Other novelists that contributed to the literature of this period are: Elias Venezis (1904–1973) with his realistic descriptions in *Galene* (1939), *Aioliki Gi* (1943), *Number 31328* (1924), Dido Sotiriou (1909–2004) with *Matomena Chomata* among other works, Stratis Myrivilis with his romantic charm in *The Teacher with the Golden Eyes* (1932), *Vasilis Arvanitis* (1934–1943), *Small Flames* (1942), and *The Mermaid Madonna* (1955) are inspired by the Greek disaster of 1922 in Asia Minor. First loves are doomed to remain unfulfilled due to the Turkish massacre and ensuing mass migration or sadly coincide with the introduction to the German Resistance.

Kosmas Politis with his insight into the character of women in his *Lemonodasos* (1928), *Hekate* (1933), and *Eroica* (1938); George Theotokas (1905–1968) with his *Demon* (1938) and *Leonis* (1940) also celebrates the first love which in classical mode afflicts the limbs as well as the mind of the enamoured. Kostas Varnalis (1884–1974) introduced in poetry a spirit of destruction that was to characterize poets of the First World War, like Romos Filyras (1889–1942), the pseudonym of J. Ikonomopoulos, who published his first works in 1911. Despite his eroticism and idealism, his poetry is ruled by grief and a sense of loss. Nostalgia for lost prospects is also expressed in the poetry of neo-Romantic Kostas Ouranis (1890–1953) while melancholy and despair dominates the mature works of Napoleon Lapathiotis (1888–1943). The greatest representative of this movement is Kostas Karyotakis (1896–1928) with his *Pain of Man and Things* (1919), and *Nepenthe* (1921). Just before his suicide he published the *Elegies and Satires* (1928); his poetry expresses an overflowing desire for life in stark contradiction with a sense of vanity. Tellos Agras (the pseudonym of Evangelos Ioannou, 1899–1944) belonged to the same world.

At the same period, I. Dragoumis (1878–1920) produced samples of psychological writing in his *Booldof Heroes and Martyrs* (1907), *Samothrace* (1909), and *Those Living* (1911). Penelope Delta (1874–1941) wrote historical novels such as *The Time of the Bulgar-Slayer* (1911) and *In the Secret Places of the Lagoon* (1937). In these the erotic element is larking powerfulin the background, but never finds clear expression or fulfilment. Desire and erotic promises keep the soldiers dedicated to the cause; sexual crimes excite their revenge instincts. Like most of the nineteenth-century Greek writings, in these novels the feminine embrace is the place where national heroes are born and raised; sexual memories only underline the yearning of soldiers, miles away from home, unable to materialize a simple life. Another major obstacle in the free expression of eroticism in Greek literature was the fact that authors often wrote under the spell of a European literary movement, which often meant that they were more preoccupied with 'belonging' to a specific school of writing rather than exploring love in an imaginative way. K. Christomanos (1867–1911) brought to Greece the climate of the European fin de siécle

and the aestheticism of Oscar Wilde with *The Wax Doll* (1911); here again sexual consummation is related with an ill-fated wedding and a sense of guilt in seeking a new erotic partner. Kostas Chadzopoulos (1870–1920) wrote the novels *The Tower of Akropotamos* (1909) and *Love in the Village* (1910) on social issues. In *Autumn* (1917), under the influence of Scandinavian literature, he describes the emotions of his characters by suggestion, thus introducing symbolism into prose. His work was very influential in the decade 1920–1930 on young writers like Constantinos Theotokis (1872–1923) who also had social interests (*The Convict* [1919], *Life and Death of Karavelas* [1920]).

Giorgos Seferis (real name Seferiadis) was born in 1900 in Smyrna and died in Athens in 1971. In 1931, he published the *Strophe* wishing to break free from the overshadowing figures of Palamas and Karyotakis. The collection, influenced by the style of Valéry and Mallarmé, is dominated by a long poem, *Erotikos Logos*, written in the tradition of the seventeenth-century *Erotokritos*. His second work, the lyrical *Cistern* (1932) is influenced by T.S. Eliot. His *Muthistorema* (1935) with its fusion of Modern Greek history and classical mythology is considered the most representative text of Greek Modernism. Seferis, who had a recognized diplomatic career, expressed in his poems many of his political experiences such as the Metaxas dictatorship (1936), the German occupation, his flight, along with the Greek government to South Africa and Egypt, the civil war that followed (*Book of Exercises* and *Logbook I* [1940], *Manuscript* 41, *Logbook II* [1944]). In 1947, he published his most mature work, *The Thrush,* a three-part 'musical' composition, where personal and erotic memories are freely interwoven with the traumatic memories of WWII and the tragedy of the Civil War. In 1953, Seferis discovered Cyprus and published his *Logbook III* (1955) inspired by the long history of the island. In 1963, he became the first Greek author to be awarded the Nobel Prize for Literature. His funeral, during the military junta, turned into one of the largest mass demonstrations against the regime.

Odysseus Elytis (real name Alepoudelis, 1911–1996), who won the Nobel Prize in 1979, was one of the few Greek surrealists along with Andreas Embeiricos (1901–1975) and Nikos Engonopoulos (1910–1985). His major works include *The Sovereign Sun* (1943) and *Axion Esti*

(1959). Although his war experiences dominate his work in many poems he captures young love in collections such as *Ta Ro tou Erota* (1972) and *Eros, Eros, Eros* (1998). His erotic verse is characterized by the youthful and carefree energy that Love inspires to his victims; his poetry oozes a bursting joy in which nature participates. Again the eternal theme of beauty acquires a central role in Elytis' celebration of love. From this tradition sprang Nanos Valaoritis (1921–) who composed under Andre Breton.

Numerous novels were written about the Greek Resistance movement and the ensuing civil war while Thanasis Valtinos (1932–) in his *Deep Blue Almost Black* (1992) and the poet Manolis Anagnostatis (1925–) relate the Greek experiences from the dictatorship of 1967–1974. Yiannis Ritsos (1909–1990) was mainly inspired by communistic thought, but his 1982 *Erotica* celebrate love and life in lyric tones. Erotic longing as well as loss, which often intermingle in Greek poetry, are described with great warmth, almost as if the poet whispered the words to his beloved. Novelists such as Stratis Tsirkas (1911–1980), Costas Taktsis (1927–11988), and Vassilis Vassilikos (1934–) focused on post-war Greek society. With regards to theatrical production, from the 1950s onwards plays of younger writers dealt with contemporary problems. In the late twentieth century, Modern Greek prose diversified to incorporate new perspectives. More women writers appeared, more writers challenged tradition in their works, and more authors focused on the present rather than the past. Margarita Karapanou's *O ipnovatis* (1986) challenged the status quo of the upper middle class in contemporary Greek society. Fiction writer and poet Rhea Galanaki wrote the historical novel *Life of Ismail Ferik Pasha* (1996), based on a nineteenth-century Cretan revolutionary. Meanwhile, a group of women lyric poets have gained distinction, including Victoria Theodorou (1928–), Angeliki Paulopoulou (1930–), Eleni Fourtouni (1933–), and Katerina Anghelaki-Rooke (1934–). These poets rendered erotic desire from a feminine point of view, touching upon sensitive issues of unfulfilled expectations, sexual and more. Several novelists began, in the 1950s, to turn away from fiction specifically about the war and its aftermath to novels dealing with other aspects of existence. Antonis Samarakis (1919–2003) wrote of individuals caught in the pressures of modern society, as in *The Flaw* (1965); Galatia Sarandi dealt with the contemporary psychological stress of women and her 1982 collection *Elene*, emphasized family and love relationships. Nikos Gatsos (1911–1992) and Nikos Kavadias (1910–1975) provided the lyrics for several popular songs in which erotic experiences shape people's lives and characters, haunting our memories and hopes for ever. Our deepest needs come to the front of our consciousness like sea waves that never cease coming in visions that often mingle sexual desires with the sailor's undying love for the sea, yet another common pattern of Greek poetry and thought, here rendered with novel freshness. Man is powerless in front of the sea, like he is in front of love; the ancient admiration for the power of love on men's minds and bodies is attributed here to a cosmopolitan overlay due to the foreign travels of the two poets. Nikos-Alexis Aslanoglou (1931–1996) wrote erotic poetry in melancholic tones while Andreas Anghelakis is distinguished for his prosaic and erotic style. Nikiforos Vrettakos (1912–1991) composes on love and peace while Olga Broumas (1949–) writes homoerotic poetry in the Sapphic tradition. Miltos Sahtouris (1919–) with his dark poetry, and Kiki Dimoula (1931–) are considered two of the greatest living poets of Greece.

EVANGELIA ANAGNOSTOU-LAOUTIDES

Bibliography

L. Politis (1973). *A History of Modern Greek Literature*, C.A. Trypanis (1981) *Greek Poetry from Homer to Seferis*, R. Beaton ([2]1999) *An Introduction to Modern Greek Literature*, D. Tziovas (1997) *Greek Modernism and Beyond*, R. Dalven (1994) *Daughters of* Sappho.

Further Reading

Barnstone, W. ed. (1972) *Eighteen Texts: Writings by Contemporary Greek Authors.*
Keeley, E. and P. Bien ed. (1972) *Modern Greek Writers.*
Anton, J.P. (1995) *The Poetry and Poetics of Constantine P. Cavafy.*
Dyck, K. Van. (1998) *The Rehearsal of Misunderstanding: Three Collections by Contemporary Greek Women Poets.*
Bien, P. (1972) *Kazantzakis and the Linguistic Revolution in Greek Literature* and (1983) *Three Generations of Greek Writers.*
Kostís, Nicholas (1993) *Modern Greek Short Stories.*
Leontis, A. (1997) *Greece: A Traveler's Literary Companion*, etc.

GREEK, ANCIENT: PROSE

Elephantis, Heracleides of Pontus, Longus, Lucian, Plutarch, Milesian Tales, Philaenis

The Greek-speaking authors of antiquity wrote a wide variety of literary prose that might be categorized as erotic. Forms ranged from full-length romance narratives with love as their central theme to bawdy novellas, from dramatic dialogues satirizing sexual mores to technical but still literary writing such as sexological works or astrology manuals. The earliest erotic prose works date to the Hellenistic period in the third century BCE, but their production peaked during a revival of Greek literary culture in the second and third centuries CE, the so-called 'Second Sophistic.' With their emphasis on romance, seduction, sexuality, and the erotic development of individuals, the writers of the Second Sophistic are among the first to make the sexual self a field of enquiry, and so their works now tend to be characterized *prima facie* as erotic literature. However, the extent to which all the types of writing outlined above would have been called erotic by their original authors and readers is debatable. Greek literary conventions allowed erotic and sexually explicit material to be present in many different kinds of writing, so a work's erotic content did not automatically assign it to a genre called 'erotica.' For example, a quasi-literary work like Artemidorus of Daldis' *Oneirocritica* (second century CE, *On Dream Interpretation*) refers constantly to every kind of sexual activity while not being a piece of erotic prose any more than its most famous derivative, Sigmund Freud's *The Interpretation of Dreams* (1900).

In fact, modern critics have had difficulty trying to define what ancient Greek readers regarded as erotic literature, becoming entangled in speculation about what kind of works might have aroused them sexually. It may be more helpful to think about Greek erotic writing in terms of *ta erotika*, the Greek root of the word 'erotic,' meaning all things related to love, desire, and the emotions in general. Accordingly,

literary works such as Plutarch's *Dialogue on Love* (second century CE, *Moralia*), which sets out a romantic conception of male–female relationships, could be defined as erotic literature, even though it was written as a rhetorical tour-de-force rather than to titillate. Also in this category could come the treatises on women's virtue attributed to Pythagoras' female followers, such as Perictione's *On the Balance which is Becoming in Women* (third century BCE?). This discusses how women may attain sexual and emotional harmony through controlled personal behavior. It is also worth including Greek pseudo-scientific writing, such as physiognomic manuals and the astrological or magical texts. The last could certainly be seen as pieces of erotic literary prose in their own right. Some types of spells intersperse ritual instructions with literary passages, especially the so-called 'leading spells for attraction' (*agogai*) and 'genital unlocking spells' (*physikleidia*).

This capacious notion of erotic literature had another aspect: the ancient Greeks seem to have had little sense that reading it or listening to it might have bad moral or psychological effects. On the contrary, some erotic prose works were praised for their medical benefits, because they could stimulate impotent men and enable them to have sex normally. The idea of erotic prose as medicine is a reminder of how differently the ancient Greeks conceived literature. It is true that in ancient times certain books were censured for being excessively licentious, among them the short stories by Aristeides of Miletus known as the *Milesiaka* (second century BCE, *The Milesian Tales*), and the sexological work attributed to the mythical prostitute Philaenis. However, criticisms of these books are usually embedded in broader critiques of excessive or unbalanced behavior, and an interest in *erotika* is not singled out as being especially bad *per se*.

Such criticisms probably did not represent ancient opinion on a wider scale. Indeed, the numerous papyrus texts containing fragments of previously unknown Greek erotic works show just how many of them must have circulated at one time. Knowledge of erotic prose in Greek, especially romantic fiction, has been greatly augmented by these papyrus books, preserved in the dry climate of Egypt. Fragments of at least 24 prose romances or 'novels' are now known from papyrus, and almost certainly others wait to be identified. One of the most tantalizing narratives revealed in this way is Lollianus' *Phoinikika* (second century CE, *The Phoenician Story*), which seems to be a picaresque tale with an ego-narrator. Among the surviving parts of the story are scenes of a woman sexually initiating the hero, a riotous festival, and a human sacrifice followed by a communal sex orgy. Another interesting papyrus contains scraps of the so-called *Iolaos* (author unknown). Here a young man tries to get access to the secluded women's quarters by masquerading as a eunuch priest who poses no sexual threat, but is caught up in awkward situations of mistaken identity. Both of these works are too fragmentary to yield much more than vignettes of their plot and action. None the less, more is known of *The Phoenician Story* and *Iolaos* than of many once-famous Greek erotic works that are now lost entirely, such as Aristeides of Miletus' *Milesian Tales*. Others survive only when quoted or referred to by other ancient writers who still had access to the texts. At all events, knowledge of ancient Greek prose erotica is still extremely patchy, despite the papyrus finds.

One of the erotic prose works most frequently mentioned by ancient authors was attributed to Philaenis, a legendary courtesan from the island of Samos who is supposed to have lived in the third century BCE. Early Christian bishops singled out Philaenis' book as an illustration of the worst extremes of pagan sexual folly, and it was thought to have been destroyed, but research into the papyrus finds has yielded its scrappy remains. These provide a glimpse into an almost vanished sub-genre of ancient Greek prose: *pornographoi*, literally 'writings about prostitutes.' Again these works elude any single modern literary category. They incorporate at once pseudo-scientific, biographical, antiquarian, and even quasi-medical elements, because prostitutes were thought to know as much as doctors about the inner workings of the female body. Various quasi-legendary women were supposed to have authored other such books, from famous prostitutes like Cyrene, Lais, and Elephantis to Astyanassa, Helen of Troy's maid. Although supposed to be the last word in erotic sophistication, Philaenis' book seems as matter-of-fact as an information manual. Philaenis outlines her intent in a brief introduction. She will give advice to men in need of instruction so that they will not have to waste time in sexual trial and error. She proceeds immediately to giving tips on how to make successful advances, one of which is that men hoping to seduce women should look untidy so that they will not be thought unduly keen. Philaenis also supplies examples of chat-up lines appropriate for various types of women: plain women should be flattered as the equal of the goddesses, old women as young girls, and ugly women as fascinating. The surviving text breaks off just after a section entitled 'How To Kiss.' From what the ancient sources tell of the rest of the book, it continued systematically with lists of different positions for heterosexual lovemaking, also arranged according to different female types. Some copies of these erotic manuals may have had illustrations. The Roman Emperor Tiberius (reigned 14–37 CE), a notorious erotomaniac, is supposed to have displayed a *de luxe* copy of Elephantis' manual which could be referred to when some sexual inspiration was required.

Prostitutes like Philaenis and Elephantis, writing from the viewpoint of their own extensive sexual experience, were obvious figures to instruct inexperienced Greek men about making love. Sexual initiation of both women and men was clearly of great interest to Greek prose writers, to judge from the frequency with which it appears in the full-length prose romances where Greek erotic fiction found its most elaborate and sophisticated form. The romances developed from diverse branches of Greek literature, not only comic poetry and love lyrics, but also prose forms such as rhetorical composition, which was an important part of elite male education in Greek. Rhetoric suffuses the five prose romances that have survived more or less intact: those of Chariton (mid-first century CE, *Chaereas and Callirhoe*), Xenophon of Ephesus (mid-second century CE, *A Tale of Ephesus*), Achilles Tatius (late second century CE, *Leucippe and Cleitophon*), Longus (c. 200 CE, *Daphnis and Chloe*) and Heliodorus (third or fourth century CE, *An Ethiopian Tale*). Not much is known about any of these authors, and even the dates when they wrote are quite uncertain. Artful, rhetorical, and full of literary allusions, the romances were perhaps intended as lighter reading for the educated. Since reading in antiquity was usually done aloud, however, they must have reached a wider audience than the literate who could read them for themselves. Although these five romances have very different situations, characters and plots, they share a certain number of common elements that also appear in the fragmentary 'novel' texts. These common elements are integral to developing the narratives' erotic component and to making love and sex their motivating themes. The centrality of love, desire, sex and, emotions to these romances is reflected in the ancient Greek term for them as a genre. They were apparently known as *erotikas hypotheseis*, perhaps translatable as 'romantic stories' or 'narratives of love.'

While not in any sense formulaic, the prose romances observe certain conventions of plot and characterization. Their heroes and heroines are young, virginal, and aristocratic. They fall in love and prepare to marry, but are parted in some melodramatic way just before they can do so. The adventures that follow put their mutual sexual devotion to extreme tests. In Xenophon's *A Tale of Ephesus*, for instance, the protagonists Anthia and Habrocomes take vows of chastity and fidelity when they are about to be separated. Anthia is eventually sold into slavery abroad. She is bought by a brothel keeper and forced into prostitution, but avoids sex with the clients by pretending to have epilepsy. This is not the first time that Anthia had struggled to save herself for Habrocomes. Earlier in the story, she drank poison rather than marry another man, but the poison only put her into a coma and she recovered - to have her virtue tested again. The apparent murder or suicide of the heroine, later revealed as a subterfuge, is another trope of the prose romances. It enables the writers to explore the poignancy and eroticism that Greek culture attached to the deaths of young women who die virgins. Instead of a living bridegroom, the only lover they will know is death. Alternatively, the heroine's false death may be accompanied by ritualized sexual violence that now seems disturbingly misogynistic, and is perhaps still concerned with the young heroine's defloration. For example, Achilles Tatius describes how his heroine Leucippe is kidnapped and bound to

posts before being disembowelled and having her heart ripped out. The killers then eat her entrails in an orgiastic communion.

The hazardous separation of the hero and heroine also involves them traveling to one or more of the eroticized spaces of antiquity, especially Egypt, the ancient world's site of sensual visioning *par excellence*. This journey is a suitable backdrop for meetings with various characters who discourse on sexual conduct and erotic life in general. Sometimes the relative merits of heterosexual versus male–male relationships are discussed, such as the set-piece debate Achilles Tatius puts into the mouths of his hero Cleitophon and the traveler Menelaus. Cleitophon says that women's bodies are more appealing and that their beauty lasts longer than that of boys. Also, women can be used sexually like boys, allowing men two possible avenues for pleasure. Menelaus counters with the argument that women are sexually false and their beauty is all artifice: only boys are honest, both physically and emotionally. Love of boys therefore belongs to a higher emotional order. This comparison of sex with women and boys is a rhetorical trope that occurs in quite a number of ancient Greek works, and indicates how far the romance authors were influenced by training in the rhetorical schools. This form of Greek erotica, then, may be regarded as a kind of rhetoric. Despite Menelaus' defence of male–male homosexuality, erotic relationships between men and women are the central focus in the prose romances. That of the hero and heroine is paradigmatically perfect, but there are also relationships with sexually experienced women who teach a male character about love. The romance authors are much more ambivalent about the quality of these relationships. In Longus' *Daphnis and Chloe*, the eponymous hero is seduced by an older woman, Lycaenion. Daphnis' encounter with her is good in that it gives him the sexual expertise to optimize the sexual relationship he and Chloe will eventually enjoy. Achilles Tatius suggests the same thing in an episode when Cleitophon has sex —one time only—with the rich widow Melite. However, the romances imply that too much sexual involvement with experienced women is dangerous because they are likely to turn out to be predators who consume men. Lycaenion, the name of Daphnis' seducer, hints at this: it means 'she-wolf.' And in Heliodorus' *An Ethiopian Tale*, the traveler Kalasiris describes how he became infatuated with the vampish courtesan Rhodopis and was subsequently ruined.

After all these sexual trials and discussions of erotic behavior, the hero and heroine will eventually be reunited. The novelists make it clear that their devotion to each other will be rewarded by the promise of a mutually affective and satisfying sexual relationship. The emphasis on romance and mutually enjoyable erotic relationships between men and women seems new to Greek prose writing and may reflect the changing sexual ideology of the time. How this ideology was different becomes clearer if Philaenis' assumptions about sex are compared with those of the novelists writing several centuries after her. Philaenis assumes that men only need to know about sex in order to please themselves; the novelists assume that men need to know in order to please both themselves and their wives.

An alternative view of sex and relationships from the refined and cultured discourse of the prose romances comes in the anonymous Greek novella known as *Lucius or the Ass*. This is sometimes attributed to the prolific writer and satirist Lucian of Samosata (c. 115–180 CE), but its authorship is uncertain. Much shorter than the romances, its tone, vocabulary, and content is more frankly sexual and its picaresque plot totally different. Generically, *Lucius or the Ass* probably has more in common with Aristeides of Miletus' lost *Milesian Tales*, and may even have been intended as a parody of the *erotikas hypotheseis*. Certainly it contains some of their conventions, such as the hero's journey into an eroticized foreign space. *Lucius or the Ass* takes place in Thessaly, a wild border area of Greece famed for the skill of its witches. The hero, Lucius, travels there on business, but is more interested in the region's magical and supernatural associations than work. In Thessaly he stays with Hipparchus, whose wife is an expert witch. In order to find out more about her magical powers, Lucius seduces her maid Palaestra ('gymnasium'), and their intercourse is described at length in a parody of technical terms from athletics. With Palaestra's help, Lucius watches Hipparchus' wife change into an owl after stripping and rubbing herself with magic ointment. Fascinated, he tries the same experiment on himself, but the wrong ointment is used and he changes into an ass. That same night, robbers steal him and a series of degrading adventures begins when various cruel and degenerate people purchase him. His owners include eunuch priests of the Syrian goddess Cybele, who prey on young village boys. Lucius' adventures culminate in a beautiful woman paying to have sex with him while he is still in his animal shape. She is compared to Pasiphae, the mythical Queen of Crete who gave birth to the Minotaur after having sex with a bull—an illustration of how myth was part of the cultural currency of sexual relationships in antiquity. The long description of Lucius' animal–human sexual encounter is uncomfortable for modern readers but may not have been so in ancient times, when the human and animal worlds were less demarcated than they are now, and animals were sometimes worshipped as the incarnations of gods. This scene may also be part of the satire on prose romances. Generally, *Lucius or the Ass* pokes fun at their polite sensibility and emphasis on sexual restraint by describing the excesses of human sexuality, which here exceed the boundaries of humanity. After this episode, Lucius regains human shape by magical means. The satirical point about sexual extremes is forced home when the woman who enjoyed sex with Lucius as an ass rejects him when she sees him in his human form.

Whether or not Lucian of Samosata was the author of *Lucius or the Ass*, his satirical dialogues give a similar worm's eye perspective on sexual relationships. Lucian was a great stylist who prided himself on writing correct and elegant Greek, but the satiric form enabled him to present sexual life in a way that is impossible in more self-consciously high-art genres like the prose romance. Both humans and the gods were Lucian's targets. In *Dialogues of the Gods*, Lucian satirizes the myth of Zeus' abduction of the boy Ganymede, who cannot understand why Zeus should want to have him as a bedfellow because he wriggles. In *Dialogues of the Prostitutes*, Lucian's lively satirical treatment of low-life female stereotypes like old madams, mannish lesbians, and naïve call-girls gives an insight into male fantasies about the sexual world of women. His presentation of women as sexually insatiable and deceitful is the conventional Greek literary one, but *Dialogues of the Prostitutes* still contains all sorts of interesting details not found elsewhere, such as the use of sex toys like leather dildos. Lucian's satires, along with the romances of Heliodorus, Longus, and Achilles Tatius, were much read and translated during the European Renaissance and early modern period, with a consequent influence on western authors.

DOMINIC MONTSERRAT

Further Reading

Anderson, Graham. *Lucian's Comic Fiction.* Leiden 1976.

Betz, Hans Dieter, editor. *The Greek Magical Papyri in Translation, including the Demotic Spells, Volume One: Texts*, 2nd edition, Chicago: The University of Chicago Press, 1992.

Goldhill, Simon. *Foucault's Virginity: Ancient Erotic Fiction and the History of Sexuality.* Cambridge: Cambridge University Press, 1995.

King, Helen. "Sowing the Field: Greek and Roman Sexology." In *Sexual Knowledge, Sexual Science: The History of Attitudes to Sexuality*, edited by Roy Porter and Mikulas Teich. Cambridge: Cambridge University Press, 1994.

Konstan, David. *Sexual Symmetry: Love in the Ancient Greek Novel and Related Genres.* Princeton, New Jersey: Princeton University Press, 1994.

Lambropoulou, Voula. "Some Pythagorean Female Virtues." in *Women in Antiquity: New Assessments*, edited by Richard Hawley and Barbara Levick. London: Routledge, 1995.

Montague, Holly. "Sweet and Pleasant Passion: Male and Female Fantasy in Ancient Romance Novels." In *Pornography and Representation in Greece and Rome*, edited by Amy Richlin. Oxford: Oxford University Press, 1992.

Morgan, John R. and Stoneman, Richard, editors. *Greek Fiction: The Greek Novel in Context*, London and New York: Routledge, 1994.

Parker, Holt. "Love's Body Anatomized: The Ancient Erotic Handbooks and the Rhetoric of Sexuality," in *Pornography and Representation in Greece and Rome*, edited by Amy Richlin. Oxford: Oxford University Press, 1992.

Reardon, B.P. editor. *Collected Ancient Greek Novels.* Berkeley, Los Angeles and London: University of California Press, 1989.

Richlin, Amy, editor. *Pornography and Representation in Greece and Rome.* Oxford: Oxford University Press, 1992.

Stephens, Susan A. and Winkler, John J. editors. *Ancient Greek Novels: The Fragments.* Princeton. New Jersey: Princeton University Press, 1995.

Tatum, James, editor. *The Search for the Ancient Novel.* Baltimore and London: The Johns Hopkins University Press, 1994.

Zeitlin, Froma. "The Poetics of Eros; Nature, Art, and Imitation in Longus' *Daphnis and Chloe*." In David Halperin et al. (editors). *Before Sexuality: The Construction of Erotic Experience in the Ancient Greek World.* Princeton, New Jersey: Princeton University Press, 1990.

GREEK, ANCIENT: VERSE

Aristophanes, Agathias, Alcman, Anacreon, Archilochus, Asclepiades, Meleager, Paul the Silentiaru, Philodemus, Sappho, Sophocles, Sotades, Strato

For the poets of ancient Greece, the erotic experience was thought to have two very distinct configurations. In one incarnation of *eros,* or erotic desire, two lovers share a reciprocal feeling of harmonious love. This type of love, with its mutual consummation of erotic longing, is described by the Greek poets as a singularly pleasurable experience and celebrated in lines of joyous verse. But it is the second type of *eros* that is much more frequently represented in the verses of the ancient Greeks, that is, the unrequited desire a lover feels for an absent or unresponsive beloved. This *eros* suggests an unfulfilled and perhaps even unfulfillable feeling of erotic desire, and is denoted by the absence of the beloved, the lack of satisfaction, and the impossibility of erotic realization. In this kind of *eros,* ubiquitous in the erotic verse of the ancient Greeks, the lover's desire is difficult, painful, and ultimately devastating.

Implied in the Greek poets' literary representations of love is the concept of absence, insufficiency, and deficit. The Greek terms *eros* "desire," *himeros* "longing," and *pathos* "yearning," all indicate this notion of want for something missing. The poets of ancient Greece characterize this feeling of lack attacking both gods and mortals equally, as no one is invulnerable to the troublesome and agonizing pangs of love. *Eros* is a dangerously compelling force that imposes itself on the lover from an external position of power, and from there controls the lover's miserable fate. The images the Greek poets employ in their verses to portray the disturbing and eventually overwhelming experience of erotic desire all emphasize these detrimental effects: love is like war, disease, madness, and even death.

The Greek poets figure the torment of unsatisfied erotic desire as a uniquely corporeal suffering, and they often depict *eros* assaulting the lover's body, inflicting severe physical pain and robbing the limbs of health and substance. With the body so weakened under the onslaught of erotic desire, the mind of the lover is also exposed to attack: the poets delineate in almost clinical detail the loss of normal mental capabilities as *eras* assails the lover's organs of thought and reason. Thus a metaphorical language emerges from this idea of destructive love: *eros* is a *nosos* ("sickness") and a *mania* ("madness") afflicting the unsuspecting lover. The ancient Greek poets tend to focus on the harmful qualities of erotic desire, and it is this negative experience that they most often illustrate in their verses with images of physical trauma, wounding, bodily dissolution, and mental incapacitation.

Greek poetic conceptions about *eros* began to take shape in the earliest literary documents that survive from their civilization. The idea that erotic desire is a kind of physical attack is first articulated in the Homeric epics, the *Iliad* and the *Odyssey,* orally composed epic poems attributed by tradition to Homer and probably written down sometime in the eighth century B.C. Although the Homeric poems do not focus on love in the explicit way that some later Greek poetry does, they offer several early accounts of how *eros* can have an effect on the bodies and minds of lovers, and how the feeling of erotic desire can influence the lover's course of action. In this respect, certain important erotic episodes deserve particular attention. Homer's *Iliad* narrates the events in the tenth and final year of the Trojan War, a conflict initiated by one of the most powerful erotic incidents of Greek legend, the seduction of the beautiful Helen of Sparta by the Trojan prince, Paris, with the help and persuasion of the Greek goddess of love, Aphrodite.

In Book 3 of the *Iliad,* Aphrodite recreates their initial love affair, as she coerces Helen and Paris to come together in their bedroom at Troy for an afternoon of passionate lovemaking. Paris graphically describes how he is "seized" by sexual longing for Helen, and how his senses are "completely veiled" by the sensation of *eros* (*Iliad* 3 .441–446). The gods themselves are not immune to the uncontrollable feeling of erotic desire, as evinced by the episode in Book 14 of the *Iliad,* the *Dios Apate,* or "Seduction of Zeus," arguably the most erotic passage in the entire poem. When the goddess Hera decides to lure her husband Zeus away from the Trojan battlefield, she does so by planning and accomplishing a sexual conquest of the great god: she adorns herself in beautiful clothes and jewelry, and borrows a love-charm from Aphrodite (*Iliad* 14.160–223). Upon seeing her, Zeus is overwhelmed by *eros:* his wits are "veiled," his heart is "melted all around," and he is "seized" by sexual desire for his wife (*Iliad* 14.294–328). Both of these erotic scenes describe the effects of a forceful *eros* that is about to be satisfied and comprise interludes in the continual warfare that is the primary theme of the *Iliad.* The *Odyssey* also presents the theme of *eros* waiting to be fulfilled, in the depiction of the intense longing of Odysseus and Penelope for each other over a twenty-year separation. Odysseus is described as "wasting away" as he yearns for his wife (*Odyssey* 5.151–158), and Penelope is constantly portrayed as weeping and longing for her missing husband (e.g., *Odyssey* 11.181–183, 16.37–39, 19.204–209). Finally, the epic allows for the satisfaction of their deep erotic desire when the couple is blissfully reunited at the end of the poem (*Odyssey* 23.205–343). The way these episodes in the Homeric poems portray the feeling of *eros* in both language and imagery had a significant influence on later Greek poets' depiction of the erotic experience as a strong physical force that attacks, occupies, and overcomes the body and mind of the lover.

The two narrative poems of the archaic Greek poet Hesiod, the *Theogony* and the *Works and Days,* belong to the same Ionian tradition as the Homeric poems, and were probably composed late in the eighth century B.C. Like the Homeric epics, Hesiod's poems also describe the erotic experiences of both gods and mortals, illustrating human as well as divine reactions to the feelings of love and longing. While the poems of Hesiod embrace the Homeric conception of a violent and powerful *eros* that can conquer the lover, his verse offers a further exploration of how erotic desire can be experienced as it invades the lover's body. In the genealogical lists of the *Theogony,* a poem that explains the genesis of all the Greek gods, Hesiod depicts the heavenly couplings of various immortals with language reminiscent of the Homeric images for the might of *eros,* but with a bold and personal characterization of the forces at work in the feeling of erotic desire. The god Eros is one of the four original deities in Hesiod's account (*Theogony*, 116–122). As a primordial entity, Eros is introduced at an early point in the poem in order to unite the many generative pairs essential to Hesiod's genealogical model: without erotic desire, Hesiod says, the cosmogonic structure cannot emerge and take its divine shape. Eros is described as "the most beautiful among the deathless gods" (*Theogony*, 120), but he is also dangerous to the physical and mental well-being of lovers: "he loosens the limbs, and subdues the mind and sensible thought in the breasts of all gods and all humans" (*Theogony*, 121–122). This vigorous and masterful Eros, together with the personified Himeros, or 'Longing," are later depicted as the companions of Aphrodite, as the goddess of erotic desire is born from the seafoam awash around the severed genitals of the Sky god, Ouranos (*Theogony*, 201–202). Aphrodite is also accompanied by the Charites , or Graces, daughters of Eurynome, whose erotic beauty is portrayed by Hesiod in a striking description: "From their glancing eyes dripped *eros* the limb-loosener, and beautiful was their glance from beneath their brows" (*Theogony*, 910–911). In this passage, erotic desire emanates in a liquid manifestation from the eyes, a place where the power of love in Greek poetry is traditionally thought to reside. Here the images of desire and desirability are confounded, as the alluring look of the Graces' eyes, melting with *eros,* arouses longing in the limbs, dissolving and destabilizing those who meet their gaze. The appearance of the first female, Pandora, narrated by Hesiod at length in his other poem, the *Works and Days* (42–105), also offers an erotic crisis of interpretation: she is "an evil men will enjoy embracing" (*Works and Days*, 57–58). Pandora is endowed with exquisite grace and beauty by the goddess Aphrodite, as well as "painful yearning (*pothos*) and cares that devour

the limbs" (*Works and Days*, 65–66). As in the figure of the beautiful god Eros, Hesiod contrasts the outward loveliness of the woman Pandora with the underlying erotic perils that her beauty masks, an alluring exterior that arouses strong physical desire, both painful and pleasurable. Through the story of Pandora and the deadly dowry of evils stored in her jar (*pithos*), Hesiod proposes an erotic mythological explanation for the existence of suffering among humankind, where the woman herself is the embodiment of the experience of intense sexual longing.

The *Homeric Hymn to Aphrodite* was composed probably in the eight or seventh century CE by a poet using a poetic language similar to Homer's; and like the Hesiodic poems, the *Hymn* represents a shift towards verse about mythological subject matter. As a story of seduction, the *Hymn to Aphrodite* contains many elements of structure and language that are parallel to those shaping epic scenes of sexual encounters, yet the primary theme of the *Hymn* is specifically and explicitly erotic. The *Hymn* narrates the sensual love between the goddess and her mortal lover, the Trojan prince Anchises, using images of *eros* as a violent force that subdues almost all who experience its power. Aphrodite is described as the instigator of erotic desire in the world: she "stirs sweet longing (*himeros*) in the gods and subdues the races of mortal men" (*Hymn* 2–3). But her ability to cause *eros* does not protect her against its effects: when the goddess sees Anchises in the midday sunshine, "strikingly longing (*himeros*) seized her heart" (56–57). The Trojan youth experiences a similar violent onset of love upon seeing her, cleverly disguised as a young virgin, as the poet says *"eros* seized Anchises" (91), but Aphrodite feels compelled to make certain the job is done right: "the goddess hurled sweet longing (*himeros*) in his heart, and *eros* seized Anchises" (143–144). This erotic trajectory, with its emphatic repetition of phrases, culminates in their lovemaking, followed by an exhausted post- coital nap (153–170). When they awaken, Anchises is astonished to find he has just had sex with the divine Aphrodite (181–190), but she assures him he is in no danger, and in fact promises him a glorious line of descendants through their son, the brilliant hero, Aeneas (196–197). The *Hymn to Aphrodite* portrays the elemental essence of an erotic desire that leads ultimately to a particular kind of immortality for the lovers, human and goddess.

The lyric poets of the Greek archaic period (c. 700–500 BCE.) described the pangs and passions of erotic love using imagery familiar from earlier epic and mythological narrative poetry: love is depicted as a powerful force that seizes and possesses the lover, leaving him wounded, weakened, and gasping for breath. But in the genre of personal lyric poetry, where the main purpose is to grasp and articulate succinctly the immediacy of individual experiences and emotions, the nature of this violent and compelling *eros* enjoys a conspicuous position and figures prominently as the explicit focus in much of these poets' verses. The tendency of the lyric mode towards the expression of the lover's direct confrontation with erotic desire is exemplified in the poetry of Archilochus of the island of Paros (c. 680–640 BCE.). The extant fragments of his verses occupy a unique status in the Greek poetic tradition, as they represent the earliest surviving examples of the work of a monodic lyric poet. Although Archilochus was most famous in classical antiquity for his poems of invective, the target of which was apparently the family of a certain Neoboule, the woman who was said to have jilted him, a few fragments of his poetry reveal his deliberate interest in describing the effects of sexual longing. The poetry of Archilochus gives first-person voice to stricken lovers, who delineate the languid yet overwhelming physical control they experience under the onslaught of erotic love. In one fragment, Archilochus describes how "limb-loosening" desire (*pothos*) "conquers" the speaker (Fragment 196); in another fragment, again *pothos* attacks a paralyzed lover, who says he is "wretched, breathless" and "pierced right through the bones" because of longing (Fragment 193). The invasion of the lover's body is dramatically represented in another verse, where *eros* is "coiled up beneath the heart" of the lover, and steals out of his breast "the soft wits" (Fragment 191). The innovation of Archilochus in the language of erotic poetry is to concentrate and enumerate in his verse such vivid images of the destructive power of unsatisfied sexual desire.

Like Archilochus, the Spartan poet Alcman was active during the seventh century BCE. While Alcman was primarily a composer of choral lyric poetry, including hymns to gods and heroes as well as ritual songs designed for choirs of voices, a few fragments of his verses remain that belong to the category of personal love lyric. These fragments suggest Alcman's intention to explore the debilitating effects of erotic longing upon the mind and body of the lover. In one fragment, Alcman personifies the god Eros as a playful but "insane" child, trampling down the delicate meadow grass, where an anxious speaker seems to be fearful of the mad god's boisterous and potentially harmful arrival (Fragment 58). The physical damage done by *eros* is represented as being more subtle in another fragment of Alcman's love poetry: here the poem's speaker depicts erotic desire as being "sweet," while it "drips down" and heats his heart (Fragment 59a), in a complex synthesis of images for warmth and liquidity. In a choral fragment, the young female singers describe the beautiful gaze of one of their group: "with limb-loosening desire (*pothos*), she glances more meltingly than sleep or death" (Fragment 3.61–62). Alcman suggests that the contiguous ideas of sleep and death simultaneously express both the dangerous and enticing qualities of the erotic experience.

The Greek archaic poets of the sixth century BCE continued the portrayal of *eros* as an aggressive, unpredictable, and ultimately inescapable force. The representation of erotic desire in these poets' fragments assumes the character of an elemental power: love has the power of a storm, wind, or fire, first assaulting its victims with unexpected violence, and then proceeding to drown, parch, melt, or bum them in their vulnerable condition. Bruised and battered by contact with this extrinsic outburst of natural energy, the lover's weakened body is then effortlessly possessed by the irresistible feeling of erotic desire. The poet Alcaeus (c. 620–550 BCE) lived in the city of Mytilene on the island of Lesbos, near the coast of Asia Minor, an area famous for its poetic tradition as well as its luxurious Eastern lifestyle. Although the outstanding feature of Alcaeus' poetry is its political character, in verses intended for performance during the communal experience of the *symposium,* a few passages of his poetry also indicate a concern for the capricious and threatening nature of *eros*. In a fragment of a drinking song, Alcaeus describes the sizzling heat of the Dog Days of summer as the time when "women are most lustful, while men are fragile" (Fragment 347), and recommends the refreshment of wine as a cure for the harmful effects of parching sexual fever. Elsewhere, in a few lines on a scrap of papyrus, Alcaeus retells the erotic causation of the Trojan War, and depicts the mental state of a love-struck Helen as she sailed off from Sparta with her lover, Paris: "in her breast her heart was shaken, and she was driven mad by the Trojan man" (Fragment 283.3–6). While the references to erotic experience in extant Alcaean fragments are few, they are consonant with other early Greek literary and lyric descriptions of the damaging effects of the onset of *eros*.

Contemporary with Alcaeus was the poet Sappho (c. 620–550 BCE), whose poetry is unmistakably and graphically erotic. Sappho was also born on the island of Lesbos, although unlike Alcaeus, she shows scant interest in recording the tumultuous political events of the period in her verses. According to tradition, Sappho lived most of her life in relative peace and urbane comfort in the city of Mytilene, surrounded by an intimate circle of female mends for whom she composed her lyric poetry and with whom she celebrated its performance. Although she also wrote wedding songs, hymns, and other mythological verses, Sappho's poetic specialty appears to have been the short monodiclyric poem, in which the first-person expression of intense personal emotions is most prominent: it is in these lyrics that the destructive passion of love finds an exalted and profound articulation. Throughout her poetry, with its explicit focus on the erotic experience, Sappho uses traditional poetic elements to describe the dangerous power of *eros,* yet she boldly applies original images and metaphors in her verse that reveal her brilliant conception of love's immediacy and potentially toxic effect. Sappho was famous in antiquity as a prolific lyric innovator, and an analysis of her sharp poetic language and lucid imagery reveals a complex melodic design and an intricate rhetorical structure that tends to contradict any romantic idea of her work's simplicity or naiveté. As a poet, Sappho controls every aspect of her art: it is only her poetic persona that exhibits itself as mad, unrestrained, and abandoned to the ravages of erotic desire. For Sappho, the fulfillment of love is blissfully sweet, while the longing of an unsatisfied desire or the pain of separation from an absent beloved destroys the mind and body of the lover. In one fragment, she describes desire (*pothos*) as having the power to subdue (Fragment 102); in another, *eros* "pours over" the face of a beautiful bride (Fragment 112.4);

still another fragment depicts *eros* as the "limb-loosener," and vividly, "a sweet-bitter irresistible creature" (Fragment 130). A number of Sapphic fragments portray the urgent assault of erotic desire upon the individual lover: a speaker complains that *eros* "shakes my wits like a wind" (Fragment 47), while another speaker describes the arrival of her beloved fanning the flames in her yearning heart "on fire with longing (*pothos*)" (Fragment 48). In a hymn to Aphrodite, almost certainly a complete poem, Sappho herself summons the goddess to be her ally in the warfare of love, and to protect her from the deleterious and overpowering effects of erotic desire (Fragment 1). But nowhere in Greek poetry is there a more striking and detailed description of the devastation of *eros* than in Sappho's fragment 31: in this poem, all the possible physical disorders induced by sexual desire are exhaustively indexed in what has been called the definitive catalogue of the symptoms of lovesickness. One by one a distressed first-person speaker lists her reactions to the sight of her beloved in close conversation with someone else: her heart pounds, she can't speak, her skin feels feverish, her vision blurs, her ears buzz, she is seized by cold sweat and trembling, and her skin pales, until she says, "I seem to be a little short of death" (Fragment 31.15–16). The experience of erotic desire is terrifying, crippling, even near fatal, yet the pain and wreckage can be overcome: the lover portrayed in Sappho's lyric verses recuperates and lives on to pursue another love.

Such imagery to portray the harmful consequences of desire can also be found in the erotic verses of the western Greek poet, Ibycus. Born in the Greek city of Rhegium in southern Italy, Ibycus eventually went east to Samos, where he joined the artistic circle financed by the wealthy tyrant Polycrates; the ancient tradition about his life and work places his poetic activity securely in the second half of the sixth century CE Ibycus wrote two types of poetry, arranged later in the Alexandrian period into seven books: long narrative choral poetry on mythological themes, and personal erotic lyric verses celebrating the beauty of boys. In the few fragments that remain of his love poetry, Ibycus combines striking expressions and lavish sound texture to describe the destructive elemental power of erotic desire. One fragment, which may be a complete poem, dynamically contrasts the calm regularity of the arrival of spring with the fitful disorder of elemental *eros:* while the flowering season brings with it predictable and welcome growth, for the agitated speaker of this poem, the feeling of erotic desire never changes its intense momentum and offers no quiet symmetry, "for me *eros* is at rest during no season" (Fragment 286.1–7). Ibycus then equates the attack of this restless eros with a blast of Boreas, the exceptionally turbulent North Wind, depicted as "shadowy and undaunted," who "with parching fits of madness masterfully and thoroughly batters my senses" (Fragment 286.8–13). Like the violent gust of wind, love is a harsh natural force, swift, sudden, hostile, resulting in physical injury and mental confusion. In another piece of Ibycus' erotic verse, again perhaps a complete poem, a first-person voice figures *eros* as a dangerously attractive youth with dark, seductive eyes, who "with spells of all sorts drives me into Aphrodite's inextricable nets" (Fragment 287): the image of being entangled in an erotic ambush proves love's overwhelming physical control over the enthralled lover. In these two poems, Ibycus confirms and expands the Greek lyric conception of the devastating primal force of erotic desire.

The erotic verses of Anacreon (c. 560–480 BCE), Ibycus' contemporary in the late sixth century, also portray the pure violence delivered by sexual desire, and continue to delineate an ever more specific vocabulary of arresting images to describe love's harmful effects. Anacreon was born in the Ionian town of Teos on the coast of Asia Minor, and is said to have been entertained at the courts of the Samian tyrant Polycrates and the Athenian tyrant Hipparchus. The main focus of Anacreon's poetry is the conviviality of wine-drinking at the *symposium,* along with the love affairs and erotic intrigues that take place in such a setting. As is the (usually undeserved) fate of other poets whose work deals with such themes, Anacreon acquired a reputation in antiquity that capitalized on his poetic persona: he was thought to have been a self-indulgent drunk and sexual libertine. In the remaining fragments of his five books of poetry, Anacreon displays a meticulous lyric style colored by a subtle spirit of irony and a tone of intellectual refinement. Yet there is nothing inhibited about this poet's voice: the fragments of Anacreon present an innovative and imaginative portrayal of the risks inherent in the game of love. Anacreon's *eros* is often personified as a robust contender, throwing a ball at the lover (Fragment 358), engaging the lover in a boxing match (Fragment 396), or gambling at dice (Fragment 398). The natural aggression of this athletic *eros* accords well with other Greek literary representations of the erotic experience as one full of jeopardy: *eros* offers a taunting challenge, and the lover can expect either a physically exhausting escape or a painful defeat. In other fragments, Anacreon describes the feeling of sexual desire as one of inebriation, "drunk with love" (Fragment 376); he calls love "melting" (Fragment 459) and a "subduer" (Fragment 357); and he compares *eros* to a blacksmith who strikes him with a hammer blow (Fragment 413). More than any other lyric poet, Anacreon emphasizes the psychological effects of erotic mania, dramatizing in his verses the convulsive state of a mind confused by sexual longing (Fragments 359, 398, 429). All the erotic fragments of Anacreon explore the consequences of contact with the hostile power of *eros:* intoxication, madness, and competitive struggle.

Later Greek poetry continued to echo and develop the vocabulary of images describing the erotic experience in terms of its extreme dominance over lovers. During the late sixth and early fifth centuries in Attica, dramatic festivals were instituted at which tragedies and comedies were performed in celebration of the god Dionysus. In the fifth century, the Athenian playwrights composed dramas for performance in an outdoor communal setting for a sophisticated audience of citizens and political allies. Although the principal themes in the genres of Athenian drama were not exclusively or even explicitly erotic, a few of the extant plays presented on stage in a dramatic context the visible spectacle of individuals under the influence of uncontrollable erotic longing. The performance of tragedy in particular, with its primary focus on the individual in the grip of an overpowering destiny, offered an unique forum in which to explore the consequences of frustrated *eros.* The tragedian Sophocles (496–406 BCE) was famous both as a model citizen and soldier of the Athenian democracy, and also as one of the three canonical Attic playwrights. One of Sophocles' earliest surviving dramas is the *Trachinian Women* (c. 450–440 BCE), a play that deals with the devastating effects of erotic desire in the axes of passion between the great hero Heracles, his wife Deianira, and his new captive, Iole. When Deianira discovers that her husband sacked the city of Iole's father only to possess the girl, for whom he has incurred a violent lust (*Trachiniae* 351–374), the hero's wife decides to win back his love by means of a secret remedy, drops of blood given to her long ago by the centaur Nessus (531–587). But the love charm turns out to be a fatal poison, a ruse by the dying beast to exact revenge on Heracles, who killed him as Nessus tried to rape Deianira (672–722). The centaur's thwarted *eros* for Deianira is made manifest in the toxic charm, which the queen administers out of a desperate passion for her husband, who has aroused her suicidal anguish because of his fierce sexual desire for the younger girl. Infected with a virulent sickness (*nosos*), Heracles is exposed onstage, ranting and raving (971–1043), and is delivered from his agony by being carried off in the final scene to be burned alive (1259–1278). Throughout the play, Sophocles draws a close network of images with *eros,* the poison, the wild *nosos* of Heracles, his cruel madness, and the brutality of beasts. The pernicious power of this agonistic *eros* is personified by the chorus of the *Trachinian Women* in the figure of Aphrodite, as both victor and umpire in the contest of love (497–498, 515–516), and the goddess is named "the clear instigator of all these things" (860–861).

The playwright Euripides (c. 480–406 BCE) treated the theme of love's contamination most memorably in his *Hippolytus* (428 BCE), in which two distinct levels of action, divine and human, are evident. Aphrodite, powerful and pitiless as the force she represents, reveals in the prologue that she will punish the young Hippolytus, son of the hero Theseus, for his rejection of sexual love, by making him the object of his stepmother's erotic passion (*Hippolytus* 1–57). Out of shame, Phaedra tries in vain to conceal her desire, but when her lovesickness (*nosos*) overwhelms and threatens to kill her (170–267), an anxious and well-intentioned Nurse tries to secure the sexual favors of Hippolytus as a remedy for Phaedra's wasting disease, but he violently refuses (601–615). Phaedra resolves to commit suicide to preserve her reputation as the king's wife (680–731), as she realizes, "I am beaten by bitter love" (727); but to avenge the extremism of her chaste stepson, she leaves a note for Theseus accusing Hippolytus

of raping her (856–886). Mad with grief, Theseus curses his son and casts him into exile (1045–1101), where he is attacked by a monstrous bull sent by Poseidon and is carried back onstage to die in torment; but at the end of the play the goddess Artemis appears *ex machina* to explain the truth to Theseus, that the terrible events were directed solely by Aphrodite (1282–1341). The fatal network of tainted *eros* binding the human characters, Hippolytus, Phaedra, and Theseus, is dramatically framed by the divine conflict between the two opposed goddesses, yet the victory over those who would deny her essential power goes unequivocally to Aphrodite, who "drives the unbending heart of gods and mortals" (1268–1269). The notion of a destructive and irresistible *eros* is a dominant motif in the *Hippolytus* and the *Trachinian Women,* as it moves through both of these plays with relentless tragic force.

The power of *eros* to sway the course of human action is well represented in the *Lysistrata* (411 BCE), a play by the greatest of the Athenian comic poets, Aristophanes (c. 448–c. 380 BCE). In this famous comedy, the women of Athens and Sparta, dismayed that the men have failed to bring an end to the Peloponnesian War, band together under the leadership of Lysistrata ("Dissolver of Armies") to impose peace with a two-pronged strategy: first, they seize and occupy the Acropolis, the civic heart of the city where the treasury is located, and second, they refuse to have sexual relations with their husbands until they reconcile with the Spartans (*Lysistrata* 1–253). The play offers a basically hedonistic calculus, starkly contrasting the deficiency of sexual relations caused by the war, with the restoration of erotic satisfaction in peacetime. As Lysistrata says, "We want to get laid, to put it briefly" (715). Aristophanes indulges in a great deal of visual comedy and humorous banter in this play, easily capitalizing on the many opportunities for sexual innuendo inherent in the plot. In one scene, a chorus of feeble and impotent old men try to take back the Acropolis by ramming the gates with logs they can barely lift, and by setting siege fires they can't keep lit (254–386); in another scene, Myrrhine teases her sex-starved and obviously ithyphallic husband, Kinesias, by promising to sleep with him, running off to obtain a series of erotic enhancements, then abandoning him still unsatisfied (837–958).

Finally as the men and women are reunited, the comedy suggests that peace is restored through an act of war—the sex-strike—and reinforces the concept that although erotic love can be a struggle, the mutual fulfillment of sexuality, of gratified *eros,* is a stabilizing force in society.

During the Hellenistic period (c. 323–331 BCE), the Greek poets carry on the notion oferotic damage as they concentrated on a new group of literary genres, in particular epyllion (short epic), mime, pastoral poems, and epigrams. The most detailed and compelling depiction of the power of *eros* comes in the third book of the *Argonautica* by Apollonius of Rhodes (c. 295–215 BCE). An epyllion in four books, the *Argonautica* narrates the tale of Jason and his journey to acquire the Golden Fleece; Book 3 recounts the explicitly erotic events in Colchis where Jason is loved by the princess, Medea, and is then aided in his quest by her gifts of sorcery. Hoping to secure help for her favorite, Jason, Hera asks Aphrodite to persuade her son Eros to make Medea fall in love with him (*Argonautica* 6–166); the winged god shoots her, "and the arrow burned inside the girl, deep down under her heart, like a flame" (286–287). Throughout this episode, the poet uses vocabulary and images that evoke the tangible immediacy of earlier Greek poetic descriptions of harmful *eros,* especially the erotic language of Sappho and the lyric poets, and adds to that the dramatist's interest in exploring the ethical consequences of such a crushing sexual desire. The result is an intimate psychological portrait of a destabilized Medea that presents her fatal longing for Jason as an attack on her judgment, as she realizes, "My mind is entirely at a loss" (772): *eros* deprives Medea of the ability to make reasoned decisions, and envelops her in a ruinous lack of clarity about her own doomed circumstances.

The epigrammatists of the Hellenistic age return to an explicit focus on erotic themes in their short occasional poems, as the epigram is raised to perfection as an independent literary genre. These epigrams were assembled in ancient times in different anthologies, including the famous Palatine Anthology; all the extant poems are now collected in a modem edition called simply "The Greek Anthology," representing over six thousand epigrams ranging in date from the seventh century BCE to the tenth century CE and covering a wide array of topics, in particular the joy and anguish of love. While the writers of epigram inherited and revived earlier poetic conceptions about *eros* as a destructive force, a tone of playfulness, irony, and even humorous detachment becomes more evident in erotic verses during this period. Asclepiades of Samos (*floruit* c. 290 BCE) was known for the elegant simplicity of his style, and his epigrams often describe the power of love with a distinctly light-hearted and mocking voice. In one epigram, he addresses the god Zeus who rains on him as he waits at his lover's door, reminding Zeus of his own amours: "The god who compels me is your master, too" (*Palatine Anthology* 5.64). A love poet famous for exquisite style and grace, Meleager of the Syrian Greek town Gadara (*floruit* c. 60 BCE) was also known as the compiler of an early anthology of epigrams, entitled *Stephanos,* or "The Garland." His own numerous epigrams describe love in dynamic images reminiscent of earlier lyric poets, as winged *eros* the wild-eyed conqueror is equated with the boy whom Meleager desires (*Palatine Anthology* 12.101). The erotic epigrams of Philodemus (born c. 110 BCE), also from Gadara, reveal his interest in Epicurean ideals, and are noted for their particular amusing frankness and dramatic approach. Philodemus celebrates a woman named Xanthippe in a series of amatory verses, saying it is for her that "a fire smolders in my insatiable heart" (*Palatine Anthology* 11.41). For the Hellenistic epigrammatists, *eros* was still full of implacable and antagonistic energy, a bittersweet event summed up in brief, incisive poems. The poets of ancient. Greece explored the idea of *eros* as a dangerous force, and defined the experience of sexual desire as an essentially overwhelming and ultimately destructive physical feeling. To come into contact with erotic longing was to be seized, melted, frozen, beaten, invaded by sickness, and driven mad. While some verses do depict the return to health and sanity that accompanies the fulfillment of shared *eros,* the Greek poets essentially agreed that there is no real drama in blissful love, only in love's torment.

MONICA SILVEIRA CYRINO

Further Reading

Austin, Norman. *Helen of Troy and Her Shameless Phantom: Myth and Poetics.* Ithaca, New York: Cornell University Press, 1994.

Bing, Peter and Rip Cohen. *Games of Venus: An Anthology of Greek and Roman Erotic Verse from Sappho to Ovid.* New York: Routledge, 1992.

Burnett, Anne Pippin. *Three Archaic Poets: Archilochus, Alcaeus, Sappho*. Cambridge, MA: Harvard University Press, 1983.

Calame, Claude. *The Poetics of Eros in Ancient Greece*. translated by Janet Lloyd. Princeton, NJ: Princeton University Press, 1999.

Cameron, Alan. *The Greek Anthology from Meleager to Planudes*. Oxford: Oxford University Press, 1993.

Campbell, David. *The Golden Lyre: The Themes of the Greek Lyric Poets*. London: Duckworth, 1983.

Carson, Anne. *Eros the Bittersweet: An Essay*. Princeton. NJ: Princeton University Press, 1986.

Cyrino, Monica S. *In Pandora's Jar: Lovesickness in Early Greek Poetry*. Lanham, MD: University Press of America, 1995.

Davidson, James. *Courtesans and Fishcakes: The Consuming Passions of Classical Athens*. New York: St. Martin's Press, 1998.

DuBois, Page. *Sappho Is Burning*. Chicago, IL: University of Chicago Press, 1995.

Friedrich, Paul. *The Meaning of Aphrodite*. Chicago, IL: University of Chicago Press, 1978.

Gentili, Bruno. *Poetry and Its Public in Ancient Greece: From Homer to the Fifth Century*. Translated by A. Thomas Cole. Baltimore and London: Johns Hopkins University Press, 1988.

Goldhill, Simon. *Foucault's Virginity: Ancient Erotic Fiction and the History of Sexuality*. Cambridge: Cambridge University Press, 1995.

Halperin, David M. *One Hundred Years of Homosexuality and Other Essays on Greek Love*. New York and London: Routledge, 1990.

Halperin, David M., John J. Winkler and Froma I. Zeitlin editors. *Before Sexuality: The Construction of Erotic Experience in the Ancient Greek World*. Princeton, NJ: Princeton University Press, 1990.

Henderson, Jeffiey. *The Maculate Muse: Obscene Language in Attic Comedy*. New Haven and London: Yale University Press, 1975.

Konstan, David. *Sexual Symmetry: Love in the Ancient Novel and Related Genres*. Princeton, NJ: Princeton University Press, 1994.

Licht, Hans. *Sexual Life in Ancient Greece*. New York: Dorset Press, 1994.

Powell, Anton, editor. *Euripides, Women, and Sexuality*. London: Routledge, 1990.

Rayor, Diane. *Sappho's Lyre: Archaic Lyric and Women Poets of Ancient Greece*. Berkeley and Los Angeles: University of California Press, 1991.

Rousselle, Aline. *Pomeia: On Desire and the Body in Antiquity*. Translated by Felicia Pheasant. Oxford: Oxford University Press, 1980.

Thornton, Bruce S. *Eros: The Myth of Ancient Greek Sexuality*. Boulder, CO and Oxford: Westview Press, 1997.

Williamson, Margaret. *Sappho's Immortal Daughters*. Cambridge, MA: Harvard University Press, 1995.

Winkler, John. *The Constraints of Desire: The Anthropology of Sex and Gender in Ancient Greece*. New York and London: Routledge, 1990.

Zeitlin, Froma I. *Playing the Other: Gender and Society in Classical Greek Literature*. Chicago, IL: University of Chicago Press: 1996.

GRISETTE

The word *grisette* originally appeared in France in the seventeenth century and designated the grey dress worn by young French women of the lower class. By metonymy and disdain, the term came to mean the women of that class while the original reference to the grey garment disappeared. During the eighteenth and nineteenth centuries, the grisette is sometimes assimilated with a young woman of limited means and easy virtue.

Jean de La Fontaine, in 1665, is the first author to report the connection made between these poor girls and a particular practice of sexual hunting by the aristocratic males, in France: "se faire une grisette" [to have sex with a grisette]. In his short story, *Joconde ou l'infidélité des femmes*, La Fontaine tells the story of a king and a handsome nobleman seducing all the women in the kingdom and keeping track of them in a book. At the conclusion of the tale, they share a bed with the same grisette, unaware of the sudden irruption of a third aficionado who, alone, enjoys the grisette's ardor! The text supports the idea that all women are unfaithful.

La Fontaine's grisette is a promiscuous girl, astute and fun, faithful while a virgin, unfaithful after the loss of her virginity and her abandonment. The grisette is a sexual object that can easily be bought. The *grisette* is particularly associated with an undergarment, an object of

596

fetishism, the *cotillon* (a poor woman's under-skirt), to which we need to add an important specific expression: *la mine chiffonnée* [the weathered face]. This idiom, as with the previous term, assumes a sexual function: the grisette and the cotillion can be crumpled [*chiffonné*] for sexual exploitation with no worry about a spoiled skirt. La Fontaine's story is labeled the *Joconde's genre* and often copied.

In the eighteenth-century texts, the grisette participates in a coming-of-age ritual for young nobles who try to take her virginity away. The grisette hopes, innocently and vainly, that all the wedding promises made by the seducer (with the aid of fashionable gifts, especially of clothing) will have a matrimonial conclusion!

In 1737, the term grisette becomes associated with craftswomen's assistants of the *magasins de nouveauté* [novelty shops], to the *filles de boutique* [shop assistants], and to the *modistes* [milliners]. It is here the finery can be observed through the shop windows where they work assiduously. From these openings, they playfully wink to tease the passers-by. They are then compared to a seraglio or a harem and become the first sexualized female advertisement for merchandise. Lawrence Sterne made a *cliché* of them in 1768, in England and America, in his *Sentimental Journey to France*, where the grisette is a disturbing promiscuous gloves' shopkeeper.

A second representation of the grisette is found in the work of Sébastien Mercier in 1781. Mercier gives a more positive image of the grisette and locates her amidst the courageous, independent seamstresses working in the privacy of their room. This room will become an indispensable accessory of her representation, a symbol of her poverty. It is always located at the uppermost floor of the house, under the roof, in a *mansarde* or a *grenier* [attic]. This location allows lovers to visit the grisette through the roof, to take their liberties with her and to escape the same way. Mercier excuses the light morality life of these girls by hard living conditions. Mercier's grisette (as opposed to the *bourgeoise*) is an independent woman who, because of her lack of a dowry, is the only woman in France who is able to choose whom she is going to love. At the time of the French Revolution, a third representation takes place. Launay, the prostitute's tax collector, completely aware of the double lives they must lead, is abusive

to all the grisettes, and considered them as disguised prostitutes.

Under the Restoration (1815–1830), two representations dominate the discourse on grisettes. One is associated with a rather erotic literary work connected with the *tableaux parisiens*. The grisette is the subject of peeping. One can observe her through a small hole drilled in the partition wall of the *Hôtels Garnis* bedrooms (furnished lodgings). She is seen dressing, or painting the nipples of her breasts in Cuisin's descriptions of the *vie galante* in Paris. Charles Paul de Kock is considered the specialist of light grisette stories. The other is associated with the most popular French singer of the period, Pierre-Jean de Béranger. He popularized the unfaithful but excusable grisette through a sequel of songs on the *Lisette* character. She becomes a kept-woman with rich lovers (Mondor), old aristocrats or bourgeois, but will be abandoned and return to her first (poor) lover. This last representation has a political tone; the grisette becomes the prototype of the republican woman who is seduced by the old and depraved aristocrats.

Under the July Monarchy (1830–1848), the grisette primarily associates with the students of medicine and law of the Latin Quarter. She is transformed into a complete romantic and melancholic character. She passionately sacrifices herself for her lover, is abandoned, and often dies from tuberculosis.

With the *Lorette's* arrival (a kept-woman, solely money-oriented, like the *Nana* of Zola), in the 1840s, the grisette is progressively detached from the figure of the prostitute and becomes a pure angel with *Mimi Pinson*, *Les Mystères de Paris* [Sue's *Rigolette*] or *Les Scènes de la Vie de Bohème* (a Murger and Puccini adaptation) where she is a singer and is associated with penniless artists (Musette and Mimi). Jules Champfleury's realism violently reacts against this iconography, in his short story: *L'homme aux figures de cire*. A wax puppet exhibitor abandons his spouse to flee with a pretty wax grisette, with whom he sleeps; thus recycling the myth of Pygmalion. Some rare explicit erotic representations of the grisette can be found in the small booklet with lithographs of Henri Monnier, *L'étudiant et la grisette*, while the socialist Victor Hugo transforms *Fantine* into an accidental prostitute in *Les Misérables*.

In the nineteenth century, the word *grisette* rhymed with *amourette* (easy, free love without any long-term attachment) and *herbette* (love on the grass) in literature.

ALAIN LESCART

References and Further Reading

Béranger, Pierre-Jean de. *Les Infidélités de Lisette*. Paris: 1813.
Champfleury, Jules. *L'Homme aux figures de cire*. 2004 ed. Paris: Gallimard, 1849.
Cuisin, J.P.R. *La vie de garçon dans les hotels-garnis de la capitale, ou, De l'amour à la minute. Par un parasite logé à pouf au grenier*. 1880 ed. 4. Paris: Henri Kistemaeckers, Palais-Royal, 1820.
Kock, Charles Paul de. *Mon Voisin Raymond*. 4 vols. Paris: G.-C. Hubert, 1822.
La Fontaine, Jean de. "Joconde ou l'infidélité des femmes." *Nouvelles en vers tirées de Bocace et de l'Arioste*. Paris: Claude Barbin, 1665.
Launay, Florentine de, and Sylvain Bailly. *Etrennes aux grisettes pour l'année 1790*. Paris: s.n., 1790.
Mercier, Louis-Sébastien. *Tableau de Paris*. Samuel Fauche, 1781.
Monnier, Henry. *L'enfer de Joseph Prudhomme: Deux gougnottes et La Grisette et l'etudiant*. Paris: A l'enseigne du plaisir des filles, 1850.

GUAMAN POMA DE AYALA, FELIPE

d.c. 1615
Incan essayist

The sixteenth-century indigenous Andean chronicler and illustrator Felipe Guaman Poma de Ayala is not an author easily placed within the context of erotic literature, yet his work offers insights into the sexual mores prevalent in early colonial Latin America. His monumental *El Primer Nueva Corónica y Buen Gobierno* [*The First New Chronicle and Good Government*] (1615) also makes references to the conception and treatment of sexual offences during the Inca period, then still within living memory. Sexuality, rather than being celebrated, is a criterion used by the author to establish both his opposition to Spanish abuse and his ambiguous position towards pre-Columbian rule. It is an example of Bakhtin's notion of "hidden polemic," applied by Rolena Adorno (1986) to this extraordinary book, since Guaman Poma adopts anti-colonial positions through stealth and inference. It should be pointed out that this work, rather than strictly literary, relies heavily for effect on illustrations often more eloquent than the text, Spanish having been a patchily acquired second language for this Quechua-speaker.

Guaman Poma wrote to complain to King Philip III of the abuses suffered by his people as a direct result of the Spanish conquest and colonial administration. His 1,200-page manuscript unsurprisingly never reached the King, but miraculously survived and became a precious source of data for historians and ethnographers.

The work was conceived not only as a denunciation of Spanish rule but also an affirmation of autochthonous cultural values, as such, sex is viewed in terms of its demographic and historical consequences for the indigenous peoples of the Andes–of particular concern to the author, the growth of *mestizo* (mixed Indian and European) and mulatto populations. Guaman Poma deplored what he saw as a destructive encroachment upon indigenous ways of life, both culturally and genetically. He advocated segregation, a position he shared with many contemporary commentators who also feared and distrusted those of mixed descent. Mercedes López-Baralt (1993) perceptively examines the coded sexual imagery in two depictions of gatherings where men of varied social positions and, crucially, ethnic backgrounds, meet to broker power. She perceives a denunciation of illicit fornication, particularly as practiced by the clergy. One perhaps unintentionally humorous reference here (574) shows a priest's illegitimate children being carried on horseback, in saddlebags, as if they were vegetables going to market.

In order to enhance his own credibility with his reader, Guaman Poma denounces certain aspects of Inca rule. The Incas' very origins are tainted since the founding couple, Mama Huaco and Manco Capac, are also mother and son (in other versions they are siblings). As well as incestuous, Mama Huaco is a sorceress, idolater, and devil-worshipper; yet she is also described as beautiful, learned, and generous (1981, p. 99). The Inca genesis is based on the falsehood that she is daughter of the sun and moon: she wins and maintains her power by making stones move and speak. Part of the section on superstition and witchcraft (252) displays naked supine figures of Indians mounted by horned devils.

If this partial vilification of the pre-Columbian world serves to establish Guaman Poma's Catholic credentials, he also stresses various instances of Inca morality with a paradoxical affirmation of the rectitude lost since the conquest. A list of crimes punishable by death, includes adultery, abortion, prostitution, rape, and incestuous marriage, this latter being reserved for the rulers (1981, pp. 164–165). All this contrasts with the sexual abuse in which the Spanish indulge with impunity, simply helping themselves to any female they choose. A particularly graphic drawing depicts a young woman innocently sleeping, her breasts, anus, and vagina (the Spanish *vergüenza*, shame) exposed, as men in authority scout for women to sate their lust: "They fornicate with married women and deflower virgins," thus producing the bugbear of *mestizos* (467). The rape and abduction of girls continues. Guaman Poma insists, because of the web of intrigue and bribery among the establishment (489).

For Guaman Poma, the abuse of power by Spanish authorities is so severe, and so corrosive of public morality, that regional segregation is the only way to prevent the contamination of indigenous peoples. Unabated miscegenation is the cause of a general malaise in Peru that he sees metaphorically as the World Upside-Down. This inversion of the natural order is borrowed from European tradition and blended with an indigenous notion of cataclysm, the *pachacuti* or periodic world-inversion seen in many pre-Columbian cosmologies as bringing essential regeneration. However, this is an inversion that will not recover any sense of natural equilibrium. Hence it retains the carnival element of grotesque upheaval, the overturning of any normal sense of social order, but sheds any sense of ribald, Rabelaisian delight.

However, despite the sorrow and complaint that pervades Guaman Poma's opus, there are several moments in which the erotic is celebrated in the section dealing with pre-Columbian fiesta, song, and music. One instance of this is the reproduction of a Quechua language (290) *harawi* (a form of plaintive appeal) likening a noblewoman to a flower reflected in water, a transient image despite its permanence in the lover's mind. A more earthy, mundane song in Aymara humorously asks whether the beloved is as sweet when drunk as when sober. No lyricism is admitted here; the woman is doubtless accessible because of her more humble origins. Another Aymara song quoted by Guaman Poma boasts of the author's sister's 'fabulous' legs, which are beautiful enough to win bets. One drawing in this section shows two naked women in a river, pointing toward the cliff above where two men sit playing flutes and with whom they sing in dialogue. Thus an ingenuous, bucolic pre-Columbian sexuality is contrasted with its abusive, rapacious Spanish counterpart.

Biography

Guaman Poma de Ayala was born a few years after the Spanish conquest of the Andes. As an Inca noble he was allowed to be raised among the colonizers, baptized a Christian, and educated. In his early years he served as an interpreter and assisted church officials in eradicating Inca spiritual practice. After a crisis of conscience he began teaching Incas to read and write so they could submit legal complains concerning their condition. From 1585 to 1615 he carefully composed his own claim, titled Nueva corónica y buen gobierno, to King Philip III of Spain. The manuscript went unread for centuries until it was discovered by a researcher at the Royal Library of Copenhagen in 1908.

Further Reading

Adorno, Rolena. *Guaman Poma: Writing and Resistance in Colonial Peru*. Austin University of Texas, 1986.

Guaman Poma de Ayala. Felipe. *El primer nueva corónica y buen gobierno*. Mexico Siglo Veintiuno, 1981 [1615].

López-Baralt, Mercedes. *Icono y conquista*. Hiperión, Madrid 1988.

———. *Guaman Poma, Autor y artista*. Pontificia Universidad Católica del Perú, Lima 1993.

GUÉRIN, RAYMOND

1905–1955
French writer

L'Apprenti [The Apprentice]

The apprentice is 19-year-old 'Monsieur Hermès'—always called that way with no indication whether Hermès is his first name, family name, or a nickname. The book relates his tribulations whilst training in a prestigious Parisian luxury hotel in the late 1920s. That unwelcome apprenticeship was his father's ('Monsieur Papa') sole decision: Monsieur Hermès would much rather study literature or stay in his native Portville near the Spanish border, playing rugby with his friends and writing theatertheater plays or a literary review. Right from the start he just cannot stand the hotel's posh and oppressive atmosphere, its underpinning of social injustice and the daily humiliation from other staff members and guests alike. He successively works at the lowest rank in the kitchen (cleaning the greasiest plates), in the restaurant (carrying dishes), and as a night attendant in charge of a floor (answering guests' silliest requests in the middle of the night, such as opening a window for a cantankerous old lady or bringing bottles of champagne for smashed aristocrats who ignore his very presence in the room). Just before being sent to a partner hotel in London, he is eventually fired after overtly rebelling against one of his cruellest mentors, putting a salutary end to twelve months of daily unhappiness and persistent victimization. After a few days of leisure in Paris, he takes the train back home, just after meeting Delorme, a fashionable playwright to whom he gives a copy of 'La joie au coeur,,' the theater play he has just written himself.

Amidst the systematic recording of his duties, problems, and feelings are reminiscences of more pleasant times and nostalgic memories, especially of his past erotic adventures: his first experience in a brothel, the various girls he fancied in Portville, his doomed yet lasting infatuation with the mysterious Nina Brett and a romantic holiday love story in San Sebastian with Alice Elvas, a married, older woman whose few presents he still cherishes. Monsieur Hermès' love-life in Paris is more frustrating: despite an almost constant obsession with women, during his whole year at the hotel he has only gone out with the nice and plain Angélique for a couple of months, and with his loose chambermaid colleague Totoche for a couple of weeks. Yet in spite of some appreciated times of sexual gratification, those two partners have left him unsatisfied and unfulfilled. His apprenticeship is not just professional but emotional as well: he discovers the complex relationship between love, sex, pleasure, and intimacy—and indeed the book was originally entitled *L'Apprenti psychologue*. As an easier, more reliable source of sexual satisfaction, Monsieur Hermès much prefers to masturbate. The book is rich in descriptions of his masturbatory techniques (preferably lying on his belly, rubbing on the sheets without touching himself) and accounts of his fantasies (usually picturing he is a woman taken by a man, either the imaginary Lily or a desirable woman he has seen in the hotel, in the street, or in a film). This largely explains why *L'Apprenti* created quite a scandal when it was published in 1946: it was heavily pilloried for its underlying thesis that masturbation is a normal stage of sexuality and not some form of sexual perversion. Most critics then focused on that aspect of the book on the triple ground that it openly described, condoned, and validated masturbation, long before discourses of sexual liberation and popular psychoanalysis started to legitimize masturbation.

In terms of eroticism, *L'Apprenti* is also interesting because it documents how a rather typical heterosexual young man explores his developing sexuality, from minor cross-dressing (when he cannot help surreptitiously stealing and trying on a female neighbor's underwear) to voyeurism (when he observes through the keyhole a couple having sex) to pornography (with his growing collection of pictures of nude women). That strong focus on the visual is a key element of his discovery of sexual desire, with his gaze eroticizing most women, all becoming potential sexual partners, whether they sit near him at the theater, pass by him in the street, or happen to stay in the hotel rooms he is responsible for. Numerous situations and characters are thus presented in a rather original language reaching its best expression in *Les poulpes* but already significant in *L'Apprenti*. Somehow reminiscent of Céline and maybe also Rabelais, Guérin's idiosyncratic style is one that mixes all levels of language, building upon vernacular phrasing and slang, adding occasional references to commercials and songs, as well as parodies of some of the texts that Monsieur Hermès himself reads in his few moments of leisure (Vicente Blasco Ibañez, Pierre Loti). The result is highly heterogeneous and polyphonic, ranging from the cynical to the burlesque via the humorous and the lyrical, cleverly combining accents of realism and existentialism, perhaps precisely corresponding to what Monsieur Hermès himself calls '*l'esthétique du caleçon et du bidet*' ('the aesthetics of pants and bidets,' p. 249).

LOYKIE LOÏC LOMINÉ

Biography

Guérin planned and drafted most of his books in the four years he spent as a war prisoner in a nazi camp near Baden. He is mainly remembered for his *Ébauche d'une mythologie de la réalité* [*Sketch of a Mythology of Reality*], a Bildungsroman of over 2000 pages, composed of three books: *L'Apprenti* (1946) about early adulthood in the interwar, *Parmi tant d'autres feux...* (1949) about married life and most importantly *Les Poulpes* (1953) about life in captivity. He died of pleurisy at age 50 before completing two books, one about civil life back from the camp and one about recovering to mental and physical sanity. Other significant texts of his include *Quand vient la fin* (1941), *La confession de Diogène* (1947), and *Le pus de la plaie, journal de maladie* (posthumous, 1982). All have been published by Gallimard and most are being reprinted.

Further Reading

Alluin, B. & Curatolo, B. (2000) La Revie Littéraire, Dijon: Le Texte et l'Edition.
Curatolo, B. (1996a) *Humeurs*, Paris: Le Dilettante.
———. (1996b) *Raymond Guérin: Une écriture de la Dérision*, Paris: L'Harmattan.

GUIBERT, HERVÉ

1955–1991
French journalist, novelist, and screenwriter

Guibert's works all germinated in and were ultimately pruned from his journal, published posthumously as *Le mausolée des amants* and to which he referred as his "spinal cord." They can be divided between those written with a concern for style, tied also to the failure of fiction, and those where writing is made as communicative, as experientially transparent as possible. They raise difficult questions, demolish stereotypes of masculinity, subjectivity, and socialization, reveal secrets, blend fiction with nonfiction, and often problematize the relationship between the textual, the visual, and the pathological. In *Compassion protocol*, for example, the rhetorical narrator, virtually indistinguishable from Guibert himself, observes that his works are permeated with truth, falsehood, betrayal, and nastiness. Moreover, Guibert was obsessed with bodies—both living and dead—, with their dissolution and fragmentation, as he admits in his journal, and with sex. As a result, he brings his public into intimate contact with his own body and those of others, while blurring the division between fiction and autobiography, his own position as voyeuristic spectator and subject of disease. The year of his death, Guibert admitted that he had always had the impression of being his own character but also of being a body in narrations, situations, relationships, and that for him it was always a question in his works of a body, whether aging, sick, ruined, reborn, monstrous, or deformed. AIDS changed his status, from character to hero, by way of tragedy.

L'image fantôme

Written around the absence of a photograph, the despair of the image, L'image fantôme [Ghost Image] privileges the relationships between photography, truth, fetishism, desire, and the artefact. It also highlights the differences between the erotic, the pornographic, the erotically unreadable, and the sexually unmarked. As he unveils the bonds between visual representation, writing, reading, and readability, Guibert subverts the ideas about referential emanation first articulated by Roland Barthes in La chambre claire (Camera obscura). As Hughes notes, he literalizes and incorporates them into a narrative of homoerotic desire with the photographic gesture turning on an erotically penetrative act and the erotic impulses and instincts of the photographic subject "legibilized."

Les chiens

In Les chiens, the violent and explicit work referred to by the narrator of Fou de Vincent as a "pornographic little book," a woman's body is a foil for a hyperrealist story of male loves, sadomasochistic fantasies and practices, and heightens the erotic interest. Sexual and narrative pleasure are indistinguishable, and the boundaries between fantasy, reality, reader, author, and characters are ultimately broken down. As a result, the reader consumes the fantasies of the protagonists, entering into the text's "pornotopia," as Heathcote observes, with feet and wrists bound.

Vous m'avez fait former des fantômes

Divided into three parts, the postmodern novel, Vous m'avez fait former des fantômes, eroticizes

cruelty and death. Loathsome men haunt crèches and orphanages to capture innocents and train them for combat in which children replace bulls to recount bullfights. The text parodies male-to-male violence with intertextual references at the same time as exposing the complicity between phantoms and fantasies, acting and obsession, the ritual and the natural.

To the friend who did not save my life

The first of the novels directly and primarily to focus on AIDS and the book, Boulé claims, is the climax and point of implosion of Guibert's œuvre, A l'ami qui ne m'a pas sauvé la vie [To the Friend Who Did Not Save My Life] was hugely controversial when it first came out in 1990, the year before Guibert's death. It was read as a roman à clés: the philosopher named Muzil was recognized as Guibert's recently deceased friend, Michel Foucault; similarly, Marine was identified as Isabelle Adjani, Stéphane as Daniel Defert, Eugénie as Yvonne Baby, Hector as Hector Bianciotti, and Melvil Mockney as Jonas Salk. It recounts the struggles of Muzil and the narrator with AIDS and the medical establishment. In its intertwining of contagion and eroticism, voyeurism and hallucination, betrayals and commemoration, it reveals the creation and destruction inherent in writing. According to Guibert, it provides keys to understanding what is in all his other books. His seropositivity allowed him further to radicalize certain narrative systems, the relation to truth, and the staging of himself beyond what he ever thought possible.

Although Guibert had said that he would not write again, To the Friend Who Did Not Save My Life was followed by Compassion protocol, his second AIDS novel, in which he explores the erotic, sadomasochistic, and pathological possibilities of the relationship between a rhetorical narrator and his 28-year-old female doctor. The insidious progress of AIDS is also reflected in works by Guibert posthumously published or aired the year following his death. Whereas Cytomégalovirus, a brief diary of Guibert's hospitalization for the opportunistic infection that gives the book its title and Le mausolée des amants, which systematically spans a quarter century, both respect chronology, Le paradis disrupts it, and disorientation forms a metaphor for illness. L'homme au chapeau rouge [The Man

In the Red Hat], marketed as the last of Guibert's AIDS novels, is more a meditation on delusion and the fake, a reflection on the relationship between reality and fiction, life and art. *La pudeur et l'impudeur*, shot between June 1990 and March 1991 and turned down by all the French television stations except TF1, was ultimately broadcast after Guibert's death. As Boulé underlines, it stands more as the third, final, and penultimate volume on AIDS than *The Man In the Red Hat*. Considered crude and exhibitionist by some and a logical continuation of Guibert's pursuit of truth by others, in his video-diary Guibert anachronistically rehearses his suicide attempt while playing Russian roulette with the poison Digitaline. In the video's final scene of the writer walking away from his desk, he ultimately becomes a specter of himself.

Biography

Born on December 14, 1955 in Saint-Cloud, just outside of Paris. Although he failed the Conservatoire and entrance examination for the Institut des Hautes Études Cinématographiques, he was multi-talented: he combined photographic sensibility with writing flair, brought a photographic writing to literature, and was the author of nearly thirty creative works, some of them published posthumously. Many of Guibert's texts are considered erotically explicit. Indeed, many stirred controversy. Examples include: *L'homme blessé*, co-scripted with Patrice Chéreau, which won a César but upset the homosexual community; *Des aveugles* [*Blindsight*], based on his volunteer work as a reader at the Institut National des Jeunes Aveugles in Paris, which gave rise to heated exchanges over how best to care for the blind; *Les chiens* which outraged many, most notably writer Marguerite Duras who, Guibert claimed, developed a negative fixation about him because of it; *La pudeur ou l'impudeur*, which provoked a great debate in the French media both before and after its broadcast. Guibert gained the widest recognition while suffering from AIDS and following the publication of *A l'ami qui ne m'a pas sauvé la vie* and *Le protocole compassionnel*. He appeared and seduced the French public on the television programs *Apostrophes* and *Ex libris*, admitting on the latter to living in a "very problematic" state of "total erotic desire." The night before his thirty-sixth birthday, he unsuccessfully attempted suicide. He died from complications two weeks later at the Beclère hospital in Clamart, near the French capital.

BRIAN GORDON KENNELLY

Selected Works

L'image fantôme. 1981; as *Ghost image*, translated by Robert Bononno. 1998.
Les aventures singulières. 1982.
Les chiens. 1982.
L'homme blessé (with Patrice Chéreau). 1983.
Vous m'avez fait former des fantômes. 1987.
Fou de Vincent. 1989.
A l'ami qui ne m'a pas sauvé la vie. 1990; as *To the Friend Who Did Not Save My Life*. translated by Linda Coverdale. 1991.
Mon valet et moi. 1991.
La mort propagande et autres textes de jeunesse. 1991.
Le protocole compassionnel. 1991; as *Compassion protocol*. translated by James Kirkup. 1994.
Vice. 1991.
Cytomégalovirus. 1992.
L'homme au chapeau rouge. 1992; as *The man in the red hat*. translated by James Kirkup. 1993.
Le paradis. 1992.
La pudeur ou l'impudeur. 1992.
Photographies. 1993.
La piqûre d'amour et autres textes, suivi de *La chair fraîche*. 1994.
La Photo, inéluctablement. 1999.
Le Mausolée des amants: Journal. 1976–1991, 2001.

Further Reading

Antle, Martine. "The Frame of Desire in the Novel of the 1980's and the 1990's." In *Articulations of Difference: Gender Studies and Writing in French*, edited by Dominique D. Fisher and Lawrence R. Schehr. Stanford, CA: Stanford University Press, 1997.
Apter, Emily. "Fantom Images: Hervé Guibert and the Writing of 'sida' in France." In *Writing AIDS: Gay Literature, Language, and Analysis*, edited by Timothy Murphy and Suzanne Poirier. New York: Columbia University Press, 1993.
Boulé, Jean-Pierre. A l'ami qui ne m'a pas sauvé la vie *And Other Writings*. Glasgow: University of Glasgow Press, 1995.
Boulé, Jean-Pierre. *Hervé Guibert: L'entreprise de l'écriture du moi*. Paris: L'harmattan, 2001.
Caron, David. *AIDS in French Culture: Social Ills, Literary Cures*. Madison, WI: University of Wisconsin Press, 2001.
Heathcote, Owen. "*Les chiens* d'Hervé Guibert: analyse d'une 'plaquette pornographique.'" *Nottingham French Studies*, 34.1 (1995): 61–69.
Heathcote, Owen. "L'érotisme, la violence et le jeu dans *Vous m'avez fait former des fantômes*" in *Au jour le siècle 2, le corps textuel d'Hervé Guibert*.

Edited by Ralph Sarkonak. Paris: Lettres modernes, 1997.

Hughes, Alex. *Heterographies: Sexual Difference in French Autobiography*. New York and Oxford: Berg, 1999.

Sarkonak, Ralph. *Angelic Echoes: Hervé Guibert and Company*. Toronto: University of Toronto Press, 2000.

Schehr, Lawrence R. *Alcibiades at the Door: Gay Discourses in French Literature*. Stanford: Stanford University Press, 1995.

Worton, Michael. "En (d)écrivant le corps en imaginant l'homme: le 'vrai corps' de Guibert." In *Au jour le siècle 2, le corps textuel d'Hervé Guibert*. edited by Ralph Sarkonak. Paris: Lettres modernes, 1997.

GUIDO, BEATRIZ

1924–1988
Argentine novelist

In her novels, Guido presents an evocative portrayal of upper-class Argentinean life, a milieu she know well from her childhood and adolescence. Her characteristic heroine is a young upper-class woman whose innocence is shattered when confronted with unexpected, sometimes unwelcome, sexual experiences. Her heroines' innocence is exacerbated by upbringings in the hands of fanatically religious mothers or aunts who equate knowledge about matters of the flesh with sin, forcing them to depend on half-truths and innuendos in lieu of a proper sexual education. Through the sagas of her traumatized deflowered virgins, ambivalent about sexuality yet eager for experience, Guido creates profound tensions in her texts while offering the reader titillating instances of elegantly described seductions or subtly eroticized rapes.

In *La casa del angel*, the young protagonist, intrigued by the figure of a friend of her father's who is to fight a duel at dawn, walks into the room where he is holding his vigil and finds herself at once seduced and raped. Rushing to uncover the face of the slain man after the duel only to discover that her assailant has survived, she withdraws into a dreamlike state haunted by his guilt-ridden presence. The theme of ambivalent seduction and traumatic deflowering is also central to *La mano en la trampa*, where the protagonist discovers that an aunt has remained locked in the attic for years after being jilted on her wedding day by the boyfriend that had seduced her. Determined to find the man and persuade him to return to confront his jilted fiancée, she falls under his spell and ends up seduced in her turn. Similarly, in *La Caída*, Guido offers the claustrophobic tale of a young student, brought up in a strict Catholic home by her maiden aunt, who moves into a boarding house in which live four amoral children who become the witnesses and catalysts to her traumatic sexual awakening. Guido will bring the same erotic tension between innocence and sexual violence that characterizes her novels to her original screenplays. *El secuestrador*, for example, where the protagonists spend most of their screen time consummating their relationship, is most memorable for a scene of consensual rape staged in a mortuary. Like in *La casa del angel* and her other fiction, the blurred line between rape and consensual sex constitutes Guido's most salient repository of the erotic. This erotic quality was captured brilliantly in a film by Torre Nilsson and became one of the salient themes in their joint work.

In these texts and film scripts, Guido explores the ambivalent nature of sexual violence as a way of addressing the patriarchal and political violence that was a central element in her world. Having lived through traumatic dictatorships, coups, and labor crises, Guido was acutely attuned to the metaphoric value of images of rape, submission, and uncontrolled masculinity. As an avowed feminist and a member of a politically liberal family, she will carefully intertwine into her plots a critique of unbridled male power and violence. The subtle accumulation of socio-logical detail in her works creates a series of markers for a specific class milieu and historical period that allows the reader to see her protagonists' bodies as metaphors of a collective experience under a succession of repressive regimes, allowing the sexual violence in her novels to be interpreted as offering a critique of authoritarianism. The seducer in Guido's *Fin de fiesta*, for example, draws on the image of unbridled masculinity of Argentinean dictator Juan Domingo Perón, linking violence against women to political violence.

Biography

Beatriz Guido was born in Rosario, Argentina, in 1924, to a liberal upper-class family with advanced notions about educational opportunities for women. Consequently, she studied literature at the University of Buenos Aires and went to France and Italy for graduate studies. She started to write in her early twenties, and by the age of thirty was an accomplished and celebrated novelist and short story writer. In 1958, she embarked on a career as a film scriptwriter with *El secuestrador* (The Kidnapper, 1958), a film directed by Leopoldo Torre Nilsson (1924–1978), who had already established a reputation as Argentina's most promising young film director. They were married the following year. Their film collaboration—Guido penned most of the screenplays for her husband's films after their marriage—resulted in film versions of many of her novels and short stories. By the time of her marriage, Guido had already published three of her best novels, *La casa del ángel* (*The House of the Angel*, 1954), *La caída* (*The Fall*, 1956), and *Fin de fiesta* (*The End of the Party*, 1958). All three were filmed by the couple within a few years of their marriage, laying the foundation for the most successful film collaboration in the history of Latin-American cinema. Film versions of her subsequent novels, *La mano en la trampa* (1961), *El incendio y las vísperas* (1965), and *Piedra libre* (1976) cemented their reputation. They remained close collaborators until his premature death

in 1978 at age 54. Together they worked on acclaimed films like *La Guerra del cerdo* (1975), based on the novel by Adolfo Bioy Casares, and *Martín Fierro* (1968), based on the classic 1872 poem by Joé Hernández. She also wrote scripts for films by other directors, among them Manuel Antín's *La invitación* (Argentina, 1982), Carlos Orgambide's *Los Insomnes* (Argentina, 1986), and Fernando Ayala's *Paula Cautiva* (Argentina, 1963). Guido, considered by many Latin-American critics as one of the most important feminist writers of the second half of the twentieth century, was one of the few women writers of the Latin-American Literary Boom of the 1960s and 70s. A prolific author, she received the Konex Award for her literary achievements in 1984, the same year she was named cultural attaché to the Argentinean Embassy in Spain. She died in Madrid in 1988.

LIZABETH PARAVISINI-GEBERT

Selected Works

La caída. Buenos Aires: Losada, 1981.
La casa del ángel. Buenos Aires, Emecé, 1954.
Fin de fiesta. Barcelona: Planeta, 1971.
La invitación. Buenos Aires, Losada, 1982.
La mano en la trampa. Buenos Aires: Losada, 1961.
Piedra libre. Buenos Aires, Galerna, 1976.

Further Reading

Clifford, Joan. "The Female Bildungsromane of Beatriz Guido." *Hispanófila* 132 (2001): 125–139.
Domínguez, Nora. "Familias literarias: visión adolescente y poder político en la narrativa de Beatriz Guido." *Revista Iberoamericana* 70:206 (2004): 225–235.
Jozef, Bella. "In memoriam: Luisa Mercedes Levinson y Beatriz Guido." *Revista Iberoamericana* 54:144–145 (1988): 1021–1023.
Lewald, H. Ernest. "Alienation and Eros in Three Stories by Beatriz Guido, Marta Lynch, and Amalia Jamilis." In *Theory and Practice of Feminist Literary Criticism*, 175–185. edited by Gabriela Mora and Karen S. Van Hooft. Ypsilanti, MI: Bilingual, 1982.
Mahieu, José Agustín. "Beatriz Guido: las dos escrituras." *Cuadernos Hispanoamericanos*" 437 (1986): 153–168.

GUILLÉN, NICOLÁS

1902–1989
Cuban poet

During his lifetime Nicolás Guillén became practically synonymous both with Revolutionary Cuba and the island's Black population. As a Mulatto, however, he expressed a dual heritage, using the erotic as a vehicle for notions of ethnic and cultural miscegenation. The confluence of sexual and cultural elements is also visible in the evolution of his personal style: Gustavo Pérez Firmat (1989, pp. 67–79) sees the dichotomy in Guillén's work between classical and vernacular verse as parallel to this ethnic duality, part of the acquisition of a mature, independent voice. Guillén's early "White" verse, which uses the sonnet form and follows certain conventions of courtly love, is in marked contrast to 1930s work in which, through phonetic transcription of spoken African-Cuban Spanish, he voiced popular concerns whilst also validating this language through the very fact of its transcription. During the early 1930s, Guillén distorts written Spanish, forcing it to speak from a Black viewpoint. After the Revolution, Guillén's increasingly overt political poetry relegated the erotic to a remote corner of his concerns. However, the persistence of this declamatory public image since his death is somewhat misleading: as Keith Ellis (1994, pp. 45–87) has shown, he was capable of discreet and intimate love poems such as *In Some Springtime Place: Elegy* (1966).

A recurrent theme among critics is that of Guillén's sexual politics, which in the early twenty-first century certainly appear archaic. Pérez Firmat shows how *El abuelo* [*The Grandfather*], (1934) ironically adopts a subservient, courtly stance in reminding a blonde Cuban woman of a partial African ancestry which she had chosen to ignore. But the generic perspective is distorted: for Vera Kutzinski (1993) the poem "constructs an interracial male lineage for its near-White female figure," reducing the feminine to mere spectatorship. Similarly, in *Ballad of the two Grandfathers* (1934) the female reproductive role is excluded as African and Spanish forebears, united by the poet, unite to heal historical wounds. Where female strength is prominent, it generally takes the form of an atavistic, telluric vigor associated with fecundity and eroticism. An instance of this can be seen in *Madrigal* (1934):

Simple and erect,
like a cane in the cane field
Oh challenger of genital
frenzy

Curiously Guillén's female forms often take on a phallic and even self-fertilizing nature; a potent image that may contradict some of the charges of aberrant sexual politics. Another example is *Piedra de horno* [*Oven Stone*] (1944), which describes a woman as sensually self-sufficient:

A river of promises
runs down from your hair,
pauses at your breasts,
congeals at last in a pool of molasses at your belly,
violates your firm flesh of nocturnal secret.

Guillén was central to the Afro-Cuban movement that began in the 1920s occasioned by, and crucial to, the process of ethnic and cultural integration between African and European heritages. For Kutzinski (1987): "Almost all aspects of Guillén's poetry are deeply rooted in the cross-cultural imagination of the Caribbean." Kutzinski (1993), sees the late 1920s "mulatto" poetry as essentially a celebration and mythification of the woman of mixed descent who is nonetheless disenfranchised. She is a paradoxical figure, the traditional object of male sexual preference but also marginalized and viewed with suspicion. "The mulata may be *the* signifier of Cuba's unity-in-racial-diversity, but she has no part in it." The poem *Mulata* (1930) explicitly rejects this object of lust and voices preference (recurrent in Guillén's earlier work) for a more reliable, less pretentious Black partner. The *mulata*, long seen as dangerous temptress in Cuban literature, exerts a threatening attraction likened to the frantic and relentless rhythm of a locomotive:

> Tanto tren con tu cueppo,
> tanto tren;
> tanto tren con tu boca,
> tanto tren;
> (literally: "So much train with your body, so much train; so much train with your mouth, so much train)

Lorna Williams (1982) sees a similar objectification in another poem entitled *Madrigal* (1931). The lines "Your belly knows more than your head / and as much as your thighs" display values ill-fitting a figure of the left today. Alluding to a matriarchal sensuality ostensibly consonant with African ancestry, the poem goes on to evoke "that dark alligator / swimming in the Zambezi of your eyes." The content ironically belies madrigal's association with elite European sophistication.

The transformation during Guillén's lifetime in the configuration of Cuban nationality can be attributed not only to the Revolution but also to the gradual validation of African heritage through early twentieth-century movements such as the boom in the song form known as *son*, *négritude* in the French Caribbean and the Harlem Revival. Guillén's codified sexuality enunciates a popular consciousness celebrating the mulatto as an embodiment of the principle of blending, a basic ingredient of 'Cubanness.' For Ian Isidore Smart (1990), this is the "central creative conflict" in his poetry: engendered by interethnic sexuality, *mulatez* in turn enables an awareness of African roots which itself "engenders [...] the inevitable conflict between Eurocentered and Afrocentered realities." For Smart, the resolution of this dichotomy, which Guillén transformed from a destructive force into the very basis of his poetics, is at the core of his work. Guillén was heir to the sociologist Fernando Ortiz's pioneering re-evaluation of Cuba's African heritage for which he invented the term "transculturation," referring to the mutual influence between cultures irrespective of questions of dominance or subalternity. Metaphoric

renditions of this principle of cultural and ethnic blending abound: Ortiz also spoke of the *ajiaco* (a Cuban stew) in this context. Guillén's own term "algarabía" (rejoicing) is similar, but shows a heightened optimism crucial to his poetry. The spirit of overcoming or dissolving cultural barriers, 'algarabía' is akin to the Cuban novelist Alejo Carpentier's conception of Magic Realism: the delirious and exuberant result of the encounter between diverse elements essential to Caribbean and Latin-American cultural formation (Kutzinski 1987).

Biography

Nicolás Guillén was born in Camagüey, Cuba on July 10, 1902. He studied law and journalism at the University La Habana. His first poems appeared in Camaguey Grafico in 1922. He joined the Cuban Communist Party in 1937 and in 1940, he ran for mayor of Camaguey and in 1948 for senatorial office; both campaigns were unsuccessful. From 1953 he lived in exile in France. He returned after the revolution and Fidel Castro appointed him president of Cuba's writers' union. Guillén died in Havana on July 16 1989.

Further Reading

Ellis, Keith, ed. *Nicolás Guillén: Nueva poesía de amor = New Love Poetry.* University of Toronto Press, 1994.

Kutzinski, Vera M. *Against the American Grain: Myth and History in William Carlos Williams, Jay Wright, and Nicolás Guillén.* Baltimore: John Hopkins University Press, 1987.

———. *Sugar's Secrets: Race and the Erotics of Cuban Nationalism.* University of Virginia Press, Charlottesville 1993.

Pérez Firmat, Gustavo. *The Cuban Condition: Translation and Identity in Modern Cuban Literature.* Cambridge University Press, 1989.

Smart, Ian Isidore. *Nicolás Guillén, Popular Poet of the Caribbean.* Columbia, MO: University of Missouri Press, 1990.

Williams, Lorna V. *Self and Society in the Poetry of Nicolás Guillén.* Baltimore: John Hopkins University Press, 1982.

GULLIVER, LILI

The title of Lili Gulliver's four-book set *The Gulliver Universe* is a take on Jonathan Swift's eighteenth-century novel *Gulliver's Travels*. However, Swift's book is a series of fantasy adventures, and there is nothing erotic in them. Here, the name Gulliver is at the same time the title of the series, the author's *nom de plume* (her real name is Diane Boissonneault) and the main character's eponym, and lets the narrative be set in a travel and discovery mode.

The excuse of travel is used at the very beginning of *Paris*, the first volume, when Lili announces that she is leaving on an erotic world tour, but only in the second volume, *Greece*, is the journey's real purpose specified: "I, Lili Gulliver, am convinced that a guide to international fuck can be very useful and help track down the best lover in the world." The intention of writing such a guide, a new erotic excuse added on to the idea of a voyage of discovery, overdetermines the contents of the narratives. The *Gulliver Guide*, as parody of a travel book, is used as an alibi for having multiple sexual encounters: "As it should be, I will meet again with various types of men, of all colours and all social standings" and also for physical descriptions and sexual relationships.

The writing of the *Gulliver Guide, Guide of International Fuck* conceals a specific purpose: find the best lover in the world. And since this is an impossible goal, Lili will not stop traveling around the world and living ever renewed sexual adventures. The visited countries are described in commonplace and cliché terms which are themselves considered from a sexual viewpoint.

For instance, France is acknowledged the world over for its cuisine, therefore, in the first volume, *Paris*, Lili links cooking and sex: "I know, from a culinary standpoint, that he wants to slip me his asparagus so that I can wrap it between my hams, as the host would say. Which is a more romantic version than 'grab my sausage any way you can among the pasta.'" Lili will have four sexual partners in all in the City of Lights: Francis, a wine waiter;

Gérard, a psychoanalyst; Carl, a male escort; and Dominique, a friend's lady-friend. The relationships with Gérard and Francis are heterosexual and traditional: foreplay followed by penetration. Things are different with Carl. During a moonlight river cruise on the Seine, one of the greatest romantic clichés in feminine romantic imagination, Carl offers anal penetration to the narrator, but even though she praises the value of sodomy, she avoids the occurrence of such an act in a very prudish and conventional way. The same refusal occurs when Dominique offers Lili to sleep with her: "Lili a dyke? It depends on the attraction, but I really prefer men. Women are not very attractive to me. Surely that's just a small mental block." At the very end of the volume, the narrator affirms in regard to the basic principle of her erotic story that: "Actually, maybe I am not such a real user of dicks, no more than I am into marathon sex. Fucking with one man can suffice and satisfy me fully."

In Volume 2, *Greece*, Lili finds six lovers in all: Gino, a waiter; Vangelis, a restaurant owner; Jack, an American sailor; an anonymous lifeguard; Erick, a Norwegian; Yan, a Danish Greek; and Peter, a Briton. The contradictory dialectics of the whole of *The Gulliver Universe* are revealed here. Lili Gulliver uses the *Guide* as an excuse to have as varied sexual encounters as possible, with as many partners as possible, but her morality prevents her from enjoying without misgivings those purely physical relationships. The issue lies with the fact that her *Guide* fits a certain approach to life, and her personal values another. The book repeats erotic clichés about brute male force which is devoid of feelings with six of the men on that list, whereas Lili's ideal relationship remains monogamous and perpetual. To confirm this, in the chapter titled "Love at first sight" she meets Peter, the Briton, who will embody for a while the perfect lover; nevertheless, she will leave him a few weeks later to pursue her adventures in Asia.

In *Bangkok, Hot and Wet*, the third volume of *The Gulliver Universe*, Lili only has three sexual encounters. The first one is with a Japanese man in the plane, the second with a Thai boxer, and the third with Richard Harvey, an extremely wealthy American tourist staying at a luxurious suite in the Bangkok Hilton. As far as being a "sexplorer" is concerned, the framework of the whole adventure remains restricted and mostly predictable. The narration insists page after page on the man's wealth, whom she describes thus: "He's a natty dresser. Lacoste shirt, cream-coloured pants, crocodile belt, tennis shoes, well-kept body. He is a handsome fifty with the air of a man who has had it easy. This gentleman has class, and it shows." Here we have a modern take on the Prince Charming, who is always handsome, rich, and cultivated. And actually, the semantic network used to describe sexual relations with Richard—tenderly, marvellous, fabulous, enchantment—belong also to the fairytale universe. On learning that her lover is already married, Lili leaves again, toward the end of the world, feeling disappointed and betrayed.

In the last of the four volumes, *Australia, Down Under Without Undies*, Lili has four lovers. Joe, an architect; Jerry, a surfer; an anonymous lover; and Tarzano Rambo, a farmer. The relationships are all conventional except for a threesome at the beginning of the novel. Later on she meets Tello, nicknamed Tarzano Rambo, for obvious reasons. Lili uses and abuses that lover who gets the highest award in *The Gulliver Universe*: "The gold dick is awarded here to a rigid, enduring, and valiant steel penis." The couple goes camping and indulges in sexual activities divided into rather equal parts of cunnilingus, fellatio, and penetration.

This survey of the four volumes of *The Gulliver Universe* shows how eroticism is organized according to sequential logic: visits to several countries, encounters with several lovers, experimentation of various positions, and description of heterodox practices. All of that is presented humorously, using as many clichés as possible to describe all the situations. It is obvious that this story relies on convention. The same can be said of the male and female paradigms underlying the narrative: the man is always manly and the woman relies on him to achieve orgasm. Lili Gulliver—the 'sexplorer'—will be satisfied only when she has traveled all the countries in the world!

Biography

Lili Gulliver—born Diane Boissonneault—studied literature and screenwriting and has been a journalist and cultural critic. She lives in Montreal, Canada where she runs a bed and breakfast with her husband.

ELISE SALAÜN

Selected Works

The Gulliver Universe. Volume 1: *Paris* (1990), Volume 2: *Greece* (1991), Volume 3: *Bangkok, Hot and Wet* (1993), Volume 4: *Australia downunder without undies* (1996), Montreal, VLB Publisher. Translation: Henry C. Mera. Ph.D.

GUYOTAT, PIERRE

1940–
French writer and artist

Tombeau pour cinq cent mille soldats

A violent, erotic epic of blood, sweat, and semen, with echoes of Genet, Guibert, Noël, Sade, and Wittig, and even Malraux's *La condition humaine*. It combines an incantatory, almost biblical, tone with parody and hyperbole—and, for some, given Guyotat's troubled period in Algeria, implicit comments on the Algerian War.

Chant I

This text recounts the taking and the liberation of Ecbatane, torn between an invading army, an

609

aged chief, and his lieutenant, Iérissos, and rebels, whether soldiers or slaves. In the course of the conflict, there is much bloodshed, copulation, and torture between the main, human characters—Iérissos, the Queen of the Night, and three slaves, Mantinée, Bactriane, and Aravik—and also animals: a horse, rats, and birds.

Chant II

This section is, at first, a more episodic account of the occupied island, moving between various individuals and groups, from the violent Kment family to the picaresque adventures of the sexually liberated Crazy Horse and of the Governor, his wife Émilienne and their two children Serge and Fabienne. Licentiousness alternates with incest, infanticide, bestiality, cannibalism, and torture. The frequent spilling of blood, semen, and excrement seems, however, neither subversive or salacious but the simply savoured self-expression of a population at war. The pace then slows to register the erotic coupling of Kment and Giauhare, a cardinal's desire for adolescent boys, and the trials of Illiten, chief of the rebels.

Chant III

Here, a series of surreal tableaux moves from brothel activities and the further visitations of the cardinal to scenes of war, torture and, since blood is the sperm of battle, sex: a soldier masturbates; the narrator (intermittently in the first-person) has congress with a seagull; Serge and Émilienne make feverish love; the young General enjoys an uninhibited session with one of his kitchen-boys, Pino, before fantasizing running an S/M male brothel and an orgy of violent, incestuous pleasures. Meanwhile, it seems that the captured Illiten has escaped and the rebels are winning.

Chant IV

Apart from occasional violent episodes—as when Giauhare is almost raped by a soldier and when a rat devours a dead boy's penis—this section evokes more gentle, even tender male-to-female and male-to-male bondings, whether on the beach where the wounded Serge is tended by a devoted Émilienne or in a cave where a soldier fellates a group of men. The

section ends in one of the disputatious local brothels, where the young, drug-injected Pétrilion sodomizes, and is sodomized by, an eager and athletic dog, after which Pétrilion is borne off, wounded and Christ-like, by a solicitous admirer, Draga.

Chant V

Conflict between revolutionaries and invaders wears on, with slave-prisoners (Véronique, Xaintrailles, Thivai, and the narrator) conducting a kind of sexual ballet, adolescents fornicating in the Royal Inaménas hotel, and the General licking the wounds of dead and dying soldiers. Fabienne mourns a happier past with Serge, Kment and Giauhare are reunited, and Illiten is murdered and replaced by Béja who brings the rebels closer to victory. After the General is murdered and the Governor imprisoned, the characters of Ecbatane are even freer to change and combine sexual partners and positions as dawn breaks over the coast.

Chant VI

Preparations for the final engagement are accompanied by the soldiers' struggle over and with the seductive Niké who wants to see the battle which will involve hideous slaughter, not least in the city of Titov Veles, hitherto characterized by its failure to support the rebels and by an absence of brothels since its inhabitants prefer its own slaves, children, and animals. Faced by the marauding rebels who rape, massacre, and plunder—killing Serge and Émilienne, decapitating Pino in his kitchen, and incinerating Titov Veles—the Governor surrenders. Giauhare tells Kment she is having a child—by a rat.

Chant VII

Kment and Giauhare are now alone with nature and with animals. Kment ejaculates into the earth while Giauhare lies under a wolf. The lovers embrace.

Éden, éden, éden

In tune with Guyotat's contention that his work is not merely erotic but pornographic, this controversial, single-sentence text describes the serial and multiple copulations of a group of men, women, children, and animals in and around an Arab brothel (male and female) in an otherwise unspecified time and place. Although war is not the issue, it was in *Tombeau*, soldiers and their fatigues—usually unbuttoned or discarded—figure strongly, alongside "lubricators," herdsmen, and nomads, who gather, with their livestock (sheep and geese), to enjoy the whores and boy-whores such as Wazzag and Khamssieh who participate readily in the alternating exchanges of seminal fluids and orgiastic couplings. When a butcher and his family become involved, the sex-making becomes predictably bloodier, with the butcher fisting Khamssieh, who is also bitten by a tarantula, and with Wazzag busy with a whoremaster, a date-picker, a panel-beater, and twin apprentices until the whole group is a virtually indistinguishable mêlée of limbs, lurchings, orgasms, and excrement. The twins then separate as other previously mentioned 'characters'—nomad, herdsman, soldiers, and Blacks—return to the fray, which, now in a farm-camp, includes a cow and a baby. The adolescent herdsman is penetrated on all sides and by all comers, including the twins, Hamza and Khemissa; the latter is then sprayed with the urine and semen of the whoremaster. However insistent and even relentless these sexual encounters and however regular the orgasms, pornography's "money shot" is itself never a sexual or even verbal climax but, rather, one aspect of the eroticism of the whole body—with its other liquids such as sweat, saliva, and blood—and of the language used to describe it. Hence the body is a permanent repository of earlier, sedemented or congealed orgasms which gleam on its surfaces and form a basis for a continuum of pleasure. This ubiquitous corporeal viscosity can also be seen as redolent of the existentialist *pour soi*, of Bataille's expenditure, and also, perhaps, of the eventual threat (or promise) of erotic death. For although the text in a sense never finishes (it "closes" mid-sentence with a comma) the exchanges do become more violent—chest-hair is burnt, a vein is bitten open, an anus is lanced—and more chaotic: dogs, monkeys, goats, women, and children are drawn in to a dervish dance of sweating, groaning, and increasingly unidentifiable bodies. Despite this uninterrupted sexual activity, what seems to be missing here is desire itself, either because it is just assumed or because it is thought to be in the reader (hence possibly the association with pornography) rather than in the text itself. Guyotat's desert "Garden of Delights" thus offers a highly original and potentially disturbing oneiric, erotic epic.

Explications

Among the topics discussed here with Marianne Alphant are the relation between sex(uality) and writing and the status and significance of the prostitute (male and female). The relation between sex and writing is complex: on the one hand writing is, despite Guyotat's notorious association between writing and masturbation and general eroticization of the word, not only borne of personal chastity but constitutes a kind of anti- or counter-sex—a revolt against sex and sexuality. On the subject of prostitution and the male or female whore, Guyotat is similarly ambivalent: although he describes the whore as a "non-person," between human and animal, who is, like everything else, a saleable commodity, the brothel and its environs are clearly his preferred "real" and symbolic territory, as is shown by its recurrence in other texts such as *Prostitution* (1975 and 1987) and *Progénitures* (2000). Without necessarily allying him to the "poète maudit" tradition, Guyotat's foregrounding of the prostitute enables him to question what it is to be human, what it is to be sexual, and what are the links between carnal and familial–social relations. On the subject of sexuality and gender, Guyotat is equally ambivalent: although he has been described as a eulogist of homosexuality, some of his texts end with an epiphany of male–female bonding, and, as the title of *Progénitures* confirms, breeding, whether actual or symbolic, is a key theme in his works. Indeed, both male and female prostitutes are put forward as breeders, whether male-on-male, male-on-female, female-on-male or (more rarely), female-on-female. The urge to breed, whether in sex or in art, transcends biological sex and sexual "orientation": semen flows between sexes as it flows between orifices in a never-ending series of human/non-human erotic exchanges.

Biography

Although Guyotat's early writing includes two novels, *Sur un cheval* and *Ashby*, it was his later

Tombeau pour cinq cent mille soldats and *Éden, Éden, Éden* which brought him fame, indeed notoriety, with the latter being banned from 1970 until 1981. After publishing a number of books in the interstice, including *Prostitution* and *Le Livre*, he came to public attention again in 2000 with two further volumes: *Progénitures and Explications*. The year 2005 saw the republication of *Ashby* and *Sur un cheval* together with the first volume of his *Carnets de bord* (1962–1969) and Catherine Brun's *Pierre Guyotat. Essai biographique*. It is worth noting that Guyotat himself rejects the title 'writer' in favor of creator, artist, or even architect.

OWEN HEATHCOTE

Selected Works

Tombeau pour cinq cent mille soldats. 1967.
Éden, éden, éden. 1970 (Translated into English under the same title by Graham Fox, with an introduction by Stephen Barber. London: Creation Books, 1995).
Prostitution. 1975 and, for a new edition with appendix, 1987.
Le Livre. 1984.
Progénitures. 2000 (includes a CD of the author reading the text's opening pages).
Explications. 2000.
Ashby suivi de sur un cheval. [1961, 1964] 2005.
Carnets de bord. Vol. 1 1962–1969, 2005.

Further Reading

Brun, Catherine. "Monstruosités de Pierre Guyotat," *Critique*. No. 653 (October, 2001), pp. 785–797.
Brun, Catherine. *Pierre Guyotat. Essai biographique*. Paris: Léo Scheer, 2005.
"Pierre Guyotat: Seminal Texts." Participants Pierre Guyotat and Stephen Barber. Audio cassette no. 1403 produced by Institute of Contemporary Arts, London, 1995.
Guichard, Thierry. 'À corps perdus' and ' "Je ne suis pas un écrivain." ' *Le matricule des anges*. No. 64 (juin 2005), pp.14–17, 18–24.
Surya, Michel. "Mots et monde de Pierre Guyotat." *Lignes*. 03 (October, 2000), pp. 28–52.
Surya, Michel. *Mots et monde de Pierre Guyotat*. Tours: Farrago, 2000.
White, Edmund and Sorin, Hubert. *Sketches from Memory: People and Places at the Heart of Our Paris*. London: Chatto & Windus and Picador, 1994.

HAINTENY (MADAGASCAR)

The *hainteny* is a poetic genre composed in both Malagasy and French and most often found in written form. It originated, however, as a form of poetic oral dialogue in Madagascar, common in everyday speech. It expresses two principal themes: love and justice, and was originally used to settle disputes, as well as, more popularly, to express metaphorically sexual desire or pursuit. *The hainteny* frequently takes the form of a dialogue, which was originally improvised on the spot as a kind of verbal dual. To engage in an oral *hainteny* competition it was first necessary to know a number of commonly cited *hainteny* or *ohabolana* (the closest translation is "proverbs"), with which they have often been confused. The dialogic structure has parallels in other African forms of poetic expression, as well as in the Malaysian *pantun*. In the written form this frequently gives rise to ambiguity however, where it is frequently not clear where divisions between interlocutors lie, or even whether more than one voice is present. The Malagasy language also does not mark the gender difference in speech and so further ambiguity is often present, especially where the *hainteny* express courtship or sexual advances.

The derivation of the word "hainteny" itself has attracted considerable controversy. Their erotic content is often stressed, as in the description of them given by the Reverend James Sibree, a British Missionary who edited the *Antananarivo Annual* from 1875–1900, as "erotic proverbs" and Domenichini-Ramiaramanana's use of "mots brûlants," or "burning words." Jean Paulhan, who spent two years in Madagascar from 1908–1910 and produced a highly influential body of work on the *hainteny*, stressed rather their wisdom and artistry, calling them "mots savants" and "science du langage." Paulhan was the first outside commentator to see the *hainteny* as poetry rather than prose, as the missionaries generally had, and sought to uncover its perceived obscurity. It was through Paulhan's work and his correspondence with, among others, Guillaume Appollinaire and Lucien Lévy-Bruhl, that the *hainteny* came most prominently into view in European cultural circles, where they found an echo in the avant-garde search for a new form of poetry. They also had a resonance within the francophone African community, as part of the anti-colonial *négritude* movement, and examples can be found in

Leopold Senghor's *Anthologie de la nouvelle poésie nègre et malgache de la langue française*. Within Madagascar the rediscovery of the *hainteny* by twentieth-century poets writing in French, notably Jean-Joseph Rabearivelo and Flavien Ranaivo, should be seen as part of a literary return to Malagasy tradition though not excluding the incorporation of European language and poetic devices.

Major collections were made in the nineteenth-century by missionaries, but these were heavily censored and so tend to exclude the more overtly sexual hainteny. The Reverend Lars Dahle, a Norwegian Missionary, went as far as to include in the preface to his *Specimens of Malagasy Folklore* (1877) the warning "In spite of all care I am still not sure that in some places an unnoticed impure thought may not lurk underneath, as it is sometimes so extremely difficult to find out what notions and associations may, in course of time, have gathered round a seemingly quite innocent word or phrase." Even in collections that were not overtly censored by Western collectors it would appear that the range of *hainteny* communicated was censored in some way by the practitioners themselves. The difference in style and content can be seen when compared with the wide-ranging collection made under the reign of Queen Ranavalona I, between 1828 and 1861, and published by Bakoly Domenichini-Ramiaramana (*Hainteny D'Autrefois,* 1968) which contain more explicit sexual references. It may also be that an effect of the spreading of Christianity in Madagascar was to dilute the erotic content of commonly known and recited *hainteny*. Even so, as Dahle feared, careful analysis of seemingly innocent *hainteny* may reveal highly erotic connotations, and Flavien Ranaivo, one of the leading Malagasy poets of the mid-/late-twentieth century, has claimed that in all *hainteny* an erotic meaning can be found on some level.

The *hainteny* is associated primarily with the Merina people, although other related genres exist in Madagascar which are more overtly sexual and direct, such as the Sakalava *saimbola*. In these the part played by the woman is simply an acceptance or refusal of the man's advances, however, which may indicate a difference in the relative status of men and women in different regions of Madagascar. *Hainteny* tend to be more indirect, where the woman is fully capable of poetic expression and negotiation. Many,

such as Ranaivo's "la cousine de Magali" take the form of a dialectic of capture and escape, where the woman is able to evade the man's advances through constant deferral and transposition of the approach or question. Here the woman responds to the man's assertions of sexual possession (gathering a silver fruit) by transforming herself from an object (the fruit on the tree) to an animal (a bird which may fly away).

This indirect communication functions primarily through the use of metaphor and symbol, which frequently operate on multiple levels. These resonate strongly in Malagasy culture and language, but have frequently led during the nineteenth and twentieth centuries to the dismissal of *hainteny* as obscure and incomprehensible. The landscape of the *hainteny* is rich and populated by birds and animals which may indicate, for example, desire or availability, and by mountains, rivers and forests, all of which bear symbolic meaning. Sexual and emotive associations may also be linked to everyday objects such as the *lamba* [shawl], which often functions as a locus of desire.

The *hainteny* presents significant problems of interpretation for a non-Malagasy audience. It repays careful study however, and its subtle treatment of themes such as love, jealousy, and desire reveal layers of meaning and association, and a rare and enduring beauty.

IMOGEN PARSONS

Further Reading

Domenichini-Ramiaramana, Bakoly. *Hainteny D'Autrefois.* Tananarive: Librairie mixte, 1968.

———. *Du Ohabolana au Hainteny: Langue, Littérature et Politique à Madagascar.* Paris: Karthala, 1983.

Dahle, Lars. *Specimens of Malagasy Folklore.* Antananarivo: Kingdon, 1877.

Fox, Leonard. *Hainteny: The Traditional Poetry of Madagascar.* Salem, MA: Associated University Presses, 1990.

Haring, Lee. *Verbal Arts in Madagascar: Performance in Historical Perspective.* Philadelphia, PA: University of Pennsylvania Press, 1992.

Paulhan, Jean. *Jean Paulhan et Madagascar, 1908–1910,* Paris: Gallimard, 1982

Les Hain-teny Merinas. Paris: Geuthner, 1913.

Les Hain-tenys. Paris: Gallimard, 1939.

Les Hain-teny poésie obscure. Principauté de Monaco: Société des Conférences, 1930.

Raberivelo, Jean-Joseph. *Poèmes: Presque-Songes; Traduits de le Nuit.* Tananarive: Imprimerie officielle de Madagascar, 1960.

Raberivelo, Jean-Joseph. *Vieilles Chansons des pays d'Imerina*. Antananarivo: Editions Madprint, 1967.

Ranaivo, Flavien. *Hain-teny*. Paris: Publications orientalistes de France, 1975.

Ranaivo, Flavien. *Textes Commentés* (par J. Valette), Paris: Fernand Nathan, 1968.

Ranaivo, Flavien. "Les Hain-teny," in *Jean Paulhan et Madagascar*. Paris: Gallimard, 1982.

Senghor, Leopold. *Anthologie de la nouvelle poésie nègre et malgache de la langue française*.

"Madagascar 2: La littérature d'expression française," *Notre Librairie*. Issue No. 110, July–September 1992.

HAITIAN LITERARY EROTICISM

Since independence and up to the middle of the twentieth century Haitian society remained remarkably structured, stable, and self-contained: The citizenry was divided into a small self-perpetuating urban minority which monopolized political power and its perquisites, and a large powerless rural majority who produced the nation's wealth while receiving none of its benefits. The constant struggle for ascendancy that characterizes Haitian history concerned the contending factions of the ruling classes, was irrelevant to the illiterate peasantry, and had little influence on the elite's cultural *Weltanschauung* and its expression.

The catastrophic dictatorship of François Duvalier on the one hand, and the progress of modernization and globalization on the other, have plunged Haitian society into a continuing ever-deepening crisis. The last half-century has witnessed ecological devastation, the pauperization of a peasantry forced to abandon the land and crowd into urban slums and shanty towns, the breakdown of law and order, the disregard for human rights, and the massive emigration of Haitians of all social strata (especially intellectuals) primarily to the other West Indies, Quebec, and the United States. Traditional ways of life, social customs, intellectual values, intergenerational relationships, and modes of interaction between the sexes have been further profoundly unsettled and deeply affected by foreign ways learned in exile or through the media. These changes are necessarily reflected in literary eroticism. One should therefore distinguish between literary eroticism during the century and a half of stability, and literary eroticism as

it has been developing since the crisis. While the first is relatively easy to describe, such is not the case for the second.

Generally speaking, Haitian society is not particularly prudish. Haitians are just as fond as other West Indians of double-entendres and ribald stories. Popular songs, enjoyed by men and women of all social classes, make a specialty of this kind of racy humor, and are quite openly suggestive. But they are in Créole, the national language, in which all citizens are fluent, and not in French, the only official language up to 1987, the medium of a literature that remains accessible to only a minute percentage of the ruling classes.

> Literate Haitians have traditionally regarded French with a respect verging on idolatry. They tend to consider that their country's contributions to its literature should deal primarily with serious, lofty, socially committed themes. One theme has in fact dominated the concerns of Haitian writers (and readers) ever since independence: the viability of Haiti as a nation, and the failings of its citizenry. This obsession with the tragic destiny of the country makes the sexual life of its citizens a secondary concern. Erotic experiences are practically never included for their own sake but used to illustrate, complement, or symbolize other themes, or to flesh out the psychological makeup of a character. Thus, in Fernand Hibbert's 1905 novel *Séna*, the eponymous hero's lusting for his light-colored mistress is an expression of color prejudice rather than of conquering masculinity. In Frédéric Marcelin's 1902 *La Vengeance De Mama (Mama's Revenge)* a young woman assassinates the corrupt politician who thinks he is finally about to enjoy her favors not during a lover's quarrel but to avenge the death of her fiancée.

If we define erotica as writings primarily designed to titillate or arouse through the description of sexual acts, there is for all intents and purposes no Haitian erotica. Haitian literature in French is meant to educate and inspire, not to entertain, and thus has produced no erotica, and no (or very few) mystery or detective novels either, nor science fiction, children's books, bedroom farces, or Harlequin romances. In addition, the writer and his public belong to the same extremely narrow social group. All writers know each other personally, and it would be only a slight exaggeration to suggest that most readers also are acquainted with one another. A writer tempted to explore erotic themes, or even to compose erotic passages, would therefore hesitate for fear of scandalizing readers who, in the way of readers everywhere, readily identify authors with their fictional characters and ascribe descriptions of "unseemly" behavior to their creator's libido.

The literary genre in which Haitian authors writing in French are less reticent to evoke sexual desire and satisfaction are tales and short stories depicting, always in the facetious mode, rural or proletarian life. For example André Chevallier in *Mon petit Kodak* [*My Little Camera*] (1916), Jacques-Stéphen Alexis in *Romancero aux étoiles* [*Songbook for the Stars*] (1960), René Depestre in *Alléluia pour une femme-jardin* [*Hallelujah for a Garden-woman*] (1973), and Gary Victor in most of his collections of ribald tales: *Albert Buron* (1988), *Nouvelles interdites* [*Forbidden Tales*] (1989) etc. These texts are reminiscent of medieval and Renaissance anecdotes about cuckolded jealous husbands, ridiculous old men lusting after young women, frustrated old maids, city Casanovas bested by wily country wenches, and the like. They could be traced back to the *fabliaux* tradition that occasionally inspired La Fontaine, Voltaire, and Balzac, but they could also be considered as the adaptation into the cultured language of the Créole songs and stories that treat the same subject matter. In these tales, as in traditional French anti-clerical anecdotes, it is not uncommon to see Breton missionary priests sacrifice their vow of chastity on the altar of their lusty Black housekeepers. However, in contradistinction to the French, Haitian authors have not depicted nuns succumbing to or even having to resist temptation.

Descriptions or mere allusions to a series of sexual behaviors are practically absent from Haitian writings before the last few decades. Sexual dysfunction, be it impotence or frigidity, is not even hinted at. Male homosexuality seems not to exist. No incidence of lesbianism before a fleeting episode between two prostitutes in Jacques-Stéphen Alexis' *L'Espace d'un cillement* [*In the Flicker of an Eyelid*] (1960). No male masturbation. The first mention of female self-gratification is in Marie Chauvet's *Amour* [*Love*] (1968) (Chauvet, and to a lesser degree Alexis, are the first Haitian novelists to have scrutinized feminine eroticism). No occurrences of incest or pedophilia. No description of orgies or evocations of masculine or feminine private parts. None of the "unnatural" heterosexual activities considered sinful by the Church. No sadists or masochists (except, once again, in Marie Chauvet's novels). Not even salacious depictions of the kind inspired by the *Kama Sutra* or *The Joy of Sex* illustrations. And sexual matters are never couched in vulgar or coarse language which, be it said in passing, is particularly rich and pungent in Créole.

This is, of course, not to say that Haitian sexual mores are any less complex than any other people's—but the theme is tacitly ignored in polite society, both in its oral and written manifestations. According to the accepted piety, Haitian sexuality takes place within the bonds of "normalcy" and "morality." Deviations and transgressions are alluded to in the normal exchange of gossip, but not in open discourse. From this point of view, it would not be unfair to speak of Puritanism.

One characteristic that distinguishes French language poetry in Haiti from that of the Europeans is the obsessive identification of women with edibles. Especially, as could be expected, with fruits. A woman's breasts can be compared to "twin sapodillas" or "twin marmalade plums," her lips are "as purple as our lovely caymitos" and taste like "mammy apples"; her kisses are "honeyed pineapple," her mouth "melts like a mango"; she is "a sugar-sweet orange," "a well-ripened fruit, defenseless and full of sap"; her body is "hot citrus," her eyes can be "tamarind, but shaped like almonds" her breath "wafts the perfume of our guavas," her cheeks are "rose apples"; and when she is cruel, her heart is as hard as "Guinea coconuts." To be sure, French poets also have celebrated women's peachy complexions or their cherry red lips, but their Haitian colleagues' imagination runs riot in the pursuit of scrumptious metaphors. And other flavorful comestibles are also evoked: the kisses of the poet's beloved can be "more gooey

616

than turtle soup," they can taste of "sour ball candy," have "a salty, tangy taste," and the nape of her neck can "taste of sea-food." All Haitians know a humorous poem by Émile Roumer in which the marabout (a dark-skinned, silky-haired woman with European features) of the poem is compared to the most appetizing specialties of Haitian cuisine:

Marabout de mon cœur [*Marabout of my Heart*]:

> Marabout of my heart, with breasts like tangerines,
> You taste better to me than eggplant stuffed with crab.
> You are the slice of tripe within my gumbo soup,
> The dumpling in my beans, my tea of herbs and cloves,
> You are the bully beef whose rind my heart provides,
> The syrup and cornmeal that trickles down my throat,
> You are a steaming dish; you are mushrooms and rice;
> Cod fritters very crisp; fish fried to golden brown.
> I hunger for your love. Where you roam I will trail
> Your buttocks, bouncing boats with bounteous victuals laden.

While French poets tend to depict beautiful women in repose, and compare them to paintings or statues, movement is an essential component of Haitian feminine attractiveness. As René Depestre puts it in *Hallelujah for a Garden-woman:*

> Garden women have electric buttocks
> Garden women have cyclones in their love play [...]
> And in their movements the geometry of she-lions

The women of Haiti reveal the true essence of their beauty by moving, walking or, better yet, by dancing—and especially in dancing for the Gods, or while possessed by them during voodoo ceremonies. Since the nineteenth century, novelists and poets have often described such ceremonies, sometimes realistically, sometimes imaginatively. And the focus is generally on the dancing woman, and on "her nimble loins" and "the savage play of her undulating hips." A particularly suggestive description is found in Milo Rigaud's 1933 novel *Jésus et Legba*:

> In the glow of the fire a woman started to dance. Half naked, dressed only in a skirt tied on her hips by a red sash, she stormed into the circle like a dusky Fury. She went through terrible contortions. A man with the limbs of a panther came after her, and while she sang:

> Zaguidi, zaguidi
> I am more of a man than a woman,
> Zaguidi, zaguidi,
> I'm more of a woman than a man

> her black partner pressed upon her with domineering gestures. While the woman kept sticking out her bouncing haunches, they mimed a mad pursuit, which the man won. (p. 109).

It should be noted that in most cases only dark-skinned peasant or working class women are compared to edibles or displayed in the performance of wild or suggestive dances. Their aristocratic light-skinned counterparts, on the other hand, are generally compared, like European women, to objets d'art and admired while dancing dignified waltzes and two-steps in well-appointed ballrooms.

Similarly, writers draw a modest veil when society ladies are about to enjoy sex. They are somewhat more daring when dealing with peasant or proletarian girls. Such scenes are not necessarily meant to be demeaning or prurient. On the contrary, they are generally described in poetic language; they take place in the open air, and the girl is identified with the motherly and bountiful earth. Jacques Roumain's evocation in *Gouverneurs de la rosée* [*Masters of the Dew*] (1944) of Manuel and Annaïse's first coupling by the side of the spring is particularly skillful, even in translation, and has inspired many imitators:

> Their lips touched.
> "My sweet," she sighed.
> She closed her eyes and he laid her down. She was stretched out on the ground and the low rumble of the water echoed within her in a sound that was the tumult of her own blood. She didn't defend herself. His hand, so heavy, transmitted an intolerable sweetness.
> "I'm going to die!"
> Beneath his touch, her body burned. He unlocked her knees, and she opened herself to him. He entered, a lacerating presence, and she gave an injured groan.
> "No! Don't leave me—or I'll die!"
> Her body went to meet his in a feverish surge. In her an unspeakable anguish was born, a terrible delight, which absorbed the movements of her body. A panting which rose to her lips.
> Then she felt herself melt in the deliverance of that long sob that left her prostrate in man's embrace.

As previously mentioned, all of the above hardly applies to most Haitian writings of the last few decades. The economic, political, and social deterioration of the country is reflected in its literature and its depiction of eroticism. Contemporary writings are the texts of despair, be they composed and published in Haiti or, increasingly, in French or Quebecois exile. Haitian authors, as their colleagues in the Western world, are now free of the censorship that used to inhibit the representation of eroticism. To be sure, some authors nevertheless hold to the old-fashioned standards of allusiveness and delicacy when depicting physical love. But the sensuous, happy descriptions of "fruit women" and of cheerful lusty encounters now seem old-fashioned. Henceforth, the erotic is at best wistfully associated with more humane bygone days or, more usually, with present deprivation and torture. Given the trials of the country and the suffering of its citizens, to evoke the *Joys of Sex* seems irrelevant if not downright offensive. As Louis Neptune put it:

> For us the stink of prison has replaced the fragrance of bosoms
> The cold wind of stone walls my Caribbean girl's soft breath.

Also, the last decades have seen Haitians broadening their literary horizon until then limited to the latest French productions. More and more Haitian readers and authors have now become familiar with and influenced by English, Spanish, and "Francophone" writings. Many have been exposed to avant-garde schools of literary criticism which regard all means of expression, even pornography, as equally respectable. Under these various influences, the modesty and seemliness of old has all but disappeared.

A particularly representative and impressive example of the new literary vision is Gérard Étienne's 1974 first person narrative *Le nègre crucifié* [*The Crucified Negro*]. In a semiconscious hallucinatory state, a prisoner who has suffered the most abject forms of torture at the hands of François Duvalier's henchmen imagines himself crucified at a street crossing in Port-au-Prince. He screams invectives at those who have debased him and the country he loved. His ranting denunciation of life under the terrorist regime makes for painful reading. Blood, excrement, garbage, vermin, scabs, the screams of prisoners, the stink of unwashed bodies, of rotting food, and of clogged latrines are the stuff of his vociferations. Humiliating sexual submission, for pubescent boys and girls as well as for men and women, is at best a survival tactic.

Eroticism has been replaced by obscenity. Even presumably tender moments are reminiscent of the nightmares painted by Hieronimus Bosch:

> Nounou is beautiful. He wants to take her. Lie down, he says. More than twenty mice run into her mouth, inspect her guts, and tumble out through a hole in her pelvis. Do the mice hurt you? No, replies the girl, they feed on my tuberculosis. [...]
> He throws himself on Nounoune, licks her skin, bites her eyes. She sighs. He lifts her dress, touches her vagina and makes a face. What a strange animal, he says. Look at its cockscomb. It looks like a grass snake's tongue. Nounoune, does it have teeth? Why don't we make love in your mouth? (pp. 56–57)

Voodoo used to be, if not respected, at least admired for its artistic components. In Étienne's phantasmagoria, this is what happens to practitioners:

> They have cavorted so long that they end up fucking their own daughters on straw mats where dogs and fleas cavort. [...] Their slobber and their food foam up. Their sweat foams with their spittle and the pus of their wounds.
> It's like a clump of meat rotting in sorcery, hunger and orgies. (p. 29)

The Crucified Negro is an extreme example, and few texts equal its apocalyptic vituperations. But it seems that, while Haitian authors used to seek inspiration in the sentimentalism of Lamartine or the committed idealism of Victor Hugo, they now turn to the Marquis de Sade and the pessimism of Céline. Be that as it may, erotic passages are now certainly more explicit, but it would take a peculiar sensibility to be aroused by novels such as Daniel Supplice's novel *Karioka* (1999), where a young girl passes out under *tonton-makout* torture. When she returns to consciousness:

> She brought her hand to her vagina, and the abundance of sperm that oozed out of it revealed that she had been raped repeatedly. (p. 89)

Such a passage would have been all but inconceivable before the Duvalier era. Rape, which used to be taboo, is now a common literary occurrence. In Marie Chauvet's *Colère* [*Anger*] (1968) the young mulatto Rose submits to the *makout* chief to protect her family.

In Jean-Claude Fignolé's *La dernière goutte d'homme* [*The Last Human Drop*] (1999) among other horrors perpetrated by Duvalier's goon is described:

a woman, her tongue cut out, her breasts ripped and mangled, after having been raped by two unidentified individuals. (p. 23)

This is the first Haitian novel in which sexual love between two men is evoked, and with respect. It is also the first one in which an episode of fellatio is described, as well as incest between a mother and her son and the homosexual rape of a child by his brother. For such daring, even though it avoids any prurience, Fignolé would probably have been run out of town in the more decorous past.

In Anthony Phelps' *Mémoire en colin-maillard* [*Memory Plays Hide-and Seek*] (1976), a sexual encounter between Claude, a well-to-do young mulatto, and his Black servant Mésina is described in poetic and very precise details. It seems at first that we are witnessing the joyful coupling of consenting adults, but we soon realize that we are dealing with an oneiric sequence, that Claude has been crippled (and possibly unmanned) by Duvalier's thugs and that the whole daydream is nothing but wishful compensation. The climax comes when Claude imagines himself as a sadistic voodoo spirit mounting the young woman (in voodoo parlance, a person possessed is a "horse" "mounted" by the spirit) and bringing her to painful climax with his whip and spurs:

-Buck, now, Mésina. Buck!
-I'm bucking, M'sieu Claude. And your whip is flaying me. I'm bucking again and your spurs bite into me. Aïe!... I'm going to die, m'sieu Claude. Aïe!... you are a god, m'sieu Claude. You are the devil himself.

In French as in Elizabethan English, "to die" is a euphemism for "to climax." And so it is here. But at the same time the primary meaning of the verb is emblematic: for most writers, sex in today's Haiti is perversely linked with death, and release can only be attained through inflicting pain. Sex in Haitian literature will become erotic again only when peace and justice return to this much abused country.

LÉON-FRANÇOIS HOFFMAN

Selected Works

Alexis Jacques-Stéphen. *Romancero aux étoiles*. Paris, Gallimard, 1960.

Alexis, Jacques-Stéphen. *L'Espace d'un cillement*. Paris, Gallimard, 1960. [*In the Flicker of an Eyelid*, tr. by Carroll F. Coates and Edwidge Danticat., Charlottesville, VA, University of Virginia Press, 2002].

Chauvet, Marie. *Amour, Colère et folie*. Paris, Gallimard, 1968. [*Amour*, the first book of the trilogy novel *Amour, colère et folie* tr. by Joyce Marie Cogdell-Travis, Ann Arbor, Mich., University Microfilms International, 1983].

Chevallier, André. *Mon petit Kodak*. Port-au-Prince, Impr. Chenet, 1916.

Depestre, René. *Alléluia pour une femme-jardin*. Ottawa, Leméac, 1973.

Étienne, Gérard. *Le nègre crucifié*. Montreal, Éditions francophones, 1974.

Fignolé, Daniel. *La dernière goutte d'homme*. Montreal & Port-au-Prince, Regain & CIDIHCA, 1999.

Hibbert, Fernand. *Séna*. Port-au-Prince, Impr. de l'Abeille, 1905.

Hoffman, Léon-François. *Haitian Fiction Revisited*. Washington, DC: Passeggiata Press, 1999.

Marcelin, Frédéric. *La vengeance de Mama*. Paris, Ollendorf, 1902.

Phelps, Anthony. *Mémoire en colin-maillard*. Montreal, Nouvelle Optique, 1976.

Rigaud, Milo. *Jésus et Legba*. Poitiers, Amis de la poésie, 1933.

Roumain, Jacques. *Gouverneurs de la rosée*. Port-au-Prince, Impr. de l'État, 1944 *Masters of the Dew*, tr. By Langston Hughes and Mercer Cook, Heinemann, London, Kingston, Port of Spain, 1978 [1947].

Supplice, Daniel. *Karioka*. Port-au-Prince, Ed. H. Deschamps, 1998.

Victor, Gary. *Albert Buron* (1988). *Nouvelles interdites* (1989).

Further Reading

Auguste, Yves L. "L'amour dans la littérature haïtienne." *Présence africaine*. 60 (4), 1966, pp. 159–171.

Carré Crosley, Bernadette. "Haïtianité et mythe de la femme dans *Hadriana dans tous mes rêves*. de René Depestre, Montreal, CIDIHCA, 1993.

Chancy, Myriam J.A. "*Léspoua Fè Viv*: Female Identity and the Politics of Textual Sexuality in Nadine Magloire's *Le Mal de vivre*." *Critical Studies* (Amsterdam), 7, 1996.

Dorsinville, Max. "Violence et répression féminine dans le roman haïtien." In Fratta, Carla (ed.), *La deriva delle francofonie*. Bologna, Cooperative Lib. Univ., 1992.

Étienne, Gérard. "La Femme noire dans le discours littéraire haïtien." *Présence francophone* (Sherbrooke, P.Q.), 18, 1979.

Fonseca, Maria Nazareth Soares. "Misticismo e erotismo em dicções pós-coloniais." *Revista de letras*. (Lisbon), 39, 1999.

Lapaire, Pierre Guy. "L'érotisme baroque, le *télédiol* et les femmes-jardins de rené Depestre." *Essays in French Literature* (University of Western Australia), 27, Nov. 1990.

Laroche, Maximilien. "Images de la femme dans la lyrique populaire haïtienne." *Études littéraires*. Québec, 25 (3), 1992–1993.

Latortue, Régine. "The Black Woman in Haitian Society and Literature." In Filomena Steady, ed. *The Black*

Woman Cross-culturally. Cambridge, MA: Schenkman Publishing Company Co., 1981.

Mahéo, Marie-France. "Le Climat érotique: Obsession et ambiguïté dans *Chronique d'un faux-amour* de Jacques-Stéphen Alexis." *Francofonia* (Bologna), 14 (27) 1994.

Marty, Anne. "Climat socio-psychologique et images de la femme dans la poésie haïtienne: la génération de *La Ronde*." Collectif paroles (Montreal), 28, mars/avril 1984.

Spear, Thomas C. "Carnivalesque Jouissance: Representations of Sexuality in the Francophone West Indian Novel." *Jouvert* (Electronic publication), 2 (1), 1998.

HALL, RADCLYFFE

1880–1943
English novelist and poet

The Well of Loneliness

Radclyffe Hall's *The Well of Loneliness* (1928) is arguably the most notorious lesbian novel in English, whereby its fame stems partly from its early ban in Britain. Subdivided into five books, the work portrays the life and loves of the female invert Stephen Gordon, who has often been wrongly assumed to be based on Hall herself. The masculine English upper-class girl, Stephen, discovers at the age of seven that she is attracted to women when she develops a crush on the housemaid. Aged twenty-one, she then has her first sexual encounter with another woman, the married Angela Crossby. The passionate affair ends when Angela confesses it to her husband, who in turn informs Stephens's mother about her sexual inclination. This results in Stephen leaving the family's country estate. She settles in London together with her teacher–companion Puddlington, or Puddle, who is herself a closeted invert. Hall modelled Puddle in part upon her earlier fictional creation, Elizabeth Rodney from *The Unlit Lamp* (1924), which was one of Hall's more overtly feminist works. Here she had condemned expectations that women had to fulfil the traditional role of womanhood, which allowed them no personal choices or development. Like Rodney, but quite unlike Stephen, Puddle suppresses her sexuality. In London, Stephen establishes herself as a successful writer.

With the outbreak of Word War I, she joins a women's ambulance unit in France, where she meets the young Welsh woman Mary Llewellyn. After the war, the two become lovers. Their first sexual union is alluded to in the now famous line "...and that night they were not divided" (316). They set up house together in Paris and become part of a colorful set of male and female homosexual intellectuals and artists, which Hall loosely based on her own Parisian circle of friends, especially on Natalie Barney. The narrative spirals towards its dramatic ending when Stephen's old friend Martin Hallam reappears and falls in love with Mary. Stephen decides that she should give up Mary to Martin. She devises a ploy whereby the unwitting Mary is directed into leaving Stephen, to be taken away by Martin. *The Well of Loneliness* ends with a quasi-religious scene in which Stephen, now alone, has taken on the grand role as representative for the millions of inverts on earth, in whose name she demands recognition and the right to existence.

The Well of Loneliness is a candid document of Hall's (at the time) radical understanding of lesbianism—or sexual inversion, as it was also known—which she perceived to be a naturally occurring sexual variation. This idea was based on the newly developed theories of sexology, for which Hall had an avid interest. Two of the leading nineteenth-century sexologists, the German lawyer and homosexual activist Karl Heinrich Ulrichs, and the German psychiatrist Richard von Krafft-Ebing, are actually mentioned in the novel. Their theories had in common that they distinguished between congenital and acquired homosexuality, and that they linked sexual inversion to gender inversion. These ideas feature prominently in *The Well of Loneliness*, especially through the portrayal of the protagonist. Stephen Gordon is characterized by her overt masculinity, which marks the fact that she is born an invert, in contrast, for example, to her first lover, Angela Crossby, for whom inversion was an acquired habit. Hall inscribes erotic tension into the narrative by repeatedly and in detail describing Stephen's masculine body, and then contrasting it with the feminine features of Stephen's lovers. The most erotic moments in the narrative are thus constructed by conjuring up certain bodily imagery, rather than through the use of explicit sexual language.

Hall had wanted *The Well of Loneliness* to be bolder than any other lesbian novel in English before. The book, written in the style of the *bildungsroman*, followed in the footsteps of recent developments in English literature, whereby lesbian themes had gained increasing, albeit tentative, attention at the turn of the last nineteenth century (see entry on lesbian literature). However, Hall was the first to sympathetically portray a sexually active invert. This bestowed almost instant notoriety upon both the work and its author. First published in May 1928 by the London-based Jonathan Cape publishing house, *The Well of Loneliness* was tried under the Obscene Publications Act of 1857 in November of the same year. It was found guilty of obscenity and banned in England. The novel was subsequently published in America where it was also tried, but cleared of obscenity charges. The British ban on *The Well of Loneliness* was only lifted in 1959 with the passing of a new Obscene Publications Act.

The ban of *The Well of Loneliness* did not end Hall's literary production. She published two more novels, *The Master of the House* (1932) and *The Sixth Beatitude* (1936), as well as a collection of short stories entitled *Miss Ogilvy Finds Herself* (1934). None of the works engaged with the subject of female sexual inversion. Hall's lover Una Troubridge claims to have given *The Well of Loneliness* its famous title. It appears rather tongue-in-cheek, as the protagonist of the novel leads anything but a lonely life.

In the 1980s, *The Well of Loneliness* suffered much critical condemnation for allegedly reinforcing narrow stereotypes about the masculine lesbian. A decade later, there has been a marked change in critical opinion and the novel has been reassessed as a subversive and empowering piece of writing. The erotic allure of Hall's narrative continues to appeal to generations of readers.

Biography

Born August 12, 1880 in Bournemouth, Hampshire as Marguerite Radclyffe-Hall, she renamed herself John in adult life and adopted Radclyffe Hall as her literary name. Privately educated, she spent 1898–1899 in Dresden, Germany, and on return attended lectures at King's College, University of London. Her life was dominated by three major relationships (the last two chronologically overlapping) with Mabel 'Ladye Batten,' Una Troubridge, and Evguenia Souline. Her friends and acquaintances included May Sinclair, Rebecca West, Natalie Barney, Colette, Havelock Ellis, and W. B. Yeats. She was a keen traveller, but rooted in England, where she died in London on 7 October 1943.

Hall published five volumes of poetry and seven novels. Her literary acclaim was established with the novel *Adam's Breed* (1926), which won the Prix Femina Vie Heureuse, and the James Tait Black Memorial Price. Her first publication, a book of poetry entitled *A Sheaf of Verses*, came out in 1908. Her first two novels *The Forge* and *The Unlit Lamp* were both published in 1924.

HEIKE BAUER

Editions

The Well of Loneliness. London: Jonathan Cape, 1928; London: Virago Press, 1992.

Selected Works

'Twixt Earth and Stars. 1906.
A Sheaf of Verses. 1908.
The Forge. 1924.
The Unlit Lamp. 1924.
A Saturday Life. 1925.
Adam's Breed. 1926.
The Master of the House. 1932.
Miss Ogilvy Finds Herself. 1934.
The Sixth Beatitude. 1936.

Further Reading

Baker, Michael. *Our Three Selves: A Life of Radclyffe Hall*. London: Hamish Hamilton, 1985.

Bauer, Heike. "Krafft-Ebing's *Psychopathia Sexualis* as the sexual sourcebook for *The Well of Loneliness*. *Critical Survey*, vol. 15, no.3, 2003, 23–28.

Brittain, Vera. *Radclyffe Hall: A Case of Obscenity?* London: Femina, 1968.

Cline, Sally. *Radclyffe Hall: A Woman Named John.* London: John Murray, 1997.

Glasgow, Joanne, ed. *Your John: The Love Letters of Radclyffe Hall.* New York: New York University Press, 1997.

Souhami, Diana. *The Trials of Radclyffe Hall.* London: Virago, 1999.

Troubridge, Una. *The Life and Death of Radclyffe Hall.* London: Hammond and Hammond, 1961.

Taylor, Leslie A. "'I Made Up My Mind to Get It': The American Trial of *The Well of Loneliness*. New York City, 1928–1929," *Journal of the History of Sexuality.* 10 (2), 2001.

HARRIS, FRANK

1856–1931
Irish memoirist, short story writer, and journalist

My Life and Loves

Frank Harris' five-volume work *My Life and Loves* is a biography with sexual elements present throughout and not (like the anonymous *My Secret Life*, for example) a sexual autobiography with no other matter covered.

This autobiography is his only enduring work, one that deliberately steps outside the contemporary restraints of the genre, provocatively setting a standard against British and American sexual prudery. Harris determines to tell the truth about his sex life, declaring "If all the ways of love are beautiful to me, why should I not say so? All the girls and women I have met and loved have taught me something."

In the forward he sets down the ultimately mournful theme of the book, of how the power to enjoy and give sexual pleasure is keenest in early life, while the understanding of how to do it well develops later, "when the faculties are already on the decline."

He creates a revealing analogy to illustrate this: when he was a child his father gave him a single-barrelled gun; when he had learned to use it he was given a double-barrelled shotgun; and in later life he took to using a magazine gun. "My Creator, or Heavenly Father, on the other hand, gave me, so to speak, a magazine gun of sex, and hardly had I learned its use and enjoyment when he took it away from me forever, and gave me in its place a double-barrelled gun: after a few years, he took that away and gave me a single-barrelled gun with which I was forced to content myself for the best part of my life. Towards the end the old single-barrel began to show signs of wear and age; sometimes it would go off too soon, sometimes it missed fire and shamed me, do what I would." The story gives much of the book: the self-important while at the same time self-pitying tone but with more than a hint of mockery; the neatness of expression over a limited field; the mechanical view of sex and the analogy with hunting game.

Harris tells of sexual experience from the earliest years: in the classroom when he was under five and would drop his pencil to be able to bend down and see the legs of the big girls; and his sisters showed him their developing breasts.

Born in Ireland, Harris was sent to school in England; he describes the sexual bullying of the public school system where 'fags' were forced to masturbate older boys. Harris believes unreservedly in the 'vital force' theory of masturbation as an enervating activity and as evidence cites the case of one boy who masturbated frequently, "All of us knew he had torn a hole in his pocket so he could play with his cock...the little fellow grew gradually paler and paler until he took to crying in a corner, and unaccountably nervous trembling shook him for a quarter of an hour at a time. At length, he was taken away by his parents."

He tells how at thirteen as a boy in the choir who sang solos, the organist would summon him to practice with local girls, one of whom also sang alto so she was placed next to him. He cautiously slips his hand up her skirt, at which "she did not move or show any sign of distaste." He examines her vagina with his fingers, "Gently I rubbed the front part of her sex with my finger. I could have kissed her a thousand times out of gratitude... as I went on, I felt her move, and then again; plainly she was showing me where my touch gave her most pleasure."

The lesson finished and they had to leave. The following week Harris tries to repeat the experiment but the girl refuses and Harris in his distress sings so badly he loses his position as soloist. Like most of Harris' sexual tales, the story has a ring of truth—a tale with pornographic intent would have had the episode leading to copulation or at least orgasm, not humiliated disappointment. Though there was no success, Harris remarks in a characteristically blunt metaphor, "I had tasted blood and could never afterwards forget the scent of it." He determined "No more self-abuse for me; I knew something infinitely better."

With the inquiring intellect that was to make him a successful newspaperman, Harris learns from older boys such lessons as "girls love kissing" and, from his sister, "you must say that the girl you are with is the prettiest girl in the room." He begs sexual advice from a man known locally as a Lothario who tells him, "When you can put a stiff penis in her hand and weep profusely the while, you're getting near any woman's heart. But don't forget the tears."

He describes in detail how he gets to fondle three other girls, one of them, Jesse, on the boat crossing from Liverpool to New York after he has run away from school at the age of fifteen. He exclaims, "She yielded again to my hand with a little sigh and I found her sex all wet, wet!" When, in New York, they are together and naked, he notices, with a disappointment very characteristic of his sexual quest, "she was too broad for her height; her legs were too short, her hips too stout. It all chilled me a little. Should I ever find perfection?"

Physically, Harris was short of stature, very short-sighted and considered himself ugly but says he discovered that qualities such as "strength and dominant self-confidence" are those most attractive to a woman. His gifts were his conversation, his brilliant memory (he could recite a book of Swinburne's verse by heart after reading it once) and a driving will which enabled him to achieve such feats as shutting himself up for three months to become fluent in a new language when he needed to do so.

In the United States, Harris' first extensive sexual experiences are at the age of eighteen with an older woman, the passionate wife of an acquaintance who, after his advances, takes the lead in the relationship, "My second orgasm took some time and all the while Lorna became more and more responsive, till suddenly she put her hands on my bottom and drew me to her forcibly while she moved her sex up and down awkwardly to meet my thrusts with a passion I had hardly imagined." She introduces him to sexual variety, riding him and also giving him his first experience of fellatio with the words, "Your seed, darling, is dear to me: I don't want it in my sex; I want to feel you thrill and so I want your sex in my mouth, I want to drink you essence."

New loves come to excite him, which he explains with the proverb "Fresh cunt, fresh courage," and he seduces the daughter of his landlord. Aware that the narrative structure implies a series of conquests, he insists "my half dozen victories were spread out over nearly as many years and time and again I met rebuffs and refusals." Still, he wishes to emphasize that "success in love, like success in every department of life, falls usually to the tough man unwearied in pursuit." In sex as in business and education, he is the ultimate self-made man.

His high intellect and thirst for knowledge lead him to be taken up as a student by Byron Caldwell Smith, a professor at Kansas University. In return, Harris says he tried to cure Smith of nocturnal emissions, which were enervating the classics scholar, by a regime of tying up his penis at night which Harris himself had found helpful.

With a scholar's dedication, Harris plunges into the mechanics of sex which he finds endlessly fascinating. He has himself circumcised because he believes that a toughened skin of the cuticle makes it more difficult to catch syphilis, and that toughening the head of the penis would allow him to prolong copulation.

Harris does not wear his knowledge lightly and feels moved to explain female anatomy and the process of conception to women with whom he has sex. He uses immediate post-coital douching as a method of contraception, helping his lovers to insert the device.

He is full of sexual lore and is ever interested in adding to it. He feels the heat of a woman's lips are an indication of the lubricity of her vagina; he remarks that the French think "small bones indicate a small sex; but I have found the exceptions are very numerous." His kindness to a black woman leads her daughter to offer herself to him, at which he remarks, "To my astonishment her sex was well formed and very small: I had always heard that Negroes had far larger genitals than white people; but the lips of Sophy's sex were thick and firm...My admiration of Sophy cleansed me of any possible disdain I might otherwise have had of the Negro people."

Some techniques are too advanced for the young man, however: when a French woman asks him to *faire minette* (give her cunnilingus) saying "I prefer in a meal the hors-d'oeuvres to the pièce de resistance like a good many other women." Harris refuses with "the ordinary English or American youth's repugnance to what seemed like degradation."

Some years later, however, in Athens, he is in bed with a woman who so fears conception that she begs him to give her cunnilingus, and out of his passion for her he consents "I opened the lips of her sex and put my lips on it and my tongue against her clitoris. There was nothing repulsive in it; it was another and more sensitive mouth." He is delighted at the experience and builds its possibilities into his sexual world, "I could give pleasure to any extent without exhausting or even tiring myself. It thus enabled me to atone completely and make up for my steadily decreasing virility. Secondly, I discovered that by teaching me the most sensitive parts of the woman, I was able even in the ordinary way to give my mistresses more and keener pleasure than ever before." Harris seems unable to have a sexual experience without drawing a moral from it, from this one he learns, "how superior art is to nature."

He travels to Europe, chiefly in Paris and Germany where he studies in Heidelberg where he discovers that "absolutely complete chastity enabled me to work longer hours than I had ever worked" and resolves to have sex only when he is truly in love. The problem with this resolution is that Harris falls in love very easily. He has sex with women in Austria and Ireland and learns through his experiences that he most enjoys sex the more he gives pleasure to women

He falls in love with Laura Clapton, a beautiful and intelligent Anglo-American with scheming, impoverished parents. He hopes to marry her but waits until he has made his fortune, but she has had liaisons with other men and he sets her up in an apartment as his mistress. Though she protests love for him, he has great difficulty in bringing her to orgasm, "I would pose her sideways so as to bring out the greater swell of the hip and the poses would usually end with my burying my head between her legs, trying with lips and tongue and finger and often again with my sex to bring her sensations to ecstasy and if possible to love-speech and love thanks!"

By hard work and by importuning editors he becomes a successful journalist in London, and rises rapidly to become one of the greatest popular newspaper editors of his generation. He described his success to his ability to see the world through the eyes of a teenager, "kissing and fighting were the only things I cared for at thirteen or fourteen, and those are the themes the English public desires and enjoys today."

In Paris, he picks up a coquette, Jeanne, by leaping into her carriage. She is no longer young nor a beauty but is a refined, well-read woman who offered the speciality of 'casse noisettes': a vagina "with the contractile strength of a hand." She has saved a good deal from her life as a mistress and offers to take Harris away to Algeria and keep him while he pursues his writing. Jeanne uses her adopted daughter of around twelve, Lisette, as bait, encouraging Harris to see her in the bath and to be alone with her. Later Harris takes the opportunity, while Jeanne is dressing, of kissing and fondling Lisette but does not have full sex with her.

He never ceases to ponder the mysteries of sexual attraction, remarking on his "adoration of virginity" which is as inexplicable to him as an old man as it was fifty years previously. "Even now a well-made girl's legs of fourteen make the pulses beat in my forehead and bring water into my mouth."

He marries in 1887 in the hope that this will advance his intended political career. His autobiography omits details of sexual relations of this and a later marriage to Nellie O'Hara, his true soul-mate, whose name does not even occur in the book.

While on honeymoon in the first marriage he chances to see his old love Laura on a station and feels a choking pain, "in one moment I realised I had bartered happiness for comfort and a pleasant life, that I had blundered badly and would have to pay for the blunder and pay heavily." He resumes the relationship with Laura while attempting, unsuccessfully, a parliamentary career.

Harris seems to tire of the chronological story by the time he has described his life to his mid-forties, and the book becomes increasingly more fragmented with chapters given over to accounts of famous people he has known or to sexual adventures.

One story is of what he calls "The greatest amatory experience of my life" after he has bought a villa in San Reno and falls in with his gardener's suggestion of a beauty contest where five local girls are invited to the villa, encouraged to strip, and rewarded with prizes by Harris who is posing as an English lord. Word gets around of these frolics and another week the gardener procures twenty girls willing to take off their clothes for the chance of winning a hundred francs.

Having made their choices, Harris and a friend work on a refinement of the game to determine the winner of winners. They then make close examinations to see who has "the smallest and best made sex" and stimulate the girls to test their reaction to sensation, though Harris' favorite, Flora, "disdained the test and said she felt more at something said, at a beautiful thought or fine deed than she ever felt by mere sexual excitement."

The contests inevitably turn into orgies, and the girls become close enough friends for some to express their disgust, "'I hate these comparisons,' cried Adriana, 'They degrade one to the level of the mere animal; surely there's more to me than round limbs and a small sex?'"

A Frenchman joins the group and introduces them to the use of dildos and to whipping, saying that by whipping a girl's bottom "he could bring her to a passion of desire." Harris remarks that, "nothing prettier could be imagined than three or four girls being excited in this way."

Harris encourages the girls to tell the stories of their sex lives. Flora talks of having what she calls "naked thoughts" from the age of seven, and of sex games she played with other girls as a young teenager. Adriana is much more passionate and

says she was given to masturbation from ten or eleven years old until at the age of thirteen when she was told it was bad for the health and then restricted herself to masturbate only on Saturday nights. She was raped at the age of sixteen by the manager of a hotel where she worked, and then had no sex for two years in disgust at the experience.

One of the most attractive features of Harris is his genuine interest in the stories of women, even when their experience undermines his world view of the joy of seduction for both male and female. Thus he prints a long letter from a woman who wrote in response to the publication of his first volume. She had met men like him and her experience of seduction was humiliation and abandonment, of venereal disease, and of becoming an unmarried mother.

Harris tries drugs and sex, sampling opium, ether, and cocaine, but finds no advantage; and also tries 'cock rings' aimed at a higher stimulation of the woman. He meets a procuress on a voyage to India who caters for his desire for young girls by supplying him with child widows (the result of Indian marriage customs). "The second evening she brought me a girl of twelve—a widow—rather pretty but childish. Her sex was naturally very small but she had little response to passion in her; she seemed afraid to complain and didn't enjoy it greatly. She was happy for the first time when I paid her." After several such encounters he remarks, "The experience cured me of my liking for the immature. For even the best of them never gave me the thrill I experienced with older girls. The sex was often very small, but it had not the gripping, pumping power of the mature older woman."

By the end of the biography his memory and stamina are failing him and he baulks at relating the decline of his sexual performance. Desire was as keen at sixty as at forty, he says, but by then he had become "a mediocre performer in the lists of love, but had never been shamed by failure." It is a shock when for the first time even desire fails him, when a servant comes who is looking for work and though she is pretty, he is not aroused by her.

For all its structural failings, the obvious exaggerations and some pure invention, *My Life and Loves* remains one of the most vivid memoirs of the nineteenth century, reading it gives the impression of a long conversation with a well-read Victorian libertine.

Putting aside Harris' extravagant claim that this is "the first book ever written to glorify the body and its passionate desires and the soul as well as its sacred, climbing sympathies," the development of biography as a form in the twentieth century vindicated his conviction that no biography can claim to be honest unless it deals with a character's sex life.

Biography

Frank Harris was born James Thomas Harris in Galway, Ireland, February 14, 1856. He immigrated to the United States in 1869 and studied at the University of Kansas. In 1878, he was married to a woman who would die the following year. She was the first of three wives he would have.

In 1882, Harris returned to England where he worked as editor at a number of publications and edited the work of H. G. Wells and George Bernard Shaw. From 1916 to 1922, he edited the U.S. edition of Britain's *Pearson's Magazine* in New York. He died in France on August 27, 1931, of a heart attack.

JAD ADAMS

Editions

Harris, Frank. *My Life and Loves.* Vol.1, privately printed, Paris 1922; Paris, Obelisk Press, 1930. First four volumes privately printed, Paris, 1930; Paris, Obelisk Press 1945. A partly spurious 'fifth volume' was issued by the Olympia Press, Paris, 1958, containing some material from Harris with additions by Alexander Trocchi. John F. Gallagher (editor) volumes 1–5, New York, Grove Press, 1963; London, W.H. Allen, 1964. The fifth volume, not published in Harris' life, was based on Harris' final typescript which is in the University of Texas.

Further Reading

Bain, Linda M. *Evergreen Adventurer.* London: Research Publishing, 1975.
Bertolini, John. "Frank Harris" in Cevasco, G.A. (editor) *The 1890s: An Encyclopaedia of British Literature, Art and Culture.* New York: Garland Publishing, 1993.
Brome, Vincent. *Frank Harris.* London: Cassell, 1959.
Caldwell Smith, Gerrit and Mary. *Lies and Libels of Frank Harris.* New York: Antigone Press, 1929.
Kingsmill, Hugh. *Frank Harris.* London: Biografia, 1932.
Pearsall, Robert B. *Frank Harris.* New York: Twayne, 1970.
Pullar, Philippa. *Frank Harris: A Biography.* New York: Simon & Shuster, 1976.
Root, Edward Merril. *Frank Harris.* New York: Odyssey, 1947.
Roth, Samuel. *The Private Life of Frank Harris.* New York: William Faro, 1931.
Tobin, A.I. and Gertz, Eleanor. *Frank Harris: A Study in Black and White.* Chicago, IL: Madelaine Mendelsohn, 1931.

HAWKES, JOHN

1925–1998
American novelist

Lauded by critics and scholars alike, and sometimes called "Gothic" or "experimental," Hawkes' darkly comic fiction, characterized by disjunctions in the traditional novel components of character, plot, setting, and theme, was never popularly received in the United States. Hawkes placed an emphasis on structure, what he called "verbal and psychological" coherence. This attention manifests itself in poetically imagistic and dreamlike sections, often narrated in the first person. The texts frequently confront human nature in all its ugliness and human failings in all their magnitude, but do so with a self-reflexive comedy and a beauty of language meant to recuperate those shortcomings. Hawkes' attempt to elucidate the unconscious desires of his characters entails frequent interrogation of the erotic components of the unconscious and thus aligns him with other writers of darkly erotic literature, including the Marquis de Sade, Georges Bataille, Angela Carter, and Flannery O'Connor.

Though he published his first novel, *Charivari*, in 1949, Hawkes did not begin to fully engage in theories of the erotic through his fiction until 1970 with the publication of *The Blood Oranges*. *The Blood Oranges* is the first novel in what Hawkes would come to call "the triad," centering upon explorations of male sexuality; the others are *Death, Sleep and the Traveler* (1974) and *Travesty* (1976). Following upon publication of these works, Hawkes began to explore female sexual subjectivity in two novels: *The Passion Artist* (1979) and *Virginie: Her Two Lives* (1981).

Set in the fictional Illyria and modeled upon Ford Madox Ford's *The Good Soldier* and Shakespeare's *Twelfth Night*, *The Blood Oranges* relates the story of Cyril and Fiona's encounter with Hugh and Catherine, and their daughter, Meredith. Cyril claims that the "only enemy of the mature marriage is monogamy." In order to introduce this ideal, Cyril impresses partner swapping upon his guests. Characterized by a truncated arm, symbolically suggestive of his failure to fully engage in his desires, Hugh serves as the "castrated" and therefore incomplete male. Hugh manifests his sexuality in two distinct ways. First, he partakes in photographing "peasant nudes" in order to build his private collection of pornography. Second, he confines Catherine in a rusty chastity belt the quartet finds in a deserted cave to prevent her union with Cyril. What Cyril takes to be Hugh's sexual impotence eventually ends in Hugh's accidental suicide from auto-erotic asphyxiation, an event that precipitates Catherine's catatonia and Fiona's departure to care for Meredith. While he prides himself on his role as a "sex singer," this dissolution of the quartet reveals Cyril's ironic inability to account for sexuality in all guises.

Like Hugh, Allert Vanderveenan in *Death, Sleep and the Traveler* experiences much of his erotic stimulation through pornographic imagery. The novel manifests Hawkes' typical technique of narrative fragmentation with the use of numerous short segments chronologically disjoined to narrate events occurring in two locales: his land home and a cruise on which Allert embarks. In each locale Allert participates in a *menage à trois*, reluctantly on land with Ursula and his best friend and therapist, Peter, and exuberantly at sea with the diminutive Ariane and the ship's wireless operator, Olaf. Through the presentation of these locales, Hawkes sets up

the dichotomy between motion and stasis, between life and death, and reveals male psychological fears concerning impotence, performance, and endowment. Over the course of the novel, Allert attempts to emotionally exonerate himself from the death of Ariane, of whose murder he has been acquitted, and through Allert's narration, Hawkes explores societal experience of repression and guilt in the arenas of sexuality and the consequent human need to control desire.

Travesty (1979) narrates a short murder-suicide ride in narrator Papa's car. Accompanying Papa are his daughter, Chantal, and her boyfriend, the poet Henri, who has been having an affair with Papa's wife, Honorine. The themes of marital infidelity and male control over sexual expression emerge in Papa's first person narration. This novel, however, takes the male desire for control to its extreme of insecurity through the murder-suicide plot, which suggests the toll inherent upon the suppression of erotic desire in marriage. While the erotic lives of all the characters prior to marriage find locution, the act of marital infidelity finally cannot be countenanced within the narrative.

Hawkes turns to an attempt to liberate female sexuality in his next two novels. While *The Passion Artist* (1979) tells the story of Konrad Vost's sexual awakening, Hawkes moves to third person narration to explore Vost's encounter with feminine sexuality. Vost, along with other men in the community La Violaine, attempt to quell a riot at the women's prison for which the community is named. During the altercation, Vost participates in brutal, disfiguring violence against some of the women, giving narrative voice to subconscious erotic desires that transgress into violence. Despite the men's efforts, the women prevail and Vost becomes himself prisoner in La Violaine. In his prison cell, he encounters writing on the walls indicating that women, too, sustain violent erotic fantasies. The prison experience constitutes Vost's awakening to the vagaries of sexuality, and suggests for many critics the liberation of female sexuality and desire because the women claim power and Vost experiences subjugation.

The same power over sexuality is granted to Virginie, the narrator of the *Virginie: Her Two Lives* (1981), because as voyeuristic witness and narrator of scenes of sexuality, she controls the reader's perception of sexuality. Eleven-year-old

Virginie recounts her two lives, one in 1740 when in the home of Seigneur she witnesses the training of women to be mistresses to members of the aristocracy and the other in 1945 where she recounts "charades of love" in the Parisian home of her brother Bocage. While the novel presents sexuality from the female perspective utilizing a diminutive, girlish figure resonant within the Hawkesian oeuvre, the reader experiences female sexuality only voyeuristically as Virginie never engages in sex. Despite the successful depiction of female *subjectivity*, this voyeuristic approach to narration ultimately signals the male authorial inability to enter feminine *sexuality* and therefore functions adroitly as Hawkes' final foray into explorations of the erotic.

Biography

John Clendennin Burne Hawkes, Jr. was born on August 17, 1925 in Stamford, Connecticut, and spent his youth in Connecticut and Alaska. Hawkes entered Harvard University in 1943, but soon failed out and served as an ambulance driver in Italy and Germany during World War II, 1943–1945. After the war, Hawkes returned to Harvard where he earned his B.A. in 1949. Hawkes worked for Harvard, first for the University Press (1949–1955) and then as an instructor for three years. In 1958, Hawkes became a professor in the English Department at Brown University in Providence, Rhode Island, where he worked until his retirement in 1988. Hawkes married Sophie Tazewell in 1947 and the couple had four children. Over the course of his career, Hawkes was awarded a Guggenhiem and a Ford Foundation Fellowship, grants from the National Institute of Arts and Letters and from the Rockefeller Foundation, and a Lannan Foundation Award. He utilized his prize monies to support travel to the various locales comprising the settings for his novels, including the West Indies, France, and Italy. His novel *Second Skin* (1964) was runner-up for a National Book Award and *The Blood Oranges* (1971) received the Paris Prix du Meilleur Livre Etranger. Hawkes was a member of the American Academy of Arts and Letters. Hawkes died during heart bypass surgery in a Providence hospital on May 15, 1998, four days after having suffered a stroke.

JON ROBERT ADAMS

Selected Works

The Blood Oranges. New York: New Directions, 1970.
Death, Sleep and the Traveler. New York: New Directions, 1973.
Travesty. New York: New Directions, 1976.
The Passion Artist. New York: Harper and Row, 1978.
Virginie: Her Two Lives. New York: Harper and Row, 1981.

Further Reading

Allen, C.J. "Desire, Design and Debris: The Submerged Narrative of John Hawkes' Recent Trilogy." In *Modern Fiction Studies,* (Winter 1979–1980): 579–592.
Busch, Frederick. *John Hawkes: A Guide to His Fictions.* Syracuse, NY: Syracuse University Press, 1973.
Ferrari, Rita. *Innocence, Power, and the Novels of John Hawkes.* Philadelphia, PA: University of Pennsylvania Press, 1996.
Greiner, Donald J. *Comic Terror: The Novels of John Hawkes.* Memphis, TN: Memphis State University Press, 1973.
Greiner, Donald J. *Understanding John Hawkes.* Columbia, SC: University of South Carolina Press, 1985.
Kuehl, John. *John Hawkes and the Craft of Conflict.* New Brunswick, NJ: Rutgers University Press, 1975.
Murphy, Peter F. "Male Heterosexuality in John Hawkes' *The Passion Artist.*" In *Fictions of Masculinity: Crossing Cultures, Crossing Sexualities,* ed. Peter F. Murphy. New York: New York University Press, 1974.
O'Donnell, Patrick. *John Hawkes.* Boston: Twayne, 1982.

HAWKESWORTH, JOHN

1720–1773
British writer, moralist, editor and translator

Almoran and Hamet

Hawkesworth originally wrote the oriental tale *Almoran and Hamet* (1761) as a play, but its exotic trappings proved too costly to stage. The dedication to King George III places the tale in the tradition of fictional works of advice to princes like Fénelon's *Aventures de Télémaque*, which Hawkesworth later translated. The self-control of Hamet, who faces off against his evil twin Almoran, provides a model of princely behavior. Yet the eroticism of magically trading bodies with another (and thus of experiencing sexual pleasures reserved for one's twin) undermines the tale's explicit moral lesson about "the suppression of desire" through rational self-mastery.

Mixing "oriental" ornament with a calculated elevation of tone, the story begins with the death of the old king who has decreed that his twin sons share rulership of Persia. Raised to value the "prerogative of his birth," the older of the twins, the "volatile, impetuous and irascible" Almoran, initially dissimulates his hatred of Hamet, immersing himself in sensual pleasures while surrounding himself with flatterers. Accustomed to deferring to his twin, the "gentle, courteous and temperate" Hamet lives a regulated life while serving the people. Both subscribe to a system of laws proposed by the wise Omar, who seeks to quash Almoran's tyranny and stimulate Hamet's submerged capacities for leadership.

This equilibrium reaches a crisis when Hamet rescues Almeida, the incomparably beautiful daughter of the Circassian ambassador, from a palace fire. Resisting an initial temptation to ravish her while she is unconscious, Hamet proclaims, "I do not want a slave, but a friend; not merely a woman, but a wife . . . if her mind corresponds with her form, and if . . . she can give her heart to Hamet, and not merely her hand to the king; I shall be happy." Giving one's heart to Hamet proves difficult indeed in a tale in which mind and body constantly shift out of proper correspondence.

Predictably, Almoran wants Almeida because she belongs to his brother: "with dominion undivided and Almeida, I should be Almoran; but without them, I am less than nothing." A "Genie" appears to Almoran and promises to help him achieve his desires. At the marriage of Hamet and Almeida, an ominous voice declares from the thick of a cloud that "Fate has decreed to Almoran, Almeida." Nonetheless, Omar persuades the people that the tyrannical Almoran has deployed occult forces and Hamet receives popular acclaim. The Genie then counsels Almoran to go before the people where a mysterious voice proclaims him king. The credulous masses reverse their position, Hamet flees, and Almoran claims his prize. Almeida resists, arguing that God has not made her love Almoran and so cannot have willed her to be his; God cannot have condemned her to "a joyless prostitution."

The Genie presents the frustrated Almoran with a magic talisman enabling him to exchange forms with another person. Assuming the appearance of Hamet, Almoran enjoys Almeida's passionate caresses, but she refuses to have sex outside of marriage despite all his persuasion. Reacting to his dishonorable arguments, she reflects that the ominous voice assigning her to Almoran must have been divine rather than occult. Since he still bears the form of Hamet, however, Almoran cannot take advantage of her change of heart.

When the exiled Hamet realizes that he looks like Almoran, he returns to court. Almeida greets him as Almoran, declaring that she is ready to marry him. Hamet registers her apparent betrayal and, consumed by desire for her and hatred of his brother, considers marrying and taking her while still in the form of Almoran. Conquering his passions, however, he reveals who he actually is. At that very moment, Almoran reassumes his own form in order to marry Almeida, so Hamet is transformed before

Almeida's eyes. Almoran then finds the two lovers reconciled, imprisons Hamet, and despairs of ever possessing Almeida.

The Genie invites Almoran to present Hamet with a means of committing suicide. Almoran, who has taken on the form of one of two subaltern rivals in order to deliver a dagger, is poisoned by the other, while Hamet resists the temptation to kill himself. At last suspicious of the Genie, whose every gift has stymied him, the dying Almoran hides in Hamet's prison and overhears the Genie presenting Hamet with a magic scroll that will allow him to invoke a secret life-giving lamp. As Hamet wavers over the morality of employing occult forces, Almoran assumes the form of Omar and steals the scroll in order to save his own life. Just as Almoran is transfixed into stone, the Genie reappears, revealing that he is in fact a divine emissary commissioned to "perfect virtue" and "entangle vice."

Almoran and Hamet has sometimes been framed as a lesser work in imitation of Samuel Johnson's *Rasselas* (1759). The genre of oriental tale to which both tales belong has often been dismissed in traditional criticism as a curious but passing fashion or, following the work of Edward Said, assimilated to the larger category of western Orientalist cultural discourse.

Current reevaluations view the oriental tale, for all its orientalism, as a popular early transnational genre contrasting with the self-conscious formation of national identity in the novel (Aravamudan), forming "a counterpart of sorts to the great male tradition" represented by the *Aeneid* and its rewritings (Mack), and acting a privileged site for materialist thought about bodily drives. Within this context, *Almoran and Hamet* may be seen as a text which, through its thematics of twinning, impersonation, and brotherly voyeurism, unwittingly undoes mind–body dualism in favor of a new psychology of self conceived as the performance of the other and as contingent on the incorporation of the other's desires. By presenting lawful and unlawful possession of a woman as an allegory for just rule or tyranny and as a talisman for differentiating the divinely chosen ruler from the pretender, the tale also hopelessly eroticizes the body politic in a move typical of the eighteenth-century oriental tale. Against the tale's own grain, the populace that gives its hand freely and that which is condemned to a "joyless prostitution" ultimately amount to identical twins. Only mildly sexualized by the standards set by the eighteenth-century pornographic novel, and not nearly as explicit in its depictions of sexuality as the notorious Tahitian passages in Hawkesworth's *Account* of voyages to the South Seas, the tale nonetheless erotically trades on the conventions of the exotic harem, the dynamics of sexual dominance and subordination, and the provocative theme of inhabiting another's body to perform one's own desire.

Biography

A respected man of letters, Hawkesworth spent most of his life in London and Bromley, Kent. His earliest literary activity in 1741 was as compiler of parliamentary debates and contributor of poetry to the *Gentleman's Magazine,* for which he later became the literary and dramatic editor. With Samuel Johnson, he wrote and edited the periodical *Adventurer* beginning in 1752. His works include plays and adaptations for the stage, moral essays, criticism, and oriental tales that appeared in periodicals, the *Life of Swift* (1755), and the controversial *Account* of eighteenth-century British voyages to the South Pacific (1773). Contemporaries imputed his death in 1773 to disappointment over the damaging reception of the *Account*, which was viewed as improper in its treatments of divine providence and Tahitian sexuality.

PAMELA CHEEK

Editions

Almoran and Hamet; An Oriental Tale. London, H. Payne and W. Cropley, 1761; London, Harrison and Co, 1786, 1790, 1803; Burlington, N.J., David Allinson, 1808; Reprint of 1761 edition, New York and London: Garland Publishing, 1974.

Selected Works

Hawkesworth, Samuel Johnson, et al. *The Adventurer.* 1752–1754.
Amphitryon (alteration of Dryden's work). 1756.
Oroonoko (rewriting of Southerne's stage adaptation of Behn's novel). 1759.
Edgar and Emmeline. 1761.
Life of Swift. 1766.
Adventures of Telemachus (translation of Fénelon's *Les aventures de Télémaque*). 1768.

An Account of the Voyages . . . by Commodore Byron, Captain Wallis, Captain Carteret, And Captain Cook. 3 vols., 1773.

Further Reading

Abbott, John Lawrence. *John Hawkesworth: Eighteenth-Century Man of Letters.* Madison, WI: University of Wisconsin Press, 1982.

Aravamudan, Srinivas. "In the Wake of the Novel: the Oriental Tale as National Allegory." *Novel* 33 no. 1 (Fall 1999), 5–31.

Caracciolo, Peter L., ed. *The Arabian Nights in English Literature: Studies in the Reception of the Thousand and One Nights into British Culture.* London: Macmillan, 1988.

Cheek, Pamela. *Sexual Antipodes: Enlightenment Globalization and the Placing of Sex.* Stanford, CA: Stanford University Press, 2003.

Conant, Martha Pike. *The Oriental Tale in England in the Eighteenth Century.* 1908; New York: Octagon Books, Inc., 1966.

Kolb, Gwin. *Rasselas and Other Tales.* New Haven, CT, 1990.

Mack, Robert L. "Introduction." *Oriental Tales.* Oxford and New York: Oxford University Press, 1992.

Mayo, Robert D. *The English Novel in the Magazines, 1740–1815.* Evanston, IL; Northwestern University Press, 1962.

HAWTHORNE, NATHANIEL

1804–1864
American novelist

The Scarlet Letter

Originally hailed as "the most moral book of the age" after its 1850 publication by literary critics, *The Scarlet Letter* appeared at a time when readers were looking for an example of moral and community values. Viewed as a book that encouraged self-restraint and adherence to conventional community values in a non-intrusive manner, *The Scarlet Letter* tackles the need for self-denial and social responsibility in the pitfalls and shortcomings of its main characters, Reverend Arthur Dimmesdale; Hester Prynne; Pearl; and Roger Chillingworth. Seen through the prism of Pearl, the daughter of Dimmesale and Hester, the novel also incorporates the perspectives of Hester, her lover, Dimmesdale, and her husband, Chillingworth, providing a discourse on social, moral, spiritual, and legal legitimacy. From the beginning, the novel follows a clear plan, beginning with the illusion of illicit sex to the accompanying psychological implications of this act, with Reverend Dimmesdale as the exemplar of all socially unacceptable qualities and Hester as the embodiment of public property. Hester, however, did not completely fit the personification of the "fallen woman," since her strength, selflessness, and positivity allows her to overcome her previous actions. Consequently, Hawthorne seems to implicitly encourage readers to condemn Dimmesdale rather than identify with his suffering, which essentially reinforces the nineteenth-century moral conservatism.

Hawthorne struggled to justify romance in a culture of pragmatism; Hester's entrance into the marketplace after her implied illicit act marks her conflicting role. While wearing the scarlet letter "A," signifying the opposing concepts of pride and shame, as well as both achievement and alienation, Hester must play two roles, that of mother and partner in the wake of adultery, in a society that viewed illegitimacy as a moral sin. Puritanical society required public confession of sin before forgiveness, yet, despite the pain of seeing Hester on the scaffold and suffering public humiliation, Dimmesdale could not bring himself to confess his adultery. Tortured by his conscience, Dimmesdale lamented, "...were I an atheist,—a man devoid of conscience,—a wretch with coarse and brutal instincts,—I might have found peace, long ere now." The request for him to speak "drove the blood from his cheek, and made his lips tremulous," which related to Hawthorne's depiction of

Dimmesdale in feminine terms, and the psychological distress led to weight loss and a distrust in his spirituality, reducing him to a "poor, forlorn creature." In contrast, despite the public humiliation in the marketplace, Hester exists in isolation, yet she somehow sustains her strength "without a friend on earth who dared to show himself." She never experienced public conflict, and earned the townspeople's respect with the "blameless purity" of her life. She maintained a subsistence living with her daughter, Pearl, and occasionally took on sewing jobs for the townspeople. Due to her position as an outcast, she somehow regains the townspeople's sense of respect.

Hester's struggle between desire and her culturally conditioned sense of social responsibility is very much a physical expression, and she uses her body as a stage for her sexuality. For example, Hawthorne describes her "art" of sewing for the townspeople, in which Hester's hands are described as repeatedly moving to her lap. Hawthorne, in his discussion of this scene, tactfully diverts the reader's attention from Hester's "sinful hands" used to touch "the spot [which] never grew callous; it seemed, on the contrary, to grow more sensitive with daily torture." This description, while not explicitly sexual, does suggest that Hester is still a sexualized being. Her clothing, normally a coarse gray cloth, was interrupted by the scarlet "A," which revealed a sense of autoeroticism. When she emerged from prison, for example, this reflected her own emergence from a physical confinement, as well as an emotional, spiritual, and sexual confinement.

While *The Scarlet Letter* may be interpreted as the rise of Hester from ruin and the demise of Dimmesdale from moral superiority, the novel can also be described as the tale of Chillingworth's fall and redemption, as well as his efforts to claim Pearl as his child. The reader's first view of Chillingworth, seen through the filter of Hester's disgust, is his appearance in the marketplace after a two-year absence. Hawthorne describes his reaction as one of repulsion, manifested as a "writhing horror." Incorporating this connection, literary critic T. Walter Herbert defines Chillingworth's reaction as practically masturbatory, with the "snake-like writhing" personifying the "erotic energy invested both in the hidden feelings and in the compulsion to

keep them concealed." Herbert contends that Chillingworth's reaction imitates Hester's sexual transgression. In many ways, Hawthorne deals with Chillingworth ambivalently, although he does give Chillingworth a name, "Roger," that was a colonial epithet for adulterous intercourse or rape, and provide Chillingworth with a new name, the pseudonym Chillingworth, in substitution for his given name, Prynne.

Self-recognition plays an important role in *The Scarlet Letter*, including Chillingworth's attempts to gain recognition from the daughter he tries to claim as his own. In his first attempt, when Pearl is three years old and refuses to be catechized by the Puritan elders, and Hester could potentially lose her daughter, she refuses the assistance of Chillingworth. In the second attempt, four years later, while Pearl and Hester stand at midnight with Dimmesdale, Pearl twice withdraws her hand from Dimmesdale's hand to point at Chillingworth, and it is in this scene that Dimmesdale first conceives of Chillingworth as an "arch-fiend." After this scene, when Hester confronts Chillingworth on the shore, he undergoes a sort of spiritual awakening. Both Chillingworth and Dimmesdale look at Pearl, perhaps dreading what image they would see reflected in Pearl's eyes. Hester does the same, expecting to see Dimmesdale's reflection, but instead seeing Chillingworth, suggesting that perhaps a solid family unit would be important. Yet, by leaving Pearl without a father, Hawthorne confronts illegitimacy and self-doubt. In the scene in which Dimmesdale acknowledges his daughter, Pearl kissed her father's lips, and "a spell was broken." His confession, however, is only part of the attempt to establish legitimacy for Pearl. The kiss may have enabled her to become a woman, but it is not until she inherits Chillingworth's legacy of his estate in England that she comes into her own as a woman. This, in many ways, further destroys Dimmesdale's reputation, and provides legitimacy to Chillingworth.

Similarly, the conclusion of *The Scarlet Letter* is fraught with meaning; Hester seems to have perfected an image of self-denial and has become the woman to whom many of the townspeople brought their complaints. Where she was once the pariah for her lack of self-constraint, Hester is now the model of restraint, counseling others on the importance of social conformity.

Biography

Nathaniel Hawthorne was born on July 4, 1804, in Salem, Massachusetts. After graduating from Bowdoin College he tried unsuccessfully to make a living as a writer. In 1942, Hawthorne married Sophia Peabody and moved to Concord, where he was introduced to the Transcendentalist circle that included Ralph Waldo Emerson and Henry David Thoreau. More lean times followed, forcing a return to Salem. Success finally came with the publication of the hugely popular *The Scarlet Letter* (1850) and *The House of the Seven Gables* (1851). Hawthorne died on May 19, 1864, in Plymouth, New Hampshire on a trip to the mountains with his friend, former President Franklin Pierce.

JENNIFER HARRISON

Further Reading

Coleman, Robert Lloyd. "The Rhetoric of American Fiction: Figures of Romance." New Brunswick, NJ: Rutgers University, May 1998. Ph.D. dissertation.

Egan, Ken. "The adulteress in the market-place: Hawthorne and *The Scarlet Letter*." *Studies in the Novel* 27.1 (Spring 1995): 26–42.

Herbert, T. Walter. *Dearest Beloved: The Hawthornes and the Making of a Middle-Class Family*. Berkeley: The University of California Press, 1993.

Johnson, Merri Lisa. "Fallen Women, Joyful Girls: The Liberatory Female Body in Nineteenth- and Twentieth-Century American Literature." Ph.D. dissertation. Binghampton: State University of New York, 2000.

HAYWOOD, ELIZA

c.1693–1756
English novelist

Eliza Haywood, dubbed the "Great arbitress of passion" by contemporary James Sterling, was perhaps the most successful writer of sensational amatory fiction in Britain in the 1720s. Her work has enjoyed considerable critical attention since the 1980s, though for generations she was chiefly familiar as an object of Alexander Pope's satire in *The Dunciad* (1728), in which she is offered— "Two babes of love close clinging to her waist" (II. 158)—to the winner of a pissing contest: "His be yon Juno of majestic size,/With cowlike udders, and with ox-like eyes" (II. 163—164). In a note, Pope justifies this attack by identifying her as the "authoress of ... most scandalous books."

Haywood was one of the most popular authors of her time. Her career spanned four decades and she produced more than 80 texts— although she at times published anonymously and no full list exists—in an astonishing array of genres, novels, shorter prose, essays, plays, and conduct literature among them. *The Female Spectator* (1744–1746), which she published anonymously, was one of the first English periodicals by women, for women. Of particular interest is her amatory fiction, a genre distinguished from erotic narrative by its emphasis on subjectivity, and from romance by its emphasis on sexuality. Her first novel, *Love in Excess* (1719–1720) was, with Defoe's *Robinson Crusoe*, arguably one of the two most popular novels of the early eighteenth century. She followed with 38 original works in the following decade, most of them short novels—"secret histories"—following the French model. Her novella "Fantomina" (1725), the story of a young woman who successfully disguises herself in various ways in order to maintain a connection with an inconstant man, is frequently anthologized. She is credited, with Delarivier Manley, of developing the novel of seduction in English (Spencer). Often framed as "scandalous memoirs," these episodic narratives of innocence defrauded frequently criticize courtly culture, with their middle-class heroines and upper-class heroes, and contemporary politics, with sexual libertines standing in for corrupt politicians.

Through most of the 1730s, Haywood concentrated on the theater, then she returned to prose fiction in the 1740s. It has been suggested that attacks such as Pope's temporarily drove her from publishing, but it would seem that she instead was drawn to the stage, at least until the political situation under Walpole made a theatrical career difficult. In the 1740s and 50s, Haywood turned to writing didactic novels such as *The History of Miss Betsy Thoughtless* (1751), but with its plain language and frank depictions of pregnancy and prostitution, even this unexceptionable narrative is considerably racier than the novels of female education of subsequent decades. Later generations, while rejecting her more unregenerate contemporaries, lauded Haywood for having "repented of her faults" (Reeve, 285), though it is generally agreed now that rather than "reforming," Haywood was particularly attuned to the nuances of the literary marketplace. This interpretation is supported by recent scholarship which identifies Haywood as a translator of Crébillon fils's erotic novel, *Le Sopha, conte moral*, as late as 1742 (Spedding).

During her lifetime and following, Haywood was seen as a successor to Aphra Behn and Delarivier Manley in "the fair triumvirate of wit," all of whom were women writers considered expert in love. Her critical reputation waned over the nineteenth century until her reclamation by feminists, in the twentieth century, as a "mother of the novel" (Spender). More recently she has been studied for her contributions to popular literature, her attacks on the sexual double standard, her interweaving of political satire with amatory fiction, her representations of female desire and subjectivity, and her "creation of environments radiant with the possibility of transgression and provocatively in counterpoint to [her] explicit moral arguments" (Pettit, 244).

Biography

Haywood is reported to have instructed her friends not to reveal details about her life, "from a supposition of some improper liberties being taken with her character after death, by the intermixture of truth and falsehood with her history" (Blouch, 545). As a consequence there is little reliable information about her, though recent research has uncovered new material and exposed the falsity of some long-standing stories, such as the rumor that Haywood was the runaway wife of a minister (Blough, Beasley). Her life after she became published is better documented, though many questions remain. She would seem to have had an unusually good education for a woman, as she published various translations; she made her acting debut 1715; she was arrested in 1749 for publishing political works; she had liaisons with Richard Savage and William Hachett, the former who referred to her in print as "a cast-off dame" and the latter with whom she lived for twenty years. She was an active member of a busy literary circle and had connections to Henry Fielding and other notable writers of the day. At the end of her life, although a successful writer herself and rumored to be wealthy, her death duties remained unpaid.

MIRIAM JONES

References

Beasley, Jerry C. "Introduction." In *The Injur'd Husband; or, the Mistaken Resentment* and *Lasselia; or, The Self-Abandon'd*. Lexington, KY: University Press of Kentucky, 1999.

Blouch, Christine. "Eliza Haywood and the Romance of Obscurity." In *Studies in English Literature* 31 (1991): 535–551.

Pettit, Alexander. "Adventures in Pornographic Places: Eliza Heywood's Tea-Table and the Decentering of Moral Argument." In *Papers on Language and Literature: A Journal for Scholars and Critics of Language and-Literature*, 38.3 (Summer 2002): 244–69.

Reeve, Clara. From *The Progress of Romance, through Times, Countries, Manners*, 1785, *Love in Excess; or, the Fatal Enquiry*. Eliza Haywood. Edited by David Oakleaf, 2nd ed., Peterborough, Ont: Broadview, 2000.

Spedding, Patrick. "Shameless Scribbler or Votary of Virtue? Eliza Haywood, Writing (and) Pornography in 1742." In *Women Writing, 1550–1750*, edited by Jo Wallwork and Paul Salzman, Bundoora, Australia: Meridian, 2001.

Spencer, Jane. *The Rise of the Woman Novelist: From Aphra Behn to Jane Austen*. Oxford: Basil Blackwell, 1986.

Spender, Dale. *Mothers of the Novel*. New York: Pandora, 1986.

Reprints of Haywood's Works

The Adventures of Eovaai: Princess of Ijaveo. Edited by Earla Wilputte, Peterborough, Ont: Broadview, 1999.

Anti-Pamela. In Anti-Pamela *and* Shamela. Edited by Catherine Ingrassia. Peterborough, Ont: Broadview, 2004.

The British Recluse in *Popular Fiction by Women 1660–1730*. Edited by Paula R. Backscheider and John J. Richette. New York: Oxford UP, 1996.

The Distress'd Orphan; or, Love in a Mad-House. New York: AMS/Augustan Reprint Society, 1995.

Fantomina and *Other Works*. Edited by Alexander Pettit, Margaret Case Croskery, and Anna C. Patchias. Peterborough, Ont: Broadview, 2004.

The History of Miss Betsy Thoughtless. Edited by Christine Bloch. Peterborough, Ont: Broadview, 1998.

The Injur'd Husband; or, the Mistaken Resentment and *Lasselia; or, The Self-Abandon'd*. Edited by Jerry C. Beasley. Lexington: University Press of Kentucky, 1999.

Love in Excess; or, the Fatal Enquiry. Edited by David Oakleaf. 2nd ed. Peterborough, Ont: Broadview, 2000.

The Masquerade Novels of Eliza Haywood. Edited by Mary Anne Schofield. Delmar, NY: Scholars' Facsimiles and Reprints, 1986.

Miscellaneous Writings, 1725–1743. Edited by Alexander Pettit. London: Pickering and Chatto, 2000.

Selected Fiction and Drama of Eliza Haywood. Edited by Paula R. Backscheider. New York: Oxford University Press, 1999.

Selected Works of Eliza Haywood. Edited by Alexander Pettit. 6 vols. London: Pickering and Chatto, 2000–2001.

Selections from The Female Spectator *by Eliza Haywood*. Edited by Patricia Meyer Spacks. New York: Oxford University Press, 1999.

Three Novellas. Edited by Earla A. Wilputte. East Lansing, MI: Colleagues Press, 1995.

Further Reading

Backscheider, Paula. "The Shadow of an Author: Eliza Haywood." *Eighteenth-Century Fiction* 11.1 (Oct. 1998): 79–102.

Ballaster, Ros. *Seductive Forms: Women's Amatory Fiction from 1684–1740*. Oxford: Clarendon, 1992.

Benedict, Barbara M. "The Curious Genre: Female Inquiry in Amatory Fiction." in *Studies in the Novel*, 30.2 (Summer 1998): 194–210.

Black, Scott. "Trading Sex for Secrets in Haywood's *Love in Excess*." In *Eighteenth-Century Fiction* 15.2 (Jan. 2003): 207–226.

Bowers, Toni O'–Shaughnessy. "Sex, Lies, and Invisibility: Amatory Fiction from the Restoration to Mid-Century." In *The Columbia History of the British Novel*. Edited by John Richetti, New York: Columbia UP, 1994.

Collins, Margo. "Eliza Haywood's Cross-Gendered Amatory Audience." In *Eighteenth-Century Women: Studies in Their Lives, Work, and Culture*. 2 (2002): 43–60.

Hollis, Karen. "Eliza Haywood and the Gender of Print." *The Eighteenth Century*, 38.1 (1997): 43–62.

Ingrassia, Catherine. "Fashioning Female Authorship in Eliza Haywood's *The Tea-Table*." In *The Journal of Narrative Technique*. 28.3 (Fall 1998): 287–304.

King, Kathryn R. "Spying upon the Conjurer: Haywood, Curiosity, and 'the Novel' in the 1720s." In *Studies in the Novel*, 30.2 (Summer 1998): 178–93.

Nestor, Deborah J. "Virtue Rarely Rewarded: Ideological Subversion and Narrative Form in Haywood's Later Fiction." In *Studies in English Literature*, 34 (1994): 579–598.

Potter, Tiffany. "'A God-Like Sublimity of Passion': Eliza Haywood's Libertine Consistency." In *Eighteenth-Century Novel*, 1 (2001): 95–126.

Saxton, Kirsten T. and Rebecca P. Bocchicchio, editor. *The Passionate Fictions of Eliza Haywood: Essays on Her Life and Work*. Lexington, KY: UP of Kentucky, 2000.

Schofield, Mary Anne. *Eliza Haywood*. Boston: Twayne, 1985.

———. *Quiet Rebellion: The Fictional Heroines of Eliza Fowler Haywood*. Washington, DC: UP of America, 1982.

Spedding, Patrick. *A Bibliography of Eliza Haywood*. London: Pickering and Chatto, 2004.

HECHT, BEN AND BODENHEIM, MAXWELL

Hecht, Ben

1893–1964

Bodenheim, Maxwell

1892–1954
American novelists, poets, and playwrights

Cutie: A Warm Momma

Maxwell Bodenheim describes this brief narrative as a "satire on ultra-prudish hypocritical censors and assailers [sic] of sexual candor and incisiveness in literary and pictorial work. . . ." It was published in 1924; its story spans the years 1922–1930.

In 1922, Covici-McGee published Hecht's *Fantazius Mallare: A Mysterious Oath*. Pascal Covici had just started as a Chicago publisher, and asked Hecht for a book which could be sold by subscription. It was to be attractively printed and illustrated, with the black boards and red end papers which were code for an upscale sex book. Covici wanted the kind of sexual content that would be desirable to people with money and fantasies of being considered avant garde, sexually sophisticated, and aware of the most daring fiction and poetry available. Covici's audience, therefore, was no different from those Sylvia Beach had in Paris for Joyce, or Pino Orioli in Florence for Lawrence and Norman Douglas: collectors, literati, booksellers with trusted customers. All had an interlocking interest for modernism, explicit language, and erotica. *Mallare* was in the decadent style of Huysmans' *A Rebours*. The protagonist is a cynical dandy with no interest in sex. He trains a gypsy girl to adulate him. Frustrated, she gives herself to his servant; only then does he realize he has lost what he most desired, and can never retrieve. Recognizing the result of his alienation from his sexual nature, his grip on sanity weakens.

Impotence and self-lacerating voyeurism are deliciously fascinating vices for prurient imaginations to contemplate—at least, Hecht must have thought so. He was disappointed that no moral guardian arose to censor his novel, the illustrations and decorations for which might easily have offended one. Wallace Smith's work included penises surrounded by thorny branches, and writhing naked figures, apparently modeled after those of Egon Schiele, one of which was obviously having intercourse with a tree. Not even when Covici had copies placed in his bookshop's windows, opened to pages with the most shock value, did the outrage develop.

Finally, postal authorities intercepted copies sent to subscribers and prosecuted. It was a federal case, and if Hecht and Bodenheim had been convicted they might have gone to jail. Hecht had trumpeted his intention to gain an acquittal and then break "the censorship" by suing and therefore bankrupting his accuser, whom he hoped would be John Sumner of the New York Society for the Suppression of Vice, but was more likely to be Philip Yarrow of the Illinois Vigilance Association (Hecht knew considerably less about how obscenity law worked than one would expect for a practicing journalist). He tells us that a dozen fellow writers reneged on promises to testify that he was a serious artist who should be allowed to express himself in language he felt necessary.

Consequently, one look at the solid citizens awaiting jury duty was all it took for him to insist that his lawyer plead *nolle contendre*. He and his illustrator were fined 1,000 dollars each. The guardians of decency could be excused for thinking that the blasphemers had been sent packing with their tails between their legs. And so could the literati who read D.H. Lawrence's contemptuous review: Lawrence opined that the book's text and illustrations, by encouraging titillation, solidified the impression that sex was dirty. Mallare might "hang his [penis] on his nose-end and a [testicle] under each ear, and definitely testify that way that he'd got such appendages, [and] it wouldn't affect me."

Hecht did not give up on *Mallare*, writing a "continuation" (*The Kingdom of Evil*) in 1924. *Cutie*, published the same year, was Hecht and Bodenheim's revenge on the censors. Bodenheim had not yet produced *Replenishing Jessica* or *Georgie May*, for which he was to encounter obscenity charges, but he was well known as a bohemian firebrand poet and reviewer. Hecht was a friend and admirer; the two co-edited *The Chicago Literary Times* and were part of the impressive group of writers and artists who congregated around Covici and McGee's bookshop. The 8,000 word satire, privately printed ("Heckshaw Press"), had appeared in installments in *The Literary Times*. In his Introduction, Bodenheim expresses his hatred for privately-organized decency societies which cannot distinguish between gratuitous vulgarity and art which must, to be honest, include frank depiction of sex and sexual experience in all its varieties and motives. Hecht and Bodenheim personify these censors in Herman Pupick, "a prude with one glass eye and splintered pieces of glass in what passed for his heart." Herman is a federal employee who sniffs out immorality everywhere and anywhere he sees it. As such, he is an amalgam of the postal inspector and the police-deputized agent of an anti-vice group, as were Sumner and Yarrow. In Yiddish, "pupik" means bellybutton. Leo Rosten defines a pupik as an inconsequential person, or "nudnick" (a bore or pest) who worries about what is not worth worrying about. Since "prepice" is the fold of foreskin over the head of an (uncircumcised) penis, Herman is also just a prick.

Herman knew nothing of life when he became besotted with Cutie. He was married, but to a woman who "couldn't pass a bathroom without blushing." Herman first noticed Cutie when she was being helped by a policeman after skinning her knee. He was outraged that the officer was exposing Cutie's leg in public. He's another Willy Wet Leg, ironically similar to Fantazius. Pupick's crusades close down *The Chicago Literary Times*, all the libraries, and the "abdominal belt displays" in the drugstore windows. He also gets rid of many of Chicago's authors, and the bookleggers (actually, he did not get the ones who later pirated *Cutie*). The story ends with Mrs. Pupick, seeing Herman with Cutie and two other flappers, stabs Cutie and Herman with a hat pin. The story is told as if the writers were entertaining fellow customers at Schlogl's, a favorite literary hangout. There are lots of topical references as well as period argot: "lost manhood advertisements," the famous cross-dressing entertainer Julian Eltinge, Gilda Grey, Ruth St. Denis, and Freudian psychoanalysis.

In 1930, the pirate publisher Samuel Roth issued his *roman à clef* about an oppressive censor from New York, *Hugh Wakem: The Diary of a Smuthound*. The smuthound is probably modeled on Sumner. Many titles of banned books are mentioned, as are six booksellers, all of whom are most likely real people with slightly disguised names.

Biographies

Hecht: Important figure in the Chicago Literary Renaissance; writer for the stage and films whose screenplays included *The Front Page* and *A Farewell to Arms*; journalist, activist for Israeli causes; satirist.

Bodenheim: Poet who won early acclaim for his work; novelist, vagabond, literary critic, and brilliant conversationalist who suffered an emotional decline near the end of his life which reduced him to selling verses in Greenwich Village bars. Some important themes in his novels were prostitution, urban life, derelicts. Well

respected by Ezra Pound, Conrad Aiken, William Carlos Williams.

JAY A. GERTZMAN

Editions

Cutie: A Warm Momma. Chicago: Heckshaw Press, 1924; New York: Boar's Head Books [Samuel Roth], 1952.

Selected Works

Hecht

Eric Dorn. 1921.
A Thousand and One Nights in Chicago. 1922.
Count Bruga. 1926.
The Front Page. 1928.
A Jew in Love. 1931.
Twentieth Century. 1932.
A Guide for the Bedeviled. 1944.
Collected Stories. 1945.
Hazel Flagg. 1953.
A Child of the Century (autobiography). 1954.
The Sensualists. 1959.

Bodenheim

Against This Age. 1923.
Replenishing Jessica. 1925.
Georgie May. 1928.
A Virtuous Girl. 1930.
Bringing Jazz! 1930.
Naked on Roller Skates. 1930.
Selected Poems. 1946.

Further Reading

"Ben Hecht, 1893–1964." <http://www.kirjasto.sci.fi/bhecht.htm>
Bisbort, Alan. "Mad Max: Death of a Bohemian King," <http://www.gadfly.org/lastweek/bondenheimfeature.html>
Boyer, Paul. *Purity in Print: The Vice-Society Movement and Book Censorship in America*. New York: Scribner, 1968.
"Fantazius Mallare Walloped for One Row of Ash Cans." *Chicago Literary Review* (15 February 1924): 1–2.
Gertzman, Jay A. *Bookleggers and Smuthounds: The Trade in Erotica, 1920–1940*. New York: University of Pennsylvania Press, 1999.
Moore, Jack B. *Maxwell Bodenheim*. New York: Twayne, 1971.
McAdams, Will. *Ben Hecht: The Man Behind the Legend*. New York: Scribner, 1990.

HERMAPHRODITISM

Hermaphroditism is a word used to denote a condition in which both male and female sexual characteristics are combined in one body. So-called 'perfect hermaphroditism,' in which male and female characteristics co-exist in equal proportions, very rarely exists. Throughout history hermaphroditism has been both real (based on some form of genital irregularity) and imagined (drawing from a range of sexual and social ambiguities). The blurring of male and female has, in many cultures, been celebrated as a spiritual ideal but embodied sexual ambiguity has also provoked fear and many supposedly hermaphroditic individuals have been reviled as monsters.

From eastern celebrations of the mystical eroticism of hermaphroditic sexuality to Antonio Beccadelli's fourteenth century Latin poem, *Hermaphrodite*, hermaphroditism has been the subject of erotica. The erotic allure of sexual ambiguity is encapsulated in a famous series of Hellenistic sculptures that depict 'The Sleeping Hermaphrodite.' Within these images a beautifully ambiguous reclining nude is represented. When viewed from behind, the soft, languid lines of the body appear to be female but when seen from the front a penis comes into view.

The hermaphrodite has often been represented as a primary symbol of sexual union. In Plato's *Symposium* Aristophanes relates how humans were originally created as 'Androgyni,' doubled beings which circled like wheels in a condition of wholeness and perfection until the god, Zeus, grew jealous and spilt them down their centers. Henceforth, the desolate remaining parts of the original whole search the earth for their lost other halves. Plato's text privileged the reunion of male/male parts of the complete original beings but the fable became disseminated in later times as a parable that demonstrated the power of heterosexual love and erotic desire. A similar story emerged within medieval Jewish literature as some mystics believed that Adam was originally hermaphroditic. Heterosexual sex thereby symbolized a return to the primal Edenic moment of unity.

Ovid's story of 'Salmacis and Hermaphroditus' in *Metamorphoses* influenced many subsequent representations of sexual ambiguity, from the Renaissance and beyond. The story relates how Hermaphroditus, the child of Hermes and Aphrodite (or Mercury and Venus), a youth of exceptional beauty, met the nymph Salmacis. Salmacis becomes overwhelmed by her passion for the indifferent Hermaphroditus and forces him to unite in a violent embrace. As Ovid describes it:

> When their limbs met in that single clinging embrace the nymph and the boy were no longer two, but a single form, possessed of a dual nature, which could not be called male or female, but seemed to be at once both and neither. (Ovid, 1955, p.104)

On seeing his transformation into 'half a man,' Hermaphroditus prays to his parents to curse the pool. The prayer is granted and the curse is passed on to all men who enter the pool of Salmacis forever more.

Ovid's representation of the sexually ambiguous, solipsistic youth has resonated throughout artistic and literary history. Hermaphroditus was one of a series of mythical youths who were the consummate objects of erotic appeal (Narcissus, Adonis, Ganymede, and Leander). Such figures were the focus of a particularly homo-erotically charged gaze as they were represented in the visual images of Renaissance artists (such as Correggio's *The Rape of Ganymede*) and the poems of William Shakespeare, Christopher Marlowe, and others. For these artists and poets the aestheticization of young male sexual ambiguity was to be delighted in. The beautiful youth was, as Shakespeare put it in sonnet 20, 'the master-mistress' of their creator's passions.

Hermaphroditism was associated with a number of social transgressions ranging from same-sex erotic desire to effeminacy, transvestism, and sodomy. According to George Sandys, writing in 1632, for example, the fountain of Salmacis was reported to have both effeminized the ancient Carians and led them into various forms of sexual debauchery. Hermaphrodites were accused of deviancy, not because they were of both sexes, but because they "defiled themselves with either" (Sandys, 1632). A later text, *The Wandering Whore*, is even more explicit, describing hermaphrodites as, "effeminate men, men given to much luxury idleness, and wanton pleasures, and to that abominable sin of sodomy, wherein they are both active and passive in it" (anon, 1660).

Throughout the seventeenth century there are a number of case-histories that are reported in medical, paramedical, and legal treatises, as well as in erotica, that connect hermaphroditism in women to the existence of an enlarged clitoris. Many stories of prodigious female members were drawn from stories about exotic and eroticized non-European lands. Writers of medical and paramedical texts exploited the titillating effects of describing how women 'abused' these enlarged members by engaging in tribadic activities with other women. Giles Jacob, for example, (whose *Treatise on Hermaphrodites* was printed in 1718 with Edmund Curll's explicitly erotic *A Treatise of the Use of Flogging at Venereal Affairs*) was typical in his exploration of erotic lesbian escapades.

By the eighteenth century, so-called hermaphrodites were increasingly viewed as objects of scientific scrutiny. But medical enquiry could not always be separated from popular entertainment and during this period many sexually ambiguous individuals were displayed as curiosities. The focus on genital anomalies in hermaphroditic cases inevitably led to ostensibly 'scientific' studies being charged with erotic excitement. During the nineteenth and early-twentieth centuries such displays reached a peak as male–female hybrids such as 'Josephine–Joseph' and 'Robert–Roberta' were regularly shown in 'freak shows' and fairground entertainments.

The late-nineteenth-century sexologists developed a discourse whereby a range of ambiguities in sex and gender were defined as 'pseudo-hermaphroditism' and pathologized. In 1978, Michel Foucault published *Herculine Barbin*, the memoirs of a nineteenth-century hermaphrodite. Foucault presented a dossier of medical and legal documents alongside Herculine's tortured first person account that conveyed the agonies of living with a confused sexual identity. The story of Herculine marked the inception of critical and theoretical interest in exploring histories of marginal lives and erotic identities.

In the early-twentieth century there is still a popular and academic fascination with issues of transsexualism and gender dysphoria. However, sexually ambiguous individuals themselves are now beginning to claim identities as intersexuals rather than accepting the surgical mutilation, pathologization, and erotic objectification that has characterized their representation throughout history.

RUTH GILBERT

Further Reading

Daston, Lorraine and Katharine Park. "The Hermaphrodite and the Orders of Nature: Sexual Ambiguity in Early Modern France." *Gay and Lesbian Quarterly*. 1 (1995): 419–438.

Delcourt, Marie. *Hermaphrodite: Myths and Rites of the Bisexual Figure in Classical Antiquity*. Translated by Jennifer Nicholson. London: Studio Books, 1961.

Epstein, Julia. "Ambiguous Sexes." In *Altered Conditions: Disease, Medicine and Storytelling*. London: Routledge, 1995.

Fiedler, Leslie. "Hermaphrodites." In *Freaks: Myths and Images of the Secret Self*. New York: Simon and Schuster, 1979.

Foucault, Michel, editor. *Herculine Barbin, Being the Recently Discovered Memoirs of a Nineteenth Century French Hermaphrodite*. Translated by Richard McDougall. Harmondsworth, Penguin, 1980.

Gilbert, Ruth. *Early Modern Hermaphrodites: Sex and Other Stories*. Basingstoke: Palgrave, 2002.

Kesler, Suzanne, J. *Lessons from the Intersexed*. New Jersey: Rutgers University Press, 1998.

Laqueur, Thomas. *Making Sex: Body and Gender from the Greeks to Freud*. Cambridge, MA: Harvard University Press, 1990.

Ian McCormick. *Secret Sexualities: A Sourcebook of 17th and 18th Century Writing*. London: Routledge, 1997.

Ovid. *Metamorphoses*. Translated by Mary M. Innes. Harmondsworth: Penguin, 1955.

Sharrock, Cath. "Hermaphroditism; or, 'the Erection of a New Doctrine': Theories of Female Sexuality in Eighteenth-Century England." *Paragraph*. 17 (1994): 34–48.

HERRGOTT, ELISABETH

1947–
French writer

Transports amoureux

The title is a play on words, referring to the metaphoric use of the word 'transport' in the classical French phrase 'transports amoureux,' as clarified by the epigraph, an entry from the *Lexique de la langue du XVIIᵉ siècle*: 'transport amoureux' are 'violent and pleasant agitations of the heart; rushes of love, lust and passion; mislayings of the body and the soul.' The tone is set: the whole book is about 'amorous transports' in both meanings of the word, as erotic scenes are usually set in particular transport contexts, from local buses to inter-continental aeroplanes. Sex with strangers during weekly commuting high-speed train journeys, sex with an air hostess on the way to Rio, sex with a gondolier in Venice: the bisexual female narrator never seems able to travel without initiating or encountering sexual adventures, even in elevators or in the underground.

Transports amoureux is a not a long book: it is composed of twenty-one short sections of four pages on average. The sections can be presented as short stories; their titles are usually explicit about the location: 'Parking' for the section about sex in a car park, 'Transports en commun' for the section about being fingered by unknown hands at rush hour in the underground. One can distinguish between two types of short stories: fifteen are directly about sex and transport together (sex in particular means of transport), six others are about sex without reference to transport. Falling into that latter category is the most intriguing short story, which is also the longest one (nine pages): entitled 'La grande abbesse de l'abbaye de P.,' it presents a filthy nun called Bénédicte de G., her private emasculated priest Ignacio, and their friend Hildegarde. It is not easy to interpret how this short story fits within the overall economy of the book, located as it is

between 'Le 83' (two pages about masturbating a man in the bus 83) and 'Anales Ferroviaires' (seven pages about having sex on the train to Paris).

Elisabeth Herrgott trained as a Lacanian psychoanalyst—and it shows, through some transparent references to youth episodes accounting for bouts of fetishism, such as the young man obsessed by buttons on women's dresses (because his mother was a school teacher who asked him to button up her blouse), or the narrator's discovery of fellatio when, aged nine, she sucked a man (an Indian Catholic priest) in an elevator (Catholicism is a recurrent sub-theme of the book). In terms of sexual activities, other interesting components of *Transports amoureux* are the instances of auditory voyeurism, masturbation with a silver dildo, and lesbian group sex. The overall atmosphere of the book is one of mild decadence, but its voluptuous universe is far from cheap: women always wear Dior perfume and expensive fur-coats (whilst being usually naked under the fur); men are lawyers or scientists who drive a Mercedes or a BMW and eat in the most expensive restaurants; holidays are spent in Brazil or Venice, and one travels first-class in aircrafts or in private yachts.

In terms of erotic literature, one can appreciate the creativity of the author with her witty focus on transportation means, as well as the way some short stories lend themselves well to queer readings, for instance the very last one: entitled 'Dédicace' ('Dedication'), starts with the epigraph 'A Vladimir mon amant lesbian,' [To Vladimir my male lesbian lover] (Vladimir was also mentioned in the 'Postface,' witch came just before the 'Dédicace'; like all other characters in the book, he only has a first name, like Daniele, Germain, Guy, Julien, Juliette...). This fair attempt to start blurring boundaries between sex, gender, and sexuality is another interesting feature of *Transports amoureux*, and Elisabeth Herrgott further develops this in her other books.

Biography

Elisabeth Herrgott, who mainly works as a journalist, has published several books of erotic literature as well as the semi-autobiographic *Mes hiérodules* (2000). That latter book caused an unexpected, dubious, and widely publicized scandal that started in the provincial town of Dole (in the Jura region of France) when local doctors identified a local colleague of theirs as the inspiration for one of the key female characters of the book (a bisexual woman keenly into sado-masochism). They successfully had that highly respected pediatrician suspended for three months, arguing in court that she had failed to follow principles of morality and ethics in her private life. Elisabeth Herrgott narrated that scandal in *Les Sorcières du Val d'Amour* (2003), which made erotic literature enter the public debate in France.

LOYKIE LOÏC LOMINÉ

Selected Works

Le gynécée. 1989.
Lettres d'amour. 1991.
Le dieu et l'amant déchu. 1992.
Transports amoureux. 1994.
L'Amant de la vierge Marie. 1996.
Mes hiérodules. 2000.

HERVÉ, GÉRALD

1928–1998
French novelist and philosopher

Questioning

The question of the masculine Eros runs through Gérald Hervé's novels and philosophical works. In 1956, he described it as "the great and naturally free male principle. Sex. Erect sex. And sperm spurting out in the sun because it is necessary to man." But unlike those in the 1950's who fictionalized homosexuality, Gérald Hervé's Dionysian imagery is the result of constant philosophical questioning. Therefore, this underrated work may be considered as the first where homosexuality "and as an indirect consequence homophobia" are not "doubly secondary problems" (P. Zaoui, "Philosophie" in *Dictionnaire de l'homophobie*, Paris: PUF, 2003). The 1956 quote comes from a text written one year after his expulsion from the Navy for homosexuality. At its source is homophobic violence against what we cannot deny, our being. This leads to the necessity of exceeding the ontological rupture by returning to the source of the repression and to confront one's homosexuality in its singularity. The author completed *Orphée interdit* in 1960. This essay on homosexual phenomenology is not a treaty for eroticism or a hedonistic plea. Some of the theses which are defended in it do lead to homoeroticism which, at the opposite extreme from the theory of androgyny turn the union of the similar into the only way out for the incompleteness of the otherness of the sexes approached from the angle of dominant relationships. The homosexual relationship tends towards psychophysical fusion. Moreover, this essay denounces the neurosis of civilization by installing a complete break between antiquity and Christianity responsible for mad Eros (in the Nietzsche sense). It is not the intention of the author to promote any kind of Greek golden age but is thinking of a way of being a full being before the alienating dualism. He therefore reveals homo-sensual forms of collective sublimation such as the Church or the Army. These erotico-ethical totalities produce some of the most significant characters in novels. The concept of heresy as a necessary product of repressive orthodoxy occupies a central role in it. By indicating and exceeding the world of fault, the homosexual writer is a heretic who proffers

641

truths which are impossible to say or intolerable. The free creation evokes this absolutely free Eros.

Fictionalizing

The drama of 1955 produced the autobiographical statement, which was published in 1971. The transposition of the real begins lately, via several novels that highlight complex characters and situations. In an episode of *Hérésies imaginaires*, the author uses a double metaphor, that of a mutilated soldier of the first world war who yells for having been deprived of his "torch." But Gérald Hervé accords a significant role to the joyful body. We may be tempted to oppose the world of infantile sexuality with that of adults. Faced with their eroticism often covered by pretexts that may not even be able to be decided, adolescent sexuality is lived through figures in games and rituals, in the happy transgression of that which is forbidden, this obstacle that provides an image to desire, which suggests a happy Eros as opposed to the incomplete, frustrated adult Eros. The friendship between Bernard and Philippe in *Le soldat nu* is accomplished through physical love but ends in a sudden break-up; the carefree and happy pederasty of J. Lambègue in *Les feux d'Orion* is threatened; the coitus of Romain Saint-Sulpice and the young Gildas is the peak of eroticism but as the subject of blackmail in an ecclesiastical pedophile scandal in which he becomes indirectly involved, the adult commits suicide. The tragic or disappointing outcomes suggest the curse hanging over male homosexuality. However, we should not look on this as a simple transposition of the drama of 1955. Eros is polymorphic. More than a dichotomy between happy fictional love and unhappy real love, the erotic experiences are indicated by intensity and abnormality. They cannot be the subject of any normative discourse: "In terms of sex, the mere Montmartre fraud knows more than esteemed university professors," he wrote in 1999. The author defines perversity as the meaning of hidden correspondences. On several occasions he recounts the relationship of two men with one woman. This is a figure of a significant relationship of this perversity, which reveals the transversality of homosexual desire. The most heretical of all the figures illustrates the crucial aspect of the theory of homosexuality that was formulated in 1960 as ontological incest: the actions of the father Cham on his son Bohor in *Les hérésies imaginaires*.

Moreover, this novel shows itself to be extraordinarily rich and original in the way it tells of love between children, which takes place away from the eyes of adults. The eroticism which is revealed in the first part culminates in episodes which highlight figures of uninhibited and non-narcissistic adolescent sexuality: homosexual cruising, mutual masturbation, discovery of the erect phallus, heterosexual deflowering, erotic purifications, anal eroticism, substitution of sexual possession by body to body contact or rectal injection. Real and realized fantasy fill up this universe where fear and attraction, pleasure and pain indicate paradoxical forms of erotic intensity: terror caused by ithyphallic beings, fear of castration, ejaculation following flagellation. This freedom culminates in nudity in front of a group of children or adults. The male nudes in the work translate the necessary link, which is also nostalgic love for a lost unity, of beauty and truth. Its end is therefore less sexual pleasure as the search for joy by reconciliation in the eyes of others.

Genital coitus constitutes above all a polymorphic, even queer figure of sexuality or an initiatory cerebra-sensorial experience mode, thus, the magnificent deflowering scene between Cyril and Barbara in les *Hérésies imaginaires*. But anal coitus is the subject of the strongest narrations. The last novel, *Les aventures de Romain Saint-Sulpice*, dedicated to the under-20s, combines the excremental vision, in the Norman Brown sense, with didactic proselytizing in favor of sodomy. Only this coitus, which is slow and tender, leads to the full accomplishment of male desire. Romain leads about sexual completeness through heterosexual sodomy, then with a boy. This love is perfect but tragic and ephemeral. The comment that Gérald Hervé made to Alberto Moravia, that sex is the key to his work, also applies to his own.

Biography

Gérald Hervé was born in Marseilles, France, December 13, 1928. He studied law and political science in Paris, was awarded a post as Navy officer and initially drafted near to Saigon in September 1954. In May 1955, the victim of an anti-homosexual purge, he spent two months in jail and was dismissed from the Army. He worked in Paris in insurance until he moved to Perros-Guirec (Brittany) in 1971 to teach economic sciences. In 1993, he retired to Nice. He died in Miami, USA, June 06, 1998, from injuries caused in a motorboat accident in Paradise Island (Nassau, Bahamas).

HERVÉ BAUDRY

See also **Gay (Male) Writing**; **Pedophilia/Pederasty**; **Philosophy and Eroticism in Literature**; **Psychoanalysis**; **Queer Theory**; **Religion and Sex**; **Sodomy**

Selected Works

Kerruel, Yves. *des Pavois et des fers*. Paris: Julliard, 1971.
———, *Le soldat nu*. Paris: Julliard, 1974.
Les Hérésies imaginaires. Lausanne: L'Âge d'Homme, 1989.
La nuit des Olympica. Essai sur le national-cartésianisme, Paris: L'Harmattan, vol. 3 et 4, 1999.

Les feux d'Orion. Soignies: Talus d'approche, 2003.
Les aventures de Romain Saint-Sulpice. Soignies: Talus d'approche, 2003.
Orphée interdit. Preceded by *Le Paradis perdu by Pierre Loti* (essay) and *Le Jeune Homme et le soleil ou les hérésies imaginaires* (short story). Soignies: Talus d'approche, 2004.

Further Reading

Hervé Baudry. "Fin d'empire et mac-carthysme sexuel : *Des Pavois et des fers* (1971) by Yves Kerruel ou la chronique d'un drame en Indochine après les accords de Genève" (ASCALF Annual Conference, London, 2001), Amsterdam : Homodok, 2002 (dactylogr.).
"Hervé, Gérald" in *Companion to Modern French Thought*, (ed. Chris Murray), New York: Fitzroy Dearborn, 2004.
"Hétérosexualités queer dans l'œuvre romanesque de Gérald Hervé," in *Masculinités queer*, ed. Lawrence Schehr, Amsterdam: Rodopi, 2005.
"*Les Aventures de Romain Saint-Sulpice* de Gérald Hervé: ballets bleus et tragédie amoureuse" in *Amour, passion, volupté, tragédie : le sentiment amoureux dans la littérature française du Moyen Age au XXIe siècle*, ed. Annye Castonguay and Jean-François Kosta-Thiefaine éd., Anglet: Atlantica-Séguier, 2005.

HISTOIRE D'I

This novella was published in 1974, in the climate of intellectual freedom that followed the "events" of 1968, a time of onslaught against literary conventions and sexual stereotypes. It employs a gender twist to parody formulaic models.

Published the same year as Belen (alias Nelly Kaplan)'s *Mémoires d'une liseuse de draps* [*Memoirs of a Sheet Reader*], *Histoire d'I* is equally literate and shares its basic strategies of reversal, but limits itself to a straightforward caricature. Beyond the title's obvious reference, the story line takes up specific episodes of *Histoire d'O* (1954) and constructs I as O's male counterpart, while relentlessly deflating the programmatic verticality of his name through a systematic inversion of male and female stereotypical positionings. Everything is described from the point of view of I's consciousness, but the author's signature, with its telluric connotations, is that of Gaëtane, the protagonist's tormentor, a fact that underscores her absolute agency, thus diverting the erotic significance of the female signature in pornography.

I, an innocuous, conceited playboy, is picked up by a stunning beauty in a café and becomes her passive prey. Gaëtane takes him to her own car where she initiates some foreplay, and then to her house, a setting where all the slaves are male and whose baroque trompe l'œil will be the stage of I's voyage into loving self-immolation, and physical and mental torture. At once comical, violent, and nauseating, Gaëtane's parody does not spare any aspect of high and low erotic literature. Gaëtane, the dominatrix, is both ultra-feminine and virilized, curvaceous but bristling with a panoply of sharp appendages, starting with her clitoris and her breasts "beautiful like iron and ice." Her monstrous cohort of women, who enthusiastically assist her in I's tormenting, embody menacing fantasies of the feminine: dentate or gaping vaginas, mountains of flesh and spiked heels that crush or pierce I's flesh, in short, engulfing and castrating sexuality.

Betrayed by the intensity of his desire, I fails to satisfy Gaëtane during their first sexual encounter. This introduces the motif of punishment. I understands that he deserves the whipping that Gaëtane instantly administers—not, as in the case of O, for some obscure flaw inscribed in nature—but because, as a man, he has "lost face and made a fool of himself." Nevertheless, the effect is the same: "The punishment did him good, absolved and purified him." I soon realizes that his total submission will take him "beyond the limit" (Bataille) and, like O with Sir Stephen, he accepts the prospect of dying for Gaëtane's sake. Like O, he is put on a leash and, unlike her, made to sleep on a litter; he has to wear high cothurni and must leave his "genital clutter" uncovered and available at all times; and he gratefully suffers Gaëtane's voyeurism of his worst tortures. In a twofold replica of O's labia pierced and chained and her buttocks branded with Sir Stephen's initials, he undergoes circumcision and Gaëtane embroiders her name on his breast, making sure not to forget the two dots on the 'e'. The accumulation of concrete minutiae in this episode points to a *mise en abyme*, from Pauline Réage to Barthes and then to Sade. In *Sade, Fourier, Loyola*, published in 1971, Barthes commented on the detail of he "red thread" with which the daughter sews the mother's vagina in *Philosophy in the Bedroom*. The parody devises all sorts of niceties in Gaëtane's needlework, thus embroidering on Barthes's clever association of *écriture* with sewing ("the sure way to horror is metonymy: the tool is more terrible than the torture").

Direct references to Sade are the roasting of a young boy (an allusion to the roasting of Juliette's daughter in *The Story of Juliette*), followed by the consumption of his penis by the "ogresses"; and the banquet scene, during which some of the slaves are temporarily transfixed into contorted poses thanks to an injection and

have their organs turned into candlesticks and inserted with candles (a function provided by women's vaginas in Sade's novel).

Constantly raped and sodomized by hideous women, when not forced to participate in sodomic "trains" with other slaves, I can achieve an erection only through repeated whippings and finally becomes unusable. After failing to attract any buyer during the slave market which provides an outlet for Gaëtane's discarded slaves, he is free to return to the outside world, but feels incapable of renouncing his voluntary servitude. He awaits death, but his punishment will be worse than death: Gaëtane forces him to witness her sexual embrace with another woman: "A woman's pleasure (*jouissance*) with another woman cannot, must not be told. It would burst the world open and would reduce it to powder. The two women did not even bother to cut I's tail. But ... he knew full well that his organ was useless. They did not even look at him. I left with his tail between his legs, as ashamed as a fox ensnared by a hen." (the latter simile a direct quote from La Fontaine's fable "The Fox and the Stork"). With this final burst of laughter, little is left of O's pathetic consent to her own death.

No doubt, beyond the male slant of the porno-/erotic genre, Gaëtane's target is the complacent earnestness that characterized its higher forms even when they were not devoid of humor, as in Klossowski, Bataille, Barthes, and their followers, all harking back to Sade. But *Histoire d'I* at times could pass for "the real thing," in its few lyrical passages and with its medley of ludicrous postures and curvilinear settings—an excellent pastiche of the burlesque vein that runs from the Ancients through Sade to the present. There remains the question of the effectiveness of such a parody, whether in terms of its erotic value or as a feminist satire, or merely as a joke. To this reader at least, the latter are far more potent than the first, an opinion that still leaves open the question of *Histoire d'I*'s readership (and authorship).

LUCIENNE FRAPPIER-MAZUR

Editions

Histoire d'I. Paris: Filipachi, 1974, 89 p.; 2nd edition Paris: Éd. Blanche, 2001.

HOUELLEBECQ, MICHEL

1958–
French novelist and poet

Les particules élémentaires

Michel Houellebecq's *Les particules élémentaires* proved to be one of the most controversial French novels of the 1990s. The storm this book provoked was rapidly christened the "Houellebecq Affair," and was largely the result of three elements: the novel's highly charged sexuality coupled with its deep-seated pessimism concerning contemporary Western society, and the author's penchant for the outrageous interview statement. In a conversation with a reporter from the distinguished French newspaper, *Le Monde,* Houellebecq once expressed his admiration for Stalin because "he killed lots of anarchists" (Van Reuterghen). With comments such as this, along with his apparent distrust of France's immigrant population, Houellebecq fueled the arguments surrounding his novel, and in doing so, positioned himself as a latter-day Céline.

Les particules élémentaires is the story of two half-brothers who try to come to terms with their lives in contemporary, post-May '68 France. They were both in their early teens in 1968, and thus were not active in the strikes and demonstrations during the spring of that year. Yet each in his own way must experience what the novel portrays as the dire consequences of the break with tradition and a new, uncontrolled liberalism.

As the novel begins the brothers are facing their early forties. Michel is a biologist utterly lacking in affect, yet a brilliant researcher. Part of the disturbing effect Michel's theories have on readers comes from the apparent verisimilitude of the description of his scientific activities. This is largely due to Houellebecq's own scientific background and knowledge. Before becoming a writer, he trained as an agronomist and received a diploma in that discipline in 1980. Michel's half-brother, Bruno, is a hedonistic high school literature teacher who tries to find solace, if not meaning, in unbridled sexuality. Their mother, Janine, who later Americanizes her name to Jane after a period in a California hippy community, is a trained physician who becomes a counter-culture fanatic; over the course of the novel she experiments with an impressive number of alternative religions, life styles, and men. Just before her death she converts to Islam, much to Bruno's chagrin.

Bruno is the sexual center of the novel. Obsessed with women, particularly young ones, and by the smallness of his phallus, he turns out to be, in an age of putative sexual liberation, a spectacularly unsuccessful seducer. He winds up mostly paying for the sexual release he so desperately seeks. However, his erotic misadventures take place against the background of the new sexual permissiveness in post-May '68 France. He visits Paris's sex clubs, participates with indifferent results in the sex parties, *les partouzes*, springing up all over France, and fails as a husband and father. Bruno's fixation with all things sexual eventually costs him his job, when he is removed from the school where he works for making advances to a teenage Arab girl. Another nasty offshoot of Bruno's frenzied pursuit of sexual release is his burgeoning racism. His contempt for young African males stems from his conviction that their penises are larger than his own.

Bruno's luck changes briefly when he spends time at the Espace du possible [the Space of the Possible]. This is a New Age vacation spot run by former and would-be hippies who shrewdly exploit the younger generation's (forty and below) desire for casual sex coupled with self-help seminars; this is a place where a "sensitive gestaltmassage" can be followed by fellatio. At the Espace du Possible a chance encounter changes Bruno's life. He meets Christiane, a woman in her early forties, with whom he has sex and discovers love. Together they plunge into a world of sexual licence, the clubs, *les partouzes*, etc., but this time Bruno mostly enjoys himself. For the first time he is relatively at ease with his life and his world. Unfortunately, his happiness is short-lived. Christiane falls victim of a non-sexually transmitted disease and dies painfully. Bruno's only recourse is to check himself into a mental institution.

Unlike his brother, Michel has practically no libido. He is all intellect; his sexual experiences are scant, and occur with little pleasure and less emotion. Yet Michel is a very successful biologist who has done distinguished research on cloning. As a youth he was a very close friend to a beautiful girl named Annabelle, but this adolescent romance went nowhere. At forty Michel takes a sabbatical leave from his research institution, and during this period he meets Annabelle again. They try being together, but the effort is a failure. Annabelle's effort to have a child with Michel results only in the discovery that she has ovarian cancer. When the cancer metastasizes, she commits suicide. Michel then takes leave from his research facility, and accepts a position in Ireland where he continues his work on cloning. It is in this setting that he will also take his life, but not before developing theories that will lead to the creation of a new race that will be asexual and immortal. When the novel ends in 2029 this new breed has largely replaced the older, human model.

Houellebecq uses sex in *Les Particules élémentaires* as a metaphor for all that is wrong in post-May '68 France and, by extension, the Western world. Unbridled sexual licence signals the collapse of traditional moral values, while it remains at the same time the only source of pleasure, and the sole means of briefly escaping life's total meaninglessness. Bruno's activities represent the pathetic attempt to be part of this new age, while Michel's scientific activities constitute an effort to curtail the era's horrors. One brother struggles to accept the contemporary world, while the other labors to reject it. Yet in the end they both fall victim to a world wherein they can find no place for themselves.

Biography

Born in 1958 on the island of the Reunion. He published his first book, a biography of H.P. Lovecraft in 1991. He has written essays, poetry, and novels. He received the Tristan Tzara Prize for his first collection of poetry, *La poursuite du bonheur* (1992), the Flore Prize for his second collection, *Le sens du combat* (1996), and the November Prize for his second novel, *Les Particules élémentaires* (1998). Houellebecq has his own website,

WILLIAM CLOONAN

Editions

Les Particules élémentaires. Paris: Flammarion, 1998; as *The Elementary Particles*, translated by Frank Wynne. New York: Knopf, 2000.

Selected Works

Extension du domaine de la lutte. 1991.
Rester vivant. 1997.
Interventions. 1998.
Renaissance. 1999.
Lanzarote. 1999.
Plateforme. 2001.

Further Reading

Badré, Frédéric. "La nouvelle tendance en littérature," *Le Monde* (3 October 1998): 14.
Noguez, Dominique. "La Rage de ne pas lire." *Le Monde* (29 October 1998): 1.
Tillinac, Denis, editor. *Atelier du Roman* (June 1999): 17–82 (Pages devoted to *Les Particules élémentaires*).

HUANG

1316–1368
Chinese writer

The Records of Green Bowers.

In Chinese *Qinglouji*, variously translated *Green Lofts Collection* (W. Idema), *Green Mansions* (Chung-wen Shi) or *Green Bower Collection*, "bower" in the singular being a literary reference to the entertainments bureau at the time of the Mongol empire. Besides, the "seventy" is in fact the round number of entries telling the biographies of many more people, a hundred and twenty female entertainers, and some thirty males introduced as their relatives. What are recounted are their activities as dancers, singers, poetesses, or comedians rather than as courtesans of unforgettable beauty. The avowed ugliness of some of them is redeemed by their gifts. Concise and matter-of-fact, the biographies range from thirty to three hundred words. According to the author's statement in his preface, the stories originate from both second-hand sources of questionable reliability and from first-hand, personal experiences.

A source-book for the early history of Chinese theater

The major value of the work is as a source-book for the early history of Chinese operatic drama. Fortunately, it has been preserved in more than half a dozen collections, in various, incomplete states, the best available text being the one included by Yze Dejun (1864–1927) in his *Shuang-mei jing'an congshu*, first published in 1903. Newer modern editions are based on it, completing and annotating it critically, mainly through the discovery of a unique manuscript, from a probable second edition prepared by the author himself after 1366.

A public service

"The brief biographies of the *Qing-lou-chi* show how varied the careers of those girls were, they mirror the confused and uncertain times. Some singing-girls were bought as concubines by wealthy men, then left them to join a private theatrical troupe owned by another man, and finally married their master or drifted back to their original profession. Others became Taoist nuns and roamed all over the larger cities of the Empire, earning their living now as actresses, then as prostitutes, to end in misery or in a harem of a Chinese or Mongol official. We also read about male actors, a lowly profession that was badly paid; their wives and daughters often had to earn extra-money as prostitutes." These limited images translated by Robert van Gulik may represent the whole picture.

In Mongol times (1276–1368), entertainments were a public service provided by the state not only to the court but also to officials and occasionally to affluent merchants. There was no clear dividing line between sexual or artistic services. Brothels of lower status were private enterprises not taken into account in the celebrity ranks. Indeed, though admired, entertainers belonged to a despised social stratum, maintained in a servile status through heredity or penalty. Nevertheless, their attractiveness tended to deplete their numbers, as the powerful tried to take hold of their persons. Repeated biographies insisted on the prohibition of intermarriage with "good people," albeit unsuccessfully. Take as example the case of Gu Shanshan:

"As she was the fourth child, she was called 'Miss Ku Number Four.' Though from a good family, she lost her status because of her father. Gifted and witty, she was an unrivalled artist. First married to the musician Li Little Big Man, she became, when her first husband died, a concubine of the district magistrate of Huating, *Kharabukha* (a probable Mongol name) for thirteen years, before returning to her former status of entertainer. She is now in her sixties, aging in Sung-chiang (Songjiang, a city not very far from present-day Shanghai), but has kept the charm of her youth when performing in dramas the role of flowery female lead. The new generation profits from her guidance and still many are her admirers."

A Multifaceted Gallery of Portraits Drawn in Sober Style

On the other hand, nothing is said about the charm of "La Petite" Shi, so "good in reciting chantefable (what we call these days 'small talks, prose interspersed with verses). Her delivery is like a ball running down hills, like water gushing out of a bottle. Her daughter, 'La Toute Petite,' was too skilled in tongue twisting. She married the male lead Qing the Bountiful but did not outstrip her mother's art."

Yang Mai-nu, "the daughter of Yang the Colt had a beautiful and charming face. Good at singing, an addicted drinker, she was the idol of high officials, dukes and princes. She married later a musician; Kicking devils Chang the Fourth, and died of gloominess. Guan Yunshi (1286–1324) wrote the lines 'Her hair twisted like a black conch, her skirts trailing like a white belt' deriding her, probably because she suffered from the 'white-belt disease' (leucorrhoea, a form of vaginitis)."

In an unaffected style the author managed to avoid repetitiveness even when dealing with loyal courtesans' cases, for example that of Truthful Fan: "A famous beauty from the capital. She became the favourite of the Councillor Zhou Zhonghong. When he returned home in the South, she saw him off at the gate of Universal Transformation. 'After our separation, keep yourself in check and behave so that people won't scoff at us,' said Chou. Throwing wine on the ground, she swore: 'If I am unfaithful to you, I'll gouge out one eye in repentance!' Some time later a powerful potentate appeared. Her mother was afraid and tempted by his wealth. The daughter resisted at the beginning but finally gave up. When Chou returned to the capital, she told him: 'It is not that I did not wish to behave after you left, it's the pressure of his wealth and power. The oath of former days, how could I have taken it in vain?' She drew a metal comb and pierced her left eye. Blood gushed out, drenching the ground all around. It was such a shock for Chou that he loved her as much as he used to before. Some amateur made a play out of it, quite successful, under the title An eye pierced with a metal comb."

Biography

The name Huang comes from a misreading in a preface dated 1364. His identity has been clearly established as Xia Tingshi, born about 1316, a renowned composer of arias. A member of a wealthy and powerful clan famous for its huge collection of books, he was patron to a number of well-known amateurs of stage entertainments. Of his writings, only one thin collection of short biographies is known. He died around 1368.

ANDRÉ LÉVY

Editions

Qinglouji, in *Chung-kuo ku-tien his-ch'ü lun-chu chi-ch'eng* (Compendium of treatises on classical Chinese theatre). Vol 2, Peking: Chung-kuo his-chü 1959, p. 1–84.

Translations

Waley, Arthur. *"The Green Bower Collection"* in *The Secret History of the Mongols, and other pieces*, London 1968, p. 89–107.

References and Further Reading

Gulik, Robert van. *Sexual Life in Ancient China: A Preliminary Survey of Chinese Sex and Society from c. 1500 B.C. till 1644 A.D.* Leiden. E.J. Brill 1961, p.252–253.

Idema, Wilt and Stephen West. *The Chinese Theatre 1100–1450, A Source Book*, Wiesbaden: Frank Steiner 1982, p.89–107.

HUNEKER, JAMES GIBBONS

1857–1921
American journalist and novelist

Painted Veils

At the time *Painted Veils* was published, a draconian censorship regime prevailed in the United States. Works by such established authors as Arthur Schnitzler and D.H. Lawrence were routinely condemned to the incinerator by the New York Society for the Suppression of Vice. The New York publishing firm of Boni and. Liveright decided to proceed with prudence, and issued Huneker's novel in a subscription edition of some 1,300 copies for which the author received $1,800. Although the book escaped prosecution, within a short while it had become an underground classic and second-hand copies were trading for as much as eighty dollars. Scholars should be aware that some later editions, including those issued by the book's original publisher, are expurgated versions.

The action is located during an eighteen-month period some time in the late 1890s. The story itself centers on Ester Brandès, a talented but impecunious young woman from Virginia, and the various cultural intermediaries whom she meets when she comes to New York to study music. These include Alfred Stone, a slightly world-weary theater and music critic, who helps her enroll in the Conservatoire Cosmopolitain as a student of Frida Ash; Ulick Ulvern, a restless, Paris-born American writer with considerable prospects; Paul Godard, a millionaire dilettante who tries to seduce her shortly after her arrival in New York; and the various women friends of these men. At the end of the novel, Ester, who has moved on to Berlin to complete her musical training, returns to New York following her triumphant operatic début.

Although *Painted Veils* contains little which might be described as erotic, there are a number of intentionally sensational episodes. One of these is the flashback "Holy Yowler" incident that occurs early in the novel during which Ester and Ulick (then unknown to each other) become involved in a drunken orgy organized by a Pentecostal sect. Although at the time Ulick believes he has sexual congress with Esther, it is later revealed that his partner was, in fact, an alcoholic black woman and that Ester had had congress with the itinerant leader of the group. Given the laws of racial segregation in force at the time, this revelation makes the episode even more scandalous than the Black Mass episode in J.-K. Huysmans's *Là-bas* (1891) which, presumably, provided the original model for the scene. Another celebrated incident also concerns a drunken orgy, this time organized for the benefit of young men-about-town in the studio of a New York painter. Once again, the selection of this episode is prompted by a close reading of Huysmans (the Black Banquet in *A Rebours*, 1884) though the scene itself is closely modelled on the notorious Pie Girl Dinner (so-called because a sixteen-year-old model emerged from a giant pie) given by millionaire Henry W. Poor in 1895. Huneker had probably been present. But even without these two set pieces, there are many other scandalous admissions in the novel, notably the lesbianism of the heroine. Indeed, it is implied that one consequence of Ester's increasing artistic prowess is a shift in her sexual orientation such that she shows rather more sexual interest in Ulick's various female partners than in Ulick himself.

As a novel, more than eighty years after its initial publication, *Painted Veils* makes little intellectual sense without an appreciation of the author's long fascination with European culture, his particular interest in music, and the problematic nature of the cultural relationship he had spent a lifetime trying to forge between the New World and the Old World. One theme that is very pronounced in the novel, for example, is that of deracination, a subject much discussed by the French writer Maurice Barrès. Similarly, Huneker would seem to have looked to Nietzsche for a justification of the philandering of his central male character, Ulick Ulvern. Likewise, although one reading of the novel would suggest that Ester Brandès is simply ambitious, opportunistic, and immoral, a more sophisticated view would be that it is only by freeing herself from the normal conventions of her time that she is permitted to attain the highest artistic development. The extent that Huneker was exploring the contradictions of his own life by reference to the individualistic philosophy of Nietzsche is further indicated by the author's identification which Ulick Ulvern whose death, like that of the German philosopher, is ascribed to a sudden syphilis-induced paralytic stroke.

At the very least, *Painted Veils* is an interesting though flawed attempt by an American writer to create a work of fiction using themes and techniques developed by European modernists and to explore their relevance within this new cultural setting. Paradoxically, given the operatic background of the novel, it is sometimes considered to be the first novel of the Jazz Age.

Biography

Though intended for the law, Huneker devoted much of his adolescence to the study of music and literature. After marrying in 1878, he and his wife spent nine months in Paris before returning to their native Philadelphia. In 1886, this time alone, he decamped to New York, where he worked as a journalist and music teacher. From 1900 to 1917, he wrote for the New York *Sun* on art, literature, drama, and music. The various collections of essays and articles he published in book form exhibit his overriding fascination with European culture. These include: *Iconoclasts. A Book of Dramatists* (1905), which is largely devoted to Scandinavian, French, and German theater; *Egoists. A Book of Supermen* (1909), which focuses on the writings on Stendhal, Baudelaire, Flaubert, Anatole France, Huysmans, and Nietzsche; and *Unicorns* (1917), in which Chopin, Wagner, Brahms, George Sand, Cézanne, and others pass under review. In contrast to his critical works, Huneker's prose fiction is often considered labored as well as unduly Continental. The latter include collections of short stories such as *Melomaniacs* (1902) and *Visionaries* (1905), both of which deal largely with the musical world, and the 'erotic' novel *Painted Veils* (1920), which though considered controversial at the time of publication managed to avoid prosecution. *Steeplejack* (1920) is an autobiographical work.

TERRY HALE

Editions

Painted Veils. New York: Boni and Liveright, 1920.

Further Reading

Arnold T. Schwab. *James Gibbons Huneker. Critic of the Seven Arts*. Stanford, CA: Stanford University Press, 1963.

HUNGARIAN

Erotic literature is defined here as a genre with three progressively explicit types of text: the erotic, the sexual, and the pornographic imaginary in its linguistic expressions and versions; progressively explicit is understood as the representations of the erotic imaginary from the implicit (i.e., erotic) to the more explicit (i.e., sexual) to the most explicit (i.e., pornographic) in content and form. Erotic literature is thus employed as an umbrella term and is understood by the levels of linguistic explicitness of the imaginary from the erotic to the sexual to the pornographic.

Similar to other Central and East European literatures (e.g., Czech, Slovak, Slovene, Romanian, Croatian, etc.), erotic literature in Hungarian is scarce in all periods of literary history. As a result of the scarcity of the genre, there is limited scholarship available on the topic beyond a few articles and László Kemenes Géfin and Jolanta Jastrzobska's *Erotika a huszadik századi magyar regényben, 1911–1947* (*Erotica in the Hungarian Novel of the Twentieth Century, 1911–1947*) (1998).

Explicit erotic, sexual, and pornographic imagery and language exist aplenty in Hungarian oral literature, common in the countryside where wedding songs in particular have been and still are today heavily erotic to pornographic. Here is an example from a suitor's song: "Kérem, alázatossan,/ Eresszen be, kisasszony,/ Ha igazán nem baszom,/ Törjék bele faszom"/ "I beg you most humbly,/ give me leave to enter, young miss,/ if I don't fuck you real well,/my cock should break off in the effort" or in a song of unmarried men to the bride: "Kelj fel menyasszony/ Itt a volegény,/ Tapogasd meg a faszát,/ Hogy milyen kemény!" / "Get up bride,/ here comes the groom,/ feel his cock,/ how hard it is") (qtd. in Vasvári at <http://clcwebjournal.lib.purdue.edu/clcweb99-4/vasvari99.html>). Also, pornographic language and imagery occurs in many folk tales passed down orally.

The situation is markedly different in written literature, canonical or popular. From the seventeenth to the mid-nineteenth centuries there are only few texts with any erotic content: examples include Mihály Csokonai Vitéz (1773–1805), whose *Lilla* songs and the comic epic *Dorottya* contain erotic symbolism; or Pál Németi (eighteenth century) whose poetry is infused with erotic tones. After the birth of the novel in Hungarian literature with the mid-nineteenth century, eroticism appears in prose but only implicitly as authorial instigation for the reader to imagine the sexual situation and in almost all cases a consummation of sexual desire is described as exemplification of the consequences of sexual repression, as a punishment for transgressions of social codes, usually by the woman. Examples of this genre of erotic literature include texts—poetry and prose—in the work of canonical authors such as Zsigmond Justh (1863–1894), Zsigmond Móricz (1879–1942), Margit Kaffka (1880–1918), Gyula Krúdy (1878–1933), Józsi Jeno Tersánszky (1888–1969); Mihály Babits (1883–1941), Dezso Kosztolányi (1885–1936), Géza Csáth (1887–1919), Zsolt Harsányi (1887–1943), Mihály Földi (1894–1943), Béla Révész (1876–1944), Erno Szép (1884–1953), and Sándor Márai (1900–1989).

An exception to the status quo is the prose of Renée Erdos (1879–1956) who published a number of novels with explicit descriptions of sexuality such as in *A nagy sikoly* (*The Great Moan*) (1923), a novel about sexual repression similar to the novels of canonical authors mentioned previously but here it is the female voice that is given prevalence, often women of the gentry in widowhood after World War I. Another exception is the verse of Árpád Löwy (pseudonym of László Réthy, 1851–1914) whose sexual and pornographic poetry remained unpublished during his life, though it was distributed in hand-written copies or orally. A few years after his death, in 1919, a private edition of his texts appeared in print while the next publication of his texts occurred, again in a private edition, in Germany in 1983, edited anonymously by "J.H.J." His verse is arguably of interest because it is with humor and irony about social matters including the pillorying of pretension and repressive social codes and mores of the time and expressed in pornographic language and imagery (including scatology and blasphemy, the latter a characteristic of Hungarian colloquial language). Rumor has it that János Arany (1817–1882), one of Hungary's most revered national writers, compiled a secret collection of pornographic verse. It is said that a relative of the author guarded the text that was then destroyed during the bombing of Budapest in World War II. Also, Arany's epic *Toldi*, a verse trilogy published 1847–1854, has an anonymously published short version of pornographic and scatological verse narration, at times attributed to Arany himself. Here is an example from this pornographic version from the epic: "Egy csak egy legény van, aki nem hág: Toldi, / Pedig rofös faszát talicskán kell tolni. / Legénytoll sem fedi bár hatalmas pöcsét, / Egyensúlyoz rajta három tonna rozsét. / Vele o az ipart csak en-gross-ban ⟨zi, / Farkára a noket hármassával f⟨zi; / Egy krónikás mondta, aki mindent látott, / Jókedvében egyszer hét megyét meghágott" / [There's only one guy who doesn't fuck now: Toldi, / Though it takes a wheel-barrow for his dick to carry. / His huge prick youthful without pubic hair yet, / He balances on his dick three loads of wood on a bet. / With this prick he does business en-gross exclusively,/ And so Toldi fucks women by the three exemplarily; / A chronicler who saw it all reported, / In a good mood Toldi once summarily in all seven provinces fucked] (my translation). What has made the text offensive in Hungarian culture in the opinion of the general reading public as well as with scholars and intellectuals is not only the pornographic language and imagery of the text but the fact that the pornographic version ridicules a national and canonical epic much revered then and now.

Further examples of erotic-pornographic poetry include verse by Ádám Valagh (alias of the literary historian and translator Tibor Szilágyi, "valag" is arse in Hungarian) published during World War II or Zoltán Somlyó (1882–1937) with his "Milléva" series published in Transylvanian Romania in 1926. In prose, of some interest are the texts published by the critic, writer, and poet Pál Ignotus (pseudonym of Hugó Veigelsberg, 1869–1949) who under the pseudonym "Emma"—it is of much discussion why he chose a female persona—published between 1893 and 1906 fictitious letters about the situation and daily life of women, embracing a feminist point of view including the right of women to eroticism and the enjoyment of sexuality. Other rare texts of sexual and pornographic contents include Tivadar Zichy's (1908–1945) novel *Orgia Rt.* [*Orgy Inc.*] and of particular note is Attila József's (1905–1937) recently published *Szabad ötletek jegyzéke* [*Notebook of Unbound Ideas*] (1991), a text categorized today as auto-psychoanalysis about the dreams and imaginings of one of Hungary's most prominent poets of modernity. In his text, József describes, among others, in sexual and pornographic language his imaginary relationship with his mother. The canonized writer Józsi Jeno Tersánszky (1888–1969), listed above, wrote a pornographic short novel that remains unpublished in a literary museum, the Petofi Irodalmi Múzeum, in Budapest.

While translations of French or other Western erotic literature are extremely rare to nonexistent until recently, of interest is the free translation of François Villon's ballads by György Faludy (1913–), *Villon balladái* (1937), a masterful rendition of the original with explicit sexual language and imagery. Faludy also translated erotic poetry of canonical authors such as Verlaine, Baudelaire, and Rimbaud.

In contemporary Hungarian literature, it is in exile literature where the first text of prose with pornographic content and language was written and published: László Kemenes Géfin's

Fehérlófia nyolcasa. Hardcore szerelem cirkusz [*The Eight Circles of the White Stag: Hardcore Circus of Love*] (1978–1981; 1995). Although not paid virtually any attention to in Hungarian scholarship, the novels of Kemenes Géfin represent the first postmodern text of Hungarian literature, not the least because of the novels' daring irony about Hungarian patriotism and history, presented in a sexual and pornographic context and language. While Kemenes Géfin's novels are still today, in the context of post-1989 Hungarian culture and literature, innovative and worthy of serious study, his sexual and pornographic writing is from a strongly patriarchal point of view; and so is his and Jolanta Jastrzo;bska's study, *Erotika a huszadik századi magyar regényben, 1911–1947* (*Erotica in the Hungarian Novel of the Twentieth Century, 1911–1947*) (1998). Here is an example of Kemenes Géfin's sexual and pornographic writing:

"He finally took his clothes off, kicked his shoes off, and told me to stand up and that I must take that goddam pantyhose off. I too took my shoes off now and quickly rolled down the offensive stockings although I put them on especially for him, they were of a nice smoky color, and now I should be glad that he did not rip them off. I wanted to crouch down in front of him, I had only the blouse left on me, it had a décolletage that my tits spilled almost out of them. But he was uninterested in this daring pose and I suddenly felt lost. He then said that he wants me to stand in front of him, so I did, my Venus just in front of his face, weak in my knees. He embraced my hips, took my ass into his hands and burrowed into my groin. I felt his tongue inside me, he was slurping, his tongue was in my cunt and for minutes I lost time, I don't know what he was doing, and felt his finger, too, in my cunt, with another one caressing my anus, and I returned to time and place when I heard his voice telling me that one does not have the chance to lick such a nice and clean cunt everyday. Then he took my clitoris into his mouth and all presence left me, if he hadn't been holding me I would have crumpled to the floor. The next I remembered I was on the bed, he was bending my legs backward, licking me, digging his tongue into my cunt, sucking my juices out, then sucking on my anus, licking it and I realized that I was making noises, babbling and sighing with short shrieks. I never experienced such pleasure. Then something burning hot and enormous began and swept through me" (1995, 62–63).

After the dissolution of the Soviet empire in 1989–1990, in Hungary, similar to all other countries of communist regime, erotic literature began to be published en masse. In canonical prose, the two most prominent examples are the novels of Péter Nádas (1942–), especially his novel *Emlékiratok könyve* (abridged and censored 1986, unabridged 1998) [*A Book of Memories*, trans. Ivan Sanders and Imre Goldstein, 1997] and *Égi és földi szerelemrol* [*Of Heavenly and Earthly Love*] (1991), a collection of essays about sexuality and language and Péter Esterházy (1950–), whose novel *Egy no* (1995) [*She Loves Me*, trans Judith Sollosy, 1997] is unremarkable although his daring of pornographic descriptions of the loves and affairs of a fictitious alter ego—similar to the work of Kemenes Géfin in a strongly patriarchal and male chauvinistic voice—nevertheless represent innovation in Hungarian literature. Here is an excerpt from Esterházy's novel:

"A Woman (64). I saw her breasts from the side, they bounced and moved about, jumped elasticized; happy breasts, this is how they can be summarized. ... I saw her ass, too, when she walked, consequently from afar, moving away, bum, ass, I don't know what to call it. Apart from all these I would like yet to see her hair in my life, her ears (cleanliness and control), her neck (from the front, I saw it fleetingly when she, excited, swallowed something, and something moved there as if she had an Adam's apple), I would like to see her collar bone, her ribs, her shoulder blades (like stumps of wings), altogether her bones, from her skull to her toes' middle bones, I would like to see her stomach, the youthful rolls of fat, altogether all her fat, her belly button, and all her holes, the hair under her belly, and altogether all her hair. I don't want to see anything else, that's what I keep my eyes for. She squeezes the champagne bottle between her legs, that's how she opens it. It's as if it were her penis. I will have to pay for this, says one of us as the champagne overflows. It's more from the champagne than from the joke that I suddenly remember: and I would like to see her cunt, face to eye" (124, my translation).

In the visual arts of Hungary, similar to literature, there is very little erotic material and virtually none exists when it comes to sexual and pornographic art (there was no impact in Hungary of the highly erotic and sexual visual arts of the Viennese art nouveau of such as Klimt or Schiele). However, of international renown are the erotic and in some instances pornographic drawings of Mihály Zichy (1827–1906), a prominent representative of romantic painting, illustrator, and portraitist. In accordance with the general sensitivity about the sexual and the pornographic with regard to national symbols and texts altogether and with regard to literature, in contemporary Hungary sexual and pornographic depictions are rare as in previous periods. An example of the contemporary situation is the following: a serious offence with legal implications was the depiction of the post-1989 reinstalled official coat-of-arms of Hungary, with two angels on each side of the escutcheon where an artist in opposition to the decision to reinstate pre-war religious symbolism, depicted the two angels masturbating. The intention of the artist was, indeed, to ridicule religious and historical symbolism albeit the humor of the alternate depiction was in whole not accepted by the general public and the picture was understood as desecration and only after a lengthy trial was the artist acquitted.

As introduced above, it is in the years after the end of the communist regime and Soviet colonialism in 1989 when an increase of productivity in Hungarian erotic literature occurred. In addition to the examples presented above, the publishing enterprise *Nappali Ház* invited in 1998 prominent authors such as Péter Esterházy, Lajos Parti-Nagy, Zsuzsa Forgács, and Ildikó Szabó (the film director of renown), to write short stories where a sexual act is described. Parallel to such publications, it has become accepted that young poets in particular publish verse in eroticized to pornographic language (e.g., János Dénes Orbán, Attila Sántha, Endre Wellmann). Akin to the practice of authors in contemporary literature elsewhere, there are examples of canonical writers who write unpublished texts such as diaries with much pornographic material as is the case with one of contemporary Hungary's prominent poets, Endre Kukorelly (1951–), who lists and describes his amorous adventures and escapades in his diaries in much detail. Further examples of contemporary texts with erotic-pornographic content include the poetry of László Lator (1927–) or Tibor Papp's "Kurvák Ilosfalván" ("Whores in Ilosfalva"), a short story in the style of stream of consciousness about amorous adventures with pornographic detail, published in the literary journal *Az Irodalom Visszavág* (1999).

Overall, the significance of the increased production of erotic culture rests on the fact that the genre of the erotic text thus attains legitimacy in Hungarian culture and literature. Of note is that homoerotic writing, gay or lesbian, is virtually nonexistent in Hungarian. Since the mid-1990s, in Hungary as elsewhere, there has been productivity of erotica in both text and visuals in new media on the World Wide Web and there are signs that in Hungary, too, it may be in new media where writers experiment with erotic and pornographic writing.

STEVEN TOTOSY DE ZEPETNEK

Further Reading

Kemenes Géfin, László, and Jolanta Jastrzobska. *Erotika a huszadik századi magyar regényben, 1911–1947*

[*Erotica in the Hungarian Novel of the Twentieth Century, 1911–1947*]. Budapest: Kortárs, 1998.
Lukacs, John. *Budapest 1900: A Historical Portrait of a City and Its Culture*. New York: Grove Weidenfeld, 1988.
Totosy de Zepetnek, Steven. *Comparative Literature: Theory, Method, Application*. Amsterdam: Rodopi, 1998.
Vasvári, Louise O. "A Comparative Approach to European Folk Poetry and the Erotic Wedding Motif." *CLCWeb: Comparative Literature and Culture* 1.4 (1999): <http://clcwebjournal.lib.purdue.edu/clcweb99-4/vasvari99.html>.

HUYSMANS, JORIS-KARL

1848–1907
French novelist

Marthe: histoire d'une fille

Huysmans completed the draft of *Marthe*, drawing on his experiences in 1867–1870 with a minor actress at the Bobino theater, in 1876; out of fear of censorship but also to anticipate Edmond de Goncourt's novel about a prostitute, *La fille Elisa* (1877), he traveled to Brussels to have it published there in 1876; almost all the copies were seized at the French border. After establishing himself in the group of Naturalist writers with *Les Sœurs Vatard* and some polemical art criticism, Huysmans was able to have a second edition of *Marthe* published in Paris in 1879, the same year as Zola's *Nana*. It met with little immediate critical and generally hostile response (one critic viewed it as an "obscene publication") and little success.

The prostitute was to preoccupy Naturalist writers with her complex linkage of sexuality with power, class, and money. Huysmans's provocative choice of subject for a first novel—the subtitle refers to the heroine bluntly as "a whore"—on a blatant contemporary social phenomenon represents the first attempt in French

to break both with the Romantic stereotype of the prostitute redeemed through love (*La dame aux camélias* of Alexandre Dumas *fils*) and with heroic and self-sacrificing figures like Fantine in *Les Misérables*, and to give an unsentimental portrayal of the life of a prostitute in contemporary Paris. The narrator stresses its demythificatory side when observing that Marthe's initial loss of her virginity to an older and richer man is due, not 'as novelists say,' to her senses, but to pride and curiosity.

The novel opens in the wings of the Bobino theater where Marthe is being prepared by the actor Ginginet for the opening night of a second-rate review; her performance attracts a young journalist, Léo. A flashback then traces Marthe's past: orphaned at 15, she had followed her mother's trade as a worker in false pearls which both undermined her health and exposed her to the corrupting conversation of her fellow workers. She yielded to an older man, but left him, disgusted. With no trade she slid into occasional prostitution, then formed a liaison with a young man. Both he and their premature child died; she sought refuge in a brothel. Slipping out one day she was noticed by Ginginet in a bar.

Marthe now begins an affair with the would-be writer who had picked her out at the theater.

After an initial idyllic period, life together and poverty erode the relationship. He grows frustrated in his literary ambitions; she suffers from his lack of interest in her as an individual. She begins to sell herself again, but stops, afraid of being caught by the police as a fugitive from a licensed brothel, and turns to drink. Léo, called to the sickbed of his mother, leaves Marthe with relief. In despair she contemplates suicide and returns to the brothel. Back in Paris, Léo seeks her out again, and finds her as the mistress of Ginginet in the sordid bar he now owns: the actor's intervention has had her struck off the police register, and he is using her to attract customers. She escapes from the mutually brutalising relationship with Ginginet, and a former woman friend helps her to acquire a lover, young, rich, and idle, who sets her up in her own apartment. Her contempt for him and sexual dissatisfaction soon drive her back to Léo. Léo, though still drawn to her sensually, is reminded by her bruises of her other life and they part definitively after a single night. She returns to a series of lovers. A coda which opens in the morgue of the Lariboisière hospital rounds off the brief novel with the triumph of bourgeois order: a smug letter from Léo to a student friend reveals him about to enter a conventional marriage, and cynically predicting for Marthe, now back in the brothel, a death from drink or in the Seine; a surgeon performs an autopsy on Ginginet to demonstrate the effects of alcoholism.

The slice of life offered by Huysmans switches between the three central figures, but Marthe remains the most ambiguous, set between the jocular cynicism of the self-destructive and exploitative Ginginet and the egoistic Léo, who is drawn to Marthe as a stimulus to his imagination, but becomes rapidly bored by the real woman beneath the actress and frustrated by the petty frictions of cohabitation.

Marthe's career allows Huysmans to portray dispassionately the varied forms that prostitution had taken in nineteenth-century Paris: the controlled world of the *maison close*, with its protection, routine, and comforts, which however imposes an "odious job" that allows neither revulsion nor fatigue; the unofficial prostitution that seeks clients in dance-halls or bars; the woman kept by a rich lover as an object of display and a sexual convenience, and her life of races, parties, and boredom. Huysmans is no

social reformer; if he is an invaluable source of information, he also betrays pervasive social attitudes (Alain Corbin), and his presentation of the prostitute's life remains intriguingly ambivalent. It offers initially the Naturalist scenario of a vulnerable individual from a sickly family corrupted by the physical squalor and moral laxity of a destructive environment, and ineluctably drawn back into the world of the brothel: "Every woman who has lived this life plunges back into it one day or another." But Marthe, though attractive and physically responsive to Léo, is not driven by sexual desire: she is full of self-loathing, and, unlike Zola's Nana, unable to use her sexuality as a weapon against others. Her point of view offers a protest against the brutality, vulgarity, and arrogance of men and against male contempt for the prostitute. On the other hand the sympathy Huysmans shows for one individual does not really call into question the exploitation of women in this society: the availability of venal sex, the dual standard, and the evocations of women in the brothel reveal on occasion a voyeuristic fascination.

Huysmans also wrote two aggressively obscene sonnets for the *Nouveau Parnasse satyrique du XIXe siècle*.

Biography

Charles-Marie-Georges Huysmans was born in Paris, 5 February 1848. Educated at Lycée Saint-Louis, Paris, 1862–1865; studied law at Faculté de Droit et de Lettres, Paris, 1866–1867. He earned his living as a minor civil servant at the Ministry of the Interior from 1866, then, after serving in the Garde Nationale Mobile in the Franco-Prussian War in 1870, in the Ministries of War (1870–1876) and the Interior (1876–1898). In 1892, undertook a retreat to a Trappist monastery and returned to the Roman Catholic church, spending nearly two years as a Bendictine oblate in a monastery in Ligugé (Poitou); returned to Paris in 1901 when the monks left France. His first book, the collection of prose poems *Le drageoir à épices* [*The Spice Bowl*], was published in 1874, signed Jorris-Karl Huysmans; he used J.-K. Huysmans for subsequent works. As well as a series of novels that chart a progression from Naturalism through an interest in Decadence and Symbolism (*A rebours* [*Against Nature*]) and in Satanism (*Là-bas* [*Down There*]) to conversion to

Roman Catholicism, he wrote art criticism. Died of cancer of the jaw and mouth in Paris, May 12, 1907.

PETER COGMAN

Editions

Marthe: histoire d'une fille. Brussels: Gay, 1876; Paris: Derveaux, 1879; as *Marthe*, translated by Robert Baldick, Fortune Press, n.d. [1958].

Selected Works

A rebours. 1880; as *Against Nature*, translated by Robert Baldick, 1959; as *Against Nature*, translated by Margaret Mauldon, 1998.
Certains. 1889.
Là-bas. 1891; as *Down There*, translated by Robert Irwin, 1986; as *The Damned*, translated by Terry Hale, 2001.

Further Reading

Antosh, Ruth B. *Reality and Illusion in the novels of J.K. Huysmans.* Amsterdam: Rodopi, 1986.

Baldick, Robert. *The Life of J-K. Huysmans.* Oxford: Oxford University Press, 1955.
Bernheimer, Charles. *Figures of Ill-repute: Representing Prostitution in Nineteenth-Century France.* Cambridge, MA: Harvard University Press, 1989.
Brandreth, Henry R.T. *Huysmans.* Lodon: Bowes and Bowes, 1963.
Corbin, Alain. *Les Filles de noce: misère sexuelle et prostitution au XIXe siècle.* Paris: Aubier Montaigne, 1978; as *Women for Hire: Prostitution and Sexuality in France after 1859*, translated by Alan Sheridan. Cambridge, MA: Harvard University Press, 1990.
Lloyd, Christopher. *J.K. Huysmans and the Fin-de-siécle Novel.* Edinburgh: Edinburgh University Press, 1990.
Olrik, Hilde. '*Marthe*: une prostituée du XIXe siècle.' *Revue des Sciences Humaines.* Nos. 171–172 (1978), 273–283.
Zayed, Fernande. *Huysmans peintre de son époque.* Paris: Nizet, 1973.
Robert Ziegler. 'Feminized Reality/Male Realism: The Case of Huysmans' *Marthe.*' *Australian Journal of French Studies*, 31 (1994), 188–199.

HYVRARD, JEANNE

1945–
French novelist, poet, short story writer, and essayist

A crucial figure in contemporary French literature, Jeanne Hyvrard nonetheless remains largely unexplored outside the critical truisms that categorize her œuvre as 'écriture féminine' (women's writing) and/or autobiography. However, the complexities of her writing in fact place her œuvre beyond restrictive generic parameters. Although her later, more structured work displays a measure and control absent from the fragmented narrative of her early texts, the initial novels are those which display a fascinating engagement with intertextual, maternal, and morbid eroticism.

The first evidence of erotic writing in Hyvrard comes in her novel, *Les prunes de Cythère* [*The Plums of Cythera*, Paris, Minuit, 1975, hereafter cited as *Prunes*]. While the novel's preoccupations with maternity, social injustice, and madness have been treated by various critics, Hyvrard also draws heavily on Charles Baudelaire's poem 'Un Voyage à Cythère' ('A Voyage to Cythera'), published in the collection *Les fleurs du Mal* [*The Flowers of Evil*]. Jeanne, the narrator, can be seen as a reincarnation of Jeanne Duval, Baudelaire's 'Muse Malade' ('Sick Muse'), his mulatto mistress and the inspiration for a number of poems in which the sensual and the necrophilial are disturbingly intertwined in the poet's erotic portrayal of his muse. The silent scapegoat of Baudelaire's passion, Duval is liberated from the mute role in which the poet imprisoned her via Hyvrard's impassioned and liberating narrative, which witnesses a woman's refusal to remain bound within stereotyped notions of femininity. Indeed Jeanne, Hyvrard's narrator, claims that 'Je crie par mille bouches' ('I cry out from a thousand mouths,' *Prunes*), thus emphasizing the universal and intertextual relevance of the narrator. However, it is not a male lover who is subjectivising and eroticizing Jeanne, but a phallic mother figure. Like Baudelaire's polarized visions of Duval, Hyvrard offers a dual representation of the mother. The first is that of a suffocating monster whose invasion of her daughter's body is likened to a rape: 'elle s'est étendue sur moi et m'a enfoncé son phallus dans la bouche' ('she spread herself over me and forced her phallus into my mouth,' *Prunes*. These violently sexual images demonstrate a morbid eroticism that is all the more sinister given the maternal provenance of the physical abuse, and the unsettlingly vivid imagery of the phallic female. The maternal rape is seen to be cannibalistic: 'elle m'étouffe et me digère' ('she suffocates me and digests me,' *Prunes*), and the repressive maternal relationship is also depicted metaphorically as quasi-sexual: in *Prunes*, as well as the 1976 novel *Mère la mort* [*Mother Death*], the mother is likened to an octopus, stifling her child in a pseudo-amorous embrace, and in the 1990 novel *La jeune morte en robe de dentelle* [*The Dead Girl In a Lace Dress*] she is likened to mistletoe, the plant which symbolizes romantic love but which suffocates and poisons the plant it wraps around.

By taking such negative qualities away from the narrator or muse, and instead incarnating them in the oppressive othered figure, Hyvrard shows Baudelaire's description of Duval to be a projection of the self onto the other. However, the representation of the positive mother figure is no less eroticized. For example, the narrator addresses her 'real' mother (an eco-feminist Mother Earth), saying that 'quand je rentre en toi, j'y disparais [...] [;] tu m'embrasses jusqu'à ce que mes plaies touchent les tiennes et qu'elles en guérissent' ('when I go back inside you, I disappear there [...]; you kiss me until my wounds touch yours and are healed by the touch,' *Prunes*). The blurring of mother and earth echoes the narrator's desire to 'rentrer dans la terre jusqu'à devenir le sexe du monde' ('return inside the earth until I become the world's entrails' *Prunes*, p. 208). The overt erotic implications suggest a communion with the earth that is powerful and life-enhancing, and

the eco-feminist nature of this eroticism is picked up and developed in Hyvrard's 1998 text *Ton nom de végétal* [*Your Plant Name*]. The return to the earth's core also symbolizes a return to the womb, thus pulling out the pro-maternal eco-feminist strand in Hyvrard's writing. The eroticized vision of childbirth is represented here from the perspective of the child, whose fulfillment is achieved by a symbolic return to the womb. However, while the backward-looking process of returning to the 'ventre' ('womb/core') is evident, we can also identify a forward-visioned re-working of Hyvrard's sexualized view of childbirth. It is in becoming a mother herself that she feels physical fulfillment reaches its zenith: projecting forwards towards a positive and life-affirming view of motherhood, and rejecting the sadistic and morbid eroticism that defines her textual relationship with her (negative) mother, Hyvrard's narrator describes the birth of her own daughter in physical, visceral terms: '[l]'enfant qui me faisait l'amour, avec tout son corps. Venu de l'intérieur de moi-même. Glissant entre mes cuisses. L'enfant nu traversant mon sexe . [...] Toi, ma petite fille, tu m'as fait l'amour mieux que tout autre.' ('[t]he child who made love to me, with its whole body. Come from my own core. Slipping between my thighs. The naked child passing across my vagina. [...] You, my little girl, you made love to me better than any other,' *Prunes*). Hyvrard's eroticized view of motherhood corresponds to the positive feminist position of viewing childbirth as the height of sexual pleasure, and thus she liberates herself from the physical and maternal restrictions of a negative female genealogy, through this orgasmic experience of childbirth.

It is thus not through a heterosexual love or relationship that Hyvrard re-works traditional or Baudelairean representations of the fetishized or eroticized female figure, but rather through a pro-life affirmation of the mother–daughter relationship. The female-centered nature of Hyvrard's texts is particularly evident in the raw and urgent emotion of her cry 'Je te crie ma haine et mes amours castrées' ('I cry out to you my hate and my castrated loves,' *Prunes*), the feminine plural 'castrées' feminizing and sexualizing the loves of which the narrator speaks. Therefore, despite her own strongly heterosexual beliefs, which she describes as a political position as well as a personal choice, the polarized representation of the female in Hyvrard is redeemed through woman-to-woman love, and via a subjectivized re-working of traditional, male-authored representations of the woman as sexual or sexualized object.

Biography

Born in Paris in 1945, Jeanne Hyvrard trained as an economist and lawyer, and claims to have come to writing 'by chance': having entered the teaching profession in the early 1970s, she was posted to Martinique for two years, and was outraged by the injustice and inequality she witnessed there, particularly in the treatment of women. She decided to write a social report about this in order to raise awareness—although she points out now that this was a naive hope—of the injustices in francophone post-colonial society. However, the text that she wrote was disturbingly poetic, and blended literary narrative with social comment. *Les Prunes de Cythère* [*The Plums of Cythera*] was thus published as a novel with the Éditions de Minuit in 1975.

Since 1975, Hyvrard has produced a substantial corpus of novels, poetry, social commentary, and philosophical short stories. She maintained her teaching job in a technical college in Paris until the age of 60, retiring in summer 2005. She still lives in Paris with her husband, and has one daughter and two grandchildren, with whom she maintains a strong family link.

HELEN VASSALLO

Selected Works

Le fichu écarlate. Paris: des femmes, 2004
Ordre relativement chronologique suivi de *La Grande Fermaille*. Paris: L'Harmattan, 2003.
La formosité. Inventaire de la beauté et de toutes les formes de forme. Liège: Atelier de l'Agneau, 2000.
Ton nom de végétal. Quebec: Trois Guinées, 1998.
Au présage de la mienne. Quebec: Le Loup de Gouttière, 1997.
La jeune morte en robe de dentelle. Paris: des femmes, 1990.
La pensée corps. Paris: des femmes, 1989.
Le cercan. Paris: des femmes, 1987.
Canal de la Toussaint. Paris: des femmes, 1985.
La baisure suivi de *que se partagent encore les eaux*. Paris: des femmes, 1984.
Le corps défunt de la comédie: Traité d'économie politique. Paris: Seuil, 1982.
Le silence et l'obscurité: Requiem littoral pour corps polonais 13-28 décembre 1981. Paris: Éditions Montalba, 1982.
Les doigts du figuier. Paris: Minuit, 1977.
La meurtritude. Paris: Minuit, 1977.
Mère la mort. Paris: Minuit, 1976.
Les prunes de Cythère. Paris: Minuit, 1975.

Further Reading

Cauville, Joëlle. *Mythologie hyvrardienne: analyse des mythes et symboles dans l'œuvre de Jeanne Hyvrard*. Québec: Presses de l'Université de Laval, 1996.
Kosta-Théfaine, Jean, ed. *Ut Philosophia Poesis: Études sur l'œuvre de Jeanne Hyvrard*. Amsterdam-New York: Rodopi, 2001.
Saigal, Monique. *L'écriture: lien de mère à fille chez Jeanne Hyvrard, Chantal Chawaf et Annie Ernaux*. Amsterdam-Atlanta: Rodopi, 2000.
Vassallo, Helen. "Passion et pulsions: la volupté baudelairienne chez Jeanne Hyvrard." in *Amour, passion, volupté: le sentiment amoureux dans la litterature française du Moyen Age jusqu'au XXIème siécle*. edited by Annye Castonguay and Jean-François Kosta-Théfaine, Paris: Atlantica, 2005.
——— "Retour à Cythère: Baudelairean intertext in Jeanne Hyvrard." *The French Studies Bulletin* 93 (Winter 2004): 10–12.
Verthuy-Williams, Maïr and Jennifer Waelti-Walters. *Jeanne Hyvrard*. Amsterdam-Atlanta: Rodopi, 1988.
Waelti-Walters, Jennifer. *Jeanne Hyvrard: Theorist of the Modern World*. Edinburgh: Edinburgh University Press, 1996.

IBN AL-HAJJĀJ

c. 932–1001
Pre-modern Arab poet

Relatively unknown nowadays except in literary circles and among specialists, Ibn al-Hajjāj was of great fame in his time, in later epochs, and up until the modern period. He is considered one of the major poets of the Būyid period (932–1062), known for its political tumult but vibrant cultural production. He secured the patronage of the most powerful men of the age, as the panegyrics he composed for them attest, and was also active in many elite circles. Ibn al-Hajjāj was praised by literary critics and admired by contemporaries, and secured many a mention in anthologies for his unique style and for pioneering a new mode of scatological parody and obscene frivolity termed *sukhf*, which became synonymous with his name and person(a).

While certainly talented and unique, Ibn al-Hajjāj and his poetry did not appear ex nihilo. The time was ripe for such a trajectory, and Ibn al-Hajjāj's *sukhf* can be seen as a natural culmination of an established and hallowed tradition which produced the potential for parody. There had already been parodic trends of the conventions of Arabic poetry before Ibn al-Hajjāj's time. In addition, the shift to urban centers and a courtly culture with a new set of sociopolitical functions and surroundings had already produced a variety of specialized genres and subgenres of poetry (ascetic, bacchic, nature, and hunting poetry, to name a few). The status and function of the poet, too, had changed from that of hero and spokesperson of his tribe in pre-Islamic times to court entertainer and, at times, even ritual clown. This urban and urbane poetry had already reveled in parodying the classical literary (and social) conventions, motifs, and values attached to and celebrated in older bedouin poetry. *Mujūn* (licentious and hedonistic poetry), with which *sukhf* at times overlaps or is coupled, saw its apex in the poetry of the libertine master Abū Nuwās (755–813). Ibn al-Hajjāj incorporated all these trends, as well as the obscene and scatological motifs and diction of invective poetry, known as *hijā*, and redeployed them with added force in a full-fledged parody of all that was conventional in literary and sociocultural spheres, to become, as many have noted, the most obscene and irreverent poet in pre-modern Arabic poetry.

Not surprisingly, the body (and its functions) is the main vehicle through which Ibn al-Hajjāj carries out his scatological parody. One of the essential motifs of Arabic poetry was the elegiac pause of the poet in remembrance of his beloved's abandoned encampments. Ibn al-Hajjāj's poetic persona reenacts this ritual, but it is his cock, rather than his eye, which cries over the abandoned encampments. Moreover, instead of a real or imagined space, the object of his tears is usually the abandoned vagina or anus of a grotesquely old woman. Not unlike parody in general, all motifs are inverted in the world of *sukhf*. If the beloved is not a hyperbolically old hag, she is at times a pre-pubescent girl, and the poetic persona is an impotent old man lamenting his lost virility. Ibn al-Hajjāj's descriptive prowess is focused on the lower parts of the body so that in lieu of the conventional imagery highlighting the upper part and face of the beloved, we find hilarious microscopic descriptions of orifices, bodily fluids, odors, and functions. The latter usually interfere with and disrupt attempts at intercourse. Even in panegyrics, it is not the patron's generosity that is (traditionally) hailed, but his virility and the length and width of his cock. The patron's enemies are not threatened with military defeat, but with Ibn al-Hajjāj's own excrement, which he threatens to hurl at them. Much in the tradition of *mujūn,* but going much further than any of his predecessors, Ibn al-Hajjāj was extremely irreverent in parodying religious themes as well. In describing a beloved's clitoris, for example, he likens it to a bent-over imam. To portray a lengthy intercourse, he writes "my cock calls for the morning prayer inside her anus and stays until the forenoon."

Ibn al-Hajjāj was well aware of the niche he had found for himself and the poetic mode he had established. There are numerous examples in his poems where he boasts of this, calling himself "the prophet of frivolity: a man claiming prophecy in frivolity/and who dare doubt prophets?/He brings forth his own miracles and calls upon people to follow/So answer all ye frivolous ones." He even likened his oeuvre to a privy, without which life is impossible.

What further distinguishes Ibn al-Hajjāj is his fame and popularity outside of literary and literate circles. He fused poetic modes but also linguistic registers. His extensive and deliberate use of vulgar street language (he started to collect and write down Baghdadi colloquial obscenities

and curses while still a boy) ensured that his audience would not be restricted to the elite. A manual for teachers from the 14th century, three centuries after Ibn al-Hajjāj's death, instructs its readers to punish boys if they are found reciting his poetry. Ibn al-Hajjāj was emulated by many poets in later centuries. By the 15th century, he himself had become a topos, and anecdotes about him and his poetry appear in other works of erotica, such as *Nuzhat al-albāb* [*The Sojourn of the Hearts*] by al-Tīfāshī.

Biography

Abū Abdullāh al-Husayn Ibn al-Hajjāj was born in Baghdad in 932 CE to a Shīī family of government officials. He was trained by the famous Abū Ishāq al-Sābī to be one himself and worked as a secretary for a short period. However, realizing that his poetic talent promised a more lucrative career and future, he quit his post and pursued a highly successful career as a poet. He was briefly appointed the market inspector of Baghdad (973–977). He died in Baghdad and was buried near the shrine of the imam Mūsā al-Kazim.

SINAN ANTOON

Selected Works

Abdelghafur, A.A., ed. *Der Dīwān des Ibn al-Haggāg, Teilausgabe: Der Reimbuchstabe nūn.* Giessen, Germany: Universitat, 1977.

Al-Tāhir, 'Alī J. *Durrat al-tāj min shi'r Ibn al-Hajjāj* [The Crown's Pearl of Ibn al-Hajjāj's Poetry]. Complementary thesis, Sorbonne, 1953.

Mustafā, Najm 'Abdallah, ed. *Taltīf al-mizāj min shi'r Ibn al-Hajjāj* [Lightening the Mood with Ibn al-Hajjāj's Poetry]. Sūsa, Tunisia: Dār al-Ma'ārif, 2001.

References and Further Reading

Antoon, Sinan. "The Poetics of the Obscene: Ibn al-Hajjāj and Sukhf." Ph.D. dissertation, Harvard University, 2006.

Gelder, Geert J.V. *The Bad and the Ugly: Attitudes Towards Invective Poetry in Classical Arabic Literature.* Leiden: E.J. Brill, 1988.

"Sukhf" and "Ibn al-Hajjāj." In *Encyclopaedia of Islam* (new edition). Leiden: Brill, 1954–.

Manna, Hashim. "Al-Husayn Ibn Al-Hajjāj: His Life and Verse." Ph.D. dissertation, University of London, 1986.

Meisami, J.S. "Arabic *mujūn* Poetry: The Literary Dimension." In *Verse and the Fair Sex: Studies in Arabic Poetry and in the Representation of Women in Arabic Literature,* edited by Fredrick De Jong. Utrecht: M. Th. Houtsma Sticchting, 1993.

Mez, Adam. *The Renaissance of Islam.* Translated by D.S. Margoliouth and S. Khuda Bakhsh. Patna, 1937.

IBN HAZM

994–1064
Muslim jurist, theologian, and man of letters

Ibn Hazm is in the West the epitome of the Muslim theorist of profane love—as distinct from divine or even mystic love—who tried to describe natural or passionate love. Ibn Hazm's only attempt in the field of literature was the book *Tawq al-hamâma fî-l-ulfa wa-l-ullâf* [*The Dove's Neck-Ring, or on Love and Lovers*].

One should distinguish between the essays, epistles, or treatises dealing with natural love and the essays that integrate natural love—*tabî'î*—into a larger approach to love, including spiritual and divine love. It was not rare for authors to blur the line between natural and divine love, so that the lover loved an anonymous Beloved, who was in fact God.

Although it may sound strange that a Muslim theologian dealt with sex and love, neither of these can be separated from God's creation, and are allowed in married life. Outside of marriage, passion is not forbidden, but sex is. A famous *hadith*—an authorized report on the Prophet's words and attitudes—holds that "the one who loves remains chaste, keeps his secret, and dies," that one is a love's martyr, *'achîq chahîd*. Erotology is a matter for a theologian to expand upon, teach, and imagine in the name of God. Besides, one and the same word, *nikâh*, means coitus and marriage.

The Dove's Neck-Ring is a prosimeter of 30 chapters which theoretically relate the successive moments of a love's story, from the beginning to the fateful and necessary end. The book is introduced by a narrator in Játiva who meets the desire of a dearest friend in Almeria by writing an epistle on truthful love, its various meanings, causes, and accidents, "neither adding anything nor embroidering anything."

Ibn Hazm anonymously records his life in Córdoba, describes each loving phase, illustrates it by supposedly edifying stories, drawn from personal experiences, hearing, and reading. Theory and example are always intertwined with poems reiterating the chapter's thesis. Ibn

Hazm also quotes other Muslim writers' poems but distinguishes himself from mystics by inserting his own verses and expressing his own subjectivity. Ibn Hazm, a theorist of profane love, soberly and perceptively analyzes the outer manifestations of natural love. However, his vision of love is not devoid of any spirituality, as it partly derives from Plato's *Symposium* and *Phaedrus*'s idealized view of love.

Sex does not automatically translate to passion, but is alluded to in various stories. The narrator can't always avoid details that awaken, entertain, titillate, or even ignite his reader's desire or erotic imagination. He concludes his epistle with two chapters that sum up Islam's prohibition of sex and illustrate the author's moralism. Still, he reports an old lady's narrative which is indirectly far from being exemplary:

> [N]ever have too good an opinion of any woman. . . . I took ship many years ago now, returning from the pilgrimage, for I had already renounced the world; with me on the same vessel were fourteen other women, all of whom had likewise been to Mecca. . . . Now one of the crew was a fine upstanding fellow. . . . On the first night out I saw him come up to one of my companions and show off his virility to her. She surrendered to his embraces on the spot. On the following nights each of the rest accepted his advances in turn, until only I was left. I said to myself, "I will punish you for this, you scoundrel." With that I took a razor and grasped it firmly in my hand. He came along as usual that evening and behaved precisely as he had done on the preceding nights. When he approached me I brandished my razor, and he was so scared that he would have run off. I felt very sorry for him then, and grasping him with my hands I said, "You shall not go until I have had my share of you." So, the old lady concluded, he got what he wanted, God forgive me! (Chap. 29)

The narrator aims at stigmatizing sin, but each sequence of the story might develop into an erotic sketch. He refrains from going further but can't help taking delight in relating such stories, which take place mostly in the Umayyads' time, for which Ibn Hazm is nostalgic.

Ibn Hazm's *The Dove's Neck-Ring* was by no means the first book on profane love in the history of Arabic or even Muslim literature. It was preceded by *Kitâb az-zahra* [*The Book of the Flower*] of Ibn Dâwûd al Isfâhâni (d. 909), the forerunner of profane love theory and possibly of Western courtly love, who tackles all the items of love to be found in later epistles, including the ideal passion that leads to death, as well as boy-love poetry by other poets.

Ibn Hazm's work belongs among a number of writings that constitute a genre characterized by the structural fact they don't infringe upon the sphere of divine love or, if so, only by metaphor. Conversely, mystic works certainly tend to use metaphors of profane love to evoke divine love, and erotic effects may arise, but these don't forge a theory of profane love in its own right (although the mixed character of all of these texts makes any strict generic classification difficult).

In natural love, through loving the beloved [*mahbub*], the lover [*muhibb*] loves nobody but himself and the act of love, *hubb al-hubb*. In spiritual love, the lover loves both himself and the beloved, who can also be and mostly is the Beloved, that is God—hence, the difference between Ibn Hazm's mundane epistle and, for example, Ibn Arabi's (d. 1240) essay on sacred love in chapter 178 of *Kitâb al-Futûhât al-Makkiyya* [*Meccan illuminations*].

Biography

Ibn Hazm al-Andalusi was born in 994 in Al-Andalus (Spain), a Muslim territory dominated from 756 until 1031 by the Umayyad Caliphs in Córdoba. He witnessed the decline of the Umayyads, vainly devoting his short political career to their dynasty, his lifelong love's object. Then he retired from political life in 1024. A large part of his work, probably written between 1025 and 1030, was concerned with law and theology. He died in 1064.

GÉRARD SIARY

Editions

Tawq Al Hamâma. Beirut: Dar Al Marefah, 2003 (in Amharic). *Le Collier du pigeon*. Translated into French and edited by Léon Bercher. Paris and Beirut: Les Éditions de la Méditerranée et les Éditions Kitaba, 1981.

The Ring of the Dove: A Treatise on the Art and Practice of Arab Love. Translated by A.J. Arberry. London: Luzac Oriental, 1996.

De l'amour et des amants. Translated by G. Martinez-Gros. Paris: Sindbad, 1992.

References and Further Reading

Arazi, Albert. *Amour divin et amour profane dans l'Islam médiéval à travers le dîwân de Khalid Al-Katib*. Paris: G. P. Maisonneuve et Larose, 1990.

Arnaldez, Roger. *Grammaire et théologie chez Ibn Hazm de Cordoue: Essai sur la structure et les conditions de la pensée musulmane*. Paris: Vrin, 1981 (1956).

Ben Slama, Raja. "Les 'Sphères divisées' d'Aristophane à Ibn Hazm." *Anales del Seminario de Historia de la Filosofia* 19 (2002): 39–51.

Charles-Dominique, Paule. "Tawq al-Hamâma." In *Dictionnaire universel des littératures*, edited by Béatrice Didier, vol. 3, 3726. Paris: PUF, 1994.

Chebel, Malek. *Encyclopédie de l'amour en Islam. Érotisme, beauté et sexualité dans le monde arabe, en Perse et en Turquie*, 605–9. Paris: Payot, 1995.

Corbin, Henry. *Histoire de la philosophie islamique*. Paris : Gallimard, 1986 (1964). Section VIII.2 on Ibn Hazm, p. 313–19.

Giffen, Lois Anita. *Theory of Profane Love Among the Arabs: The Development of the Genre*. New York: NYU Press, 1971.

Goodman, Lenn E. *Islamic Humanism*, 61–5. Oxford: Oxford University Press, 2003.

Ibn Dawud. *The Book of the Flower*. Translated by A.R. Nikl. Chicago: University of Chicago Press, 1932 (bilingual edition).

Jahiz, al-. "Boasting Match over Maids and Youths." In *Nine Essays of al-Jahiz*, translated by William M. Hutchins, 139–66. New York: Lang, 1989.

Martinez-Gros, Gabriel. "L'amour-trace. Réflexions sur le *Collier de la Colombe*." *Arabica* 34 (987): 147.

———. "Les Femmes dans le *Collier de la Colombe*." In *Atalaya* I, 5–14. Paris: Presses de la Sorbonne nouvelle, 1991.

———. "L'Amour en miroir dans le *Tawq al-hamâma*." In *Al-Qantara*. Paris: Institut du Monde Arabe, 1996.

Michot, Yahia. "Un célibataire endurci et sa maman : Ibn Taymiyya (m. 728/1328) et les femmes." *Acta Orientalia Belgica* 15 (2001): 165–90.

Mújica Pinilla, Ramón. *Collar de la paloma del alma. Amor sagrado y amor profano en la enseñanza de Ibn Hazm y de Ibn 'Arabi*. Madrid: Hiperión, 1990.

Toelle, Heidi, and Katia Zakharia. *A la découverte de la littérature arabe du VIe siècle à nos jours*. Paris: Flammarion, 2003.

IHARA SAIKAKU

1642–1693
Japanese short story writer and poet

The authorship of several of the works of prose fiction attributed to Ihara Saikaku has been questioned by some modern critics, one theory alleging that all but the first, *Kōshoku ichidai otoko* [*The Life of an Amorous Man*] (1682), are by his followers and disciples. Be that as it may, we can discern two main divisions of subject matter in his writings: erotic works [*kōshokubon*] in the period 1682–1687, and fiction centering on the lives of ordinary city dwellers and their financial and economic worries [*chōninmono*] from 1688 to 1693. There are also other groupings of a variety of stories, such as *Shokoku banashi* [*Tales from the Provinces*] (1685).

The Life of an Amorous Man gained Saikaku a great reputation. It describes the sexual adventures of its hero, Yonosuke, and the women (and on a few occasions the youths) with whom he has passionate but fleeting affairs. The son of a rake and a courtesan, Yonosuke finds his sensual vocation early when, at the age of seven, he becomes fixated on love to the great amusement of the maids in his household. While still a youth he and a companion escape from a wily courtesan who has tried to entrap them with too well-worn a story, comparing him to a handsome prince who once threw snow into her bosom to match its whiteness. At age fifteen, in the first year of his manhood, he has some sexual encounters with a group of kabuki actors who are going around the villages looking for clients. When in bed, his lover tells how these activities will help to purchase his freedom but that he is meanwhile obliged to accept any male who comes along, just as he has already made love to a woodcutter in the forest and a naked sailor on the beach, and even an old man covered in sores could not be refused. Yonosuke cannily suspects that this tale, like the courtesan's, is largely invented, but this does not spoil his pleasure. The narrative is picaresque, following Yonosuke through his many and varied encounters:

there are well-observed details of courtesans, prostitutes, and ordinary women both young and old, married and free, together with depictions of their behavior, conditions of life, dress, and demeanor in many expected and unexpected places of assignation. Teahouses feature prominently, but so also do bathhouses, tumble-down shacks, and dilapidated cottages in the countryside. The series of events moves swiftly from the story of a widow who develops too great a familiarity with her servants, to how Yonusuke becomes the business manager for groups of effeminate wandering youths—an ignoble trade, he feels, though despite his poverty, the hiring of amorous women never fails to attract him. A pretty, young girl, who disguises herself as an ugly old woman at a village religious orgy to escape the attentions of the local youths is seduced by Yonosuke. They live together in penury for a while, and then go their separate ways.

Yonosuke is now twenty-eight. Even when thrown into prison, he fraternizes with the roughs and glimpses a woman there through the bars of his cell. The story develops a strange, macabre, and almost whimsical quality at moments: he writes to the woman with ink made of the prison cobwebs, then she is violently reclaimed by her husband when Yonosuke and she are unexpectedly released. Yonosuke later comes across some grave robbers hard at work, who explain that they need only the corpse's nails and hair, since the courtesans in the nearby town pay good prices for the supply of allegedly personal love tokens they can give to their clients. The corpse, is, of course, that of the woman from the prison, thus eliciting Yonosuke's comment, which seems appropriate to many of the incidents narrated in the book, "How frail indeed is life."

Ghosts of Yonosuke's past loves to whom he falsely vowed fidelity come one night to attack him in frightening shapes—half woman, half monster: "There is no fury like a woman deceived, especially *after* she has been driven to suicide." But the narrative is not overtly ironic. Yonosuke refuses to be manacled by amorous ties to any woman. He is always on the move, and is by now widely admired for the enviable notoriety of his erotic adventures. An encounter with another band of kabuki actors results in the unexpected and amusing sight of an amorous priest hidden in the branches of a tree waiting for his lover to acknowledge him. Yonosuke puts the pair together: "Dallying with these youths is like seeing wolves beneath scattering cherry blossoms, whereas going to bed with prostitutes gives one the feeling of groping in the dark beneath the new moon without a lantern." The narrative ends with a short chapter that foreshadows, it seems, a sort of erotic utopia for worn-out reprobates. Yonosuke has become gray haired and ugly—but so too, he reflects, have all the women he has known. Together with some companions in a like state of decrepitude, he builds a tiny ship to sail to the island of Nyogo, where all the women will aggressively seize hold of them. The sail is made from the silken inner garments of his former courtesan wife, and the ropes are fashioned from prostitutes' hair. There is to be no return. This is a witty summation of Yonosuke's amorous life and his convivial wantonness, for which he is not condemned. It seems strangely like an apotheosis. The book is "meant obviously to be understood as a plebeian version of the courtly lover Prince Genji in *The Tale of Genji*" (Schalow), though it may be doubted that its overall tone is parodic.

The second book, *Shoen Ōkagami* [*The Great Mirror of Loves*] (1685), chronicles the amorous adventures of Yonosuke's son. The third book, *Kōshoku gonin onna* [*Five Women Who Loved Love*] (1686), narrates in separate stories based on actual events the fates of five heroines enmeshed in romantic love. Respectability is sacrificed to the pursuit of passion, and four of the affairs terminate in death. Even the fifth affair/story, "The Tale of Gengobei," was probably based on a real-life event which ended in suicide. But here it is given an upbeat ending, and also provides a wry twist on the theme of the woman who captures her beloved by adapting her strategy to his tastes. The hero, twenty-six-year-old Gengobei, worships in succession two incomparably beautiful youths who both unfortunately soon die. Unlike women, Gengobei swears that he will not take a new lover (but, of course, we see the irony that he has already been unfaithful to the memory of his first love). However, a young girl named Oman is consumed with love for him and, having noticed a book on male love in his collection, dresses as a boy and seduces him. The vicissitudes of life are again deftly caught in this narrative, and Gengobei concludes that there is little difference between being in love with men or women. He is thereafter happy and sorrowful in turn.

The fourth book, *Kōshoku ichidai onna* [*The Life of an Amorous Woman*] (1686), is another picaresque novel, plausibly interpreted as a parody of Buddhist confessional literature. At the start, the narrator comes to the "Hermitage of Voluptuousness," according to the sign that an old crone has put up on her dilapidated retreat in the wilderness. He overhears the story of her life, which she tells to two unexpected (but evidently very welcome) male visitors. This female "Rake's Progress" charts her fall from prosperity to destitution and from youth to old age through a series of erotic adventures and sexual employments. She is first dismissed for making love to her handsome prospective father-in-law while his ugly wife lies asleep in bed with them. She takes this with a light laugh. Then she is wrongly blamed by fellow concubines, who are erotically overheated, for causing her new lord's impotence. At sixteen she is sold to a teahouse because her father is heavily in debt. Here she learns how to conduct herself as a courtesan, describing both her pleasant and her disagreeable duties and experiences. Her clients are varied and demanding—many are inexperienced and need to be aroused; one snores heavily; what is going on in adjacent rooms seems far more sexy.

Next on the downward path she becomes a courtesan of the middle rank, reduced to social humiliation, fewer clients, and only two layers of mattress. She learns the rule that men will often ruin themselves with courtesans, but in her case three of her clients are business failures and she is left alone when she starts to lose her hair. On the next level in her descent, she is down to one layer of mattress and has blunt, vulgar clients. She now learns more tricks to inveigle men. In a hurry she services shop assistants and, following the rules of the house, bundles her clothing quickly out of sight. At one point she is so glad to have a customer that she does not even ask what he looks like.

She is sold again into even cheaper prostitution. Later she establishes a writing school for girls, though this is a front for composing love letters to order for young men, since she knows how a girl's passion works. She becomes a maid-servant and seduces her employer when he is dressed up for a Buddhist ceremony. She joins a group of singing "priestesses," who are in reality prostitutes. She mistakenly tries to seduce an old man, who turns out to be a woman in disguise.

In many of these episodes a delicate form of ribaldry is fused with cutting observations on the vulnerable state of women who fall too low and have to survive. Toward the end of her story— and now, of course, of her life—she reflects on the quantity and quality of her lovers and seems, perhaps, poised for repentence. It was, she candidly but no doubt shrewdly admits, a shameful and demanding career. Since she could not possibly save enough from her small earnings, she simply made a companion of her *sake* bottle. And now that her beauty has faded, she still has hopes that there are "worms who prefer nettles." But as the story ends, it is far from obvious that the old woman regrets her past, except in the sense that she cannot experience it all over again. In what has every appearance of mock innocence, she asks her male visitors: "You may call it a trick of my old trade, but how could my heart be so impure?"

The fifth book, for which Saikaku is perhaps now chiefly remembered, particularly in the West, is *Nanshoku Ōkagami* [*The Great Mirror of Male Love*] (1687), which, by its title, could be thought to form a pendant to *Shoen Ōkagami.* The author states that he has tried to reflect in this "Great Mirror" the various examples of the love of men which his readers may all too soon perhaps forget. This large collection of short stories is divided into two main parts, the whole comprising eight sections of five stories each. In a mythological preface, Saikaku wittily outlines the origin of the love of youths, which is held to have precedence chronologically and aesthetically over the love of women. This idea is developed in Story 1.1 which poses the question why, in Saikaku's time, people remained unaware of the subtle and elegant pleasures afforded by such love. After narrating several examples of lovers of boys, including the priest Yoshida Kenkō, who tarnishes his reputation by writing one love letter to a lady when his friend

has asked him to do so, an amusing and sophisticated list is made of the comparative charms of girls and boys. Which should be preferred: the young girl preening herself before a mirror? or a lad of the same age cleaning his teeth? No comment is offered, though in this example, artifice is set against natural cleanliness. Judgment is left to the connoisseurship of the (male) reader. The parallels conclude with the observation that a woman's heart is twisted like the wistaria with all its lovely blooms, whereas a youth may have a thorn or two, but he possesses the fragrance and beauty of the plum tree's early blossom.

The first 20 stories focus on the Samurai ethic of nobility, loyalty, and honor. They describe other examples of selfless devotion, too, as in Story 1.2, which narrates an idyll of boy love shared by two students at school. Their mutual devotion inspires watchful anxiety in their misogynistic teacher and admiring passion in the heart of an eighty-year-old Buddhist priest. An episode in Story 2.1 captures with some irony the moment of freedom when a youth has just passed the peak of his good looks, which are now beginning to fade. His lord, who would not previously have allowed him to commit *sepputu* (ritual suicide), has now transferred his affections to another boy, thus making suicide allowable but no longer honorably motivated. Another story (2.2) well illustrates the code of love, honor, and revenge. Here, a boy's unadorned beauty strongly attracts his lord, who declares himself willing to die for him. But the boy proudly responds that forcing him to yield is not true love: his heart remains his own; and should he ever find a true lover, he will lay down his life for him. A lover materializes and the lord cuts off the youth's arms and head. Later the lover himself cuts off the lord's arms and kills him before committing *sepputu* in a temple at the age of twenty-one. Those who hear the story of such deep love approve strongly of the conduct of the two lovers.

The tales in this section come from traditional literary sources. The love which men and youths swear to uphold, though erotically charged, was intended to last in this world and the next— hence the nobility attached to *sepputu,* which provides an honorable conclusion to several of the tales and the justification for exacting revenge which springs from outraged honor. The relationships are usually between an attractive youth (*wakashu,* up to the age of nineteen) and an older man. One lord can have several youths who all owe him social and sexual allegiance, but as a consequence they dare not respond to another's love without risking severe punishment. In this world, emotional and sexual bonds create obligations of trust which cannot be violated without danger, though transgressions are sometimes pardoned, as in Story 3.5, which tells how an impoverished Samurai falls in love with the handsome favorite of a powerful lord. After many years he declares his passion by means of an account of the long history of his feelings. The youth is therefore in a quandry and tells his master that if he refuses the man's affection, he will betray his honor as a follower of boy love. On the other hand, if he responds, he betrays his lord. He therefore asks to be allowed to commit *sepputu.* The lord is, however, magnanimous: he forgives the youth and gives money and robes to the Samurai, who then says farewell to his lover and becomes a monk. The second part of the collection focuses on the love of youths among kabuki actors and male prostitutes in the "floating world" of the pleasure districts of Saikaku's own time, which he knew firsthand. By 1651 boys and women had both been banished from the stage, so adult male actors alone remained. Saikaku's stories wittily paint this milieu, with its love intrigues between actors and youths, its thirty-year-olds archly pretending to be young, its sexual exploitation, its sufferings, and its shabbiness.

The stories in this section are peopled by city dwellers, unsophisticated provincials, greedy tradesmen, and hypocritical priests. With dry humor and irony they show both the good and the bad sides of the picture as complementary elements of human life. In Story 6.1 a lover of the handsome Itō puns on the youth's name, calling him a "burial ground" because his fee for a single night is three pieces of silver. Another tale (6.3) relates how a man has such lifelike pictures of the actors that he can enjoy himself all day long in solitude at home. But soon he falls in love with a kabuki prostitute and the intrigue develops from there. A more facetious story is told in 6.4: the beautiful female impersonator Kichiya sells his own attractive brand of face powder to many eager women, one of whom very discreetly invites him to her house. He is disguised in his woman's clothes, but the lady's husband returns unexpectedly and takes him for what he is not. In bed with him,

however, the husband is more than delighted at his mistake and the two men spend the night together to their mutual satisfaction.

In Story 7.1, the problems encountered by a boy prostitute are narrated with sophistication and: on one occasion he is with a group of pilgrims, who draw lots, as a result of which he is assigned to a repulsive old man. He resorts to using his "secret thigh technique" but fears his ruse will be discovered. The narrator adds that none of his efforts ever brought him in much money, since his manager took it all. In the same tale a cloud of fireflies, which are emblematic of sodomy, are let loose by a priest at a party, reminding the revelers of an incident in bygone days when the insects were placed in the palanquin of a certain lady. The narrator comments that it seemed suspiciously like an unusually refined confession of love. In Story 7.4 a group of high-spirited actors, who, being well over twenty-two dare not reveal their true ages, are with their lovers when an uncouth Samurai arrives on the scene and demands to pair off with Tamamura Kichiya, the most beautiful among them. Kichiya temporizes before craftily shaving off half of the Samurai's beard. Saikaku's urbane narratives describe a connoisseurship of the love of youths which signals a high measure of sophistication and culture in his society. Although some of the male admirers of male beauty are portrayed as misogynists, perhaps for ironic or humorous effect, this is not a widespread attitude, and the stories demonstrate that a variety of sexual tastes was accommodated in 17th-century Japan.

In modern times Saikaku has found new fame. Rediscovered toward the end of the 19th century, along with the introduction of realism into Japanese literature by writers such as Ozaki Kōyō (1869–1903) and Kōda Rohan (1867–1947), he has benefited from the lifting of censorship and from more open attitudes since 1946. The appreciations of Takeda Rintarō (1904–1946) and Oda Sakunosuke (1913–1947) mark a significant moment in the renewal of public interest in Saikaku, and in the West a selection of stories from *The Great Mirror of Male Love,* translated with an appreciative and explanatory preface by Ken Satō, appeared in French in 1927 (this shortened version was translated into English in 1931). In recent years a number of his works have become available in English. His attraction for us is not so much as an historical witness to a certain moment in the development of social attitudes in Japanese culture toward hedonism and erotic experience, but as a refined and witty teller of tales who leaves salacious details understated and sensual enjoyment understood.

Biography

Ihara Saikaku was born in Osaka when it was a recently developed busy trading town, and belonged to the mercantile middle class. His real name was probably Hirayama Tōgo. He used several aliases in the course of his career as a famous composer of *haikai,* for which he was especially renowned, and, from the 1680s to the end of his life, as a successful writer of fiction. He adopted the style "Saikaku" [West Crane] in 1673. His wife died in 1675. In 1677 he is reported to have taken the tonsure, without it necessarily implying the profession of Buddhist vows, and to have journeyed throughout central Japan as a mendicant for several months at a time. This is allegedly the period when he gathered the stories which were to supply the material for his collections of tales. The Genroku period under the Tokugawa regime when he was writing was a time of growing prosperity and relaxed hedonism after the rigors and uncertainties of four centuries of civil war. Saikaku was a contemporary of several great artistic men: Hishikawa Moronobu (1618–1694), the artist who perfected the technique of woodblock illustration and incidentally provided the erotic pictures for a number of Saikaku's novels, adapting Saikaku's original witty designs and also pirating an edition of the *Life of an Amorous Man* in Edo in 1684; Matsuo Bashō (1644–1694), the poet in whose hands the haiku reached its zenith; Chikamatsu Monzaemon (1653–1725), the great dramatist; and Ejima Kiseki (1667–1736), following in Saikaku's footsteps, a writer of stories and anecdotes describing fugitive pleasures (e.g., *Yakusha Kuchi-Jamisen*

[*The Actor's Vocal Samisen*] 1699, which deals with the lives of kabuki actors, and *Fūryū Kyoku-Jamisen* [*The Elegant Samisen Virtuosities*], which is in the form of a confessional by a decrepit ex-courtesan and an old man who was formerly an effeminate kabuki youth). It was also the time when pleasure districts (*yūri*) were set up in the larger cities of Kyōto, Osaka, and Edo. In these *yūri*, which were separated from the main urban area and provided with independent access, teahouses afforded sexual relaxation in the context of formal etiquette, together with a strict and complex hierarchy of courtesans (*tayu,* the predecessors of the modern geisha) and prostitutes ranging from the very exclusive to the cheap and unsophisticated girls and women of the back streets. Those who could be found there have been brought back to life by Saikaku's piquant anecdotes.

PATRICK POLLARD

Selected Works

Five Women Who Loved Love. Translated by W.T. de Bary. Rutland, VT: Charles E. Tuttle, 1956.

The Great Mirror of Male Love. Translated with an introduction by P.G. Schalow. Stanford, CA: Stanford University Press, 1990. Complete translation, with bibliography.

The Life of an Amorous Man. Translated by Kengi Hamada. Rutland, VT: Charles E. Tuttle, 1964.

The Life of an Amorous Woman and Other Writings. Edited and translated by Ivan Morris. London: Chapman and Hall, 1963. Abridgment, with extracts from several works.

Further Reading

Danly, R.L. *In the Shade of Spring Leaves.* New Haven, CT: Yale University Press, 1981.

Hibbett, H. *The Floating World in Japanese Fiction.* London: Oxford University Press, 1959.

Leupp, G.P. *Male Colors: The Construction of Homosexuality in Tokugawa Japan.* Berkeley and Los Angeles: University of California Press, 1995.

Struve, D. *Ihara Saikaku. Un Romancier japonais du XVIIe siécle.* Paris: Presses Universitaires de France, 2001.

İLHAN, ATTILA

1925–
Turkish poet, novelist, and essayist

Attila İlhan, a very prominent Turkish intellectual and author, has published novels, film scripts, and collections of poetry and of critical essays on politics and literature. His politically engaged work focuses on the establishment and progress of the nation-state in Turkey and unconventional sexual attitudes. His works blend popular genres and politically and sexually charged themes, making him the most controversial Turkish author of the last six decades. The role of sexuality in his works distinguishes Attila İlhan from other Turkish socialist realist intellectuals. İlhan's several visits to Paris beginning in the 1940s determined his approach to literature and politics, as well as sexuality.

In his poetry, Attila İlhan employs an original stock of images involving female same-sex desire. In his poem "Triangle," a lesbian relationship was depicted for the first time in Turkish poetry, and lesbian sexuality is also featured in "The Kingdom of Cem the Second." In "A Country named Claude," a poem of nine stanzas, the title character, a woman, faces her desire for other women:

> A country named Claude where black palm trees
> change and kiss young girls every night
> that Raphael draws in the form of young boys
> with doubtful lips lined with down
> . . . .
> a country named Claude, nobody has visited
> its silence that is deeper than oceans;
> it is cut out of the map of the world
> a howling dog is put in its place

Beginning with *Kurtlar Sofrası* [*The Feast of Wolves*] (1963), which contains a severe criticism of the relations between the Turkish state and newly forming corporations, he started a five-volume series of novels with the general title *Aynanın İçindekiler* [*Those Inside the Mirror*] (1973–1987), in which he developed characters that not only are politically involved, but also have unconventional sexual identities. These

novels, though still widely read and discussed, had a mixed reception by critics due in large part to their unfamiliar and blunt sexual content.

In a period when sexuality was perceived as secondary in status to the problem of social inequality by rightist and leftist intellectuals, Attila İlhan depicted women characters who explored their sexuality without any limitations. Indeed, they appear as dominant partners in sexual relations. In his novels, sexual identity itself doesn't determine the political convictions of a character; however, it may have consequences on personal development. This discrepancy between the political and the sexual morality of the protagonists creates a tension that is never resolved by the author. Marxist critics harshly criticize his distinguishing sexual and political personae, since this is against a holistic perception of the individual.

The novel in which Attila İlhan develops his conviction of the necessary destruction of the dualism between femininity and masculinity is the highly controversial *Fena Halde Leman* [*Leman Badly*] (1980). Due to its unfamiliar sexual content, *Leman* met with hostile reviews, as many critics condemned İlhan for exploiting sexual themes to make profit.

This subversive novel starts as the protagonist, a famous businesswoman, Leman Korkut, strikes a deal with a French company just after the military intervention of 1971 in Turkey. A left-wing journalist witnesses the making of this deal and decides to investigate further. He later meets with Leman, who is disturbed by his investigations; but far from being dissuaded from pursuing them, he is intrigued by the juxtaposition of Leman's coarse, manly voice and her beauty. The journalist realizes that Leman Korkut is the wife of a deceased politician, Ekrem Korkut, who had committed suicide in Paris, where he exiled himself after the 1960 military coup. He also finds out that she was originally named Jeanne and is a half-Jewish French woman who later married Ekrem during the 1950s, changed her name, and settled in Turkey.

After Leman Korkut's sudden death in a car accident, the journalist receives her memoirs, which tell the story of a few months during an unspecified period between 1964 and 1970 when Leman went to Paris, lured by a mysterious letter concerning her husband's suicide.

With the memoirs the dry and measured narration of the journalist is replaced by a confusingly ornate narrative in which we learn the story of Leman Korkut's whole life through flashbacks. During her stay in Paris, she also meets some of her late husband's friends: the narcissistic Cécile, daughter of a rich family, who never lets anyone touch her but enjoys having someone else watching her masturbate; Lili, alias George, a blond, femme-fatale transvestite with a taste for physical pain, who is trying to raise money for a sex-change operation; Bobby, alias Victoire Kaunda, an African woman of male gender who is a sadist and impersonates women in night clubs; Pasha Nuri, an ex-communist Turk who is a masochist and surrenders to the tortures of an old woman for money; and finally Madame Pellegrini who pursues very young boys and pimps Lili.

As the narrative unfolds, even Leman appears as a sexually complex character, and we learn how she fell for her mother-in-law Haco Hanım during the early years of her marriage to Ekrem Korkut. Haco Hanım, who dies while making love to Leman, was the third wife of an Ottoman officer, whose earlier life and initiation into lesbian sex by one of her co-wives in her husband's harem are recounted by Attila İlhan in another historical novel, *Haco Hanım Vay* (1984).

In Paris, while simultaneously attracted to the two transvestites—Lili, the femme-fatale man-to-woman, and Bobby, the muscular woman-to-man—Leman starts to lose her sense of self, and she finds out that her husband has always wanted to have her as a boy, while she had strived to be a "real" woman for him, and that, never becoming conscious of each other's desire, they ruined a possibly harmonious relationship. She escapes back to Turkey to a dream world, in which the journalist would meet her as a businesswoman.

Curiously, although *Fena Halde Leman* is crowded with polysexual characters, the phallus is conspicuously missing in the novel. Apart from Lili's penis, which is mentioned once in a passive mood, and Bobby's rubber penis, the presence of the phallus is always made known by its conspicuous absence. Even though Ekrem's homosexual tendencies are implied, his sexual relationships with Cécile and Lili, are never fully depicted in the novel; nor are Leman and Ekrem's lovemaking scenes. In fact, Attila İlhan clearly focuses on the feminine sexual potential of women in his novels, while men, with suppressed feminine tendencies, are sexually silent.

In *Leman*, İlhan's belief that femininity and masculinity one day will merge into each other, erasing gender difference, is unabashedly put forth. While expressing this conviction, he creates one of the most intriguing explorations of gender confusion. Attila İlhan expressed his ideas on gender in two volumes of essays: *Hangi Cinsellik* [*Which Sexuality?*] (1976) and *Yanlış Kadınlar Yanlış Erkekler* [*Wrong Women, Wrong Men*] (1985). In these essays İlhan, exploring the progression of the merging of genders in world history, produced the first balanced work about diversity of gender roles in Turkey.

Unfortunately İlhan's work has yet to be translated into any of the European languages. This is possibly due to Attila İlhan's creative use of Turkish. Ornate with unconventional metaphors and archaisms and incorporating local usages and social codifications in order to reflect class and generational differences, Attila İlhan's language, as well as his innovative approach to sexuality, continues to have a profound impact on modern Turkish literature.

Biography

Attila İlhan was born in Menemen, Turkey. His first book of poetry, *Duvar* [*The Wall*], appeared in 1948.

SELIM S. KURU

IRELAND

Ireland is not a country readily associated with the erotic. Censoriousness and repression in the modern period, both pre- and post-independence, have colored perceptions of the island as a place deeply inimical to writings on the pleasures of the flesh. Yet, from the earliest mythological tales to the writings of James Joyce and Edna O'Brien, the erotic has been an area of continuous preoccupation and interest for the Irish writer. The centerpiece of the eighth-century Ulster cycle of mythological tales is the epic account of a giant cattle raid, *Táin Bó Cuailgne*. The *Táin* is held to be a masterpiece of early Irish literature and is important in giving us insights into the mores of pre-Christian Ireland. A central character in the tale is the Queen of Connacht Medb, who is explicit in asserting her right to her own sexual pleasure and makes love to one of her captains, Fergus, with the approval of her husband, Ailill, and indeed the tale ends with Medb urinating and menstruating three lakes. As Medb tries to recruit warriors to fight against her deadly foe, Cú Chulainn, she frequently offers the "companionship of [her] thighs" to her allies; and her daughter, Finnabair, is similarly free with her sexual favors. Such was the discomfort caused by the sexual frankness of the *Táin* that it would be 1976 before the first full, uncensored edition of the greatest epic in Old Irish would appear in English translation.

In another set of stories from the Ulster cycle on the birth of Cú Chulainn we are introduced to Fergus, whose name has been translated as "Male Ejaculation Son of Super Stallion." His virility was quantified by the claim that seven fists fit into his penis and that his scrotum was the size of a bushel bag. Such was the voraciousness of his sexual appetite that it took "seven women to curb him" unless he slept with Medb or with Flidais (the Deer Goddess), who used to "change thirty men every day or go with Fergus once."

One of the obstacles facing the transmission of erotic writing from earlier periods is that a considerable amount of secular literature was in fact written down by monks in the highly active centers of learning that were Irish monasteries in the early medieval period. The new patriarchal culture of Christianity viewed with deep suspicion the matricentered elements of pre-Christian Irish culture, and many early Irish lyrics depict monks heroically resisting the sexual allure of women. The shadowing of pleasure by the strictures of the evangelists can be seen in the ninth-century poem "A Bé Find" [Lovely Lady], where the poet situates his utopia in the sexual license of pagan Ireland but is aware of the finger-wagging of the Christian present, "Srotha téithmilsi tar tīr / rogu de mid ocus fín / doïni delgnaidi cen on / combart cen peccad, cen chol [All around gentle streams entwine / Mead is drunk, the best of wine / The people have not learned to hate / It's not a sin to copulate]. The erotic in the early and late medieval period often finds its outlet in the displacement from the secular to the religious domain, with poems to Mary and the goddess-turned-saint Bridget particularly common in the Irish literary canon. Another motif is the monk who finds himself transformed into a woman, with the erotic confusion and excitement that ensues from this morphological twist. The influence of the *amour courtois* tradition from continental Europe makes itself keenly felt in late medieval Ireland, and many of the recensions of tales from the period, particularly the *Fiannaíocht* cycle, bear the traces of the oblique ecstasies of courtly love. In the most famous love story from the period, *Tóraigheacht Dhiarmada agus Ghráinne* [*The Pursuit of Diarmaid and Gráinne*], Diarmaid, a bosom companion of the warrior chief Fionn, elopes with Fionn's young fiancée, the lovestruck Gráinne, who has placed Diarmaid under a spell. Initially, Diarmaid puts a fishbone between himself and Gráinne to prove to the pursuing Fionn that they have not been unfaithful to him. However, one day as they are crossing a stream, a spurt of water strikes Gráinne's leg and she notes that it is bolder than Diarmaid, and it is not long before they become lovers.

Their story became inscribed in the Irish landscape as the *dolmens* (ancient burial portals), which consist of one flat stone raised on top of two others, often referred to as the "beds of Diarmaid and Gráinne."

As a result of the Anglo-Norman invasion, English and French were spoken as minority languages in late medieval Ireland, and it is from the latter half of the thirteenth century that we get an English-language text written down in Kildare, *The Land of Cockaygne,* which is an anticlerical satire in verse, with copious couplings between various members of the clergy. Prominent in this text, as in Irish-language texts of the period, is an exuberant celebration of orality, with eating, drinking, and fornication linked in a charmed circle of excess. The Tudor and Cromwellian conquest of Ireland, which would begin in earnest in the late sixteenth century and see the final military pacification of the native population by end of the seventeenth century, causes the collapse of the Gaelic and Anglo-Norman aristocracy who were patrons of the Gaelic-language poetic elite. Irish still remained the majority language of the population, and the eighteenth century would witness the production of the great erotic masterpiece in Irish of the period, the 1,026-line *Cúirt an Mheán Oíche* [*The Midnight Court*], by the schoolteacher and poet Brian Merriman. However, as English became the sole language of public life, an English-language literature began to emerge which would eventually bring Irish eros to the forefront of world literature.

A spate of English-language translations of French drama for the Dublin theatre in the late seventeenth century provided the impetus for the work of Irish dramatists who began to form and exploit the genre of Restoration drama. Foremost among these dramatists were George Farquhar and Richard Brinsley Sheridan. In George Farquhar's "Love and a Bottle" (1698), his first play staged in London at the Drury Lane Theatre, we meet Wildair and Roebuck, "Irish Gentlemen of wild, roving temper," who ally libertinage and economic self-advancement. In Sheridan's most successful plays, *The Rivals* (1775) and *The School for Scandal* (1777), the plots are rich in sexual suggestiveness, and much use is made of metaphor and figurative language to signal erotic subtexts and subplots to the audience. Indeed, part of the popular success of these dramatists related to their manipulation of

theatrical conventions as a way of testing the sexual proprieties of the period. The Irish tradition of gothic fiction in the nineteenth century, from Charles Mathurin's *Melmoth the Wanderer* (1820) to Sheridan Le Fanu's *In a Glass Darkly* (1872) and Bram Stoker's *Dracula* (1897) would explore transgression and extreme mental states in their various forms. Sexual tension and the erotic would be central to much of the speculation of Irish gothic novelists on the relationship between the sexes; and a constant preoccupation, articulated most fluently by Stoker, is the undermining of conventional reason by powerful, transgressive sexual urges.

Oscar Wilde, who was related to Mathurin, professed his strong admiration for *Melmoth the Wanderer* (1820), and gothic elements are strongly to the fore in *The Picture of Dorian Gray* (1889). Wilde, who was much influenced by writers of the French Decadent era, used the theme of the double in *The Picture of Dorian Gray* to explore the highly ambiguous nature of Gray's sexuality, and in Wilde's essay on Shakespeare, "The Portrait of Mr. W.H.," he explicitly addresses the question of Shakespeare's alleged homosexuality. His earlier *Poems* (1881) had already hinted at the erotic possibilities of forbidden love. Wilde's biblical drama *Salomé* was refused a license in London in 1892, partly on the grounds of the undisguised eroticism of the relationship between Salomé and St. John the Baptist, and would not be staged until 1896 in Paris. Wilde would endure, of course, imprisonment and public opprobrium for his homosexuality, but his defense of homoeroticism both at his trial and in his posthumously published letter to Lord Alfred Douglas, *De Profundis* (1905), made him an emblematic figure for gay-rights activists in the twentieth century.

Wilde was not the only Irish literary figure who would attract the attention of the courts for what was deemed an unseemly interest in the erotic. In *Ulysses* (1922) Joyce explored the manifold varieties of the erotic and situated sexuality at the heart of the quotidian preoccupations of his Dublin men and women going about their daily lives. Molly Bloom's soliloquy which ends the book was found to be particularly shocking because a female character was frankly assuming her sexuality and describing its pleasures. The Society for the Prevention of Vice had the serial publication of *Ulysses* in the *Little Review* stopped in 1920 on the grounds that it was pornographic. As a result, Joyce was forced to publish *Ulysses* in Paris in 1922.

That same year, the Irish Free State came into being, strongly influenced by the moral teachings of the Catholic hierarchy. The Censorship of Publications Act of 1929 initiated a period of sustained censorship of any material that was deemed to be "indecent" or even remotely touching on the erotic. A trenchant critic of the new legislation was William Butler Yeats, who in *The Winding Stair and Other Poems* (1933) gave voice (particularly in the "Crazy Jane" poems) to the full power of the erotic and deplored the baleful influence of life-denying prudery. Kate O'Brien, who broached lesbian sexuality in her writing, had two of her novels, *Mary Lavelle* (1936) and *The Land of Spices* (1941), banned in Ireland. Another pioneer in the literary exploration of the sexuality of women, from a heterosexual perspective, was Edna O'Brien, whose novel *The Country Girls* (1960) also fell foul of the Irish censor. The passing of a new Censorship of Publications Act in 1967 coincided with the beginnings of the liberalization of Irish society, which would gain momentum throughout the 1970s, 1980s, and 1990s. Writers now dealt much more freely with erotic experiences in different-sex and same-sex relationships in both English and Irish-language writing. Nuala Nï Dhomhnaill, Caitlïn Maude, and Biddy Jenkinson have all explored variations of the erotic in their Irish-language poetry. Colm Tóibïn in *The South* (1990), Desmond Hogan in *Leaves on Grey* (1980), Keith Ridgway in *Standard Time* (2001), and Jamie O'Neill in *At Swim Two Boys* (2001) have given expression to the subtle permutations of pleasure in the lives of their gay characters. Emma Donoghue in *Stir Fry* (1994) and *Hood* (1995), Mary Dorcey in *The Noise in the Woodshed* (1989), and Cherry Smyth in *When the Lights Go Up* (2001) have detailed the coming-of-age of the sexual awareness of their lesbian heroines and narrative personae.

Two distinctive notes on contemporary Irish writing on the erotic are, firstly, the foregrounding of a darker side to human sexual encounters and, secondly, the continuing presence of the satirical or the parodic. The first feature is exemplified by the writing of Dermot Bolger, in which the sexual is often a potent metaphor of frustration and failure; in novels such as *A Woman's Daughter* (1987), the malignant consequences of a deeply repressive religious culture express themselves in exploitative and demeaning sexual relationships. The second feature is to be found in the work of writers such as Anne Enright, John Banville, and Aidan Mathews, in which the erotic is often the occasion for high comedy and, as in late medieval satire, the ridiculous and the sublime are to be found in close proximity. Constipated solemnity in the presence of eros is not often to be found, and there is frequently a kind of Beckettian wryness in the observation of human ecstasies. The Irish erotic tradition in literature has withstood the repeated assaults of church and state over the centuries to produce more than one thousand years of written celebration of the endless transfigurations of bodily pleasure.

MICHAEL CRONIN

Further Reading

Carlson, Julia, ed. *Banned in Ireland: Censorship and the Irish Writer*. London: Routledge, 1990.

Condren, Mary. *The Serpent and the Goddess: Women, Religion and Power in Celtic Ireland*. New York and London: Harper and Row, 1989.

Ellmann, Richard. *Oscar Wilde*. London: Hamilton, 1987.

Kilfeather, Siobhán. "Origins of the Irish Female Gothic." *Bullán: An Irish Studies Journal* 1 (1994): 35–47.

Marcus, David, ed. *"The Irish Eros": Irish Short Stories and Poems on Sexual Themes*. Dublin: Gill & Macmillan, 1996.

McKone, Kim. *Pagan Past and Christian Present in Early Irish Literature*. Maynooth: An Sagart, 1990.

Nic Eoin, Máirín. *B'ait leo bean: Gnéithe den idéolaïocht inscne i dtraidisiúin literartha na Gaeilge*. Dublin: An Clóchomhar, 1998.

O'Toole, Fintan. *A Traitor's Kiss: The Life of Richard Brinsley Sheridan*. London: Granta, 1997.

Rosenstock, Gabriel, ed. *Irish Love Poems / Dánta Grá*. New York: Hippocrene Books; Dublin: Roberts Books, 1996.

Seymour, St. John D. *Anglo-Irish Literature, 1200–1582*. Cambridge: Cambridge University Press, 1929.

IRIARTE, TOMÁS DE

1750–1791
Spanish dramatist, poet, and translator

The Erotic Poems

Cerezo and Millares Carlo-Hernández Suárez have attempted to clarify the textual status of poems scattered in manuscript and miscellaneous printed editions, but Iriarte's erotic poems have yet to be properly edited or seriously studied. The main sources are (1) Biblioteca Nacional (Madrid) Ms. 3744, entitled *Poesïas lúbricas* [*Lubricious Poems*] (probably added by a cataloguer), which brings together 19 texts, sometimes repeated and in different hands, and (2) the poems contained in *Cuentos y poesïas más que picantes* (1899). The latter includes the outstanding "Perico y Juana," copied in various contemporary manuscripts and reproduced in printed collections from 1872 onward and recently the object of serious textual and critical attention. Though attributed to José Iglesias de la Casa in some early collections and appearing under alternative titles ("El siglo de oro" [The Golden Age], Iriarte's authorship now seems secure.

Written in the Italianate meter of the *octava*, used for pastoral or lyric poetry, "Perico y Juana" exhibits features of a popular style in its fluent narrative manner and simple, though refined, poetic language. The 24 stanzas move from a quarrel between Perico and Juana to their eventual reconciliation through making love. The context is pastoral, since the encounter takes place in the countryside, and the moral of the couple's behavior is drawn by the shepherd, who praises the value of reconciliation to girls from the nearby village. The original break in the relationship is provoked by Juana, but she equally initiates the action which leads to their making up. Her elegance and attractiveness is highlighted by the narrator as she makes her way to the shady valley where she asks to meet Perico. While waiting, she ties a garter to her leg,

erotically lifting the lace-edged petticoats. A voyeuristic pleasure is transmitted through the narrator's voice, in exclamatory and even broken phrases, but without lowering the linguistic tone; thus when her underwear is raised, she reveals the "maravilla octava" [eighth wonder of the world]. The wonderment transfers to Perico, as he arrives, unseen by Juana, and admires the beauty of her body, which under thin clothing appears almost naked. Again her beauty, which the restrained, unexplicit description extends to hips, waist, thighs, and breasts, indirectly communicates her capacity to arouse. Perico's arousal affects both his imagination and his senses, and he embraces Juana with a "dulce fuego" [sweet fire] burning in his veins. His words focus on her breasts and mouth as he expresses the pleasure he receives from her embrace. But his boldness angers her, and ashamed at having caused offense, he retreats.

Once alone, Juana meditates on the capacity of love to blind; women who play hard to get and ignore their natural impulses fail to enjoy the pleasures which love offers. She attempts to rejoin Perico but catches up to him when he is "meando" [pissing], against a tree. This unexpected, and sole, use of a vulgar word is prepared for by the narrator's doubts as to whether to use it. The earlier voyeurism of Perico now transfers to Juana, who hides in order to see the previously covered parts of her lover's anatomy, the poem reverting to euphemism ("crecidas insignias de varón" [swollen male attributes])—and not without erotic literature's customary exaggerations about size. Rushing to clasp Perico, Juana makes the pair fall to the ground with their now bare lower parts coming into contact. Commenting that the couple enjoyed a golden age that morning, the narrator turns away from physical details to evoke the simplicity of lovemaking in the open and then, surprisingly, to note that the so-called frail sex readily sustains a male body in such circumstances. The physical responses become more passionate, and their coupling, in which Juana leads, is conveyed in terms of boats entering narrow straits. The intensity of movements and caresses leads to a climax which reduces Juana to silence. Perico, taken aback, speaks to restore her to normality, whereupon Juana slaps him, inducing a temporary faint. After further movements, they both fall asleep with Juana on top. A shepherd appears and marvels at the harmonious outcome of what earlier was disagreement and discord. The moral lesson addressed to the village girls seems male-centered, suggesting that Juana used her beauty to bring the reconciliation. The previous narration, however, revealed her as protagonist and equal participant in the lovemaking, while the mutuality of their feelings and pleasure are stressed.

Iriarte's other erotic poems are slighter pieces, many in shorter forms such as sonnets or the popular, 10-line *décimas*. Several are improvisations or responses to challenges from other poems, mostly belonging to what Spanish literature terms "festive poetry." The "Casóse el mayordomo" *seguidillas* (popular songs) exploit, in their light, rapid meter, the legendary insatiability of women, provoking a smile in the hearer. The sonnet "Con licencia, señora," a response to the question as to the finest feature of a woman's body, plays on the reader's expectations during the quatrains to end up answering in the tercets that it is her fine bottom. The sonnet "Cuando estoy del Amor, Filis, picado" is a spirited celebration of male pleasure in penetration. The *redondilla,* or round, "Dos finos amantes," concerning a pair of lovers who make love in a toilet, is not erotic, but merely stresses the power of passion to achieve satisfaction. The popular "En viendo la recatada" explains why different types of women yield to and enjoy sex. The sonnet "A una dama que fingió desdenes" rejects women's false show of disdain at being the object of sexual attention and at their capacity to arouse men. The sonnet "La resistencia" is a witty monologue by a woman during clandestine lovemaking, apparently not keen on it, but equally not resisting; it moves to a climax in appropriately halting phrases, ending with her desire for a repeat performance the following day. The sonnet, "La semana adelantada" wittily points up sexual inequality between an elderly husband and young, nubile wife—he claims he can be of service only once a week, which she accepts, thinking the situation could be worse, but ends up asking for a week on account. The thoughts contained in these poems belong to a

venerable tradition, which Iriarte expresses with wit and in polished verse. An acceptance of sexual appetite is evident, as is the mutual enjoyment of both sexes, and hypocrisy is rejected.

Biography

Tomás de Iriarte belonged to a family of intellectuals hailing from the Canary Islands; his uncle Juan was Royal Librarian in Madrid, and his cultured brothers Bernardo and Domingo were prominent in cultural, political, and diplomatic life. Tomás was famed as a dramatist, poet, and translator, achieving celebrity outside Spain in translations of his literary fables and didactic poem on music. His linguistic skills gave him access to philosophical writings in English, French, and Italian, and an Inquisitorial investigation of him in 1779 confiscated works by Voltaire (*L'Évangile de la raison, Dictionnaire philosophique portatif*) and d'Holbach (*Le Bon-Sens, Système de la nature*), as well as a representative selection of erotic narratives in French (*L'Académie des dames, Thérèse philosophe, Les délices du cloître,* among others). His interest in materialist philosophy extended to sexuality, finding literary expression in a series of poems which were unpublished—and unpublishable, given government and Inquisitorial censorship—in his lifetime.

PHILIP DEACON

Editions

Poesías más que picantes. Las Palmas: Ultramarino, 1992. Anthologies including texts by Iriarte.
Cancionero de amor y de risa. Madrid: Joaquín López Barbadillo, 1917; facsimile edition, Madrid: Akal, 1977.
Cancionero moderno de obras alegres. London: H. W. Spirrtual, 1872; facsimile edition, Madrid: Visor, 1980.
Cuentos y poesías más que picantes (Samaniego, Yriarte, anónimos). Edited by "un rebuscador de papeles viejos" [an antiquarian researcher]. Barcelona: L'Avenç, 1899.

Further Reading

Cerezo, José Antonio. "José Iglesias de la Casa" and "Tomás de Iriarte." In *Literatura erótica en España: Repertorio de obras 1519–1936.* Madrid: Ollero y Ramos, 2001.
Gies, David T. "El XVIII porno." In *Signoria di parole. Studi offerti a Mario Dï Pinto,* edited by Giovanna Calabrò. Naples: Liguori, 1999.

Millares Carlo, Agustín, and Manuel Hernández Suárez. "Tomás de Iriarte." In *Biobibliografía de escritores canarios (Siglos XVI, XVII y XVIII)*. Vol. 4. Las Palmas, Grand Canary Island, Spain: El Museo Canario, 1981.

Palacios Fernández, Emilio. "'Los amores de Perico y Juana': Notas a un poema erótico del siglo XVIII." In *Eros literario. Actas del Coloquio celebrado en la* *Facultad de Filología de la Universidad Complutense en diciembre de 1988*. Madrid: Universidad Complutense, 1989.

Pinta Llorente, Miguel de la. "Problemas de cultura española. Decadencia y enciclopedismo." In *Aspectos históricos del sentimiento religioso en España. Ortodoxia y heterodoxia*. Madrid: CSIC [Consejo Superior de Investigaciones Científicas], 1961.

ISTARÚ, ANA

1960–

Costa Rican poet and dramatist

Istarú's work—both her poetry and her plays—is characterized by her fiercely political commitment to the political and sexual liberation of women in Central America. It is marked by its erotic content, its subtle humor, and its giving of voice to women who have been victimized by political intolerance, economic injustice, and gender-based oppression. Istarú is an outspoken critic of social conventions that limit women's potential and of the political neglect that has imposed on women a greater burden of poverty and lack of opportunity.

Istarú's poetry is best known for its erotic content. Her goal, as she has argued frequently, has been to produce an erotic poetry that breaks away from the objectification of the female body that has characterized male erotic poetry in Latin America. This male-centered poetry has led to the creation of stereotypical images of the sexual woman, the most positive of which depict women's bodies as passive recipients of men's desire. Her objective as a poet has been to eschew these male patterns of female erotic representation by linking women's sexuality to both their inner lives (love, emotions, conflicts) and external concerns (politics/nation, economics). Her poetry, as a result, has been described by critics as work that seeks to sever connections to established molds, by extending women's erotic life to encompass most aspects of their being in society. Sexual delight, explicitly described, is never separated from the oppressive sexual mores of Latin American machismo, never far from a critique of the double standards applied to women as sexual beings, and never forgetful of Istarú's responsibility to strive for political and sexual freedom for women. In its celebration of women's sexuality and openly expressed desire, Istarú never forgets that the expression of women's erotic freedom is linked to political freedom and economic power.

Istarú's most mature plays are satiric comedies that sparkle with mordant wit, intelligent dialogue, and plenty of double entendres. *Madre nuestra que estás en la tierra* [*Our Mother Who Art on Earth*] (1996), with its irreverent feminist take on the Lord's Prayer, had its first performance at the Compañía Nacional de Teatro in Costa Rica in 1988. *Baby Boom en el paraíso* [*Baby Boom in Paradise*] (1996) is a one-woman show which Istarú has performed herself on many occasions, narrating the adventures of the female egg from ovulation to conception and then through pregnancy, detailing a woman's changing emotions and their impact on others. Its impudent comedic approach to pregnancy and labor has earned it admirers throughout Latin American and Europe.

In 2000, Istarú wrote and performed in her most critically lauded play to date, *Hombre en escabeche* [*Men in Prickling Brine*], a biting portrayal of Latin American sexual morality. The satire, whose main character is a young woman looking for love in all the wrong places, follows her relationships with the many men in her life (all played by the same actor) as they disappoint her, abandon her, or crush her heart. The gallery of men—which include her father, brother, first boyfriend, and most recent lover—constitutes an assembly of social types in familiar situations which Istarú dissects with sharp irony and satiric wit. The play, whose point of departure is a father's inability to love, allows Istarú to argue that men's disassociation of sexuality and love ultimately condemns them to incomplete lives and contributes to women's feelings of lovelessness and sexual frustration. These themes are linked in the text to Costa Rica's search for political stability in the tricky terrain where Marxism, neoliberalism, and a benevolent despotism lurk.

Biography

Ana Istarú was born in San José, Costa Rica, in 1960. She received a degree from the School of Dramatic Arts of the University of Costa Rica and is well known as a poet, actress, and dramatist. Istarú gained recognition as a poet at the age of fifteen, in 1975, when she won a national competition for young poets with *Palabra nueva* [*New Word*]. Her second book, *Poemas para un día cualquiera* [*Poems for Just Any Old Day*], was published in 1977, when she was just sixteen, followed by her third, *Poemas abiertos y otros amaneceres* [*Open Poems and Other Dawns*], in 1980. *La estación de fiebre* [*Season of Lust*], a collection of highly erotic verse, won the EDUCA (Editorial Universitaria Centroamericana) prize in 1983 and became a best seller in Costa Rica and throughout Latin America. It has been translated into several languages. Her other collections include *La muerte y otros efímeros agravios* [*Death and Other Ephemeral Grievances*] (1989), *Verbo Madre* [*Mother Verb*] (1995), and *Raíces del aire* [*Roots of the Air*] (1996). Her poetry has appeared in translation in highly regarded journals and anthologies in the United States and Europe. A selection of her poems, *Poesía escogida*, appeared in 2002.

Istarú is equally known for her work as an actress and dramatist. She claims to have learned to love poetry through her father and to have drawn her passion for the theater from her mother. As an actress, she has performed in her own plays as well as in Latin American and European classics and is the recipient of several awards, chief among them the Costa Rican National Award for a Beginning Actress in 1990, the National Award for a Lead Actress in 1997, and the Áncora Theater Award for the 1999–2000 season.

Besides the dramas mentioned earlier, Istarú also wrote *El vuelo de la grulla* [*The Flight of the Crane*] (1984). She has earned accolades internationally as the recipient of the María Teresa León Prize for Dramatists (1995), given by the Spanish Association of Stage Directors, for *Baby Boom en el paraíso*, and the Machado Theater Prize (1999), given by the municipal government in Seville, Spain, for *Hombre en escabeche*. Her work has been performed in Spanish and in translation in Costa Rica, Spain, Mexico, France, and the United States. She penned the script for *Caribe*, an award-winning 2004 Costa Rican film directed by Esteban Ramírez.

LIZABETH PARAVISINI-GEBERT

Selected Works

Baby boom en el paraíso. Madrid: Publicaciones de la Asociación de Directores de Escena de España, 1996.
La estación de fiebre y otros amaneceres. Madrid: Visor, 1991.
La muerte y otros efímeros agravios. San José: Editorial Costa Rica,1988.
Poemas abiertos y otros amaneceres. San José: Editorial Costa Rica, 1980.
Verbo madre. San José: Editorial Mujeres, 1995.

Further Reading

Chen Sham, Jorge. "La insurrección de la mujer y su estrategia liberadora en Ana Istarú: El poema III de *La estación de fiebre*." *South Eastern Latin Americanist* 44 (2000): 19–27.
Hernández, Consuelo. "Feminidad y feminismo en la poesía de Ana Istarú." *Alba de América* 20 (2001): 209–20.
———. "Poetas centroamericanos de fin de siglo: Ana Istarú y Otoniel Guevara: Cuerpo y autoridad." *Ístmica: Revista de la Facultad de Filosofía y Letras* 5–6 (2000): 26–42.
Krugh, Janis L. "La erótica fiebre feminista de Ana Istarú en La estación de fiebre." In *Afrodita en el trópico: Erotismo y construcción del sujeto femenino en obras de autoras centroamericanas*, edited by Oralia Preble-Niemi, 198–208. Potomac, MD: Scripta Humanistica, 1999.
Moyano, Pilar. "Reclamo y recreación del cuerpo y del erotismo femeninos en la poesía de Gioconda Belli y Ana Istarú." In *Afrodita en el trópico: Erotismo y construcción del sujeto femenino en obras de autoras centroamericanas*, edited by Oralia Preble-Niemi, 135–52. Potomac, MD: Scripta Humanistica, 1999.
Zavala, Magda. "Poetas centroamericanas de la rebelión erótica." In *Afrodita en el trópico: Erotismo y construcción del sujeto femenino en obras de autoras centroamericanas*, edited by Oralia Preble-Niemi, 245–59. Potomac, MD: Scripta Humanistica, 1999.

J

JAHIZ, AL-

---

c. 776–c. 868
Arab essayist

Abu 'Uthman 'Amr, known as al-Jahiz, wrote prose works on a variety of subjects, including a number of erotic-polemical works that provide a striking contrast to the "libertine" literature of his time. Al-Jahiz's erotic writings must be understood in the context of the extraordinary flowering of Arabic literature in the early Abassid period (749–945), in which authors devoted serious attention to the conflicts between their desire to follow the dictates of the Qur'an and their love of pleasure. While writers like the poet Abu Nuwas extolled the joys of drunkenness and the pleasures of sexual relations with young men, al-Jahiz's work shows his unease with this love of pleasure. One finds him praising women and love, but condemning adultery and homosexual activity. He did not hesitate to write frankly of sexual matters, and even provided justifications for doing so when it suited his purposes. Elegant and ironic, the writings of al-Jahiz ultimately defended a conventional Islamic morality and a relatively strict interpretation of

Qur'anic law, in contrast (and in reaction) to the libertine writings of many of his contemporaries.

Much of al-Jahiz's work on sexual themes (including his "Difference Between Men and Women" and his "Diatribe Against Fornication") is lost. Surviving compositions are often known only from fragments; thus his "Diatribe Against Sodomy" appears to have been part of a larger lost diatribe on schoolteachers and follows the general trend of al-Jahiz's writings against homosexual relations. The most important of al-Jahiz's surviving works on sexual themes are four compositions that secure his position as an important figure in the history of erotic literature. They are significant in part because they are so frequently cited and quoted in later Arabic works. The writings of al-Jahiz had a profound impact on the shaping of erotic discourse in the medieval Islamic world.

Love and Women

In *Love and Women,* al-Jahiz articulated his theory of the nature of love between men and women. He distinguished between affection and passionate love, seeming to praise the latter, although his analogies make it clear that there is a certain irony at work and that he is, in fact, satirizing the excesses to which many of his contemporaries went in pursuit of their passion. Al-Jahiz devotes much of this work to a discussion of women as love objects—their natures, the differences between free women and slaves, and the ideal appearance of a woman—but displays a viewpoint that is more sympathetic to women than was customary in his time.

Epistle on the Singing Slave Girls

This work is in the form of an open letter, ostensibly a defense of the institution of the *qiyan:* female slaves trained as singers and hired out as companions. The letter begins with a detailed justification of relations between men and women, appealing to pre-Islamic and early Islamic social practices as a seeming justification for the companionship of the singing female slaves. Al-Jahiz then gives a detailed description of these women, their talents, and their training. The real intention of al-Jahiz's epistle becomes clear toward the end: it is, in fact, a criticism of the merchants who own, train, and sell the services of these women. Pretending admiration for their sharp practices, al-Jahiz satirizes the owners of these slaves and, by extension, the men who deal with these slave traders. The work concludes with an ironic postscript disclaiming responsibility for the reader's possible offense.

Boasting Match between Girls and Boys

This composition, along with *Superiority of the Belly to the Backside* described below, is part of a tradition of literature debating the respective merits of young men and women as objects of sexual desire. It begins with al-Jahiz's famous defense of the use of "obscene" words by citing the use of such terminology by famous religious figures. He then places his work into the context of other such debate literature, abruptly leading into the actual debate between the lovers of young women and the lovers of young men ("fornicators" and "sodomites," respectively). The lovers of young men alternate between praising their beauties and making misogynistic observations, while the lovers of young women frequently invoke Islamic law and custom. Both

debaters make frequent quotation of favorite authors, in some cases turning the same author to different purposes (as when the poet Abu Nuwas is first cited in favor of young men, then of young women). Al-Jahiz's sympathies were clearly with the lovers of young women, whom he permitted to have the final say. Al-Jahiz concluded this work with a series of anecdotes about sex to illustrate various aspects of the foregoing debate; these stories include jokes about sexual positions, penis size, gendered differences in the enjoyment of sex, and homosexual activity.

Superiority of the Belly to the Backside

This brief work purports to be a response by an uncle to his nephew's treatise in praise of the backside (and, by extension, the love of young men) and is written in a high-blown, elaborate style. It begins innocuously enough with a general comparison of the relative importance and beauty of the belly over the back in nature, and the narrator elaborates on his theme of the general superiority of bellies to backsides (for example, one cuts with the "belly" of a knife, not with its back, whereas the backside is what is always beaten or chastened). All this is, of course, a prelude to the main thrust of the argument: the superiority of sexual intercourse with women (via the ventral position) over sex with men (focusing on the dorsal) and, by extension, love of women over the love of men. The overall tone of the work is highly moralistic, with frequent appeal to the Qur'an and Islamic law presented as familial advice, and, in contrast to the *Boasting Match* described above, the language of the text is restrained and nonspecific. Al-Jahiz takes advantage of his avuncular narrator to present the argument in a condescending way, as the affectionate but firm scolding of a wayward young nephew, attempting to talk him out of his love of men.

Biography

Al-Jahiz was born Bahr al-Kinani al Fuqaimi al-Basri, in Basra (in modern Iraq) around 776. Educated in Basra; despite lack of literary background, decided to become an author. Early writings attracted the attention of the Abassid caliph al-Ma'mun in 817–8; moved to Baghdad shortly thereafter. Worked briefly as a scribe and teacher, but apparently held no official posts and relied on income from the dedications of his writings and (possibly) a governmental allowance. Retired to Basra in 861 in ill health, and died there in 868/9.

T.G. WILFONG

Selected Works

Pellat, Charles. *The Life and Works of Jahiz*. London: Routledge & Kegan Paul, 1969.

Beeston, A.F.L., ed. *The Epistle on Singing-Girls of Jahiz*. Warminster: Aris and Philipps, 1980.

Hutchins, William M., trans. *Nine Essays of al-Jahiz*. New York: Peter Lang, 1989.

Further Reading

Pellat, Charles. "Al-Jahiz." In *Encyclopedia of Islam*, edited by C.E. Bosworth, E. van Donzel, B. Lewis, and C. Pellat. 2nd ed. 11 vols. Leiden: Brill, 1954–2001.

———. "Al-Jahiz." In *Abbasid Belles-Lettres*, edited by Julia Ashtiany et al. Cambridge: Cambridge University Press, 1990.

Rosenthal, Franz. "Male and Female, Described and Compared." In *Homoeroticism in Classical Arabic Literature*. Edited by J.W. Wright, Jr., and Everett K. Rowson. New York: Columbia University Press, 1997.

Rowson, Everett K. "The Categorization of Gender and Sexual Irregularity in Medieval Arabic Vice Lists." In *Body Guards: The Cultural Politics of Gender Ambiguity*. Edited by Julia Epstein and Kristina Straub. London: Routledge, 1991.

JAPANESE: MEDIEVAL TO NINETEENTH CENTURY

The Archaic Period to the Nara Period (710–794)

At the time when the Shintô, the way of the Gods, the ethereal cult of nature, was the unique identity of the Japanese, we note the parallel existence of *Norito,* a body of earthy rituals and magical formulas for down-to-earth problems, such as those collected during the *Engi* era in 927, dating back sometimes to the 7th century. For example, the "ritual of great purification" lists such offensive acts as cutting the skin, incest, or being subjected to the calamity of crawling worms. From the beginning, ugly reality is opposed to a quest for purity.

The *Kojiki* [*The Book of Things That Are Now of the Past*], published at the beginning of the 8th century, relates, among other facts, the birth of the Japanese islands in a cosmic sexual act, followed by the union of Izanagi and Izanami, each child being a new island in the archipelago.

More than in the *Nihongi,* the mythical image of a supernatural feminine figure can be found in the *Kojiki* with Amaterasu, an "angry mother," in a Jungian sense, angry because she was the victim of sexual violence, but at the same time

showing her genitals, dancing in a naturist ecstacy. Unveiling her genitals, or her breast, can paralyze the enemy or stimulate the warrior's courage. Amenouzume's dance can awaken the whole of nature. These primitive representations of feminine sexual power will be later found in modern literature.

The *Manyôshû* was collected around 760 and contains *sômonka* [love poems] and *banka* [elegies]. Passion is expressed in a very subtle manner, but directly. Most of *Manyôshû* focuses on the private relations between men and women. The *Azuma no uta* (poems from the oriental provinces) show how lovers met various obstacles. Above all, love was supposed to increase the harmony of the group.

The Heian Period (794–1186)

The Heian was the period when the ideal of Japanese civilization was seen. During the 10th century, life reached a high degree of refinement, especially in literature. Poets and aesthetes were numerous, as were amorous affairs. These behaviors were very open, though a mere sensual passion was never the ideal. The lover is aware of the seasonal changes, and feels a deep melancholy.

Poetry is present with the *Kokinshû* (collected in 905); popular poetry, such as the Iroha-uta, along with prose about both genders, such as the first tales (the *Taketori, Ise,* and *Yamato Monogataris*). In the *Kokinshû,* one of the main lyrical themes is love, but it is quite different from the transitive, physical love of foreplay and sexual intercourse, as appears in the *Man'yoshû.* Rather, the Heian period presents an intransitive, contemplative love [*mono omou*] which is the subject of abstract reflection. This tradition presents the image of the lover in a dreamworld, with the best-loved poems being descriptions of misty landscapes. But there were some exceptions, such as poems written by court ladies like Ono no Komachi and Izumi Shikibu in the *Shinkokinshû* and in the *Goshûishû* (11th century), which treat more practically of a psychology of sexual relations.

Fujiwara no Akihira compiled the *Honchô monzui* in the middle of the 11th century. It contains several pornographic pieces, such as the "Danjo kon'in fu," which begins by describing the sentimental attractions, then proceeds to a detailed description of sexual acts. Another example from this collection is the "Tettsuiden," which is a parodic discussion of the penis in the formal manner of a biography from Confucian wise men whose names are all suggestive of the male organ. These themes come from Chinese literature, in which pornography appeared in both prose and poetry.

In numerous tales in the *Ise Monogatari* (905–951), sometimes funny, mostly sentimental, are related the amorous exploits of a *mukashi no otoko,* an ex-lover, an "old boyfriend," supposedly Ariwara no Narihira (825–880), a nobleman and great seducer of women. He is known for his libertinage and for his poetic talent. He is never ashamed of his passion and always takes great pleasure in sex with many partners. This stance is historically significant, because the *Ise Monogatari* expresses for the first time an individual ideal of hedonism between the sexes. The *Ise Monogatari* gave birth to an aesthetic form and a Don Juan–like figure essential to understanding the Heian culture. Love is possible on both single and multiple levels, is never to be refused, doesn't decrease with age, and is not divided into carnal and sentimental love. This foundation will be reaffirmed and integrated into the modern age.

Upper-class women in the Heian period had two options to escape from boredom: love and literature. Hence, the masterpieces of the Heian were written by women, in pure Japanese syllabary, both as novels and diaries. The *Makura no sôshi* of Sei Shônagon (first years of 11th century), for example, is not chronological in the sense of being a *nikki* (diary), but is a *sôshi,* more like a journal capturing the feelings and fantasies of the writer. Both the *Makura* and the *Genji Monogatari* [*Tale of Genji*] (c. 1000) depict Japanese eros at length. The famous *Tale of Genji,* by court lady Murasaki Shikibu, tells of the love affairs of the radiant and handsome Prince Genji, focusing on his amorous adventures and on the court intrigues surrounding him and his son after him. The *Tale* is supposed to be illustrative of the vanity of all things human, especially human love. The sexual act is always suggested in an indirect way, and love is manifested in terms of psychology and emotion. In the poems, instead of using explicit terms for coitus, the verb "to chat" is often used.

The *Genji Monogatari* is an invaluable source for analyzing Japanese eros. For example, the best-loved part of feminine beauty is long hair, and the naked body is appreciated even less than a "nice hand," that is, beautiful calligraphy. The ideal of feminity is then crystallized, and the *Tale* is precisely a quest for the essence of women. We see this quest echoed in Ihara Saikaku's character Yonosuke, who seeks an encounter with femininity through cultural criteria. Prince Genji is not a Don Juan, despite his numerous relations with at least ten featured female characters and plenty of anonymous ones. The Heian organization of relations was based on polygamy. Concubines didn't arouse jealousy, and the women benefited from a relative sexual freedom. Love experience was merely part of the transient nature of human life. It was also an aesthetic one and a cultural emotion, as much as a pure physical pleasure. Pleasure was connected to clothing and to a stagecraft of love. Infidelity was neither definitive nor absolute. Feelings were enriched by a subtle balance between faithful and unfaithful love.

These works were written by and for literary and highbrow courtiers. By contrast, the *Konjaku Monogatari* (c. 1120) is based on anecdotes belonging to popular literature. The *Konjaku* gives us a very raw image of everyday life during the Heian, with no subject forbidden. It is written in a cinematic way, showing the reality of death and physical love, which would have been in extreme bad taste according to the criteria of the lady Murasaki Shikibu, for example. And yet, though explicit, the *Konjaku* is not perverse—in contrast to the swing toward treatments of sexual perversion in court literature after Lady Murasaki's *Genji Monogatari*. The world of the *Konjaku* is one of quick action—one story inspired Akutagawa Ryûnosuke to write *Yabu no naka,* which became the basis for Kurosawa's film *Rashômon*. The sexual organs are a matter of general interest. The most vile love is described, such as sexual intercourse between the empress and a demon in front of the court, including the emperor. Heichû, the famous libertine and poet, is driven by his interest in scatology, and all sorts of excess are described in the 30th book, devoted to love stories. Especially of note are those tales devoted to the couplings of monks and beautiful ladies of the capital, which inspired popular songs.

The violence and crudity of these pictures of a society at this point in time can be linked to the fact that this society was at the end of its existence. The noble and idealized world of the court is reverted to real life, full of lust and violence. The Heian period ends with the reign of uncultured warriors from the provinces, such as the first *shôgun,* who ruled Japan from Kamakura. From Heian to Edo culture, the warriors seemed more inclined to homosexuality or wild sex and didn't pay much attention to faithful women—except to sentence adulterous women to death, an idea that will not be shared by the middle class.

The Kamakura Period and Beyond (1186–1603)

During the Kamakura (1186–1332), poetic creation continues with the *Shinkokinshû* (1205), among many other poetry books, and the most famous collection of all, the *Hyakuninisshû* [*One Hundred Poems by One Hundred Poets*] (c. 1235). The semiotics of love are common to both this and the Heian period. The frozen or wet sleeve in the winter night, the grass, the wind, and the cold dawn express indecision— a sleeve wet with tears is also the image suggested by archbishop Jien (Kamakura period) to indicate separation

and longing. Sorrow at parting with one's lover is expressed through images such as damp or fallen flowers. And although life is short, Ki no Tomonori writes: "to meet you / I would give it without regret" (*Kokinshû* 12, 615). In short, what is exalted above all is a romantic image of love suffering through separation and wait. The pleasure of love and the sensual aspects of it are rarely expressed in these poems.

The Nambokuchô period (1332–1392) and the Muromachi period (1392–1603), like the Kamakura before it, are not rich in literature, though the monk Kenkô's *Tsurezurekusa* (c. 1335) is an original essay about many feelings and ideas, especially women and the sensual desire of men. Even those most attuned to spiritual life can't escape the lusts of the flesh: incense, white legs, and beautiful hair arouse sexual desire. But the monk is mainly misogynistic.

Beginning with the Heian period, neither homosexual nor heterosexual relations were mentioned, except rarely. But in the *haikai renga,* the Muromachi period, and there alone, allusions to male and female sexual organs are numerous, in total contrast with Heian court poetry. The effect is humorous and iconoclastic, and these poems were very popular. The ballads called *ko uta* are love songs, some of which treat of sexual passion.

The Tokugawa Period (1603–1868)

The moralist Kaibara Ekiken (1630–1714) represents the vulgar pleasures as quickly changed into sufferings, and is well known for his educative role. He published the *Onna Daigaku,* which was an aristocratic manual for girls education. This kind of book was quickly adopted as sexual education books later on. According to the Confucian idea, women should be submissive to their husbands and should not have any kind of intimacy with any other men. If they deviated from these rules, they were ostracized and subject to great community shame. This strict code is apparent in the coming novels, especially those of Ihara Saikaku.

The Edo (1603–1686) and Genroku (1688–1704) Periods

The *chônin* [merchants] were the premier literati of 17th-century Japan, their novels describing the real social life of that time. In an urban culture, the new meeting points for artists and writers were usually in the "pleasure world," which included prostitution districts like Shimabara in Kyôto and the Yoshiwara in Edo. Ihara Saikakuto (1641–1691) dedicated himself above all to erotic stories, and described thoroughly the life of debauchery in these places.

Kôshoku ichidai otoko (1682), one of the first *ukiyo-sôshi* ["social novels," *romans de moeurs*], is a portrait of Yonosuke, a middle-class erotomaniac of the Edo period, obsessed with sex, women, and beautiful young boys. He paid for sex thousands of times with women in *kuruwa* [brothels]. The novel has no direction except for what is provided by the multiple sexual episodes, but it does describe the somnambulism and brutality of clients. This is also a feature of *Kôshoku ichidai onna* (1686), which is the story of a voluptuous woman—a courtesan and a whore—detailing the events of her generally picaresque life.

Kôshoku ichidai otoko ends with a trip on a boat called "Yoshi-no-maru" [The Voluptuous Boat], sailing to the "women's island" [*Nyogo no shima*], a no-return trip into sensual exhaustion. This finale is linked to the Buddhist philosopher's island—a device also found in Nosaka Akiyuki's *Pornographers* (1966) and in some masterpieces of the filmmaker Imamura Shohei. The seducer in the "Maboroshi" [ghost, illusion] chapter of the *Genji Monogatari* comes to a similar end.

Yonosuke is looking to seduce as many women as possible; he is a maniacal collector of spoils (as was usual for clients of courtesans), but he has no emotions. He is incapable of affection—compared with Prince Genji, who aimed at knowledge about women more than at sensuality. Prince Genji experiences variety to find the ideal, which would not be far away from the coming ideal of the geisha. He savors the passing of time in a positive way to remember his many loves fondly, while Yonosuke is never satisfied with time. His accounts as a "collector" and fetishist is done in a negative way. Among the perversions presented is sacrilege, in the depiction of the profanation of priestesses in a Shintô temple, but this is considered a game and a social gaffe rather than a sin. There are few perversions expressed in the *Genji Monogatari*; one of these is Genji incestuous desire for his absent mother. Although he never actually passes to the act of incest. The myth of the androgyne is not present, but there is a narcissism rooted in the original incest of Izanami and Izanagi (myth of the origins of the country). Yonosuke has only one major perversion, and that is fetishism (hair, nails, underwear, images). In the *Genji Monogatari*, signs such as calligraphy, poetry, music prepare the erotic encounters. The most intimate encounter is with the face of a woman, not with her naked body. Clothes are particularly erotic, and the feminine body is a fictive one, of phantom-like beauty, as will be suggested later on by Tanizaki Jun'ichirô in *In'ei raisan* [*Praise of Shadow*] (1933). Eroticism is cultural, and linked to dream and illusion. The naked body is not attractive, but clothes enable it to be explored in an extension of foreplay in the darkness, sometimes leading to mistakes, but pleasure nevertheless.

Clothes and perfumes are means for the conquest of the other. Modesty is another essential part of the erotic code—for example, the woman hiding the lower part of her face, or her mouth. Shame (*haji*) excites male desire. The term *hazukashii* ["I feel ashamed"] is often used by women to entice desire, and is a medium for sexual pleasure. The physical act is never described precisely by Saikaku, the reader is able to perceive it indirectly. Often, there is no communication, and coitus takes place in silence, with a sleeping beauty (anticipating the necrophilia of Kawabata or Tanizaki). It is a fundamental aspect of Japanese eros. Through drunkness, too, a distance is created, and there is no significant contact with the other's soul.

The story of Yonosuke can be seen as a parody of the *Genji Monogatari*, in so far as the hero similarly fades into legend. The way the hero argues about the qualities and defects of women is related to a systematic erotic quest; Yonosuke, like Genji, can be subject to melancholy. The difference lies in a new challenge: create an authentic love with courtesans trained to pretend to be in love. In the literary point of view, the celebration of natural beauties (flowers or moonlight) has to be replaced successfully by the description of the *kuruwa*. An idealization of courtly behavior–the *sui*, or *iki*-emerges. It is an art of life with pleasure, elegance, and ostentation. One sex is striving toward the other, in a pre-orgasmic eroticism. This code of gallantry, *iki*, evolved into *ikiji*, courage, which was borrowed by the *bushido* [the way of warriors], and into *akirame* [resignation to a situation].

Sexual desire was to be cultivated without any genuine affection, which was a departure from the Heian ideal of love. The Edo ideal was a gallantry based on a fantasy. The perversion lay in the consciousness that the venal love was only an elegant comedy. The *sui* spirit was a perverted heroism and mysticism, because the middle class had no political power. To spend one's money and energy with courtesans was the only challenge available.

However, the novels of Saikaku contain a bitter charge against prostitution: he denounces the violence under its erotic refinement. The relation between sex and money came to obsess the author. After his death, five posthumous books were published, among which was *The Moon of That Floating World* (1693). It deals with the destiny of brothel clients, and is a testimony to the "floating world" (*ukiyo*) he described so well. One theme of these short stories is the client ruined because of courtesans. The book strongly condemns the hypocrisy of the *kuruwa*: theatricality based on money. The complete destruction of the client is the only way to put an end to the farce. The prestige of the pleasure districts is replaced by disillusionment and misery. This universe is one of ruin and solitude, but it also leads to detachment and freedom. In *The Life of Wankyu*, the title character is inspired by the kabuki theater and by a real Osaka merchant. The debauchery leads to ruin and insanity. He becomes a champion of eros. Symetrically, the merchant's ethic is no longer unidimentional (accumulate a fortune or be ruined). In the pleasure world, the merchants have acquired a sense of elegance, or sacrifice. The ruined client, banned from the courtesans' districts, has a free mind like the warrior ready to die.

Yonosuke was also a ruined *daijin*. The kabuki theater created a type of the ruined young man rejected by his family, which is not the *daijin* type. Yonosuke, thanks to a large fortune, becomes a super-*daijin* (dai-dai-daijin) and is desperate because he cannot put an end to his money with courtesans. Yoden, in *The Great Mirror of All Pleasures*, can be considered the prototype of the *daijin*. In the end, he immolates himself over a fire made with all the letters he received from courtesans. We can deduce that at the end of the 17th century, money took over male seduction in the pleasure districts. *Sui* could not be attained since financial ruination would come long before.

The middle class tends to appropriate the trappings of aristocratic culture. It takes its inspiration from Urabe Kenkô, a retired aristocrat, and to his *Hours of Idleness,* where it is considered that love is an essential experience for sensitivity.

The warrior ethic has as its finale death or entry into Valhalla, but homosexual love introduces an internal contradiction. As for *nanshoku* [homoeroticism, or male-to-male love], we can note the success of *Nanshoku ôkagami* [*The Great Mirror of Male Love*] (1687) published simultaneously in Osaka, Kyôto, and Edo. The men in power, the samurai, could only approve the entry of *nanshoku* into the Japanese literature tradition. It is not synonymous with homosexuality in a Western sense, because neither homosexuality, heterosexuality, nor sodomy were operant concepts in the Japanese 17th century.

Nanshoku is opposed to *joshoku* [woman-to-woman love]. *Nanshoku* is the sexual pleasure experienced between men. It is neither a court model, like that of the Chinese, nor a popularized version of the kabuki *nanshoku* pattern. In the Heian period, *nanshoku* was considered as immature and was marginalized.

The Great Mirror of Male Love is divided into two parts. The first is dedicated to monks and samurai; the second to the prostitute-actors of kabuki theater (where the female roles were played by *onnagata,* men). The social intermixing through sex, above all hierarchy, was intensive, but the perfect *nanshoku* way is expressed by warriors and monks.

The Japanese tradition goes back to the Chinese model (*nanfeng,* or "passion of the cut sleeve"), and extended through the urbanization of Japan. The feudal model was based on seniority, and the cadet was subordinate to the elder. Young men, sometimes vassals, were used as domestics. Around 1600, the young partners were educated to be passive and to look like women, without behaving like them. A common pattern was for a samurai to become a pariah (*hinin*) or a wanderer (*rônin*) but still be in love with his master (*daimyô*).

Middle-class men in this context are presented as having no other interest than money and sexual adventures. They experience *ukiyo* or *hakanai,* the ennui of world. The warriors have to wear a mask or hide their nature, but *nanshoku* is for them an ideal: the perfect warrior is young and part of the *nanshoku.* Many realities are to be understood under that term: bisexuality; *onnagirai* [pure homoeroticism]; the taste for young men [*shôjinzuki*]; homophilia; or love of beautiful or girlish young boys. The physical appearance of the warrior is strictly defined. The hair is cut on the sides of the head [*maegami*], and a codified langage is used (e.g., *kiku* [chrysanthemum] = anus).

As for monks, *nanshoku* became a main pattern of monastic life—the Buddhist Kûkai (Kobo Daishi) is said to have introduced the first coitus between men, in the monastery town of Mount Koya. For the monks, it was a compromise between abstinence and heterosexual love, the worst investment for Buddhism, and of less energetic cost in *yang* (i.e., maleness, creation, solar power). The *chigo* (novice) who enters a temple as a trainee becomes a partner in a fraternal and at the same time homosexual link [*kyôdaichigiri*].

No moral objections are made to male–male love, apart from those of Confucianism (one does not marry, one squanders the family fortune, one contributes to public disorder). On the contrary, the warriors deprived of glory in war could spend their fighting energy in that way. *The Great Mirror of Male Love* thus becomes Saikaku's *roman de moeur* [*ukiyo-sôshi*] serving as the mirror of what was expected by a society that mainly approved of *nanshoku*.

After the *ukiyo-sôshi*, came the *kusa-sôshi* [graphic novel] and the *sharebon* [the "smart," or witty novelette or pun book], such as those of Santô Kyôden in 1787–1791, whose licentious tales were forbidden.

Two publishers in Kyôto, Ando Jishô and Ejima Kiseki, from Hatchimonjiya, published many licentious novels at the beginning of the 18th century, and then the movement spread to Edo with the *sharebon*, which would be forbidden by the government in 1711. Then the *ninjôbon* [books about human feelings] appeared, above all in the first half of the 19th century with Tamenaga Shunsui (1789–1842), but they were also quickly prohibited, as their basis was pornography.

At the same time Jippensha Ikku (1765–1831), introduced the comic novel [*kokkei-bon*] who would publish no less than 331 books. The *Hizakurige* (1802) is a well-known travel narrative on the Tokaido road. His gallic spirit and strong, realistic genius can be compared to that of Rabelais. Shikitei Samba (1775–1822) wrote early in his life naturalistic and then comic novels. Among many works, the *Ukiyo-buro* (1809–1811), about the world of the public baths, and the *Ukiyo-doko* (1811–1812), about the world of the barber's, are composed of encounters and chats in the promiscuity of naked bodies of many kinds of people. In the *Ukiyo-buro*, Samba uses *kyôbun* [crazy prose].

Drama

The kabuki theater is the popular and vulgar version of the Nô theater. It made its appearance in the Muromachi period. It can be linked to the *kyôgen* component of Nô. The origin of it is Okuni, a former Ise priest who fled to Kyôto, then went to Edo with a troupe of actors, and was considered to be of low morality. The women were no longer allowed to play in the kabuki theater from 1629. The courtesans' theater was then replaced by a young boy's theater, which was forbidden again. Chikamatsu Monzaemon (1653–1724) wrote more than a hundred plays and is considered to be the creator of the Japanese popular drama. Historical dramas were full of suicides, murders, and violent events; the comedy of manners related sensual passions. Takeda Izumo (1688–1756) was the direct descendant of Chikamatsu.

The love quest can become a death quest, if affected by dark impulses from the unconscious. Lovers sometimes have to escape, and this is a common theme of novels, such as those of Saikaku, like *Kôshoku gonin-onna*, and many dramas. Lovers are often sentenced to death, according to the bushido ethic, but readers and the public didn't approve of it. They often commit *shinjû* [double love suicide]. The government censored dramatists like Chikamatsu who made of *shinjû* the turning point in their dramas. Saikaku never showed *shinjû* because he denounced its idealization through the influence of the theater. The heterosexual love described by Saikaku is subversive according to the Tokugawa criteria: it is a total love, independent in death, like that of O-Sen and Maemon. The subversive heterosexual love of Oshichi, for example, may be traced back to the heretical celebration of love by the monk Ikkyû (1394–1481), author of erotic poems written under Zen influence. The experience of love in Saikaku's works is at the margins of official Buddhist thought.

Manuals and Poetry

Two essential fields are to be mentioned, because they were long-term cultural facts, and because they were so popular that they concerned the major part of the society: the *makura-e* [pillow book], *shunga* [spring illustrations], and *higa* [secret drawings]. They are mentioned as early as the 10th century, and are not made for laughter, as may be suggested by one meaning of the term *warai-e* or *warai-bon*. They were intended to give a sexual education. In the classical sense, *warau* means sexual pleasure. The aim of these books was to show how the couple's affection can be expressed bodily, according to the *Kojiki* (the 8th-century tale of Creation), and to the first coitus of Izanagi and Izanami. Coitus expresses the natural pleasure within the lover's happiness. During the Edo period, these books were published especially for young people in order to give them precise help and advice for sexual life. This was particularly relevant for girls, who were supposed to be virgins and thus completely ignorant of the physical nature of men. The young men have to decipher the words uttered by girls during coitus. These books were anatomically precise, describing organs, as well as showing them in action. The qualities of the vagina are connected to the appearance of the face [*rokkaisen*]. Technical pages are devoted to dildos (or olisbos) and various accessories, while proper nutrition and medicines for the sex act are explained. In the spirit of the *kyôka*, or burlesque poem, noble classical langage is subverted into an erotic one. It is not a sense of modesty that determines why figures are drawn not entirely unclothed, but rather a sense of aesthetics, for complete nudity was not considered to be sexually attractive.

For example, the *Manual to Have a Hard-On Like Shimekawa in Order to Possess Women* is a parody of a famous book for female instruction, *The Teaching Letter of Imakawa for Women*, written in 1394 by Imakawa Ryôshin. The former book is attributed to Takeda Kichi, and was republished more than 20 times between 1687 and 1865; dozens of other books were published under a similar title during the same period. So, the meaning of the parodic title was common knowledge.

The second fact is that haiku was associated with comical poetry: parody, pun, and comical situations were their basis. After Saikaku's novels, around 1700, everything seems to be a subject for poems. The topic (*maeku*) given by a master receives an answer (*tsukeku*) written by the client. It is a new exercise called *maekuzuke*, which becomes a craze all over the country. Senryû, born in Edo in 1718, becomes the master of it, in 1757, under that pen name. From 1844, after the death of that master, *maekuzuke* was designated as *senryû*. Any kind of subject could become a *senryû*, such as the neighbor's life, conjugal life, and the Yoshiwara courtesans. The themes—"husbands-lovers, domestics, courtesans"—were placed inside the books in parallel series. The erotic *senryû* deal with the monastic world, the inaccessible court ladies (known through the olisbos they ordered, for example), the widows, couples, courtesans, and domestics. To give an idea of the importance of *senryû*, the Yoshiwara was the theme of at least 110,000 of them, among those selected by masters. The authors could know by experience the life of a monk or warriors but the life of court ladies had to be imagined, as a fantasy world. The main books published in Japan during this period were *Yanagidaru* [*The Willow's Barrel*] (1765–1838) and *Suetsumuhana* [*The Flower of the End*] (erotic *senryû* written from 1776 to 1801). The erotic poems were related to real places of Edo and the surroundings of Yoshiwara. At a time when Christianity was being implanted in Japan, and with it the idea of "sin" and "purity of the body," the writing and reading of these poems was a kind of antidote.

MARC KOBER

Further Reading

On Japanese literature in general

Katô, Shuîchi. *Histoire de la littérature japonaise*. "Intertextes" series vols. 1 and 2. Paris: Fayard, 1986.

Lévêque, Pierre. *Le Japon des mythes anciens. Colère, sexe, rire*. Paris: Les Belles Lettres, 1982.

Revon, Michel. *Anthologie de la littérature japonaise des origines au Xème siècle*. Paris: Vertiges, 1986.

On Japanese erotic literature

Faure, Bernard. *Sexualités bouddhiques. Entre désirs et réalités, l'homosexualité féodale*. Editions le Mail, 1994.

Leupp, Gary P. *Male Colors: The Construction of Homosexuality in Tokugawa Japan*. Berkeley, Los Angeles, and London: University of California Press, 1995.

Plugelder, Gregory M. *Cartographies of Desire: Male-male Sexuality in Japanese Discourse, 1600–1950.* Berkeley and Los Angeles: University of California Press, 1999.

Pons, Philippe. *D'Edo à Tôkyô. Mémoires et modernités.* Paris: Gallimard, 1988.

Struve, Daniel. *Saikaku, un romancier japonais du XVIIème siècle.* "Les Orientales" collection. Paris: PUF, 2001.

Walter, Alain. *Erotique du Japon classique.* Paris, NRF Gallimard, 1994.

JAPANESE: TWENTIETH AND TWENTY-FIRST CENTURIES

It is difficult to separate the 19th and 20th centuries in any study of Japanese lierature, as the turning point in modern Japanese history is marked by the beginning of the Meiji period, which spanned from 1868 to 1912. This was the real starting point of modern Japanese literature, and of Western influence. On the other hand, Japanese literature is very coherent, and traditions are passed on from one period to another and developed with continuity. Ueda Akinari is a good example of this process, in his *Ugetsu Monogatari* [*Rain and Vague Moon Stories*], published in 1776, and his *Harusame* [*Spring Rain Tales*], which was published prior to the 20th century. Both deal with abnormal or supernatural events. Ueda was very talented in describing ghosts and beautiful women of fantasy. Mori Ogai is another case of an author of the Meiji and the succeeding Taishô period (1912–1926). In 1890, his short story *Mahiimé* [*The Dancer*], a love story of a Japanese student and a young girl from Berlin, marked a sudden change in Japanese literary tradition and caused a significant aesthetic quarrel.

Young writers were attracted by Zolaesque Naturalism, which was taken to be a holistic system of understanding life, especially the sensual awakening of the individual through sexual feelings. The first work in the Zola manner was *Jigoku no hana* [*Hell's Flower*] (1902) by Nagai Kafû. Writers began to use their own experiences in first-person novels [*watakushi shôsetsu*]—e.g., Shimazaki Tôzon, whose actual relationship with his niece was revealed in his novel *Shinsai* [*New Life*] (1918) and caused a scandal. Also scandalous were the life and works of Tayama Katai (1872–1930), whose taste extended to detailed observations and raw descriptions of life. Though he didn't seek immoralism, his *Futon* (1907) was a form of defiance against traditional morals. Considered obscene at the time of its publication, it describes the repressed love between young Yoshiko from the country and Tokio, a writer who is supposed to teach her the art of writing. Tokio has a moral choice between satisfying his desire for Yoshiko and fulfilling his social role as a protector. Tokio is jealous of Yoshiko's lover, Tanaka, and the crux of the novel is whether Yoshiko and Tanaka have slept together. As a modern "Meiji girl," Yoshiko probably has. Mori Ogai deals with various themes, from love to the description of sexual experiences, in *Vita Sexualis* (1910). He reacted to Naturalism in a negative way, calling it "impudent." *Vita Sexualis* was for him an anti-Naturalist manifesto, with his medical knowledge employed to create a parody of realism, but the book was temporarily forbidden as immoral.

In the margins of Naturalism, around 1910, writers like Kafû Nagai (1879–1959) began to appear. He published short stories with a poetical aesthetic linked to cynicism, a perspective to be further developed by Tanizaki Jun'ichirô (1885–1965). Kafû was unable to reconcile the social pressures he observed at the end of the Meiji period, and a sort of renunciation led him to cynicism. Proclaiming himself the heir of Edo Ukiyo-sôshi and the "Gesaku" (entertainment) authors of the Meiji, Kafû dedicated his works to the description of the new pleasure districts, trying to capture some of Edo's old prestige. He embodied the "man of taste" [*fûryûjin*] and the *bunjin* tradition of refined cultivation. At 37, he dedicated himself completely to literature, as a sort of refuge, and to elegant works for the theater, like *Sumida River* (1909) and *The Nights of Shimbashi*. Kafû wasn't driven to suicide out of a sense of regret, like Arishima Takeo, who wrote about his deep love affair and struggle against hypocrisy in *Aru Onna* [*A Woman*] (1919)—rather, Kafû fell in love with a married woman and commited suicide with her. This act was reminiscent of the dramas of Chikamatsu, at a time when *shinjû*, or suicide pacts between lovers, was still popular. Yet, in *Waidan* [*A Squalid Affair*], Kafû examines the circumstances of and condemns adultery. A libertine, he was proud to have had sexual relations only with geishas, or professionals, of whom he wrote accurate observations. He could not understand the experience of Arishima. His play *Sumida River* represented an escape to the Yoshiwara "village" of pleasure houses. In the face of the Occidentalization of Japan at the end of the Meiji, his final answer was to become a *gesakusha*, or entertainment writer, so as to lose himself in dealing with only the world of pleasure.

Tanizaki Jun'ichirô was strongly encouraged by Kafû, and professed an amorality he called "diabolism," which was rather provocative. Tanizaki was a prolific twentieth-century writer and compared himself to Kafû, whose conception of "art above all" won his admiration. However, he disapproved of Kafû's erratic sexual life and charged that Kafû despised women as inferior and doll-like—an observation also made by Nosaka Akiyuki. Tanizaki himself, on the contrary, considered women to be superior to men. He spent most of his life as a married man, and his writings explored love in middle-class society. Although both he and Kafû took male–female relations as their primary source of inspiration, the two writers belonged to different cultural traditions—Kafû to the *bunjin* and Tanizaki to the *joruri* [chanted recitative]. The *bunjin* were delighted with *iki*, or being "chic," and hated falling in love; love and suicide was exalted by their dramatists, like Tsuruya Namboku (1758–1829), who celebrated the impulses of cruelty and submission. These elements were to be the basis of Tanizaki's literary

world. He was drawn to his beautiful mother with an almost oedipal force. The beauty of her skin in particular and her way of walking attracted him. As a little boy, he had been a victim of sadism, which may have forced a predilection for masochism into him. His first sex-maniacal works may be traced back to Western models, such as those of Poe, Baudelaire, and Wilde.

Shisei [*The Tattoo*] (1910) is characteristic both of Tanizaki's Decadent inspiration and of diabolism. The work is about a woman with a spider tattoo on her back who is a kind of femme fatale. The tattoo master Seikichi takes pleasure in having his clients suffer through needles. Then, he introduces the soul of a dead cruel Chinese princess into the tattoed girl, and becomes the first victim of that beautiful monster.

In *In'ei Raisan* [*In Praise of Shadow*] (1933), Tanizaki describes woman's beauty as being like a ghost, with her fragile body wrapped in the kimono. He develops also the idea that Japanese skin is slightly colored from the inside, and his explanations refer to a very peculiar erotic taste. He establishes a contrast between Western and Japanese cultures in terms of the explicit and the implicit, the liberated and the repressed. From 1935 to 1938, he was engaged to translate the *Genji Monogatari* [*The Tale of Genji*] into modern Japanese, but he had to expurgate the amorous passages, and he had to interrupt the serialized publication of his own *Sasameyuki* [*The Makioka Sisters*] (1943–48), because military censorship during this time was all-powerful.

In representative Tanizaki works such as *Shunkin shô* [*Story of Shunkin*] (1933) and *Kagi* [*The Key*] (1956), affective and sexual relations are examined out of any social or economic context. Two kinds of relations can be observed. In the first one, a man is devoted to a woman, or becomes attached to her, and takes pleasure in the sufferings she gives him (e.g., *Chijin no ai* [*An Idiot's Love*], 1924). In this scenario, a woman may have several lovers. The second kind is a detached observation through fictional narrative of the sexual relations of a couple, from *Tadekuumushi* [*Some Prefer Nettles*] (1928–29) to *Kagi*. In this scenario, a third person, usually a man, is introduced into the triangle. In *Kagi*, jealousy arouses sexual desire. The husband wants to give and receive suffering at the same time. For instance, as an aphrodisiac, he puts his drunken wife into a scalding hot bath before taking pictures of her. He asks a young man to develop the photos in a shared voyeurism; he also encourages adultery, with the help of his own daughter. He is driven to his death through oversexed sexual activity, using drug injections to be able to have intercourse until the last moment. The point is that he and his wife share hidden diaries, and the key to their diaries is also the key to their sexual and unconscious worlds. This bold treatment of the amorous was a first step toward freedom in the Japanese literary expression of sex. The elements of perversion must be distinguished from mere pornography because they are treated with artistic detachment.

With *Fûten Rôjin Nikki* [*Diary of an Old Man*] (1961–62), Tanizaki takes up the subject of sex in old age, a variation on his earlier themes. The diary is that of a decrepit old man, suffering from high blood pressure. Though impotent, he is attracted to his daughter-in-law, and takes pleasure in kissing her feet and biting her toes. The story reaches a climax when he identifies her with a Kan'non figure and takes a print of her foot dabbed in red ink to be carved on his tombstone. The nearly dead man indulges in a masochistic fantasy of being walked on by a holy femme fatale. This dream of the old man is a summary of Tanizaki's lifelong concern with the quest for eternal womanhood. We see this fixation also suggested in *Haha o kouru ki* [*Yearning for Woman*] (1919), in the form of an idealized figure who arouses foot fetishism. Tanizaki managed to describe various types of sexual love which he then applied, macrocosmically, to Japan. For example, he dealt with peculiar subjects, such as the daydreams of a blind man about feminine beauty, or sex between a young blind woman and a man who becomes blind in his turn. The novels where sadomasochistic relations are described are numerous, and the male characters often behave in fetishistic ways.

Women are able to attract and master men, whereas men seem to identify and fulfil their lives through a woman's body. These carnal relations are not presented in terms of the Christian dichotomy of body and soul. The flesh is not sinful, and sex has no diabolical origin. The Buddhist disgust for life's pleasures is not present either. Man has to grasp the physical nature of his life. The Confucian ideological system began to collapse during the Meiji period, worn

out by individualists such as Kafû. It then became possible to represent characters living an absolute love. Other heroes, by being very close to death, are likewise delivered from social constraints and can let a hedonistic sexuality come out.

Inspired by the *Konjaku Monogatari* [*The Tale of Konjaku*] and other stories, Akutagawa Ryonôsuke (1892–1927) was obsessed with madness, before he commited suicide, and his "vague uneasiness" became everybody's concern. The insanity of his mother produced in him the fear of becoming himself insane. Mixing the images of his mother and his sister as a composite, he idealized an eternal female figure. While still a student, he published *Rashômon* (1915). The director Kurosawa combined it with another tale, *Yabu no naka* [*In the Grove*] (1922) for his renowned film. In these novels begins Akutagawa's obsession with the infernal, a central theme in *Jigoku* [*The Hell Screen*] (1918). Set in pre-feudal imperial Japan, the story focuses on the painter Yoshihide, nicknamed *Saru-hide*, "monkey-like face," who finds difficulty in finishing a work in which the central scene is of a woman enveloped by flames in a carriage. The model of the woman is his own daughter. His demonic passion predominates; he has no attachment to the lives of others and sacrifices his daughter to the desires of Lord Horikawa. This same infernal vision of life is seen in the classic Rashomon story *Yabu no naka,* in which although the fact is clear that the bandit Tajomaru raped the wife of a warrior, who is found dead, so many variations of interpretation are woven in the narrative. Akutagawa didn't expose his real life in the sadomasochistic manner of the Naturalists. He was talented in creating historical fiction drained of the context of his own life. To him has been attributed an erotic tale called *Akaibôshi no onna* [*The Red Hat Girl*], and to Kafû *Yojôhan fusuma no shitabari* [*The Secret of the Small Room*]. The first was published by Seisaburô Oguro in his review *Sôtai,* which between 1913 and 1930 published the works of the *Sôtaikai* group of about 300 writers doing research in sexology. The second was first published in 1940, and then in 1947. The story of their publications is enmeshed with that of censorship and interdiction.

In the life and works of Kawabata Yasunari (1899–1972), a tension exists between life and death, between abstraction and sensuality; the author's consciousness of beauty is melancholy. His *Yukiguni* [*Snow Country*] (1934–1947) follows a very coherent plot. Shimamura, a married man, is attracted to two different types of women in a mountain resort. Yôko is inaccessible, in the manner of the childlike entertainer in the author's earlier *Izu no odoriko* [*Izu Dancer*] (1926), toward whom the protagonist is compelled to feel only brotherly affection. In contrast, the geisha Komako gives herself to him. Thus, Shimamura lives a tension between his entirely physical love for Komako and his ethereal love for Yôko. But ironically, it is Komako who belongs to the world of transience, while Yôko is made of flesh and blood. Kawabata's sensual approach to beauty not only is related to the feminine body, but spreads to objects like a piece of Chijimi linen and to the snowy landscape. His sensibilities, like those of haiku poets, are sharp and precise. And the precision becomes suggestive. In a *Nô* perspective, Komako appears like the *shite*, or main character, and Shimamura as the *waki*, or foil. The last scene, in which Komako rushes to embrace the body of Yôko, who has burned in a fire, has the powerful effect of a *Nô* drama's ending. Even the stars in the night sky and the play of lights can have an erotic effect on the narrator. Kawabata was especially interested in the connection between the beauty of young girls and traditional arts, as in the novel *Sembazuru* [*A Cloud of White Birds*]. He describes the beauty of a cup as if the light would give it a sensual aspect, like a woman's skin. The same type of images can be found in *Yukiguni*. The woman can be fondled like porcelain, and the objects become sensual. This aesthetic attitude toward women is continuous. Women are always beautiful objects. The extreme of this attitude is reached in *Nemureru bijo* [*The Sleeping Beauties*] (1960–61), in which, in a strange house, an old man contemplates and caresses a drugged young woman.

Other stories by Kawabata, like *Tampopo* or *Kataude*, express the idea that women have to be seen (and cannot see their lovers during orgasm), or are reduced to the most erotic part of their bodies. He used the short story to express his peculiar sensuality and his sense of beauty. Women and men are only one aspect of various sensual impressions.

The Sleeping Beauties is a farewell to what Kawabata loved: the female body. The girl is completely anonymous and is offered for caresses and longing. After a few hours, the client will enjoy the pleasure of dreams, remembering forgotten loves and faces, thanks to drugs. This is a deep meditation on women's mystery. Eguchi concludes by thinking that they are infinite. Another aspect is that the old man feels that his virility is going away. He can scarcely bear his impotency, in a country where the phallic symbol is so very important. His loss of potency is mirrored by the girls limp body. Beauty and sadness are closely linked. Kawabata may belong to the genre of tender and feminine literature [*taoyameburi*], but as the woman is at the center of Japanese literature, even the self-styled *masuraoburi*—virile literature—is rather feminine.

This is exemplified in the works of Mishima Yukio (born Kimitaka Hiraoka, 1925–1970), a psychological and aesthetic writer. *Kamen no Kokuhaku* [*Confession of a Mask*] (1952) is the autobiography of a homosexual. It has been said that Mishima glorified erotic death. In fact, he associated eroticism and death in the precious style of the Japanese romantic school. He represents the emotional and Eros-related part of Japanese culture, as in *Yukoku* [*Patriotism*] (1961), one of his many works made into films. The integrity of the lieutenant and of his wife through death is identified with their passionate lovemaking. Mishima was influenced by Georges Bataille's theory of Eros. In *The Sailor Who Fell from Grace with the Sea,* a young widow, a sailor, and a teenager meet. Voyeuristic activity is featured on the part of the teenager, who observes the sailor nude, in a scene in which male nudity is exalted over that of the female. Discovered, the young peeping tom is disgusted by the sailor's lack of a virile reaction, and he decides to kill him. Mishima became immersed in bodybuilding and built himself a more manly body by lifting weights. He strove for a moral strength in Japanese society which he saw as having been eroded by Dazai Osamu, who succeeded at last in commiting suicide with his last girlfriend. Mishima too killed himself with his male lover. He created his own right-wing army, the *Tate no Kai,* a sort of harem of young men drawn from among the Jietai (the Japanese Self-Defense Forces). He considered that Japan without an army was like a woman that could be raped by anybody, whereas an army would be a phallus for a reconstituted man. He dreamt about the young samurai of the Tokugawa period, who hoped to restore imperial power in an erotic love for their master. Through his *seppuku,* or ritual suicide, he found union with one of his obsessions, the martyrdom of Saint Sebastian, for which he posed in a carefully staged scene. The beautiful body suddenly driven to death is a very sensitive theme, linked to the love for cherry blossoms, the symbol of the samurai.

It is easy to detect literary elements in Mishima's works: he was fascinated by Mauriac, Radiguet, and the sadism and satanism of Baudelaire. The morbidity and frailty of Mishima were disguised, contrary to Dazai Osamu, Mishima's contemporary and rival. Mishima wore a mask. Yet, *Confession of a Mask* treats clearly of sexual perversion. Mishima was drawn to Joan of Arc, whom he misconceived as a man. His perversion was connected to death through a fascination with soldiers. The picture of Saint Sebastian by Guido Reni led him to his first experience of ejaculation. Death, love, and eternity stand out from the beginning in his works. His sensual perversion and inability to love women emerge from other characteristics. The mask may be the hero himself who pretends to love women and yet is unable to do so. *Kinkakuji* [*The Golden Pavilion*] (1956) is the story of a satanic criminal. He adheres to beauty as an ideal aesthetic value, and therefore, he cannot attain the fullness of life, and is again unable to make love to a woman. *Shiosai* [*The Sound of the Waves*] (1954) finds a positive value in the perfection of physical beauty. In that short story, the main character embodies the fullness of life through an ideal of physical strength.

Among postwar writers, Kobo Abé and Oe Kenzaburô produced important works. Both of them deviate from Japanese tradition. The novels of Kobo (born in 1928) present the alienation of the individual trapped by society like an insect, beginning with *Suna no onna* [*The Woman in the Dunes, 1962*]. The Kafkaesque allegory depicts how a man, in a state of deprivation, takes on beast-like instincts as he metamorphosizes. The woman is associated with an animal and with sand, or nature. Teshigahara's film shows well the mineral appearance of her skin and focuses on the grain of her naked body. The insect catcher falls into the sand-hole where

she lives, and the two become sexually intimate, out of any sentimental love. The sand-hole can be associated with a vagina. Kobo Abe likes to describe how a man can be driven to a complete loss of identity. For example, the insect catcher doesn't want to go back home anymore after he knows that the woman is pregnant. In the story, Japan and Japanese society play no role, except in terms of a peculiar sensuality. The woman is for him at the same time a liberation and a destruction through sexuality. He is swallowed, and the images become repetitive, in an archaic way of life, similar to the return to the origins, the forest in the island in Oe Kenzaburô's works, like *M.T. and Other Stories of the Forest.* Born in 1935, Oe Kenzaburô received the Akutagawa rize for *Game Raising* (1966). He is representative of the youthful spirit after the war.

MARC KOBER

Further Reading

Bonneau, Georges. *Histoire de la littérature japonaise contemporaine (1868–1938)*. Paris: Payot, 1940.

De Vos, Patrick, ed. *Littérature japonaise contemporaine.* Brussels and Paris: Editions Labor/Editions Philippe Picquier, 1989.

Forest, Philippe. *Oé Kenzaburô - légendes d'un romancier japonais.* Paris: Editions Pleins Feux, 2001.

Griolet, Pascal, and Michael Lucken, eds. *Japon pluriel: Actes du cinquième colloque de la Société française des études japonaises.* Paris: Picquier, 1995.

Literature d'extrême-orient au Xème siècle. Paris: Picquier, 1993.

Magazine littéraire, nos. 216–217, March 1985. Special issue on Japanese literature.

Nishikawa, Nagao. *Le Roman japonais depuis 1945.* Paris: PUF/Ecritures, 1988.

Pérol, Jean. *Regards d'encre - Ecrivains japonais 1966–1986.* Paris: La Différence, 1995.

Rimer, J. Tomas. *Modern Japanese Fiction and Its Traditions.* Princeton, NJ: Princeton University Press, 1978.

Shuichi, Katô. *Histoire de la littérature japonaise.* "Intertextes" collection, vol. 3. Paris: Fayard, 1985.

Sieffert, René. *La Littérature japonaise.* Paris: POF, 1986.

Snyder, Stephen, and Philip Gabriel, eds. *Oe and Beyond: Fiction in Contemporary Japan.* Honolulu, HI: University of Hawai'i Press, 1999.

Walker, Janet A. *The Japanese Novel of the Meiji and the Ideal of Individualism.* Princeton, NJ: Princeton University Press, 1979.

Yamanuchi, Hisashi. *The Search for Authenticity in Modern Japanese Literature.* Cambridge: Cambridge University Press, 1978.

JAYA DEVA

Twelfth-century
Indian poet

Gita Govindam

The *Gita Govindam* is a highly acclaimed poem which opens with the description of the ten *avatars* (reincarnations) of Vishnu, the god in Hindu mythology who nurtures and sustains all living beings in the world. Its author, Jaya Deva, was a dedicated devotee of Lord Jagannath, the deity of Puri in Orissa, and was also a disciple of Nimbarka, founder of the Radhavallabha sect, whose members gave hitherto unknown prominence to Radha as the loving consort of Lord Krishna. Legends claim that Padmavathi would sing with him the verses of the *Gita Govindam* at the newly built temple in Puri, and it was the only song to be sung in front of the Elder Lord (Balarama) and the younger lord (Jagannath) during their ritual bedtime worship, a practice continued to this day. The *Gita Govindam*'s fame has spread to every corner of India, inspiring great mystic saints like Chaitanya Prabhu and Bhakta Meera Bhai and a host of others all over India, and is part of the daily chant at the Rameswaram temple in the southernmost tip of India.

The *Gita Govindam* enjoys a unique position in Sanskrit literature due to the fluid cadences of its lyric sequences and a perfectly knit poetic structure, which together create a peerless combination of poetry and music. The song's cadences are based on alliteration, rhymes, and captivating words that enthrall the reader. The book features the springtime love play of Radha and Krishna, featured in various *ragas* (fully developed melodies) and strung together as richly orchestrated symphonies. The poem is divided into twelve *sargas,* or chapters, of 24 songs, including the first 2 invocatory songs in praise of Lord Vishnu's 10 avatars, titled *Dasavatara stuti,* enumerating the 10 avatars: Matsya (fish), Kuurma (tortoise), Varaha (boar), Narasimha (man-lion), vamana (dwarf), parasurama (divine), Rama (virtuous one), Balarama (Lord Krishna's brother), Buddha (Gautama Buddha), and finally, Kalki (mighty warrior). Each incarnation addressed a particular human need and the divine, benevolent response to it, which always showed unlimited compassion and infinite variations of mood, temperament, and ability, and emphasized the ultimate truth—the goal of a final communion with the divine being.

Blending devotion and mystical experience, the songs feature only three characters, Radha, Krishna, and the girlfriend-cum-messenger. An enchanting lyrical drama, the *Gita Govindam* depicts the divine lovers' inevitable estrangement and final reconciliation. The songs essentially are distributed between the three of them as their speeches, and the links of the story are provided by verses introducing each *sarga.* Using familiar rhythm and rhyming verses, Jaya Deva evokes a picturesque narration depicting the three stages of love between the divine couple: incidences of Lord Krishna's flirtation with the Gopi (cowherd) women of Brindavan, which is reported to his consort Radha by the girlfriend, followed by Krishna's penitence and Radha's rejection of him despite her inner longing. Finally, due to Krishna's entreaty and her friend's advice, Radha forgives Krishna, and thus brings about their reunion and the final consummation of their love. All human emotions associated with love—jealousy, desire, hurt, anger, separation, persuasion, and reunion—are expressed in full lyrical ebullience, and inimitably connote humans' quest for a spiritual union with God.

The open eroticism, lucid descriptions of the attractions of the female body, and graphic recital of the various aspects and details of the love play between Radha and Krishna are unique features of this poem, which evidently symbolize the final union of the individual soul [*atman*] with that of the universal [*paramatma*], achieved through total abandonment and complete surrender. The language and imagery are truly indicative of the intensity of the devotee's love in all its multifarious moods. The true value of the poem rests in its rich devotional content and the spiritual expression it gives to the devotee's yearning for the blessings of Lord Krishna and Radha. A highly original composition, the *Gita Govindam* is a trendsetter in its use of simple Sanskrit (devoid of the classical rigor that characterizes the language of earlier poetry), new idioms, and extensive melodious rhyme, and its break from the classical mould in form and metrical formation. It also served as a precursor to later Bhakti (devotional) poetry that came to be written in Indian vernacular languages and which was characterized by the effusion of love for the godhead. The *Gita Govindam* perfected and popularized the idea of Radha as the eternal consort of Krishna. Through the depiction of their amorous love play, the *Gita Govindam* established the pivotal role of Radha, and thereafter the idols of the celestial couple were installed and worshipped at several temples in eastern India.

The verses of the *Gita Govindam* have inspired dance forms, specifically *Odissi,* in which the lyrics are set to different *ragas* and have evolved into great musical compositions, which to this day delight enthralled audiences. Jaya Deva's poetry also animates Rajput and Pahari miniature paintings, the temple architecture of Orissa, and a host of other art forms all over India.

Biography

A native of Orissa-Bengal in the northeastern regions of India, Jaya Deva lived during the latter half of the twelfth century CE and served as the court pundit of Sri Lakshmana Sena, the king of Bengal. Born to Bhojadeva and Bamadevi, Jaya Deva was raised in the Birbhum district of West Bengal in a village called Kendubiva Gram, and was married to a temple dancer, Padmavathi. An annual festival called Jaya Deva Mela marks the anniversary of his death, which falls on Pausha Sankranti Day and is still celebrated today at the Puri Jagannath temple.

RAVI KOKILA

Editions

Love Song of the Dark Lord: Jaya Deva's Gita Govindam. Edited and translated by Barbara Stoler Miller. New York: Columbia University Press, 1977.

Further Reading

Ayengar, N.S.R. *Gita Govindam: Sacred Profanities: A Study of Jayadeva's Gita Govinda.* Original Sanskrit text with English translation. New Delhi: Penman Publishers, 2000.

Chandra, Moti. *Gita Govindam: Paintings.* New Delhi: Lalit Kala Akademi, 1965.

Siegel, Lee. *Sacred and Profane Dimensions of Love in Indian Traditions as Exemplified in the Gita Govindam by Jaya Deva.* New Delhi: Oxford University Press, 1978.

JAYE LEWIS, MARILYN

1960–
American writer and anthologist

Marilyn Jaye Lewis (1960–) is a prolific writer and editor of erotica, working in several genres from queer erotica and bondage-discipline/ sadomasochism (BDSM) to heterosexual erotic romance novels. She worked as a singer-songwriter in New York City folk clubs over a thirteen-year period in the 1980s and early '90s, meeting with minimal success. During the queer zine explosion of the early 1990s, she began writing erotic short stories with same-sex and BDSM themes. Her first published story,

"Draggin' the Line," a lesbian BDSM story, was published in *Bad Attitude* in 1990, and "The Urge Toward Jo," in which two girls experiment with spanking and masturbation, was published in *Frighten the Horses* the same year. She published several stories in queer zines during the following years and later was frequently published in anthologies.

Continuing to write mostly queer-oriented fiction, she worked in 1996–97 as head writer for *Dada House,* a bisexual CD-ROM game that won Best Adult Game of 1997. Becoming interested in electronic media, she began a website, *Other Rooms,* in 1997, featuring the work of several well-known erotica writers. Following this, she produced *Marilyn's Room,* a multimedia website, in 1998–2000. The site featured erotic stories, art, films, photography, and nonfiction, and at its peak was attracting 3–4,000 visits daily. She founded the Erotica Author's Association, with an accompanying website, in 2002, though the group became moribund by the end of the following year. She currently has a personal website at http://www.marilynjayelewis.com

Lewis worked as a Web producer for the New York erotica publisher Masquerade Books, which published her first book, *Neptune and Surf,* in 1999. The book contained three erotic novellas, including the title piece, set in Coney Island, about a romantic entanglement between a prostitute and a client.

Her writing won her the Erotic Writer of the Year award in the UK in 2001; the *Mammoth Book of Erotic Photography,* which she coedited with Maxim Jakubowski, was nominated as Erotic Book of the Year in the same competition in 2002. She was also a finalist in the William Faulkner Writing Competition in 2001 and won the New Century Writer's Award that year.

Working from time to time as an editor of anthologies, like her collaboration on *The Mammoth Book of Erotic Photography,* she also presented *The Big Book of Hot Women's Erotica* and *That's Amore!,* a collection of four erotic novellas to which she contributed as a writer as well. In 2003 Lewis began working in the erotic romance market, with her first three books in that genre—*When Hearts Collide, In the Secret Hours,* and *When the Night Stood Still*—published by Magic Carpet Books. In 2004, Alyson Publications published *Lust: Bisexual Erotica,* collecting the best of Lewis's short stories,

many of them previously published in anthologies during the preceding ten years.

Lewis's work always features a superb use of pacing. Writing at lengths of from 1,500 words to novels, she shows a marked ability to bring a scene up to speed with economy and focus, but also to weave a multitude of character threads into a scene to give it context and weight. Unhesitant to use the most bawdy or direct language when necessary, she gives a scene erotic tension by making it clear why an encounter matters to the characters, what they're risking, and what they stand to gain. Lewis's writing is also marked by a willingness to push her characters' comfort levels. Many of her stories feature a heroine whose sex life is varied and experienced but who in the course of the story discovers an unexplored area (often anal sex, sex with another woman, or both) and embraces it. Other stories feature interplay between an innocent and more experienced, older lovers; but contrary to the reader's expectations, the ingenue's combination of simplicity and purity winds up confounding the more experienced characters even as they seduce her. Another striking feature of Lewis's work is that no matter how outré the sexual acts, they are rarely depicted as horrid or filthy. Alienation and depravity are rare. Even when one of the characters is taken aback by another's desires, the desired act invariably is an expression of love.

Biography

Born July 22, 1960 in Columbus, Ohio; educated in Ohio public schools, graduating high school in Columbus in 1978; studied recording and audio engineering 1981–83; moved to New York City and worked as a professional singer-songwriter in folk clubs 1982–94 under her maiden name, Marilyn Jaye, and later as Marilyn Jaye Lewis.

MARK PRITCHARD

Editions

The Mammoth Book of Erotic Photography, with Maxim Jakubowski. New York: Caroll & Graf, 2001; London: Constable Robinson, 2002.
The Big Book of Hot Women's Erotica. New York: Venus/Book of the Month Club, 2003.
That's Amore! New Milford, CT: Magic Carpet Books, 2004.
Lust: Bisexual Erotica. Los Angeles: Alyson Books, 2004.

JELINEK, ELFRIEDE

1946–
Austrian author

Elfriede Jelinek's third novel, *Die Ausgesperrten* [*The Excluded*] was originally published in 1980 and started life as an audio play produced by and for German radio in 1978. In 1979 the text was also worked into a film script by the author and the director Franz Novotny, although the cinematic production was not released until 1982, with Jelinek herself in a cameo as a stern schoolteacher.

In some ways, Jelinek's novel is reminiscent, both in conception and style, of Bataille's *Story of the Eye*—and the French philosopher is intermittently (mis)quoted by the book's protagonist—yet it draws much more extensively on the meanderings of internal monologues (direct speech is the exception, which greatly reduces the relational dimension of the book's language) and is more broadly concerned with formulating a critique of sociopolitical constellations and a certain type of mass-market ideology. *Die Ausgesperrten* is also less overtly pornographic than Bataille's work (although descriptions of sexual acts are by no means absent), and its eroticism is predominantly situated in its panegyric of the intellectual and sensual pleasures of senseless violence. In its depiction of eroticism as a self-serving expression of interpersonal cruelty, emanating from deep-seated emotional and ideological discontents, the book induces a more complex and less negotiable set of effects than the erotic literature of transgression, and is more profoundly disturbing than explicit novels in the pornographic genre.

In *Die Ausgesperrten*, Jelinek draws upon an actual 1960s case of a Viennese high school student who brutally assassinated his entire family after reading the work of Albert Camus, in order to portray the hopelessness, despair, and estrangement of four youths who embark upon a project of senseless violence as a means of escaping the suffocating hypocrisy and absurdity of their social living conditions. Set in Vienna in the late 1950s, when the promising future of the *Wirtschaftswunder* (the postwar economic "miracle") left many people hopeful yet also alienated and in search of new securities, the novel offers an extraordinarily bleak picture of the degradation of a traditional class society. In addition, it makes the reader privy to the difficult gestation of a new Americanized culture and the self-delusional aspirations of adults and youngsters, parents and children, regardless of class and background. In this fragile network of relationships, violence is shamelessly eroticized, eroticism is selfishly instrumentalized, and cruelty is either trivialized as a pleasant pastime or glorified as a sublime aesthetic value, all in the service of pseudo-philosophical ideals of annihilation. Tragically and mercilessly, love is reciprocal only in the narcissistic fantasies of the protagonists. Outside these fantasies it is merely a deceitful commodity, which is used either as a ransom or as a pretext for the pursuit of self-aggrandizing goals.

The group of "misfits" around which Jelinek's narrative revolves is made up of the unbearably pretentious Rainer Maria Witkowski; his talented but not very attractive twin sister, Anna; the ethereal rich kid, Sophie (von) Pachofen; and the working-class hero Hans Sepp: four disenchanted adolescents representing three social classes and one personal ideal, that of transcending the meaninglessness of their existence through the paradoxical affirmation of the virtues of non-meaning. Under the supposed leadership of Rainer, the group's individuals detach themselves, each in their own way, from what they experience as the ideologically tainted norms and values of their social world. Like most adolescents, they hate their parents, despise rules and regulations, and believe themselves to be intellectually superior, above the law, and endowed with a unique critical sense. What makes them different, however, is that they express their sense of entitlement (and the emotional unease associated with it) through random acts of violence and, especially in the case of the Witkowski twins, a progressive mental detachment from communal, "massified" life. Yet Jelinek also shows how the most self-absorbed withdrawal and the most deeply felt hatred for social conventions is hidden behind a deceitful, mendacious mask of compliance. This is especially conspicuous in the case of Rainer Witkowski, although it is difficult to gauge which of Rainer's two faces (his private persona of solipsistic nihilism or his public appearance of materialistic indulgence) is the most truthful one.

Perhaps inevitably, the group's antisocial pact and the specific internal dramas of each of its members are also an obstacle to the development of solid relationships within the group and to the maintenance of the group as such. Rainer is in love with Sophie, and so is Hans, yet Sophie is not interested in either of them, despite the fact that both Rainer and Hans are convinced that she is. Hans has sex with Anna, who is in love with him and who believes that the feelings are mutual, yet Hans is interested only in sex, and really only in sex with Sophie. Shockingly, Rainer has to admit that he cannot plant a bomb in the school because he cannot jeopardize his final exam, and so Sophie and Hans do what the "weak leader" is incapable of doing because of his conventional concern for his own academic future. Equally shockingly, Rainer does not take revenge on Sophie and Hans, but brutally assassinates his twin sister, his father, and his mother in a cold-blooded orgy of death and destruction, before turning himself in.

In 1990, Jelinek's book was translated into English with the ironic title of *Wonderful, Wonderful Times*. Despite the international acclaim her work has received (culminating in the 2004 Nobel Prize in Literature), Jelinek's literary oeuvre, and especially *Die Ausgesperrten*, remains rather understudied in the Anglo-American world. Most of the secondary literature (criticism, textual analysis, and biographical research) is in German and awaiting translation.

Biography

Elfriede Jelinek was born on October 20 in the town of Mürzzuschlag in the Austrian province of Styria. Her father was of Czech-Jewish origin and her mother came from a prosperous Viennese family. She studied music at the Vienna Conservatory and theatre and art history at the University of Vienna. She was, controversially, awarded the Nobel Prize in Literature in 2004.

DANY NOBUS

Selected Works

Die Ausgesperrten. Reinbek bei Hamburg: Rowohlt, 1980; as *Wonderful, Wonderful Times*, translated by Michael Hulse, London: Serpent's Tail, 1990.
"Die Ausgesperrten." Radio play. In *Das Wunder von Wien. 16. österreichische Hörspiele*, edited by Bernd Schirmer, 225–61. Leipzig: Reclam, 1987.

Further Reading

Claes, Oliver. *Fremde. Vampire. Sexualität, Tod und Kunst bei Elfriede Jelinek und Adolf Muschg*. Bielefeld: Aisthesis Verlag, 1994.
Enslinn, Astrid C. "'Artistic Performance Is Not for Women'—Contemplation on the Work of Elfriede Jelinek." *Journal of Literature and Aesthetics* 4 (2004): 74–84.
Fiddler, Allyson. *Rewriting Reality: An Introduction to Elfriede Jelinek*. Oxford: Berg, 1994.
Hoffmann, Yasmin. *Elfriede Jelinek: Sprach- und Kulturkritik im Erzählwerk*. Opladen: Westdeutscher Verlag, 1999.
Janke, Pia, ed. *Die Nestbeschmutzerin: Jelinek & Österreich*. Salzburg-Vienna: Jung und Jung, 2002.
Janz, Marlies. *Elfriede Jelinek*. Stuttgart: Metzler, 1995.
Johns, Jorun B., and Katherine Arens, eds. *Elfriede Jelinek: Framed by Language*. Riverside, CA: Ariadne Press, 1994.
Konzett, Matthias. *The Rhetoric of National Dissent in Thomas Bernhard, Peter Handke, and Elfriede Jelinek*. Rochester, NY: Camden House, 2000.
Mayer, Verena, and Roland Koberg. *Elfriede Jelinek: Ein Porträt*. Reinbek bei Hamburg: Rowohlt, 2006.
Strobel, Heidi. *Gewalt von Jugendlichen als Symptom gesellschaftlicher Krisen: Literarische Gewaltdarstellungen in Elfriede Jelinek's "Die Ausgesperrten" und in ausgewählten Jugendromanen der neunziger Jahre*. Frankfurt am Main: Peter Lang, 1998.
Vis, Veronika. *Darstellung und Manifestation von Weiblichkeit in der Prosa Elfriede Jelineks*. Frankfurt am Main: Peter Lang, 1998.

JEWISH EROTIC LITERATURE

Judaism is a tradition built on archaeological strata of textual sources, and each of these layers reflects the interaction of Jewish culture with the cultures that surrounded it. For the Bible, the foundational text of Judaism, which was composed when ancient Israel was a small, beleaguered nation, the predominant issue connected to sexuality was fertility. The repeated stories of infertility, especially in Genesis, may well reflect the need of this small nation to ensure its survival. Thus, the priestly author of the first creation story has God utter a blessing of fertility on the first man and woman: "Be fruitful and multiply" (Genesis 1:26).

In the second creation story, human beings are created immortal, and when they acquire knowledge of sexuality, they become mortal. While later traditions, both Jewish and Christian, understood the expulsion from the Garden of Eden as a "fall from grace," for the Bible itself it seems that the story came to explain the difference between humans and God: while human beings procreate and die, God does neither, a fundamental difference between the biblical deity and the gods of other ancient Near Eastern religions.

Erotic attraction was not considered problematic in biblical culture; the Song of Songs, in which two unwed lovers pursue each other with something close to gender equality, represents one of the greatest works of erotic literature. The sexual prohibitions in the Bible are generally to be found in the priestly laws of purity, where they may be understood as part of the priests' preoccupation with guaranteeing fertility through proper unions. At the same time, some key narrative texts subvert these strict laws. This is particularly true of the various stories of King David's ancestors in which strong women (Tamar and Ruth) violate the laws in order to become pregnant and ensure David's line.

In the first centuries of the Common Era, a body of literature parallel to the Bible, the Talmud (called the Oral Law or "rabbinic law"), was formulated and set in writing by scholars called rabbis. The attitude toward sexuality and the body in rabbinic literature can best be understood in the context of late antiquity. For Greco-Roman thinkers, such as the Stoic philosophers, the body itself posed less of a problem than did the passions, which could overpower one's reason. The rabbis were also preoccupied with the passions, especially the sexual drive, which they called the *yetzer ha-ra* [evil impulse]. They held that the law is designed to restrain and challenge erotic passions—which might otherwise lead to evil—into constructive activities. But, like the Stoics, they generally viewed the body itself as a neutral vessel.

The rabbis held that all men must marry and father children (the law in this case is directed only toward men). Men also have an additional obligation to give sexual pleasure to their wives. At the same time, the rabbis had ambivalent feelings about male sexuality. Their position seemed to be that the sexual desires of the body are legitimate and even holy, but only if the sexual act is performed with the proper restraint. Sex must be potentially procreative, hence masturbation, for example, is labeled a capital crime, something unknown to the Bible. Nevertheless, all sexual positions are "legal," if perhaps not desirable from a medical point of view: in discussing this issue, the Babylonian Talmud unabashedly describes different sexual practices. While the rabbis never endorsed celibacy, as did the Christian Church fathers, there is evidence that they were also attracted by scholarly abstinence. In some texts, the study of Torah (i.e., biblical and rabbinic law) is invested with eroticism, suggesting that intellectual activity might compete with the desires of the body.

In the Middle Ages, under the influence of Greek philosophy, Jewish thinkers often denigrated the body as representing the purely material. Moses Maimonides (twelfth century) denounced sexuality, condemning the sense of touch as the lowest of all human faculties. Yet, as a physician and expounder of Jewish law, Maimonides recognized the importance of the body's desires and tried to strike a middle ground, emphasizing moderation and self-control.

A different school of medieval thought was the mystic (often called "Kabbalah"). A thirteenth-century erotic text called the *Iggeret ha-Kodesh* [*Letter of Holiness*] criticizes Maimonides by asking how the sense of touch could be evil, since God had created the body and called it "good"? The text insists that Adam and Eve had had sexual relations in the Garden of Eden and had done so without any sinful pleasure.

However, the *Letter of Holiness* also places severe limitations on sexuality and the body. According to the mystic tradition, God consists of male and female elements which are engaged in a kind of spiritual intercourse: the thirteenth-century *Sefer ha-Zohar* [*Book of Splendor*] contains elaborate descriptions of divine eroticism. Proper human sexuality can be directed toward God by the correct thoughts, causing the male and female elements in God to unite sexually. But improper sexuality or improper thoughts cause these elements to break apart. Sex without the proper intention is "idolatry," since it causes a rupture within the divine.

This doctrine from the thirteenth century was to have tremendous implications for Jewish thought in the subsequent centuries. In the eighteenth century, a pietistic Jewish movement in Poland, called Hasidism, created a popular theology based on the earlier Kabbalah. Some Hasidic doctrines celebrated the material world and spoke of worshipping God through the material. Others, on the other hand, saw the purpose of the worship of God as emptying the material of its divinity. These latter led to a much more ascetic approach to the body, particularly in the realm of sexuality: any sexual act that involved pleasure was sinful.

The Zionist movement, starting in the late nineteenth century, attacked these attitudes. Traditional Judaism, the Zionists argued, had denigrated the body in favor of pure spirituality, and as a result, Jews had become physically weak and politically impotent. They wished to return bodily vigor to the Jews by creating what

the Zionist ideologue Max Nordau called "muscular Judaism." They also favored an erotic revolution that would liberate the Jews from the sexual constraints of both traditional Judaism and bourgeois conventions. Some of the radical communes that the Zionists established in Palestine in the early twentieth century opposed the institution of marriage. But while many suspected these communes of fostering free love, the reality was often highly ascetic, as the members were exhorted to put collective values above the satisfaction of individual desires.

Far from negating Jewish tradition, this secular nationalism reproduced the historical tensions over sexuality and the body. At times affirmed and denied, the many genres of Jewish literature never ignored the erotic: the "people of book" can never be divorced from the "people of the body."

DAVID BIALE

Selected Works

Bible. Book of Genesis: chs. 1 and 2.
———. Book of Leviticus: chs. 15, 18, and 20
———. Song of Songs
Babylonian Talmud. Yevamot 63b
Letter of Holiness
Book of Splendor

Further Reading

Biale, David. *Eros and the Jews: From Biblical Israel to Contemporary America*. New York: Basic Books, 1992.
Biale, Rachel. *Women and Jewish Law: An Exploration of Women's Issues in Halakhic Sources*. New York: Schocken Books, 1984.
Boyarin, Daniel. *Carnal Israel: Reading Sex in Talmudic Culture*. Berkeley and Los Angeles, CA: University of California Press, 1993.
Cohen, Jeremy. *Be Fertile and Increase, Fill the Earth and Master It: The Ancient and Medieval Career of a Biblical Text*. Ithaca, NY: Cornell University Press, 1989.
Eilberg-Schwartz, Howard. *People of the Body: Jews and Judaism from an Embodied Perspective*. Albany, NY: State University of New York Press, 1992.
Fraade, Steven. "Ascetical Aspects of Ancient Judaism." In *Jewish Spirituality*, edited by Arthur Green. Vol. 1, 253–88. New York: Crossroad, 1986–7.

JIN PING MEI [*PLUM IN THE GOLDEN VASE*] AND *GELIAN HUAYING* [*FLOWER SHADOWS BEHIND THE CURTAIN*]

Seventeenth-century Chinese erotic novel and sequel

Jin Ping Mei

Jin Ping Mei, first published in 1618 or shortly thereafter, is the first major Chinese novel to have a cohesive narrative, to be written by a single author, and to be an original creation. It is unlike almost all earlier Chinese novels—which developed from the repertoire of professional storytellers—engaging in new modes of literary representation. *Jin Ping Mei* is acutely aware of its divergence from the established form of the vernacular novel in China, which allowed it to incorporate an almost encyclopedic range of texts and genres, such as jokes, popular songs, comic skits, and short stories, which were all made available to a wider audience than ever before because of the boom in commercial publishing. The novel is a rich historical source for those interested in daily life in Ming China, and is an entertaining story of deceit, revenge, jealousy, and retribution.

Jin Ping Mei [*Plum in the Golden Vase*] (also known as *The Golden Lotus*), is a milestone in the development of narrative fiction in world literature. With the possible exceptions of *The Tale of Genji* (1010) and *Don Quixote* (1615), there is no earlier work of prose fiction of comparable sophistication and depth. It is notorious in China and abroad as a work of pornography, recounting the many sexual exploits and perversions of Ximen Qing and his wives. While "Plum in the Golden Vase" is a provocative image, the sound of the title in Chinese also puns, through near homophones, with "The Glory of Entering the Vagina." Both titles are recalled in an episode

when the male protagonist ties one of his wives to the bedposts using the wrappings of her bound feet, and then throws frozen plums into her vagina from across the room. Despite its notoriety as a work of pornography, *Jin Ping Mei* is also counted among the six great novels of the premodern period due to its quality, complexity, length (about 2,000 pages), and sophistication.

The novel was circulating in manuscript among a small group by 1595, and good arguments have been made for an original publication date of 1610. The characters are taken from another novel, *Shui Hu Zhuan* [*Outlaws of the Marsh*], which itself is an aggregate of many well-known tales. The action of *Jin Ping Mei* takes place between chapters 23 and 27 of *Shui Hu Zhuan,* but, as many critics have pointed out, *Jin Ping Mei* is much more sophisticated in structure, creativity, and literary innovation than its predecessor, on which it is only very superficially dependent. The narrative is tightly structured (though occasionally containing contradictions that could be textual corruptions as easily as authorial error). It certainly is the first major work of long fiction in the Chinese vernacular tradition that has the sort of unified cohesion that allows it to bear criticism under the rubric of a novel.

The plot of *Jin Ping Mei* essentially chronicles the rise and fall of Ximen Qing, a wealthy urban merchant, his household, and all but one or two of its residents. Most spectacularly, it focuses on the moral decline of Ximen Qing and the three female protagonists who lend their names to the title (Pan *Jin*lian, Li *Ping*er and Pang Chun*mei*). The most notorious of these, Pan Jinlian (whose name in translation serves as the title of the Clement Egerton translation, *Golden Lotus*), kills her first husband so that she may marry into the Ximen Qing household. Ximen, along with most of his wives, has many affairs with those in and outside of his house. Additionally, Ximen Qing has accrued great wealth—not through the traditional means of gaining official employment by taking rigorous exams, but through currying favors, double-dealing, and bullying those in office. He is attended by various sycophantic friends, who advise him and try to benefit from his patronage.

The story takes a turn when Ximen meets a strange foreign monk, who is described as looking quite like a bloated male member. The Buddhist monk uncharacteristically eats meat at a banquet that Ximen has prepared for him and then offers Ximen a powerful aphrodisiac, which he keeps in a penis-shaped pill box. With each pill, Ximen is given sexual potency, but is warned never to take more than one at a time. Over the course of the novel and his many sexual exploits, it seems that the pills in the box represent Ximen's vital essence and its corresponding diminution over time. Ximen ignores traditional medical wisdom that the vital *yang* essence will safeguard his health and spends it frivolously, leaving him susceptible to harmful influences of ghosts, spirits, and the elements.

One night, coming home drunk from an evening of lovemaking with a friend's wife, Ximen thinks he sees the ghost of a man he killed. He is exhausted and is taken to bed with the help of assistants. His lascivious wife, Pan Jinlian, finding him too inebriated to maintain an erection, gives him an overdose of the monk's medicine and takes the last remaining pill for herself. After some coaxing, she straddles him, and eventually he ejaculates all of his semen, followed by blood. Ximen Qing then slips in and out of consciousness. The following day he is dizzy and his scrotum swells. His member still firm, Pan Jinlian continues to pleasure herself on it. Various physicians are unable to effect a cure, and finally his scrotum bursts, and he dies shortly after.

In *Jin Ping Mei,* most of the characters meet deaths that are also clearly retribution for their misdeeds. The house falls into disarray, the remaining members are scattered, and some of Ximen's wives remarry. Pan Jinlian is killed by the brother of her first husband, and Li Pinger bleeds to death from vaginal hemorrhaging. In the last chapter of the novel, the reader finds out that most of the characters have been redeemed from their suffering and reincarnated. Although

there is a crisis in the text that suggests two alternatives for Ximen Qing, none of the situations seem particularly odious and it does indeed seem that the characters have been redeemed through their deaths.

Jin Ping Mei employs themes of jealousy, mismanagement, and retribution strategically, conflating health and coin in terms of a sexual economy. Its themes and conceits are drawn largely from the corpus of fictional, medical, and sexual texts of its day. It incorporates and develops rhetoric from previous works of fiction, particularly those passages that describe the body in detail. It also appropriates older notions from medical texts warning of dangerous female sexuality. *Jin Ping Mei* is indebted to sexual manuals, and in particular what seems to be the earliest (early 16th century) and most well known piece of narrative erotica with graphic sexual depictions, *Ruyijun Zhuan* [*The Lord of Perfect Satisfaction*].

The general use of refined, lyrical language to describe sexual acts (with notable exceptions) has helped apologists defend the *Jin Ping Mei* against accusations of pornography. The most common defense is that the lascivious and selfish characters die prematurely, violating in most instances the Confucian dictum to procreate. The revelation in the last chapter of the novel, that Ximen Qing has been reincarnated as his own son, born shortly after his death, suggests that he has not yet redeemed himself but that he has a second chance to be a filial son and a good father.

Few novels that give an account of quotidian experience have been subject to such extremes of contrasting interpretation as *Jin Ping Mei*. One of the most interesting of these interpretations is that *Jin Ping Mei* was written as an act of filial piety. The 1695 text of *Jin Ping Mei* includes a preface that suggests that its author was one of the leading poets and essayists of his time, Wang Shizhen (1526–90). The story goes that Wang wrote the novel in order to avenge the death of his father, for which the evil minister Yan Song was mainly responsible. Yan Song died in 1568, but Wang set his sights on Yan's son, Yan Shifan (?–1565), who had risen in rank and was a model of corruption. While Yan was cunning and managed to escape many of the assassination plots against him directed by Wang, his fatal flaw was his penchant for licentious literature. So, Wang Shizhen set himself to writing a novel that would be of interest to Yan. Some accounts say that he finished the 100-chapter novel in a matter of days, others say it took him three years, but when he finished, he soaked the pages in poison and hired a merchant to sell the book to Yan. Yan, falling prey to his desires, bought the book, and as he licked his finger to turn the page, over the course of the long novel, he eventually ingested enough of the poison from the pages to fall ill and die. The legend endured at least up to the time of Lu Xun, who taught it as legend in his lectures at Beijing University between 1920 and 1924. Wang's authorship of the *Jin Ping Mei* is almost certainly as fictional as the story of how he avenged his father's death, but the Confucian moral of filial revenge and retribution is embedded in the novel's prefaces and commentary and has formed an important school of criticism.

Related to the story of Wang and Yan is the interpretation that the novel is a work of social and political satire, meant to expose and dispose of corrupt officials and mock the current members of the Ming court by comparing them to their counterparts of an unsuccessful late Northern Song dynasty. Another extreme considers the work a result of Buddhist devotion and an effort to demonstrate the workings of karmic retribution and reincarnation. Defending the novel against accusations that it is solely a work of pornography has also become a well-established endeavor of *Jin Ping Mei* scholars and apologists, though it to some extent undermines the Wang Shizhen story, which relies on the novel's erotic aspects to exact revenge. A common way to defend literature against accusations of pornography is to liken the work to history, a strategy that works well with *Jin Ping Mei* because of its encyclopedic nature and its focus on the particular fortunes of characters.

Novels in premodern China were usually read in variorum-type editions, with the text of the novel surrounded by printed commentary in the margins, in between lines and at the end of chapters. They would often contain lengthy prefatory essays and appendices. Zhang Zhupo (1670–98) added an important commentary and many prefatory materials to *Jin Ping Mei* in 1695 that guided interpretation for centuries. Notably, his edition contains a preface entitled "Why *Jin Ping Mei* is Not a Work of Pornography."

Lately, *Jin Ping Mei* criticism has considered the novel as having a complex relationship with

a society in which men interacted with women on the basis of domination, disdain, cruelty, and power. Traditional criticism is being reconsidered from standpoints of misogyny and sexual politics. Its representations of the "body" are also being reevaluated through material and medical considerations of physicality.

Gelian Huaying [*Flower Shadows Behind the Curtain*]

One of the prefaces to *Jin Ping Mei*, written by "Dongwu Nongzhuke" [Pearl-Juggler of Eastern Wu], possibly a pseudonym of Feng Menglong, the famous connoisseur and purveyor of vernacular stories, argues that it is the reader's responsibility to interpret the novel correctly, "He who reads *Jin Ping Mei* and feels pity and compassion is a bodhisattva; he who feels apprehension is a noble-minded man; he who feels enjoyment is a petty man; and he who feels the desire to emulate the vices portrayed is a beast."

Ding Yaokang wrote *Gelian Huaying* as a sequel to *Jin Ping Mei,* with seemingly the notion in mind that its readers hitherto had not clearly understood its moral of worldly retribution for indulgence, depravity, and treachery. This notion is made explicit in a preface to *Gelian Huaying* by "Xihu Diaoshi" [Angling Historian of West Lake], who argues that since *Jin Ping Mei* depicted much sumptuousness and depravity, its readers often "witnessed its descriptions without knowing its hidden meanings, saw its recklessness without knowing its restraint, and enjoyed its showing off without knowing its satire." *Gelian Huaying* is consequently more obviously didactic than its predecessor, *Jin Ping Mei.*

Ding Yaokang (c. 1599–c. 1669) probably wrote the 64 chapter version of *Xu Jin Ping Mei* [*Sequel to Jin Ping Mei*] late in life, putting its creation sometime in the 1660s. *Gelian Huaying* is a shortened version (48 chapters) that seems to have appeared for the first time in 1880 and was attributed to the same author. The primary differences from *Xu Jin Ping Mei* are that the names of characters are changed. While in the *Xu Jin Ping Mei*, the original names of the characters are retained, the recension *Gelian Huaying* changes these names to those which thinly mask the originals. Certain place names are changed as well. There is little agreement as to why these changes were made. Lengthy passages of historical and philosophical reflections were excised and the discussion of retribution is curtailed from the original, though it is obvious that the workings of karma to punish the wicked is the governing theme of the work.

The premise of the novel is to follow most of the main characters of Jin Ping Mei through their subsequent incarnations to witness all of the troubles that befall them as karmic punishment for their actions in *Jin Ping Mei*. The travails of Ximen Qing's primary wife, Wu Yueniang, who survives *Jin Ping Mei*, make up a large part of the story, followed and interspersed with reports of Ximen Qing, Pan Jinlian, and others. *Gelian Huaying* ignores the details of the characters' new names and families presented in the last chapter of *Jin Ping Mei* in favor of more explicitly undesirable circumstances. Ximen Qing is reborn as a blind boy who becomes a beggar, Li Pinger's new family is tricked into selling her into a brothel, and Pan Jinlian is reborn into a military family, loses her father when he dies in battle, and marries the man to whom she was betrothed at age six, who is now poor and paralyzed from a blow to the head.

Gelian Huaying states explicitly in the first few pages that the characters' early deaths have not fully atoned for their sins. An important distinction is made between retribution that happens during a lifetime and the workings of karma that follow particularly evil persons into the next. This is a fundamental difference between *Jin Ping Mei* and its sequel. While in the original, characters simply die early for their misdeeds, in *Gelian Huaying*, they must go on paying for them in a second, more miserable incarnation. There is a fairly simple reversal of fortune employed to depict the workings of karmic retribution. What was done by a character in *Jin Ping Mei* is done to him or her in *Gelian Huaying*. Those characters that were rich or lustful in a previous lifetime are denied wealth and intimacy in this one.

In addition to more explicit moral didacticism, *Gelian Huaying* presents fewer instances of sexual intercourse than does *Jin Ping Mei*, and those that it does represent are depicted using flowery, indirect language. While *Jin Ping Mei* seems to revel in some of the scenes of sexual debauchery, including lyrical descriptions of anatomy and occasional vulgar terms; the sequel seems to present sex primarily either as something for which the character will later have to atone or as karmic punishment in the form of violence, as is the case with one of the more explicit sex scenes when Li Pinger sleeps with the coarse but wealthy man to whom she has been married. The narrative does not employ sexual metaphors of combat or economy as *Jin Ping Mei* does. The general lack of sexual interaction in *Gelian Huaying* seems misleading given the title, which implies catching fleeting glimpses of beautiful maidens hidden behind a screen, and the subsequent lust that such an image would normally produce.

Ding Yaokang relies heavily on Daoist and Buddhist texts to advise and warn his readers, while the author of *Jin Ping Mei* incorporates a wider variety of materials into the body of the novel. Ding plays the role of a preacher, claiming on the title page that his name is the "Recluse of the Purple Brilliance," and refers to himself in the novel and to his previous incarnations. Ding shows that he is a living example of the ongoing cosmic process of reincarnation, thereby lending further authority to the Daoist and Buddhist messages he is promulgating. He also seems to grant the characters ultimate escape from the wheel of karmic retribution, as most pay penance for their misdeeds and attain enlightenment.

Biography

The author of *Jin Ping Mei* calls himself "Lanling Xiaoxiao Sheng" [The Scoffing Scholar of Lanling], which would make him probably the Confucian philosopher Xun Zi of the third century BCE. Xun Zi was appointed magistrate in Lanling and is now buried there, according to the *Shi Ji* [Records of the Grand Historian]. Although he did not refer to himself as the "scoffing scholar," an image of him as scoffing at corrupt officials is presented in Liu Xiang's (79–8 BCE) preface to Xun Zi's works, the only early biography of him other than that in the *Shi Ji*. Xun Zi's (greatly simplified) philosophy centers on the belief that human nature is evil and is redeemable only through arduous attention to reform.

See also **Hong Lou Meng; Xiuta Yeshi; Zhulin Yeshi**

Editions

The Plum in the Golden Vase or Chin P'ing Mei. Vol. 1: *The Gathering*, 1993; Vol. 2: *The Rivals*. Edited and

translated by David Tod Roy. Princeton, NJ: Princeton University Press, 2001.
The Golden Lotus. Translated by Clement Egerton. London: Routledge, 1939.
Flower Shadows Behind the Curtain. New York: Pantheon, 1959.
Jin Ping Mei Cihua [1618], reprint Tokyo: Daian, 1963; Hong Kong: Yiyuan Chubanshe, 1993.

References and Further Reading

Ding, Naifei. *Sexual Politics in Jin Ping Mei*. Durham, NC: Duke University Press, 2002.

Hsia, C.T. *The Classic Chinese Novel*. New York: Columbia University Press, 1968.
Plaks, Andrew. *The Four Masterworks of the Ming Novel*. Princeton, NJ: Princeton University Press, 1987.
Rolston, David L. *How to Read the Chinese Novel*. Princeton, NJ: Princeton University Press, 1990.
Stone, Charles. *The Fountainhead of Chinese Erotica: The Lord of Perfect Satisfaction*. Honolulu: University of Hawaii Press, 2003.

JINGU QIGUAN [*THE OIL VENDOR WHO CONQUERS THE QUEEN OF BEAUTY*]

Nineteenth-century Chinese short story

This Chinese short story in colloquial language came early to the notice of a readership curious about Chinese mores when it was translated into French and published in 1877 by the Dutch interpreter and Sinologist Gustav Schlegel (1840–1903). He appended to his translation, together with the Chinese text, an account of his visit to a Cantonese "flower boat" in 1861. It was more recently praised as being informative about brothel life by van Gulik (*Sex Life*). The Chinese text, in more than 20,000 characters, is the seventh of 40 chapters of the so-called anthology *Wonders of the Present and the Past*, completed around 1640 by an unknown compiler out of 200 short stories from a series of five 40-chapter volumes, published between 1620 and 1633, the first three by Feng Menglong (1574–1646) and the last two by Ling Mengchu (1580–1644). *The Oil Vendor Who Conquers the Queen of Beauty* is to be found in the third chapter of the third volume of Feng Menglong, but was probably penned by one of his contemporaries and friends, the unidentified "Langxian" [Libertine Immortal], perhaps enlarging an earlier tale in classical Chinese. Another story, possibly by Feng Menglong, included in chapter 5 of *Jingu qiguan*, "The Courtesan's Jewel Box," offers a number of comparable features with *The Oil Vendor*, paradoxically opposing true love to venal love. "The Pearl-sewn Shirt," likely penned by Feng Menglong, who published it as the first chapter of his first volume, had more explicit sex descriptions. It was retained in the *Jingu qiguan* as chapter 23. The most famous tale of a big-hearted courtesan in classical Chinese is attributed to Bai Xingjian (776–826), of which Dudbridge (*The Tale of Li Wa*) gives the best study, translation, and critical edition.

The Story

The story is set some five hundred years before its publication, when the Northern Song capital, Kaifeng, fell unto the hands of barbarians (1126), sending a flow of refugees south to Hangzhou, the city which became the provisional capital of the Southern Song dynasty. The two main characters of the tale, a girl and a boy, are among them, soon to be lost and forsaken children. The girl is sold to a brothel and becomes at twelve a "Queen of Beauty." The boy is bought by a childless old oil merchant but is slandered by a jealous shop assistant and is forced to become an oil peddler. Now a young man, but still poor, he falls madly in love with the courtesan at first sight. Though nubile at thirteen, she had been deflowered when fifteen, and ever since has been in so great demand that a night spent with her would cost ten ounces of silver. The youth saves patiently for a year to accumulate the necessary amount, plus another six ounces of silver with which to buy the proper attire in which to be presented to her. Still the brothel "mother" has to introduce him stealthily, as the pampered girl would not have received a client of such low status. But on the appointed evening, the courtesan is so sick from overdrinking that the peddler, instead of demanding what he has paid for, soothes her with great care, wiping her vomit with his new clean clothes. She is deeply moved by the gallantry of the poor, but handsome lad. Later he saves her from a rich bully who abandons her helpless and barefoot on a river bank. Grateful, and in love, she brings to him her savings, enough to buy her out of prostitution, marry her, and turn the peddler into a wealthy merchant and landlord. The term "oil peddler" actually became then in the area a popular nickname for any considerate lover.

The Dedicated Lovers

The plot of the story is cleverly unfolded, without any unaccountable coincidences, rather sparing in erotic explicit descriptions, as requested by the mood of sentimental pathos, for, though not promoting love without sex, the tale denounces sex without love. Never coarse or crude, it may have contributed to the birth of the sentimental short novel *Caizi jiaren xiaoshuo,* about a "talented young scholar and the beautiful learned girl," in vogue between the mid-17th and mid-18th centuries in China. The oil peddler did not conquer the Beauty through poetry, as is usual in those codified novels, and find happiness in turning into a respected married merchant. Besides reproving social snobbery, the story gave a new currency to the theme of the big-hearted courtesan (the "whore with the heart of gold," in Western terms), so much so that Li Yu (1611–1680) disclosed its romantic fallacy in one

of his ironic short stories (translated by Kaser as "Reine de cupidité").

Numerous singers, storytellers, and dramatists over the centuries have reworked the story of the *Jingu qiguan* and brought it to the attention of ever-larger audiences. It has been translated or retranslated many times in Japanese, Russian, German, and other languages. The original edition of the *Jingu qiguan* is lost, but hundreds of early and later ones testify to its steady popularity.

ANDRÉ LÉVY

Editions

Feng Menglong. *Le Vendeur d'huile qui seul possède la reine de beauté.* Translated under the direction of and edited by Jacques Reclus [1976]. Préface by Pierre Kaser. Arles: Philippe Picquier, 1990.

Ma Y.W. and Joseph S.M. Lau. "The Oil Peddler Courts the Courtesan." In *Traditional Chinese Stories, Themes and Variations, Traditional Chinese Tales,* 177–208. New York: Columbia University Press.

Schlegel, Gustav. *Le Vendeur d'huile qui seul possède la Reine-de-Beauté, ou splendeurs et misères des courtisanes chinoises.* Leyden and Paris 1877.

Wang Chi-chen. "The Oil Peddler and the Queen of Flowers." In *Traditional Chinese Tales.* New York: Columbia University Press, 1944.

Yang Hsien-yi and Gladys Yang. "The Oil Vendor and the Courtesan." In *The Courtesan's Jewel Box,* 272–332. Peking: Foreign Language Press, 1967.

"Le Marchand d'huile conquiert seul la reine des fleurs." In *Spectacles curieux d'aujourd'hui et d'autrefois* (Jingu qiguan). Translated, edited, and annotated by Rainier Lanselle, 201–79. Paris: Gallimard, 1996.

Further Reading

Dudbridge, Glen. *The Tale of Li Wa: Study and Critical Edition of a Chinese Story from the Ninth Century.* London: Faculty of Oriental Studies, Oxford University/Ithaca Press, 1983.

Hanan, Patrick. *The Chinese Vernacular Story.* Cambridge, MA: Harvard University Press 1981.

Lévy, André. *Inventaire analytique et critique du conte chinois en langue vulgaire.* Vol. 8-2, 582–86. Mémoire de l'Institut des Hautes Etudes Chinoises. Paris: Collège de France, 1979.

Li Yu. "Reine de cupidité." In *A mari jaloux femme fidèle,* translated by Pierre Kaser, 135–61. Arles: Philippe Picquier, Arles 1990.

Van Gulik, Robert. *Sex Life in Ancient China.* Leiden: Brill, 1961.

JOANOU, ALICE

1966–
American novelist

Alice Joanou's career in erotic writing began with her interest in extreme expression. As an artist, she wants to go where people generally do not: deep into the roiling id. Her first forays into the genre were assignments to rewrite formulaic erotica for Richard Kasak at Masquerade Books in New York. She convinced him that she could write a better novel, and the result was her debut collection of stories, *Cannibal Flower* (1991), available, as are all of Joanou's books, through Rhinoceros Publications. In those 13 stories, she adapts myth and fairy tale—Salome, Penelope, Delilah, Rapunzel—to modern themes. Like Borges, she is interested in a psychosexual rearrangement of reality.

Tourniquet (1992), a collection of 24 stories, opens with "A," a wicked comedy of adultery. In it, transgression is the stimulus for passion. Through a web of dream and memory, the narrator describes a single act of adulterous sex that she commits with the husband of a woman who has passed out drunk, in her wedding dress, on the kitchen floor. Next to her prostrate body the narrator makes love to the bride's husband, moving between rhapsody and exact physical description, between observation and participation in the tragicomic farce she has created. "L'Enfer" means "hell" in French, and it is also the name of a chillingly unusual nightclub in France as imagined by a female Rimbaud. In this story, the narrator is a gigolo whose mistress is married to a rich old man. Fancying that his mistress is a beautiful woman in front but a boy from behind, he proposes a gender-switching game.

Black Tongue (1995) is Joanou's third book of short stories, a dozen fractured narratives à la J.G. Ballard and Kathy Acker which take us to horrifying places in the imagination of lust. The first story, "Spain 28," is forensic poetry married to science fiction in which the narrator describes her adolescent malaise, controlled by the mass media.

Joanou's first novel, *Maya 29*, was published in England in the Eros Plus series in 1995. In it she examines the erotological relationship between doctor and patient, and the transformative nature of each sexual emotion. Dr. Lazar is a psychiatrist who is visited by a schizophrenic Sheherazade named Maya. As she confesses to him, he is drawn into her nightmare, and when he meets a literary agent named William St. John, he is drawn deeper into a murderous reality. Maya is forced to work her way through 29 personas in an attempt to heal herself. *Maya 29*'s exploration of feminine madness is reminiscent of Paul Ableman's *I Hear Voices*.

The Best of Alice Joanou (1998) contains 17 stories taken from her three story collections. Joanou writes disturbing prose poems and longer, complex, experimental narratives in which unbridled sexuality can lead to disaster—or into an alternate universe of lust in which anything can happen and usually does. People make love in a crowded subway car ("Scylla and Charybdis") and no one notices; a famous Andy Warhol–style photographer has a most Dorian Gray–like finish after he has sucked up the souls of 20 young models.

As much a romantic as Anne Rice or Anaïs Nin, Joanou is a delicate, deadly poet of eros. Each inlaid paragraph of her exotic stories provides the reader with that combination of mystery, experiment, explicit sexuality, erotic intelligence, and lyrical emotionalism that are the ingredients of a distinctive literary voice.

Biography

Born in Los Angeles. She attended the Los Angeles Art Center College of Design, and took an MA in sculpture at Yale in 1990. She teaches in San Francisco.

MICHAEL PERKINS

JONG, ERICA

1942–
American novelist, poet, short story writer, essayist

Although not all of Erica Jong's works are erotic, the concern of all of them has been sexuality: Many of her works focus on female sexuality as a means for gauging, exploring, and developing identity as well as the interrelationship between writing and sexuality. The intermingling of sexuality and identity is a constant theme, and writing is a way of discovering it. As she herself said in 1999 of Anthony Burgess's erotic Shakespearean fantasy, "without language, Eros is dumb."

Even in her first book, *Fruits and Vegetables*, there is a celebration of the body that is both physical and intellectual. The central poem of this volume, "Arse Poetica," intertwines inspiration and intercourse, depicting the poet as female sitting upon the passive male muse, so that "penetration" can be "at its deepest." The other poems in this volume are less blatantly sexual, but are imbued with the spirit of this seduced muse. Thus a Chaucer class in "The Teacher" becomes the arena for erotic attention concentrated on the instructor, who is "naked before them" and is eventually devoured by the students. The final line instructs the reader to relate to literature in the same way: "Eat this poem." *Fruits and Vegetables* was followed by *Half-Lives* in 1973. The poems in this book already betray Jong's sensitivity to the virulent criticism of her erotic/literary propensities. "Beware of the man who denounces women writers," she writes as warning 3 in "Seventeen Warnings in Search of a Feminist Poem," "his penis is tiny & cannot spell." But despite the public reactions that might have made another writer fall silent or hide, many of these poems develop the open erotic vulnerability of her previous work. "Touch," for example, exposes the secrets of "the house of the body," and "Gardener" focuses entirely on the womb, its processes and demands. Jong combines the characteristically American "confessional" mode of Theodore Roethke, Anne Sexton, Robert Lowell, and Sylvia Plath with the openly erotic search for self. Like her friend Sexton, she writes about sex, but unlike Sexton, she uses sex metaphorically as well as graphically and as a means to communication. More significantly, she is different from the "confessional" poets in her embrace of life. As John Ditsky notes, Jong is "a Sexton determined to survive." Sexuality for Jong is not an escape from confrontation but the confrontation itself, and the graphic descriptions in her verse are means to this confrontation. Her poems have garnered awards from *Poetry* magazine (Chicago), the Poetry Society of America, and the Borestone Mountain Poetry Anthology, and were praised by Louis Untermeyer as "sly but penetrating, witty but passionate, bawdy and beautiful."

But it was her groundbreaking first novel, *Fear of Flying*, which pushed her name, as well as the entire concept of open and active female sexuality, into the limelight. In *Fear of Flying*, Jong quotes a prominent work of 1967, *The Normal Woman*, as summing up sex in "three P's: procreation, pleasure, and pride." Pleasure, however, is considered superfluous, "the prize in the cereal box." It is this assumption, so basic to American society of the time, that Jong's entire novel is aimed at disproving, and it for this reason that Henry Miller hailed *Fear of Flying* as "a female *Tropic of Cancer*." "This book will make literary history," said Miller in the *New York Times,* "because of it women are going to find their own voice and give us great sagas of sex, life, joy, and adventure." His words proved right.

Isadora Wing—young, bookish, beautiful, Jewish, and frustrated—goes to a convention in Vienna with her conventional psychiatrist husband and meets a Laingian psychiatrist, Adrian Goodlove. Seeking in Adrian and in the Laing alternative alleviation for the frustration of women's role, she embarks on a passionate but unsatisfying relationship. Her fantasies may be of sex for its own sake, but her experiences are different. Despite the fact that Isadora's term, "zipless fuck," is associated with this book, her desires are far more extensive and all-encompassing than the term has come to mean. Isadora's husband, Bennett, though silent and boring and antithetical to the colorful Adrian, is the better lover. Although *Fear of Flying* traces Isadora's every sexual encounter from the age of fourteen, the conclusion of the book has her disappointed with Adrian and trying to transcend the need for relationships as the means to self-fulfillment. "People don't complete us. We complete ourselves." This is an answer to Freudian theories of psychiatry which stress the adjustment of women to their supplementary roles and incomplete anatomy, as well as a response to the marginalization of female sexuality and fulfillment in the popular contemporary depiction of the "normal woman."

Although the positive reception was not unmitigated, and critics like Alfred Kazin and Paul Theroux found the book "vulgar," *Fear of Flying* was greatly praised by numerous writers, such as John Updike, who compared the novel to Chaucer and *Catcher in the Rye*. *Fear of Flying* catapulted Jong to international fame and became one of the top ten best-selling novels of the 1970s, selling more than 12.5 million copies worldwide, 6.5 million in the United States. It has been translated into 15 languages and was reissued in 1997.

The affirmative Whitmanesque poem which begins *Loveroot* (1975) and inspired the title of the book opens with "I, Erica Jong," having endured "three decades of pain ... declare myself now for joy." The poems of this collection explore this search for joy, its pitfalls, and the possibilities of success. Identifying the coldness of men as danger and torture in the section entitled, "In the Penile Colony," "Sexual Soup" presents a man whose illness is defined by his lusts "for nothing," and is therefore destructive to the giving woman. She will be destroyed by masochistic relationships as many female icons have been destroyed. In the next poem, "Sylvia Plath Is Alive in Argentina," Sylvia Plath, Norma Jean, and Zelda Sayre are "done in" by men. Yet the final poem, dedicated to Anne Sexton, "Eating Death," reaffirms the salvation of erotic love.

Selected by Anthony Burgess as one of the 100 best novels since 1939, *How to Save Your Own Life* (1975) develops the idea of the author as character, as self, as object and subject. Isadora

Wing, heroine of Jong's previous novel, is now herself the author of an semi-autobiographical erotic best seller, *Candida Confesses,* and bears the freedom fame has bestowed upon her as well as the self-consciousness and responsibility inherent in the role of representative woman she has acquired. Isadora, Jong's own creation, examines the ways in which Candida Wong (Isadora's creation) is similar to and different from Isadora herself, just as Jong in her life examined in interviews her own biographical comparisons to Isadora. The point of this postmodern analysis is the ancient one of developing self knowledge, just as the books to come featuring Isadora will present the protagonist as a representative woman in a stage of contemporary development. As "representative" heroine, Isadora must of necessity experiment with as many options as possible, even if they appear strained and artificial to her as she experiences them. Jong repeatedly notes in interviews that her novel is satirical and is not therefore limited by facts. Yet many critics judge her works in general by "realistic," pop-culture novelistic standards, not satirical and picaresque ones.

The structure of this novel is clearly picaresque and leads to an affirmative conclusion. Isadora leaves her husband, goes to Hollywood, widens her sexual repertoire, and experiences some of the devastations undergone by her friend Jeannie Morton (Anne Sexton). But while Morton commits suicide, Isadora chooses love as a positive alternative, and the novel ends in violent passion.

The poetry books that alternate with her novels are often conclusions drawn from the previous novel and direct expressions of stages the next novel will illustrate. In *At the Edge of the Body* (1979), Jong describes poetry as a Zen experiment beginning with "Letting the mind go, / letting the pen, the breath" ("Zen & the Art of Poetry"). This book deals with matured sexuality. "Flesh is merely a lesson. / We learn it / & pass it on," she notes in "The Buddha in the Womb." As Benjamin Franklin V notes, "She has repeatedly stated her openness to all experience, and once she accepts life's totality, as she does explicitly in *Loveroot*, then death becomes a topic she has to address." Experience, release, sense of self, and the future: these are the topics of her next "confessional" work. In "Without Parachutes," she even invokes this next direction: "Send parachutes & kisses! /Send them quick! / I am descending into the cave / of my own fear."

Transcending the cave of her fear in her next work, however, Jong works with a very different direction and perspective. *Fanny, Being the True History of the Adventures of Fanny Hackabout-Jones* (1980) is a, feminist, mock-eighteenth-century novel of a woman seeking independence and erotic fulfillment, and a revisionist view of John Cleland's *Fanny Hill*. As a thinking, feral, female Tom Jones, Fanny does not stumble once and fall forever like traditional women in the English novel, but develops from virgin to whore to mother to writer. By reconceptualizing women characters of the past, Jong creates new potential for women characters in the present. By rewriting the stereotype of the pornographic heroine as masochistic victim, Jong has opened the way for the vast potential for female erotica.

In her preface to her next book of poems, *Ordinary Miracles* (1983), Jong notes the interrelationship between her poetry and prose, that the poetry foreshadows the novels and that "my poems and my novels have always been very much of a piece." This is a significant indication of how to read her work as a chronological whole. In "Poem for Molly's Fortieth Birthday," Jong reveals her role as provider of previously hidden information for the next generation to learn from: the author not as role model but as source material. Her next novel, *Parachutes and Kisses* (1984), embodies this concept of source material about being forty rather than the woman as role model. It returns to Isadora Wing, now a maturing libidinous heroine, reexperiencing and reevaluating erotica and placing its function differently in existence. Her numerous erotic encounters (with, among others, a real estate developer, a rabbi, an antiques dealer, a plastic surgeon, and a medical student) are attempts to seek love within the context of her identity, and not confirmation of her identity.

Although it might appear that *Shylock's Daughter* (1987) is the antithesis of *Ordinary Miracles*, with its escape into the past and the romanticism of Venice, this novel actually humanizes and domesticates the Jewish ghetto of the Renaissance as well as Shakespeare's own gigantic character. Jessica Pruitt, a middle-aged actress, returns to the past in Venice to become the dark lady of Shakespeare's sonnets and come to terms with her mother's death, her own middle age, and her need for direction. In *Any Woman's*

Blues (1990), however, maturity is far more complex and less easily achieved. The middle-aged Leila Sand, an artist, is an obsessed self-termed sexaholic. Her downward spiral into alcoholism, sexual dissoluteness, and drugs recalls the blues songs of Billie Holiday, but her analytic maturing vision enables her to eventually take back control of her life. Sexual obsession in older women is common, unique in its manifestations, and very rarely discussed. *Any Woman's Blues* opens the discussion.

The poems in *Becoming Light* (1991) concern the development of sexuality in the light of maturing wisdom. It is this that makes the combination of selected and new poems unique—they integrate the erotic vision of the earlier work into the present mellow vision. The opening poem, "Lullaby for a Dybbuk," has the dybbuk "tweak my clit, / hoping that my sexaholic self / will surface / and take, me back, back, back / to the land of fuck," and her response is to love the dybbuk into submission, including the past turbulence in her present, rather than rejecting or forgetting it.

In recent years Jong's range and control of the subject of sexuality has increased, and her analytic skills have become focused upon explaining erotica in literature and society as well as telling good stories about herself. In *Fear of Fifty* (1994) she talks candidly about her own passionate experiences, successes, and failures, revealing her weaknesses as well as her strengths. She continues dialogues with writers who were influenced by her, such as Susie Bright, in subjects that have become popular as a result of *Fear of Flying*, such as female fantasies. She also continues dialogues with those who influenced her, even her mother. If *Fear of Flying* was intended to help herself and others overcome their flying fears, *Fear of Fifty* intends to prove that there is life in middle age—a growing, sexual, and exciting life—and the individual does not cease to grow and desire. This is also a major function of her long look at Henry Miller in *The Devil at Large* (1994). A friend, teacher, and inspiration, Miller's influence on Jong continues here in essays, stories, and an imaginary dialogue.

The novel *Inventing Memory* (1997) continues the broader reach and the attempt at a greater scope of the same subject. Three generations of women are depicted—in their continuity, rebellion against continuity, and interrelationship. At least two of the essays in *What Do Women*

Want? Power, Sex, Bread & Roses (1999) deal with the subjects introduced in previous work. Questions of the mother–daughter dialectic and its influence on feminism, sexuality, and backlash relate back to *Inventing Memory*, and an essay on Henry Miller develops the subject of pornography and creativity. But her scope continues to expand. It is the nation's sexuality that interests her here: the significance of the Clinton marriage in "The President's Penis," the puritanical reception of the film of Nabokov's *Lolita*, the reception of Viagra. Jong's future work includes a book about the quintessential erotic poet, Sappho. Clearly she has more to say on this subject.

Biography

Born March 26 in New York City to Seymour and Eda (Mirsky) Mann, Erica graduated from Barnard College in 1963, completed an MA at Columbia University in 1965, and, turning her back on doctoral studies, continued postgraduate study at the Columbia School of Fine Arts, 1969–70. Married Michael Werthman, 1963 (divorced, 1965); married Allan Jong, 1966 (divorced, 1975); married Jonathan Fast, 1977 (divorced, 1983); married Ken Burrows, 1989; children: Molly Miranda Jong-Fast. English faculty, City College of the City University of New York, 1964–65 and 1969–70; faculty, University of Maryland, Overseas Division, Heidelberg, Germany, 1966–69; instructor in English, Manhattan Community College, 1969–70; instructor in poetry, YM/YWCA Poetry Center, New York City, 1971–73; instructor, Bread Loaf Writers Conference, 1981, and Salzburg Seminar, 1993. Judge in fiction, National Book Award, 1995. Member, New York State Council on the Arts, 1972–74. Awards include: American Academy of Poets Award, 1963; New York State Council on the Arts grant, 1971; Borestone Mountain Award in poetry, 1971; Bess Hokin prize, *Poetry* magazine, 1971; Madeline Sadin Award, *New York Quarterly*, 1972; Alice Faye di Castagnolia Award, Poetry Society of America, 1972; Creative Artists Public Service (CAPS) award, 1973, for *Half-Lives*; National Endowment for the Arts fellowship, 1973–74; Premio International Sigmund Freud, 1979; and United Nations Award of Excellence.

KAREN ALKALAY-GUT

Selected Works

Fruits and Vegetables. New York: Holt, Rinehart and Winston, 1971; London: Secker and Warburg, 1973.
Half-Lives. New York: Holt, Rinehart and Winston, 1973; London: Secker and Warburg, 1974.
Fear of Flying. New York: Holt, Rinehart and Winston, 1973 ; London: Secker and Warburg, 1974.
Here Comes and Other Poems. New York: New American Library, 1975.
Loveroot. New York: Holt, Rinehart and Winston, 1975; London: Secker and Warburg, 1977.
The Poetry of Erica Jong. New York: Holt, Rinehart and Winston, 1976.
How to Save Your Own Life. New York: Holt, Rinehart and Winston, and London: Secker and Warburg, 1977.
Four Visions of America, with Others. Santa Barbara, CA: Capra Press, 1977.
Selected Poems. 2 vols. London: Panther, 1977–80.
At the Edge of the Body. New York: Holt, Rinehart and Winston, 1979; London: Granada, 1981.
Fanny, Being the True History of the Adventures of Fanny Hackabout-Jones. New York: New American Library, and London: Granada, 1980.
Ordinary Miracles: New Poems. New York: New American Library, 1983; London, Granada, 1984.
Parachutes and Kisses. New York: New American Library, and London: Granada, 1984.
Shylock's Daughter. Boston: Houghton Mifflin, and London: Bantam, 1987; New York: HarperCollins, 1995.
Any Woman's Blues. New York: Harper, and London: Chatto and Windus, 1990.
Becoming Light: Poems, New and Selected. New York: HarperCollins, 1991.
Fear of Fifty: A Midlife Memoir. London: Chatto & Windus, 1994.
Erica Jong on Henry Miller: The Devil at Large. London: Vintage, 1994.
Inventing Memory: A Novel of Mothers and Daughters. New York: HarperCollins, 1997.
What Do Women Want? Power, Sex, Bread & Roses. London: Bloomsbury, 1999.

Further Reading

Butler, Robert J. "The Woman Writer as American Picaro: Open Journeying in Erica Jong's *Fear of Flying.*" *Centennial Review* 31 (Summer 1987).
Ferguson, Mary Anne. "The Female Novel of Development and the Myth of Psyche." In *The Voyage In: Fictions of Female Development*, edited by Elizabeth Abel, Marianne Hirsch, and Elizabeth Langland, 232–46. Hanover, NH: University Press of New England, 1983.
Hite, Molly. "Writing and Reading—The Body: Female Sexuality and Recent Feminist Fiction." *Feminist Studies* 14 (Spring 1988): 121–42.
Kazin, Alfred. "The Writer as Sexual Show-off; or, Making Press Agents Unnecessary." *New York Magazine*, June 9, 1975, 36–40.

Mandrell, James, "Questions of Genre and Gender: Contemporary American Versions of the Feminine Picaresque." *Novel* 20 (Winter 1987).

Nitzsche, Jane Chance. "'Isadora Icarus': The Mythic Unity of Erica Jong's Fear of Flying." *Rice University Studies* 64 (1978): 89–100.

Ostriker, Alicia Susan. *Stealing the Language: The Emergence of Women's Poetry in America.* Boston, MA: Beacon Press, 1986.

Shepherd, Kenneth R. "Erica Jong." In *Contemporary Authors New Revisions Series.* Vol. 26. Detroit, MI: Gale Research Inc., 1988.

Schmidt, Daniel Wayne. *Rewriting the American Picaresque: Patterns of Movement in the Novels of Erica Jong, Toni Morrison, and Marilynne Robinson.* Carbondale, IL: Southern Illinois University, 1993.

Showalter, Elaine, ed. *The New Feminist Criticism: Essays on Women, Literature, and Theory.* New York: Pantheon Books, 1985.

Suleiman, Susan Rubin. "(Re)Writing the Body: The Politics and Poetics of Female Eroticism." *In The Female Body in Western Culture: Contemporary Perspectives,* edited by Susan Rubin Suleiman, 7–29. Cambridge, MA: Harvard University Press, 1985.

Templin, Charlotte. *Feminism and the Politics of Literary Reputation: The Example of Erica Jong.* Lawrence, KS: University of Kansas Press, 1995.

Theroux, Paul. "Hapless Organ." *New Statesman,* April 19, 1974, 554.

Updike, John. "Jong Love." *New Yorker,* December 17, 1973, 149–53.

JOUHANDEAU, MARCEL

1888–1979
French writer

Écrits secrets

The first volume of this trilogy, *Le voyage secret,* chronicles a journey the author made away from his wife, Élise, in the company of a group of men, designated by capital letters only, including particularly H and X. In a series of dense, poetic meditations the author reflects on the emotional and moral implications of living his obsessive passion for X: how can or should such a fascination be realized and how could X—and others in their entourage—be expected, if they knew, to react to it? Given that the very intensity of his passion depends on a taboo which prevents its resolution or reciprocation, he returns home both relieved and reenergized.

The second volume, *Carnets de Don Juan,* contains analytical or anecdotal reflections on the body—its pleasures, its affects, and its expressiveness—and a lyrical hymn to an irresistible love of men which combines mysticism and eroticism, the abject and the sublime. Then follow the author's fraught, impassioned encounters with a series of youths: Raoul, a gauche

literary admirer; the elusive, imperious Jean-Pierre; the potentially dangerous Albert; the well-proportioned, golden-haired, and uninhibited Louis, who, according to the ever-watchful Élise, plays that season's Giton to Marcel's Socrates. However brief or seemingly reprehensible Marcel's relationships, he remains, however, an unregretful and unapologetic Don Juan. In final sections, he claims to endow himself, his partners, and their pleasures with the respect and the nobility their beauty deserves. As before, the abject plays host to the sublime.

The third volume, *Tirésias,* is a paean to the bathhouse boys who, in their twenties, gave Marcel, around sixty, his greatest joys, initiating him magisterially into the pleasures of sodomy (hence the sexual ambivalence of the Tirésias of the title) and developing a sense of mutual respect and friendship. Although Richard, Philippe, "The Dwarf," and Pierre are in a sense interchangeable, this very interchangeability strengthens their semi-mystical animal appeal: cumulatively they represent not just men but "Man." Each boy is an unself-conscious sexual athlete, with his own physique and personality, and together they transform the author's sexual, moral, and emotional life. He remains unrepentant—and free from disease. If the reappearances of one of the boys disconcertingly near his home means that the boy is the Devil, then he is a Devil whose fascination warrants the threat of exposure, in the same way that the pleasure of sodomy repays the initial pain of penetration.

Chronique d'une passion

Very different in tone and focus, this work charts Marcel's passion for J.St. (Jacques), a man some twenty years his junior whom he sees regularly over a period of time and who, as it happens, has painted a portrait of him before they met: the *Prélat*. Although clearly physical, this relationship is more important for the all-consuming and thus, in a sense, purifying effect it has on Marcel and for its devastating impact on his wife, Élise, who destroys the painting and vows to murder the lover. She eventually changes her mind when she realizes this may play into the couple's hands, but, in return for her restraint, Marcel promises never to see J.St. again. The passion that hitherto had superseded the divine finally seems to present an image of Hell.

De l'abjection

Like *Chronique*, *De l'abjection* is a heady mixture of the ecstatic and the detached, the sacred and the profane, the visionary and the documentary, the pure and the erotic. The author alternates between aphoristic explorations of his inner world and emotive accounts of his early sexual experiences which eventually reveal his "different" sexuality whose association with evil gives it—and him—both excitement and insight: his vice and his virtue is Man. After further lyrical evocations of a naked male lover, the book closes with an apologia of the poignancy and the nobility of abjection.

Bréviaire; Portrait de Don Juan; Amours

In the first of these short texts, *Bréviaire*, Jouhandeau's "Je ne regrette rien," the elderly author recalls the joys of his meetings with the anonymous but appreciative men of Mme Made's *maison close*: if homosexuality is an ethic and an art, desire for men and virtuoso sex are the mainsprings of his life. The second, *Portrait de Don Juan et son esprit retrouvé chez un homosexuel*, chronicles the variety of homoerotic pleasures available to the author who, as *flâneur-voyeur*, savors chance sightings of men in the streets or who, as solitary dream-lover, recaptures the beauty of partners such as "The Swimmer" and Jean-Pierre. A third text, *Amours*, contains letter-poems for men, whose charisma not only defies both reality and imagination but exceeds any distinction between reality and imagination, presence and absence. Marcel's erotic experiences have an almost mystical, magical force, taking his life to its uttermost limits and placing him on a par with the angels.

Biography

Jouhandeau was a prolific novelist, essayist, and diarist. The writings he acknowledged include novels set in the fictional town of "Chaminadour," portraying Monsieur Godeau and the Pincengrain family (1936–1941), and an account of his turbulent marriage to Élise in *Chroniques maritales* (1935 and 1938). Unsigned writings include *De l'abjection* and the three texts of *Écrits secrets*.

OWEN HEATHCOTE

Selected Works

Écrits secrets I: Le Voyage secret. 1954 (repr. 1988).
Écrits secrets II: Carnets de Don Juan. 1954 (repr. 1988).
Écrits secrets III: Tirésias. 1954 (repr. 1988).
Chronique d'une passion. 1949 (repr. 1964).
De l'abjection. 1939 (repr. 1999).
Bréviaire; Portrait de Don Juan; Amours (1981).

Further Reading

Bowman, Frank Paul. "The Religious Metaphors of a Married Homosexual: Marcel Jouhandeau's *Chronique d'une passion*." In *Homosexualities and French Literature*, edited by George Stambolian and Elaine Marks, 295–311. Ithaca and London: Cornell University Press, 1979.
Larivière, Michel. *Pour tout l'amour des hommes. Anthologie de l'homosexualité dans la littérature.* Paris: Delétraz, 1998.
Meyer, Bernard. *Éros Jouhandelien. L'Attrait de l'homme dans les premières œuvres de Marcel Jouhandeau.* Paris: L'Harmattan, 1994.
Missotten, Geert. "L'Écriture spéculaire dans les romans donjuanesques de Marcel Jouhandeau, homme sans nom." *Nottingham French Studies* 38.1 (1999): 24–34.
Robinson, Christopher. *Scandal in the Ink. Male and Female Homosexuality in Twentieth-century French Literature.* London: Cassell, 1995.

JOUISSANCE

The idea of orgasm as heightened pleasure during sexual intercourse was prevalent even in classical cultures. For example, in his account of human reproduction, the second-century anatomist and medical scholar Galen described how the act of conception was accompanied by "a great pleasure." Aristotle too noted that the processes of procreation were "usually accompanied by pleasure in man and woman alike." Although these descriptions might be recognizable to us as depicting orgasms, the medical theory behind these sensations differed strongly from our understanding of orgasm today. The nature and function of orgasm produced divergent and sometimes opposing views in the classical period; but broadly speaking, orgasm was considered to be the culmination of bodily (specifically genital) heating, during which substances were emitted by both partners. These substances (and thus orgasm itself) were deemed necessary for procreation, a view which endured until the end of the eighteenth century. Thomas Laqueur has attributed the popularity of this understanding of orgasm to the predominance of the "one-sex body": the view that the female body was an inverted (and imperfect) "copy" of its male counterpart.

Even though the physical manifestations of orgasm were widely documented even by classical authors, it would be centuries before this phenomenon became as well defined linguistically in the English language. Indeed, it was not until the early nineteenth century that the term *orgasm* shifted its sense from its seventeenth-century meaning of "violent excitement" and became widely used to describe sexual pleasure. Although the exact cause of this change is not known, the French language is the most likely influence: the word *orgasme* had been used in French to describe sexual pleasure since 1777. The necessity to express the concept of orgasm at all may have been provoked by the political, social, and intellectual revolutions which took place in France during the eighteenth century. In addition to the growing strength of feminist calls for sexual equality which sought to overturn ideas of a hierarchy of the sexes, an increasing amount of medical evidence demonstrated that female orgasm was not necessary for procreation, as had been believed since antiquity. This separation of sexual pleasure and procreation opened up a range of possibilities of sexual behavior which required definition in language. It is important to note that irrespective of this discovery, conception and female orgasm continued to be linked until the beginning of the twentieth century. Indeed, the nineteenth century did not see great advances in the understanding of female orgasm partly because researchers tended to overlook the idea of female sexual pleasure.

Studies on sexual behavior published in the twentieth century have ensured that orgasm has been transformed into one of the most discussed aspects of human sexuality. At the dawn of the twentieth century, Freud threw out the conventional wisdom of female sexuality by privileging the vaginal orgasm as the norm amongst adult women, an aspect of female sexuality which had hitherto been ignored in favor of the clitoral orgasm. Freud's work would have a lasting influence on attitudes to sex and would serve to obscure the predominance of the clitoral orgasm until its "rediscovery" by feminists in the latter half of the century. Kinsey's studies on male sexuality (1948) and female sexuality (1953) shocked America by laying bare previously hidden aspects of sexual experience, including graphic descriptions of the physiology of male and female orgasms. Some conservative social commentators hold Kinsey responsible for initiating the so-called sexual revolution. This period of comparative sexual liberation which began in the 1960s and 1970s was facilitated by changes in the laws concerning homosexuality and abortion, as well as the advent of more reliable forms of birth control. These events widened still further the contexts in which orgasms were described and discussed and it is in this period that the first use of the verb *to orgasm* was recorded. It is important to recognize, however, that not all studies of sexuality have placed orgasm at the center of their focus. Shere Hite adopted a different methodology in her study of the family (1994), described by the author as "a combination of sociology, psychology, and cultural history, together with innovations relating to feminist methodology." The breadth of experiences represented in the report implicitly challenged the presumed centrality of orgasm in human sexual behavior.

The French language adopted a term denoting pleasure in general and sexual pleasure in particular, much earlier than did English. The term *jouissance* and its associated verb *jouir* derive from the classical Latin *gaudere* (to please), which became *gaudire* in the Vulgar Latin used in Gaul. Initially spelled *goïr*, then *joïr*, the word *jouyr* was recorded from the thirteenth century. Its initial primary sense was "to take pleasure in," with its secondary (legal) meaning being "to enjoy" (as in possess). Its connotation as a noun describing sexual pleasure was present from its earliest uses. Evidence of its sexual connotation from these times can be found in the sixteenth-century works of François Rabelais, who uses the phrase "jouir de leurs amours" to connote lovemaking. However, it is unlikely that all such occurrences of *jouissance* connoted sexual orgasm in the sense that it is understood today. It is not until the modern period that this became its predominant sense, to the point where the erotic values of *jouissance* have almost excluded its use in nonsexual contexts. The word *jouissance* is rarely encountered in current usage, as the French language adopted *orgasme* as a synonym in the late eighteenth century, as has already been mentioned. Today *jouissance* is

also a term used in psychoanalysis to connote an extreme pleasure indistinguishable from pain, gained from obtaining an object or condition which has been strongly desired. First used by Jacques Lacan, it has become a key concept in contemporary French feminist thought, where it has been particularly important in the work of Julia Kristeva and Hélène Cixous. Here it represents a feminine pleasure distinct from pleasure in general.

POLLIE BROMILOW

References and Further Reading

Aristotle. *Generation of Animals*. Translated by A.L. Peck. London and Cambridge, MA: Heinemann, 1953.

Galen. *On the Usefulness of the Parts of the Body*. Translated by Margaret Tallmadge May. 2 vols. Ithaca, NY: Cornell University Press, 1968.

Gallop, Jane. "Beyond the Jouissance Principle." *Representations* 7 (1984): 110–15.

Hite, Shere. *The Hite Report on the Family: Growing Up Under Patriarchy*. London: Hodder and Stoughton, 1995.

Jeffreys, Sheila. *Anticlimax: A Feminist Perspective on the Sexual Revolution*. London: The Women's Press, 1990.

Kinsey, Alfred, C. *Sexual Behavior in the Human Male*. Philadelphia and London: W.B. Saunders Company, 1948.

———. *Sexual Behavior in the Human Female*. Philadelphia and London: W.B. Saunders, 1953.

Laqueur, Thomas. *Making Sex: Body and Gender from the Greeks to Freud*. Cambridge and London: Harvard University Press, 1990.

Oxford English Dictionary. Oxford: Clarendon Press, 1989.

Rey, Alain, et al. *Dictionnaire historique de la langue française*. 2 vols. Paris: Dictionnaires Le Robert, 1992.

JOYCE, JAMES

1882–1941
Irish fiction writer, dramatist, and poet

Ulysses

Along with D.H. Lawrence's *Lady Chatterley's Lover* and the works of Henry Miller, Joyce's *Ulysses* is probably the most famous example of a 20th-century work that vividly illuminated the conflict between the wish to honor literary value on the one hand and the wish to censor erotic or obscene writing on the other. The entire novel of 600-odd pages takes place on a single day, June 16, 1904, in Dublin. It follows the lives of Stephen Dedalus, the protagonist of *A Portrait of the Artist as a Young Man*, a while after the close of that book, and of Leopold Bloom, a Jewish advertising canvasser, and his wife Molly. Where Stephen is a brilliant intellectual obsessed by guilt for having left the religion of his dead mother, Bloom is a middle-aged father of a son who died shortly after his birth; he and his wife have not had "normal sexual relations in over ten years." On this day, Molly has an assignation with "Blazes" Boylan, and Bloom is staying away from home so as not to interfere.

Although the US Attorney's Office marked as obscene some 250 passages from the novel in preparation for the 1933 trial before Judge John M. Woolsey, the government's main objections were to two scenes: one where Bloom, watching one Gerty MacDowell leaning back at the seashore and exposing her "drawers," masturbates, and a group of passages from Molly Bloom's final soliloquy as she lies in bed thinking about her experience with Boylan and reviewing her life as a girl and as Bloom's wife. But neither of these passages in fact is very satisfactory as pornography. The first has a very strong comic element—Bloom's climax is only implied by a description of the fireworks bursting over the nearby fair—while in Molly's reminiscences there is no real continuous narrative, so that at times it is difficult even to tell which man she is thinking about.

On the other hand, she is, even by contemporary standards, strikingly frank in her thoughts about sexuality and very direct in her language. Indeed, passages from the soliloquy, such as the closing "yes I said yes I will Yes" have entered popular consciousness as an emblem of erotic affirmation. Nevertheless, Judge Woolsey's decision, recognizing the literary value of the book, pronounced that while in many places the effect of *Ulysses* on the reader "is somewhat emetic, nowhere does it tend to be an aphrodisiac."

Biography

Born in 1882 in Dublin, Joyce was raised a Roman Catholic; his adolescent rebellion against that faith is a major theme of his first novel, *A Portrait of the Artist as a Young Man* (1916). An important factor in his apostasy was his early sexual experience with prostitutes. After graduating from University College Dublin with a BA degree, he met Nora Barnacle, a hotel chambermaid from Galway with whom he was to spend the rest of his life. In 1904 the two left Ireland for Trieste without benefit of marriage, because of Joyce's refusal to acknowledge the church or state's involvement in the most intimate of relationships. Although they returned for brief visits, neither would live in Ireland again, instead making their home in Trieste, Rome, Zurich (during both world wars), and Paris. But despite his self-imposed exile, all of Joyce's fiction remained set in his native Dublin. Since 1904 Joyce had been working on a series of stories which he collected in 1909 under the title *Dubliners*, but the publisher who had originally accepted them changed his mind and Joyce was unable to publish the collection until 1914. This first, frustrating experience of censorship had less to do with any explicit erotic content of the stories than with Joyce's naturalistic use of existing Dublin locations and businesses. His subject matter is also at times debased, including the portrayal of a man whose pederastic tastes are clearly implied and a woman who tacitly encourages her daughter to become sexually involved with a man so that she can blackmail him into marrying the girl.

Meanwhile, Joyce had been working on a semi-autobiographical novel that Ezra Pound arranged to appear serially in *The Egoist* magazine. It was published in New York in 1916 as *A Portrait of the Artist as a Young Man*. Although he had no censorship problems with this book, some critics found aspects of it shocking—one complained that on the very first page Joyce outraged decency with a reference to a child wetting the bed. Although it is clear that the protagonist Stephen Dedalus patronizes prostitutes, only one encounter is narrated within the book, and with such lyrical and metaphorical density that it is difficult to tell what is happening. Still, the boy's intense emotional experience of the erotic impulse is rendered with unprecedented vividness.

Although *Portrait* is now acknowledged as one of the most important novels of the century, Joyce's reputation was really made by his masterpiece, *Ulysses*, written roughly between 1914 and 1922 in Trieste, Zurich, and Paris and supported by grants from Harriet Shaw Weaver. Starting in 1918, the book was serialized in *The Egoist* and *The Little Review*, and in 1920 the latter magazine was enjoined from publishing further installments of the work on a complaint by the Society for the Prevention of Vice that it was pornographic. The book was published in Paris by the bookstore Shakespeare and Company in 1922 but could not be sold in the United States until Joyce's representatives won the landmark court case in 1934.

Immediately following the furor that greeted the publication of *Ulysses*, Joyce began work on his last book, which was identified only as "work in progress" up until its publication as *Finnegans Wake*. Written in a dense, experimental, and obscure prose that combined elements of many languages besides English, it features characters whose names and identities might change from one sentence to the next and whose "stories" shifted equally often. In the near-total absence of what Joyce called "go-ahead plot," the *Wake* presents a dreamlike world in which everything is subject to change, and a majority of the words are puns of some sort. Thus, although it is likely that passages of the book might well have offended the sensibilities of the same authorities who wished to deny publication to *Ulysses*—passages hinting at an incestuous passion of the protagonist for his daughter, for instance, or those discussing the "depravity" of the artist figure Shem—the *Wake* was immune to prosecution because of its very obscurity. When he died suddenly in 1941, Joyce left a legacy of work whose difficulty, as he himself noted, would keep generations of scholars busy.

R. Brandon Kershner

Selected Works

Dubliners. Edited by Robert Scholes and Richard Ellmann. New York: Viking, 1967.

A Portrait of the Artist as a Young Man. Edited by Chester G. Anderson. New York: Viking, 1968.

Ulysses. Edited by Hans Walter Gabler et al. New York: Garland, 1984.

Finnegans Wake. London: Faber and Faber Ltd., 1939.

Further Reading

Brown, Richard. *James Joyce and Sexuality*. Cambridge: Cambridge Unversity Press, 1985.

Budgen, Frank. *James Joyce and the Making of "Ulysses."* Bloomington, IN: Indiana University Press, 1960.

Ellmann, Richard. *James Joyce*. New York: Oxford University Press, 1982.

Vanderham, Paul. *James Joyce and Censorship: The Trials of "Ulysses."* New York: New York University Press, 1998.

JUNNOSUKE YOSHIYUKI

1924–1994
Japanese writer

Like Henry Miller, some of whose texts he translated, Junnosuke Yoshiyuki is attracted by the red-light districts, the world of prostitution, and the nightclubs where women can easily be met. He describes erotic relations very precisely, between a feeling of loneliness and the urge of desire. His writing traces its influence back to the *Shi-shosetsu* tradition. The cycle of stories *Fui no Dekigoto* [*Are the Trees Green?*]—written in a style known as *rensaku*, which links themes and characters of stories but allows the book to be more flexible than a novel—reflects well the art of this writer. In *Yûgure made* [*Toward Dusk*] (1978), a middle-aged man yearns obsessively for emotional rather than physical virginity in his mistress. *Anshitsu* [*The Dark Room*], *Shûu* [*Sudden Shower*], and *Genshoku no machi* [*The Main Colors Town*], develop the theme of physical relationships as a quest for emotional purity. A peculiar bond appears when the narrator associates with prostitutes, because this kind of relationship remains uncluttered by egotism or heavy demands. The ideal relationship for this writer is one in which tenderness develops within an exclusive and sensual link, far away from any kind of social censorship. As a matter of fact, the male characters are either unmarried or separated from their wives, and they do not expect any kind of recognition through a professional career. The writer Nakata in *Anshitsu* has no professional obligations and is able to focus entirely on different kinds of sensual and erotic relationships. According to this writer, and maybe as a personal experience and idiosyncrasy, the essence of love is mainly sensual. As a consequence, far away from sentimental and social lies, it is the body that remains at the center of the human experiences described in the narratives.

However, he is not interested at all in describing sexual intercourse or fantasies (apart from lesbian relations). The casual relation with a prostitute is intended as an experimental method to improve his understanding of what love really is, and a way to get more knowledge about the women he meets. Through sexual relations an emotional sensitivity increases, and the narrator comes to feel very deeply a few sensations related to sexual intercourse, or to the vision of a naked woman's body. These sensations may mean nothing more than the perfect achievement of the sensual relation: a blend of physical sensations where mere sexual pleasure is overwhelmed by the symptoms of it. The consequences of pleasure, or the side effects, become more important and tend to be analyzed like an enigma, the full distinctiveness of the individual experience inside the very universal frame of sexual intercourse. Then, sensual desire and pleasure are only the first steps in a wider quest for pure physical love, and a basic experiment in order to find the very truth of bodies and hearts. It is a quest for wisdom and knowledge, though not at all written in an abstract or intellectual way. On the contrary, the knowledge comes from the physical experience.

For example, in *Are the Trees Green?*, the main character, Iki Ichirou, realizes that he is in love with his student, Asako. A common theme is the double identity of the woman, as Asako is a barmaid and behaves like a prostitute toward clients. Her makeup is just like a painted mask to hide her true self. Iki wants to decipher her face's enigma and true identity. Sometimes, Yoshiyuki Junnosuke tries to understand the truth about the role of a client and lover in relation to a prostitute, and his importance for her. This is the case in *Fui no Dekigoto*, where a triangular relationship between Yukiko; Masuda, a weak Yakuza; and the narrator is described. One day, he smells on Yukiko's body a mix of emotion, makeup, and sweat. The smell expresses the inside being of Yukiko, though he seeks and finds an external cause. He can also read a vertical wrinkle between her eyes as a sign of climax, as if she were suffering. These side effects arouse his desire and remind him of other signs seen on women's bodies, such as a green and vivid line on a prostitute showing the

715

lips of her sex. The narrator splits his life between an underpaid career in journalism and the solace he seeks in the evenings spent in contemplation of women. Yukiko's body fragrance disappears as well as the pleasure wrinkle when she moves in with Masuda. The narrator understands through physical experience the strength of his pleasure and its limitations.

Anshitsu is a good example of how Yoshiyuki tends toward an absolute of sexual relation in the unique space of a bedroom. A famous writer, Nakata, meets Natsue, who has dark sides and other lovers. He himself has several relations at the same time, and yet ends up having relations with Natsue alone, in search of absolute sexuality in the dark room. As a result of that quest, a rose blossom replaces the female sexual organ, and the two lovers are linked by an invisible golden thread.

The style of Yoshiyuki is nearly clinical, and in all his works, he alternates realistic description of Japanese characters and places with very unusual and magical details, such as the meaningful blossom of flowers, or external phenomena. It is altogether the expression of a singular experience, a quest for pure pleasure and a profound analysis of prostitution, homosexuality, and marriage.

Biography

Born in Okayama, but raised in Tokyo, Yoshiyuki was exempted from military service because of ill health and was plagued most of his life by respiratory problems. He studied English literature at Tokyo University for a time but, unable to finance his studies, opted for a career in journalism. His father, Yoshiyuki Eisuke, was one of the main writers of the modernist school influenced by Dadaism at the beginning of the Showa era. Yoshiyuki Junnosuke received the Akutagawa award in 1954 for *Shûu*. The author

has won awards and recognition for such works as *Hoshi to tsuki wa ten no ana* [*The Moon and Stars Are Holes in the Sky*], (1966), *Anshitsu* (Tanizaki Prize, 1969), and *Yûgure made* (Noma Award, 1978). He belongs to a line of sensual writers, from Ihara Saikaku to Nagai Kafû and Tanizaki, and was often compared to the French writer André Pieyre de Mandiargues.

MARC KOBER

Selected Works

Bara no hanbainin [*The Rose Seller*]. 1950.
Shûu [*Sudden Shower*]. 1954.
Genshoku no machi [*The Town with Fundamental Colors*]. 1956.
Kigi wa midori ka? [*Are the Trees Green?*]. 1958.
"Ajisai" [*Hortensias*]. 1964.
Fui no dekigoto [*An Unpredictable Event*]. 1965.
Hoshi to tsuki wa ten no ana [*The Moon and Stars Are Holes in the Sky*]. 1966.
Onna no dobutsuen [*The Women Zoo*]. 1968.
Anshitsu [*The Dark Room*]. 1969.
Hadaka no nyoi [*Smell of a Naked Body*]. 1971.
Kaban no nakami [*The Bag Content*]. 1974.
Onna no katachi [*The Woman Shape*]. 1975.
Yûgure made [*Toward Dusk*]. 1978.

Essays

Sei to sei [*Living and Sexuality*]. 1971.
Machikado no tabako-ya e no tabi [*The Journey to the Corner of the Street*]. 1979.

Recent Translations

"Kinjû chûgyo" [Birds, Beasts, Insects and Fish]. *Japan Quarterly* 28 (Jan–March 1981).
"Shokutaku no kôkei" [Good Table Manners]. *Japan Echo* 12 (1985).

Further Reading

Pons, Philippe. "Yoshiyuki à l'assaut du ciel." *Le Monde*, January 4, 1991.

K

KALYANA MALLA

Indian author of *Ananga Ranga,* medieval marital sex manual

The *Ananga Ranga* by Kalyana Malla is one of the three major Indian erotic texts, the other two being *Kamasutra* by Vatsyayana and *Ratirahasya* by Kokkaka. Liberally translated, *Ananga Ranga* means the art of love. In fact, the first English translation of the work by Sir Richard F. Burton and F.F. Arbuthnot published in 1885 was appropriately titled *The Hindu Art of Love.* It is written in Sanskrit, the classical language of India. The work is available in translation in many Indian languages. It was also translated into Arabic, Persian, and Turkish under the title '*Lizzat-al-Nissa*' [*The Pleasure of Women*] before it was translated into English, which points to its popularity not only in the Indian subcontinent but also in other Eastern countries. It has also been translated into Japanese and French.

The period of the author and the date of the text are not known. The author Kalyana Malla describes himself in the text as a poet of repute. By reference to *Kavi-charika,* a biography of famous Indian poets, Kalyana Malla is identified by some as the Brahmin poets from Kalinga (present Indian state of Orissa on the east coast of India) and a contemporary of the Oriya king Anangabhima. Going by the date of one of Anangabhima's inscriptions, the date of Kalyana Malla and *Ananga Ranga* would be around 1172 CE. However, all manuscripts of *Ananga Ranga* examined by Burton and Arbuthnot contained a verse indicating that it was written for the amusement of Lad Khan, son of Ahmed Khan, who was a viceroy of the Lodhi dynasty (1450–1526) in Gujarat, a state in western India. By this reckoning, the date of Kalyana Malla and *Ananga Ranga* has to be placed somewhere between the late 15th and early 16th centuries. Kalyana Malla refers to *Kamasutra* and *Ratirahasya* in *Ananga Ranga,* which indicates that it was certainly the latest among these three well-known erotic texts.

In concluding the book, Kalyana Malla states that he wrote the *Ananga Ranga* because no one till then had written a book to prevent separation of married couples or to show them how they could live through their lives happily together. He notes that if husband and wife can live together as one soul, they will be happy in this world and in that to come. He further notes that the main reason for separation of husband and wife and their each seeking other partners and committing adultery is monotony and lack of variation in married life. He claims that after fully understanding the way quarrels take place, he has shown in the book that by varying the enjoyment of the wife, the husband may live with her as if living with 32 different women and how the wife may also become pleasing to the husband by learning what is taught in the book. *Ananga Ranga* is a unique erotic text that aims at enhancing pleasure within marriage, ensuring lifelong married bliss and preventing promiscuity and conjugal infidelity. Kalyana Malla's work is no doubt based on the pre-existing literature on the subject, but he has introduced many innovations in his prescription for erotic enjoyment which are not found in the earlier texts. He emphasizes ethics and spirituality, and envisages a happy couple with their passion cooling with advancing age devoting themselves to the study of divine knowledge.

Ananga Ranga is well structured, comprising an introductory chapter, ten textual chapters dealing with separate topics, and two appendices. The topics include characteristics, qualities, and temperaments of women of different kinds as well as of different regions. Kalyana Malla notes that desires of women are slower to rouse and that unlike men, they are not easily satisfied by a single act of congress. They require prolonged embraces, and if denied, women feel aggrieved. There are chapters dealing with various centers of passion in women, the days and periods of their excitement, classification of men and women into four classes, and the matings from among these classes in marriages that are ideal. Part of the text and the appendices deal with the use of recipes for potions for erotic purposes and with astrology in securing greater pleasure between husband and wife. The text contains elaborate prescriptions of herbal and other medicines for conditions like premature ejaculation and menstrual disorder, as well as preparations for uses as perfumes, bathing pre-

parations, mouth fresheners, and beauty aids. One chapter deals with charms and mantras, through the use of which a man can win over the love and affection of his wife. The last two chapters deal with external and internal enjoyments, with advice of a practical nature. The first of these emphasizes the role of foreplay and deals with it in some detail. The last chapter deals with various ways of sexual congress, including *Purushayita*, where the woman plays an active role in pleasing the man. The following provides a flavor of Kalyana Malla's writing:

> At all times of enjoying *Purushayita,* the wife shall remember that without a special effort of will on her part, the husband's pleasure will not be perfect. To this end, she must ever strive to close and constrict her *yoni* until it holds her husband's *linga,* as with a finger, opening and shutting at her will and finally acting as the hand of the cowherd girl who milks the cow. This can be learned only by long practice, and especially by throwing the will into the part to be affected, even as men endeavor to sharpen their hearing and their sense of touch. While so doing, she will mentally repeat the name of the Lord of Love in order that a blessing may rest upon the undertaking. And she will be pleased to hear that the art, once learned, is never lost. Her husband will then value her above all women, nor would he exchange her for the most beautiful queen in the three worlds. So lovely and pleasant to man is she who constricts. (The translation follows Burton and Arbuthnot.)

CHITTARANJAN SATAPATHY

Further Reading

Bhandari, V., ed. *Ananga Ranga.* Benares: Haridas Sanskrit Series No. 9, 1923.

Burton, R., and F.F. Arbuthnot, trans. *Ananga Ranga: The Hindu Art of Love.* New Delhi: Orient Paperbacks, 1998.

———. *Kamasutra.* New Delhi: Orient Paperbacks, 2001.

Comfort, A. *Koka Shastra.* London: Mitchell Bleazley, 1997.

De, S.K. *Ancient Indian Erotics and Erotic Literature.* Calcutta: Mukhopadhyay, 1959.

Dutta, A., ed. *Encyclopaedia of Indian Literature.* Vol. 3. New Delhi: Sahitya Academy, 1996.

Ray, T.L. *Kalyana Malla's* Ananga Ranga. Calcutta: Medical Books, 1960.

KĀMASŪTRA

Classical Indian erotic text

The Kāmasūtra of Vātsyāyana was composed sometime around the third to fourth centuries CE and is the earliest extant work of erotic science from South Asia. Written in Sanskrit prose and verse, the text is attributed to a scholar named Vātsyāyana, whose name is connected to no other texts and about whom we know nothing other than what we can extrapolate from the Kāmasūtra. Vātsyāyana relies upon the now lost work of earlier specialists in the field of erotic science, whom he cites by name, sometimes agreeing and sometimes disagreeing with their theories. In turn, later works of erotic science, such as the *Ratirahasya/Kokaśāstra*, the *Nāgarasarvasva*, the *Pañcasāyaka*, the *Anaṅgaraṅga*, and the *Kandarpacūḍāmaṇi*, defer to the authority of the Kāmasūtra, explicitly modeling themselves upon it or citing it often in their treatments of the subject.

Accordingly, the Kāmasūtra is the most well known and authoritative text in a genre known as *kāmaśāstra*, the "discipline" (*śāstra*) of pleasure (*kāma*). Śāstric texts are academic and theoretical, rather than artistic and literary. They tend to be extremely dense and allusive in nature, apparently written for a scholarly audience able to comprehend their jargon-laden statements and their style of argumentation. While there are śāstric texts devoted to a whole range of techno-practical sciences (e.g., medicine, architecture, animal husbandry, astrology, physiognomy), a distinct body of śāstric inquiry developed around a conceptual trio known as the trivarga, a "group of three" with apparent claims to humanistic comprehensiveness. This group is comprised of *kāma, dharma* (duty, moral order) and *artha* (acquisition, profit); study of these three subjects taken together comprises a sort of "life science," enabling the educated person to cultivate a fruitful existence.

Each member of the trivarga has theoretical texts devoted to it, as well as an extensive commentarial tradition. Only one Sanskrit commentary on the Kāmasūtra has been edited and published to date, the *Jayamaṅgalā* of Yaśodhara, most likely composed in the thirteenth century CE, almost a thousand years after the probable composition of the Kāmasūtra. Yaśodhara's commentary is extremely erudite, standing as both an invaluable verse-by-verse interpretation of the frequently obscure Kāmasūtra and an original reflection on the subject of erotic pleasure. Yaśodhara, as a commentator, always defers to the authority of the Kāmasūtra, but his lengthy exposition necessarily exceeds the spartan language of the original. In the face of compact statements like "From [their] connection with that," Yaśodhara elaborates philosophical concepts deployed by the Kāmasūtra, provides details of stories alluded to by it, refers to medical evidence, and expands upon the text's many typologies. His explanations may range far from the meaning of the original text, but they are always worth taking seriously.

A second Sanskrit commentary, the *Prauḍhapriyā* of Bhāskara Narasiṃha, was composed in eighteenth-century Benares, India; it has been neither edited nor published, let alone translated. Written at even greater historical remove from the Kāmasūtra, the *Prauḍhapriyā* is highly philosophical in its orientation, and cites numerous works of scholarship and literature in its explanation of the text. Interestingly, the *Prauḍhapriyā* seems ignorant of Yaśodhara's *Jayamaṅgalā* or any other Kāmasūtra commentary, and so represents a distinctly eighteenth-century perspective on the field of erotic science. A number of commentaries in Indian vernacular languages were written and published in the twentieth century, including an unnamed commentary by Devadatta Śāstrī, Paṇḍit Mādhavācāryya's *Puruṣārthaprabhā,* Rāmānand Sharmā's *Jayā,* and Pārasanāth Dvivedī's *Manoramā,* all in Hindi, as well as commentaries in Bengali, Kannada, Marathi, Oriya, Tamil, and Telugu.

The text was first published in a European language in 1883, as an English translation by Sir Richard F. Burton and F.F. Arbuthnot (with the unacknowledged assistance of Indian scholars Bhagavanlal Indrajit and Shivaram Parashuram Bhide). In the preface to this translation, Burton presents the Kāmasūtra as providing valuable scientific knowledge capable of remedying woeful and injurious British ignorance of sexual matters, thus initiating the tendency to consider the Kāmasūtra as representative of putative Indian sexual license, in opposition to European sexual repression. Burton's translation is frequently inaccurate, and often incorporates without acknowledgement segments of the *Jayamaṅgalā* into the text of the Kāmasūtra, an unfortunate trend followed by many subsequent translators of the text. Nevertheless, Burton's translation was the most widely available for over one hundred years, until the publication in 2002 of an excellent translation by Wendy Doniger and Sudhir Kakar, who carefully separate the Kāmasūtra from the *Jayamaṅgalā,* passages of which they include as footnotes, in addition to selections from Devadatta Śāstrī's Hindi commentary. To date, the only complete translation of both the Kāmasūtra and the *Jayamaṅgalā* is the German translation by Richard Schmidt, first published in 1897 (subsequently revised on several occasions). The Burton translation has been retranslated into numerous European languages. An original but highly inaccurate French translation by Alain Daniélou appeared in 1992; this translation was translated into English in 1994.

The Kāmasūtra

The Kāmasūtra is cosmopolitan in outlook; it takes for granted its applicability to any civilized social context. Because the pursuit of social and sexual pleasure necessarily involves other people, the text advises its audience in the means of negotiating a highly sophisticated social world. In this world, male–female social interaction is normative, with courtesans playing an important role in the pursuit of pleasure. At the same time, the text assumes the sequestered status of married women, though it provides justifications and means for overcoming this obstacle. While the text attends to a whole host of constraints that might prevent the accomplishment of one's erotic goals (those of class, caste, and family, for example), it takes as its ideal social actor one who is educated, wealthy, and good-looking, with plenty of leisure time in which to pursue

a rich and rewarding life. It is also highly significant that the text makes no mention of the relationship between sex and reproduction, as if pregnancy were not a possible outcome of the sex acts described.

The Kāmasūtra is probably most famous for its systematization of the varieties of sex acts. While the Kāmasūtra takes sex between a man and a woman to be normative, it should be noted that the text does recognize the existence of a "third sex," a man who takes on the appearance and behavior of a woman and who performs fellatio on other men. It also describes sex acts between women, a behavior said to take place when male sexual partners are unavailable. The text mentions group sex (with multiple men and with multiple women), as well as anal intercourse, though this last is said to be a regional variant. Scratching, biting, and striking are considered to be key elements in sexual play, because they incite passion both during lovemaking and afterward, when the marks they leave prompt memories of sexual encounters. As Doniger and Kakar translate:

There are no keener means
of increasing passion
than acts inflicted
with tooth and nail. (Kāmasūtra 2.4.31)

Vātsyāyana is careful to caution his audience against excessive use of these acts, noting instances when they resulted in mutilation or even death. Nevertheless, hitting, biting, and otherwise marking the body of one's lover are taken to be key elements in sexual union.

But the Kāmasūtra's descriptions of sex acts are merely one small portion of its investigation of the subject of pleasure. The Kāmasūtra organizes its subjects into seven chapters, each further subdivided by topic. The first chapter of the Kāmasūtra opens with a theoretical discussion of pleasure in relation to the other primary objectives of human existence: duty and acquisition. The text defends the importance of pleasure, as well as the need for scholarly texts devoted to the subject. It then enumerates 64 fine arts that mark the cultivated man or woman, ranging from singing, dancing, and poetry to metallurgy, woodworking, and architecture. It also describes the lifestyle of the cosmopolitan man and his friends, including details of his toilette, the furnishing of his house, garden, and bedroom; his daily schedule, with particular attention to his leisure activities; and his conduct at public festivals. These descriptions have been highly influential in the history of Indian literature, encapsulating the ideal behavior of heroes, heroines, and their sidekicks for the duration of Sanskrit literary history.

The second chapter contains, among other things, the detailed lists and descriptions of sexual positions for which the Kāmasūtra is most famous. It classifies men and women according to the dimensions of their genitalia, the degree of their passion, and the time taken to reach sexual climax. This last division contains a notable debate regarding the existence and nature of female orgasm. This chapter also enumerates, labels, and describes sexual postures (17 varieties), sexual strokes (ten for the man and three for the woman when she is on top), and ways of kissing (16 varieties), embracing (12 varieties), scratching (eight varieties), biting (eight varieties), slapping (eight varieties), and screaming and moaning (eight varieties), as well as regional variations and sexual preferences, unusual sex acts (including group sex and anal sex), sex with the woman playing the part of the man, oral sex (with a detailed description of same-sex fellatio), protocols for before and after sex, and typical behaviors during lovers' quarrels.

The third chapter gives recommendations for courtship and seduction of potential marriage partners; it is addressed primarily to men seeking brides but also advises women in the seduction of potential husbands. It outlines the signs and signals by which one comes to know the mindset of one's intended, and by which a man or woman makes his or her intentions clear to a desired partner. It describes in great detail the ways in which one can captivate the potential partner. It also suggests means of tricking, and indeed, forcing young women into the marriage bed.

The fourth chapter is devoted to the behavior of wives, especially those in a polygamous household. Here the emphasis is upon specialization, with co-wives advised to assume distinct roles, each designed to maintain the attention of the husband, while the husband is advised to treat each individually. The "senior wife," the "junior wife," the kept woman, and the "wife unlucky in love" are all advised how best to behave with respect to one another and to their husband.

This is the chapter that will seem most conservative to the modern reader, as the freedom of women is tightly circumscribed. Nevertheless, the behavior of wives in Sanskrit literature strongly conforms to the descriptions found in this brief chapter.

The fifth chapter is concerned with the seduction of married women. It includes criteria for determining the likelihood of success, and a sympathetic inventory of the many reasons a woman might reject a would-be lover. It describes the types of men likely to succeed with women and provides a psychologically rich catalogue of women who are easily seduced. It provides strategies for producing intimacy with the woman, the various signals employed to convey intent, and the means of testing her feelings. It also describes in great detail the all-important role of the messenger in bringing about a love affair; this role is of central importance in South Asian erotic literature. The fifth chapter also contains several sections devoted to the sex life of men in power, such as kings and ministers of state, and of the women living in the harems of such powerful men.

The sixth chapter of the Kāmasūtra is addressed to courtesans, and details the criteria for selecting or rejecting a lover, as well as how to acquire, keep, extract money from, cast off, and reunite with him. It also offers the means to calculate advantage and disadvantage in any union. Within the Kāmasūtra's social world, courtesans are expert both in generating pleasure and in using it for profit.

The final chapter is devoted to various pharmacological, mechanical, and magical aids to sex and love, including aphrodisiacs, philters for making oneself sexually desirable or for bringing another under one's sexual sway, and aids to virility (including means of increasing the size and endurance of the penis, as well as dildos and piercing). There are also recipes to eliminate passion for a particular person, to make the vagina expand or contract, and to alter one's appearance.

The Kāmasūtra and Erotic Literature

Since its first European translation in 1883, the Kāmasūtra has occupied an important place in the erotic imaginary of the modern West, representing sexual license and titillation, a means of arousal disguised as sexology or Indology. However, it is doubtful that the Kāmasūtra was composed as erotic literature, if by that term we mean literature designed to arouse erotic feelings. The text does advise a man to talk about the Kāmasūtra in the presence of a woman he would like to seduce, but, contrary to its depiction (and use?) in the modern West, there is no historical evidence that the text itself was used to stimulate an erotic response.

Nevertheless, its descriptions and prescriptions are designed to facilitate an eroticized lifestyle, in which one's private and public activities can be oriented toward the maximization of pleasure. Such pleasure is created not through indulging some otherwise-thwarted sexual instinct, after the model of liberation from sexual repression. Rather, the Kāmasūtra suggests that with proper application, the reader of the text can achieve an existence in which pleasure has a prominent place. It also implies that real pleasure is achieved with full knowledge of the range of erotic possibilities, so that the actor can identify the situation at hand and determine the appropriate course of action. For the Kāmasūtra, as for other Sanskrit textbooks, textualized knowledge has absolute authority; real-life success is that which approximates what is contained in the text. The Kāmasūtra does not deny the possibility that people can find erotic pleasure without knowledge of the text, but understands such achievement to be purely fortuitous, based upon knowledge that has "trickled down" from those educated in erotic science.

While the Kāmasūtra itself may not be erotic literature, it has exercised a profound influence upon the literatures of the Indian subcontinent, particularly upon Sanskrit literature, in which the erotic is arguably the dominant aesthetic mode. The typologies of sexual actors, situations, and modes of intercourse systematized in the Kāmasūtra have been deployed in a vast array of dramatic, poetic, sculptural, and two-dimensional artworks. According to Sanskrit poetic theory, true aesthetic enjoyment can be produced only by representation of situations that conform to established norms; for erotic poetry, to a great extent, this means conforming to the norms depicted in the Kāmasūtra.

While the rule-bound nature of the śāstric universe should not be underemphasized, the Kāmasūtra nevertheless envisions circumstances in which an erotic situation might exceed the strictures of the text:

> To the extent that men are of weak passion, there is scope for textbooks.
> But when the wheel of erotic delight is in motion, there is no textbook and no logical order. (Kāmasūtra 2.2.31)

LAURA S. DESMOND

See also **Kalyana Mala; Koka Pandit; Sex Manuals**

Editions

Kāmasūtra, with *Jayamaṅgalā*. Edited and with Hindi commentary by Devadatta Śāstrī, 1964, Varanasi: Caukhambhā Sanskrit Sansthan, fifth edition, 1996.

The Kama Sutra of Vatsyayana, Translated [by Sir Richard Burton and F.F. Arbuthnot] *from the Sanscrit. In Seven Parts, with Preface, Introduction and Concluding Remarks*. Cosmopoli: 1883.

Das Kāmasūtram des Vātsyāyana, Die Indische Ars Amatoria nebst dem Vollständigen Kommentare (Jayamaṅgalā). Translated by Richard Schmidt. Leipzig, 1897 (subsequently revised on numerous occasions).

Kama Sutra of Vatsyayana. Translated by S.C. Upadhyaya. Bombay: Taraporevala, 1961.

The Complete Kāma Sūtra. Translated by Alain Daniélou. Rochester, VT: Park Street Press, 1994.

Vatsyayana Mallanaga Kamasutra. Translated by Wendy Doniger and Sudhir Kakar. Oxford: Oxford University Press, 2002.

References and Further Reading

Chakladar, Haran Chandra. *Social Life in Ancient India, Studies in Vātsyāyana's Kāmasūtra*. Second revised edition. Calcutta: Susil Gupta, 1954.

De, Sushil Kumar. *Ancient Indian Erotics and Erotic Literature*. Calcutta: Firma K.L. Mukhopadhyay, 1969.

Doniger, Wendy. "The Kamasutra: It Isn't All About Sex." *Kenyon Review* 25 (2003): 18–37.

Hampiholi, Vishwanath K. *Kāmashāstra in Classical Sanskrit Literature*. Delhi: Ajanta Publications, 1988.

KAMENSKII, ANATOLII

1876–1941
Russian novelist and playwright

Zhenshchina [*The Woman*]

Anatolii Kamenskii's short story *The Woman* is indicative of the writer's interest in the inevitability of human enslavement to the call of the flesh, although it is much lighter in tone than some of his other writings.

This story, written in the 1910s and published in a collection of stories about love entitled *Moi garem* (Berlin, 1923), tells of a young man, Nezhdanov, who comes to St. Petersburg from a provincial town on a business trip, lodges at his sister's apartment, and gets swept up by the excitement of a big city. One day, as he sits in the empty apartment, he looks at himself in the mirror and thinks that he is a handsome, albeit slightly feminine-looking, man. For fun, he puts on some makeup he finds in his sister's bedroom and tries out some of her clothes on top of his suit. He enjoys seeing himself in feminine attire and decides to get dressed completely as a woman and go out into the city. He buys himself a wig of beautiful blonde hair and puts on his sister's underwear, stockings, and dress. He finds his new clothes to be very comfortable. Nezhdanov is both captivated by his prank and fascinated by his own body in its feminine guise, and gets an erotic thrill from seeing himself in the mirror. He is in love with his body. As he leaves the building, he finds himself enjoying the comedy of deception and self-deception that he is now playing.

As he walks down the street, he notices the attention he is getting from several men, some of whom follow him and make remarks to him, thinking that he is a beautiful woman. One man continues following him after Nezhdanov catches a carriage for the train station. As he rides in the carriage, pursued by the stranger, Nezhdanov conjures for himself different life stories, alternatively those of a cocotte, or sporting lady; an adventuress; a mistress on her way to a rendezvous; an innocent girl; and an abandoned wife. He is astonished to what extent he is mentally taken over by each of these imagined personae.

In the train compartment, riding toward a popular concert park, Nezhdanov attracts the attention of all the men, and particularly of his pursuer. The young man follows him to the concert hall and strikes up a conversation. After a while, Nezhdanov responds, first in a coquettish way, and then more seriously. They converse for a long time, and Nezhdanov surprises his interlocutor, a young lawyer, with his literary tastes and knowledge. The lawyer assumes that Nezhdanov is a progressive woman and invites him to his place, saying that the inevitable would happen sooner or later and that the two of them are too modern to play silly games of pursuit. While Nezhdanov tries to decline the invitation, which would reveal him as a man, he instinctively realizes that the lawyer seriously takes him for an extraordinary and modern woman, just the kind of a woman who would attract Nezhdanov himself. Inwardly Nezhdanov sympathizes with the lawyer, seeing in him a kindred spirit to his own male self. He declines the lawyer's offer of a rendezvous, telling him that they would never meet again. The lawyer struggles to comprehend this "woman's" secret before letting "her" disappear forever. Amazed at the depth of feelings that he has evoked in the young lawyer and in himself, Nezhdanov rhapsodically imagines that he is a manifestation of spiritual and sexual longing, of a missed chance, and in this state mounts the train platform to go back to the city, leaving the lawyer behind.

The question of homosexuality is alluded to rather elusively in *The Woman*. Underpinning this story is Otto Weininger's theory of sexuality as described in his *Eros und Psyche*, a widely read text at that time. According to Weininger, normal men's character is composed of 75 percent virility. Fifty percent virility in a man points toward homosexual tendencies. While Nezhdanov doesn't surpass this percentage, and remains a man, he enjoys his role as a woman. Nezhdanov's sympathy for the young lawyer is ambiguous—is it because he understands him, or is it because the lawyer appeals to him sexually? Kamenskii left this question unresolved, and at least one late-20th-century critic found this story to be a light and absurdist comedy on gender roles.

Kamenskii was a popular writer in the early part of the 20th century, although he was seen by critics as not quite on the literary level of Leonid Andreev, Valerii Bryusov, Mikhail Kuzmin, and other writers of the Silver Age who wrote about sexuality. Some critics recognized the strength of his evocation of city life: *The Woman* provides an exuberant description of the excitement of St. Petersburg, with its smells, crowds, fast-paced transportation, and chance encounters, and of the deterioration of bourgeois gender norms. Nevertheless, Kamenskii often got satirized and demonized in the highbrow literary press. This is particularly true of his novel *Leda* and of his story *Chetyre* [*The Four*], which alternatively dealt with transcending and succumbing to sexual needs. Maksim Gor'kii wrote that Kamenskii's plots were inappropriate in a period following the failed 1905 Revolution. Kamenskii, however, felt that an artist needed to be above the madness of politics. Many critics dismissed Kamenskii as pathologically weak and perverse in character, who basely took advantage of controversial topics in his writings. To this day Kamenskii is considered to have stopped developing in a literary sense around 1908, despite the fact that he wrote and published quite a bit after this date. Novopolin, in his 1909 book on the pornographic elements in Russian literature, dismissed Kamenskii for cynically and self-servingly propagating the idea of the supremacy of the sexual instinct over other human endeavors. Kamenskii was all but

forgotten after his death, and very little has been written about him afterward.

Biography

Anatolii Pavlovich Kamenskii was born in Novocherkassk. He came from minor nobility and worked as a civil servant. Kamenskii started publishing in Russian literary periodicals in 1896 and wrote scripts for Russian silent films in the early 1910s. After staging the play *Reigen* [The Round Dance] by Arthur Schnitzler, which was considered pornographic, Kamenskii faced censure and lived in Berlin from 1920 to 1924. He returned to Soviet Russia in 1924, was arrested in 1937, and died in a prison camp in Komi.

RUTH WALLACH

Editions

"Zhenshchina." In *Moi garem; rasskazy o liubvi*. Berlin: I. Blagov, 1923.
"Ideal'naia zhenshchina." In *Erotizmy*. Moscow: EKSMO-Press, 2000.

Selected Works

Rasskazy [*Discussions*]. 1908–1910.
Liudi [*The People*]. 1910.
Leda. 1918.
Nichego ne bylo [*Nothing to It*]. 1918.
Belaia noch [*White Night*]. 1928.
Peterburgskii chelovek [*Petersburg Man*]. 1936.

Further Reading

Novopolin, G. *Pornograficheskii element v russkoi literature*. St. Petersburg: M.M. Stasiulevich, 1909.
Persi, Ugo. "Les Recits erotiques d'Anatolij Kamenskij: Leda, Cetyre, Zenscina." In *Amour et erotisme dans la litterature russe du XXe siècle / Liubov' i erotika v russkoi literature XX-go veka*, edited by Leonid Heller, 64–72. Bern: Peter Lang, 1992.
Russkie pisateli 1800–1917. Biograficheskii slovar'. Moscow: Sovetskaia entsiklopediia, 1989–1994.

KESSEL, JOSEPH

1898–1979
French novelist and journalist

Belle de jour

Kessel intended this psychological novel (1928) as a representation of "the terrible divorce between the heart and the flesh, between a true, immense, and tender love and the implacable demands of the senses" (translations throughout are by the author of this article from the French original of *Belle de jour*). In a preface, he expresses his belief that this antagonism belongs to all people in varying degrees and that—echoing a premise of nascent psychoanalysis—"an exceptional situation" is required in order to uncover it fully: "just as one studies the sick in order to know the healthy, the mentally ill in order to penetrate the workings of intelligence." The situation he has found is that of Séverine, a young society woman who deeply loves her husband but is inexorably drawn to a secret life of prostitution. In order to conceal her activities, she works in a discreet brothel and limits her presence there from two to five o'clock in the afternoon, hence the sobriquet "Belle de jour" (daytime girl).

Both by direct appeal in the preface and by the third-person, internally focused narration, *Belle de jour* continually calls upon the reader to feel compassion for a protagonist who falls victim to her own deep and uncontrollable desires. A prologue dramatizes an incident from Séverine's childhood that is clearly intended to account for the conflict between love and desire that will devastate her as an adult: As an eight-year-old, she is molested in her home by a plumber. When her governess finds her on the floor, it is thought that she slipped—and she too believes this explanation. This incident is central to the novel's principal innovation. Venturing well beyond conventional story lines that relate the hidden lives of upright women, *Belle de jour* depicts its heroine as suffering from a psychosexual pathology with origins in repressed childhood trauma.

When the main action begins, Séverine has been married to Pierre, a young surgeon, for two years, but her physical attitude toward him seems maternal, and she feels only rebellion and lassitude when she detects his desire. He has concluded that carnal passions are inaccessible to her, and she no doubt shares this view until an acquaintance, Husson, kisses her insolently— filling her with disgust, but also with brief, intense pleasure. This kiss is the first sign that Séverine, who still thinks she exerts perfect control over herself, is instead subject to "essential, dormant forces" from within. The subsequent revelation that a woman from her own circle secretly works as a prostitute fires her imagination. Soon thereafter, as she repeatedly fantasizes about a strange man who pursues her lustfully along dark alleys, she is terrified and overcome with desire.

Until only recently, Séverine was repulsed by anything that strayed from social norms. Now, as she moves from one erotically charged fantasy or encounter to another, eventually making her way to the brothel operated by Madame Anaïs, she feels "prohibited desires" which affirm her resemblance to all other human beings according to the narrator. From Pierre she receives tenderness and trust; what he cannot give her, and what she finds in coarse, even vulgar, men, is "that exquisite animal pleasure." As Belle de jour, she takes pleasure in forced obedience and verbal and physical domination. Initially, the need to play her new role consumes her, but soon a kind of intoxication sets in and habit displaces desire. When she realizes that her behavior has become servile—not only as Belle de jour but in general—she uses her afternoons to forget her troubles. In a dramatic denouement, her two lives intersect when Husson makes an unexpected appearance in Madame Anaïs's establishment. Lest her hidden identity be revealed to her husband and others, she turns to an underworld client for help, and the narrative accelerates toward its tragic end.

Belle de jour attempts to represent both an extraordinary experience—childhood molestation, prostitution for pleasure—and a universal tension between "true love" and the "demands of the senses." It describes Séverine's desires as common to all human beings while also offering her up as a pathological case that can shed light on normal function. Just how all of this works is not immediately apparent. Occasional clues, however, suggest that the novel conforms to a single, overall conception of love and desire. It may be inferred that as a result of Séverine's traumatic experience, her "two essential poles" of the heart and flesh have become strictly non-overlapping realms; whereas for people who have not endured a similar trauma, they may be united within a single love relation. It is true that Séverine resumes a sexual relationship with her husband after becoming a prostitute, but it never becomes satisfying in the manner of her other encounters. The long-term effect of her repressed memory is to dissociate feelings of love from those of desire and to make desire possible only as a reenactment of the traumatic event.

Luis Buñuel's brilliant film adaptation (*Belle de jour*, 1967) is greatly indebted to Kessel's novel and also makes several notable departures. The basic story line remains (with a modified ending), along with virtually all the characters and the childhood incident. The filmmaker eschews direct access to Séverine's feelings, however, in favor of a rigorously external perspective. He also creates a complex fantasy life for her which he dramatizes in alternation with real-life scenes. The effect is to open a window to Séverine's psyche at once more tenuous and more profound than the perspective provided by the novel. In the film, moreover, her life as a prostitute ultimately serves a therapeutic function, allowing her to work through her condition and to remove the impediments to a fulfilling relation with Pierre. As a result, her uncontrollable fantasies, which serve as indicators of her pathology, have all but ceased as the ending draws near. This evolution—which is more coherent and more convincing than the treatment by Kessel—is particularly compelling in the light of certain tendencies in psychoanalysis, in particular Sigmund Freud's repetition compulsion (*Beyond the Pleasure Principle*, 1920), Melanie

Klein's psychoanalytic theory (*Love, Hate and Reparation*, 1937), and Jessica Benjamin's notion of identificatory love (*The Bonds of Love*, 1988).

Biography

Born in Clara, Argentina, to Russian–Jewish emigrés, and died in Avernes, France. Childhood spent in France and Russia. Studied literature in Russia, at the lycée of Nice and at Paris's Lycée Louis-le-Grand, 1914. Served as editor of the *Journal des débats* and reporter for *Le Matin*, later for *France-Soir*. Earned a degree in literature from the Sorbonne, 1915. Studied acting and became an actor at the Odéon.

Like Ernest Hemingway and André Malraux, Kessel was a writer and man of action. His 80 novels and numerous *reportages* are inspired by personal experiences in World War I aviation, the Spanish Civil War, the French Resistance during World War II, the birth of the state of Israel, and by extensive travels throughout five continents. In 1925 he was awarded the Grand prix du roman de l'Académie française for *Les rois aveugles* [*Blinded Kings*]. Following the immense success of *Le Lion* [*The Lion*] (1958), he received the Prince Rainier of Monaco Prize. He was elected to the French Academy in 1962.

L. Scott Lerner

Editions

Belle de jour. Paris: Gallimard, 1928. Reprint, 1972, Folio Collection 125. *Belle de jour*. Translated by Geoffrey Wagner. New York: St. Martin's Press, 1962.

Selected Works

La Steppe rouge. 1922.
L'Equipage. 1923.
Les rois aveugles. 1925.
Le journal d'une petite fille sous le bolchévisme. 1926.
Nuits de princes. 1927.
Le coup de grâce. 1931.
Nuits de Montmartre. 1932.
Bas-fonds. 1932.
Fortune carrée. 1932.
Vent de sable. 1934.
L'Armée des ombres. 1946.
Le tour du malheur. 1950.
Le lion. 1958.
Discours de réception, at l'Académie française. 1962.
Tous n'étaient pas des anges. 1963.
Terres d'amour et du feu. 1966.
Les cavaliers. 1967.

Further Reading

Buñuel, Luis, dir. *Belle de jour*. Paris: Paris Film Productions, 1967.

Courrière, Yves. *Joseph Kessel, ou, sur la piste du lion*. Paris: Plon, 1985.

Reiner, Silvain. *Mes saisons avec Joseph Kessel*. Levaloie-Perret: Manya, c. 1993.

Tassel, Alain. *Création romanesque dans l'oeuvre de Joseph Kessel*. Paris: Harmattan, 1997.

———, ed. *Présence de Kessel: Colloque de Nice, 2–3 avril 1998*. Nice: Université de Nice-Sophia Antipolis; Paris: C.I.D. Diffusion, 1998.

Wood, Michael. *Belle de Jour*. London: BFI Film Classics, 2001, U of Calif P. 2001. Includes bibliography relating to the film by Luis Buñuel.

KHARJAS

This poetic composition is known as *jarcha* in Spanish, and refers to the last lines that close an Arabic *muwashshaha,* a strophic poem flourishing—broadly speaking—from the 10th to the 12th century, elaborated in Al-Andalus (Muslim territory of medieval Spain, present-day Andalucía). While the main body of the poem had classical and refined attributes, the *jarcha* would be composed in a more popular register either in colloquial Arabic, in Romance, or in a mixture of the two languages. In 1948, the scholar Samuel Stern came upon 20 *jarchas* written in Romance, figuring as the last strophes of classical Arabic or Hebrew poems. Subsequent discoveries confirmed the *jarcha* as an expression of a hybrid and more personal lyric poetry in early Spanish literature. These hybrid Romance *jarchas* are the focus of the following entry. It must, however, be noted that to look at *jarchas* as Romance lyric is to offer a limited perspective. For a thorough discussion of the Arabic *kharjas* and the history of criticism on these, especially in relation to their Romance counterparts, the reader should start by consulting Rosen ("The muwashshah"). The debate on the relationship between the two is complex and rather technical but of great interest to anyone with some training either in medieval Spanish or in classical Arabic.

The Spanish *jarchas* are composed in Mozarabic, the dialect spoken by Christians living in Muslim Spain as well as the Jewish population and any bilingual residents of Al-Andalus. Brief and highly evocative, these compositions often center upon a girl's fleeting musings on requited or unrequited love, longing, and absence; this feminine voice is quite characteristic of the Romance *jarcha*. The addressee is often the mother, who, biological or not, represents a number of differing postures: confidante, guard, silent listener, accomplice. The compositions also address the lover at times as well.

In the Romance *jarchas,* the tone of the female speaker is frank, filled with sensuality, and clearly centered upon physical feeling. The strength of musical and folkloric tradition is apparent in the rhythm, imagery, and focus of the brief songs. As love songs identified with the feminine voice, these Spanish *jarchas* recall the other medieval lyric traditions of women's love songs found in German and English, for example. In the Spanish *jarchas,* the mother–daughter relationship is also touched upon, either as a vehicle for the expression of the daughter's longing or rebellion or as the mother's advice on amorous matters. As a genre embracing folklore, Romance languages, Arabic, and classical elements, the sensuality of these brief compositions is direct and often very evocative.

LEYLA ROUHI

Edition (the Romance *jarchas*)

Lírica española de tipo popular. Edited by Margit Frenk. Madrid: Cátedra, 1986.

Further Reading

Armistead, Samuel G. "A Brief History of Kharja Studies." *Hispania* 70 (1987): 8–15.

Compton, Linda Fish. *Andalusian Lyrical Poetry and Old Spanish Love Songs: The Muwashshah and*

Its Kharja. New York: New York University Press: 1976.

Frenk, Margit. *Las jarchas mozárbes y los comienzos de la lírica románica.* Mexico City: El Colegio de México 1975. Repr. 1975.

Liu, Benjamin, and James T. Monroe. *Ten Hispano-Arabic Strophic Songs in the Modern Oral Tradition: Music and Texts.* Berkeley and Los Angeles: University of California Press, 1989.

Rosen, Tova. "The muwashshah." In *The Literature of Al-Andalus,* edited by María Rosa Menocal, Raymond P. Scheindlin, and Michael Sells, 165–89. Cambridge History of Arabic Literature. Cambridge: Cambridge University Press, 2000.

KIRKUP, JAMES

1918–

British poet, translator, autobiographer, short story and travel writer, dramatist, novelist, and essayist

James Kirkup's autobiography, *I of All People: An Autobiography of Youth* (1988) pictures the extremely conservative academic and literary world in the United Kingdom of the 1940s and 1950s. The themes that Kirkup chose for his poems as well as the many sexual and scatological allusions they contain guaranteed that they would be received with some hostility. Nevertheless, his friendship with J.R. Ackerly, the editor of *The Listener,* enabled Kirkup to print some of his more daring poems in that magazine. These included "The Drain," which contains both voyeuristic and homoerotic images as the narrator watches young workmen wield their "well-oiled tools" while repairing the drain in the road outside his room, and "The Convenience," about a urinal, describing how men seek "passionate relief" with "voluptuous ferocity," which was, however, considered too much by *The Listener*'s typists, who refused to prepare the copy for print. Kirkup's poems treat a wide range of erotic scenarios, including the heterosexual ("An Indoor Pastoral"), the homosexual ("Gay Boys"), and the autoerotic ("Ode to Masturbation"). Kirkup was later to argue in his autobiographies that his treatment of such topics showed the Continental influence on his poetry (he translated a number of French and German poets), and he fiercely condemned the stuffiness of both English poetry and the English literary scene. He claimed that his outsider status made him persona non grata with the British Council, which did all it could to block his employment opportunities both at home and abroad.

By today's standards, the sexual references in Kirkup's poetry seem unremarkable. However, the poem that has continued to create controversy is "The Love That Dares to Speak Its Name," the publication of which in issue 96 of *Gay News* resulted in the newspaper's editor, Denis Lemon, being successfully prosecuted for blasphemy. It remains illegal to either publish or circulate the poem in the UK, and as late as 1997, a lesbian and gay Christian group was investigated by the police for providing a hypertext link to the poem on their website. The title refers to the poem "Two Loves" by Lord Alfred Douglas, onetime companion of Oscar Wilde, in which homosexuality is referred to as "the love that dare not speak its name." In Kirkup's poem, the love that dares to speak its name is Christ's love "for all men," which is described in explicitly sexual terms. Kirkup was later to disown the poem (on artistic, not moral grounds) and it has never been serialized in any of his collections.

Kirkup's prose works, too, feature scenes of erotic intensity. His description of his attraction to, and eventual seduction by, an American student in Spain in *A Poet Could Not But Be Gay* (1991) is particularly effective. His short story "The Teacher of American Business English" provides a witty description of a sexual encounter between a foreign teacher and one of his Japanese students. However, the novel *Gaijin on the Ginza,* which is full of graphically described and somewhat perverse sexual acts, seems written to offend several barely disguised members of the British Council in Japan whom Kirkup believed had sullied his name with the Japanese administration.

Kirkup will be remembered as much for the flamboyant life described in his autobiographies as for the daring nature of his poetry, which will no doubt live on in volumes of lesbian and gay verse.

Biography

James Kirkup was born in South Shields, England, on April 23, 1918. He graduated with a degree in modern languages from Durham University in 1941, after which, as a conscientious objector during the Second World War, he worked as an agricultural laborer. It was at this time that he published his first poems. He published many poems in the BBC's arts magazine *The Listener* from 1949 to 1965 and became a good friend of its editor, J.R. Ackerly. Kirkup's early poetry collections included *The Drowned Sailor and Other Poems* (1947), *The Submerged Village and Other Poems* (1951), *A Correct Compassion and Other Poems* (1952), *A Spring Poem and Other Poems* (1954), and *The Descent into the Cave and Other Poems* (1957). During this time he held several positions as writer in residence, including Leeds University (1950–52). However, the sexual, homoerotic, and scatological overtones in many of his poems made him a controversial and unpopular figure in the conservative literary and academic world of the 1950s. In the late 1950s he left England to teach abroad, including a spell in Sweden and Spain before settling in Japan, where he taught

at universities in Sendai, Tokyo, Nagoya, and Kyoto. His exposure to Japanese literature had a profound effect on his own poetic output, and his collections from this time show the influence of Japanese poetic forms, including haiku. In the 1970s, he was on the move again, this time teaching in the United States, Morocco, and Ireland. In 1977 his poem "The Love That Dares to Speak Its Name," which imagines a Roman guard in a sex act with the dead Christ, resulted in the first blasphemy trial in the UK since 1922. In the late 1970s, he settled in the Principality of Andorra in the Pyrenees, where he has continued to produce poetry, travel diaries, essays, and, in the 1990s, a series of autobiographies.

Selected Works

The Descent into the Cave and Other Poems. London: Oxford University Press, 1957.
Gaijin on the Ginza. London: Peter Owen, 1991.
I, of All People: An Autobiography of Youth. London: Weidenfeld and Nicolson, 1988.
A Poet Could Not But Be Gay. London: Peter Owen, 1991.
Me All Over: Memoirs of a Misfit. London: Peter Owen, 1993.
"Gay Boys" and "The Love of Older Men." In *The Penguin Book of Homosexual Verse*, edited by Stephen Coote. Harmondsworth, UK: Penguin, 1983.
"The Love That Dares to Speak Its Name." Poem banned in the UK but available on the Internet at http://petertatchell.net/religion/blasphemy.htm among other websites.
"The Teacher of American Business English." In *The Penguin Book of Gay Short Stories*, edited by David Leavitt and Mark Mitchell. London: Viking, 1994.

KLOSSOWSKI, PIERRE

1905–2002
French novelist, literary critic, and philosopher

In *Roberte ce soir* [*Roberta Tonight*] and *La révocation de l'edit de Nantes* [*The Revocation of the Edict of Nantes*], the author's interpretation

of the rules of hospitality may at first seem confusing. Octave, an elderly professor of scholastics, presses the sexual favors of his wife, Roberte, onto their guests, in order that he may see into her mystery. She is an inspector of censorship, whose own fantasies include seducing her young nephew, Antoine.

Clearly we are not in Kansas. We are about to enter a labyrinth of mirrors, led by a lean, priestly figure in black. We scramble to keep up. He turns occasionally to give us a thin smile of amused encouragement. He winks.

This saturnine guide is Pierre Klossowski, the older brother of the painter Balthus, son of a minor Polish nobleman and an artist whose friendship with Rilke was such that she asked the poet to introduce young Pierre, just come to Paris, to André Gide. Gide generously took the twenty-year-old under his wing, finding him an apartment and paying his college tuition. Klossowski studied scholastic philosophy with the Dominicans, and attended the Collège de Sociologie, which was directed by his friend Georges Bataille. His novels, translations of the classics, and literary essays—particularly his study of de Sade—influenced the French postmodernists. Klossowski's own literary antecedents include the classic Greek, Roman. and French authors; he has affinities with Lautreamont, Gide, Andre Breton, Celine, Queneau, and of course Bataille. The dark figure of de Sade looms over all.

Klossowski published *Roberte ce soir* and *La révocation de l'edit de Nantes*—two strange and singularly fascinating novels—in the 1950s. Existentialism reigned on the Left Bank, and his formal inventiveness and unsettling metaphysical comedy must have made him seem an odd duck indeed: an avant-gardist from the seventeenth century.

The time to enter Klossowski's mirrored labyrinth is now; he was wise to exploit the popular genre of erotic writing to make the approach to it as broadly appealing as possible. (Similarly, according to Robert Darnton, erotic novels were also employed as vehicles for political expression in eighteenth-century Paris.)

But pity the poor masturbator who comes to these pages for a peep and a wink—and finds Klossowski winking back at him! It is no use asserting that these novels are fully accessible to all. They are destined to delight most those readers who think it possible that perversity may be one of the paths to transcendence. Klossowski is an erotic writer in the sense that Italo Calvino talks about in *The Uses Of Literature*: "In the explicitly erotic writer we may . . . recognize one who uses the symbols of sex to give voice to something else, and this something else, of a series of definitions that tend to take shape in philosophical and religious terms, may in the last instance be redefined as another and ultimate Eros, fundamental, mythical, and unattainable."

The ideal reader of Klossowski's subversive masterpiece will possess a capacious literary intelligence that includes a more than passing acquaintance with French history, philosophy, and art; medieval theology; familiarity with erotic literature, along with an ungrudging interest in the ideas of the Marquis de Sade; a sense of humor equal to Klossowski's sly, ironic wit; and—this is essential—an awareness of "the connection between metaphysics and the flesh," in Yukio Mishima's phrase.

Fortunately for the less-than-ideal reader, Klossowski is a master of literary seduction. He is hospitable. He employs—and explodes—the conventions of the erotic and suspense genres as he draws us deeper into his labyrinth, utilizing a variety of narrative techniques, from eighteenth-century philosophical dialogues to Surrealist dream strategies. (Mishima has written perceptively about our seducer's methods: "The writers I pay most attention to in modern Western literature are Georges Bataille, Pierre Klossowski, and Witold Gombrowicz. . . [Their] works reveal an anti-psychological delineation, anti-realism, erotic intellectualism, straightforward symbolism, and a perception of the universe hidden behind all these.")

In precise and elegant language, Klossowski leads us, through theological and philosophical arguments, political debates and aesthetic ruminations, elaborate jokes, nightmares, tableaux vivants, and diary entries, into sacrilege, war crimes, and murder. His tone is always mocking, often mysterious, and sometimes, especially in his seriocomic erotic scenes, grimly hilarious. He is the writer playing God whose characters seek God; his subject, in the largest sense, is creation.

He offers pleasures for his readers in surprising contexts. One of the greatest surprises he provides is typical of his jokes: the book we are reading has been officially banned by Roberte, the inspector of censorship; her hospitable husband, Octave, is none other than the book's author, Pierre Klossowski.

Roberte ce soir opens with Antoine's view of his uncle and aunt in "the house where I spent such a trying adolescence." Small wonder: his uncle Octave "suffered from his conjugal happiness as though from an illness, firm in the belief he would be cured of it once he made it contagious," and his aunt Roberte's "beauty was of that somber sort which so often conceals pronounced tendencies to frivolity." Frivolity?

Winning Antoine—adopted by them at age thirteen—is the first objective in the couple's struggle for dominance. "My aunt treated me like a brother, and the professor had turned me into his favorite disciple; I served as the pretext for the practice of that hospitality which was practiced at my aunt's expense."

Octave has hung in his guest room, framed under glass, "The Rule of Hospitality," a parody of medieval theology which is both funny (well, it's a churchy wit) and an introduction to some of Klossowski's ideas. In making love to Roberte, a proper guest grants actuality to her—brings her from potentiality to essence—and illuminates her mystery for Octave. Eros becomes a direct route to hypostasis; the metasexual leads to the metaphysical.

While their main contention is religious, Roberte and Octave also debate philosophical, political, and artistic issues. Each has an agenda. Roberte is a left-wing humanist, and Octave is a Catholic, an aesthete, a sensualist. The couple argues a lot about ideas which are of the utmost importance to their creator. In fact, Roberte and Octave come to life in our minds to the extent that we are willing to engage with the ideas that drive them. Then they step off the page. They act for themselves.

Klossowski, in the character of Octave, believes that he is creating Roberte, a creature made of her own elements, "which first took draft form in my mind." But Roberte, in a diary entry, denies that "he is at the origin of my temperament." She is capable of devilishness unaided by her husband's machinations. And he can never know her, for one of Klossowski's themes is the unknowability of others.

But it is possible, sometimes, to glimpse the spirit through the flesh. The temptations of Eros are the temptations of love that reveal the soul. Thought wears the garments of skin and bone.

In one dialogue ("The Denunciation," Klossowski's homage to Corneille), uncle and nephew debate Thomist ideas about the soul while illustrating them with humor and sex. One minute we are following an intricate argument made by Octave about the mystery of hypostatic union, and the next he is showing Antoine a film in which Roberte's skirt catches fire and her rescuer molests her. (Antoine exclaims, "My stars, there in her panties is the outline of her bottom.") Klossowski's use of erotic elements is the more powerful for being deft, spare, and ironic—a glimpse of a bare thigh, a momentary encounter—often with dream figures made manifest by Roberte's rambunctious libido.

Roberte the censor is ravished by spirits she refuses to give voice to. Either speak the unspeakable, as de Sade warned, or suffer the demons. In his essay on de Sade, Klossowski writes of the natural order of things, "Only motion is real; creatures are nothing but nature's changing phases." The temptations of Eros allow the transcendence of this natural order. And for the novelist, as Milan Kundera says, "I have the feeling that a scene of physical love generates an extremely sharp light that suddenly reveals the essence of characters. . . . [C]ertain erotic passages of Georges Bataille have made a lasting impression on me. Perhaps it is because they are not lyrical but philosophical."

It has been suggested by symbolists that some labyrinths should be interpreted as diagrams of heaven. Perhaps that is how Klossowski would like us to see this splendidly intricate maze. When we come to the end of it, and bid him farewell, we emerge blinking into unfamiliar light, looking up at the heavens.

Biography

Born in Paris, August 9. Attended the Collège de Genève, the Lycée Janson de Sailly (Paris), then the École des sciences politiques, the Facultes catholiques (Lyon), and the Institut catholique (Paris). Wrote novels, philosophy, and literary criticism. His novel *Le Baphomet* won the Prix des Critiques.

MICHAEL PERKINS

Editions

La Révocation de l'Edit de Nantes [1959]. Les Editions de Minuit. Translated by Austryn Wainhouse. New York: Grove Press, 1969; Dalkey Archive Press, 2002.
Roberte ce soir. Paris: Les Editions de Minuit, 1953.

Selected Works

La vocation suspendue.
La bain de Diane.
Un si funeste desir.
Le Baphomet.
Sade mon prochain.

KOKA PANDIT

Ninth-century Indian poet

Koka Shastra

The *Koka Shastra*, the "Scripture of the Koka," also widely known as *Rati Rahasya*, "The Secrets of Rati" (spouse of the love god, Manmadha, in Hindu mythology), was composed in the 9th century by the poet Kokkoka to whet King Vainyadatta's curiosity concerning the art of love. *Kama Sutra*, compiled by Vatsyayana, reigned as the classic treatise on love and sex for several years in India, but Koka Pandit saw the need to address the theme again, as India's moral values had changed significantly since the composition of *Kama Sutra*. The *Ananga Ranga* of Kalyana Malla, composed in the 15th century, is another subtle and detailed treatise that followed the tradition set by Vatsyayana and Koka Pandit, and served as a guide on love and sexual behavior for men and women of subsequent generations. While acknowledging that ultimate wisdom on this topic has been achieved by Vatsyayana in *Kama Sutra*, Koka Pandit justifies the significance of his work by addressing the systems of Nandikesvara and Gonikaputra, who had made significant contributions to identifying the basic categories of women and their anatomical features, sexual preferences, and personality traits, determined by four individual physical types (*Padmini,* a "lotus woman"; *Sankhini,* a "conch shell woman"; *hasthini,* an "elephant woman"; and *citrini,* a "varied and fancy woman").

Koka Shastra is a manual that equips a man with the knowledge and skill to master the arts and technique of love and empowers him with the essential knowledge about the various habits, preferences, customs, and manners of women hailing from various regions within India, the different bodily types, gestures, positions, and techniques appropriate to specific occasions and types of women, and the suitable times for coition. Besides invoking the work of Nandikesvara and Gonikaputra, Koka Pandit's treatise widens the scope of the subject to include later traditions, the astrological systems of physical types and lunar calendars for courtships and the influence of Tantrism reflected in spells, *japas* (chants), and far-fetched recipes like those which require both wings of a bee which has rested on a petal blown from a funeral wreath. While *Kama Sutra* established the code of conduct for lovers of both sexes, *Koka Shastra* is written more for the husband, thus establishing the transition from a permissive, "free" approach to sex in ancient India to a rigid code of conduct and sex being circumscribed within marriage. The book begins with an invocation to the muse, establishes the treatise in the context of existing works of erotic literature, and defines the significance of the work in light of the changing moral customs and beliefs. Chapter 2, "Chandrakala" (about the lunar calendar), identifies the specific body parts of the woman that are touched by the arrows of the love god (Manmadha) during the light and dark halves of the month and how the suitor must gradually proceed with the woman in the art of lovemaking. In chapter 3, Koka Pandit delineates the physical types of men and women determined by their anatomical characteristics, which in turn determine ways by which the women can be satisfied. A woman may be characterized as a gazelle (*mrgi*), a mare (*vadava*), or an elephant (*hasthini*) and a man as a hare (*sasa*), a bullock (*vrsa*), or a stallion (*asva*). Chapter 4 discusses women by their ages, temperaments, and dispositions. Chapter 5 deals with specific social customs and practices of women relating to love and sex based on their locales, and the appropriate ways to solicit their attention. Chapter 6 describes the various methods of foreplay, or the "outer" modes of lovemaking (beginning with embraces), and chapter 7 discusses the preparation, positions, conduct, and methods of sexual intercourse. Chapter 9 deals with coition and various coital postures, chapter 10 with love cries and blows, and chapter 11 with the wooing of a bride, delineating the principles of choosing a bride and the successful ways to court her and win her love and affection completely. While chapter 12 outlines the duties of a wife, chapter 13 deals with relations concerning women other than one's wife.

Biography

It is believed that Koka Pandit hailed from a Kashmiri Brahmin family and was the protégé of King Vainyadatta, who lived from 830 to 960 CE.

KOKILA RAVI

Edition

Kokkoka. *The Koka Shastra; being the Ratirahasya of Kokkoka and other Medieval Indian Writings on Love.* Translated and with an introduction by Alex Comfort. Preface by W.G. Archer. New York: Stein and Day, 1965.

Further Reading

The four known untranslated commentaries on *Rati Rahasya* are by Kancinatha, Avantya Ramacandra, Kavi Prabhu, and Srngarasabandha Pradhipika.

KUPRIN, ALEXANDER

1870–1938
Russian novelist and short story writer

Alexander Ivanovich Kuprin's *Iama* [*The Pit*] is the longest and most notorious of prerevolutionary Russia's literary works devoted to the problem of prostitution. It is a virtual catalogue of all the motifs and clichés associated with the topic in the previous half-century, but it also goes many steps further than its predecessors. If prostitutes had previously been either supporting characters in a larger story devoted to other issues and themes (Fyodor Dostoevsky's *Notes from Underground* [1864], Nikolai Chernyshevsky's *What Is to Be Done?* [1863]), the subjects of shorters works (Vsevolod Garshin's "An Occurence" [1875], "Nadezhda Nikolaevna" [1885]), or the embodiment of the male protagonist's own moral dilemma (Lev Tolstoy's *Resurrection* [1899]), *The Pit* allows the prostitutes themselves to share center stage with the men: in at least a few of the large, extended chunks that compose the novel, these women are the heroines of their own stories.

Part of the novel's immense popular appeal was that it purported to give an unvarnished account of daily life in a brothel. Most of Part 1 of the novel verges more on documentary than on fiction, with the male and female characters serving largely as vehicles for the author's almost journalistic descriptions of the prostitute's

world. As in Chekhov's 1888 short story, "A Nervous Breakdown," the reader follows a group of young men on an expedition to the brothels in a notorious red-light district. Like Chekhov's young men, the protagonists of *The Pit* represent a carefully selected cross section of Russian professional and intellectual life: Yarchenko the classicist, Ramzes the lawyer, Sobashnikov and Likhonin the students, and Platonov the reporter. As they talk each other into visiting the brothel, they, with no small amount of irony, discuss their project as if it were a scientific expedition: prostitution is a crucial social problem that must be investigated by members of the intelligentsia. And indeed, their discussions of prostitution go into a greater detail and greater depth than any previous representations of sex-for-hire trades in Russian fiction: from the relationship between the prostitutes and the madam to the relationships among the prostitutes themselves, even making a reference to the frequency with which these women's disgust for their male clients pushes them toward lesbianism. Yet this scientific veneer can easily be seen as an exercise in self-justification, not only for the characters, but by extension for the author and even the readers: the journey to the brothel is not the result of anything so vulgar as mere sexual desire, while the literary depiction of the topic is therefore scientific rather than pornographic.

These men are clearly far more informed than any of their literary predecessors. But it is precisely their level of knowledge that only increases the irony of their encounter with the prostitutes and calls into question the value of their discussions. Not only does Kuprin have the benefit of his familiarity with the earlier Russian literature on the question, but so do his male characters: their visit to the brothel is inevitably colored by the fact that they have read the same books on the subject as Kuprin's readers. Thus they tend to approach the subject as an abstract, philosophic, and even aesthetic phenomenon. One of the men even points out that to date, Russian literature's engagement with the problem has been woefully inadequate, since the best it could produce was Sonya Marmeladova, the saintly prostitute who saves the hero's soul in Dostoevsky's *Crime and Punishment* (1866). As the same man argues, the prostitute has heretofore remained unknown and unknowable to the Russian intellectual, along with that other eternally mysterious figure, the Russian peasant (also the frequent subject of semidocumentary exposés throughout the nineteenth century). And even as they go to the brothel, they lament the impossibility of ever actually discovering the "truth" about the prostitutes: the women are used to being asked how they got to their sorry state and are used to providing standard-issue lies as a response. Moreover, there is even an acknowledgment on one of the men's parts that they have no right to expect any more: why should the women be expected to tell the men anything?

Once the men become involved with the prostitutes, their self-consciousness does them little good, and despite themselves they begin to behave according to the standard literary script. Inevitably, one of the men tries to "rescue" a young woman from the brothel, and soon the rest join in what becomes a veritable orgy of liberal interventionism. No cliché is left untouched: there is even talk of buying poor Lyubka a sewing machine, which was the standard instrument for the prostitute's by-her-bootstraps redemption since Chernyshevsky's *What Is to Be Done?*

Instead, the uniqueness of *The Pit* lies in the careful attention paid to the women themselves, to the world of the brothel. In scenes reminiscent of Defoe's *Moll Flanders*, Kuprin almost overwhelms the reader with a wealth of detail about the women's expenses, income, and rules of conduct. More gripping are his plots that center on the women themselves. Kuprin tells the story of Zhenka, a prostitute who, when she realizes she has syphilis, decides to take revenge on the entire male sex by infecting as many clients as she can before dying. Here as elsewhere, Kuprin walks a fine line between the standard sentimentalization of the prostitute as victim and the male fantasy of the vengeful, demonic female. Ultimately, Zhenka resolves her situation in a way far more typical of Russian heroines: she kills herself, and her death is mourned publicly by all the prostitutes, as, in a rare demonstration of solidarity, her body is accompanied to the cemetery by women from all the brothels in the district. But nothing changes for the better in the women's lives: the entire district is closed as a result of a virtual pogrom against prostitutes on the part of a group of angry sailors who complain that they were overcharged, forcing the prostitutes to live and work on the streets.

The novel's rather abrupt ending can be attributed to the vagaries of serial publication: six years passed between the publication of the first and last parts, and Kuprin may well have finished the book hastily after another author published his own conclusion to the story. Yet despite the novel's unevenness, it has had a lasting appeal among Russian readers. Still in print during Soviet times because of Kuprin's status as a canonical author, it was one of the few "erotic" texts readily available in the USSR.

Biography

Born August 26 in Narovchat, Penza oblast. Studied at the Second Moscow Military High School (Cadet Corps) from 1880 to 1888, followed by the Alexander Military Academy from 1888 to 1890. Served in the army from 1890 through 1894, whereupon he began to write for various newspapers in Kiev. In the 1890s he made a name for himself as an author who focused on Russia's social problems, most notably in *Poedinok* [*The Duel*] (1905) and *Iama* (1908–1915). After the 1917 Revolution, he emigrated to France, where he continued to write, although with far less critical and commercial success. He returned to the Soviet Union in 1937 and died of cancer the following year.

ELIOT BORENSTEIN

Selected Works

Sobranie sochinenii. 9 vols. Moscow, 1970–1973.
The Pit: A Novel in Three Parts. Translated by Bernard Guilbert Guerny. Westport, CT: Hyperion Press, 1977.

Further Reading

Borenstein, Eliot. *Men Without Women: Masculinity and Revolution in Russian Fiction, 1917–1929.* Durham, NC: Duke University Press, 2000.

Luker, Nicholas J.L. *Alexander Kuprin.* Boston: Twayne Publishers, 1978.
Matich, Olga. "A Typology of Fallen Women in Nineteenth Century Russian Literature." *American Contributions to the Ninth International Congress of Slavists.* Vol. 2, 325–43. Columbus, OH: Slavic Press, 1983.
Siegel, George. "The Fallen Woman in Nineteenth Century Literature." *Harvard Slavic Studies* 5 (1970): 81–108.

KUZMIN, MIKHAIL

1872–1936
Russian poet, prose writer, playwright, and critic

Primary Work: *Wings*

A musician turned poet and prose writer, Mikhail Alekseevich Kuzmin created a sensation with the publication of *Kryl'ia* [*Wings*], a novella that dealt openly with the subject of same-sex desire and that helped earn Kuzmin the epithet "the Russian Oscar Wilde." *Wings* first appeared in the journal *Vesy* [*Scales*] in 1906 and was published in book form in 1907. It went through several editions, including a post-revolutionary one published in Berlin in 1923. Its frank treatment of homosexuality made a Soviet edition unthinkable, and it was not republished in Russia in book form until 1994. Initial reception of *Wings* was varied. It was criticized by a number of critics and writers as pornographic but was praised by others, although positive reviews tended to ignore or play down the central theme of homosexuality.

The novella is divided into three parts, and its structure combines elements of the *Bildungsroman,* or novel of self-education, and the philosophical novel in the tradition of Voltaire's *Candide* (Bogomolov, 21). Against the backdrop of Vania Smurov's coming of age, Kuzmin offers philosophical discussions on the nature of love and the relationship of the body and the spirit. The novella opens with Vania, a recently orphaned adolescent, being sent to live with the Kazanskii family in St. Petersburg. There he meets the elegant and charismatic Larion Dmitrievich Stroop, who is part Russian and part English, suggesting a vague association with Oscar Wilde and aestheticism. It soon becomes clear that Stroop is homosexual. *Wings* traces Vania's gradual acceptance of Stroop as his male "guide"—a recurring theme in Kuzmin's work—and of his own homosexual desires.

Vania's journey of self-discovery is predicted early in the novella by Stroop when he tells the adolescent that he has it in him "to become a completely transformed being" (Granoien and Green, 14). His personal transformation mirrors that of Russian society in the tumultuous first years of the twentieth century, when, in the words of Mr. Kazanskii, "everything is awakening" (6). The loosening of censorship restrictions made possible relatively frank representations of sexuality and eroticism, creating the impression that Russia—like Vania—was experiencing a sexual awakening.

While Vania is initially fascinated by Stroop, he is horrified—and perhaps jealous—when he discovers that Stroop is having an affair with Fedor, a bathhouse attendant who has been hired by Stroop as his servant. This relationship, founded on Stroop's physical lust and Fedor's desire for money, is associated with death and decay. In fact, Vania first encounters Fedor after reading a saint's life about a hermit who was shown a vision of rotting corpses to cure him of his lustful thoughts. Later, Ida Holberg, a young woman infatuated with Stroop, discovers the relationship between Stroop and his manservant and kills herself in Stroop's home.

Punctuating this rather sordid melodrama are discussions of same-sex desire among the ancient Greeks and Romans. A key figure in Vania's development is his instructor of Greek, Daniil Ivanovich, who is homosexual and serves as a confidante and adviser to Vania. Both Stroop and Daniil Ivanovich are lovers of Greek culture, and for them homosexuality in the ancient world—symbolized by the love between Antinous and the Roman emperor Hadrian—represents an ideal. For Stroop, ancient Greece was a time "when men saw that beauty and love in all their forms are of the gods, and they became free and brave, and they grew wings" (22). Later, in the company of his closest friends, Stroop explains to Vania: "We are Hellenes" (32).

In part 2, Kuzmin introduces another philosophical perspective on sexual desire when Vania goes on vacation with his friend Sasha. Sasha's family are Old Believers, members of a religious sect that broke from the Russian Orthodox Church in the seventeenth century over proposed revisions to Church books and practices. Like the ancient Greeks—and the authors of the gnostic gospels, who so influenced Kuzmin— the Old Believers in *Wings* refuse a simplistic morality based on the dichotomy of natural/ unnatural. "Sin," one Old Believer explains, "doesn't lie in the act itself, but in its relation to other things," a paraphrase of a verse from St. Paul's Letter to the Romans (14:14). Sasha will later tell Vania that "a man ought to be like a river or a mirror—whatever is reflected in him he should make part of himself."

While, in part 1, Kuzmin associates death with lust ("possessing without loving"), in part 2 he associates death with asceticism ("loving without possessing"). On vacation, Vania witnesses the recovery of the body of a boy his own age—sixteen—who lost his life while crossing the Volga River. He had run away from home to join a monastery (an idea that had attracted Kuzmin himself for many years). Vania reacts with horror to the slimy corpse.

Acknowledging both his own physical beauty and its perishability, he asks, "Who will save me?". He then makes clear that the person to save him is not a woman, when he cruelly rejects the advances of Sasha's widowed aunt.

In part 3, Vania finds himself in Italy with Daniil Ivanovich. There, he is introduced to a third important philosophical influence: Italian Catholic culture, which, for Kuzmin, also represents the integration of the sensual and the spiritual. "Asceticism is," according to Ugo, an Italian acquaintance, "a highly unnatural phenomenon." Crossing paths with Stroop in Italy, Vania believes that he offers him the possibility of a fuller life and decides to accompany him on his travels, continuing the theme of life as a journey. When Vania accepts Stroop's invitation, he throws open his apartment window onto a street that is bathed in sunlight.

In contrast to typical descriptions of homosexuals as decadent and unnatural—characterized by Vasilii Rozanov as "People of the Moonlight" (1911)—Kuzmin repeatedly associates his homosexual characters with sunlight and the natural world. "Somewhere," Stroop declares to his homosexual friends, "lies our ancient kingdom, full of sunlight and freedom, of beautiful and courageous people." *Wings* is the story of one orphan's journey to that symbolic home.

Biography

Born in Saratov, Russia, Kuzmin spent most of his life in St. Petersburg, where he studied music composition with Nikolai Rimsky-Korsakov. His first publications appeared in 1905 in *Zelenyi sbornik* [*Green Miscellany*], but Kuzmin established his literary reputation in 1906 with the publication of a cycle of poems, *Aleksandriiskie pesni* [*Alexandrian Songs*], and a novella, *Kryl'ia* [*Wings*], in the journal *Vesy* [*Scales*]. Both works invoke the theme of homosexual love.

Kuzmin published poems, prose works, plays, and criticism. He also worked as a translator and a musician, setting many of his own lyric poems to music. Kuzmin remained in the Soviet Union after the Bolshevik Revolution but found it increasingly difficult to publish his works. He died of a chronic illness.

BRIAN JAMES BAER

Editions

Kryl'ia. Moscow: Skorpion, 1907; Berlin: Petropolis, 1923.

Granoien, Neil, and Michael Green, ed., trans. "Wings." In *Wings: Prose and Poetry*. Ann Arbor, MI: Ardis, 1972; in *Selected Prose and Poetry*, edited and translated by Michael Green, Ann Arbor, MI: Ardis, 1980.

Selected Works

Fiction

Prikliucheniia Eme Lebefa. 1907.

Pervaia kniga rasskazov. 1910; selected stories as "Aunt Sonya's Sofa." "From the Letters of the Maiden Clara Valmont to Rosalie Tutelmaier," "The Shade of Phyllis," and "Florus the Bandit" in Green, 1980.

Vtoraia kniga rasskazov. 1910.

Tret'ia kniga rasskazov. 1910, selected story as "The Story of Xanthos" in Green, 1980.

Pokoinitsta v dome. Skazki. 1914.

Zelenyi solovei. 1915.

Voennye rasskazy. 1915.

Plavaiushchie-puteshestvuiushchie. 1915.

Antrakt v ovrage. 1916.

Babushkina shkatulka. Rasskazy. 1918.

Devstvennyi Viktor i drugie rasskazy. 1918; selected stories as "Virginal Viktor" and "The Education of Nisa" in Green, 1980.

Chudesnaia zhizn' Iosifa Bal'zamo, grafa Kaliostro. 1919.

Poetry

Seti: Pervaia kniga stikhov. 1908; selections as "Alexandrian Songs" in Green, 1980.

Kuranty liubvi. Slova i muzyka. 1910.

Osennie ozera. Vtoraia kniga stikhov. 1912.

Glinianye golubki. Tret'ia kniga stikhov. 1914.

Vozhatyi. Stikhi. 1918.

Dvum. 1918.

Zanaveshennye kartinki. 1920.

Ekho: Stikhi. 1921.

Nezdeshnie vechera. Stikhi. 1914–1920. 1921.

Paraboly. Stikhotvoreniia 1921–22. 1923.

Novyi Gul'. 1924.

Forel' razbivaet led. 1929, as "The Trout Breaks the Ice" in Green, 1980.

Drama

Venetsianskie bezumtsy. Komediia. 1915; as "The Venetian Madcaps. A Comedy" in Green, 1980.

Further Reading

Bogomolov, Nikolay. *Mikhail Kuzmin: Stat'i i materialy*. Moscow: 1995; "Mikhail Kuzmin i ego ranniaia proza," in *Mikhail Kuzmin. Plavaiushchie Puteshestvuiushchie. Romany, povesti, rasskaz*, edited by N.A. Bogomolov, 7–40. Moscow: Sovpadenie, 2000.

Engelstein, Laura. *The Keys to Happiness: Sex and the Search for Modernity in Fin-de-Siecle Russia*. Ithaca and London: Cornell University Press, 1992.

Gillis, Donald S. "The Platonic Theme in Kuzmin's *Wings*." *Slavic and East European Journal* 22 (1978): 336–47.

Granoien, Neil. "'Wings' and the 'World of Art.'" *Russian Literature Triquarterly* 11 (1975): 393–405.

Malmsted, John, and Nikolay Bogomolov. *Mikhail Kuzmin: A Life in Art*. Cambridge and London: Harvard University Press, 1999.

Pevak, E.A. "Proza i esseistika M.A. Kuzmina." In *Mikhail Kuzmin. Proza i esseistika: V 3-kh t. T. 1. Proza 1906–1912gg.*, edited by E.G. Domogatskoi and E.A. Pevak, 5–68. Moscow: Agraf, 1999.

INDEX

E

Men (*cont.*)
  fidelity of, 318
  fire/water principals and, 78–79, 81
  Fowles and, 471, 472, 473
  Harvey, Pauline, on, 501
  Hite on, 435
  hysteria in, 146
  impersonation of, 1308–1311
  infertility in, 82
  Istarú and, 675–676
  Japanese, Nosaka on, 961
  kidnapped by women, 304
  Latin American, 429
  "lion-like," 1456
  Nafzâwî on, 943–944
  Nin on, 1409, 1410
  in nineteenth-century France, 490, 496
  old, Kawabata and, 1447, 1448–1450
  passive, 353, 1163
  peasant, 446, 447, 963
  as readers, 530
  Rossetti, Ana, and, 1135
  Sacher-Masoch and, 1148
  self-aggrandizement of, 76–77
  as sex slaves, 304, 353
  sexual hygiene of, 7
  short stories for, 1226
  single, lonely, 102
  submissive, 526
  suicide by, 315
  as travelers, 441
  Victorian, 529
  violence by, against women, 28, 44, 71, 161–162, 347, 366, 403, 404, 618–619, 627, 1378
  women writing as, 138, 139
  women's bodies owned by, 1409
  women's underclothes and, 1309
  in work of women writers, 1403
  writers, fairy tales rewritten by, 451
  writers, using female pseudonyms, 1399
  writers, women writers v., 459
  young, older married women and, 491
  young white, Mailer on, 434
  younger, with older women, 485, 499, 1193, 1417
  Zayas and, 1455, 1456
Ménage à trois. *See* Triangles, love
Menander, 364
Ménard, Philippe, 446
Menchu, Robert, 1428
Mendès, Catulle, 885–887, 1391, 1392
Mendes, Peter, 1048
Menelaus, 424, 586
Menstruation, 36, 965, 1024
  blood, fetish for, 294
  blood, sperm and, 423
  blood, taboo of, 404
  Chinese sexual alchemy and, 1209, 1210
  di Giorgiò on, 344
  as pollution/disorder, 79
  Qur'an on, 868
  sex during, 1205
  taboos and, 1274
Mental illness. *See also* Madness
  Akutagawa and, 688
  Eminescu's, 410

  in *Journal d'une femme soumise*, 859–860
  medical science and, 799
  in *Rougon-Macquart, Les*, 1466
Mérat, Albert, 298
Méray, Antony, 489
Mercado, Tununa, 1229–1230
Merchant of Venice, The (Shakespeare), 1215, 1216
Mercier, Henri, 297
Mercier, Sébastien, 597, 1157
Mercury, 754
Merkin, 413
Merlin (magazine), 312, 1313
Mermaids, 240
Mernissi, Fatima, 949
Merril, Judith, 1190
Merriman, Brian, 671
Merryland Displayed (Stretzer), 1259, 1260
Merteuil, Madame de, 1281, 1330
Mes amours avec Victoire [*My Love with Victoria*] (E.D.), 397
Mes etapes amoureuses [*My Loving Stages*] (E.D.), 398
Meslier, Jean, 375
Mesopotamian literature, 551–552, 887–891
  Akkadian, 890–891
  love poetry, Sumerian, 400, 889–890
  myths, Sumerian, 888–889
Metamorphoses (Ovid), 425, 638, 763, 772, 892–893, 981, 987–989, 990, 991, 1213
Metamorphoses (*The Golden Ass*) (Apuleius), 41–42, 140, 426, 761–762, 892
Metamorphosis, 892–893, 1138
Metaphor(s)
  Aretino on, 1242
  botanical, 1259, 1260
  dance as, 501
  deterritorializing, for Latin America, 1428
  female body, 39, 188, 1242–1243, 1259–1260, 1380
  intercourse as ploughing, 1380
  penis, 39, 447, 506, 998, 1259, 1380
  Renaissance use of, 1242
  Sea, 240
  somatopia as, 1242–1243
Metaphysical poetry, 354–356
Metaphysics, 426, 436
Metasex, Mirth and Madness (Vassi), 1342
"Metasexual Manifesto, The" (Vassi), 1342
Metasexuality, 1342
Metge, Bernat, 210
Methodists, 418, 807
Meung, Jean de, 369, 506–507, 826–828
Meusnier de Querlon, Ange Gabriel, 894–895
Mexican literature, 157–159, 429–430, 433, 1001–1003, 1228, 1229, 1428, 1432, 1433
Mexico
  Esquivel and, 429–430
  Mistral in, 911
  Paz and, 1001, 1002
  Torrid Tales and, 741–742
Meyer, Detlev, 543
Mi hermano el alcalde [*My Brother the Mayor*] (Vallejo), 1337–1338, 1338
Miallat, Henriette, 1005
Michael, in *Mind Blower*, 1341, 1342
Michel, Albin, 162
Michelet, Jules, 491
Micromegas (Voltaire), 1372

INDEX